HANDBOOKS

D0283804

CHILE

WAYNE BERNHARDSON

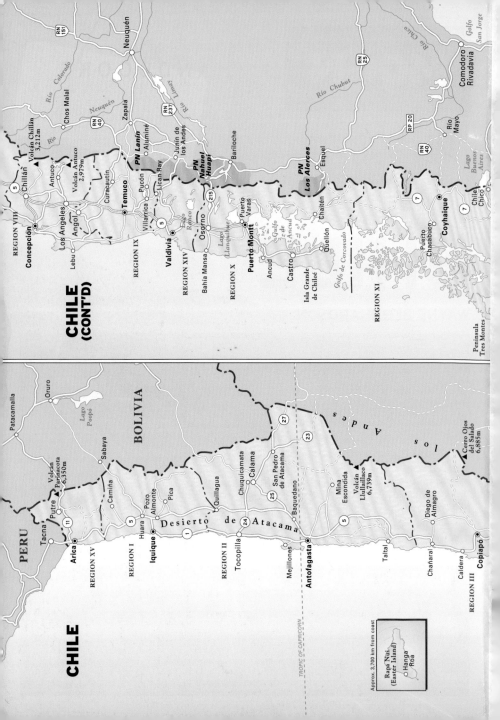

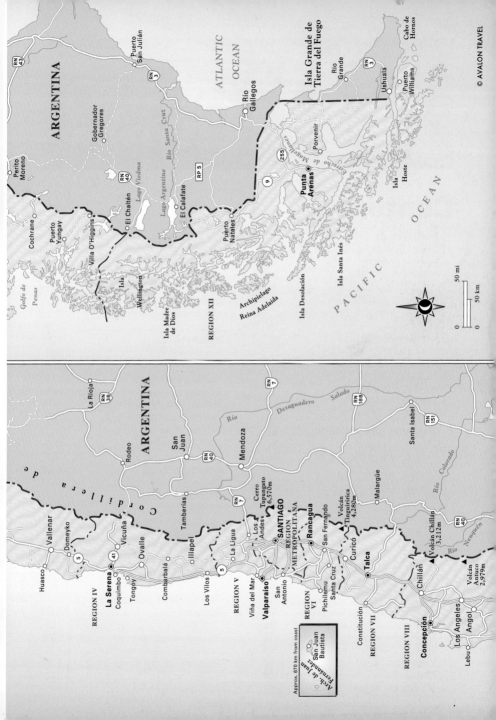

Contents

Discover Chile

In Benjamín Subercaseaux's memorable phrase, Chile embodies *una loca geografía* – literally, "a crazy geography." Less literally, it's "a geographical extravaganza" whose northern deserts, Mediterranean heartland, deep mountain lakes and soaring volcanoes, temperate rainforests, and Patagonian wildlands all occur within a land area only a little larger than Texas.

Dotted with archaeological sites, the arid north and its uplands were outliers of the Inka and other Andean civilizations. The Spaniards left their colonial churches and chapels, but indigenous llama and alpaca herders have outlasted them in wildlife-rich steppes at the foot of snow-topped cones. Desert rats find the Atacama's crumbling ghost towns irresistible; farther south, the world's clearest skies have made the Norte Chico a stellar site for astronomers.

Central Chile is wine country and home to one of South America's most progressive capital cities. The port city of Valparaíso is Chile's San Francisco, and the California-like coastline has its own surfers' mecca at Pichilemu. In winter, South America's best skiing is barely an hour from downtown Santiago.

Home to the indigenous Mapuche, the southern mainland is a land of lakes and forested mountains, where national parks abound along both sides of the Chile–Argentina border. The archipelago of Chiloé is a verdant outlier with a unique cultural heritage.

Farther south, the Patagonia steppes, mountains, fjords, and ice fields are some of the world's wildest country. Getting there is more than half the fun on the Carretera Austral, the scenic southern highway, and the ferries through the channels that parallel it. Rafting and kayaking on the Río Futaleufú offer some of the world's greatest adrenaline rushes.

Glaciers still reach the sea here and on Tierra del Fuego, while whales and penguins cavort in the Strait of Magellan. The region's highest-profile destination, Torres del Paine, provides exhilarating scenery and hiking.

In the distant western Pacific, Easter Island (Rapa Nui) is an iconic destination for its megalithic, enigmatic monuments. Nearer the continent, the Juan Fernández archipelago helped bring world literature the story of Robinson Crusoe, but its modern treasure is its luxuriant flora and fauna.

About 8 hours from Miami, 10 hours from New York, or 14 hours from Los Angeles, Chile is close enough for short-term visitors focused on special interests in specific regions, but large and diverse enough that longer-term travelers will find plenty to see and do along the entire length of the country.

Planning Your Trip

► WHERE TO GO

Physiographically, culturally, and economically, Chile divides into several vernacular regions, which roughly coincide with political boundaries.

Santiago and Vicinity

Chile's capital is an underrated metropolis of quality museums, lively neighborhoods and nightlife, and outstanding restaurants; major ski resorts are less than an hour from downtown. Vineyards in the vicinity complement its gastronomic progressivism, but the metropolitan region also has a high wild backcountry where white-water rafting and kayaking are barely an hour away.

Just off the Alameda, Cerro Santa Lucía is one of downtown Santiago's top garden spots.

The Chilean Heartland

Nearly surrounding Santiago, the heartland stretches from the Río Aconcagua south to the Biobío. A transect would pass from its rugged coastline over the rounded coastal range

Ascensor Espíritu Santo, Cerro Bellavista

oficinas (company towns) that are now ghost towns. It's even more different from pre-Columbian times, when the population clustered in coastal fish camps, farmed the valleys, and tended llamas and alpacas in the altiplano (which some still do).

Norte Chico

As a holiday destination, the "Land of 10,000 Mines" sounds inauspicious, but the semi-arid region north of Santiago has some of Chile's best beaches, a scenic shoreline with abundant wildlife and unique flora, and skies so clear that international astronomical organizations have built observatories on their fog-free heights. Near picturesque villages like Vicuña, its irrigated valleys are the source of pisco, Chile's powerful grape brandy, while its highlands offer genuine solitude. Foreign visitors to this region are few, but the open-minded come away satisfied and often thrilled.

and through the alluvial central valley to the Andean heights.

Northwest of Santiago, the hillsides and winding alleyways of Valparaíso offer one of the continent's greatest urban experiences. The nearby beach resort of Viña del Mar may be overrated, but the unassuming Pichilemu is one of South America's top surf spots.

Several transverse river valleys have become well-traveled wine routes for visitors from around the world. Almost unknown to non-Chileans, their Andean backcountry would draw hordes of hikers if it were so close to urban populations in North America or Europe.

Norte Grande

Chile's "Great North" comprises the arid Atacama coast, the precordillera "foothills" (reaching nearly 4,000 meters), and the altiplano or high steppe (punctuated with soaring volcanoes over 6,000 meters).

Most of the population lives in coastal cities like Arica and Antofagasta, and oases like Calama (a mining town) and San Pedro de Atacama (a tourist-magnet colonial village). That's changed from a century ago, when many lived in nitrate

pre-Columbian geoglyphs at Cerro Pintados

Volcán Villarrica looms over its namesake lake at Pucón.

Chilean Lakes District

Known popularly but imprecisely as Chile's "Lakes District," south of the Río Biobío, the Sur Chico ("Lesser South") is a wonderland of rivers, lakes, forests, and volcanoes, and the homeland of the Mapuche Indians. Within this vernacular region lies the Chiloé archipelago, a UNESCO World Heritage site rich in scenery, architecturally distinctive houses and churches, and extravagant folklore.

The Sur Chico is popular with Chilean and foreign visitors alike, and it's common to cross the Andes into Argentine Patagonia here. It's also the official starting point for the Carretera Austral, the discontinuous southern highway that's linked previously inaccessible parts of southern Chile to the mainland, and for the ferries whose services help fill the gaps.

Northern Patagonia

Chile's most thinly populated region, Aisén (Region XI, formally speaking) is islands-and-highlands country that resembles British Columbia and the Alaska panhandle. For purposes of this book, it also includes the southernmost part of Los Lagos (Region X), often known as "continental Chiloé," where the tiny ferry port of Caleta Gonzalo is the de facto (as opposed to the official) starting point of the Carretera Austral.

The Carretera Austral is one of Patagonia's greatest road trips, but off-the-highway sights like Laguna San Rafael (accessible by boat or air taxi) are highlights in their own right. There are numerous national parks and reserves along or near the highway, and Parque Natural Pumalín may be South America's most audacious private conservation initiative.

Reserva Nacional Villa Cerro Castillo

Southern Patagonia and Tierra del Fuego

South of Aisén, Chilean Patagonia consists of jagged, forested mountains and uninhabited islands bordering inland seas battered by Pacific storms; rain and snow feed surging rivers and the sprawling glaciers of the Campo de Hielo Sur, the southern continental ice field.

The major city is the regional capital of Punta Arenas, but Puerto Natales is the gateway to the igneous spires of Torres del Paine. Across the Strait of Magellan, Chile and Argentina share the broad steppes and mountainous grandeur of Tierra del Fuego, where Ushuaia is the world's southernmost city.

Most of Chilean Tierra del Fuego is thinly settled, and its most scenic parts are almost inaccessible, but across the Beagle Channel from Ushuaia, local cruise ships now visit Isla Navarino and Cape Horn, South America's southernmost point.

The Chilean Pacific Islands

For aficionados of the exotic and the romantic, it's hard to imagine destinations any more exotic or romantic than the Juan Fernández archipelago—a World Biosphere Reserve that also gave literature the Robinson Crusoe story—and Easter Island (Rapa Nui), whose enigmatic stone statues are instantly recognizable anywhere in the world.

Both islands are small, dormant volcanoes that have risen out of the ocean. Castaway Alexander Selkirk's lonely exile, fictionalized by Daniel Defoe, put Juan Fernández on the map, but its unique flora and fauna are equally noteworthy. Despite a tumultuous history that nearly destroyed its natural environment, Easter Island remains an open-air archaeological wonderland whose contemporary South Pacific ambience tenuously blends the culture of Polynesia with the South American continent.

IF YOU HAVE . . .

- **ONE WEEK:** Visit Santiago / Valparaíso, San Pedro de Atacama, and Torres del Paine.

- **TWO WEEKS:** Add the wine country and Tierra del Fuego (including the Cruceros Australis cruise from Punta Arenas to Ushuaia), and Argentina's Moreno Glacier. Alternatively: Add Laguna San Rafael (including parts of the Carretera Austral and Termas de Puyuhuapi, or the ferry from Puerto Natales to Puerto Montt).

- **THREE WEEKS:** Consider additional time in the desert north, including Iquique and its nearby ghost towns and geoglyphs, and Parque Nacional Lauca, and/or the Lakes District, including Pucón and Puerto Varas, and their backcountry.

- **FOUR WEEKS:** Add both the desert north and the Lakes District, plus Chiloé and its vicinity.

- **SIX WEEKS:** Add a road trip, along the entire Carretera Austral (Chile) with a possible detour into Argentina to reach southernmost Chile.

church at Parinacota, Parque Nacional Lauca

► WHEN TO GO

The fact that the Southern Hemisphere's seasons are opposite those of the Northern Hemisphere, where most overseas visitors live, adds to Chile's appeal. Still, it remains a year-round destination, where urban exploration, winter skiing, and desert trekking are all possible.

Santiago's urban appeal defies the seasons, but business travelers should avoid January and February, when many Santiaguinos abandon the capital for their summer vacations. The relatively mild winter sees some stretches of warm, brilliant weather.

Because Chile extends from the tropics of the Atacama to sub-Antarctic Tierra del Fuego, seasonality can vary not only according to latitude, but also with altitude. Beach resorts like Viña del Mar and La Serena can be uncomfortably crowded in the summer months (January–February) but ideal when the coastal fog recedes in March and April.

In the northernmost Andean highlands, summer is the rainy season. That may mean only an afternoon thundershower, but occasional downpours can cause flash floods and cut off roads, reducing access to areas of interest; at the highest altitudes, it can even mean snowstorms. Winter's warm, dry days, by contrast, can be ideal for exploring the backcountry, despite cold nights.

The heartland's wineries are open most of the year, but the fall harvest season (March–April) is ideal for tours and tasting. Summer is the time for mountaineering throughout most of the country, while winter is ski season at Portillo and other resorts.

The southern Lakes District is a traditional summer destination, but from October to April it's also a magnet for fly-fishing. In Patagonia, the season is lengthening, especially among foreign visitors who come to view South Atlantic wildlife such as penguins and natural attractions like the pinnacles of Torres del Paine.

As an extension of Patagonia, Tierra del Fuego is still primarily a summer destination, though it also has a ski season. Also featured in this book, the Argentine city of Ushuaia is a gateway to Antarctica, where the spring breakup of pack ice determines the season.

a close-up of Chilean Tierra del Fuego's Glaciar Pía

► BEFORE YOU GO

When planning a trip to Chile, remember that distances are great and logistics can be complicated. Unless your trip is an open-ended overland excursion, this means choosing among numerous options both as to destinations and means of transport. Santiago and the heartland are compact and easy to travel around, but visiting other high-profile destinations like San Pedro de Atacama and Torres del Paine can require two- to three-hour flights or 24-hour bus trips. Driving is an option, but for most visitors this will require a rental car from a provincial airport or city.

Passports and Visas

U.S. and Canadian citizens traveling to Chile and Argentina (whose southernmost provinces get coverage in this book) need passports but not advance visas. Passports are also necessary for checking into hotels, cashing travelers' checks, or even credit card transactions. Both countries routinely grant foreign visitors 90-day entry permits in the form of a tourist card. Chile collects a variable "reciprocity fee" from U.S., Canadian, Australian, and Mexican citizens at Santiago's international airport; Argentina has considered this but appears to have backed off for the moment.

Vaccinations and Health Insurance

Theoretically, Argentina and Chile demand no proof of vaccination, but if you are coming from a tropical country where yellow fever is endemic, authorities could ask for a vaccination certificate. Traveling to Chile or Argentina without adequate medical insurance is risky. Before leaving home, purchase a policy that includes evacuation in case of serious emergency.

bridge over the Río Paine, Parque Nacional Torres del Paine

Transportation

GETTING THERE

Most visitors arrive in Chile by air, via the Aeropuerto Internacional Arturo Merino Benítez (SCL). Some will arrive overland and others by ship.

Overland travel from the north can be challenging, but once you reach Argentina or Chile, it's easy enough. Argentina and Chile share numerous border crossings; in both countries' Andean Lakes Districts, trans-Andean bus service is fairly common, but many southerly crossings lack public transportation. For those choosing an aquatic route, the main option is the cruise between Punta Arenas and Ushuaia.

GETTING AROUND

Chile has several domestic airports making air travel convenient.

Buses along the principal highways are frequent, spacious, and comfortable—sometimes even luxurious. Rail service is limited and slow. If you're visiting for several months, renting or buying a vehicle is worth consideration.

Explore Chile

► THE BEST OF CHILE

For first-time visitors, the key sights are the Atacama Desert and Torres del Paine, but both mean considerable flying time on a relatively short holiday. Except for Santiago to Punta Arenas (about 3 hours, a little more with a stopover) and Easter Island (5 hours) flights are less than 2 hours.

This is usually a summer itinerary—the arid but relatively cool Atacama can be ideal at any season, but most people prefer Patagonia in summer. That said, the Paine season is lengthening and some accommodations remain open all year; there are fewer visitors in spring (when days are longer but the weather is blustery) and autumn (when days are shorter but the weather often calmer). At any time of year, though, unpredictable Patagonian weather can short-circuit even the best-planned itinerary.

At some point, the first-timer should take at least a day to visit the World Heritage Site of Valparaíso and sample the goods at one or more heartland wineries. An overnight would be better.

Day 1

Arrive at Aeropuerto Internacional Arturo Merino Benítez and transfer to a Santiago hotel. In the afternoon, visit central sites such as the Barrio Cívico, Plaza de Armas, and poet Pablo Neruda's La Chascona home.

Day 2

Take an early flight to Calama and overland transfer to San Pedro de Atacama. After an afternoon's sightseeing around town, including the Museo Arqueológico Padre Gustavo Le Paige, plan on an early evening

the Tatio geysers steam at daybreak

departure for a red-rocks sunset at Valle de la Luna. After dinner, it's off to bed for an early morning excursion to El Tatio.

Day 3

Rising early—no later than 3:30 A.M.—is essential for a sunrise arrival at the steaming Geysers del Tatio. Return in early afternoon to San Pedro; after lunch and perhaps a nap, take a shorter excursion to visit the nesting flamingos at Laguna Chaxa, including a stop at the village of Toconao.

Day 4

Plan a full-day excursion to the altiplano lakes of Laguna Miscanti and Laguna Miñiques, as well as scenic salt lakes with abundant wildlife.

Day 5

Depart early for Calama and the return flight to Santiago, then an onward flight to Punta

LINES IN THE DESERT

In the world's driest desert, the evidence of human activity weathers but is slow to disappear. The Norte Grande, in particular, is a wonderland for desert rats who want to wander through pre-Columbian archaeological sites and ghost towns that date from the nitrate era of the late 19th and early 20th centuries. Most of the archaeological sites are inconspicuous, at least compared with Peru's Machu Picchu and Bolivia's Tiwanaku, but they're abundant and almost always scenic.

OFICINA HUMBERSTONE

Alongside the Panamericana, east of **Iquique,** Humberstone is the best preserved of the hundreds of nitrate company towns that sprouted, like dormant flower seeds after an unexpected rain, in the flats of Chile's northernmost provinces. For photographers, it's a dream, and since it was named a UNESCO World Heritage Site, informational panels have made it the educational experience it always should have been. Nearby **Santa Laura** is part of the attraction.

CERROS PINTADOS

On the western edge of the **Pampa del Tamarugal,** only a short drive from Humberstone, pre-Columbian people covered more than four km of the the "Painted Hills" with more than 1,000 abstract and figurative designs – one of the world's biggest canvases – in nearly a millennium from A.D. 500. Archaeologists have restored and maintained these geoglyphs, originally made by scraping the hillsides clear and arranging loose rocks, but small-scale sulfur miners have damaged some of them.

OFICINA CHACABUCO

Like Humberstone, Chacabuco was an important nitrate company town and, like Humberstone, it's become part of Chile's historical heritage – buildings like its elaborate theater are a marvel in such an apparently inhospitable environment. What sets it apart is the fact that this was a prison camp in the Pinochet dictatorship and, unlike most Chilean historical museums even today, it doesn't refrain from telling unpleasant truths. The fenced minefield that nearly surrounds it says even more.

PUKARA DE QUITOR

On the outskirts of **San Pedro de Atacama,** Quitor is one of many fortifications suggesting that pre-Columbian times were not a festival of peace, love, and understanding. Advancing over the terraced walls, in the face of armed defenders who would have seen their opposition well in advance, would have been risky.

ruins of Oficina Santa Laura, near Humberstone, east of Iquique

Arenas. If an early-afternoon arrival permits, take a boat excursion to the Magellanic penguin colony at Isla Magdalena with accommodations at Punta Arenas; otherwise, transfer overland to Puerto Natales. It's now possible to fly directly into or Puerto Natales as well.

Day 6

If the previous night was spent in Punta Arenas, take an overland transfer to Puerto Natales, stopping over at the Otway penguin colony; after lunch in Natales, hike to the ridge of Cerro Dorotea. If the previous night was spent in Natales, schedule a full-day motor launch or catamaran excursion to Balmaceda Glacier.

Day 7

Depart early for Torres del Paine, with an afternoon hike to the Torres themselves. Stay at Hostería Las Torres, its cheaper but still comfortable refugios, or camp outdoors. An alternative is a hike to Refugio Los Cuernos, with overnight accommodations there.

Day 8

Hike from Hostería Las Torres to Paine Grande Mountain Lodge for overnight accommodations.

Day 9

Boat from Paine Grande Mountain Lodge to Lago Pehoé, followed by overland transfers to Puerto Natales and Punta Arenas. Catch an evening flight to Santiago.

Day 10

Leave midmorning for Valparaíso, by rental car or public transportation, with a stop at one or more Casablanca Valley wineries. After exploring the winding streets of Valpo's hills neighborhoods, have lunch with a harbor view.

Return to Santiago, with evening departure from Aeropuerto Internacional Arturo Merino Benítez.

▶ CHILEAN WINE COUNTRY

Chile's underrated capital of Santiago offers fine hotels and restaurants, plus a surrounding landscape where (during some seasons) it's possible to ski in the morning and surf in the afternoon. Wine-oriented visitors can almost simultaneously enjoy the port city of Valparaíso (a UNESCO World Heritage Site) and its neighboring beach resort Viña del Mar, the ski centers of Portillo and Valle Nevado, and rafting on the Río Maipo. Complex logistics make a rental car desirable, if not quite imperative, for winery visits.

Day 1

Arrive at Aeropuerto Internacional Arturo Merino Benítez and transfer to a Santiago hotel. In the afternoon, Viña Cousiño Macul is open for tours and tasting within the city limits.

Day 2

Depart midmorning for Viña Concha y Toro, Chile's largest winery, in the suburb of Pirque. After a tour and tasting, drive up the Cajón del Maipo for lunch at San Alfonso, followed by white-water rafting down the Río Maipo. Alternatively, hike to a glacier at Monumento Natural El Morado, with a late afternoon return to Santiago.

In winter, skiing at Valle Nevado can substitute for the Cajón del Maipo excursion.

Day 3

Leave in the early morning, by rental car, for

Viña Santa Cruz occupies a placid site in the Colchagua Valley, midway between the towns of Santa Cruz and Lolol.

the Aconcagua Valley. Plan on tours and tasting at Viña San Esteban (Los Andes) and/or Viña Errázuriz (San Felipe), continuing to the Pacific coast for Maitencillo's luxury Marbella Resort or other more economical accommodations. In wintertime, stay in Los Andes for a day's skiing at Portillo.

Day 4

Start a leisurely day at Maitencillo, with a midday excursion to Zapallar (take binoculars to view the Humboldt penguins at nearby Monumento Natural Isla Cachagua). A longer and more strenuous alternative could be an excursion to Parque Nacional La Campana, climbing its namesake peak for Andes-to-the-Pacific panoramas.

Day 5

Take an almost equally leisurely drive south through Viña del Mar, Chile's traditional summer vacation destination, to Valparaíso; in winter, come directly from Los Andes to Viña and Valpo. Take an afternoon to explore the historic hills and back-streets of Chile's main port, a UNESCO World Heritage Site that includes Neruda's La Sebastiana residence.

Day 6

Depart midmorning for the Casablanca Valley, southeast of Valparaíso, home to Chile's finest white wines. Lunch at a winery restaurant such as Viña Indómita or House of Morandé before a late afternoon return to Valparaíso. Alternatively, stay at Viña Matetic's secluded neocolonial guesthouse.

Day 7

Leave early for Neruda's Isla Negra home, now a museum. It's a fairly slow drive by paved back roads or a longer one by four-lane freeway to the Colchagua Valley wine district. Look for accommodations in San Fernando, the gateway to Colchagua, or Santa Cruz; if it's not too late, take the day's last tour at Viña Montes to enjoy the sunset over the valley.

Day 8

Plan on a full day for Colchagua Valley wineries, with a possible extension to the surfing capital of Pichilemu.

Day 9

Return to Santiago, with possible excursions en route to the historic mining town of

Sewell or to Viña Santa Rita, just south of Santiago.

Day 10

Sightsee for a full day in Santiago, with options such as the Museo Chileno de Arte Precolombino, including lunch at the Mercado Central or in Barrio Bellavista. Depart in the evening from Aeropuerto Internacional Arturo Merino Benítez.

▶ LAKES, PEAKS, AND FORESTS OF THE ANDES

This itinerary tours Chile's favorite vacation area, the lakes and volcanoes south of the Río Biobío. The region resembles Oregon and Washington, with glacial lakes beneath soaring volcanoes, picturesque villages like Puerto Varas, and the intensely traditional archipelago of Chiloé, the heartland of Chilean folklore.

Lago Villarrica is one of the gems of Chile's southern Lakes District, and the town of Pucón is its adventure travel capital. At the lake's east end, beneath the looming, smoldering, snowcapped Villarrica volcano, it's a blend of traditional resort and youthful energy.

All along the route, it offers a wide range of outdoor activities, including hiking, climbing, cycling, mountain biking, and white-water rafting. As in the Pacific Northwest, the weather can be changeable and you may need to be flexible to take best advantage of the finest days.

Day 1

Arrive at Aeropuerto Internacional Arturo Merino Benítez and transfer to a Santiago hotel. In the afternoon, visit central historic sites such as the Barrio Cívico, Plaza de Armas, and poet Pablo Neruda's Bellavista home, La Chascona. After enjoying Santiago's sights, take a comfortable overnight sleeper bus to the city of Temuco, or take an early morning flight.

Day 2

In Temuco, take a rental car to the Lago Villarrica town of Pucón, Chile's adventure travel capital; if you've taken the overnight bus, pick up your car downtown rather than at the airport. Spend the afternoon enjoying the views and relaxing or, alternatively, rafting the Río Trancura. For a little more peace and quiet, consider staying in the nearby town of Villarrica instead of Pucón.

Day 3

Plan an excursion to nearby Parque Nacional Huerquehue, where a steep but well-kept trail climbs from Lago Tinquilco to Lago

An Araucaria seedling sprouts on the flanks of Volcán Llaima.

Verde, a wooded alpine lake. Alternatively, take a guided day hike to the forests of the private Santuario Cañi.

Day 4

A strenuous climb will bring you to the rim of smoking Volcán Villarrica, a snow-capped peak where the sight of the active volcano and the surrounding panorama makes it all worthwhile. Sliding down the snow is much quicker than the ascent.

Day 5

Depart midmorning for the all-inclusive Termas de Puyehue, a European-style spa dating from 1908, but with up-to-date infrastructure. About an hour east of the city of Osorno, the gateway to its namesake national park, the site enjoys a mild climate all year but is near enough to high Andean hiking trails, lakes, and streams for fishing and, in winter, a ski resort. Cheaper alternative accommodations are available.

Day 6

Pack a lunch for a hike to the crater of Volcán Puyehue, a stiff four-hour climb from a small inholder farm known as El Caulle, about 15 kilometers from Termas de Puyehue. The lower part of the trail passes through dense

CHILE'S RING OF FIRE

From its Peruvian border to Patagonia, Chile is part of the Pacific "Ring of Fire" that, running 25,000 km from New Zealand through East Asia and the west coast of the Americas to Antarctica, includes some 450 volcanoes and accounts for 90 percent of the world's earthquakes. It's also given Chile some of the continent's greatest scenery and, serendipitously, an abundance of hot springs resorts. Following is a rundown of some of the most impressive.

VOLCÁN PARINACOTA AND VICINITY

It's not active, but the snow-covered cone of 6,350-meter Volcán Parinacota lends real majesty to the wildlife-rich steppes and swamps that surround it in Parque Nacional Lauca. Its slightly shorter sibling, **Pomerabe,** measuring 6,232 meters, is also dormant, but nearby Volcán Guallatire (6,071 meters) last erupted in 1960, but it's constantly smoking.

VOLCÁN LLAIMA

Chile's second most active volcano, 3,125-meter Llaima has, in the words of the Smithsonian Institution, experienced "frequent moderate explosive eruptions with occasional lava flows... since the 17th century." The latest came on New Year's Day, 2008, when its ash plume reached an altitude of about 12.5 km above sea level, and a lahar forced the closure of the northern access road to **Parque Nacional Conguillío.**

VOLCÁN VILLARRICA

Widely considered Chile's most active volcano, 2,847-meter constantly threatens the nearby resort of **Pucón,** and a lahar from its flanks nearly obliterated the town of **Coñaripe** in 1964. Nevertheless, hundreds of hikers slog through the snow to the edge of its smoldering caldera every summer (when it's too active, though, Conaf closes excursions down), and the surrounding countryside benefits from vulcanism through at dozen hot springs resorts (including the striking **Termas Geométricas,** near Coñaripe).

VOLCÁN CHAITÉN

In May 2008, Chaitén made global headlines around the world when its inconspicuous 1,122-meter dome – which had never erupted in historic times – expelled enormous clouds of ash and also flooded its namesake village, forcing an emergency evacuation and probable relocation. In the meantime, the town is open for business – at your own risk. Nearly a year later, as this book went to press, the volcano was still smokin'.

Valdivian rainforest, but at higher altitudes the volcanic landscape is utterly barren.

Day 7

At the south end of Lago Llanquihue, Puerto Varas is one of the district's most picturesque towns, and a close second to Pucón for adventure tourism. Because Puerto Varas is less than 100 kilometers from Puyehue, try a leisurely drive through Puerto Octay and the east side of the lake for a backroads perspective, with views of Volcán Osorno and a stop at the village of Ensenada.

In the afternoon, tour the streets of Puerto Varas and its historic neobaroque, neo-Gothic, and neoclassical houses, eight of which are national monuments.

Day 8

After breakfast, drive east toward Parque Nacional Vicente Pérez Rosales and its centerpiece, Lago Todos los Santos, a glacial finger lake extending more than 30 kilometers to the east. For a leisurely afternoon, take the catamaran to Peulla, which has a grand old hotel that needs an upgrade and a newer hotel that's just opened, or return to accommodations at Petrohué or Puerto Varas.

Day 9

Following breakfast, take a Class III rafting trip down the Río Petrohué and, afterward, a drive southeast toward the village of Ralún, where the Río Petrohué enters the fjord known as the Estero de Reloncaví. If time permits, continue south toward the equally scenic village of Cochamó before returning to Puerto Varas.

Day 10

The southern Lakes District's largest city is Puerto Montt, only half an hour south of Puerto Varas; its port of Angelmó has the area's largest crafts market, lining both sides of the street for several blocks, and seafood restaurants that are modest in decor but rich in fish and shellfish.

After an early lunch at Angelmó, take the highway southeast to Parque Nacional Alerce Andino, whose hiking trails lead to large groves of alerce trees, the "Chilean redwoods." Return to Puerto Varas, which has better accommodations.

Day 11

From Puerto Montt, head southeast overland and a short ferry trip to the verdant archipelago of Chiloé. This is Chile's most "traditional" area, still isolated from the continent by the Canal de Chacao, the strait that separates the largest island from the mainland. Perhaps visit the Puñihuil penguin colony near the city of Ancud, where you will spend the night.

Day 12

The city of Castro, with its landmark cathedral and stilted *palafito* houses over the water, is a brief stop before continuing to the southern Chanquín sector of Parque Nacional Chiloé, on the island's wild Pacific coast. Return to Castro for the night.

Day 13

Travel overland to Puerto Montt and catch a return flight to Santiago. Since flights to North America leave around 10 P.M., you'll have most of the day to spend sightseeing between Castro and Puerto Montt. The market village of Dalcahue is the place to load up on crafts souvenirs, especially woolens; if there's time, take the frequent short ferry crossing to the offshore island of Quinchao and drive to the scenic, typical village of Achao.

WILDLIFE ENCOUNTERS

From the Pacific to the Andes, and from the desert north and the sub-Antarctic south, Chile abounds in wildlife that, for most visitors, will be utterly novel. Following is a list of destinations for prime wildlife viewing.

PARQUE NACIONAL LAUCA

Nudging the Bolivian border, east of the city of Arica, Lauca is a UNESCO World Biosphere Reserve where populations of the endangered vicuña, whose fine wool clothed Inka royalty, have recovered spectacularly; the larger guanaco, also a relative of the domestic llama and alpaca, is also found here. Lauca's heights and wetlands also boast 130 bird species, including the majestic Andean condor and the lesser rhea.

an endangered vicuña on the Bofedal de Parinacota, Parque Nacional Lauca

PARQUE NACIONAL TORRES DEL PAINE

Its scenic horns and towers are a big attraction, but the steppes of Chile's best known national park are also home to tens of thousands of grazing guanacos, as well as flocks of rheas that sprint as fast or faster than the automobiles touring the park's roads. The condor is only the most conspicuous bird among abundant bird populations that include flamingos and Patagonian parakeets.

MONUMENTO NATURAL LOS PINGUINOS

In the Strait of Magellan near Punta Arenas, reached by ferry or rigid inflatable, Isla Magdalena is so saturated with Magellanic penguins that the surplus has started to colonize nearby Isla Marta, but cormorants, gulls, skuas, steamer ducks, and other birds nest here as well. On the 35 km ferry trip through the Strait, visitors are likely to see dolphins, black-browed albatrosses, terns, and many other birds.

PARQUE MARINO FRANCISCO COLOANE

One of Chile's first maritime reserves, this park was created to investigate the southern humpback whale's feeding grounds. Orcas, Magellanic penguins, sea lions, cormorants, and many other southern seabirds populate the 67,000-hectare park.

▶ MAGALLANES AND TIERRA DEL FUEGO

Combining the extreme south of Chile and Argentina, this itinerary devotes ten days to two weeks to such destinations as Chile's Torres del Paine, Argentina's Parque Nacional Los Glaciares, penguin reserves near the city of Punta Arenas, and "the uttermost part of the earth" near the Argentine city of Ushuaia, Tierra del Fuego.

Day 1

Arrive at Aeropuerto Internacional Arturo Merino Benítez and transfer to a Santiago hotel. In the afternoon, visit sites such as the Barrio Cívico, Plaza de Armas, and poet Pablo Neruda's La Chascona home.

Day 2

Take a morning flight to Punta Arenas. If

Cruceros Australis passengers set off on an excursion in a Zodiac.

Cuernos del Paine

monument to Magellan, Plaza Muñoz Gamero, Punta Arenas

the timing is right, catch a penguin-watching excursion to Isla Magdalena with accommodations at Punta Arenas; if not, visit the regional museum and transfer overland to Puerto Natales. It's now possible to fly directly to Puerto Natales as well.

Day 3

If the previous night was spent in Punta Arenas, take a bus or rental car to Puerto Natales, gateway to Parque Nacional Torres del Paine. If the previous night was spent in Natales, plan a full-day motor launch or catamaran excursion to Balmaceda Glacier; otherwise, hike in the afternoon to Cerro Dorotea for panoramas of Natales and Seno Última Esperanza (Last Hope Sound).

Day 4

Depart early for Torres del Paine, with an afternoon hike to the tarns beneath the Torres. Stay at Hostería Las Torres, its cheaper but still comfortable *refugios,* or a campsite. Alternatively, hike to Refugio Los Cuernos, with overnight accommodations there at Las Torres or Los Cuernos.

Day 5

Hike from Hostería Las Torres to Paine Grande Mountain Lodge for overnight accommodations.

Day 6

Boat from Paine Grande Mountain Lodge to Lago Pehoé, followed by transfer to Puerto Natales.

Days 7-8

Depart in the morning by bus or rental car for El Calafate (Argentina), gateway to Parque Nacional Los Glaciares. The next morning, leave early for the Moreno Glacier, followed by a visit to a nearby *estancia* for a barbecue before returning to El Calafate for the night.

With two or three extra days, consider a side trip to trail-rich El Chaltén, in the park's northern Fitz Roy sector, before returning to Chile.

Day 9

Return to Puerto Natales and Punta Arenas; if you couldn't do it on the way out, make a short detour to the penguin colony at Seno Otway or, preferably, the larger Isla Magdalena colony. Alternatively, catch a direct flight from El Calafate to Ushuaia, in Argentine Tierra del Fuego, and take an afternoon wildlife-watching excursion on the Beagle Channel.

Days 10-11

Catch a morning flight to Ushuaia, in Argentine Tierra del Fuego, followed by a wildlife-viewing excursion on the Beagle Channel. The next morning, plan a full-day excursion to Parque Nacional Tierra del Fuego, with multiple short hiking trails, but don't miss the Museo Marítimo de Ushuaia. If you arrived in Ushuaia on Day 9, use the extra day here for a full-day trip to Estancia Harberton, where a few gentoo penguins breed among the more numerous Magellanics.

Day 12

Fly back to Punta Arenas and on to Santiago, with the afternoon free for sightseeing and a seafood lunch at the Mercado Central, followed by an evening departure from Santiago's Aeropuerto Internacional Arturo Merino Benítez.

▶ ESCAPE TO THE SOUTH PACIFIC ISLANDS

This itinerary combines four days on Rapa Nui (Easter Island), known for its enigmatic statues, with three days on the Juan Fernández Islands, the real-life location where castaway Alexander Selkirk spent four years that would be immortalized in Daniel Defoe's *Robinson Crusoe*. The trip starts and ends in Santiago.

moai heads at Rano Raraku, Parque Nacional Rapa Nui

Day 1

After a five-hour flight from Santiago's Aeropuerto Internacional Arturo Merino Benítez, the sight of triangular Rapa Nui is nearly as welcome as it must have been to the first Polynesians who crossed the Pacific in open canoes. Stay in Hanga Roa, a sprawling, subtropical seaside village that's home to every islander and nearly all services.

On an afternoon stroll, visit the Museo Antropológico Padre Sebastián Englert and close-in archaeological sites such as Ahu Tautira and Ahu Tahai (one of the best places to catch the sunset).

Day 2

After breakfast, hire a cab to the stunning Rano Kau Crater and Orongo, a ceremonial village perched between the marshy crater's rocky edge and steep cliffs that drop vertiginously to the ocean. Return to Hanga Roa via the Sendero de Chile heritage footpath and, after lunch in town, hire a car to visit Ahu Vinapu, the obsidian quarry of Maunga Orito, and Playa Anakena (also an archaeological site).

Day 3

Circling most of the island by road, the itinerary's single busiest day passes a string of archaeological sites on the rugged south coast, including Rano Raraku Crater, where the great *moai* were carved, and the restored Ahu Tongariki; the north coast's Ahu Te Pito Kura shows the largest *moai* ever raised.

Day 4

Some *moai* got their reddish topknots at Puna Pau quarry, just east of Hanga Roa. From there, a road — more a track, really — goes north to Ahu Akivi and its seven standing *moai*, and the coastal Ahu Tepeu, then returns to Hanga Roa. The summit of Maunga Terevaka, the highest and most northerly of three volcanoes that coalesced to form Rapa Nui, is reachable by foot.

Day 5

Morning is available for souvenir shopping before an early afternoon flight back to Santiago. Given late arrival on the mainland, around 7:30 P.M., you'll probably want to go straight to the hotel, shower, and head out for dinner.

Day 6

Leave by midmorning air taxi for Isla Robinson Crusoe, a two-hour flight to an extraordinary combination of subtropical verdure and arid desolation, depending what side of the island you're on. After landing, a covered passenger launch skirts vertical volcanic cliffs to arrive at San Juan Bautista, the island's only settlement.

After settling into accommodations, a walk around the village leads to late colonial ruins, remains of an early Chilean penal colony, and a fascinating cemetery. Alternatively, hike from the airstrip to San Juan, with a stop at the Tierras Blancas fur seal colony (the boat's crew will deliver your bags to your accommodations).

Day 7

If you didn't walk from the airstrip, take a morning hike to the Mirado de Selkirk for spectacular views of both sides of the island; weather and time permitting, continue to Tierras Blancas, but note that the hike back is a long one. Alternatively, consider the strenuous hike to El Camote, through some of the best island's preserved forests.

Day 8

Ask for a box lunch before hiring an open motor launch for a full day's excursion around the island. From Cumberland Bay you'll sail toward Puerto Francés, site of

moai at Ahu Nau Nau, at Playa Anakena

a brief French encampment, and around the island's eastern cape to Islote El Verdugo, a vertical volcanic stack.

The most entertaining sights, other than the vertical cliffs, are the several colonies of Juan Fernández fur seals that bask on the rocks and frolic in the water. Before returning to San Juan, stop at Puerto Inglés, where there's a reconstruction of Selkirk's shelter.

Day 9

Because weather sometimes delays flights to and from Robinson Crusoe, it's wise to include an extra day. If things go according to schedule, though, a midafternoon arrival in Santiago allows further sightseeing explorations.

Day 10

Since northbound international flights don't leave until around 10 P.M., there's plenty of time for a full day's sightseeing. One alternative is a winery excursion followed by a drive up the Cajón del Maipo, a scenic Andean canyon barely an hour from downtown. There are two good, well-known wineries near the town of Pirque, southeast of Santiago: Viña Concha y Toro and Viña Santa Rita, both of which offer English-speaking tours and tasting.

SANTIAGO AND VICINITY

Few world capitals can match the setting of Santiago de Chile, with its Mediterranean hillsides at the base of the snow-covered Andean crest. Skiing, hiking, climbing, and whitewater rafting and kayaking opportunities are barely an hour beyond the city limits.

Since the return to constitutional government and an economic expansion, the city itself has improved dramatically. Tasteful contemporary apartments have replaced unsalvageable structures in a downtown construction boom, and both families and businesses have restored or rehabbed houses and buildings in once rundown neighborhoods such as Barrio Brasil. Barrio Bellavista has become a gastronomic and nightlife center, and international commerce flourishes in Providencia and Las Condes.

Five million people, more than a third of all Chileans, live in Gran Santiago (Greater Santiago). The locus of political and economic power, the capital has grown at the expense of the regions, but unevenly so—some *comunas* have become prosperous, others remain desperately poor.

Class-based residential segregation is still striking. There are also environmental costs, as well; more than a million automobiles sometimes clog narrow colonial streets. Along with the smokestacks of local industry, they aggravate one of the world's worst smog problems, especially in the calm autumn months of March and April.

A new transport system has mostly replaced sooty diesel buses but, unfortunately, has been less successful in moving Santiaguinos

© WAYNE BERNHARDSON

HIGHLIGHTS

Museo Chileno de Arte Precolombino: In an elegant colonial building, this museum houses an irreplaceable assortment of indigenous artifacts from throughout the Americas (page 39).

Mercado Central: North of the Plaza de Armas, this onetime colonial rubbish tip became a produce market and, more recently, a tourist draw for its *simpático* seafood eateries (page 39).

Palacio de la Moneda: Santiago's colonial presidential palace survived the 1973 headlines, and the public is welcome to stroll its passages (page 41).

Cerro Santa Lucía: In the late 19th century, visionary mayor Benjamín Vicuña Mackenna started the transformation of a barren quarry, where Pedro de Valdivia founded Santiago, into a true garden spot (page 41).

La Chascona (Museo Neruda): On a cul-de-sac in bohemian Barrio Bellavista, Nobel poet Pablo Neruda's whimsical Santiago residence is a literary pilgrimage site that delights everyone (page 51).

Viña Cousiño Macul: Though surrounded by the sprawling capital, the surviving vineyards and subterranean bodegas of this classic winery are conveniently close for tours and tasting (page 54).

Valle Nevado: Few cities around the globe can boast world-class slopes so close to a city center (page 75).

Cajón del Maipo: When the snow melts in the spring, the Río Maipo is nearly as close to downtown Santiago as the ski resorts, but its canyon has hiking, hot springs, and many other activities as well (page 77).

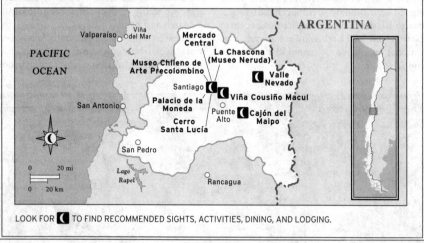

LOOK FOR (TO FIND RECOMMENDED SIGHTS, ACTIVITIES, DINING, AND LODGING.

between home and work. Still, it's one of the continent's most livable cities for its blend of cultural life, entertainment, personal security, and efficiency.

Most points of interest are in downtown Santiago, the city's colonial nucleus; the adjacent boroughs of Recoleta, Independencia, Quinta Normal, and Estación Central; and the eastern suburban boroughs of Providencia, Las Condes, and Ñuñoa.

PLANNING YOUR TIME

Presuming only two days, visitors should see the central Plaza de Armas and vicinity, including the Mercado Central and the Museo Chileno de Arte Precolombino; the Palacio de la Moneda and its new cultural center; Cerro Santa Lucía; poet Pablo Neruda's La Chascona house; and a winery or two. With an additional day or two, there's time for activities-oriented excursions such as hiking or rafting in the Cajón del Maipo, or wintertime skiing.

GEOGRAPHY AND CLIMATE

Santiago is 32 cities in one—each of its *comunas,* or boroughs, has a separate municipal government. The national government, though, controls services overlapping municipal boundaries, such as transportation.

Between the high Andes and the lower coast range, Gran Santiago sprawls from north of the Río Mapocho to south of the Río Maipo; the meandering Mapocho joins the Maipo near the town of Talagante, in the southwestern corner of the Región Metropolitana. The city sits on a southwest-sloping sedimentary plain 550 meters above sea level, but Andean outliers such as 635-meter Cerro Santa Lucía and 869-meter Cerro San Cristóbal are scattered throughout.

The Mediterranean climate includes a pronounced dry season (November–April) and wet winters (though droughts are not unusual). The daily maximum temperature averages 28°C in January, but the elevation helps keep nights cool. In July, the coolest month, the daily maximum averages 10°C.

HISTORY

Pedro de Valdivia himself founded "Santiago del Nuevo Extremo" on February 12, 1541, in a place where "The land is such that there is none better in the world for living in and settling down...because it is very flat, very healthy, and very pleasant." It had to be, since, unlike Spaniards in already densely populated Peru, Valdivia's settlers were occupying a thinly populated frontier zone.

Establishing good relations with the Araucanians, Valdivia decreed the platting of a basic grid, and his men, with indigenous help, built some simple houses. In his absence, though, the Spaniards began to abuse the indigenes, whose rebellion nearly destroyed the settlement; though rebuilt with sturdier adobes, it became a precarious armed camp. Still, the site he chose for the capital proved an enduring one, but not without problems.

One problem was the Mapocho, which often flooded with the spring runoff. Another was the Araucanian presence, which made it costly to maintain—after the initial Araucanian assault, according to historian John A. Crow, "the meager garrison of Santiago held body and soul together on a starvation diet, working, thinking, living only for the future." Between 1600 and 1606, the governing Viceroyalty of Lima had to quadruple Chile's military budget just to maintain its presence. By the late 16th century, according to Chilean historian Eduardo Solar Correa, Santiago's "appearance was sad and miserable: narrow streets, dusty in summer and impassable with mud in winter, low-lying houses of clay and adobe, whose meager and only half-finished rooms were lighted at night by a tallow candle."

The abundance of Spanish soldiers and absence of Spanish women left an evident and enduring legacy. Many Spaniards formed both fleeting and permanent unions with indigenous women, their mestizo children forming the foundation of a new society, but one in which class distinctions became critically important. Landed proprietors, successors to *encomenderos,* dominated Santiago society, though the countryside was their economic and political power base.

With the 18th century came material improvements such as a cathedral, creation of the Casa de la Moneda (colonial mint) to spur economic activity, *tajamares* (dikes) to contain the Mapocho's floods, and improved roads to the countryside and to the port of Valparaíso. Cultural life improved with establishment of the Universidad de San Felipe (founded in 1758 as a law school), later to become the Universidad de Chile.

By the time of Chile's independence, Santiago was a modest city that made mixed impressions. On her first visit to the capital, in 1822, the Englishwoman Maria Graham remarked that:

> The disposition of the houses, though pleasant enough to the inhabitants, is ugly without, and gives a mean, dull air to the streets, which are wide and well paved, having a footpath flagged with slabs of granite and porphyry; and through most of them a small stream is constantly running, which, with a little more attention from the police, might make it the cleanest city in the world: It is not very dirty; and when I recollect Rio de Janeiro and Bahia, I am ready to call it absolutely clean.

Mrs. Graham, of course, reflected the perspective of Santiago's elite and the British community, so her experience barely touches the situation of laborers and peasants (there were country estates in areas now decidedly urban) who lived beyond those enclaves. Darwin, more than a decade later, found the city equally nondescript:

> It is not so fine or so large as Buenos Ayres, but it is built after the same model.

Part of the reason for Santiago's nondescript aspect was seismic; earthquakes, which often destroyed landmark buildings, discouraged elaborate construction.

Post-independence Santiago, though, was

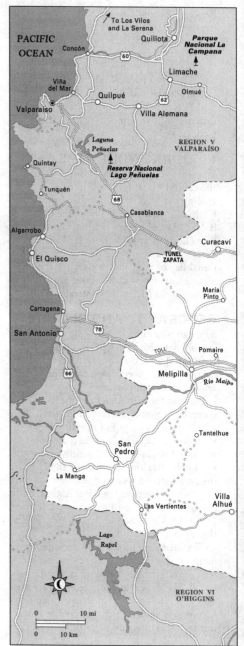

poised for a boom. The mid-19th century California gold rush opened a market for Chilean wheat, wine, and other produce; the beneficiaries were a landed elite who could build splendid city mansions, furnish them with extravagant imports, and support exclusive institutions such as the Club Hípico (Racing Club). By the 1870s, progressive mayor Benjamín Vicuña Mackenna was transforming areas such as Cerro Santa Lucía into magnificent public parks, but at a cost—displacing less fortunate residents from convenient central areas.

At the same time, the city progressed culturally, thanks largely to the efforts of Venezuelan-born scholar Andrés Bello, who turned the moribund Universidad de San Felipe into the present-day Universidad de Chile and taught many of the country's 19th-century leaders. Figures such as the exiled Argentine politician and educator Domingo Faustino Sarmiento, later his country's president, also enriched the intellectual life of a city whose midcentury population exceeded 100,000.

Conflict with Peru and Bolivia in the War of the Pacific (1879–1884) brought dramatic changes, in ways that were not immediately apparent. Chilean interests grew wealthy with control of the nitrate-rich Atacama Desert, bringing revenue to the government treasury and financing a new round of conspicuous consumption by mining magnates. At the same time, lack of land forced small farmers to the city, just as the failure of the nitrate mines in the early 1900s drove a militant labor force to the capital. For a time, industrialization absorbed the excess labor, but continued rural chaos exacerbated urban immigration and resulted in spontaneous peripheral squatter settlements known as *callampas* (mushrooms). These exploded with activism during the Unidad Popular years, but after the 1973 coup they had to bide their time as wealthy eastern suburbs such as Las Condes literally reached for the skies in high-rise apartments and office blocks.

The dictatorship's economic policies—largely intact despite nearly 20 years of

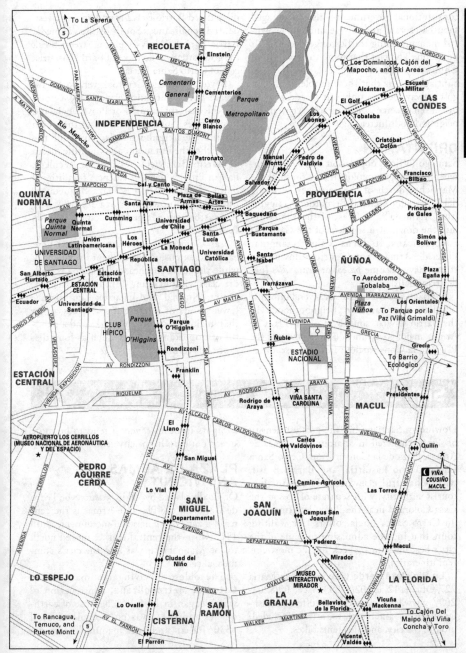

constitutional government—also encouraged suburban sprawl and private automobile ownership, aggravating traffic congestion and air pollution. The fact that more than a third of Chile's 15 million inhabitants live in Gran Santiago means that these problems are not going away, but it's only fair to add that an urban renaissance is making some central city neighborhoods increasingly livable.

ORIENTATION

Santiago (official population 4,658,687) centers on a triangular colonial core south of the Mapocho, north of the east–west Avenida del Libertador General Bernardo O'Higgins (the "Alameda"), and east of the Vía Norte Sur, the downtown segment of the Carretera Panamericana. Its focus is the rectangular Plaza de Armas. Some narrow downtown streets have become *paseos* or *peatonales* (pedestrian malls).

Santiago Centro consists of several informal but distinctive barrios or neighborhoods. In the Barrio Cívico, southwest of the Plaza de Armas, major government offices surround the Plaza de la Constitución; farther west, once-dilapidated Barrio Brasil is undergoing a residential renaissance. South of the Alameda, Barrio París Londres's winding streets break the grid pattern, as do those of Barrio Lastarria, east of Cerro Santa Lucía.

Beyond Santiago Centro, several other *comunas* have sights and services, most notably the easterly suburbs of Providencia and Las Condes. Some of these boast their own distinctive neighborhoods: north of the Mapocho, the restaurant and nightlife mecca of Barrio Bellavista lies half in Recoleta, half in Providencia. Providencia's traditional point of demarcation is Plaza Baquedano, universally known as Plaza Italia, where the eastbound Alameda becomes Avenida Providencia.

Las Condes and Vitacura are affluent eastward extensions of affluent Providencia, while the more southeasterly Ñuñoa is middle-class without being dull. Independencia, Quinta Normal, and Estación Central have fewer points of interest and services, other than major museums and parks and a handful of important services (such as long-distance bus terminals).

Sights

Downtown Santiago has the greatest density of sights, clustered in or around the Plaza de Armas, Plaza de la Constitución, Cerro Santa Lucía, Barrio Lastarria, and Barrio Brasil, with a handful elsewhere. The municipal tourist authority, with separate offices at the Casa Colorada near the Plaza de Armas and on Cerro Santa Lucía, offers free walking tours that include admission to some of the city's best museums; check for the most current itineraries.

La Bicicleta Verde (Avenida Santa María 227, Oficina 12, tel. 02/5709338, cel. 09/8202-2097, www.labicicletaverde.cl) offers English-language foot and bicycle tours (bike included) around the city, and also rents bikes.

Sights in other *comunas* tend to be more spread out than in the city center.

PLAZA DE ARMAS AND VICINITY

Originally platted by Valdivia's surveyor, Pedro de Gamboa, the Plaza de Armas is the center of a *zona típica* national monument. Until 1821, when the central market moved north to the Mapocho, it was also the city's commercial center.

The oldest surviving landmark is the **Catedral Metropolitana,** construction of which began in 1748 but, because of earthquakes and fires, was not completed until 1830. Italian architect Joaquín Toesca de-

© WAYNE BERNHARDSON

Santiago's Catedral Metropolitana is the city's main ecclesiastical landmark.

signed its neoclassical facade, since modified with late-19th-century Tuscan touches.

The next oldest structure is the **Municipalidad de Santiago** (1785). Immediately west, the **Palacio de la Real Audiencia** (1804) houses the Museo Histórico Nacional; at the corner of Paseo Puente, the Francophile **Correo Central** (Post Office, 1882) replaced the colonial government house.

Commerce monopolized the plaza's south side; after the market moved, the handsome 19th-century arcade known as the **Portal Fernández Concha** replaced it, though its current hot dog and sandwich stands make it less prestigious than it once was. Half a block east, dating from 1769, the **Casa Colorada** (Merced 860) houses the municipal tourist office and the city museum. Another block-plus east, the national monument **Iglesia de la Merced** (Merced and MacIver) dates from 1795; housing an assortment of ecclesiastical art, its adjacent **Museo de la Merced** (MacIver 341, tel. 02/6649189, www.museolamerced

.cl) is open 10 A.M.–6 P.M. Tuesday–Saturday, 10 A.M.–2 P.M. Sunday. Admission costs US$2, but is free on Sundays.

One block west of the plaza, bounded by Bandera, Catedral, Morandé, and Compañía, Chile's legislature occupied the former **Congreso de la República** until the 1973 coup. The building suffered a whole series of setbacks, however, from its inception under President Manuel Montt in the 1850s: death of an architect, shortages of funds, and a fire. Finally finished in 1876, a great part of it was again destroyed by fire in 1895; by 1901, it was rebuilt and reinaugurated in its present neoclassical style. It suffered earthquake damage in 1985, but has since had a seismic upgrade; until recently, the Foreign Ministry occupied the building.

Immediately north of the ex-Congreso, the Foreign Ministry trains both Chilean and foreign diplomats at its Academia Diplomática Andrés Bello (Diplomatic Academy, Catedral 1183) in the renaissance-style **Palacio Edwards** (1888).

One block from the plaza's southwest corner, the **Palacio de la Real Aduana** (Royal Customs House, Bandera 361) now accommodates the exceptional Museo Chileno de Arte Precolombino (Chilean Museum of Pre-Columbian Art). Immediately across the street and south of the Congreso, but facing Compañía, stand the neoclassical **Tribunales de Justicia** (Law Courts, 1912–1930). Another block west, at Compañía 1340, Chañarcillo mining tycoon Francisco Ignacio Ossa Mercado inhabited the Moorish-style **Palacio La Alhambra** (1862), which now serves as an art gallery and cultural center.

Half a block north of the plaza, on Paseo Puente, the French-style **Cuerpo de Bomberos** (completed in 1893) resembles the post office. One block north of the plaza, built of massive blocks, the **Templo de Santo Domingo** (1747–1808) stands at 21 de Mayo and Monjitas; two blocks north, on a lot once known as the "Dominicans' trash dump," stands the **Mercado Central,** the landmark central

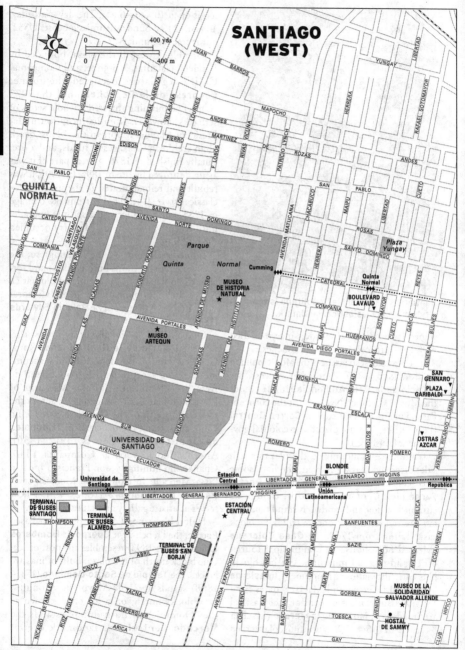

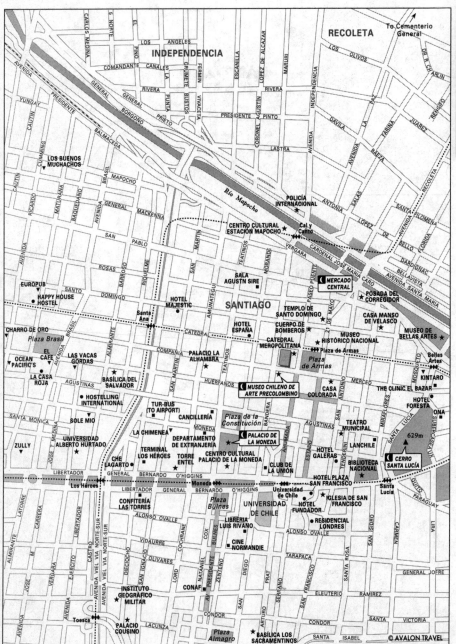

© AVALON TRAVEL

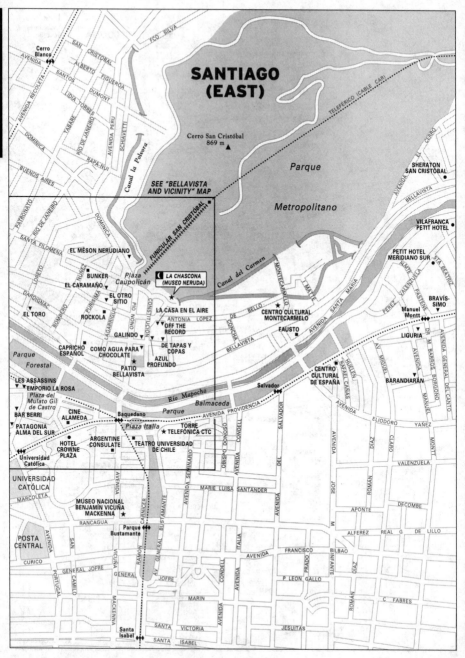

SANTIAGO (EAST)

Cerro San Cristóbal 869 m ▲

Parque

Metropolitano

TELEFERICO (CABLE CAR)

SHERATON SAN CRISTÓBAL ●

VILAFRANCA PETIT HOTEL ●

PETIT HOTEL MERIDIANO SUR ●

BRAVÍSIMO ▼

SEE "BELLAVISTA AND VICINITY" MAP

Cerro Blanco

Canal la Pehovra

FUNICULAR SAN CRISTÓBAL

EL MESON NERUDIANO ▼

Plaza Caupolicán

BUNKER ■
EL CARAMAÑO ■
NUÑEZ ■

EL OTRO SITIO ▼

ROCKOLA ▼

GALINDO ▼

CAPRICHO ESPAÑOL ■

COMO AGUA PARA CHOCOLATE ▼

PATIO BELLAVISTA ★

EL TORO ▼

LA CHASCONA (MUSEO NERUDA)

LA CASA EN EL AIRE ★
ANTONIA LOPEZ
OFF THE RECORD ▼

DE TAPAS Y COPAS ▼

AZUL PROFUNDO ★

Canal del Carmen

CENTRO CULTURAL MONTECARMELO ★

FAUSTO ★

LIGURIA ▼

Manuel Montt ●

CENTRO CULTURAL DE ESPAÑA ★

BARANDIARÁN ▼

Parque Forestal

LES ASSASSINS ▼
EMPORIO LA ROSA ▼

Plaza del Mulato Gil de Castro

BAR BERRI ●

PATAGONIA ALMA DEL SUR ▼

CINE ALAMEDA ●

Baquedano

Río Mapocho

Parque   Balmaceda

Salvador ▲

Plaza Italia

ARGENTINE CONSULATE ■

HOTEL CROWNE PLAZA ●

Universidad Católica

TORRE TELEFÓNICA CTC ★

TEATRO UNIVERSIDAD DE CHILE ★

AVENIDA PROVIDENCIA

UNIVERSIDAD CATÓLICA

MARCOLETA

MUSEO NACIONAL BENJAMÍN VICUÑA MACKENNA ★

Parque Bustamante

POSTA CENTRAL

Santa Isabel

Cerro San Luis
710 m

Canal Santo Domingo

CRISTAL DE ABELLI

HOTEL
INTERCONTINENTAL
SANTIAGO

UNITED STATES EMBASSY
AND CONSULATE

LA
VINOTECA

TAVELLI

RADISSON PLAZA
SANTIAGO HOTEL

FRAGOLA

CAFÉ MELBA

DON CARLOS

Río Mapocho

AKARANA

REYES LAVALLE

Parque de las
Esculturas

ROGER DE FLOR

HOTEL
RITZ CARLTON

HAPPENING

AV APOQUINDO

El Golf

SKY
AIRLINE

BOOMERANG

BRANNIGAN'S

AVENIDA PROVIDENCIA

Tobalaba

SEBASTIÁN

CINE TOBALABA

NAPOLEON

Los
Leones

STUDENT
FLIGHT CENTER

EL HUERTO

PÍO

HOTEL
ORLY

CALLAO

SANTIAGO PARK
PLAZA HOTEL

CORONEL

AVENIDA

LOTA

HOTEL
NERUDA

PHONE
BOX PUB

PROVIDENCIA

Pedro de
Valdivia

SERNATUR

B ERRAZURIZ

JUANA DE ARCO

AVENIDA CARMEN SILVA

TRAIGUEN

COPIHUE

CARLOS   ANTÚNEZ

LAS   HORTENSIAS

LAS HORTENSIAS

EZEQUIAS   ALLIENDE

Cristóbal
Colón

AVENIDA   ELIODORO   YAÑEZ

CASTILLO

EL   VERGEL

EL   VERGEL

SILVINA HURTADO

BIARRITZ

LAS   VIOLETAS

LA BRABANZONE

Parque Inés
de Suárez

AVENIDA   POCURO

CALIFORNIA

0   500 yds

Plaza de la
Alcaldesa

0   500 m

Plaza Pedro
de Valdivia

AVENIDA   FRANCISCO   BILBAO

MARIATEGUI

Plaza El
Bosque

BUSTOS

EDWARDS   MATTE

CARLOS WILSON

GUILLERMO   ACUÑA

ALMAGRO

© AVALON TRAVEL

market that's also a major tourist draw for its seafood restaurants.

From 1913 until 1987, trains to Valparaíso, northern Chile, and Mendoza (Argentina) used Eiffel-influenced architect Emilio Jecquier's monumental **Estación Mapocho;** closed in 1987 and reopened as a cultural center, it hosts Santiago's annual book fair and other special events. In the nearby Cal y Canto Metro station, excavations have exposed parts of the foundations of the colonial **Puente Cal y Canto** bridge over the Mapocho.

Northeast of the Templo de Santo Domingo stand two remaining colonial residences. The mid-18th-century **Posada del Corregidor** (Esmeralda 749) is an adobe with colonial features such as a corner pillar and balconies but no interior patios. Despite its name, no Spanish colonial official ever worked or lived within; for nearly a century after 1830, it went by the ironic nickname "Filarmónica" because of the dance hall that operated within its walls. At Santo Domingo and MacIver stands the **Casa Manso de Velasco** (1730), named for José

Manso de Velasco, governor of Chile (1737–1744) and later viceroy of Peru.

Museo Histórico Nacional (Palacio de la Real Audiencia)

After 1609, the Real Audiencia housed Chile's colonial supreme court, but earthquakes destroyed its quarters in both 1647 and 1730. Architect Juan José de Goycolea y Zañartu designed the current neoclassical building (1808), but its clock tower dates from Mayor Benjamín Vicuña Mackenna's late-19th-century term.

Three years later, during the independence struggle, the first Congreso Nacional met here, but royalists restored the Real Audiencia from 1814 to 1817. That same year, the Cabildo of Santiago met here to make Argentine general José de San Martín head of state, but San Martín declined in favor of Bernardo O'Higgins. After President Manuel Bulnes moved government offices to the Casa de la Moneda, the building became municipal offices and then a museum.

Following a professional makeover, this

In the Estación Mapocho cultural center, November's Feria del Libro attracts authors and book dealers from throughout Latin America and the world.

once moribund museum (Plaza de Armas 951, tel. 02/4117000, www.dibam.cl/historico_nacional) now deserves a visit. Thematically, its collections encompass Mapuche silverwork, colonial and republican furniture and art, material folklore, textiles, weapons, and photography. Chronologically, it traces Chile's development from indigenous times through Spanish colonial rule, the subsequent establishment of church and state, collapse of the Spanish empire, the early republic and its 19th-century expansion, the oligarchy that ruled parliament, and the failed reforms that resulted in the 1973 coup—when the story abruptly ends.

Also hosting special exhibits, the museum is open 10 A.M.–5:30 P.M. daily except Monday; admission costs US$1.20 except Sunday, when it's free.

Museo de Santiago

Perhaps Santiago's best-preserved colonial house, the Casa Colorada was home to Mateo de Toro y Zambrano, who became Chile's interim governor, at age 83, after the colonial governor resigned. Named for its reddish paint, it hosted both José de San Martín and Bernardo O'Higgins after the battle of Chacabuco (1817), and the famous mercenary Lord Cochrane later lived here. Abandoned for many years, it underwent restoration after 1977.

Only the two-story facade facing Merced, with its forged iron balconies, is truly original. The museum itself chronicles the city's development from the pre-Columbian past through its founding by Valdivia, the evolution of colonial society, the independence era, and its transformation under 19th-century mayor Benjamín Vicuña Mackenna. The history is particularly vivid in the models of historic buildings and dioramas of events such as the 1863 fire that destroyed the Iglesia de la Compañía.

The Museo de Santiago (Merced 860, tel. 02/6330723) is open 10 A.M.–5:45 P.M. weekdays except Monday, 10 A.M.–4:45 P.M. Saturday, and 11 A.M.–2 P.M. Sundays and holidays. Admission costs US$0.85.

◖ Museo Chileno de Arte Precolombino

The late architect Sergio Larraín García-Moreno donated a lifetime's supply of acquisitions to stock this exceptional museum in the late colonial Real Casa de Aduana (Royal Customs House, 1805). Following independence, the neoclassical building became the Biblioteca Nacional (National Library) and then the Tribunales de Justicia (Law Courts) until a 1968 fire destroyed most of its interior and archives. Flanked by twin patios, a broad staircase leads to the upstairs exhibits.

The permanent collections from Mesoamerica and the central and southern Andes are impressive; there are smaller displays on the Caribbean, the Amazon, and Andean textiles. Particularly notable are the carved wooden *chemamull,* larger-than-life-size Mapuche funerary statues. The museum also possesses Aguateca's Stele 6, from a Late Classic Maya site in Guatemala's Petén lowlands that's suffered severe depredations from looters.

The Museo Chileno de Arte Precolombino (Bandera 361, tel. 02/6887348, www.precolombino.cl) is open 10 A.M.–6 P.M. daily except Monday; it closes during Semana Santa (Holy Week) and on May 1, September 18, Christmas, and New Year's Eve. Admission costs US$6 but is free for students and children.

◖ Mercado Central

In 1817, Bernardo O'Higgins himself shifted the disorderly market on the Plaza de Armas to an area once known as "the Dominican garbage dump" on the Mapocho's south bank, a few blocks north. When fire destroyed the informal installations on the new Plaza de Abasto in 1864, municipal authorities hired Manuel Aldunate to create more permanent facilities, but the current structure (1872) is mainly the work of Fermín Vivaceta.

Streetside storefronts have concealed the original facade except on the Ismael Valdés Vergara side, where it faces the river and opens onto a new plaza; there are entrances, however, on San Pablo, Paseo Puente, and 21 de Mayo. From the interior, the wrought-iron

© WAYNE BERNHARDSON

The Mercado Central features some of the world's most diverse fish and shellfish.

superstructure, embellished with the Chilean flag's recurring lone star, provides an airy setting for merchants to display their fresh fruit, vegetables, and seafood—according to journalist Robb Walsh, "a display of fishes and shellfish so vast and unfamiliar that I felt I was observing the marine life of another planet."

Lunching and people-watching at tables set among the produce is a popular pastime for foreigners and tourists alike. The smallish restaurants on the periphery are cheaper and nearly as good as the two or three that monopolize the prime central sites.

BARRIO CÍVICO AND VICINITY

Straddling the Alameda, southwest of the Plaza de Armas, the Barrio Cívico is Chile's political and administrative center. Facing the **Plaza de la Constitución,** the late-colonial **Palacio de La Moneda** is the locus of presidential authority. At 10 A.M. on even-numbered days, there's a presidential changing-of-the-guard ceremony here.

In a development that infuriated Pinochet diehards, a dignified statue of former president Salvador Allende overlooks the plaza's southeast corner, with a plaque inscribed with words from his last radio address: "I have faith in Chile and her destiny," September 11, 1973.

On the west side of the plaza, at Teatinos 120, the sturdily elegant doors of the **Ministerio de Hacienda** (1933) seemingly signify the solidity of the Chilean treasury; immediately to its north, the former Hotel Carrera now houses the **Cancillería** (Foreign Ministry). **Codelco,** arguably the government's single most influential agency for its control of the copper industry, has its headquarters at Paseo Huérfanos 1276.

At Moneda and Morandé, the **Intendencia de Santiago** (1914–1916) features a spectacular cupola. Today, ironically enough, it houses regional government offices in a building that once headquartered *El Diario Ilustrado,* a newspaper founded by the Partido Conservador (Conservative Party)—and a persistent critic of various administrations to occupy the Moneda.

One block east of the plaza, Augustine nuns owned the entire block bounded by Bandera, Ahumada, Moneda, and Alameda until the early 20th century, when they subdivided some of Santiago's most valuable real estate, keeping only the mid-19th-century **Iglesia de las Agustinas** (restored in 1994). Mammon supplanted Jehovah with French architect Emilio Jecquier's flatiron **Bolsa de Comercio** (La Bolsa 84), begun in 1914 but delayed when World War I disrupted the arrival of materials from New York. Immediately south, reached by a cobbled Y-patterned passageway but fronting on the Alameda, the members-only **Club de la Unión** (1925) gave stockbrokers a place to schmooze on their lunch hours.

Immediately south of the Moneda, a new cultural center lies beneath the fountains of the **Plaza de la Ciudadanía** (Citizens' Plaza), dedicated by outgoing president Ricardo Lagos in 2006. Across the Alameda, General Pinochet had once placed the sepulchre of Chilean liberator General Bernardo O'Higgins beneath an eternal natural gas flame at the so-called "Altar de la Patria" at **Plaza Bulnes,** where Lagos opened a new mausoleum to reclaim O'Higgins's legacy from the dictatorship. One block west, dating from 1976, the 128-meter **Torre Entel** communications tower (Alameda and Amunátegui) resembles London's Post Office Tower.

◖ Palacio de la Moneda

Never intended as the seat of government, the neoclassical Moneda became the presidential palace in 1846, when Manuel Bulnes moved his residence and offices to the former colonial mint. It made global headlines in 1973, when the Chilean air force strafed and bombed it in General Pinochet's coup against President Salvador Allende, who shot himself to death before he could be taken prisoner.

Around 1730, during a deep economic depression, the Cabildo de Santiago requested the Spanish crown to establish a local mint, but it took another half century for Governor Agustín Jáuregui to propose a purpose-built building under the direction of Italian architect Joaquín Toesca. Construction began in 1784; its cement came from Hacienda Polpaico (north of Santiago, still a functioning factory today), sand came from the Río Maipo, colored stone came from a San Cristóbal quarry, and oak and cypress came from Chile's own Valdivian forests. Details such as forged iron came from Spain. Toesca died six years before the building's completion in 1805.

Pinochet's regime restored the building to Toesca's original design by 1981, but it's no longer the presidential residence. Shortly after taking office in 2000, President Ricardo Lagos (the first Socialist elected since Allende) opened the main passageway for one-way public traffic from the Plaza de la Constitución entrance to the Plaza de la Ciudadanía exit, accessible 10 A.M.–6 P.M. weekdays only. The new plantings that have replaced the withered orange trees on its interior Patio de los Naranjos will take a while to mature, but walk-through visitors can still enjoy sculptures such as Roberto

Matta's *El Toromiro* (named for a tree now extinct on its native Easter Island).

For a more thorough guided tour, contact the Dirección Administrativa del Palacio de La Moneda (Morandé 130, tel. 02/6714103, visitas@presidencia.cl) at its office beneath Plaza de la Constitución. Normally, arranging a visit takes a couple of days with a written or emailed request.

The Moneda's most impressive addition, new in 2006, is the subterranean **Centro Cultural Palacio La Moneda;** between the palace and the Alameda, beneath the lawns and reflecting pools of the Plaza de la Ciudadanía, broad pedestrian ramps descend to a luminous subterranean facility with a gigantic atrium flanked by special exhibit galleries and other facilities.

◖ CERRO SANTA LUCÍA

East of Paseo Ahumada and north of the Alameda, the promontory called Welén by the Mapuche was where Pedro de Valdivia held out against the indigenous forces that threatened to expel the Spaniards from the Mapocho Valley. Nearly three centuries later, in 1822, Scotswoman María Graham marveled at the view:

From Santa Lucía we discovered the whole plain of Santiago to the Cuesta de Prado, the plain of Maypu stretching even to the horizon, the snowy Cordillera, and beneath our feet the city, its garden, churches, and its magnificent bridge all lit up by the rays of the setting sun...what pen or pencil can impart a thousandth part of the sublime beauty of sunset on the Andes?

In the winter of 1834, Darwin seconded Mrs. Graham's opinion in a more matter-of-fact manner:

It is an inexhaustible source of pleasure to climb Cerro Santa Lucía, a small hill that rises up in the center of the city, from which the view is truly impressive and unique.

It took Benjamín Vicuña Mackenna to realize Santa Lucía's potential, as his efforts transformed a barren quarry into an urban Eden with more than 60 hectares of gardens, fountains, and statuary. His own tomb is the **Capilla La Ermita,** a tiny chapel just beneath the summit.

From the summit, approached by meandering footpaths and reached by a steep climb to a tiny parapet, there are stupendous Andean views—at least on a rare clear day—and panoramas of the city and Cerro San Cristóbal. A lower but broader terrace offers less panoramic but almost equally impressive views toward Providencia and the Andes.

Royalists built **Fuerte Hidalgo** (1816) toward the park's north end to defend against Chilean revolutionaries. On its lower northeastern slope, the **Jardín Japonés** (Japanese Garden) is a recent addition; along the Alameda, look for the inscription of Pedro de Valdivia's letter to the king and the tile mural of Nobel Prize–winning poet Gabriela Mistral.

Fenced except around its lowest periphery and steepest slope, Santa Lucía has two main entrances: from the Alameda just east of Plaza Vicuña Mackenna, where twin staircases climb around the fountains of **Plaza Neptuno,** and by a cobbled road from the east end of Agustinas. There's also a modern glass elevator, at the east end of Huérfanos, that's often shut for lack of personnel (authorities apparently do not trust the citizenry to press buttons on their own). In an exaggerated attempt to improve security, they now require all visitors to sign in (as if muggers would do so), but the park is not dangerous.

Hours are 9 A.M.–8 P.M. daily, but the best introduction is a guided tour (English and Spanish) starting from its municipal tourist-office branch at 11 A.M. Thursday. Tours include Vicuña Mackenna's tomb and the still-functioning gun emplacement (neighbors' complaints once halted the customary midday cannon shot, but broader public pressure restored the tradition at a lower decibel level).

Between Santa Lucía and Paseo Ahumada lie several landmarks of mostly republican vintage. The most imposing is the classicist **Biblioteca Nacional** (National Library, 1914–1927) on the Alameda between MacIver and Miraflores, which also houses the **Archivo Nacional** (National Archive). Two blocks north, the neoclassical **Teatro Municipal** (Municipal Theater, 1857) has survived fires and earthquakes with most of its original features intact. High-culture figures who have performed here include Sarah Bernhardt, Igor Stravinsky, Plácido Domingo, Anna Pavlova, and Chilean classical pianist Claudio Arrau.

One block west, dating from 1784, the once baroque **Templo de San Agustín** (Agustinas and Estado) fell on hard times during the early republican years, when its convent was even used as military barracks. In 1863 architect Fermín Vivaceta salvaged it and applied a more contemporary facade, which survives to the present.

BARRIO PARÍS LONDRES AND VICINITY

South of the Alameda, dating from 1618, the major landmark is the **Iglesia y Convento de San Francisco** (Alameda 834), Chile's oldest colonial building. A survivor of repeated fires and earthquakes, the former convent is also home to an ecclesiastical colonial art collection.

Until the early 1920s, the Franciscans controlled much of this area, but a financial crisis forced them to sell 30,000 square meters to developer Walter Lihn. Lihn demolished several buildings and patios, and their gardens, but architects Roberto Araya and Ernesto Holzmann created an intimately livable neighborhood of meandering cobbled streets in their place.

Betraying the neighborhood's legacy, the house at **Londres 40** was a torture center during Pinochet's reign of terror. Two blocks west of Iglesia San Francisco, the **Casa Central de la Universidad de Chile** (1863–1872), the state university's main campus, stretches along the Alameda. Several blocks south, Ricardo Larraín Bravo designed the **Basílica Los Sacramentinos** (Arturo Prat 471) after Paris's Eglise de Sacre Coeur. The 1985 earthquake caused damage that still awaits repair.

Iglesia y Convento de San Francisco

Pedro de Valdivia himself established the Ermita del Socorro to house an image of the Virgen del Socorro—to which he credited Santiago's survival from Mapuche attacks—that he had brought to Chile. In 1554, in exchange for 12 city lots, the Franciscan order built a church to house the image, but a quake destroyed the original structure in 1583. After finishing the present church in 1618, they built a pair of cloisters and gradually added patios, gardens, a refectory, and other structures. Earthquakes toppled the original towers in 1643 and 1751, but Vivaceta's 19th-century clock tower has withstood every shock since. The interior is notable for its Mudéjar details and carved cypress doors.

Over four and a half centuries, the Franciscans have kept faith with Valdivia by continuing to host the Virgen del Socorro. In addition, their **Museo de Arte Colonial** boasts 42 separate canvases, representing the life of St. Francis of Assisi, from the late 17th-century Cuzco school. A later wall-sized painting chronicles the Franciscans' lineage and their patrons.

The Museo de Arte Colonial (Londres 4, tel. 02/6398737, www.museosanfrancisco.cl) is open 9 A.M.–1:30 P.M. and 3–5 P.M. Tues.–Sat., 10 A.M.–2 P.M. Sun., but it's closed January 1, May 1, Good Friday, September 11, 18, and 19, and Christmas. Admission costs US$2 for adults, US$1 for children.

BARRIO LASTARRIA AND VICINITY

East of Cerro Santa Lucía, between Parque Forestal and the Alameda, Barrio Lastarria is a neighborhood of narrow streets and cul-de-sacs that's home to several intimate restaurants and bars.

The barrio's main axis is its namesake street, José Victorino Lastarria, which is a pedestrian mall between Rosal and Merced. Its **Plaza del Mulato Gil de Castro** is an adaptive reuse uniting several early-20th-century buildings into a commercial/cultural cluster with two notable museums: the **Museo Arqueológico de Santiago** and the eye-catching **Museo de Artes Visuales.**

One long block east, originally built for a nitrate baron between 1916 and 1921, the Italian renaissance **Palacio Bruna** (Merced and Estados Unidos) soon became the U.S. ambassador's residence; it later served as the consulate, until the new embassy was built in Las Condes.

To the north, the Mapocho's banks and floodplain were home to slums and rubbish dumps until the early 20th century, when Mayor Enrique Cousiño turned it into the **Parque Forestal,** stretching from Estación Mapocho on the west to the Pío Nono Bridge on the east. Shaded with mature trees and dotted with statues and fountains, it's a verdant refuge from the midday heat.

Toward the west, directly north of Cerro Santa Lucía, the **Palacio de Bellas Artes** is the city's traditional fine arts museum. South of the Plaza del Mulato Gil, dating from 1858, the neoclassical **Iglesia de la Vera Cruz** (Lastarria 124) is a national monument designed by French architect Brunet des Baines.

On the Alameda's north side, east of Lastarria proper is the **Edificio Diego Portales** (1972), which became the dictatorship's seat of government after the air force's bombing and strafing left La Moneda unusable for eight years. A March 2006 fire destroyed part of this building. Because of its association with the dictatorship, there's pressure to permanently relocate its defense ministry offices and turn the site into a contemporary art museum. Just across the Alameda is the central campus of the **Universidad Católica** (1913).

Museo de Artes Visuales

With a permanent collection of 1,400 pieces by 400 contemporary Chilean artists, among them Roberto Matta and Alfredo Jaar, Santiago's visual-arts museum, in the Plaza del Mulato Gil complex, opened in early 2001. About 140 of these pieces, ranging from engravings to paintings, photographs, and sculptures, are on display at any one time.

Architect Cristián Undurraga's design incorporates 1,400 square meters of display space. Flawless lighting accentuates each piece's individual qualities in the museum's half dozen spacious galleries, which feature high ceilings and polished wooden floors. The English translations are better than at some Chilean museums, but a reliance on cognates makes some of them a bit vague.

Privately owned and financed, the Museo de Artes Visuales (Lastarria 307, tel. 02/6649397, www.mavi.cl) is open 10:30 A.M.–6:30 P.M. daily except Monday; it's also closed January 1, September 17 and 18, and December 25. Admission costs US$2 for adults, US$0.50 for children 8–12, but is free Sunday.

The MAVI now subsumes the **Museo Arqueológico de Santiago** (Lastarria 321, tel. 02/6383502). With excellent but stagnant exhibits on Chile's indigenous peoples from pre-Columbian times to the present, Santiago's archaeological museum ("ethnohistorical" might be more accurate) is worthwhile for an introductory visit, but repeat visits are unlikely to reveal new material.

Palacio de Bellas Artes

Built for Chile's centennial and fashioned after Paris's Petit Palais, Santiago's neoclassical fine-arts museum is the pride of Parque Forestal. Collections range from colonial and religious art to nearly contemporary figurative and abstract works by artists like the late Roberto Matta. It also has a sample of French, Italian, and Dutch painting, and prestigious special exhibits. While Bellas Artes is a traditional museum, its ambitious website is making the works of 2,000 Chilean artists accessible to the world in a "museum without walls."

The Museo de Bellas Artes (José Miguel de La Barra s/n, tel. 02/6330655, www.mnba.cl) is open 10 A.M.–6:50 P.M. daily except Monday. It's also closed January 1, Good Friday, May 1, September 18, November 1, and December 25. Admission costs US$1.20; the children's rate is US$0.60.

BARRIO BRASIL AND VICINITY

West of the Vía Norte Sur, Barrio Brasil was a prestigious early-20th-century residential area that fell upon hard times but has recently rebounded without losing its character. The best way to approach the barrio is the Huérfanos pedestrian suspension bridge that crosses the Vía Norte Sur to an area where recently constituted private universities have rehabbed buildings, salvaged libraries, built collections, and introduced a youthful vigor. It's also good for moderately priced accommodations and food.

The barrio's focus is its lovingly landscaped namesake, **Plaza Brasil.** Dating from 1892, its most impressive landmark may be the neo-Gothic **Basílica del Salvador** (Huérfanos 1781), if only because it's still standing after the 1985 earthquake. Dating from 1926, the most idiosyncratic building is the German Gothic **Universidad Albert Hurtado** (Cienfuegos 41), whose grinning gargoyles and smiling skulls, jutting out from its facade, always attract attention.

On Santiago Centro's western edge, beyond Barrio Brasil proper, wooded **Parque Quinta Normal** offers relief from a densely built area and is home to several museums.

Basílica del Salvador

After the Jesuit Iglesia de la Compañía burned to the ground in 1863, Archbishop Rafael Valdivieso decreed what became one of Santiago's longest ongoing construction projects: It took seven years to lay the cornerstone, three more to start building in earnest, and 19 more until its formal inauguration in 1892. Now a national monument, the massive church has the potential to hold 5,000 worshippers in an area 89 meters long, 37 meters wide, and 30 meters high.

Elevated to *basílica* status in 1938, the neo-Gothic structure also contains murals by Aristódemo Lattanza Borghini, bronzes by Virginio Arias, and altars and altarpieces by Onofre Jarpa. Large sections of it tumbled in the 7.8 earthquake of March 1985, though, and reinforced concrete columns have replaced some finely decorated originals. Rigid metal buttresses support some exterior walls as well, and restoration will be a long and expensive process. Its main entrance is at Huérfanos 1781.

Parque Quinta Normal

At the western edge of Santiago Centro, Parque Quinta Normal is a traditional open space whose 40 hectares constituted the city's first de facto botanical garden. It also provides playgrounds, soccer fields, tennis courts, skating rinks, and pools, and a cluster of museums.

The most notable museum is the **Museo Nacional de Historia Natural** (Natural History Museum), a research facility with public exhibits on archaeology, ethnography, physical anthropology, mineralogy, paleontology, botany, and zoology. Dating from 1830, when the government contracted French naturalist Claude Gay to inventory Chile's natural resources, the Museo de Historia Natural (tel. 02/6804615, www.mnhn.cl) is open 10 A.M.–5:30 P.M. Tuesday–Saturday, 11 A.M.–6:30 P.M. Sunday. Admission costs US$1.20 for adults, US$0.60 for kids, but is free Sundays and holidays except January 1, Easter Sunday, May 1, September 18–19, November 1, and December 25, when it's closed.

A private concessionaire operates three additional museums. The interactive **Museo de Ciencia y Tecnología** (Mucytec, tel. 02/6816022, www.corpdicyt.cl) is open 10 A.M.–6 P.M. Tuesday–Friday and 11 A.M.–6 P.M. weekends and holidays. Admission costs US$1 for adults, slightly less for children.

Trainspotters will enjoy the **Museo Parque Ferroviario** (tel. 02/6814627), with more than a baker's dozen of antique locomotives, additional railcars, and an audiovisual salon. It's open 10 A.M.–6 P.M. Tuesday–Friday all year; 11 A.M.–6 P.M. weekends and holidays. Admission costs US$1.60 for adults, US$1.30 for children.

© WAYNE BERNHARDSON

The handsome Museo Nacional de Historia Natural occupies a site within Parque Quinta Normal.

The **Museo Infantil** (tel. 02/6818808) is more oriented toward groups of school-children and requires reservations. It's open 9 A.M.–5:30 P.M. weekdays only; admission costs US$1.30.

The main entrance to the park, which now has its own Metro station, is on Matucana at the west end of Compañía, with other gateways on Avenida Portales, Santo Domingo, and Apóstol Santiago. Grounds are open 8 A.M.–8:30 P.M. daily except Monday.

Museo de la Solidaridad Salvador Allende

Many of the works in this contemporary-art museum—created in 1971 with donations by artists who identified with Chile's Marxist experiment—spent 17 years of military dicta-torship in anonymous storage. Among those represented are Roberto Matta, Joan Miró, David Alfaro Siqueiros, and Alexander Calder; despite the artists' leftist sympathies, few of those works are explicitly political.

Since the return to constitutional gov-ernment, the museum (República 475, tel. 02/6817542, www.museodelasolidaridad .cl) moved several times but it's finally settled into permanent quarters in what was once the Spanish Embassy and later, ironically enough, belonged to Pinochet's DINA secret police. Hours are 10 A.M.–6 P.M. daily except Monday; admission costs US$1 but is free Sundays. It closes on major holidays.

OTHER SANTIAGO CENTRO SIGHTS

While most downtown sights are fairly central, a handful are scattered elsewhere.

Palacio Cousiño

South of the Alameda, 19th-century Calle Dieciocho was an area of pseudo-Parisian man-sions long before the oligarchy moved to the eastern suburbs. One of its keystone families was the Cousiños, Portuguese immigrants who made fortunes in wine and mining.

Funds for the Palacio Cousiño (1878) came from the estate of art collector Luis Cousiño,

who inherited his father's mining fortune (Luis Cousiño died young, in 1873, but his widow Isidora Goyenechea continued construction). Architect Paul Lauthoud, also responsible for the Museo Nacional de Historia Natural, de-signed the three-story house with marble stair-cases, a music hall, a winter garden, and even a one-person elevator (the country's first).

Decorative touches included baroque cab-inets made for Russian czar Nicholas II and freestanding Ming vases. Spanish landscape architect Miguel Arana Bórica fashioned ex-tensive formal gardens, but urban growth has steamrolled most of them. The palace re-mained in family hands until 1941, when the city bought it to use as a museum and as a guesthouse for high-profile visitors such as Charles DeGaulle, Marshal Tito, and Golda Meir. A 1968 fire, which destroyed the 3rd-floor interior, kept England's Queen Elizabeth II from spending the night.

The Palacio Cousiño (Dieciocho 438, tel. 02/6985063, www.palaciocousino.co.cl) is open 9:30 A.M.–1:30 P.M. daily and 2:30–5 P.M. weekdays only. Admission, including guided tours in Spanish or English, costs US$3.50 for adults, US$1.30 for children. Photographers and videographers may shoot the gardens and exterior, but not the interior.

Parque O'Higgins

As Mayor Benjamín Vicuña Mackenna used political influence to transform Cerro Santa Lucía into a city park, Luis Cousiño used pri-vate resources to turn barren southwestern Santiago into a pastoral showcase—but at a price. Today's Parque O'Higgins had its origins as La Pampilla, an area of truck gardens and military parade ground where, in mid-Septem-ber, Chileans of all social classes gathered to celebrate their patriotic holidays.

Cousiño admired Europe's great public parks and, after acquiring 90-plus hectares in 1870, proposed donating it to the city. He hired Spanish landscaper Miguel Arana Bórica to make the wasteland an urban woodland, but Cousiño died in 1873, well before its comple-tion. When the 80 Chilean laborers hired for the project went to war in the north, 140 Peruvian POWs took their places.

Vicuña Mackenna named the final product after its late benefactor, but the improvements created an unspoken social segregation in a place that once belonged to all Chileans. It reached its peak around Chile's 1910 centennial, when the procession of elegant horse-drawn carriages led one observer to remark that:

> Not in London's Hyde Park, New York's Central Park, nor Buenos Aires's Palermo would you find better presented teams than those that parade through Parque Cousiño.

The park's development stimulated construction of graceful mansions in what became a garden barrio, but the automobile's arrival sparked an eastward movement into the open spaces of Providencia and Ñuñoa before and after World War II. As the elite moved out, the area declined economically, but the park was once again accessible to working-class Chileans.

In the early 1970s, the park's name was changed in favor of Chile's independence hero, it was fenced, and new developments devoured its green spaces—from its original 91.7 hectares, the park has shrunk to 76.7. Parts are still rundown, but it remains a favorite weekend outing for families who can't escape the capital.

Recalling the days of La Pampilla, but dating from the 1970s, **El Pueblito** re-creates a (stereotyped) vision of 19th-century agrarian Chile, as do the menus at its inexpensive *picadas*. It also holds the folkloric **Museo del Huaso** (tel. 02/5550054), paying homage to Chile's traditional horsemen, open 10 A.M.–noon and 1–5 P.M. weekdays, 10 A.M.–2 P.M. weekends. Admission is free.

Also on the park grounds, the children's theme park **Fantasilandia** (tel. 02/4768600, www.fantasilandia.cl) opens noon–9 P.M. daily in summer, during winter holidays, and for September's patriotic holidays. The rest of the year, hours are noon–7 P.M. weekends and holidays only except from mid-November to

Christmas, when it's closed. General admission, including unlimited rides, is US$13 per person; children shorter than 140 centimeters pay US$8 and those shorter than 90 centimeters get in free (as do conspicuously pregnant women).

Just west of the Vía Norte Sur, Parque O'Higgins is a short walk from its namesake Metro station, on Línea 2.

Club Hípico

Immediately west of Parque O'Higgins, the more exclusive of Santiago's two major racetracks dates from 1870, when it marked a major social change—discarding the Chilean custom of linear racing, riders now ran their mounts around an oval track. Like an outing in Parque Cousiño, horse racing became an elite privilege rather than a peasant pastime.

Today much of that has changed—the windows accept bets from anyone with cash to place them—but the elegance of architect Josué Smith Solar's Francophile design, based upon the Bois de Boulogne's Longchamps track, has survived. An 1892 fire destroyed the original club and grandstands, but Smith's replacement (1918), surrounded by Guillermo Renée's French baroque gardens, accentuated the views across the track to the Andean front range.

Races at the Club Hípico (Av. Blanco Encalada 2540, tel. 02/6939600, www .clubhipico.cl) usually take place Sunday, Monday and Friday, but check the website to be certain. It's within walking distance from the Unión Latinoamericana and República Metro stations.

ESTACIÓN CENTRAL

West of Santiago Centro, Estación Central is partly residential and partly industrial, most notable as a transit point because the city's train and bus stations are here. The *comuna* takes its name from the 1897 **Estación Central** (Alameda 3322), a train station built in Paris on a design by Gustave Eiffel. Shipped in pieces across the Atlantic, it was first proposed in 1885 by then-senator Benjamín Vicuña Mackenna.

© WAYNE BERNHARDSON

Parisian Gustave Eiffel designed the Estación Central, Santiago's only surviving train station.

Immediately across from the station, the **Planetario de la Universidad de Santiago** (Alameda 3349, tel. 02/7182900, www .planetariochile.cl) is part of the Universidad de Santiago campus. While light-polluted Santiago is not an ideal place to view the night skies, the audiovisuals here can simulate the astronomical sophistication in the Norte Chico and Norte Grande. These take place at 11:30 A.M., and 3 and 4:30 P.M. weekends, but in summer there are also weekday events; the cost is about US$4.50 for adults, US$3.30 for children ages 3–10.

Directly across from Parque Quinta Normal, the **Museo Artequín** (Av. Portales 3530, tel. 02/6825367, www.artequin.cl) is an interactive art museum dealing exclusively in reproductions of (mostly) European art; the building itself, built for the 1889 Paris Exhibition, then dismantled and shipped across the Pacific to be erected here, is more interesting than the family-oriented exhibits themselves. It's open 9 A.M.–5 P.M. Tuesday–Friday, 11 A.M.–6 P.M. weekends and holidays except in February, when it's closed; it's also closed January 1, May

1, and December 25. Admission costs US$1.60 for adults, US$1 for kids.

PROVIDENCIA AND VICINITY

At the east end of the Alameda, lively **Plaza Italia** (formally known as Plaza Baquedano) marks the boundary of the *comuna* of Providencia, the westernmost of the affluent eastern suburbs that also include Las Condes, Vitacura, and Ñuñoa. While mostly staid and middle- to upper-middle-class, it also has Bohemian enclaves like Barrio Bellavista (Santiago's main restaurant and nightlife area) and bar-hopper zones like Avenida Suecia. Except in compact Bellavista, points of interest are more spread out than in Santiago Centro.

From Plaza Italia, the northbound Puente Pío Nono (Pío Nono Bridge) crosses the Mapocho to **Barrio Bellavista.** The most conspicuous landmark is the 31-story **Torre Telefónica CTC** (Av. Providencia 111), the company headquarters in the form of a 140-meter cell phone! While the company's architectural aesthetic may be questionable, its **Sala de Arte Telefónica** (tel. 02/6812873) is open

10 A.M.–8 P.M. daily with rotating exhibits of Chilean and foreign artists. Admission is free.

South of Plaza Italia, Avenida Vicuña Mackenna separates the *comunas* of Santiago Centro, on the one hand, and Providencia and Ñuñoa, on the other. On the Providencia side, the **Museo Nacional Benjamín Vicuña Mackenna** (Av. Vicuña Mackenna 94, tel. 02/2229642) honors the mayor, historian, journalist, and diplomat responsible for the capital's 1870s modernization. Hours are 9:30 A.M.–1 P.M. and 2–5:50 P.M. daily except Sunday; admission costs US$1.20 for adults, half that for students and seniors.

On the Mapocho's north bank between the Padre Letelier and Pedro de Valdivia Bridges, the open-air **Parque de las Esculturas** (Av. Santa María 2201, tel. 02/3407303) showcases abstract works by contemporary Chilean sculptors on the order of Federico Assler's *Conjunto Escultórico* (Sculpture Group), Sergio Castillo's *Erupción* (Eruption), Marta Colvín's *Madre Tierra* (Mother Earth), José Vicente Gajardo's *Sol y Luna* (Sun and Moon), and Osvaldo Peña's *Verde y Viento* (Green and Wind). Open 10 A.M.–7 P.M. daily, it also has an enclosed gallery with rotating exhibitions.

Providencia's newest art facility is the **Museo de Arte Hispanoamericano** (Av. Costanera Andrés Bello 1877, tel. 02/2441430, www.museomaha.com), a private collection of more than 400 paintings, drawings, and sculptures from throughout the region and selected other Spanish-speaking areas. Artists on display include Picasso, Dalí, and the Mexican muralists José Clemente Orozco, David Alfaro Siqueiros, and Diego Rivera, as well as Rivera's wife, Frida Kahlo. Hours are 10 A.M.–6 P.M. daily except Monday; admission costs US$4 per person except Sunday (US$3) and for seniors and students (US$2).

The Municipalidad de Providencia offers free open-air bus tours of the *comuna*, visiting sites such as the Museo Nacional Benjamín Vicuña Mackenna, Neruda's La Chascona house in Barrio Bellavista, and the Parque Metropolitana. These leave from the borough's Centro de Información Turística (Av. Providencia 2359, tel. 02/3742743, www.citi.providencia.cl); schedules and itineraries change from month to month.

Barrio Bellavista and Vicinity

At the foot of Cerro San Cristóbal, compact Bellavista is a walker's delight. In the daytime, Santiaguinos cross the Pío Nono Bridge to stroll its leafy streets, parks, and plazas and enjoy modest lunch specials at innovative restaurants. At night, they crowd the same places for elaborate dinners before a night at nearby bars, discos, theaters, and other diversions. Daytime visitors may not even realize that this is a nightlife nucleus—most dance clubs, for instance, do not *open* until 1 A.M. or so, and few have prominent signs.

While most visitors see Bellavista as a single neighborhood, there's a clear demarcation—Avenida Pío Nono—between the two *comunas* that comprise the barrio. To the west, roughedged Recoleta has more rundown buildings

The Pío Nono bridge links downtown Santiago and bohemian Barrio Bellavista.

© WAYNE BERNHARDSON

and a lower density of fashionable restaurants than wealthier Providencia, which makes more conspicuous efforts to prevent auto burglaries and other petty crime in what is generally a safe neighborhood. Especially on weekends, crowds are on the street day or night—well into the wee hours.

North of the river, the first major landmarks are **Parque Gómez Rojas,** with a weekend crafts market stretching up the west side of Avenida Pío Nono, and the **Facultad de Derecho de la Universidad de Chile** (law school) to the east. On weekends, **Avenida Pío Nono** has been a frenetic blend of crafts market, cheap sidewalk restaurants, and beer joints

but a recent makeover closed the gap between it and the side streets.

For a notion of Bellavista's best, relax on a bench at **Plazuela Camilo Mori,** a small triangular plaza at Antonia López de Bello and Constitución. Walking north, turn into the Márquez de la Plata cul-de-sac where poet Pablo Neruda lived at the house he called **La Chascona.** A short stroll northwest, **Plaza Caupolicán** is the main entry point to the 722-hectare **Parque Metropolitano,** a hillside and hilltop public park.

On the Recoleta side, at the north end of Avenida La Paz, famous figures from Chile's past, as well as many ordinary Chileans, are among the two million who repose in the **Cementerio General** (General Cemetery), whose imposing frontispiece dates from 1897.

(La Chascona (Museo Neruda)

Inconspicuous from the street side of its cul-de-sac, Pablo Neruda's hillside house is by no means extravagant—in fact, despite its idiosyncracies, it may be the most conventional of his three houses (the others are in Valparaíso and the beach community of Isla Negra). Opposite the house, a small amphitheater tucked into the slope complements the residence, restored since its military sacking in 1973 (Neruda, a committed Allende partisan, died about a month after the coup).

The Fundación Neruda (Márquez de La Plata 0192, tel. 02/7378712, www.fundacionneruda.org) offers hour-long guided tours by reservation, 10 A.M.–6 P.M. daily except Monday. Guided tours in Spanish cost US$5 per adult, US$1.50 for children; in English, German, or French, it's US$7 per person. The museum also operates a café, bookstore, and souvenir shop.

Parque Metropolitano

When 1870s mayor Benjamín Vicuña Mackenna envisioned Santiago's beautification, he thought of Cerro San Cristóbal as well as Cerro Santa Lucía, but he lacked the means to implement his plans for larger hill. The idea resurfaced around 1909, when Mayor Pablo Urzúa began a modest afforestation program; widespread support developed shortly thereafter under Ramón Subercaseaux's administration, which expropriated property and built roads and canals. Despite improvements, it did not officially become Parque Metropolitano until 1966.

From Plaza Caupolicán, the **Funicular San Cristóbal,** built with support from Santiago's Italian community 1922–1925, gains 240 meters in elevation en route to its upper terminal at **Terraza Bellavista.** At the midway point, there's a stop at the improved **Jardín Zoológico** (zoo, tel. 02/7776666, www

.zoologico.cl), which opened about the same time as the funicular. Now emphasizing native fauna such as puma, *pudú,* and *ñandú,* it's open 10 A.M.–6 P.M. daily except Monday; admission costs US$4 for adults, US$2 for children.

Above Terraza Bellavista, a 14-meter statue of the Virgin Mary with a 10-meter armspan, atop an eight-meter pedestal, towers over the amphitheater of the **Santuario Inmaculada Concepción** (which owes its own conception to the 50th anniversary of that particular papal dogma). Workers placed the cornerstone for the Paris-built statue, designed by Italian sculptor Jacometti and based on a similar work in Rome, in 1904. After the 1906 earthquake, though, they altered plans to anchor the 36,000-plus kilogram monument to bedrock, and it was finally inaugurated in 1908.

From the nearby **Estación Cumbre,** a modern two-kilometer **Teleférico** (cable gondola) connects the summit sector with Providencia's Avenida Pedro de Valdivia Norte, an alternative route to and from the park. About two-thirds of the way, passengers can descend at **Estación Tupahue** to visit the **Piscina Tupahue** (swimming pool), the **Casa de la Cultura Anájuac** (art museum, open 9 A.M.–5 P.M. daily but with free concerts Sunday at noon), the **Enoteca** (a wine museum/restaurant), and the **Jardín Botánico Mapulemu** (an erstwhile quarry reclaimed as a botanical garden). The even larger **Piscina Antilén** is within walking distance.

The Funicular San Cristóbal (www.funicular.cl, tel. 02/7376669) operates 1–8 P.M. Monday, 10 A.M.–8 P.M. the rest of the week; the *teleférico* operates 2:30–7:30 P.M. Monday and Tuesday, 12:30–7:30 P.M. other weekdays, and opens two hours earlier on weekends. Both have slightly reduced winter hours. The funicular-*teleférico* combination costs about US$5 for adults, US$3 for children. The funicular alone costs US$1.60 to Estación Cumbre, US$3 for a round-trip, again with discounts for children; the *teleférico* costs US$3 round-trip, US$1.80 for children. Buses from Plaza Caupolicán also make the loop to Avenida Pedro de Valdivia Norte.

Cementerio General

Among the cemetery's Gothic, Greek, Moorish, and Egyptian-style sepulchres, all but two of the country's presidents are interred: Bernardo O'Higgins's remains rest beneath Plaza Bulnes and Gabriel González Videla was buried in his native La Serena. The notable figures buried here include diplomat Orlando Letelier (killed by a car bomb in Washington, D.C., by army terrorists under orders from Pinochet's henchman General Manuel Contreras), Venezuelan-born scholar and educator Andrés Bello, and cultural icon folksinger and songwriter Violeta Parra. Nobel Prize poets Gabriela Mistral and Pablo Neruda were both interred here as well, but Mistral's body was moved to her Elqui Valley birthplace and Neruda's to his Isla Negra coastal residence.

Salvador Allende moved in the other direction—after 17 years in Viña del Mar, following the end of the Pinochet dictatorship, he regained his freedom to travel to a monumental memorial here. Another indicator of change is sculptor Francisco Gazitúa's *Rostros* (Faces), a memorial to the regime's detained and executed victims.

LAS CONDES AND VITACURA

Because of its conspicuous wealth and high-rise apartments, Las Condes has acquired the semi-ironic nickname of "Sanhattan," though it can't come close to the cultural offerings of New York City's most famous borough. While Las Condes does have a good (and improving) selection of hotels and restaurants, its sights are less significant than those in other parts of the city.

On Américo Vespucio just north of Avenida Apoquindo, where the Metro's Línea 1 ends, high fences and lack of cover on the expansive lawns should discourage any assault on the **Escuela Militar** (Army War College); the building is imposing enough from a distance, but a closer inspection reveals cracked walls and weeds wedging apart the patios.

Vitacura's **Museo Ralli** (Alonso de Sotomayor 4110, tel. 02/2064224, www .rallimuseums.org) is one of several transnational museums dedicated to contemporary Latin American art; it has other locales in Uruguay, Spain, and Israel. Completely noncommercial—lacking even a museum shop—it showcases painting and sculpture from many American countries, with a handful of items from well-known Europeans, in a custom-built facility of 2,900 square meters. It's normally open 10:30 A.M.–5 P.M. daily except Monday, and open weekends only in January, but closed for all of February. Admission is free; any bus out Avenida Vitacura will drop you at the corner of Candelaria Goyenechea, where it's just one block to the north.

Professionally organized, the new **Museo de la Moda** (Av. Vitacura 4562, tel. 02/2193023, www.museodelamoda.cl) takes the topic of fashion a little too seriously—in special theme exhibits such as "War and Seduction," for instance, the sensationalist publicity contrasts with the analytical focus. The content is ultimately trivial, but the sprawling ranch house—built for clothier Jorge Yarur and inspired by Frank Lloyd Wright—is worth a visit. Whether it's worth the US$6 admission is another issue. Hours are 10 A.M.–6:30 P.M. daily except Monday.

Los Dominicos

One of few survivals from colonial Las Condes, the **Iglesia y Convento San Vicente Ferrer de los Dominicos** sits on lands that Pedro de Valdivia seized from Mapuche cacique Apoquindo for Valdivia's mistress Inés de Suárez. Eventually willed to the Dominican order, the property deteriorated during a century-plus of litigation, but the Dominicans managed to add its twin Byzantine domes in 1847.

Alongside the church, where Avenida Apoquindo dead-ends at Padre Hurtado, **Los Graneros del Alba** (Av. Apoquindo 9085) is Santiago's biggest crafts market, also popular for its country cuisine and impromptu entertainment. Popularly known as "Los Dominicos," it's open 10 A.M.–7:30 P.M. daily all year. Several buses out the Alameda, Avenida Providencia, and Avenida Apoquindo go directly there; the quickest alternative is

Línea 1 to Metro Escuela Militar and then either the bus or a taxi (about US$5).

ÑUÑOA

South of Providencia and east of Santiago Centro, middle-class Ñuñoa has few obvious landmarks, but the vigorous cultural life on and around **Plaza Ñuñoa,** thanks partly to nearby university campuses, has made it a growing attraction. There are good but unpretentious restaurants, bars, and dance clubs.

With the Andean front range as a backdrop, Ñuñoa's sole unforgettable landmark is the **Estadio Nacional** (National Stadium, Av. Grecia 2001). Famous for the 1962 World Cup, it became infamous after the 1973 coup, when Pinochet's regime incarcerated some 7,000 Allende sympathizers (and suspected sympathizers) in an impromptu prison camp here. Many suffered torture and more than a few were executed (including folksinger Victor Jara

and U.S. citizens Charles Horman and Frank Teruggi). Within walking distance of Línea 5's Ñuble station, the stadium hosts the country's most important soccer matches and megaconcerts.

OUTER COMUNAS

Most outer *comunas* have few points of interest, but some are very worthwhile. They are mostly toward the southeastern part of the city.

Viña Santa Carolina

Santiago's most accessible winery is a short subway ride from downtown—at its creation in 1875, though, Luis Pereira's Viña Santa Carolina was *puro campo* (countryside). Santiago gradually enveloped it and there are no more vineyards here, but the original house remains, complete with its galleries and patios, along with impressive subterranean vaults where the wine ages in French oak.

THE TRANSFORMATION OF VILLA GRIMALDI

During General Pinochet's 17-year dictatorship, when more than 3,000 people were murdered or disappeared and as many as 400,000 others were detained and tortured, no single site evoked more fear than **Villa Grimaldi,** the largest detention and torture center.

Before the 1973 coup, Villa Grimaldi, in the geographically peripheral *comuna* of Peñalolén, was a retreat popular with leftists and intellectuals. Appropriated by the dictatorship, between 1973 and 1980 it was the site of the death or disappearance of well over 200 people – though no bodies have been found there – and more than 5,000 detentions.

Villa Grimaldi also served as a training center for General Manuel Contreras's infamous Directorio de Inteligencia Nacional (DINA, National Intelligence Directorate) and its successor, the Centro de Inteligencia Nacional (CNI, National Intelligence Center). It was also the Chilean headquarters for Operación Cóndor, a covert alliance with the so-called "security

forces" of military dictatorships in Argentina, Uruguay, and Brazil.

When it became apparent that Pinochet had lost his bid to extend his "presidency" for another eight years, military authorities tried to eradicate all evidence of Grimaldi's violent past and sold the property. Outraged community members, though, lobbied President Patricio Aylwin's incoming Christian Democrat administration to buy back the land and turn it into a contemplative memorial.

A book titled *Grito mi Silencio* (*I Shout My Silence;* Santiago: Librería Pax, 2001), written under the pen name Rodrigo by a Spanish-Chilean businessman who was inexplicably detained after an innocent inquiry about some family property, recounts conditions at Villa Grimaldi. Just as inexplicably released, the detainee waited 25 years before he could feel comfortable enough to tell his story, even though he was not tortured. His book caused a minor sensation as the trend toward accountability accelerated.

Santa Carolina's main white varietals are chardonnay and sauvignon blanc, while the reds include cabernet sauvignon, carmenere, merlot, and syrah; there are also both red and white blends. The vineyards themselves are in the Cachapoal, Colchagua, and Casablanca Valleys.

In the *comuna* of Macul, Viña Santa Carolina (Av. Rodrigo de Araya 1431, tel. 02/4503000, www.santacarolina.com, tours@santacarolina.cl) is only a 10-minute walk from Metro Rodrigo de Araya (Línea 5). It offers basic tours and tasting (one hour, two varietals, US$14 pp) in Spanish (10 A.M.) and English (12:30 P.M.) daily except Sunday; if demand is sufficient, there's a 3 P.M. tour in either language. A more elaborate tour, with three premium wines and a corkscrew (US$30 pp, 1.5 hours), takes place at 4:30 P.M. weekdays.

Museo Nacional de Aeronáutica y del Espacio

Santiago's former international and domestic airport, Aeropuerto Los Cerrillos, closed in early 2006, but one former hangar survives as Chile's air and space museum. It harbors a hodgepodge of historic planes such as DC-3s, and also covers Chile's tiny role in space exploration—in 1971, Apollo 14 carried the Chilean flag to the moon. The Museo Nacional de Aeronáutica y del Espacio (Av. Pedro Aguirre Cerda 5000, Cerrillos, tel. 02/4353030, www.museoaeronautico.cl) is open 10 A.M.–5:30 P.M. daily except Monday. Admission is free.

Templo Votivo de Maipú

After victory over the Spaniards at the battle of Maipú in 1818, Bernardo O'Higgins himself proposed construction of a tributary temple to the Virgen del Carmen, Chile's patron saint. Begun shortly thereafter, the original temple went unfinished until 1887, then suffered such serious earthquake damage that this new modernist—some might say brutalist—church was constructed of reinforced concrete. The project began in 1944, but not until 1974 was it complete.

Still, the Templo Votivo draws throngs of the faithful, especially around July 16 for the Fiesta de la Virgen del Carmen. Standing ruins of the earlier church are fenced off; the adjacent **Museo del Carmen** (tel. 02/5317067, www.museodelcarmen.cl) displays patriotic and ecclesiastical artifacts.

The Templo Votivo (Av. 5 de Abril s/n, Maipú, tel. 02/5312312) is open 9:30 A.M.–8 P.M. daily, while the museum (admission US$0.85) is open 9 A.M.–2 P.M. Tuesday–Friday, and 10 A.M.–1 P.M. and 3–6 P.M. weekends and holidays. From the Alameda, Transantiago bus No. C-19 goes directly to the Templo; *taxi colectivos* leave from Alameda and Amunátegui.

Viña Cousiño Macul

In the southeastern *comuna* of Peñalolén, Cousiño Macul is one of Chile's oldest wineries, in the same family since Matías Cousiño purchased the vineyards in 1856. Its cellars and Museo del Vino (Wine Museum) are open for English-language tours weekdays at 11 A.M., with Spanish-language tours weekdays at 3 P.M. and Saturday at 11 A.M. Tours cost US$10; the accompanying tasting, held in an attractive bar cum sales room, include one varietal and one reserve vintage, in a souvenir glass. The house produces cabernet, merlot, chardonnay, sauvignon blanc, and riesling.

Viña Cousiño Macul (Av. Quilín 7100, tel. 02/3514135, www.cousinomacul.cl, sschotte@cousinomacul.cl) is a 20-minute walk from Quilín station, on the Metro's Línea 4.

Parque por la Paz

The most subtly eloquent memorial to the Pinochet dictatorship's victims, Peñalolén's Parque por la Paz (Park for Peace) occupies the grounds of the former Villa Grimaldi, the principal torture center for the Directorio de Inteligencia Nacional (DINA), General Manuel Contreras's ruthless intelligence service. Before it closed, more than 200 political prisoners died at the isolated mansion, and many more were interrogated and tortured.

In the regime's final days, the military bulldozed nearly every building to destroy evidence, but the nonprofit Fundación Parque por la Paz has transformed the property into a pilgrimage site that commemorates the victims without any overt political posturing. It has permanently locked the original streetside gates, by which prisoners entered the grounds, with a declaration that they are "never to be opened again."

Parque por la Paz (Avenida Arrieta 8401, tel. 02/2925229, www.villagrimaldicorp.cl) is open 10 A.M.–2 P.M. and 3–6 P.M. daily; admission is free. Several Transantiago bus lines pass nearby, including D08 (Metro Grecia), D09 (Metro Los Leones), and D11 (Metro Los Orientales).

Chip Travel (Av. Santa María 227, Oficina 12, tel. 02/7775376, www.chip.cl) is the only operator offering alternative "Human Rights Legacy" tours that take in Parque por la Paz, the Cementerio General, and the Fundación Pinochet.

Barrio Ecológico

In upper Peñalolén, Santiago's most nonconformist community occupies a conflictive area alongside middle-class suburban subdivisions and working-class squatter settlements where the militant leftist Movimiento Izquierdista Revolucionario (MIR) is loath to let the police even enter. Nevertheless, the residents of the self-consciously environmentally correct community have fashioned a neighborhood where campesinos once toiled to eke out low yields from barren soils.

In the 1960s, as Chilean peasants clamored for land, President Eduardo Frei Montalva's cautious redistribution program had hesitated to tackle the powerful landowners of the fertile lowlands, preferring to acquire less desirable areas such as Peñalolén, where landowners were more amenable to a buyout. After most peasant farmers failed, naive but sincere back-to-the-land types supplanted them, living—camping, really—without utilities, but gradually planting trees and gardens and creating their own spontaneous architecture. Eventually, municipal authorities accepted the barrio as a permanent buffer against suburban sprawl, and it now enjoys running water, electricity, and telephone service—but not paved streets. The houses themselves, while atypical, have acquired an air of greater permanence, and many individuals from the arts and literary communities now live here.

Transantiago route D02, from Estación Irrarrázaval, goes directly to the Barrio Ecológico. An ideal walking area, it has a small handicrafts market (best on weekends) and good but simple eateries.

Museo Interactivo Mirador

South of Peñalolén, in the *comuna* of La Granja, everything is meant to the touched at the Museo Interactivo Mirador—it's primarily for kids, though many adults enjoy it as well. With little textual explanation, it relies on seeing and doing.

It's good not only in the physical sciences, including water and its properties, and plate tectonics, but also in the psychology of perception. The building is a two-story concrete block with an open floor plan and curved lath ceilings where, unfortunately, pigeons have taken up residence. One unique exhibit lets you choose your daily diet as in a cafeteria line and then provides nutritional information on the menu chosen.

The museum (Sebastopol 90, tel. 02/2943955, www.mim.cl; Metro Mirador Azul) is open 9:30 A.M.–6:30 P.M. daily except Monday, when it closes at 1:30 P.M. It also closes January 1, May 1, and December 25. Admission costs US$6 for adults, US$4 for children.

Entertainment and Events

As with restaurants, Barrio Bellavista is the focus of the city's nightlife—in a neighborhood where most clubs don't *open* until midnight or 1 A.M., and hardly anybody goes before 2 A.M., it seems unbelievable that, during the dictatorship, the city endured an 11 P.M. *curfew.*

There are also nightspots in and around Santiago Centro, around Providencia's Avenida Suecia, and near Plaza Ñuñoa. Many bars and dance clubs, especially gay venues, have no obvious public signs except during the hours that they are open.

ENTERTAINMENT
Bars

Barrio Lastarria's **Bar Berri** (Rosal 321, tel. 02/6384734) is an unpretentious neighborhood bar that also serves fixed-price lunches.

Bellavista's **La Casa en el Aire** (Antonia López de Bello 0125, tel. 02/7356680, www.lacasaenelaire.cl) is a direct descendant of 1960s and 1970s *peñas,* with folkloric music, storytelling, films, and the like in an alternative milieu. Down the block, **Altazor** (Antonia López de Bello 0189, tel. 02/7779651, www.baraltazor.cl) is a blues-and-folk venue, while **Peña Nano Parra** (Ernesto Pinto Lagarrigue 80, tel. 02/7356093) is more traditional.

The consistently best rock-music locale is Plaza Ñuñoa's **La Batuta** (Jorge Washington 52, tel. 02/2747096, www.batuta.cl). Improbably enough, one of Chile's most popular acts is the homegrown reggae band Gondwana; when it's not in town, Santiago's wannabe dreads hang out to hear Bob Marley at Bellavista's **Jammin' Club** (Antonia López de Bello 49).

The **Club de Jazz El Perseguidor** (Antonia Lopez de Bello 0126, tel. 02/7776763, www.elperseguidor.cl) offers live jazz nightly except Sunday.

North of Avenida Providencia, Avenida Suecia and its cross streets sport a swarm of theme bars that tend toward kitsch, but the drinks are good, often imaginative, and a

bargain during happy hours that can last until midnight. Among them are Australian-run **Boomerang** (General Holley 2285, tel. 02/3345081, www.boomerang.cl), which has managed to survive and even sustain its popularity in a highly competitive environment; the roughly comparable **Brannigan's** (Av. Suecia 035, tel. 02/2325172, www.brannigans.cl); and **Wall Street** (General Holley 99, tel. 02/2325548). Many of these places are also popular for light meals, though the food is only ordinary.

The food is far better than ordinary at Ñuñoa's **Borne 19** (19 de Abril 3550, tel. 02/3563077, www.borne19.cl), a subdued tapas bar with great drinks (happy hour until 9:30 P.M.) and moderately priced Spanish food.

Discos and Dance Clubs

Blondie (Alameda 2879, tel. 02/6817793, www.blondie.cl; Metro Unión Latinoamericana) is a four-floor dance club, featuring occasional live acts, that accommodates up to 2,000 people at a time—two-thirds of those on the main floor. Admission starts around US$4–5 pp.

Bellavista's **Rockola** (Antonia López de Bello 56, tel. 02/7351167, www.rockola.cl) has both live music (including the likes of Argentina's Charly García) and recorded music for dancing, Thursday–Saturday. The cover cost is US$5–7.

Nightclubs

Several venerable venues hold stage and floor shows, often featuring clichéd cultural staples such as the *cueca,* along with typical cuisine such as *pastel de choclo* and *cazuela de ave.* The most interesting is **Confitería Las Torres** (Alameda 1570, tel. 02/6986220, www.confiteriatorres.cl), a magnificent 19th-century building that hosts live tango on weekends. If you can't visit Buenos Aires's Café Tortoni, this is Santiago's best option.

South of the Alameda, the garish **Los**

© WAYNE BERNHARDSON

The pisco sour is Chile's national cocktail.

Adobes de Argomedo (Argomedo 411, tel. 02/2222104, www.losadobesdeargomedo.cl) is popular for foreign tour groups' farewell dinners, but it gets plenty of Chileans as well. The floor show is participatory—get ready to *cueca*.

In the same location since 1939, Barrio Brasil's cavernous **Los Buenos Muchachos** (Av. Ricardo Cumming 1031, tel. 02/6980112, www.losbuenosmuchachos.cl) seats up to a thousand people for lunch or dinner and floor shows with its own orchestra. The above-average food is not *that* far above average; prices are farther above average. The service is excellent, and there's an effectively isolated tobacco-free dining room.

Gay and Lesbian Venues

Bellavista's Recoleta side is home to most of Santiago's gay clubs. The most discreet is **Capricho Español** (Purísima 65, tel. 02/7777674), whose patrons often meet for a quiet drink and/or dinner before a night on the town.

Open every night, **Bokhara** (Pío Nono 430, tel. 02/7321050, www.bokhara.cl) is home to a lively scene that looks bigger than it is, as plenty of hangers-on crowd the entrance without actually entering. A bit less central, **Fausto** (Av. Santa María 0832, tel. 02/7771041, www.fausto.cl) draws a mixed-age crowd on separate levels linked by broad staircases that encourage interaction.

Holding up to a thousand partygoers on Thursday, Friday, and Saturday nights, the gigantic **Bunker** (Bombero Núñez 159, tel. 02/7773760, www.bunker.cl) appeals to those who can afford the US$10-plus cover charge; for lesbians, it operates **Femme by Bunker** (Bombero Núñez 169, tel. 02/7382301), immediately next door. Several other gay clubs and bars dot the same street.

Cultural Centers

New in 2006, the **Centro Cultural Palacio La Moneda** (Plaza de la Ciudadanía 26, tel. 02/3556500, www.ccplm.cl) is in a class of its own. In addition to its gigantic atrium and special exhibit galleries, facilities include the **Cineteca Nacional** (national film archive, with regular repertory programs) and a sprawling crafts shop displaying museum-quality pieces from artisans around the country (not all of these are for sale). General admission costs US$1 for adults, half that for children.

After the former Valparaíso train station closed in 1987, it took seven years to become the **Centro Cultural Estación Mapocho** (Plaza de la Cultura s/n, tel. 02/7870000, www.estacionmapocho.cl). With several performance spaces, restaurants, and bookstores, it also hosts major events such as November's annual Feria del Libro (book fair).

The **Instituto Chileno-Norteamericano de Cultura** (Moneda 1467, tel. 02/6777070, www.norteamericano.cl) sponsors art exhibits and other events, and has an English-language library. The most elaborate and active foreign cultural center, though, is Providencia's **Centro Cultural de España** (Av. Providencia 927, tel. 02/7959700, www.ccespana.cl), which sponsors events nearly every night.

Cinema

Several multiscreen cinemas, both in Santiago Centro and outlying *comunas,* show current films, often in English with Spanish subtitles. Children's films and animated features, however, usually appear in Spanish.

Santiago's traditional cinema district is downtown along Paseo Huérfanos and nearby streets, where many formerly large theaters have been modified into multiplexes. Elsewhere in town, newer custom-built multiplexes are the rule. Most theaters offer half-price discounts on Wednesdays.

Independent films generally show at smaller venues scattered around town. Wednesday discounts are also available.

Performing Arts

Santiago has many live theater and music venues, with a range of offerings from serious classical and contemporary drama to burlesque, and from classical music to traditional folk and rock; the best place to find a listing of current offerings is the entertainment section of the daily *El Mercurio* and especially its Friday supplement *Wikén.*

The landmark **Teatro Municipal** (Agustinas 794, tel. 02/4638888, www.municipal.cl) is Santiago's most prestigious performing-arts venue, hosting classical music, opera, and occasional popular musicals. Only opening performances are truly formal, and Santiaguinos sometimes appear in surprisingly casual clothes; during operas, a translation of the libretto is projected above the stage so that it's easier to follow the plot (if you read Spanish).

Musicians rave about the acoustics at the **Teatro Universidad de Chile** (Av. Providencia 043, tel. 02/9782480, http://teatro.uchile.cl), best known for ballet and classical music, though it hosts the occasional rock event.

Occupying the restored former northern railway station, the **Centro Cultural**

© WAYNE BERNHARDSON

Santiago's opera, ballet, and other performing arts companies use the Teatro Municipal.

Estación Mapocho (Plaza de la Cultura s/n, tel. 02/7870000, www.estacionmapocho.cl) has several performing arts venues within. Other Santiago Centro locales include the **Teatro Nacional Chileno** (Morandé 25, tel. 02/6961200, www.tnch.uchile.cl); the Universidad de Chile's **Sala Agustín Sire** (Morandé 750, tel. 02/6965142, www.agustinsire.uchile.cl); and the smallish **Teatro La Comedia** (Merced 349, tel. 02/6391523). South of the Alameda, the capacious **Teatro Caupolicán** (San Diego 850, tel. 02/6991556, www.teatrocaupolican.cl) showcases rock and pop.

Repertory groups play small Bellavista venues like **Teatro Bellavista** (Dardignac 0110, tel. 02/7356264), **Teatro El Conventillo** (Bellavista 173, tel. 02/7774164), and **Teatro La Feria** (Crucero Exeter 0250, tel. 02/7377371).

EVENTS

In even-numbered years, March's **Feria Internacional del Aire y del Espacio** (www.fidae.cl), at the international airport at Pudahuel, draws big crowds interested in general aviation; it's also a showcase for international weapons manufacturers.

September's patriotic holidays are an excuse for parties and parades, but the month can be contentious—September 11, the date of Pinochet's coup, often sees disturbances around Providencia's Avenida 11 de Septiembre. September 18, **Día de la Independencia** (Independence Day), sees cheerful barbecues in the parks, but September 19's **Día del Ejército** (Armed Forces Day) is more divisive.

Halloween (October 31) is not a Chilean holiday, but in nonconformist Bellavista it's one of the year's biggest nights. Chileans customarily honor their dead on **Día de los Muertos** (Day of the Dead), November 2.

At the Estación Mapocho, November's 10-day **Feria de Libro** (book fair, www.camlibro.cl) draws both Chilean writers and internationally recognized authors.

SHOPPING

Santiago may not be a global shopping mecca, but quality Chilean handicrafts and antiques are widely available. Many visitors, of course, take home local wines.

Books and Music

The **Feria Chilena del Libro** (Huérfanos 623, tel. 02/6396758, www.feriachiladellibro.cl) is a chain with several branches elsewhere. For academic and antiquarian tastes, try downtown's **Librería Luis Rivano** (San Diego 111, Local 7, tel. 02/6723164) or Providencia's **Librería Chile Ilustrado** (Av. Providencia 1652, tel. 02/2358145), in the same complex as the Phone Box Pub. At the same address, **Books** sells used English-language paperbacks at fairly high prices.

Vitacura's **Librería Eduardo Albers** (Av. Vitacura 5648, tel. 02/2185371, www.texto.cl) has a selection of guidebooks and other general-interest books in English and German.

For CDs or tapes of present and past Chilean music, try the **Feria del Disco** (Ahumada 286, tel. 02/5928921, www.feriadeldisco.cl).

Handicrafts and Souvenirs

Downtown's best souvenir shops are **Chile Típico** (Moneda 1025, Local 149, tel. 02/6965504) and **Huimpalay** (Huérfanos 1162, tel. 02/6721395), with premium prices. Cerro Santa Lucía's **Centro de Exposición de Arte Indígena** (Alameda 499, tel. 02/6323668), in the semisubterranean Grutas del Cerro Welén, has Mapuche, Aymara, and Rapanui crafts; it's open 10 A.M.–6 P.M. daily except Sunday, closing an hour later in summer.

Bellavista is best for lapis lazuli jewelry, at locales like **Lapiz Lazuli House** (Bellavista 04, tel. 02/7321419, www.lapislazulihouse.cl).

In the Bellas Artes neighborhood, **Ona** (Victoria Subercaseaux 299, tel. 02/6321859, www.onachile.com) carries a wide selection of quality Andean handicrafts from throughout Chile and even parts of Bolivia and Peru, commissioned from notable artisans. The best include delicately carved and painted wooden birds, *krin* (woven horse-hair items including dolls and butterflies), Mapuche silver, textiles, and pre-Columbian reproductions.

In a category of its own, **The Clinic El Bazar** (José Miguel de la Barra 459, tel. 02/6320736, www.theclinicelbazar.cl) is the souvenir store for the iconoclastic bimonthly that's Chile's most-read magazine. This is the place to buy your Pinochet mugshot sleeveless T-shirt.

Wine

If visiting wineries isn't on your agenda but buying wine is, **La Vinoteca** (Isidora Goyenechea 2966, tel. 02/3341987, www.lavinoteca.cl) is one of several wine outlets in the Las Condes area.

SPORTS AND RECREATION

Santiago and environs offer a diversity of options for both personal recreation and spectator sports.

Soccer

Like other Latin Americans, Chileans are passionate about soccer. Major matches take place in Ñuñoa's **Estadio Nacional** (Av. Grecia 2001), built for the 1960 World Cup and then used, 13 years later, for incarcerating, torturing, and executing political prisoners in the aftermath of the Pinochet coup.

Accommodations

Nearly all the budget to midrange accommodations are in and around Santiago Centro, with luxury hotels in Providencia and Las Condes. Most midrange and top-end hotels discount IVA for foreign visitors. Many upper-range hotels belong to international chains.

Unless otherwise indicated, hotels listed here are in Santiago Centro; some of them are more closely defined by barrio. Many hotels in other *comunas* are oriented towards business travelers, but still welcome ordinary travelers or tourists.

US$10-25

South of the Alameda, U.S.-run **Hostal de Sammy** (Toesca 2335, tel. 02/6898772, www.hostaldesammy.com, US$10–17 pp) is gradually transforming a rundown mansion in a lively university neighborhood, around the corner from the new Allende museum, into comfy backpackers' accommodations. Rooms range from six-person dorms to doubles with private baths; amenities include a self-serve breakfast, kitchen access, laundry privileges, WiFi, local phone calls, a game room with pool tables and table tennis, and a shady patio with a barbecue. Its main drawback is the shortage of restaurants

and nightlife in the immediate vicinity, but it's close to two Metro stations.

US$25-50

A dull burgundy facade masks the interior of Barrio Brasil's **(La Casa Roja** (Agustinas 2113, tel. 02/6964241, www.lacasaroja.cl, US$13 pp, US$40 d), a sprawling 19th-century mansion that bids to become a backpackers' boutique hostel—though with 85 or so beds, it's perhaps a bit too large for that. Australian owner Simon Shalders has restored period details while modernizing the baths and creating a contemporary kitchen—not to mention a garden pool with a swim-up bar and a batting cage (for cricket, but adaptable for baseball). Even the eight-bed dorms don't feel cramped, and with large common areas scattered through the building, the place never seems crowded. There are also private rooms with or without private baths.

Directly across from the Los Héroes bus terminal, the casual HI affiliate **Che Lagarto** (Tucapel Jiménez 24, tel. 02/6991493, www.chelagarto.com, US$14–22 pp) occupies a rehabbed older building.

In the winding cobbled streets south of the

Alameda, such good value that reservations are imperative, **(C Residencial Londres** (Londres 54, tel. 02/6339192, www.londres.cl, US$14–15 pp with shared bath, US$32 d with private bath) has real charm but may not be able to keep pace with some of the newer backpacker favorites. Breakfast costs extra.

Used mostly by groups and an influx of independent foreigners, **Hostelling International** (Cienfuegos 151, tel. 02/6718532, www.hisantiago.cl, US$16 pp) has spacious common areas (including a bar), dorm-style accommodations (four beds per room), free Internet and WiFi, and laundry service. Its cafeteria has lunches and dinners in the US$4–6 range, and the Saturday night *asado* (US$8 pp, wine and salad included) is a bargain. It has also added a few doubles (without and with private bath, US$48–54 s or d); those with private baths also have plasma TVs with cable.

In the renovated ex-Residencial del Norte, the gleaming **Happy House Hostel** (Catedral 2207, tel. 02/6884849, www.happyhousehostel.cl, US$22 pp, up to US$62 s or d with breakfast) hasn't managed to silence the ancient building's creaky floors, but it's upgraded already spacious rooms, added commodious common areas including a kitchen and a bar, and even installed a sauna adjacent to the sunny rooftop deck.

US$50-100

At the north end of Cerro Santa Lucía, the underrated **(C Hotel Foresta** (Subercaseaux 353, tel. 02/6396262, hforesta@terra.cl, US$45 s, US$56 d with breakfast) offers excellent value for money. In the past, it's suffered from traffic noise, but recent street improvements have helped.

Magnificently modernized, **(C Hotel España** (Morandé 510, tel. 02/6966066, www.hotelespania.com, US$60 s, US$75 d) has spacious cheerful rooms with contemporary baths, exceptional natural light on the 4th floor in particular, plus cable TV, Internet connections, and electronic strong boxes.

Few traditional townhouses survive among Providencia's high-rises, but a Catalan couple

has converted two of them into the tobacco-free **(C Vilafranca Petit Hotel** (Pérez Valenzuela 1650, tel. 02/2351413, www.vilafranca.cl, US$68 s, US$80 d with breakfast), whose only drawback is the rush-hour drone from nearby Avenida Andrés Bello. Engagingly furnished, the eight rooms vary from cozy attic doubles to spacious suites, all with private baths, plus amenities such as cable TV and WiFi; the common areas include a comfortable living room, with plenty of reading material, and a shady patio.

Decorated with museum piece artifacts from the Chilean countryside, downtown's **(C Hotel Galerías** (San Antonio 65, tel. 02/4707400, www.hotelgalerias.cl, US$70–200 s or d) is a theme hotel that, despite its romantic ruralism, has contemporary conveniences including WiFi and a terraced pool. With 162 rooms, its deceptively inconspicuous streetside entrance leads to spacious facilities that are an enclave of calm in a busy neighborhood.

Hotel Acacias de Vitacura (El Manantial 1781, tel. 02/2118601, www.hotelacacias.cl, US$89 s or d) is a family-run hotel whose gardens and foyer feature an astonishing assortment of antique machinery and artifacts from around the world. The building lacks character, but the 37 rooms are comfortable, the service impeccable, the recreational facilities outstanding, and it's convenient to summer hiking and winter skiing in the Cajón del Mapocho.

US$100-150

Despite its inauspicious location half a block east of the busy Vía Norte-Sur, the Indian-owned **Hotel Majestic** (Santo Domingo 1526, tel. 02/6958366, www.hotelmajestic.cl, US$100 s, US$110 d with buffet breakfast), a 50-room Best Western affiliate, offers good value for the cost; double-paned windows keep out the noise, and there's a pool. Just two blocks from Metro Santa Ana, its restaurant is Chile's only exclusively Indian eatery, featuring items such as samosas and curries. Discount rates are available through its website.

In recent decades, many high-rises have replaced handsome French-style buildings that once graced Providencia's streets. One survivor is the 23-room (**Hotel Orly** (Av. Pedro de Valdivia 027, tel. 02/2318947, www.orlyhotel .com, US$95 s, US$110–140 d), whose ornate facade and mansard roof denote midsize rooms with breakfast and assiduous service.

New in late 2008, the **Petit Hotel Meridiano Sur** (Santa Beatriz 256, tel. 02/2353659, www .meridianosur.cl, US$78 s, US$125 d) is a mansion retrofitted into a design hotel in an appealing neighborhood with outstanding restaurants within walking distance. The rooms are on the small side—especially one single that goes for US$60—but a spacious loft can sleep up to five or six people for US$260.

US$150-200

A converted apartment building, **Hotel Neruda** (Av. Pedro de Valdivia 164, tel. 02/6790700, www.hotelneruda.cl, US$150–240 s or d) is a business-oriented facility, with contemporary conveniences including free WiFi, plus a gym, sauna, and rooftop pool in an adjacent building.

At Providencia's **Hotel Santiago Park Plaza** (Ricardo Lyon 207, tel. 02/3724000, www.parkplaza.cl, US$126–241 s or d), the antique-studded foyer belies the modernity of its wired rooms and recreational facilities, including a glassed-in rooftop plunge pool. The 104 rooms in this European-style hotel vary considerably in size, however.

In Barrio París-Londres, business-oriented **Hotel Fundador** (Paseo Serrano 34, tel./fax 02/6322566, www.hotelfundador.cl, US$134–218 s or d with buffet breakfast in its Winter Garden restaurant) has undergone a makeover under the supervision of award-winning architect Germán del Sol, designer of Puerto Natales's landmark Hotel Remota. Painted in pastels, its 147 rooms, in two buildings linked by a fourth-floor bridge, enjoy fine lighting and stylish wooden furniture, but WiFi is available in common areas only.

Las Condes's **Radisson Plaza Santiago Hotel** (Av. Vitacura 2610, tel. 02/2036000, www.radisson.cl, US$159–213 s or d) caters primarily to business travelers; each room comes with its own cell phone, for instance, and it occupies part of Santiago's World Trade Center. There are also, of course, amenities such as a rooftop pool, a gymnasium, and whirlpool tubs, and views of the Andes to the east.

Alongside the Parque Arauco shopping center, Las Condes's skyscraping (**Marriott Santiago Hotel** (Av. Kennedy 5741, tel. 02/4262000, www.marriott.cl, US$169–219 s or d) is one of Santiago's tallest buildings. It projects a contemporary gentility, especially in its luminous atrium, but nonconformist celebrity guests are often among its clientele—check to see if Ozzy Osbourne's in the adjacent room.

Virtually self-contained, downtown's business-oriented **Hotel Crowne Plaza Santiago** (Alameda 136, tel. 02/6381042, www.crowne-plaza.cl, US$189–359 s or d) features recreational facilities including a gymnasium, swimming pool, dozens of shops, and even its own post office. All the 293 rooms in this

© WAYNE BERNHARDSON

In Las Condes, The Ritz-Carlton is widely considered Santiago's top hotel.

22-story hotel have luxury furniture, marble baths, and free Internet access.

MORE THAN US$200

Business-oriented **Hotel Plaza San Francisco** (Alameda 816, tel. 02/6393832, www.plazasanfrancisco.cl, US$200–230 s or d) often gets celebrity clientele such as Mia Farrow, Plácido Domingo, and even the Dalai Lama (appropriately enough, some of its 148 rooms have Asian design touches). In the summer off-season, there may be discounts for "standard" rooms.

Overlooking the Mapocho from the base of Cerro San Cristóbal, with garden space that other luxury hotels lack, Providencia's **Sheraton San Cristóbal Hotel & Convention Center** (Av. Santa María 1742, tel. 02/2335000, www.sheraton.cl, US$309–349 s or d with buffet breakfast) is where Bob Dylan holes up when he plays Santiago. The superb rooms are stylishly decorated and feature beautiful views, but for those who want to explore the city, this hotel is a little isolated and definitely not pedestrian-friendly.

In Las Condes, the 310-room high-rise **Grand Hyatt Santiago** (Av. Kennedy 4601, tel. 02/9501234, www.hyatt.cl, US$389 s or d) has made *Condé Nast Traveler*'s top 10 list of Latin American hotels; its lofty atrium, topped by a glass dome, lets natural light stream inside. Rates for midsize to capacious rooms, some with stupendous Andean panoramas, also include access to a gymnasium, a swimming pool, and tennis courts.

Well-placed for almost everything, **The Ritz-Carlton Santiago** (El Alcalde 15, tel. 02/4708500 www.ritzcarlton.com, US$399–599 s or d) has reached the apex of Santiago's luxury hotels—in both quality and price. With 205 rooms, rising 14 stories above Las Condes, it enjoys city and Andean views, but it's barely a minute from the Metro and also easy walking distance to some of the city's best dining.

Food

On a global level, Santiago's diverse and innovative gastronomy is an underappreciated secret. The distribution of restaurants mirrors that of hotels, with cheaper eateries downtown and most upscale restaurants in Providencia and Las Condes—though Barrio Bellavista, across the Río Mapocho, offers the most original dining and congenial ambience.

SANTIAGO CENTRO

Santiago cafés have finally broken through the "coffee with legs" barrier to become places such as **Emporio La Rosa** (Merced 291, tel. 02/6389257), which serves excellent breakfasts and lunches, with outstanding juices and Argentine-style *medialunas* (croissants) and empanadas.

For whimsical decor, traditional Chilean food, and equally reasonable prices (about US$4–5 for most lunches), there's **La Chimenea** (Príncipe de Gales 90, tel. 02/6970131, www.lachimenea.cl); in the same location since 1952, it also hosts live jazz Wednesdays at 9 P.M. and sponsors theme-based film programs, free of charge, Saturdays at 8 P.M.

In Barrio Lastarria, near Cerro Santa Lucía, **Patagonia Alma del Sur** (José Victorino Lastarria 96, tel. 02/6643830) is making the shift from a café with a creative sandwich menu to a full-fledged restaurant and wine bar; it's probably still best for sandwiches, but it has the advantage of one of the neighborhood's most spacious sidewalks for outdoor dining.

At the north end of the Lastarria pedestrian mall, **Les Assassins** (Merced 297-B, tel. 02/6384280) is a tiny venue that gets crowded around lunchtime, but it's an excellent value for French food.

Kintaro (Monjitas 450, tel. 02/6382448) is one of Santiago's cheapest sushi options, with large fresh fish and shrimp plates—more than most diners can consume in a sitting—in the US$10 range. Sashimi and rice-based plates like *donburi* are also on the menu. Not quite so good or diverse, but notably cheaper, is **Izakaya Yoko** (Merced 456, tel. 02/6321954).

BARRIO BRASIL AND VICINITY

Barrio Brasil's dining options are getting steadily better but, unfortunately, many of them are free-fire zones for tobacco junkies, with no smoke-free areas.

For breakfast, espresso drinks, exceptional sandwiches (large enough for two), and rich desserts, it's hard to top **El Café** (Huérfanos 2064, tel. 02/6880352), a cheerful corner place that also provides the morning newspapers. **Europub** (Maturana 516, tel. 02/6721016) has excellent lunch specials (around US$8) in hip surroundings but favors smokers.

The misleadingly named **Peperone** (Huérfanos 1934, tel. 02/6879180) is not a pizzeria but rather a tobacco-free *empanadería* with fillings that are far more diverse than most of its Chilean counterparts—baked rather than deep fried, the empanadas can include items such as crab and scallops for around US$2.50. Fresh fruit juices are also a house specialty.

Long after its opening, **Las Vacas Gordas** (Cienfuegos 280, tel. 02/6971066, closed Sun. evening) still manages to combine high standards with high volume and low prices, but it's almost always crowded and noisy except Sunday night—when it's closed. The fare is primarily *parrillada,* but pasta and fish are also on the menu. Service is exceptional for such a busy place, but go early or late to avoid the crowds. It has a large, well-segregated tobacco-free area.

Prepared to a soundtrack of *narcocorridos,* the bargain-priced Mexican tacos, *antojitos* (short orders such as enchiladas), and more elaborate dinner plates at **Charro de Oro** (Av. Ricardo Cumming 342-A, tel. 02/6972695) are too spicy for some Chilean palates, but those who have eaten Mexican food elsewhere will probably not be bothered. Its main drawback

is the erratic hours, though it's ostensibly open for lunch and dinner daily except Sunday, and until 3 A.M. Friday and Saturday.

The best Mexican option, **Plaza Garibaldi** (Moneda 2319, tel. 02/6971418) continues to draw diners who at one time wouldn't be caught dead in this area. Brightly decorated, it's operated by the improbably named Jane Holmes, a Chilean who lived many years in exile in Mexico City and once cooked for Salvador Allende's widow, Hortensia Bussi. The diverse regional Mexican menu merits a visit even for those who live in areas where such food is common. Entrées are mostly in the US$6–10 range; the margaritas and Mexican beers are authentic.

Under the same ownership, **San Gennaro** (Av. Cumming 132, tel. 02/6889063) has moderately priced pastas in more spacious surroundings—a mansion with spectacular beamed ceilings and walls painted in Mediterranean pastels—not to mention a walk-in fireplace. While it hasn't yet caught on like Garibaldi, it's at least as good and has begun to offer some Mexican dishes, such as *camarones al mojo de ajo* (garlic shrimp) that Garibaldi's small kitchen can't handle.

Sole Mio (Moneda 1816, tel. 02/6726342) is a stylish but moderately priced Italian choice, in a spectacularly recycled building; the mezzanine is stunning (though its acoustics are a little *too* good). Unlike many Chilean restaurants, it offers ample distance between tables, and the ground floor is tobacco-free. Also unusual for a Chile restaurant, the ground-floor kitchen is open to public view.

Ocean Pacific's (Av. Ricardo Cumming 221, tel. 02/6972413) is another seafood restaurant with higher prices than it had in the past, thanks to an expanded menu that includes deep-sea fish and lobster from Juan Fernández and Rapa Nui, as well as nonseafood game dishes such as wild boar and rhea (around US$14). While there are good values such as the *reineta* (US$7), the expansion and larger menu suggest the restaurant is trying to do too much, but it is open Sunday evenings, when most other barrio restaurants are closed.

Ostras Azócar (Bulnes 37, tel. 02/6816109 or 02/6822293, www.ostrasazocar.cl) has retained its traditional approach to serve a more affluent clientele; before being seated, everyone enters the oyster bar for freshly shucked samples accompanied by a shot-plus of Chardonnay. A wide selection of sauces accompanies very fresh fish dishes, and the Peruvian-style pisco sours are outstanding.

The barrio's star, and one of the city's best is **Zully** (Concha y Toro 34, tel. 02/6961378, www.zully.cl), an audacious restoration/modernization of a once-crumbling mansion in Barrio Concha y Toro, an intriguing maze of streets just off the Alameda. Its Michigan expat owner has created an intimate destination-in-itself bar/restaurant with multiple dining rooms, plus a spectacular basement wine bar with an adjacent sunken patio and an equally impressive rooftop terrace; the furniture and place settings, though, are ultra-modern. That's not to mention a creative, visually spectacular menu that changes frequently but includes entrées

such as "ostrich" (rhea, US$17). Open for lunch and dinner weekdays, dinner only Saturday, it's expensive, with entrées in the US$13–18 range, but the weekday business lunch costs just US$12 (entrée plus dessert only). Starters and desserts both cost in the US$6–7 range, and there's a big wine list (including a good by-the-glass selection).

In a similar vein, **Boulevard Lavaud** (Compañía 2789, tel. 02/6825243, www.boulevardlavaud.cl, closed Sun.) has recycled an 1868 building into a combination bar/restaurant that also serves, in daytime hours, its historic function as a barbershop (for men and women). Even that doesn't say everything, as it has also integrated an antiques shop into the restaurant—much of the decor along its redbrick interior walls is for sale. With all that, the food might seem an afterthought, but dishes such as *dados de filete en salsa de frutas secas* (beef chunks in a red wine and dried fruit sauce, US$10) are both moderately priced and imaginative. Drinks are fairly expensive—the

© WAYNE BERNHARDSON

In the picturesque Barrio Concha y Toro, Zully is one of Santiago's most creative restaurants, in both menu and décor.

US$4.50 pisco sour costs twice what it might elsewhere—but Lavaud is still deservedly popular. Unlike most restaurants of its class, it also serves breakfast, plus a midday menu for US$7.

BARRIO BELLAVISTA

North of the Mapocho via the Pío Nono Bridge, Barrio Bellavista is Santiago's gourmet ghetto, with dozens of first-rate restaurants virtually side-by-side—but not on Pío Nono itself, where most of the options are little better than greasy spoons. The bulk of the choices are east of Pío Nono, on the Providencia side of the barrio, but there are still fine options on the Recoleta side, to the west.

Surviving in the midst of rampant gentrification by serving outstanding sandwiches and simple but well-prepared Chilean dishes to a Bohemian clientele, **Galindo** (Dardignac 098, tel. 02/7770116) is one of the Providencia side's oldest eateries. With its bright new facade, **El Caramaño** (Purísima 257, tel. 02/7377043) is less casual than it once was—in the past, it lacked even a street sign and you used to need to bang on the door to get in, lending it a slumming sort of "members only" atmosphere. In the back rooms, diners can still scribble on the walls.

One of Santiago's best in any category, the Peruvian **◖ El Otro Sitio** (Antonia López de Bello 53, tel. 02/7773059, www.elotrositio .cl) is slightly expensive (US$10–15 and up for entrées) but worth the splurge. The upstairs tables, with views over the atrium, are the most pleasant (on weekends, it's entirely tobacco-free, but on weeknights smokers have the upstairs).

Dining at **Azul Profundo** (Constitución 111, tel. 02/7380288) must be the closest possible experience to eating at Pablo Neruda's; its whimsical decor, including its signature deepblue exterior, a doorway bowsprit, and maritime memorabilia within, could have come straight from the poet's beloved Isla Negra residence. Seafood, of course, is the specialty, and they've put as much effort into its kitchen as its character; with entrées at US$10 and up, it's worth the price.

Serving unconventional—at least for Santiago—Japanese and Vietnamese specialties, popular **Etniko** (Constitución 172, tel. 02/7320119) is more of a scene than a restaurant, but the food is better than merely palatable. One block east, **Muñeca Brava** (Mallinkrodt 170, tel. 02/7321338) looks like a scene—or scenes from the films evoked by its elaborate cinematic decor—but the menu, especially the seafood, is consistently excellent. Entrées start in the US$9–11 range.

Occupying a classic Bellavista mansion, with a small shaded terrace offering views of densely wooded Cerro San Cristóbal, **El Mesón Nerudiano** (Dominica 35, tel. 02/7371542, www.elmesonnerudiano.cl) prepares exceptional fish (especially corvina) and seafood dishes, as well as pastas with seafood sauces, in the US$10–13 range. Downstairs, it has live music, ranging from folk to jazz, several nights per week.

De Tapas y Copas (Dardignac 0192, tel. 02/7776477, www.detapasycopas.cl) has a broader Spanish menu ranging from the obvious small and inexpensive dishes to fish and seafood entrées in the US$10 and up range; the food is above average in concept, less so in execution. Despite a large wine list, its name is misleading in that it offers only a handful of those wines by the glass.

Looking like a set from the movie based on its Mexican namesake novel, **◖ Como Agua Para Chocolate** (Constitución 88, tel. 02/7778740, www.comoaguaparachocolate .cl) is one of Bellavista's smartest restaurants. Mexican-Caribbean–style entrées start around US$10; try the *reineta a la plancha* (grilled fish) with coconut sauce. The dessert menu is elaborate, the wine list large.

New on the scene, **Santería** (Chucre Manzur 1, tel. 02/7329316, www.santeria .cl) sports a Latin American fusion food with Peruvian, Mexican and Caribbean touches— the *santo mero* (sea bass) with shrimp, its Peruvian rice flavored with fresh corn, is ideal for fish and seafood lovers. The openair patio, with wicker furniture, is comfortable and stylish, but the non-smoking area is

The traditional restaurant Galindo bucks the trends of trendy Bellavista.

relatively small (though effectively segregated). Most entrées fall into the US$12 and up range, complemented by a variety of sours—including the spicy Mapuche *merkén*.

It's stretching things to call it Bellavista—it's really in Recoleta's Patronato garment district—but Argentine-run 🌙 **El Toro** (Loreto 33, tel. 02/7375937, www.eltororestoran.cl) has earned a loyal following for its crepes, moderately priced lunches, and nonconformist sidewalk atmosphere.

One of Bellavista's best is politically conscious **Off the Record** (Antonia López de Bello 0155, tel. 02/7777710, www.offtherecord.cl), a bar/restaurant whose wood-paneled walls sport photos of the Chilean arts community. Excellent meat, seafood, and pasta entrées, and combinations, fall into the US$6–10 range, with wines by the glass (about US$3).

Amongst Bellavista's inventive eateries, Italian *cucina* might seem the odd man out, but **Il Siciliano** (Dardignac 0102, tel. 02/7372265) has surmounted the stodginess of its upscale competitors elsewhere in town. Three-course lunches (around US$9–10 pp) are the best bet.

On the Providencia side, the latest development in neighborhood gastronomy is **Patio Bellavista** (Pío Nono 73, tel. 02/7774582, www.patiobarriobellavista.cl), a refashioned interior patio between Avenida Pío Nono and Constitución that's home to new branches of several successful restaurants as well as some new establishments. The Peruvian institution **Barandiarán** (Constitución 38, Local 52, tel. 02/7370725) and the nearby, well-established **La Casa en el Aire** (Constitución 40, Local D) have locales here, while **PizzaSí** (www.pizzasi.cl) is a serviceable pizzeria that doubles as **Backstage,** a bar and Saturday night blues club.

PROVIDENCIA

Liguria (Av. Providencia 1373, tel. 02/2357914) is a hangout with plain but reliable Chilean meals at moderate prices (around US$5). **Eladio** (Av. 11 de Septiembre 2250, 5th floor, tel. 02/2314224) specializes in beef, but its varied menu will satisfy almost anyone, with inexpensive entrées (US$5–8) and good, cheap pisco sours (about US$1.50).

Within a surprisingly secluded cluster of bookstores and other specialty shops on an otherwise hectic avenue, the **Phone Box Pub** (Av. Providencia 1670, tel. 02/2359972) is a pub-

© WAYNE BERNHARDSON

grub kind of place with a shady grape arbor and lunches in the US$6–8 range, plus imported beers on tap and in the bottle.

El Huerto (Orrego Luco 054, tel. 02/2332690) is a landmark vegetarian restaurant, with dishes so appetizing that even dedicated carnivores don't seem to notice the lack of meat. Its adjoining café, **La Huerta,** has a limited menu but lower prices—try the fresh fruit bowl with yogurt, granola, and honey (about US$5).

In an old but spacious Providencia house, painted in exuberant primary colors, **Barandiarán** (Manuel Montt 315, tel. 02/2366854, www.barandiaran.cl) prepares tangy appetizers and ceviches, spicy Peruvian entrées (US$10–12), and a diverse dessert menu. The corvina with mango sauce rates high, but the lamb dishes are too heavy on the cilantro.

It's no longer a secret—go early for dinner or call ahead for reservations at **Puerto Perú** (Av. Condell 1298, tel. 02/3639886, www .puertoperu.cl), a once-modest Peruvian place that put the neighborhood south of Avenida Providencia, near the border with Ñuñoa, on the gastronomic map. Prices have risen, but so has the quality.

Another fine Peruvian option is **Alto Perú** (Seminario 38, tel. 02/2230713, www.altoperu .cl), which puts a twist on the traditional *ají de gallina* by substituting squid, shrimp, and octopus for chicken, thus turning it into *ají de mariscos* (US$12). The Peruvian-style pisco sours are first-rate.

Providencia has some of the city's best ice creameries, including **Bravíssimo** (Av. Providencia 1406, tel. 02/4217601) and **Sebastián** (Andrés de Fuenzalida 26, tel. 02/2319968).

LAS CONDES AND VITACURA

For Sunday brunch and fine lunches, the hands-down choice is Kiwi-run **Café Melba** (Don Carlos 2898, tel. 02/2324546), just around the corner from the British Embassy on Avenida Bosque Norte. There's sidewalk seating, and the omelettes, fresh juices, and similar breakfast fare are unmatchable in their category.

Under the same ownership, in the shadow of Las Condes's Ritz-Carlton Hotel, **Akarana** (Reyes Lavalle 3310, tel. 02/2319667, www .akaranarestaurant.cl) is an elegant, full-service restaurant. Occupying one of the area's few surviving WWII vintage houses, with both interior and stylish open-air seating, it serves entrées ranging from pumpkin ravioli (US$12) to New Zealand fish and chips (US$13), Moroccan-style lamb filets (US$18), and Juan Fernández crayfish (US$31). Appetizers include calamari salad (US$7.50) and Cajun carpaccio (US$8); there are also individual gourmet pizzas (around US$7.50) and a midday business lunch (US$12.50) with choice of entrées and dessert, along with a soft drink or glass of wine.

Except for a few boned cuts, nearby **Happening** (Av. Apoquindo 3090, tel. 02/2332301) imports its beef directly from Argentina (sanitary regulations prohibit shipping boned meats across the border). The results are well above average, as are the prices, with the cheapest entrées around US$12 and most substantially higher. There are a couple of fish dishes, the odd pasta, very fine desserts (try the dark and white chocolate mousse with a mild mint sauce, US$7), and a gigantic wine list. The building itself is an older house, its interior walls demolished to form a spacious, luminous dining room, with a small nonsmoking section.

The Hyatt Regency Santiago's highly regarded **Anakena** (Av. Kennedy 4601, tel. 02/3633177) has one of a handful of Thai menus in town. Popular with the diplomatic corps, **Shoogun** (Enrique Foster Norte 172, tel. 02/2311604) is an upscale Japanese venue.

Las Condes now has two fine ice creameries within sight of each other: **Fragola** (Av. El Bosque Norte 0166, tel. 02/3332029) and **Tavelli** (Isidora Goyenechea 2891).

Information and Services

Santiago is home to Chile's central tourism agency but also to municipal authorities and some private information sources. Like accommodations and restaurants, most of the major tourist services are concentrated in Santiago Centro, Providencia, and Las Condes, though a few important addresses are elsewhere in the city.

TOURIST OFFICES

The national tourism service **Sernatur** (Av. Providencia 1550, tel. 02/7318300, www.sernatur.cl) has competent English-speaking personnel who distribute maps and information on city attractions and services, and brochures on the rest of the country; hours are 8:30 A.M.–6 P.M. weekdays, 9 A.M.–2 P.M. Saturdays. Its international airport office (tel. 02/6019320) is open 8:15 A.M.–9:30 P.M. daily.

Half a block east of the Plaza de Armas, the municipal **Oficina de Turismo** (Merced 860, tel. 02/6327785, turims@entelchile.net) also has a satellite office on Cerro Santa Lucía (tel. 02/6644206). Both are open 10 A.M.–6 P.M. Monday–Thursday, 10 A.M.–5 P.M. Friday.

The borough of Providencia has its own **Centro de Información Turística** (Av. Providencia 2359, tel. 02/3742743, www.citi.providencia.cl), open 9 A.M.–8 P.M. weekdays and 10 A.M.–7 P.M. weekends.

NATIONAL PARKS

South of the Alameda, the **Corporación Nacional Forestal** (Conaf, Av. Bulnes 291, tel. 02/3900282 or 02/3900125, www.conaf.cl) provides information on national parks and other protected areas; it also has inexpensive maps, as well as books and pamphlets. Hours are 9 A.M.–1 P.M. and 2–4:30 P.M. weekdays only.

MAPS

Though it no longer comes in a compact and relatively durable paperback book format, Telefónica CTC's *Plano de Santiago* is indispensable for its full-color coverage and detailed index of city streets. The format now resembles a Sunday newspaper supplement, on flimsy newsprint.

JLM Cartografía's *Santiago* covers most of the city well, but lacks a scale; it also includes a country map at a scale of 1:3,000,000. Widely available overseas, ITM's *Santiago de Chile* (scale 1:12,500) is good for getting around and has a street index, but it has numerous misspellings.

NEWSPAPERS AND LIBRARIES

The notoriously conservative—many would say reactionary—daily *El Mercurio* still publishes paeans to Pinochet, but now does it through guest columnists rather than its own editorial department. It partially compensates for that with broad international, business, cultural, and entertainment coverage. The tabloid *La Nación* is the official government daily, but its editorial line seems more diverse and independent. The dailies *La Tercera, Últimas Noticias,* and the squalid *La Cuarta* are all conservative tabloids—the first has some credibility, but the latter focus on sensationalist celebrity, crime, and sex stories (often simultaneously).

The online *Santiago Times* (www.santiagotimes.cl) provides an excellent digest of the Spanish-language press, but full access requires a paid subscription.

The **Biblioteca Nacional** (Alameda 651, tel. 02/3605200), the national library, also has frequent special exhibitions on history, archaeology, and art.

MONEY

ATMs are so abundant that exchange houses have become virtual dinosaurs except for changing travelers checks or leftover cash. Most exchange houses are downtown on Agustinas, between Bandera and Ahumada, but there are others in Providencia and at the airport (where rates are notably lower).

For replacing lost or stolen travelers checks, contact the AmEx representative (Blanco Viajes, Carmencita 20, Las Condes, tel. 02/3459500, www.blanco.cl) or Thomas Cook representative.

POSTAL SERVICES

The **Correo Central** (Plaza de Armas 983) is open 8 A.M.–10 P.M. weekdays, 8 A.M.–6 P.M. Saturday. In addition to poste restante (general delivery), it has a philatelic office here and branch offices around town.

For courier service, try **Federal Express** (Av. Providencia 1951, tel. 02/2315250).

COMMUNICATIONS

Long-distance *centros de llamados* are so abundant that none needs individual mention any more. Many of these provide Internet access as well, but there are also countless Internet specialists charging US$1 per hour or even less.

IMMIGRATION

For visa extensions, visit the **Departamento de Extranjería** (Moneda 1342, Santiago Centro, tel. 02/6725320), open 8:30 A.M.–3:30 P.M. daily. Replacing a lost tourist card requires a trip to the **Policía Internacional** (General Borgoño 1052, Independencia, tel. 02/7371292), across the Mapocho from the old railroad station. Hours are 8:30 A.M.–12:30 P.M. and 3–7 P.M. weekdays.

LAUNDRY

Laundries include Santiago Centro's **Lavandería Autoservicio** (Monjitas 507, tel. 02/6321772), Barrio Brasil's **Lavandería Lolos** (Moneda 2296, tel. 02/6995376), and Providencia's **Laverap** (Av. Providencia 1645).

TRAVEL AGENCIES

Las Condes's **Blanco Viajes** (Carmencita 20, tel. 02/3459500, www.blanco.cl) is the AmEx representative. The **Student Flight Center** (Hernando de Aguirre 201, Oficina 401, Providencia, tel. 02/3350395, fax 02/3350394, www.sertur.cl) provides discounts for both students and the general public.

PHOTOGRAPHY

For simple camera repairs and service, try **Von Stowasser** (Santa Magdalena 16, Providencia, tel. 02/2315559). For more complex needs, visit **Photo Service** (Av. Suecia 84, 8th floor, Providencia, tel. 02/3354460).

LANGUAGE SCHOOLS

Perhaps because Chilean Spanish is so distinctive and Santiago is distant from the language study centers of Mexico and Central America, it lacks the critical mass of language schools that some other Latin American capitals have. Still, the number of schools has increased; most work with small groups of students but offer one-on-one classes for higher fees.

Usually the minimum fee is around US$150–170 per week for 4–6 hours of instruction per day; longer periods are cheaper by the hour, but more intensive courses may be more expensive. Most language schools either offer housing or can help arrange homestays with a Chilean family.

Among the options are the **Bridge Linguatec Language Center** (Los Leones 439, Providencia, tel. 02/233-4356, tel. 866/574-8606 in the U.S. and Canada, www .bridgechile.com); the **Escuela Violeta Parra** (Ernesto Pinto Lagarrigue 362-A, Recoleta, tel. 02/7358240, www.tandemsantiago.cl), which is particularly strong on field excursions that tie in with its political and social commitment; the **Instituto Chileno-Suizo de Idioma** (José Victorino Lastarria 93, 2nd floor, tel. 02/6385414, www.chilenosuizo.cl); and the **Natalis Language Center** (Vicuña Mackenna 6, 7th floor, tel./fax 02/2228721, www.natalislang.com).

MEDICAL

The **Posta Central** (Av. Portugal 125, Santiago Centro, tel. 02/6341650) is a public clinic; the private **Clínica Universidad Católica** (Lira 40, tel. 02/3846000, www.clinicauc.cl) is nearby. The private **Clínica Alemana** (Av. Vitacura 5951, Vitacura, tel. 02/2129700, www.alemana.cl) is highly regarded.

Getting There

Santiago enjoys international air service from most South American capitals and some provincial cities, and from Europe, North America and the Caribbean, and across the Pacific. Domestic air service is available from Arica, near the Peruvian border, to Punta Arenas, in the far south, and to Easter Island (Rapa Nui) and the Juan Fernández archipelago.

International and domestic overland passengers arrive by bus from Peru, Argentina, and many destinations throughout the country. Regular passenger train service connects Santiago with the southern cities of Temuco and Concepción; a separate line runs from Temuco to Puerto Montt. In the summer of 2009, though, authorities suspended all long-distance rail service.

AIR

Domestically **LAN** (Huérfanos 926, tel. 02/5263000) flies northbound to Arica and intermediates, and southbound to Punta Arenas and intermediates. Its competitors, **Sky Airline** (Andrés de Fuenzalida 55, Providencia, tel. 02/3533100) has fewer destinations and flights, but is growing steadily.

BUS

Santiago's four bus terminals are all on or near the Alameda; some companies have offices at more than one.

Tur-Bus and **Pullman Bus** are based at the **Terminal de Buses Alameda** (Alameda 3750, tel. 02/2707500; Metro: Universidad de Santiago) and travel to a wide variety of destinations. Most southbound carriers use nearby **Terminal Santiago** (also known as Terminal de Buses Sur, Alameda 3848, tel. 02/3761755).

Northbound long-distance carriers use **Terminal San Borja** (San Borja 184, tel. 02/7760645, www.terminalsanborja.cl; Metro: Estación Central). Some northbound carriers also use **Terrapuerto Los Héroes** (Tucapel Jiménez 21, tel. 02/4200099, www .terrapuertolosheroes.co.cl), where some Terminal Santiago buses pick up additional passengers. Most international carriers use Terminal Santiago, but the handful that use Terminal los Héroes are specifically mentioned as follows.

Fares can fluctuate both seasonally and among companies, so comparison pricing is advisable. Correlation between distance and price is imperfect—some longer trips can be cheaper because competition is greater to certain destinations.

Sample domestic destinations, fares, and journey times include Valparaíso or Viña del Mar (US$7, 2 hours), La Serena (US$23–35, 7 hours), Copiapó (US$41–63, 10 hours), Antofagasta (US$57–84, 19 hours), Calama (US$61–92, 22 hours), Iquique (US$65–91, 24 hours), Arica (US$71–92, 28 hours), Chillán (US$18–23, 5 hours), Concepción (US$22, 7 hours), Temuco (US$33–51, 9 hours), Villarrica (US$36–61, 11 hours), Valdivia (US$33–62, 12 hours), and Puerto Montt (US$38–69, 15 hours).

The Argentine city of Mendoza (US$32, 6 hours), just across the Andes via the Libertadores tunnel, is the most frequent foreign destination; Mendoza's massive bus terminal has frequent onward connections throughout Argentina and to Brazil, Uruguay, and Paraguay.

From Terminal Santiago, Mendoza-bound carriers include **Covalle Bus** (tel. 02/7787576), **El Rápido Internacional** (tel. 02/7790316), **Transportes Automotores Cuyo** (TAC, tel. 02/7796920), and **Tur-Bus,** tel. 02/4907500). There are also *minibuses* to Mendoza with **Coitram** (tel. 02/7761891), which are an hour faster and now a bit cheaper (around US$27).

Also to Mendoza, **Buses Ahumada** (tel. 02/6969337) uses Terminal los Héroes, where **Pullman del Sur** (tel. 02/7795243) goes to Asunción, Paraguay (US$83, 30 hours), on Tuesday and Friday at 1 P.M.

Nar-Bus (tel. 02/7781235) goes to Argentina's Patagonian cities of Junín de los Andes, San Martín de los Andes, and Neuquén, with a change of buses in Temuco. **Cruz del Sur** (tel. 02/7790607) also goes to Bariloche, but this requires changing buses in Osorno.

EGA (tel. 02/7793536) goes to Montevideo, Uruguay (US$100, 30 hours), with onward connections to Brazil. **Pluma** (tel. 02/7796054) goes weekly to Rio de Janeiro, Brazil (US$142, 62 hours), a direct service that does not allow stopovers in Argentina. **Chile Bus** (tel. 02/7765557) goes four times weekly to São Paulo (US$130, 54–56 hours) and to Rio de Janeiro; it also goes to La Paz, Bolivia, but this requires changing buses in Iquique.

Ormeño (tel. 02/7793443) goes to Lima, Peru (US$120, 56 hours), twice weekly, continuing to Quito, Bogotá, and Caracas—certified by the *Guinness Book of Records* as the world's longest bus route, it actually starts in Buenos Aires.

TRAIN
Estación Central (Alameda 3322, tel. 02/3768500), **EFE** (Empresa de los Ferrocarriles del Estado, www.efe.cl) normally has direct service to Chillán, Concepción, and Temuco (with connections to Puerto Montt), but operational problems in the summer of 2009 meant limited service only as far south as Talca. For updates, check EFE's website.

Getting Around

AIR
Serving all international and virtually all domestic flights, the state-of-the-art **Aeropuerto Internacional Arturo Merino Benítez** (tel. 02/6019001, 02/6019709) is 26 kilometers west of Santiago Centro, in the *comuna* of Pudahuel.

Flights to and from the Juan Fernández archipelago use the international airport and **Aeródromo Tobalaba** (Av. Larraín 7941) in the southeastern *comuna* of La Reina.

The new domestic airline, **Principal Airlines** (San Sebastian 2839, Oficina 611, Las Condes, tel. 02/6150600) flies to Iquique and Antofagasta.

For airport transport to Pudahuel, the cheapest option (US$1.75 pp) is **Centropuerto** (tel. 02/6019883), which has some 40 buses daily from Plazoleta Los Héroes, just off the eastbound lanes of the Alameda outside Los Héroes Metro station. The slightly more expensive Tur-Bus has similar services.

For shuttle services, it's best to call a day in advance. **Transvip** (tel. 02/6773000) provides door-to-door service for the entire city, starting around US$6 to Santiago Centro; Providencia, Las Condes, and other eastern *comunas* are slightly more expensive. This is the best option for travelers with heavy luggage, or those who arrive late at night.

Hotels can help arrange taxi or radio-taxi service, which can be cost-effective if shared by several people.

METRO
Carrying upwards of 200 million passengers per year, Santiago's quiet, clean, and efficient Metro (www.metrosantiago.cl) would be the pride of many European cities. Four interconnected lines cover most points of interest; others, and extensions of existing lines, are under construction.

For most visitors, Línea 1, running beneath the Alameda, Avenida Providencia, and Avenida Apoquindo, is the most useful; it will soon continue east to Los Dominicos. Línea 2 connects Cerro Blanco, north of the Río Mapocho, with the southern La Cisterna station. Línea 4 (there is no Línea 3 as yet) links Tobalaba with the southeastern suburb of Puente Alto and with La Cisterna via the lateral Línea 4-A. Línea 5 connects Quinta Normal with the southeastern *comuna* of La Florida.

There are seven transfer stations: Los Héroes (Línea 1 and Línea 2), Baquedano (Línea 1 and Línea 5), Santa Ana (Línea 2 and Línea 5), Tobalaba (Línea 1 and Línea 4), La Cisterna (Línea 2 and Línea 4-A), Vicuña Mackenna (Línea 4 and Línea 4-A), and Vicente Valdés (Línea 4 and Línea 5).

Hours are 6:30 A.M.–10:30 P.M. daily except Sundays and holidays, when it's open 8 A.M.–10:30 P.M. Fares depend on the hour of the day. A *punta* (peak hour) ticket, good 7:15–9 A.M. and 6–7:30 P.M. weekdays, costs US$0.70; during the day and on weekends, the *valle* (low hour) fare is about US$0.65. The turnstile swallows the ticket, which is not needed to exit the system.

Multivía (multitrip ticket) purchasers get small discounts, but the electronic ticket itself requires a US$3 investment that's almost pointless for short-term users. More than one person, though, may use a *multivía* ticket by passing it back across the turnstile (this is not illegal).

BUS

Traditionally, Santiago city buses *(micros)* have been numerous and cheap, and have run all day and all night to virtually every part of town—often faster than they should. They have also spewed black diesel clouds into Santiago's already smoggy skies, but the Lagos administration's Transantiago plan to replace those dilapidated yellow-and-whites with smart new, cleaner-burning articulated buses has proved better in theory than in practice.

Along the Alameda are dedicated bus lanes and fixed stops, intended to speed up traffic, and the hope is that the new system will reduce traffic congestion, but this has not yet happened. After the Metro closes, it's the main means of getting around town.

Destinations are marked on window signs and at fixed stops. Boarding requires exact change or an electronic *bip* ticket (interchangeable with the Metro's Multivía).

© WAYNE BERNHARDSON

In recent years, Transantiago's sharp articulated buses have replaced most of its smoky diesels, but the system has drawn criticism for not being user-friendly.

TRAIN

From the Estación Central, **Metrotrén** runs 28 trains to Rancagua (US$2) between 6:45 A.M. and 10:05 P.M. every weekday, three fewer on weekends. Eleven of these weekday trains continue to San Fernando, the last of which leaves at 8:45 P.M.; there's one fewer San Fernando train on weekends.

TAXI

Black with yellow roofs, regular taxis charge about US$0.50 to start the meter and US$0.15 more for every subsequent 200 meters. There is also a system of radio taxis with fixed fares within certain zones; among the choices are **Radio Taxi Arauco** (tel. 02/2461114) and **Radio Taxi Alameda** (tel. 02/7764730).

TAXI COLECTIVOS

Designated by illuminated roof signs, *taxi colectivos* carry up to four or five passengers on fixed itineraries. Slightly more expensive than regular buses, they cover many of the same routes but are often quicker.

Vicinity of Santiago

An extraordinary number of interesting sights are near Santiago, suitable both for day trips and overnights. Among the many activities are winery tours, winter skiing and summer hiking, horseback riding, and white-water rafting and kayaking.

ADS Mundo (El Golf 99, Las Condes, tel. 02/3877070, www.adsmundo.cl) has the widest variety and greatest frequency of day tours for Santiago and its vicinity, including coastal excursions to places like Valparaíso and Isla Negra.

U.S.-run **Santiago Adventures** (Guardia Vieja 255, Oficina 403, tel. 02/2442750, www.santiagoadventures.com) arranges a variety of excursions focusing on city tours, skiing, and wine, both within and beyond the immediate metropolitan area.

Activities-oriented operators include **Cascada Expediciones** (Don Carlos 3219, Las Condes, tel. 02/2329878, www.cascada.travel), which specializes in the Cajón del Maipo, and **Altué Active Travel** (Encomenderos 83, Las Condes, tel. 02/2321103, www.chileoutdoors.com), though its day excursions are substantially more expensive.

In addition to its human-rights focus, **Chip Travel** (Av. Santa María 227, Oficina 12, tel. 02/7775376, www.chip.cl) offers more traditional historical and cultural tours, winery excursions, and trips to Pablo Neruda's Isla Negra house.

CALEU

In a secluded coast range valley on the border between the Metropolitan Region and Region V (Valparaíso), northwest of Santiago, the village of Caleu has attained a certain rustic chic among Santiago's elite—including ex-president Ricardo Lagos, who owns a weekend house here. Perhaps because it has avoided the more garish aspects of Chile's economic transformation, Caleu is widely regarded as symbolic of a simpler past, with its modest artisans' market and November's equally modest Feria Artesanal y Gastronómico (Crafts and Food Fair).

There's little to do in Caleu except kick back, walk, ride, and go birding in the nearby mountains (Parque Nacional La Campana is just across the regional border to the west, via the serpentine road over the pass known as Cuesta la Dormida). **La Cabaña de Steve** (cel. 09/9517-7222, US$60) can sleep up to five people on orchard grounds with a small swimming pool.

Caleu is about 75 kilometers northwest of Santiago via Ruta 5 (the Panamericana), the town of Tiltil, and a northbound lateral off the road over the Cuesta la Dormida. An alternative route leaves the Panamericana at Rungue and heads directly east to Caleu. The only regular public transportation is via **Buses Colina** (Av. La Paz 350, Independencia, tel. 02/7374572), which leaves at 4 P.M. daily (US$3, 1.5 hours).

SKI RESORTS

From the eastern *comuna* of Lo Barnechea, a narrow paved road climbs gradually up the Río Mapocho Canyon, past the entrance to the massive La Disputada copper mine, and then snakes up dozens of switchbacks before branching into separate routes to Santiago's best ski areas. On this winding road with numbered curves, some people suffer motion sickness—so much so that some even take medication.

Some skiers have remarked that, unlike forested areas in most of Europe and North America, the barren Chilean skiscapes make depth perception difficult, so it's best to be prepared for a different kind of experience.

Note that, during ski season, there are road restrictions on weekends and holidays: Traffic goes uphill only 8 A.M.–2 P.M., downhill only 4–8 P.M., and both directions at all other hours. Carabineros may require chains beyond a certain point.

At the upper end of the Cajón del Mapocho, barely an hour from Santiago in the area known as Tres Valles, there are three major resorts: El Colorado, La Parva, and Valle Nevado. Where the road forks, the left fork goes to El Colorado and La Parva, while the right fork goes to Valle Nevado.

While Chilean ski areas enjoy high elevations, the start of the rainy (and snowy) season can be erratic in this Mediterranean climate; it generally runs from June to early October. For this reason, Chilean resorts now have snowmaking equipment to help augment the natural snowfall at the beginning of the season; for current snow conditions, see the online English-language news service *Santiago Times* (www.santiagotimes.cl).

Full equipment rentals—boots, skis, poles—cost around US$30 per person per day, but high-performance equipment costs US$37 per person per day. Snowboards and boots cost US$30 per day. Both lift tickets and rental equipment are marginally cheaper when purchased from Skitotal in Las Condes.

Skitotal (Av. Apoquindo 4900, Local 42-46, Las Condes, tel. 02/2460156, www.skitotal .cl) also runs shuttles to El Colorado (US$15), La Parva (US$15), and Valle Nevado (US$16). Shuttles depart around 8:15 A.M. daily, returning around 5 P.M. from each site. Skitotal can also arrange three-day budget packages, with lift tickets, all gear, dorm accommodations, most meals, and transport, for US$451.

El Colorado

Just 39 kilometers east of Santiago, with a maximum elevation of 3,333 meters, El Colorado has 18 lifts from a base elevation of 2,750 meters. Daily lift tickets are more expensive on weekends (US$61) than on weekdays (US$46) except for the mid-July to mid-August period, when there is no differential. There are discounts for children and seniors.

The nearby Swiss-style **Hotel Posada de Farellones** (tel. 02/2013704, www.skifarellones.com, US$180–300 s or d) has packages whose rates include breakfast, dinner, and lift tickets, while El Colorado has its own apart-hotel accommodations.

For additional information in Santiago, contact **Centro de Ski El Colorado** (Av. Apoquindo 4900, Local 47-48, Las Condes, tel. 02/2463344, www.elcolorado.cl); this is a major departure point for minibuses from Santiago.

La Parva

Only a short distance north of El Colorado, La Parva's skiable runs range from 2,662 to 3,630 meters above sea level—nearly a 1,000-meter vertical drop. Lift tickets cost are a bit cheaper than at El Colorado, US$47 on weekends and US$38 on weekdays.

Accommodations are available on a weekly basis through the **Centro de Ski La Parva** (Av El Bosque Norte 0177, 2nd floor, tel. 02/3398482, Las Condes, Santiago, www .laparva.cl).

◖ Valle Nevado

Highest of the three resorts, 14 kilometers beyond the Farellones junction, Valle Nevado reaches 3,670 meters above sea level, though its base is 2,860. There are 37 kilometers of trails, even more for those who can afford to indulge in helicopter dropoffs that aren't accessible by lifts.

Valle Nevado is a full-service resort, with multiple hotels, restaurants, a cinema, bars, day care, and many other amenities. For nonguests, weekend and holiday lift tickets cost US$50; weekday tickets run US$37.

Valle Nevado has three luxury hotels: **Hotel Valle Nevado** (US$244–438 pp with half board per night, varying between low and high season), **Hotel Tres Puntas** (US$150–257 pp), and **Hotel Puerta del Sol** (US$181–371 pp).

Among the restaurants, **La Trattoria** has reasonably priced pizza with thin crust and a fair number of toppings, including scallops and artichoke, but the buffet is expensive. **Slalom** is its fast-food outlet.

For more information, contact **Valle Nevado** (Av. Vitacura 5250, Oficina 304, Vitacura, tel. 02/4777000, www.vallenevado.com). Valle Nevado has toll-free numbers in the United States (tel. 800/669-0554) and Canada (tel. 888/301-3248).

SANTUARIO DE LA NATURALEZA YERBA LOCA

Just before the road begins its final ascent to the major ski resorts, it passes the entrance to Yerba Loca, one of Santiago's best hiking and mountain biking options. Even in winter much of this scenic high mountain area remains snow-free. Donated to the *comuna* of Las Condes by former *fundo* owner Hans von Kiesling and now under Conaf management, this national monument gets fewer visitors than it deserves.

Geography and Climate

In the Andean front range 27 kilometers east of Santiago, the sanctuary comprises 39,029 mountainous hectares between the parallel Andean ridges of El Plomo–La Parva to the east and Yerba Loca to the west; the Estero de la Yerba Loca is a U-shaped valley between the two that drains south into the Mapocho.

Elevations range from about 1,500 meters on the Mapocho itself to 4,910 meters on the summit of Cerro La Paloma.

Yerba Loca's climate is Mediterranean, with long dry summers and short wet winters that include snow at the highest elevations. Because of its elevation, seasonal and diurnal temperature variations are greater than in Santiago proper.

Flora and Fauna

Yerba Loca's vegetation consists of spiny shrubs and sclerophyllous (glossy-leaved) trees at lower elevations, with sparse bunch grasses at higher altitudes. The remaining native fauna include mostly rodents, but there are also many birds, including predators such as the peregrine falcon and *carancho* (crested caracara), the striking *bandurria* or buff-necked ibis, and the occasional scavenging Andean condor.

Sights and Recreation

From the ranger station at Curva 15, the former vehicle road is now a 4.2-kilometer trail that takes about 1.5 hours to walk to **Villa Paulina,** the former *fundo* headquarters and site of a Conaf campground. Mountain bikers leave their cars at the park entrance and ride to Paulina and beyond.

Continuing north from Paulina, the **Sendero al Glaciar** is a 30-kilometer round-trip to an ice field at the base of Cerro La Paloma; the shorter **Sendero Interpretativo La Leonera** is a 45-minute nature trail.

Practicalities

Conaf's campground (US$2.50 pp), or at least part of it, occupies an aging pear orchard where it's possible to collect fresh fruit in the fall. There are picnic tables and clean flush toilets, but no hot water.

Conaf's Guardería at Curva 15 collects a US$2.50 per person admission charge.

VIÑA UNDURRAGA

In the Lower Maipo Valley, between Peñaflor and Talagante, Undurraga is one of Chilean wine's traditional big names;

dating from the 1880s, its original brick cellars and the wooded gardens—the latter designed by French landscape architect Pierre Dubois—are a national historical monument. Surrounded by one of its four vineyards, the contemporary processing and bottling plants produce mostly cabernet sauvignon, carmenere, and chardonnay.

All the facilities are open for exhaustive guided tours (US$12 pp), which conclude with a sample of three reserve wines and a complimentary glass to take home. The tasting room is also a store with a complete selection of Undurraga wines and souvenirs.

Reservations are essential to visit Viña Undurraga (tel. 02/3722850, www.undurraga.cl), which is 34 kilometers southwest of Santiago via the Autopista del Sol (Ruta 68). Hour-plus tours take place weekdays 10 A.M.–3:30 P.M., weekends and holidays 10 A.M.–1 P.M.

If driving, take the Malloco exit, turn right after paying the toll, and then left at the first traffic light, continuing about two kilometers to the vineyard. From Santiago's Terminal San Borja (San Borja 184), **Buses Peñaflor** (tel. 02/7761025) passes the vineyard entrance.

POMAIRE

About 70 kilometers southwest of the capital via Ruta 68, the dusty village of Pomaire produces many of the clay pots that contain *cazuela de ave, paila marina,* and *pastel de choclo* in homes and restaurants throughout the country. Foot-powered potters' wheels and wood-heated kilns are still the rule, but electrical equipment is supplanting some of the traditional technology. Before attempting to haul any of this fragile material home, get it well and tightly packed.

Pomaire is busiest on weekends, when excursionists from Santiago crowd the streets and fill good but unpretentious eateries. Traditional hearty Chilean dishes such as *pastel de choclo* are the standard—no Santiago pseudo-sophisticates here.

From Santiago's Terminal San Borja (San Borja 184), **Buses Melipilla** (tel. 02/7763881)

has frequent bus service to Pomaire, continuing to Melipilla.

◖ CAJÓN DEL MAIPO

Barely an hour southeast of downtown Santiago, the Río Maipo has cut a deep canyon through more than 70 kilometers of the Andean foothills before it meanders onto the plains near the town of Pirque. Once the border of the Kollasuyu, the Inka empire's southernmost limits, the Cajón del Maipo (Canyon of the Maipo) is one of urban Santiago's great escapes, barely an hour from the Plaza de Armas.

Starting with fine wineries at Pirque and Santa Rita, the canyon just gets better as it climbs toward the Andean crest. While parts of the main road are cluttered with cabañas, campgrounds, and restaurants, it still provides access to plenty of high and wild country—not to mention the river itself. Paved as far as Romeral, it and a parallel road from Pirque are good enough for road bikes, but other routes are suitable for mountain bikers, and hikers and horseback riders can explore the trails of Monumento Natural El Morado and the private nature reserve Cascada de las Ánimas.

The Class III–IV Río Maipo provides plenty of thrills for rafters and kayakers even though diversions for irrigation works and even more from sand and gravel quarrying have taken their toll. At day's end, rustic hot springs are suitable for a soak. While the area gets crowded in summer and on weekends and holidays, especially from December to March, the rest of the year it's pretty sedate.

Transportation to the Cajón del Maipo is good and getting better—though perhaps not so interesting as when, half a century ago, a military train carried passengers from Puente Alto to El Volcán. From the Puente Alto Metro station, **Buses Cajón del Maipo** (tel. 02/8611518) ascends as far as San José de Maipo every eight minutes, to San Alfonso (US$1) every half hour, and to San Gabriel (US$2) hourly. From the Bellavista de La Florida station, it also goes to Baños Morales (US$7.50 round-trip) Saturday and Sunday at

8:30 A.M. all year; in summer, departures are daily. *Taxi colectivos* also shuttle up and down the canyon from the Puente Alto Metro.

Viña Santa Rita

Bernardo O'Higgins and 120 of his troops hid from the Spaniards in the catacombs at Hacienda Santa Rita, a distinguished winery that named its main line of wines—120—after the event. Today, its main house is a hotel, the former colonial house (a national monument) is a restaurant, and the grounds and cellars (also a national monument) are open for tours (US$13 pp with tasting) at 11:30 A.M. and 4 P.M. weekdays except Monday. On weekends and holidays, tours are free with lunch (which costs around US$28) but do not include sampling the produce.

Santa Rita's 16-room **Hotel Casa Real** (tel. 02/8219966, hotelcasareal@santarita.cl, US$350–465 s or d) is open by reservation only; its restaurant, **La Casa de Doña Paula** (tel. 02/3622520) is open 12:30–3:30 P.M. daily, also by reservation.

Though it's not quite in the Cajón del Maipo proper, Viña Santa Rita (Camino Padre Hurtado 0695, Alto Jahuel, tel. 02/3622594, www.santarita.com, rrivas@santarita.cl) is part of the Maipo drainage, east of Buin and southwest of Pirque; buses from Pirque to Buin pass the front gates. For obligatory reservations, contact them at least a few days in advance.

Viña Concha y Toro and Vicinity (Pirque)

On the Maipo's south bank, 30 kilometers from Santiago, Pirque is a tranquil community that's resisted the cookie-cutter suburbanization that mars much of southeastern Santiago. Its key attraction is Viña Concha y Toro, one of Chile's largest and oldest wineries, but it also boasts a weekend crafts fair and is the starting point for a scenic but narrow paved road that climbs the canyon before rejoining the main road via a bridge at El Toyo.

Viña Concha y Toro (Victoria Subercaseaux 210, tel. 02/4765269, www.conchaytoro.cl) offers guided English-language tours with tasting

(US$10 pp) of its vineyards, estate grounds, cellars, and museum at 10 and 11:30 A.M., noon, and 3 P.M. daily except Sunday. Spanish-language tours take place 10:30 and 11 A.M. and noon and 4 P.M. daily, but there's a good chance a bilingual guide may be able to handle English-speakers on these tours as well. While reservations are desirable, it's often possible to join an existing group that might include—who knows?—figures such as Mick Jagger, Bono, Helmut Kohl, Nicaraguan poet Ernesto Cardenal, and others who have toured the grounds and sampled the results.

After the tour, look for lunch at any number of eateries along Ramón Subercaseaux, the main road up the Maipo's south bank. **La Vaquita Echá** (Ramón Subercaseaux 3355, tel. 02/8546025) can seat up to 500 people indoors and outdoors for country cuisine such as *pastel de choclo* and *cazuela de ave*.

Reserva Nacional Río Clarillo

In the precordillera southeast of Pirque, Río Clarillo is a 10,185-hectare unit of glossy-leaved Mediterranean scrub woodland, plus denser gallery forest along the course of its namesake river, a Maipo tributary. While Conaf does not allow camping here, it does permit picnicking and hiking.

Two short nature trails have interpretive panels: the 1.2-kilometer **Sendero Interpretativo Quebrada Jorquera** and the 1.7-kilometer **Sendero Interpretativo Aliven Mahuida,** a more biologically diverse path. Conaf collects a US$4 per person admission charge.

Reserva Nacional Río Clarillo is 45 kilometers southeast of Santiago and 18 kilometers from Pirque.

Las Vizcachas

At the western approach to the main road up the north side of the Cajón del Maipo, just beyond the Carabineros police post at Las Vizcachas, note the informal shrine for the folk saint **Difunta Correa,** strongly identified with Argentina's San Juan province but with a distinctly binational twist here. According to legend, the young mother Deolinda Correa died of thirst in the desert in the 19th century, but her baby survived at her breast; her need for water explains the bottles left by her devotees.

On the south side of the highway, a bit farther on, **Vinícola Cavas del Maipo** (tel. 02/8711508, www.cavasdelmaipo.co.cl) offers guided winery tours US$7) by reservation only, preferably made a day ahead of time. The visit includes half a dozen samples of their wines, accompanied by cheese and crackers.

Geo Expediciones has a climbing wall at its Centro de Escalada (Camino al Volcán 07910, tel. 02/8712110, www.geoexpediciones .cl). It also organizes hiking, mountain biking, horseback riding, rafting, and paragliding excursions.

La Obra

A short distance east of Las Vizcachas, 790 meters above sea level, La Obra was a stop on the military railroad that once climbed from Puente Alto to El Volcán; its **Estación La Obra** is a national monument. Directly on the highway, seating up to 200 people for lunch or dinner, **Hostería El Tucán** (La Obra 675, tel. 02/8711089, www.eltucan.cl, US$44 pp with full board) appeals to the masses.

Just east of La Obra, the rise known as Cuesta las Chilcas was the site of the Frente Patriótico Manuel Rodríguez's 1986 assassination attempt on General Pinochet as he returned to Santiago from his El Melocotón country house. Five of Pinochet's bodyguards died in a hail of bullets and a rocket launcher attack, but his chauffeur's skilled driving saved the dictator's life. Pinochet's admirers have commemorated the event with a monument honoring his bodyguards.

El Manzano

With sunny outdoor seating overlooking the river, **Trattoria Calypso** (Camino al Volcán 5247, tel. 02/8711498) is an outstanding Italian restaurant that makes a great stop on the way up the canyon. The menu, of course, concentrates on pasta, but with greater variety than in many Italian restaurants in Santiago proper, and it offers an exceptional dessert menu. Befitting its weekend business, it's only open Friday–Saturday 12:30–10 P.M., and Sunday 12:30–6 P.M. Figure about US$10–12 for most entrées.

Guayacán

At a bend in the river, a few kilometers north of San José de Maipo, **Casa Bosque** has the most extravagant decor of any Cajón del Maipo restaurant—the twisted trunks of polished cypress that hold it up seem like something from Grimm's most nightmarish tales or an early Disney misadventure. Unfortunately, the putatively simple menu based on beef, plus a few chicken and pork dishes, falls short of what might be called imaginative architecture. Most entrées are in the US$10–18 range. Still, Casa Bosque (Camino El Volcán 16829, tel. 02/8711570, www.casabosque.cl) is worth seeing for the spectacle; it has recently added an 18-room hotel whose interior is less preposterous than the restaurant.

San José de Maipo

The canyon's largest town, 967 meters above sea level, San José has a leafy Plaza de Armas focused on its **Iglesia y Casa Parroquial,** a national monument dating from late colonial times. Its former **Estación de Ferrocarril,** also a national monument, was a stop on the military railroad from Puente Alto to El Volcán.

Centro de Ski Lagunillas

From a turnoff just south of San José, a winding dirt road leads 19 kilometers northeast to Lagunillas, a scenic but no-frills beginners' ski area rather than a high-powered resort such as Valle Nevado or Portillo. At the final approach, there's an oddball sculpture 3–4 meters high apparently intended to portray Jesus Christ, but it could as easily be a Rasta (someone even scribbled "legalize it" on one of its legs).

In ski season, lift tickets cost around US$20 weekdays, US$25 on weekends. For details, including accommodations information, contact the **Club Andino** (Alameda 108, Local 215, cel. 09/9825-3578, www.skilagunillas.cl), which also provides transportation from San José de Maipo.

El Melocotón

About five kilometers south of San José de Maipo, El Melocotón is most famous—or notorious—as the site of General Pinochet's riverfront home (the first recreational kayakers to descend the Maipo, in the 1970s, faced automatic rifles pointed at them from the shore). It briefly made the news again in 2001 when it was discovered that a former FPMR guerrilla had rented a house just a few hundred meters from the general's residence.

San Alfonso

San Alfonso, about six kilometers southeast of El Melocotón and 1,106 meters above sea level, made news in 1997 when local residents successfully forced relocation of a natural gas pipeline from Argentina by establishing a private nature reserve at Cascada de las Ánimas. A short distance up a tree-lined dirt road before the entrance to Cascada de las Ánimas, look for the scale miniature railway circling the house and gardens of José Sagall ("Pepe Tren"), as well as his assortment of full-scale antique railcars. About 100 meters farther south, the former **Estación San Alfonso** is a national monument as part of the military short line that also hauled Santiaguinos to their weekend getaways from the capital.

Hostería Posada Los Ciervos (Camino el Volcán 31411, tel. 02/8611581, US$37 d for bed and breakfast) is an aging, somewhat ramshackle place that still manages to exude personality. Its restaurant has good desserts.

New on the scene **Hotel Altiplánico** (Camino al Volcán 29955, tel. 02/8612078, www.altiplano.cl, US$200 s, US$300 d) is the latest effort of the boutique hotel chain that now has properties in Puerto Natales, San Pedro Atacama, and Easter Island.

Santuario de la Naturaleza Cascada de las Ánimas

In the midst of a multiyear struggle to divert a natural gas pipeline from Argentina,

the Andean precordillera of the Astorga family's former *fundo* Cascada de la Ánimas became one of Chile's first private nature reserves in 1995. Only two years later, though, did the owners manage to definitively defeat the pipeline.

In practice, the official designation hasn't made much difference, but it allows them to continue, without disruption, the activities-oriented recreation that has made the 3,600-hectare property a prime destination for hikers, riders, and especially white-water rafters and kayakers. Descending the Maipo (US$31 pp) is a Class III–IV experience that's normally suitable for novices, but the river can get wild enough for more experienced white-water lovers, especially during the spring runoff. Elevations range from about 1,100 meters along the river to 3,050 meters on the highest summit.

Many Santiaguino families come here for picnicking (US$5 per adult, US$3 per kid) and swimming (another US$10 pp for adults, US$7 for kids) at Cascada's large outdoor pool on the river's more developed north side. Most other activities take place on the south side, where the **Sendero Cascada de las Ánimas** is a short guided hike to its namesake waterfall. More foreigners than Chileans undertake the two- to three-hour guided climb to the summit of **Cerro Pangal.** While horseback riders will enjoy this scenic terrain, much of it is very steep and novice riders should be particularly cautious. Cascada also offers longer two- to three-day rides into the backcountry.

The campground charges US$10 per person for camping for adults, US$7 for children; after the first night, though, the price drops by a third. Cabaña accommodations cost US$73 double, US$110 for up to four people; larger cabañas are also available. These prices include pool access and a guided hike to the waterfall.

In addition, Cascada's restaurant **La Tribu** offers a diverse menu ranging from Chilean standards such as *cabrito* (kid goat) and *pastel de choclo,* as well as Thai and other international dishes. The new terrace has unobstructed river views.

For information on all activities and camping, contact **Cascada de las Ánimas** (tel. 02/8611303, www.cascada.net).

MONUMENTO NATURAL EL MORADO

Beyond San Gabriel, where the Río Yeso joins the Maipo and the paved road ends, it's 23 kilometers farther to one of the canyon's finest excursions, a taste of the high Andes at Monumento Natural El Morado. Only 92 kilometers from downtown Santiago, it overlooks the valley of the Río Volcán, a Maipo tributary that joins the main river a few kilometers south of San Gabriel.

Despite its modest size—only 3,009 hectares—El Morado gets hikers into the high country fast, with easy access to Andean lakes and glaciers. Though it's a feasible day trip from the capital, the camping and accommodations make it a good overnight option as well.

Geography and Climate

At altitudes ranging from about 1,750 meters in the Río Morales Valley to the 5,060-meter summit of Cerro El Morado, this is an alpine environment shaped by flowing ice and running water. It's also been shaped by tectonics—over 100 million years, the rising Andes have lifted marine fossils upward of 3,500 meters at Cerro Rubillar.

El Morado's climate is Mediterranean, with a pronounced dry summer and temperatures ranging up to 25°C, but more than two meters of snow can accumulate in winter. Because of the altitude, even summer nights are cool.

Flora and Fauna

Vegetation covers only about 20 percent of the park's otherwise rocky and icy surface, mostly in the form of Andean steppe. There are few shrubs and almost no trees, but where water accumulates the vegetation is more diverse.

Mammals are few, though foxes and skunks are occasionally seen, along with hares introduced from Europe. Waterfowl inhabit parts of the marshes, hummingbirds flit amongst the Andean scrub, and the occasional raptor or condor soars overhead.

Sights and Recreation

From the visitors center at the **Baños Morales** hot springs, the **Sendero El Ventisquero** is a six-kilometer trail that climbs steeply at the outset before leveling off at **Aguas Panimávida**, a series of small thermal springs. It continues to Laguna El Morado, a small lake at 2,400 meters, and on to the tongue of the **Ventisquero San Francisco.** From here, all further travel is cross-country.

Visitors disinclined to walk can rent horses cheaply at Baños Morales.

Practicalities

Conaf has a small rustic campground (US$3 pp) at Laguna El Morado; at Baños Morales, there is the inexpensive **Camping del Valle** and simple accommodations as well in summer.

The best option, though, is across the valley at the **Refugio Alemán** (Camino El Volcán s/n, cel. 09/9220-8525, www.refugiolovaldes.com,

© WAYNE BERNHARDSON

the Andean crest, east of Santiago

US$28 pp). Also known as Refugio Lo Valdés, this popular poplar-studded hillside hotel is no luxury lodging, but it's had a loyal public for both accommodations and food since the 1930s. There is also budget backpacker space in the attic (US$17 pp, sleeping bag essential, and bring your own towel). Both guests and nonguests can also take breakfast, lunch, dinner, or *onces* at the restaurant.

Rangers collect an admission charge of US$2.50 for adults, US$0.85 for children, at Conaf's **Centro de Información.**

At 7:30 A.M. Wednesday, Friday, Saturday, and Sunday, **Turismo Montaña** (tel. 02/8500555) buses leave for El Morado and Baños Morales (US$12 pp round-trip) from Parque Bustamante, Providencia, alongside the CTC telephone headquarters; they return at 6 P.M.

BAÑOS COLINA

At the end of the road, 12 kilometers from Baños Morales and 2,500 meters above sea level, barren Baños Colina is a no-frills hot springs with rocky, exposed campsites charging about US$4 per person. Summer pack trips across the Andes to Argentina start here (only organized tour companies such as Cascada Expediciones can easily handle the logistics), but there are opportunities for shorter rides in the vicinity.

Several companies offer transportation (about US$20 pp including access to the baths), usually on weekends, occasionally during the week, with frequently changing schedules. Most leave around 7 or 7:30 A.M. and return around 5 or 6 P.M. Space permitting, it's possible to stay overnight and return another day.

Carriers include **Expediciones Manzur** (tel. 02/7774284, turismomanzur@gmail. com), which leaves from Plaza Italia; **Buses Cordillera** (tel. 02/7773881), from Marcoleta and San Ysidro; and **Alicia Miranda** (tel. 02/7372844), from Alameda and Santa Rosa.

THE CHILEAN HEARTLAND

For most foreign visitors, Chile's Mediterranean heartland has played second fiddle to Torres del Paine's Patagonian grandeur, the forested Andean lakes and peaks, and the Atacama Desert's vast wastes. This is changing, though, as they discover appealing destinations such as the port of Valparaíso, a marvel of vernacular architecture and spontaneous urban growth that so entranced poet Pablo Neruda that he built homes there and at the beachfront community of Isla Negra.

Chile's coastline, from Valparaíso and its twin city Viña del Mar, north to Papudo and south to Cartagena, is a traditional summer destination for Chileans and for Argentines from over the Andes. Overseas travelers may find its Mediterranean headlands beautiful but the beaches crowded and the water cold even in summer; committed surfers, though, find the breaks at small resorts like Pichilemu irresistible even in midwinter.

For those reluctant to brave the water, the coast range backcountry of Parque Nacional La Campana is barely an hour from Viña; east of the Panamericana, from Rancagua south to Los Angeles, hikers have the underrated Andean scenery almost to themselves, thanks to the progress of the Sendero de Chile, a recreational path due to cover the length of the country.

The biggest news, though, is that Chilean wineries are now welcoming visitors for tours, tasting, dining, and even accommodations. Multiple "Rutas del Vino," each with distinctive characteristics, have become reason enough to travel the heartland.

© WAYNE BERNHARDSON

HIGHLIGHTS

◖ Hills of Valparaíso: With their funky funiculars and quasi-medieval streets, the port city's hills are the main reason it's a UNESCO World Heritage Site (page 95).

◖ Isla Negra: Poetry pilgrims and Chilean romantics stand in long lines to tour Neruda's beach house on the shoreline south of Valparaíso (page 108).

◖ Parque Nacional La Campana: From the summit of its namesake peak, this compact but ecologically diverse national park offers views from the vast Pacific to the peak of Cerro Aconcagua, the highest point in the Americas (across the Argentine border) (page 120).

◖ Portillo: Nudging the Argentine border, the snows of Portillo have seen downhill speed skiing records, but there are options for all skill levels (page 130).

◖ El Teniente (Sewell): Bidding for World Heritage Site status, the model company town of Sewell was the residential sector of the El Teniente copper mining complex, east of Rancagua (page 135).

◖ Museo de Colchagua: In the town of Santa Cruz, this highly professional museum helps put the surrounding wine country in historical context (page 139).

◖ Pichilemu: The water's cold all year, but the breaks bring surfers from around the world even in midwinter (page 144).

◖ Reserva Nacional Altos del Lircay: In the Andes east of Talca, Altos del Lircay is the best approach to the Sendero de Chile and wild backcountry that offers far more solitude than highly publicized Torres del Paine (page 152).

◖ Escuela México: In the city of Chillán, Mexican muralists David Alfaro Siqueiros and Xavier Guerrero left their politically committed legacy on the walls of a school financed by their government (page 156).

◖ Nevados de Chillán: East of its namesake city, hot-springs hotels and heavy snowpack make this Andean resort a year-round destination (page 158).

LOOK FOR ◖ TO FIND RECOMMENDED SIGHTS, ACTIVITIES, DINING, AND LODGING.

GEOGRAPHY AND CLIMATE

Chile's Mediterranean heartland, known to geographers as "Middle Chile," stretches from the northerly Río Aconcagua to the southerly Río Biobío drainage, where the rainfall regime changes gradually from the dry summer/wet winter profile to the more evenly distributed precipitation of a marine west coast climate.

The physical geography features a rugged Pacific coastline at the foot of coastal mountains that reach upward of 2,000 meters. To the east, millions of years of Andean runoff have deposited fertile sediments in the long but narrow Central Valley—really a structural depression rather than a single watershed—making it Chile's most productive agricultural region, suitable for grains, orchards, and vineyards. Beyond the Central Valley, which is barely 70 kilometers across at its widest, the Andes, dissected by several transverse rivers, rise dramatically.

Separated from the Central Valley by the coastal cordillera, the seashore enjoys a mild year-round climate, but the cool Humboldt Current keeps swimmers from staying too long in the sea. The *camanchaca,* which may obscure the sun until early afternoon, is a further deterrent to beachgoers, but even winter's cold waters don't deter surfers who bring proper wet suits.

Politically, the heartland consists of Santiago's Región Metropolitana, Region V (Valparaíso), Region VI (O'Higgins), Region VII (Maule), and Region VIII (Biobío). In addition, this chapter includes a couple Region IX (Araucanía) localities that are most easily accessible from the Panamericana in Region VIII.

Nearly three-quarters of all Chileans live in the densely populated heartland (including the capital), and most economic activity—industrial and agricultural—takes place here. The ports of Valparaíso, San Antonio, and Talcahuano connect the Central Valley's cities and the cordillera's copper mines to the rest of the world, while the Libertadores tunnel links them to the Argentine city of Mendoza.

PLANNING YOUR TIME

From the ocean to the Andes, the heartland is a geographically diverse region where time spent depends on individual preferences. Anyone with a sense of history and an appreciation of unique urbanism could spend several days or more exploring Valparaíso's recesses and, when walking the hills becomes tiring, spend a few afternoons nearby Viña del Mar's beaches or explore the scenic coastline to the north. With its cultural resources, Valparaíso makes an ideal location for an extended stay studying Spanish.

Most of the coastline, from Viña north, is the traditional choice for beach holidays, but intercontinental visitors are uncommon—the headlands are scenic enough, but the beaches and cool foggy weather can't match balmy Brazil or the Caribbean. Surfers are the exception, as they spend weeks or months at a time, often in winter, to ride the breaks at Pichilemu.

Meanwhile, the western Andean slopes, from Rancagua south to Los Angeles, are home to a series of high altitude national parks and reserves that, in many parts of the world, would be overrun with hikers. Here, though, the longitudinal Sendero de Chile is a long-distance footpath where hikers can find solitude and scenery to last for weeks—unlike the fabled but overcrowded Torres del Paine.

The Andes also have surprising cultural resources, most notably the historic mining ghost town of Sewell and the massive underground copper mine of El Teniente, now open to visitors.

In winter, two high Andes locations draw skiers from around the world: the record-setting venue of Portillo, near the Argentine border northwest of Santiago, and the hot-springs-and-snow combination of Termas de Chillán, east of its namesake market town. Weeklong packages are the rule, though it's possible to make day trips from below the snow line.

All year, though, Chilean wines provide reason enough to visit the heartland, though spring, summer, and fall are best. With well-

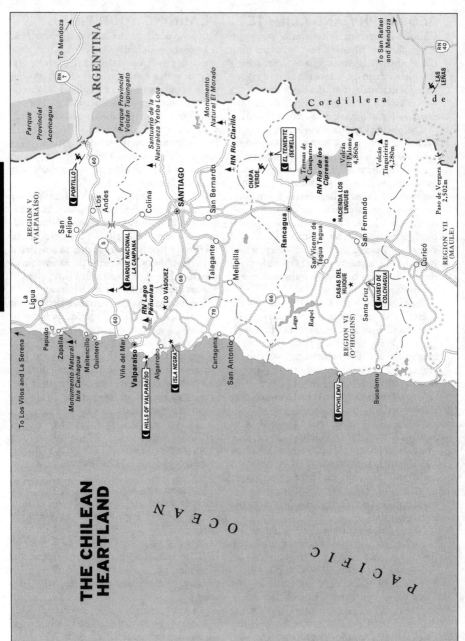

THE CHILEAN HEARTLAND

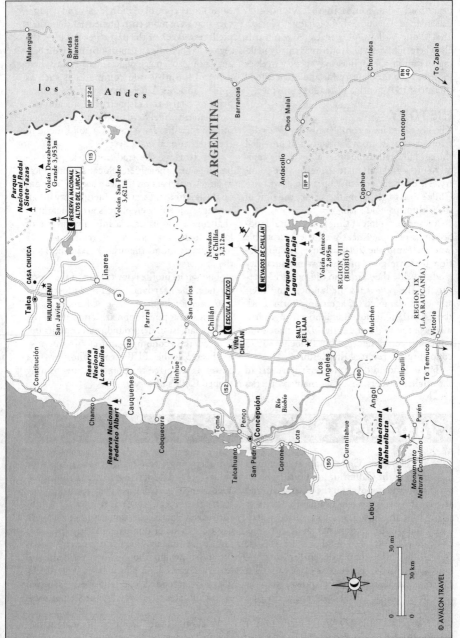

© AVALON TRAVEL

organized wine routes in the Aconcagua, Casablanca, Cachapoal, Colchagua, Curicó, and Maule Valleys, plus scattered vineyards elsewhere, Chilean wine tourism is finally making an impact. Oenophiles may spend a week or more touring the countryside and often extend their trips to Argentina's Mendoza province.

HISTORY

The heartland has a complex history that's difficult to separate from Santiago, as it provided the agricultural surplus that allowed the capital to grow and dominate the rest of the country. Through the port of Valparaíso, it was also Chile's link to global markets from the time of the California gold rush.

A legacy of colonial times, large rural landholdings occupied nearly all the best arable land well into the 20th century. As population pressure grew on the low-productivity lands outside the *fundos,* so did political pressure on the *fundos,* as the landless and their advocates clamored for agrarian reform. Both the Christian Democrat and Socialist governments of the 1960s and early 1970s made solid but controversial reforms, but Pinochet's 1973 coup abruptly reversed these efforts.

Those lands did not necessarily revert to the original owners, though—many properties came under control of individuals and companies that were more entrepreneurial than their predecessors. Over the past three decades, the region has become an export-oriented fruit basket, taking advantage of Northern Hemisphere demand for off-season commodities such as apples, apricots, blueberries, cherries, grapes, peaches, pears, and raspberries. Chilean vineyards, meanwhile, have proliferated, and their improved wines have gained a solid niche in the international market.

Nevertheless, the tradition of large landholdings and their hierarchical structure left as large an impact on Chilean society as it did on the landscape. Even in contemporary urban settings, underling employees are reluctant to challenge authority or take initiative for fear of losing their jobs—just as, on the *fundo,* they might have found themselves expelled from the property.

Though its profile is lower than in the Norte Grande, the heartland's mining industry has also been influential. East of Rancagua, El Teniente's copper deposits constitute the world's largest underground mine, and its impact on the economy—and environment—has been palpable. El Teniente's ghost town of Sewell is *the* place to appreciate how mining shaped Chile's history.

Valparaíso

Like San Francisco, Chile's main seaport owes its growth to the California gold rush, when it was a strategic stopover on the passage around the Horn. Also like San Francisco, it has so many hills that a walking tour of its streets, steps, and winding footpaths can be a productive cardiovascular workout. For those who tire of walking, more than a dozen funiculars—comparable to San Francisco's cable cars—lift Porteños (as city residents are known) from the downtown financial and commercial districts to their hillside neighborhoods.

Declared a UNESCO World Heritage Site for its unique urban geography, Valparaíso is undergoing a real-estate renaissance as the values of its distinctive traditional houses—Victorian-style structures clad with *calamina* (corrugated metal)—rise as steeply as the hills themselves. Trash collection has improved with the placement of dumpsters at key locations but, unfortunately, this has driven street dogs into other neighborhoods where residents still leave wet garbage in plastic bags. The streets, alleyways, sidewalks, and staircases are dappled with canine *soretes*—watch your step or wash your feet.

Valparaíso's rundown port, its least attractive area despite two kilometers of prime ocean frontage, is undergoing an overdue privatization and modernization of its docks to improve their handling capacity and tourist appeal. In addition, construction of a new southern access route has reduced heavy truck traffic through downtown's congested core and is opening the waterfront to the public.

HISTORY

European Valparaíso dates from the winter of 1536, when Juan de Saavedra, who had split off from Diego de Almagro's expedition and reached the coast at Concón, miraculously met Almagro's supply ship *El Santiaguillo* at the indigenous settlement of Quintil, the site of present-day Plaza Echaurren. Despite selection by Pedro de Valdivia as Santiago's port, it suffered from Madrid's mercantile policy, which restricted direct commerce with any other Spanish South American port except Lima. This, of course, encouraged both contraband, which couldn't compensate for lack of an orderly trade, and piracy, which damaged the economy.

Madrid finally granted a *cabildo* (town council) in 1791 and formal recognition as a city in 1802, but by then the irregular terrain and spontaneous growth had defeated the Spanish ideal of a quadrangular city plan. Despite its port status, the first pier was not finished until 1810, the year of Chile's independence.

War with Spain continued into the 1820s, but Valparaíso soon became a vibrant immigrant city of North Americans, British, Germans, Italians, Yugoslavs, and other ethnic communities. The Englishwoman Maria Graham, who spent several months in Valparaíso as the war with Spain raged into the 1820s, described its bustling commerce:

The English shops are more numerous than any. Hardware, pottery, and cotton and woolen cloths form of course the staple articles....

The Germans furnish most of the glass in common use. It is of bad quality to be sure, but it, as well as the little German mirrors,

which are chiefly brought to hang up as votive offerings in the chapels, answers all the purposes of Chileno consumption....

English tailors, shoemakers, saddlers, and inn-keepers hang out their signs in every street, and the preponderance of the English language...would make one fancy Valparaíso a coast town in Britain.

The North Americans greatly assist in this, however. Their goods, consisting of common furniture, flour, biscuit, and naval stores, necessarily keep them busier out of doors than any other set of people. The more elegant Parisian or London furniture is generally despatched unopened to Santiago, where the demand for articles of luxury is of course greater.

Valparaíso remained simple for some years— Graham remarked that the Iglesia Matriz (predecessor of today's church of the same name) "like all other buildings here, appears mean from without." It boomed after midcentury, though, as the main port for commercial vessels rounding Cape Horn, with wheat exports to gold-mad California, completion of the railroad to Santiago in 1863, and rapid advances in banking.

Thanks to its immigrants, Valparaíso became Chile's most cosmopolitan city and a leader in modern infrastructure such as tramways, electricity, and gas. Like San Francisco, the Americas' other cosmopolitan Pacific port, Valparaíso suffered a crippling 1906 earthquake. The opening of the Panama Canal was even more devastating—it became a terminal rather than an intermediate port, as European shipping could avoid the longer and more dangerous route around the Horn. The collapse of nitrate exports, thanks to synthetic substitutes, followed by the Great Depression of the 1930s, nearly paralyzed the economy until after World War II, when copper exports recovered.

Even with the economy's post-1970s recovery, Valparaíso has lost its primary port status to San Antonio, southeast of and rather closer

THE CHILEAN HEARTLAND

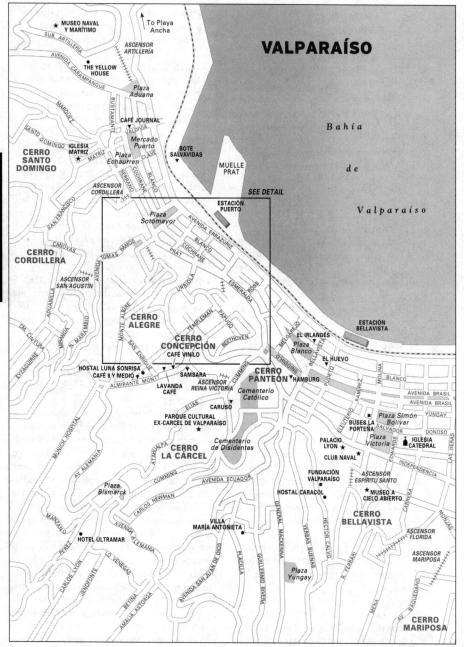

VALPARAÍSO

Bahía

de

Valparaíso

★ MUSEO NAVAL Y MARÍTIMO

To Playa Ancha

SUB. ARTILLERÍA

ASCENSOR ARTILLERÍA

AVENIDA CARAMPANGUE

● THE YELLOW HOUSE

MARQUEZ

SANTO DOMINGO

BUSTAMANTE

Plaza Aduana

CAFÉ JOURNAL ▼

VALDIVIA

IGLESIA MATRIZ ★

Mercado Puerto

CERRO SANTO DOMINGO

MATRIZ

Plaza Echaurren

CLAVE

COCHRANE

BLANCO

SERRANO

● BOTE SALVAVIDAS

MUELLE PRAT

ESTACIÓN PUERTO

SEE DETAIL

SAN FRANCISCO

ASCENSOR CORDILLERA

CANOVAS

CERRO CORDILLERA

ADUANILLA

MIRANDA

N. MARAMBIO

AVENIDA TOMAS RAMOS

MONTE ALEGRE

SAN ENRIQUE

Plaza Sotomayor

AVENIDA ERRAZURIZ

BLANCO

PRAT

COCHRANE

ESMERALDA

URRIOLA

ROSS

ASCENSOR SAN AGUSTÍN

TEMPLEMAN

PAPUDO

CERRO ALEGRE

CERRO CONCEPCIÓN

CAFÉ VINILO

BEETHOVEN

CUMMING

ESTACIÓN BELLAVISTA

MELGAREJO

O'HIGGINS

EL IRLANDÉS ▼

Plaza Blanco

BELLAVISTA

PUDETO

● EL HUEVO

RAMÍREZ

MOLINA

BLANCO

EYZAGUIRRE

CM. CINTURA

ALMIRANTE MONTT

HOSTAL LUNA SONRISA ● CAFÉ 8 Y MEDIO ●

LAVANDA CAFÉ

SAMSARA

ASCENSOR REINA VICTORIA

CERRO PANTEÓN

▼ HAMBURG

Cementerio Católico

AVENIDA BRASIL

AVENIDA BRASIL

YUNGAY

ELEUTERIO

DONOSO

MUNICH HOSPITAL

ELIAS

CARUSO

PARQUE CULTURAL EX-CARCEL DE VALPARAÍSO ★

Cementerio de Disidentes

SALVADOR

Plaza Simón Bolívar

■ BUSES LA PORTEÑA

Plaza Victoria

LAS HERAS

ATAHUALPA

AV. ALEMANIA

CERRO LA CÁRCEL

PALACIO LYON ★

● CLUB NAVAL

IGLESIA ▲ CATEDRAL

EDWARDS

INDEPENDENCIA

Plaza Bísmarck

CUMMING

AVENIDA ECUADOR

FUNDACIÓN VALPARAÍSO

● HOSTAL CARACOL

ASCENSOR ESPÍRITU SANTO

★ MUSEO A CIELO ABIERTO

CARRERA

MONJAS

MANZANO

CARLOS NEWMAN

AVENIDA ALEMANIA

VILLA MARÍA ANTONIETA ●

GENERAL MACKENNA

YERBAS BUENAS

HÉCTOR CALVO

CERRO BELLAVISTA

ASCENSOR FLORIDA

PEREZ

● HOTEL ULTRAMAR

LO VENEGAS

PLACILLA

AVENIDA SAN JUAN DE DIOS

GUILLERMO RIVERA

R. FERRARI

ASCENSOR MARIPOSA

CARLOS LYON

JERONIMO

BETINA

AMALIA ASTORGA

Plaza Yungay

MESA

AV. BAQUEDANO

CERRO MARIPOSA

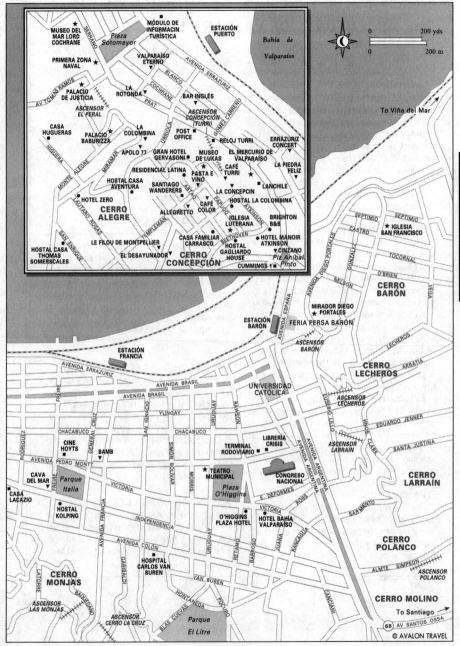

THE CHILEAN HEARTLAND

0   200 yds
0   200 m

To Viña del Mar

Inset map (Cerro Alegre / Cerro Concepción):

Bahía de Valparaíso

- MUSEO DEL MAR LORD COCHRANE ★
- Plaza Sotomayor
- MÓDULO DE INFORMACIÓN TURÍSTICA
- ESTACIÓN PUERTO
- PRIMERA ZONA NAVAL ★
- VALPARAÍSO ETERNO
- AVENIDA ERRAZURIZ
- BLANCO
- SERRANO
- AV TOMÁS RAMOS
- PALACIO DE JUSTICIA ★
- LA ROTONDA ▼
- COCHRANE
- PRAT
- BAR INGLÉS ■
- ASCENSOR EL PERAL
- ASCENSOR CONCEPCIÓN (TURRI)
- GÓMEZ CARREÑO
- CASA HUGUERAS ●
- PALACIO BABURIZZA ★
- LA COLOMBINA ▼
- URRIOLA
- POST OFFICE ■
- RELOJ TURRI ■
- ERRÁZURIZ CONCERT ★
- HIGUERA
- MONTE ALEGRE
- MIRAMAR
- APOLO 77 ●
- GRAN HOTEL GERVASONI ●
- MUSEO DE LUKAS ★
- EL MERCURIO DE VALPARAÍSO
- LA PIEDRA FELIZ ▼
- RESIDENCIAL LATINA ●
- CAFÉ TURRI ●
- PASTA E VINO ●
- LANCHILE ■
- AUTARO ROSAS
- HOSTAL CASA AVENTURA ●
- SANTIAGO WANDERERS ★
- BEAYO
- LA CONCEPCIÓN ▼
- HOSTAL LA COLOMBINA ●
- HOTEL ZERO ●
- CERRO ALEGRE
- ALLEGRETTO ●
- CAFÉ COLOR ●
- PAPUDO
- ATKINSON
- IGLESIA LUTERANA ■
- BRIGHTON B&B ▼
- SAN ENRIQUE
- TEMPLEMAN
- LE FILOU DE MONTPELLIER ▼
- CASA FAMILIAR CARRASCO ●
- BEETHOVEN
- HOTEL MANOIR ATKINSON ▼
- HOSTAL CASA THOMAS SOMERSCALES ●
- EL DESAYUNADOR ●
- CERRO CONCEPCIÓN
- HOSTAL GAGLIARDO HOUSE ●
- CINZANO ▼
- Plz Aníbal Pinto
- CUMMINGS 1 ■

Main map:

- SEPTIMIO
- SEPTIMIO
- CASTRO
- GONZÁLEZ
- IGLESIA SAN FRANCISCO ★
- TOCORNAL
- O'BRIEN
- NELSON
- AVENIDA DIEGO PORTALES
- CERRO BARÓN
- VEGA
- MIRADOR DIEGO PORTALES ★
- FERIA PERSA BARÓN
- ESTACIÓN BARÓN
- AVENIDA ESPAÑA
- ASCENSOR BARÓN
- LECHEROS
- CERRO LECHEROS
- ARRATIA
- ESTACIÓN FRANCIA
- AVENIDA ERRAZURIZ
- EUSEBIO LILLO
- ASCENSOR LECHEROS
- HNOS. CLARK
- EDUARDO JENNER
- FREIRE
- AVENIDA BRASIL
- AVENIDA BRASIL
- YUNGAY
- UNIVERSIDAD CATÓLICA
- SANTA JUSTINA
- ASCENSOR LARRAÍN
- RODRÍGUEZ
- CHACABUCO
- GENERAL CRUZ
- SAN IGNACIO
- URUGUAY
- RAWSON
- CHACABUCO
- CINE HOYTS ▼
- BAMB ▼
- AVENIDA PEDRO MONTT
- LIBRERÍA CRISIS ■
- TERMINAL RODOVIARIO ■
- AVENIDA ARGENTINA
- CERRO LARRAÍN
- CAVA DEL MAR ●
- Parque Italia
- VICTORIA
- SIMÓN BOLÍVAR
- MORRIS
- TEATRO MUNICIPAL ★
- Plaza O'Higgins
- CONGRESO NACIONAL
- SARMIENTO
- CASA LACAZIO ■
- HOSTAL KOLPING ●
- INDEPENDENCIA
- AVENIDA FRANCIA
- E. DEFORMES
- VICTORIA
- ROSS
- CERRO POLANCO
- AVENIDA COLÓN
- O'HIGGINS PLAZA HOTEL ●
- HOTEL BAHÍA VALPARAÍSO ●
- RETAMO
- BARROSO
- JUANA
- TRANZAGUA
- ALMTE. SIMPSON
- GARIBALDI
- HOSPITAL CARLOS VAN BUREN ●
- VAN BUREN
- ASCENSOR POLANCO
- CERRO MONJAS
- LATORRE
- BAQUEDANO
- BLAS CUEVAS
- FOCURO
- HONTANEDA
- CERRO MOLINO
- ASCENSOR LAS MONJAS
- ASCENSOR CERRO LA CRUZ
- Parque El Litre
- To Santiago
- 68 AV SANTOS OSSA
- SANCIANI

© AVALON TRAVEL

THE *ASCENSORES* OF VALPARAÍSO

Nothing else distinguishes Valparaíso so much as its hillside *ascensores*, or elevators, once 33 in number but now down to 14 or so. Such a part of the city are they that the Fundación Valparaíso uses the slogan "Un ascensor es un barrio" ("An elevator is a neighborhood," as their intimacy encourages interaction).

Only Ascensor Polanco is an elevator in the strictest sense of the word – the rest are funiculars. They date from the late 19th century; as the port, commercial, and financial districts quickly occupied the city's limited level terrain, residential neighborhoods climbed and spread up the canyons and over the nearby hillsides.

English, German, French, Yugoslav, and other immigrants who had made their fortunes in business, finance, and mining built mansions and houses in the hills, but the precipitous topography and complicated street plan created access problems. The elegant solution was the *ascensores*, which carried residents quickly and directly to their neighborhoods.

At their peak, more than 13 million people used them every year; during the second half of the 20th century, though, roads and vehicles invaded the hills, so that only about 3.3 million per year use them now. Without operating subsidies, many would probably close.

As Valparaíso achieved World Heritage Site status, the remaining *ascensores* were one of the attractions that made the city unique. Improving the surrounding areas with better sidewalks, ornamentation, lighting, and landscaping has encouraged a vigorous street life in areas that, until recently, were marginal neighborhoods.

Here is a list of the most widely used *ascensores* with their main characteristics. All charge small fares, usually less than US$0.25; some are privately operated, while others are public. For more detail, those who can read Spanish should see Juan Cameron's *Ascen-sores Porteños* (Viña del Mar/Santiago: Ediciones Altazor, 1998).

ASCENSOR ARTILLERÍA

From Plaza Aduana, also known as Plaza Wheelwright, Ascensor Artillería extends for 175 meters with a 30-degree gradient. One of the most popular tourist funiculars, it carries passengers 50 meters above the port to Cerro Playa Ancha, with panoramic views from Paseo 21 de Mayo toward Viña del Mar; the Museo Naval (Naval Museum) is nearby. It dates from 1894.

ASCENSOR BARÓN

Offering some of the best views of any of the city's funiculars, the recently restored Ascensor Barón (1906) overlooks the east end of the waterfront, immediately behind the Feria Persa flea market. It ascends a gradient of nearly 60 degrees over its 98-meter length before arriving at Paseo Diego Portales for panoramas of the entire harbor; this is the best approach to the landmark Iglesia San Francisco.

ASCENSOR CONCEPCIÓN (TURRI)

Dating from 1883, Valparaíso's oldest funicular is also one of the most popular, climbing 69 meters at a 45-degree gradient to Paseo Gervasoni, home to a popular hillside restaurant and the starting point for walking tours of Concepción and Cerro Alegre. Its lower station entrance is opposite the Reloj Turri clock tower, from which it takes its popular name, Ascensor Turri.

ASCENSOR CORDILLERA

Known also as Ascensor Serrano, for the street that its lower station faces, Ascensor Cordillera is one of Valpo's shortest funiculars, climbing just 60 meters up the side of its namesake hill to Plaza Eleuterio Ramírez, easy walking distance from the Museo Lord Cochrane. Dating from 1887, it has a gradient of 32 degrees.

ASCENSOR EL PERAL

From a nearly hidden entrance just off the Plaza de Justicia, but easily found by a conspicuous sign, Ascensor El Peral climbs 52 meters at a 48-degree gradient to Cerro Alegre's Paseo Yugoslavo and the Palacio Baburizza. This is one of the best walking areas in the hills, easily linking up to Cerro Concepción and its namesake *ascensor*. It dates from 1902.

ASCENSOR ESPÍRITU SANTO

Immediately southwest of El Almendral's Plaza Victoria, Espíritu Santo is the best approach to Cerro Bellavista, home to the open-air Museo al Cielo Abierto, the nonprofit Fundación Valparaíso, and the late Pablo Neruda's Valparaíso residence, now a museum and cultural center. Dating from 1911, it's officially known as Ascensor del Cerro Bellavista; it climbs 66 meters, at a gradient of nearly 45 degrees, to its upper terminus at Paseo Rudolph.

ASCENSOR FLORIDA

One of Valpo's best-kept secrets, at the south end of Carrera, also in El Almendral, Ascensor Florida is an alternative route to Cerro Bellavista and to Neruda's La Sebastiana house, via Calle Ferrari. Built in 1906, with a length of 138 meters, it has a gentle gradient – by Valpo standards – of just 19 degrees. One unique feature is a tiny pedestrian walkway that crosses over the railway.

ASCENSOR POLANCO

The only true elevator of them all, at the southeast end of town and reached by a 140-meter tunnel from Calle Simpson, Ascensor Polanco

climbs vertically for 60 meters, stopping at an intermediate station at Carvallo, 34 meters above the base. Dating from 1916, its size only permits eight passengers.

ASCENSOR REINA VICTORIA

One of the city's most entertaining funiculars, Cerro Concepción's Ascensor Reina Victoria (1902) climbs 40 meters of rails at a 57-degree gradient in cars holding only seven passengers. Reached from Plaza Aníbal Pinto via Cumming and Quebrada Elías, it has its upper station at Paseo Dimalow, another good starting point for walking tours of Cerro Concepción and Cerro Alegre.

© WAYNE BERNHARDSON

Ascensor Reina Victoria, in Cerro Concepción

THE CHILEAN HEARTLAND

to Santiago, over easier terrain. It has, however, gained political influence with the transfer of the Congress under Pinochet's custom constitution (Pinochet was a Valparaíso native) despite strong sentiments, and many practical reasons, for moving it back to Santiago.

Traditionally, Valparaíso has played second fiddle to nearby Viña del Mar in the tourist trade, but its World Heritage Site status has spawned interest in the city. With the opening of ever more tourist hotels, B&Bs, and restaurants, it's become a viable alternative to Viña.

ORIENTATION

For nonnatives of Valparaíso (population 276,000), 120 kilometers northwest of Santiago via Ruta 68, orientation can be a challenge. Along the curving waterfront, built largely on fill, the relatively regular downtown area consists of long east–west streets and avenues, crossed by short, mostly north–south streets and alleyways.

Northwest of Cerro Concepción, marked by the Reloj Turri clock tower and the *Mercurio de Valparaíso* newspaper headquarters, this narrow coastal strip is generally known as the Barrio Puerto; to the east, the broader level area is El Almendral. Merval, the regional rail transit system, parallels the shoreline.

In the gridless hills, all bets are off. A free but basic map, available at the tourist office, is essential, but a more detailed version is advisable. Even the best map, though, can't cover every winding medieval staircase and passageway.

SIGHTS
Barrio Puerto

Valparaíso's maritime orientation is palpable in the Barrio Puerto, where the main public buildings cluster around remodeled **Plaza Sotomayor,** nearly vehicle-free after construction of an underground parking garage; while it's an improvement over the previous parking lot, its barrenness is still disconcerting.

Facing the plaza, the former Intendencia Regional (1910) has become the **Primera**

Zona Naval, the national naval headquarters that symbolizes the service's influence. Built to replace an earlier structure that had a shaky foundation, this French-inspired, five-story building was the work of architect Ernesto Urquieta, whose design won a contest for a building that served as the provincial governor's residence and a summer house for presidents.

On the harbor side, the **Monumento a los Héroes de Iquique** is the crypt of Arturo Prat, Ignacio Serrano, and other casualties of the *Esmeralda*'s ill-advised assault on the Peruvian ironclad *Huáscar* at Iquique, during the War of the Pacific. After recovering the bodies from a common grave and then saving them from a parish church that burned down, the government sponsored a contest to build the monument here; French architect Diogene Ulysse Mayllard created the general design and French sculptor Denis Pierre Puech the statuary (according to an unverified account, the judges rejected Rodin's sculpture *La Defensa,* now at Viña's Palacio Carrasco). The Chilean Virginio Arias, who supervised the work, sculpted the bas reliefs.

At the foot of the plaza, **Muelle Prat** is the passenger pier, the departure point for occasional harbor tours. The pier is also home to a so-so crafts market and a replica of the *Carabela Santiaguillo,* the tiny vessel that first brought the Spaniards from Lima. Facing each other across the plaza are the current **Aduana Nacional** (Customs House) and the former **Estación Puerto,** a gallery that was once the terminus for suburban commuter trains (note the colorful murals); the new station, integrated into a new shopping mall, is slightly to the southeast.

Marking the approximate border between the Barrio Puerto and El Almendral, the **Reloj Turri** clock tower, at the narrow end of a flatiron at Prat and Carreño, is directly across from Ascensor Concepción. One block east, dating from 1903, the neoclassical headquarters of **El Mercurio de Valparaíso** (Esmeralda and Ross) belongs to Chile's most venerable newspaper (first published in 1827).

El Almendral

East of Cerro Concepción, also bounded by the port, Avenida Argentina, and Avenida Colón, El Almendral is Valpo's commercial heart. When Maria Graham lived here in the 1820s, though, it was "full of olive groves, and of almond gardens, whence it has its name."

El Almendral still has fewer conspicuous architectural landmarks than the Barrio Puerto, but its several plazas—**Plaza Simón Bolívar, Plaza de la Victoria, Parque Italia,** and **Plaza O'Higgins** (home to Chile's finest antiques market)—are the axes of Porteño street life.

At the barrio's west end, dating from 1888, the almost rococo **Palacio Ross** (Salvador Donoso 1337) was home an elite Valparaíso family before they moved to Viña; it is now the **Club Alemán,** the German community center.

Dating from 1881, the neoclassical **Palacio Lyon** (Condell 1546) holds both the **Museo de Historia Natural** (Natural History Museum) and the **Galería de Arte Municipal** (Municipal Art Gallery). Two blocks north, on Avenida Brasil, the **Arco Británico** honors the British colony.

At the southwest corner of Plaza de la Victoria, the **Club Naval** (1895) shows French influence. At Avenida Brasil and Avenida Argentina, Urquieta designed the **Universidad Católica.**

On Avenida Pedro Montt, between Barroso and Avenida Argentina, Valpo's most conspicuous single monument is the pharaonic **Congreso Nacional** (1990); Pinochet's custom constitution dictated the national legislature's move from Santiago.

[HILLS OF VALPARAÍSO

Valparaíso is a walker's city, so long as those walkers are willing to test their legs and lungs on its steep staircases and narrow alleyways—though they may prefer to use the *ascensores* whenever possible. The following paragraphs

© WAYNE BERNHARDSON

On Sunday, Valparaíso's Plaza O'Higgins is home to what may be the country's best antiques fair.

detail the main hill neighborhoods from west to east (unofficial estimates put the total number of hills at about 45).

While the most prominent landmarks are mentioned here, there is much more to see, as the city's typical constructions, with *calamina* siding and remarkable if unexpected architectural flourishes, seemingly occupy every square inch of declivitous lots that would be considered unbuildable almost anywhere else. There's a surprise around every corner, but the most famous feature is poet Pablo Neruda's **La Sebastiana** home on Cerro Bellavista.

Cerro Artillería

At the base of Cerro Artillería, **Plaza Aduana** (also known as Plaza Wheelwright) is the site of the former **Aduana de Valparaíso** (Customs House, 1854), a national monument since superseded by a newer building on Plaza Sotomayor. The **Ascensor Artillería** climbs to **Paseo 21 de Mayo,** a harbor-view terrace that's home to the Museo Naval y Marítimo (1893), the naval and maritime museum.

Cerro Santo Domingo

Several blocks north of Plaza Sotomayor, at the base of Cerro Santo Domingo, **Plaza Echaurren** is the likely spot of Saavedra's 1536 landing. Almost immediately west, overlooking the **Plaza Matriz,** the **Iglesia la Matriz del Salvador** (1842) is one of several successors to the original 16th-century chapel. Designed by parish priest José Antonio Riobó, the basilica-style construction is a national historical monument and the heart of Valpo's oldest barrio; the neighborhood has a reputation for petty crime, but Sunday mornings are safe enough, as the faithful gather for Mass and most delinquents are sleeping off their Saturday night debaucheries.

Cerro Cordillera

From the top of Calle Hurtado, midway between Plaza Echaurren and Plaza Sotomayor, the **Ascensor Cordillera** (1887) climbs to **Plaza Eleuterio Ramírez,** a short stroll from the Museo del Mar Lord Cochrane, which

occupies a colonial-style house dating from 1841. This was also the site of Chile's first astronomical observatory.

Cerro Alegre

From the **Plaza de Justicia,** immediately behind Plaza Sotomayor and the Primera Zona Naval, **Ascensor El Peral** (1902) is the access point to Cerro Alegre, a picturesque neighborhood that served as a backdrop for a Chilean TV soap opera some years ago.

From El Peral's upper exit, **Paseo Yugoeslavo** leads directly to the **Palacio Baburizza,** a former mansion being rehabbed as the city's Museo de Bellas Artes (Fine Arts Museum). Almost directly south, toward Cerro Concepción, the passageway steps known as **Pasaje Bavestrello** pass between separate wings of an apartment building, a nearly perfect integration of public and private space; on occasion, locals project movies onto the apartment walls. Calle Urriola marks the border between Cerro Alegre and Cerro Concepción.

© WAYNE BERNHARDSON

one of Cerro Alegre's most distinctive houses

POLISHING THE PEARL

Valparaíso is Chile's most unusual city, but much of its distinctive architecture declined with the city's economy after the opening of the Panama Canal undercut its once-thriving port. The nitrate era's end was another blow – the houses and mansions of its hills neighborhoods deteriorated, as there was no money to maintain them. Fortunately, there wasn't enough money to tear them down either, and much of that heritage remains on the steep slopes behind the port.

In its heyday, Valparaíso sported the nickname La Perla del Pacífico (Pearl of the Pacific), as much for its incomparable setting and vernacular distinction as for any genuine glitter. Over the past decade or so, though, municipal officials and private organizations have begun to appreciate what Valparaíso has to offer and have made enormous progress in salvaging and restoring what remains.

One of the leaders in this effort is the Fundación Valparaíso, a nonprofit that helped the city earn UNESCO World Heritage status. Already, with help from the World Monuments Fund, it has restored and adapted a magnificent building on Cerro Bellavista as its headquarters, and it is attempting to identify and restore the facades of buildings dating from 1914 or earlier – before the Panama Canal. The foundation is able to help restore rusted *calamina* (metal siding) in the original style, insulate the buildings while the *calamina* is off, repair roofs, and provide scaffolding and donated paint. It's hoping for a spinoff effect with other neighbors to improve their prop-

erties, even though those properties may be more recent.

Cities seeking World Heritage Site status, such as Venice, Rome, Prague, Saint Petersburg, Istanbul, Cuzco, and Cartagena (Colombia), are chosen for their historical, cultural, architectural, and urban merits. While such comparisons might not seem obvious to those unfamiliar with Valparaíso, its historic status in the golden age of Pacific trade around Cape Horn, its spontaneous growth and eclectic architecture, and its immigrant ethnic diversity combine to make a strong case for its inclusion.

The Fundación Valparaíso, along with its other activities, is attempting to reclaim public space for community use, tourism, and cultural purposes. It has also helped restore the Museo al Cielo Abierto, participated with the state arts agency Fondart in promoting the annual Festival de Cine de Valparaíso (Valparaíso Film Festival), and opened its own space to the public with a bookstore/café, which hosts literary events, and with an international restaurant.

To visit the **Fundación Valparaíso** (Héctor Calvo 205, Cerro Bellavista, tel. 032/2593156, www.fundacionvalparaiso.cl), take Ascensor Espíritu Santo to the top and walk to its headquarters, painted a cheerful yellow with a blue mansard and extraordinary details. The website contains details of its numerous projects, but visitors can also keep up with its cultural activities on its portal site (www.capitalcultural.cl).

Cerro Concepción

The city's first funicular, **Ascensor Concepción** (1883) climbs from an inconspicuous entrance at the upper end of Carreño, just off Prat, to Paseo Gervasoni. Among the sights in this *zona típica* are the **Museo El Mirador de Lukas,** memorializing cartoonist and caricaturist Renzo Pecchenino; Chile's second Protestant church, dating from 1858, the **Iglesia Anglicana San Pablo** (Pilcomayo 566; classical organ concerts take place every

Sunday at 12:30 P.M.); and the 1897 Gothic-style **Iglesia Luterana** (Beethoven and Abtao). **Paseo Atkinson** and **Paseo Dimalow** are typical hillside promenades, the latter linking with **Ascensor Reina Victoria** (1902), an easy route to or from Plaza Aníbal Pinto.

Cerro Panteón

Reached by a series of steep streets and staircases, but no *ascensores,* Cerro Panteón is home to three ridgetop cemeteries, of which the most

THE CHILEAN HEARTLAND

© WAYNE BERNHARDSON

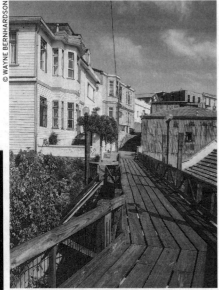

A boardwalk links Valparaíso's Ascensor Reina Victoria with Paseo Dimalow.

interesting is the **Cementerio de Disidentes,** where non-Catholic immigrants found their final resting place. Immediately east is **Cerro Cárcel,** site of the former city prison, where bureaucratic hangups finally forced Brazil's famed architect Oscar Niemeyer (born 1907) to bow out of a project for a new cultural center; the city, sitting on a US$12 million budget for the center, will hold a contest to choose another architect.

Cerro Bellavista

At the upper end of Huito, reached by **Ascensor Espíritu Santo** but also by streets and staircases, Cerro Bellavista is the site of the **Museo al Cielo Abierto** (Open Air Museum), a series of mostly abstract murals in strategic sites by more than a dozen well-known Chilean artists, including Roberto Matta, Nemesio Antúnez, and Roser Bru.

Cerro Bellavista is also the focus of city renovation efforts by the **Fundación Valparaíso** (Héctor Calvo 205, tel. 032/2593156, www .fundacionvalparaiso.org), which has renovated

an abandoned and dilapidated house into its "campus." Families in several historical houses here have taken advantage of the foundation's technical and financial assistance to restore the facades of their homes.

On Bellavista's uppermost reaches, poet Pablo Neruda bought La Sebastiana, one of his three outlandish houses (the other two are in Santiago and at Isla Negra, south of Valparaíso). Like the others, La Sebastiana is open to the public.

Cerro Barón

One of Valpo's more easterly neighborhoods, Cerro Barón is home to one of its most conspicuous landmarks: for arriving vessels, the towering **Iglesia San Francisco** (Blanco Viel and Zañartu), a national historical monument dating from 1845, was their first glimpse of the city (Valpo's historical nickname "Pancho," a diminutive of Francisco, derives from the church). The imposing **Universidad Técnica Federico Santa María** (1931) overlooks Avenida España from Cerro Los Placeres.

From the Feria Persa Barón, a working-class flea market at the north end of Avenida Argentina, the **Ascensor Barón** (1906; the city's first electric funicular) climbs to the **Mirador Diego Portales,** a scenic overlook that's the best starting point for exploring the neighborhood.

MUSEUMS
Museo Naval y Marítimo

Housed in Cerro Artillería's former Escuela Naval (Naval Academy), this museum is more naval than maritime, focusing on military figures such as Bernardo O'Higgins, the mercenary Lord Thomas Cochrane, and Admiral Manuel Blanco Encalada, and nationalistic explanations of events such as the War of the Pacific (including its foolhardy hero, Arturo Prat). It pays exaggerated homage to Diego Portales, the authoritarian political operative who promoted Chilean seapower in early independence times, at the expense of early exploration and discovery. There's even less on the significance of maritime resources in the contemporary Chilean economy.

Surrounding an immaculately landscaped patio, the Museo Naval (Paseo 21 de Mayo s/n, tel. 032/2437651, www.museonaval.cl) is open 10 A.M.–6 P.M. daily except Monday; admission costs US$0.85 for adults, US$0.35 for children. From Plaza Aduana (Plaza Wheelwright), Ascensor Artillería climbs almost to the entrance.

Museo del Mar Lord Cochrane

In a colonial-style structure dating from 1842, this misleadingly named museum has little to do with Lord Cochrane (one of South America's most colorful figures) but much to do with ships in bottles—the Club de Modelismo Naval de Valparaíso exhibits its best work here. There are also occasional special exhibitions and events, and the views from the terrace alone are worth the trip.

Reached by Ascensor Cordillera from Calle Serrano, near its intersection with Plaza Sotomayor, the Museo del Mar (Merlet 195, tel. 032/2939587, free) is open 10 A.M.–6 P.M. daily except Monday.

Museo de Bellas Artes (Palacio Baburizza)

Designed by architects Arnaldo Barison and Renato Schiavon, this art nouveau chalet (1916) on Cerro Alegre bears the name of Croatian-born nitrate baron Pascual Baburizza, who began his career selling meat and fish in the *oficinas* around Iquique; he lived here until his death in 1946. The city acquired the building, now a national monument, in 1971.

Having cashed out of the nitrate industry before its crash, Baburizza donated more than 90 19th- and 20th-century paintings to the municipal art collections, among them historic landscapes by Thomas Somerscales and Alfredo Helsby.

Its collections in storage, the Museo de Bellas Artes (Paseo Yugoeslavo 166, tel. 032/2213124) has been undergoing a prolonged renovation; the building itself, with remarkable details in its woodwork, wrought iron, and central

turret, is an artifact of its era. Presuming the restoration ever ends, its theoretical hours are 10 A.M.–6 P.M. daily. Admission is free.

Museo El Mirador de Lukas

On Cerro Concepción, this unique museum is the legacy of Italian-born Renzo Pecchenino, an honorary Porteño who worked in several different media—cartoons and caricatures of his adopted country and sketches of Valparaíso's cityscape. Published in newspapers such as *El Mercurio de Valparaíso,* he went by the pseudonym "Lukas." Some of his cartoons are displayed on brief videos.

Easily reached by Ascensor Concepción, the Museo de Lukas (Paseo Gervasoni 448, tel. 032/2221344, www.lukas.cl) is open 11 A.M.–6 P.M. daily except Monday; admission costs US$1 for adults, half that for children.

Museo de Historia Natural

In the resplendent Palacio Lyon, Valparaíso's natural-history museum does much of what the Museo Naval y Marítimo has abdicated, emphasizing the future of the oceans from an ecologically analytical—rather than simply strategic—viewpoint. It also depicts the diversity of pre-Columbian Chile and its culture through dioramas, but the natural-history specimens are a routine and disappointing effort at taxidermy. From an anthropological perspective, the museum holds ceramics from Peru, the Norte Grande, and the Mapuche borderlands.

The Museo de Historia Natural (Condell 1546, tel. 032/2544840, www.museodevalparaiso.cl) is open 10 A.M.–1 P.M. and 2–6 P.M. weekdays except Monday, 10 A.M. to 2 P.M. weekends and holidays only. Admission costs US$1, US$0.50 for children and seniors, but is free Wednesday, Sunday, and holidays. In summer, it stays open until 8 P.M. weekdays.

In the building's basement, reached by a separate entrance, the **Galería de Arte Municipal** (Condell 1550, tel. 032/2939567) features rotating fine-arts exhibitions. Hours are 10 A.M.–7 P.M. daily except Sunday; admission is free.

THE CHILEAN HEARTLAND

La Sebastiana

With his love of the sea, Pablo Neruda could hardly resist a residence in Valparaíso, and bought this five-story house in 1961. He also loved the city's informality and spontaneity:

> Valparaíso grabbed me, she subjected me to her will, to her absurdity: Valparaíso is a mess, a cluster of crazy houses.

The Fundación Neruda opened La Sebastiana to the public in 1992, and in one sense it's the best of his three houses—unlike Santiago's La Chascona and Isla Negra, with their relatively regimented guided tours, visitors can roam through the house more or less at will. Like La Chascona and Isla Negra, it displays a whimsical assortment of artifacts the poet collected on his global travels. In addition to the house, the Fundación Neruda operates a café, cultural center, and souvenir shop.

La Sebastiana (Ferrari 692, tel. 032/2256606, www.fundacionneruda.org) is open 10:10 A.M.–6 P.M. daily except Monday—except in January and February, when hours are 10:30 A.M.–6:50 P.M. for the same days. If either Monday or Tuesday is a holiday, closing time can change. Admission costs US$4.

The most direct route to La Sebastiana is to walk up Cerro Bellavista and follow the signs from the Museo de Aire Libre; alternatively, take a *taxi colectivo* from Plazuela Ecuador or the No. 612 bus (which locals still refer to as the "O") from Plaza Sotomayor to the 6900 block of Avenida Alemania, from which the house is a short walk.

ENTERTAINMENT

Bars

Valparaíso has a vibrant nightlife, thanks to re-development immediately southeast of the port and in hillside neighborhoods such as Cerro Concepción.

La Piedra Feliz (Av. Errázuriz 1054, tel. 032/2256788, www.lapiedrafeliz.cl) is a live music venue that alternates jazz, rock, tango, and salsa. Nearby **Errázuriz Concert** (Pasaje Ross 51, tel. 032/2595954, www

.errazurizconcert.cl) also features live music in a variety of styles. The legitimately Irish **El Irlandés** (Blanco 1279, tel. 032/2593675) claims to stock 161 different beers.

The biggest downtown venue, though, is **El Huevo** (Blanco 1386, tel. 032/2257534, www .elhuevo.cl), a multistory pub that, on any given night, can feature a variety of acts on the main stage and in its several separate lounges.

Cerro Concepción's **Café Color** (Papudo 526, tel. 032/2746136) is more a teahouse but has the ambience of a classic neighborhood bar, its walls plastered with photographs of people and paintings and postcards of Valpo. Stocking a selection of menus from restaurants around town, it's a good place to go to decide where to eat if the simple sandwich fare here isn't enough for you; lively without being noisy, it's small and intimate, with *simpático* staff.

Cinema

The five-screen **Cine Hoyts** (Pedro Montt 2111, tel. 032/2594709) is a conventional commercial cinema. Cerro Alegre's **Café 8 y Medio** (Almirante Montt 462, tel. 032/2493223) shows repertory movies in a more intimate setting.

Theater

The **Teatro Municipal** (Av. Uruguay 410, tel. 032/2214654, www.teatromunicipal.cl) is the main performing arts venue, with both drama and live music.

Spectator Sports

Valparaíso's first-division soccer team, **Santiago Wanderers** (Independencia 2053, tel. 032/2217210, www.santiagowanderers.cl) plays home matches at Playa Ancha's Estadio Regional Chiledeportes.

EVENTS

Hundreds of thousands of Chileans converge on the port city to see the massive fireworks display at **Año Nuevo** (New Year's Eve). April 17 marks the **Fundación de la Ciudad,** commemorating the city's official founding in 1791.

The annual **Festival Cinematográfico de Valparaíso** (Valparaíso Film Festival) takes place in August.

SHOPPING

Valparaíso is home to a horde of crafts, antiques, and flea markets. The most commercial is Muelle Prat's **Feria de Artesanías**, at the foot of Plaza Sotomayor.

On weekends and holidays, at Plaza O'Higgins, the **Feria de Antigüedades y Libros La Merced** is an extraordinary but expensive antiques and book market comparable—except for the lack of tango—to the famous Feria de San Telmo on Buenos Aires's Plaza Dorrego. **Casa Lacazio** (Independencia 1976, tel. 032/2255111) is a permanent antiques outlet.

Bookstores

Librería Crisis (Av. Pedro Montt 2871, tel. 032/2218504) offers a good stock of used books on Chilean history and literature. For local maps and local guidebooks, try **Librería Ivens** (Plaza Aníbal Pinto 339, tel. 032/2213707).

Cummings 1 (Subida Cumming 1, cel. 09/8606-1605) is a gallery/bookstore with a good selection of English-language titles. Hours are noon–9 P.M. Monday, 11:30 A.M.–2:30 P.M. and 4:30–9 P.M. Tuesday–Saturday.

ACCOMMODATIONS

Nearby Viña del Mar still has more accommodations, but Valpo's new boutique hotels and even its hostels are more interesting than anything there. For the most part, they occupy sites in scenic hill neighborhoods with fine dining and entertainment nearby.

US$10-25

On Cerro San Juan de Dios, **Villa María Antonieta** (Bernardo Vera 542, tel. 032/2734336, www.hivalparaiso.cl, US$11–13 pp) is the Hostelling International affiliate; in addition to dorms, it has slightly more expensive doubles and triples.

Cerro Alegre's **(Hostal Casa Aventura** (Pasaje Gálvez 11, tel. 032/2755963, www

.casaventura.cl, US$12 pp, US$16 s, US$30 d) has rooms with high ceilings, burnished wooden floors, and one, two, or three beds, as well as two shared baths, and kitchen facilities. Rates also include an outstanding breakfast, with bread, fresh cheese, and fresh fruit; its major drawback, despite its charming location, is that it faces busy Calle Urriola, which gets lots of downshifting cars, buses, and trucks.

US$25-50

Facing Plaza Victoria, **Hostal Kolping** (Francisco Valdés Vergara 622, tel. 032/2216306, www.kolping.cl, US$17–20 s, US$25–30 d with breakfast) may not have kept up with the times, but its small rooms with shared baths and larger rooms with private baths are still more than acceptable.

On Cerro Concepción, **Casa Familiar Juan Carrasco** (Abtao 668, tel./fax 032/2210737, US$20 s, US$37 d with shared bath and breakfast) has been one of Valpo's finest values, in a four-story house furnished with antiques and capped by a rooftop terrace with sensational panoramas of the harbor and coastline. Reached via Ascensor Concepción (Turri), it's still a good choice, with an affable family atmosphere, but other nearby places have overtaken it.

Owned and operated by a knowledgeable rival guidebook author, with a lively (but not rowdy) international atmosphere, Cerro Alegre's Anglo-Chilean **(Hostal Luna Sonrisa** (Templeman 833, tel. 032/2734117, www.lunasonrisa.cl, US$12.50–15 pp, US$30 s, US$37 d) is friendly and provides a fine breakfast. Rooms range from dorms to doubles with private baths, plus one spacious (and significantly more expensive) apartment with a loft bedroom, living room, kitchen, and enormous bath.

Immediately beneath the Lutheran church, friendly **Hostal Gagliardo House** (Beethoven 322, tel. 032/2459476, www.gagliardohouse .cl, US$15 pp, US$42 d) has one claustrophobic single and several more spacious doubles, all with shared baths.

Cerro Bellavista's cheerful and spacious **Hostal Caracol** (Héctor Calvo 371, tel. 032/2395817, hostalcaracol@gmail.com, US$13 pp, US$45 d) has one dorm with a shared bath and several doubles with private baths. It has large and comfortable common spaces, along with a book exchange.

US$50-100

On Cerro Artillería, run by an Australian-Chilean couple, **The Yellow House** (Capitán Muñoz Gamero 91, tel. 032/2339435, www .theyellowhouse.com, US$30 s, US$54 d) is a cheerful new B&B in an up-and-coming area. Its seven rooms, each with a private bath, vary considerably in size and style.

Nearby **Casa Hostal 199** (Artillería 199, tel. 032/2369054, www.artilleria199.cl, US$40–63 s or d) is a well-run B&B at the upper end of Ascensor Artillería. It has glistening common areas with high ceilings, a front deck with harbor views, and a diverse breakfast including fresh fruit and juices. Rooms vary considerably in size, though, and some have exterior private baths.

Aspiring to be a boutique hotel, Cerro Concepción's renovated **Casa Latina** (Papudo 462, tel. 032/2494622, www.casalatina.cl, US$39 s, US$59–89 d with breakfast) gets high marks for cheerful decor and for quiet; some rooms are very large and well-lighted. It has a small terrace but no views.

Cerro Concepción's **Hostal la Colombina** (Concepción 280, tel. 032/2234980, www .lacolombina.cl, US$50–68 d) has large rooms furnished with antiques, plus a restaurant that's worth a look.

Some architects adore Cerro Concepción's **Hotel Brighton** (Paseo Atkinson 151, tel./fax 032/2223513, www.brighton.cl, US$53–71 s or d), which mimics traditional Valparaíso in contemporary accommodations built from salvaged materials—but others really detest its retro style. Overlooking Plaza Aníbal Pinto, rooms with harbor views command the highest prices; nonguests can savor the view during lunch or dinner at its terrace restaurant.

© WAYNE BERNHARDSON

Cerro Concepción's Hotel Brighton is a new construction in traditional style.

In the eastern Almendral area, near the Congreso Nacional, there are two decent and comparably priced places: the **O'Higgins Plaza Hotel** (Retamo 517, tel. 032/2235616, www .restaurantohiggins.cl, US$62 s, US$77 d) and **Hotel Bahía Valparaíso** (Victoria 2380, tel. 032/2230675, www.bahiavalparaiso.cl, US$68 s, US$77 d).

Behind the brick Italianate facade of a century-old building, Cerro Cárcel's 17-room ❰ **Hotel Ultramar** (tel. 032/2210000, www.hotelultramar.cl, US$72 s, US$88–117 d with buffet breakfast) is a luminous hotel with scant contemporary decoration. In what was once a private residence, the rooms vary in size and shape (some baths are a bit small, in particular), but it's quiet and comfortable. One budget single goes for US$48, while a penthouse suite goes for US$157; off-season rates are about 20 percent lower in all categories. It lacks a restaurant, but its café serves sandwiches and snacks until 10 P.M.

US$100-200

Decorated with period or retro furniture, though the facilities are otherwise contemporary, Cerro Alegre's eight-room **◖ Hotel Casa Thomas Somerscales** (San Enrique 446, tel. 032/2331006, www.hotelsomerscales.cl, US$113–130 s or d with breakfast) was in fact the artist's house, a classic Anglophile mansion. It's easy walking distance to the Alegre/Concepción restaurant and nightlife district, but far enough to guarantee a good night's sleep. Some baths have whirlpool tubs.

The 15 rooms at Cerro Concepción's **Gran Hotel Gervasoni** (Paseo Gervasoni 1, tel. 032/2239236, www.hotelgervasoni.com, US$116–140 s or d) offer satellite TV, WiFi, a wine cellar, and beautifully terraced gardens, but downtown buildings have obstructed some of the views.

Also on Cerro Concepción, **Hotel Manoir Atkinson** (Paseo Atkinson 165, tel. 032/2351313, www.hotelatkinson.cl, US$150–240 s or d) is a seven-room boutique hotel with vivacious Quebecoise-Chilean ownership, a rooftop deck ideal for viewing the New Year's fireworks, and easy access to the city's finest restaurants. The rooms vary in size, however.

More than US$200

Cerro Alegre's **Zero Hotel** (Lautaro Rosas 343, tel. 032/2113113, www.zerohotel.com, US$230–320 s or d) is nine-room boutique hotel that's drawn extravagant praise for having preserved the lines of a classic Victorian-era house while installing all contemporary comforts. On top of that, it's one of few buildings in the hills that offer unobstructed panoramas of the harbor, and its terraced gardens are magnificent—in a building that would not be out of place in San Francisco's prestigious Pacific Heights.

Nearby **Casa Higueras** (Higueras 113, tel. 032/2497900, www.casahigueras.cl, US$203–383 s or d) is a restored 1920s mansion whose 20 guestrooms vary in size but most of them have bay views. Its polished interior woodwork,

THE CHILEAN HEARTLAND

© WAYNE BERNHARDSON

Cerro Alegre's Zero Hotel (second from left) is one of several new small, but sophisticated, hotels in the hills of Valparaíso.

with huge dark beams, is traditional, but the rooms and baths are a functional blend of the historic and the contemporary. Like The Zero, it has terraced gardens, as well as a pool, but the views are not quite so panoramic.

FOOD

In the flatlands and the hills, Valparaíso's improving restaurant scene is quickly overtaking Viña del Mar's for both style and quality.

Puerto and El Almendral

There are still many traditional and inexpensive seafood restaurants, such as the 2nd-floor *marisquerías* at the **Mercado Puerto** (Port Market), bounded by Cochrane, Valdivia, Blanco, and San Martín.

More expensive but also traditional and broadly similar seafood alternatives include the **Bar Inglés** (Cochrane 851 but with a separate entrance at Blanco 870, tel. 032/2214625); **La Rotonda** (Prat 701, tel. 032/2217746); and **Bote Salvavidas** (Muelle Prat s/n, tel. 032/2251477), a favorite with tour groups.

Café Journal (Cochrane 81, tel. 032/2596760, www.cafejournal.cl, lunch daily and Thurs.–Sat. dinner) is a more mature version of its Viña del Mar sibling, with Peruvian food and live music. Reasonably priced, with lunches around US$6, **Valparaíso Eterno** (Señoret 150, 2nd floor, tel. 032/2255605) has more Porteño personality than any other flatlands dining spot. Alternatively, in new quarters **Bambú** (Avenida Independencia 1790, tel. 032/2234216, www.bambuvegetariano.cl, 10:30 A.M.–8 P.M. daily in summer, 10:30 A.M.–5:30 P.M. daily except Sun. the rest of the year) serves vegetarian specials.

Weeknights can seem moribund at **Cinzano** (Plaza Aníbal Pinto 1182, tel. 032/2213043), but it serves good Chilean food at moderate prices, along with cheap mixed drinks and a good selection of beers. From Thursday to Sunday, it has live tango music; on other nights, the selection of recorded material is excellent.

Around the corner, loaded with maritime memorabilia, **Hamburg** (O'Higgins 1274, tel. 032/2597037) has excellent German food.

Opposite Plaza Italia, ◖ **Cava del Mar** (Independencia 2099, tel. 032/2210471, www.cavadelmar.cl) occupies the 2nd and 3rd floors of a mansion that once belonged to miner/philanthropist Santiago Severín. It is a wine bar that focuses on a limited but evolving menu of beef, fish, and Peruvian dishes, with a wide selection of wines. Architecturally, its circular atrium, topped by a domed skylight, and burnished wood floors and staircases lend it a turn-of-the-20th-century ambience.

Cerro Concepción

For breakfast, sandwiches, and desserts, the best choice is the informal **El Desayunador** (Almirante Montt 399, tel. 032/2365933, www.eldesayunador.cl). In the same neighborhood, lunchgoers pack the French-run **Le Filou de Montpellier** (Av. Pedro Montt 382, tel. 032/2224663, www.lefiloudemontpellier.cl, lunch daily except Mon., dinner Fri.–Sat.) for well-prepared but inexpensive meals (about US$6–7).

For high-quality, moderately priced Italian standards—don't miss the gnocchi—try **Allegretto** (Pilcomayo 529, tel. 032/2968839), a casual British-Chilean project that includes an early Space Age jukebox with an eclectic mix of 45 rpm singles ranging from Sandro (the Argentine Elvis) to The Clash.

At Paseo Gervasoni's east end, near the Ascensor Concepción exit, **Café Turri** (Templeman 147, tel. 032/2252091) is still one of Valpo's top restaurants known for its view, with spectacular panoramas from its terrace, and new personnel has helped it recover some of its former luster.

Adjacent to the Turri, **La Concepción** (Papudo 541, tel. 032/2498192, www.restaurantlaconcepcion.cl, Wed.–Sat. lunch, Fri.–Sat. dinner) has an almost equally spectacular terrace, but the food varies—a nice ceviche with watercress and lúcuma mousse dessert, for instance, but the *jabalí* (wild boar) stew is mediocre. There are good wines by the glass, and well-meaning but erratic service.

Up the hill, though, one of Chile's top restaurants is **(Pasta e Vino** (Templeman 352, tel. 032/2496187, pastaevino@hotmail.com). Offering exactly what it says—every entrée is made-to-order pasta in the US$10 and up range—it does serve nonpasta starters and has a superb wine list. During the week, it's possible to make reservations in the morning for dinner that night, but for the weekend call no later than Monday; otherwise, the only option is dining at the bar. Its only drawback is conversational noise; the music volume is only moderate.

Cerro Alegre

Possibly the best lunch specials (around US$6) in town can be found at the creative **(Café Vinilo** (Almirante Montt 448, tel. 032/2230665), which takes its name from the record-album decor covering the walls. The menu is eclectic, but the bread deserves special mention; the service is casual but attentive, the music good but unintrusive.

Reached by Ascensor El Peral, **La Colombina** (Pasaje Apolo 91, Paseo Yugoeslavo, tel. 032/2236254, www.lacolombina.cl) has fine food and an even finer panoramic dining room, open Tuesday to Saturday for lunch and dinner, Sunday for lunch only; it also has a pub open Thursday to Saturday. Immediately downhill, **Apolo 77** (Pasaje Apolo 77, tel. 032/2734862, www.restauranteapolo77.cl) has an excellent reputation.

Though it has attractive ambience and fine service, **Samsara** (Almirante Montt 427, cel. 09/92513467, www.samsararestaurante.cl, open Wed.–Sat. dinner, Sun. lunch only) falls short of the best Thai food; the surprisingly bland three-course dinners (US$15–21 pp) feature a single entrée only, but do include salad, rice, and dessert.

Other Neighborhoods

Cerro Cárcel's **Caruso** (Av. Cumming 201, tel. 032/2594039, www.caruso.cl, lunch daily except Mon., dinner Thurs.–Sat.) gets high marks for seafood but low marks for keeping irregular schedules—phone before going, even on a Friday or Saturday evening.

On Cerro Bellavista, serving an international menu that includes Thai and Indian dishes, as well as vegetarian specialties, the Fundación Valparaíso's **(El Gato Tuerto** (Héctor Calvo 205, tel. 032/2734328) is part of the nonprofit's effort to reinvigorate the city. It also has a bookstore/café.

Toward Viña del Mar, on Cerro Esperanza above Avenida España, **Portofino** (Bellamar 301, tel. 032/2621464) still has its adherents, but it's lagging behind some newer Italian options.

INFORMATION AND SERVICES

The waterfront **Módulo de Informaciones Turísticas** (Muelle Prat s/n), at the foot of Plaza Sotomayor, offers basic information and some guided walks. There is a satellite office at the Terminal Rodoviario (bus station, Avenida Pedro Montt and Rawson, tel. 032/2213246).

Downtown ATMs are abundant; for **exchange houses,** try Inter Cambio (Plaza Sotomayor 11, Local 8) or Cambio Exprinter (Prat 895).

Correos de Chile (Prat 856) is the **post office.** There are numerous long-distance offices, including Telefónica CTC (Esmeralda 1054, Avenida Pedro Montt 2023).

Café Riquet (Plaza Aníbal Pinto 1199, tel. 032/2213171) is a traditional Porteño favorite that's moved into the cyber age, but there are many others.

Cerro Alegre's **Lavanda Café** (Av. Pedro Montt 454, tel. 032/2591473) does the **laundry** and, meanwhile, steams your espresso.

For **medical treatment,** contact **Hospital Carlos van Buren** (San Ignacio 725, tel. 032/2204000).

For **language instruction,** consider the Escuela Español Interactivo (Prat 725, Oficina 414, cel. 09/9286-4973, www.interactive-spanish.cl), just uphill from Hostal Casa Aventura.

Several neighboring and overseas countries have **consulates** here: Argentina (Cochrane 867, Oficina 204, tel. 032/2213691); Germany (Blanco 1215, Oficina 1102, tel. 032/2256749); Peru (Av. Errázuriz 1178, Oficina 71, tel. 032/2253403, conpeval@entelchile.net); and Great Britain (Blanco 1199, 5th floor, tel. 032/2213063, con.britanico@entelchile.net).

GETTING THERE

Except for suburban commuter rail, transport in and out of Valparaíso is exclusively by bus; though LAN (Esmeralda 1048, tel. 032/2251441) sells tickets and confirms reservations, Santiago has the nearest commercial airport.

Unless otherwise indicated, all buses depart from Valparaíso's aging **Terminal Rodoviario** (Av. Pedro Montt 2800, tel. 032/2213246). Regional, long-distance, and international services from Valparaíso and Viña del Mar are almost identical, so most details appear here and only those that differ (such as some telephone numbers) appear in the listing for Viña's much newer Terminal Rodoviario. Some northbound long-distance buses link up with departures from Santiago, which can mean waiting at the Panamericana junction for a transfer.

Regional Buses

From its own terminal, **Buses La Porteña** (Molina 366, tel. 032/2216568) serves coastal and interior destinations in northern Region V, including La Ligua (US$5) and Los Vilos (US$7.50) every 30 minutes from 6 A.M.–7:15 P.M.

Every half hour until early evening, from the main terminal, **Sol del Pacífico** (tel. 032/2281024) serves Quintero and other northern Region V beaches, including Papudo (US$3); it continues to La Ligua and Cabildo.

Several carriers, most notably **Pullman Bus** (tel. 032/2253125) go to Los Andes (US$7.50, 2.5 hours) via Limache, Quillota, and San Felipe.

Pullman Bus Lago Peñuelas (tel. 032/2224025) goes to southern Region V beach towns including Algarrobo and nearby Isla Negra (US$4), the site of Pablo Neruda's most famous house, every 20 minutes between 6:15 A.M. and 10 P.M.

Buses to Santiago

To the capital (US$7, two hours), **Tur-Bus** (tel. 032/2212028) has the most frequent service, but there are several other carriers.

Interregional Buses

Tur-Bus (tel. 032/2212028), **Pullman Bus** (tel. 032/2253125), and several others ply northbound routes on the Panamericana to Arica and intermediates and southbound to Puerto Montt and intermediates.

Southbound Panamericana carriers, to Puerto Montt and intermediates, include **Buses Norte** (tel. 032/2258322) and **Sol del Pacífico** (tel. 032/2213776).

Sample northbound destinations, with approximate times and fares, include La Serena (US$23–33, 8 hours), Copiapó (US$41–63, 12 hours), Antofagasta (US$58–84, 19 hours), and Iquique (US$65–91, 25 hours). Southbound destinations include Talca (US$12, 7 hours), Chillán (US$17, 9 hours), Concepción (US$19–38, 11 hours), Temuco (US$34–52, 12 hours), Osorno (US$37–58, 14 hours), and Puerto Montt (US$38–65, 16 hours).

International Buses

International buses to Argentina bypass Santiago but usually pass through Viña del Mar. Nearly all leave early, between 8 and 8:30 A.M., and stop in Mendoza (US$30, 7 hours); the exception to early departures is **Buses Ahumada** (tel. 032/2216663), which leaves at noon and 9 P.M. daily; for Buenos Aires (US$67, 22 hours), it's sometimes necessary to change buses at Los Andes). **Buses TAC** (tel. 032/2257587) and **Fénix Pullman Internacional** (tel. 032/2681785) also go to Mendoza and/or Buenos Aires.

GETTING AROUND

Easily the most interesting and entertaining way to get around town is on foot and via the funiculars, but there are other mechanized alternatives.

Bus and *Taxi Colectivo*

Numerous local buses and *taxi colectivos* connect Valparaíso with Viña del Mar, only a few kilometers north. They also thread in and around the hill neighborhoods, necessarily via very indirect routes.

Train

From the new Estación Puerto (Av. Errázuriz 711), the **Metro Regional de Valparaíso** (Merval, www.merval.cl, tel. 032/2381510) is a suburban commuter line that goes to several stations in town and onward to Viña del Mar, El Salto, Quilpué, Villa Alemana, Peñablanca, and Limache. It requires purchasing an inexpensive rechargeable plastic card.

© WAYNE BERNHARDSON

THE CHILEAN HEARTLAND

The Valparaíso Metro, which connects to Viña del Mar and other suburbs, has been greatly improved and partly undergrounded.

Vicinity of Valparaíso

East and south of Valparaíso are several excursion options, including Casablanca Valley wineries and Pablo Neruda's Isla Negra beachfront home.

LO VÁSQUEZ (SANTUARIO DE LA INMACULADA CONCEPCIÓN)

Ruta 68 between Santiago and Valparaíso is one of Chile's busiest highways, but motor vehicle traffic miraculously vanishes every December 8, as up to half a million faithful congregate at the Santuario de la Inmaculada Concepción, one of the holiest Catholic shrines in Chile.

After the 1906 Valparaíso earthquake destroyed the original chapel, it took more than 30 years to build the present church, dating from 1940. The 4,000-square-meter amphitheater can accommodate nearly 3,000 worshippers. To reach the shrine, 26 kilometers southeast of Valparaíso and 84 kilometers northwest of Santiago, pedestrian pilgrims literally take over the highway. Many start days earlier from Santiago and even farther away, sleeping outdoors en route; some even crawl the final five or six kilometers.

On arrival, they attend open-air masses, which take place from 6 P.M. the afternoon of the December 7 until 8 P.M. the evening of the 8th; the festivities close with a procession led by the bishop of Valparaíso. In the interim, authorities divert Valparaíso- and Viña-bound traffic north through Ruta 5 and Ruta 60 to Quillota.

Throughout the event, hawkers sell prodigious quantities of food and souvenirs—though there are almost-permanent eateries and the sanctuary has its own souvenir shop—and pilgrims deposit tons of trash. At other times, they leave small monetary offerings in hopes of avoiding traffic accidents or perhaps speeding tickets, as Carabineros patrol this stretch of highway zealously.

THE SOUTH-CENTRAL COAST

There is no direct road south from Valparaíso, but the paved road west/southwest from the Casablanca Valley passes through a series of popular beachfront towns. Regular bus service from Valparaíso is with Pullman Bus Lago Peñuelas, and from Santiago with several companies.

Algarrobo

Home to many Santiaguino summer houses, the beach resort of Algarrobo (population 6,628) hosts the **Regata Mil Millas Náuticas** for yachties every February; the postcolonial adobe **Iglesia de la Candelaria** (1837) is a national historical monument. Out of season, it can be mortuary-silent, though business increases on weekends.

In a quiet cul-de-sac, friendly **Hotel Uribe** (El Teatro D, tel. 035/481035, clarisa33@hotmail.com, US$25 s, US$47–57 d) is spacious and comfortable enough, with a decent breakfast. Rates at the best hotel, **Hotel Pacífico** (Av. Carlos Alessandri 1930, tel. 035/482855, www.hotel-pacifico.cl, US$79 s, US$105 d with breakfast) have stabilized after recent increases.

La Regata (Av. Carlos Alessandri 2108, tel. 035/482590, www.laregatapub.cl) is a bar that has pizza, sandwiches, and live music (mostly salsa) on weekends. It has a fireplace for cool nights, and also an adjacent cybercafé.

C Isla Negra

About 10 kilometers south of Algarrobo, Isla Negra—which is not an island—has become famous for the **Casa de Pablo Neruda,** the poet's favorite beachfront house and burial site. Built to entertain his friends and hold his whimsical collections of nautical memorabilia, including bowsprits, ships-in-bottles, and wood carvings, the house has been open to the public for more than a decade. The Fundación Neruda, which administers the site, has added a room originally planned by Neruda but never completed, to house his huge assortment of sea snails, clam shells, and narwhal spikes.

Unfortunately, because Isla Negra is Neruda's most popular house, the half-hour guided tours are so rushed that the guides sometimes find themselves talking over each other. No photography is permitted in the house itself, but after the tour is over, visitors may remain on the grounds and photograph the exterior.

In summer, reservations are imperative at Isla Negra (tel. 035/461284, www.fundacionneruda.org), which is open 10 A.M.–8 P.M. daily except Monday. The rest of the year, when hours are 10 A.M.–6 P.M. daily except Monday, it's easier to join a tour on a drop-in basis. Admission, including the tour, costs US$5 for adults, half that for children and seniors, but tours in English cost about US$1 per person more.

Most people come to Isla Negra for the day, but for those who stay longer, down the road is **Hostería La Candela** (Calle de la Hostería 67, tel. 035/461254, www.candela.cl, US$80 s or d), which belongs to people who befriended Neruda in his later years. Past its prime, but still interesting, the rambling building also has a restaurant. The best rooms have ocean views.

The Fundación Neruda's own **El Rincón del Poeta** (tel. 035/461774, open museum hours) has good seafood lunches for about US$8–10.

From Valparaíso, **Pullman Bus Lago Peñuelas** (tel. 032/2224025) stops at Isla Negra (US$4, 1.5 hours) en route to San Antonio, frequently between 6:15 A.M. and 10 P.M.

Viña del Mar

Famous for white-sand beaches that stretch from Caleta Abarca north through the suburbs of Reñaca and Concón, Viña del Mar is also Chile's Ciudad Jardín (Garden City) for its Mediterranean cityscapes—one of its signature symbols is the Reloj de Flores, the "Clock of Flowers" at the Avenida Marina approach from Valparaíso.

In the immediate post-independence times, though, today's Viña was *puro campo,* a bucolic countryside that was part of the Carrera family's Hacienda Las Siete Hermanas. The Carreras, one of Chile's founding families, sold the hacienda to the Alvares-Vergara family, who, as the Santiago–Valparaíso railroad increased land values, sold off parts of the property to wealthy Valparaíso businessmen, marking a transition from semi-rurality to elegant residential suburb and beach resort.

Throughout the latter half of the 20th century, though, Viña became a more democratic destination and even began to pull Argentine tourists from across the Andes—even though its constant fogs, cool sea breezes, and cold Pacific currents can make entering the water without a wet suit a forbidding experience. Once Chile's prestige beach resort, Viña has lost ground to competitors such as La Serena (whose seaside climate is only slightly milder) but still gets plenty of weekend and summer beachgoers from metropolitan Santiago.

ORIENTATION

Viña del Mar (population 287,000) is 120 kilometers northeast of Santiago via Ruta 68 and about 10 kilometers north of Valparaíso via Avenida España, which hugs the coastline. The Estero Marga Marga, a potentially stunning riverbank asset that's been turned into a disgraceful backhoe parking lot crossed by a series of parallel bridges, divides the city's northern and southern sectors. There is an ambitious plan to transform the westernmost Marga Marga into a commercial marina within a decade.

THE CHILEAN HEARTLAND

© WAYNE BERNHARDSON

The Estero Marga Marga separates the newer northern sector of Viña del Mar from its traditional southern sector.

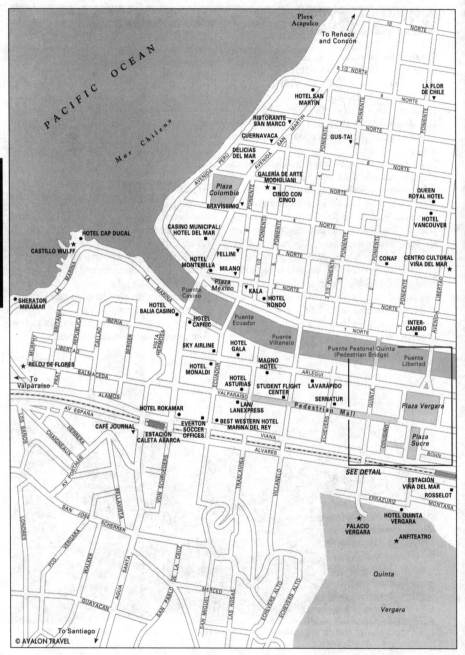

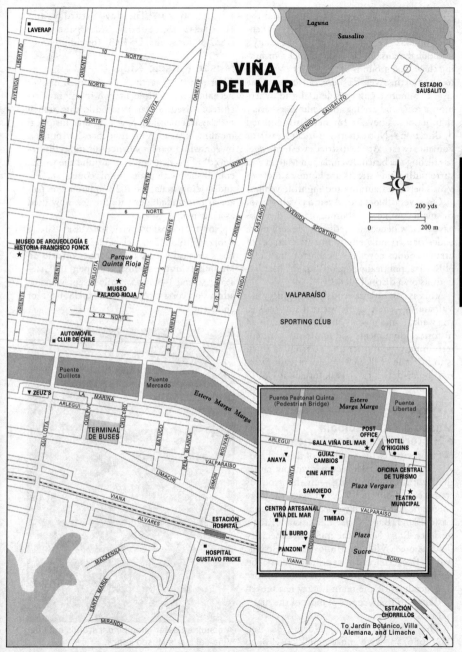

To the south, between the estuary and the railroad tracks, the commercial district is centered on Plaza Vergara, with many of the city's traditional mansions beyond the tracks, including the fabled grounds of the Quinta Vergara; to the north, Avenida Libertad crosses the river to a more regular residential grid, where most streets and avenues bear numbers rather than names. They are further distinguished by direction—Norte (north), Oriente (east), or Poniente (west). At the district's western edge, paralleling the beach, Avenida San Martín and surrounding side streets are home to most of Viña's better restaurants and nightlife venues.

On several blocks of Avenida Valparaíso, the main commercial thoroughfare, sidewalks have been widened and retiled to create a more pedestrian-friendly environment. Terraces of luxury condos cover the beachfront hillsides of Reñaca, politically part of Viña del Mar but with its own distinct identity.

Viña is less spontaneously engaging than Valparaíso—there are fewer real surprises as you walk around town—but there are scattered historical monuments and museums. One entertaining way of orienting yourself to town is to hire one of Plaza Vergara's elegant *victorias* (horse-drawn carriages), for about US$15 per hour.

MUSEUMS
Museo de Arqueología e Historia Francisco Fonck

For most visitors, the highlight of this archaeological and historical museum is without rather than within the building—on the grounds stands one of only half a dozen *moai,* the large enigmatic statues, to have been removed from Easter Island (Rapa Nui), Chile's distant Pacific territory. Rapa Nui is the museum's specialty (its Biblioteca William Mulloy has one of the world's finest collections of printed material on the island), along with Chilean natural history in general; while the main library has moved to Rapa Nui itself, copies of most of the material remain here.

The **Museo Fonck** (4 Norte 784, tel. 032/2686753, www.museofonck.cl) is open 10 A.M.–6 P.M. Tuesday–Saturday and 10 A.M.–2 P.M. Sunday. Admission costs US$2.50 for adults, US$0.35 for children.

Museo Palacio Rioja

After the 1906 earthquake, Spanish banker Fernando Rioja hired French immigrant architect Alfredo Azancot to build this French neoclassical mansion, now a national historical monument, as his Viña residence. Surrounded by sprawling gardens (since substantially reduced) of exotic trees from around the world, embellished with pools, tennis courts, stables, and a riding arena, the 1620-square-meter palace also included a private theater, now used as a cinema.

Now municipal property, the Museo Palacio Rioja (Quillota 214, tel. 032/2483664) also hosts musical events at its **Conservatorio de Música Izidor Handler.** It's open 10 A.M.–1:30 P.M. and 3–5:30 P.M. daily except Monday; admission costs US$1 for adults, US$0.50 for children.

A genuine Easter Island *moai* stands outside Viña del Mar's Museo Fonck.

Palacio Carrasco (Centro Cultural Viña del Mar)

In 1912, nine years after buying an entire block fronting on Avenida Libertad, nitrate magnate Emilio Carrasco Alliende hired Palacio Rioja designer Alfred Azancot to build this two-story structure, whose facade features a portico with three Norman arches, topped by a mansard roof.

Carrasco died in 1923, before actually moving in, and the following year his heirs sold the building. In 1930, Viña mayor Manuel Ossa Sainete acquired it for the city and, despite 1965 quake damage, it served as city hall until another quake in 1971. Condemned in 1975, it somehow escaped demolition; since 1977, this national historical monument has housed the Centro Cultural de Viña del Mar. The grounds include Rodin's sculpture *La Defensa,* supposedly rejected in a competition for Valparaíso's Plaza de los Héroes de Iquique.

The Centro Cultural Viña del Mar (Av. Libertad 250, tel. 032/2269721) hosts exhibitions of painting and sculpture. It's open 9 A.M.–7 P.M. weekdays, 9 A.M.–2 P.M. Saturday. Admission is free except for special summer exhibitions, when there's a modest charge.

Castillo Wulff

Now an exhibition hall, this extravagant structure dates from 1906, when Valparaíso businessman Gustavo Adolfo Wulff Mowle indulged himself by building atop a rocky headland at the mouth of the Marga Marga. In 1920, Wulff added its signature tower and a section of transparent floor to see the waves breaking on the rocks below.

After Wulff's death in 1946, the castle passed through several different hands, including the city of Viña and the Chilean navy, before finally coming under control of the national Dirección de Bibliotecas, Archivos y Museos, which made it into a museum and then a Sala de Exposiciones. Near the Marga Marga's outlet, the Castillo Wulff (Av. Marina 37, tel. 032/2269728) is open 10 A.M.–1:30 P.M. and 3–5:30 P.M. daily except Monday. Admission is free.

QUINTA VERGARA

Originally part of the colonial Hacienda Las Siete Hermanas, Viña's famous public park and performing arts venue passed through the hands of the Carreras, one of Chile's founding families, before being sold to Portuguese businessman Francisco Alvares, whose granddaughter Mercedes married Viña's founder José Francisco Vergara.

Spectacularly landscaped, thanks to the Alvares family's imports of exotic tree species from their overseas travels, the Quinta's grounds feature the Venetian-style **Palacio Vergara** (1908), which replaced the original house destroyed in the 1906 earthquake; within the *palacio,* Viña's **Museo de Bellas Artes** (Fine Arts Museum, Errázuriz 563, tel. 032/2269431) is open 10 A.M.–1:30 P.M. and 3–5:30 P.M. daily except Monday. Adult admission costs US$1, and the rate for children is half that.

The Quinta's 15,000-spectator **Anfiteatro** (amphitheater) is the principal venue for the annual Festival Internacional de la Canción (International Song Festival), as well as other concert events throughout the year. There is no admission charge to the grounds, entered from the south end of Calle Quinta and open 7 A.M.–6 P.M. (7 P.M. in summer) daily.

JARDÍN BOTÁNICO NACIONAL

At the east end of town, Chile's National Botanical Garden owes its existence to Croatian nitrate entrepreneur Pascual Baburizza, who acquired Fundo El Olivar in the early 20th century and donated it to the Compañía del Salitre with the stipulation that, on the company's dissolution, the city of Viña would acquire it for public use. While it's been a public recreational area for most of its existence, in the past two decades Conaf and the Instituto de Desarollo Agropecuario (Indap, the governmental Agrarian Development Institute) have paid greater attention to its research and educational missions; it has since come under control of a private foundation with continued state assistance.

RUTA DEL VINO DE CASABLANCA

Midway between Valparaíso and Santiago, several wineries have united to promote the **Casablanca Valley,** one of Chile's fastest-growing and most accessible wine regions. Best known for its whites, the Ruta del Vino de Casablanca (www.casablancavalley.cl) enjoys a cool oceanic climate, though afternoons can get warm. As nearly all the wineries are on or near Ruta 68, they are convenient to public transportation; several have accommodations and restaurants.

CASAS DEL BOSQUE

In a striking building at one of the route's westernmost vineyards, Casas del Bosque produces a diversity of varietal and reserve versions of whites (sauvignon blanc and chardonnay) and reds (merlot, cabernet sauvignon, pinot noir, syrah, and the occasional blend). Tours of the winery itself, a visitor-friendly place combining contemporary technology with tasting at its **Living Wine & Bar,** cost US$12 per person.

If the visit is combined with dining at the **Tanino** restaurant, Casas del Bosque is suitable for spending an afternoon, rather than just tasting and running. While the kitchen and service can both be slow, and the portions small (more like a tasting menu), the food quality is undeniable.

To reach the winery, take the main Casablanca exit south off Ruta 68 and follow the signs through town. Casas del Bosque (Hijuela 2, Ex-Fundo Santa Rosa, tel. 032/3779431, www.casasdelbosque.cl) is open 10 A.M.-5:30 P.M. daily except in winter, when it closes at 5 P.M. It also closes January 1, Good Friday, December 8, and December 25, and the restaurant is closed Mondays.

CENTRO ECUESTRE PURO CABALLO

It's not really part of the wine circuit, but the ranch at Puro Caballo (Lagunillas, Casablanca, tel. 032/2740156 or 099/3346524, www.purocaballo.cl) is close to the Matetic winery. Throughout the year, it offers riding excursions for aficionados and rodeos for spectators, as well as a crafts fair. On-site there is an independently run restaurant, **El Estribo** (cel. 09/9438-5788), which specializes in Chilean country cooking such as *parrillada* and *pastel de choclo.*

HOUSE OF MORANDÉ

While the Morande winery is not open for tours and tasting, its vineyard restaurant has become a landmark for both its eye-catching contemporary architecture and its cuisine. With an arching roof and clean Scandinavian lines, this luminous restaurant offers panoramic vineyard views on two sides and wine-barrel porthole peeks through a third wall. In reality, the line of demarcation between interior and exterior seating is a fluid one (though the interior dining room can get a little noisy when full).

Chef Christopher Charpentier has created a menu of nouvelle Chilean cuisine, including versions of standards such as *pastel de jaiva* (crab casserole) and game dishes such as *costillas de jabalí* (boar chops), and desserts such as chirimoya mousse with a chardonnay sauce. The wine list includes not just Morandé but other area wineries. Fresh − not bagged − herbal teas are available.

Immediately west of Veramonte, House of Morandé (Ruta 68, Km 64, tel. 032/2754700, www.morande.cl) is open 11 A.M.-5 P.M. daily except Monday (when it's closed) and Friday (when it stays open until midnight).

VIÑA INDÓMITA

Its kitschy turret towering above the valley from a flattened hilltop site just east of Viña Mar, Indómita is Casablanca's most conspicuous winery. It cultivates 200 hectares of its chardonnay and sauvignon blanc whites here, but also has 400 hectares of reds − cabernet sauvignon, carmenere, and merlot − in the Maipo Valley. All are processed here, however.

In addition to its wines, Indómita's becoming well-known for its namesake restaurant, with spectacular valley views and a creative menu that's strong on seafood but also includes regional Chilean specialties such as Patagonian

© WAYNE BERNHARDSON

The Valle de Casablanca is one of Chile's up-and-coming wine regions.

lamb (US$19) and grilled mahimahi from Easter Island (US$10).

Viña Indómita (Ruta 68, Km 64, tel. 032/2754400, www.indomita.cl) is open for tours and tasting (US$5 pp, applicable to lunch at the restaurant) at 10 A.M., noon, and 3 and 4:30 P.M. daily. The restaurant is open daily for lunch.

VIÑA MAR

On the south side of the highway, Viña Mar took over the unsuccessful Cuvée Mumm champagne plant in 2002 and has begun to produce fine varietals and blends from cabernet sauvignon, carmenere, merlot, pinot noir, chardonnay, and sauvignon blanc. While it's not what it once was – it's much better – it still makes sparkling wines via champenoise and charmat methods.

On the south side of the highway, Viña Mar (Ruta 68, Km 72, tel. 032/2754300, www .vinamar.cl) is open for tours 10 A.M.-2 P.M. and 3-5 P.M. daily except Sunday, when hours are noon-5 P.M. There is a branch of Viña del Mar's Italian institution, **Ristorante San Marco,** on the grounds.

VIÑA MATETIC

One of Casablanca's newest wineries, discreetly built into a hillside in the San Antonio Valley southwest of Casablanca, Matetic is a glisteningly modern winery that produces organic pinot noir and syrah, a merlot/malbec blend, sauvignon blanc, and chardonnay. Sprawling over the coast range, the scenic grounds contain a crumbling early winery bursting with antique equipment that should become a museum.

Viña Matetic (Fundo El Rosario, Lagunillas, tel. 032/2741500, www.mateticvineyards.cl) is open for guided tours and tastings (starting at US$12 pp) at 11 A.M. and 3:30 P.M. daily except Monday; make reservations 24 hours in advance. In addition to the winery, it has a stylish adobe guesthouse with palm-studded gardens (US$320 s, US$400 d) and a restaurant **Equilibrio** (cel. 09/8920-2066), open daily except Monday for lunch.

VIÑA VERAMONTE

Immediately west of the Zapata tunnel, Veramonte is a 1,000-hectare vineyard surrounded by a 10,000-hectare greenbelt. Run by the Huneeus family, who also operate the Napa Valley's Franciscan Vineyards, it produces sauvignon blanc, cabernet sauvignon, carmenere, and merlot, but its pride is the Primus premium blend of the three reds.

Led by well-informed guides, Veramonte's tours (not always available in English, US$10 pp) visit the production facilities and vineyards, but also its museum of antique presses, corkscrews, and other wine technology. They end with a generous tasting, at shaded picnic tables, that includes several varietal and reserve wines, including the Primus, as well as goat, parmesan, and sheep cheeses, with crackers and nuts to accompany them. In addition, Veramonte's on-site wine shop carries books, souvenirs, and premium agricultural products.

On the north side of the highway, Viña Veramonte (Ruta 68, Km 66, tel. 032/2742421, www.veramonte.com) is open 9:30 A.M.-6:30 P.M. daily except Sunday for visits to its cellars, bottling plant, and wine shop.

THE CHILEAN HEARTLAND

From downtown Viña's Calle Alvarez, eastbound bus No. 203 goes almost directly to the entrance of the Jardín Botánico (tel. 032/2672566, www.jardin-botanico.cl). From September to March, the grounds are open 9 A.M.–7 P.M. daily; the rest of the year, hours are 10 A.M.–6 P.M. Admission costs about US$1.50, half that for seniors, and a bit less for children.

ENTERTAINMENT

Viña del Mar is one of Chile's entertainment and events hotbeds.

Pubs

El Burro (Pasaje Cousiño 12-D) draws weekend crowds. **Café Journal** (Agua Santa 2, tel. 032/2666654), an outlier of Bohemian Valparaíso, has both pub grub and live entertainment.

Discotheques

Scratch (Quillota 898, tel. 032/2381381), a longtime local favorite, occupies new quarters toward the north end of town. **Zeuz's** (Arlegui 829, www.zeuzs.cl) is a large gay disco directly behind Hotel O'Higgins.

Galleries

The **Sala Viña del Mar** (Arlegui 683, tel. 032/2680633) offers visual-arts exhibitions. The **Galería de Arte Modigliani** (5 Norte 168, tel. 032/2684991) displays local and regional paintings and sculpture.

Cinema

At the north end of town, the eight-screen **Cinemark** (15 Norte 961, Local 224, tel. 032/2993391) is Viña's main commercial cinema. The **Cine Arte** (Plaza Vergara 142, tel. 032/2882798) is a repertory house.

Theater

The **Teatro Municipal** (Plaza Vergara s/n, tel. 032/2681739, www.culturaviva.cl) hosts live theater, concerts, and occasional films.

Spectator Sports

Viña's soccer team **Everton** (Viana 161, tel. 032/2689504, www.evertonchile.cl) holds its matches at Estadio Sausalito (Av. Sausalito s/n, tel. 032/2978250). The **Valparaíso Sporting Club** (Av. Los Castaños 404, tel. 032/2689393) is the site for horse racing.

Gambling

Stylistically it's not Las Vegas—¡gracias a Dios!—but Viña's **Casino Viña del Mar** (Av. San Martín 199, tel. 032/2846100, www.casinodevinadelmar.cl) is still the place where risk addicts can fritter away their finances on bingo, cards, roulette, slots, and other money-losing diversions (those with an elementary knowledge of statistics and probability can limit themselves to dinner, drinks, and live entertainment). Now part of the adjacent Hotel del Mar, open from 6 P.M. into the wee hours, the casino charges a US$5 cover for those visiting the main floor (formal attire is the rule; hotel guests get in free). For bingo and the slots (known in Spanish as *tragamonedas,* "coin-swallowers"), hours start at noon or 2 P.M.

EVENTS

For two weeks in January, sponsored by the Cámara Chilena del Libro (Chilean Book Chamber), Viña's **Feria del Libro** attracts literary figures such as novelist Alberto Fuguet, playwright and novelist Marco Antonio de la Parra, and essayist Pedro Lemebel. Regionally oriented, it includes live readings, interviews, theater and music performances, and children's shows.

Viña's single biggest event, though, is February's **Festival Internacional de la Canción,** where nearly 100,000 ticketholders crowd the Quinta Vergara to hear Spanish-speaking acts from around the Americas and the Mediterranean, plus some over-the-hill international acts; it fills TV screens throughout the country and the Latin American TV network Univisión broadcasts part of the event overseas. Since it's partly a competition, the highlight is the best song award, which usually seems to go to the most pedestrian tune by the dreariest diva or a cheerless crooner, but the regular programming has become more audacious with acts including *narcocorrido* bands such as Mexico's Los Tigres del Norte and rockers such as Argentina's brilliant but erratic Charly García.

During mid-September's **Fiestas Patrias,** the Estadio Sausalito is the site of an informal Chilean food festival with folkloric music.

SHOPPING

The crafts booths along **Paseo Cousiño** hawk run-of-the-mill jewelry, but the leather and copper goods are more interesting. The larger **Centro Artesanal Viña del Mar** (Quinta 220) is also worth a visit.

ACCOMMODATIONS

Despite Viña's historical reputation as an elite beach resort, there are several economical alternatives south of the Marga Marga. Chile's weak peso has increased demand, though, as Argentines returned in 2009 after six years in the wilderness of their own country.

US$25-50

Hotel Capric (Von Schroeders 39, tel. 032/2978295, hivinacapric@hostelling.cl, US$12–15 pp) is the longtime Hostelling affiliate, but the newly affiliated **Hostel Make Out** (Viana 147, tel. 032/3174150, www.makeout .cl, US$15–20 pp) is hipper and livelier, with its own bar/restaurant. The highest prices correspond to weekend accommodations.

In addition to its dorm-style hostel facilities, improved **Hotel Capric** (Von Schroeders 39, tel. 032/2978295, www.hotelcapric.cl, US$30 s, US$33 d) has rooms with private baths that are really better value.

Though it no longer offers hostel facilities, **Hotel Asturias** (Av. Valparaíso 299, tel. 032/2711565, hotelasturias@chile.com, US$30 s, US$42 d) has good private rooms. Parking costs extra.

Adjacent to the grounds of Viña's famous performing arts venue—a disadvantage during the weeklong summer song festival— **Hotel Quinta Vergara** (Errázuriz 690, tel. 032/2685073, www.hotelquintavergara .cl, US$30 s, US$47 d) offers a traditional Francophile style with some contemporary amenities such as WiFi.

Near the Miramar Metro station, **Hotel Rokamar** (Viana 107, tel./fax 032/2690019, www.hotelrokamar.cl, US$37 s, US$47 d with breakfast) occupies a handsome older building.

Owned by a Chilean long resident in Canada, **Hotel Vancouver** (5 Norte 650, tel. 032/2482983, www.hotelvancouvervina .cl, US$30 s, US$49 d) is a good value—cozy and friendly, with cable TV, Internet, and parking.

At the reddish stucco **Queen Royal Hotel** (5 Norte 655, tel. 032/2682450, www.queenroyal .cl, US$37 s, US$47 d), rates include a buffet breakfast and WiFi access.

Hotel Monaldi (Arlegui 172, tel. 032/2881484, www.hotelmonaldi.cl, US$22–40 pp, US$37 s, US$50 d with breakfast) is the refurbished Residencial Villarrica. Some rooms are small, though, and others have too many beds.

US$50-100

A bargain for the price **C Magno Hotel** (Arlegui 372, tel. 032/2713816, www.magno-hotel.cl, US$45 s, US$70 d) is a beautifully modernized downtown hotel.

North of the river, well-regarded **Hotel Rondó** (1 Norte 157, tel./fax 032/2977157, www.hotelrondo.cl, US$55 s, US$70 d with breakfast) is a tidy, old-fashioned B&B. It's on a busy street, but the back rooms are quiet and the staff are gracious.

In recent years, the classic **C Hotel O'Higgins** (Plaza Vergara s/n, tel. 032/2882016, www.panamericanahoteles.cl, US$65 s, US$82 d) has undergone a remodel that's restored some of its lost luster, but it still lags behind some other ostensible luxury hotels.

© WAYNE BERNHARDSON

Viña del Mar's Sheraton Miramar Hotel replaced the historic Hotel Miramar, demolished in 2004.

US$100-150

A couple blocks west of the Rondó, across from the casino, **Hotel Monterilla** (2 Norte 65, tel. 032/2976950, www.monterilla.cl, US$91–114 s, US$104–131 d) is a cozy (19-room) luminous hotel, with midsize to large rooms. Despite the busy location, it's quiet, friendly, and has abundant parking.

With the sound of the surf literally outside the window—pray there's no tsunami—the unique **Hotel Cap Ducal** (Av. Marina 51, tel. 032/2626655, www.capducal.cl, US$119 s, US$140 d) exploits its nautical theme to the max. The more expensive rooms are suites, some with two bedrooms, and some with whirlpool tubs, but decades of oceanic weather have left the exterior looking worn.

Hotel Marina del Rey (Ecuador 299, tel. 032/2383000, fax 032/2383001, www.marinadelrey.cl, US$140 s or d) is a Best Western chain affiliate.

The 64-room **Hotel Gala** (Arlegui 273, tel. 032/2321500, www.galahotel.cl, US$110–130 s, US$126–145 d) is a highrise overlooking the Estero Marga Marga, with a contemporary style accentuated by its modern Chilean art collection. All the rooms (also decorated with modern art) have WiFi, most have small balconies, and it has both a pool and restaurant.

More than US$200

With its 155 rooms, the remodeled high-rise **Hotel San Martín** (Av. San Martín 667, tel. 032/2689191, www.hotelsanmartin.cl, US$130 s, US$225 d) offers beachfront convenience but an impersonal style.

Overlooking the ocean near Caleta Abarca, the luminous **Sheraton Miramar Hotel & Convention Center** (Avenida Marina 15, tel. 032/2388600, www.sheraton.com/vinadelmar, US$225–349 s or d) is a more-than-worthy, state-of-the-art replacement for an earlier landmark hotel that had deteriorated. The service is assiduous, with a management that ensures attention to detail. In Viña, this 142-room gem is the best that money can buy.

Facing the Pacific, part of the Enjoy casino consortium, the 60-room **Hotel del Mar** (Av. Perú and Avenida Los Héroes, tel. 032/7705190, www.hoteldelmar.cl, US$200–465 s or d and up) has enormous luxury rooms with sprawling balconies and baths that are larger than entire rooms at some midrange accommodations. The buffet breakfast is spectacular, with fresh Chilean fruits and juices, but the in-room Internet (both Ethernet and WiFi) can be balky. The casino's air quality is positively toxic.

FOOD

Viña's dining scene has lost ground to Valparaíso's, but there are still some decent choices. For breakfast, snacks, and *onces,* try cafés such as **Anayak** (Quinta 134, tel. 032/2680093) and **Samoiedo** (Av. Valparaíso 637, tel. 032/2684610).

Fellini (3 Norte 88, tel. 032/2975742) is a fine but relatively expensive Italian option with large portions and exemplary service, but it suffers from a high decibel level.

Divino Pecado (Av. San Martín 180, tel. 032/2975790) is a pasta specialist in tobacco-free surroundings, with creative options such as lamb in merlot sauce over fettucine. The desserts are also good, but the service can be a little overbearing.

Other Italian choices, tending toward the upscale and pretty good, include **Milano** (6 Poniente 121, tel. 032/2698839, www.mangiarbene.cl) and **Ristorante San Marco** (San Martín 597, tel. 032/2975304).

Delicias del Mar (Av. San Martín 459, tel. 032/2901837) is a fine Basque seafood restaurant with entrées in the US$10 and up range and an owner who, to judge from the decor, might be stalking Marilyn Monroe were she still alive. Unlike many Chilean restaurants, it firmly discourages cell phones, and the service is exemplary.

La Flor de Chile (8 Norte 601, tel. 032/2689554) is the best choice for Chilean specialties. **Gus-Tai** (3 Poniente 537, tel. 032/2684367) is the only option for Thai dishes (available only at night).

For Mexican food a bit more complex than the standard *antojitos* such as enchiladas and burritos, there's popular **Cuernavaca** (San Martín 501, tel. 032/2739083), but the noise factor is notable.

Viña has two fine ice creameries: **Bravíssimo** (Av. San Martín 302, tel. 032/2681862) is a chain, while **Timbao** (Av. Valparaíso 670) is more strictly artisanal.

Peruvian food isn't quite the fashion here that it is in Santiago, but **Kala** (2 Norte and 6 Poniente, tel. 032/2687340, weekdays dinner, weekends lunch and dinner) is a credible choice, with fish dishes and fine service at reasonable prices (starting around US$8).

INFORMATION

Viña's municipal **Oficina Central de Turismo** (Arlegui s/n, tel. 032/2269330, www.visitevinadelmar.cl) occupies new offices on the south side of Hotel O'Higgins. Summer hours are 9 A.M.–9 P.M. weekdays, 10 A.M.–9 P.M. weekends and holidays, but the rest of the year it's open 9 A.M.–2 P.M. and 3–7 P.M. weekdays, and 4–7 P.M. on weekends and holidays. Its monthly newsletter, *Todo Viña,* is an exhaustive calendar of events and entertainment in Viña, Valparaíso, and suburbs; it also offers a free city map.

At the bus station, there's a privately run **Oficina de Informaciones** (Av. Valparaíso 1055, tel. 032/2752093), open 8 A.M.–8 P.M. daily.

Sernatur's regional office (Valparaíso 507, 3rd floor, tel. 032/2882285, fax 032/2684117, infovalparaiso@sernatur.cl) is open 8:30 A.M.–7 P.M. daily in summer; the rest of the year, hours are 8:30 A.M.–2 P.M. and 3–5 P.M. weekdays except Friday, when it closes half an hour earlier.

The **Automóvil Club de Chile** (Acchi, 1 Norte 901, tel. 032/2689505) helps motorists.

The regional office of **Corporación Nacional Forestal** (Conaf, 3 Norte 541, tel. 032/2970108) has information on Parque Nacional La Campana and other protected areas.

SERVICES

Banco de Chile (Av. Valparaíso 667) has an ATM, but there are many more. Exchange houses include **Guiñazú Cambios** (Arlegui 686) and **Inter-Cambio** (1 Norte 655-B).

Near the municipal tourist office, **Correos de Chile** (Plaza Latorre 32) is the post office.

Cinco con Cinco (5 Norte 182) has both long-distance telephone and Internet connections.

The **Student Flight Center** (Villanelo 180, Oficina 514, tel. 032/2881330) can help arrange flights.

Viña has two convenient laundries: **Lavarápido** (Arlegui 440, tel. 032/2688331) and **Laverap** (Libertad 902).

Hospital Gustavo Fricke (Alvares 1532, tel. 032/2680041) is south of the tracks and several blocks east of the main Merval train station.

GETTING THERE

Like Valparaíso, Viña del Mar relies exclusively on bus transportation to and from the city.

Air

Viña's Aeropuerto Torquemada has no commercial flights, but **LAN** (Av. Valparaíso 287, tel. 032/2690365) and **Sky Airline** (Ecuador 78, tel. 032/2695345) both fly out of Santiago.

Bus

Viña's modern **Terminal Rodoviario** (Av. Valparaíso 1055, tel. 032/2752000) is about 300 meters east of Plaza Vergara. Carriers and services are almost identical to those from Valparaíso; all northbound and international buses from Valpo stop in Viña.

GETTING AROUND
Train

Merval trains between Valparaíso and Limache make several Viña stops, at Estación Caleta Abarca, Estación Viña del Mar, Estación Hospital, and Estación El Salto.

Bus and *Taxi Colectivo*

From Arlegui, west of Plaza Vergara, local buses marked "Aduana" or "Puerto" connect Viña with Valpo, as do *taxi colectivos*.

Car Rental

Options include **Rosselot** (Alvares 762, tel. 032/2382888) and **Mach Viña** (Viana 33, tel. 032/2381095).

Vicinity of Viña del Mar

From Viña north, a string of beach towns corresponding to various social classes stretches among the headlands. To the interior, the towns of Limache and Olmué are gateways to Parque Nacional La Campana, one of the region's underappreciated gems; a northern park access point from the Panamericana is near the town of Hijuelas.

In January, Olmué hosts the **Festival del Huaso de Olmué,** honoring Chile's counterpart to Argentina's gaucho. The country's largest folk festival, it's far less commercial than Viña's international song competition.

◖ PARQUE NACIONAL LA CAMPANA

Rising above the fertile coastal plain of Quillota, La Campana comprises 8,000 hectares of sheer-sided scrubland, scattered "oak" forests, and the greatest remaining concentration of the rare Chilean palm. A UNESCO World Biosphere Reserve since 1984, the former Jesuit hacienda of San Isidro is the place where temperate southern Chile's forests reach their northernmost, overlapping the Norte Chico's desert scrub.

Noteworthy for a network of integrated hiking trails that cross ridges and scale summits with spectacular views from the Pacific to the summit of Aconcagua (across the border in Argentina), it is also a historic site. Trekking toward the Andes from Valparaíso in the winter of 1834, Charles Darwin detoured to climb the summit of Cerro La Campana, an experience that he detailed in *The Voyage of the Beagle:*

The evening was fine, and the atmosphere so clear, that the masts of the vessels at anchor in the bay of Valparaíso, although no less than twenty-six geographical miles distant, could be distinguished clearly as little black streaks. A ship doubling the point under sail, appeared as a bright white speck....

The setting of the sun was glorious; the valleys being black, whilst the snowy peaks of the Andes yet retained a ruby tint....

We spent the day on the summit, and I never enjoyed one more thoroughly. Chile, bounded by the Andes and the Pacific, was seen as in a map. The pleasure from the scenery, in itself beautiful, was heightened by the many reflections which arose from the mere view of the Campana range with its lesser parallel ones, and of the broad valley of Quillota directly intersecting them....

Geography and Climate

In the coastal range east of Viña del Mar, La Campana consists of three sectors: the adjacent Sector Granizo and Sector Cajón Grande are about 45 kilometers east of Viña via Ruta 62 through Villa Alemana, Limache, and Olmué, while Sector Ocoa is about 110 kilometers northwest of Santiago via the Panamericana.

Elevations range from about 400 meters near the park entrances to 2,222 meters on Cerro El Roble, the park's highest summit; the rugged topography can be challenging even for very strong hikers. Like coastal Southern California, La Campana enjoys a mild Mediterranean climate, cooled by the maritime influences of the Pacific. While the annual precipitation is only about 800 millimeters, it nearly all falls between May and September; the dry summer and autumn are fire season. Winter can bring snowfall to the summits, but even in summer a sweater or light jacket is a good idea at upper elevations.

Flora and Fauna

La Campana has more than 300 different plant species forming several different associations. In the relatively well-watered ravines, between about 300 and 1,000 meters above sea level, there are gallery forests of species such as

THE CHILEAN PALM

Also known as the *palma de coquitos* because its tiny fruits resemble coconuts, the Chilean palm *(Jubaea chilensis)* was once abundant in the Chilean heartland. Indiscriminate cutting for its sap, which yields what Chileans call *miel de palma* (palm honey), reduced this abundance; the ruined ovens scattered around La Campana's Sector Ocoa, used to boil down the sap into treacle, are evidence of the palm honey trade. Each mature tree could yield up to 200 liters of sweetener.

In fact, their diameter can exceed a meter and a half, and they can reach a height of 25 meters. They are slow-growing, though; around age 60, when their height is usually less than 10 meters, they yield their first fruit. Thanks to a planting program begun by the Hacienda Las Palmas de Cocalán in the 1940s and continued by Conaf after La Campana became a national park in 1967, there are now about 100,000 specimens in Sector Ocoa.

patagua lingue, and *belloto.* On south-facing slopes, up to about 1,000 meters, sclerophyllous forests of *peumo boldo,* and *quillay* tolerate the annual summer drought.

At higher altitudes, above 800 meters, deciduous forests of *roble de Santiago* (*Nothofagus obliqua,* referred to by Chileans as an "oak") constitute the most northerly species of this "false beech" genus. There are also communities of Chilean palm *(Jubaea chilensis),* punctuated with occasional cacti, and open thorn forests of acacia and smaller shrubs.

In addition, on north-facing slopes, shrub communities known as *matorrales* resemble California's chaparral, relying on natural fires to renew themselves at regular intervals. Above 1,500 meters, similar but more widely spaced communities occupy thin soils. Clusters of cacti also punctuate the landscape.

Guanacos once roamed the park, but today's fauna are smaller and less conspicuous—foxes, vizcachas, skunks, and tinier rodents, along with more than 50 species of birds, most notably quail, pheasant, owls, and hummingbirds.

Sights and Recreation

Most of the sights are accessible by trails that crisscross the park or loop through it. Near the Granizo entrance, the **Sendero La Canasta** provides a good introduction to the forest, looping past several labeled trees and shrubs in the course of half an hour's walk (the identifications on this nature trail, though, do not place the information in an ecological context).

More gratifying, if more strenuous, is the seven-kilometer **Sendero Andinista,** from the Granizo entrance to the 1,880-meter summit of Cerro La Campana, where hikers enjoy the same views that entranced Darwin. While the distance may not seem great and the climb is not technical, the 1,507-meter elevation gain means an average grade of almost 22 percent. For most people, it's a full-day excursion, more tiring than Patagonia's famous Torres del Paine. The hard-baked trail can be slippery even when dry, so wear suitable shoes.

Fortunately, most of the hike passes through shady forest and three cool springs with potable water: **Primera Aguada,** 580 meters above sea level, about an hour along the trail; **Segunda Aguada,** around the midway point, where camping is possible; and **La Mina,** the drive-in campground at the abandoned mine site, where the trail continues to the summit (in dry weather, with a high-clearance vehicle, it's possible to reach La Mina by road).

Beyond the mine site, the trail becomes narrower and steeper; here, 1,500 meters above sea level, the Sociedad Científica de Valparaíso and the city's British community placed a commemorative plaque on the 101st anniversary of Darwin's ascent (which he reached August 17, 1834, having camped below the summit on the previous day). Another plaque, dedicated by the Club Montañés de Valparaíso, remembers climbers who died when an earthquake triggered a landslide in 1868.

Sector Ocoa, at La Campana's northern approach, is its largest sector, about 5,440 hectares. From Casino, two kilometers beyond the entrance station, the **Sendero El Amasijo** climbs gradually up the Estero Rabuco's palm-filled gorge to the Portezuelo de Granizo saddle, where it bifurcates: the southern **Sendero Los Robles** descends to Sector Cajón Grande, while the **Sendero Los Peumos** heads west to Sector Granizo. Either route is a feasible day trip, but it's also possible to camp in Estero Rabuco. Carry plenty of water since, except for a spring just below the Portezuelo de Granizo, livestock have made the streams unpotable.

Also at Sector Ocoa, the **Sendero La Cascada** is a four-hour round-trip to an attractive waterfall; there are other shorter trails in the area.

Accommodations and Food

Within the park, camping is the only option. Organized camping for up to six people costs US$10 at Conaf's **Sector Granizo** (tel. 033/443067, 23 sites), **Sector Cajón Grande** (22 sites), and **Sector Ocoa** (16 sites). Backcountry camping is possible, but in areas that are steep, rocky, or fire-prone, Conaf permission is required.

Half a block off Olmué's Plaza de Armas, **Hostería Copihue** (Diego Portales 2203, tel. 033/441544, www.copihue.cl, US$81–100 s, US$117–157 d with breakfast) is a sprawling 40-suite resort with pool, tennis courts, and other amenities. Its main clientele is Chilean families but, given its access to Las Campanas, it also gets foreigners who go hiking in the park. Half-board and full-board packages are also available; For fairly conventional Chilean cuisine, the quality is well above average. Off season, major discounts are possible.

Also in Olmué, **Parador de Betty** (Av. Eastman 4801, tel. 033/441511) does Chilean country cooking—*pastel de choclo, humitas, cazuelas* and the like—at a high level. The last weekend in March, it hosts the annual *Festival de la Comida del Huaso* to showcase the best of rural food and other products, to the accompaniment of folkloric music and dance.

Information

At each park entrance, Conaf rangers collect a US$2.50 admission fee (seniors and children pay half). The Granizo ranger station occasionally has maps, for a small charge, and usually has books on flora, fauna, and other conservation topics. Visitors specifically interested in flora can buy Rodrigo Villaseñor Castro's inexpensive (Spanish-only) *Guía para el Reconocimiento de las Especies Arbóreas y Arbustivas en el Parque Nacional La Campana* (1998), a joint publication of Conaf and Valparaíso's Universidad de Playa Ancha.

Getting There and Around

La Campana is readily accessible from Valparaíso and Viña del Mar, less so from Santiago. From Valpo's Estación Puerto, Merval trains take an hour to reach Limache, where *taxi colectivos* shuttle back and forth to Olmué and the Granizo entrance.

From Santiago, any northbound bus along the Panamericana can drop passengers at Hijuelas, where an ill-marked gravel road heads south just before the main highway bridge over the Río Aconcagua. There is no regular public transportation on this gravel road, which is 12 kilometers from the Ocoa entrance.

NORTHERN BEACH RESORTS

From the Viña suburb of Concón to Papudo, the northern beach towns offer visitors the same general sorts of attractions, but they are not quite cookie-cutter resorts—in fact, in terms of clientele, there is considerable diversity among them.

Concón

Contiguous to Viña but politically separate, Concón has been a holiday destination since construction of a coastal highway and the first beach houses in 1917. From Reñaca, Avenida Borgoño follows the coastline past **Playa Amarilla,** the preferred beach for swimmers and sunbathers; **Playa Negra** gets body-boarders.

Concón's greatest appeal, though, is the gaggle of seafood *picadas* at Caleta Higuerillas,

near the Club de Yates, and at Playa La Boca, near the Río Aconcagua estuary. At Caleta Higuerillas, reached via a staircase from Avenida Borgoño, **La Picá Horizonte** (San Pedro 120, tel. 032/2903665) is an established favorite, but **Picá los Delfines** (San Pedro 130, tel. 032/2814919) and other nearby places are by no means inferior. At Playa La Boca, one of the top choices is **La Perla del Pacífico** (Av. Borgoño 25007, tel. 032/2812330).

Quintero and Vicinity

About 16 kilometers north of the Río Aconcagua, a paved road heads west to Quintero, a working-class isthmian beach town that once was Lord Cochrane's hacienda (Maria Graham was Cochrane's guest during the 1822 earthquake). Before turning inland to Quillota and La Campana, Darwin rode here to see "the great beds of shells, which stand some yards above the level of the sea, and are burnt for lime." A few kilometers south, Chilean surfing got its start at the hamlet of **Ritoque.**

Like Concón, Quintero has a score or more of seafood *picadas,* lining 21 de Mayo, for family-style dining, but it lacks any accommodations worth mentioning.

Las Ventanas

Across Bahía Quintero, in what otherwise appears to be an industrial sacrifice area with a major power plant, the **Estero de Puchuncaví** is a wetland reserve that appears to be a environmental mitigation project. Just to its north, at the tiny fishing port of Las Ventanas, salvage crews have finally finished pulling scrap metal off a grounded LPG tanker whose rusting rim barely sticks above the water. Despite the coal-fired power plant nearby, this is one of the north coast's primo surfing spots.

Horcón

About five kilometers north of Las Ventanas, on its namesake harbor and off the main highway, the community of Horcón is a combination fishing port and artisans'/artists' colony with a holdover reputation as a hippie hideaway. Its single main street dead-ends at the small but sheltered beach, where fisherfolk sell their catch directly to waterfront *picadas.*

Just to the south, **Playa Cau Cau** was a onetime nude beach that is now a more conventional destination for sunbathers, surfers, and swimmers. The only remaining nude beach is **Playa La Luna,** immediately south.

Maitencillo

At Maitencillo, 12 kilometers north of Horcón, rocky outcrops along Avenida del Mar separate the long sandy beaches of **Playa Aguas Blancas** and **Playa Larga,** among the region's best. Maitencillo's dominant tourist institution, though, is the sprawling **◖ Marbella Resort** (Km 35, Carretera Concón-Zapallar, tel. 032/2772020, US$194 s or d), which also has more expensive apartments for rent.

Occupying most of the broad hilltop above Avenida del Mar, Marbella is an all-inclusive resort with a conference center, restaurants, and bars, with recreational facilities that include swimming pools and tennis courts, an 18-hole golf course, a 9-hole par 3, and polo grounds (Chile has few public golf courses, but guests can play here).

For everything it offers, the rates are not excessive, and there's a variety of weekend and weeklong packages; for more details contact Marbella's Santiago headquarters (La Concepción 81, Oficina 303, tel. 02/4385300, www.marbella.cl).

Cachagua

Filled with Santiaguino weekenders, 10 kilometers north of Maitencillo, Cachagua is an upscale village where kids ride docile ponies and plump burros over hardpacked sandy roads. There are no accommodations, but the beachfront restaurant **Los Coirones,** reached via a staircase at the south end of Avenida Los Eucaliptos, is a good lunch alternative.

Opposite the west end of the beach, bring binoculars to view the Humboldt penguins and other seabirds at Conaf's **Monumento Natural Isla Cachagua,** separated from the mainland

by a 100-meter channel. Measuring only 300 by 150 meters, the nearly barren granitic island harbors a breeding population of 1,000 to 2,000 Humboldt penguins, roughly 10 percent of the global population and 15 percent of the Chilean population. There are also brown pelicans, cormorants, oystercatchers, Dominican gulls, and other birds, while sea lions and otters (who subsist on shellfish) frolic offshore. While divers take some sea urchins and other shellfish, the human disturbance is minimal.

Zapallar

Three kilometers north of Cachagua and 80 kilometers from Viña, curving tree-lined streets nearly block the view of the ocean at Zapallar (population 5,700), originally part of Francisco Javier Ovalle's Hacienda Catapilco. After inheriting the property in 1884 and making a tour of European beach resorts, his son Olegario began to give away lots to his friends on the condition that they build houses within two years, and Zapallar quickly became an outpost of monied Santiaguinos.

Zapallar's sandy beach is a summer hangout, but in the off-season it's almost deserted.

The 1906 earthquake destroyed many early buildings, but Zapallar's inhabitants rebuilt with a vengeance, creating some of the coast's largest, most elegant properties. Now a *zona típica* national monument, Zapallar is an eclectic mix of colonial-style *casas,* neo-Gothic mansions, and fashionably rustic villas, on large lots with extensive gardens. The **Rambla,** a broad footpath, follows the coastline.

Many founding families still own properties here. Among the notable mansions are those of Manuel Vicuña Subercaseaux (1912) and Carlos Aldunate Solar (1915), both designed by Josué Smith Solar; the extravagant castle of painter Álvaro Casanova; and María Luisa MacClure's Bavarian-style Casa Hildesheim.

Directly on the highway, the 42-room **Hotel Isla Seca** (Camino Costero s/n, tel. 033/741224, www.hotelislaseca.cl, US$155–345 s or d) consists of two separate structures a short distance apart; despite the roadside location, traffic is not heavy and most of the rooms face the ocean and have balconies. Some have whirlpool tubs. There's also a handsome bar/restaurant.

On the beachfront **César** (Rambla s/n, tel. 033/741507) is an upscale seafood restaurant with outdoor as well as indoor seating. To the south, reached either by the curving Rambla or by road, **Chiringuito** (Caleta de Zapallar s/n, tel. 033/741024) has better views, more charm (with its crushed-shell terrace and asymmetrical tables), and even fresher fish straight off the boat.

PAPUDO

Seven kilometers north of Zapallar, Papudo's sheltered harbor is a more egalitarian destination than its snobbish southern neighbor. Its natural assets sparked an extravagant enthusiasm from Pedro de Valdivia, who, in a letter to Spain's King Carlos V in 1545, wrote:

Among all the new world's lands, the port of Papudo has a greater abundance of good things than any other, it is like God's paradise; it has a mild climate, great and rugged mountains, fertile expanses covered with cattle, herds of horses, abundant grains, delicious fruits, inexhaustible amounts of fish, crabs, and shellfish, saturated with milk and rennet and wines, and rich with honey, timber, salt and other minerals, and products that make life worthwhile.

Fertile Papudo (population 4,700) was the port for colonial Hacienda La Ligua, but became part of Fernando Irarrázaval Mackenna's Hacienda Pullalli in the mid-19th century and shortly thereafter an official port. With the railway's arrival in 1898, it took off as a beach resort, its landmark Gran Hotel (since destroyed by fire) designed by architect Josué Smith. After 1927, it became a separate municipality from La Ligua, forsaking its port status for the tourist trade.

Sights

The main highway, known in town as Avenida Irarrázaval, parallels the central **Playa Chica** and the more extensive **Playa Larga,** which stretches northeast. At Avenida Irarrázaval and Avenida Latorre, the main remaining landmark is the neocolonial **Iglesia Nuestra Señora de las Mercedes** (1918), a national monument with a baroque facade by architect Alberto Cruz Montt.

Beyond the Club de Yates, at the west end of Playa Chica, brown pelicans hang out on rocky outcrops where the town has created an informally landscaped **Camino del Conquistador** footpath to trace Pedro de Valdivia's steps. There are more formal beachfront promenades along Avenida Irarrázaval.

Accommodations and Food

Though the rooms are a little cramped, the family-run **Residencial La Plaza** (Chorrillos 119, tel. 033/791391, US$17 pp) maintains year-round rates with private baths and breakfast. Upgraded **Hotel Carandé** (Chorrillos 89, tel. 033/791105, www.hotelcarande.cl, US$47 d) may be overpriced in summer, but for US$18 per person with breakfast off-season, it's not bad. Rooms are heated, the service is decent, and the hot water abundant and easy to regulate.

Playa Chica's **Gran Azul** (Av. Irrarrázaval 86, tel. 033/791584) prepares fine fish and seafood, with attentive service, at moderate prices (US$7–10 for entrées); in a dining room with high ceilings and natural wood beams, large windows face the sea and surf.

LA LIGUA

About 15 kilometers inland from Papudo and just east of the Panamericana, the farming town of La Ligua is famous for its *dulces de La Ligua*. On both sides of the highway, platoons of handkerchief-waving, white-coated vendors flag down passing vehicles to sell their cakes, cookies, meringues, and other typical sweets. About 20 companies employ more than 300 people in their manufacture, and another 2,000 depend indirectly on the trade.

La Ligua is also known for its textiles, and at 1997's annual **Feria del Tejido** (Weavers' Festival), the world's largest vest made the *Guinness Book of Records*. More normal sizes are available in stores and at the artisans' market on the Plaza de Armas.

For northbound motorists, La Ligua (population 35,000) is the starting point for an adventurous but not difficult backcountry alternative through the Andean foothills via the abandoned railroad line, now mostly a dirt-and-gravel road, to Ovalle.

Museo de La Ligua

Occupying the erstwhile abattoir, La Ligua's municipal museum might not justify a trip in its own right, but its exhibits on the early Molle and Ánimas cultures, through the Aymara, Mapuche, and Diaguita/Inka who successively dominated the area, merit at least a brief stopover. The museum also deals with issues of cultural change during colonial times through institutions such as the *encomienda,* the 19th-century mining industry, and 20th-century urban development.

Six blocks north of the Plaza de Armas, the Museo de La Ligua (Pedro Polanco 698, tel. 033/712143, www.museolaligua.cl) is open 9:30 A.M.–1 P.M. and 3–6 P.M. weekdays, 10 A.M.–2 P.M. Saturday; admission costs US$0.85.

Accommodations and Food

La Ligua has inexpensive but pleasing lodgings at **Residencial Regine II** (Condell 360, tel. 033/711916, US$13–20 pp); rates vary depending on shared or private bath. A block west of the Plaza de Armas, surrounding a sunny atrium, some rooms at **Hotel Anchimallén** (Ortiz de Rosas 694, tel. 033/711685, hotelanchimallen@hotmail.com, US$28 s, US$43 d) are worn, but they're also spacious, luminous, and clean. Rates include breakfast, cable TV, and parking.

Lihuén (Ortiz de Rosas 303, tel. 033/711143) offers snacks, sandwiches, homemade ice cream, and more elaborate meals in its formal restaurant next door.

Information and Services

The museum has become La Ligua's de facto tourist office, with basic maps and brochures, and helpful personnel.

Banco de Chile (Ortiz de Rosas 485) has an ATM. There's a **Centro de Llamados** on the west side of the Plaza de Armas.

Getting There and Around

Terminal La Ligua (Papudo between Pedro Polanco and Uribe, tel. 033/711101) is a block south of the Plaza de Armas. Tur-Bus, Pullman Bus, and Sol del Pacífico have services north and south on the Panamericana, and down the coast to Viña del Mar.

The Aconcagua Valley

East of Quillota and north of metropolitan Santiago, but politically part of Region V, the Río Aconcagua's main attraction is the ski resort of Portillo, near the Argentine border. The lower part of the valley, though, is home to colonial towns with a growing wine industry and its own nascent Ruta del Vino.

SAN FELIPE AND VICINITY

Encircled by mountains, at an altitude of 630 meters, San Felipe El Real is the political and commercial center of a valley that exports grapes and wine thanks to its favorable microclimate. Founded in 1740 by José Manso de Velasco, who later became viceroy of Peru, its core retains a colonial ambience; in addition to its attractive Plaza de Armas, several smaller *plazuelas* mean greenery and open space to the otherwise densely built downtown.

San Felipe (population 64,000) is 94 kilometers north of Santiago via Ruta 57, the northbound highway to Argentina, and a secondary paved highway that passes through Rinconada. It's a little farther, about 117 kilometers, via the Panamericana and Ruta 60, the international highway from Concón to the Argentine border. It's 18 km west of Los Andes.

Sights

The centerpiece of San Felipe's shady **Plaza de Armas** is a multileveled fountain resembling the rocky Andes, visible in the distance to the east. Embellished with statuary, the plaza has a permanent artisans' market.

Historical monuments include the **Catedral de San Felipe** on the plaza's north side, the **Iglesia y Claustro del Buen Pastor** (Av. Yungay between Av. O'Higgins and San Martín), alongside the bus terminal, and the colonial **Casa Mardones** (Av. Yungay 10).

On the plaza's west side, the **Teatro Municipal** (Salinas 203, tel. 034/509066, www.teatrosanfelipe.cl) keeps a solid calendar of cultural events, from films to jazz and art exhibits.

Curimón

Arriving in the late 17th century at Curimón, seven km east of present-day San Felipe, Franciscan fathers soon began to build a church and convent, but both fell to earthquakes. Dating from 1727, the current **Iglesia San Francisco de Curimón** has 1.2-meter-thick adobe walls and a three-arched, 19th-century portico topped by a two-tiered bell tower. While it's impressive, parts are suffering serious termite damage. The gardens, surrounding a cypress tree reportedly 400 years old, deserve a look.

In 1740, José Manso de Velasco signed San Felipe's founding papers here, and José de San Martín's Army of the Andes lodged here before its decisive 1817 victory over Spanish royalists at Chacabuco.

An adjacent museum (www.conventocurimon.cl, tel. 034/531020, US$0.85 for adults, US$0.35 for children) romanticizes Franciscan evangelism but also features anonymous ecclesiastical paintings impressive in both size and detail. It's open 9 A.M.–noon and 3:30–6:30 P.M. Tuesday–Saturday; on Sunday, it keeps afternoon hours only. In summer, it stays open until 8 P.M.

Accommodations and Food

San Felipe is short on accommodations; the cheapest are also the best, starting with cheerful **Hotel Residencial Aldo's** (Salinas 67, tel. 034/512356, US$17–30 s or d), which also has parking. Friendly **Hotel Reinares** (Carlos Condell 75, tel./fax 034/510359, US$15 pp, US$25 s, US$40 d) has both utilitarian rooms with shared baths and slightly better rooms with private baths, as well as a large and popular restaurant.

Half a block east of the Plaza de Armas, the **Club Arabe** (Prat 124, tel. 034/536549) serves standard Chilean fare plus Middle Eastern dishes, such as stuffed grape leaves, in the US$6 range. In the historic Casona Mardones, the **Club Social San Felipe** (Av.

Yungay 10, tel. 034/510402) is the traditional night-out choice.

Services

Several banks on the Plaza de Armas have ATMs. **Entel** (Combate las Coimas 186) has long-distance service. **Ciber Link** (Merced 106, tel. 034/511067) has the best Internet facilities.

Getting There and Around

San Felipe's **Terminal de Buses** (Avenida Yungay 300, tel. 034/509085) has frequent southbound buses to Santiago, along Ruta 60 west to Viña del Mar and east toward Los Andes and the border.

LOS ANDES

Los Andes, Chile's main overland port of entry, is a crossroads where international Ruta 60 from Viña del Mar meets Ruta 57 from Santiago. Founded in late colonial times (1791) by Ambrosio O'Higgins, the Chilean liberator's father, its central core retains some of that earlier atmosphere. Like San Felipe, it's the center of a fruit- and wine-growing area.

Los Andes (population 67,000) is 77 km north of Santiago via Ruta 57, 144 km east of Viña del Mar via Ruta 60, and 67 km west of the actual border post. A bypass from Santiago now allows eastbound motorists to avoid the town.

Sights

In the center of the city's colonial core, an area seven blocks square that constitutes a *zona típica* national monument, the shady **Plaza de Armas** remains the focus of urban life. On its north side, the neoclassical **Gobernación Provincial** (1888–1891) was the provincial governor's residence until 1964; today government offices cluster around the central patio, but the arched portal beneath its facade is a popular gathering place. Half a block east is the former **Colegio de Niñas** (Girls' School, Esmeralda 246), where Nobel Prize–winning poet Gabriela Mistral taught in the early 20th century.

Emphasizing local cultures, the **Museo Arqueológico de Los Andes** (Av. Santa Teresa 398, tel. 034/420115, museo_losandes@hotmail.com) displays collections of funerary items, stone tools, pottery, and petroglyphs from Molle times (around A.D. 1–800) through the Aconcagua culture (about A.D. 800–1500) and the brief Inka presence (A.D. 1450 to the Spanish takeover). Horse gear and household goods are more recent, and there are some Mapuche items. The English translations are far better than in most small provincial museums. Advertised hours are 10 A.M.–6 P.M. daily except Monday, but the real schedule can be erratic; admission costs US$1.50.

Across the avenue, the 19th-century **Museo Antiguo Monasterio del Espíritu Santo** (Av. Santa Teresa 389, tel. 034/421765, US$0.50 admission) was once a cloister for Carmelite nuns. The Chilean Santa Teresa de los Andes, beatified in 1993, lived at this national monument (rebuilt in the 1920s), and many of the faithful undertake pilgrimages here. The museum also commemorates Santiago-born Laura Vicuña, whose widowed mother took an Argentine lover in order to keep the family together after they fled across the Andes to avoid political persecution; according to legend, Laura's deteriorating health was an attempt to persuade her mother to change her ways. Hours are 9:30 A.M.–1 P.M. and 3–6 P.M. weekdays, 10 A.M.–6 P.M. weekends.

At the north end of Avenida Santa Teresa, the waiting room of the former **Estación Ferrocarril del Estado,** the rail line that ran erratically to the Argentine city of Mendoza between 1910 and 1984, now holds judicial offices; Gregorio de la Fuente's mural *A la Hermandad Chileno–Argentina* (To Chilean–Argentine Brotherhood) is visible from outside. Railroad historian Ian Thomson referred to the line, subject to avalanches and rockslides, as "a marvel to engineers, a disaster to accountants."

Accommodations

The best value may be well-furnished **Hotel Olicar** (Papudo 385, tel. 034/424106,

RUTA DEL VINO ACONCAGUA

While the Aconcagua Valley is not Chile's highest-profile wine route, four of its wineries (one near Los Andes and three near Panquehue, west of San Felipe) are open to visitors.

At Rinconada, south of San Felipe, the route's **Museo del Vino** (Carretera San Martín 235, tel. 034/401121) occupies a traditional tile-roofed adobe, open daily except Monday. For organized tours and general information on the route, contact María Soledad Latorre (Ruta del Vino Valle Aconcagua, tel. 099/4790278, www.aconcaguavinos.cl). **Santiago Adventures** (Guardia Vieja 255, Of. 403, Providencia, Santiago, tel. 02/2442750, cel. 09/8230-0025, www.santiagoadventures.com), which charges US$155 pp for a full day tour, with an English-speaking driver, that includes two wineries and lunch at a historic hacienda.

VIÑA ERRÁZURIZ

Dating from 1870, Errázuriz is one of Aconcagua's oldest wineries. It has several vineyards in the San Felipe area, but the flagship is its Don Maximiano estate, which produces a variety of whites (chardonnay and sauvignon blanc) and reds (cabernet sauvignon, merlot, pinot noir, sangiovese, and syrah). In the past, it has partnered with California's Robert Mondavi.

More accessible than in the past, Errázuriz has a magnificent bodega and tasting room that also serves meals. The two-hour tour (US$28 pp) includes a hike to the hills above the estate and a tasting of two or three premium wines.

West of San Felipe, Viña Errázuriz (Antofagasta and O'Higgins, Panquehue, San Felipe, tel. 034/591089, tel. 02/2036688 in Santiago, www.errazuriz.com) is open for guided tours 10 A.M.–6 P.M. daily except Sunday and Monday, but it's best to make reservations.

VIÑA SAN ESTEBAN

Just north of Los Andes, Viña San Esteban retains the style of the colonial hacienda it once was, but its contemporary installations date from 1994. About 800 meters above sea level, with vines on steep slopes as well as the alluvial flats, it experiences hot days and cool nights. Carmenere is its reserve specialty, but it also produces sauvignon blanc.

Guided tours (US$5 pp, some English spoken) include a respectable tasting of its sauvignon blanc and reserve carmenere. Guests can also hike to a series of hillside petroglyphs on the property.

Viña San Esteban (La Florida 2220, San Esteban, tel. 034/481050, www.vse.cl) is amenable to drop-in visits, but phone ahead. Local buses from Los Andes pass the entrance, but the route is roundabout and slow; consider a taxi instead.

VIÑA SÁNCHEZ DE LORIA

Directly on Ruta 60, west of San Felipe, dating from 1890, Sánchez de Loria is almost a stereotype of a traditional winery, what with its 50,000-liter wooden barrels – no shiny stainless steel here – and a local population that stops to purchase its jug wines directly from the producer. Of its 40 hectares, about 10 are devoted to fine wines, including cabernet sauvignon, sauvignon blanc, and late harvest. Higher arbors of table grapes surround the wine grapes (also used to produce *chicha*), while nearby orchards produce toasted almonds that are also for sale here.

Owner Felipe Cruz Sánchez de Loria himself shows visitors around the property and treats them to a generous tasting at no charge. Viña Sánchez de Loria (Camino San Roque s/n, Panquehue, tel. 034/591054, www.sanchezdeloria.cl) is open to drop-ins, but it's still best to phone ahead if possible.

VIÑA VON SIEBENTHAL

Less than a decade old, within easy walking distance from Errázuriz, Swiss-run Viña von Siebenthal (O'Higgins s/n, Panquehue, tel. 034/591827, www.vinavonsiebenthal.com) can't match the maturity of its venerable neighbor in landscape or product. Its varietal carmenere and blends of cabernet sauvignon, syrah, merlot, and other minor grapes, though, have made strong first impressions. Tours and tastings (US$10 pp) take place Thursday and Friday 9 A.M.–5 P.M.

gloria.zamorano@gmail.com, US$27 s or d), which lacks amenities other than private baths and cable TV. Some rooms are dark, though. Uphill from the plaza, the well-located and immaculate **Hostería Rucahue** (General del Canto 98, tel. 034/406366, www.hosteriarucahue.cl, US$37 s, US$40 d) is also friendly and quiet. Amenities include WiFi, cable TV, parking, and a bar/restaurant.

On the road to San Felipe, **Hotel Los Andes** (Av. Argentina 1100, tel. 034/428199, hotellosandes@tie.cl, US$43 s, US$48 d) is newer but not dramatically better than the Olicar. **Hotel Plaza** (Rodríguez 370, tel. 034/421169, www.hotelplazalosandes.cl, US$50 s, US$57 d with breakfast) offers cozy rooms (some with small patios) with cable TV, WiFi, and parking. Ironically enough, it no longer has a Plaza de Armas entrance.

Food

Several reasonable eateries line Avenida Santa Teresa, among them **Lomo House** (Av. Santa Teresa 194, tel. 034/422422), which serves huge sandwiches at low prices, plus lunch or dinner entrées in the US$7–8 range, with attentive service. **Donde El Guatón** (Av. Santa Teresa 240, tel. 034/423596) serves traditional dishes such as *pastel de choclo.*

Half a block east of the museum, the local classic **Centro Español** (O'Higgins 674, tel. 034/424885) has excellent three-course lunches for US$6.

On the eastern outskirts, well-regarded **La Table de France** (Ruta 60, Km 3, tel. 034/406319, www.latabledefrance.cl) is open daily except Monday for lunch and dinner.

In new quarters opposite the plaza, **Pastelería Marcam** (O'Higgins 400, Local 33, tel. 034/404461) makes fine homemade ice cream and other desserts.

Information and Services

The private consortium **Turismo Aconcagua** (Av. Santa Teresa 333, tel. 034/902525, www.turismoaconcagua.cl) is open 9 A.M.–3:30 P.M. daily; it focuses on the services of its members but is helpful with other matters.

Several banks opposite the Plaza de Armas have ATMs. **Correos de Chile** (Esmeralda 387) is the post office.

Entel (Esmeralda 423) has long-distance phones. There are several Internet outlets near the plaza.

Hospital San Juan de Dios (Av. Argentina and Av. Hermanos Clark, tel. 034/421121 or 034/421666) is the local hospital.

Getting There and Around

At the north end of Avenida Santa Teresa, the **Rodoviario Internacional Los Andes** sits alongside the former train station. **Pullman Bus** (tel. 034/421262) has the most frequent schedules to Santiago, while **Buses JM** (tel. 034/422009) goes to Viña and Valparaíso. Mendoza-bound international buses may stop here, but reservations are advisable—these are often full.

Buses Ahumada (Yerbas Buenas 650, tel. 034/424896) has its own, more central terminal.

🄲 PORTILLO

For more than half a century, Portillo has been a prestige ski resort, and while more luxurious facilities closer to Santiago have been expanding, Portillo retains its reputation for quality dry powder and steep slopes that yield downhill speed records—in 1987, Michael Prufer reached 217.68 kilometers per hour. Its 23 different runs vary from beginner and intermediate to advanced and expert, the longest of which is 3.2 kilometers. Altitudes range from 2,590 to 3,322 meters, and it averages six meters of snow every winter.

Accommodations and Food

Housing up to 500 skiers, **Hotel Portillo** hosts weeklong packages only, starting at US$1,200 per person in low season, rising as high as US$5,300 per person in peak season; prices include four meals daily, but not taxes (nonresidents are exempt from the 19 percent IVA). Perks include a cinema, day-care facilities, a gymnasium (full-court basketball, anyone?), game rooms, a discotheque, and live music;

© WAYNE BERNHARDSON

In winter, Hotel Portillo hosts skiers, but guests can take a dip in the heated pool in any season.

extras include a ski school, sauna and massage, WiFi, and a beauty salon. It overlooks **Laguna del Inca,** a cobalt blue alpine lake.

For budget skiers, the **Inca Lodge** and **Octagon Lodge** offer ski weeks, with bunk-style accommodations starting around US$590 to US$890 per person; both options have four bunks to a room, but the latter offers private rather than communal baths.

For nonguests, lift tickets cost around US$44–57 daily, depending on the date; the highest rates correspond to weekends and the period from mid-July to mid-August. For US$8 more, the hotel restaurant (with superb views of Laguna del Inca) provides a midday meal. Cheaper accommodations are available in the city of Los Andes, 69 kilometers west.

There are now efforts to promote Portillo as a year-round destination; in summer, the resort rents chalet accommodations for US$93 d, with breakfast. The main hotel, though, is closed except to large groups with special arrangements.

Getting There and Around

Almost directly on the international border via Ruta 60 from Los Andes, Portillo is 164 kilometers from Santiago and about 200 kilometers from Viña del Mar. For transportation from either the airport or the capital, contact the **Centro de Ski Portillo** (Renato Sánchez 4270, Las Condes, Santiago, tel. 02/2630606, www.skiportillo.com), near Metro Escuela Militar. There are toll-free contacts in the U.S. (tel. 800/829-5325) and Canada (800/514-2579).

The Southern Heartland

Besides Region V (Valparaíso), the southern heartland consists of Region VI (Rancagua), Region VII (Maule), and Region VIII (Biobío). This is wine country, with a great and growing density of vineyards, but its rugged coastline will appeal to surfers in particular.

Its real secret, though, is the Andean backcountry—if the cordillera from Rancagua south past Curicó, Talca, and Chillán were in North America or Europe, its meadows, forests, and summits would swarm with hikers every summer. Instead, it gets just a handful of outdoor recreationists compared with the Sur Chico lake district, not to mention Patagonia's Torres del Paine.

RANCAGUA

For most visitors, Rancagua may be a brief stop or a day trip rather than an overnight, but its nearby Andean attractions—the historic mining town of Sewell, the luxury hot springs of Termas de Cauquenes, and the wild high country of Reserva Nacional Río de los Cipreses—are grossly underappreciated.

Colonial Rancagua was ranch and farming country, and it's still an agricultural service center and home to Chile's annual rodeo championships. As capital of Region VI, it has key administrative functions and several historical sites, but the economy's true motor is the El Teniente copper mine, in the Andes to the east.

History

Rancagua dates from 1743, when colonial governor José Manso de Velasco established the city as Villa Santa Cruz de Triana, on lands relinquished by Tomás Guaglén, the last Picunche cacique. Here, in October 1814, Bernardo O'Higgins's army suffered the Desastre de Rancagua (Disaster of Rancagua), resulting in the exile of many of its leaders to the Juan Fernández archipelago and delaying independence by several years.

Orientation

Rancagua (population 206,971) is 87 kilometers south of Santiago via the Panamericana, which bypasses the city to the east. The Plaza de los Héroes is the focus of its original grid, eight blocks square, but many services are west of Avenida San Martín, one of that grid's boundaries. Between Plaza de los Héroes and Avenida San Martín, Calle Independencia, the central business cluster, is a pedestrian mall; so is Calle Estado, which leads south off the plaza past most of Rancagua's historic buildings.

Sights

Rancagua's historic center is the **Plaza Los Héroes;** though no colonial buildings remain, it is pleasantly car-free. Its main landmarks are the neoclassical **Gobernación Provincial** (1889), a national monument, and the **Iglesia Catedral** (1861) at the south end. On and around the plaza are several monuments, including a banal equestrian statue of Bernardo O'Higgins and a hideously stylized stone sculpture of city founder (and later viceroy of Peru) José Manso de Velasco.

One block north is the late 18th-century **Iglesia de la Merced** (Estado and Cuevas), which was occupied by O'Higgins and his troops during the battle of Rancagua. From the tile-roofed adobe structure's tower, O'Higgins watched hopefully for reinforcements, but two-thirds of his troops perished here.

At opposite corners of Estado and Ibieta, two late colonial houses, both national monuments, together form the **Museo Regional** (tel. 072/221524, www.museorancagua.cl). The more distinctive is the **Casa del Pilar de Esquina** (Estado 684), with exhibits on local prehistory, mining, and agriculture. Named for the corner pillar often used as a colonial architectural flourish, it was owned by independence figure Fernando Errázuriz Aldunate, Rancagua's representative to the Congress of 1811. Hours are 10 A.M.–6 P.M. weekdays except

THE *HUASO* AND THE RODEO

Less celebrated than the Argentine gaucho, the Chilean *huaso* resembles his trans-Andean counterpart in many ways, but differs dramatically in others. Both are horsemen, but the gaucho arose from a background of fierce independence on the Pampas, while the subservient *huaso* originated on the landed estates that dominated economic and social life in colonial and republican Chile.

Though the *huaso* was a hired hand or even a peon attached to the property, he and his colleagues could blow off steam by racing their horses, betting, and drinking on Sundays. As the spontaneous rodeo grew too raucous, though, it drew the disapproval of landowners, who responded by organizing competitions that, over time, became more genteel versions of their *huaso* origins.

Though Chilean rodeo remains popular, it is now, according to historian Richard Slatta, a nostalgic exercise that's "a middle- and upper-class pastime, not a profession" as it has become in North America. Riders wear colorful ponchos, flat-brimmed hats, over-sized spurs, and elaborately carved wooden stirrups.

Chilean rodeo's signature event is the *atajada*, in which a pair of *jinetes* (riders) guide and pin a calf or steer to the padded wall of the *medialuna*, the semicircular rodeo ring. Since it's harder to control the steer by the body than the head – the chest is best – the horsemen get more points for this. They lose points if the steer strikes any unpadded part of the wall, or escapes between the horses.

There are no cash prizes, though the event ends by acknowledging the champions and other riders with wine and empanadas. Compared to Canada, the United States, and even Mexico, Chilean rodeo is truly *machista* – women prepare and serve food, dress in costume, and dance the traditional *cueca* with the men, but they do not ride.

Rancagua is the Chilean's rodeo capital, drawing thousands of spectators to the national festival in March. In small settlements along the Carretera Austral, the rodeo probably comes closest to its historic roots.

Monday, 9 A.M.–1 P.M. weekends and holidays. Admission costs US$1 for adults, US$0.50 for children, but Tuesday and Sunday it's free.

The **Casa del Ochavo** (Estado 685) is filled with period furniture and colonial religious art, as well as an almost equally devotional tribute to O'Higgins's role in Chilean independence. Hours and admission fees are the same as the Casa del Pilar de Esquina.

One block south, the **Casa Patronal del Ex Fundo El Puente** (Av. Millán and Av. Cachapoal, tel 072/584269) was the landowner's residence that housed royalist Colonel Mariano de Osorio during the Battle of Rancagua (Osorio's victory earned him the viceroy's appointment as governor of Chile, a position whose power he wielded ruthlessly). Also a national monument, it now holds the city's Casa de la Cultura, which occasionally exhibits paintings and photographs; hours are 9:30 A.M.–5:30 P.M. daily.

Events

In mid- to late March, visitors swarm Rancagua for the **Campeonato Nacional de Rodeo** (national rodeo championships) at the Medialuna de Rancagua (Av. España and Germán Ibarra; the rodeo ring holds up to 12,000 spectators).

November 1's **Encuentro Criollo** folkore festival also draws crowds.

Accommodations

Accommodations are few, and expensive compared with those in other comparably sized cities; for the annual March rodeo, prices can skyrocket. The best value is **Hostal Yaiman** (Bueras 655, tel. 072/641773, US$19 s, US$26 d with breakfast), but **Hotel España** (Av. San Martín 367, tel. 072/230141, US$25 s, US$37 d) is a good alternative with private bath and breakfast.

Midrange choices include modest **Hotel Rancagua** (Av. San Martín 85, tel. 072/232633,

THE CHILEAN HEARTLAND

www.hotelrancagua.cl, US$37 s, US$53 d) and **Hotel Aguila Real** (Av. Brasil 1045, tel. 072/222047, hotelaguilareal@terra.cl, US$45 s, US$65 d). **Hotel Turismo Santiago** (Av. Brasil 1036, tel. 072/230860, www.hotelsantiago.cl, US$66–74 s, US$78–105 d) is ostensibly a four-star facility.

Food

Best for breakfasts and sandwiches, **Bavaria** (Av. San Martín 255, tel. 072/233827) is the local representative of the reliable nationwide chain. **Reina Victoria** (Independencia 667, tel. 072/239867) has moderately priced lunches and fine ice cream.

Carnivores can try **Torito Parrilla** (Zañartu 323, tel. 072/222704, www.toritoparrilla.cl, lunch and dinner daily), which has an attractive dining room. The sophisticated downtown favorite Guy has closed, but its French Basque chef has moved to **Doña Emilia** (Diego de Almagro 440, tel. 072/239483, www.donaemilia.cl).

Though not so good as the Santiago ice creamery it displaced, **Fiorella** (Astorga 307, tel. 072/230596) is the best in town.

Information

The regional office of **Sernatur** (Germán Riesco 277, 1st floor, tel. 072/230413, inforancagua@sernatur.cl) is open 8:30 A.M.–5:15 P.M. weekdays. In summer, it also opens 9 A.M.–1 P.M. Saturdays.

Motorists can contact the **Automóvil Club de Chile** (Cuevas 011, tel. 072/239930).

Conaf (Cuevas 480, tel. 072/297505) handles national parks and reserves.

Services

Ifex (Campos 363, tel. 072/244499) can change foreign cash and travelers checks. Several banks have ATMs on and around the Plaza de Armas.

Correos de Chile (Campos 322) is the post office. **Entel** (Independencia 468) has long-distance phones, while **@Net** (Independencia 591), at the back of a gallery of shops, offers fast Internet access.

Lava Express (Av. San Martín 270, tel. 072/241738) offers laundry facilities.

The **Hospital Regional** (Av. O'Higgins 611, tel. 072/239555) handles medical matters.

Getting There and Around

Rural and regional bus companies use the **Terminal Rodoviario** (Doctor Salinas 1165, tel. 072/225425), just north of the Mercado Central. **Pullman del Sur** (tel. 072/222245) and **Nilahue** (tel. 072/222361) go to coastal destinations such as Pichilemu (US$6, two hours).

Tur-Bus (O'Carrol 1175, tel. 072/241117) has frequent service to Santiago (US$4, 1.5 hours) and extensive long-distance routes. Other Santiago-bound buses leave from Terminal O'Higgins (Alameda 0480, tel. 072/222740).

From **Estación Rancagua** (Av. Viña del Mar between O'Carrol and Ignacio Carrera Pinto, tel. 072/225239), **Metrotrén** runs 28 commuter trains to Santiago (US$2, one hour or more) every weekday, between 6:05 A.M. and 9:43 P.M., with fewer services on weekends. Long-distance passenger trains to Chillán, Concepción, and Temuco (with connections to Puerto Montt) normally stop here.

VICINITY OF RANCAGUA

Rancagua's Andean backcountry, little visited even by Santiaguinos, offers some exceptional excursions.

Termas de Cauquenes

Ever since the Jesuits first established themselves at the foothills' hot springs in the 17th century, Termas de Cauquenes has pulled in prestigious passengers such as Bernardo O'Higgins, José de San Martín, and Charles Darwin. In their day, though, it wasn't the luxurious retreat it is now—in 1834, Darwin described it as "a square of miserable little hovels, each with a single table and bench."

In 1876, Copiapó nitrate magnate Apolinario Soto modernized the facilities, creating a Vichy-style pavilion with tubs of Carrara marble, and Termas de Cauquenes has retained its elite image ever since. Temperatures in the pools range 42–48°C.

On the Río Cachapoal's south bank, 760 meters above sea level on beautifully landscaped grounds, **(Hotel Termas de Cauquenes** (tel. 072/899010, US$113 d with breakfast, US$200 d with full board) has pools and tubs, modern conference facilities, and a fine—if arguably overpriced—riverview restaurant. The rooms are more than comfortable.

Termas de Cauquenes (tel. 02/6381610 in Santiago, www.termasdecauquenes.cl) is 31 kilometers east of Rancagua via the paved highway to Coya and a six-kilometer gravel road to the south; there is no longer any public transport, but the hotel does its own transfers. Both the restaurant and individual tubs are open to nonguests. Lunch or dinner costs US$25; an hour's simple soak costs US$8 per person, while a whirlpool tub visit costs US$11 single, US$20 double.

(El Teniente (Sewell)

Part of state-run Codelco, 55 kilometers east of Rancagua, El Teniente is the world's largest underground mine; its more than 2,400 kilometers of tunnels yield more than 400,000 metric tons of refined copper per year. It dates from 1905, when the U.S.-based Braden Copper Company began operations; after its acquisition by Kennecott Copper Company and World War I's outbreak, production increased and the company became enormously wealthy. Widespread resentment of its dominant role pressured the state and, by 1967, the government had acquired majority shareholdings; in 1971, Salvador Allende's Unidad Popular government expropriated the entire industry, including El Teniente.

Until the late 1960s, El Teniente's residential community of Sewell (named for Braden's first president) was a classic company town and a thriving (but residentially segregated) community of North American managers and technicians, their Chilean support staff, a mass of miners and their families, and many single miners as well. At that time, though, President Eduardo Frei Montalva's Operación Valle began to transfer all of Sewell's 15,000 workers and their families to Rancagua because the

THE CHILEAN HEARTLAND

© WAYNE BERNHARDSON

Sewell, the historic company town for the massive El Teniente mine east of Rancagua, is now open for guided tours.

prevailing winds carried toxic sulfur hydroxide fumes from the Caletones smelter.

Parts have been dismantled or demolished, such as the so-called Barrio Americano where North American technicians lived with their families, but many structures, such as the hospital, the Escuela Industrial (Industrial School, now home to the museum), the theater, a four-lane bowling alley (Chile's first, dating from 1917), and the Club Social, remain intact. All these were connected by a warren of concrete steps and walkways that gave the town its nickname, "Ciudad de las Escaleras" (City of Staircases).

Codelco has nominated Sewell for UNESCO World Heritage status, intending to develop a cultural and tourism project emphasizing the historic, economic, and social significance of copper mining in the region. Both the mine and Sewell are open to the public for guided tours that are expanding in scope—at present, for instance, buses carry visitors into the labyrinth of underground tunnels to view a subterranean cavern of spectacular crystals uncovered in the course of extracting copper ore. Guests also view the massive ore-crusher in action, and in coming years tours will expand to include the actual mining and the smelter.

Full-day tours to El Teniente and Sewell, 2,600 meters above sea level, take place weekends only through **VTS** (Manuel Montt 192, Rancagua, tel. 072/210290, www.vts.cl); Sewell on its own costs US$25 per person; combined with a descent into El Teniente, the price is US$33. Lunch is US$6 extra. Tours include transport from Rancagua's train station, easily reached by Metrotrén from Santiago, or from any Rancagua hotel. For an additional US$5 pp, they provide bus transport from Santiago.

Aside from the privately contracted tours, Codelco maintains a separate informative website on Sewell (www.sewell.cl).

Centro de Esqui Chapa Verde

One of the perks of Codelco's presence is the Chapa Verde ski area, part of the El Teniente complex. Open to the general public in the winter, 3,100 meters above sea level, the 1,200-hectare area has four lifts and 22 separate runs, rated from beginner to expert. There is limited night skiing on one illuminated run.

Adult lift tickets at Chapa Verde (tel. 072/294255, www.chapaverde.cl) cost US$23 weekdays, US$30 weekends; the rate for children is half that. There is also a ski school (US$12 pp for group lessons, US$32 for individual lessons), rental equipment (US$23 per day), a café, and a restaurant. The Chapa Verde road is not a public highway; visitors must take Codelco buses (US$11 round-trip) from Rancagua's Lider Vecino home improvement store (Av. Manuel Ramírez 665). Departures are at 9 A.M. weekdays, or between 8 and 9:30 A.M. weekends.

RESERVA NACIONAL RÍO DE LOS CIPRESES

Immediately south of El Teniente, rarely visited other than by locals, the forested foothills, rushing rivers, hanging valleys, and volcanic summits of Reserva Nacional de Los Cipreses are grossly underappreciated. Even locals, though, rarely venture into the backcountry beyond the road and picnic areas.

Orientation

Fifty kilometers southeast of Rancagua via the paved road to Coya and a gravel road that passes through Termas de Cauquenes, Los Cipreses is a 36,882-hectare unit ranging from 900-meter foothills to the 4,850-meter summit of Volcán El Palomo.

Flora and Fauna

The flora of Los Cipreses includes not just the endangered native conifer from which it takes its name, but also stands of *hualo, olivillo, peumo,* and other native trees. The endangered *flor de la araña* (literally, spider's flower) is an endangered bloom that bears an eye-catching resemblance to a daddy longlegs.

The fauna includes guanaco, fox, vizcacha, Andean condors, owls, parrots, small reptiles, and controversially reintroduced pumas, which local farmers assume attack their livestock.

Sights and Recreation

Several sites near park headquarters have petroglyphs; Conaf can provide directions. Near the Ranchillo campground, the **Sendero de Excursion Los Peumos** is a short nature trail that also passes near small mines from pre-reserve days.

One longer trail, suitable for at least an overnight backpacking trip, climbs the Río de los Cipreses Valley to a basic Conaf *refugio* at Urriola, about 20 kilometers from road's end; the road itself is gated past Ranchillo, and motorists must get Conaf permission to continue to the trailhead (hikers or cyclists can easily bypass the gate).

Practicalities

Six kilometers south of park headquarters, Conaf's 35-site **Camping Ranchillo** (tel. 072/297505, US$8 for up to seven people) is the only alternative, but it's a good one. Sites have picnic tables, barbecues, water, some shade, and there's even a swimming pool. Bring all food from Rancagua—there's nothing for sale here.

At the park entrance, Conaf's **Centro de Visitantes** collects US$3 admission per person and displays a scale model of the reserve, along with material on flora and fauna, including full skeletons of guanacos and foxes, taxidermy specimens of birds and reptiles, and display cases of insects. It also has motivated and helpful personnel. Unfortunately, public transportation is non-existent.

SAN FERNANDO

About half an hour south of Rancagua, 142 kilometers from Santiago and west of the Panamericana, the agricultural service center of San Fernando (population 24,582) is the gateway to Colchagua Valley wineries. Colonial landowner Juan Jiménez de León donated the lands for its founding, in the mid-18th century.

Sights

Several San Fernando landmarks are national monuments. On the north side of the Plaza de Armas, the two-story, neoclassical **Liceo de Hombres Neandro Schilling** (boys' school,

© WAYNE BERNHARDSON

On the grounds of its namesake winery near San Fernando, Viña Casa Silva's guesthouse is the gateway to the Colchagua Valley's Ruta del Vino.

Argomedo and Valdivia) dates from 1846. Three blocks south, the 1891 **Iglesia de San Francisco** (Valdivia and Manuel Rodríguez) has a clock tower with an unusual onion-shaped dome.

Several blocks northwest of the plaza, adjacent to the hospital, the 1899 **Capilla San Juan de Dios** (Negrete s/n), a brick building with elaborate filigree cornices, suffered serious damage in the 1985 earthquake. Two blocks north, the **Casa Patronal del Fundo de Lircunlauta** (Jiménez and Av. Manso de Velasco) belonged to Juan Jiménez de León; now a museum (tel. 072/717326), it's open 10 A.M.–5:30 P.M. Tuesday–Saturday, 10 A.M.–1 P.M. Sunday. Admission costs US$0.85 for adults, US$0.15 for children.

Accommodations and Food

The best accommodations and food are at the **Viña Casa Silva** winery (hotel tel. 072/913091, US$130 s, US$205–260 d). Its restaurant, considered the best in San Fernando, is closed to non-guests Sunday evenings and all day Monday. Another option for lodging is **Hotel Marcano** (Manuel Rodríguez 968, tel. 072/714759, US$30–37 pp).

Getting There and Around

The **Terminal de Buses** (Rancagua 1009, tel. 072/713912) is four blocks east of the Plaza de Armas. **Tur-Bus** (tel. 072/712923) has extensive schedules north- and southbound on the Panamericana, while regional services connect the city with destinations west, including Santa Cruz (for the wine route) and Pichilemu (on the Pacific).

For rail service, **Estación San Fernando** (Querecheguas s/n) is three blocks south of the bus terminal. **Metrotrén** runs 11 commuter trains to Santiago every weekday 6:10 A.M.–9:10 P.M.; there's one fewer on weekends. Long-distance **EFE** (Empresa de los Ferrocarriles del Estado) trains from Santiago also stop here.

VICINITY OF SAN FERNANDO

Rural San Fernando has no eye-popping attractions, but Hacienda Los Lingues is one of South America's elite—though not totally elitist—resorts, and those exploring the countryside will find some pleasant surprises in addition to the wineries.

Hacienda Los Lingues

Short of time travel, the easiest way to grasp the sum and substance of life on a colonial hacienda—at least from the perspective of a *latifundista* (owner of a large estate)—is to visit or, preferably, spend a night at Hacienda Los Lingues. It was founded in the 16th century, though the present buildings date from the 17th, and it's one of the best-preserved units of its kind. It is also the only Chilean affiliate of the international Relais & Chateaux luxury accommodations group, and one of few on the entire continent.

Decorated almost exclusively with antiques, Los Lingues's 18 guestrooms retain colonial style but also have contemporary comforts such as private baths—but not TV. Set among sprawling but manicured gardens, surrounded by a working farm, it also has a colonial chapel, a rodeo ring, and breeding stables. It took years for Germán Claro Lyon, who manages the resort, to convince his parents to open it to tourists.

In addition to accommodations, Los Lingues offers activities such as tennis and swimming, hiking, mountain biking, riding, and fly-fishing. Those who can't afford the luxury accommodations can book a day tour (US$66) that includes a tour of the main house, lunch (but not wine), pool access, and a rodeo at the *medialuna* (rodeo ring). Most of the grounds, though, are closed except to hotel guests.

Lodging at ◖ **Hacienda Los Lingues** (Panamericana Sur, Km 124; Av. Providencia 1100, Torre C de Tajamar, Oficina 205, Providencia, Santiago, tel. 02/2352458, www.loslingues.cl, US$194–491 s or d) is about 20 kilometers north of San Fernando and 32 kilometers south of Rancagua, a short distance east of the Panamericana by a well-marked gravel road; rates do not include breakfast or any other meals, but meal packages are available.

North–south buses can drop you at the

junction, where it's possible to find a cab to the hacienda. Los Lingues also provides round-trip transportation from Santiago or from the international airport, but this would be very expensive for individuals or couples.

San Vicente de Tagua Tagua and Vicinity

At the town of **Pelequén,** about 20 kilometers north of San Fernando on the Panamericana, the outstanding landmark is the sparkling copper dome of the **Iglesia y Santuario de Santa Rosa de Lima,** site of an annual festival for its patron saint every August 30. From here, a paved two-lane road heads west along the valley of the Estero Zamorano, a Río Cachapoal tributary, to the town of San Vicente de Tagua Tagua.

Regional authorities are promoting this area as the Ruta Huasa, a repository of peasant tradition. In the cultural landscape, the object of interest is the succession of traditional *azudas* (waterwheels), which lift water from the river and divert it through wooden *canaletas* (flumes or chutes) to the fields.

Mostly in the vicinity of **Larmahue,** these Muslim-style structures date from colonial times. Measuring 6–8 meters in diameter, fitted with 16–32 wooden spokes of poplar, *roble, raulí,* or eucalyptus, they need frequent repairs but are cheaper to operate than gasoline-powered pumps. Of the several dozen in the area, 17 of the older ones are national monuments; unfortunately, for photographers at least, some farmers have found it expedient to replace rotting wooden buckets with cheaper plastic milk cartons to draw water from the river.

At San Vicente itself, **Hostería San Vicente de Tagua Tagua** (Diego Portales 222, tel. 072/571336, andreacornejo@hotmail.com, US$42 s, US$58 d with breakfast) provides accommodations.

SANTA CRUZ AND VICINITY

Thanks largely to the efforts of a single man—the controversial arms dealer Carlos Cardoen—the town of Santa Cruz has become the locus of a burgeoning tourist industry that takes advantage of the country's best-organized *Ruta del Vino,* incorporating vineyards from San Fernando almost to the coast and a wine train that's gradually advancing westward.

Studded with Araucarias, palms, peppers, ginkgos, and conifers, surrounding a small central plaza, the Plaza de Armas is the focus of Santa Cruz's street life. At the southwestern corner, an intriguing clock tower reveals its inner workings.

Santa Cruz (population 18,603) is 37 kilometers west of San Fernando via a smooth paved road.

Shopping

Casa Espíritus de Colchagua (Nicolás Palacios 221, tel. 072/822754, www.espiritus-decolchagua.cl) produces homemade liqueurs from fruit and herbs, including raspberry, blueberry, cherry, peach, mint, cinnamon, and other local flavors.

◖ Museo de Colchagua

Most Ruta del Vino tours take in the Museo de Colchagua, Chile's largest nonpublic museum, but it's worth a detour off the Panamericana even for those with no interest in wine. Rapidly expanding, it displays Cardoén's collections of paleontological specimens, pre-Columbian art, and local historical materials, including a remarkable assortment of antique carriages and farm machinery. Its professional organization matches or surpasses that of Santiago's Museo Chileno de Arte Precolombino.

Open 10 A.M.–7 P.M. daily except Monday in summer, the Museo de Colchagua (Errázuriz 145, tel. 072/821050, www.museocolchagua .cl) closes an hour earlier the rest of the year. Admission costs US$5 per person, but only US$3 for seniors and US$1.50 for students and children; for another US$5, visitors can rent an electronic audio guide in English or Spanish. Ruta del Vino tours usually include the admission price.

Casas del Huique

Donated to the army by the Sánchez Errázuriz family in 1976, the hacienda house of San José

RUTA DEL VINO DE COLCHAGUA

West of San Fernando, Colchagua is the best organized of Chile's emerging wine routes. Working out of a common office in the town of Santa Cruz, the **Ruta del Vino** (Plaza de Armas 298, tel. 072/823199, www.rutadelvino.cl) comprises 14 different wineries. Several open on a drop-in basis or short notice, others by reservation only.

Some of the most prestigious winemakers have located here; the area is best known for its reds, especially but not exclusively carmenere. Starting around 10:30 A.M., full-day Ruta del Vino tours usually visit two or three wineries; in addition to lunch at one of the vineyards, they may also visit either Santa Cruz's Museo de Colchagua or the Casa de Huique, north of town. Rates vary depending on the number of guests – US$141 per person for 2, US$125 per person for 3-4, US$110 per person for 6-9. Half-day "express tours" range US$45-125 per person, again depending on the number of clients.

Several wineries now have their own restaurants and accommodations along the "Carretera del Vino," which runs west from San Fernando. Some also offer activities such as hiking and astronomy, in addition to the **Tren del Vino,** a Saturday steam train that leaves from San Fernando and stops at one or more wineries before returning to its starting point. Tours range from US$40-250 per person, depending on whether the excursion leaves from Santiago, how many wineries it visits, and whether it includes meals. For details, contact **Tren del Vino** (San Antonio 65, Oficina 106, Santiago, tel. 02/4707403, www.trendelvino.cl).

RESIDENCIA HISTÓRICA DE MARCHIHUE

It's not a winery, but this 18th-century Jesuit hacienda, recently restored and upgraded as a 22-room hotel, lies at the west end of the Colchagua Valley, about midway between Santa Cruz and Pichilemu. In its first year, it already attracted high profile clientele such as Chilean President Michelle Bachelet to its cool adobe rooms; even after subdividing the rooms to create modern baths, the sleeping quarters are huge, with a mix of contemporary and historic styles in their furnishings.

The Residencia Histórica (Fundo Los Maitenes, Marchihue, tel. 072/831199, www.residenciahistorica.com, US$183 s, US$200-310 d) is a quiet getaway that eschews television but does provide WiFi. It also has a pool, and offers excursions such as horseback rides.

VIÑA BISQUERTT

West of Santa Cruz, Bisquertt is a contemporary winery with a diversity of reds, whites, and blends; its shiraz and gewürztraminer are uncommon in the Colchagua Valley. Dating from 1991, it's a young winery, but one of its highlights is a spectacular set of carriages, restored to mint condition by a German craftsman from Santa Cruz. One of these belonged to President Federico Errázuriz Echaurren (1896-1901).

Viña Bisquertt (Carretera del Vino, Km 50, tel. 072/821792, www.bisquertt.cl) is open for tours at 10:30 A.M. and 12:30, 3:30, and 4:30 P.M. weekdays, and 10 A.M., and 12:30 and 3 P.M. Saturday. Prices vary according to the wine tasted: With varietals it's US$13, with reserve wines US$17, and with premium wines US$20.

VIÑA CASA SILVA

Santa Cruz is the hub of Colchagua's wine route, but Casa Silva is its gateway – barely off the Panamericana, it makes the otherwise forgettable city of San Fernando an ideal break for north-south sojourners lacking time for a longer detour. Only a small percentage of its grapes come from these vineyards – most grow nearer the coast or closer to the Andes – but some come from vines nearly a century old. The winery itself is a capacious colonial-style building with contemporary technology.

Casa Silva produces most of the usual Chilean reds and whites, including carmenere, but also less common varietals such as shiraz (syrah) and the whites sauvignon gris and viognier. Blends, both red and white, are also on the list.

Viña Casa Silva (Hijuela Norte, Angostura, San Fernando, tel. 072/913117, www.casasilva.cl) offers tours and tasting at 10:30 and 11:30 A.M., and 12:30, 3, 4, and 5 P.M. daily. The tour without tasting costs US$8; with one reserve wine US$15, and with three wines US$20.

In addition, it operates the adjacent, seven-room **Casa Silva Hotel** (tel. 072/913091, US$130 s, US$205–260 s or d); dating from the 1820s, it's a handsome adobe with traditional furnishings but modernized baths. Its namesake restaurant has become a popular dining option – easily the best in San Fernando – and both food and service have improved. It's closed to non-guests Sunday evenings and all day Monday.

VIÑA LAPOSTOLLE

Built by the French family responsible for Grand Marnier, Lapostolle is a state-of-the-art gravity-fed winery built into an Apalta hillside, only a short distance from Montes. At this facility, it produces only the award-winning Clos Apalta blend of carmenere, merlot, cabernet sauvignon, and petit verdot. So painstaking is the process that, during the fall harvest, 80

women select the grapes individually – there's no machine processing here. The tours, which take place at 10 A.M., and 1 and 3 P.M., are the valley's most expensive (US$33 pp) but, at the end of the tour, this means sampling wine that goes for US$100 or more per bottle.

The winery's **Lapostolle Residence** (Camino Apalta Km 4, tel. 072/953355, www.casalapostolle.com, US$450 s, US$550 d for B&B) consists of four *casitas* (small houses) with wraparound decks and almost total privacy on a promontory above the winery; the common areas, at the winery level, include a restaurant. With lunch or dinner included, rates rise to US$550 s, US$650 d. For hotel guests, the tour and tasting are included.

VIÑA MONTES

A short distance northeast of Viu Manent via a gravel road, Viña Montes is the work of Aurelio Montes, one of Chile's best known winemakers. Montes drew lots of flack for planting syrah on south-facing, 45-degree slopes with thin soils, but his "Montes Folly" label has been a resounding success.

In addition to syrah, Montes produces di-

(continues on next page)

© WAYNE BERNHARDSON

Viña Lapostolle is one of the Colchagua Valley's elite wineries and accommodations.

THE CHILEAN HEARTLAND

RUTA DEL VINO DE COLCHAGUA (continued)

verse wines including merlot, malbec, pinot noir, chardonnay, and a late harvest blend of gewürztraminer and semillon. Grapes for the pinot noir and the whites come from the Casablanca or Curicó regions, however.

Viña Montes (Parcela 15, Millahue de Apalta, tel. 072/825417, www.monteswines.com) is about 6.6 kilometers northwest of Santa Cruz. It offers 1.5-hour tours and tastings (US$24 pp) in either Spanish or English at 9:30 A.M., noon, and 3 P.M. daily, with later schedules in summer; if possible, save the best for the last – the tasting takes place on a deck in the uppermost vineyards, to the accompaniment of spectacular sunsets over the Colchagua Valley.

In addition to its tours and tasting, Montes now offers a botanical hiking trail through its Mediterranean scrublands and *hualo* (deciduous white oak, Nothofagus glauca) forests on the slopes of Cerro Divisadero.

VIÑA MONTGRAS

West of Santa Cruz on the Pichilemu highway, dating from 1992, MontGras is a modern winery that exports nearly all its production; focusing on reds such as carmenere, syrah, and cabernet sauvignon, as well as blends, it also produces an outstanding sauvignon blanc. It was among the first Chilean vineyards to plant mountaintop wines, a technique that others have since adopted.

Like Viu Manent, Viña MontGras (Camino Isla de Yáquil s/n, Palmilla, tel. 072/822845, www.montgras.cl) uses horse carts for vineyard tours (US$10-25 pp, depending on the wines tasted) at 10:30 A.M. and 12:30 and 3 P.M. weekdays, and 10:30 A.M., and 12:30 and 3 P.M. weekends. Tasting follows in its modern production facilities.

VIÑA SANTA CRUZ

In a colonial-style building off the main highway, about 25 km southwest of town, Viña Santa Cruz is Cardoen's modern boutique winery, producing limited quantities of reserve reds such as cabernet sauvignon, carmenere, syrah, and malbec, plus a few blends. Tours here are more than just a walk-through and tasting, though: Cardoen has also installed a *teleférico* (cable gondola) that climbs to a small hilltop events center and a cluster of museums that include prototype indigenous villages from throughout Chile (Aymara from the Norte Grande, Mapuche from the southern heartland, and Rapa Nui from Easter Island).

In addition, evening tours include a professional lecture on the southern hemisphere skies at the Centro Astronómico, followed by a peek at the planets and stars through several telescopes. On weekends, the restaurant **Mirador de Lolol** serves a buffet comparable to that of Hotel Santa Cruz's *Los Varietales*. Whenever the winery is open, the Sala de Ventas offers Cardoen's wines and *huaso* souvenirs.

Viña Santa Cruz (tel. 02/2219090, Carretera I-72 Km 25, Lolol, www.vinasantacruz.cl) offers tours and tasting at 10 A.M., noon, and 3 and 4:30 P.M. daily. Rates are US$25 pp except for the nighttime astronomy tour, which costs another US$16 pp.

VIÑA VIU MANENT

A short distance east of Santa Cruz on the highway from San Fernando, Viu Manent produces almost as great a variety of blends and varietals as Casa Silva, but focuses on reds, including carmenere, malbec, and merlot. Tours include a horse-and-carriage spin through the vineyards, followed by a tasting at its La Llavería wine shop and visitors center.

In addition to the winery, Viu also operates a Club Ecuestre (cel. 09/9847-1751), which offers riding classes (including polo preparation, US$20 per hour) and more traditional horseback rides through the vineyards (US$67 pp).

Viu Manent (Carretera del Vino, Km 37, tel. 072/858751, www.viumanent.cl) is open for tours and tastings (US$17 pp) that take place at 10:30 A.M., noon, and 3 and 4:30 P.M. daily except Monday. Open noon-6 P.M. daily except Monday, its restaurant **La Llavería** (tel. 072/858350) makes an ideal lunch break; with both indoor and outdoor seating, it's part of a restored 19th-century building decorated with artifacts from Cunaco's rural past.

del Carmen de El Huique dates from 1828, though the hacienda itself was a 17th-century creation. Having spent more than two centuries in the same family, it's one of the best survivors of its kind; it's also one of the largest, its facade measuring 250 meters across.

Most of the building and its patios remain intact, but agrarian reform gave the westernmost wing to a peasant cooperative that's not been able to maintain it. For that matter, the army's maintenance has been imperfect, though the house itself is richly decorated with period art and furniture, plus family heirlooms and photographs.

One of Huique's owners, Federico Errázuriz Echaurren, served as president from 1896 to 1901. Through most of its existence, the house hosted Santiago's elite on their summer vacations as they arrived in horse-drawn carriages or, from the early 20th, in automobiles.

Open Tuesday–Sunday 10 A.M.–6 P.M., but closing half an hour earlier in winter, Casas del Huique (tel. 072/933083, www.museoelhuique.cl) is 19 kilometers north of Santa Cruz. Admission costs US$3, half that for seniors and children.

Accommodations and Food

In-town accommodations are few. A couple blocks east of the plaza, **Hostal del Valle** (21 de Mayo 0317, tel. 072/821297, www.valledecolchagua.cl/hostaldelvalle, US$25–47 s, US$40–50 d) is a new six-room B&B, offering either shared or private baths.

Though its private baths look like an improvisation, the upstairs rooms at **Hostal Santa Cruz** (Carvacho 40, tel. 072/822046, hostalsantacruz@terra.cl, US$17–30 pp) are spacious and comfortable, and the management is friendly. The breakfast is forgettable (try negotiating a discount without it) and the street is busy, but it quiets at night.

A few blocks west of the plaza, **Hostal D'Vid** (Alberto Edwards 205, tel. 072/821269, www.dvid.cl, US$30 s, US$44 d with shared bath, US$68 s or d with private bath) is a stylish new place with WiFi and a pool.

Cardoen's ◖ **Hotel Santa Cruz Plaza** (Plaza de Armas 286, tel. 072/821010, www.hotelsantacruzplaza.cl, US$172–235 s or d with a diverse buffet breakfast) sets the accommodations standards here. Rooms in the new rear wing overlook the museum grounds and, in some cases, have views into exhibit rooms. It has WiFi throughout, a souvenir shop, a wine shop, and the restaurant **Los Varietales**, where the weekend lunch buffet is exceptionally popular. There is also a weekend pizzeria on the grounds, and it has recently acquired a (separately managed) casino.

Beneath a fine grape arbor, the **Club Social de Santa Cruz** (Plaza de Armas 178, tel. 072/822529) is a traditional dining favorite for winery tours. **Sushi Plaza Santa Cruz** (General del Canto 5, tel. 072/822059) is neither cheap nor up to Santiago sushi standards, but it's popular with local winemakers looking for some variety in their diet.

Information and Services

The de facto tourist office is the privately run headquarters of the **Ruta del Vino** (Plaza de Armas 298, tel. 072/823199, www.rutadelvino.cl), which does an excellent job of providing information on the entire Colchagua Valley, especially but not exclusively on wines (some of which it sells). Hours are 9 A.M.–6:30 P.M. weekdays; it opens an hour later on weekends.

Correos de Chile (Diaz Besoain 96) is the post office.

Getting There

From the capital's Terminal de Buses Santiago (Alameda 3750), the main carriers are **Pullman del Sur** (tel. 02/7762424) and **Nilahue** (tel. 02/7785222); it's about three hours (US$6) to Santa Cruz's own **Terminal Municipal** (Casanova s/n), about four blocks southwest of the Plaza de Armas. A slower alternative would be **Metrotrén** to San Fernando and a local bus (**Expreso Santa Cruz** or **Jetsur**) for the last 37 kilometers.

◀ PICHILEMU

In the early 20th century, Pichilemu was an aristocratic Pacific resort thanks to Agustín Ross Edwards, who bought Fundo Petrén in 1885 with the idea of making it a commercial port; despite his parliamentary influence, the project failed and he settled for a beach getaway with European pretensions.

Pichilemu owes its current celebrity, though, to the left break at Punta de Lobos, six kilometers south of town, where the **Campeonato Nacional de Surf** (National Surfing Championship) takes place every summer. In these notoriously chilly seas, though, a warm wetsuit is imperative.

Other good surf spots include the point break at La Puntilla, right in town (the breaks are too far offshore for spectators to see well without binoculars); the smaller point break at Infiernillo just to its south; and Cahuil, 15 kilometers south of town at the mouth of Estero Nilahue.

Orientation

Pichilemu (population about 12,000) is 126 kilometers west of San Fernando via Santa Cruz. At the north end of town, Playa Terrazas is a long sandy beach, but rocky headlands dot the curving coast toward the south. Unlike most Chilean cities, Pichilemu's grid is irregular in spots, though the Avenida Costanera follows the shoreline.

Sights

Directly on Playa Terrazas, the restored **Parque Ross,** with broad lawns, a pool, and palm-lined walkways, is Pichilemu's de facto Plaza de Armas and a national monument. Across the street, Ross built the **Edificio Casino** (1906), consisting of a pair of two-story pavilions topped by a mansard level that lodged the staff; after losing its casino license to Viña del Mar in 1932, it served as a hotel. It's undergoing restoration as a library and cultural center.

At the north end of town, the former **Estación de Ferrocarriles** (railroad station, 1925), a national monument, is now a cultural center.

A surfer rides the point break at Punta de Lobos, Pichilemu.

© WAYNE BERNHARDSON

Accommodations and Food

Residencial Antumalal (Aguirre 64, tel. 072/841004, antumalal@costapichilemu.cl, US$11 pp with private bath and cable TV) is a friendly family-run place with plain but comfortable rooms surrounding a shady central patio.

Some rooms at moribund **Hotel Asthur** (Av. Ortúzar 540, tel. 072/841072, www.hotelasthur .cl, US$42 pp with full board) are dark, but it does have a restaurant and a pool with a view.

At surfer-friendly **Hotel Chile España** (Av. Ortúzar 255, tel./fax 072/841270, www.chil-eespana.cl, US$33 s, US$50 d), some ground-floor rooms are unavoidably dark. All have cable TV and a private bath, and include breakfast.

A self-anointed "surf lodge," **Posada Punta de Lobos** (cel. 09/8154-1106, www .posadapuntadelobos.cl, US$70 s, US$92 d) is walking distance to its namesake break, and offers rental gear, a pool, and a bar/restaurant. On a per-person basis, its cabañas are cheaper than the lodge proper.

Up the block from Hotel Chile España, **El Balaustro** (Av. Ortúzar 289, tel. 072/842369) is a pub/restaurant that serves both beef and seafood.

Hostería La Gloria (José Joaquín Prieto 980, tel. 072/841052, www.lagloria.cl) has a big seafood menu.

Information and Services

Pichilemu's municipal **Oficina de Información Turística** (Angel Gaete 365, tel. 072/841017, ext. 246, www.pichilemu.cl, turismo@pichilemu.cl) is open 8 A.M.–1 P.M. and 2:30–7 P.M. weekdays.

Opposite Parque Ross, the private **Cámara de Turismo** (Av. Ross 568, tel. 072/842367, www.camaraturismopichilemu.cl), open 9 A.M.–1 P.M. and 2:30–9 P.M. daily, is more reliable and helpful.

Correos de Chile (Av. Ortúzar 498) handles the mail. **SurfNet** (Aníbal Pinto 105, tel. 072/841324) has both telephone and Internet service.

Hospital Pichilemu (Av. Errázuriz s/n, tel. 072/841022) handles medical matters.

Getting There

Pullman del Sur (Aníbal Pinto 213, tel. 072/843008) and **Nilahue** (Aníbal Pinto 108, tel. 072/841104) buses from the Terminal de Buses Santiago drop passengers at Pichilemu's **Terminal Municipal** (Millaco 534). The US$8 trip takes 3.5 hours.

CURICÓ

In some ways a model garden city—or at least known as one for its magnificently landscaped Plaza de Armas—Curicó is seeing the early dividends of a major tree-planting program. The surrounding area is known for its wineries and for Parque Nacional Radal Siete Tazas, a small but interesting park in the Andean foothills.

Like other Central Valley towns, San José de Buena Vista de Curicó owes its origins to a military base intended to protect settlers on the colonial frontier. Founded in 1743, along with Rancagua and San Fernando, by José Antonio Manso de Velasco, the town center was moved

a few years later when the original site proved prone to flooding.

Orientation

Curicó (population 157,876) is 195 kilometers south of Santiago via the Panamericana. Like many colonial Chilean cities, its core is a rectangle seven blocks square, centered on the Plaza de Armas.

Sights

Curicó's **Plaza de Armas** and its surroundings are a *zona típica* national monument. After the city became a provincial capital in 1865, local authorities began to beautify what had been a parking lot for horses, planting Canary Island palms around the perimeter and placing a pool known as *Las Tres Gracias* (The Three Graces) at its center; on occasion, black-necked swans paddle around the fountain.

Several modern sculptures embellish the plaza, also shaded by araucarias, robles, *boldos,* and *tilos,* along with other native and exotic trees; one dead trunk has been carved into a representation of the Mapuche legend of Lautaro. The **Quiosco Cívico** (1905) is a forged-iron bandshell modeled after one a Curicó mayor saw in Santiago.

On the west side of the plaza, restoration architect Jorge Squella managed to salvage some original walls of the earthquake-damaged **Iglesia Matriz** (Merced and Yungay). Six blocks east and one block south of the Plaza de Armas, opposite Plaza Luis Cruz, the soaring brick neo-Gothic **Iglesia San Francisco** is also a national monument.

Vinícola Miguel Torres

Just a few kilometers south of Curicó, Vinícola Miguel Torres is a Spanish vintner that began buying Chilean properties in the late 1970s. With wines that vary from cabernet sauvignon and rosé to chardonnay, sauvignon blanc, and riesling, as well as sparkling wine, it's also one of Chile's largest wineries. Its modern Curicó bodegas are open on a drop-in basis for hour-long tours (US$8) that begin with a video that emphasizes the company's operations in Spain

THE CHILEAN HEARTLAND

and California, followed by a visit to the local facilities for a sample tasting.

In addition to tours, visitors can lunch at **Restaurant Viña Torres,** set among the vines; it features a set daily lunch menu, each of whose four courses comes with an appropriate wine, for US$32 per person (US$18 without wine). There's also an à la carte menu, and the wine list includes a wide variety of by-the-glass options at modest prices. In summer, it offers a Friday night dinner.

Vinícola Miguel Torres (Panamericana Sur, Km 195, tel. 075/564100, www.migueltorres.cl) is open 10 A.M.–7 P.M. daily, but closes two hours earlier in autumn and winter. From the corner of Avenida Camilo Henríquez and Manuel Rodríguez in Curicó, Molina-bound *taxi colectivos* will drop passengers almost at the entrance; if driving, it's necessary to pay attention to the vineyard's signs at Maquehua, which has a dirt road off the highway (technically, it's not a freeway exit). Tours are hourly in French and English.

Entertainment and Events

Curicó is a quiet provincial town, but the local branch of the **Centro Cultural Universidad de Talca** (Merced 437) shows movies and stages concerts, as does the **Centro Cultural Universidad Católica** (Prat 220).

Centered on the Plaza de Armas, Curicó's biggest annual event is late March's **Festival de la Vendimia** (Wine Harvest Festival), which has grown since Catalan winemaker Miguel Torres began operations here in 1986.

Accommodations

Hotel Prat (Peña 427, tel. 075/311069, hotelpratcurico@yahoo.es, US$12 pp with shared bath, US$17 pp with private bath) is a traditional budget favorite. **Hostal Pehuen** (Prat 83, tel. 075/310461, US$16 s, US$24 d) is also good.

Better than its drab original exterior would suggest, **Hotel Comercio** (Yungay 730, tel. 075/310014, www.hotelcomercio.cl, US$41–57 s, US$46–79 d with breakfast) has 120 rooms that vary substantially in size. The higher prices correspond to the newer of its two buildings, and it has a pool, WiFi, and other amenities.

Despite its name, **Hotel Turismo** (Arturo Prat 301, tel. 075/543440, hturismo@tnet.cl, US$57 s, US$75 d) is more accurately the business traveler's favorite, though tourists will feel just as much at home in its large rooms and spacious, stylish common areas.

Some rooms are on the small side, but **Hotel Palmas Express** (Membrillar 728, tel. 075/320066, www.villaeldescanso.com, US$56–78 s, US$78–85 d) is in primo condition. Given the minimal price difference, the more expensive suites are worth consideration; amenities include cable TV, a/c, parking, and a buffet breakfast.

Food

Curicó's dining scene is not quite so bleak as in past years; easily the area's best is the vineyard restaurant at Vinícola Miguel Torres.

The standard is the fire station's **Casino de Bomberos** (Membrillar 690), a reliable choice in most Chilean cities. Meals served at the dining room at **Hotel Turismo** (Prat 301, tel. 075/543440) are only so-so despite attractive surroundings.

The best choices otherwise are the local *parillas:* **Entre Barrricas y Copas** (Las Heras 423, tel. 075/221081) and **Los Cisnes** (Rodríguez 1186, tel. 075/313576).

Information and Services

Sernatur has no office here and the municipality is unreliable, but the office of the **Ruta del Vino de Curicó** (Prat 301-A, tel. 075/320972, www.rutadelvinocurico.cl), in the Hotel de Turismo, is open 9 A.M.–2 P.M. and 3:30–7 P.M. weekdays only. Though imperfect in some regards, it's helpful in arranging visits to local wineries that, except for Miguel Torres, are harder to organize here.

Banco de Crédito (Merced 315) and **Banco Santander** (Estado 336) have ATMs.

Correos de Chile (Carmen 556) is on the

east side of the Plaza de Armas. In Prat and Yungay streets, various telephone centers and Internet venues keep long hours.

The Hospital de Curicó (Chacabuco 121, tel. 075/206200) handles medical matters.

Getting There and Around

All buses now leave from the Terminal de Buses de Curicó (Prat s/n), opposite the train station. Long-distance carriers include **Pullman del Sur** (tel. 075/310387) and **Tur-Bus** (tel. 075/312115). **Talmocur** (tel. 075/311360) goes to Molina and Talca, the regional capital, as well as Santiago.

Transportation to Parque Nacional Radal Siete Tazas leaves from nearby Molina.

EFE trains between Santiago and Talca, and other points south, stop at **Estación Curicó** (Maipú 657, tel. 075/310028), four blocks west of the Plaza de Armas.

PARQUE NACIONAL RADAL SIETE TAZAS

In the Andean precordillera southeast of Curicó, the Río Claro plunges steeply over basalt bedrock into a series of pools known as the Siete Tazas (Seven Teacups), a feature that has given its name to this 5,026-hectare reserve. When the water is high with spring snowmelt, skilled kayakers have made this one of their favorite stops, but the reserve still gets relatively few foreign visitors. Even when Chileans crowd it in summer and on weekends, areas off the main road are almost people-free.

Ecologically, distributions of drought-tolerant Mediterranean plants overlap southern Chile's evergreen forests here. Ranging 600–2,156 meters above sea level, the park does not reach the high Andean summits to the east.

Nonkayakers can view the Siete Tazas via a short trail off the main road; a slightly longer footpath leads to an overlook to the **Salto de la Leona,** a tributary waterfall that plummets more than 50 meters into the Río Claro.

Longer hikes up the **Valle del Indio** and **Cerro El Fraile** are also possible. The lengthy trek north across the Claro to Reserva Nacional Altos del Lircay traditionally requires a guide, as multiple tracks make route-finding difficult for those who don't know the area, but advancements in signing on the Sendero de Chile are making this simpler.

Accommodations and Food

At Radal and Parque Inglés, there are rudimentary campgrounds with basic services; the former is community-run, the latter administered by Conaf. Sites at Conaf's **Camping Los Robles** (tel. 071/228029, US$13) sleep up to six people.

Near Parque Inglés, **Hostería Flor de la Canela** (tel. 075/491613, US$37–42 pp with full board) offers accommodations December–March.

Basic supplies are available at Parque Inglés, but there's a better selection in Curicó or Molina.

Information

Conaf collects a US$2.50 entrance fee (US$0.85 for kids) at Parque Inglés, where its **Centro de Información** also offers Saturday nature talks.

Getting There

The Parque Inglés entrance is 50 kilometers east of Molina via a mostly unsurfaced road. In January and February, from Molina, **Buses Hernández** (Maipú 1723, tel. 075/521303) goes as far as Parque Inglés (US$2.50) six or seven times daily from 8 A.M.–7:45 P.M.; the rest of the year, it goes only as far as Radal (US$1.50), at 5:30 P.M. daily except Sunday.

THE CHILEAN HEARTLAND

Talca

Like Rancagua and Curicó, the midsized city of Talca makes an ideal base for exploring a key wine- and fruit-growing area, with easy access to an Andean backcountry that's drawing a select number of foreign visitors who realize they can hike through spectacular mountain scenery without the crowds of Torres del Paine. While it's settled into the comfortable roles of political capital (of Region VII, Maule) and service center, it does not lack a cultural component—especially since the 1981 founding of the Universidad de Talca, the arts have flourished here.

Tomás Marín de Poveda founded Talca in 1690, but after a major earthquake, José Manso de Velasco refounded it in 1742 under the name Villa San Agustín de Talca. Bernardo O'Higgins signed Chile's declaration of independence here.

ORIENTATION
Wedged between the Río Claro to the west and the Panamericana to the east, Talca (population 193,755) is 257 kilometers south of Santiago. Unlike most Chilean cities, its streets are numbered rather than named, but the central core still has a colonial grid.

SIGHTS
In 1818, Bernardo O'Higgins signed Chile's declaration of independence at what is now the **Museo O'Higginiano y de Bellas Artes,** built in 1762 by Portuguese merchant Juan Albano Pereira y Márquez; Pereira and his wife, Bartolina de la Cruz, were in fact O'Higgins's godparents, and O'Higgins spent part of his youth in the house, now a national historical monument. Unfortunately, the exhibits on O'Higgins here are marginal; more substantial are the archaeological and numismatic exhibits, the five rooms of Chilean art from colonial times to the 20th century, and materials on the origins of local journalism.

As of writing, the Museo O'Higginiano

(1 Norte 875, tel. 071/227330, www .museodetalca.cl) was undergoing restoration, but it's normally open 10 A.M.–6:30 P.M. weekdays except Monday, 10 A.M.–2 P.M. weekends and holidays. Admission costs US$1 for adults, half that for children and students, but is free Wednesdays.

The **Casa del Arte** (1 Norte 931) is a contemporary art space, open 10 A.M.–1 P.M. and 4–7 P.M. weekdays; admission is free.

ENTERTAINMENT
Run by the Universidad de Talca, the **Centro de Extensión Pedro Olmos Muñoz** (2 Norte 685) sponsors films, lectures, and art exhibitions.

For commercial movies, try the **Cine Star 2** (1 Sur 1278).

ACCOMMODATIONS
Talca's budget accommodations have improved considerably, but some midrange choices are outstanding values.

New in 2008, **Hostal Los Pastaños** (8 Oriente 1481, tel. 071/684531, loscastanostalca@gmail.com, US$15 s, US$25 d) is a cozy five-room B&B (shared bath only) with conscientious English ownership, and an above-average breakfast.

Hostal del Río (1 Sur 411, tel. 071/225448, www.hostaldelrio.co.cl, US$25 s, US$33 d) enjoys a quiet location on a dead-end street where the only steady noise is the flow of the Estero Piduco, a Río Claro tributary. There are slightly more costly suites as well.

Alongside Hostal del Río, all rooms have private baths at **Hostal del Puente** (1 Sur 407, tel. 071/220930, www.hostaldelpuente.cl, US$22 s, US$38 d with breakfast). The amiable English-speaking management is a bonus.

Close to the plaza and small restaurant/ nightlife sector that runs just off it, **Hostal Serana** (1 Sur 532, tel. 071/, www.hostalserana.cl, US$23 s, US$33 d) has made good early impressions.

RUTA DEL VINO DEL MAULE

Like other heartland wine areas, the Maule Valley has a rapidly developing tourist circuit, with 15 wineries open to the public, from Talca south toward San Javier and west toward Constitución. Few, though, are open on a drop-in basis; most require advance arrangements.

Like the Casablanca and Colchagua wine routes, the Maule has an increasing number of accommodations and restaurants. To arrange a more extensive itinerary, contact the Ruta del Vino del Maule (Villa Cultural Huiquilemu, Km 7 Camino San Clemente, Talca, tel. 073/246460, www.valledelmaule.cl).

CASA DONOSO

Acquired in 1989 by French-Tahitian interests, Casa Donoso was an over-the-hill family winery (some vines dated from 1905) that has since replanted substantially and begun to focus on fine wines, including cabernet sauvignon, merlot, chardonnay, and carmenere for export, as well as some blends; it's also growing cabernet franc and malbec. Completely upgraded without losing its colonial style, the winery now includes a restaurant and guesthouse.

Casa Donoso is the closest winery to downtown Talca; directly east of the Panamericana, at the 2.4-kilometer point just past the Easy home improvement store, a gravel road leads south for 3.5 kilometers to its grounds. Tours with tasting (US$12) and affable attention are available 10 A.M.–6 P.M. weekdays only, by reservation; contact Casa Donoso (Fundo La Oriental, Camino a Palmira s/n, Talca, tel. 071/242506, www.casadonoso.com).

Accommodations at Casa Donoso's colonial-style **Guest House Casa Donoso** (tel. 071/242506, ext. 210, US$235 s or d with breakfast) are by reservation only; meals at its restaurant, for both guests and nonguests, also require reservations a day in advance.

VIÑA BALDUZZI

South of Talca, where the Panamericana crosses the Río Maule canyon, the parallel **Puente Ferroviario Maule** (1885) is a landmark 442-meter railroad bridge that still carries trains to Chillán, Concepción, and Temuco.

Another two kilometers south is San Javier's modern Viña Balduzzi (Av. Balmaceda 1189, tel. 073/322138, www.balduzzi.cl), a boutique winery that produces mostly chardonnay, sauvignon blanc, cabernet sauvignon, and carmenere. It's open daily except Sunday 9 A.M.–6 P.M. for guided tours; there are many buses from Talca's Rodoviario Municipal.

VIÑA CALINA

Likewise close to Talca, Calina is a project of California's Kendall-Jackson winery, producing high-quality cabernet sauvignon, carmenere, merlot, and blends, along with chardonnay. With the Andes as a backdrop, the vineyards and winery are contemporary in style with all the latest technology.

While the wines are impressive, the tours themselves (US$10 pp with one reserve wine), if not quite perfunctory, lack Casa Donoso's conviviality. Viña Calina (Fundo El Maitén, Camino Las Rastras, tel. 071/263126, www.calina.com) is about 15 kilometers east of Talca; turn left instead of right at the Casa Donoso turnoff and follow the road (which turns from paved to gravel) to the grounds.

VIÑA TABONTINAJA (GILLMORE WINERY & VINEYARDS)

Southwest of San Javier, across the Río Loncomilla on the road to Constitución, Tabontinaja is a boutique winery, specializing in reds such as cabernet sauvignon, cabernet franc, and merlot, that produces only about 20,000 bottles per year.

Viña Tabontinaja, formally known as Gillmore Winery & Vineyards (Km 20, Camino a Constitución, San Javier, tel. 073/1975539, www.gillmore.cl) is open for call-ahead tours (personnel is limited). In addition to the winery, the grounds at Gillmore also include the **Casa de Huéspedes El Tabonkö** (tel. 073/1975539, www.tabonko.cl, US$200 d), a modern 14-room guesthouse and spa that concentrates on multiday packages. Its restaurant, **La Cava de Francisco**, is open to the public. There is also a zoo of native animals.

Hotel Cordillera (2 Sur 1360, tel. 071/221817, www.cordillerahotel.cl, US$27 s, US$42–50 d) has simple rooms with shared bath and others with private baths and cable TV.

More expensive, but not *that* much better than Hostal del Río, are **Hotel Nápoli** (2 Sur 1314, tel. 071/227373, US$31 s, US$52 d with breakfast and private bath) and **Hotel Terranova** (1 Sur 1026, tel. 071/239608, hotelterranova@entelchile.net, US$48 s, US$54 d, also with breakfast).

The modern **Hotel Marcos Gamero** (1 Oriente 1070, tel. 071/223388, www.marcosgamero.cl, US$48 s, US$69 d), though, is a step up.

One block west of the plaza, the contemporary **Hotel Terrabella** (1 Sur 641, tel./fax 071/226555, terrabella@hotel.tie.cl, US$65 s, US$79 d) has spacious wooded grounds and a swimming pool—both unusual in this part of town.

FOOD

For truly cheap eats, there are the several *cocinerías* in the **Mercado Central,** bounded by 1 Norte, 1 Sur, 4 Oriente, and 5 Oriente. The chain **Bavaria** (1 Sur 1330, tel. 071/227088) has sandwich fare and some more elaborate dishes.

El Gobelino (1 Sur 770, tel. 071/233980) serves fixed-price Chilean lunches in the US$4–5 range—good enough, but unexceptional. Alongside the fire station, the **Casino de Bomberos** (2 Sur 1160, tel. 071/212903) is a reliable choice in almost every Chilean city.

Facing the plaza, **Restaurant Chilote** (1 Norte 717, tel. 071/215267) has good seafood at moderate prices; the combination shrimp-and-scallops empanadas are unusual. To its northwest, a shady diagonal is home to Talca's budding gourmet ghetto of restaurants such as the Italian **⟨ Vivace** (Isidoro del Solar 50, tel. 071/238337), which serves upscale pastas and other dishes in the US$7–8 range, and doubles as a wine bar with a good by-the-glass selection. The kitchen, though, can be slow even when it's not crowded.

Across the block, **Isidora** (Isidoro del Solar

97, tel. 071/217320, www.isidora-resto.cl, Tues.–Fri. lunch, Tues.–Sat. dinner) is a well-designed restaurant with a sushi bar and a fusion menu of homemade pastas, fish, and game dishes.

Arguably Talca's best, **⟨ Rubén Tapia** (2 Oriente 1339, tel. 071/237875, www.rubentapia.cl) has just one small upstairs dining room, so reservations are advisable. It's getting competition, though, from **Russo** (7 Oriente between 2 and 3 Sur, tel. 071/511051, www.russo.cl), which occupies new designer surroundings.

INFORMATION

In new quarters opposite the plaza, the helpful regional office of **Sernatur** (1 Oriente 1150, tel. 071/233669, infomaule@sernatur.cl) has some English-speaking staff; it's open 8:30 A.M.–5:30 P.M. weekdays only.

Motorists can get advice from the **Automóvil Club de Chile** (Acchi, 8 Orente 1154, tel. 071/235339).

Conaf's Patrimonio Silvestre office (2 Poniente and 3 Sur, tel. 071/228029) specializes in protected areas such as Altos del Lircay.

SERVICES

Conveniently located in the same building, the only exchange houses are **Afex** (2 Oriente 1131) and **Cambios Macelo Cancino** (2 Oriente 1131). **Banco de Crédito** (1 Sur 732) has an ATM on the south side of the Plaza de Armas.

Correos de Chile (1 Oriente 1150) is on the east side of the Plaza de Armas. Telephone centers and Internet outlets are abundant on and around the Plaza de Armas.

The **Hospital Regional** (1 Norte 1990, tel. 071/209100) is just east of the tracks.

GETTING THERE

Talca has no air services, but buses are frequent and it's a stop on the EFE railroad line between Santiago, to the north, and Chillán and Temuco to the south—but as of summer 2009, operational problems prevented this travel south from Talca. It also has Chile's last operating short-line passenger train, to the Pacific port/resort of Constitución.

Bus

Talca's **Rodoviario Municipal** (2 Sur 1920, tel. 071/243270) is east of the tracks; **Tur-Bus** (3 Sur 1940, tel. 071/265715) has a separate terminal one block south. Both have frequent north-south services along the Panamericana.

From the municipal terminal, **Buses Vilches** has three buses daily, at 7:30 A.M. and at 1 and 4:50 P.M., to Vilches Alto and Reserva Nacional Altos del Lircay (US$2).

Pullman Contimar (tel. 071/613594) goes frequently to and from the coastal town of Constitución (US$3, 2 hours), as does **Interbus** (tel. 071/613146).

Sample destinations and fares include Chillán (US$5, 2 hours), Santiago (US$7–11, 3.5 hours), Temuco (US$11, 6.5 hours), Valdivia (US$19, 9 hours), Osorno (US$21–32, 11 hours) and Puerto Montt (US$23–37, 12 hours).

Train

From Santiago, nine EFE trains stop daily at **Estación Talca** (11 Oriente 1100, tel. 071/226254), at the east end of Avenida 2 Sur; eight of these continue to Chillán. Services to the south were suspended as of summer 2009 due to operational problems; for more information check EFE's website at www.efe.cl.

At 7 A.M. and 4:30 P.M. daily, a narrow-gauge train goes to the port/beach resort of Constitución (US$2.50, 2.5 hours).

Vicinity of Talca

From the coast to the cordillera, the Talca countryside has abundant recreational opportunities, even more than Curicó. Casa Chueca is the best single source of information for backcountry trips and other excursions, such as winery visits, in the vicinity.

HUILQUILEMU

Across the Panamericana from Talca, the former *fundo* of Huilquilemu is one of Chile's single most impressive big houses, with its long corridors, thick adobe walls, multiple patios, wooden ceilings, and extensive gardens of native and exotic trees. Under the administration of the Universidad Católica, it boasts a religious art museum, an assortment of historic farm equipment, an elegant library honoring regional writers including Neruda and Pablo de Rokha, and a spectacular display of folk art from throughout the Americas. The sprawling, forested gardens include specimens of sequoias, deodar cedars, and palms.

Huilquilemu (Ruta 115, Km 10, tel. 071/242474) is 10 kilometers east of Talca on the San Clemente road; hours are 9 A.M.–1 P.M.

and 3–8 P.M. daily except Monday in summer; the rest of the year, hours are 10 A.M.–1 P.M. and 3–6:30 P.M. weekdays except Monday, 3–7 P.M. Saturday, and 11 A.M.–2 P.M. Sunday; adult admission costs US$0.85, the rate for children is US$0.35. All San Clemente–bound micros from Talca's Rodoviario Municipal pass the site.

CASA CHUECA

In a quiet location on the Río Lircay's south bank, just across the Panamericana from Talca, German-Austrian Casa Chueca is a fashionably decorated colonial-style guesthouse with all the essential comforts—firm beds, hot showers, clean toilets, a library, and even a small gym—and none of the inessential (no TV, for instance). Set among sprawling lawns with a large swimming pool, it's become a destination in itself for weekenders from Santiago and vagabonds along the Panamericana.

The **(** **accommodations** themselves are impeccable, with spacious rooms (US$30 s, US$57 d) and an abundant breakfast. Backpackers will find equally classy dorm accommodations (US$14 pp, six or eight bunks to a room, with private bath). Primarily vegetarian lunches and dinners cost US$5 and up, and mixed drinks and wine are equally reasonably priced. On a separate property only a short distance away, new "Divino Suites" (US$120 s, US$150 d) include whirlpool tubs and other amenities.

In addition to accommodations, Casa Chueca offers well-guided excursions into the Andean backcountry of Altos del Lircay, Radal Siete Tazas, and the upper Río Maule toward the Argentine border, all areas greatly underappreciated by Chileans and foreigners alike. The owners and staff are also generous with information to independent travelers and speak Spanish, English, German, Swedish, French, and Portuguese. Rental cars—including camper vans—and bicycles are available here.

To reach Casa Chueca from Talca's bus terminal, take the local Taxutal A micro to the end of the line at the Toro Bayo restaurant, about a 10-minute ride, and walk another 20 minutes along the dirt road. Casa Chueca will also provide the first transfer free from Toro Bayo—contact Casa Chueca (Viña Andrea s/n, Sector Alto Lircay, tel. 071/1970096, tel./fax 071/1970097, cel. 09/9419-0625, www.trekkingchile.com, casachueca@trekkingchile.com).

◖ RESERVA NACIONAL ALTOS DEL LIRCAY

In the precordillera southeast of Talca, Altos del Lircay is another of Chile's hidden secrets, a forested wilderness of 12,163 hectares with multiple options for backcountry hiking and camping in canyons, valleys, and summits that range 600–2,448 meters above sea level. Part of the Sendero de Chile passes through here, but it's not the only hike of interest. The reserve has warm, dry summers, but serious snowfall can accumulate in winter.

Flora and Fauna

Closely resembling the forests of nearby Radal Siete Tazas, Lircay's woodlands consist of species toward the northern limits

of their range, such as the southern beech *coigüe,* overlapping central Andean species such as *lingue, boldo,* and *peumo.* They have abundant birdlife, including the burrowing parrot, black woodpecker, thrush, and California quail (an introduced species). The largest mammal is the puma, a reintroduction under a joint program between Conaf and the Talca branch of the conservation organization Codeff.

Sights

Lircay's aboriginal population ground their grains at the **Piedras Tacitas,** a series of creekside mortars reached by a short signed trail from Conaf's Centro de Información Ambiental. On the north side of the former logging road that leads east from the park entrance, the **Mirador del Indio** offers views of the Lircay Valley; it's possible to hike across the Lircay drainage to the Río Claro and Parque Nacional Radal Siete Tazas; with improved signage along the Sendero de Chile, route-finding is less difficult than it used to be.

Two kilometers east of Mirador del Indio, a signed trail climbs north and then east to **El Enladrillado,** a sprawling tableland where weathering has uncovered columns of hexagonal basalt formed millions of years ago beneath the earth's surface. This tiring hike, which Conaf suggests should take two days, is possible in one day, but carry adequate water and high-energy snacks. Views of the Río Claro Valley, 3,830-meter Volcán Descabezado Grande, and the Andean ridge along the Argentine border are among the country's best.

More ambitious hikers can consider a five-day trek on the **Sendero Valle del Venado** to the summit of Descabezado Grande and back; the less ambitious can do a day hike to **Mirador Venado,** which gives fine views from a platform at the junction with the Sendero de Chile.

For details on current conditions and further suggestions, contact Casa Chueca in Talca; their *Condor Circuit* map, at a scale of 1:50,000 with some details at 1:25,000, is the best available guide to the area.

© WAYNE BERNHARDSON

A heaven for hikers, Reserva Nacional Altos del Lircay gets only a handful of Talca's backcountry visitors.

Accommodations and Food

Conaf's **Camping Antahuaras,** near the entrance to the reserve, charges US$13 for up to six persons, with hot showers. There are also private campgrounds along the dusty road just prior to the entrance, with a few small shops nearby, but supplies are cheaper and more abundant in Talca.

Information

At the park entrance, Conaf collects an admission charge of US$2.50 for adults, US$0.85 for children. Its **Centro de Información Ambiental** contains exhibits on natural and cultural history.

Reasonably priced rental horses are available just outside the park entrance.

Getting There

Altos del Lircay is 66 kilometers southeast of Talca via paved Ruta 115 and a 29-kilometer side road, whose unpaved upper half billows with dust in the dry summer and splatters mud in winter, when the last few kilometers can be difficult. From Talca's Terminal Rodoviario, **Buses Vilches** goes to the Administración (park office) at 7:30 A.M. and at 1 and 4:50 P.M.,

returning at 7:15 and 9:15 A.M., and 6:15 P.M. There are usually additional buses in summer; the fare is US$3. The day's last bus from Talca returns the next morning.

CONSTITUCIÓN

West of Talca, at the mouth of the Maule, the town of Constitución lives on paper pulp, port traffic, and weekenders who take launch excursions on the estuary. It has a handful of handsome colonial houses with tiled roofs, but the main reason for coming here is getting here—the picturesque railroad from Talca is the last operating line of its kind in the country. In truth, it makes a better day trip than an overnight.

Sights

The admirably landscaped **Plaza de Armas** features a distinctive wrought-iron bandshell dating from 1923; on its south side, the **Iglesia Parroquial San José** wears a neoclassical facade. The **Edificios Públicos** (Civic Center) on the plaza's west side include the 1950s-style **Teatro Municipal** (Municipal Theater).

At the west end of town, the 90-meter summit of **Cerro Mutrún** should offer views over the town, out to sea, and south toward the Celulosa Arauco (Celco) pulp mill. Fast-growing pines have blocked views of the mill, but your nose knows where it is.

Accommodations and Food
The best budget choice is **Residencial Alameda** (Avenida Enrique Donn 734, tel. 071/671896, US$13 pp with breakfast).

Along the estuary, **Hostería Constitución** (Echeverría 460, tel. 071/671450, US$42 s or d with breakfast and cable TV) is past its peak. Garden rooms are slightly cheaper than those with river views.

Otto Schop (Oñederra 601), at the southeast corner of the Plaza de Armas, has good sandwiches and other short orders.

Services
On the north side of the Plaza de Armas, both Banco de Chile and Banco Santander have ATMs. Also on the plaza, **Entel** (Cruz and Freire) has both long-distance telephone services and Internet access.

Getting There and Around
Easily the most entertaining way to Constitución is the morning train from Talca, the Ferrocarril Constitución, Chile's last operating short-line passenger spur.

Still, it's advisable to take a bus or *taxi colectivo* back to Talca—though a little farther, it's faster and takes a different route.

The train and bus station are alongside each other on Rozas between Echeverría and Bulnes, several blocks northeast of the Plaza de Armas. Frequent buses with **Pullman Contimar** (tel. 071/672929) and **Interbus** connect Constitución with Talca (US$3, two hours).

Chillán

Beset by natural disasters throughout its history, Chillán lacks even the limited colonial character of heartland cities such as Talca. But the birthplace of Chilean liberator Bernardo O'Higgins compensates with museums, its renowned Mexican murals—reason enough for stopping in the city—and the most vibrant fruit-and-vegetable market in the entire country. In addition to O'Higgins, Chillán has recently honored internationally known concert pianist Claudio Arrau with his own museum.

HISTORY
Initially established as a Spanish fortress in 1565, Chillán dates officially from 1580, when Chilean governor Martín Ruiz de Gamboa decreed the founding of the city of San Bartolomé de Gamboa. Almost destroyed by fire in 1655 and earthquake in 1751, it was rebuilt at what is now Chillán Viejo, a few kilometers southwest, but moved to its current site after yet another quake, in 1835. In 1939, though, a truly cataclysmic temblor leveled most of the city; rebuilding proceeded on the same site with improved seismic safety standards. Chillán Viejo, ironically, survives to this day.

ORIENTATION
Chillán (population 148,015) is 407 kilometers south of Santiago and 270 kilometers north of Temuco by the Panamericana, which bypasses the city to the west. Between the Río Ñuble to the north and the Río Chillán to the south, its unstable alluvial soils have probably contributed to its repeated natural disasters.

Bounded by Libertad, 18 de Septiembre, Constitución, and Arauco, Plaza Bernardo O'Higgins marks the city center; there are several satellite plazas. The divided, tree-lined Avenidas Ecuador, Brasil, Collín, and Argentina circumscribe the central core, an area 12 blocks square. Three blocks west of the plaza, Avenida O'Higgins provides access to the northbound Panamericana (toward

Santiago) and the southbound Panamericana (toward Los Ángeles and Temuco) via Chillán Viejo.

SIGHTS

Produce from throughout the region converges on the **Feria de Chillán,** a vigorous fruit-and-vegetable market that fills the entire Plaza de la Merced, southeast of the Plaza de Armas, and overflows onto nearby streets. Also boasting an impressive assortment of handicrafts, it's open every day but is most active on Saturday.

Part of its eponymous church on Plaza General Lagos, the **Museo Franciscano** (Sargento Aldea 265, tel. 042/211634) honors the contributions of colonial Franciscan missionaries who used Chillán as a base to evangelize the Mapuche to the south (even after Chilean independence, this was the northern limit of the area commonly known as "La Frontera," much of it under effective indigenous control). It's open 2–6:30 P.M. daily except Monday.

One of few structures of any antiquity, the 1874 **Capilla del Hospital San Juan de Dios** (Av. O'Higgins 1661) is the remaining chapel of the former main hospital; a few blocks south of Avenida Collín, this historical monument is rapidly deteriorating.

Museo Claudio Arrau León

Opened in December 2005, Chillán's newest museum is an interactive facility on the site of the classical pianist's boyhood home (only two remodeled rooms, filled with Arrau's personal effects, remain of the original house, which suffered severe damage in the 1939 quake). A work in progress, with a 300-seat auditorium still under construction, the museum contains several exhibits detailing how musical instruments work.

Born in Chillán, Arrau (1903–1991) spent much of his adolescence and youth in Berlin before fleeing Nazi Germany (after using a diplomatic passport to help many Jews escape the Hitler regime) and settling in New York.

He frequently toured Chile and other South American countries, however, and was buried in Chillán's Cementerio General.

The Museo Claudio Arrau León (Claudio Arrau 564, tel. 042/433390, www.museoarrau .cl) is open 8:30 A.M.–1 P.M. and 3–7:30 P.M.

THE FERROCARRIL CONSTITUCIÓN

Chile's last operating short-line passenger spur, the Ferrocarril Constitución, owes its shaky existence primarily to state subsidies. Departing Talca early every morning, it's the only Chilean rail line with no parallel highway, as it pauses at many settlements and whistlestops that have no other regular public transport – Colín, Corinto, Curtiduría, González Bastías, Toconey, Pichamán, Forel, Huinganes, and Maquehue – before finally shuddering to a stop at Constitución.

For most of the route, on a narrow one-meter track, the 1961-vintage FerroStaal railbus (the first car is also the locomotive) follows the north bank of the Río Maule. There are several bridges and one tunnel; just before arrival at Constitución, the line crosses to the south bank of the broad Maule estuary.

Most of the passengers are peasants with no other mode of transport; flat-brimmed sombreros, rather than nylon baseball caps, are the headgear of choice. Conversation runs from "look at that pasture" and "look at those melons" to "how are the grapes this year?" as you pass the fields near Talca and proceed between the coast range peaks.

As the train approaches Constitución station, plantations of Monterey pine cover the hillsides – at least where they haven't been clearcut – betraying the importance of the city's main employer, the Celulosa Arauco y Constitucion (Celco) pulp mill. Soon enough, the scent gives it away.

weekdays except Monday, 10:30 A.M.–1 P.M. and 4–7 P.M. Saturday, and 10 A.M.–2 P.M. Sunday. Admission is free.

◖ Escuela México

Now enjoying historical monument status, the Escuela México (Av. O'Higgins 250) probably gets more attention than any other local attraction because of its famous frescos by Mexican muralist David Alfaro Siqueiros and his countryman Xavier Guerrero. The school itself was part of a relief effort by Mexican president Lázaro Cárdenas's government after the 1939 earthquake.

Like other Mexican muralists and many other artists of his time, the outspoken Siqueiros was a Communist. His library murals, collectively titled *Muerte al Invasor* (Death to the Invader), reveal his commitment to the rebel and the underdog. Dedicated to Mexico, the north wall depicts individuals such as Aztec emperor Cuauhtémoc, revolutionary priest Miguel Hidalgo, President Benito Juárez (a Zapotec Indian), 20th-century revolutionary Emiliano Zapata, and President Cárdenas himself—not to mention Spanish conquistador Hernán Cortés. Devoted to Chile, the southern wall features Mapuche leaders Caupolicán, Lautaro, and Galvarino (the latter's bleeding hands amputated on the orders of Pedro de Valdivia, also depicted here), independence hero Bernardo O'Higgins, and reformist president José Manuel Balmaceda, who committed suicide after defeat in the civil war of the 1890s.

Less obviously political, Guerrero's *Hermanos Mexicanos* (Mexican Brothers) fill the library's stairwells and their ceiling with muscular figures symbolizing their country's dedication to the relief effort. Unfortunately, Siqueiros's murals in particular are in serious need of restoration. Though the Escuela México is still a public school, the library is open to the public 10 A.M.–13 P.M. and 3–6 P.M. weekdays; hours are 10 A.M.–6 P.M. on Sundays and holidays. Admission is free.

ENTERTAINMENT

Performing arts events, as well as film showings, take place at the **Teatro Municipal** (18 de Septiembre 590, tel. 042/231048, ext. 334). It also has a gallery for special exhibits, open 9 A.M.–2 P.M. and 3–6 P.M. weekdays.

Cine El Roble (El Roble 770, tel. 042/239022) is a twin-screen cinema in the Plaza El Roble shopping mall.

ACCOMMODATIONS

Well-established **Hospedaje Sonia Seguí** (Itata 288, tel. 042/214879, US$7 pp with breakfast) has a cheerful aspect and a quiet location, but shared baths only. More central, the drab **Claris Hotel** (18 de Septiembre 357, tel. 042/221980, www.clarishotel.net, US$8 pp with shared bath, US$14 s US$22 d with private bath) will do in a pinch. It has recently added WiFi.

Hotel Floresta (18 de Septiembre 278, tel. 042/222253, US$23 s, US$32 d with private bath and breakfast) is a good choice in its range.

Hotel Javiera Carrera (Carrera 481, tel./fax 221175, tel. 042/244360, hotel.javiera. carrera@terra.cl, US$25 s, US$37 d) has tiny rooms and truly claustrophobic showers, but also remarkably attentive staff for an inexpensive hotel.

Quiet despite its busy corner location, **Hotel de la Avenida Express** (Av. O'Higgins 398, tel. 042/430672, www.hoteldelavenida.com, US$38 s, US$45 d) has just eight smallish rooms, but it's almost immaculately kept and offers IVA discounts to foreign tourists. Rates include a forgettable breakfast, WiFi, and parking.

At a busy intersection at the southeast corner of the plaza, family-run **Hotel Cordillera** (Arauco 619, tel. 042/215211, www.hotelcordillera.cl, US$41 s, US$51 d) is a comfortable option that readily grants IVA discounts to foreigners.

Hotel Las Terrazas (Constitución 664, 5th floor, tel. 042/227000, fax 042/227001, www.lasterrazas.cl, US$78 s, US$84 d) is a nice place with a business center; it also operates a slightly cheaper across-the-street annex. Rates fall about 10 percent on weekends.

Facing the plaza, **Gran Hotel Isabel Riquelme** (Arauco 600, tel. 042/213663, www.hotelisabelriquelme.cl, US$79 s, US$95 d) is a traditional favorite; foreigners should ask for IVA discounts.

FOOD

For inexpensive traditional Chilean food, including some of the country's finest *pastel de choclo* in summer and outstanding *pastel de papas* (potato pie) at almost any season, try any of the several simple *cocinerías* in the **Mercado Central,** a rejuvenated landmark on Maipón between 5 de Abril and Isabel Riquelme. If the market's closed, the **Casino Cuerpo de Bomberos** (El Roble and 18 de Septiembre) is a good alternative.

On the pedestrian mall south of the plaza, the **Fuente Alemana** (Arauco 661, tel. 042/212720) specializes in sandwiches and desserts, including decent ice cream.

Two restaurants with different menus occupy the same space at Rosas 392: the pizzería **Ficus** (tel. 042/212176) and the beef-oriented **La Parrillada de Córdoba** (tel. 042/233522).

There are only a handful of upscale restaurants, among them the traditionally elegant **Centro Español** (Arauco 555, tel. 042/216212) and **Kuranepe** (O'Higgins 0420, tel. 042/221409), north of the bus station.

INFORMATION

In summer, the local delegation of **Sernatur** (18 de Septiembre 455, tel./fax 042/223272, infochillan@sernatur.cl) is open 8:30 A.M.–7 P.M. weekdays and 10 A.M.–2 P.M. weekends. The rest of the year, hours are 8:30 A.M.–1 P.M. and 3–6 P.M. weekdays only.

At the train station, a small but helpful private **Centro de Información Turística** (Av. Brasil s/n, tel. 042/244837) is open 11 A.M.–11 P.M. daily.

SERVICES

The main exchange house is **Schüler Cambios** (Constitución 608). **Banco de Crédito** (Av. Libertad 677) and **Banco Concepción**

(Constitución 550), both on the plaza, have ATMs.

Correos de Chile (Libertad 505) is the post office. **Telefónica CTC** (Arauco 625) and **Entel** (Arauco 623) both have call centers on the pedestrian mall. Down the block, **Planet Cybercafé** (Arauco 683, 2nd floor, tel. 042/222797) provides Internet access seven days a week.

Lava Matic (Prat 357-B) handles the washing.

Hospital Herminda Martín (Av. Francisco Ramírez s/n, tel. 043/208000) is six blocks east of the plaza.

GETTING THERE AND AROUND

Chillán has bus service, but as of summer 2009, rail service was temporarily suspended.

Bus

For long-distance services, the main facility is the **Terminal María Teresa** (Av. O'Higgins 010, tel. 042/272149), just north of Avenida Ecuador. A few companies, such as Tur-Bus, also use the dingy **Terminal de Buses Interregionales** (Constitución 01, tel. 042/221014), and several others have ticket offices in the immediate vicinity.

At the Interregionales, **Línea Azul** (tel. 042/211192) goes daily at 8 A.M. to Las Trancas for Termas de Chillán, returning at 6 P.M. For other rural and regional services, try the **Terminal Paseo La Merced** (Maipón 890, tel. 042/223606). **REM Bus** (tel. 042/224087) also goes to Las Trancas.

Typical destinations, fares, and times include Concepción or Los Ángeles (US$2.50, 1.5 hours), Angol or Talca (US$5, 2.5 hours), Temuco (US$8–11, 4 hours), Valdivia (US$11, 7 hours), Puerto Montt (US$19–35, 8 hours), Santiago (US$9–14, 5 hours), and Valparaíso/ Viña del Mar (US$15, 7 hours).

Train

Normally, eight EFE trains daily arrive at and leave from **Estación Chillán** (Av. Brasil s/n, tel. 043/222267), at the west end of

Avenida Libertad; in 2009, though, service was temporarily stopped due to operational problems. EFE trains from Santiago and Temuco (one daily) should also stop here. For more information, visit EFE's website at www.efe.cl.

Car

For rental cars, try **Rent Car** (18 de Septiembre 380, tel. 042/212243, rentacarchillan@edntel-chile.net) or **Econorent** (Av. Brasil s/n, Local 3, tel. 042/229262, www.econorent.cl), at the train station.

Vicinity of Chillán

Chillán's suburbs and surrounding country-side traditionally get little attention except for the Termas de Chillán ski area, but that's changing.

PARQUE MONUMENTAL BERNARDO O'HIGGINS

In Chillán Viejo, a few kilometers southwest of modern Chillán, the outstanding element in this park and museum complex is an impressive tiled mural—60 meters long—depicting scenes from the liberator's life. What works in an artistic context, though, doesn't work in the colonial-style center itself, where the romanticized perspective is misleading—even if illegitimate, the viceroy's son was no rustic.

The park grounds are open 8 A.M.–8 P.M. daily December–March, but close at 6 P.M. the rest of the year; its **Centro Histórico y Cultural** (Av. O'Higgins s/n, tel. 042/201575, cultura@chillanviejo.cl) offers guided tours throughout the day. Admission is free.

VIÑA CHILLÁN

Commercial Chilean wine production occurs almost as far south as Temuco, but only recently have the source of fine wines shifted southward at vineyards such as the Italo-Swiss Viña Chillán, in the Itata Valley south of Chillán. In business only since 1999, it produces standards such as sauvignon blanc and cabernet, but also oddities including a white carmenere (probably not to everyone's taste).

The establishment is open for drop-in tours but, even better, it also serves meals at its cheerfully airy restaurant. However, ownership has recently changed hands, so it's best to contact them before going.

Seven kilometers west of the Panamericana via the Bulnes exit, just west of the village of Tres Esquinas, Viña Chillán (Camino Tres Esquinas s/n, tel. 042/1971573, www.tierray-fuego.cl) also has an appealing six-room guest-house with a swimming pool.

◀ NEVADOS DE CHILLÁN

Southeast of Chillán, campgrounds, cabañas, and country-style restaurants line much of the paved highway to **Valle Las Trancas,** where a gravel road continues through southern beech forests for the last few kilometers to the **Nevados de Chillán Mountain Resort** (tel. 042/206100, www.nevadosdechillan.com), the only southern Chilean ski resort that can match Portillo and Valle Nevado in terms of accommodations and snowfall—while not so far above sea level as its northern counterparts, it enjoys a climate with higher precipitation.

Beneath the slopes of the 3,122-meter Volcán Chillán, at a base elevation of 1,600 meters, ski season extends from mid-June to mid-October. It is also a summer destination, though, thanks to its luxury lodgings and hot springs.

Nevado's de Chillán's 28 separate ski runs range 90–700 meters in vertical drop, and 400–2,500 meters in length. For nonguests, lift tickets cost US$42 per person.

Unaffiliated with Nevados, the adjacent hot springs resort of **Termas de Chillán** offers day use of its heated pools, open all year; a full-day program including lunch costs US$45 for adults, US$35 for kids.

Accommodations and Food

For those who can't afford to stay at the extravagant Hotel Termas de Chillán or its slightly cheaper neighbor, Pirimávida, **Albergue Las Trancas** (Km 73, tel. 042/423718 or 042/244628, hostellinglastrancas@gmail.com, US$11–13 pp in summer) has rooms with 1–6 beds whose prices rise only moderately in ski season. Affiliated with Hostelling International, it's a bargain in this resort area, especially for a hostelry with natural wood decor throughout and a homey fireplace in its restaurant and bar.

Hotel Parador Jamón, Pan y Vino (Km 74, Las Trancas, tel./fax 042/432100, www.paradorjamonpanyvino.cl, US$75 d) offers hotel and cabaña accommodations set among sprawling lawns surrounding a swimming pool and a wading pool. It also has good food.

Also at Las Trancas, in a quiet woodsy setting just off the main highway, **Hotel Robledal** (Km 72.5, tel. 042/214407, www.hotelrobledal.cl, US$80 s, US$90 d with half board) has fine midsized rooms in a building that, despite its prefab exterior, is stylish enough inside. The restaurant has very fine desserts, in particular.

In ski season, weekly accommodations at Termas de Chillán's luxury **Hotel Pirimávida** start at US$750 per person and reach US$1,265 per person, double occupancy with half board; rates include lift tickets and other amenities. Weekly four-to-a-room bunk accommodations range US$600–860 per person with half board, including lift tickets. At the even more sumptuous **Gran Hotel Termas de Chillán,** the range is US$1,450–4,800 per person weekly.

In summer, nightly hotel rates at the Pirimávida start at US$76/134 s/d with full board; the Gran Hotel starts at US$181 s, US$292 d, also with full board. Centro de Ski Termas de Chillán (San Pío X 2460, Providencia, tel. 02/2331313, www.termaschillan.cl) also has a regional office (Panamericana Norte 3651, Chillán, tel. 042/434200).

Meanwhile, the Hotel Nevados de Chillán (tel. 042/206100, www.nevadosdechillan.com, US$68 pp in summer, with full board) has similar ski packages to those of Termas de Chillán, in newer but by no means superior facilities.

Getting There and Around

Termas de Chillán is 82 kilometers east of the city of Chillán. In summer only, the resort offers its own transportation for US$25 per person from the city. From Chillán's Terminal de Buses Interregionales, **Línea Azul** (tel. 042/211192) goes as far as Las Trancas at 8 A.M. daily, returning at 6 P.M.

Concepción

For much of its history, the capital of Region VIII (Biobío) has been Chile's industrial powerhouse, thanks to its navigable river, convenient coal resources, the Huachipato steel plant, and sheltered port of Talcahuano. Fishing and forestry contribute to the regional economy, but the economy suffered a hit with the end of coal mining at nearby Lota. A hoped-for tourism boom is doubtful, but the presence of several universities and upwards of 30,000 students gives it an active cultural life and a cosmopolitan feel, as many foreigners are exchange students here.

HISTORY

For more than three centuries from its founding in 1550, Concepción was a frontier city in a war zone. What Mapuche raiders could not destroy in the Guerra del Arauco, plate tectonics did—after major earthquakes and tsunamis in 1730 and 1751, the city moved to the Valle de la Mocha from its original site at Penco, about 12 kilometers to the north (city residents are still known as *penquistas*).

Spaniards first saw the area in 1544, when Juan Bautista de Pastene and Jerónimo de

THE CHILEAN HEARTLAND

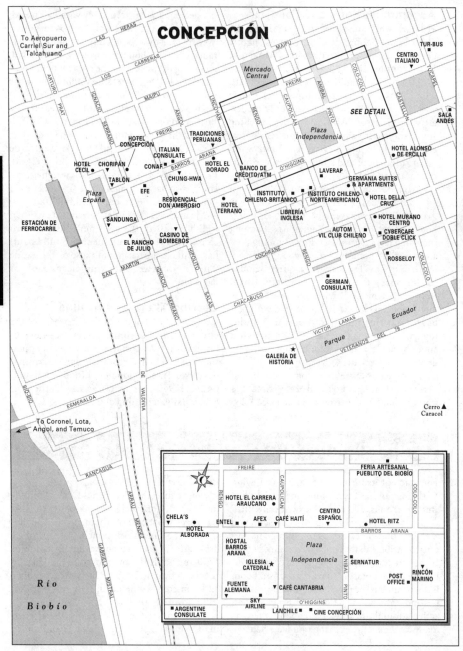

CONCEPCIÓN

To Aeropuerto Carriel Sur and Talcahuano

LAS HERAS
CARRERAS
MAIPU
FREIRE
ANIBAL
COLO-COLO

TUR-BUS
CENTRO ITALIANO

Mercado Central

SALA ANDES

SEE DETAIL

Plaza Independencia

ARTURO PRAT
IGNACIO SERRANO
LINCOYAN
RENGO
CAUPOLICAN
PINTO
CASTELLON
TUCAPEL

HOTEL CONCEPCIÓN
ITALIAN CONSULATE
TRADICIONES PERUANAS
CONAF
BARROS
ARANA
HOTEL EL DORADO
O'HIGGINS
HOTEL ALONSO DE ERCILLA

HOTEL CECIL
CHORIPÁN
TABLÓN
CHUNG-HWA
BANCO DE CRÉDITO/ATM
LAVERAP
GERMANIA SUITES & APARTMENTS

EFE
Plaza España
RESIDENCIAL DON AMBROSIO
HOTEL TERRANO
INSTITUTO CHILENO-BRITÁNICO
INSTITUTO CHILENO-NORTEAMERICANO
HOTEL DELLA CRUZ

SANDUNGA
LIBRERÍA INGLESA
HOTEL MURANO CENTRO
CYBERCAFÉ DOBLE CLICK

ESTACIÓN DE FERROCARRIL
EL RANCHO DE JULIO
CASINO DE BOMBEROS
AUTOM VIL CLUB CHILENO
ROSSELOT

SAN MARTIN
IGNACIO SERRANO
HIPOLITO
SALAS
COCHRANE
RENGO
COLO-COLO

GERMAN CONSULATE

CHACABUCO

VICTOR LAMAS
Parque Ecuador
VETERANOS DEL 79

BIOBÍO
ESMERALDA
P. DE VALDIVIA

GALERÍA DE HISTORIA

Cerro Caracol

To Coronel, Lota, Angol, and Temuco

RANCAGUA
ARRAU MENDEZ
GABRIELA MISTRAL

Río Biobío

FREIRE
FERIA ARTESANAL PUEBLITO DEL BIOBÍO

RENGO
CAUPOLICAN
COLO-COLO

HOTEL EL CARRERA ARAUCANO
CENTRO ESPAÑOL

CHELA'S
ENTEL
AFEX
CAFÉ HAITÍ
HOTEL RITZ

HOTEL ALBORADA
BARROS ARANA

HOSTAL BARROS ARANA
Plaza Independencia
SERNATUR

IGLESIA CATEDRAL
ANIBAL
PINTO

FUENTE ALEMANA
CAFÉ CANTABRIA
POST OFFICE
RINCÓN MARINO

SKY AIRLINE
O'HIGGINS

ARGENTINE CONSULATE
LANCHILE
CINE CONCEPCIÓN

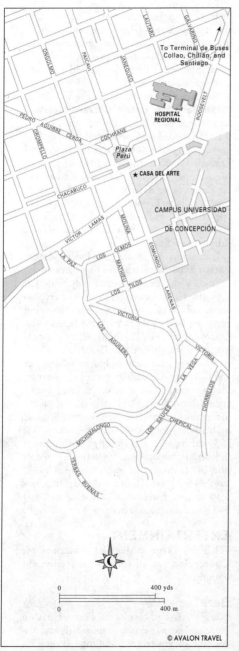

LAUTARO
GALVARINO
ONGOLMO
PAICAVI
JANEQUEO
To Terminal de Buses
Collao, Chillán, and
Santiago
ROOSEVELT
PEDRO AGUIRRE CERDA
OROMBELLO
COCHRANE
HOSPITAL
REGIONAL
Plaza
Perú
★ CASA DEL ARTE
CHACABUCO
CAMPUS UNIVERSIDAD
DE CONCEPCIÓN
VICTOR LAMAS
MOLINA
LA PAZ
LOS OLMOS
MATHIEU
EDMUNDO
LOS TILOS
LOS
LARENAS
VICTORIA
LOS AGUILERA
VICTORIA
LA VEGA
CHORRILLOS
LOS SAUCES
CHEPICAL
MICHIMALONGO
YERBAS BUENAS
0   400 yds
0   400 m
© AVALON TRAVEL

Alderete sailed up the Biobío. Pedro de Valdivia made it here in 1550, founding Concepción de María Purísima del Nuevo Extremo at the southeast corner of the Bahía de Concepción, a sheltered harbor formed by the Península de Tumbes.

The move did not end the city's vulnerability to earthquakes, as its tiled adobe construction fell well short of seismic safety standards. When Darwin visited the city after an 1835 tsunami, he found:

> ...the whole coast being strewed over with timber and furniture as if a thousand ships had been wrecked. Besides chairs, tables, book-shelves etc. in great numbers, there were several roofs of cottages, which had been transported almost whole. The storehouses at Talcahuano had been burst open, and great bags of cotton, yerba, and other valuable merchandise were scattered on the shore.

Concepción remained remote from the rest of Chile until the railroad arrived in 1872; by that time it had developed its own industrial base and identity, thanks partly to the presence of undersea lignite seams at Lota. When the Mapuche wars finally ended in the 1880s, the railroad bridged the Biobío and the city became a gateway to the southern lake district.

Midway between Concepción and Talcahuano, the Huachipato steel plant helped revive prosperity after World War II, but the catastrophic 1960 earthquake, combined with the exhaustion of Lota's coal deposits, began a gradual economic decline from which the area has only partly recovered. The militant local labor movement and even more militant university community helped Salvador Allende and the Unidad Popular to power in 1970 and suffered heavy repression during the subsequent Pinochet dictatorship.

ORIENTATION

On the navigable Biobío's north bank, Concepción is 519 kilometers south of Santiago via the Panamericana and Ruta

THE CHILEAN HEARTLAND

152 from Chillán, and 287 kilometers north of Temuco via the Panamericana and Ruta 180 from Collipulli and Angol. It is part of a sprawling urban area that includes the port of Talcahuano, 15 kilometers northwest on the Bahía de Concepción; Penco, to the northeast at the other end of Bahía de Concepción; and San Pedro, connected by several bridges across the Biobío.

Plaza Independencia is the focus of Concepción's central grid, which trends northeast–southwest. Southeast of the plaza, Parque Ecuador and the 256-meter summit of Cerro Caracol mark the edge of the downtown area, while the riverfront to the southwest is the subject of ambitious redevelopment plans.

SIGHTS

Concepción's repeated earthquakes have leveled nearly all its colonial structures—the last remaining one is the **Muro de la Merced,** a crumbling convent wall on Castellón between Maipú and Freire that's a national monument.

Surrounded by architecturally drab but seismically sensible buildings such as the **Catedral de la Santísima Concepción, Plaza Independencia** is still the city's heart. Its centerpiece is the **Pileta de la Plaza,** a fountain originally planned in 1750 but unfinished until 1856. Lavishly landscaped, the plaza serves as a stage for mimes, musicians, and other street performers. The Barros Arana and Aníbal Pinto *peatonales* encourage foot traffic; west of the plaza, Barros Arana's widened sidewalks still allow one lane of automobile traffic.

Southwest of Plaza Independencia, where Barros Arana intersects Arturo Prat, the **Barrio Estación** is an area of trendy pubs and restaurants on and around **Plaza España.** A new railroad station has replaced the former **Estación de Ferrocarril** (1941–1943), notable for the columns on its facade, the work of modernist architect Luis Herreros; the former station's waiting room features Gregorio de la Fuente's spectacular mural *Latidos y Rutas de Concepción,* depicting scenes from pre-Hispanic regional history, the Araucanian wars, Chilean rural society, the mining industry, and its manufacturing offshoots. They also show the natural disasters—earthquakes, fires, and tsunamis—that have devastated the city throughout its history.

Northeast of downtown, in the vicinity of **Plaza Perú,** the **Barrio Universitario** enjoys a vigorous cultural and student life. On the Universidad de Concepción campus, the university's **Casa del Arte** (Chacabuco and Eduardo Larenas, tel. 041/2204126) features Mexican muralist Jorge González Camarena's *La Presencia de América Latina,* along with smaller galleries of portraits and landscapes. It's open Tuesday–Friday 10 A.M.–6 P.M., Saturday 10 A.M.–4 P.M., and Sunday 10 A.M.–1 P.M. Admission is free.

Four blocks southeast of Plaza Independencia, **Parque Ecuador** stretches for nine blocks along Avenida Víctor Lamas; immediately behind it, the Cerro Caracol's woodsy summit offers panoramas of the city. At the park's southwestern edge, the **Galería de la Historia** (Lamas and Lincoyán, tel. 041/2231830) relates regional history through Rodolfo Gutiérrez's dioramas of pre-Columbian Mapuche subsistence and their post-Columbian guerrilla resistance, the garrison origins of Spanish colonial society at nearby Penco, negotiations between the indigenous nation and the invaders, Spanish soldier-poet Alonso de Ercilla, the catastrophic 1939 earthquake, and the city's 20th-century industrial development. Unchanged since its mid-1980s debut, the gallery is open weekdays 3–6:30 P.M., Tuesday–Friday 10 A.M.–1:30 P.M., and weekends 10 A.M.–2 P.M. and 3–7 P.M. Admission is free.

ENTERTAINMENT

With its large university community, Concepción has all sorts of entertainment options.

Bars

Many watering holes in the Barrio Estación come and go; of a dozen or more bars and discos, the survivors are **Sandunga** (Prat 438, tel. 041/2935504), **Tablón** (Prat 528), and **Choripán** (Prat 546, tel. 041/2253004).

Cinema
Downtown's **Cine Concepción** (O'Higgins 650, tel. 041/2227193) also hosts live performances.

Several binational cultural centers also show occasional films: the **Instituto Chileno-Norteamericano** (Caupolicán 315, tel. 041/2225506), the **Instituto Chileno-Británico** (San Martín 531, tel. 041/2242300), and the **Instituto Chileno-Español** (San Martín 450, 2nd floor, tel. 041/2244573).

Performing Arts
Downtown's **Teatro Concepción** (O'Higgins 650, tel. 041/2227193) hosts live theater and music as well as movies. Other venues include the **Sala Andes** (Tucapel 374, tel. 041/2227264) and the Barrio Universitario's **Casa del Arte** (Chacabuco and Larenas, tel. 041/2234985).

Spectator Sports
Concepción's first-division soccer team is the Universidad de Concepción, which plays at **Estadio Collao,** on Avenida General Bonilla near the Terminal de Buses Collao (Puchacay).

EVENTS
Lasting two weeks in mid-January, Parque Ecuador's **Feria Internacional de Arte Popular** (International People's Art Festival) has drawn artists and artisans from as far away as Russia, Egypt, and Senegal. In early October, the weeklong **Fiesta de la Primavera** (Festival of Spring) celebrates the city's founding in 1550.

SHOPPING
For handicrafts, from basketry and ceramics to woolen goods and leather, try the **Mercado Central,** fronting on Caupolicán between Maipú and Freire, or the **Feria Artesanal Pueblito del Biobío** (Freire 755).

The **Librería Inglesa** (San Martín 585,

Local 21, tel. 041/2232887) sells English-language titles.

ACCOMMODATIONS
Concepción has only a handful of good budget accommodations, a greater number of midrange options, and good but relatively expensive places that focus on business travelers. Because of the city's business orientation, prices have very little seasonal variation.

US$10-25
Close to the Barrio Estación restaurant and entertainment district, in a rambling labyrinth of a building, most rooms at **Residencial Don Ambrosio** (Salas 452, tel. 041/2951096, oliviadecastro@hotmail.com, US$10 pp–US$17 s, US$25 d) are spacious, and even the small but otherwise adequate singles have private baths; breakfast costs extra.

Across from the railroad station, the 1938 landmark **Hotel Cecil** (Barros Arana 9, tel. 041/2739981, santamariaclaramuntja001@chilnet.cl, US$20 s, US$23 d with private bath and breakfast) has cleaned up its exterior with a fresh paint job, but a sore-thumb mansard has destroyed its deco integrity. The interior upgrade is lagging a bit.

US$25-50
On the *peatonal* near Plaza Independencia, **Hotel Ritz** (Barros Arana 721, tel. 041/2226696, www.hotelritz.cl, US$27 s, US$35 d with breakfast) has simple but renovated rooms with private baths. It also offers a late checkout of 2 P.M. with no additional charge.

Looking better at street level than it does upstairs, **Hostal Barros Arana** (Barros Arana 521, tel. 041/2254207, residencialcolocolo@hotmail.com, US$27 s, US$40 d) has some small rooms with two beds so close together that it requires you to shuffle sideways between them. Each room, though, has a private bath, and by city standards it's decent value for the price.

Also on the mall, just a few doors away, **Hotel Bío Bío** (Barros Arana 751, tel. 041/2223212, casaorellana@surnet.cl, US$27–35 s, US$35–45 d with breakfast) occupies the upstairs interior of a gallery building; this means that some rooms of this older hotel are dark, but they're also sheltered from street noise. Rates vary for medium-sized "B" rooms, with shared baths and including breakfast, and "A" rooms with private baths, but can be lower with discounts.

Increasingly worn around the edges, all rooms at the cheerful but cramped **Hotel della Cruz** (Aníbal Pinto 240, tel./fax 041/2240016, US$38 s, US$48 d with breakfast) have private baths, and there's ample parking. The WiFi is erratic.

US$50-100

Hotel Concepción (Serrano 512, tel. 041/2620851, hotelconcepcion@entelchile.net, US$45 s, US$55 d with breakfast) is decent but unremarkable.

Room sizes vary dramatically at **Hotel Murano Centro** (Aníbal Pinto 180, tel. 041/2936825, www.hotelmurano.cl, US$25–45, US$56 d). The lower rates correspond to 4th-floor rooms, reached by a narrow spiral staircase, with shared bath. It has friendly and efficient service; amenities include an unremarkable breakfast, WiFi, and limited parking.

Only a short stroll from the plaza, the modern **Hotel Alonso de Ercilla** (Colo Colo 334, tel. 041/2227984, www.hotelalonsodeercilla.co.cl, US$43–55 s, US$55–65 d with breakfast) has comfortable but undistinguished rooms with private baths, cable TV, WiFi, covered parking, and responsive service. The lower rates correspond to tiny "B" singles, but even those have recently modernized baths.

Friendly **Hotel El Dorado** (Barros Arana 348, tel. 041/2229400, www.hoteleldorado.cl, US$59 s, US$68 d) is a contemporary downtown hotel. Business-oriented **Hotel Alborada** (Barros Arana 457, tel. 041/2911121, www.hotelalborada.cl, US$72 s, US$80 d with buffet breakfast) is a smartly kept and managed place.

The also business-oriented **Hotel Terrano** (O'Higgins 340, tel./fax 041/2240078, www.hotelterrano.cl, US$69 s, US$85 d with breakfast) has a good gym and sauna access. **Germania Suites & Apartments** (Aníbal Pinto 295, tel. 041/2747000, www.hotelgermania.cl, US$80 s, US$86 d) is an upgraded hotel for business-oriented visitors, but also has apartments suitable for families.

More than US$100

Hotel Carrera Araucano (Caupolicán 521, tel. 041/2740606, www.hotelaraucano.cl, US$97 s, US$116 d) is a central highrise with nonsmoking rooms and all of the traditional business amenities; rates include an airport pickup.

FOOD

For typical Chilean food such as *pastel de papas* and *pastel de choclo,* at bargain basement prices, try the sit-down *cocinerías* at the cavernous (3,600-square-meter) **Mercado Central** (Caupolicán s/n), two blocks west of Plaza Independencia.

Only slightly more formal, the **Casino de Bomberos** (Salas 347, tel. 041/2227535) is a reliable choice that can be found throughout the country, including in Concepción. **Chela's** (Barros Arana 405, tel. 041/2243367) serves Chilean dishes as well as sandwiches and desserts.

The **Fuente Alemana** (O'Higgins 513, tel. 041/2228307) is comparable to Chela's, but with a wider selection of kuchen and cold beer on tap. Once the only choice for espresso drinks, **Café Haití** (Caupolicán 511, Local 7, tel. 041/2230755) serves sandwiches in addition to coffee drinks. In recent years, Concepción's widened sidewalks have sprouted more sidewalk cafés such as **Café Cantabria** (Caupolicán 415, 041/2252693).

Concepción's Spanish and Italian communities have downtown club restaurants at the **Centro Español** (Barros Arana 675, tel. 041/2230685) and the **Centro Italiano** (Barros Arana 935, 2nd floor, tel. 041/2230724).

Argentine-owned **El Rancho de Julio** (O'Higgins 36, tel. 041/2239976) comes closer to the Argentine experience in ambience and quality—the beef dishes, although pricier than at most of its competitors, are well worth a try. **Rincón Marino** (Colo Colo 486, tel. 041/2230311) is a seafood locale where beef, though available, is secondary.

It doesn't look like much from outside—the illuminated store-width plastic sign doesn't help—but the ceviche at the Peruvian █ **Tradiciones Peruanas** (Barros Arana 337, tel. 041/2799140) is to die for. Dine early to try the *ají de gallina* (US$7), as this popular dish can run out early.

Café Rometsch (Barros Arana 685, tel. 041/2747040) has some of Chile's finest ice cream with flavors, such as chocolate almond and white chocolate, that are hard to find outside the capital.

INFORMATION

Sernatur (Aníbal Pinto 460, tel. 041/2741337, infobiobio@sernatur.cl) has upgraded its regional office. In summer, it's open 8:30 A.M.–8 P.M. weekdays and 10 A.M.–4 P.M. Saturday; the rest of the year, hours are 8:30 A.M.–1:30 P.M. and 3–6 P.M. weekdays only.

Concepción has several foreign **consulates,** most notably neighboring Argentina (O'Higgins 420, Oficina 82, tel. 041/2230257), Germany (Chacabuco 556, tel. 041/2730744), Italy (Barros Arana 243, 2nd floor, tel. 041/2229506), and Spain (Barros Arana 675, tel. 041/2224249).

For motorists, the **Automóvil Club de Chile** (Acchi, Aníbal Pinto 143, tel. 041/2259038) can help with information.

While Region VIII has relatively few protected areas, **Conaf** (Barros Arana 215, tel. 041/2220094) is happy to handle inquiries.

SERVICES

Afex (Barros Arana 565, Local 57) changes cash and travelers' checks. **Banco de Crédito** (O'Higgins 399) is one of several downtown banks with ATMs.

Correos de Chile (O'Higgins 799) is the post office. **Entel** (Barros Arana 541, Local 2)

is the best call center. **Ciberc@fe Doble Click** (Chacabuco 707, tel. 041/2210458) has shown staying power, but there are many other Internet options.

Laverap (Caupolicán 334) washes the clothes.

The **Hospital Regional** (San Martín and Av. Roosevelt, tel. 041/2237445) is eight blocks northeast of Plaza Independencia.

GETTING THERE
Air

Aeropuerto Internacional Carriel Sur (Jorge Alessandri 5001, tel. 041/2732000) is five kilometers northwest of downtown on the Talcahuano road.

LAN (O'Higgins 648, tel. 600/5262000) averages three to four flights per day to Santiago. It flies less frequently to Temuco and Puerto Montt, and to Valdivia.

Sky Airline (O'Higgins 537, tel. 041/2218941) flies north to Santiago and, on occasion, south to Puerto Montt.

Bus

Most long-distance buses use the **Terminal de Buses Collao** (Tegualda 860, tel. 041/2749000), near the soccer stadium on Avenida General Bonilla (Ruta 148), the old Chillán toll road; unless otherwise detailed, buses leave from this terminal, which is also known as Terminal Puchacay. All companies except **Tur-Bus** (Tucapel 530, tel. 041/2237409) have closed their downtown ticket offices.

Destinations, fares, and times include Chillán or Los Ángeles (US$3.50, 1.5 hours), Angol (US$5, 2 hours), Talca (US$7, 4 hours), Temuco (US$10, 4 hours), Valdivia (US$13, 6 hours), Puerto Montt (US$18–31, 10 hours), Santiago (US$13–18, 6 hours), and Valparaíso/Viña del Mar (US$17–26, 9 hours).

From **Terminal Jota Ewert** (Lincoyán and Manuel Rodríguez, tel. 041/2229212), southbound buses go to the Costa del Carbón cities of Arauco, Lebu, Cañete, Tirúa, and Contulmo.

Train
As of writing, rail service was temporarily suspended, but **EFE** maintains a local ticket office (Barros Arana 164, tel. 041/2226925). For the most current information, visit www.efe.cl.

GETTING AROUND
To the Airport
Airport Service (cel. 09/7862-8762) provides door-to-door service to Carriel Sur for about US$8 per person.

To the Bus Terminal
From downtown Concepción, both buses and *taxi colectivos* go to Terminal Collao (Puchacay) via Calle San Martín; to Terminal Chillancito, they leave from the corner of Maipú and Rengo or Barros Arana.

Car Rental
Rental agencies include **Hertz** (Prat 248, tel. 041/2797461, **Avis** (Salas 29, tel. 041/2887420), and **Rosselot** (Chacabuco 726, tel. 041/2732030).

Vicinity of Concepción

Concepción is not a tourism hotbed, but most nearby attractions are accessible by public transportation. **Esquerré Tour Operador** (Barros Arana 185, tel. 041/2749920, www.turismoesquerre.cl) arranges tours and activities nearby.

TALCAHUANO
Fifteen kilometers northwest of Concepción, Talcahuano is the city's main port and the site of the Segunda Zona Naval, one of Chile's largest naval bases. For Chilean nationalists, it's the harbor of the **Museo Huáscar,** a floating museum dedicated to naval icon Arturo Prat.

In his assault in Iquique Harbor on May 21, 1879, Prat died on board the *Huáscar,* a British-built ironclad, captured from the Peruvian navy at the battle of Angamos less than three weeks later. Today, anchored at Talcahuano, *Huáscar* is the mummy of maritime museums, a monument on which naval conscripts, under their officers' stifling oversight, bestow the same attention that Soviet morticians did on Lenin's cadaver.

From Calle San Martín in downtown Concepción, buses with "Base Naval" placards go to the Puerta los Leones gate at the end of Avenida Villaroel. You leave your passport at the gate; small launches shuttle from the jetty to the ship. Photographing the *Huáscar* is permitted, but this does not apply to other naval

ships or the base itself. The Museo Huáscar (tel. 041/2745715) is open 9:30 A.M.–noon and 2–5 P.M. daily except Monday. Admission is US$1.50 for adults, US$0.75 for children.

MUSEO FUNDO HUALPÉN (PARQUE PEDRO DEL RÍO ZAÑARTU)
At the mouth of the Biobío, 18 kilometers west of Concepción, businessman, farmer, whaler, nitrate baron, and writer Pedro del Río Zañartu (1840–1918) inhabited this late-19th-century mansion, set among extensive grounds planted with native and foreign trees and crisscrossed by numerous footpaths (Del Río stipulated in his will that no tree be removed, only pruned).

A chronic globetrotter, Del Río circled the world four times before his death, when he left his travel mementos—not to mention Hualpén and its grounds—to the city of Concepción. Opened to the public as a museum in 1938, it remains partly as it did when Del Río lived here, with information on his voyages and family history, plus bedrooms, a dining room, and a music conservatory with period furniture. Visibly warping because of deferred maintenance, the house encloses a central patio, but a sunny east- and north-facing gallery runs around part of the exterior.

In addition, several exhibit rooms show

off his eclectic assortment of artifacts from Europe, the Near East, ancient Egypt (including a mummy), the Far East, Chile, and Easter Island, along with 18th-century weapons, religious icons, and materials on American ethnology, history, and folklore. The grounds extend to the coast, where there's a small island and several guano-covered rocks.

Museo Hualpén (tel. 041/2426399) is open daily except Monday 9 A.M.–5:30 P.M. Museum and park admission are free, but there is a cost of US$2.50 for parking.

Food
At the mouth of the river, the **Casino Club de Caza y Pesca** (cel. 09/9442-0921 or 09/9828-2737) offers ample, simply prepared fish dishes in the US$7–8 range. The club, too, is part of Del Río's legacy—the area was to be left open for hunting and fishing, though there can't be much game left on the periphery of an urban area of more than half a million people.

Getting There and Around
No regular public transportation reaches Hualpén except on summer Sundays, when Flota Centauro leaves from downtown Concepción's Calle Freire. Otherwise, Concepción city buses to Avenida Las Golondrinas go within a few kilometers of the entrance, where a cab is the best alternative.

LOTA
Across the Biobío from Concepción, Lota's lignite seams have given their cachet to the Costa del Carbón (Coast of Coal), a string of towns that once relied on this regionally rare fossil fuel for their livelihood (in the entire Southern Cone, the only other coal deposits are at Peket, near Punta Arenas, and Río Turbio, in the Argentine province of Santa Cruz). Today, undergoing a difficult transition from an entrenched mining culture, this is one of Chile's most economically depressed areas—with high unemployment and poverty rates.

Nevertheless, the coast is a popular weekend destination for working-class beachgoers. For foreign visitors, the towns of Coronel and Lota,

with their company town architecture, Mina Chiflón's sloping coal shafts, and the remarkable Parque de Lota, are the major points of interest. Lota has its own informative website (www.lotasorprendente.cl).

Parque de Lota Isidora Cousiño
In the mid-19th century at Lota, 30 kilometers south of Concepción, mining magnate Matías Cousiño began to transform a 14-hectare headland into a lavish garden that his daughter-in-law, Isidora Goyenechea, would finally complete after the deaths of both her father-in-law and his son, Luis Cousiño. British landscapers designed the flowered and wooded grounds and studded them with neoclassical statues of figures such as Neptune, Venus, and Diana the Huntress, plus, incongruously, the Mapuche warrior Caupolicán. The tomb of Matías Cousiño's son (and Luis's brother) Carlos Cousiño is also found here.

One of the area's biggest attractions, Parque Cousiño (Av. del Parque s/n, tel. 041/2871549) is open 9 A.M.–6 P.M. daily except Monday; in summer it's open until 8 P.M. every day of the week. Now operated by the private Fundación Chile, it charges US$2.50 admission for adults, US$2 for kids. Guides in 19th-century dress, known as Isidoras after the founding family's matriarch, lead tours around the park.

Mina Chiflón Carlos
Adjacent to Parque de Lota, Mina Chiflón Carlos (El Morro, Barrio Arturo, tel. 041/2871565) offers the opportunity to descend into the pits beneath the sea as local miners once did. Guided by former miners themselves, visits (US$7 pp) take place 9 A.M.–8 P.M. daily November–March, 9 A.M.–6 P.M. the rest of the year.

CAÑETE
About 97 kilometers south of Lota via Ruta 160, Cañete is the site of the improved **Museo Mapuche de Cañete Juan Antonio Ríos Morales** (tel. 041/2611093, www.museomapuchecanete.cl), which provides a good cartographic introduction to the region's indigenous

geography, along with displays on subsistence activities, mortuary customs, and silverwork and other art. Directly on the highway, the museum is open 9:30 A.M.–7 P.M. weekdays, 11 A.M.–7 P.M. weekends, in summer. The rest of the year, hours are Tuesday–Friday 9:30 A.M.–5:50 P.M., Saturday 11 A.M.–6 P.M., and Sunday 1:30–6:30 P.M. Admission costs US$1 for adults, US$0.50 for kids or seniors.

MONUMENTO NATURAL CONTULMO

One of Conaf's smallest protected areas, 38 kilometers southeast of Cañete, Contulmo's native forest occupies 82 hectares of a rugged southerly spur of the Cordillera de Nahuelbuta, directly contiguous to the paved highway to Angol. Barely half a kilometer across at its widest, it still boasts a 3.2-kilometer loop trail through verdant moist forest (the park gets nearly two meters of rainfall per year), punctuated with tree ferns whose fronds reach two meters or more in height. Contulmo has an information center and a picnic ground, but no camping; admission fee is US$2.50 for adults, US$1.25 for children.

LOS ÁNGELES

A farm-and-forestry town with few attractions in its own right, the city of Los Ángeles is strategically located for access to the coast range, the upper Biobío, and Parque Nacional Laguna del Laja, in the Andes to the east. It was also strategically located when, in 1739, it was founded as a military outpost against the Mapuche.

Less than a decade later, in 1748, it received official recognition from Chilean governor José Antonio Manso de Velasco as Villa de Nuestra Señora de Los Ángeles de la Alta Frontera del Reino de Chile. The city began to prosper with the railroad's arrival in 1875, but it has a distinct contemporary aspect, as major public buildings date from the 1940s. It has recently acquired a massive new casino, with a highrise hotel due to open alongside it.

Orientation

Los Ángeles (population 123,445) is 517 kilometers south of Santiago and 110 kilometers south of Chillán via the Panamericana; it is 162 kilometers north of Temuco, also via the Panamericana. Most major public buildings surround the handsomely renovated Plaza de Armas, bounded by Lautaro, Valdivia, Caupolicán, and Colón. Most businesses and services are on or near Colón, from the plaza north.

Museo de la Alta Frontera

Except for an extraordinary assortment of traditional Mapuche silverwork—unfortunately, it lacks space to display all 600 pieces in the collection—Los Ángeles's municipal museum would be truly mediocre. Even then, the lack of text accompanying the artwork makes it seem more like a jewelry store before the price tags have been affixed, but, as it's rare to see this much quality jewelry in one place, it's well worth a detour from the Panamericana.

The museum (Colón 195, 2nd floor, tel. 043/408641) is open 8:15 A.M.–1:45 P.M. and 2:45–6:30 P.M. weekdays only. Admission is free.

Accommodations

Ilo's Residencial (Rengo 459, tel. 043/630398, US$13) is probably the best of the cheapest, with shared bath only. **Hotel Océano** (Colo Colo 327, tel. 043/342432, hoteloceanola@hotmail.com, US$17–39 pp) has rooms with either shared or private baths; some of the private baths, though, are separate from the room proper.

On the west side of the Plaza de Armas, **Gran Hotel Müso** (Valdivia 222, tel. 043/313183, www.hotelmuso.cl, US$56 s, US$74 d) is a business-oriented hotel that offers discounts up to 25 percent off these rack rates for payment in cash—a better bargain than the usual IVA discounts. Just off the plaza, **Hotel Mariscal Alcázar** (Lautaro 385, tel. 043/311725, www.hotelalcazar.cl, US$75 s, US$93 d) has 60 renovated rooms, the quieter of which face the interior garden and a well-regarded restaurant.

Food

Two blocks south of the plaza, the **Casino Cuerpo de Bomberos** (O'Higgins 119) is almost always a good bet for reasonable lunches and dinners. The German-run **Tu Café** (Colo Colo 378, tel. 043/325814) has both good coffee and European-style pastries. **Julio's Pizza** (Colón 452, tel. 043/314530) serves pasta as well. The **Centro Español** (Colón 482, tel. 043/311669) is a traditional club-style restaurant. Likewise, the **Club de la Unión** (Colón 261, tel. 043/322218) has prix-fixe lunches and dinners for US$7–10.

El Alero (Colo Colo 235, tel. 043/312899) is a *parrilla* (grill), while **Donde Anitamaría** (Colón 782, tel. 043/315812) specializes in seafood.

Information

The municipal **Oficina de Información Turística** (Colón 195, tel. 043/408641, cbravo@losangeles.cl), on the 2nd floor of the museum, is open 8 A.M.–1:45 P.M. and 3–5 P.M. weekdays only, except for Friday, when it closes an hour earlier. In summer, it operates a separate kiosk (tel. 043/310886) on the Plaza de Armas, open 10:30 A.M.–1 P.M. and 3–7 P.M. weekdays only.

Conaf (José Manso de Velasco 275, tel. 043/322126) has national parks information.

Services

Inter-Bruna (Caupolicán 350, tel. 043/313812, www.interbruna.cl) is a reliable travel agency that also changes money; **Banco de Chile** (Colón 299) and several other banks have ATMs.

Correos de Chile (Caupolicán 464), the post office, is on the south side of the Plaza de Armas. **Entel** (Colo Colo 489, Local 1) has a long-distance telephone center, while the nearly adjacent **Cibertel** (Colo Colo 489, Local 4) provides Internet access until midnight.

The **Hospital Regional** (Av. Ricardo Vicuña 147, tel. 043/321456 or 043/409720) handles medical matters.

Getting There and Around

Most long-distance buses use the modern **Terminal Rodoviario** (Av. Sor Vicente 2051), northeast of downtown via Avenida Villagrán. **Tur-Bus** (Av. Sor Vicenta 2061, tel. 043/315610) has a separate terminal next door.

From Terminal Santa Rita (Villagrán and Rengo), **ERS** goes to Antuco, near the entrance to Parque Nacional Laguna del Laja, six times daily on weekends, three times each weekday. Other rural services leave from the Terminal Vega Techada (Villagrán and Tucapel).

Sample destinations, fares, and times include Angol (US$2.50, 1 hour), Chillán (US$3, 1.5 hours), Temuco (US$7, 3 hours), Puerto Montt (US$13, 8 hours), and Santiago (US$15, 8 hours).

Inter-Bruna (Caupolicán 350, tel. 043/313812) rents vehicles.

VICINITY OF LOS ÁNGELES

Los Ángeles is centrally located for excursions to several protected areas, including Parque Nacional Laguna del Laja and Parque Nacional Nahuelbuta (though the latter is closer to Angol). The waterfall at Salto del Laja is a traditional Chilean holiday destination, while a couple of rural accommodations are destinations in themselves.

German-run El Rincón does tours in and around the area, as does Kumbre Turismo Aventura (cel. 09/9460-5103 or 09/9720-4393, www.kumbre.cl).

El Rincón

On two hectares of secluded riverside property 15 kilometers north of Los Ángeles, El Rincón is not so much a place to stay as a destination in itself, where guests remain several days to relax among densely wooded grounds studded with fruit trees, complemented by vegetable and flower gardens. At night the only sounds are wind in the trees and a low traffic hum from the Panamericana.

THE CHILEAN HEARTLAND

Lodging at the B&B costs US$16–30 per person in four cozy double rooms (two of which have private baths) in the main accommodations; there is one single with shared bath. A separate cabaña holds up to six people for US$68. Rates include an abundant breakfast; there's no lunch service, but excellent dinners (US$20 pp) take place on the patio or in the main house's dining room; the food is fresh, diverse, and filling, and the wine is reasonably priced. There's a large German-language library and a smaller book exchange (mostly in English).

El Rincón (Ruta 5, Km 494, cel. 09/9441-5019, 09/9082-3168, www.elrinconchile.cl) is reached from the Perales exit off the Panamericana Norte. It's a couple kilometers farther east via a gravel road (follow the sign toward El Olivo) and a private dirt road, but owners Winfried and Elke Lohmar can arrange pickups at the highway, or in Los Ángeles. English, Spanish, and German are spoken.

The Lohmars also offer Spanish lessons costing US$350 weekly per person, minimum two people, with room and full board; there is a US$120 single supplement. They also offer full-day excursions (US$110 pp for up to four persons) to Parque Nacional Laguna del Laja, Parque Nacional Nahuelbuta, and Concepción and vicinity. Ask for copies of their excellent informational brochures on the geology of Laguna del Laja and Nahuelbuta, in Spanish, English, and German.

Salto del Laja

With its kitschy clutter of campgrounds, cabañas, hotels, and souvenir stands, Salto del Laja is Chile's mini-Niagara. After descending from the Andes, the Río Laja drops more than 50 meters over a broad escarpment before flowing on toward its confluence with the Biobío at La Laja, 40 kilometers west. Like Niagara, though, Salto del Laja is vulnerable to irregular releases from upper drainage reservoirs, and power needs may or may not coincide with tourists' desire to view the spectacle. In dry years, the flow can slow to a trickle.

One positive development is the relocation of the Panamericana, now a four-lane divided toll road, to the west. No longer do long-distance buses, overloaded 18-wheelers, and speeding SUVs clog the former Panamericana, a two-lane road that bridges the river—though walking in the middle of it is still inadvisable. The falls are close enough to the highway that, when the water's high, it justifies a brief stopover—but not an overnight stay.

Fundo Curanilahue

Part of a growing trend toward rural tourism, this Anglo-Chilean property is a 500-hectare *fundo* that specializes in wheat and sugar beets, but it also raises beef and dairy cattle, and alfalfa to feed them. While not a dude ranch in the North American sense—guests are not expected to participate in farm activities—it does offer garden cabañas with fireplaces and private baths, and diverse recreational options both on and off the farm.

Open mid-November to mid-March, accommodations cost US$160 per person with full board, including wine, aperitifs, beer, and soft drinks. Most of the food comes from Curanilahue's own organic gardens. Basic rates also include horseback riding through its eucalupytus and pine plantations, swimming in the heated pool, laundry service, access to tennis, and motorboat excursions up the Río Laja.

Curanilahue also arranges excursions into the Andean backcountry and the coast range, including day trips to Parque Nacional Laguna del Laja, Parque Nacional Nahuelbuta, or Termas de Chillán (US$100 per group), and the Laja Golf Club or the Chillán market (US$80 per group). Transfers to or from the Concepción airport cost US$80; transfers to or from the Temuco airport are US$100.

Reached by a turnoff from the Panamericana a few kilometers north of Salto del Laja and a gravel road that leads east from the Carabineros police station through the hamlet of Chillancito, Curanilahue is open all year, but reservations are essential. For more information, contact John or Louisa Jackson at Fundo Curanilahue (Casilla 1165, Los Ángeles,

tel. 043/1972819, 043/1972829, www.cura-
nilahue.com, louisamayhew@gmail.com).

PARQUE NACIONAL LAGUNA DEL LAJA

Barren can be beautiful, and Laguna del Laja's
harsh volcanic landscape proves it's so. The
park's centerpiece Volcán Antuco is actually a
volcano within a volcano, rising from the caldera that exploded cataclysmically about 6,000
years ago. Though its last major eruption was
in 1869, Antuco has been one of Chile's most
active volcanoes, with 11 separate episodes
in the 19th century. When Darwin visited
Concepción a couple of weeks after the calamitous earthquake and tsunami of 1835, he
observed that locals had, in their own way, in-
ferred a cause-and-effect relationship between
that event and Antuco's relative silence:

> The lower orders in Talcahuano thought
> that the earthquake was caused by some
> old Indian women, who two years ago
> being offended stopped the volcano of An-
> tuco. This silly belief is curious, because
> it shows that experience has taught them
> to observe, that there exists a relation be-
> tween the suppressed action of the volca-
> noes, and the trembling of the ground. It
> was necessary to apply the witchcraft to
> the point where their perception of cause
> and effect failed.

Whatever its role in this and other earthquakes,
over the past 130,000 years Antuco's avalanches
and its basaltic lava flows helped form Laguna
del Laja and have, at various times, raised and
lowered its surface level. There are still weak
fumaroles in the crater, but no indication of a
major eruption any time soon.

In May 2005, though, Antuco's slopes were
the site of a controversial incident in which
Chilean army officers marched 45 ill-equipped
conscripts to their deaths in a training exercise
in brutally cold, snowy conditions. In the aftermath, several officers were court-martialed
and imprisoned.

The highway from Los Ángeles to Laguna
del Laja now continues to the border at 2,062-
meter Paso Pichachén and the Argentine town
of Chos Malal, but it is open in summer only.
Parts of the route can be tricky for vehicles
with low clearance during the spring runoff—
in one spot, the road goes right through the
channel of the Río de los Pinos.

Geography and Climate

In the upper Río Laja basin, 96 kilometers east
of Los Ángeles, the 11,600-hectare park takes
its name from Laguna del Laja, a natural lake
transformed by hydroelectric development. It
ranges in altitude from 976 meters in its western precordillera to 2,985 meters on Antuco's
conical summit. To the southwest, but beyond
the park boundaries, the glacial Sierra Velluda
rises even higher.

In winter, enough snow accumulates to
support a ski season from June to October.
Summer is dry, especially late in the season on
the Antuco circuit, so hikers must carry plenty
of water.

THE CHILEAN HEARTLAND

© WAYNE BERNHARDSON

waterfalls on the Rio Laja, Parque Nacional
Laguna del Laja

Flora and Fauna

Antuco's slopes and the shores of Laguna del Laja are almost completely barren except for some pioneer grasses and shrubs, but coniferous forests of mountain cypress *(Austrocedrus chilensis)* and monkey puzzle tree *(Araucaria araucana)* cover parts of the well-watered precordillera. The nearly 50 bird species are the most conspicuous fauna, most notably the Andean condor, but there are also vizcachas, pumas, and some smaller cats.

Sights

At Sector Chacay, from a parking area just off the main road near Conaf's Centro de Información Ambiental, a short hike leads to **Salto Chilcas,** which topples over multiple falls in a basalt flow into the Laja gorge; reached by a spur off the main trail, the **Salto de Torbellino** is a smaller and shorter but thunderous cascade from a tributary creek. When the sun is out, Torbellino usually sports a rainbow.

For more ambitious hikers, a three-day **Volcán Antuco** circuit from Chacay offers views of the Laguna del Laja, the Sierra Velluda, and the opportunity to climb the summit itself. The last part of the circuit returns along the road back to Chacay, so it may be possible to catch a lift back to the park entrance or even Los Ángeles.

Accommodations and Food

Within the park proper, the only option is **Camping y Cabañas Lagunillas,** now under concession to Lidia López (cel. 09/7454-2184). Wooded campsites here cost US$17 with running water, hot showers, and electricity, while three-bedroom A-frame cabañas with kitchen facilities cost US$75 for up to six people.

At Abanico, only 5 kilometers from the park entrance and 12 kilometers from the lake, the simple but appealing **Hostería El Bosque** (tel. 043/1972719, hosteriaelbosque@yahoo.com) delivers more than its modest prices (US$17 pp for lodging with breakfast, with half board and full board options) would suggest. On attractive grounds, with hospitable owners and a small swimming pool, it's one of the region's best values. In fact, it's a better choice than the nearby and more expensive eight-room **Hotel Malalcura** (tel. 043/1972720, US$17 pp), which does boast both larger grounds and a larger pool.

For food, the ski area's **Casino Club de Ski Los Ángeles,** open all year, is marginal at best. Supplies are cheaper and more diverse in Los Ángeles than in either Antuco or El Abanico.

Information

Conaf's **Centro de Información Ambiental** at Chacay, 11 kilometers east of Abanico, is rarely open. Conaf does, however, collect a US$1.15 admission fee per person at the park gates, five kilometers east of Abanico.

Getting There and Around

From Los Ángeles's Terminal Santa Rita (Rengo and Villagrán), **ERS** buses go five times daily to El Abanico (US$2, 1.5 hours) via Antuco. Departure times are 11:30 A.M. and 1:30, 2:45, 5:30, and 7:15 P.M. daily except Sunday, when departures are at 11:30 A.M. and 1:30 and 7:15 P.M. only.

From El Abanico, there's no public transportation for the five kilometers uphill to the park entrance; the park office is six kilometers farther.

ANGOL

A true frontier fortress, Angol de los Confines suffered devastation at least six times during the three-century Guerra del Arauco before outlasting the tenacious Mapuche in the late 19th century. Now known for its annual folklore festival and kitschy knickknacks created by local ceramicists, it's the main access point for the coast range's Parque Nacional Nahuelbuta, with extensive Araucaria (monkey puzzle) forests.

Orientation

Between the Panamericana and the Cordillera de Nahuelbuta, Angol (population 43,801) belongs politically to Region IX (Araucanía), but it's most easily accessible from Los Ángeles, 60 kilometers to the northeast; it is 608 kilometers south of Santiago.

Angol's colonial core, centered on the lavishly landscaped Plaza de Armas, lies west of the Río Vergara, while the newer part of the city has sprawled eastward.

Sights

On the Plaza de Armas, the central fountain and its four marble sculptures, imported from Italy and representing Europe, Asia, Africa, and America, are a national historical monument. Several blocks northeast, 1863's **Iglesia y Convento San Buenaventura** (Covadonga and Vergara) is the region's oldest church.

Five kilometers east of town, 19th-century Anglo-Chilean landscaper Manuel Bunster created El Vergel, a horticultural nursery that, after Methodist missionaries took it over in the 1920s, became the **Escuela Agrícola El Vergel,** an agricultural school. Its **Museo Dillman S. Bullock** is the legacy of Michigan Methodist Dillman S. Bullock (1878–1971), who willed his natural history and archaeological collections to the Angol school.

First visiting Angol in 1902, Bullock served as U.S. agricultural attaché in Buenos Aires before returning to take charge of El Vergel in 1924; one of the first foreigners to study the Mapuche systematically, he also learned their language. An enthusiastic ornithologist, he also proposed creation of Parque Nacional Nahuelbuta as early as 1929 (it finally happened in 1939) and worked tenaciously to preserve the region's Araucaria forests.

Among Bullock's greatest contributions was to study the Vergel I and II complexes of the pre-Mapuche Kofkeche, between the Biobío and the Río Toltén, south of Temuco. His Vergel discoveries, designated a national monument, suggested a dispersed settlement pattern, primarily agricultural but with some hunting and gathering; from about A.D. 1200, there are dramatic improvements in burial patterns, with bodies interred in ceramic urns rather than surrounded by clusters of stones.

From Angol's Plaza de Armas, *taxi colectivo* No. 2 drops passengers at the gate to El Vergel's grounds, which are open 9 A.M.–7 P.M. daily; admission is free. Admission to the museum (tel. 045/711142), which is open 10 A.M.–7 P.M. daily, costs US$0.85 for adults, US$0.35 for children.

Events

Since the early 1980s, Angol has hosted **Brotes de Chile,** a folkloric song festival with cash prizes that also features dance, traditional Chilean food, and artisanal crafts. It takes place the second week of January.

Accommodations

Just east of town, on the grounds of the Escuela Agrícola El Vergel, the slowly declining **Hostal El Vergel** (Camino Angol–Collipulli, Km 5, tel. 045/712103, ext. 209, fundoelvergel@ hotmail.com, US$15 pp with shared bath, US$33 d with private bath) is probably the quietest option.

Hotel Millaray (O'Higgins 1037, tel. 045/711570, www.millarayinn.com, US$38 s, US$53 d with breakfast) has 11 sharply decorated rooms. Northwest of the plaza, the **Hotel Club Social** (Caupolicán 498, tel. 045/711103, clubsocialangol@yahoo.com, US$40 s, US$57 d) boasts a swimming pool, a bar, and a restaurant.

Food

Lomitón (Lautaro 146, tel. 045/717675) is a fast-food *sandwichería.* For pizza, try **Pizzería Sparlatto** (Caupolicán 418, tel. 045/716272).

At the agricultural college's hotel, **El Vergel** does less with its abundant fresh produce than it could or should. Other options include the **Club Social** (Caupolicán 498, tel. 045/711103), at its namesake hotel; **Las Totoras** (Ilabaca 806, tel. 045/712275); and **La Rueda** (Lautaro 176, tel. 045/714170).

Information

Just east of the bridge over the Río Vergara, Angol's motivated **Oficina Municipal de Turismo** (Av. Bernardo O'Higgins s/n, tel. 045/201571, www.angolturismo.es.tl,

THE CHILEAN HEARTLAND

turismo@angol.cl) is open 8:30 A.M.–5:30 P.M. weekdays all year.

Conaf (Prat 191, 2nd floor, tel. 045/712191) should have the latest on transportation to Parque Nacional Nahuelbuta.

Services
West of the plaza, **Banco de Chile** (Lautaro 2) has an ATM. For cash or travelers checks, try **Nahuel Tour** (Pedro Aguirre Cerda 307, tel. 045/715457).

Correos de Chile (Chorrillos and Lautaro) is at the northeast corner of the plaza.

Just west of the plaza, **Entel** (Lautaro 317) has a call center, while Net-Café (Lautaro 465) has Internet access.

Getting There and Around
Angol's long-distance **Terminal Rodoviario** (Oscar Bonilla 428, tel. 045/711854) has moved east of the river. Sample destinations, fares, and times include Los Ángeles (US$2.50, 1 hour), Temuco (US$4.50, 2 hours), Concepción (US$5.50, 2.5 hours), and Santiago (US$16–28, 8 hours).

For rural and regional carriers, the **Terminal Rural** (Ilabaca 422, tel. 045/712021) is three blocks east of the plaza.

PARQUE NACIONAL NAHUELBUTA
In the coast range west of Angol, 6,832-hectare Nahuelbuta is the last major coast range sanctuary for the Araucaria (monkey puzzle) tree, a rare conifer also known as the *paragua* (umbrella) for the shape of its crown (the Mapuche refer to it as the *pewen*). Dramatically undervisited, except on summer weekends, the park features a series of medium-length loop trails through the forest; from the highest summits, reaching almost 1,600 meters, several Andean volcanoes are visible to the east and south.

Geography and Climate
At the northern edge of Region IX (La Araucanía), in Malleco province, the igneous Cordillera de Nahuelbuta comprises a mostly rolling plain, about 950 meters above sea level,

Araucaria forests cover the coastal mountainsides at Parque Nacional Nahuelbuta.

but also cut by steep ravines and punctuated by craggy summits such as the 1,530-meter Cerro Alto Nahuelbuta.

Nahuelbuta is open all year, but the steeper segments of the gravel and dirt road can get muddy and even impassable when it rains. Summers are mild and nearly rainless, but higher elevations can get a dusting of winter snow. Nearly all the rainfall, about 1,000 millimeters per year, falls May–September.

Flora and Fauna
In addition to *Araucaria araucana,* whose largest specimens measure 50 meters in height and 2 meters in diameter, dense woodlands of *coigüe* (*Nothofagus dombeyi,* southern beech) cover Nahuelbuta's steeper hillsides.

In these dense forests, rare and endangered mammals including the *pudú* (the dwarf Chilean deer), *zorro chilote* (Chiloé fox), and puma are present but rarely seen. The endangered peregrine falcon is the rarest bird species.

Sights and Recreation

Camping and hiking are the main activities. From the park Administración at Pehuenco, a twisting four-kilometer footpath climbs through monkey puzzle forests to 1,379-meter **Piedra del Aguila,** a granodiorite pinnacle with awesome panoramas of the snow-topped Andean volcanoes from Antuco in the north to Villarrica, Lanín, and sometimes as far as Osorno in the south (Nahuelbuta occupies a transitional zone between the clear and almost cloudless Mediterranean climate to the north and the drizzly marine west coast climate to the south). To the west, the Pacific stretches to infinity. Rather than returning by the same route, follow the trail that zigzags south into the valley of the Estero Cabrería from the west side of Piedra del Aguila; just beyond the main stream crossing, the trail becomes a road that leads back to Pehuenco.

From the picnic ground at Coimallín, a shorter footpath through flatter terrain reaches the 1,450-meter summit of **Cerro Anay,** which offers comparable vistas. The park's highest point, 1,530-meter **Cerro Alto Nahuelbuta,** is open to hikers after being closed for a puma reintroduction project several years ago.

Accommodations and Food

Near the park administration, **Camping Pehuenco** (US$12 for up to six people) has 11 secluded sites; all have picnic tables, flush toilets, and (cold) showers. There are no concessionaires in the park, so buy supplies before coming here.

Information

At Los Portones, the park's eastern entrance, 35 kilometers from Angol, Conaf rangers collect an admission charge of US$7 for adults, half that for children. At Pehuenco, five kilometers farther west, Conaf's **Centro de Informaciones Ecológicas** includes a small museum where rangers sometimes provide slide shows or video shows on park ecology.

Getting There and Around

From Angol's Terminal Rural (Ilabaca 422, tel. 045/712021), daily except Sunday, **Buses Nahuelbuta** (tel. 045/715611) and **Buses Carrasco** (tel. 045/715287) alternate service to Vegas Blancas (US$2.50), seven kilometers west of the Los Portones entrance, at 6:45 A.M. and 4 P.M.; return times are 9 A.M. and 5:45 P.M. There is no more direct service to the park.

THE CHILEAN HEARTLAND

NORTE GRANDE

From the Peruvian border south to Taltal, the Atacama Desert of Chile's "Greater North" may be the world's greatest wasteland. Flowing along the sandy beaches and dramatic headlands of the Tarapacá and Antofagasta regions, the cool Humboldt or Peru Current moderates the tropical temperatures and produces the *camanchaca,* the dense fog that condenses on the barren coastal mountains. Real rainfall is so rare that, for several hundred kilometers, only runoff from sporadic Andean rains moistens its sandy watercourses.

Despite its superficial desolation, the Norte Grande's highlights are startlingly spectacular: The dry climate has preserved prehistory on valley slopes, whose pre-Columbian geoglyphs depict the llama trains that passed en route to and from the Andean highlands, and in the *tambos* (way stations) and *pukarás* (fortresses) whose ruins dot the ancient routes. In some areas, hikers may even come across mummies desiccated by the dry air and tanned to leather by centuries of tropical sunshine.

At higher elevations, scattered Andean hamlets, their colonial chapels surrounded by stone-faced agricultural terraces, testify that this was an outlier of the central Andean civilizations that came under colonial Spanish control. At the highest altitudes, among immense plains punctuated by snowcapped volcanic cones, indigenous Aymara herders still tend their llamas and alpacas in areas now protected as national parks.

On the rainless coast itself, nearly endless beaches have begun to draw visitors from the Chilean heartland, but the real appeal is the Victorian architecture of 19th-century ports

© WAYNE BERNHARDSON

HIGHLIGHTS

◖ Museo Arqueológico San Miguel de Azapa: The Chinchorro mummies alone are reason enough to visit, but this professional museum puts it all in context, in Arica's lushly irrigated Azapa Valley (page 188).

◖ Parque Nacional Lauca: East of Arica, wildlife-rich Lauca covers the steppes and volcanic summits of the high Andes, but it's also home to Aymara villagers, with their llama and alpaca herds, and a plethora of colonial churches and chapels (page 194).

◖ Paseo Baquedano: With the removal of automobiles and restoration of its boardwalks, the views of Iquique's Victorian historic district are now unobstructed (page 204).

◖ Oficina Humberstone: The atmospherically weathering ruins of this nitrate mine east of Iquique include a landmark theater, rusting rail lines, and even a cast-iron (waterless) swimming pool(page 212).

◖ Geoglifos de Cerros Pintados: Pre-Columbian earth art, both abstract and figurative, stretches for several kilometers of the arid hillsides of the Pampa del Tamarugal southeast of Iquique (page 222).

◖ Oficina Chacabuco: Declared a national historical monument shortly before the 1973 Pinochet coup, this former nitrate mine soon became a prison camp. Today it's a museum (page 236).

◖ Museo Arqueológico Padre Gustavo Le Paige: The Belgian Jesuit priest for whom this museum is named put San Pedro de Atacama on the archaeological map (page 250).

◖ Geisers del Tatio: In the altiplano north of San Pedro, the otherworldly Tatio may be the world's highest geyser field (page 257).

◖ Valle de la Luna: In the desert just west of San Pedro, the sunsets at this polychrome valley help make it the area's most popular excursion (page 259).

LOOK FOR ◖ TO FIND RECOMMENDED SIGHTS, ACTIVITIES, DINING, AND LODGING.

NORTE GRANDE

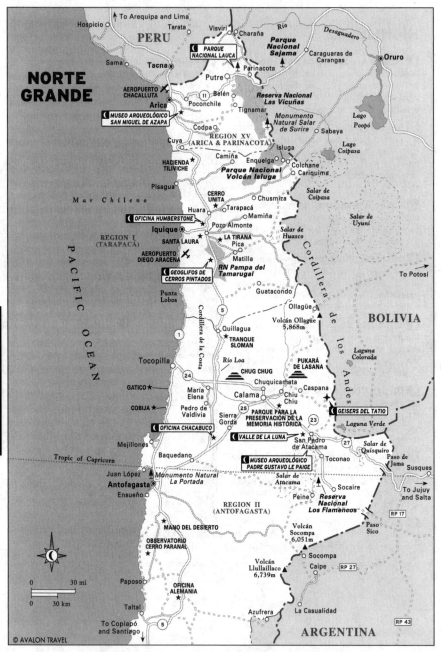

NORTE GRANDE

© AVALON TRAVEL

such as Iquique. Desert rats will glory in exploring the nitrate ghost towns, now a collective UNESCO World Heritage Site, that just decades ago were thriving communities.

Infrastructural improvements are making access to all these attractions easier, especially in the highlands, where a planned "Camino del Inca" is beginning to link settlements from Visviri, near the Peruvian and Bolivian borders, through the altiplano to the landmark village of San Pedro de Atacama (the authentic Inka road from Cuzco ran through the precordillera foothills).

PLANNING YOUR TIME

In the sprawling Norte Grande, great distances separate many sights and an automobile is advisable for those with limited time. The best bases are San Pedro de Atacama, Iquique, and Arica; Iquique is the most central, but San Pedro is the most popular. From any one of them, though, at least a week would be essential; two weeks or more would be desirable to see any two of them, and their backcountry, thoroughly. For those with flexibility, a month or more would be rewarding.

Because of its dry gentle climate, the Norte Grande can be an all-year destination, though winter nights get cold at higher elevations. Except on paved roads, access to those elevations may be difficult in the summer months (December, January, and February), known colloquially as the *invierno boliviano* (Bolivian winter) or *invierno altiplánico* (altiplano winter). Nearly all the rain falls during this period.

While most Chileans enjoy the region's beaches in summer, both Chilean and foreign surfers prefer the winter, when Pacific storms bring the biggest waves.

HISTORY

Around 10,000 B.C., the first hunter-gatherers occupied the central Andean highlands; eventually, several thousand years later, they found their way down the transverse river valleys to the arid Pacific littoral, where they thrived on the abundant fish and shellfish, and swapped guano for maize with their kinfolk in the precordillera, where irrigated agriculture was possible. They also obtained meat and wool from the altiplano, where llamas and alpacas grazed the high Andean steppe.

In the valleys and the precordillera, farmers cultivated native crops such as the potato and quinoa, a nutritious grain that's recently begun to earn a niche in international markets. While northern Chile was beyond the nucleus of the great central Andean civilizations, both Tiwanaku (after about A.D. 800) and the Inkas of Cuzco (from about A.D. 1450) left lasting imprints.

Precisely because of its extreme aridity, the Atacama has been a source of riches since pre-Columbian times, and remains so today—its mineral wealth was undisguised by vegetative growth. When 16th-century Spaniards invaded the Americas, of course, they sought gold and silver, but with few exceptions, their expectations were unrealistic (the Huantajaya silver mine, east of present-day Iquique, was one of these exceptions). Still, the real wealth of the Americas was the surprisingly numerous indigenous populations, who provided labor and tribute to the Spaniards until ecologically exotic diseases such as smallpox decimated their numbers.

From the mid-19th century, when the region was under Peruvian and Bolivian sovereignty, the strip mining of mineral nitrates—nicknamed *oro blanco* (white gold)—brought unheard-of wealth and precipitated the War of the Pacific (1879–1884), in which Chile expanded its continental territory by nearly a third.

After the Chilean victory, workers from the Chilean heartland streamed into the underpopulated region, and their presence resulted in Chile's first organized labor movement despite growing pains—among them the massacre of more than several hundred peacefully protesting nitrate workers in Iquique in 1907.

Mineral nitrates made Chile wealthy until, after World War I, synthetic nitrates supplanted them in European and North American agriculture. When nitrates failed, copper filled the economic vacuum and has retained its economic dominance to the present. Chuquicamata's open-pit mine, near Calama, is the world's largest.

Arica

Though not a major destination in its own right, Arica is the northern gateway to Chile (for arrivals from Peru) and to the altiplano (an excellent paved highway climbs east toward several national parks and the Bolivian border). Meanwhile, it's a beach resort that draws Bolivians from their own frigid highlands, in addition to Chileans, to the relatively warm Pacific waters, so it can be more than just a stopover en route elsewhere.

It's also a historic city, once the port for the legendary silver mine at Potosí in present-day Bolivia and later the stage for dramatic battles between Peruvian and Chilean forces during the War of the Pacific, on the spectacular headland of El Morro. In the nearby Azapa Valley, a first-rate archaeological museum provides more than just an introduction to the region's pre-Columbian heritage.

Now the capital of its new namesake region, Arica still lags behind Iquique and its Zona Franca duty-free zone, but it remains a major port for Bolivian imports and exports (though landlocked Bolivia continues to lobby for a territorial outlet to the Pacific, its access to the ocean is probably better than it's ever been).

ORIENTATION

At the foot of the historic Morro, Arica (population 175,441) is 316 kilometers from Iquique via the southbound Panamericana and a westbound lateral near Pozo Almonte, though it's a significantly shorter distance as the crow flies. It's 2,062 kilometers north of Santiago via the inland Panamericana, though many buses and drivers take the coastal route through Iquique.

Arica's central core is a compact grid that roughly parallels the southwest–northeast shoreline (the port area is built entirely on fill). Streets perpendicular to the Costanera, such as Maipú, 18 de Septiembre, and 21 de Mayo,

The historic El Morro headland rises above the city of Arica.

© WAYNE BERNHARDSON

are one-way thoroughfares that carry most of the traffic, though 21 de Mayo is a *peatonal* between Calle General Lagos and Avenida Comandante San Martín, where renovated Plaza Colón marks the old shoreline.

From the foot of the Morro, Avenida Comandante San Martín rounds the headlands and passes popular beaches before ending abruptly nine kilometers to the south. To the northeast, the Tacna-Arica railway line and Avenida General Velásquez head toward the Panamericana Norte, Aeropuerto Chacalluta, and the Peruvian border.

SIGHTS

For an overview, climb **El Morro de Arica,** an imposing natural headland whose 110-meter summit offers expansive views north toward the Peruvian border and south toward the beaches. Beneath the Morro's northern face, fronting on Avenida Comandante San Martín, a cluster of verdant public parks and palm-shaded plazas adjoin each other: **Plaza Vicuña Mackenna, Parque General Baquedano,** the **Plazoleta Estación,** and **Plaza Colón.** Many architectural landmarks stand nearby, but the trees are suffering from the droppings of the countless cormorants and turkey vultures that perch there.

On Plazoleta Estación, a German Esslingen locomotive (1924) faces the **Estación Ferrocarril Arica-La Paz** (1913) from which, for most of a century, it and other Bolivia-bound trains chugged across the high Andes. The occasional freight still climbs into the altiplano.

At the east end of Plaza Colón rises the prefab **Iglesia San Marcos de Arica** (1875), the work of Frenchman Alexandre Gustave Eiffel (yes, *that* Eiffel!). Brick walls cover an iron superstructure at the well-restored **Aduana de Arica** (Arica Customs House, 1874), which now serves as the municipal Casa de la Cultura (tel. 058/206366); it sponsors special exhibitions in its 2nd-floor gallery, with access from a spiral staircase.

At Colón and Yungay, at the eastern foot of the Morro, the **Casa Bolognesi** was Peru's

© WAYNE BERNHARDSON

Gustave Eiffel's Iglesia San Marcos de Arica

military headquarters during the War of the Pacific and still belongs to the Peruvian consulate. Below the Morro's western face, along the Costanera, the former guano island of **Isla de Alacrán** was fortified against pirates during colonial times and still contains some ruins from those times. United with the mainland by fill since 1967, it's now home to the local yacht club.

El Morro de Arica

Atop El Morro's summit, most notable for its panoramic views, the **Museo Histórico y de Armas del Morro de Arica** recalls the bloody combat between Chilean and Peruvian forces on June 7, 1880; in taking the high ground, Chile lost nearly 500 troops, while the Peruvians lost 1,250, including commanding officer Colonel Francisco Bolognesi.

More recently, in the interest of better relations between the two countries, the 11-meter **Cristo de la Concordia,** by the late Chilean sculptor Raúl Valdivieso, extends a symbolic embrace toward Peru. From the south end of Colón, a sandy trail switchbacks up the Morro,

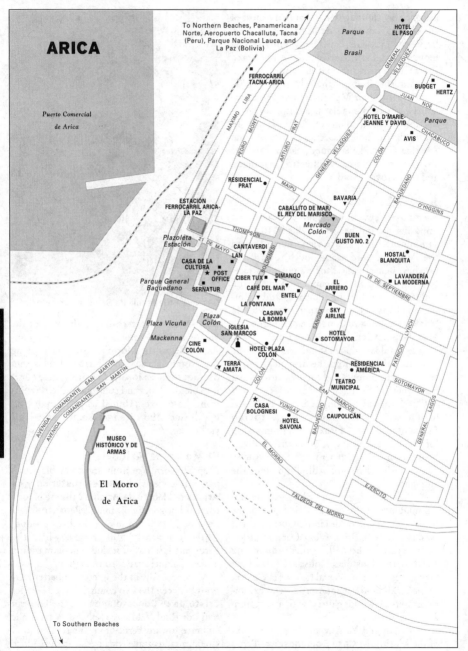

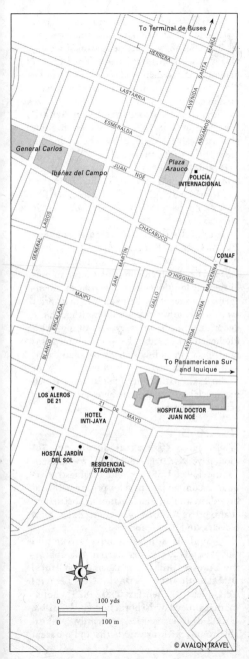

which is also accessible by a paved road from the east end of Sotomayor. The museum (tel. 058/229192, www.museomorrodearica.cl) sits atop the Morro and is open 8:30 A.M.–8 P.M. weekdays, 9 A.M.–8 P.M. weekends; admission costs US$1.

Iglesia San Marcos de Arica

Famous for his tower in the French capital, the celebrated Parisian engineer Alexandre Gustave Eiffel designed numerous prefabricated wrought-iron structures for Peru and other Latin American countries in the late 19th century; several of his works are among the few remaining buildings from Arica's Peruvian period. Initially planned for Lima's beach resort of Ancón, then assembled here after an earthquake destroyed its predecessor, Eiffel's church survived the 1877 tsunami on its existing foundations.

BEACHES

Arica is one of few Chilean beach towns where the cold Humboldt Current does not preclude or discourage swimming, surfing, and the like. Some beaches, though, have dangerous rip currents.

South of the Morro, along Avenida Comandante San Martín, are **Playa El Laucho,** which draws a young crowd, **Playa La Lisera,** popular with families, and **Playa Corazones,** which is pretty but not suitable for swimming. **Isla Alacrán, La Capilla,** and **Playa Brava** offer outstanding surfing. North of downtown, **Playa Chinchorro** is fine for both swimming and surfing, while **Playa Las Machas** is too rough for most swimmers but suitable for experienced surfers. In wet years, when the Río San José and Río Lluta reach the ocean, they may deposit debris that spoils the northerly beaches, at least temporarily.

In early July, Chilean surfers compete in the **Maestros del Gringo** championship at Isla Alacrán; local surfers have their own website, **Arica Surf** (www.aricasurf.cl). There's also a handful of surf shops, including Gringo Surf Shop (Bolognesi 440).

NORTE GRANDE

ENTERTAINMENT AND EVENTS

Arica has a gaggle of downtown pubs and similar hangouts, such as **Café 303** (Bolognesi 303). The liveliest, though, may be **Cantaverdi** (Bolognesi 453, tel. 058/258242), where spontaneous live music often breaks out to accompany the beer and sandwiches.

For current movies, go to **Cine Colón** (7 de Junio 190, tel. 058/231165). The **Teatro Municipal** (Baquedano and Sotomayor) is the municipal performing arts venue.

Carnaval is not the wildly colorful occasion here that it is in Brazil, but late February's **Carnaval Ginga** reveals the syncretism between indigenous Andean and imported European customs in a parade down Avenida Comandante San Martín. More strictly local, June's **Semana Ariqueña** does include the **Concurso Nacional de Cueca,** celebrating Chile's national folkloric dance.

SHOPPING

Barely wider than a condor's wingspan, the pedestrian **Pasaje Bolognesi,** between Sotomayor and Thompson, features a spirited crafts market nightly.

ACCOMMODATIONS

Arica offers a wide variety of accommodations in all categories. The best budget accommodations are in the area southeast of the 21 de Mayo *peatonal* and Colon, mostly along Sotomayor between Baquedano and Arturo Gallo. Most upscale hotels are outside the crowded downtown—both along the beaches and in the Azapa Valley.

US$10-25

Hostal Blanquita (Maipú 472, tel. 058/232064, residencialblanquita@hotmail.com, US$7.50 pp without breakfast) is a good choice in its range, with shared bath only. It's plain, but **Residencial Stagnaro** (Gallo 294, tel. 058/231254, arica_hostalstagnaro@hotmail.com, US$8-12 pp with breakfast) has the advantage of a quiet neighborhood; rates vary according to private or shared bath.

Nearly faultless in its facilities, 🄲 **Residencial América** (Sotomayor 430, tel. 058/254148, www.residencialamerica.com, US$17 d with breakfast) has suffered from a haughty management style but appears to be more responsive recently. All rooms now have private baths.

Tidy, friendly **Residencial Don Genaro** (Prat 521, tel. 058/232813, US$8 pp) has singles with cable TV and private baths, but no other frills—not even breakfast.

Residencial Prat (Arturo Prat 545, tel. 058/251292, US$17 s or d) has immaculate rooms with private baths and cable TV. Rates do not include breakfast, but there is kitchen access.

Arica's HI affiliate is **Casa de Huéspedes Doña Inés** (Manuel Rojas 2864, tel. 058/226372, casadehuespedes@hotmail.com, US$9-11 pp), which compensates for an out-of-the-way location with truly hospitable management, some of the best facilities in its price range—including spacious rooms (though the decor may not be to everyone's liking) with kitchenettes and cable TV—and ample common spaces including a shady patio and a casual bar. Take *taxi colectivo* Línea 4 or 6, or Radio Taxi Pirámide (tel. 058/264040), which has special rates for guests here. HI members get the lower rates.

US$25-50

Well-located 🄲 **Hostal Jardín del Sol** (Sotomayor 848, tel. 058/232795, www.hostaljardindelsol.cl, US$15 pp with breakfast) offers quiet accommodations with private bath and breakfast, and an ample patio for socializing. It also offers WiFi, has kitchen facilities, rents bicycles, and does laundry.

Though it adjoins a busy street and the grounds are rather barren, the charming Franco-Chilean management at **Hotel D'Marie-Jeanne y David** (Av. General Velásquez 792, tel./fax 058/258231, hotelmariejeanneydavid@hotmail.com, US$18 s, US$32 d) offers spotless, generally comfortable rooms with private baths and a decent breakfast.

Rehabbed, well-located **Hotel Sotomayor** (Sotomayor 367, tel. 058/585761, www.hotel-sotomayor.cl, US$30 s, US$40 d) is the former Hotel San Marcos, with improved services including WiFi.

Rooms at the rejuvenated **Hotel Plaza Colón** (San Marcos 261, tel. 058/254424, www.hotelplazacolon.cl, US$30 s, US$40 d) may be a bit less sizable than is claimed, but all come with a private bath, cable TV, telephone, and frigobar.

Slowly recovering from years of neglect, **Hotel Bahía Chinchorro** (Avenida Luis Beretta Porcel 2031, tel. 058/260676, www.bahiahotel .cl, US$30 s, US$50 d) enjoys a nearly silent beachfront location. There remain some imperfections but, for the price, it's an excellent deal, and the breakfast is above average.

Possibly Arica's best value, on a quiet street but still easy walking distance from everywhere, **Hotel Savona** (Yungay 380, tel. 058/232319, www.hotelsavona.cl, US$31–45 s, US$40–52 d) boasts friendly service, soothing gardens, and comfortable rooms with private baths, cable TV, and breakfast.

US$50-100

Hotel Inti-Jaya (21 de Mayo 850, tel. 058/230536, www.hotelintijaya.cl, US$30–40 s, US$53 d) wins no points with its kitsch decor, but the rooms are spacious and comfortable. Only cash is accepted, however.

Snuggled between the expansive grounds of Parque Brasil and the Universidad de Tarapacá campus, just north of downtown, **Hotel El Paso** (General Velásquez 1109, tel. 058/231041, www.hotelelpaso.cl, US$67 s or d) has the distinction of having hosted General Pinochet and Monty Python's Michael Palin—on the same day.

More than US$100

South of downtown, fronting on the crescent beach at Playa el Laucho **Hotel Arica** (Av. Comandante San Martín 599, tel. 058/254540, www.panamericanahoteles.cl, resarica@entelchile.net, US$100 s, US$120 d) has amenities such as swimming pools and tennis courts. Reports suggest, though, that it's past its peak.

FOOD

For breakfast, sandwiches, and fresh fruit drinks (ask them to hold the sugar, though), perpetually crowded **(Buen Gusto No. 2** (Baquedano 559) has been a personal favorite for more than 25 years. It has bar-style seating only. **Caupolicán** (San Marcos 444, tel. 058/254915) serves the tangy Bolivian empanadas known as *salteñas*.

Fire stations offer reliable food throughout Chile, but Arica's **Casino La Bomba** (Colón 357, tel. 058/255626) is one of the best of its kind, serving a variety of Chilean dishes, especially lunchtime specials, at modest prices. In a country where seasonings are generally bland, its *ají* is one of Chile's spiciest fresh condiments.

Chifa Shao-Lin (Sotomayor 275, tel. 058/231311) serves good Chinese dishes in the US$5–8 range, with excellent service and, unusual for many Chilean restaurants in its category, no TV or loud music.

Within a few blocks of each other, Arica has a pair of popular *parrillas:* **El Arriero** (21 de Mayo 385, tel. 058/232636) and **Los Aleros de 21** (21 de Mayo 736, tel. 058/254641). The former (closed Monday) is casual, the latter more formal, but both have good meats.

At Colón and Maipú, the **Mercado Colón** fish and produce market also holds several good seafood restaurants, including the midrange **Caballito del Mar** (Colón 565, tel. 058/252570) downstairs and the pricier **El Rey del Marisco** (Colón 565, tel. 058/229232) upstairs.

Most of the places in the commercial downtown are mediocre, but **Café del Mar** (21 de Mayo 260, tel. 058/231936, www.cafedelma-rarica.cl) adds a touch of sophistication even in its fixed-price lunches. Around the corner from Eiffel's church, open for lunch and dinner except Sundays, **Terra Amata** (Yungay 201, tel. 058/259057) is the best new high-quality restaurant in town, offering dishes that blend Andean and Mediterranean styles.

In summer, when sunset coincides with the dinner hour and the surf breaks on the rocks, the outdoor seating at **☕ Maracuyá** (Av. Comandante San Martín 321, tel. 058/227600) offers unmatchable ambience. It's less than perfect, though—while the entrées, desserts, drinks, and wine list are good enough, the menu is simply too large and ambitious to do everything well. Still, local fish dishes such as corvina, in the US$10–15 range, are worth the price.

DiMango (21 de Mayo 244, tel. 058/224575) offers fine ice cream, but the best ice creamery in town, loaded with imaginative tropical fruit flavors, is **La Fontana** (Bolognesi 320, tel. 058/254680).

INFORMATION

Sernatur (San Marcos 101, tel. 058/252054, infoarica@sernatur.cl) is open 8:30 A.M.–7 P.M. daily in summer, weekdays only the rest of the year, when closing time is 5:30 P.M. except Friday (4 P.M.). Each day, it also closes 2–3 P.M. for lunch.

For motorists, the **Automóvil Club de Chile** (Acchi, 18 de Septiembre 1360, tel. 058/252878) is open 9 A.M.–7 P.M. weekdays, 9 A.M.–1 P.M. Saturday only.

For national park information, contact **Conaf** (Vicuña Mackenna 820, tel. 250207, tarapaca@conaf.cl), open 8:30 A.M.–5:15 P.M. weekdays only.

SERVICES

There are fewer exchange houses than there were before the advent of ATMs (abundant along the *peatonal*), but try **Turismo Sol y Mar** (Colón 610, Oficina 4) for U.S., Argentine, Bolivian, or Peruvian cash, or for U.S. travelers checks.

Correos de Chile (Prat 305) handles the mail. For long-distance phone service, go to Entelchile (21 de Mayo 270).

Internet outlets are many, but the most comfortable is **Ciber Tux** (Bolognesi 370), which doesn't have rowdy video gamers.

The **Policía Internacional** (Angamos 990, tel. 058/250377) is open 8:30 A.M.–12:30 P.M. and 3:30–6 P.M. weekdays. It's possible to obtain a replacement tourist card or renew one here, but a brief trip to Peru or even Bolivia is almost certainly cheaper than Chile's US$100 renewal charge.

There are **consulates** for the neighboring countries of Peru (18 de Septiembre 1554, tel. 058/231020) and Bolivia (Patricio Lynch 292, tel. 058/231030).

Lavandería La Moderna (18 de Septiembre 457, tel. 058/232006) does the washing.

Hospital Dr. Juan Noé (18 de Septiembre 1000, tel. 058/229200) is Arica's public hospital.

GETTING THERE

As a border city, Arica has international connections by air (limited), bus, taxi, and train (to nearby Tacna, Peru, only). Domestic air and bus services are abundant.

Air

Aeropuerto Internacional Chacalluta (tel. 058/211116) is 18 kilometers north of town, near the Peruvian border.

LAN (Arturo Prat 391, tel. 058/252600) flies several times daily to Santiago, usually stopping in Iquique. **Sky Airline** (21 de Mayo 356, tel. 058/251816) also flies south to Iquique, Antofagasta, and Santiago, with connections south of the capital.

Bus and *Taxi Colectivo*

Arica's main **Terminal de Buses** (Diego Portales 948, tel. 058/241390) is northwest of downtown, at the corner of Avenida Santa María. Immediately adjacent to it on Portales, the deceptively named **Terminal Internacional** (tel. 058/248709) has both domestic and international services, and some international buses leave from the main terminal, as well. Most regional bus companies have separate offices nearer downtown.

On the regional routes, **Bus Lluta** (Chacabuco and Vicuña Mackenna) has six departures daily to Poconchile, between 5:45 A.M. and 8 P.M. At the Terminal Internacional, **Buses La Paloma** (tel. 058/222710) offers service to the altiplano villages of Parinacota (Parque Nacional Lauca) and Visviri (across from the Bolivian border town of Charaña) Tuesday and Friday at noon. Fares are US$6 to Parinacota, US$8 to Visviri.

Buses La Paloma (Germán Riesco 2071, tel. 058/222710) goes daily at 6:30 A.M. to Putre (US$4.50, three hours), and also to the northern precordillera villages of Socoroma (Tues. and Sat. at 6:30 A.M., US$4) and Belén (Tues. and Fri. at 6:30 A.M.). La Paloma also has Monday and Friday service, at 8 A.M., to the southern precordillera hamlet of Codpa (US$4.50, four hours). La Paloma's terminal is 12 blocks east of the hospital, but it may arrange hotel pickups.

Several bus companies shuttle frequently between Arica and Iquique, along with faster *taxi colectivos* such as **Tamarugal** (tel. 058/222609), **Turiscargo** (tel. 058/241052), and **Turis Auto** (tel. 058/244776).

Numerous long-distance carriers link Arica with Santiago and intermediate points, some with cushier but more expensive *semi-cama* and *salón cama* seating to Santiago. Sample fares and durations include Iquique (US$13, 4 hours), Calama (US$22, 9 hours), Antofagasta (US$22–30, 10 hours), Copiapó (US$49–64, 17 hours), La Serena (US$65–76, 22 hours), and Santiago (US$71–91, 29 hours).

The simplest way to Tacna, 55 kilometers north, is by *taxi colectivo* from the Terminal Internacional with **San Remo** (tel. 058/255038) or **San Marcos** (tel. 058/260513). Charging about US$3.50 per person, these international carriers leave whenever they have five passengers. From Tacna, there are multiple options north to Lima.

Overland transportation to Bolivia is simpler than in the past, thanks to improving diplomatic relations and infrastructure, but heavy summer rains can still cut the paved highway to La Paz (US$15, seven hours). **Pullman Bus** (tel. 058/241972) has daily service at 10 A.M.; Lauca-bound passengers can take these buses, but they will have to pay full fare to Bolivia.

Train

Near the port, the **Ferrocarril Arica-Tacna** (Máximo Lira 889, tel. 058/231115) crosses the Peruvian border (US$2) at 9:30 A.M. and 7 P.M. daily. Arrive early for immigration paperwork.

GETTING AROUND
Airport Transfers

Several radio taxi companies carry passengers to Aeropuerto Chacalluta for US$4 per person shared or US$10 single. Among them are **Radio Taxi Pirámide** (tel. 058/264040), **Radio Taxi Futuro** (tel. 058/233566), and **VJC Servicios Turísticos** (tel. 058/254311).

Local Transportation

Buses and faster *taxi colectivos* (the latter distinguished from other cabs by illuminated signs that indicate their routes) link downtown Arica with the bus terminal, the Azapa Valley, and other destinations.

Car Rental

Rental agencies include **Hertz** (Baquedano 999, tel. 058/231487); **Avis** (Chacabuco 314, tel. 058/584821); **Budget** (Colón 996, tel. 058/258911); and **Cactus** (Baquedano 635, Local 40, tel. 058/257430 or 099/5417067, cactusrent@latinmail.com).

Bicycles

Hostal Jardín del Sol (Sotomayor 848, tel. 058/232795) rents bikes.

NORTE GRANDE

Vicinity of Arica

The transverse valleys, precordillera, and altiplano in and around Arica all have their attractions. Many of them, such as the Azapa Valley and Tacna (Peru), are easily accessible by routine public transportation, but time constraints and awkward logistics can make organized tours a good alternative for some more remote sights.

Note that, while the operators may also offer tours to more distant destinations such as Parque Nacional Lauca and Parque Nacional Volcán Isluga, they will often double up with other agencies in the interest of economy. In some instances, guides may be essentially drivers with limited knowledge and ability to communicate in any language other than Spanish.

Among established Arica operators are: **Ecotour Expediciones** (Bolognesi 362, tel. 058/250000, eco-tour@ctcinternet.cl), **Geotour** (Bolognesi 421, tel. 058/253927, www.geotour.cl), **Transportes La Paloma** (Bolognesi 470, tel. 058/255030), and Belgian-run **Latinorizons** (Bolognesi 449, tel./fax 058/250007, www.latinorizons.com; French and English spoken).

VALLE DE AZAPA

In pre-Columbian times, the Río San José Valley—commonly known as Azapa—was one of the main transport routes between the altiplano and the coast, and the geoglyphs on its barren hillsides are a palpable reminder of the llama pack trains that once climbed and descended the canyon. Since colonial times, it has produced premium olives, citrus, and vegetables in an area where cultivable land, and water to irrigate it, is scarce.

A smooth paved road ascends the valley from Arica to beyond the hamlet of Sobraya, where it becomes a gravel surface and gradually peters out as it approaches the precordillera. The old and roughly parallel Azapa road, along with a few secondary loops, provides access to the geoglyphs and other archaeological sites in the vicinity.

For a thorough introduction to regional prehistory and an orientation toward the valley's impressive archaeological resources, visit the remarkable **Museo Arqueológico San Miguel de Azapa.** To see the valley's attractions in situ, follow the museum's **Circuito Arqueológico del Valle de Azapa,** which visits a dozen of the most notable sites. The most impressive are probably Cerro Sombrero's **Geoglifos Atoca,** representing a llama train and its guide, from about A.D. 1300; the Tiwanaku-influenced **Pukará San Lorenzo,** a 12th-century fortress on the opposite side of the valley from the museum; and the Incaic **Geoglifos Cerro Sagrado,** dating from around A.D. 1400. Nearby are the **Túmulos Alto Ramírez,** a cluster of funeral mounds dating from 1000 B.C. to A.D. 300.

◖ Museo Arqueológico San Miguel de Azapa

Under the auspices of the Universidad de Tarapacá, one of the country's finest museums traces the region's cultural evolution from the earliest hunter-gatherers to present-day Aymara agropastoralists through a series of generally chronological exhibits; in the surrounding gardens, the rock art of its **Parque de Geoglifos** was salvaged from the valley's urban and agricultural development. It also guards the remarkable Chinchorro mummies, the world's oldest and among the most elaborately prepared. Heather Pringle relates the story of these infant mummies, found at the base of Arica's El Morro headland, in her outstanding book *The Mummy Congress* (New York: Hyperion, 2001).

In addition, the museum boasts a bank of interactive computer exhibits, a shop with books and crafts, and a Web page that's nearly as good as an in-person visit. In January and February, the museum (Km 12, tel. 058/205555, www

.uta.cl/masma) is open 9 A.M.–8 P.M. daily, while during the rest of the year its hours are 10 A.M.–6 P.M. Admission costs US$1.50 per person, half that for children under age 10.

Accommodations and Food

Azapa's only hotel, a favorite with Arica visitors, is the (**Azapa Inn** (Guillermo Sánchez 660, tel. 058/244517, www.azapainn.cl, US$116 s or d), a tranquil getaway on four hectares of gardens and olive orchards, with recently remodeled rooms. It also has a swimming pool and a good restaurant.

For Ariqueños, Azapa is also a weekend getaway, where they go for Sunday *asados* at spots such as the **Club de Huasos** (Km 3.5, tel. 058/223991, www.clubdehuasos.cl); hours are noon–5 P.M., but it sometimes closes for private functions.

If it's not open, try the **Club Italiano** (Km 2). Museum visitors may enjoy **La Picá del Muertito** (Km 13, tel. 058/227437), alongside the cemetery.

Getting There and Around

Azapa has no regular bus service, but *taxi colectivos* from Arica's Parque Chacabuco, at the corner of Chacabuco and Baquedano, shuttle up and down the valley 7 A.M.–10 P.M. daily. Since these *colectivos* use the main road, visiting some of the sites would mean hiking in the hot sun; a good option would be a mountain bike, as this part of the valley rises only gradually toward the east.

PANAMERICANA SUR

From Arica south, the Panamericana turns inland, alternately climbing and dipping steeply through spectacular barren canyons separated by even more barren plateaus. Though the seemingly vertical walls of Quebrada Vitor and the Río Camarones Valley are the most impressive, there are points of interest in unexpected places.

Presencias Tutelares

From Arica, the Panamericana relentlessly ascends the hillside of the Quebrada de Acha until, leveling out at the summit of Cuesta de Acha, 27 kilometers south of town, it intersects a smooth dirt road that heads east to the precordillera village of Tignamar. At the junction, the state arts council Fondart has funded the creation of the *Presencias Tutelares* (Guardian Spirits, 1996), a cluster of desert sculptures evoking the region's pre-Columbian civilizations. A subsequent addition to the group, Arica sculptor Juan Gustavo Díaz Fleming's *Nacimiento del Inti* (Birth of the Sun), symbolizes the burning disk's emergence above the eastern horizon.

Camarones

Some 110 kilometers south of Arica, the hamlet of Cuya is an agricultural sanitation checkpoint and wide spot in the road that's also the administrative center for the *comuna* of Camarones, home to one of the country's few Afro-Chilean communities, dating back to Peruvian times. According to four-time mayor Sonia Salgado:

> There is evidence that people of African descent have existed in the north of the country ever since that territory was conquered. Our ancestors arrived here together with the conquerors.

Eleven kilometers west of Cuya via a dirt road, at the outlet of the Río Camarones, **Caleta Camarones** is a fishing settlement that is also a fine place to view migratory birds. About 20 kilometers south of Cuya, the restored **Geoglifos de Chiza** blanket the hillsides for several kilometers.

VALLE DE LLUTA

About nine kilometers north of Arica, the paved Ruta 11 climbs east up the valley of the Río Lluta to a junction where a paved lateral heads to the village of Molinos, while the main highway zigzags steeply into the precordillera and the altiplano, eventually reaching the Bolivian border near Lago Chungará. For most of the 20th century the railway, which parallels the highway as far as Molinos before heading northeast to Visviri, was the main way to Bolivia, but it now it's used to haul freight rather than passengers. Local buses carry passengers as far as Molinos, but frequent regional and international buses carry passengers up Ruta 11 to Putre, Parque Nacional Lauca, and over the border to the neighboring capital city of La Paz.

One of few northern Chilean rivers that regularly reach the sea, the Lluta flooded tremendously in February 2001, when the altiplano runoff washed out roads, rails, and bridges all the way to Poconchile, 35 kilometers up the valley. It even destroyed the ostensibly sturdy bridge over the Panamericana, briefly isolating Arica from its airport at Chacalluta and from the nearby Peruvian city of Tacna.

Poor water quality, though, has limited Lluta's agricultural growth to lower-value crops and livestock. Like Azapa, it was a major pack train route well into the 20th century, and the enormous series of **Geoglifos de Lluta,** visible from the highway, embellish its southern hillsides only a few kilometers up the valley. They date from around A.D. 1000–1300.

At Poconchile, 37 kilometers from Arica, the unadorned 17th-century **Iglesia San Jerónimo** is one of Chile's oldest churches, but its antiquity is deceptive, since it was rebuilt in the 19th century and refurbished in the 20th century. After the highway leaves the Lluta Valley, it switchbacks up **Cuesta El Aguila** before emerging onto a plateau and then entering, at around kilometer 73, the **Quebrada Cardones.**

Here, between 2,000 and 2,800 meters, grows the *cactus candelabros (Browningia candelaris),* so called because, in specimens taller than about two meters, its trunk divides into multiple branches resembling a candelabra. Interestingly, the upper branches are almost spineless, while the main trunk is almost covered with vicious needles. It grows at what is roughly the western limit of the summer rains, mostly along dry watercourses, but it also benefits from the high *camanchaca* that penetrates from the coast.

Just west of kilometer 100, one of the route's unlikeliest sights is the antique rail car, acquired from a nitrate *oficina* near Antofagasta, that marks **Pueblo Mailiku.** Zealously convinced that visitors to the altiplano need to break their journey precisely at this point to adapt to the altitude, Alexis Troncoso and Andrea Chellew are raising their family here and offering delectable fresh bread, soothing *mate de coca* (coca leaf tea), three guest beds (US$5 pp), camping, solar-powered hot showers, clean toilets, and excruciatingly sincere convictions.

Almost precisely at kilometer 100, 3,270 meters above sea level, the 12th-century hilltop fortifications of the **Pukará de Copaquilla** guarded the pre-Columbian agricultural terraces in the upper drainage of the Río San José, immediately below. Altiplano tours usually take a break at the site, restored by the Universidad de Tarapacá in 1979.

At kilometer 102, the tight-fitting stonework of the **Tambo de Zapahuira** was an Inka posthouse on the road that ran north to Cuzco and south toward San Pedro de Atacama. Ironically, the nearby contemporary crossroads of Zapahuira, where a lateral road heads southeast into the precordillera of Belén, serves much the same function, as Bolivian truckers stop for lunch or dinner before continuing toward Arica or heading back to La Paz.

Below a turnoff at kilometer 116, deep in its namesake valley and surrounded by pre-Columbian terraces, the village of **Socoroma** is known for its 16th-century **Iglesia de San Francisco** (damaged but still standing after the June 2005 earthquake) and the fresh *tumbo* (Andean passionfruit *Passiflora mollisima Bailey*) juice at the house of Emilia Humire, who also offers inexpensive lodging in two cabañas with external baths. About three kilometers west, the **Pukará de la Calacruz** is an Incaic ruin.

PRECORDILLERA DE BELÉN

From the Zapahuira junction, a gravel road built primarily for the modern Chapiquiña hydroelectric plant follows, in part, the precordillera Inka highway that once linked northern

Despite its non-traditional corrugated roof, Belén's church dates from the 18th century.

© WAYNE BERNHARDSON

NORTE GRANDE

Chile with Peru. At Murmuntani, midway to Chapiquiña, a secondary road switchbacks vertiginously up to the altiplano, an alternative route to Parque Nacional Lauca and Reserva Nacional Las Vicuñas.

On the main road, surrounded by terraces where Aymara farmers still cultivate indigenous crops such as quinoa, the villages of Belén and Tignamar Viejo both feature colonial churches; the former's is in better condition. Belén's July 24 **Fiesta de Santiago** is worth a visit for those already in the area.

There are also several Inka fortifications, all of them national monuments: the **Pukará de Belén** (six kilometers west of the town and the road), the **Pukará de Lupica** (at the hamlet of the same name), and the **Pukará de Saxamar** (at the confluence of the Río Saxamar and the Río Tignamar).

Beyond Tignamar Viejo, to the southwest, the road passes through a dusty gorge before emerging onto the broad but equally dusty Pampa de Chaca, eventually intersecting the Panamericana at the Presencias Tutelares, 21 kilometers south of Arica. An alternative route back to the Panamericana leaves the road across the Pampa de Chaca and heads south to the village of Codpa, a better choice for southbound travelers.

Reached by a road barely wide enough for a single automobile in some stretches, **Codpa** is a scenic oasis in a bowl surrounded by barren cliffs where boulders loosened by the June 2005 earthquake still perch tenuously above town. A steep paved highway climbs south out of the valley and onto the Pampa de Camarones, where it intersects the Panamericana about 65 kilometers south of Arica.

Beyond reach of falling rocks, Codpa has solid accommodations on landscaped grounds, with a large pool, at the 15-room **Ecolodge Codpa** (General Salvo 159, Oficina 209, Santiago, tel. 02/2351519, www.codpavalleylodge.cl, US$80 s, US$100 d with breakfast). Under new professional management, it also has activities-oriented packages, and serves lunch and dinner (US$20 each) at its restaurant.

Getting There and Around

For travelers without their own motor vehicles or mountain bikes (an interesting alternative despite the shortage of drinking water between Tignamar Viejo and the Panamericana), transportation options are limited. Arica's **Empresa La Paloma** (Germán Riesco 2071, tel. 058/222710) goes to Belén Tuesday and Friday at 6:30 A.M. (US$3.50), to Tignamar Tuesday and Friday at 7 A.M. (US$4), and to Codpa Monday, Wednesday, and Friday at 8:30 A.M. (US$4.50, four hours). Covering the distance between Belén and Tignamar or Codpa depends not only on the schedules, but also on negotiating at least 13 kilometers with no public transport.

PUTRE

Gateway to the altiplano, beneath the 5,800-meter massif of the Nevados de Putre, Putre is the village-sized capital of the thinly populated province of Parinacota. Given its picturesque colonial style, scenic surroundings, and access to the altiplano and its national parks, some have speculated that Putre will be the next San Pedro de Atacama. The critical mass of visitors to sustain that sort of popularity is lacking, but services are improving.

Many visitors take advantage of Putre's intermediate altitude—3,500 meters above sea level—to acclimatize before tackling oxygen-poor Parque Nacional Lauca and other areas higher than most of the highest summits of North America and Europe. Increasing numbers, though, are spending more time at Putre itself, for activities such as hiking and horseback riding.

As the provincial capital, Putre boasts a burgeoning bureaucracy. In a sense, though, this marks a continuity rather than a break with the past—centuries ago, this Aymara settlement was a Spanish colonial *congregación* or *reducción,* created to control the indigenous population through tax, tribute, and religious indoctrination.

Orientation

Putre (population 1,235) is 150 kilometers east/northeast of Arica by paved Ruta 11, the international route to La Paz, and a paved spur that dips into town. The town itself, a relatively regular grid based on the Plaza de Armas and sloping toward the west, is compact enough that finding one's way is easy.

Sights

Facing the Plaza de Armas, the **Iglesia de Putre** (1670) is a colonial adobe, though its facade is a later stone addition. Numerous other colonial and early republican buildings have maintained their facades, some of them surprisingly ornate, but their interiors have deteriorated and the June 2005 earthquake damaged some of them seriously. Valentina Aliave leads hour-plus village tours that include new murals with Aymara cultural themes.

For specialty birding and natural history tours of the altiplano and other fauna- and flora-rich areas, contact Putre-based Barbara Knapton's **Alto Andino Nature Tours** (Baquedano 299, cel. 09/98907291, www.birdingaltoandino.com). Destinations include Arica, Reserva Nacional Pampa del Tamarugal, Parque Nacional Lauca's Las Cuevas, Parinacota, Laguna Cotacotani, and Lago Chungará; Reserva Nacional Las Vicuñas; Monumento Natural Salar de Surire; Parque Nacional Volcán Isluga; and coastal wetlands around Pisagua. Accommodations can include either camping at Conaf *refugios* or staying at hotels; tours can start and end in Arica, Iquique, or Putre.

Events

For a small Andean village, Putre's annual **Carnaval,** in February or March depending on the date of Easter, is remarkably extroverted and participatory—locals and outsiders alike may find themselves showered with flour and adorned with colorful paper dots *(chaya).* Music, rather like the brass bands in Arica's Carnaval Ginga, comes from the youthful *tarqueada* and the more venerable *banda;*

celebrations culminate with the burning of an effigy known as the *momo*.

Accommodations and Food

Putre has several modest but better-than-adequate accommodations and one that's more elaborate. Most of them also serve meals but none have in-room heating (though they usually provide plenty of blankets).

The cheapest is **Residencial La Paloma** (O'Higgins 353, cel. 09/9197-9319, US$8 pp with private bath). **Residencial Cali** (Baquedano 399, 09/9282-1152, US$10–15 pp) has one shared-bath single; all other rooms have private baths.

Hotel Kukuli (Baquedano 301, cel. 09/9161-4709, 09/8368-2250, www.translapaloma.cl, US$20 s, US$34 d with breakfast), is a sharp new place with no frills but good furniture, and each room has a balcony or terrace.

Hostal Pachamama (Cochrane s/n, tel. 058/231028 in Arica www.chileanaltiplano .cl, ukg@entelchile.net, US$12 pp with shared bath and breakfast) has made good first impressions. Under the same management, catering to both the mining industry and the general public, the 112-room **Hotel Las Vicuñas** (Baquedano 80. tel. 058231028 in Arica, www.chileanaltiplano.cl, akg@entelchile.net, US$30 s, US$42 d) sits at the eastern approach to town. In addition to the usual amenities, it has Mac-incompatible WiFi and electric heaters.

New on the scene, operated by the owners of Talca's Casa Chueca, **Chakana Mountain Lodge** (cel. 09/9745-9519, www.la-chakana .com, US$13 pp, US$45 s, US$57 d) is about a 10-minute walk west of town. The lower rates correspond to hostel-style dorms, the higher rates for private rooms.

La Paloma (O'Higgins 353), and **Rosamel** (Latorre 400-C) prepare simple meals for tour groups and casual visitors. The Arica pub/restaurant **Cantaverdi** has opened a branch on the Plaza de Armas, but it keeps erratic hours.

Putre's only other nightspot is **⬛ Kuchu Marka** (Baquedano 351, cel. 09/9011-4007), which has good food and drinks in surprisingly fashionable surroundings, with live Andean music. The menu is not extensive, but it's creative enough to include Andean specialties such as quinoa.

Information and Services

On the Plaza de Armas, Putre's **Oficina de Información Turística** faces the bank but keeps erratic hours.

Nearly all other services are directly on the Plaza de Armas, including **Banco del Estado** (changing U.S. cash only, no ATM) and **Correos de Chile** (the post office). **Restaurant Rosamel** (tel. 058/300051) has telephones that work with phone cards, while there's good Internet service at **Quipunet**, on the plaza's north side.

Opposite the army base downhill from the plaza, **Conaf** has an information office open 8:30 A.M.–1 P.M. and 2–5:30 P.M. daily. It can provide information on Parque Nacional Lauca and other protected areas in the altiplano.

Cali Tours (Baquedano 399, cel. 09/8518-0960 or 09/8536-1242, www.calitours.cl) goes to Parque Nacional Lauca, does bike and hiking tours, changes money, and will shuttle clients to the highway junction to meet Bolivia-bound buses.

Getting There and Around

From Arica, **Buses La Paloma** (Germán Riesco 2071, tel. 058/222710) goes daily to Putre at 6:30 A.M. (US$4.50, three hours), returning at 1:30 P.M.

The Altiplano of Arica

Well above 4,000 meters, the highlands beyond Putre consist of sprawling freshwater lakes and well-watered alluvial plains, encircled by rounded hills and punctuated by soaring volcanic cones and calderas, some of them perpetually snowbound. Aymara shepherds herd llamas, alpacas, and sheep at scattered homesteads. In drier, more southerly areas, copious flocks of flamingos and other birds feed at shallow saline lakes.

Most of the same operators who offer tours in and around Arica also offer altiplano tours; some offer day trips, but many if not most people prefer to spend at least a night acclimatizing at an intermediate destination such as Putre to avoid *soroche* (altitude sickness); if going for the day, be certain the operator carries oxygen. Dehydration and sunburn are also serious matters at this altitude—carry plenty of water, use sunglasses, and apply a powerful sunblock. The combination of altitude sickness and the nearly

WARNING

Because of the altiplano's elevations, often well above 4,000 meters, *soroche* or *apunamiento* (altitude sickness) is a potentially serious matter in the Norte Grande – even young and vigorous individuals have fallen gravely ill. Before heading to the heights, get familiar with the warning signs, which include intense headaches, vertigo, either drowsiness or insomnia, and shortness of breath.

In the mildest cases, rest and relaxation can help relieve symptoms as the body adjusts to the reduced oxygen level. If symptoms persist or worsen, moving to a lower elevation should have the desired effect. It is better to stay at an intermediate altitude than to climb directly from sea level to such high elevations. Avoid or limit alcohol consumption, do not overeat, and drink extra fluids.

direct tropical rays is particularly dangerous. Do not hesitate to return to lower elevations—unacclimatized visitors have died here.

One of northern Chile's most interesting excursions is the loop from Arica to Putre, Parinacota, and Lago Chungará, then south to Reserva Nacional Las Vicuñas, Monumento Natural Salar de Surire, and Parque Nacional Volcán Isluga, then back to Arica (or Iquique) via Pozo Almonte and the Panamericana. This is possible either with private or rented vehicles, or with an Arica tour operator. During the summer rainy season, though, it may be impossible to continue south of Guallatire even with four-wheel drive.

◖ PARQUE NACIONAL LAUCA

Near the Bolivian border, Parque Nacional Lauca is a top-of-the-world experience—flamingos fly above cobalt blue lakes and Aymara shepherds tend flocks of llamas and alpacas more than 4,000 meters above sea level, at the foot of snow-clad volcanic cones at least 2,000 meters higher. The recovery of the endangered wild vicuña, whose wool a Spanish chronicler called "finer than silk," is one of Latin America's great conservation successes.

Occupying 137,883 hectares of soaring volcanoes, rolling hills, sprawling lakes, and marshy bogland—the Aymara word *lawq'a* means "swamp grass"—Parque Nacional Lauca has been a UNESCO World Biosphere Reserve since 1981. Between 3,200 and 6,342 meters above sea level, the park is home to abundant wildlife, including 130 bird species and 21 mammal species, such as the vicuña, a wild relative of the domestic llama and alpaca.

Lauca's high altitude makes it less suitable for long hikes without acclimatizing at "foothill" villages such as Putre—*only* about 3,500 meters above sea level. Well-equipped climbers, in top physical condition, can attempt to scale the 6,320-meter Volcán Parinacota.

Lauca is accessible all year but best from

September to April; the December to February rainy season brings afternoon thunderstorms.

Since 1983, the park has been reduced from its original 520,000 hectares, though it's only fair to say that part of these disaffected areas became Reserva Nacional Las Vicuñas and Monumento Natural Salar de Surire. Water diversions for hydroelectricity facilities in the precordillera and agriculture in the Azapa Valley have desiccated parts of the high-altitude wetlands; at the same time, mining interests have pressured the government to remove additional areas near Putre, at the northwestern edge of the park.

Ironically, the return to democracy has contributed to these problems. At the park's creation in 1970, authorities apparently assumed that all the land belonged to the state, when in fact many Aymara have held individual titles since Peruvian times. Records in Arica's land registry indicate that altiplano land was freely bought and sold, and that some pastoralists also regularized their de facto occupancy with legal documents. Conaf and other government agencies have acknowledged the legitimacy of these claims, but have not yet managed to reconcile indigenous rights with park management plans—an issue that couldn't even come up during the Pinochet dictatorship.

Flora and Fauna

The Lauca altiplano has two principal types of vegetative associations. The first, and more abundant, is the dry steppe, or *puna,* which consists of Compositae shrubs and of perennial bunch grasses of the genera *Stipa, Poa, Festuca,* and others; known collectively as *icchu* in Aymara or *paja brava* in Spanish, the grasses form a discontinuous cover that increases with the summer rains. The second is the well-watered alluvial depressions known locally as *bofedales, vegas,* or *ciénegas;* here, dense cushion plants completely cover the soil and, with dwarf annuals and perennial grasses, offer permanent grazing for wild and domestic livestock.

Some plant species are unique to the Andean highlands. Though it appears, from a distance,

Andean teal, Ciénagas de Parinacota, Parque Nacional Lauca

to be a spongy moss, the prostrate *llareta (Azorella compacta)* is a rock-hard shrub whose branches are so densely packed together that the Aymara must use a pick to break open dead plants, which they use as fuel for cooking and heating. In the past, the slow-growing *llareta* was depleted in parts of the altiplano because miners collected it for fuel.

The woody *queñoa,* growing up to five meters in height at altitudes up to 4,500 meters or even a bit higher, survives in scattered forest clusters. Once used for fuel and lumber (despite its crooked trunk), it thrives in cold and shady ravines.

Lauca is an extraordinary destination for birds and birders. The most conspicuous are the Andean condor, the flightless, ostrichlike *ñandú* or *suri,* and aquatic species such as the Chilean flamingo, *tagua gigante* (giant coot), the *guallata* or *piuquén* (Andean goose), and the *gaviota andina* (Andean gull). The puna tinamou is an occasional sight.

One primary reason for Lauca's creation was the vicuña, the wild camelid that's kin to the domestic llama and alpaca, both of which are herded by the Aymara shepherds. According to a 2007 census, vicuña numbers—only about 1,000 in the 1970s—have reached 14,455,

NORTE GRANDE

thanks to effective park management and the virtual cessation of poaching.

Other mammals include the rarely seen puma (the park's largest predator), the even rarer *taruca* or northern *huemul*, foxes, and the plump rodent *vizcacha*, a chinchilla relative inhabiting scattered rookeries. The domestic sheep, a Spanish introduction that survives in part on forage that llamas and alpacas cannot tolerate, is also numerous.

Sights and Recreation

Nine kilometers east of the park's western entrance, where Ruta 11 emerges from the narrow Quebrada Taipicahue onto the altiplano, 4,300 meters above sea level, **Las Cuevas** is one of the best places to view both vicuñas and vizcachas. Nearby, look for a rock shelter inhabited by hunter-gatherers nearly 10,000 years ago, a *chacu* whose tapering rock walls trapped vicuñas in pre-Columbian times, and where the temperature of enclosed thermal baths hovers around 31°C. A short distance to the east, the primary colors of a sore-thumb sculpture of an Andean *zampoña* (panpipe) mar the view at the **Mirador Llano de Chucuyo**, a Conaf-constructed observation point.

From the observation point, toward the east, are the Llanos de Chucuyo (Plains of Chucuyo) and the well-watered **Ciénegas de Parinacota**, the marshes or *bofedales* that comprise the park's most productive pasturelands and most diverse assemblage of flora. Augmented by a network of irrigation canals, the marshes provide a habitat for wild geese, ducks, coots, and other waterfowl. At the village of **Chucuyo**, where roadside restaurants cater to passing truckers and tourists, there's a small colonial chapel and a weavers' cooperative selling locally produced alpaca woolens.

Just beyond Chucuyo, a dirt road follows the *bofedal*'s edge north toward the rejuvenated village of **Parinacota**—4,400 meters above sea level—a national monument for its traditional architecture. During festival dates, such as August 30's Fiesta de Santa Rosa de Lima, Aymara throngs crowd in and around

© WAYNE BERNHARDSON

Indigenous statuary tops the walls and bell tower of the church at Parinacota, Parque Nacional Lauca

the 17th-century **Iglesia de Parinacota**, a national architectural monument in its own right. Surrounded by adobe walls that are themselves topped by an offbeat mix of ecclesiastical and phallic statuary, the church features a separate two-story bell tower at its southwest corner. Five meters wide and 22 meters long, with two lateral chapels, the building is roofed with *icchu*. Local vendors sell alpaca woolens and other crafts, not all of them locally made, outside the walls.

Interestingly, the church's interior murals, by an indigenous artist in colonial times, portray Spanish soldiers leading Christ to the cross, alongside a graphically disconcerting *Final Judgment* in which sinners suffer gruesome tortures before being led to the jaws of a fire-breathing dragon. Experts from Cuzco have recently begun a restoration project on the deteriorating paintings.

Conaf's Refugio Parinacota no longer provides accommodations, but rangers stationed here can provide information on nearby excursions such as 5,097-meter **Cerro Guane Guane,** an extinct volcano whose summit offers astounding panoramas. The climb takes at least four hours, and the last several hundred meters involves a particularly tiresome assault through volcanic ash and sand.

Less strenuously approached, just east of Parinacota, **Laguna Cotacotani** is really a series of small lakes whose water levels vary according to diversions toward the precordillera's Central Chapiquiña hydroelectric plant. These diversions have also desiccated parts of the *bofedales,* but there are still crested ducks, Andean geese, and other wildlife, including foxes, at the base of the scattered cinder cones and congealed lava flows that surround it.

East of Chucuyo, toward the Bolivian border, **Lago Chungará** is a shallow but biologically thriving lake formed when Holocene lava flows dammed the Río Lauca. At 4,517 meters above sea level, covering an area of 21.5 square kilometers to a maximum depth of only 37 meters, Chungará supports abundant populations of wetland birds such as the Andean goose, the Andean gull, several species of ducks, and even flamingos. Giant coots, about the size of domestic turkeys, build seemingly floating nests near the shoreline.

North of Chungará, Lauca's most imposing natural landmarks are the twin Pallachata volcanoes, known individually as Parinacota (elevation 6,350 meters) and Pomerabe (6,232 meters). Both are climbable for truly well-equipped parties but require permission from the Dirección de Fronteras y Límites (Difrol) in Santiago, since they are directly on the border. Their snowy cones are dormant but, only a short distance south of the highway, Volcán Guallatire (6,061 meters) smolders constantly.

Conaf maintains a ranger station, as well as a *refugio* and campground, at Chungará, where crafts vendors meet tour buses in the early afternoon; as in Parinacota, not all of the items for sale are locally produced. To the east, directly on the border, the **Feria Tambo Quemado,** taking place on alternate Fridays, is where local Aymara go to exchange goods with their kin from across the line.

Accommodations and Food

Conaf's **Camping Parinacota,** in its namesake village, offers two small but sheltered tent sites for free, but there are no bathroom facilities. At Lago Chungará, its somewhat more elaborate and considerably more scenic **Camping Chungará** is higher and colder; it has picnic tables, and the **Refugio Chungará** is also open to guests (US$7 pp).

At Parinacota, **Albergue Uta Kala Don Leo** (tel. 058/261526 in Arica, leonel_parinacota@ hotmail.com, US$5 pp) offers the best accommodations the village has ever had—though all the rooms are dorms and the baths are shared, it's a brand new construction that's suitable for more than just hard-core backpackers.

At Chucuyo, directly on Ruta 11, there are several truckers' restaurants, including **Copihue de Oro** (ask for *chairo,* a Bolivian soup/stew with alpaca, quinoa, and vegetables) and **Restaurant Doña Mati,** which also offers inexpensive beds. Limited supplies are available in both Chucuyo and Parinacota; it's better to bring food from Arica or Putre.

Information

In addition to its Parinacota facilities, Conaf keeps **Centros de Información Turística** at Las Cuevas and Lago Chungará. But because the rangers are often working in the field, there may not always be someone on duty. Because Lauca is on a major international transit route, unlike most other Chilean parks, it does not collect an admission fee.

Getting There and Around

From Arica's Terminal Internacional, **Transporte La Paloma** (tel. 058/222710) goes to Parinacota and the Bolivian border at Visviri at 9 A.M. and 9 P.M. Tuesday and Friday, but schedules are subject to change. Bolivia-bound buses will drop passengers at Chucuyo (the turnoff for Parinacota) and Lago Chungará,

NORTE GRANDE

but expect to pay the full fare as if going to to La Paz.

Motorists should bring extra gasoline, though it may be available at premium prices at Putre (where construction of a station has stalled) and at Chucuyo. Remember that vehicles at high altitudes consume at least 20–30 percent more fuel than at sea level.

RESERVA NACIONAL LAS VICUÑAS

Part of Parque Nacional Lauca until, under pressure from mining interests, it was recategorized to permit exploitation of existing tailings from the gold mine at Choquelimpie, 209,131-hectare Reserva Nacional Las Vicuñas gets far fewer visitors than its northern neighbor—most tours and tourists do not stray far from the paved international highway. Less populated than Lauca, it boasts abundant wildlife and a string of Aymara hamlets and shepherds' outposts en route to points south.

Sights

East of Las Cuevas and west of Chucuyo, separate gravel roads leading south merge to continue southeast, passing the junction to the Central Chapiquiña hydroelectric plant in the precordillera and continuing past **Choquelimpie,** a colonial gold mine that closed just a few years ago; for a brief period in the late 1980s and early 1990s, tailings were processed under new technology that permitted exploitation of lower-grade deposits.

From Choquelimpie the road, troublesome or even impassable in the wet summer, heads southeast toward **Ancuta** (with a small colonial chapel) and the village of **Guallatire,** at the foot of its smoking namesake volcano. The last substantial settlement for several hours, Guallatire has an impressive 17th-century church with a freestanding bell tower and some of the Chilean altiplano's most productive *bofedales.* Motorists must stop at the Carabineros checkpoint here.

Just south of the village, on the west side of the road, are the ruins of the colonial **Trapiche de Guallatire,** a hydraulic silver mill and

smelter. Beyond here, vicuñas and rheas are common sights, but summer rains can make the road south difficult even for skilled motorists with four-wheel drive despite good bridges over the Río Viluvio and the Río Lauca—avoid the slippery yellow clay if at all possible. Only the occasional isolated shepherd, in a small adobe, is around to lend a hand.

Accommodations and Food

Accommodations options are limited. In Guallatire, the no-frills **Casa de Hospedaje Guallatire** (tel. 058/242482, guallatire@hotmail.com, US$4 pp) also serves meals for US$3 per person, with homemade bread. Conaf's **Refugio Guallatire** (US$7 pp) offers bunks in a comfortable building, but if planning to stay here, make advance inquiries at Conaf in Arica or Putre—rangers are not always present.

Getting There and Around

There is no public transportation whatsoever and few private vehicles, but loop tours from Arica do pass through the area. In summer, four-wheel drive may not be sufficient for areas south of Guallatire; the rest of the year, it's not necessary, though high clearance is a good idea.

MONUMENTO NATURAL SALAR DE SURIRE

Home to three species of flamingos, 4,295 meters above sea level, the 11,298-hectare Salar de Surire is an awkward reserve comprising roughly 70 percent of the sprawling, blindingly white salt lake from which it takes its name. Its Aymara name means "place of the rhea," which, though they are present in the area, attract less attention than the flamingos, which feed on microorganisms in pools created by the summer rains.

Created in 1983, when commercial mining interests forced the dismantling of Parque Nacional Lauca into three separate units, it does *not* include 4,560 hectares granted to the Sociedad Química Industrial de Borax in 1989, only months before the formal end of the Pinochet dictatorship, for a surface borax mine.

Ironically, of Conaf's various land-use categories, *monumentos naturales* presumably receive the highest level of protection, but conservationists have complained vigorously about the miners' disturbance of nesting birds.

Still, up to 10,000 birds spend the year here. Most are Chilean flamingos, but the smaller James flamingo *(Phoenicoparrus jamesii)* and the larger, rarer Andean flamingo *(Phoenicoparrus andinus)* are also present. Vicuñas and rheas are also common sights.

Sights
Wildlife, primarily the large flamingo colonies at the **Lagunas Salar de Surire,** is the main attraction. Just outside the door of Conaf's ranger station on the west side of the reserve, there's a large vizcacha rookery that's ideal for photography. Rheas are also common.

Some 16 kilometers southeast of Conaf's ranger station, the **Termas de Polloquere** is a small geyser field with a handful of large pools suitable for soaking.

Accommodations
On the west side of the Salar, Conaf's **Guardería y Refugio Salar de Surire** (US$7) has sleeping accommodations in a converted freight container. There are kitchen facilities, plus solar-powered electricity and hot showers; the rangers who run it welcome visitors and can give essential information for those heading south toward Isluga. Tour groups from Arica often stay here, so it's best to make reservations in Arica.

Camping is possible at **Termas de Polloquere** in an exposed location with no fresh water.

Getting There and Around
The Salar de Surire is roughly 126 kilometers southeast of Putre via either Las Cuevas (Parque Nacional Lauca) or the less traveled alternative via the Portezuelo de Chapiquiña, and 48 kilometers south of Guallatire. Again, there is no public transport, so renting a vehicle or taking a tour from Arica is pretty much the only option.

Segments of the road to Parque Nacional Isluga and Colchane, 79 kilometers to the south, can be tricky in wet weather, and distances on Turistel's highway map are grossly inaccurate. Beyond the well-marked Polloquere junction, the road grows faint over **Cerro Capitán,** then becomes clearer toward **Mucomucone,** where there's a disconcerting river crossing that makes you feel as if you are diving into a pool—high clearance is imperative, though the bottom is now paved and four-wheel drive is not essential. The road then passes through the villages of Enquelga, Isluga, and finally the bleak border post of Colchane.

PISAGUA
From its appearance, it's hard to conceive that sleepy Pisagua, at the end of a precipitous zigzag road that descends from the pampa, once was one of northern Chile's principal ports. A town whose population numbered several thousands in the early 20th century has only about 200 inhabitants today, though it's slowly reviving with the export of sea urchins and increasing tourist traffic. There are even new houses being built alongside the historical monuments that remain from its nitrate heyday.

In 1973, though, Pisagua became a synonym for terror. Its remote location—only one road in or out, through unrelentingly arid and shadeless terrain—made it a natural prison after Pinochet's 1973 putsch (some prisoners were forced to run barefoot up the hot barren hillsides, as if to teach them how futile any escape attempt would be). After Chile's return to democracy in 1989, investigators found a mass grave at the town's historic cemetery.

The handful of native-born Pisaguans who still live here keep to themselves, having little to do with recent arrivals. While it's a languid backwater during the week, it can fill up with visitors on weekends.

History
Pisagua was a minor port until the exploitation of nitrates at Zapiga, in the coast range, made it a convenient export point. It was the site of a major battle during the War of the

© WAYNE BERNHARDSON

The cemetery at Pisagua dates from Peruvian times, in the 19th century.

Pacific, when Chilean troops came ashore on November 2, 1879, to defeat allied Peruvian and Bolivian forces. Under Chilean rule, it became the country's third major nitrate port, after Antofagasta and Iquique.

At its peak, Pisagua had two daily newspapers, three banks, and seven piers—three belonging to the Nitrate Railways Company, two to nitrate baron John Thomas North, one to the Compañía Salitrera La Aguada, and one to the Chilean state. After the nitrate collapse, it became a penal colony and continued for many years as the terminus of the Longino, the longitudinal railway that connected the north with the south. It languished for many years thereafter, before achieving unwanted notoriety during the Pinochet regime.

Sights

Several striking landmarks from Pisagua's nitrate boom are national architectural monuments. Pisagua's gaily painted, 12-meter wooden **Torre Reloj** (Clock Tower, 1887) stands sentinel on a bedrock outcrop above

the town, but its clock no longer functions. Immediately south, built on fill, the two-story **Hospital de Pisagua** (1906–1909) began to slip down the hillside not long after its construction and was finally abandoned in 1958. It is due to become a museum.

Along the shore—overhanging it, really—the **Teatro Municipal** (1897) was an extravagant performing arts facility for a town of Pisagua's size, complete with private box seats, bench seating for the proles (proletariats), and an immense stage. While the regional government has helped with some preservation and restoration, the peeling ceiling murals need urgent attention. The building's northern half once housed a market, city offices, the Banco de Londres, and, during the dictatorship, many female prisoners. For access to the theater, visit the library alongside it.

Half a block east of the plaza, the Georgian-style **Cárcel Pública de Pisagua** (1909) served as a standard prison for decades and as a political prison during President González Videla's 1947 anti-Communist purge. After

September 1973, though, so many prisoners filled its cells—roughly half the size of a modest bedroom—that they could not even sit down. After a German crew filmed these appalling conditions clandestinely, the military shifted half the prisoners into the market building, separating the women upstairs. The administrators' rooms at the front of the building served as hotel accommodations until recently, while those toward the back, ironically, hosted banquets.

North of the theater, the rails are gone from the **Estación Ferrocarril de Pisagua,** where nitrates and passengers once arrived, and the station itself is at risk—posted notices beg people not to carry off any of the remaining lumber. On Pisagua's northern outskirts, the **Monolito Centenario** memorializes the 1879 Chilean landing.

Beyond the cemetery, two kilometers north of town, rusting metal and rotting wooden crosses mark gravesites at the **Cementerio Municipal;** nearby, a recent marker memorializes the victims exhumed from a mass grave with the vow:

> Although footprints may tread this site for a thousand years, they will not cover the blood of those who fell here.

As of early 2006, the Chilean government had declared its intention to make these unmarked graves a national historical monument. Two new memorials have recently been built.

North of the cemetery, the road climbs the steep headland of Punta Pisagua and drops into **Pisagua Vieja,** the adobe remains of the town's original site (and also the site of a pre-Columbian cemetery). The nearby **Quebrada de Tana** estuary is a breeding site for shorebirds, but the dirt road that once ascended the Quebrada to Hacienda Tiliviche is no longer passable.

Accommodations and Food

At Playa Blanca, north of the police station, Pisagua's free **Camping Municipal** can draw lots of weekend visitors but hardly anybody during the week. It has flush toilets and warm-to-hot showers with water funneled from the former Oficina Dolores, on the Panamericana, but maintenance has declined. If it gets too crowded, there are wild sites farther north, near the Monolito Centenario.

Hostal Don Gato (Prat 129, tel. 057/731511, dongato@chilesat.net, US$8 pp with shared bath) has simple accommodations and is also a sea-view *picada* with excellent fish dishes at moderate prices, though the aging proprietors sometimes seem overwhelmed. Ask for the fish *a la plancha* (grilled) instead of fried.

Hostal La Roca (Manuel Rodríguez 20, tel. 057/731502, viejopisagua2@hotmail.com, US$19 s, US$28–43 d with an above-average breakfast that includes omelettes) has four rooms, two with ocean views, with private bath. French-speaking Catherine Saldaña also prepares meals (for guests only), and is a good source of information.

Getting There and Around

Roughly midway between Arica and Iquique, Pisagua is accessible only by a recently repaired paved road that leads directly west from the Panamericana at a junction 85 kilometers south of Cuya (Camarones) and 47 kilometers north of Huara. There is no regular public transportation from the junction and vehicles along the route are few, but rumors persist that Iquique travel agencies may start service.

NORTE GRANDE

Iquique

Sometimes called—only semi-facetiously—the "Miami of Chile" for its high-rise beachfront hotels and condos, the port city of Iquique and its Zona Franca (Zofri) duty-free zone were the main motor of import-led growth during the Norte Grande's 1980s economic boom. While that boom has slowed, Iquique stands alone as Tarapacá's political capital, major port, and tourist destination, pulling even Argentines and Paraguayans over the Andes for duty-free shopping.

For nonshoppers, though, the main attraction is its late-19th- and early-20th-century architecture, its fire-prone Georgian and Victorian mansions built of so-called *pino oregón* (literally, "Oregon pine"). This timber is in fact Douglas fir *(Pseudotsuga mienziesii)* shipped from California and the Pacific Northwest during the nitrate boom.

Iquique is also a center for outdoor activities, most notably surfing and parasailing *(parapente),* both of which bring in overseas visitors, and cruise ships are also beginning to visit here. As for the Miami connection, well, Iquique does maintain a "sister city" relationship with the Dade County metropolis.

HISTORY

In colonial times and even after independence, the port of Iquique played second fiddle to Arica; it was, remarked Darwin in 1835:

> ...most gloomy; the little port, with its few vessels, and small group of wretched houses, seemed overwhelmed and out of proportion to the rest of the scene.

Nitrates changed everything. Arica enjoyed a direct route to Potosí via the Lluta and Azapa Valleys, but several deeply incised canyons separated it from the broad nitrate pampas that lay behind the coast range, from Pisagua in the north to Taltal in the south.

Some nitrate ports, such as Pisagua, stagnated and even died, but Iquique flourished and adapted, as fishing complemented and then replaced nitrates in the local economy. It was, however, the backdrop for one of the most infamous incidents in Chilean labor history when, in 1907, police and military fired upon and killed hundreds of nitrate strikers holed up in the Escuela Santa María (a school of that name still occupies the site, south of the Mercado Central, but it replaced the historic structure).

In the mid-1970s, creation of the Zofri spurred a new immigration boom. As Iquique's population exceeded 140,000 and occupied nearly all available space on its narrow coastal shelf, the ridgetop community of Alto Hospicio—which two decades ago comprised just a handful of farmers who grew vegetables with irrigation water squeezed from the *camanchaca*—mushroomed to accommodate tens of thousands of low-wage workers.

ORIENTATION

On a narrow shelf at the foot of a 600-meter escarpment that parallels the Pacific Ocean, Iquique (population 214,586) is 1,850 kilometers north of Santiago via the Panamericana and coastal Ruta 1 via Antofagasta. It is 315 kilometers from Arica via paved Ruta 16, which runs east–west to and from a junction near the nitrate ghost town of Humberstone, and the Panamericana; it is 410 kilometers from Calama via Ruta 16, the Panamericana, and paved Ruta 24, the Tocopilla–Calama highway.

Historically, Iquique's center is Plaza Prat, but the city has spread north and, to a greater extent, south along the Pacific beaches. North of the old railroad station, the Barrio Industrial is also home to the commercial Zona Franca; the areas south and east, toward Cerro Dragón's towering dunes, are largely residential. On the escarpment above the city, the working-class suburb of Alto Hospicio has sprawled spontaneously over the surrounding pampa.

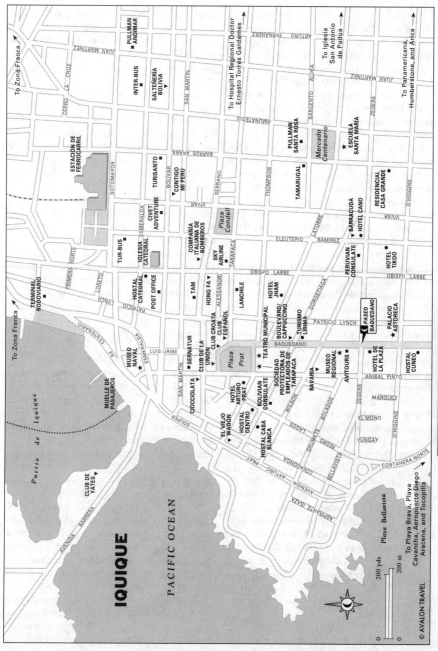

IQUIQUE

PACIFIC OCEAN

Puerto de Iquique

© AVALON TRAVEL

NORTE GRANDE

To Playa Brava, Playa
Cavancha, Aeropuerto Diego
Aracena, and Tocopilla

Playa Bellavista

200 yds
200 m

SIGHTS

Dating from the nitrate era, central Iquique's characteristic Victorian and Georgian architecture makes it a walker's delight, while the city's popular beaches extend south. The Peruvian-era **Torre Reloj** (Clock Tower, 1877) remains the centerpiece of recently remodeled **Plaza Prat,** surrounded by a cluster of other historic structures, several of them national monuments.

On the plaza's south side, the **Teatro Municipal** (1890) has been the city's premier performing arts venue for parts of three centuries; immediately alongside it, Iquique's workers literally and figuratively flexed their muscles in building one of the country's first organized-labor social clubs, the **Sociedad Protectora de Empleados de Tarapacá** (1913)—only a few years after the 1907 massacre.

Designed by architect Miguel Retornano in a Moorish style, the two-story **Casino Español,** at the northeast corner, dates from 1904; home to one of Iquique's best traditional restaurants, it features early 20th-century oil paintings based on *Don Quijote* by Spanish painter Vicente Tordecillas and other scenes from Spanish history by Chilean artist Sixto García. Immediately north, the **Club Yugoeslavo** also dates from this period.

Along with Plaza Prat, the eight blocks of **Paseo Baquedano** directly south comprise a *zona típica* national monument. Just beyond the district is the imposing **Iquique English College** (Balmaceda and Patricio Lynch).

Iquique has fewer religious landmarks than most other Chilean cities, but a pair of them are noteworthy national monuments: the **Iglesia San Antonio de Padua** (Latorre and 21 de Mayo), distinguished by its twin bell towers, and its adjacent **Convento Franciscano;** and the **Catedral de la Inmaculada Concepción** (1885) at Obispo Labbé and Bolívar, which replaced an earlier church that burned to the ground. It did not acquire cathedral status until 1929, with the establishment of the bishopric of Iquique.

One block north of the cathedral, at Ramírez and Sotomayor, trains from the Georgian gingerbread **Estación Central** linked Iquique with Santiago as late as the mid-1970s. Along with the adjacent **Casa del Administrador,** a couple of antique locomotives and passenger and dining cars, it is also a national monument.

There's a cluster of historic landmarks on and around the waterfront four blocks north of Plaza Prat. The most significant is the former **Edificio de la Aduana,** which holds the well-kept Museo Naval and another minor museum. Immediately west, seaborne passengers landed and disembarked at the **Muelle de Pasajeros** (1901), also known as Muelle Prat, a covered pier with concrete steps to accommodate the tides. Harbor tours still leave from here, visiting the **Boya Conmemorativa del Combate de Iquique,** which marks the spot where Chilean naval officer Arturo Prat's corvette *Esmeralda* sank in a confrontation with Peruvian officer Miguel Grau's ironclad *Huáscar.* (Later captured by the Chileans, the *Huáscar* survives as a museum piece in the naval base at Talcahuano, near Concepción.)

◖ Paseo Baquedano

Between Calle Serrano to the north and Calle J. J. Pérez to the south, rows of wooden Georgian and Victorian buildings and houses with airy second-story balconies line both sides of Iquique's revived historic district. Thanks to recent municipal initiatives, it's now a car-free mall where pedestrians can appreciate the city's architectural heritage from elevated boardwalks, while a battery-powered tramcar carries passengers along its length.

Many structures along Baquedano—some painted with bright contrasting colors, others stained and varnished to accentuate their natural wood exteriors—are becoming restaurants and hotels, but most remain private residences. Among the landmarks are the former **Tribunales de Justicia** (1892), now housing the Museo Regional, near the corner of Zegers; the **Palacio Astoreca** (1904), a nitrate-era mansion at the corner of O'Higgins; and the Chilean army's former headquarters, now the

Iquique's Palacio Astoreca is a monument of the nitrate era.

Museo del Primer Cuerpo del Ejército at the corner of Riquelme.

Originally called Huancavelica, after a highland Peruvian city, the street acquired its present name for General Manuel Baquedano after Chile's victory over Peru in the War of the Pacific.

Museo Regional

Housed in the former law courts, the regional museum chronicles the evolution of local cultures, in the context of their basic geography and environment, from early Chinchorro times (4000–2000 B.C.) to the present.

The Chinchorros, a coastal people, used three-log kayaks (of a sort) and rafts crafted from sea lion pelts for inshore subsistence fishing; some mummies, intentionally deformed skulls, and great numbers of adornments also date from this period.

With the rise of agriculture in the valley oases, precordillera, and the Andes, there developed an intricate system of contacts between the coast and the interior, which intensified during Tiwanaku times (around A.D.

1000)—geoglyphs and other rock art in the transverse river canyons are the most spectacular proofs of this—and during the Inka conquest (around A.D. 1450). There's an impressive assortment of Tiwanaku and Inka pottery, basketry, and textiles, and Inka mummies (probably sacrifices of girls 18 or 19 years old) found at Cerro Esmeralda, near Iquique.

In addition to pre-Columbian Tarapacá, exhibits on the nitrate era offer interpretive accounts of items such as *fichas,* the tokens used in lieu of cash in nitrate *oficinas,* mines, haciendas, hotels, stores, restaurants, and transportation (*fichas* were outlawed in 1924). There is also a model of Oficina La Palma (the current ghost town of Humberstone, east of Iquique), along with a full-scale ersatz Aymara village scene from the altiplano.

Hours at the Museo Regional (Baquedano 951, tel. 057/544710) are 9 A.M.–5:30 P.M. weekdays, 10 A.M.–5 P.M. weekends and holidays. Admission is free.

Palacio Astoreca

Built for nitrate baron Juan Higinio Astoreca

© WAYNE BERNHARDSON

in 1904, Iquique's most impressive surviving mansion is a Georgian-style edifice whose owner inhabited it for only a few years before his death in 1908. His heirs sold it to the regional government, and until 1976 it housed generations of bureaucrats before being restored and opened to the public.

Now sparsely furnished—it's used primarily as a museum and cultural center with exhibitions by local artists—the Palacio Astoreca is architecturally notable for its 27 capacious and high-ceilinged rooms, embellished with natural wood trim, immense chandeliers, stained glass, and second-story verandas. Constructed mostly of Douglas fir, it's probably the work of Miguel Retornano, designer of the Club Español.

Now an events center for the Universidad Arturo Prat, the Palacio Astoreca (O'Higgins 350, tel. 057/425600) is open during normal weekday business hours.

Museo del Primer Cuerpo del Ejército

In an immaculately maintained historic district building, Iquique's military museum reveals more than you probably care to know about military tactics used in War of the Pacific battles at the Morro de Arica, the port of Pisagua, and the nitrate *oficinas* of Dolores and Pampa Germania. While it includes many artifacts of these battles, including heart-wrenching soldiers' letters home, it plays the same role that Gettysburg does for U.S. Civil War zealots.

A courteous military guide does his best to give a thorough explanation—from the Chilean viewpoint—of the issues behind the war. The Museo (Baquedano 1396, tel. 057/431555) is open 10 A.M.–1:15 P.M. and 4:15–7:15 P.M. weekdays except Wednesday, when hours are 10 A.M.–1:30 P.M. only. Admission is free.

Edificio de la Aduana (Museo Naval)

Begun in 1871 to replace its predecessor, which was destroyed by a tsunami in 1869, the former Peruvian customs house was and still is the port area's major landmark. Its 18th-century colonial design consists of a two-story rectangle with an interior patio surrounded by corridors on each level; reached by a marble staircase, the second floor is covered by a freestanding roof on four gables that extrude from the flat roof and is crowned by an octagonal watch tower.

Within its meter-thick walls, the Naval Museum exalts the life and courage—some might say recklessness—of naval captain Arturo Prat, who died in 1879 while storming the Peruvian ironclad *Huáscar* after it sunk his own *Esmeralda* (whose mast and other artifacts are on display here). Later that same year, though, Chilean forces managed to take Iquique and made the building their headquarters; during the 1891 civil war, Balmaceda's presidential forces besieged congressional rebels who were holed up here.

The Museo Naval (Esmeralda 250, tel. 057/402121) is open 9:30 A.M.–12:30 P.M. and 3–6 P.M. Tuesday–Saturday, and only 10 A.M.–1 P.M. Sunday and holidays. Admission is free.

RECREATION

For most people, Iquique's beaches are its prime recreational attraction, offering swimming, surfing, and sunbathing. The city's ideal geographic and atmospheric conditions have also made it an international destination for *parapente* (paragliding).

Water Sports and Activities

The crescent beach of **Playa Cavancha,** beginning around the intersection of Avenida Balmaceda and Amunátegui and curving south toward its namesake peninsula, is the city's most popular, thanks largely to its convenience and calm waters. There are boardwalks and bikepaths, a small but well-designed zoo/aquarium, and hordes of cyclists, skateboarders, joggers, and surfers.

South of Cavancha, paralleling Avenida Arturo Prat, **Playa Brava** lives up to its name (Wild Beach), but it's good for sunbathing. A bit farther south, **Playa Huaiquique** is a good **surf** site and is also the landing point for paragliders who have leapt off the coast range precipice east of Cerro Dragón.

Within the city, surfers can also test the breaks at Cavancha's **Sector Saint Tropez,** almost directly at Balmaceda and Amunátegui, and **Playa Bellavista,** near the Intendencia Regional at Avenida Balmaceda and O'Higgins. South of town, along Ruta 1, there are good breaks at **Punta Gruesa, Punta Aguila,** and **Caleta Loa,** but these would constitute a full day trip out and back by bus or rental car. For information, gear, surfboard repairs, and the like, visit Playa Cavancha's **Vertical Store** (Av. Balmaceda 580, tel. 057/391077, www.verticalstore.cl).

From Muelle Prat, there are hour-long **tours** (US$2.50) past the fishing boats, the buoy where the *Esmeralda* went down, and the sea lion colony of **Isla de los Lobos;** contact **Lanchas Turísticas Muelle Prat** (cel. 09/9368-5676). **Nautitour** (Thompson 107, tel. 057/421551 or cel. 09/92182543, nautitour@yahoo.es) does more extensive tours for US$8 per person and up.

Parapente

Because of its fine, dry weather and late-morning thermals, Iquique is widely considered the best place in South America for paragliding. The city has responded by welcoming paragliders—even to the point of building a takeoff pad on the cliff at the top of the road to Alto Hospicio where, watching the turkey vultures soar when the coastal breeze comes up, participants can judge when to take off. Experienced gliders can conceivably soar for more than 200 kilometers down the coast toward Tocopilla; novices can try short tandem flights over the downtown area, taking in spectacular views of the city and the dunes of Cerro Dragón before landing at Playa Huaiquique.

The **Escuela de Parapente Altazor** (tel. 057/380110, www.altazor.cl) is the best-established operator in Iquique, and also offers camping and accommodations with private baths in its "Flight Park" at the south end of town.

ENTERTAINMENT

The main performing arts venue is the **Teatro Municipal** (Plaza Prat s/n, tel. 057/471621).

In a restored building with a burnished wooden bar, one of Iquique's best nightlife choices is lively **Taberna Barracuda** (Gorostiaga 601, tel. 057/427969, www.tabernabarracuda.cl), which has fine Peruvian-style pisco sours and an 8–10 P.M. happy hour daily. The kitchen serves excellent Mexican and Peruvian specialties.

SHOPPING

For most Chileans, the main shopping destination is the **Zona Franca,** where it's possible to find reasonably priced cameras, camping equipment, and the like. Price differences with the rest of Chile, though, are smaller than they once were.

Artesanía Tocornal (Baquedano 1035, tel. 057/410592) sells a sample of crafts and souvenirs from throughout the region.

Artesanías Urbanas Miski (Plaza Prat 570, tel. 057/473742) specializes in crafts made from regional materials, such as alpaca and vicuña wool, copper, and even salt.

ACCOMMODATIONS

Iquique has plentiful accommodations in all categories, but be selective in choosing budget lodgings—the difference in quality is often greater than minor difference in price.

US$10-25

Hostal Centro (Pedro Lagos 631, tel. 057/421030, hostalcentro@hotmail.com, US$13 s, US$23 d) is simple but well-located on a quiet downtown block.

Part of the historic district, though lacking the architectural style of the neighborhood, **Hostal Cuneo** (Paseo Baquedano 1175, tel. 057/428654, US$12 pp, US$19 s, US$30 d) is still good value, but there's just a single hot shower for the cheaper, shared-bath rooms.

Across from the cathedral, the patio rooms at perennially popular **Hostal Catedral** (Obispo Labbé 233, tel. 057/391296, US$12 pp, US$22 s, US$30 d) are clean and quiet, with either shared or private baths.

US$25-50

The classic exterior at **Hotel Anakena** (Orella 456, tel./fax 057/330063, www.hotelanakena .cl, US$21 s, US$29 d) is deceptive; the modern hotel proper sits behind the historic house, still family-occupied, and the only original area open to the public is the dining room.

Only minutes from Playa Cavancha, the HI affiliate is the justly popular **(Backpacker's Hostel Iquique** (Amunátegui 2075, tel. 057/320223, www.hosteliquique.cl, US$9–15 pp). The transition from what was once a spacious single-family house has been almost faultless, with common spaces—bar, kitchen, and living room—that encourage interaction. The accommodations, meanwhile, are well segregated from the common areas; one minor glitch is that the luminous 3rd-floor double shares a window with an adjacent dorm room. Parking is limited.

Hotel de la Plaza (Paseo Baquedano 1025, tel. 057/417172, www.kilantur.cl, US$17 s, US$28 d) is a historic-district home with a handsome balcony, though the rooms themselves, with private baths and cable TV, are part of a modern annex invisible from the street. Still, the owners are friendly, the common areas are immaculate, and it has WiFi.

Tidy, friendly **Residencial Casa Grande** (Barros Arana 1071, tel. 057/426846, casa-grande@tie.cl, US$18 s, US$30 d) is a fine choice in its price range, though the location is not the best. All rooms have private baths.

In a partially modernized older house, each guestroom at **Hostal Casa Blanca** (Gorostiaga 127, tel. 057/420007, US$23 s, US$34 d) is clean and comfortable with a private bath,

breakfast, telephone, and cable TV; some older rooms have multiple beds.

Near Playa Cavancha, the equally friendly and modern **Hostal Beach** (Vivar 1707, tel. 057/429653, www.hostalbeach.tk, US$17–25 pp) has spacious rooms with either shared or private baths.

Family-run **Tikoo Hotel** (Ramírez 1051, tel. 057/475031, tikoo@ctcinternet.cl, US$26 s, US$35 d) is an older Iquique house with a modern addition in the back. The rooms are compact but well-designed, with private baths and cable TV, but the breakfast is only so-so and the WiFi is erratic.

Though a little worn around the edges, the friendly **Palm Hostal** (Los Rieles 285, tel. 057/333885, www.palmhostal.cl, US$23 s, US$39 d with private bath) has a great Península Cavancha location, reliable WiFi, and limited parking. Unusual for budget accommodations in Chile, staff will prepare an early breakfast on request. One single room without a private bath is a bargain at US$14.

Hotel Costa Norte (Aníbal Pinto 1150, tel./fax 057/423899, US$30 s, US$39 d) is a newish facility offering rooms with private baths, cable TV, telephone, and breakfast.

Near Playa Cavancha, **Hotel Manuel Rodríguez** (Manuel Rodríguez 550, www .hotelmanuelrodriguez.cl, tel. 057/427524, US$28 s, US$43 d) is an old Georgian that's been divided up into small rooms, but with a bit more integrity than some other comparably priced places. It offers WiFi throughout and an above-average breakfast.

The beachfront hotels along Playa Cavancha, some but not all of them high-rises, contribute to Iquique's "Miami Beach" image. A few blocks inland from them, **Hotel Cano** (Ramírez 996, tel. 057/315580, www.hotel-cano.cl, US$32 s, US$47 d) is a contemporary hotel whose rates are far lower than its beachfront counterparts.

US$50-100

Hotel Jham (Latorre 426, tel. 057/415457, www.hoteljham.cl, US$42 s. US$56 d) is a contemporary 40-room downtown hotel with numerous amenities, including WiFi, and professional service.

Iquique's traditional favorite, **☾ Hotel Arturo Prat** (Aníbal Pinto 695, tel. 057/427000, www.hotelarturoprat.cl, US$55–73 s, US$58–78 d) consists of a "classic" sector and a newer wing with larger rooms and greater amenities, but also higher prices. Rates include a buffet breakfast.

US$100-150

Near Playa Brava at the south end of town, catering to both business travelers and tourists, the **Holiday Inn Express** (Av. Arturo Prat 1690, tel. 057/433300, www.ichotelsgroup .com/h/d/EX/hd/iqqex, US$120–130 s or d) is an affiliate of the North American chain. The higher rates are for sea-view rooms.

Hotel Cavancha (Los Rieles 250, tel. 057/431007, www.hotelcavancha.cl, US$94 s, US$106 d) has relatively modest but well-designed rooms with balconies overlooking the beach.

Where the Baquedano mall ends at the beach, the high-rise **☾ Hotel Gavina** (Av. Arturo Prat 1497, tel. 057/393030, www .gavina.cl, US$120 s, US$131 d) stands alone, combining views north and south with easy access to the historic downtown. The rooms themselves are spacious, with balconies and all modern conveniences, including WiFi in the rooms). One unique feature is a seminatural swimming pool formed by closing off the entry point of a natural tidal pool.

At Playa Cavancha, the high-rise **Hotel Terrado Suites** (Los Rieles 126, tel. 057/437878, US$125–200 s, US$141–225 d) is widely considered the city's best, but the most spacious—and expensive—rooms face the ocean and have large balconies.

FOOD

Cioccolata (Aníbal Pinto 487, tel. 057/413010) is a good breakfast and *onces* choice for its espresso and pastries, and a good lunch option for its sandwiches and fixed-price meals.

Cappuccino (Baquedano 798) has good coffee and ice cream.

A bit different from fire station restaurants elsewhere in the country, the **Compañía Italiana de Bomberos** (Serrano 520, tel. 057/527520) emphasizes its Italian roots. **Bavaria** (Aníbal Pinto 926, tel. 057/427888) is the Iquique branch of the nationwide chain.

In an inviting garden setting, **El Tercer Ojito** (Patricio Lynch 1420-A, tel. 057/426517, www.eltercerojito.cl) serves vegetarian food, fresh tropical and temperate zone juices, Peruvian dishes, sushi, and regional specialties such as quinoa. **Contigo Mi Perú** (Bolívar and Vivar, tel. 057/527128) is a Peruvian restaurant and nightspot.

As the key port for the Norte Grande's fishing industry, Iquique has numerous seafood options, such as the **Club de Yates** (Jorge Barrera s/n, tel. 057/471968), on the water just west of the Muelle de Pasajeros, and the Hotel Terrado Suites' upscale **El Sombrero** (Los Rieles 126, tel. 057/437878).

For cheaper but still excellent seafood, though, try any of the 2nd-floor *cocinerías* in the **Mercado Centenario,** the central market bounded by Barros Arana, Sargento Aldea, Amunátegui, and Latorre.

Several classy restaurants are clustered in historic buildings around Plaza Prat: the **Club Croata** (Plaza Prat 310, tel. 057/416222), the **Club de la Unión** (Plaza Prat 278, 3rd floor, tel. 057/413236), and the resplendent Moorish-styled **Casino Club Español** (Plaza Prat 584, tel. 057/423284), a landmark in its own right. Across the plaza, the almost equally distinctive but more proletarian **Sociedad Protectora de Empleados de Tarapacá** (Thompson 207, tel. 057/421923) has inexpensive lunches.

El Viejo Clipper (Baquedano 1393, tel. 057/320228) occupies a vintage house in the historic district, specializing in seafood dishes such the *trilogía de mar* (US$12) of shrimp, scallops, and squid. The Peruvian chef also prepares specialties from his own country.

Just off the south end of the Baquedano mall, the popular **Neptuno** (Riquelme 234, tel.

057/323264) is a casual seafood *picada* with appropriately nautical decor and midrange prices (around US$8–10) for abundantly sized fish and shellfish specialties, plus large, strong pisco sours.

Under new ownership, **(Boulevard** (Baquedano 790, tel. 057/413695) remains an outstanding but expensive French restaurant where entrées range upwards of US$10 but everything else, including salads and sides, is à la carte—making it easy to blow upwards of US$40 per person on dinner. The budget-conscious can sample their lunchtime fare for about US$8 prix fixe.

In an archetypically historic Iquique building with magnificent natural wood-work and great decor, **(El Viejo Wagón** (Thompson 85, tel. 057/411647) serves regional specialties, mostly fish and seafood, in the US$8–10 range but, as at Boulevard, à la carte items can steepen the bill up. One dining room is decorated in an early cinema motif, another with nitrate relics better than some museums have. Its *pebre* is tastier and spicier than most.

On the peninsula, Playa Cavancha's **(Don Rodrigo** (Filomena Valezuela 221, tel. 057/433011) is at or near the top of Iquique's culinary choices, especially for seafood. In attractive surroundings, including tile floors, gleaming wood, and a canvas roof that's open in fine weather—i.e., most of the time—it offers the usual standards plus Peruvian variations on fish and seafood. It has a modest selection of wines by the glass, an unusual practice in regional restaurants.

Also on the peninsula, **El Viejo Iquiqueño** (Los Rieles 299, tel. 057/483318) is a new seafood restaurant whose outstanding scallops appetizer (US$8) is large enough—not to mention tasty enough—for a lunch in itself.

INFORMATION

Better staffed, and better stocked with maps and brochures than it used to be, **Sernatur** (Aníbal Pinto 436, tel. 057/419241, infoiquique@sernatur.cl) is open 9 A.M.–5 P.M.

weekdays and 10 A.M.–1 P.M. Saturday; in summer, it may keep longer hours.

Motorists can consult the **Automóvil Club de Chile** (Acchi, Héroes de la Concepción 2855, Locales 11–12, tel. 057/527333) for both general and driver information.

SERVICES

Downtown ATMs are numerous, but **Afex** (Serrano 396) is the only exchange house (there are other ATMs and *cambios* at the Zona Franca).

Correos de Chile (Bolívar 458) handles the mail.

Telefónica CTC (Plaza Prat 614) and **Entelchile** (Tarapacá 476) are among many long-distance offices.

For laundry service, **Lavarápido** (Obispo Labbe 1446, tel. 057/424691) is reliable.

Hospital Regional Doctor Ernesto Torres Galdames (Av. Héroes de la Concepción 502, tel. 057/422370) is about 10 blocks east of Plaza Condell.

Two neighboring countries have **consulates** here: Peru (Zegers 570, tel. 057/411466) and Bolivia (Gorostiaga 215, Departamento E, tel. 057/527471).

GETTING THERE
Air

Aeropuerto Diego Aracena (tel. 057/410684) is 41 kilometers south of Iquique via coastal Ruta 1.

LAN (Tarapacá 465, tel. 057/427600 or 057/413038) flies to Iquique several times weekly from La Paz, Bolivia; domestically, it flies at least three times daily to Iquique from Arica and three or four times daily from Santiago. Some southbound flights stop in Antofagasta and La Serena.

Transportes Aéreos Mercosur (TAM, Serrano 430, tel. 057/390600) flies several times weekly to Asunción, Paraguay.

Sky Airline (Tarapacá 530, tel. 057/415013) covers most of the same domestic destinations as LAN, with slightly lower fares but sometimes erratic service.

Bus
Despite the need for a new bus terminal, Iquique's down-in-the-mouth **Terminal Rodoviario** (Patricio Lynch and Av. Centenario, tel. 057/426492) will have to do for the foreseeable future. Many carriers also pick up passengers at their own separate ticket offices around the Mercado Centenario.

Tur-Bus (Esmeralda 594, tel. 057/472984), which has the country's most extensive services, has remodeled a traditional landmark as its own separate terminal.

Domestic northbound services via the Panamericana to Arica are frequent; almost all southbound buses use coastal Ruta 1 to Tocopilla (for Calama and San Pedro de Atacama) and Antofagasta (for Santiago and intermediates). There are regional services to Pica with **Pullman Santa Angela** (Barros Arana 971, tel. 057/423751) and **Pullman Santa Rosa** (Sargento Aldea 884, tel. 057/431796), but most other interior destinations are served by *taxi colectivos*.

Typical destinations, fares, and times include Arica (US$13, 4 hours), Calama (US$17, 6 hours), Antofagasta (US$19–23, 6 hours), Copiapó (US$33–49, 15 hours), La Serena (US$40–57, 18 hours), and Santiago (US$50–70, 24 hours). The higher fares correspond to *salón-cama* services.

International buses to the altiplano border town of Colchane, continuing to Oruro and La Paz, Bolivia (US$30–33), include **Pullman Andimar** (Juan Martínez 182, cell tel. 099/5434393), **Interbus** (Esmeralda 978, tel. 057/424940), and **Copacabana** (Esmeralda 990, tel. 057/419932).

Pullman's Calama services connect with buses across the Andes to the Argentine cities of Jujuy and Salta.

Taxi Colectivo
Shared taxis to Arica cost about US$15 per person with **Tamarugal** (Barros Arana 897-B, tel. 057/482330), and **Turisanto** (Barros Arana 295, tel. 057/412191). Tamarugal also goes to Mamiña (US$6), as does **Turismo Mamiña** (Zegers 1611, cell. 09/8286-4774).

GETTING AROUND
Airport Transportation
Aerotransfer (18 de Septiembre 1919, tel. 057/310800) provides door-to-door lifts to Aeropuerto Diego Aracena for about US$7.50 per person.

Bicycle
Rent A Cycle (Baquedano 1440, tel. 057/417599) offers alternative transportation.

Car Rental
Rental agencies include **Hertz** (Aníbal Pinto 1303, tel. 057/510432); **Avis** (Manuel Rodríguez 734, tel. 057/472392); **Budget** (Bulnes 542, tel. 057/416332); and **Auto's Procar** (Serrano 796, tel. 057/470668).

NORTE GRANDE

Vicinity of Iquique

Like Arica, Iquique provides urban amenities for travelers and good access to excursions in the coastal range, precordillera, and altiplano. Many of these excursions are possible by public transportation or rental car, but there are also organized options starting around US$30–40 for destinations such as the Quebrada de Tarapacá (including Huara, the Gigante de la Atacama, and possibly Parque Nacional Volcán Isluga), the hotsprings hill stations of Mamiña and/or Pica (including stops at the nitrate ghost towns of Humberstone and Santa Laura, the pilgrimage site of La Tirana, and the colonial village of Matilla), Reserva Nacional Pampa del Tamarugal (including the spectacular geoglyphs at Pintados), and even truly off-the-beaten-track destinations such as the Quebrada de Guatacondo. It's also possible to organize tours to Pisagua.

Among Iquique travel agencies offering excursions are **Avitours** (Baquedano 997, tel. 057/527692, www.avitours.cl), **Turismo Lirima** (Gorostiaga 301, tel. 057/391384), and **Extremo Norte** (Filomena Valenzuela 712, Oficina 102, tel. 057/760997, www.extremonorte.cl). **Civet Adventure** (Bolívar 684, tel./fax 057/428483, civetcor@vtr.net) offers customized adventure trips to highland destinations.

RUTA 1 BEACHES

Since it opened in the early 1990s, paved Ruta 1 has improved access to beaches as far as Tocopilla and shortened travel times to Antofagasta and other points south. That access has come at a price—uncontrolled camping and lack of municipal services beyond Aeropuerto Diego Aracena have resulted in trash accumulation and other environmental problems on what was, not so long ago, a nearly pristine coastline.

At Río Seco, a developing settlement with limited services 95 kilometers south of Iquique, the roadside **Museo Parque** displays pre-Columbian Chango objects and relics from nitrate *oficinas*. Only 29 kilometers north of the regional border, the adobe ruins of **Huanillos** were a 19th-century guano port that saw a major battle in the War of the Pacific and exported guano until the 1930s; the ruined but still imposing headland castle here was the residence of its English manager. Nearby tidal pools teem with crabs, conger eel fry, sea urchins, and starfish, while lizards scamper over the dry rocks.

At the **Río Loa** border between Region I (Tarapacá) and Region II (Antofagasta), 148 kilometers south of Iquique, there's an internal customs post for merchandise from the Zofri and surfing possibilities at the beach. The Río Loa estuary is the only place in the Norte Grande where fresh water consistently reaches the Pacific ("fresh" is a relative term here, as heavy metals from upstream mining make its human use unwise).

◖ OFICINA HUMBERSTONE

From Iquique, paved Ruta 16 climbs steeply east to the suburb of **Alto Hospicio,** which barely two decades ago was home only to a handful of truck farmers who watered their gardens with condensation from the *camanchaca*. Today, on the broad escarpment overlooking Iquique, it's home to working-class families and squatters who can't afford to live in costly Iquique.

Passing the site of the abandoned colonial silver mine at Huantajaya, northeast of Alto Hospicio, the highway continues to a junction with the Panamericana, 45 kilometers east of Iquique. Here Humberstone and Santa Laura are two of Chile's few remaining nitrate ghost towns, together forming Iquique's single most popular excursion.

Both are national monuments, a largely symbolic protection, but in 2005 they received World Heritage Site status from UNESCO; restoration work is under way despite a strong earthquake (7.8 on the Richter scale) that

© WAYNE BERNHARDSON

a rusting rail crane at Oficina Humberstone

damaged some of its surviving structures on June 13 of that year.

After a long legal struggle, the Chilean government has handed control of Humberstone to the Corporación Museo del Salitre, which has a 50-year concession to manage the former company town and its landmark buildings. In 2001, Humberstone enjoyed a renaissance in public attention as Televisión Nacional (TVN) filmed part of its miniseries *Pampa Ilusión,* based on life in the *salitreras* circa 1935, here. This brought some benefits—TVN tidied the Plaza de Armas, replanting it with bougainvilleas, iceplant, and geraniums, and repainted the sun-bleached facades of several buildings for the shoot. There were also questionable decisions, though—since the plants in the plaza didn't grow fast enough for filming, TVN imported plastic shrubbery, hung bogus foliage from dead trees, and even painted the concrete columns of the pergolas to look like brick. The network even built a full-scale facade of its conception of an administrator's residence, since donated to the nearby town of Pozo Almonte.

However ill-advised the creation of an instant tourist attraction was, the site proves its authenticity with November's weeklong **Semana del Salitre,** when former residents and employees gather to celebrate what was a community as well as a company town. The event sometimes includes a train from Iquique, as the line is still functional.

History

Founded in 1872 by the Peruvian Nitrate Company, Oficina La Palma was one of Tarapacá's largest nitrate mines within a couple decades; at its peak, the town had a population of 3,700 and shipped 46,000 quintals of nitrate and 100 quintals of iodine every month. Functioning until 1960 despite a brief stoppage with the early 1930s global depression, it was one of the last surviving nitrate settlements.

Humberstone's name derives from La Palma's precocious British manager, James Humberstone (1850–1939), who arrived in Pisagua at the age of 25 (before the Chilean takeover); in the course of a long career, he refined the "Shanks system" for obtaining maximum yields from the low-grade caliche (hardpan) of the Atacama's sprawling pampas. After his retirement, the Compañía Salitrera de Tarapacá y Antofagasta renamed the town in his honor, and Britain's King Edward VIII honored him with an Order of the British Empire. Humberstone himself now reposes in the British Cemetery at Hacienda Tiliviche on the Panamericana, north of the Pisagua turnoff.

Sights

More remains of Humberstone's residential core than of the surrounding industrial plant. The museum now offers self-guided routes, with explanatory plaques, that make it easier to understand how the settlement was organized and worked.

Around the Plaza de Armas, itself partially transformed by TVN, stand the restored **Iglesia Jesús Obrero;** the **Teatro Humberstone** (built of Douglas fir, its stage and seating have undergone an impressive makeover; the famous folksinger Violeta Parra once performed here; the well-restored **Hotel;** the **Recova,** or market building; the **Pulpería** (company store, now an excellent museum despite some recent earthquake damage); and housing for management and workers. The most incongruous sight, a block east of the plaza, is the **Piscina,** an enormous cast-iron swimming pool, now empty but with an intact diving board. There were also tennis and basketball courts.

Most of these buildings date from the 1930s (Humberstone reached its zenith as the Great Depression waned), but the Victorian-style **Casa del Administrador** dates from 1883. West of the residential zone, the former power plant, railyards, and other industrial relics have suffered from depredations by scrap dealers, but there are still locomotives, narrow-gauge rails (a dozen kilometers of track helped link Humberstone to nearby Santa Laura), and dozens of the rail carts that hauled caliche from the fields to the processors. In the distance are stupendous piles of *tortas* (tailings) left after the extraction of the nitrates; some of these are being reprocessed, with new technology, for products such as iodine.

Mornings are the best time to explore Humberstone, before the sun gets too hot, but late afternoon breezes can make that time of the day pleasant enough.

Practicalities

The **Museo del Salitre** (www.museodelsalitre.cl) now charges US$1.50 admission, with guides available for tours. Hours are 9 A.M.–6:30 P.M. daily except New Year's day, when it's closed. There are limited supplies—cold drinks, etc.—and a simple restaurant across the highway from the entrance.

While Iquique agencies make Humberstone a regular stop on their tours, it's easy enough to arrive on public transportation. Any Panamericana-bound bus, those to precordillera destinations such as Mamiña and Pica, as well as *taxi colectivos* to Pozo Almonte, will drop passengers at Humberstone, only half an hour from the city. It's easy enough to flag down a return bus to Iquique as well.

OFICINA SANTA LAURA

Just across Ruta 16, within reasonable walking distance, Humberstone's sister *salitrera* is home to the *in situ* **Museo Santa Laura,** housed in the partially restored **Casa del Administrador.** Several of its rooms have been outfitted with period furniture and other nitrate-era artifacts, but there is lamentably little historical narrative. The June 13, 2005, earthquake caused some damage.

Santa Laura's most impressive surviving structure is the **Planta de Chancado** (ore crusher), with its soaring smokestack, but the building itself suffered serious damage in 1999, when chainsaw vandals cut and sold 31 Douglas fir beams (the thieves were caught by police, however). Parts of the building are fenced off—it's no longer possible, for instance, to climb among the rafters. Craftsmen have restored several of the old horse-and-mule carts that used to haul ore to the processors.

In late October, folk musicians of the stature

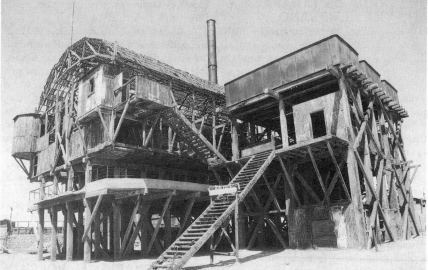

© WAYNE BERNHARDSON

ruins of Oficina Santa Laura, near Humberstone, east of Iquique

NORTE GRANDE

of Patricio Manns perform at the **Festival Canto a la Pampa** (Pampa Song Festival). Like Humberstone, Santa Laura is open 9 A.M.–6:30 P.M. daily except New Year's Day.

PANAMERICANA NORTE

North of Humberstone, the highway has a handful of roadside attractions starting at the town of **Huara,** the junction for the international highway into the altiplano. Some 33 kilometers from Humberstone, hard hit by the 2005 earthquake, Huara doesn't merit a long stopover, but try to visit its **Farmacia y Drogueria Libertad** (Arturo Prat s/n), an old-fashioned apothecary that opened in 1906 but was acquired by the Municipalidad in 1993 as a museum; unfortunately, the business so rarely keeps its designated hours that it's not even worth mentioning them. The nearby church dates from 1890. While there are no accommodations here, you could do worse than to lunch at **La Flor de Huara** (Donato Zanelli s/n, tel. 057/752253), which keeps long hours on the west side of the highway.

A few kilometers north of Huara, at kilometer 1,853 of the Panamericana, the **Geoglifos Ex-Aura,** named for the nitrate *oficina* that once existed here, consist of what appears to be a sun and a human figure.

About 57 kilometers north of Huara and 10 kilometers north of the Pisagua turnoff, **Hacienda Tiliviche** is a British-founded farm nestled in its namesake oasis canyon; the present occupant, Santiago Adán Keith, generally welcomes visitors who want to take a look around, but check in at the *casco* (big house) before doing so. The inconspicuously signed entrance road is on the south side of the river.

On the river's north side, readily visible from the highway but reached by crossing from the main house, Tiliviche's **Cementerio de los Ingleses** (British Cemetery), enclosed by a wrought-iron fence, is a national monument dating from 1876. James Humberstone, a legendary figure in the nitrate industry, is among those buried here. The June 2005 earthquake did serious damage to the tombs here, and repairs have been slow to get underway.

QUEBRADA DE TARAPACÁ AND THE ALTIPLANO

From Huara Ruta 55, the international highway to Oruro, Bolivia, passes a number of archaeological and historical sites en route to the bleak border post of Colchane. While the repaving process has been slow, this scenic road is much improved over recent years, despite potholes and ongoing construction. From the altiplano it's possible to travel the spectacular circuit north toward Parque Nacional Lauca and on, or back to Arica through wild and still rarely visited backcountry.

Only 14 kilometers east of Huara, a short distance north of the highway, the isolated hillock of **Cerro Unita** is famous for the 86-meter geoglyph known as *El Gigante de Atacama* (Giant of the Atacama), the world's largest anthropomorphic representation (it is 39 meters wide as well). Dating from about A.D. 900, it probably depicts an indigenous authority of the time; unfortunately, it's becoming hard to distinguish the geoglyph from the tire tracks that disrespectful drivers have left here. Everyone cautions against walking on the figure, and that's good advice, but that can't do nearly the damage that uncontrolled SUVers and dirtbikers have.

Nine kilometers east of Cerro Unita, a paved side road descends into the Quebrada de Tarapacá, where somnambulant **San Lorenzo de Tarapacá,** an oasis village surrounded by irrigated fields, belies its status as one of colonial Peru's most important local towns and the site of a major battle during the War of the Pacific. The entire town is a *zona típica* national monument.

Tarapacá's most notable landmark is its national monument **Iglesia San Lorenzo,** a fragile adobe begun in 1717 and finished in 1720. Thanks partly to the Cerro Colorado mining company, the church and its freestanding *campanario* (bell tower, 1741) have undergone restoration since the June 13, 2005, earthquake put their survival at serious risk. At the approach to town, a monument maps the November 27, 1879, Battle of Tarapacá, a bloody but indecisive encounter between Chilean forces under Eleuterio Ramírez (who died here) and a joint Peruvian-Bolivian army.

At **Chusmiza,** 75 kilometers east of Huara and 3,200 meters above sea level, the former hot-springs hotel has closed for the foreseeable future, but the bottling plant that produces one of Chile's premium mineral waters remains open. Passing numerous pre-Columbian hillside terraces, the highway climbs out of the precordillera and onto the altiplano, where there are several access points to Parque Nacional Volcán Isluga. It ends at **Colchane,** which, though it is the capital of its *comuna,* deserves no more than a brief visit unless the border's closed or you need a basic bed and food. At 3,750 meters above sea level, on a plain with nothing to stop the wind and weather, its nights get bitterly cold. The border is open 8 A.M.–8 P.M. daily.

PARQUE NACIONAL VOLCÁN ISLUGA AND VICINITY

Not quite so high as Parque Nacional Lauca to the north, Isluga's 174,744 hectares incorporate environments similar to Lauca's summits, steppes, and marshes, with comparable wildlife, but it also encompasses several scenic Aymara villages in what is one of their most traditional indigenous strongholds. Its literal high point, though, is 5,218-meter Volcán Isluga, which gave the park its name.

Sights

Six kilometers west of Colchane, the village of **Isluga,** a settlement of about 200 houses that's primarily an Aymara ceremonial center, is a national monument. Its outstanding feature is its spectacular 17th-century **Iglesia Santuario,** perhaps the altiplano's finest single church, bedecked with a traditional tiled roof and complemented by a freestanding bell tower.

Six kilometers west of Isluga, at the village of **Enquelga,** the road crosses the river and follows the south shore of **Laguna Arabilla;** summer rains often cut an alternative road west through a series of small villages. The more reliable southerly road continues west to **Latarana,** where it intersects the northbound

church at Isluga, altiplano of Iquique

road to Parque Nacional Lauca, which passes through **Mucomucone** en route to the Salar de Surire.

Reached by a narrow road from a signed turnoff from Ruta 55, roughly midway between Chusmiza and Colchane, **Termas de Puchuldiza** is a small but active geyser field 3,800 meters above sea level. In the past, when the condensed steam froze overnight to form an ice dome, it was a fascinating sight, but seismic activity has apparently altered these dynamics. Puchuldiza is also accessible by a separate southbound lateral from a junction on the Latarana road, which passes through the village of **Mauque.**

Immediately west of the Isluga turnoff, there's an interesting backcountry route to Pica via the village of **Cariquima,** which has an impressive 17th-century church and simple accommodations, and the **Salar de Huasco,** a sprawling salt lake with large populations of flamingos. Highway signs warn against the dusty road down from Salar Huasco directly

to Pica, but it's easily passable for any passenger vehicle in good condition.

Accommodations and Food

Within the park proper, Conaf's **Refugio Enquelga** (US$7 pp) is up to its usual standards, but make advance arrangements before coming here. Conaf has put up shelters with roofs and picnic tables at the free-of-charge **Camping Aguas Calientes,** sited at thermal baths about one kilometer east of town, which is cleaner than in past years but less than impeccable. One pool is large enough for swimming, the other for a warmer soak.

The only other regular accommodations are at Colchane, beyond park boundaries, where visitors driving from Putre or Parque Nacional Lauca often spend the night. **Residencial Rogelia Castro** (sumauta@yahoo.es, US$10 pp with half board) has simple rooms with shared baths. **Hostal Camino del Inca** (cel. 09/7694-7583, US$15 pp with half board) has rooms with either shared or private baths, and exceptionally friendly ownership. Nonguests can take meals at its adjacent **Pensión Gómez,** which serves llama steaks and quinoa, among other altiplano specialties.

Information

Colchane's **Municipalidad** (Av. Teniente González s/n, tel. 057/794312, turismocolchane@yahoo.es) will help out with tourist inquiries and responds quickly to emails (Spanish only). Conaf's Enquelga ranger can provide park information.

Getting There and Around

Bolivia-bound buses from Iquique pass through Colchane, which is 180 kilometers northeast of Huara, but there is no regular public transportation into the park proper. Both Arica and Iquique travel agencies offer loop excursions through Isluga and Lauca; it's probably easier to arrange these in Arica.

PANAMERICANA SUR

Between the Humberstone junction and the regional border with Antofagasta, most areas of interest are east of the Panamericana in the precordillera and its canyons. The exception is the Reserva Nacional Pampa de Tamarugal, most of which straddles the highway south of Pozo Almonte, though it has discontinuous sectors north of Huara and in the vicinity of La Tirana.

Pozo Almonte

Just five kilometers south of the Humberstone junction, in the midst of the pampa, bustling Pozo Almonte (population 7,202) is the largest town along the Panamericana between Arica and the regional border. Founded as a colonial watering hole (*pozo* means "well"), it owes its present prosperity to the copper boom at Cerro Colorado, 59 kilometers northeast on the Mamiña road, and at Collahuasi, high in the southeastern Andes near the Bolivian border.

Not many people plan to stay here, but if night falls while you're in town, you could do far worse than the impeccable **Hotel Estancia Inn** (Comercio 132, tel. 057/752242, hotelestanciainn@live.cl, US$22 s, US$27 d), which also has a restaurant. That said, it's easy to catch buses either north- or southbound on the Panamericana, or *taxi colectivos* to Iquique, Mamiña, La Tirana, or Pica.

Salar de Huasco

From Pozo Almonte, a smooth paved highway climbs east and then southeast to the Collahuasi copper mine near the Bolivan border. At a junction 96 kilometers from Pozo, a gravel road leads slightly northwest for 10 kilometers to the Salar de Huasco, a sprawlingly colorful salt lake 3,700 meters above sea level that teems with flamingos, Andean geese, other waterfowl, and many small birds. Iquique travel agencies often include this as part of their tours from the city.

From the Salar de Huasco, it's possible to drive north via a series of gravel roads, some of them badly washboarded, through scarcely populated backcountry to the border crossing of Colchane. From Colchane, it's possible to continue north to the Salar de Surire, Parque Nacional Lauca, Putre, and Arica.

From the same paved highway junction, it's possible to descend via a broad but dusty road to the oasis town of Pica. In the summer rainy season, this road may be difficult to manage, but during the rest of the year it's generally passable.

La Tirana

About 19 kilometers southeast of Pozo Almonte, along the paved road to Matilla and Pica, the otherwise placid village of La Tirana erupts with activity between July 12 and 18, when tens of thousands of pilgrims celebrate the annual **Festival de la Virgen del Carmen.** The most important day is July 16, but the entire week is an orgy of frenzied activity from spectators and organized participants who, clad in kaleidoscopic costumes, fill the streets with folkloric music and dance.

The Norte Grande's single most important devotional site, whose permanent population is only about 250, is also a national monument, largely but not exclusively because of its **Santuario de la Tirana.** Fronted by the **Iglesia de la Tirana** (1886), an outlandish structure that replaced an earlier counterpart destroyed by earthquakes, this broad but barren ceremonial plaza is the main venue for the July celebrations. The church itself, distinguished by a central dome, twin bell towers, and metal siding, is undergoing a seismic retrofit.

While the July celebrations are the primary attraction, La Tirana also draws plenty of pilgrims during **Pascua de Negros** (January 5–6, Epiphany, when black slaves in colonial times celebrated Christ's birth), **Semana Santa** (Easter), and the **Fiesta de la Oración por Chile** (Chilean Prayer Festival, the last Sunday in September).

On the north side of the plaza, La Tirana's **Museo del Salitre** displays a chaotic collection of objects from the nitrate era. While many of the exhibits are visible from the sidewalk, the entrance is through Almacén El Progreso, the local general store.

THE TALE OF THE TYRANT

Legend says that Ñusta Huillac, an Inka priest's daughter, had fled with her father from Diego de Almagro's return expedition to Cuzco. Hiding in the forests, the princess led raids against passing Spaniards, torturing her prisoners and earning her the nickname "La Tirana del Tamarugal" (Tyrant of the Tamarugal).

When, however, Ñusta fell in love with the Portuguese captive Vasco de Almeyda, tried to save him, and accepted Christianity, her followers considered it treason. Condemning both to death, they nevertheless granted her wish to place a cross on her grave.

Again according to legend, an 18th-century priest found Ñusta's cross in the forest, and her cult grew with construction of an Andean-style temple destroyed by an 1866 earthquake. Today, pilgrims honor her indirectly with dances that postdate the War of the Pacific, when local residents began to honor the Virgen del Carmen de La Tirana, the local version of Chile's patron saint.

La Tirana's cult has spread through 200 cofradías (brotherhoods), rooted in remote Andean times. Geographically based in Arica, Iquique, Tocopilla, Chuquicamata, and other cities, they converge on La Tirana every July for the annual festivities.

Canadian writer Lake Sagaris, a longtime Chilean resident, recounts the story of Ñusta Huillac, with references to contemporary Chile, in *Bone and Dream: Into the World's Driest Desert* (Alfred A. Knopf Canada, 2000).

La Tirana has no hotels (Pozo Almonte and especially Pica are better choices for a room), but pilgrims camp without restriction in the open areas on the east side of town. For food, several simple *comedores* circumfuse the plaza in front of the church.

MAMIÑA

Directly northeast of Pozo Almonte via 73 kilometers of paved two-lane blacktop, the precordillera hot-springs resort of Mamiña has long been a popular "hill station" for Iquiqueños, especially on winter weekends. These days, though, it also houses large numbers of miners from nearby Cerro Colorado.

Despite Mamiña's local tourist appeal, the Aymara presence is still palpable, and the abundant pre-Columbian terraces reinforce its indigenous character. In pre-Columbian times, it was a fortified way station on the route between the Inka capital of Cuzco and its southern satellites.

Orientation

Though Mamiña's official elevation is 2,700 meters above sea level, its rugged topography makes any such statistic misleading. The compact upper sector of town sits atop an isolated rocky scarp, while the lower sector, site of most of the hot-springs hotels, stretches along the Quebrada de Mamiña beneath Cerro Ipla and several other parallel ridges. Winding streets and footpaths link the two sectors.

Sights

Mamiña's **Iglesia de Nuestra Señora del Rosario** dates from the 17th century but has undergone modifications such that only the adobe facade is obviously colonial; the flanking twin bell towers, built of symmetrical stone blocks and topped by blue-painted wood framing, seem incongruous. It suffered relatively minor damage in the mid-2005 earthquake. There is free public WiFi on the square in front of the church.

Inka influence is evident in the several *pukarás* in and around town.

Accommodations and Food

Mamiña offers decent accommodations, at a variety of prices, but winter weekends can challenge their capacity. So can the mining industry, whose occupancy often takes places off the market for months at a time, especially during

NORTE GRANDE

the week. Rates often include full board, and virtually every place has large thermal tubs and WiFi.

Street addresses and house numbers are really pretty meaningless—all are either on the hilltop or in the valley below, on or near Ipla. Except for cell phones starting with 09, telephones are Iquique numbers—Mamiña has no landlines.

Hotel Niña de Mis Ojos (Ipla s/n, tel. 057/519132, US$12 pp room only, US$30 pp with full board) has comfortable rooms with nearly new beds and tubs long enough for an NBA forward, but its barren grounds need more greenery.

Hotel Los Cardenales (Ipla s/n, tel. 057/517000, US$46 pp with full board) offers the most complete services of any accommodations here: subtropical gardens (despite the altitude), a covered and heated pool, and a whirlpool tub in every room.

Hotel Termas Llama Inn (Sulumpa 85, tel. 057/419893, www.termasdemamina.cl, US$92 s, US$115 d with full board) has more contemporary style than other accommodations here; its restaurant is open to nonguests for lunch and dinner, but when it feeds the miners the fare is mediocre.

Las Chacras de Pasquito (Ipla s/n) is a *picada* with a limited Chilean menu, but everything in its fixed-price lunches and dinners—salad, soup, and entrée—is skillfully done.

Getting There and Around

Minibuses from Iquique arrive at and depart from the church plaza. Departures take place early, around 7:30 A.M. daily except Sunday, and late, around 6 P.M. daily.

PICA

Along with Mamiña, the oasis of Pica is the most popular weekend getaway for Iquiqueños, and has been since the early 20th-century nitrate boom. Unlike Mamiña's canyon country, it occupies a relatively open site on the cusp between the pampa and the precordillera, irrigated by a series of Spanish-built tunnels that

reduced evaporation and, according to the late geographer Isaiah Bowman, watered its gardens "with scrupulous economy."

Pica was one of Spain's earliest settlements in what is now Chile—both Diego de Almagro and Pedro de Valdivia passed through there, and by 1550 it was the center of an important *encomienda*. Its orchards and vineyards supplied produce to both Arequipa and the silver city of Potosí, in present-day Bolivia.

When Bowman visited Pica, as the nitrate era faded, the Tarapacá Water Company had long since diverted water from Pica to Iquique, to the local system's detriment. Pica's citrus and subtropical fruits—limes, oranges, grapefruits, mangos, and guavas—have maintained their reputation throughout the country, but the last wine harvest took place in 1937.

Orientation

Pica (population 4,674), 1,325 meters above sea level, is 42 kilometers southeast of La Tirana and 61 kilometers southeast of Pozo Almonte via a smooth paved road. It features an elongated street plan whose main thoroughfare, Avenida Balmaceda, enters town from the west. A parallel thoroughfare two blocks north, Avenida Presidente Ibáñez, links the center with the popular east-end pools.

Sights

On the south side of the well-landscaped Plaza de Armas, Pica's **Iglesia San Andrés** (1886) is a national monument that supplanted a colonial structure leveled by earthquakes; a neoclassical facade of galvanized iron covers its wooden framing. The **Hospital de Pica** (Balmaceda s/n) is also a national monument. Most Chileans, though, come to enjoy the warm natural pools (30°C) at **Cocha Resbaladero** (Av. Presidente Ibáñez s/n), which collects a modest admission charge.

In the same building as the tourist office and public library, the nearly new **Museo de Pica** (Av. Balmaceda 178) has a professional look but is still a work in progress. Among the exhibits are material on dinosaur tracks at Chacarillas, in an isolated canyon southwest of Pica; the region's early human presence; more recent archaeology, including ceramics, mummies, and burial customs; the nitrate era (including the role of the oasis in feeding the *oficinas*); and the contemporary agricultural economy. It focuses appropriately on the local and regional, with a fine collection of historical photographs. Hours are 9 A.M.–1 P.M. daily except Sunday, and 4–8 P.M. weekdays only.

In the village of **Matilla,** three kilometers west of Pica, there are two national monuments. The **Iglesia de San Antonio** replaced an earlier church destroyed around the same time as that of Pica, but its freestanding bell tower is original; after repairs following the June 2005 earthquake, it looks far less original. Built in colonial times, restored by the Universidad de Chile in 1968, the **Lagar de Matilla** was a working winepress as late as 1937.

Accommodations

Spartan but spotless, **Hostal Casa Blanca** (Av. General Ibáñez 75, tel. 057/741410, US$23 d with private bath but without breakfast) is friendly enough; cheaper shared-bath singles are claustrophobic and the beds vary in quality.

New in 2008, **Hostal La Noria** (Avenida Ibáñez 598, tel. 057/741167, lanoria.hostal@gmail.com, US$15 s, US$28 d) is a friendly family-run accommodation offering half a dozen immaculate rooms with private baths and cable TV, and a rambunctious Shar-Pei for additional entertainment.

At the western approach to town, **Hostería O'Higgins** (Av. Balmaceda 6, tel. 057/741524, hohiggins@123mail.cl, US$25 s, US$31 d without breakfast) has good furniture, but some baths have been awkwardly carved out of once bathless rooms.

Ask for a quieter garden room at **Hostal Café Suizo** (Av. General Ibáñez 210, tel. 057/741551, cafesuizo@latinmail.com, US$25 s, US$31 d), which fronts on a busy avenue but is otherwise delightful, with immaculate and comfortable rooms with first-rate furnishings. Breakfast costs extra but includes fresh local fruit juices and is well worth the price.

Food

For sandwiches and especially fresh juices and fruit-flavored ice cream, try any of the stands along the north side of Avenida General Ibáñez, immediately below the Cocha Resbaladero.

El Sabor Andino (Esmeralda and San Martín, tel. 099/1328194) specializes in altiplano dishes, such as llama steaks and quinoa omelettes, adapted to local tastes.

Los Naranjos (Barbosa 200, tel. 057/741318) is a spotless eight-table *picada* that does a lot with a little, with fine service and imaginative preparation even of routine dishes such as *pollo a la plancha* (grilled chicken, marinated in local lime juice). Dinners cost around US$8–10 with salad.

El Socavón (Arturo Prat 208, tel. 057/741576) serves meat, fowl, and seafood dishes in the US$8–11 range; the US$5–6 lunches offer a choice of well-prepared, visually appealing entrées. It has spacious patio seating, but the giant TV can be distractingly noisy at dinnertime.

Information and Services

Pica's **Oficina Comunal de Turismo** (Balmaceda 299, tel. 057/741310, Anexo 17, www.pica.cl, turismo@pica.cl) is open 8:30 A.M.–1:30 P.M. and 3–5 P.M. daily in summer, but weekdays only the rest of the year.

Pica has free public WiFi on the Plaza de Armas, but it's not always functional; there's a **Centro de Llamados** (Blanco Encalada 500) that also has Internet access. **Correos de Chile** (Balmaceda s/n) is the post office.

Getting There and Around

Two blocks north of the Plaza de Armas, Pica's **Agencia de Buses** (Esmeralda between Barbosa and Maipú) sells tickets for Pullman Santa Angela, Pullman Santa Rosa, and Pullman Chacón. Pullman Santa Rosa has a separate office at Balmaceda and Barbosa.

There are 13 buses to Iquique (US$3.50, two hours) via La Tirana, Pozo Almonte, and

Humberstone daily except Sunday, when there are only 11. There are also *taxi colectivos.*

RESERVA NACIONAL PAMPA DEL TAMARUGAL

Before the Spanish invasion, dense forests of the mesquite-like *tamarugo (Prosopis tamarugo)* covered much of the arid pampa between the coastal escarpment and the precordillera, from about 20° south latitude to the Río Loa, the present-day boundary between the regions of Tarapacá and Antofagasta. Deforested for fuel for the colonial Huantajaya silver mine and the post-independence nitrate *oficinas,* this narrow endemic species has made a remarkable comeback in the last half century.

Conaf's Reserva Nacional Pampa del Tamarugal preserves the last great stands of *tamarugo* trees in a thriving plantation. The forest alone is impressive enough in this desert context, but the major sight is the geoglyphs at Pintados, a national archaeological monument that's one of the continent's most impressive concentrations of pre-Columbian rock art. Twitchers should look and listen for the rare tamarugo conebill *(Conirostrum tamarugense)* near Conaf's visitors center.

Orientation

Reserva Nacional Pampa del Tamarugal comprises 102,264 hectares in three sectors: one north of Huara, one east of La Tirana, and another, the largest and most widely visited, south of Pozo Almonte.

◖ Geoglifos de Cerros Pintados

About 43 kilometers south of Pozo Almonte, at a junction with a paved but potholed road that heads east toward Pica, a westbound gravel road leads past an abandoned nitrate rail station to the Geoglifos de Cerros Pintados, where nearly 1,000 abstract and figurative designs blanket four kilometers of otherwise barren hillsides surrounding the crumbling adobe ruins of a former *oficina.* Many of the figures, which date between A.D. 500 and A.D. 1450, represent humans and animals, including birds, fish, and llamas, suggesting shared beliefs and frequent contact with the pre-Columbian cultures of highland Peru and Bolivia.

At the site itself, Conaf has installed a ranger station, erected a gate, built picnic sites and some shaded parking, and instituted a US$1.50 admission fee. Frequently, though,

THE WOODLAND IN THE DESERT

The utterly rainless nitrate pampas might seem an improbable place for any forest, but the Pampa del Tamarugal's peculiar geography has provided a favorable environment for *Prosopis tamarugo.* Despite saline soils, low humidity, thin cloud cover, and dramatic day-to-night temperature oscillations, the pampa is an interior drainage basin where, for millennia, the penetrating flow from transverse river valleys and the westward movement of fresh groundwater created an enormous subterranean aquifer.

A relative of the common mesquite, the taprooted *tamarugo* is uniquely adapted to this environment. Unfortunately, the colonial and post-colonial mining industry nearly eradicated it until a successful 1950s replanting program. The goal was to provide fuel for rural residents and forage for their sheep and goats, who eat the tree's seedpods. While most of the dense groves straddling the Panamericana are plantations rather than primary forest, they are a remarkable achievement.

That achievement, though, is under threat. Ever since Atacameño times, the pampa's fossil waters had been used for irrigation and, during the nitrate boom, the *oficinas* drew up to 40,000 gallons per day from wells at Dolores (east of Pisagua) and Pozo Almonte. Today, though, wells drilled to slake Iquique's thirst have lowered the water table from 4 to 15 meters below the surface; this makes it difficult for existing trees to survive and impossible for seedlings to establish themselves.

Surreptitious sulfur miners, unfortunately, have defaced part of the pre-Columbian geoglyphs at Cerro Pintados.

no one's there to collect the charge. This can be a mixed blessing; when the gate's locked, it means walking farther in the hot sun to reach the geoglyphs. *Pirquineros* (small-scale miners) have damaged some of the designs while digging for sulfur.

Other Sights

East of the Panamericana, directly opposite the Pintados road, there's a paved but potholed alternative route to Pica and a turnoff to **Colonia Agrícola Pintados,** an oasis community that began in the 1960s as a religious community but developed into a flourishing horticultural settlement. Pumping 80 liters of irrigation water per minute out of the aquifer, it has established markets in Pozo Almonte and Iquique for its carrots, celery, chard, lettuce, tomatoes, maize, onions, peppers, melons, and watermelons.

At kilometer 1,750 of the Panamericana, 57 kilometers south of Pozo Almonte, the town of **Victoria** was a working *oficina* until 1980 but was almost totally dismantled in 1981–1982. Now barely a facade along the highway, it could have been another Humberstone; instead, it retains only a few storefronts and services, including a restaurant and gas station.

Accommodations and Food

West of the Panamericana, 24 kilometers south of Pozo Almonte and opposite its Centro de Información, Conaf's **Área de Recreación y Refresco** provides *tamarugo*-shaded campsites with picnic tables, clean toilets, and (cold) showers for US$7 per site. East of the highway, its **Casa de Huéspedes** offers beds (US$9 pp).

At Victoria, 33 kilometers south of Conaf's Centro de Información and directly on the highway, tidy **El Rotito** is a surprisingly good eatery, with shaded parking to boot. Restaurant owner Jaime Armando Godoy Henríquez, who owns most of the rest of the town, provides simple accommodations here.

Information

About 24 kilometers south of Pozo Almonte, Conaf's **Centro de Información Ambiental** (tel. 057/751055) is open 8:30 A.M.–6 P.M. daily. It has small but informative displays on the pampa environment, notably the *tamarugo*.

Getting There and Around

Southbound Panamericana buses pass near all the major attractions in the Pintados sector and nearby, but it's still a hot dry walk of about seven kilometers in the desert sun—carry plenty of water. Organized tours from Iquique to Humberstone and Pica regularly stop at Pintados.

QUEBRADA DE GUATACONDO

Foreign visitors anticipating kaleidoscopic desert country like the box canyons of the southwestern United States sometimes find themselves disappointed by the Atacama's mainly monochromatic landscapes, but the isolated Quebrada de Guatacondo, in the southeastern corner of Tarapacá, lives up to expectations.

From a point on the Panamericana, 63 kilometers south of Pintados and 66 kilometers north of the regional border at Quillagua, a broad dusty road crosses 40 kilometers or so of barren pampa, where dust devils swirl across the landscape, before dropping into and then ascending a serpentine canyon to the oasis of Guatacondo. Tours rarely go here, so a rental vehicle, preferably with four-wheel drive, is almost the only possibility.

At kilometer 40, just before the route begins descending into the Quebrada, the hillside **Geoglifos El Vado** depict a llama pack train. In the canyon itself, at kilometer 49, the **Petroglifos de Temantica** is a remarkable assortment of engraved stone surfaces reflecting a succession of cultures from Tiwanaku times (A.D. 500–1000), post-Tiwanaku regional development (A.D. 1100–1400), and the relatively brief Inka dominion (A.D. 1450–1530).

Beyond Temantica, the road ascends a dappled sedimentary canyon whose beds have been folded almost vertically over the ages, before arriving at **Guatacondo,** a village so isolated that, in event of rain, it can remain cut off for months on end. In dry weather, with permission from Carabineros here, it's possible to continue east toward the copper mine at Collahuasi and the paved highway back to Pozo Almonte, but flash floods can make this route—and indeed the entire canyon—dangerous during the summer rainy season.

Antofagasta

Antofagasta, a 19th-century city that superseded the colonial port of Cobija with the rise of the nitrate and copper industries, is mainly a service center for the region's mines, though there are several interesting excursions in the vicinity. With nearly 300,000 people straining regional water resources, the city could collapse before the mines run out of ore.

HISTORY

Originally known as Peña Blanca, then as La Chimba, Antofagasta was barely a prospectors' base camp when, in 1865, José Santos Ossa discovered mineral nitrates in the Salar del Carmen, about 20 kilometers east of the city. Together with Francisco Puelma and Manuel Antonio de Lama, he formed the Sociedad Explotadora del Desierto de Atacama, which obtained a 15-year concession to exploit, process, and sell its nitrates. It acquired the name Antofagasta in 1870 from Bolivia's President Mariano Melgarejo.

Melgarejo's name stuck, but Bolivian jurisdiction did not, because of Chile's triumph in the War of the Pacific. With the ascendancy of nitrates and then copper, Antofagasta's status was assured, despite a brief period when nearby Mejillones threatened to take over—as it does

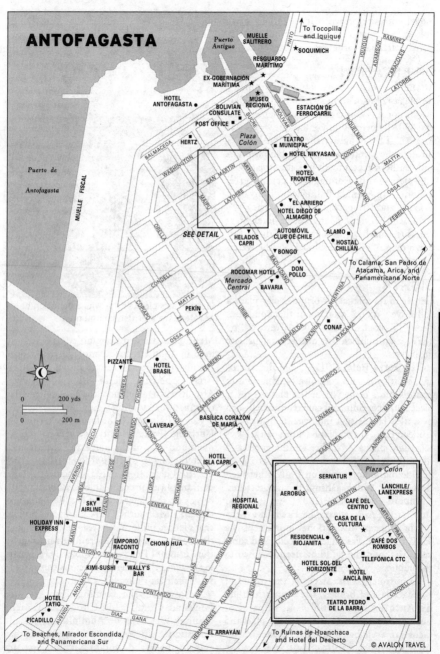

NORTE GRANDE

© AVALON TRAVEL

today, with the present Megapuerto project linking the region with the Mercosur countries Brazil, Paraguay, Uruguay, and Argentina.

ORIENTATION

At the foot of the coast range escarpment, Antofagasta (population 295,792) is 1,350 kilometers north of Santiago via the Panamericana and 490 kilometers south of Iquique via coastal Ruta 1. The Panamericana actually runs through the pampa east of town, but northern and southern access roads link it to the city.

Streets within Antofagasta's central grid, bounded by Avenida Balmaceda, Bolívar, J. S. Ossa, and Uribe, contain most of the city's sights and services. Many better hotels, restaurants, and bars, though, are southwest of downtown, within a few blocks of the waterfront Avenida Grecia.

SIGHTS

Center of Antofagasta's original city plan, a collective national monument that comprises about 17 blocks, **Plaza Colón** featured, by 1872, a church, banks, and several private businesses.

The **Torre Reloj** (1912), a Big Ben surrogate built by British community donations to honor Chile's centenary, is the plaza's centerpiece; built of reinforced concrete, embellished by a tiled facade that interweaves British and Chilean flags, the scale model stands 13.5 meters high, plus a 2.7-meter weathervane, and sounds just like its London counterpart.

One block northeast, on Bolívar between Balmaceda and Washington, the restored **Estación Ferrocarril** (1887) was the final stop for the Antofagasta–La Paz railway; the second story of this national monument is a 1900 addition. Passenger service ceased some years ago, and the building itself is closed to the public.

Almost across the street at the corner of Balmaceda and Bolívar, the former **Aduana de Antofagasta** (1866) is a Valparaíso-built prefab with a U-shaped floor plan and Georgian-style balconies, balustrades, moldings, and other features. First assembled in

Plaza Prat's clock tower was a donation of Antofagasta's British community.

Mejillones, then disassembled and moved here in 1888 because Antofagasta's booming nitrate exports required it, the two-story structure housed Chilean customs until 1966. After its 1976 restoration, the Museo Regional occupied the building.

Across Balmaceda, the former **Gobernación Marítima** (Port Authority) is a national monument and part of the museum. Almost next door, the onetime **Resguardo Marítimo** (Port Security) dates from 1910. Immediately to its east, freight trains once unloaded their nitrate cargos on the deteriorating **Muelle Salitrero** (1872), a Melbourne Clark Company project that's fenced off for safety reasons. Just beyond the pier, brown pelicans scramble for scraps at the **Terminal Pesquero** (wholesale fish market), where the budget-conscious can sample fresh shellfish right off the boat.

Across from the Terminal Pesquero, the Sociedad Química de Chile (Soquimich) maintains its **Casa de Administración** (administrative offices), a national monument that was originally the Lautaro Nitrate Company and then became the Anglo Lautaro Nitrate Company before its 1968 nationalization.

South of the plaza, there are fewer architectural landmarks, but the former **Municipalidad de Antofagasta** (Latorre 2535) is a national monument that now houses the municipal **Casa de la Cultura**. In 1999, Pope John Paul II declared the baroque-Byzantine **Iglesia Corazón de María** (21 de Mayo and Cochrane) a minor basilica.

Museo Regional de Antofagasta

Gradually expanding to fill Antofagasta's historic customs house, the remodeled regional museum emphasizes mineral wealth, the cornerstone of the regional economy. At the same time, it explains regional biogeographical diversity and traces the development of cultures that adapted to the near-total aridity and, in some areas, high elevations and brutally cold temperatures. The museum has moved beyond generally antiquarian topics such as early man and the Inka dominance to tackle subjects such as the nitrate era, its connection to the War of the Pacific, urban development, and contemporary mining.

The Museo Regional (Balmaceda 2786, tel. 055/227016, www.museodeantofagasta.cl) is open 9 A.M.–5 P.M. weekdays except Monday, and 11 A.M.–2 P.M. weekends and holidays. Admission costs US$1 for adults, US$0.50 for kids, but it's free Sunday and holidays.

Ruinas de Huanchaca

Starting in 1888, under a British-Bolivian-Chilean consortium that owned the large Pulacayo silver mine near Potosí (Bolivia), construction of this major refinery on the hillslopes above Playa Blanca took four years to complete. The ore itself made a 500-kilometer rail trip to arrive at the plant, which was capable of processing 100 tons per day to produce 20 tons of silver monthly. In addition to the industrial plant itself, the complex included workers' housing, a church, hotel, and shops, but its very expense and falling silver prices resulted in its closure by 1902.

Until recently, only the plant's foundations remained, at the south end of Avenida Angamos, but a joint effort by the Universidad Católica del Norte and the nearby Hotel del Desierto has turned it into a historical site that includes the former **Museo Geológico Profesor Humberto Fuenzalida V,** which stresses the region's mineral resources. As of deadline, the finishing touches were not yet complete, and its hours and contacts uncertain.

ENTERTAINMENT

As a university town, Antofagasta has reasonably good performing arts alternatives, and the foreign mining presence helps support a fair amount of nightlife.

Bars

Wally's Pub (Antonino Toro 982, tel. 055/223697) is an expat miners' hangout—next to the Servicio Nacional de Geología y Mineralogía (Sernageomin)—where U.S., Canadian, and Australian engineers try to calculate conversions from Celsius to Fahrenheit under the influence of multiple pisco sours.

Emporio Raconto (Antonino Toro 995, tel. 055/741576) is a *peña* with live music.

Cinema and Theater

Cinemundo Antofagasta (Zenteno 21, tel. 055/490348) is a six-screen multiplex.

The principal performing arts venues are **Teatro Pedro de la Barra** (Condell 2495, tel. 055/263400) and the **Teatro Municipal** (Sucre 433, tel. 055/264919).

Spectator Sports

The local soccer team, **Deportes Antofagasta** (Baquedano 482, Oficinas 24–25, tel. 055/373708, www.deportesantofagasta.cl) remains in the second division. Matches take place at the Estadio Regional (Av. Angamos and Homero Ávila).

ACCOMMODATIONS

Most of Antofagasta's budget accommodations are mediocre at best, while the midrange to upscale places offer better value.

US$10-25

Friendly **Residencial Riojanita** (Baquedano 464, tel. 055/410693, US$6 pp) is the best of the cheapest downtown choices. South of town at its namesake beach, **Residencial Playa Huáscar** (US$10 pp) has half a dozen rooms with private baths; kitchen facilities cost another US$1.50 per person, and lunch and dinner are also available for around US$4. Owner Hugo Cerda of Desértica Expediciones (Avenida Jaime Guzmán 06250, Playa Huáscar, cel. 09/9718-6772, www.desertica.cl) has negotiated free admission for his guests at nearby pubs and provides one free transfer from downtown. It's also close to beachfront restaurants.

In the same general area, uphill from the Kamikazi discotheque, **Casa El Mosáico** (El Huáscar C-18, cel. 09/9938-0743, www.chilegreentours.com, US$12 pp) is a new hostel that also organizes trips in the Antofagasta backcountry.

Though the location is good for a budget hotel, and the rooms are spacious, **Hotel Isla Capri** (Copiapó 1208, tel. 055/263703, antoniosierra@elsotano.cl, US$15 s, US$25 d) has stagnated and parts of it are rundown. Rates include a marginal breakfast.

US$25-50

At downtown **Hotel Nikyasan** (Latorre 2743, tel. 055/221297, US$20 s, US$28 d) there's no price difference between good upstairs rooms and not-so-good downstairs rooms; breakfast is included. Well-located **Hotel Brasil** (J. S. Ossa 1978, tel. 055/267268, hluna@vtr.net, US$12–23 s, US$18–32 d) has large but otherwise ordinary rooms with either shared or private baths; breakfast costs extra. Under the same management, the more central **Hotel Frontera** (Bolívar 558, tel. 055/281219, hluna@vtr.net, US$11–20 s, US$18–28 d) has spotless utilitarian rooms with cable TV—a mixed blessing, since all the rooms are fairly close together.

Central **Hostal Chillán** (Sucre 823, tel. 055/227237, US$23 s, US$30 d) has smallish but comfortable rooms with private baths and breakfast. The **RocoMar Hotel** (Baquedano 810, tel. 055/261139, US$29 s, US$36 d) is a modern and mostly well-kept accommodation whose rooms offer better natural light than most competitors in its range.

Hotel Sol del Horizonte (Latorre 2450, tel. 055/449207, www.hotelhorizonte.cl, US$39 s, US$45 d) is a respectable choice of recent vintage, but some downstairs rooms are dark; rates include private bath, cable TV, and telephone.

Some rooms at placid **Marsal Hotel** (Arturo Prat 867, tel. 055/268063, www.marsalhotel.com, US$45 s, US$48 d) come with attractive balconies, but other parts show signs of deferred maintenance.

US$50-100

Well-run **Hotel Ancla Inn** (Baquedano 508, tel. 055/357400, www.anclainn.cl, US$55 s, US$63 d) has smallish rooms, but it offers plenty of perks, including breakfast, a business center, two pools, a gym, a whirlpool tub, and sauna.

All 30 rooms at **Hotel Tatio** (Av. Grecia 1000, tel. 055/419111, www.tatio.cl, US$53 s, US$66 d with breakfast) have ocean views, and the common areas are attractive. While it also fronts on the busy Costanera, it's one of the city's best values.

Hotel Diego de Almagro (Condell 2624, tel. 055/268331, US$50 s, US$/68 d with breakfast) has upgraded in recent years and is good value in its range.

A few blocks north of the Tatio, the highrise **Hotel Holiday Inn Express** (Av. Grecia 1490, tel. 055/228888, front.anf@talbot.cl, US$87 s or d) provides multinational chain conventionality.

More than US$100

Downtown's waterfront **Hotel Antofagasta** (Balmaceda 2575, tel. 055/228811, www.hotelantofagasta.cl, US$115 s, US$148 d) is a traditional business and holiday favorite that belongs to the reliable Panamericana chain, and is recovering something of its former glory. Weekend specials can be a bargain.

During the filming of *Quantum of Solace*,

"James Bond" (Daniel Craig) was a celebrity guest at the **Florencia Suites** (Avenida República de Croacia 0126, tel. 055/775687, www.florenciasuites.cl, US$83–250 s, US$95–300 d). Had it been filmed a few months later, though, he probably would have stayed at the spectacular new **Hotel del Desierto** (Av. Angamos 01455, tel. 055/356000, www.enjoy .cl, US$214–518 s or d), the accommodations for the city's new casino. With its spacious sea-view rooms, and opposite the restored Huanchaca ruins, it's the city's new prestige hotel—even for non-gamblers.

FOOD

Low-priced **Bongo** (Baquedano 743, tel. 055/263697) serves perfectly good sandwiches. So does **Café del Centro** (Prat 470, tel. 055/227551), which scores points for coffee as well, along with **Café Dos Rombos** (Latorre 2528, cel. 09/9839-6737). Grilled chicken with fries is virtually the entire menu at **Don Pollo** (J. S. Ossa 2594, tel. 055/263361).

Partially tobacco-free **Pizzanté** (J. M. Carrera 1857, tel. 055/268115, www.pizzante .cl) serves tasty, sizable pizzas and sandwiches in agreeable surroundings.

Chinese food is popular throughout the north, and Antofagasta is no exception. Among the established choices are **Chong Hua** (García Lorca 1468, tel. 055/251430) and **Pekín** (J. S. Ossa 2135, tel. 055/260833).

The nationwide chain **Bavaria** (J. S. Ossa 2424, tel. 055/266567) serves everything from sandwiches to *parrillada,* while **El Arriero** (Condell 2644, tel. 055/268759) is a traditional Chilean *parrilla,* with midrange to upscale prices.

The cheapest fresh seafood alternatives are the market stalls at the **Terminal Pesquero** (Aníbal Pinto s/n), north of the Muelle Salitrero, and the **Mercado Central** (bounded by J. S. Ossa, Uribe, Matta, and Maipú).

Kimi-Sushi (Antonino Toro 904, tel. 055/777111) has decent sushi at moderate prices—combination plates (around US$12) are large enough for two but fall short of

Santiago's best. **Picadillo** (Avenida Grecia 1000, tel. 055/247503, www.picadillo.cl), has good *tables* of smoked meats and cheeses.

For more elaborate seafood, try ☾ **Puerto Caliche** (Ejército 0809, tel. 055/241048), a premium restaurant that's moved to the southern edge of town. Another outstanding seafood choice is **El Arrayán** (Díaz Gana 1314, tel. 055/240220).

Antofagasta's best ice cream is available at **Heladomanía** (Baquedano 508), in the same building as Hotel Ancla Inn. A close second, with other desserts as well, is **Helados Capri** (Baquedano 632), just down the block.

INFORMATION

For general information on the city and region, **Sernatur** (Prat 384, tel. 055/451818, infoantofagasta@sernatur.cl) is open 8:30 A.M.–1 P.M. and 3–7:30 P.M. weekdays.

Motorists can consult the **Automóvil Club de Chile** (Acchi, Prat 770, tel. 055/449495).

For information on national parks and other protected areas, visit **Conaf** (Av. Argentina 2510, tel. 055/383332, antofaga@conaf.cl).

SERVICES

Downtown ATMs such as **BankBoston** (Arturo Prat 425) are abundant. For cash or travelers checks, there are **Cambio Ancla Inn** (Baquedano 508) and **Cambio San Marcos** (Baquedano 508).

Facing Plaza Colón, **Correos de Chile** (Washington 2613) is the post office. **Telefónica CTC** (Condell 2529) has long-distance service, but there are many others. **Sitio Web 2** (Latorre 2404) has good Internet access.

Laverap (14 de Febrero 1802, tel. 055/251085) can handle the washing.

For medical assistance, try the **Hospital Regional** (Av. Argentina 1962, tel. 055/269009).

Two neighboring countries have **consulates** here: Argentina (Blanco Encalada 1933, tel. 055/220441) and Bolivia (Washington 2675, Oficina 1301, tel. 055/259008).

NORTE GRANDE

GETTING THERE

Antofagasta has excellent air and overland connections north and south, and overland connections to the interior of the region.

Air

Aeropuerto Cerro Moreno is 25 kilometers north of town on Ruta 1, at the south end of Península Mejillones.

LAN (Arturo Prat 445, tel. 055/265151) flies north to Iquique and Arica, east to Calama, and south to Copiapó (infrequently), La Serena, and Santiago. **Sky Airline** (General Velásquez 890, Local 3, tel. 055/459090) flies south to Santiago, north to Iquique and Arica, and also to Calama.

Bus

As of 2009, Antofagasta was about to inaugurate its new Terminal Carlos Oviedo Cavada, at the north end of town. This should help reduce downtown congestion, but will also be slightly more inconvenient in terms of reaching the city center and its services.

The local carriers Fepstur, Maravilla Bus, and Corsal all go to Mejillones (US$3.50, one hour). Many long-distance carriers use Ruta 1 north toward Iquique and Arica, and have southbound services on the Panamericana.

Pullman Bus (tel. 055/262315) and **Tur-Bus** (tel. 055/266691) both have extensive services northbound, southbound, and east toward Calama and San Pedro de Atacama. **Flota Barrios** (tel. 055/268559) has somewhat less ambitious schedules along most of the same routes, as does **Buses Géminis** (tel. 055/231968); Flota Barrios also stops at the nitrate towns of María Elena and Pedro de Valdivia.

Typical destination fares and times include Arica (US$32–40, 10 hours), Iquique (US$28–31, 6 hours), Tocopilla (US$11–13, 2.5 hours), Calama (US$8–11, 3 hours), Taltal (US$11, 4 hours), Chañaral (US$25, 5 hours), Copiapó (US$20–36 7 hours), La Serena (US$30–46, 12 hours), Valparaíso/Viña del Mar (US$45–52, 20 hours), and Santiago (US$46–60, 19 hours).

International services to the Argentine cities of Jujuy and Salta (US$45, 15–16 hours) are available through Géminis Tuesday, Friday, and Sunday at 7 A.M. Pullman makes connections with its Argentine services in Calama.

GETTING AROUND
Airport Transportation

For US$4 per person, **Aerobús** (Baquedano 328, tel. 055/262727) offers door-to-door service to Cerro Moreno. For the financially challenged, bus 15 leaves from the Terminal Pesquero, charging just US$0.50, but only every two hours between 7:30 A.M. and 10:30 P.M.

Car Rental

Rental agencies include **Alamo** (Av. Argentina 2779, tel. 055/261864), **Budget** (Av. Pedro Aguirre Cerda 13358, tel. 055/214445), **First** (Bolívar 623, tel. 055/225777), **Hertz** (Balmaceda 2492, tel. 055/269043), and **Automotriz La Portada** (Av. Argentina 2761, tel. 055/263788).

Vicinity of Antofagasta

While Antofagasta isn't the obvious choice for excursions that San Pedro de Atacama is, it can still be a good base for trips up and down the coast and some destinations on and around the Panamericana.

The most ambitious and imaginative excursion from the city is a full-day tour and transport to San Pedro de Atacama via the Baquedano railroad museum and then across the southern end of the Salar de Atacama, visiting the villages of Peine and Socaire, the altiplano lakes of Miscanti and Miñiques, and the town of Toconao before arriving in San Pedro de Atacama in time for the sunset at Valle de la Luna.

Antofagasta's **Desértica Expediciones** (cel. 09/9718-6772, www.desertica.cl, desertica@gmail.com) charges US$100 per person for the 12-hour excursion, which leaves at 8 A.M. and includes breakfast and lunch. While the trip is unique, the elevation gain from sea level to above 4,000 meters at Miscanti and Miñiques may cause problems for some individuals.

CALETA COLOSO (MIRADOR ESCONDIDA)

At present, the highway south stops a short distance beyond Caleta Coloso, where copper concentrate arrives for processing via a subterranean pipeline from the Escondida mine, 170 kilometers to the east, 3,100 meters above sea level in the Andes. The Mirador Escondida overlook doesn't exactly offer tours, but some sophisticated exhibits explain the copper mining process 10 A.M.–7 P.M. daily.

At **Dunas de Coloso,** where the new road continues south toward an eventual link with Taltal, Desértica offers sandboard excursions and instruction for US$20—though the climb back up the steep dunes is pretty brutal.

MONUMENTO NATURAL LA PORTADA

Crowned by Miocene sedimentary strata eroded into a graceful natural arch, Monumento Natural La Portada stands alone on a volcanic platform of Jurassic rocks in the Pacific, opposite a broad sandy beach beneath steeply rising headlands 25 kilometers north of Antofagasta. Unfortunately, because of frequent seismic activity, the headlands are so unstable that descending to the beach of the 31-hectare reserve is prohibited.

Even so, this symbol of the Norte Grande coastline is probably one of Conaf's most visited units because of its scenery and accessibility. A short distance west of Ruta 1, easily reached by bus 15 from Antofagasta's Terminal Pesquero, La Portada also offers a good concentration of seabirds (boobies, gulls, oystercatchers, and pelicans), occasional marine mammals (dolphins, sea lions, and otters), and a decent seafood restaurant at the parking lot. Drivers should lock their cars.

RESERVA MARINA LA RINCONADA

Established under fishing laws by Servicio Nacional de Pesca (Sernap), this 332-hectare protected zone is a key habitat for the *ostión del norte* (northern scallop)—*Agropecten purpuratus* has a high genetic diversity and long reproductive season here, from end of spring to middle of autumn. On the south side of the Mejillones peninsula, the reserve is 31 kilometers northwest of Antofagasta on the paved road to the beach town of Juan López.

JUAN LÓPEZ

In sheltered waters at the south end of Península Mejillones, at the east end of Bahía Moreno, Juan López is a working-class beach resort that vibrates with street life—and deafening amplified music—in summer and on weekends. To the west—toward the coastal village of Bolsico—Conaf, several other agencies, and the Municipalidad de Mejillones are cooperating on a project to create a reserve to protect large offshore pelican colonies.

For accommodations or lunch, try **Hostal**

NORTE GRANDE

Restaurant Vitoco (tel. 055/487510) where, however, the live salsa on weekends is loud enough to set off car alarms in the street.

In summer, from Juan López, it's possible to approach the offshore stack at Monumento Natural La Portada with the motor launch *Rica Ventura* (US$8 pp) daily at 10 A.M.

Taxi colectivos link Antofagasta with Juan López in summer and on weekends.

PANAMERICANA SUR

The thinly populated area south of Antofagasta in and around the Panamericana has few conspicuous sights, but visitors with time and transportation will find it worthwhile.

Observatorio Cerro Paranal

About 51 kilometers south of Antofagasta, the Panamericana swerves southeast, while a newly paved road heads directly south to the European Space Organization's Cerro Paranal facility, in an isolated coast range locale, 2,664 meters above sea level.

© WAYNE BERNHARDSON

Cerro Paranal's smaller telescopes are on mobile tracks.

Opened in March 1999, Paranal's state-of-the-art observatory features four eight-meter Very Large Telescopes (VLTs). Even more distant from light pollution sources than Chile's Norte Chico observatories, it offers ideal conditions for viewing the northern night skies. Guided tours, which take place 2–4 P.M. the last two weekends of every month except December, visit one of the four major telescopes, the control room, and some parts of the hotel (used to house visiting researchers), it went up in cinematic flames in the recent James Bond film, *Quantum of Solace*).

Cerro Paranal (tel. 055/435335, www.eso.org) is 126 kilometers south of Antofagasta, at the end of a short paved westward lateral off the main road. Reservations are advisable, preferably well in advance, but it's sometimes possible to join a group if you're fortunate enough to pass by at the right time. The main road, paved until it enters the canyon known as the Quebrada de Despoblado, continues south and then west toward Paposo and Taltal.

Antofagasta's Desértica Expediciones (cel. 09/9718-6772) arranges full-day excursions to the observatory (US$58, lunch included) and vicinity, as does Taltal's **Empresa Gali** (San Martín 641, tel./fax 055/611008).

Sierra de Remiendos

Only 14 kilometers south of the same Panamericana junction that leads to Cerro Paranal, a vertiginous gravel road heads southwest through wild desert country to Caleta El Cobre, a now-abandoned copper mine and smelter on the Pacific coast. Eventually, a coastal road may link Caleta El Cobre with Antofagasta, but in the meantime, this is an adventurous alternative through the "Patchwork Sierra" for southbound travelers with their own vehicles. The total absence of water makes this route inadvisable for cyclists.

Mano del Desierto

At kilometer 1,310 of the Panamericana, 70 kilometers south of Antofagasta and 1,100 meters above sea level, Santiago sculptor Mario

© WAYNE BERNHARDSON

At regular intervals, Santiago sculptor Mario Irarrázabal scours the graffiti off his "Hand in the Desert," south of Antofagasta.

Irarrázabal erected this enigmatic sculpture of a hand protruding about 12 meters above the barren pampa, on the west side of the highway. Finished in 1992, the hollow structure supports an exterior of *ferrocemento* (literally, "iron cement") only eight centimeters thick. It took two months for three people to build the structure in Santiago and, after it was shipped north, two weeks more to finish the job.

Financed by a group of Antofagasta businessmen—as individuals, rather than as corporate representatives—the sculpture reflects the artist's intention to give passing motorists "a reason to stop in the middle of nowhere" and "feel the silence and the breeze." Unfortunately, lesser "artists" have often felt the need to deface this graceful landmark with pointless graffiti; the artist himself professes not to be too bothered, but he cleans it off whenever he visits his wife's family in Antofagasta. Irarrázabal has installed other sculptures in Puerto Natales, Punta del Este (Uruguay), Madrid, and Venice.

Oficina Alemania

At kilometer 1,175, about 280 kilometers south of Antofagasta, Oficina Alemania was a key nitrate *oficina* that, unfortunately, was dismantled for scrap only a few years ago. At the turnoff, Héctor Cuadra's Fondart-sponsored sculpture is dedicated to the Shanks-system nitrate workers who, according to Cuadra, "surrendered their lungs" to the nitrate industry.

TALTAL

Taltal, the Norte Grande's only sizable town south of Antofagasta, was even more sizable when, in the early 20th century, it was one of the region's main nitrate ports, well served by rail to the rest of the pampas. Today, it's an obscure fishing port and beach town, studded with nitrate-era monuments, but the greatly improved road from Antofagasta and Cerro Paranal may help rejuvenate the town, as the route is shorter and more scenic than the Panamericana.

NORTE GRANDE

History

As a settlement, Taltal dates from about 1850, when mining pioneer José Antonio Moreno first began to exploit its nitrate deposits and ship them from its early port. After a border treaty with Bolivia in 1866, it was Chile's most northerly outpost; by 1877, the government had platted a town and port that grew rapidly with nitrate exploitation here and at nearby Aguas Blancas. After the 1950s, when the last remaining nitrate *oficinas* fizzled, much of the infrastructure was dismantled, but government preservation decrees and the bankruptcy of the last remaining enterprises salvaged part of this irreplaceable heritage.

Orientation

Taltal (population 9,564) is 325 kilometers from Antofagasta via the Panamericana and a paved northwest lateral that descends the Quebrada de Taltal between the Sierra Vetada and the Sierra de Tipias; however, via the new road that passes Cerro Paranal, it's only 234 kilometers from Antofagasta. It's 170 kilometers north of Chañaral via the Panamericana and the same paved lateral.

Entering town from the southeast, Calle O'Higgins divides Taltal into two: to the southwest, Calle Prat, one block inland from the beach, is the main commercial strip of a regular grid; to the northwest, the grounds of the former Taltal Railway Company hold most of the town's historic monuments.

Sights

Starting operations in 1882, the London-based Taltal Railway Company reached its terminus at Cachinal, 149 kilometers to the east, but it had branch lines to all the region's *oficinas*. On the east side of O'Higgins, between Esmeralda and Prat, its petroleum-burning **Kinston Meyer Locomotora No. 59** entered service in 1906; along with two railcars filled with historic photographs, it's an *in situ* museum and national monument that keeps irregular hours.

The company's port infrastructure, covering 15 hectares, once included five piers, warehouses, turntables, fuel storage tanks, platforms, and 22 locomotives with 560 cars. The remaining structures include its **Oficinas Generales** (general offices), the **Casa Administrador** (administrator's house), and the 120-meter **Muelle Salitrero** (nitrate pier), now missing many sleepers, though its corroded 1903 cranes, from Stothert and Pitt in Bath, England, still stand.

In the downtown area, overlooking the rejuvenated Plaza Prat mall, the Gothic-style **Iglesia San Francisco Javier** (1897) recently succumbed to fire, while the restored **Teatro Alhambra** was finished in 1921. The plaza itself bears the form of the Union Jack, a reminder of the Anglo-dominanted nitrate epoch.

One block seaward, between Torreblanca and Ramírez, the waterfront **Plaza Riquelme** is a gathering place behind the **Balneario Municipal** or city beach, but better beaches are north of town.

Accommodations

At **Muelle de Piedra,** two kilometers north of town on the Paposo road, there are free beach campsites with shade, toilets, and showers. Ignore the peeling exterior paint at cheerful **Residencial Paranal** (O'Higgins 106, tel. 055/613604, US$12 pp, US$23 s or d without breakfast), a spacious period house with high ceilings that's kept most of the original configuration. The cheaper rooms have shared contemporary baths, while the more expensive ones have private baths and cable TV.

Despite its pleasing beachfront location, continued deferred maintenance at **Hostería Taltal** (Esmeralda 671, tel. 055/611173, www.taltalhosteria.galeon.com, US$31 s, US$33 d) suggests that it's passed its peak, and mining companies often use it to house their personnel.

Though it's fairly new and well-kept, some rooms at **Hotel Gali** (San Martín 637, 2nd floor, tel. 055/611008, galihotel@123.cl, US$29 s, US$54 d) have too much furniture and lurid red bedspreads. The 2nd-floor singles lack exterior windows, though they get some hallway light.

Taltal's best, by far, is **Hotel Mi Tampi** (O'Higgins 138, tel. 055/613605, www .hotelmitampi.cl, US$39 s, US$44 d), which has 14 spacious, luminous garden rooms in impeccable condition, with amenities like cable TV, WiFi, and breakfast. It's also exceptionally friendly.

Food

Dining options are limited. For inexpensive breakfasts and sandwiches, there's **Pastelería La Central** (Prat 649, tel. 055/611519).

For a more elaborate menu, don't miss the **Club Social Taltal** (Torreblanca 162, tel. 055/611064, open lunch and dinner daily). While it's not the fashionable place it was when founded as the Club Inglés in 1893, it preserves spectacular woodwork (despite visible termite damage), a library, a poker room, and even an imported pool table dating from the reign of Edward VII. The fish and seafood entrées, in the US$7–10 range, may have changed little since Edwardian days, but they're well-executed and as fresh as can be.

Information and Services

In a kiosk on Plaza Prat, Taltal's **Oficina de Información Turística** (www.taltal.cl) is open in summer only. **BancoEstado** (Ramírez 247) has an ATM.

Valentina (Prat 456) has decent telephone and Internet connections. Facing Plaza Prat, **Correos de Chile** (Prat 515) is the post office.

The **Hospital de Taltal** (O'Higgins 450, tel. 055/611077) handles medical services.

Getting There and Around

Tur-Bus (Prat 631, tel. 055/611426) serves destinations north and south along the Panamericana and Ruta 1. Typical destinations, fares, and times include Antofagasta (US$12, 4.5 hours), Calama (US$16, 6 hours), Iquique (US$40, 14 hours), Arica (US$45, 18 hours), Chañaral (US$10, 3 hours), La Serena (US$23, 7 hours), and Santiago (US$35–45, 13 hours).

VICINITY OF TALTAL

North of Taltal, coastal Ruta 1 is due to reach Antofagasta by 2010, but as of 2009 goes only as far as Caleta El Cobre, where a steep, truly remote road turns northwest to intersect the Panamericana about 50 kilometers south of the regional capital. The first 20-plus kilometers are paved; there are an estimated 300 archaeological sites between Taltal and Caleta El Cobre, the oldest of which dates back 6,000 years during hunter-gatherer times. There are also relatively recent Inka sites.

The only town along the route, the fish camp of **Paposo,** has a modernized park and plaza and fishing pier, but not much else. **Reserva Nacional Paposo,** in the slopes of the coast range, is more easily reached from the pampa above, where there are numerous pre-Columbian rock art sites. Antofagasta's Desértica Expediciones (cel. 09/9718-6772) leads trips into this area.

Beyond Paposo, the northbound road is washboarded, but there are no washouts; another road turns inland up the Quebrada del Despoblado and intersects a road that leads to the Cerro Paranal observatory; after about 22 km, this is smoothly paved all the way to the Panamericana junction. About 85 kilometers north of Paposo, the inland route from Caleta El Blanco is closed but there is no warning sign—be sure to continue to Caleta El Cobre and then turn east toward the Sierra de Remiendos and the Panamericana at the first turn past the abandoned mining camp.

PANAMERICANA NORTE

From Antofagasta, the Panamericana trends northeast, crossing the **Hito de Capricornio,** marking the Tropic of Capricorn; after about 70 kilometers, it passes through the rail junction town of Baquedano before turning north again near the ruins of Oficina Chacabuco and continuing to the regional border at Quillagua. While dozens of other abandoned *salitreras* dot both sides of the Panamericana, only Chacabuco and the recently closed or closing mines at Pedro de Valdivia and María Elena have avoided nearly complete dismantling for scrap.

Where the Panamericana turns north, paved Ruta 25 continues to Calama, the gateway to interior destinations such as San Pedro de Atacama, in an area that is Chile's widest geographical point.

Baquedano

At the desert junction of Baquedano, the Ferrocarril a Bolivia (FCAB) between Antofagasta and La Paz crossed the Longino (Longitudinal Railway) that once connected Iquique with Santiago. The Longino is long since defunct, but the FCAB still hauls freight to Bolivia and another freight line reaches the Argentine border at Socompa.

For most visitors, though, the more accessible attraction is Baquedano's open-air **Museo Ferroviario,** conserving the Longino's legacy with half a dozen vintage locomotives and deteriorating antique railcars at a roundhouse that's a national monument. In early 2008, the mayor of Baquedano drove his car onto the set of the James Bond flick *Quantum of Solace* to protest the fictional film's portrayal of the station as part of Bolivia.

All buses on the Panamericana pass through Baquedano, so it's easy to stop for a look at the station and the roundhouse. There are also several basic but decent restaurants for meals and temporary luggage storage.

◖ Oficina Chacabuco

Just four kilometers north of the junction between the Panamericana and Ruta 25, the Calama highway, Oficina Chacabuco is second only to Humberstone in terms of preservation among the Atacama's nitrate ghost towns. It also has a darker recent history: In the Pinochet dictatorship's first year, it was a prison camp, but International Red Cross intervention prevented executions. Ironically enough, one detainee was Salvador Allende's education subsecretary Waldo Sánchez, who only a few months earlier had declared Chacabuco a national monument.

Almost equally ironically, Chacabuco's former caretaker, Roberto Zaldívar, was one of the more than 2,200 people incarcerated in the former workers' housing. While Chacabuco was less obviously secure than geographically isolated Pisagua, the military surrounded the town with minefields, which have still not been removed, to keep prisoners in. These fields are well-signed, and visitors should take them seriously.

Built by the Lautaro Nitrate Company in 1924, Chacabuco was the last and largest of those using the Shanks system—even as it was under construction, synthetic nitrates were supplanting mineral nitrates, and United States–based Guggenheim Brothers was experimenting with a new system to increase nitrate yields from lower-quality ores.

At its peak, Chacabuco could produce 15,000 metric tons of nitrate per month, but that peak was brief. Still, technological obsolescence brought about its closure by 1940. Though it suffered depredations by scrap thieves, it remains one of Chile's best-preserved *oficinas.* The industrial plant included workshops, warehouses, ore crushers, and 54 enormous liquification tanks under a single roof.

Really a city in itself, Chacabuco occupied an area of 36 hectares, its wide streets forming a grid pattern, and reached a maximum population of about 5,000. It boasted a hospital, theater, hotel, school, market, gymnasium, swimming pool, athletic fields, a tree-lined plaza, and long blocks of adobe housing for workers. Beyond the industrial plant, there remain huge piles of low-grade tailings.

Chacabuco's theater, the beneficiary of painstaking restoration work funded by the German Embassy and Santiago's Goethe Institute, is even larger than Humberstone's. Its 2nd and 3rd floors feature a photographic exhibit of Chacabuco in its heyday; note also the well-preserved murals above the stage. Other notable structures include the train station, the general store, the employees' casino, and its tennis courts.

Caretaker Zaldívar had a large but disorganized collection of artifacts from the nitrate era. Admission to the Museo de Salitre (tel. 055/412516 in Antofagasta, corporacionchacabuco@gmail.com) costs US$1.50 for adults, half that for kids. It's open 10 A.M.–5 P.M. Wednesday–Saturday, and 10 A.M.–7 P.M. alternate Sundays.

Chacabuco is only a short distance east of the Panamericana, but since it's four kilometers north of the main highway junction, Calama-bound buses do not pass nearby. All other northbound buses on the Panamericana come within easy walking distance, however.

Pedro de Valdivia

Founded in 1931 by Guggenheim Brothers, the nitrate *oficina* of Pedro de Valdivia was a working company town until 1996. Because the Guggenheim process of extracting nitrates from the hardpan caliche was so superior to the Shanks system that preceded it, both Pedro de Valdivia and nearby María Elena managed to survive long after Shanks-dependent *oficinas* collapsed.

Officially a *zona típica* national monument since its closure, Pedro de Valdivia is 75 kilometers north of the Calama junction via the Panamericana and a short paved westbound lateral.

María Elena

One of Chile's last working *oficinas*, also founded by Guggenheim Brothers (1926), María Elena processed more than a million tons of caliche per year at its peak, in conjunction with Pedro de Valdivia. Today, though, it clings tenuously to life despite its imminent closure. The mine installations belong to the Sociedad Química Chilena (Soquimich), successor to the Guggenheim dynasty, but the town itself is an independent municipality, about 38 kilometers north of Pedro de Valdivia via a paved road that parallels the Panamericana. There is also a paved lateral that leads west from the Panamericana.

On the dusty streets surrounding María Elena's Plaza de Armas, several buildings comprise the **Barrio Cívico,** a *zona típica* national monument. Among them are the former **Escuela Consolidada** (school), the **Pulpería** or general store, the **Mercado** (market), the **Teatro Metro** (Metro Theater), the **Iglesia San Rafael Arcángel, Sindicato No. 3** (union headquarters), the **Baños Públicos** (public baths), **Banco del Estado,** and the **Asociación Social y Deportiva** (Social and Sports Association).

Also on the plaza, the **Museo del Salitre** (Ignacio Carrera Pinto s/n, tel. 055/639172) recalls the region's pre-Columbian past and the historic nitrate era. It's open 8 A.M.–1 P.M. and 4–10 P.M. weekdays, 10 A.M.–2 P.M. and 4–10 P.M. weekends and holidays. Admission is free.

The only places to stay are **Residencial Chacance** (Claudio Vicuña 4338, tel. 055/639524, US$8 s, US$12 d) and **Hotel Jor** (Av. Osorno 3080, tel. 055/639195, US$10 s, US$13 d); both with private baths. There are various simple *comedores* for a meal.

Several Antofagasta bus companies, including Camus, Flota Barrios, and Pullman Bus, serve María Elena.

Tranque Sloman

Built between 1905 and 1911, this sloping 36-meter-high dam in the Río Loa Canyon once supplied electricity to several nearby *oficinas,* but nowadays the quarried stone structure merely regulates the release of irrigation water to the fields near Quillagua, about 20 kilometers to the north. Reached by a gravel lateral that leads about three kilometers east from the Panamericana, it is now a national monument that contains a **Casa de Máquina** with three rusting turbines, plus several other constructions.

In 1997, when heavy altiplano rains caused downstream floods, Tranque Sloman was the site of a major fish kill, as the rushing waters apparently stirred up toxic sediments deposited through decades of upstream mining (even naturally, the Río Loa has such high arsenic levels that it must be heavily treated to be potable). The dam's national monument status—not to mention the expense—complicates any cleanup efforts, and it is unfortunately closed to the public for the time being.

Quillagua

Flowing through Quillagua, the Río Loa marks the border between Region I (Tarapacá) and Region II (Antofagasta). Until coastal Ruta 1 opened in the early 1990s, this was always a crowded internal customs check because of merchandise moving back and forth to the duty-free Zofri, but now it plays second fiddle to the seaside post at the Loa estuary.

While it's a conspicuous oasis in the Atacama wastes, Quillagua is a virtual ghost town, but it's worth stopping to view the remarkable collection of pre-Columbian and historic mummies in the **Museo de Quillagua.** It keeps no fixed hours, but it's easy to find the custodian in her nearby house.

About 10 kilometers south of the regional border, conspicuous geoglyphs line both sides of the Panamericana.

The Northern Coast

From Antofagasta, coastal Ruta 1 heads north past the Mejillones peninsula, the copper port of Tocopilla, and several ghost towns and numerous desert beaches before arriving at the Río Loa estuary, where there's an internal customs check. Open for only about 15 years, the paved highway linking Tocopilla with Iquique now carries most of the traffic between Region II and Region I.

MEJILLONES

Calm Pacific waters lap the long but steep and relatively narrow beaches of sheltered Mejillones, whose shady coastal promenade provides protection from the hot midday sun. Founded when the region was part of Bolivia, the town lapsed into subtropical torpor as Antofagasta boomed with nitrate exports, but it still boasts some nitrate-era landmarks. It has long been popular with Antofagastinos as a weekend retreat.

Mejillones's peacefulness is under siege, though. Construction of a multimillion-dollar *megapuerto* (megaport) at its east end is supposed to establish the town as the terminus of a transcontinental trade route, oriented toward the Pacific Rim, from Brazil and Paraguay through Argentina and across the Andes to Chile. Despite delays due to environmental damage mitigation, the megaport opened in October 2003 and handled 1.5 million tons of cargo, mostly copper for export in 2004 (the last year for which statistics are readily available). As the megaport grows, Mejillones may regain its economic primacy from Antofagasta.

Orientation

Facing its namesake bay and protected from most ocean swells by the Punta Angamos peninsula to the west, Mejillones (population 7,888) is about 80 kilometers north of Antofagasta via coastal Ruta 1 and a paved northwestern lateral. Another paved access road connects to Ruta 1 to the northeast.

Avenida Latorre, two blocks south of the beach, is the main thoroughfare, while Avenida San Martín faces the beach. Most services are on or near one or the other.

Sights

Mejillones has no national monuments, but several buildings, all dating from the early 20th century, would be worthy candidates. At the foot of Francisco Pinto, topped by a lighthouse, stands the handsome **Capitanía del Puerto** (Port Authority). One block south, the **Museo Histórico y Natural** (Francisco Pinto 110, tel. 055/621289, US$0.50) occupies the former **Aduana de Mejillones,** which replaced an earlier landmark customs house that was dismantled and moved to Antofagasta. While the museum posts hours of 10 A.M.–8 P.M. weekdays, it rarely keeps them; exhibits include material, including photography, on marine fauna, historical figures, and local institutions.

The **Locomotora** in the median strip on Manuel Rodríguez, just south of Avenida Latorre, is one of the original locomotives of the Ferrocarril a Bolivia (Mejillones was the terminus of a spur line). Five blocks west, at Avenida Latorre and Avenida Castillo, the soaring **Iglesia Corazón de María** is the major ecclesiastical landmark.

At the corner of Avenida Latorre and Las Heras, there's a summer **mercado artesanal** (artisans' market).

Accommodations
Though some places shut down in winter, Mejillones offers modest lodgings at **Residencial Elizabeth** (Latorre 440, tel. 055/621500, US$4 pp with shared bath) and **Residencial Mis Nietos** (Riquelme 323, tel. 055/623989, US$13 s, US$17 d with shared bath and breakfast).

Though a bit Spartan, **Hotel París** (Pasaje Iquique 95, tel. 055/623061, iseche2@hotmail.com, US$20 s, US$33 d) has cheerful management and reasonable rates for rooms that include TVs, private baths, and breakfast.

Hostal Miramar (San Martín 650, tel. 055/621638, US$25 s, US$33 d with private bath) is quiet and tidy. Though scuffed and worn in spots, **Hotel Capitanía** (Av. San Martín 410, tel. 055/621542, hotelcapitania@entelchile.net, US$25 s, US$33 d with private bath and breakfast) has sea-view rooms that may be worth haggling for.

Close to the beach, **Hotel Mejillones** (Manuel Montt 086, tel. 055/621590, www.hotelmejillones.cl, US$40 s, US$47 d) has immaculate rooms with all contemporary conveniences, but ask for IVA discounts.

Food
Zlatar (Manuel Rodríguez 125, tel. 055/621580, lunch and dinner daily) is a fine, moderately priced seafood locale. **Hotel Mejillones** (Manuel Montt 086, tel. 055/621590) has a street-level cafeteria and the 4th-floor **Playa Blanca** for more elaborate meals.

Getting There and Around
There are frequent bus connections to Antofagasta (US$3.50, one hour) with **Corsal Bus** (Latorre 647) and **Megatur** (Latorre 753, tel. 055/621528). Long-distance carriers include **Pullman Bus** (Latorre 799, tel. 055/622179) and **Tur-Bus** (Latorre 583, tel. 055/622816).

TOCOPILLA
Once the end of the road, until Ruta 1 opened the coastal trail more than a decade ago, Tocopilla's dilemma is to get passersby to stop en route north to their sunbathing, swimming, and shopping sprees at Iquique. There is potentially good surfing in the area, and little competition for waves.

Traditionally, Tocopilla exports nitrates from María Elena and Pedro de Valdivia (an electric railway carries the cargo to the port), and its massive Central Termoeléctrica powers the copper mine at Chuquicamata, 143 kilometers to the east. Still, unemployment is a serious issue.

In an offbeat way, Tocopilla is a sports hotbed. About 20 kilometers north of town, just before the Túnel Galleguillos, the Tocopilla Golf Club is the *literal* Pebble Beach—the "greens" consist of crushed black volcanic rock; most of the rest of the course is one big sand trap (except for planted, or rather emplaced, plastic palms). Unfortunately for duffers hoping to challenge these unique conditions, it's not a public course.

Even more improbable, though, is Tocopilla's downtown baseball park. The seaside diamond has grand views, but this is true sandlot ball—the entire field is a hard dirt surface—you don't want to dive for balls, and you certainly don't want to crash into the concrete outfield walls. Baseball has been played here since 1928; in 2005, on its home field, Tocopilla defeated Iquique for the national championship. As of

2009, though, it's the site of improvised housing for victims of the 2005 earthquake.

Orientation

On narrow wave-cut terraces above the Pacific, at the foot of the coast range, Tocopilla (population 23,352) is 188 kilometers north of Antofagasta and 244 kilometers south of Iquique. It is 143 kilometers west of Chuquicamata via another paved highway that intersects the north–south Panamericana about midway to Chuqui.

Tocopilla has an elongated city plan in which thoroughfares such as Ruta 1 (known as Arturo Prat through town) and 21 de Mayo (the downtown business district) are crossed by shorter streets that rise steeply from west to east.

Sights

Bounded by 21 de Mayo, Aníbal Pinto, Sucre, and Bolívar, **Plaza Carlos Condell** is the focus of Tocopilla's street life. Other than its industrial installations, the main landmark is the **Torre Reloj** (Av. Prat), a wooden clock tower moved from Coya, a former nitrate *oficina* midway between María Elena and Pedro de Valdivia.

Accommodations

Friendly, spotless **Hotel Croacia** (Bolívar 1332, tel. 055/810332, US$20 s, US$25 d) may not be the cheapest, but it's perhaps Tocopilla's best value.

Modern **Hotel Chungará** (21 de Mayo 1440, tel. 055/811036, US$20 s, US$25 d) has decent, good-sized rooms with cable TV, but downstairs rooms can be dark. There's a rowdy bar two doors south, but the sound doesn't seem to carry.

Rooms at **Hotel Vucina** (21 de Mayo 2069, tel. 055/813088, US$20 s, US$30 d) are spacious and luminous, but also well-worn. Set back from the street, the hotel has its own on-site parking, unusual in Tocopilla.

Hotel Atenas (21 de Mayo 1448, tel. 055/813650, US$30 s, US$40 d) is the most high-class of Tocopilla's accommodations, with contemporary rooms and services.

Food

The chain **Bavaria** (21 de Mayo 1999, tel. 055/811160) is good for breakfast and standard Chilean fare of reliable quality.

Club de la Unión (Prat 1354, tel. 055/813198) retains the atmosphere of the bygone nitrate era, with good seafood at modest prices. **Chifa Jok San** (21 de Mayo 1848, tel. 055/811458) serves Chinese meals.

At the south end of downtown, **La Casa de Don Julio** (Serrano 1336, tel. 055/816129) passes for haute cuisine here, but it would be considered a decent restaurant just about anywhere in Chile, with pleasant outdoor seating on a quiet block. Seafood dinners cost around US$10.

Services

BCI (Arturo Prat 1401) has an ATM.

Correos de Chile (21 de Mayo and Aníbal Pinto) is the post office. **Entel** (21 de Mayo 2066) and **Telefónica CTC** (21 de Mayo 1829) have long-distance telephone service. **Cyberworld** (21 de Mayo 1893) and other locales provide Internet access.

Tocopilla's **hospital** (Santa Rosa and Matta, tel. 055/821839) is a short distance northeast of downtown.

Getting There and Around

Tocopilla has no central bus terminal, but many lines pass through town en route between Santiago, Antofagasta, and Iquique. Among them are **Buses Camus** (21 de Mayo 1940, tel. 055/813102), **Flota Barrios** (21 de Mayo 1720, tel. 055/811861), **Tur-Bus** (21 de Mayo 1491, tel. 055/811581), and **Pullman Bus** (21 de Mayo 1812, tel. 055/815340).

From the corner of 21 de Mayo and Manuel Rodríguez, *taxi colectivos* connect Tocopilla with Chuquicamata and Calama at 3 and 9 P.M. (US$7, 2.5 hours). Camus also goes to Calama, Monday–Saturday at 7:20 A.M. and 4:50 P.M., with an additional Sunday departure at 7:50 P.M.

Sample destinations and fares include Antofagasta (US$10, 2.5 hours), Calama (US$8, 3.5 hours), Iquique (US$15, 4.5 hours), Chañaral (US$20, 7.5 hours), Copiapó (US$30,

Parts of the James Bond film *Quantum of Solace* were shot among the crumbling adobes of Cobija.

11 hours), La Serena (US$40, 15 hours), and Santiago (US$55, 21 hours).

COBIJA

It's only a cluster of crumbling adobes today, but in the early 19th century the port of Cobija was the *salida al mar* (outlet to the sea) for which Bolivian governments have clamored ever since losing their maritime frontage to Chile in the War of the Pacific.

About 130 kilometers north of Antofagasta, between Punta Guasilla in the south and Gatico on the north, the shoreline around Cobija constitutes a *zona típica* national monument for its plaza, church, graveyard, and some otherwise mostly unidentifiable structures. Colorful jellyfish float in the tidal pools on its rocky peninsula. Scenes from the 2008 James Bond flick *Quantum of Solace* were shot here.

Though Cobija's population reached 1,500 in the mid-19th century (despite perpetual water shortages), a massive 1868 earthquake and an 1877 tsunami delivered its death blows. A handful of fishing families now reside here; the more modern ruins at **Gatico,** to the north, were once a guesthouse for a nearby mine.

Calama

Billing itself as the "land of sun and copper," fast-growing Calama is mainly a crossroads and service center for the mining industry, the foundation of the local economy. While many travelers pass through en route to the famous desert village of San Pedro de Atacama, the main staging post for visits to the altiplano, Calama does boast nearby sights such as the open-pit copper mine of Chuquicamata, the colonial hamlet of Chiu Chiu, and the pre-

Columbian fortress ruins of the Pukará de Lasana. It also offers alternative routes to some destinations more commonly visited from San Pedro.

One reason Calama is growing is the closure of nearby Chuquicamata as a residential community—thanks to Codelco's Plan Calama, by which all the miners now commute to Chuqui for work and their families live here. The construction of 2,500 houses, all on Codelco land, has had some glitches, but there was no alternative to moving residents from heavily polluted Chuqui.

While tourism takes a back seat to mining, as there's little to see in the city proper—though founded in the 1850s when the area was Bolivian territory, it's really a 20th-century town. Visitors may find it hard to believe, but parts of Calama were under water during the early 2001 floods.

ORIENTATION

Calama (population 136,600) is 213 kilometers northeast of Antofagasta via the Panamericana and paved Ruta 25. On the banks of the Río Loa, 2,250 meters above sea level, it has a compact core with a slightly irregular street plan. Calle Ramírez, leading east off the plaza, is a *peatonal* that's a popular meeting place.

SIGHTS

Calama's geographical and symbolic center is **Plaza 23 de Marzo,** commemorating the date of its occupation by Chilean troops in the War of the Pacific. It has undergone a complete remodel: The mature pepper trees still extend their shade, but there are also patches of neatly mown grass, tiled walkways, numerous benches, and tidy trash receptacles. Its bandshell has a copper roof, its church a copper steeple, and a copper plaque memorializes the 34 Calameños who were executed or who "disappeared" during the infamous Caravan of Death.

Parque El Loa

On the southern outskirts of town, irrigated by its namesake river, Parque El Loa is a favorite afternoon and weekend retreat for Calameños, with shady picnic grounds, sports fields, and a pair of museums.

The more established museum is the **Museo Arqueológico y Etnológico** (Museum of Archaeology and Ethnology, tel. 055/531770), strong on materials but weak on explanations of the Atacameño peoples and their environment.

This may change as it's undergoing renovation, with content and hours uncertain as yet.

At the private **Museo de Historia Natural y Cultural del Desierto** (Museum of Natural and Cultural History of the Desert, cel. 09/8245-6497, museocalama@vtr.net), across the river footbridge from the Museo Arqueológico, there are exhibits on mineralogy, paleontology (especially notable), Andean ecology and environment, Atacameño culture (outstanding), regional history (including one of the better accounts of the War of the Pacific), and mining culture. Hours are 10 A.M.–1 P.M. and 3:30–7 P.M. daily except Monday; admission costs US$0.75.

ENTERTAINMENT AND EVENTS

The **Teatro Municipal** (Ramírez 2080, tel. 055/531704, teatromunicipal@calamacultural.cl) offers live theater and concerts, and hosts art exhibits. Some larger concerts take place at the **Estadio Techado,** one block west.

Calama's first-division soccer team, **Cobreloa** (Abaroa 1757, tel. 055/341775, www.cobreloa.cl) plays at the 20,000-seat Estadio Municipal, on Avenida Matta east of the train station.

Every March 23, Calama commemorates the city's occupation by Chilean troops during the War of the Pacific.

ACCOMMODATIONS

Because Calama depends on trade from the booming mining industry, hotel prices here are higher than in many other Chilean cities. In all categories, selectivity is the rule—there is significant variation even within individual hotels.

US$10-25

Passable but past its prime, on the *peatonal,* **Hotel Atenas** (Ramírez 1961, tel. 055/342666, www.hotelatenas.cl, US$13–21 s, US$24–29 d) has good beds and large baths. The more expensive rooms have private baths.

US$25-50

Friendly **Residencial Gran Chile** (Latorre 1474, tel. 055/317455, US$15 s, US$26 d) is one of the region's best bargains—all rooms are spotless and spacious, with private baths and cable TV. Its only drawback is the utterly barren exterior, which needs landscaping.

Exceptionally quiet for a cheap sleep, **Hotel El Loa** (Abaroa 1617, tel. 055/341963, US$12 pp, US$27 s or d) now has rooms with private baths, but the shared-bath singles are better value. All rooms, even the singles, have cable TV, but the beds vary in quality. The upstairs rooms have better natural light.

Congenial **Hostal Camino del Inca** (Bañados Espinoza 1889, tel. 055/349552, US$17 pp) offers no frills in its simple but well-maintained quarters.

At the modern, well-run **Hotel Alfa** (Sotomayor 2016, tel. 055/342496, www.hotelalfa.cl, US$42 s, US$50 d), rooms differ substantially—if the first room shown seems too small, ask for a larger one. Rates include an ample buffet breakfast.

US$50-100

The starkly modern **Hotel Olimpo** (Santa María 1673, tel. 055/319075, holimpo@starmedia.com, US$49 s, US$57 d) still needs greenery; IVA discounts are possible for its utilitarian, relatively small rooms.

Easily Calama's most stylish accommodation, **Hotel El Mirador** (Sotomayor 2064, tel. 055/340329, www.hotelmirador.cl, US$48 s, US$65 d) occupies a flawlessly restored historic building just half a block off the plaza.

Directly on Plaza 23 de Marzo, **Hotel Quitor** (Ramírez 2116, tel. 055/314716, US$41 s, US$60 d, hotelquitor@entelchile.net) has undergone a significant remodel.

Hotel Punakora (Santa María 1640, tel. 055/345539, www.hotelpunakora.cl, US$51 s, US$60 d) is a modern, spacious, comfortable, and attractive establishment that, astonishingly, can't be bothered to give IVA discounts to foreign visitors. Rates include breakfast,

cable TV, telephone, gym access, and similar amenities.

Hotel Universo (Sotomayor 1822, tel. 055/361640, US$63 s, US$66 d) is friendly and newish but not quite immaculate; rates include breakfast, private bath, and cable TV.

The traditional top-end choice, **Hostería Calama** (Latorre 1521, tel. 055/310306, hcalama@tie.cl, US$59 s, US$70 d) is often full despite its size. Friendly but kitschy **Hotel Paradise Inn Desert** (Ramírez 1867, tel. 055/341618, paradise_hotel@hotmail.com, US$59 s, US$78 d) offers large rooms with private baths, whirlpool tubs, and other amenities.

US$100-150

Alongside the airport, the **Park Hotel Calama** (Camino Aeropuerto 1392, tel. 055/447700, www.parkplaza.cl/calama/index.htm, US$110 s, US$120 d) is the city's only luxury hotel.

FOOD

Bavaria (Sotomayor 2093, tel. 055/341496), the Chilean counterpart to Denny's, is good for breakfast and sandwiches. **Cactus** (Sotomayor 1901, tel. 055/825991, lunch and dinner daily except Sun.) is a new pub/restaurant that has good lunch specials.

The **Club Croata,** alternatively known as the Hrvatski Dom (Abaroa 1869, tel. 055/342126), serves moderately priced lunches but more expensive dinners. Open for dinner only, **Fogata** (Vicuña Mackenna 1973, tel. 099/0778624) is a *parrilla*-pub with both indoor and outdoor seating.

Calama has several cheapish *chifas,* including **Grande Chong Hua** (Latorre 1415, tel. 055/363826).

INFORMATION

Calama's understaffed municipal **Corporación Cultural y Turismo** (Latorre 1689, tel. 055/345345, mirnacortes@calamaturistico.cl) tries hard but can't keep up as well as it used to; it does have English-speaking personnel who will help make reservations for Chuquicamata.

Hours are 8 A.M.–1 P.M. and 2–6 P.M. week-days only.

Motorists will find the **Automóvil Club de Chile** (Acchi, Avenida Ecuador 1901, tel. 055/310604) a good source of information.

SERVICES

Banco de Crédito (Sotomayor 2002) has an ATM, while **Moon Valley Money Exchange** (Vivar 1818) can change cash or travelers checks.

Correos de Chile (Vicuña Mackenna 2185) handles postal services. Calama has several convenient long-distance offices, including **Entelchile** (Sotomayor 2027) and **Telefónica CTC** (Latorre 1955), which also have Internet service. There are several cyber-cafés, most notably **Cybernet** (Vargas 2054), which stays open late and also has long-distance telephone service.

Neighboring Bolivia's **consulate** (Pedro León Gallo 1985, tel. 055/341976) is a moving target that manages to keep the same phone number; it's open 9 A.M.–4 P.M. week-days only.

Hospital Carlos Cisterna (Av. Granaderos between Félix Hoyos and Cisterna, tel. 055/342347) is the local hospital.

GETTING THERE

Calama has air and highway connections to the rest of Chile, and rail service to Bolivia.

Air

Aeropuerto El Loa (tel. 055/342348) is on the southern outskirts of town.

LAN (Latorre 1726, tel. 055/313927) flies around four times daily from Antofagasta and Santiago; one flight every weekday also stops in Copiapó. **Sky Airline** (Latorre 1497, tel. 055/310190) also serves Santiago, sometimes via Antofagasta.

Bus

Calama lacks a desperately needed central bus terminal, but many of the bus companies are clustered near the railroad station at the east end of town, or northwest of Plaza 23 de

Marzo. There are both regional and long-distance services as well as international connections to Bolivia and Argentina.

Buses Frontera (Antofagasta 2041, tel. 055/318543) goes nine times daily to San Pedro (US$2.50) and twice to Toconao (US$4). **Buses Atacama 2000** (Abaroa 2106, tel. 055/314757) goes twice or thrice daily to San Pedro. **Camus** (Antofagasta 2239, tel. 055/342800) serves Tocopilla (US$6, 3.5 hours) at least twice daily.

Several companies cover north- and south-bound destinations on the Panamericana, among them **Tur-Bus** (Balmaceda 1852, tel. 055/316699), which also goes to San Pedro de Atacama and leaves from its terminal at Avenida Granaderos and Manuel Montt; **Pullman Bus** (Sotomayor 1800, tel. 055/341282), which leaves from Mall Calama, Avenida Balmaceda 3242; **Ramos Cholele** (Balmaceda 2012, tel. 055/317989); and **Géminis** (Antofagasta 2239, tel. 055/341993). **Kenny Bus** (Balmaceda 2004, tel. 055/342514) serves Iquique via María Elena and Pozo Almonte.

Sample domestic destinations, times, and fares include Arica (US$22, 9.5 hours), Iquique (US$18, 6 hours), Antofagasta (US$8, 3 hours), Tocopilla (US$9, 3.5 hours), Chañaral (US$35, 8 hours), Copiapó (US$40, 11 hours), Vallenar (US$42, 13 hours), La Serena (US$46–68, 13 hours), and Santiago (US$60–92, 22 hours).

Since international buses fill up fast, reservations are advisable. **Buses Frontera** (Antofagasta 2041, tel. 055/318543) goes to Ollagüe, on the Bolivian border, Wednesday and Sunday at midnight (US$6); a connecting Bolivian bus continues to Uyuni (US$12).

Two companies cross the Andes to Jujuy and Salta, Argentina (US$45 to either city, 12–13 hours), without the necessity of changing buses. Normally, **Géminis** departs Friday and Sunday at 9 A.M., while **Pullman Bus** goes at 8 A.M. Tuesday, Friday, and Sunday, but schedules are subject to seasonal changes. With advance arrangements, it's possible to catch these buses in San Pedro de Atacama.

Taxi Colectivo

Taxis Cruceros (Balmaceda and Vargas, tel. 055/347946) has departures for the coastal city of Tocopilla (US$8, three hours) at noon and 6 P.M. daily, passing through the nitrate town of María Elena.

GETTING AROUND

Yellow *taxi colectivos* to Chuquicamata leave from a spot on Abaroa just north of Ramírez.

For the afternoon tours, leave no later than 12:30 P.M.

Car Rental

Rental agencies include **Alamo** (Félix Hoyos 2177, tel. 055/364545), **Avis** (Parque Industrial Apiac 2525, Km 2, tel. 055/363120), **Dollar** (Latorre 1510, tel. 055/318505), and **Hertz** (Granaderos 1416, tel. 055/341380).

Vicinity of Calama

Most visitors to the area start their excursions from San Pedro de Atacama, but several Calama agencies offer comparable services, including **Sol del Desierto** (Av. Granaderos 723, Local 7-A, tel. 055/330428, www.soldeldesierto.cl), and **Tungra Expediciones** (Punta Arenas 2125, tel. 055/363010, tungra@ctc.internet.cl).

CHUQUICAMATA

Sixteen kilometers north of Calama, Chuquicamata's cavernous open pit is the Grand Canyon of the copper industry. Managed by Codelco, the state mining company, everything at Chuqui exists on such a massive scale—its towering power shovels, fleet of mammoth diesel trucks, and the mountains of *tortas* (tailings) accumulated over nearly a century of operations—that it could easily be a metaphor for mining's role in the Chilean economy ever since independence, and for copper for more than a century.

In 2007, the last year for which complete statistics are available, the 896,308 tons produced by Codelco Norte (including Chuquicamata and the nearby Radomiro Tomic mine) constituted more than half the country's entire copper production, at the lowest cost of any of its divisions. Though international prices have recently fallen, copper remains Chile's single largest export and is likely to do so for the foreseeable future, despite diversification efforts.

Chuquicamata itself is a tidy company town

that, for all its controversial role in Chilean history, was also a community with a distinctive working-class culture. All this has ended, though—the need for workspace and the accumulated toxic pollution of more than eight decades of copper extraction and processing has finally forced Codelco to relocate its employees and their families to nearby Calama. Today's Chuqui is merely a work site.

History

While pre-Hispanic peoples worked Chuquicamata's copper deposits for weapons, tools, and other artifacts, it was not until around 1910 that the Guggenheim Brothers first worked the deposit through their Chile Exploration Company. In 1923, the Guggenheims sold their rights to the Anaconda Copper Company of Butte, Montana.

Anaconda controlled Chuqui for nearly half a century, building a city with housing, schools, shopping, medical services, and even entertainment—including a cinema and a full-sized soccer stadium—from scratch. At the same time, the wealthy foreign mining enclave engendered suspicion and resentment among certain sectors of Chilean society, especially as political radicalism grew in the 1960s. Reformists such as President Eduardo Frei Montalva (1964–1970) promoted greater Chilean participation in the industry, but Salvador Allende's Socialist government (1970–1973) successfully nationalized it, with congressional approval.

NORTE GRANDE

Even after the 1973 Pinochet coup, the Corporación del Cobre de Chile (Codelco) has kept Chuqui, along with other large copper mines such as El Salvador (Region III, Atacama) and El Teniente (Region VI, O'Higgins) under state control, despite occasional privatization rumors. Codelco remains the country's single most important economic player.

Sights

In Chuqui proper, the main structures date from Anaconda days, such as the **Estadio Anaconda,** where the Cobreloa soccer team played before moving to Calama; the **Auditorio Sindical,** an immense theater dedicated for labor use and embellished with a mural that recalls the death of several workers during a 1960s strike; and the freestanding **Pala Electromecánica Mundial,** the 26.5-meter, 450-ton power shovel that was the world's largest from its inception in 1949 to its retirement in 1971. Near Relaciones Públicas (Public Relations) offices, where guided tours of Chuqui begin, a striking statue dignifies the laborers who still risk their lives in the company's day-to-day operations.

The single most impressive physical feature, though, is the enormous **Yacimiento Chuqui,** the terraced oval cavity that measures 4.3 kilometers in length, 3 kilometers in width, and 750 meters in depth. A railroad once hauled copper ore from its depths, but today massive diesels, riding on tires higher than 3 meters, carry Chile's most critical commodity to the smelter, which is no longer open to the public.

Tours

In Walter Salles's 2004 movie *The Motorcycle Diaries,* a Chuquicamata foreman sarcastically scolds a young Ernesto Guevara that the mine "is not a tourist sight." In the years since "Che" and his buddy Alberto Granado passed through here, though, it's become one.

Codelco's **Oficina de Relaciones Públicas** (Av. J. M. Carrera and Avenida Tocopilla, tel. 055/322122, visitas@codelco.cl; call 8:30–11:30 A.M. for reservations) conducts tours (US$2) at 1:15 P.M. weekdays (do not pay Calama travel agencies for spots on the tour). Catch a *taxi colectivo* from Calama no later than 12:30 P.M. to be certain of on-time arrival.

Visitors must present identification (national ID card or passport). While trousers and long sleeves are no longer obligatory, sensible shoes are: no sandals, in particular. Tours start with a 10-minute Spanish-language video, followed by an English-language version; visitors then board buses for the 50-minute excursion. Dust from trucks often obscures the view of the open pit.

Getting There

From a stop on Abaroa just north of Ramírez in Calama, yellow *taxi colectivos* leave frequently for Chuquicamata.

PARQUE PARA LA PRESERVACIÓN DE LA MEMORIA HISTÓRICA

It'll probably make the pages of the timidly apolitical *Turistel* guides, but one of Chile's most moving modern monuments is a semicircle of 34 columns that rise from a sunken amphitheater about 15 kilometers east of Calama, on the north side of the road to San Pedro de Atacama. Twenty-six of these columns represent victims of army executions on October 19, 1973, by the "Caravan of Death" under General Sergio Arellano Stark.

The amphitheater itself is the site where the 26 bodies were flung. The remains were later removed as the return to representative government approached in 1990; DNA from a handful of remaining bone fragments unearthed here permitted identification of some victims. The remaining eight columns symbolize other Calama fatalities that did not correspond directly to the Caravan of Death.

The Municipalidad de Calama spent some US$65,000 to build the monument, which was dedicated October 19, 2004, the 31st anniversary of the Caravan's "visit." Some family members have added their own simple plaques in remembrance, and have planted trees that are struggling to survive despite drip irrigation.

CHUG CHUG

Between Chuquicamata and the Panamericana, the Chug Chug geoglyphs testify to the antiquity of a caravan route that once linked Chiu Chiu and Calama with the oasis of Quillagua and the coast—note the human figures, on reed rafts, harpooning fish or sea lions. There are additional human and animal figures, but also abstract designs such as the *rombos escalerados,* rhomboid shapes.

Administered by the *comuna* of María Elena, Chug Chug is on the pampa's eastern edge, 1,200 meters above sea level. It is 36 kilometers east of Chuquicamata and 30 kilometers west of the Panamericana crossroads, on the road to Tocopilla.

Chiu Chiu

At the confluence with the Río Salado, a Loa tributary, 33 kilometers east of Calama via paved Ruta 21, the village of Chiu Chiu is famous for its 17th-century **Iglesia de San Francisco;** until the early 20th century, when Calama built its cathedral, Chiu Chiu was the regional locus of ecclesiastical authority.

Chiu Chiu's church is a national monument with buttressed walls, twin bell towers, and a ceiling built of various desert woods held together with leather ties and covered with mud thatch. More than a meter thick, its sturdy adobe walls are originals, but the bell towers are reconstructions of earlier counterparts that collapsed.

Chiu Chiu has accommodations at **Hotel Tujina** (Esmeralda s/n, tel. 055/342201, US$12 pp with private bath and breakfast); in addition to breakfast, other meals are served. Try also **Restaurant Muley** (Esmeralda 948, tel. 055/692141).

Pukará de Lasana

North of Chiu Chiu, the pavement ends on Ruta 21, which continues toward Ollagüe, though the parallel route to the El Abra copper mine, which diverges about two kilometers south of Chiu Chiu, is paved for some distance. Either route leads up the Loa Valley to the Pukará de Lasana, a well-restored 12th-century defensive fortification that's a national monument.

Ayquina

Nestled in the valley of its namesake river, a Loa tributary about 35 kilometers east of Lasana, the village of Ayquina and its surrounding agricultural terraces constitute a *zona típica* national monument. Dependent on Chiu Chiu, its colonial **Iglesia de la Virgen de Guadalupe** constituted one of the earliest efforts at Catholic evangelization in the region.

Ayquina's **Museo Votivo** is an ethnographic museum that displays ex-voto offerings to its patron saint and exhibits elaborate and colorful costumes from its 29 folkloric dance groups (the village's September 7–8 festival is the best time to see them in action). The museum is open 10 A.M.–1 P.M. weekdays except Monday, and 3–7:30 P.M. daily except Monday and holidays.

Vegas de Turi

Directly east of Lasana via a reasonably good gravel road, the Vegas de Turi is a marshland that is gradually desiccating because of water demands from Calama and the mining industry. It is also the site of the hilltop **Pukará de Turi,** a four-hectare site that was the largest architectural complex of Atacameño times. Dating from about A.D. 900, influenced by immigrants from the Bolivian altiplano, northwestern Argentina and, in its latest stages, Inka Peru, it is also a national monument.

Toconce

At Toconce, a village with only about 50 permanent residents, pre-Columbian terraces climb the slopes to a hilltop site where the colonial **Iglesia San Santiago** overlooks the valley of the Río Toconce, a tributary of the Salado and the Loa. Initially part of the community of Ayquina, Toconce gradually established its own identity although it maintains strong kinship links with the other community.

Caspana

About midway between Ayquina and Toconce, a winding road drops into the Río Caspana Valley, whose picturesque namesake village nestles cosily between terraced hillsides; on a promontory above the village stands the colonial **Iglesia de San Lucas,** a national historical monument.

Organized by Maltese anthropologist George Serracino, the **Museo Etnográfico de Caspana** is an exceptional collection for a community of this size; it also sells a selection of locally produced crafts. It's open 10 A.M.–1 P.M. weekdays except Monday, and 2–6 P.M. daily except Monday and holidays; admission is free.

From Caspana, a southbound road climbs out of the valley and then intersects a zigzag eastbound road over the Cuesta de Chita toward the El Tatio geysers and San Pedro de Atacama. Only high-clearance vehicles are advisable on this route; if it's been raining, four-wheel drive is a good idea.

San Pedro de Atacama

On the surface, San Pedro de Atacama is still a serene colonial village where the aboriginal Kunza or Atacameño peoples go about the daily business of farming their fields and tending their flocks, while captivated tourists stroll the adobe-lined streets where conquistador Pedro de Valdivia and his retinue paused on their way south to Santiago. For all its charm, though, the reality is that San Pedro has become a contested space where casual backpackers, commercial interests, and indigenous cultures are struggling to get along.

Some regional officials suggest San Pedro is "reaching its carrying capacity" for tourism; if local feelings are any gauge, this may be true. The informal, easygoing street life of backpacking nomads has upset some locals to the point that relations with the community can be tense.

In this atmosphere, there have been some unpleasant incidents. In early 2001, for instance, there were mysterious twin cases of vandalism and arson in San Pedro's landmark church—despite the fact that it sits across the street from the police station and the delinquents entered by breaking windows. The main altar and several wooden saints—one the church's patron saint dating from 1737—were destroyed or seriously damaged in the blaze.

San Pedro also has problems with street dogs, despite a municipal campaign to neuter them; fortunately, though, they seem larger than most *perros callejeros,* most have good dispositions. On a lighter note, their abundance has led to the ironic nickname "San Perro de Atacama."

For all these problems, travelers of all economic strata continue to flock to San Pedro and its surroundings for their perceived

A large pepper tree shades the plaza at San Pedro de Atacama.

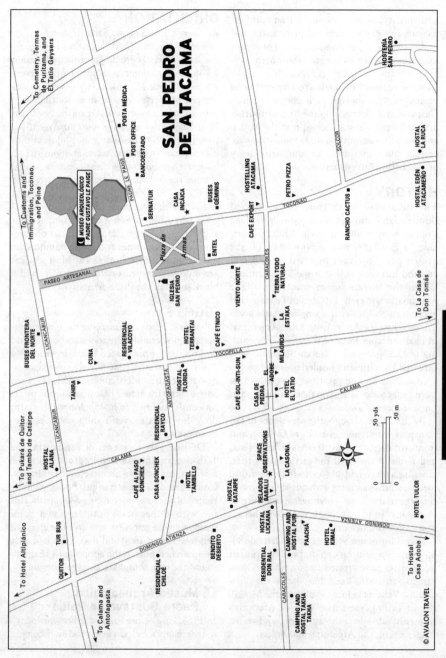

SAN PEDRO
DE ATACAMA

To Cemetery, Termas
de Puritama, and
El Tatio Geysers

To Customs and
Immigration, Toconao,
and Peine

To Pukará de Quitor
and Tambo de Catarpe

To Hotel Altiplánico

To Calama and
Antofagasta

To La Casa de
Don Tomás

To Hostal
Casa Adobe

HOSTERÍA
SAN PEDRO

HOSTAL
LA RUCA

HOSTAL EDÉN
ATACAMEÑO

POSTA MÉDICA

POST OFFICE

BANCOESTADO

SERNATUR

CASA
INCAICA

BUSES
GÉMINIS

CAFÉ EXPORT

HOSTELLING
ATACAMA

PETRO PIZZA

RANCHO CACTUS

ENTEL

TIERRA TODO
NATURAL

LA
ESTAKA

MILAGROS

EL
ADOBE

HOTEL
EL TATIO

VIENTO NORTE

CAFÉ ÉTNICO

HOTEL
TERRANTAI

RESIDENCIAL
VILACOYO

IGLESIA
SAN PEDRO

MUSEO ARQUEOLÓGICO
PADRE GUSTAVO LE PAIGE

BUSES FRONTERA
DEL NORTE

CUNA

TAHRA

RESIDENCIAL
RAYCO

HOSTAL
FLORIDA

CAFÉ SOL-INTI-SUN

CASA DE
PIEDRA

HOSTAL
ALANA

CAFÉ AL PASO
SONCHEK

CASA SONCHEK

HOTEL
TAMBILLO

HOSTAL
KATARPE

SPACE
OBSERVATIONS

LA CASONA

HELADOS
BABALU

HOSTAL
LICKANA

CAMPING AND
HOSTAL PUR

PAACHÁ

HOTEL
KIMAL

HOTEL TULOR

TUR BUS

QUITOR

RESIDENCIAL
CHILOÉ

BENDITO
DESIERTO

RESIDENCIAL
DON RAL

CAMPING AND
HOSTAL TAKHA
TAKHA

Plaza de
Armas

PASEO ARTESANAL

PADRE LE PAIGE

LICANCABUR

ANTOFAGASTA

LICANCABUR

CALAMA

TOCOPILLA

CALAMA

DOMINGO ATIENZA

DOMINGO ATIENZA

CARACOLES

CARACOLES

SOLCOR

TOCONAO

50 yds

50 m

0

0

© AVALON TRAVEL

NORTE GRANDE

authenticity, as the closest Chilean counterpart to indigenous communities and colonial survivals in Peru and Bolivia. Foreigners make up much of its clientele, but metropolitan Chileans are at least as numerous.

Some regional officials are attempting to promote off-the-beaten-path options such as Caspana and Toconce, home to new tourist-oriented enterprises, to help spread the wealth around. San Pedro, though, is more easily accessible and central to excursions, with plenty of supporting infrastructure.

HISTORY

The Inka road south from Cuzco passed through San Pedro but, while Pedro de Valdivia stopped here on his way to the Chilean heartland in 1540, it remained far enough off the beaten path to retain its architectural and cultural integrity well into the 20th century. When the nitrate boom transformed the Atacama in the early 1900s, San Pedro's oasis became an obligatory rest stop for cattle herds driven across the Andes from Salta, Argentina, to feed the labor force of the *oficinas* (according to U.S. geographer Isaiah Bowman, who explored the altiplano borderlands and passes on muleback around this time, the cattle came from as far away as Catamarca, La Rioja, San Luis, and even Córdoba).

By the 1920s, though, the prevalence of rail transport throughout the Norte Grande, and from Antofagasta across the Andes to Bolivia, had reduced the need for cattle drives that, crossing arid, frigid passes well above 4,000 meters, were even more arduous than those of the legendary Texas cowboys. According to Bowman, "In place of mule transport there is now railroad transport."

Roads for motor vehicles were a later development, but mining exploration and tourist imperatives have created improved access not just to San Pedro itself, but also to the polychrome Valle de la Luna (Valley of the Moon), the El Tatio geysers, the Salar de Atacama's immense salt lakes, the altiplano, and trans-Andean routes to Argentina and Bolivia.

ORIENTATION

At the north end of the Salar de Atacama, an immense sprawling salt lake that has nearly evaporated, San Pedro de Atacama (population 1,938) is 120 kilometers southeast of Calama via paved Ruta 23, which parallels the Salar's eastern border as it continues south before turning west toward the Argentine border at Paso Sico. An alternative route to Argentina, paved Ruta 23 to Paso Jama and Jujuy, climbs directly east from San Pedro; at about the 45 kilometer point, a short northeastern lateral reaches the Bolivian border post at Portezuelo del Cajón.

Even without a map, it's not hard to find your way around San Pedro's compact but slightly irregular grid after an initial orientation, and street names and house numbers are more common than in the past. Most services are on or around east–west Caracoles, half a block south of the Plaza de Armas.

SIGHTS

All of San Pedro is a *zona típica* national monument, but several landmarks stand out in and around the pepper-shaded Plaza de Armas.

On the east side, generally acknowledged to be San Pedro's oldest construction, the aged adobe **Casa Incáica** is often, and probably erroneously, claimed to have belonged to Pedro de Valdivia. A souvenir shop now occupies its interior.

Despite past incidents of vandalism, the 17th-century **Iglesia San Pedro** remains the town's most notable architectural landmark. Constructed with a rectangular floor plan, its thatched roof supported by *algarrobo* beams tied with leather straps, it underwent a major remodel in the mid-18th century. The attached bell tower is an 1890 addition. Breached only by an arched portal, the adobe walls that surround the compound are a reconstruction.

◖ Museo Arqueológico Padre Gustavo Le Paige

In 1955, long before San Pedro became today's tourist magnet, Belgian priest and archaeologist

Gustavo Le Paige began to acquire and organize artifacts from the surrounding desert into what has become Chile's foremost archaeological museum. By the time of his death in 1980, he had accumulated nearly 400,000 separate pieces, with the help of local villagers and Antofagasta's Universidad Católica del Norte, to help detail the region's cultural evolution and history from the earliest Paleo-Indians, about 11,000 years ago, to the 16th-century Spanish invasion.

Housed in modern facilities with well-organized display cases in three octagonal pavilions, the museum displays an assortment of stone tools, ceramics, and textiles; details the region's diverse natural environments; and replicates pre-Hispanic burial customs; the grounds feature a modest botanical garden. It continues to have one glaring shortcoming— there is nothing on post-conquest Kunza culture, whose once-thriving language has become extinct—and despite recent events there is nothing whatsoever on tourism's impact on the village. While its primary mission may be archaeological, it owes something more to the community that helped build it.

Half a block east on the Plaza de Armas, across from the post office, the Museo Arqueológico (Gustavo Le Paige 380, tel. 055/851335, www.sanpedroatacama.com/museo.htm) is open 9 A.M.–6 P.M. weekdays, 10 A.M.–6 P.M. weekends and holidays. Admission costs US$4 for adults, half that for children.

EVENTS
A traditional town, San Pedro hosts more than a handful of festivals, the most notable of which is June 29's patronal **Fiesta de San Pedro y San Pablo.** In early February, folkloric dances mark the **Fiesta de Nuestra Señora de la Candelaria,** while the Andean **Carnaval** lasts several days in February or March.

August's **Limpia de Canales** is the local version of the practice of clearing the irrigation canals, common throughout the Hispanic world, for the coming spring planting. August

30's **Fiesta de Santa Rosa de Lima** celebrates one of the Andean countries' most popular official saints.

SHOPPING
Between the Plaza de Armas and the bus plaza, San Pedro's **Paseo Artesanal** is a shaded passageway where vendors hawk crafts and souvenirs, many of them imported from Bolivia, such as alpaca woolens and wooden carvings. Individual shops include **Petroglifo** (Caracoles 190-B, tel. 055/851192), **La Manada** (Caracoles s/n, tel. 055/851480), **La Luna** (Toconao 459, tel. 055/851108), and the women's cooperative **La Mano** (Tocopilla 450-A, tel. 055/851312, www.ceramicalamano.cl), which specializes in quality ceramics.

ACCOMMODATIONS
San Pedro has abundant budget accommodations at reasonable prices, some excellent values in midrange choices, and some real high-enders. During Chilean summer and winter holidays, it can get crowded, with reservations advisable even at budget lodgings. Except in the upper ranges, few places provide breakfast.

Several accommodations are available only as part of multi-day, all-inclusive packages.

Camping
On the west side of town, **Camping Takha Takha** (Caracoles 101-B, tel. 055/851038, takhatakha@terra.cl, US$13 pp) has good sites with shade. At Solcor, just beyond the customs and immigration post east of town, the quiet **Camping Conaf** (US$9 per site) has shade, clean toilets, and cold showers, but gets little use.

US$10-25
Nearly three two decades ago, **Hostal Florida** (Tocopilla 406, tel. 055/851021, hostalflorida@sanpedroatacama.com, US$10 pp) was one of a less than a handful of places to stay in town; still living in the past, it's suitable if other places are full. Likewise, the dorm-style

Residencial Rayco (Gustavo Le Paige 202, tel. 055/851008, US$10 pp) hasn't kept pace with improvements elsewhere, but prices are fair for what it offers.

The clapboard **Residencial Vilacoyo** (Tocopilla 387, tel. 055/851006, vilacoyo@sanpedroatacama.com, US$10 pp) draws a youthful crowd of budget travelers in a hostel-style atmosphere that includes kitchen privileges.

In a rehabbed adobe with shared baths only, the HI affiliate **Hostelling Atacama** (Caracoles 360, tel. 055/851426, www.hostellingatacama.com, US$10–13 pp, US$29–33 d with shared bath) has the drawback of being next door to a popular bar, so getting to sleep early can be difficult—particularly important for the 4 A.M. Tatio excursions (unless, of course, you stay up all night). Most rooms are dorms, but there are some doubles, and it also has its own bar.

US$25-50

Once a marginal campground, with ample gardens and shade trees, **Hostal Edén Atacameño** (Toconao 592, tel. 055/851154, hostaleden@gmail.com, US$12 pp, US$29 d) has reinvented itself as standard accommodations with small shared bath singles, doubles, and triples, and significantly better rooms with private baths. It also provides parking and kitchen privileges.

In addition to its campground, **Hostal Puritama** (Caracoles 113, tel. 055/851049, hostalpuritama@sanpedroatacama.com, US$18 pp, US$25 s, US$30 d) has small singles with shared baths and has recently added larger garden rooms with private baths.

Hostal Sonchek (Gustavo Le Paige 178, tel. 055/851112, soncheksp@hotmail.com, US$10 pp, UD$45 d) has upgraded to include rooms with private baths and also has a restaurant.

(Hostal Elim (Palpana 6, tel. 055/851567, hostal_elim@terra.cl, US$12 pp, US$45 s, US$48 d) has utilitarian rooms with shared bath for the budget-conscious, and much better, finely furnished rooms with private baths and breakfast for its more indulgent guests; either choice, though, is good value. Unlike some other newer places, it has well-established gardens with ample shade.

Having reinvested its earnings in improvements, **Residencial Don Raúl** (Caracoles 130, tel. 055/851138, www.donraul.cl, US$13 pp, US$37 s, US$48 d) still offers modest rooms with shared baths, but the larger quarters with private baths are significantly better. Its barren grounds still lack greenery, though.

Likewise barren, **Hostal Lickana** (Caracoles 140, tel. 055/851940, www.lickanahostal.cl, US$45 s, US$50 d) has immaculate rooms and private baths, but there's little to distinguish it from several others.

An erstwhile budget choice, **Residencial Chiloé** (Domingo Atienza 404, tel. 055/851017, marialow02@hotmail.com, US$23–42 s, US$23–50 d) has upgraded dramatically, adding handsome adobe rooms with private baths to complement its existing shared bath wing (also improved).

US$50-100

Under new ownership, **Hotel Pachamama** (Domingo Atienza 352, cel. 09/9457-3197, pachamamatours@yahoo.com, US$48 s, US$52 d) has roomy and comfortable quarters, but it remains a work in progress. Like many others in its category, it has delayed landscaping the grounds. Nearby **Hostal Katarpe** (Domingo Atienza 441, tel. 055/851033, katarpe@galeon.com, US$45 s, US$53 d) is comparable.

Adjacent to Hostal Puritama, **Hostal Takha Takha** (Caracoles 101-A, tel. 055/851038, takhatakha@terra.cl, US$10 pp, US$51 s, US$55 d) has frills-free garden rooms with shared bath and more elaborate quarters with private baths.

Hostal La Ruca (Tocopilla 513, tel. 055/851568, laruca@sanpedroatacama.com, US$42–55 d) has spotless, well-furnished rooms with private baths, but it has sacrificed style by centering a blue plastic pool in what might have been an appealing patio. Breakfast costs extra (US$5 pp).

The best value here may be **Hotel Tambillo** (Antofagasta 159, tel. 055/851078, www.hoteltambillo.cl, US$58 s or d), a cozy place

© WAYNE BERNHARDSON

Hotel Alto Atacama is one of several new boutique hotels in and around San Pedro de Atacama.

with plain rooms but secluded interior patios. Another choice that's so small—just four rooms—that it's usually full, **Hostal Inti & Killa** (Domingo Atienza 294, tel. 055/852114, www.intikilla.cl US$50 s, US$60 d) is a modest place with shady gardens.

Hotel El Tatio (Caracoles 219, tel. 055/851092, www.eltatio.com, US$68 s or d) offers satellite TV, phone, pool, laundry, room service, and an independent power supply in a town where electricity can be spotty. Its central location, between two popular restaurants that double as nightspots, can be a drawback.

US$100-150

Having undergone a major makeover after being sold to the Diego de Almagro chain, **Hostería San Pedro** (Toconao 460, tel. 055/851011, www.dahoteles.com, US$137 s, US$145 d) is once again among San Pedro's elite accommodations, with the most extensive wooded grounds and largest pool of any in-town hotel.

◖ **Hotel Kimal** (Domingo Atienza 452, tel. 055/851030, www.kimal.cl, US$142 s, US$159 d) remodeled what was already a stylish adobe to offer even more exceptional service in some of San Pedro's most agreeable surroundings. It also boasts one of the village's best restaurants, an elevated deck for watching the night sky, and a small circular swimming pool.

US$150-200

La Casa de Don Tomás (Tocopilla s/n, tel. 055/851055, www.dontomas.cl, US$124 s, US$156 d) has comfortable rooms and attractive common areas, with rustically stylish furniture, a pool, and patio. The exterior is barren, though, and the gardens remain sparse.

On the Quitor road, but still easy walking distance from the village, ◖ **Hotel Altiplánico** (Domingo Atienza 282, Quitor, tel. 055/851212, www.altiplanico.cl, US$150 s, US$158 d) is a sprawling but strikingly designed hotel on the plan of an Andean village, with Atacameño motifs in its details. In some cases, fields with crops separate individual rooms, easily preserving privacy and quiet (as does the lack of telephones and other electronic gadgets). The reception building does have a bar/cafeteria and WiFi.

Open primarily for multi-day packages, the (**Terrantai Lodge** (Tocopilla 411, tel. 055/851045, www.terrantai.com, US$117 s, US$163 d) is an inconspicuous luxury resort whose interior mimics its village surroundings; it's open to nonpackage guests on a drop-in, space-available basis.

More than US$200

Fashioned after the indigenous architecture of its namesake *ayllu,* **Hotel Tulor** (Domingo Atienza 523, tel. 055/851027, www.hoteltulor .cl, US$203 s, US$247 d) has recovered from a period of neglect, but it's debatable whether the improvements justify price increases. The rooms are spacious and comfortable, but not quite deluxe; it also has a restaurant and a small pool.

South of San Pedro proper, **Hotel Tierra Atacama** (Camino Sequitor s/n, Ayllu de Yaye, tel. 055/555977, www.tierratacama.com, US$300 s, US$370 d) is a new spa hotel primarily oriented toward multi-day packages, but also offers overnight accommodations on a space-available basis. All rooms have views of the Andes in the distance.

North of town, **Hotel Alto Atacama** (Camino Pukará s/n, Sector Suchor, Ayllu Quitor, tel. 02/4360265 in Santiago, US$604 s, US$686 d with half-board) resembles Tierra Atacama in its offerings—primarily all-inclusive packages including excursions and spa services—but also offers overnight accommodations on a space available basis. Its canyon surroundings, though, are more immediately scenic than Tierra Atacama's.

FOOD AND ENTERTAINMENT

Several of San Pedro's restaurants double as live music venues at night. Note that, because of the local *ley seca* or alcohol control law, restaurants stop serving drinks no later than midnight weekdays and 1 A.M. on weekends; depending on the current situation, last call may be even earlier.

Tahira (Tocopilla 372, tel. 055/851296) serves cheap (US$3–4) but well-prepared Chilean meals such as turkey and rice. Similar choices include **Quitor** (Licancabur s/n, tel. 055/851492); **Café al Paso Sonchek** (Calama 310, tel. 055/851377), a popular breakfast and burger choice; and **La Casona** (Caracoles 195, tel. 055/851004), which doubles as a wine bar.

Café Étnico (Tocopilla 423), a coffeehouse and bookstore, has also reinvented itself as a wine bar with simple meals, and has free Internet access for clients as well.

Casa de Piedra (Caracoles 225, tel. 055/851271, www.restaurantcasadepiedra.cl) makes fine breakfasts and lunches, such as *pastel de papas,* in the US$4 range and à la carte dishes for US$6–10; as San Pedro has become a tourist destination, the menu has grown more sophisticated without abandoning its roots.

Tierra Todo Natural (Caracoles 271, tel. 055/851585) has some of San Pedro's best breakfasts, along with sandwiches, a wide variety of salads, and even tacos; a cozy, centrally placed earth oven warms the dining room on cool nights. For sandwiches and espresso, try **Café Export** (Toconao and Caracoles, tel. 055/851547, www.cafe-export .cl), which has transmogrified from a simple café into a popular bar and nightspot, with live music, as well.

As popular for socializing as for dining, (**La Estaka** (Caracoles 259-B, tel. 055/851201, www.laestaka.cl) remains one of San Pedro's better choices, with an à la carte international menu.

(**Café Adobe** (Caracoles 211, tel. 055/851132, www.cafeadobe.cl) is as much a meeting place—possibly San Pedro's most popular—as a dining choice. Wooden patio tables surround a blazing hearth and murals replicating regional rock art to create the village's most inviting environment. The food, from breakfasts through its US$7–10 lunch or dinner specials and à la carte entrées (US$7–10), is a worthy complement to the ambience, but the service can be sluggish even if good-natured.

In similar surroundings, **Milagro** (Caracoles 241, tel. 055/851515, www.milagro.cl) fills up early with happy hour celebrants, though it's less rowdy than that might imply. Pizza is the most popular item.

San Pedro's most ambitious restaurant is **(Cuna** (Tocopilla 359, tel. 055/851999, www.cuna.cl), which has a nightly *prix fixe* dinner (US$9) and an elaborate à la carte menu that includes homemade pastas. The spacious restored colonial building, with plenty of elbow room between tables, is a star in its own right, with a stylish bar; its gardens are the best in town for open-air dining.

Hotel Kimal's **(Paachá** (Domingo Atienza 452, tel. 055/851030), showcases a sophisticated à la carte menu and a nightly *prix fixe* dinner (US$18 pp). Following its remodel, diners can sit around the circular pool for some of the village's finest open-air dining.

New on the scene, **Bendito Desierto** (Domingo Atienza 426, tel. 055/851944) specializes in *lechón altiplánico,* a spicy suckling pig (US$10) with an equally spicy puree, in surroundings that aspire toward an art gallery. Half the seating is inside, half outside; it's open daily for lunch and dinner.

For cooling off on hot summer days, San Pedro now has one of Chile's finest ice creameries in **Helados Babalu** (Caracoles 160), which produces diverse traditional and special flavors, though only a small portion of those are on sale any given day.

INFORMATION AND SERVICES

On the east side of the plaza, **Sernatur** (Toconao s/n, tel 055/851420, sanpedrodeatacama@gmail.com) has helpful English-speaking staff. Normal hours are 10 A.M.–1:30 P.M. and 3–7:30 P.M. weekdays, 10 A.M.–2 P.M. Saturday. In summer, though, it stays open 9 A.M.–9 P.M. daily.

BancoEstado (Gustavo Le Paige s/n) now operates an ATM here, but it has an unfortunate propensity for swallowing plastic when San Pedro's erratic electricity fails—usually in the evening hours. **Money Exchange** (Toconao 492) is now just one of several informal exchange houses.

Correos de Chile (Gustavo Le Paige s/n) is half a block off the Plaza de Armas. **Entelchile** (Plaza de Armas 315-A) has long-distance and high-speed Internet services. **Café Sol-Inti-Sun** (Tocopilla 432-B, tel. 055/851178) has broadband Internet and WiFi in less institutional surroundings than Entel.

Viento Norte (Vilama 432, tel. 055/851329) does the washing for about US$2.50 per kilo and, separately, will clean salt-encrusted sneakers—a common fate in San Pedro's surroundings—separately for US$5.

San Pedro has no hospital, but the improved **Posta Médica** (Padre Le Paige s/n, tel. 055/851010) now has a full-time doctor. In a true emergency, Calama has the nearest hospital.

GETTING THERE

San Pedro lacks a central terminal, but most buses stop at a broad staging area on Licancabur just north of the Paseo Artesanal. Some companies keep separate offices.

Tur-Bus (Licancabur 154, tel. 055/851549), which leaves from the Licancabur site, has direct services to Antofagasta (US$11, 4.5 hours) and Santiago (US$54–70, 24 hours), and to Arica (US$20). **Buses Géminis** (Toconao 421, tel. 055/851538) and **Pullman Bus** (tel. 055/341282 in Calama) will pick up passengers here for their international services to Jujuy and Salta, Argentina (US$45; it's now much easier to buy tickets here if you want to board the bus in San Pedro).

Buses Atacama 2000, at the Licancabur site, goes two or three times daily to Calama (US$4), and also to Toconao (US$2) at 2:15 and 7:40 P.M. daily; the early Toconao buses continue to Peine (US$6) Tuesday and Sunday only, while all the later buses do.

Also the agent for Pullman, **Frontera del Norte** (Licancabur s/n, tel. 055/851117) goes eight or nine times daily to Calama and four times to Toconao except Sundays, when there are only three buses; its 7:30 P.M. Toconao bus continues to Socaire (US$3.50) Monday, Thursday, and Friday.

NORTE GRANDE

Transfer Licancabur (tel. 055/334194, transferlicancabur@terra.cl) provides Calama airport transfers (US$13 pp, plus an extra US$3 pp for departures between 8 P.M. and 6 A.M.).

GETTING AROUND

Bicycles are a good alternative for nearby sights such as Catarpe, Quitor, and Valle de la Luna, but carry plenty of water; for rentals (around US$10 per day), try any of several operators along Caracoles; many hotels and *residenciales* also loan or rent bikes to their guests.

For horse rentals, visit **Rancho Cactus** (Toconao 568, tel. 055/851506, www.ranchocactus.cl), across from Hostería San Pedro.

San Pedro has a new car rental agency, **Eurorentacar** (Palpana 7-D, tel. 055/555393, sanpedrodeatacama@eurorentacar.cl).

Vicinity of San Pedro de Atacama

San Pedro is the primary base for excursions into destinations such as the polychrome Valle de la Luna (Valley of the Moon), pre-Columbian ruins at Quitor and Catarpe, flamingo breeding sites at high-altitude salt lakes such as Laguna Chaxa and Laguna Miniques, and the world's highest geyser field at El Tatio. In some ways, it's a better option for exploring high altiplano environments than Parque Nacional Lauca, because its elevation (about 2,500 meters above sea level) permits more gradual acclimatization before visiting sites such as El Tatio (at about 4,000 meters).

For several of these destinations, their relative inaccessibility means either booking a tour or hiring a vehicle (preferably with high clearance and/or 4WD). Sample tours include Valle de la Luna (US$12, half day), an archaeological tour to Quitor, Catarpe, and Tulor (US$15, half day), the Salar de Atacama and Toconao (US$20, half day), El Tatio (US$33, full day), and the Altiplano lagoons (US$62, full day). At some sites, the local community collects an entrance fee that's the passenger's responsibility.

Well-established San Pedro agencies include **Atacama Connection** (Caracoles and Toconao, tel. 055/851421, www.atacamaconnection.cl), Dutch-run **Cosmo Andino** (Caracoles and Tocopilla, tel. 055/851069, cosmoandino@entelchile.net), which also boasts a fine foreign-language book exchange (for clients only); **Desert Adventure** (Caracoles and Tocopilla, tel. 055/851067, www.desertadventure.cl); and **Corvatsch Chile** (Tocopilla 406, tel. 055/851087, www.corvatschchile.cl).

Bolivian-run **Turismo Colque** (Caracoles s/n, tel. 055/851109, www.colquetours.com) has been the only San Pedro operator licensed across the border, but **Cordillera Traveller** (Toconao 447-B, tel. 055/851509) and **Pamela Tour** (Tocopilla 405, tel. 099/8770495) have broken their monopoly. That said, Colque has the biggest fleet of vehicles and, in case of breakdown, the best emergency response.

While it's not exactly a travel agency, one of San Pedro's most interesting initiatives is the **Red de Turismo Rural Licanhuasi** (Caracoles 349, cel. 09/9491-3280, www.licanhuasi.cl), an Atacameño-run organization that operates a series of ethno-tourism excursions and has opened a number of lodges in remote communities that, until recently, had little or no accommodations.

PUKARÁ DE QUITOR

Only three kilometers northwest of San Pedro, the Pukará de Quitor is a 12th-century fortification on the west side of the Río San Pedro Valley. Originally intended for defense against Aymara invaders, it consists of about 160 structures spread over 2.5 hectares. At the ruins' entrance, the eastward view from the newly dedicated **Plaza de Quitor** focuses directly on the summit of Volcán Licancabur, on the Bolivian border.

Relatively easy foot trails zigzag through the ruins—don't attempt to climb the gullied badlands, whose loose rock and soil are serious hazards, especially if no one's around to call for help. Carry water and snacks, as the area is hot and dry. Admission costs US$3.

TAMBO DE CATARPE

Four kilometers beyond Quitor, on the east side of the river, the erstwhile Inka administrative center of Catarpe really is ruins in the most literal sense of the word—there are barely any walls standing in what was once a large hilltop site, but the panoramic views make the excursion worthwhile. Here, Inka officials ran the tributary system to which all its conquered peoples were subject. Admission costs US$2.50.

TERMAS DE PURITAMA

About 30 kilometers northeast of San Pedro, just west of the road to El Tatio's famous geysers, the volcanic hot springs of Termas de Puritama now belong to the Explora company, and unlimited access comes with their packages. Reached by a precipitous road that hugs the canyon wall, its installations have undergone a long overdue refurbishment since the company obtained the concession to run them.

Unfortunately, Puritama is no longer an obligatory stop on the way back from El Tatio because San Pedro tour operators cannot justify the hefty US$17 day-use charge for brief visits. Under pressure, though, Explora has relented to provide free admission to San Pedro residents, for whom such high fees were a hardship.

LAGUNA VERDE (BOLIVIA)

For many years, the only secure way to see shimmering blue-green Laguna Verde, just across the Bolivian border from San Pedro, was by taking a three-day four-wheel-drive crossing to the town of Uyuni with a Bolivian tour operator. Chilean operators who dared to cross the line—admittedly illegally—sometimes had their tires shot out and their clients robbed by the Bolivian military.

Crossing the altiplano to Uyuni is still a popular trip. At the same time, ever since Bolivia opened a border post at Hito Cajones, directly on the border and less than an hour from San Pedro, it's been possible to cross to Laguna Verde for the day and return to Chile.

In fact, these day trips are part of the Uyuni crossings. From San Pedro, Turismo Colque, Cordillera Traveller, and other companies carry both day-trippers and Uyuni-bound passengers to Hito Cajones—one of South America's most isolated international crossings—and on to Laguna Blanca, for breakfast at a small hotel.

Day-trippers then are taxied around Laguna Blanca—home to flocks of flamingos—and then to the Laguna Verde overlook to admire its shifting colors before returning to the Laguna Blanca hotel. They then return to San Pedro with westbound passengers from Uyuni.

The day tour to Laguna Verde costs US$65 per person with breakfast, for a minimum four persons—not that much less than the three-day crossing to Uyuni. The latter, in four-wheel-drive vehicles, runs about US$100, including food and lodging at Laguna Colorada and at Hotel San Juan, near Chiguana.

◖ GEISERS DEL TATIO

Hugging the Bolivian border, 4,321 meters above sea level and 95 kilometers north of San Pedro, El Tatio's collapsed caldera is the world's highest major geyser field; at dawn, its steaming fumaroles are one of the continent's great natural spectacles. Within the sprawling ancient crater, the deposition of dissolved minerals has created many stunningly delicate individual landforms.

Long suggested as a possible national park, Tatio was the site of an experimental geothermal power project by the state Corporación de Fomento (Corfo) some decades back. Corfo shelved the project, though, because the geysers yielded inconsistent steam, and the saline water clogged the pipes and turbines; still, rusting machinery evidences the effort. There is still a large heated pool in which visitors can enjoy a swim.

In addition to its scenic value, El Tatio is

home to impressive concentrations of wildlife. Endangered vicuñas graze its pastures and vizcacha scramble among its rookeries. Conaf wanted the area for a national park, while Corfo wanted to invest in new geothermal projects, but Sernatur and the Corporación Nacional Indígena (Conadi) have initiated a project to permit the nearby indigenous communities of Caspana, Ayquina, and Toconce to manage the geysers.

In addition to collecting a fee (around US$4 pp for Chilean residents, US$6 pp for foreigners), the Conadi regime will establish fixed roads and trails through the geysers, to reduce both damage to the geysers and the number of accidents that have taken place. They will also construct and maintain bathrooms, have emergency oxygen supplies for altitude sickness, and provide accommodations.

Warning

Historically, Tatio has been a free-for-all in which visitors have strolled freely among the pools and geysers. With no formal paths or controls, four fatal accidents have taken place when the thin crust failed to hold the weight of walkers. Third-degree burns from waters whose temperatures reach 85°C are a serious hazard—err on the side of caution.

Accommodations

Camping has been possible at El Tatio, but only with the best gear—temperatures drop well below freezing every night all year. Conadi has just built a new *refugio* at which it's now possible to lodge.

Getting There and Around

Most visitors take tours from San Pedro, but some prefer to hire vehicles (high clearance is imperative, four-wheel drive advisable). To arrive by dawn, when the geysers are most active, it's necessary to leave San Pedro by 4 A.M.; while parts of the road are badly washboarded, improved signage makes it easier to follow than in the past. On the return, most tours visit the indigenous village of Machuca, spruced up by the rural tourism organization.

From Tatio, it's also possible to cross the Cuesta de Chita to the west, visiting the indigenous villages of Caspana, Ayquina, Toconce, and Chiu Chiu en route to Calama.

RESERVA NACIONAL LOS FLAMENCOS

From the Salar de Atacama's salt flats to the altiplano's azure lakes, the 73,986-hectare Reserva Nacional Los Flamencos comprises seven scattered sectors in and around San Pedro de Atacama. Its most popular single attraction is the polychrome Valle de la Luna (Valley of the Moon), but the flamingo colonies of Laguna Chaxa and the altiplano are also proving favorites.

At the *ayllu* of Solcor, just a couple kilometers outside town beyond the customs and immigration post, Conaf maintains a **Centro de Información Ambiental** with good exhibits on ecology and environment, open 9 A.M.–1 P.M.

© WAYNE BERNHARDSON

Swimmers enjoy the geyser-heated waters at El Tatio, more than 4,000 meters above sea level.

and 2–6 P.M. daily. Conaf also has a post at the village of Toconao, and a ranger station at Laguna Chaxa.

【 Valle de la Luna

Every evening at twilight, cars, minivans, and tour buses converge on the Valle de la Luna and its Cordillera de la Sal, where the natural processes of millennia have eroded the sedimentary strata into eerie forms and the early evening's slanting sun highlights their colors for spectacular sunsets. From the main highway approach to San Pedro, the Valle de la Luna provides only a taste of its polychrome glory; many if not most visitors prefer to climb the dunes at dusk for the best views to the west.

Every San Pedro travel agency offers inexpensive trips to Valle de la Luna, about 15 kilometers west of San Pedro. Some visitors prefer renting mountain bikes, at least when there's bright moonlight for the return ride, but avoid leaving the main routes—some areas still have landmines left over from the 1970s. Carry food, water, and warm clothing—days may be warm at this altitude, but temperatures drop rapidly after dark. Admission costs US$3 pp.

Laguna Cejar

In the midst of the Salar, 30 kilometers south of San Pedro via a maze of sandy roads, Laguna Cejar is a limestone lagoon similar to the cenotes of Mexico's Yucatán Peninsula, but filled with saline water that makes floating on its surface effortless. Admission costs US$3 pp.

Laguna Chaxa

On the eastern side of the Salar de Atacama, 61 kilometers south of San Pedro and directly west of the village of Toconao in the Soncor sector of the reserve, Laguna Chaxa is one of three interconnected lagoons where both Chilean and Andean flamingos, as well as Andean gulls, nest in summer. Tours to Toconao and the altiplano lakes east of Socaire usually stop here; there's an admission charge of US$3 per adult, half that for children.

Salar de Pujsa

About 100 kilometers east of San Pedro, on the paved highway to Paso de Jama and Argentina, 4,500 meters above sea level, James flamingos pair up at the 1,900-hectare Salar de Pujsa, though they nest elsewhere in the altiplano.

Salar de Tara

Los Flamencos's largest single sector, 133 kilometers east of San Pedro via the Paso de Jama road, the Salar de Tara comprises 36,674 hectares at an average altitude of 4,300 meters above sea level. It's particularly important bird habitat, with three species of flamingos, Andean gulls, ducks, and other species in its marshlands. The surrounding *puna* grasslands and rookeries support vicuñas, vizcachas, foxes, and armadillos.

Salar de Quisquiro

In the Pampa Loyoques, a short distance before the border, the Salara de Quisquiro was formerly home to breeding colonies of the Chilean flamingo, but no nest has been seen here since 1990. According to Conaf, mining activities, egg collection by locals, and an increasing human presence in general have discouraged breeding colonies. Still, it continues to serve as a feeding and resting site for the birds.

Socaire

From the village of Toconao, 33 kilometers southeast of San Pedro, paved Ruta 23 has reached the picturesque hamlet of Socaire, where broad, stone-faced pre-Columbian terraces cover the hillsides. Beyond Socaire, Ruta 23 is still a gravel road to 4,079-meter Paso Sico, an alternative route to Salta, Argentina, whose improvements are lagging behind the Paso de Jama route.

Socaire now has accommodations at the **Casa de Huéspedes Socaire** (arranged through San Pedro de Atacama's Licanhuasi, Caracoles 349, San Pedro, cel. 09/9491-3280, www.licanhuasi.cl, US$17 pp with private bath). Nearby restaurants can provide meals.

From Socaire, Frontera del Norte buses

return to Toconao and San Pedro at 6 A.M. Wednesday, Friday, and Saturday.

Laguna Miscanti and Laguna Miñiques

About 15 kilometers beyond Socaire, a short lateral leads to Laguna Miscanti and the smaller Laguna Miñiques, 115 kilometers from San Pedro, a flamingo-breeding site that's a frequent destination and lunch stop for tours from San Pedro. Admission to Miscanti and Miñiques costs US$5 per person.

The lateral eventually rejoins Ruta 23 to the border (if continuing to Argentina, don't forget customs and immigration formalities at San Pedro).

TOCONAO AND VICINITY

On the southeast side of the Salar de Atacama, several interesting destinations are accessible via increasingly good roads with public transportation.

Toconao

The townscape of Toconao, an orchard oasis southeast of San Pedro de Atacama, is like no other in the region—rather than use adobe, its skilled carvers quarried and shaped volcanic bedrock into solid blocks that form the walls of its distinctive houses. Its major landmark, the freestanding **Campanario** (bell tower) in the Plaza de Armas, is a national monument even though, curiously enough, the nearby 18th-century **Iglesia San Lucas** is not.

In the **Quebrada de Jeria** (admission US$1.50), a well-watered canyon that runs nearly through the middle of town, local growers cultivate almonds, apples, figs, grapes, pears, quinces, and other crops for San Pedro and Calama. Unlike San Pedro, its water quality is so high that, according to Isaiah Bowman's account in the 1920s, it was:

> ...celebrated not only for its fruit but for the clearness and purity of its water. About a dozen well-to-do families at San Pedro send peons to Toconao to obtain drinking water, brought in casks on mule back.

There are shoestring accommodations and meals on and around the plaza, but Toconao makes a better day trip than an overnight.

Buses Frontera del Norte goes to San Pedro three or four times daily, and to Peine at 8:30 P.M. daily. **Buses Atacama 2000** (Latorre 164) goes to San Pedro twice daily and to Peine at 8:40 P.M. daily and at 3:15 P.M. Tuesday and Sunday.

Peine

Some 102 kilometers south of San Pedro, the indigenous village of Peine sits on a elevated scarp just above the Salar de Atacama's southeastern edge. The village itself is fairly recent,

---

WATCH YOUR STEP: LANDMINES IN THE ALTIPLANO

In the 1970s, when military dictatorships were the rule, the armies of Chile, Argentina, and Bolivia felt no compunction about mining their borders. Most disputes have dissipated or disappeared, but the legacy of landmines continues, especially where the three countries' borders converge in the Region II altiplano.

While Chile has not yet removed all mines in accordance with international treaties, it has managed to mark them with *Campo Minado* (minefield) signs and to implement a program to reduce the hazards to tourists who wander the backcountry.

If you find any apparent military artifact near a designated minefield, keep your distance and contact the Carabineros (tel. 133) or the Primera División headquarters in Antofagasta (tel. 055/242392). This is not a trivial issue – tourists have been seriously injured by encounters with landmines.

though nearby are three national monuments: the **Tambo Incáico de Peine,** an Inka staging point; the **Pueblo Antiguo de Peine,** the ruins of pre-Columbian Peine; and the **Ruinas de la Capilla de Misiones de Peine Viejo,** a colonial mission chapel.

In an overhang in the canyon adjacent to Peine, only a few minutes' walk from the main drag, the **Pictografías del Alero de Peine** are a cluster of rock art representing at least three distinct styles in local prehistory. The oldest, dating from about 3000–2000 B.C., depict human hunters and their camelid prey in dark ochre, while later figures, 1200–400 B.C., suggest a transition to a more advanced pastoral society, with elaborate costumes and ritual dances. After a substantial hiatus, more geometrical and abstract designs date from pre-Inka agriculturalists (A.D. 1000–1450).

From Peine, a good but dusty westbound road traverses the unrelenting salt crystal landscape of the Salar de Atacama, crossing the Cordillera de Domeyko, to Baquedano, on the Panamericana. It has heavy truck traffic, though, and few landmarks except for the sulfur mine at Lomas Bayas, but for southbound travelers with their own vehicles, it saves time and distance over the return route via San Pedro and Calama. No gasoline is available until Baquedano—fill up in San Pedro.

Peine's only accommodation has been a rustic campground, but the **Casa de Huéspedes Peine** (arranged through Licanhuasi, Caracoles 349, San Pedro de Atacama, cel. 09/9491-3280, www.licanhuasi.cl, US$17 pp) now provides regular accommodations and food.

THE SKIES OF SAN PEDRO

Until recently, polychrome sunsets at Valle de la Luna were the main way to appreciate the skies around San Pedro de Atacama. That's mostly a matter of aesthetics, but French astronomer Alain Maury, with his knowledge of the southern heavens, has made late nights outside the village more rewarding than the occasional full-moon rave.

At his house about 15 minutes outside San Pedro, where there's little interference from artificial light, Maury has arranged a series of telescopes to observe the stars and planets as they rise and set. As he delivers clear explanations in both Spanish and English, he also can mount digital and film cameras to the telescopes so that participants can have a visual keepsake.

For more information, contact Maury at **Space Observations** (Caracoles 166, San Pedro de Atacama, tel. 055/851935, cell 099/8178354, www.spaceobs.com). Tours, around US$25, include transportation to and from San Pedro, and they have recently begun to offer lodging. Nighttime temperatures are cold at this altitude, so bring warm clothing. After the tour, there's hot chocolate in the house.

Buses Atacama 2000 (Latorre s/n, tel. 055/312435) goes to San Pedro at 6 A.M. daily and on Tuesday and Sunday afternoons.

NORTE CHICO

One of Chile's least-touristed areas, the Norte Chico has much to offer: stunning, sparsely peopled beaches in a nearly rainless climate; spectacularly clear night skies such that international astronomical observatories have flocked here; picturesque villages in remote Andean valleys; and vast, rugged high country along the Argentine border. Its national parks and reserves are reasonably accessible, and visitors are few except in the peak summer season. One highlight, in rare rainy years, is the *desierto florido,* when evanescent wildflowers carpet the desert floor in color.

Underappreciated by nationals and foreigners alike, thinly populated Region III (Atacama) has only one major city, the capital of Copiapó, but the ramshackle ports of Caldera and Chañaral—the former also a beachgoers' destination—contain a wealth of 19th-century architecture. Its national parks—Llanos de Challe and Pan de Azúcar on the coast, Nevado Tres Cruces in the *puna*—are attracting more visitors. Nudging the Argentine border, the country's highest peak, 6,885-meter Ojos del Salado, belongs to no national park but draws serious climbers.

North of the Chilean heartland, Region IV (Coquimbo) is close enough to Santiago for a long weekend, but it merits more. In summer, Chileans and Argentines flock to the beaches in and around La Serena, but spring and fall are less crowded and cheaper. Even winter, when southern Chile stays in out of the rain, Coquimbo often enjoys warm clear days—if cool nights.

Coquimbo has several protected areas, the

© WAYNE BERNHARDSON

HIGHLIGHTS

◖ Parque Nacional Nevado Tres Cruces: In the highlands east of Copiapó, where the conquistadors crossed the Andes, flamingos filter their food from shallow saline lakes as guanacos and vicuñas graze the surrounding steppe at one of Chile's least-visited national parks (page 273).

◖ Bahía Inglesa: Even in subtropical latitudes, upwelling from the Pacific depths makes the ocean cold, but the sun warms the shallow sheltered waters of Bahía Inglesa, and its sandy crescent makes it the best pure beach stopover between La Serena and Iquique. The surf is almost nil, but the strong breezes do attract windsurfers (page 278).

◖ Parque Nacional Pan de Azúcar: Just north of Chañaral, the *camanchaca*'s steady drip supports unique vegetation on stunning headlands at Pan de Azúcar, while Humboldt penguins nest on its namesake offshore island. In the afternoon, the sun usually makes an appearance for beachgoers (page 280).

◖ Parque Nacional Llanos de Challe: Northwest of Vallenar, rare but intense rains make Llanos de Challe one of the best places to view the springtime's "flowering desert" (page 284).

◖ Coquimbo: Until recently, the historic port was a rundown runner-up to nearby La Serena, but an enlightened municipal administration has helped make it the region's nightlife center (page 296).

◖ Reserva Nacional Pingüino de Humboldt: Northwest of La Serena, several offshore islands boast not just penguins, but many other seabirds and even marine mammals ranging from otters to dolphins and whales (page 298).

◖ Museo Gabriela Mistral: In the town of Vicuña, gateway to the Elqui Valley, this museum is an homage to the region that shaped the Nobel Prize–winning poet's life and work (page 301).

◖ Pisco Elqui: Pisco Elqui and neighboring communities such as Cochiguaz have a reputation for New Age culture, but that shouldn't deter visitors who enjoy spectacular scenery and sipping the region's namesake product at any of several distilleries (page 305).

◖ Hacienda Los Andes: In the Andes east of Ovalle, saddling up for the high desert is the specialty of this stylish but low-key and affordable ranch (page 313).

◖ Parque Nacional Bosque de Fray Jorge: On the headlands west of Ovalle, Fray Jorge's *camanchaca* condenses to support forests far denser and greener than similar conditions manage at Pan de Azúcar (page 315).

LOOK FOR ◖ TO FIND RECOMMENDED SIGHTS, ACTIVITIES, DINING, AND LODGING.

NORTE CHICO

best of which are Parque Nacional Pingüino de Humboldt, Parque Nacional Bosque de Fray Jorge, and Reserva Nacional Las Chinchillas. Other enticements include the Elqui Valley (home to pisco and to poet Gabriela Mistral), and the chance to scan the southern constellations on nighttime tours and learn the latest in astronomy from professionals at international observatories. Opportunities for outdoor recreation, particularly hiking, mountain biking, and horseback riding, are plentiful.

North of La Ligua and south from Parque Nacional Pan de Azúcar, Regions III and IV constitute the present-day Norte Chico. Traditionally, though, the regional boundaries are the Río Aconcagua on the south (today part of Region V, Valparaíso) and the Río Copiapó drainage, at roughly 27° south latitude. Mining is the economy's traditional backbone, and irrigated agriculture retains a hold, but tourist development has proliferated in and around La Serena.

PLANNING YOUR TIME

Internationally, the Norte Chico may have the lowest profile of any Chilean region, but there's plenty to recommend to both conventional tourists and travelers seeking off-the-beaten-path experiences. The former will enjoy beach towns such as La Serena and Caldera/Bahía Inglesa, but more demanding visitors can explore remote high country roads, survey the southern constellations in an astronomers' Mecca, ride into the Andean backcountry, and visit wildlife-rich saline lakes at oxygen-poor altitudes.

From Santiago, La Serena makes an easy weekend excursion, and with only a day or two more, there would be time to explore Vicuña and Pisco Elqui, or even take an overnight pack trip into the rugged Andean outback east of Ovalle. Good roads make it possible, in a week or so, to add more northerly destinations such as Caldera and Parque Nacional Pan de Azúcar, but the new airport between Copiapó and Caldera has made reaching this area easier and would leave more time for less celebrated but worthwhile sites. Truly independent travelers can find enough underappreciated gems to occupy them for several weeks or more.

Like the Norte Grande, the Norte Chico enjoys a mild climate that makes it a year-round option, though it gets some winter rainfall and the highest altitudes get cold in winter. The best bases for excursions are La Serena, Vicuña/Pisco Elqui, and Caldera/Bahía Inglesa, which have the best services.

HISTORY

Around 11,000 to 15,000 years ago, the Norte Chico's earliest human inhabitants were probably Paleo-Indian hunter-gatherers in the Upper Huasco Valley, near present-day Alto del Carmen. Over the following millennia, the Huentelauquén culture and their successors relied on coastal resources around present-day Chañaral and Huasco, and south to Los Vilos. Only after the beginning of the Christian era, though, were there stable encampments of coastal peoples in and around present-day Pan de Azúcar, Caldera, Bahía Inglesa, and Puerto Viejo.

First identified in the Elqui Valley site of El Molle, the El Molle culture appears in the early Christian era and ranges from the Río Salado (Chañaral) and Copiapó Valleys south to the Río Choapa. Both farmers and herders, they made the first regional advances in metallurgy and basketry, as well as rock art—Valle del Encanto, near Ovalle, is their best-preserved site.

From about A.D. 900, Diaguita peoples who probably came from Argentina established village-style settlements where they cultivated maize, beans, and squash in the well-watered valleys and potatoes and quinoa at higher elevations. They probably also herded llamas, and fished and hunted to add protein to their diet. By the early 15th century, though, the Inka empire began to expand its dominion, linking the Copiapó Valley to Cuzco via a highway along the precordillera. The Inkas extended their influence into and beyond the Chilean heartland, though their power was weak on the periphery.

Inka domination was short-lived, as the Spanish invasion of Peru quickly spread south.

NORTE CHICO

After the Pizarros took Cajamarca, Cuzco, and Quito in the early 1530s, their skeptical partner (and subsequent enemy) Diego de Almagro headed a large but ill-fated expedition of 500 Spaniards and thousands more Indians across the frigid *puna* from Argentina to the Copiapó Valley, via the 4,726-meter Paso de San Francisco.

En route, Almagro lost men, horses, llamas, and supplies to floods and cold; turning back at the Río Aconcagua, he chose an Andean foothill route rather than risk the brutal high-altitude crossing again. Disappointed in search of gold and silver, he had unknowingly passed within a day's journey of the Chañarcillo silver lode that made 19th-century Copiapó rich. A few years later, Pedro de Valdivia followed Almagro's return path southward, founding the city of La Serena en route to Santiago.

Only after independence, with the discovery of Chañarcillo in 1832, did the Norte Chico gain prominence with impressive technological developments, including one of South America's first railways. While the silver boom lasted only a few decades, copper in the highlands northeast of Copiapó brought a more enduring prosperity—at great environmental cost. Mining has also proved important in the vicinity of La Serena, but tourism has wrought an urban renaissance in what is becoming the Chilean Riviera. The cultivation of irrigated grapes for export and pisco production in the Copiapó, Huasco, and Elqui Valleys continues to be important.

Copiapó

Founded in 1744 by Francisco Cortés y Cartabio, under the name San Francisco de la Selva de Copiapó, the regional capital has always been a mining town. Most visitors spend no more than a night here, but it's a key administrative and service center that's also the gateway to rarely visited high country to the east. With the construction of a new airport closer to the coastal resort of Caldera than the city, Copiapó's share of tourist traffic is likely to decline.

HISTORY

The boom that established Copiapó came in the 1830s, when the fortuitous discovery of silver at Chañarcillo, in rugged and remote country almost directly south of the city, brought scads of prospectors, laborers, and speculators. Copiapó's silver heyday was like the California gold rush, when ordinary supplies sold for preposterous amounts.

When Darwin visited in 1835, he remarked that:

> Before the discovery of the famous silver-mines of Chanuncillo [Chañarcillo], Copiapó was in a rapid state of decay, but now it is in a very thriving condition; and the town, which was completely overthrown by an earthquake, has been rebuilt.

Still, he added, the area's limited agricultural potential—"its produce is sufficient for only three months of the year"—and transport difficulties raised prices to levels that astonished him.

Some of those difficulties were alleviated when, 16 years later, Chile's first railway linked the city to the port of Caldera. While Chañarcillo's deposits gave out in the 1870s, a more diversified mining economy, with copper and iron supplanting silver, has kept the city prosperous—at a cost. Its Universidad de Atacama is the academic equivalent of the famous Colorado School of Mines, but the copper smelter at nearby Paipote (built in 1951) bears the burden for some of the country's worst air and water pollution.

ORIENTATION

Copiapó (population 125,983) is 333 kilometers north of La Serena and 801 kilometers north of Santiago via Ruta 5, the Panamericana. Known

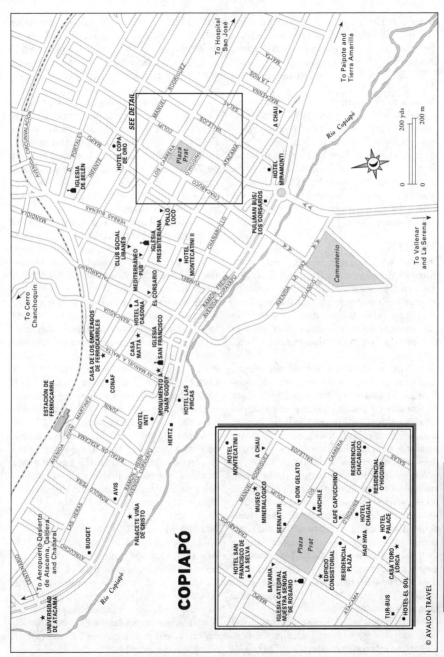

NORTE CHICO

© AVALON TRAVEL

as Avenida Copayapu as it parallels the Río Copiapó, the Panamericana turns west toward the coastal resort of Caldera and Antofagasta, another 566 kilometers to the north.

While the city has sprawled east and west along the river valley, and even up the sides of the hills to the north and south, most points of interest are within a few blocks of the central Plaza Prat. Cerro Chanchoquín, known colloquially as Cerro de la Cruz for the landmark cross placed there by Franciscan father Crisógono Sierra y Velásquez, towers above the city to the northwest. Immediately below, the Alameda Manuel Antonio Matta marks the historic barrio of Copiapó's mining magnates and its pioneer railway.

SIGHTS

Studded with massive pepper trees, shady **Plaza Prat** is downtown's focal point. Its central fountain, with a marble statue honoring the mining industry, is a national monument, as are four other marble statues representing the seasons—ironically enough, in an area that averages only 23 millimeters of rainfall per year.

At the western corner of the plaza, Englishman William Rogers built the neoclassical **Iglesia Catedral Nuestra Señora de Rosario** (1851), its elegant portico topped by a three-story bell tower, the latter in turn crowned by a cupola. Also a national monument, the structure itself consists of oak partitions, covered by cane and adobe.

Kitty-corner from the cathedral, the green-and-gold **Edificio Consistorial,** once a private home and later occupied by the Municipalidad, now hosts art exhibits and performance events as the **Casa de la Cultura Julio Aciares.** Southwest of the plaza, on Atacama between Colipí and Vallejos, the **Casa Toro Lorca** is a national monument from the historic mining era. One short block from the plaza, at the corner of Colipí and Manuel Rodríguez, is the **Museo Mineralógico.**

Besides the cathedral, Copiapó boasts several other religious monuments, including the 1890 Protestant **Iglesia Presbiteriana** (O'Higgins

391). Three blocks north, near the corner of Infante and Yerbas Buenas, the colonial **Iglesia de Belén,** rebuilt in the mid-19th century, is now the **Santuario Santa Teresa,** dedicated to a Chilean saint from the town of Los Andes, northeast of Santiago.

Several blocks west of the plaza, Chile's Consejo de Monumentos Nacionales has designated the entire neighborhood known as the **Barrio Estación** as a monument in itself. Its main landmarks are the historic **Estación de Ferrocarril** (Railroad Station), the tree-lined avenue known as **Alameda Matta,** and a scattering of other buildings, including the **Casa Matta** (home to the Museo Histórico Regional); the onetime **Casa de los Empleados de Ferrocarriles** (built in 1860 as housing for railway employees, now home to Sernageomin, the national mining service), and the **Iglesia San Francisco** (1872), built of Douglas fir and stucco.

On a small plaza facing the Iglesia San Francisco, near the south end of Avenida Matta, the **Monumento a Juan Godoy** honors the muleteer and prospector who stumbled upon Chañarcillo's silver. Mining entrepreneur Apolinario Soto built the **Palacete Viña de Cristo** as his personal mansion in 1860, but it passed through several hands before becoming property of the Universidad Técnica del Estado (now the Universidad de Atacama) in 1974.

A short distance west, the former **Escuela de Minas** (School of Mines) is also part of the Universidad de Atacama; the **Locomotora Copiapó,** the Norris Brothers steam locomotive that first linked Caldera to Copiapó, resides on the grounds.

Museo Mineralógico

Under the auspices of the Universidad de Atacama, Copiapó's mineral museum possesses a collection of more than 14,000 minerals from around the world, though only about 2,000 are on display at any one time. Among its prize exhibits are a meteorite found in the Atacama, ore from Chañarcillo's bonanza silver mine, and the ubiquitous Chilean copper, along with some fossils.

Only half a block from the Plaza de Armas, the Museo Mineralógico (Colipí and Rodríguez, tel. 052/206606) is open 10 A.M.–1:30 P.M. Monday–Saturday and also 3:30–7 P.M. weekdays only. Adults pay US$0.85 admission; children's admission costs US$0.35.

Museo Regional de Atacama

Copiapó's first-rate historical museum focuses on pre-Hispanic cultures and mining (from the truly archaic to the relatively recent Inka-Diaguita, at nearby Viña del Cerro, all the way to contemporary industrial mineral exploitation).

The displays also present key figures in regional history, from conquistador Pedro de Valdivia to prospector Diego de Almeyda, mining magnate Manuel Antonio Matta, essayist José Joaquín Vallejo (better known by his nom de plume, Jotabeche), not to mention illustrious visitors such as Darwin and Vicente Pérez Rosales.

The most imaginative single exhibit is a convincing replica of a mineshaft, complete with miners' artifacts. The interpretations are generally excellent, but in Spanish only. Built in the 1840s by the influential Mattas, the building is an attraction in its own right, a national monument whose gallery, supported by fluted neoclassical columns, surrounds an interior patio.

The Museo Regional (Atacama 98, tel. 052/212313, www.museodeatacama.cl) is open 9 A.M.–5:45 P.M. weekdays, 10 A.M.–12:45 P.M. and 3–5:45 P.M. Saturday, and 10 A.M.–12:45 P.M. Sunday and holidays. Admission costs about US$1 for adults, half that for children, but it's free Sundays and holidays.

Palacete Viña de Cristo

Born in 1808 in San Felipe, north of Santiago, Apolinario Soto moved north with his family as a child. Later, as owner of the Tres Puntas silver mine northwest of Copiapó, near the present-day site of Inca de Oro, he became one of the city's leading citizens.

Completed in 1860, Soto's Georgian-style Palacete Viña de Cristo was the region's most elaborate mansion, fronted by a four-column portico supporting a balcony that, in turn, is covered by a three-gabled roof supported by wrought-iron posts. The main floor held four reception rooms and the 2nd floor seven bedrooms, though most of these are now university offices.

All the building's decorative elements, mostly notably the elaborate wrought iron that resembles that of 18th-century New Orleans, came from the United States. Nearly all the woodwork, including the exquisitely polished staircases, consists of Douglas fir. From the 2nd floor, a spiral staircase leads to a perched *mirador* (overlook) with a 360-degree view.

Unfortunately, the two lateral wings that once flanked the building to form an inverted "U" were demolished in the late 1930s; otherwise the building and its grounds would be even more imposing. The wings held a chapel, a music room, guest bedrooms, and staff facilities, but construction of the Panamericana, which runs directly past the entrance, brought their demise; a further widening also meant an eight-meter displacement of the original wrought-iron fences and gates. Designation as a national monument, which would have saved the original configuration, did not come until 1986.

On the south side of the Panamericana (Avenida Copayapu), directly opposite its junction with Rómulo Pena, the Palacete Viña de Cristo is open to the public 8 A.M.–7 P.M. weekdays. Contrary to some guidebook accounts, it has no functioning museum.

ENTERTAINMENT AND EVENTS

For drinks, there's the **Mediterráneo Pub** (O'Higgins between Yumbel and Yerbas Buenas), a large dance club.

Beginning the first Sunday of February, the **Festival de Candelaria** is a nine-day event, celebrated with folkloric dances and religious fervor, that attracts up to 50,000 pilgrims from around the region and country. It takes place at the 19th-century Iglesia de la Candelaria (Los Carrera and Figueroa), about two kilometers east of Plaza Prat.

NORTE CHICO

Día del Minero, honoring the region's miners, takes place August 10. Copiapinos commemorate the **Fundación de la Ciudad** (Founding of the City) on December 8.

ACCOMMODATIONS

The clientele at most *residenciales* consists of single miners, and women traveling alone may feel uncomfortable about this. It's a less likely scenario in midrange and top-end categories.

US$10-25

Well-located **Residencial Plaza** (O'Higgins 670, tel. 052/212671, US$8/13–20/30 s/d) is the best shoestring choice, with friendly ownership and a well-kept patio, and has upgraded to include amenities such as WiFi. Rates vary according to shared or private bath.

Having apparently found a permanent home after several moves, **Residencial Chacabuco** (Salas 451, tel. 052/218542, US$12 pp, US$25 d) has a handful of single rooms and some doubles with baths, but it's often full.

Residencial O'Higgins (O'Higgins 804, tel. 052/363043, US$12 s, US$21 d, up to US$25 s or d) is a ramshackle place that's been turned into more and smaller rooms than it should have been, but that's why prices are low. Despite its shortcomings, the staff is friendly and attentive, and it's also the only *residencial* with on-site parking.

US$25-50

Far less than its name suggests, the well-worn **Hotel Palace** (Atacama 741, tel. 052/212852, US$28 s, US$46 d) is suitable for one night only. Surrounding a shady patio, the rooms have decent beds, recessed lighting, and cable TV, but also ragged wall-to-wall carpets. Unlike most cheaper downtown hotels, though, it has on-site parking.

Hotel Montecatini I (Infante 766, tel. 052/211363, alitor@ctcinternet.cl, US$29–39 s, US$38–50 d) has ample gardens, a small pool, and rooms that vary considerably—the singles are small, for instance, and some are dark; it lacks parking, though nearby lots are available.

US$50-100

Under the same management as its near namesake, **Hotel Montecatini II** (Atacama 374, tel. 052/211516, hotelmontecatin@ole.com, US$47 s, US$59 d) is more contemporary than its sister hotel.

Copiapó's most distinctive and intimate hotel, arguably its best value, **【** **Hotel La Casona** (O'Higgins 150, tel. 052/217277, www.lacasonahotel.cl, US$50 s, US$60 d) features comfortable, attractively furnished rooms in a colonial-style garden setting.

Hotel Inti (Av. Freire 180, tel. 052/217739, US$50 s, US$60 d, intihotel@hotmail.com) is one of the city's more modern hotels and **Hotel Copa de Oro** (Infante 530, tel./fax 052/216309, www.hotelcopadeoro.cl, US$42 s, US$59 d) is a full-service hotel.

One block from Plaza Prat, **Hotel San Francisco de la Selva** (Los Carrera 525, tel. 052/217013, www.hotelsanfcodelaselva.cl, US$60 s, US$70 d) has rooms with cable TV, telephone, and similar amenities. Despite its relative newness, though, some parts are surprisingly worn; there are a handful of smaller, cheaper rooms.

Hotel Las Pircas (Av. Copayapu 095, tel. 052/213220, www.hosterialaspircas.cl, US$84 s, US$97 d) is a Santa Fe–style motel (in the North American sense of the word) with commodious garden rooms that vary in size and quality.

More than US$100

Hotel Miramonti (Freire 731, tel. 052/210440, www.miramonti.cl, US$78 s, US$103 d) is the newest entry in Copiapó's hotel sweepstakes.

Half a block from Plaza Prat, **Hotel Chagall** (O'Higgins 760, tel. 052/213775, www.chagall.cl, US$88 s, US$108 d), a stylish contemporary option, is favored by business visitors—particularly the mining sector.

FOOD

For breakfasts, juices, pastries, and especially quality coffee, **Café Capuccino** (Colipí 484, Local F-107) is a welcome presence on the

Copiapó scene. While it's part of the Mall Plaza Real complex, it actually faces onto O'Higgins.

Bavaria (Chacabuco 487, tel. 052/217160) is the local rep of the reliable nationwide chain. Offering a diverse Chilean menu, **El Corsario** (Atacama 245, tel. 052/233659) also offers open-air dining on its central patio.

The **Club Social Libanés** (Los Carrera 350, tel. 052/212939) offers Middle Eastern specialties.

Copiapó has a wide selection of generally high-quality *chifas*—the traditional favorite is **Hao Hwa** (Colipí 340, tel. 052/213261). In spacious and sparkling quarters, **A Chau** (Chañarcillo 991, tel. 052/249826) serves good Cantonese entrées, with excellent service.

Just north of the Mall Plaza Real, the ice cream at **Don Gelato** (Colipí 506, Local 6, tel. 052/2352720) is a pleasant surprise for both its quality and diversity—try the creamy blueberry, mango, and tiramisu, or the sorbet-style pisco sour.

INFORMATION

In a sidewalk office on the east side of Plaza Prat, the local office of **Sernatur** (Los Carrera 691, tel. 052/231510, infoatacama@sernatur.cl) distributes maps and lists of accommodations and has some English-speaking staff. Hours are 8:30 A.M.–7 P.M. weekdays all year, Saturday 10 A.M.–2 P.M. in summer.

For information on national parks and reserves, visit **Conaf** (Juan Martínez 55, tel. 052/213404), open 8 A.M.–4:30 P.M. weekdays only.

SERVICES

As the regional capital, Copiapó has a complete array of services.

Cambio Fides (Colipí 484, Local B-123, tel. 052/210550) can change U.S. cash or travelers checks. Several banks or near the plaza have ATMs, including **Banco de Crédito** (Chacabuco 449).

Correos de Chile (Los Carrera 691) is in the Intendencia Regional, directly behind the Sernatur office. For long-distance telephone services, try **Telefónica CTC** (Chacabuco 505), on the north side of Plaza Prat, or **Entelchile** (Colipí 484), on the east side of the plaza.

Turismo Atacama (Los Carrera 716, tel. 052/212712) is a conventional travel agency.

Hospital San José (O'Higgins s/n, tel. 052/213474) is eight blocks southeast of Plaza Prat.

GETTING THERE

Copiapó has both air and land connections to points north and south.

Air

Some 50 kilometers northwest of Copiapó, **Aeropuerto Desierto de Atacama** is less than 25 kilometers from the port/beach resort of Caldera.

LAN (Colipí 484, Local A-103, tel. 052/213512 or 052/217406) occupies quarters at in the Mall Plaza Real. LanExpress usually flies at least twice daily to Santiago, occasionally stopping in La Serena, and most days to El Salvador (the Chilean copper mining town, not the country). **Sky Airline** (Colipí 526, tel. 052/214640) has recently entered the market.

Bus

All the major bus companies have offices two or three blocks south of Plaza Prat, with services southbound to Santiago and northbound as far as Arica. **Tur-Bus** (Chañarcillo 680, tel. 052/238612) has the most complete services. **Pullman Bus** (Colipí 109, tel. 052/215143) covers the Panamericana between Arica and Santiago, also reaching Viña and interior Norte Chico destinations such as Illapel, Salamanca, El Salvador, and Potrerillos. At the same terminal, **Los Corsarios** (Colipí 109) serves destinations throughout the Norte Chico.

Typical destinations and fares include Caldera (US$2.50, 1 hour), El Salvador (US$11–17, 3 hours), La Serena (US$13–20, 4 hours), Santiago (US$27–45, 11 hours), Antofagasta (US$33, 7 hours), Taltal (US$12,

4 hours), Calama (US$40, 10 hours), Iquique (US$42–58, 15 hours), and Arica (US$50–68, 18 hours).

GETTING AROUND
Airport Shuttle
Transfer Casther (Freire 557, tel. 052/235891) carries passengers to and from Aeropuerto Desierto de Atacama, 45 kilometers west of Copiapó via the Panamericana (US$7.50 pp). So does Transportes Aeropuerto Sergio Berrios (Felipe Pinto 865, tel. 052/244815). Alternatively, take any Caldera-bound yellow *taxi colectivo* and ask to be dropped at the airport entrance (US$3.50).

Car Rental
Rental agencies include **Avis** (Rómulo Peña 102, tel. 052/524591,copiapo@avischile.cl), **Budget** (Ramón Freire 050, tel. 052/216272, copiapo@budget.cl), **Hertz** (Av. Copayapu 173, tel. 052/213522, counter_copiapo@ autorenta.cl), and **Rodaggio** (Colipí 127, tel. 052/212153, rodaggio@entelchile.net). Budget and Rodaggio usually have the best rates.

Vicinity of Copiapó

While it's not yet an adventure travel mecca, a growing number of agencies offer excursions to the Upper Copiapó Valley, Bahía Inglesa, Parque Nacional Pan de Azúcar, and more remote backcountry destinations such as Parque Nacional Nevado Tres Cruces and Ojos del Salado. Among them are **Atacama Chile** (Maipú 580-B, tel. 052/211191, www .atacamachile.com), **Atacama Expeditions** (Colipí 484, Local B-102, cel. 09/9130-8291, www.atacamaexpedition.cl), **Gran Atacama** (Colipí 484, Local B-122, tel. 052/219271, www.granatacama.cl), and the mountaineering specialist **Aventurismo** (Atacama 240, tel. 052/247007, www.aventurismo.cl).

VALLE DE COPIAPÓ
Southeast of Copiapó, a paved highway climbs the valley of the Río Copiapó as far as Las Juntas, 97 kilometers away, where it becomes a gravel road that turns northeast toward the Argentine border. Local buses carry passengers up the valley.

The route actually begins at Paipote, eight kilometers east, where the **Fundición Hernán Videla Lira** copper smelter is a dubious landmark that, historically, is one of Chile's worst polluters. The ever-observant Darwin, in 1835, noted that:

> From having firewood, a smelting-furnace had formerly been built here; we found a solitary man in charge of it, whose sole employment was hunting guanacos.

At the mining and farming village of **Tierra Amarilla,** 17 kilometers from Copiapó, Spanish architect José Miguel Retornano designed the restored, Gothic-style **Iglesia Nuestra Señora de Loreto,** dating from 1898. Immediately to the southwest, a good gravel road climbs to the Sierra de Ojancos and the **Museo de Sitio Mina El Tránsito,** an in situ salvage project of a former gold mine that took up much of the slack when the silver deposits at Chañarcillo began to fail. Long since dismantled except for the **Casa del Administrador** (Administrator's House, retaining some historic artifacts), a scattering of rusting machinery, and some open shafts, El Tránsito makes an engrossing side trip, also offering views of the modern copper mine at Candelaria to the south. For guided visits of Mina El Tránsito, contact Tierra Amarilla's **Casa de la Cultura** (tel. 052/320098).

To the south, about 22 kilometers from Copiapó, mining mogul Apolinario Soto had his country house and built a landmark church, both in need of restoration, at

Nantoco. Soto acquired the property from Francisco Javier Ossa, also a figure in the early mining elite.

Copiapó journalist and politician José Joaquín Vallejo (1811–1858), founder of the newspaper *El Copiapino,* resided at **Casa Jotabeche,** on the former Hacienda de Totoralillo at Km 34. Noted for gentle caricatures of his Chilean compatriots and malice toward Argentine rivals such as Domingo Sarmiento, Vallejo was a member of the so-called "Generation of 1842"; he took his pen name, Jotabeche, from the initials of his friend Juan Bautista Cheneau.

The railway from Caldera and Copiapó reached **Pabellón,** a grape-growing area 38 kilometers from Copiapó, in 1854; by 1859, a spur linked Pabellón to Chañarcillo's bonanza silver mine, 42 kilometers southwest. The main line later reached **Los Loros,** 64 kilometers from Copiapó, and its terminus at **San Antonio** in 1867. Drip irrigation is transforming this area into a major source of grapes—usually the Chilean harvest's earliest—and other export-oriented crops.

Seven kilometers south of San Antonio, a eastbound lateral leads to the archaeological site of **Viña del Cerro,** a national monument where the Diaguita and Inka milled copper ore and smelted it in more than two dozen charcoal-fired ovens.

CHAÑARCILLO

Discovered on May 16, 1832, by muleteer and prospector Juan Godoy, the silver mine of Chañarcillo rendered such great wealth that, by 1860, the community that grew up alongside it (by then named for Godoy himself) boasted an infrastructure worthy of many modern Chilean towns: church, school, hospital, theater, and police station. By 1859, it had a railroad spur to Pabellón, and by 1865 it had grown to more than 7,000 inhabitants. Yields fell rapidly after 1870, though, and water in the shafts eventually made further exploitation impossible. Other than a solitary well marked by cluster of trees, all

that remains of Juan Godoy are stone foundations, a few adobe walls, and a plundered cemetery.

There are two ways to reach the ruins. The easier one is to follow the Panamericana south to Km 59, where a smooth but dusty road to Mina Bandurrias, an inactive open-pit iron mine, also leads to Chañarcillo. From Pabellón, in the Upper Copiapó Valley, a rugged dirt road, passable with high clearance and considerable skill but easier with four-wheel drive, follows the abandoned rail spur over the Portezuelo La Viuda (Widow's Pass) to Chañarcillo. Just before the *portezuelo,* a side road climbs precipitously northwest to the abandoned **Mina Tres Marías,** for some of the region's best views.

◖ PARQUE NACIONAL NEVADO TRES CRUCES

Skirting the Argentine border almost directly east of Copiapó, Parque Nacional Nevado Tres Cruces consists of two distinct sectors, totaling about 61,000 hectares about 4,500 meters above sea level. Both sectors protect high-altitude wetlands and surrounding *puna* with abundant wildlife; flamingos feed and other aquatic birds feed and nest in the shallow saline lagoons, while vicuñas and guanacos graze the surrounding grasslands.

Orientation

The northerly Sector Laguna Santa Rosa is 146 kilometers from Copiapó via Ruta 31, the international highway to Argentina, and another dusty road that leads eastward up the Quebrada de Paipote. Ruta 31 continues to the north edge of the Salar de Maricunga, where there's a Chilean immigration and customs post for those continuing to the 4,726-meter Paso San Francisco and the Argentine provinces of La Rioja and Catamarca; all vehicles must stop at immigration and customs, even those not crossing the border.

From Laguna Santa Rosa, Sector Laguna del Negro Francisco is another 85 kilometers south via a road that loops past the former Mina Marte gold mine and follows the Río Astaburuaga to the lake. From the east end of the intersection with the Mina Marte road, it's possible to continue north through the Salar de Maricunga and the mining town of El Salvador to the Panamericana at Chañaral.

Sights

The larger, more northerly **Sector Laguna Santa Rosa** consists of 49,000 hectares of which its namesake body of water is a relatively small feature; it also contains about half the sprawling **Salar de Maricunga.**

Its eponymous lagoon comprises a larger part of the 12,000-hectare **Sector Laguna del Negro Francisco,** about 50 kilometers south. While flamingos nest in Brazil, Peru, Bolivia, and Argentina, 6,000–8,000 migrate here every summer to feed on plankton and crustaceans in its shallow waters. More than half are Andean flamingos, nearly all the rest Chilean flamingos, while the rare James flamingo is present in smaller numbers. Andean geese and gulls, plus giant and horned coots, are abundant.

Practicalities

At the western edge of its sector, Conaf's small **Refugio Laguna Santa Rosa** has room to sleep and cook—but no toilet facilities.

At the upper section of Laguna del Negro Francisco, Conaf's spacious **Refugio Laguna del Negro Francisco** (US$13 pp) once belonged to the Chilean military, who equipped it with electricity, kitchen facilities, snug beds, and toilet facilities, including hot showers. Make reservations at Copiapó's Conaf office (tel. 052/213404).

Conaf's Laguna del Negro Francisco station,

which collects a US$6 admission charge, is the best source of information.

Most visitors arrive by rental car (four-wheel drive is advisable but not essential), though Conaf's Copiapó office may be able to offer transportation suggestions. Copiapó adventure travel operators occasionally offer excursions into the area.

CERRO OJOS DEL SALADO

Though it lies beyond the national park boundaries, 6,887-meter Ojos del Salado is South America's second-highest peak (after Argentina's 6,962-meter Aconcagua) and a climbers' favorite. It is also the world's highest active volcano, though the last significant eruptions were in 1937 and 1956. While top physical condition and acclimatization are essential, it is not a technical ascent except for the last 50 meters to the crater, which requires some rock-climbing skills.

For Ojos del Salado, directly on the border, the best season is October to April. Foreign climbers require permission from the Chilean Foreign Ministry's Dirección de Fronteras y Límites (Difrol) and pay a nonrefundable US$160 per person, covering support and the cost of a possible rescue, to Copiapó's **Aventurismo** (Atacama 240, tel. 052/247007, www.aventurismo.cl). Once obtained, this permission must be presented to the Carabineros outpost at the north end of the Salar de Maricunga.

At the 4,200-meter base, climbers can stay at the **Refugio Claudio Lucero.** Up to a dozen can sleep at the **Refugio Universidad de Atacama** at the 5,100-meter level, while another 24 can occupy the **Refugio César Tejos,** at the 5,750-meter level, which has kitchen facilities and chemical toilets.

Caldera

Ever since the Copiapó railway reached Caldera in 1851, the town has hosted hordes of beachgoers in January, February, and on weekends. With completion of a new airport—closer to Caldera than to Copiapó—Caldera and neighboring Bahía Inglesa seem poised for a growth spurt based on tourism to some of Chile's warmest Pacific waters.

In the past decade or so, Bahía Inglesa's broader, cleaner beaches have superseded those at Caldera, but Caldera, with its historic architecture and active summer street life, remains the more interesting of the two. Off-season, it feels more like a ghost town, and prices drop considerably, but services are fewer.

HISTORY

As a port, Caldera dates from 1850, when William Wheelwright's railway transformed a tiny fishing camp into, at least briefly, the country's second most important port. Shipping silver from Chañarcillo, it supplanted Copiapó's original port, Puerto Viejo, 35 kilometers to the south on the Bahía de Copiapó.

While Caldera faltered as silver deposits diminished, it survived Chañarcillo's collapse to become the region's most important *balneario;* the Panamericana's completion in the early 1950s made it more accessible for visitors from the north and south. Today the port ships copper concentrates from the Candelaria mine near Copiapó and spring grapes and other fruits from the Upper Copiapó Valley.

ORIENTATION

On the south shore of its namesake bay, Caldera (population 13,540) is 75 kilometers northwest of Copiapó and 92 kilometers south of Chañaral via the Panamericana. Its center is a regular grid, based on the Plaza de Armas, whose streets trend northeast to southwest.

Avenida Diego de Almeyda, the main exit from the Panamericana, becomes Avenida Carvallo as it passes through town on the way to the beaches of Bahía Inglesa.

SIGHTS

As a historic port and contemporary bathing resort, Caldera is oriented toward the Costanera (waterfront). The central **Muelle de Pasajeros** (Passenger Pier) and antique **Muelle Fiscal** (Government Pier), though, are less important than the contemporary **Muelle Mecanizado** (Mechanized Pier), to the northwest, that ships Candelaria's copper concentrates.

Restoration of Caldera's 19th-century **Estación de Ferrocarril,** Chile's oldest railroad station, is complete; it now serves partly as a museum but primarily as an events center and exhibition hall. Restoration has probably not completely arrested the termite damage; a section of one wall has been left uncovered, but glassed in, to demonstrate the wattle-and-daub—or lath-and-plaster—construction style. Unfortunately, there's no exhibit about the station's history, though there are remnants of the rails that once ran here.

Facing the Muelle de Pasajeros, the former 19th-century **Aduana de Caldera** (Caldera Customs House) once served as the British consulate and is now the **Centro Cultural Universidad de Atacama** (Gana 100-B, tel. 052/316756).

Overlooking Caldera's central **Plaza Condell,** the **Iglesia San Vicente** (1862), its Gothic tower reaching 36 meters above street level, is a distinguished landmark. The less distinguished **Municipalidad** (City Hall) dates from 1855. On summer nights, the **Peatonal Gana,** between the plaza and the Costanera, is the site of a lively crafts market.

East toward the Panamericana, along Avenida Diego de Almeyda, forged iron fences enclose the not-so-lively **Cementerio Laico** (1876), the country's oldest non-Catholic cemetery. Northern Europeans, primarily Britons and Germans, occupy most of the graves, but *feng shui* most likely played a role in siting the elaborate Chinese crypts.

Atop a rugged outcrop at the west end of town, near the rotunda at the intersection

THE CALDERA-COPIAPÓ RAILWAY

Frequently but erroneously claimed to be South America's first railway, the **Compañía del Ferrocarril de Copiapó** opened in December 1851 under the eye of President Manuel Bulnes. It was really only the continent's third – British Guyana's Demerara Railway Company opened a route from Georgetown to the suburb of Plaisance in 1848, while Peru linked its port of Callao to Lima via a 14-kilometer line earlier in 1851.

Still, completion of the 81-kilometer line in less than two years (1849-1851) was a remarkable achievement. Later extended to Pabellón (37 kilometers, by 1854, followed by a spur to Chañarcillo) and then to San Antonio (another 39 kilometers, by 1867), the railway was Copiapó's silver-boom pride.

Now resting at the Universidad de Atacama, the original steam locomotive *La Copiapó* (1850) – along with first-, second-, and third-class carriages, the differences among which are minimal – last ran in 1961. For 40 years, the engineer was one Juan O'Donovan, who left Copiapó at 9 A.M. daily, arriving in Caldera at 1 P.M., then departing Caldera at 3 P.M. to arrive in Copiapó at 6:45 P.M.

At present, the line hangs on a thread and brush has overgrown much of it. In 1986, a few years before his dictatorship ended, General Pinochet decreed removal of the rails, but nature intervened – when rare rains cut the Panamericana, only a rail shuttle kept the areas north and south in contact. Out of necessity, Pinochet annulled the first decree, but there has been no regular service since.

If local authorities have their way, the rails might sing again. The line has been the subject of a feasibility study to resurrect it as a tourist train; the cost and limited tourist traffic, though, make the project unlikely. Caldera authorities have abandoned efforts to return *La Copiapó* to their restored train station (a national monument) and have settled for a couple of trucks remodeled to resemble railcars.

of Avenida Carvallo and Canal Beagle, Colombian priest Crisógono Sierra y Velásquez built the **Gruta del Padre Negro,** a chapel that, with time and religious murals by painter Luis Cerda, has become a significant pilgrimage site. It's open 9 A.M.–1:30 P.M. daily, though it's possible to peek in at the murals at other hours.

Santuario de la Naturaleza Granito Orbicular

North of Caldera, sandy beaches alternate with rocky headlands until, at about the kilometer 12 point, the Panamericana passes this small roadside cluster of elliptical and spheroidal curiosities—an area of just 375 square meters—that are really conglomerates rather than true granites.

ACCOMMODATIONS

Unlike Copiapó, Caldera's prices are markedly seasonal, reaching their peak in January and February. The rest of the year, prices moderate, though not much at the lowest level—where accommodations are pretty dire, in any event. Bahía Inglesa has better but more expensive options (other than campgrounds, of which it has many).

Residencial Palermo (Cifuentes 150, tel. 052/315847, US$11 s, US$21 d) is cheap but marginal. **Residencial Puerto Caldera** (Riveros 411, tel. 052/316827, roboamflavio@hotmail.com, US$16 s, US$25 d), has slipped a bit, but an exceptionally cheerful place where all rooms have private baths, and most have abundant natural light; there are even handicapped facilities, including a ramp and bath.

Rooms at **Hotel Montriri** (Tocornal 371, tel. 052/319055, hotelvictoriapaz_caldera. es, US$28 s, US$35 d) are passable but less than immaculate—upstairs is better. Friendly **Hotel Costanera** (Wheelwright 543, tel. 052/316007, hotelcostanera@entelchile.net,

US$33 s or d) is a good midrange choice, offering spacious rooms with no frills except breakfast and parking.

Well-maintained despite an unimpressive exterior, **Hotel Montecarlo** (Carvallo 627, tel. 052/315388, www.hotel-montecarlo.cl, US$37–48 s, US$48–52 d) has an occasionally distracted staff and offers no IVA discounts for foreigners.

Hostería Puerta del Sol (Wheelwright 750, tel. 052/315205 or 052/315507, www.hosteriapuertadelsol.com, US$48 s, US$57 d) looks good with its small pool and gardens, and it's seen recent improvements, but the streetside rooms get a great deal of foot traffic. Ask for IVA discounts.

Hotel Jandy (Gallo 560, tel. 052/316451, www.jandy.cl US$30–40 s, US$40–50 d) is a cozy and spotless hotel that's grown to include a third floor with sea views, though the empty lots in between are an eyesore. Rates include a mediocre breakfast, parking, and WiFi, and rental bikes are also available.

FOOD AND ENTERTAINMENT

For about US$1 each, **Empanapolis** (Carvallo 616-A, tel. 052/316006) produces a wider variety of empanadas, including scallops and crab, than most Chilean kitchens; they are fried rather than baked, but still lighter and better than most other fast-food alternatives.

Most places specialize in seafood, such as **Nuevo Miramar** (Gana 90, tel. 052/315381) and **Il Piron di Oro** (Cousiño 218, tel. 052/315109).

For variety, the **Bartholomeo Pub** (Wheelwright 747, tel. 052/316413) offers an imaginative assortment of Asian dishes (including sushi) in the US$8 and up range.

El Teatro (Gana 12, tel. 052/316768) serves Peruvian ceviche, plus fish, meat, and pasta dishes, in eclectic surroundings, but the pisco sours are too sugary. In summer, it offers live music from a mezzanine stage.

INFORMATION AND SERVICES

Directly on the Plaza de Armas, **Caldera's Departamento de Turismo e Integración** (tel. 052/316076, www.caldera.cl, antonio-paez_17@hotmail.com) is open 9 A.M.–2 P.M. and 4–7 P.M. daily all year, with extended evening hours in summer.

BCI (Ossa Cerda 127) has an ATM.

Correos de Chile (Edwards 325) is the post office. **Telefónica CTC Chile** (Edwards 360) has long-distance telephone services. **El Cactus** (Ossa Cerda 462-B) keeps long hours (11 A.M.–1 A.M.) for excellent Internet service.

GETTING THERE AND AROUND

Long-distance bus services resemble those to and from Copiapó, an hour to the south, but fewer companies operate here—though some through buses will stop for passengers on the Panamericana. **Tur-Bus** (Ossa Varas 710, tel. 052/316832) and **Pullman Bus** (Gallo 160, tel. 052/316585) have the most extensive routes.

Regional carrier **Casther** (Ossa Varas 710, tel. 052/316300) and **Bahía Express** to Copiapó (US$3, one hour). Faster *taxi colectivos* also go to Copiapó (US$4.50), from a spot on Cifuentes just south of Ossa Varas.

Vicinity of Caldera

◖ BAHÍA INGLESA

From Caldera, a smooth paved highway and a parallel bicycle path lead south to Bahía Inglesa, whose sheltered crescent beach with warm, relatively shallow waters makes it a favorite family destination. While a sheltering sandspit keeps the ocean waves gentle, it gets breezy enough for windsurfers.

With the new airport closer to Caldera than Copiapó, Bahía Inglesa seems poised for rapid growth. The bay and town—really a Caldera suburb—take their name from 17th-century British privateers who anchored here. The seaside *malecón* (promenade) is the site of a summer crafts market.

Accommodations and Food

Hotel El Coral (Av. El Morro 564, tel. 052/315331, US$35 s, US$58 d) provides modern, comfortable rooms, some of which have no exterior windows.

Overlooking the *malecón,* the geodesic dome rooms and restaurant at U.S.-run ◖ **Hostería Domo Chango Chile** (Av. El Morro 619, tel. 052/316168, www.changochile.cl, US$48–60 d) initially drew skepticism from traditionalists and especially municipal officials, but it has gradually gained acceptance. Both the rooms and the restaurant (which specializes in fish and shellfish, including shrimp and locally farmed scallops) are excellent; the wafer-thin pizza crust is an agreeable surprise. Off-season rates can be considerably lower, affordable even for backpackers.

The far more elaborate **Hotel Rocas de Bahía** (Av. El Morro 888, tel./fax 052/316005 or 052/316032, www.rocasdebahia.cl, US$156 s or d with breakfast) is a handsome Mediterranean-style facility, but whether the recently doubled prices are justifiable is open to debate.

Part of its namesake hotel, **El Coral** (tel. 052/315331) has good seafood starting around US$8 for a fixed-price meal, though à la carte items are significantly dearer. On the waterfront, **El Plateao** (Av. El Morro 756) specializes in delectable fresh fruit juices, but it also offers snacks and meals.

Services

In addition to accommodations, **Chango Chile** (Av. El Morro 610, tel. 052/316168, www.changochile.cl) offers surfing and kitesurfing classes (US$33) from mid-November to mid-April, and operates a variety of four-wheel-drive excursions to more remote areas. Its restaurant also provides WiFi access.

Morro Ballena (Av. El Morro s/n, tel. 052/315115 or cel. 09/9886-3673, morroballena@hotmail.com) offers excursions in and around Bahía Inglesa, including kayak and diving trips, and goes as far afield as Reserva Nacional Pingüino de Humboldt, on the border between Region III (Atacama) and Region IV (Coquimbo).

Getting There and Around

Taxi *colectivos* run constantly between Caldera and Bahía Inglesa, which are only about six kilometers apart.

CHAÑARAL

The easiest access point to increasingly popular Parque Nacional Pan de Azúcar, the crumbling but picturesque mining port of Chañaral is otherwise interesting for all the wrong reasons—primarily the 20th-century natural and human-influenced disasters that afflicted this small city. A 1922 tsunami killed 22 people, a 1940 flood and debris flow claimed many more lives, and a 1970 earthquake reached 7.0 on the Richter scale.

Chañaral's biggest disaster, though, is evidenced in the striking white crescent beach that once began at what is now called the Costanera but now extends much farther west: Decades of runoff from the Andean copper mines at Potrerillos and El Salvador have deposited so many thousands of tons of toxic sediments that no one dares use it. The worst pollution, which began around 1920, finally ceased in 1988, when local residents obtained a court order requiring Codelco to build containment ponds at higher altitudes.

Chañaral dates from the early 19th century, when Diego de Almeyda uncovered the Las Ánimas copper deposits. Because of the proximity of the U.S.-run Anaconda mining company, and copper's strategic significance, United States Marines were stationed here during World War II. When the Allende government nationalized copper in the early 1970s, the mines passed to Codelco's administration.

Orientation

Chañaral (population 13,180) is 167 kilometers northwest of Copiapó via the Panamericana, which runs east–west as it passes through town. Set among rocky headlands at the foot of the Sierra de Las Ánimas, it has a compact center whose main streets, connected to each other by staircases, more or less follow the contours of the hills. One of few level streets, the "Costanera" formerly fronted on the beach but now sits several hundred meters inland. One short block south, Merino Jarpa is the main commercial street, while just to the north, the Panamericana follows a route that once lay beneath the sea.

Sights

Chañaral has three national monuments, two of them churches: the Catholic **Iglesia Nuestra Señora del Carmen** (1865), on the east side of the Plaza de Armas, along with its adjacent **Casa Molina** (1904); and the Georgian-style, Protestant **Iglesia Presbiteriana de Chañaral** (1861).

Chañaral's biggest surprise is the **Museo de Historia Natural Rodulfo B. Philippi** (Buin 818, tel. 052/480042). It has an engaged curator and staff who are constantly improving exhibits on entomology, marine biology, and archaeology. Raided by the Chilean military who, in the early 1980s, absconded with large parts of the collections, it still holds a remarkable computerized collection of 700 historic photographs of Chañaral, surrounding

localities, and mines, including Salvador and Potrerillos. It's open 9 A.M.–1 P.M. and 3–6 P.M. weekdays, with occasional weekend hours; admission costs US$0.60.

In recent years, the city has improved its rocky western waterfront to create a **Borde Costero** of walkways and even a large saltwater swimming pool. About two kilometers farther west via the Panamericana, the mechanized pier at Chañaral's dilapidated port of **Barquito** ships both refined copper and copper concentrate that arrives from El Salvador and Potrerillos on ancient railcars (the railway dates from 1871, though the cars aren't quite *that* old). It also imports copper ore from other Chilean ports for processing at El Salvador.

Accommodations

Hotel Marina (Merino Jarpa 562, tel. 052/480942, US$7 pp with shared bath) is plain but clean, with good beds. **Hostal Sutivan** (Comercio 365, tel. 052/489123, US$15 s, US$24 d with private bath) has small rooms with good beds, cable TV, and ample common spaces, but poorly designed bathrooms; it's popular enough that reservations are advisable. Breakfast costs extra.

The still-shiny **Hotel Portal Atacama** (Merino Jarpa 1420, tel. 052/480695, portalatacama@hotmail.com, US$47 s, US$50 d) is up to Santiago standards but does not offer IVA discounts.

Well-established **Hostería Chañaral** (Müller 268, tel. 052/480050, hosteriachanaral@yahoo.com, US$47 s, US$50 d) has small but comfortable rooms, set among quiet gardens, and friendly service. It occupies the former site of a 19th-century copper smelter; in fact, parts of the walls came from the smelter.

Food

For good sandwiches and seafood at fair prices, Chañaral has **Nuria** (Yungay 434, tel. 052/489199), but the house wines are swill. **El Rincón Porteño** (Merino Jarpa 567, tel. 052/480071) and the restaurant at **Hostería Chañaral** (Müller 268, tel. 052/480050) are also good enough. West of town, toward

Barquito, **Alicanto** (Panamericana Sur 49, tel. 052/481168) is worth the two-kilometer walk to get there.

Services

Banco Estado (Buin and Maipú) has an ATM.

Correos de Chile (Comercio 172) is the post office. **CTC Telefónica Chile** (Merino Jarpa 506) has long-distance telephone services. For Internet access, there's the **Merino Center** (Los Baños 204) at the corner of Merino Jarpa.

Turismo SubSole D'Atacama (Pinto 583, cel. 09/8304-3704) does tours to Parque Nacional Pan de Azúcar.

Getting There and Around

Many north–south buses pass through on the Panamericana, including **Tur-Bus** (Panamericana s/n, tel. 052/481012) and **Pullman Bus** (Panamericana s/n, tel. 052/480213), which also goes to the interior destinations of Diego de Almagro and El Salvador.

Turismo Chango (Panamericana Norte s/n, tel. 052/480484) provides seemingly improvised service to Parque Nacional Pan de Azúcar, though it's officially scheduled at 8:30 A.M. and 3 P.M. daily in summer. It leaves not from its offices (an auto repair shop), but from a spot opposite the Municipalidad, at Merino Jarpa and Los Baños, though it also makes a run through town looking for passengers.

◖ PARQUE NACIONAL PAN DE AZÚCAR

Copious marine wildlife, scattered rare flora, and a starkly beautiful desert coastline are the big draws to Parque Nacional Pan de Azúcar, a 43,769-hectare reserve straddling the border between the regions of Copiapó and Antofagasta. Most visitors see only the coastal sections, but those who manage to visit the fog-sodden uplands find a diversity of flora and even the occasional guanaco, at altitudes up to 900 meters.

Pan de Azúcar's humid coastal environment

brown pelicans, Parque Nacional Pan de Azúcar

© WAYNE BERNHARDSON

rarely experiences rain as such, but it's often overcast until late morning from the *camanchaca* that rises out of the ocean. Temperatures are mild—the average daytime maximum temperature is 19.3°C, while the nighttime minimum is 12.3°C. Combined with sea breezes, these temperatures can feel cooler, and a sweater or light jacket is a good idea.

Sights

At sheltered **Caleta Pan de Azúcar,** a traditional fishing camp where families have been able to maintain their livelihood despite the park's presence, fishermen fillet the day's catch on the rocks, while brown pelicans skirmish over the scraps. The area has a good beach, though the surface is steep.

Other beaches of interest are **Playa Los Piqueros,** a short distance south beneath the landmark hill of Cerro Soldado, and **Playa Blanca,** on Caleta Coquimbo, near the park's southern entrance.

The most popular excursion is to the offshore **Isla Pan de Azúcar** where, besides

2,000–3,000 Humboldt penguins and numerous brown pelicans, there are olivaceous and red-footed cormorants, blue-footed boobies, Dominican gulls, and other seabirds. There are also otters (rarely seen) and breeding colonies of southern sea lions. In summer and on weekends, launch excursions are frequent, but these are fewer the rest of the year. Landing is not permitted, but launches can go close enough to see both birds and mammals clearly.

Fewer visitors see the interior than the shoreline, but the winding eight-kilometer road to **El Mirador** ends in a spectacular panoramic overlook of Caleta Pan de Azúcar and the island; at this altitude, the *camanchaca* provides moisture to nurture a natural cactus garden and many flowering plants, as well as mosses.

Farther east, toward the park's eastern Las Bombas approach, the longer 15-kilometer road to **Las Lomitas** climbs steeply at first and then across an undulating desert surface punctuated by increasingly dense concentrations of cacti as it approaches cliffs above the coastline. At road's end, where the *camanchaca* can be so dense as to block all views, Conaf has a ranger station where mesh screens condense the fog to provide fresh water.

Excursions

At Caleta Pan de Azúcar, the Sociedad Turística Caleta Pan de Azúcar offers one-hour launch excursions along the coast of Isla Pan de Azúcar (landings are not permitted, but there are still good views of penguins and sea lions). Charges are around US$7 per person based on a 10-person voyage, but with a minimum charge around US$70; smaller groups pay more per person.

Accommodations and Food

Conaf has three campgrounds: **Caleta Pan de Azúcar, Playa Piqueros,** and **Cerro Soldado;** for visitors without their own vehicles, the Pan de Azúcar campground has better access to services. In summer, on weekends, and especially during school holidays, all campgrounds can get crowded.

Sites with fire pits, picnic tables, and shade cost US$6 pp. Sites have a daily fresh water ration and access to clean, modern toilets but no showers.

Several cabañas sleep up to six people, with kitchen facilities and solar panel electricity, for US$100 in July, September, and December–February; the rest of the year, rates fall to US$50. In summer and on weekends, make reservations through Copiapó's concessionaire **Gran Atacama** (Colipí 484, Local B-122, tel. 052/219271, www.granatacama.cl).

Several Caleta Pan de Azúcar's restaurants offer *dorado* and other fresh fish (if you don't want it deep-fried, ask for it *a la plancha*) and homemade *pan amasado* (kneaded homemade bread). There's also a small grocery, and fresh fish is available directly off the boat.

Information

Opposite Playa Piqueros, Conaf's **Centro de Información Ambiental** is open 8:30 A.M.–12:30 P.M. and 2–6 P.M. daily. Besides slide talks about park ecology, it features a cactarium for those unable to visit the uplands. At the southern approach from Chañaral, Conaf rangers usually collect an admission fee of US$6 for foreigners, US$2.50 for children up to 18 years of age. For Chilean residents, fees are US$3 for adults and US$1 for children; foreigners over age 60 may pay Chilean rates. Note that no fee is collected at the eastern entrance.

Getting There and Around

Turismo Chango runs buses to and from Chañaral, 30 kilometers south via a smooth gravel road. From Chañaral, it's also possible to hitchhike, hire a taxi (though it's necessary to pay both directions), or rent a car.

Southbound cyclists and even motorists will find it more interesting (and for cyclists, easier) to approach the park from the east, from a well-marked turnoff at Las Bombas, a wide spot in the road at kilometer 1,014 on the Panamericana, about 45 kilometers northwest of Chañaral. The good dirt road follows the Quebrada Pan de Azúcar all the way down to the coast.

NORTE CHICO

EL SALVADOR AND VICINITY

From Chañaral, a smooth two-lane blacktop road climbs the valley of the Río del Salado to El Salvador, a Codelco company town 129 kilometers to the east and 2,300 meters above sea level. The famous Brazilian architect Oscar Niemeyer devised its street plan, laid out in the shape of a Roman helmet; the city dates from 1959, when its copper deposits superseded those of nearby **Potrerillos,** which continues to operate a smelter and sulfuric acid plant. The operation was once owned by the Andes Mining Company, a subsidiary of the U.S.-based Anaconda Corporation that dominated Chile's economy for decades; it came under state control in the 1970s.

As an isolated company town, El Salvador has amenities that many larger Chilean cities lack, including an airport, a stadium with a first-division soccer team, a cinema and museum, and sports and social clubs. The presence of Potrerillos also makes it one of Chile's most polluted places and, as copper ores decline, it's due to close by 2011. About two-thirds of its 1,300 workers will retire or be reassigned.

From El Salvador and Potrerillos, a good but unpaved road goes east and then south to a customs post at the north end of the **Salar de Maricunga** and then to Parque Nacional Nevado Tres Cruces, where it turns east toward the border crossing, the 4,726-meter Paso San Francisco. From the border, the road continues to the Argentine cities of La Rioja and Catamarca, capitals of their namesake provinces. All vehicles must stop at Chilean customs, even those not crossing the border. Carry extra fuel.

Accommodations and Food

Hostería El Salvador (Av. Potrerillos 003, tel. 052/475749, US$10 pp, US$23 s, US$37 d) has rooms with either shared or private baths, but does not provide breakfast. **Hotel Camino del Inca** (Av. El Tofo 330, tel. 052/475252, www.hotelesatacama.cl, US$66 s, US$80 d with breakfast), which caters primarily to mining engineers and executives, also has a top restaurant.

Getting There and Around

Aeropuerto El Salvador is 16 kilometers west of town. **LAN** (Coquimbo 1, tel. 052/475447) flies several times weekly to Copiapó, La Serena, and Santiago.

Buses to Chañaral and other Panamericana destinations leave from the **Pullman Bus** terminal (Av. Potrerillos Norte and Av. O'Higgins, tel. 052/475439).

VALLENAR

In a valley so deep and narrow that the Panamericana passes above it on a bridge over the Río Huasco, the mining and farming service center of Vallenar stretches east toward the Andes and west toward the Pacific. It's home to one unique Chilean product, the white dessert wine known as *pajarete,* and is also known for local specialties such as olives and river shrimp.

From here, it's possible to head east toward Alto del Carmen, one of Chile's main pisco zones, or west toward Huasco and Parque Nacional Llanos de Challe, one of the best places to see the sporadic *desierto florido,* or flowering desert.

History

The Irish-born colonial governor Ambrosio O'Higgins, father of independence hero Bernardo O'Higgins and later the viceroy of Peru, chose the site for this city and reportedly named it "Villa de San Ambrosio de Vallenar" for his County Sligo hometown of Ballenary. There's some evidence, though, that he came from County Meath.

Orientation

Vallenar (population 43,750) is 145 kilometers south of Copiapó and 188 kilometers north of La Serena via the Panamericana. While the Puente Huasco across the valley bypasses the city, eastbound roads descend into the town center at each end of the bridge. At the bridge's south end, a paved highway heads west toward the fishing port and beach town of Huasco.

The city itself sits on the Río Huasco's north bank. Most services are on or near Plaza

Ambrosio O'Higgins, the city's historical center, or on east–west Avenida Prat.

Sights

Most buildings are relatively new wooden or modern concrete structures, since a 1922 earthquake destroyed most of its characteristic adobes. One that survived is the **Iglesia Parroquial San Ambrosio,** distinguished by its shiny copper dome, at the southeast corner of Plaza O'Higgins.

In new quarters, the **Museo del Huasco** (Ramírez 1001, tel. 052/610635) contains exhibits on regional mineralogy, paleontology, botany, zoology, archaeology, history, and an outstanding photo collection, which includes several images of the 1922 earthquake's aftermath. Hours are 9 A.M.–1 P.M. and 3–6 P.M. weekdays only. Admission costs US$1 for adults, US$0.35 for kids.

Over the past several years, one of the most successful efforts to improve the livability of any Chilean city has been Vallenar's reclamation of the **Paseo Ribereño,** a greenbelt on the Río Huasco's north bank. With broad lawns, shady trees, basketball and tennis courts, and barbecue pits, it's become one of the city's most popular hangouts, especially on weekends.

Entertainment and Events

Within the Centro Cultural Vallenar, the **Cine Municipal** (Prat 1094, tel. 051/611501) shows current films.

January 5's **Fundación de la Ciudad** commemorates the anniversary of Ambrosio O'Higgins's founding of the city in 1789. Another summer event, the **Festival Vallenar Canta,** is a musical celebration toward the end of the month.

Accommodations

The quality of accommodations here is better than at most comparably sized Chilean cities, even at simple budget choices such as **Residencial Oriental** (Serrano 720, tel. 051/613889, US$10–13 pp), which has singles with shared baths and others with private baths. **Residencial La Rivera** (Merced

1117, tel. 051/611906, US$13 s, US$25 d) is good and friendly, but lacks rooms with private baths.

Hotel Viña del Mar (Serrano 611, tel. 051/611478, US$12 pp with shared bath, US$20 s, US$30 d with private bath) has smallish but spotless rooms with cable TV and parking. **Residencial L&M** (Serrano 1378, tel./fax 051/611756, residencial_lym@yahoo.com, US$17 s, US$32 d) is one of the better budget picks—friendly and tidy, with responsive service.

Plain but friendly and nearly flawless, **Hotel Corona del Inca** (Aconcagua 455, tel. 051/613380, www.hostalcoronadelinca.cl, US$23 s, US$37 d) is the former Hostal Vall, offering rooms with private baths, cable TV, and parking included.

In an excellent location, amiable **Hostal Real Quillahue** (Plaza O'Higgins 70, tel. 051/619992, pedroprokurica@yahoo.com, US$23 s, US$33 d) has small but impeccable rooms with private baths, good beds, cable TV, and an ample breakfast.

Clearly the city's best choice, spacious **Hostería Vallenar** (Alonso de Ercilla 848, tel. 051/614370, www.hotelesatacama.cl, US$60 s, US$70 d, up to US$77 s or d) offers *superior* rooms with private baths (shower only), while *lujo* (luxury) rooms have tubs. Rates include breakfast.

Despite its unimpressive faux brick exterior, **Hotel Garra de León** (Serrano 1052, tel./fax 051/613753, www.hotelgarradeleón.cl, US$60 s, US$80 d) offers spacious, well-decorated, and well-maintained rooms.

Food

At the **Mercado Municipal** (Santiago and Serrano), several simple *cocinerías* offer cheap but nutritious meals.

Directly on Plaza O'Higgins, **Il Bocatto** (Prat 750, tel. 051/614609) serves moderately priced pizza, sandwiches, and other light meals. **Café del Centro** (Colchagua 550, tel. 051/611117) produces excellent oversized sandwiches that are a meal in themselves, and good fruit juices. The **Club Social** (Prat 899, tel.

051/616403) serves a variety of Chilean, international, and seafood dishes.

Information and Services
Banco de Crédito (Prat 1002) has an ATM.

Correos de Chile (Vallejos s/n), on the north side of Plaza O'Higgins, is the post office. **Entel** (Prat 1040) has long-distance telephones. For Internet access, try the **Cyber Café** (Santiago 422, tel. 051/342850).

For medical help, contact the sparkling new **Hospital Provincial del Huasco** (Av. Huasco 392, Acceso Sur, tel. 051/331500, www.hospitalprovincialdelhuasco.cl), at the southern approach to town.

Getting There and Around
All Vallenar's long-distance bus companies have finally moved from downtown offices to locales in or near the main **Terminal de Buses** (Av. Prat 137, tel. 051/611431), across from the old train station, where several companies provide frequent services north and south along the Panamericana.

Two key companies have newer terminals nearby: **Tur-Bus** (Prat 32, tel. 051/611738) and **Pullman Bus** (Prat and Atacama, tel. 051/619587). Both have extensive services in both directions.

For transportation to the village of Freirina and the port and seaside resort of Huasco, and to the Upper Huasco Valley village of Alto del Carmen, try the **Terminal de Buses Rurales** (Marañon and Verdaguer, tel. 051/612117). **Colectivo Vía Mar** (Serrano 959) provides shared taxi service to Huasco as soon as there are four passengers.

Sample destinations and times include Copiapó (US$7.50, 2 hours), La Serena (US$8, 2.5 hours), Caldera (US$8.50, 3 hours), and Santiago (US$21–39, 8.5 hours).

HUASCO
From the south end of the Puente Huasco, a smooth paved highway parallels the river west to the village of **Freirina,** founded in 1752. Its **Iglesia Santa Rosa de Lima** (1869) is a national monument, as is the neoclassical **Edificio**

Los Portales (1870), whose nine-arched portal faces the Plaza de Armas.

From Freirina, the road continues to the beach resort, and fishing and mining port of **Huasco** (population 6,445), suitable for either a day trip or an overnight, but weekends get crowded. Most locals head for the **Playa Grande,** which stretches east and north from Avenida Craig, the main commercial street, but the **Playa Chica** is closer to hotels and restaurants.

Practicalities
Ocean-view **Hostal San Fernando** (Pedro de Valdivia 176, tel./fax 051/531726, www.hostalsanfernando.dk, US$25 s, US$30 d) offers roomy accommodations with private bath. Well-worn **Hostería Huasco** (Ignacio Carrera Pinto 110, tel. 051/531026, rossanabergamasco@hotmail.com, US$53 s, US$73 d) has potential, but desperately needs modernization.

For lunch or dinner, try the seafood at **Bahía** (tel. 051/532593), perched on the second floor overlooking the Terminal Pesquero, the fisherman's pier. While plain in decor, the food is well-prepared and the service is welcoming.

Buses and *taxi colectivos* run frequently between Huasco and Vallenar.

◖ PARQUE NACIONAL LLANOS DE CHALLE
North of Huasco Bajo, a good but unpaved road parallels the coast for 50 kilometers to the dilapidated but increasingly popular beach town of **Carrizal Bajo.** En route it passes through the coastal Sector Punta Los Pozos of Parque Nacional Llanos de Challe, a 45,708-hectare unit whose main attraction is its rare but ephemeral flora. There is a contiguous inland sector of the park directly inland from Carrizal Bajo.

Recently, Carrizal Bajo has become inundated by campers from Vallenar and land sharks gambling that the vastly improved road north to Puerto Viejo and Caldera will drive real estate prices through the roof. It has a crumbling church in a state of arrested

THERE'S GOLD UNDER THAT THAR ICE

Until recently the **Upper Huasco Valley**, southeast of Alto del Carmen, was best known for its namesake pisco. Recently, though, the skyrocketing price of gold has revived a stalled mining project and contributed to one of the continent's most contentious environmental controversies.

Since 2003, the Canadian transnational corporation Barrick Gold has worked the Veladero mine in Argentina's adjacent San Juan province. With the spike in gold prices, though, the company decided to go ahead with the far larger and more complex open-pit Pascua Lama project on the Chilean side. To do so, it proposed moving 300,000 cubic meters of a border glacier – the source of irrigation water for downstream grape and olive farmers – and attempting to fuse it with larger nearby ice fields.

In an era of global warming, this unprecedented tampering with the area's natural hydrology attracted attention – in a classic guerrilla publicity stunt, protestors dumped blocks of ice on the sidewalk outside Barrick's Santiago headquarters. Even more serious, though, was Barrick's intention to use cyanide to leach the gold from the ore – a method banned in many mining areas, including the U.S. state of Montana; cyanide leakages could poison the entire Huasco drainage.

Barrick claimed its plan to create impermeable storage ponds for cyanide-contaminated tailings would overcome this problem. Under pressure, it agreed to create a 20-year, US$60 million mitigation fund to offset any negative environmental impact. Even that plan did not take into account the potential for earthquake damage in one of the Andes' most seismically active areas.

Finally, in 2006, Chile's Comisión Nacional del Medioambiente (Conama) approved the project on the condition that the glaciers be left intact, and that the company monitor them for any damage. The project was due to begin in 2009, but opposition has since cropped up on the Argentine side, where most of the ores would be processed. Environmental objections are part of the issue there, but there's also disagreement between Argentina and Chile as to distribution of tax revenues – an issue that may work to the environment's advantage.

deterioration. It's infamous for a 1986 incident in which the insurrectionist Frente Patriótico Manuel Rodríguez (FPMR) landed a load of Cuban weapons here and shipped some of them to Viña del Mar. Later that same year, the FPMR assaulted General Pinochet's motorcade in the Cajón del Maipo near Santiago, killing several bodyguards but failing to touch the general.

Flora and Fauna

In rare rainy years, Llanos de Challe is *the* place to observe the *desierto florido,* when the desert floor erupts with wildflowers. It's not a common event, though—French naturalist Claudio Gay went north in 1831 in search of this fleeting carpet of color, but he had to wait until 1840 to actually observe the phenomenon.

There were major *desierto florido* events in 1983, 1987, 1991, and 1997 (when 96 millimeters of rain fell in only 15 hours), but erratic rainfall distribution makes finding the best spots and getting the timing right a challenge. Even then, the phenomenon is brief as the rain quickly percolates into the sandy soils and the sun soon evaporates standing water on the desert floor. September is the likeliest month, but the phenomenon can happen at any time between July and November.

Llanos de Challe's signature species is the *garra de león* (lion's claw, *Leontochir ovallei*), a fleshy-stemmed creeper whose multiple flowers, either yellow or red, form a single mass. Endemic to parts of the Atacama coast and first collected by Javier Ovalle in 1866, it has been the unfortunate target of seed poachers and introduced to Japan as an ornamental. There are many other wildflowers, though, as

NORTE CHICO

well as numerous cacti, and mammals including guanacos and foxes.

Practicalities

Sites at Conaf's campground at **Punta Los Pozos** cost US$5 per person, including 20 liters of potable water, with access to toilets and showers. Many people camp informally at or near Carrizal Bajo.

Conaf charges US$3 admission per person for adults, US$1 for children.

There is occasional public transport from Vallenar to Bajo Carrizal via Huasco. Southbound motorists or cyclists now have the option of heading south directly from Bahía Inglesa, though there are also direct westbound approaches from the Panamericana.

ALTO DEL CARMEN AND VICINITY

From Vallenar, a smoothly paved but narrow and winding road climbs the scenic Río Huasco Valley, past the Santa Juana reservoir, about 40 kilometers to the mountain town of Alto del Carmen, home to its namesake pisco distillery (open for tours and tasting in summer only). Another 25 kilometers up the valley, by an equally smooth but less vertiginous road,

the equally scenic village of San Félix holds a late February **Festival de la Vendimia** (Grape Harvest Festival).

Along the entire valley, the contrast between the barren hillside and the lush Huasco Valley, with its grapes and other irrigated crops, makes a spectacular excursion. Limited accommodations and mediocre food, though, make it a better day trip than an overnight.

As scenic as it is, the Upper Huasco's resources are threatened by a dubious project sponsored by Canada's Barrick Gold Corporation, although this company has abandoned its original idea of "relocating" three high-altitude glaciers to provide access to nearly 18 million ounces of gold for its Pascua Lama mine (which straddles the Argentine border). Still, there is worry that chemical runoff from the open-pit mine could contaminate downstream irrigation waters, and the first gold has yet to be extracted. Signs of opposition are everywhere—including an elaborate mural that climbs the steeple of Alto del Carmen's church—but so are Barrick trucks and other heavy equipment.

There are borderline accommodations and food at both Alto del Carmen and San Félix.

La Serena

Despite its chill Pacific waters and the *camanchaca* that cools the city until it burns off—usually—in midafternoon, La Serena has somehow displaced Viña del Mar as Chile's prime beach resort. Chile's government is so convinced of Serena's tourist appeal that it's even proposed a new international airport at Tongoy, south of the city, to land larger jets than close-in Aeropuerto La Florida can handle, but there's been little progress so far.

With its museums, university, and other cultural resources, La Serena is also a base for excursions to regional attractions ranging from

offshore penguin colonies to astronomical observatories and the pisco-producing Elqui Valley. Its colonial appearance is deceptive—most buildings are far newer than their style suggests—but the pedestrian-friendly core has much to recommend it.

A sister city to Millbrae, in the San Francisco Bay Area, La Serena is suffering a plague of minor ills, such as ubiquitous graffiti, that have undercut its visitor appeal. The revitalized port of Coquimbo has in turn challenged La Serena with its gastronomy and nightlife, though La Serena surpasses Coquimbo in quality and quantity of accommodations.

La Serena's Iglesia Santo Domingo dates from the 17th century.

HISTORY

Originally founded as Villanueva de la Serena by Pedro de Valdivia's subordinate, Juan Bohón, some time between late 1543 and early 1545, Chile's second-oldest city burned to the ground during an indigenous revolt in which most of the resident Spaniards, including Bohón, died. It was refounded in 1549 by Francisco de Aguirre as San Bartolomé de la Serena, and by the end of the 16th century it had about 100 Spanish citizens and 800 Indians in *encomienda*.

La Serena suffered repeated 17th-century raids by French and English privateers, among them Sir Francis Drake, Bartholomew Sharp, Edward Davis, and George Anson, leading to fortifications by the end of the century (Sharp's 1680 attack destroyed the Cabildo, where many valuable records burned). While the city survived, the recurring attacks contributed to an economic stagnation that persisted until independence, when La Serena evolved into a commercial and administrative center for the Norte

Chico, and the port of Coquimbo developed to accommodate the copper industry. In the early 20th century, exploitation of iron drew workers and their families from elsewhere in the country.

While La Serena has few truly colonial remains, it has colonial character thanks to its original city grid and former president Gabriel González Videla's Plan Serena, which spawned a "colonial renaissance" architectural style. Part of a larger and less successful scheme to reduce metropolitan Santiago's political and economic dominance, González Videla's plan helped make the tourist development of the 1980s and 1990s possible.

ORIENTATION

Near the mouth of the Río Elqui, La Serena (population 147,815) is 474 kilometers north of Santiago via the Panamericana, a four-lane divided toll road for the entire way between the two cities, and 333 kilometers south of Copiapó. Its central core, bounded by the

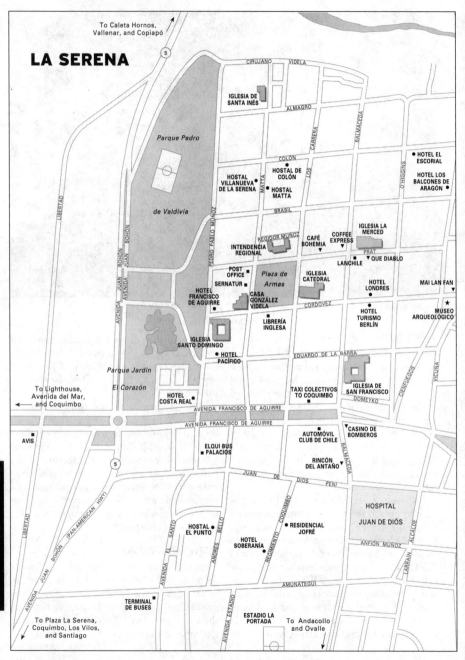

LA SERENA

To Caleta Hornos, Vallenar, and Copiapó

5

CIRUJANO VIDELA

IGLESIA DE SANTA INÉS

ALMAGRO

CABRERA

BALMACEDA

Parque Pedro

COLÓN

LOS

O'HIGGINS

● HOTEL EL ESCORIAL

HOTEL LOS BALCONES DE ARAGÓN ●

HOSTAL VILLANUEVA DE LA SERENA ●

HOSTAL DE COLÓN

MATTA

HOSTAL MATTA

de Valdivia

BRASIL

REGIDOR MUÑOZ

CAFÉ BOHEMIA

COFFEE EXPRESS

IGLESIA LA MERCED

PEDRO PABLO MUÑOZ

INTENDENCIA REGIONAL

PRAT

QUE DIABLO

LANCHILE

POST OFFICE

Plaza de Armas

IGLESIA CATEDRAL

HOTEL LONDRES

MAI LAN FAN

SERNATUR

LIBERTAD

AVENIDA

AVENIDA

JUAN BOHÓN

BOHÓN

HOTEL FRANCISCO DE AGUIRRE

CASA GONZÁLEZ VIDELA

CORDOVEZ

HOTEL TURISMO BERLÍN

★ MUSEO ARQUEOLÓGICO

LIBRERÍA INGLESA

CIENFUEGOS

VICUÑA

IGLESIA SANTO DOMINGO

● HOTEL PACÍFICO

EDUARDO DE LA BARRA

Parque Jardín El Corazón

HOTEL COSTA REAL ●

TAXI COLECTIVOS TO COQUIMBO

IGLESIA DE SAN FRANCISCO

DOMEYKO

To Lighthouse, Avenida del Mar, and Coquimbo

AVENIDA FRANCISCO DE AGUIRRE

AVENIDA FRANCISCO DE AGUIRRE

AVIS

5

AUTOMÓVIL CLUB DE CHILE

CASINO DE BOMBEROS

ELQUI BUS PALACIOS

RINCÓN DEL ANTAÑO

BALMACEDA

JUAN   DE   DIOS   PENI

LIBERTAD

JUAN BOHÓN (PAN-AMERICAN HWY)

HOSTAL EL PUNTO ●

AVENIDA EL SANTO

ANDRÉS BELLO

HOTEL SOBERANÍA

● RESIDENCIAL JOFRÉ

REGIMIENTO COQUIMBO

HOSPITAL

JUAN DE DIÓS

ANFIÓN MUÑOZ

ALCALDE

ZABRÍN

AMUNÁTEGUI

TERMINAL DE BUSES

To Plaza La Serena, Coquimbo, Los Vilos, and Santiago

AVENIDA ESTADIO

ESTADIO LA PORTADA

To Andacollo and Ovalle

© AVALON TRAVEL

streets Pedro Pablo Muñoz, Amunátegui, Justo Donoso, Castro, and Cirujano Videla, lies south of the Río Elqui and is, officially, a national monument. From its junction with the Panamericana, Avenida Francisco de Aguirre leads west to the landmark lighthouse, where Avenida del Mar hugs the southern shoreline, past the city's many beaches—not to mention hotels, restaurants, discos, and pubs.

SIGHTS

The literal centerpiece of González Videla's Plan Serena, the city's **Plaza de Armas** features subtropical plantings of palms and similar species and a central fountain by sculptor Samuel Román. On the east side, dating from 1844, the **Iglesia Catedral** (Los Carrera and Cordovez) is a national monument; the columns supporting the roof of this elegant stone edifice are particularly impressive. It is home to the **Museo de Arte Religiosa** (Los Carrera 450, tel. 051/225388), a religious art museum recently moved here from the Franciscan church; its hours are 10 A.M.–1:30 P.M. and 5–8 P.M. weekdays, as well as 10 A.M.–2 P.M. on Saturday.

Across the plaza, the former president lived for half a century (1927–1977) in the **Casa González Videla** (Matta and Cordovez), a building that dates from 1890. Also a national monument, it now houses the regional history museum that bears his name. Many nearby buildings, such as the regional government's **Intendencia** and the **Municipalidad,** reflect González Videla's influence, though the nearly indistinguishable **Tribunales** (Law Courts) date from 1938, a few years before his plan took effect.

To the west, between Pedro Pablo Muñoz and the Panamericana, **Parque Pedro de Valdivia** is one of Serena's largest open spaces, but substantial parts of it are suffering from years of deferred maintenance. The exception is the fastidiously landscaped **Parque Jardín El Corazón,** a 2.6-hectare Japanese garden that commemorated the 450th anniversary of the city's founding. Open 10 A.M.–6 P.M. daily except in winter, when it's closed Mondays, the Parque Jardín (tel. 051/217013) charges US$1 admission for adults, US$0.50 for children.

Most of Serena's other landmarks are ecclesiastical. Begun in 1585 and completed in 1627, the colonial **Iglesia de San Francisco** (Balmaceda and Eduardo de la Barra) is a national monument with meter-thick walls and graceful corbelled arches; venerable religious paintings adorn the lateral walls.

Half a block west of the plaza, on Cordovez, the **Iglesia Santo Domingo** dates from 1755, but its hexagonal bell tower is a 1912 addition. A national monument, it is also known as the **Iglesia Padres Carmelitas,** after the order that now controls it. Three blocks north of the plaza, the 19th-century **Iglesia de Santa Inés** (Almagro and Matta) is yet another national monument.

At the corner of Prat and Balmaceda, fronted by its own *plazuela,* the **Iglesia La Merced** (1709) has undergone frequent modifications; note the block construction and the unusual porthole window.

Three blocks east of the plaza, the Jesuit-built 1755 **Iglesia San Agustín** (Cienfuegos and Cantournet) came under Augustinian control after the Jesuit expulsion of 1767. Renovations since the 1975 earthquake have left it looking better than ever.

At the east end of Cantournet, on an imposing hilltop site, the neoclassical **Iglesia y Claustro de la Casa de La Providencia** (Justo Donoso 420) was built as an orphanage in 1872. One block south and one block west, dating from 1755, the **Iglesia Las Carmelitas** (Gandarillas and Manuel Rodríguez) is a national monument notable for its magnificently carved doors.

Part of its namesake hospital, the 19th-century **Capilla San Juan de Dios** (Balmaceda and Juan de Dios Peni) is a stucco-covered adobe that resembles stone blocks, while its impressive doors and columns are made of *alerce* timber. Also a national monument, its two-story bell tower, topped by a bulbous cupola, is well worth a look.

Museo Histórico Gabriel González Videla

González Videla was La Serena's native son, and this regional history museum contains personal effects, including photographs of and correspondence between the Chilean president and major international figures such as Argentina's Juan Perón, Brazil's Getulio Vargas, and U.S. president Harry Truman (some of the letters seem more formulaic than personal).

During his term, from 1946 to 1952, Chile claimed a sector of Antarctica, building icy strongholds known as Base Arturo Prat, Base Bernardo O'Higgins, and then, in 1952, Base González Videla. Chile also symbolically strengthened its Pacific presence when, on January 19, 1951, Comandante Roberto Parragué Singer flew the *Manutara* from La Serena to Hanga Roa in 20 hours—the first flight ever from the continent to distant Easter Island. More than symbolically, González Videla's administration granted women the vote in 1948.

The museum conveniently overlooks the authoritarian aspects of his presidency, during which he outlawed the Communist party (once his supporters) and even prosecuted senator/poet Pablo Neruda, who fled to Argentina for a year. Some caustic caricatures suggest that González Videla was not a great intellect, but one room is devoted to Plan Serena, the cornerstone of the president's project to combat centralism and make provincial cities more livable.

In addition to the material on González Videla, the main floor is also home to the **Pinacoteca Oscar Prager,** a collection of both abstract and figurative Chilean art from the first half of the 20th century. Among the works are portraits and, especially, a large assortment of landscapes by Osvaldo Ramírez Ossandón (1904–1990), also known as Mister Rou. The 2nd floor has exhibits on colonial and contemporary history, and also hosts special events.

At the southwest corner of the Plaza de Armas, the Museo González Videla (Matta

495, tel. 051/217189, www.museohistorico-laserena.cl) is a national monument. Open 10 A.M.–6 P.M. weekdays and 10–1 P.M. Saturday, it charges US$1 admission for adults, US$0.50 for kids.

Museo Arqueológico de La Serena

Serena's archaeological museum contains exhibit halls on geology and fossils, agricultural origins and early coastal settlements, and regional cultures. During construction of Embalse Puclaro, a sprawling reservoir behind a large new dam between La Serena and Vicuña, archaeologists salvaged many of the artifacts now on display here.

The local succession includes several distinct cultures that gradually evolved into the Inka-Diaguita hybrid the first Spaniards saw. From about 130 B.C. to A.D. 600, distinguished by its ceramics and metallurgy, the El Molle culture occupied the area between present-day Copiapó and the Río Choapa, in the vicinity of Illapel. There is a reproduction of the El Molle site known as Valle del Encanto, near Ovalle.

The successor Las Ánimas culture, dating roughly from A.D. 700 to A.D. 1000, had a more maritime orientation but also imported traits from the present-day Argentine provinces of La Rioja and Catamarca; it set the stage for the Diaguitas (A.D. 1000–1536), a settled agricultural people with more elaborate ceramics who came under Inka domination in the 16th century.

One of the museum's most prized items, in the Easter Island display, is the 2.5-meter *moai* designated number 659 by German priest and archaeologist Sebastián Englert, who spent many years in the Pacific. Donated to La Serena via González Videla, it was initially installed at the Chilean army's Regimiento Arica, then moved to a public park on Avenida Colo Colo before being shipped to exhibits in Milán, Barcelona, and Burdeos (France). In the shipping process, it suffered serious damage, but was repaired and then returned to La Serena in 1996.

On a more contemporary note, the museum contains a photographic exhibit of the city's development/evolution, as well as an excellent sample of crafts and souvenirs, including reproductions of Diaguita pottery, lapis lazuli jewelry, and also books.

The Museo Arqueológico (Cordovez and Cienfuegos, tel. 051/224492, www.museoarqueologicolaserena.cl) is open 9:30 A.M.–5:50 P.M. weekdays except Monday, 10 A.M.–1 P.M. and 4–7 P.M. Saturday, and 10 A.M.–1 P.M. Sundays and holidays. It has a reciprocal admissions policy with the Museo González Videla—what's valid for one is also valid for the other, on the same day.

Museo Mineralógico Ignacio Domeyko

Beneath a distribution map of the region's mineral deposits, wooden display cases fill one large room with samples of 2,160 minerals native to the region in this simple but orderly mineralogical museum. On the grounds of the Universidad de La Serena, it takes its name from Polish immigrant explorer and scientist Ignacio Domeyko, who explored northern Chile between 1839 and 1844 (an Andean front range that bears his name stretches from the latitude of Copiapó to that of Antofagasta).

From March to December, when the university is in session, the Museo Mineralógico (Anfión Muñoz 870, tel. 051/204096) is open 9:30 A.M.–12:30 P.M. weekdays. In January and February, it's also open Saturdays and February hours are 9 A.M.–4 P.M. Admission costs US$0.85.

BEACHES

South of the lighthouse at the west end of Avenida Francisco de Aguirre, Avenida del Mar parallels a string of more than a dozen beaches all the way to Coquimbo. Nearly all of these are reasonably safe for activities as various as sunbathing and swimming to surfing and windsurfing, but **Playa Cuatro Esquinas** (appropriately close to the Kamikaze Pub) and some others bear watching for their rip currents (authorities have erected warning signs where appropriate). Authorities have also added a segregated bike lane between beach and road, so cyclists needn't concern themselves with motorized vehicles, and frequent speed bumps protect pedestrians crossing from their hotels and cabañas to the beach.

ENTERTAINMENT

As a beach resort, La Serena has numerous bars and entertainment venues that come and go every summer. Many of these are along Avenida del Mar, while the ones that follow are downtown.

On the south side of the Plaza de Armas, the **Club de Jazz** (Cordovez and Los Carrera, te. 051/215832, teatrocentenario.blogspot.com) recently moved here from Coquimbo. **Rincón del Antaño** (Balmaceda 865) is a tango bar.

The multiscreen **Cinemark** (Av. Alberto Solari 1400, tel. 051/213103) is at the Plaza La Serena shopping center, a short distance south of the bus terminal. For live theater and concerts, there's the **Teatro Municipal** (Benavente 580, tel. 051/206554), opposite Plaza Tenri.

EVENTS

La Serena hosts a variety of mostly summertime events, many of which take place on Plaza González Videla, just north of the former president's house on the west side of the Plaza de Armas. Among the most enduring are January's **Encuentro Nacional de Artesanía,** a crafts fair; and February's **Feria del Libro de La Serena,** a book fair that attracts national and international publishers, along with mostly Chilean authors.

SHOPPING

For the best permanent display of crafts and souvenirs, visit the **Mercado la Recova** (Cienfuegos and Cantournet). There's another crafts market at the **Plazuela La Merced** (Prat and Balmaceda), directly in front of its namesake church, and a big summer crafts market at **Plaza González Videla,** just north of the Casa González Videla, on the west side of the Plaza de Armas.

For regional and national artworks, visit

Galería Carmen Codoceo (Prat 424, tel. 051/211186).

Facing the Plaza de Armas, the **Librería Inglesa** (Cordovez 309, Local 5, tel. 051/215669, www.libreriainglesa.cl) carries a selection of English-language novels.

ACCOMMODATIONS

La Serena has a wide range of accommodations options in all categories; the priciest alternatives are right on the beach.

US$10-25

Barely a block off the plaza, **◖ Hostal Matta** (Matta 234, tel. 051/210013, www.hostal-matta.cl, US$12 pp, US$ 27 s, US$30 d) is a cheerfully decorated place with ample rooms, mostly with private baths, fine new furniture, and attractive common areas including a patio and a garden. The lower prices correspond to smaller shared-bath singles.

Near the bus terminal, rates at travelers' favorite **Hostal Jofré** (Regimiento Coquimbo 964, tel. 051/222335, hostaljofre@hotmail.com, US$33 d with private bath and breakfast) include kitchen privileges, but singles are hard to come by. There are slightly cheaper rooms with shared baths.

US$25-50

Rooms at amiable **Residencial Suiza** (Cienfuegos 250, tel. 051/216092, residencial.suiza@terra.cl, US$30 s or d) are contemporary and immaculate. Despite a stellar reputation, **Hostal Croata** (Cienfuegos 248, tel./fax 051/224997, www.hostalcroata.cl, US$25 s, US$33 d) is fairly plain, but rates include breakfast, kitchen and Internet access, cable TV, and parking.

Charmingly anachronous **Hotel Pacífico** (Eduardo de la Barra 252, tel. 051/225674, www.hotelpacifico.cl US$13 pp, US$22 s, US$37 d) offers some of La Serena's best service for the price, even though some of the staff in this aging onetime mansion seem as venerable as the building itself. Rates vary according to shared or private baths; the best and newest baths are far to the back.

Just two blocks from the bus terminal, **Hotel Soberanía** (Regimiento Coquimbo 1049, tel. 051/227672, www.hotelsoberania.cl, US$25 s, US$40 d) is friendly, well-organized, comfortable, and quiet, with interior gardens and shaded parking. Off-season rates (around US$10–12 pp) are a true bargain.

In new quarters barely a block from its previous location, **Hostal Villanueva de la Serena** (Matta 269, tel. 051/550268, www.hostalvillanueva.cl, US$27 s, US$45 d) is a cozy, friendly, six-room B&B with a diverse breakfast that includes *kuchen* (breakfast pastry).

The spacious, cheerfully decorated rooms at renovated 【 **Hotel Londres** (Cordovez 550, tel. 051/219066, www.hotellondres.cl, US$35 s, US$45 d) are among Serena's best values. Services include Internet access and other perks.

Rooms at **Hotel Casablanca** (Vicuña 414, tel. 051/213070, www.hotelcasablanca.cl, US$38 s, US$45 d with breakfast) are smallish but efficiently designed—though some interior rooms lack natural light.

Easy walking distance from the bus terminal, German-run **Hostal El Punto** (Andrés Bello 979, tel. 051/228474, www.hostalelpunto.cl, US$11 pp, US$42 s, US$48 d) has both dorms and private rooms with cable TV, but the most expensive come with balconies; rates include breakfast.

Hotel El Escorial (Colón 617, tel. 051/224793, www.hotelescorial.cl, US$37 s, US$50 d) is popular in its price range, for rooms with cable TV, telephone, parking, and the like.

US$50-100

The remodeled street-level rooms at **Hotel Turismo Berlín** (Cordovez 535, tel. 051/222927 or 051/233583, hotelberlin@gmail.com, US$34–40 s, US$53–61 d) are more than agreeable; guests in the older, smaller upstairs rooms can enjoy the attractive common spaces as much as those paying higher rates. Rates include breakfast and on-site parking.

The colonial-style exterior at **Hostal de Colón** (Colón 371, tel. 051/223979, www

.hostaldecolonlaserena.cl, US$48 s, US$73 d) is a little misleading, as the hotel consists of two levels of well-kept but utilitarian rooms facing each other across a narrow patio; the upper level gets much better light. Rates include breakfast and a free airport or bus terminal transfer; parking is a block away.

Hotel Los Balcones de Aragón (Cienfuegos 289, tel. 051/211982, www.losbalconesdearagon.cl, US$65 s, US$82 d) is an excellent choice with numerous amenities in a quiet location with parking; with the 18 percent IVA discount for foreigners, it's a fine value.

La Serena's traditional luxury choice, **Hotel Francisco de Aguirre** (Cordovez 210, tel. 051/222991, www.franciscodeaguirre.tie.cl, US$65–80 s, US$78-93 d) remains one of the city's best; rates differ for "standard" rooms and "superior" units; ask for IVA discounts.

Despite its location at a busy downtown intersection, the stylishly modern 【 **Hotel Costa Real** (Av. Francisco de Aguirre 170, tel. 051/221010, www.costareal.cl, US$90 s, US$98 d) has curbside appeal, gracious management, and 51 comfortable rooms with all amenities.

US$100-150

Along the beach, with endless views to the north, the seven-story **Hotel La Serena Club Resort** (Av. del Mar 1000, tel. 051/221262, www.laserenaclubresort.cl, US$128–151 s or d) offers comfortable standard rooms and more spacious suites with private balconies at just slightly higher prices; though the mid-1990s structure is showing minor wear, everything works well and the service is efficient and friendly. Amenities include a large pool set among sprawling lawns and maturing palms, clay tennis courts, and a restaurant (whose breakfast includes fresh seasonal fruit).

FOOD

La Serena's restaurant scene has stagnated. To get creative food, served with style, it's essential to go to nearby Coquimbo, even though

La Serena's hotels are more numerous and mostly better.

For breakfast, ice cream, desserts, and coffee, try **Coffee Express** (Prat 490, tel. 051/221673) or the similar **Que Diablo** (Prat 563).

The **Casino de Bomberos** (Balmaceda and Colo Colo, tel. 051/225047) is a traditional lunch and dinner choice. Fixed-price lunches are a bargain. La Serena has several respectable *chifas*, such as **Mai Lan Fan** (Cordovez 740, tel. 051/214828).

Upstairs in the **Mercado La Recova** (Cienfuegos 370), a dozen crowded seafood eateries offer inexpensive lunches in the US$6–7 range that often include a free pisco sour. The quality is above average at places such as **Caleta Hornos** (Local 220, tel. 051/283356), but there are several others.

Grill-Bar Serena (Eduardo de la Barra 614, tel. 051/211962) serves good seafood at modest prices, especially for lunch; entrées cost around US$5–9. **Dónde El Guatón** (Brasil 750, tel. 051/211519) is a popular *parrilla* with beef dishes in the US$7–10 range, but it also serves fish.

Along Avenida del Mar, between the lighthouse and the suburb of Peñuelas, many seaside restaurants offer mostly seafood, such as **Tololo Beach** (Av. del Mar 5200, tel. 051/242656), but the food served at these establishments is not always as enjoyable as the seaside location.

Don Chuma (Av. del Mar 4661, tel. 249010) is a modest but popular place across from the beach, so it lacks the views that the literal beachfront restaurants enjoy. It does have fresh fish dishes, mostly in the US$7–10 range, and specialties such as *chupe de locos* (abalone casserole, US$10). The service is fine, but the conservative wine list includes only the biggest Chilean producers.

Bakulic (Av. del Mar 5700, tel. 051/245715) has a prime beachfront location, assiduous service, and above-average seafood specialties such as *pastel de jaiva* (crab casserole, US$10), but the seafood *parrillada* might be the best choice for a group. There are good wines by the glass.

INFORMATION

On the west side of the Plaza de Armas, **Sernatur** (Matta 461, tel./fax 051/225199, infocoquimbo@sernatur.cl) is open 8:30 A.M.–9 P.M. daily in December, January, and February; the rest of the year, hours are 8:30 A.M.–5:30 P.M. weekdays and on holiday weekends.

At the Terminal de Buses (Amunátegui s/n), the Municipalidad operates an **Oficina de Información Turística** (tel. 051/206631), open weekdays 8:30 A.M.–1:30 P.M. and 3–5:30 P.M., but it's more erratic than Sernatur.

The **Automóvil Club de Chile** (Acchi, Av. Francisco de Aguirre 447, tel. 051/550070) provides motorist information.

Conaf's **Patrimonio Silvestre** office (Ruta 41 s/n, tel. 051/272798 or 051/272799) is just west of Aeropuerto La Florida.

SERVICES

La Serena has several exchange houses, including **Herrera y Espinosa** (Balmaceda 460, Local 1) and **Cambios Talinay** (Prat 548). Numerous banks on and around the Plaza de Armas have ATMs.

On the Plaza's west side, **Correos de Chile** (Matta and Prat) is the post office. **Entel** (Prat 575) has long-distance telephone service. In the Café Bohemia complex, **Talinay Adventure Expeditions** (Prat 460) has high-speed Internet, but there are many others. Bohemia itself has WiFi.

Lavaseco Nevada (Los Carrera 635) can handle the washing.

Hospital Juan de Diós (Balmaceda 916, tel. 051/200500) occupies an entire block also bounded by Juan de Diós Peni, Larraín Alcalde, and Anfión Muñoz. Its emergency entrance is at the southeast corner of the grounds, at Larraín Alcalde and Anfión Muñoz.

GETTING THERE
Air

Only domestic flights serve close-in **Aeropuerto La Florida** (Ruta 41 s/n, tel. 051/225944), a few kilometers east of downtown; a new international airport near Tongoy remains under consideration.

LAN (Balmaceda 406, tel. 051/225753 or 051/221531) average four or five flights daily to Santiago, with a couple flights per week to Antofagasta and occasionally to Copiapó.

Bus

Most regional services and long-distance services leave from **Terminal de Buses** (Amunátegui and Av. El Santo, tel. 051/224573), but some companies also have downtown ticket offices. Elqui Valley buses also stop at the **Plaza de Abasto** (Colo Colo and Av. Cisternas).

Buses Serenamar (tel. 051/211735, www .serenamar.cl) serves the southerly Panamericana resorts of Guanaqueros and Tongoy (US$2) every 20 minutes 8 A.M.– 8:30 P.M. Several carriers go to Upper Elqui Valley destinations, such as Vicuña (US$3, 1 hour) and Pisco Elqui (US$3.50, 1.5 hours), but the main one is **Vía Elqui** (tel. 051/314710), which has eight buses daily to Vicuña, nearly all of which continue to Pisco Elqui.

Postal Bus (tel. 051/211707) goes several times daily to the pilgrimage center of Andacollo (US$2, 1 hour).

Numerous long-distance southbound and northbound Panamericana carriers stop in La Serena. Sample destinations, fares, and times include Santiago (US$17–23, 6 hours), Valparaíso/Viña del Mar (US$17–28, 7 hours), Los Vilos (US$10–13, 3 hours), Vallenar (US$9–15, 2.5 hours), Copiapó (US$13–21, 5 hours), Chañaral (US$16–23, 7 hours), Antofagasta (US$42–59, 12 hours), Calama (US$45–67, 16 hours), Iquique (US$49–69, 18 hours), and Arica (US$64–76, 21 hours).

Most international travelers bound for Argentina must change buses in Santiago, but in summer **Buses Covalle** (Infante 538, tel. 051/213127) goes directly to the Argentine cities of Mendoza and San Juan (US$42, 14 hours, the same price for either city) via the Libertadores tunnel, Tuesday, Thursday, and Sunday. **Cata** (tel. 051/218744) also goes to Mendoza.

Taxi Colectivo

Most *taxi colectivos* leave from Domeyko, a blocklong street between Balmaceda and O'Higgins, just north of and parallel to Colo Colo. Those to Coquimbo, however, leave from the north side of Avenida Francisco de Aguirre, between Balmaceda and Los Carrera.

Tacso (Domeyko 510, tel. 051/215507) serves Andacollo, Ovalle, and the Elqui Valley destinations of Vicuña and Pisco Elqui. **Línea Coquimbo-Elqui** (Domeyko 565, tel. 051/224517) also serves the Elqui Valley. **Anserco** (Domeyko 530, tel. 051/217567) goes to Andacollo as well. **Fremop** (Domeyko and O'Higgins) goes to Ovalle.

GETTING AROUND

SHE (tel. 051/295058) shuttles passengers to La Florida (US$3 pp).

Car-rental agencies include the downtown **Automóvil Club de Chile** (Acchi, Av. Francisco de Aguirre 455, tel. 051/217583) and several west of the Panamericana: **Avis** (Av. Francisco de Aguirre 063, tel. 051/227171), **Budget** (Av. Francisco de Aguirre 015, tel. 051/218272), **Econorent** (Av. Francisco de Aguirre 0135, tel. 051/220113), and **Hertz** (Av. Francisco de Aguirre 0225, tel. 051/218925).

Vicinity of La Serena

Serena-based agencies generally offer excursions to regional attractions such as Reserva Nacional Pingüino de Humboldt, the Elqui Valley, the Mamalluca municipal observatory, and international observatories such as Cerro Tololo, La Silla, and La Campana; those that don't can book them through other operators. While it's possible to do many of these excursions independently, booking them with an agency can simplify the logistics to areas where public transportation is limited or even nonexistent.

Talinay Adventure Expeditions (Prat 470, Local 22, tel./fax 051/218658, cel. 09/8360-6464, www.talinaychile.com) does full-day excursions to the Elqui Valley, Reserva Nacional Pingüino de Humboldt, and the La Silla or La Campana observatory. It also offers activity-oriented trips such as diving, horseback riding, and sea kayaking, and more demanding expedition-style excursions such as the summit of Ojos del Salado.

Other reliable agencies with similar offerings include **Ingservtur** (Matta 611, tel. 051/220165, www.ingservtur.cl), **Inti Mahina Travel** (Prat 214, tel. 051/224350, www.intimahinatravel.cl), **Turismo Lancuyén** (O'Higgins 336, tel. 051/214744, www.turismolancuyen.cl), and **Turismo Delfines** (Matta 591-A, tel. 051/223624, www.turismoaventuradelfines.cl).

Typical excursions and charges include the La Serena/Coquimbo city tour (US$20), the Valle de Elqui (US$28), Mamalluca observatory (US$25), Parque Nacional Bosque de Fray Jorge (US$42), and the Reserva Nacional Pingüino de Humboldt (US$47).

◖ COQUIMBO

At the south end of its namesake bay, on a rocky headland only 15 kilometers from La Serena, Coquimbo's tourist profile is growing, thanks partly to its vernacular blue-collar historic tradition and the beaches that stretch north and south. Only recently, though, its rejuvenated Barrio Inglés historic district has made Coquimbo a destination in its own right for nightlife, surpassing La Serena's moribund offerings.

The Romeral iron mine north of La Serena, which ships its ore to the mechanized port on the south side of the Coquimbo peninsula, remains the dominant economic force, but the Barrio Inglés evinces an infectious liveliness and optimism that bodes well for the city's future. In late 2008, the city hosted the under-20 women's World Cup at its new soccer stadium.

History

Coquimbo (population 154,316) is the region's main port, a 19th-century city that grew slowly with copper exports—in 1852, seven years after its official port designation, it had only about 40 houses of inhabitants to help service the Edwards and Lambert smelter, just north of La Serena, that became its prime economic motor. Within a few years the area had eight smelters, and the city grid, designed by French architect Jean Herbage in apparent defiance of the rugged topography, began to fill in.

Sights

Coquimbo's major contemporary landmark is the conspicuous 93-meter **Cruz del Tercer Milenio** (Cross of the Third Millennium), which sits atop Cerro El Vigía and offers 360-degree views of the peninsula. Besides three symmetrical columns symbolizing the Holy Trinity, there are a dozen pillars representing Christ's apostles, 10 smaller columns signifying the Ten Commandments, and 2,000 steps standing for the years of Christianity. It's open 9:30 A.M.–6:30 P.M. daily.

The cross is not the only monument to reach for the heavens. To the southeast, atop Cerro Dominante, the 15-story minaret of the

Centro Cultural Mohammed VI is a joint project of Morocco's king and the municipality of Coquimbo (home to a Muslim community of Lebanese origin).

On Plaza Gabriela Mistral, adjacent to the municipal tourist office, the **Museo de Sitio** is a pre-Diaguita cemetery dating from Las Ánimas times, about A.D. 900–1000. Excavations in the process of demolishing several buildings to expand the plaza unearthed evidence of a local variant that combined maritime subsistence with herding of llamas and alpacas and sacrificed domestic animals to be buried with their owners. Archaeologists from La Serena's archaeological museum also found sophisticated metallurgy, primarily copper, and ceramics, along with bone tools and projectile points.

From the Terminal Pesquero on Avenida Costanera, hour-long **harbor tours** through **Turismo Ensenada** (tel. 051/315295, www.turismo-ensenada.cl, US$3 pp) on the *Catamarán Mistral* include a visit to an offshore sea lion colony. In summer, there are hourly departures 11 A.M.–7 P.M.; the rest of the year, excursions take place at 3 P.M. weekdays and at 1, 3, and 5 P.M. weekends and holidays.

Entertainment

Coffe El Mural (Freire 387, cel. 09/9873-2761) is a combination coffee shop, bar, meeting place, and antiques outlet (though arranged with care and style, virtually all of the objects within are for sale).

Coquimbo has a plethora of contemporary pubs, but also a **Club de Tango** (Aldunate 631, tel. 051/328663), with a 30-year history of milongas and lessons. Presently it's open around 8:30 P.M. Thursday–Sunday.

Accommodations

Most people stay in La Serena, but Coquimbo has options worth consideration. In the historic Barrio Inglés, the HI affliate **Hostal Nómade** (Regimiento Coquimbo 5, tel. 051/315665, www.hostalnomade.cl, US$10–13 pp in dorms, US$17–25 s, US$23–30 d) occupies a distinctive mid-19th century residence that once housed the French consulate. It's retained the original configuration, so all the rooms are spacious and have high ceilings, and they contain many antiques including some of the beds (which have firm new mattresses). For the truly budget conscious, there's also camping (US$5 pp).

Though past its prime, friendly **Hotel Iberia** (Lastra 400, tel. 051/312141, www.hoteliberia.cl US$11–15 s, US$18–26 d) has brightened up and retains its tumbledown charm. Rates include breakfast and TV, and some rooms have balconies; the cheaper rooms have shared baths.

Hotel de la Bahía (Avenida Costanera 5351, tel. 051/423000, www.enjoy.cl, US$123–444 s or d) is the beachfront hotel for Coquimbo's new casino and, as such, closely resembles Enjoy's Hotel del Mar in Viña del Mar. All the rooms are spacious and have sea views, but the balconies are not so large as those at Viña.

Food

After a promising start, the Barrio Inglés's gourmet ghetto has become more of a pub grub scene, and one unfortunate side effect is that virtually all of these establishments are free fire zones for tobacco abusers. The most striking of them is **Fusión** (Aldunate 708, tel. 051/324816, open nightly except Sun.), which occupies an erstwhile private home with 15-foot ceilings, small balconies facing onto the street and nearby murals, and a rooftop dining room with expansive views of the Barrio Inglés, Coquimbo harbor, and La Serena's shoreline in the distance (best at sunset).

Beyond the Barrio Inglés, the Hotel de la Bahía's standard restaurants **La Barquera** and its **Hanami Sushibar** are worthwhile even for those who don't care to drop their coins into the slots.

Information

In a dome on the center of Plaza Gabriela Mistral, Coquimbo's municipal **Oficina de Información Turística** (Las Heras 220, tel. 051/322615, www.municipalidaddecoquimbo.cl) is theoretically open 9 A.M.–6 P.M. weekdays, but sometimes in summer only.

NORTE CHICO

Getting There and Around

Coquimbo's **Terminal Rodoviario** (Varela 1300, tel. 051/326651) has long-distance services similar to La Serena's. There are frequent local buses and *taxi colectivos* between the two cities and south to Guanaqueros and Tongoy.

TONGOY

About 45 kilometers south of Coquimbo, straddling an isthmus between a rocky promontory and an estuary floodplain flanked by two sandy beaches, the modest resort of Tongoy makes a fine excursion from La Serena—after a swim at the sandy northside Playa Socos, cross the isthmus for lunch at any of the beachfront *marisquerías* at the hard-packed Playa Grande.

For those who choose to stay overnight, Tongoy's well-worn **Hotel Yachting Club** (Av. Costanera 20, tel. 051/391259, yachtingclub@ hotmail.com, US$58 s or d) is less grand than it sounds. Almost next door, the modernist **Hostería Tongoy Costa** (Av. Costanera 10, tel. 051/391203, hosteriatongoycosta@yahoo. es US$80 s or d) is a better option.

Visitors jam the numerous *marisquerías,* such as **La Picá del Veguita** (Av. Playa Grande s/n, tel. 051/391220), for seafood.

Getting There and Around

Frequent buses and *taxi colectivos* from La Serena and Coquimbo continue to Tongoy.

CALETA LOS HORNOS

About 35 kilometers north of La Serena, straddling the Panamericana, Caleta los Hornos is a tumbledown fishing village that's home to several seafood *picadas* and a beach camping area with water, toilets, and cold showers. For lunch, try **Entre Rocas** (tel. 051/224393), which has fresh fish, good fried empanadas of crab and scallops, and superb sea views from a balcony that may be a little too sunny for some. Service is efficient; prices are moderate.

◀ RESERVA NACIONAL PINGÜINO DE HUMBOLDT

Increasingly popular for its prolific wildlife, which includes both birds and marine mammals, Reserva Nacional Pingüino de Humboldt comprises three islands, two of them—**Isla Damas** and **Isla Choros**—in Region IV and easily accessible from La Serena. The third, **Isla Chañaral,** belongs to Region III (Atacama) and is less frequented, while a fourth island closer to the continent, Isla Gaviotas, is the site of a deplorable real-estate scheme.

Totaling about 860 hectares of land area, surrounded by cobalt Pacific waters, the reserve is home to breeding populations of *Spheniscus humboldti,* also known as the Peruvian penguin. Other nesting seabirds include boobies, cormorants, and gulls, while mammals include bottle-nosed dolphins, sea lions, and even the occasional *chungungo* (sea otter). Humpbacks, blue whales, and orcas have been spotted around Isla Chañaral.

Sights

From Caleta los Hornos, the Panamericana switchbacks up the Cuesta de Buenos Aires, past the abandoned hilltop iron mine at **El Tofo.** At a junction near Trapiche, 77 kilometers from La Serena, a rugged gravel road heads west to olive-growing **Choros,** Chile's most southerly desert oasis. From Choros, a sandy road continues to **Caleta de Choros,** where fishing launches (US$75–85 for up to 10 people) carry passengers out to 320-hectare **Isla Choros,** whose rocky shoreline offers glimpses of the abundant birdlife (landing is prohibited). En route, pods of curious dolphins dive, surface, and criss-cross beneath and around the boat.

Of the reserve's three islands, only 60-hectare **Isla Damas** is open to landings—though no more than 50 people may visit at any one time. A one-kilometer trail links the two principal beaches: the steep, narrow **Playa La Poza** at the landing and the broader, longer, and less visited **Playa Tijeras.**

Information

At Caleta de Choros, 114 kilometers from La Serena, Conaf's **Centro de Información Ambiental** has exceptional displays on local ecology and environment. It also collects a US$2.50 admission charge, applicable to everyone except those camping at Isla Damas.

Accommodations and Food

On Isla Damas, Conaf's **Camping Playa La Poza** costs US$20 per site for up to six people, with a maximum stay of two nights; for reservations contact Conaf's Patrimonio Silvestre office (tel. 051/272798) in La Serena. The campground has toilets but no fresh water or food (though local fisherfolk will sell part of the day's catch). Campstoves are obligatory for cooking, and campers must pack out trash.

If there's no room on the island, try **Camping El Memo** at Caleta de Choros, where sites cost US$20. Some supplies are available at Caleta de Choros but, except for fresh fish, La Serena has a much wider selection.

Getting There and Around

From La Serena, **Héctor Moyano** (tel. 051/253206) provides round-trip transportation to Punta de Choros (US$13 pp); call to confirm departure times, normally around 9 A.M. but occasionally earlier in summer.

Numerous La Serena travel agencies conduct day tours. If driving, note that the gravel road from Trapiche to Choros can be hell on tires.

ANDACOLLO

Every December 26, more than 100,000 pilgrims overrun the gold- and copper-mining center of Andacollo, in a narrow canyon 53 kilometers southeast of La Serena, to pay homage to the Virgen de Andacollo. With the ambience of a colonial Mexican mountain town, Andacollo is, along with Lo Vásquez and La Tirana, one of Chile's key pilgrimage sites.

At 1,050 meters above sea level, Andacollo is cool and breezy much of the time, thanks to the influence of the coastal *camanchaca*. *Pirquineros,* small-scale gold miners, still grind their ore in more than 30 *trapiches* or artisanal mills in the vicinity; local kids will, for a small tip, lead visitors to view the miners at work.

In the shadow of Andacollo's imposing Basílica, its Plaza Pedro Nolasco Videla features a crafts market distinguished by local stone carvings, but even here, "positive energy" quartz crystals compete with mementos of the Virgen for devotion.

Except for truly dedicated pilgrims, Andacollo makes a better day trip than an overnight, though travelers with their own cars or serious cyclists might consider continuing on the decent gravel road that goes south to the Hurtado Valley, where it's possible to loop to Vicuña and back to La Serena, or else go west to Ovalle. Some newer sights, such as the nearby observatory, will appeal to more secular tastes.

Sights

Italian architect Eusebio Celli designed Andacollo's **Templo Grande** or **Basílica,** built of Douglas fir from California, in a Roman-Byzantine style. Begun on Christmas Day 1873 under Monseñor José Manuel Orrego's direction, it was inaugurated exactly 20 years later by Monseñor Florencio Fontecilla. Sited on the plaza's north side, it is now a national monument.

Including the plaza, the Basílica can hold 10,000 worshippers. It is 70 meters long, with five separate naves, and 30 meters wide for most of its length, though the cross-style floor plan reaches a maximum 40-meter width. The central arch is 24 meters high, while the twin towers reach 50 meters and the central cupola 45 meters. The 6-meter foundations work toward seismic safety; sheets of galvanized iron cover adobe walls.

On the plaza's west side, the smaller **Templo Antiguo** (1789) contains the **Museo de Ofrendas de la Virgen** (Videla s/n, tel. 051/431525, www.santuarioandacollo.cl) that holds all the adornments used in ceremonies on December 26. Open 10 A.M.–1 P.M. and 3–6 daily, it also holds ex-votos brought by believers in tribute to the Virgen, including model ships built by Coquimbo stevedores (apparently her strongest devotees).

It's housed in parochial property, but

NORTE CHICO

Andacollo's new **Sala Museográfica de Yahuin** (Urmeneta and Quitería Vargas, tel. 051/432367, www.yahuin.cl) does a fine job of chronicling the area's pre-Columbian past. The government agency Fondart and the Minería de Carmen mining company have partly sponsored these professionally mounted archaeological displays that cover local history from the earliest hunter-gatherers through the Molle, Las Ánimas, and Diaguita cultures to the Inka invasion. Admission costs US$0.50 except Sundays, when it's free.

Events

Typified by enthusiastic dancers known as *chinos,* who fill the plaza and surrounding streets in procession, the **Fiesta de la Virgen de Andacollo** takes place the day after Christmas. Many pilgrims arrive on foot from La Serena or elsewhere for the fiesta, which dates from the 16th century, when legend says a Spaniard saved her carved image from the destruction of La Serena during an indigenous rebellion. The present image of the Virgen del Rosario came from Lima in the 17th century.

In addition to the main fiesta, the Virgen also parades through town during the **Fiesta Chica,** the first Sunday in October.

Accommodations and Food

At the south end of Urmeneta, beyond the bus and *taxi colectivo* stops, are half a dozen or more roughly comparable *residenciales,* charging less than US$10 per person. During the annual fiesta, pilgrims camp just about anywhere they like.

La Rueda (Urmeneta 657, tel. 051/431600) has simple but well-prepared meals in the US$4–6 range, complemented by excellent service. **La Chilenita** (Urmeneta 534, tel. 051/431574) is similar.

Getting There

Taxi colectivos from La Serena, the fastest and most efficient way to get here, cost around US$3 per person.

Vicuña and Vicinity

East of La Serena, paved Ruta 41 climbs gradually up the Elqui Valley, through irrigated fields of citrus, chirimoya, and papaya, to the village of Vicuña, once home to Nobel Prize–winning poet Gabriela Mistral. She's still a presence here but, at the same time, it's also the site of Chile's only major municipal observatory and a prominent pisco distillery—the Upper Elqui Valley grows many of the grapes that generate the region's signature alcoholic beverage.

About midway to Vicuña, the road detours through a tunnel with a view of the Embalse Puclaro, a 80-meter-high dam whose sprawling reservoir, with a capacity of 200 million cubic meters of water, inundated several villages, parts of the Río Elqui, and the old highway.

ORIENTATION

About 62 kilometers east of La Serena, 623 meters above sea level on the Río Elqui's north bank, Vicuña (population 12,910) consists of a compact grid whose main thoroughfare, Avenida Gabriela Mistral, runs east–west. Ruta 41 from La Serena, which passes south and east of town, continues to the Argentine border at Paso Aguas Negras, where Argentina's Ruta Nacional 150 continues to the hot-springs resort of Pismanta and the provincial capital of San Juan. On the Elqui's south side, a scenic but dusty road crosses the Portezuelo Tres Cruces to the Río Hurtado Valley, a rugged but scenic alternative route to Ovalle for motorists and mountain bikers.

SIGHTS

Most sights are on or near the densely landscaped **Plaza de Armas,** with its canopy of mature peppers, palms, and other trees, and a large bandshell often used for open-air

© WAYNE BERNHARDSON

Torre Bauer, Vicuña

concerts. On the plaza's west side, at Mistral and San Martín, the offbeat **Torre Bauer** (1905) literally towers above the city—its wooden battlements resemble a medieval castle from former mayor Alfonso Bauer's ancestral Germany. Immediately to its south is the deco-style **Teatro Municipal.**

Kitty-corner from the Torre Bauer, on the foundations of the earlier Iglesia La Merced, the **Iglesia de la Inmaculada Concepción** (1909) has its own distinctive wooden tower; the ceiling murals beneath its arched roof, supported by impressive wooden columns, have benefited from recent restoration work. The church also displays Gabriela Mistral's baptismal font.

[Museo Gabriela Mistral

In some ways, Vicuña's Gabriela Mistral museum seems more a pilgrimage site, where the devout file quietly past images of the saint and

her relics. Unlike the gregarious Pablo Neruda, Chile's other Nobel Prize poet, Mistral was subdued, even dour, and this low-key museum reflects her personality as much as Neruda's three extravagant heartland houses did his.

Among Mistral's relics is a full-sized replica of her nearby Monte Grande birthplace, which, as it contains some original doors and windows, is a designated national monument. Born Lucila Godoy Alcayaga in 1889 of mixed descent—Spanish, indigenous, and perhaps African—she may have created her pseudonym by combining the names of Italian poet and novelist Gabriel D'Annunzio and French Provençal poet Frédéric Mistral (a 1904 Nobel Prize winner); an alternative explanation says she may have combined the name of the archangel Gabriel with that of Mediterranean France's cold, dry north wind.

Mistral began writing in local newspapers and Chilean magazines and fell under the influence of Nicaragua's famous poet Rubén Darío, who spent several years in South America. Like Darío, and Neruda for that matter, she occupied a variety of diplomatic posts in foreign locales; for Mistral, these include Los Angeles, Santa Barbara, New York City, Florida, Cuba, Guatemala, Brazil, Oporto, Madrid, Nice, and Italy. Some Chilean rightists accused her of being a Communist (ironically enough for someone who may have admired Mussolini's ardent partisan D'Annunzio), but she maintained public neutrality, even seeming apolitical (unlike Neruda, who proudly proclaimed his Communist beliefs).

Among the exhibits are a photographic biography, a bookstore that includes titles she donated to Vicuña's library, and a forbidding bust whose grim expression must have intimidated her students, even as her writing suggested affection for them. There's a copy of her Nobel Prize check, which bought her a house in the United States.

The Museo Gabriela Mistral (Gabriela Mistral 759, tel. 051/411223, www.mgmistral.cl) charges US$1 admission. January–February hours are 10 A.M.–7 P.M. daily. March–December, hours are 10 A.M.–5:45 P.M.

NORTE CHICO

weekdays, 10 A.M.–6 P.M. Saturday, and 10 A.M.–1 P.M. Sunday and holidays.

Museo Entomológico e Historia Natural

Proving what a dedicated, enthusiastic amateur can achieve, Guido Castillo has done a remarkable job of organizing this extensive collection of mostly South American insects, providing taxonomic details and illustrating their geographical distribution. The museum also contains a selection of regional minerals and fossils and taxidermy specimens with equally useful information.

A pleasant surprise, the Museo Entomológico (Chacabuco 334, cel. 09/93237177, insects_castilloi@yahoo.es) is open 10:30 A.M.–7 P.M. daily except in January and February, when it stays open until 8 P.M. Admission costs US$1 for adults, half that for kids.

Museo Histórico de Elqui

Stagnant in its content and approach, Vicuña's historical museum remains a "museum of the kitchen sink," with minerals, fossils, Diaguita ceramics, and a congeries of household objects gleaned from around the valley. One room displays photos of Gabriela Mistral, most of which appear, under better conditions, in the Mistral museum.

In January and February, the Museo Histórico (Prat 90, cel. 09/97438430, mhelqui@yahoo.com.ar) is open 10 A.M.–2 P.M. daily, 4–9 P.M. Monday–Saturday. The rest of the year, afternoon hours are 3:30–6 P.M. daily except Sunday. Admission costs US$0.65 for adults, US$0.35 for students, and US$0.25 for kids.

Casa de los Madariaga

Built by an influential landowning family, this historic adobe (1875) is now a private museum with eight rooms of antiques, artifacts, and photographs from the late 19th century. The Casa de los Madariaga (Gabriela Mistral 683, tel. 051/411220) is open 10 A.M.–7 P.M. daily; admission costs US$0.85 for adults, US$0.50 for seniors, and children get in free.

Cerro de la Virgen

For views of Vicuña and the Elqui Valley, follow the footpath or road up to this pilgrimage site, where an image of the Virgen de Lourdes overlooks the city. Though it's barely an hour to the top, hikers should carry water and snacks.

ENTERTAINMENT AND EVENTS

There's little nightlife in Vicuña, but try **Pub Kharma** (Gabriela Mistral 417, tel. 051/419738). In summer, the Municipalidad sponsors live concerts in the Plaza de Armas; the connecting streets may be blocked off and admission charged, but it's possible to hear the music from nearby.

Vicuña's late-summer **Festival de la Vendimia** (Grape Harvest Festival) climaxes on February 22, the city's anniversary.

SHOPPING

On the north side of the Plaza de Armas, the **Pueblo de Artesanos** is an attractive retail space for local products ranging from pisco and papaya to honey, jewelry, and leather.

ACCOMMODATIONS

Vicuña has relatively few places to stay, but quality is good to excellent in all categories. Even **Residencial Mistral** (Gabriela Mistral 180, tel. 051/411278, US$5 pp with shared bath) is okay.

The best budget choice, though, is nearby **Casa del Profesor** (Gabriela Mistral 152, tel. 051/412026, US$8 pp), which has modern garden rooms with private baths, breakfast, and TVs, situated behind a distinctive early-20th-century house with shady galleries. The gardens could be tidier, but the beds (some of them bunks) and baths are new, and the breakfast is a step above others in its price range. It's best to reserve your room at least a week in advance.

Set among gardens and orchards, **Residencial La Elquina** (O'Higgins 65, tel. 051/411317, la_elquina@hotmail.com, US$10 pp, US$30 s or d) has rooms with either shared or private baths, but too many beds clutter some of them.

Near the Mistral museum, the motel-style **Hotel Sol del Valle** (Gabriela Mistral 739, tel. 051/411078, www.hotelsoldelvalle.cl, US$23 s, US$33 d with breakfast) has decent rooms on spacious grounds, with a pool and a friendly white dog.

In an older colonial-style house with an appealing patio, **Hostal Aldea de Elqui Hermoso** (Gabriela Mistral 706, tel./fax 051/543068, www.hostalaldeadelelqui.cl US$25 s, US$42 d) has reinvented itself as a vaguely New Age hostelry that offers sitar solos on its website and, among other services, Tarot readings, WiFi, and parking.

Furnished with antiques and remodeled with colonial style, but with amenities including a swimming pool and on-site parking, **◖ Hotel Halley** (Gabriela Mistral 542, tel. 051/412070, US$47 s or d) is one of the country's best values, even more so with IVA discounts.

Hostería Yunkai (O'Higgins 72, tel. 051/411195, yunkai@latinmail.com, US$50 s or d) offers kitchen facilities and a pool. In addition to a quiet garden location at the west end of town, **Hostería Vicuña** (Sargento Aldea 101, tel. 051/411301, www.hosteriavicuna.cl, US$69 s, US$80 d) boasts amenities such as a restaurant, tennis courts, and a swimming pool.

FOOD

Vicuña has relatively few places to eat but, again, reasonable quality. The rather ordinary **Pizzería Virgo** (Prat 234, tel. 051/411090) is at least moderately priced.

The **Club Social de Vicuña** (Gabriela Mistral 445, tel. 051/411853) serves a traditional Chilean menu at above-average prices in comfortable surroundings. Across the street, **El Gelatto** (Gabriela Mistral 438) produces small batches of fruit-flavored ice cream on site.

Cabrito (grilled kid goat, US$8.50 including a large diverse salad) is the house specialty at **◖ Restaurant Halley** (Gabriela Mistral 410, tel. 051/411225), which also offers a good wine selection, good service, and indoor and outdoor

seating (the latter shaded by *totora* mats). Other entrées—a cornucopia of poultry, beef, pork, fish, and shellfish—range US$6–15.

Vicuña's most distinctive restaurant is as notable for *how* as for *what* it cooks. In the nearby village of Villaseca, easily reached by *taxi colectivo*, the **Restaurant Solar de Villaseca** (Punta Arenas s/n, tel. 051/1982184, daily for lunch and dinner except Sun.) cooks and bakes everything in simply designed but effective solar ovens that have made it a sight in itself. Run by a women's collective, who say it's "gotten us out of the vineyards," it's enormously popular for fixed-price lunches such as kid goat casserole with brown rice (US$8, including an aperitif, salad, and dessert). It's best for lunch (when the sun is highest) to see the baking in action; reservations are essential on weekends.

INFORMATION AND SERVICES

In the Torre Bauer, the municipal **Oficina de Información Turística** (San Martín s/n, tel. 051/209125, luisvigorena@123mail.cl) is open 8:30 A.M.–5:30 P.M. daily except Sunday, when hours are 9 A.M.–2 P.M.; January and February hours are slightly longer.

On the south side of the Plaza de Armas, **BancoEstado** (Chacabuco 384) changes U.S. cash and now has an ATM that works with foreign plastic.

Correos de Chile (Gabriela Mistral 270) has a post office at the Municipalidad, just west of the Plaza de Armas. **Telefónica** (Prat 378) has long-distance services. For Internet access, try **Cyber Drib** (Gabriela Mistral 604) or **Cibernauta** (Carrera 299).

Vicuña's **Hospital San Juan de Dios** (Independencia and Prat, tel. 051/411263) provides medical assistance.

GETTING THERE AND AROUND

Buses leave from the **Terminal Rodoviario de Vicuña** (Prat and O'Higgins, a block south of the Plaza de Armas). Several companies go to La Serena, including **Vía Elqui,** which also has eight buses daily to Pisco Elqui (US$2.50). **Expreso Norte** (tel. 051/411348) goes to Santiago and intermediates, but La Serena has better long-distance connections.

From the **Terminal de Taxi Colectivos** (Prat and O'Higgins), across the street from the Rodoviario, shared taxis go up the Elqui Valley to Paihuano (US$2), Monte Grande (US$2.50), and Pisco Elqui (US$3), and down the valley to La Serena (US$4).

The Upper Río Elqui

At Rivadavia, 18 kilometers east of Vicuña, two rivers converge to form the Elqui: The Río Turbio enters from the nearly uninhabited northeast, while the Río Claro descends from the south, an area marked by a series of scenic villages along a smooth paved road that goes all the way to Pisco Elqui and, as of summer 2009, was being paved to Alcohuaz. Just south of Monte Grande, a gravel road climbs southeast up the Río Cochiguaz Valley, famous (or infamous) for New Age flakiness.

Pisco producers may be complaining about competition from imported whiskey in the Chilean market, but their newly planted vines continue climbing the slopes of rocky alluvial fans; apricots also grow abundantly in the Upper Claro drainage, and huge new avocado plantings are scaling the hillsides as well.

The scenery, fresh dry climate, and clear skies are making the Upper Elqui watershed an increasingly popular destination, but it's also attracted Chile's largest concentration of New Age and UFO aficionados—to the frustration and embarrassment of the serious astronomers at area observatories.

PAIHUANO

Paihuano, 30 kilometers from Vicuña and 978 meters above sea level, is a shady riverside service center. In the Municipalidad, directly on the highway, its exceptionally helpful **Oficina de Turismo** (tel. 051/451015, odel_paihuano@ hotmail.com) has information on every locality up the Río Claro drainage, including Pisco Elqui and Cochiguaz. Hours are 8 A.M.–4 P.M. weekdays except Friday, when it closes half an hour earlier.

Paihuano has excellent new accommodations in the Diaguita-motif **[Casa Puka Yana** (Balmaceda 117, tel. 051/451037, www .casapukayana.cl, US$33 s, US$50 d with shared bath, US$58 d with private bath), with friendly English-speaking owners, fashionable and comfortable furniture, and a huge garden with a pool and fruit trees. Rates include breakfast.

MONTE GRANDE

Ten kilometers south of Paihuano, Gabriela Mistral's Monte Grande birthplace is also the site of her hillside final resting place, **Tumba de Gabriela Mistral**—though she lived most of her life elsewhere and much of it outside the country, her will stipulated that her body be interred in her "dear village" of Monte Grande in the Elqui Valley.

Monte Grande is home to the **Museo de Sitio Casa Escuela Gabriela Mistral,** a former public school that served as the local post office until its restoration in the early 1980s; with Mistral's tomb and the nearby church, it makes up a *zona típica* national monument. Though it displays many of the same photos as other regional museums, it does have some original furniture. Open 10 A.M.–1 P.M. and 3–6 P.M. daily except Monday, it charges US$0.50 admission. In January and February, hours are 10 A.M.–7 P.M.

Monte Grande is also the site of the Artesanos de Cochiguaz pisco plant, but its big surprise is **Cavas del Valle** (Fundo El Campanario, tel. 051/451352, www.cavasdelvalle.cl), a minnow of a boutique winery in an ocean of pisco producers. In a stylish rehabbed

© WAYNE BERNHARDSON

Destilería Los Nichos, near Pisco Elqui, is a small-scale pisco producer.

colonial building, with state-of-the-art equipment, it produces just 22,000 bottles per year of organic syrah and its specialty *cosecha otoñal,* a variety of late harvest. It's open for drop-in tours and tastings 10 A.M.–8 P.M. daily.

The restaurant **Mesón del Fraile** (tel. 051/1982608), directly on the highway through town, specializes in pizza.

C PISCO ELQUI

High in the Río Claro Valley, its modernized adobes fast becoming trophy houses, the hillside village of Pisco Elqui seems to be metamorphosing into a scale model of Santa Fe (New Mexico). At 1,247 meters above sea level, two kilometers south of Monte Grande on the Río Claro Canyon's steep southern slope, it boasts the area's best tourist infrastructure and a variety of activities, varying from souvenir hunting in the artisans' market to pisco tasting and horseback riding.

Formerly known as La Unión, Pisco Elqui changed names in 1939, at the urging of then-deputy (later president) Gabriel González

Videla, in the interest of product promotion—and from concern that the Peruvian city of Pisco, south of Lima, intended to register the term as an international trademark.

Sights and Recreation

Beneath the towering Gothic steeple of the **Capilla Nuestra Señora del Rosario** (1922), the shady **Plaza de Armas** is the site of summer's **Mercado Artesanal.** At the end of the block, the **Solar de Pisco Gabriela Mistral** provides tours and tasting, as does the **Destilería Los Nichos,** four kilometers farther up the valley. Six kilometers beyond Los Nichos, local government has constructed an elaborate **Pueblo Artesanal de Horcón** to give local craftsworkers a place to display and sell their goods; it's open 12:30–7 P.M. weekdays except Monday, and stays open an hour longer weekends and holidays.

Alcohuaz Expediciones (Prat s/n, tel. 051/451168, www.caballo-elqui.cl) offers horseback rides into the outback.

NORTE CHICO

PICK OF THE PISCO

Wine tourism keeps growing in the Chilean heartland, but grapes from the Norte Chico make more pisco, the potent grape brandy that's the base of the legendary pisco sour. While pisco comes from all of the Norte Chico's transverse valleys – Copiapó, Huasco, Elqui, Límarí, and Choapa – the Elqui is the best to get to know Chile's preferred spirits.

Pisco derives from muscatel grapes, which thrive in the narrow valleys, where summer harvest temperatures average around 30°C and winter rains rarely exceed 120 millimeters. After harvest, the grapes are slowly milled and then fermented under strict temperature controls. After being stored as wine for a time, it undergoes slow distillation to extract the ethyl alcohol and other chemical components that typify the product. Finally, the liquor is stored in wooden casks just long enough to stabilize it.

Pisco comes in several categories, according to its alcoholic content (proof is expressed in terms of *grados*, or degrees): *selección* (30°); *especial* (35°); *reservado* (40°); and *gran pisco* (42-43°, but sometimes as high as 50°). It comes in a variety of containers, the most distinctive of them Capel's Easter Island souvenir *moai*.

One pisco sour, though, belongs in a category of its own: On February 16, 1999, opposite the Casino at Peñuelas, 800 people mixed 11,172 bottles of pisco (7,202 liters) with 96,000 lemons, 1,800 kilograms of refined sugar, and 3,724 kilograms of ice to prepare the world's largest ever. The result of their 24 hours' labor was 200,000 servings totaling 12,500 liters in 16,000 bottles.

DESTILERÍA LOS NICHOS

Four kilometers south of Pisco Elqui, Los Nichos (tel. 051/451085) is an old-fashioned distillery where all processing is done by hand in small batches. What's most interesting is the subterranean bodega, where a collection of antique wine- and pisco-processing equipment covers the floors and dusty bottles of aging sweet wine repose in the niches that give the place its name. At one time, smaller niches held human skulls found in the hills, but these have since been given a proper burial.

Los Nichos (tel. 051/451085) offers free tastings of pisco and *pajarete* 11 A.M.-1 P.M. and 2-7:30 P.M. daily.

LAGAR ARTESANOS DE COCHIGUAZ, MONTE GRANDE

Across from Gabriela Mistral's final resting place, Capel's premium brand offers a brief view of the milling process – the distilling is done in Vicuña rather than here – along with tasting and sales. For most Chileans, the highlight is Ruperto, an ostensibly boozing burro from the company's TV commercials – everyone wants to be photographed with him.

The Lagar (tel. 051/1982534) is open 10 A.M.-1 P.M. and 2:30-6 P.M. daily. Like the Vicuña plant, it's closed January 1, May 1, September 20, November 8, and December 25.

PLANTA CAPEL, VICUÑA

Capel, a 1,500-member cooperative of Norte Chico growers, is Elqui's other main producer (Capel stands for Cooperativa Agrícola Pisquera Elqui, Elqui Agro-Pisco Cooperative). More than 80 percent of the Elqui Valley's pisco grapes, in varying strengths, are distilled and bottled at its Vicuña plant, which offers

Accommodations and Food

Pisco Elqui's landmark accommodation is its cheapest, the singularly decrepit **Hostal Don Juan** (Prat s/n, tel. 051/451087, donjuan@ piscoelqui.cl, US$10 s, US$16 d), which may remind Hitchcock fans of the house behind the Bates Motel. It has its shortcomings, but

nowhere else can so little money buy so much character. **Hotel Elqui** (O'Higgins s/n, tel. 051/451130, habiles@ gmail.com, US$20 d with breakfast) is marginally better, and has a restaurant.

Down the block from the Don Juan, **Hotel Gabriela Mistral** (Arturo Prat 59,

© WAYNE BERNHARDSON

vineyards near Pisco Elqui

tours and tasting the entire year. Among the brands produced here are the standard Pisco Capel brand and the premium Los Artesanos de Cochiguaz, known for its woody flavor, in smaller batches. The plant also turns out the dessert wine *pajarete.*

An easy walk from Vicuña, on the Peralillo road on the south side of the river, Planta Capel (tel. 051/554396, www.centroturis-ticocapel.cl) offers guided tours (US$1.50 pp) 10 A.M.-6 P.M. daily in summer, 10 A.M.-12:30 P.M. and 2:30-6 P.M. the rest of the year. Individual attention is the rule – there is no minimum group size – and there's an ample sales room. It's closed January 1, May 1, September 20, November 8, and December 25.

SOLAR DE PISCO GABRIELA MISTRAL

In the trendy village of Pisco Elqui, Tres Erres (tel. 051/1982503) is as much a museum as a distillery, what with its antique machinery and aging bodegas, and it has undergone a major expansion. Tours and tasting take place 10 A.M.-7 P.M. daily except Monday in summer; the rest of the year, hours are 10:30 A.M.-1 P.M. and 2-6:30 P.M.

NORTE CHICO

tel. 051/451086, www.hotelgabrielamistral .cl, US$23 s, US$37 d) has large but worn rooms, as well as cabañas, and a decent bar/restaurant.

At the northern approach to Pisco Elqui, **Hotel Cotinai** (Sector La Jarilla, tel. 051/451137, hotelcotinai@yahoo.com, US$34 s, US$42 d) has spacious rooms, beds that vary from too-soft to firm, and a shady balcony with panoramic valley views (a mixed blessing, as the wood squeaks loudly underfoot). It also serves an abundant breakfast and has a pool.

Just across the street from Hostal Don Juan, **Hostería Los Dátiles** (Prat s/n, tel.

© WAYNE BERNHARDSON

Pisco Elqui's Hostal Don Juan might remind Hitchcock fans of the house behind the Bates Motel.

051/451266, www.losdatileselqui.cl, US$53 s or d with IVA discount) has half a dozen attractively landscaped cabañas with decks and kitchenettes. The fixed-price meals at its bar/restaurant, with Chilean country cooking in the US$7–12 range, are also worth a try.

Still German-run, but under new ownership, **El Tesoro de Elqui** (Prat s/n, tel. 051/451069, www.tesoroelqui.cl, US$15 pp, US$57 d) has earned a reputation not just for outstanding accommodations but also for exceptional food. Rooms vary from singles with shared baths to more elaborate cabañas with private baths, and there's also a pool, a book exchange, and other amenities, and one minor shortcoming: the unpruned apricots, plums, and other trees can drop prodigious amounts of rotting fruit on the ground.

Pisco Elqui's most stylish choice, **Refugio Misterios del Elqui** (Prat s/n, tel. 051/1982544, www.misteriosdeelqui.cl, US$81 d with IVA discount), rents six hillside view cabañas in a Mexican motif. It also has an appealing restaurant, with a French chef and shady balcony seating, that's open Wednesday–Sunday only.

At Los Nichos, about three kilometers beyond Pisco Elqui, **Elquidomos** (cel. 09/7709-2879, www.elquidomos.cl, US$82 s or d with IVA discounts) is a self-described "astronomical hotel" of geodesic domes, each with its own telescope. It also has a restaurant and a larger telescope for general use, and organizes excursions such as horseback and bicycle rides.

Across from the church, **Jugos Pizzería** (Centenario and Los Carrera) has refreshingly cold fruit juices, sandwiches, and pizzas in increasingly stylish surroundings; the owners also operate the next-door pub **Lado V. Rustik@** (Los Carrera s/n) serves tacos and drinks, along with Internet access.

Just uphill from the church, **El Ranchito de Don René** (Centenario s/n, tel. 051/451303) has shaded open-air dining with Chilean standards such as *pastel de choclo* (US$6), but the pisco sours are distressingly sugary.

New on the scene is **Escuela** (Prat and Baquedano), a hybrid bar/café that looks as if it were airlifted intact from Santiago's Bohemian Barrio Bellavista.

Getting There and Around

Both buses and *taxi colectivos* run regularly up and down the canyon to Vicuña, some of them continuing to La Serena.

COCHIGUAZ

Cochiguaz, an enclave of crystals, cosmic energy, and UFO sightings, is less a nucleated geographical community—the name applies to any part of the constricted Río Cochiguaz Canyon—than it is a state of mind. Even then, it's not so flagrantly flaky as some other New Age outposts, and there's even some self-effacing humor; the landmark Refugio El Alma Zen, for instance, is a punning Spanish reference to the irony of running a practical general store (*almacén* in Spanish) and its apparent Buddhist essence (standing apart, *alma* means "soul"). Still, it's tempting to suggest that the extraterrestrial sightings here may stem, at least in part, from all the pisco produced and consumed here.

Accommodations and Food

A string of cabañas and campgrounds runs the length of the canyon to the end of the road at El Colorado. Note that rural electrification has barely begun; the cabañas have solar power or their own generators, but the campgrounds, unlike those elsewhere in Chile, lack lights and any other hookups.

Cabañas Naturistas El Albaricoque (Km 6, cel. 09/7922-4529, carmenhurtado74@yahoo.com, US$68 s or d) rents several smallish but rustically comfortable *departamentos* and larger cabañas, sleeping up to five people. Breakfast and other (vegetarian) meals are extra. It also deals in alternative therapies and meditation workshops.

Refugio El Alma Zen (Km 11, cel. 09/9047-3861, US$68 s or d) is the canyon's most self-consciously kooky choice—in addition to solar-powered cabañas with private baths, hot water, and kitchen facilities, there's a quartz crystal swimming pool; Alma Zen now has a campground (US$6 pp) as well. Meanwhile, you can also have your aura cleansed or perform Tibetan rituals to recover your youth or do aroma Tarot.

A short distance on, the rather ragged **Camping Río Mágico** (Km 11, cel. 09/9593-3943, US$7 pp) celebrates events such as the Mayan New Year and also hosts a reggae festival for the conventional New Year.

Up the hill from Alma Zen, the **Spa Cochiguaz** (Km 11.5, cel. 09/8502-2723, www.cochiguaz.com, US$42 pp) features an octagonal hotel whose eight rooms surround a central complex of tub and massage therapy facilities; there are also separate cabañas and a vegetarian restaurant at this Ecuadorian-owned spiritual resort, which has a truly spectacular mountain setting.

Camping Tambo Huara (Km 12.5, cel. 09/9220-7237, US$6 pp) is the valley's best value for its attractively designed campsites, set among a mixed landscape of native plants and cultivated fruit trees. Like other sites along the road, it has a couple of meditation gardens, but it also offers spotless toilets, potable water at every site, and hot showers 9 A.M.–noon—not to mention a good portable telescope to observe the southern skies.

Just beyond Tambo Huara, **Cabañas Casa del Agua** (Km 13, tel. 051/321371, casadelagua@gmail.com, US$83 s or d) has more luxurious cabañas and is considerably less cultish. It offers many activities, including fishing, swimming, hiking, mountain biking, and horseback riding.

Getting There and Around

There's no regular public transport up the Cochiguaz Canyon, but hitching from the Monte Grande turnoff is feasible. Working pickup trucks and other vehicles may offer lifts from Monte Grande's Los Paltos restaurant.

PASO DEL AGUA NEGRA

From Rivadavia, international Ruta 41 ascends the Río Turbio Valley northeast and then southeast for 75 kilometers to the Chilean border post of Juntas del Toro, where it's another 92 kilometers southeast to the Argentine border and the 4,765-meter Paso del Agua Negra, where it continues to the spa of Termas de Pismanta and provincial capital of San Juan. From late November until the first April snows close the pass, the border is open 7 A.M.–5 P.M. daily.

As the road is being paved, public transportation to San Juan could begin soon. The road is the best way to see the barren *puna,* glaciers, and *penitentes,* frozen snow formations that resemble lines of monks dressed in the conical headgear known as *cucuruchos.*

OVALLE

Capital of Limarí province, Ovalle is a service center for farmers and fruit growers, but it's also the closest city to Parque Nacional Fray Jorge, the hot-springs resort of Termas de Socos, and the Molle archaeological site at Valle del Encanto. It's also become the gateway to the Upper Hurtado Valley, an area of growing interest for its access to the Pichasca petrified forest and backcountry horseback excursions. It takes its name from José Tomás Ovalle, Chile's vice president at the city's founding in 1831.

Orientation

Ovalle (population 73,790) is 88 kilometers south of La Serena by the paved two-lane Ruta 43, and 37 kilometers east from the Termas de Socos turnoff on the Panamericana. Its palm-studded Parque Alameda, between Ariztía Oriente and Ariztía Poniente, separates the main city grid to the west from the newer and slightly more irregular area to the east. Most services are to the west, in and around the Plaza de Armas.

Sights

On the east side of the Plaza de Armas, restored after 1997 earthquake damage, the adobe **Iglesia San Vicente Ferrer** (1849) features a distinctive bell tower and murals on its wooden ceiling.

Across the Alameda, in the former railroad station (built 1926–1930) the **Museo del Limarí** (Covarrubias and Antofagasta, tel. 053/433680, www.museolimari.cl) houses a collection of 1,700 ceramic pieces, primarily Diaguita (some of them Inka-influenced), though there are also earlier Huentelauquén and Molle artifacts. Hours are 9 A.M.–6 P.M. Tuesday–Friday, 10 A.M.–6 P.M. Saturday, 10 A.M.–1 P.M. Sunday only. Admission costs US$1 for adults, half that for children and seniors, but Sundays are free.

Farther east, the **Feria Modelo de Ovalle** (Benavente and Maestranza) is northern Chile's largest fruit and vegetable market. On the site of the former railroad repair yard, it's open Monday, Wednesday, Friday, and Saturday 8 A.M.–4 P.M.

Entertainment

On the south side of the Plaza de Armas, **Cine Cervantes** (Vicuña Mackenna 370, tel. 053/620267) shows current movies and is one of the sites of Ovalle's late-November **Festival Nacional del Cine,** which highlights short films from around the continent but also includes some feature-length flicks.

One block west of the plaza, the **Café Pub Real** (Vicuña Mackenna 419-B, tel. 053/623926) is a stylish spot that stays open until 2 A.M. weeknights and 5 A.M. weekends, but is closed completely on Sunday.

Accommodations

Though showing its age—the electrical system is truly antique—**Hotel Roxi** (Libertad 155, tel. 053/620080, hotelroxi@gmail.com, US$15–20 s, US$23–30 d) remains one of Ovalle's better values for large rooms with shared baths or private baths (the latter with TV as well). A high grape arbor shades its enormous patio, and the hot water is abundant, but some beds are soft. Rooms toward the back are quieter.

Not far from the bus terminal, friendly **Hotel Quisco** (Maestranza 161, tel. 053/620351, jofrehoteles@gmail.com, US$13 pp, US$25 s, US$30 d) has clean, comfortable, utilitarian rooms with cable TV and private baths, but some interior rooms are dark. It also has a bar/restaurant.

The deco-style **Gran Hotel Ovalle** (Vicuña Mackenna 210, tel./fax 053/621084, hotel@

yagnam.cl, US$26 s, US$40 d) is less grand than its name implies, but management has freshened up its midsize rooms, provides a buffet breakfast, and now offers WiFi.

Frayed but friendly, **Hotel American** (Vicuña Mackenna 169, tel. 053/620159, www.hotelamerican.cl, US$28–32 s, US$45–50 d) has ground floor rooms with cable TV, private baths (with showers), and free parking; the more spacious upstairs rooms have tubs.

Under the same management, better-maintained but with similar services, **Hotel Plaza Turismo** (Victoria 295, tel. 053/623258, www.plazaturismo.cl, US$40 s, US$58 d) has upgraded its rooms, but some of the baths are still small.

Food

In and around the **Mercado Municipal** (Victoria and Independencia), there are several inexpensive eateries.

It's well past its prime, but the **Club Comercial** (Aguirre 244, tel. 053/620141) can do some dishes really well—the *ostiones al pil pil* (spicy scallops, US$7) come to mind—and the service is truly obliging. Not only that, the tart pisco sours pack a wallop.

For Middle Eastern specialties, as well as beef, chicken, and seafood, try the **Club Social Arabe** (Arauco 261, tel. 053/620015), where entrées run US$5–9. The most distinctive dining experience, though, is **El Quijote** (Arauco 298, tel. 053/620501), an Unidad Popular throwback that serves good Chilean meals with its outspoken politics.

Information

Epu-Maikoño (Independencia and Victoria, tel. 053/622108, agenciadeturismo2tortolas@gmail.com) is a commercial travel agency that also operates the municipal tourist information office at the same location. It's open 10 A.M.–6 P.M. weekdays only.

Services

BCI (Vicuña Mackenna 440) has an ATM. **Correos de Chile** (Vicuña Mackenna 330), on the south side of the Plaza de Armas, is the post office. Long-distance call centers and Internet outlets are numerous in and around the plaza.

Hospital Dr. Antonio Tirado (Ariztía Poniente 7, tel. 053/620042) provides medical assistance.

Getting There and Around

Long-distance buses use Ovalle's new **Terminal Media Luna** (Ariztia Oriente 769, tel. 053/626612) at the south end of town. Since Ovalle is less than an hour from La Serena, services are similar, although many Serena-bound buses use the Panamericana rather than pass through Ovalle. Carriers include **Tur-Bus** (tel. 053/623659), **Flota Barrios** (tel. 053/626956), **Pullman Bus** (tel. 053/627736), and several others.

Regional services mostly use the **Terrapuerto Limarí** (Maestranza 443), about four blocks east of Avenida Ariztía.

Regional carriers include **Expreso Rojas** to Combarbalá and La Serena; **Buses Serenamar** to the beach resort of Tongoy; **Expreso Norte/ Tacc Vía Choapa** (at the Media Luna) to La Serena/Coquimbo, Vicuña, Illapel, Salamanca, and Los Vilos; **Buses Vía Elqui** (at the Media Luna) to La Serena/Coquimbo, Vicuña, and Pisco Elqui; **Ciktur** (at the Media Luna) to La Serena/Coquimbo, Tongoy, and Guanaqueros; and **Horvitur** to La Serena/Coquimbo.

Sample destinations, fares, and times include La Serena/Coquimbo (US$3.50, 1 hour), Los Vilos (US$9, 2.5 hours), Vallenar (US$9, 2.5 hours), Santiago or Copiapó (US$15–20, 5 hours), Caldera (US$16, 5 hours), Chañaral (US$18, 6 hours), Antofagasta (US$42–52, 13 hours), Iquique (US$50, 17 hours), and Arica (US$68, 18 hours).

Fremop (Ariztía Oriente 218, tel. 053/626969) has shared taxis to La Serena (US$4, 1 hour).

VICINITY OF OVALLE
Monumento Arqueológico Valle del Encanto

In a granite bedrock canyon midway between Ovalle and the Panamericana, petroglyphs, pictographs, and *piedras tacitas* (mortars) evidence the presence of the El Molle culture that flourished here in the early centuries of what was, in the Old World, the Christian era. Ranging from present-day Copiapó to the Río Choapa, the Molle culture was agropastoral, probably reflecting a variety of influences from San Pedro de Atacama in the north to the Llolleo of central Chile and the Patrén of the south, not to mention trans-Andean influences from as far as present-day Brazil—the *timbeta* (lip disk) of lowland Amazonia has been found here.

The most typically Andean of the artifacts are engraved, carved, smoked, or painted ceramics, and the remains of camelids. Best seen around midday, when shadows are not a factor, Sector 2's petroglyphs represent masks or tiaralike objects typical of the Limarí region.

Administered by the Municipalidad de Ovalle, Valle del Encanto is a national monument. Any bus between Ovalle and the Panamericana will drop passengers at the turnoff, which is 19 kilometers west of Ovalle and 18 kilometers from Termas de Socos, but the Valle del Encanto itself is 5 kilometers south via a bumpy gravel road with no public transportation. The Municipalidad has an information booth where it collects US$1.35 admission charge; hours are 8 A.M.–6 P.M. daily.

Termas de Socos

Precisely at the junction of the Panamericana and the Ruta 45 turnoff to Ovalle, 370 kilometers north of Santiago and 100 kilometers south of La Serena, Termas de Socos is the most upscale hot-springs resort north of Santiago—but at the same time, it's an affordable day trip for anyone who wants to soak in the thermal baths (US$6–7 pp) or swim in the pool (US$6 for adults, US$3 for kids). Whirlpool tubs, saunas, massages, and similar services are also available; a nearby plant produces its own bottled mineral water.

Rates at the **❰ Hotel Termas de Socos** (tel. 02/2363336 in Santiago, tel. 053/1982505, www.termasocos.cl, US$78 s, US$141 d in its upper pavilion, US$70 s, US$135 d in its lower pavilion) include full board. Nonguests can also lunch or dine at the restaurant.

On the same grounds, **Camping Termas de Socos** (tel. 053/631490, fpcampingsocos@yahoo.es, US$7 pp) provides an economical alternative to the hotel.

THE RÍO HURTADO VALLEY

From an overlook about five kilometers north of Ovalle, a newly paved road reaches the village of Pichasca and, still under construction, continues as an improved but dusty road up the nearly untouristed Río Hurtado Valley to the village of Hurtado, where a serpentine northbound road crosses the Portezuelo Tres Cruces to Vicuña. In his *Canto General* (1946), Nobel Prize–winning poet Pablo Neruda described the valley's rugged landscape as an area

> ...between rough and irascible hills, bristling with spines, because here the great Andean cactus rises like a cruel candlestick.

For motorists or cyclists, though, the Hurtado Valley makes an excellent backcountry alternative approach to La Serena and the Upper Elqui Valley.

Monumento Natural Pichasca

About 45 kilometers east of Ovalle, at the village of San Pedro Viejo, a bridge crosses the river to this 128-hectare semi-desert reserve, ranging 711–1,072 meters above sea level. Once full of fossil araucarias, it suffered so much pilferage that, by the time it acquired legal protection in 1969, only a handful of specimens remained. Dinosaur bones have also been found here, though, and the so-called **Casa de Piedra,** a rock shelter, contains some smoke-blemished Molle rock art.

Open 9 A.M.–6 P.M. daily, Pichasca has picnic sites but no campground. Admission costs US$2.50 for adults, US$1 for children.

From Ovalle's Feria Modelo, two or three buses per day pass San Pedro, from where it's a two-kilometer climb along a dusty road to Pichasca, en route to Hurtado.

◖ Hacienda Los Andes

In the Upper Río Hurtado Valley—a mountainous area whose chaparral and cacti resemble parts of southern California—German operator Clark Stede and his Austrian partner, Manuel Paradeiser, created a facility for backcountry horseback trips that resembles, except for the arid surroundings, their former Campo Aventura near drizzly Puerto Varas. Near the village of Morrillos, recently sold to another German operator, the colonial-style Hacienda Los Andes offers access on sure-footed horses to vast areas of steep and rugged terrain barely touched by tourists. It also has ample river frontage for swimming and relaxing at the end of the day.

Rates for a variety of day trips (not all of them on horseback), overnight excursions, and multi-day riding trips into the backcountry that includes some nights accommodations at the hacienda. B&B accommodations in colonial-style rooms are also available from US$64 s, US$95 d, with additional reasonably priced meals available, and an improving wine list.

For more details, contact Hacienda Los Andes (Vado Morrillos s/n, tel. 053/691822, www.haciendalosandes.com).

Hurtado

In the village of Hurtado, four kilometers up the valley from Hacienda Los Andes, the **Tambo del Limarí** (Caupolicán 027, tel. 053/691854, US$15 pp) offers country-style B&B accomodations. There's also good food and cold beer at **Restaurant Benita,** open noon–10 P.M. or sometimes later. Up the block, there's also the slightly more stylish **Río del Sol** (tel. 053/691841), which has shady outdoor seating.

COMBARBALÁ

About midway between Ovalle and Illapel, the scenic mountain town of Combarbalá can be part of an adventurous backroads trek by motor vehicle or bicycle between Ovalle and

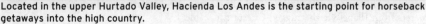

Located in the upper Hurtado Valley, Hacienda Los Andes is the starting point for horseback getaways into the high country.

NORTE CHICO

© WAYNE BERNHARDSON

SIGHTING THE SOUTHERN CROSS

Under its perpetually cloudless skies, the Norte Chico's precordillera boasts the greatest concentration of international astronomical observatories below the Equator.

Even without optical assistance, the southern heavens can be spectacular. Besides the legendary Southern Cross and other constellations that are novelties to Northern Hemisphere residents, the Small Magellanic Cloud, a galaxy orbiting the Milky Way 200,000 light years away, is one of the most distant features visible without a telescope.

Within about two hours of La Serena, there are three major research observatories: the Cerro Tololo International Observatory (CTIO) near Vicuña; the more remote European Southern Observatory (ESO) at La Silla; and the even more remote – if only because the road is unpaved – Las Campanas Observatory, run by the Carnegie Institution.

OBSERVATORIO COMUNAL CERRO MAMALLUCA

Mamalluca's popularity means that getting a spot on the nightly tours can be difficult, at least during the summer peak. If possible, try to reserve a spot (US$6 per adult, US$2.50 for children under age 12) before arriving in Vicuña or La Serena; if necessary, go through a La Serena travel agency. Summer tours in Spanish and English take place at 8:30 and 10:30 P.M. and 12:30 and 2:30 A.M.; the rest of the year, there are shows at 6:30, 8:30 and 10:30 P.M. More elaborate "Andean Cosmovision" tours (Spanish only) start 45 minutes later.

Mamalluca, 1,150 meters above sea level, is nine kilometers northeast of downtown Vicuña via a gravel road. Vehicles leave in a convoy from its Vicuña office: Observatorio Cerro Mamalluca (Avenida Gabriela Mistral 260, Oficina 1, tel. 051/411352, www.mamalluca.org).

OBSERVATORIO INTERAMERICANO CERRO TOLOLO (CERRO TOLOLO INTERNATIONAL OBSERVATORY)

Cerro Tololo is 88 kilometers southeast of La Serena via Ruta 41 and a winding gravel road to its campus just below the 2,200-meter summit. Visitors should make reservations at its hilltop La Serena campus (Colina el Pino s/n, tel. 051/205200, www.ctio.noao.edu), just east of downtown.

La Ligua. Along the abandoned highland rail route, 875 meters above sea level, Combarbalá is known for jewelry and other crafts made of *combarbalita,* a semiprecious stone of silicon, quartz, clay, and copper and silver oxides that comes in a variety of colors.

Dating from 1789, originally called Villa de San Francisco de Borja de Combarbalá, the town owed its founding to gold, silver, and copper deposits, but pisco grapes and citrus now dominate the economic landscape.

Orientation

Combarbalá (population 5,494) is 112 kilometers south of Ovalle by a good paved road via Monte Patria, 99 kilometers south of Ovalle by a 32-kilometer paved road to Punitaqui and another 67 kilometers on gravel. It is 73 kilometers from Illapel via the rugged Cuesta El Espino, but only 91 kilometers via a smoothly paved (though slightly less interesting) route through Los Pozos. It is 82 kilometers from the Panamericana via a fully paved road through Canela Baja.

Accommodations

Hostería Beltrán (Maipú 197, tel. 053/741532, hosteriabeltran@gmail.com, US$20 s, US$30 d) offers spacious rooms facing onto lush gardens. It also offers meals. Take a back room at the immaculate **Hotel Yagnam** (Comercio 252, tel. 053/741329, hotelyagnam@hotmail.com, US$21 s, US$31 d), as the front rooms face directly onto an attractive pedestrian mall that, however, gets lots of foot traffic. The rooms are even larger than the Beltrán's; rates include breakfast and cable TV.

Tours take place at 9 A.M. and 1 P.M. Saturday only. On the day of the tour, private vehicles meet at the gate near the well-signed turnoff on Ruta 41, five kilometers east of the Puclaro tunnel, where they ascend the hill in convoy.

OBSERVATORIO LA SILLA

Because of its isolation, La Silla has not had to deal with light pollution from urban development. The diameters of its 14 telescopes reach up to 3.6 meters, and there is also a 15-meter radiotelescope. Guided visits, offered every Saturday at 1:30 and 5 P.M. except in July and August, require permission from the European Space Organization (tel. 02/4633280 in Santiago, www.eso.org, recepstg@eso.org).

OBSERVATORIO LAS CAMPANAS

Las Campanas is directly on the northern regional border, via a gravel turnoff from the paved road to La Silla. Like the other research observatories, it's open Saturdays only; for reservations, contact its La Serena campus (Colina El Pino s/n, tel. 051/207304, www.lco.cl), near the CTIO campus.

OBSERVATORIO TURÍSTICO ASTRONÓMICO COLLOWARA

Only three kilometers outside the pilgrimage center of Andacollo, also offering nighttime tours, Collowara seems primed to take pressure off Mamalluca. With only basic *hospedajes*, Andacollo's shortage of accommodations is a drawback for some visitors, who will need to get back to La Serena after late-night stargazing.

Collowara visitors can purchase tickets at the central Andacollo office (Urmeneta 599, tel. 051/432964, www.collowara.cl). Tours (US$6 for adults, US$2.50 for children) start at 8:30 P.M. in summer, earlier in the off-season.

COMMERCIAL TOURS

In addition to tours to the fixed observatories, several La Serena travel agencies offer nighttime excursions with portable equipment, taking advantage of the clearest weather in the darkest locales, such as the Quebrada de Talca, southeast of the city. Visitors should time their trips within five days on either side of the new moon. Weather, however, can be a factor even here, and trips may be canceled if the skies cloud over.

Getting There and Around

From the Terminal de Buses on the south side of the Plaza de Armas, several lines connect Combarbalá with Ovalle, but there is no service south to Illapel.

◖ PARQUE NACIONAL BOSQUE DE FRAY JORGE

In the coastal range known as the Altos de Talinay, the 9,959-hectare Bosque de Fray Jorge consists of a small but dense Valdivian cloud forest, nurtured by the dripping *camanchaca* but nearly encircled by semidesert. At sea level, precipitation is only about 113 centimeters per year, but above 450 meters or so, within the forest, it ranges between 800 and 1,000 centimeters.

Because of its unique flora, of which only about 400 hectares remain, Fray Jorge has been a UNESCO World Biosphere Reserve since 1977. First reported on by a Franciscan friar in 1672, it is the subject of debate between scientists who believe these shrinking woodlands are the victims of human activities—primarily woodcutting, farming, and fire—and those who see evidence of long-term climatic change.

Flora and Fauna

The signature species of Fray Jorge's forest are *canelo (Drimys winteri), olivillo (Aetoxicon punctatum),* and *petrillo* (myrtle, *Myrceugenia correifolia*), surrounded by mosses, lichens, and ferns. As the death of old trees has left clearings colonized by opportunistic invaders, recent efforts have attempted to cultivate and replant some of these species.

Park mammals include two fox species, sea

NORTE CHICO

otters, skunks, and bats; the guanaco was reintroduced in 1995. There are about 80 bird species, including numerous seabirds and, infrequently, the Andean condor; some reptiles, including the rare Chilean iguana; and many insects associated with the Valdivian forest, normally found much farther south.

Sights and Recreation

Fray Jorge's most frequently visited attraction is the **Sendero El Bosque,** a one-kilometer nature trail that circles through the Valdivian headland forest, seven kilometers west of the Arrayancito campground via a steep exposed road. In the morning, the *camanchaca* soaks the trees and shrubs (few of which are labeled, let alone explained) until the sun breaks through. The late afternoon return of a solid wall of fog can be a spectacular sight. In the surrounding area, scattered forest patches may be relics of earlier, denser woodlands.

Three kilometers from the Centro de Información at the park entrance, the **Administración,** once the *casco* (big house) of the hacienda, now contains a *vivero* (plant nursery) that is part of the attempt to restore Fray Jorge's shrinking forests. From here, there's a 15-kilometer hike to the beach at the mouth of the Río Limarí, the park's southern boundary.

Accommodations and Food

Conaf's wooded **Camping El Arrayancito,** three kilometers from the visitors center and seven kilometers from Sector El Bosque, charges US$13 for up to six people at each of its 13 campsites, all of which have picnic tables, fire pits, and drinking water; the separate men's and women's restrooms both have flush toilets and (cold) showers. El Arrayancito also features an abandoned orchard where, in late summer, abundant pears and figs can supplement your diet; there are no supplies for sale within the park, however.

In addition, alongside the Administración, Conaf has built cabaña accommodations sleeping up to five people for US$42. For reservations, contact Conaf's La Serena office (tel. 051/272798 or 051/272799).

Information

Access hours to Fray Jorge are limited to 9 A.M.–5 P.M. in January and February, and 9 A.M.–5 P.M. the rest of the year, though it's possible to leave after that hour. Just beyond the gate, the Conaf's Centro de Información Ecológica has modest exhibits on the park's unique environment. Rangers collect an admission charge of US$3 per adult, US$1 for children.

Getting There and Around

From a highway junction 15 kilometers north of Termas de Socos via the Panamericana, Fray Jorge is another 22 kilometers west via an exposed, dusty road suitable for cyclists but probably not for pedestrians. While there is no public transportation, travel agencies in both Ovalle and La Serena offer day tours; some may allow you to camp and return another day.

LOS VILOS

Officially founded in 1894, the fishing village and seaside resort of Los Vilos is the proletarian alternative to trendy La Serena. Nobody knows the true origin of its name, but one popular legend calls it a corruption of Lord Willow, a privateer who supposedly frequented the area. Another attributes the name to an indigenous word meaning "serpent"—though Chile has few snakes of any kind. A few locals, though, ironically call it "Macondo" after Colombian novelist Gabriel García Márquez's fictional village from *One Hundred Years of Solitude.*

Orientation

Los Vilos (population 12,859) is 245 kilometers north of Santiago via the Panamericana, and 225 kilometers south of La Serena. From the Panamericana, Avenida Caupolicán leads west across the railroad tracks to the older part of town, a fairly regular grid that's home to most accommodations and services. Following

TAKING THE HIGH ROAD THROUGH THE NORTE CHICO

For motorists, bikers, and cyclists really intent on getting off the beaten track, there's no better alternative than the old highland railroad route that, until the Panamericana opened in the early 1950s, connected the Chilean heartland with the Norte Chico and the Norte Grande. Passing through five former train tunnels, with countless ups and downs along the isolated Andean foothills between La Ligua and Ovalle, it's one of the country's unappreciated gems for Chileans and foreigners alike.

From the city of La Ligua, in Region V (Valparaíso), a paved road heads east to the town of Cabildo, where the **Túnel las Grupas** continues north toward Petorca; a semaphore regulates the traffic through it, as Las Grupas is the only tunnel in a populated area. At Pedegua, 10 kilometers north of Cabildo, the main road continues northeast to Petorca, but the former rail route heads north/northwest as a paved road to the Region IV (Coquimbo) border.

Perhaps the most scenic segment is **Cuesta las Palmas,** about 20 kilometers north of Pedegua, passing newly planted avocado and citrus orchards. At the Region IV border, it penetrates the **Túnel las Palmas,** surrounded by mature palm trees in the valley, and continues as a gravel road (four-wheel drive is unnecessary) toward Salamanca and Illapel.

About 35 kilometers north of Túnel las Palmas, the largest settlement until Illapel is the strangely named **Caimanes** – there are no large aquatic reptiles here – where Diego de Almagro passed in 1536. Just north of Caimanes, in quick succession, the road passes through three tunnels; the longest is the **Túnel las Astas,** dating from 1912, whose ceilings drip with groundwater. Its length makes it the likeliest in which to encounter a vehicle heading the other direction.

At **Limáhuida,** the turnoff for the old road to Salamanca about 30 kilometers north of Caimanes, the last standing station building on the line serves as a small grocery. Along the route, *huasos* in their characteristic flat-brimmed sombreros are a common sight, as are flocks of goats on the dry hillsides, but Salamanca inhabits a lush green valley. From Salamanca, a paved highway heads northwest to the city of Illapel.

From Illapel north toward Combarbalá, evidence of the rail route is rare, though the gravel road north through Reserva Nacional Las Chinchillas passes the foundations of the station at **Aucó.** From here the road diverges from the rail embankments, which are often visible in the distance. At the reserve, a newly paved road cuts northwest to a paved highway from the coast to Combarbalá.

From Combarbalá, another paved road goes to Monte Patria and Ovalle, while a slightly shorter alternative takes a gravel road to Punitaqui and paved road to Ovalle.

Along the entire route, keep an eye out for condors – that enduring symbol of the Andes that serves as a reminder that the route was, first and foremost, an Inka road.

---

the shoreline, the Avenida Costanera is now officially Avenida Presidente Salvador Allende Gossens.

Sights and Recreation

For most visitors, the main attractions are the in-town **Playa Los Vilos** and the more northerly **Playa Amarilla;** the former gets quite a few body boarders as well as swimmers and sunbathers. At the south end of the beach, local fishmongers hawk the day's catch at **Caleta San Pedro,** where there's a gaggle of inexpensive seafood restaurants. At Avenida Caupolicán and Purén, peruse the **Feria Artesanal** for crafts and souvenirs.

A new attraction is the **Acuario Municipal** (Av. Costanera Salvador Allende 131, tel. 053/541070), the country's first saltwater aquarium. It's open 10 A.M.–2 P.M. and 3–6 P.M. Wednesday–Sunday.

NORTE CHICO

From Caleta San Pedro, there are launch excursions to the offshore seabird colonies at **Isla de Huevos** (cel. 09/85040896, US$2.50 pp) and to the more distant **Isla de Lobos,** a large southern sea lion rookery (cel. 09/89627352, US$3 pp). A dirt road also leads south of town to Isla de Lobos, which is visible across the water.

North of Playa Amarilla, at Punta Chungo, the 50.9-hectare **Santuario de la Naturaleza Laguna de Conchalí** is a wetlands haven for storks, herons, egrets, and other shorebirds. Ironically, so to speak, it owes its status to the Los Pelambres copper mine near the Argentine border, which has constructed a mechanized pier and, under pressure, established the reserve to mitigate environmental concerns over toxic wastes.

Events

February's **Semana Vileña** (Vilos Week) is the tourist season's highlight, but June's **Fiesta de San Pedro Pescador** (Festival of Saint Peter) probably has more resonance for locals.

Accommodations

The cheapest in town is **Residencial La Cabaña** (Av. Los Vilos 11, tel. 053/541318, US$10 pp); some singles, though they may have cable TV and private baths, are barely cubicle-sized. Parking is also available.

The labyrinthine **Residencial Las Rejas** (Av. Caupolicán 1310, tel. 053/541026, marco_poncem@hotmail.com, US$10–12 pp) has reasonably spacious, comfortable, and quiet accommodations with cable TV, both with and without private baths. Some rooms, though, are dark. **Residencial Jamaica** (Los Molles 354, cel. 09/9588-2929, US$10–12 pp) is also economical, with a choice of either shared or private baths. **Residencial Turismo** (Av. Caupolicán 437, tel. 053/541176, US$12 s, US$20 d) offers good value for the cost.

Rates at well-kept but otherwise ordinary **Hostería Lord Willow** (Av. Los Vilos 1444, tel. 053/541037, www.turlosvilos.cl, US$29 s, US$35 d) vary according to size and view; the cheapest rooms are tiny with interior views, midrange rooms are cramped, and pricier, more spacious rooms face the ocean. It does have a pool and bar; breakfast costs US$3 extra.

Close to the beach, **Hostal El Conquistador** (Av. Caupolicán 210, tel. 053/541663, US$25 s, US$42 d) is new and highly regarded.

Food

Los Vilos is known for hearty, if conventional, seafood restaurants with reasonable prices, such as **El Faro** (Colipí 224, tel. 053/541190) and **Las Brisas** (Av. Costanera s/n, cel. 09/9928-5507).

On the rocks near the end of the Avenida Costanera, **Caleta Las Conchas** (Salvador Allende s/n, tel. 053/543062) is a good seafood choice with indoor and outdoor seating, full meals with impeccable service for around US$7–8, and gulls and pelicans hovering for scraps.

Los Vilos's most sophisticated dining is at Uruguayan-run **Alisio** (Elicura 160, tel. 053/542173), a recycled 19th-century warehouse where fish, seafood, and international entrées run around US$12 and up. Try the corvina in a scallop sauce and the surprisingly spicy Chilean salad, along with good house wines by the glass.

Information and Services

At the junction of the former Panamericana (now a frontage road) and Avenida Caupolicán, the **Oficina Regional de Informaciones Turísticas** (tel. 053/541070) is usually open 9 A.M.–8 P.M. daily in summer only. When staffed, it's more than helpful.

Banco del Estado (Guacolda 098 at Avenida Caupolicán) is the only bank, but the Shell and Esso gas stations on the Panamericana bypass have ATMs.

Correos de Chile (Lincoyán s/n) is at the northeast corner of the Plaza de Armas. **Telefónica CTC** (Caupolicán 474) has long-distance telephone service. **Internet Express** (Caupolicán 633) has Web access.

Hospital San Pedro (Talcahuano and Arauco, tel. 053/541061) has excellent facilities.

Getting There and Around

At the west end of Avenida Caupolicán, the old railroad station serves as Los Vilos's Terminal de Buses, though most companies have separate offices and even terminals elsewhere on Caupolicán.

The main carriers, covering destinations north and south along the Panamericana, include **Tur-Bus** (Caupolicán 898, tel. 053/541312), **Pullman Bus** (Caupolicán and Av. Estación, tel. 053/541197), and **TACC Vía Choapa** (Av. Caupolicán 784, tel. 053/541032). The latter also go to interior provincial cities such as Illapel and Salamanca.

ILLAPEL

Founded in 1754 by General Domingo Ortiz de Rozas, under the name Villa de San Rafael de Rozas, the provincial agricultural town of Illapel is notable for its proximity to Reserva Nacional Las Chinchillas, only 15 kilometers northeast of town by a scenic, smoothly paved highway that continues north to Combarbalá and Monte Patria via Los Pozos. A more scenic and direct—but more rugged—route to Combarbalá crosses the Cuesta El Espino.

Illapel (population 21,826) is 53 kilometers northeast of Los Vilos via a paved highway.

Accommodations and Food

The cheapest option is friendly **Residencial Aucó** (Constitución 181, tel. 053/523368, US$13–17 pp) for spotless rooms with shared bath and kitchen privileges; for service, knock or ring at the door with the speaker diagonally across the street.

Most rooms at the worn-around-the-edges **Hotel Diaguitas Illapel** (Constitución 276, tel. 053/522587, www.hoteldiaguitas.cl, US$35 s, US$45 d) have balconies, there's a pool, and limited parking is available. If business is slow, try bargaining.

So well-maintained it looks as new as the day it opened in 1988, **Hotel Domingo Ortiz de Rozas** (Av. Ignacio Silva 241, tel. 053/522127, www.hotelortizderozas.cl, US$50 s, US$58 d) has tasteful rooms in a quiet garden setting,

with off-street parking. It does not offer IVA discounts, however.

As always, **Tap** (Constitución 382, tel. 053/522034) serves excellent sandwiches, along with beef and fish dishes. Well-regarded **Nicco** (Av. Ignacio Silva 279) has a comparable menu. Try also the **Casino de Bomberos** (Buin 540) or the Chilean chain **Bavaria** (Constitución 435, tel. 053/523338).

Services and Getting There

Entel (Constitución 301) has long-distance telephone services. **Correos de Chile** (Av. O'Higgins 220) is the post office.

From Illapel's **Terminal de Buses** (San Martín 260), TACC Vía Choapa and Pullman Bus go to Los Vilos; Tur-Bus goes straight to Santiago.

RESERVA NACIONAL LAS CHINCHILLAS

Native to the central Chilean Andes, in a rocky habitat covered with the bromeliad *chagual (Puya chilensis),* the nocturnal 500-gram rodent *Chinchilla lanigera* feeds on herbs, bushes, and cacti. Highly valued in the international fur trade, its fine grey pelt led to its over-exploitation in the early 20th century, but in 1983 the Chilean government established this 4,229-hectare reserve, 15 kilometers northeast of Illapel, to help protect the endangered species. The largest remaining colonies are here and at La Higuera, near La Serena, but the existing colonies are far smaller than the reserve itself, and the population appears to be declining.

Sights

On the west side of the highway, at El Espinal, Conaf's **Centro de Información Ambiental** displays a sample of antique chinchilla traps. Even more interestingly, it contains a *nocturnato* where half a dozen native rodent species, including the chinchilla (along with a sole marsupial), are on display in cages whose blue lights convince the animals it's nighttime. The center is open 9 A.M.–6 P.M. daily.

At El Espinal, there's also a one-kilometer

CHASING CHINCHILLAS

At least from Inka times and probably much earlier, Andean royalty treasured chinchilla stoles for their soft, dense fur, but *Chinchilla lanigera* did not feel the brunt of commercial exploitation until the late 19th century, when massive trapping and exportation began. Between 1898 and 1900, nearly 1.2 million pelts were shipped abroad, with a maximum of 450,000 in 1899; during a nine-year period around the turn of the 20th century, more than 2.5 million pelts passed through Valparaíso. The trade declined after 1910 because of overexploitation, but Chile did not prohibit hunting and trapping until 1929.

Meanwhile, in 1923, U.S. mining engineer Matthew Chapman exported nine live males and three females from Potrerillos, north of Copiapó, to North America, marking the beginning of an international chinchilla fur industry. Today there are about 150,000 breeding domestic chinchillas worldwide. With a state subsidy in 1929, Chile began its own industry, which now comprises about 40 nurseries with 3,000 females.

In the mountains east of Illapel, Reserva Nacional Las Chinchillas is the most important official conservation initiative, but it protects only a small part of the most critical habitat. The small NGO **Save the Wild Chinchillas** (www.wildchinchillas.org) is promoting community-based habitat restoration to help promote population recovery among the remaining populations.

Sendero de Interpretación (nature trail) for hikers. On the highway's east side, just the foundations survive of a former railway station at **Aucó,** once a gypsum mining village of 400 people. Only three houses stand, and a handful of inhabitants remain, in this virtual ghost town.

Practicalities

At El Espinal, Conaf charges US$10 per person for comfortable cabañas sleeping up to six. For reservations, contact Conaf's Illapel office (cel. 09/94733768).

Park rangers at the **Centro de Información,** open 9 A.M.–6 P.M. daily, collect a US$3 admission charge. Children under age 15 pay US$1.

SALAMANCA

In the verdant Choapa Valley southeast of Illapel, Salamanca enjoys a certain fame for its folkloric Fiesta Huasa, which takes place during Semana Santa, and a certain notoriety for legends of witches and witchcraft. Its Plaza de Armas, landscaped with mature Araucarias (beware of falling cones), mimosas, casuarinas, and cypresses, is the pivot of local life.

Salamanca (population 12,689) is about 30 kilometers southeast of Illapel via a paved highway.

Sights

At Salamanca's western approach, there are petroglyphs on an igneous outcrop at **Cerro Chilinga,** in the hamlet of the same name, reached by a concrete staircase and a short scramble over the granite. Beginning almost directly behind the church, the trail continues to the summit of the hill, where there are ruins of a small pre-Columbian *pirca* (dry stone wall) and a possible Inka cemetery.

Accommodations and Food

One block south of the Plaza de Armas, **Hostería Gálvez** (J. J. Pérez 540, tel. 053/551017, hosteriagalvez@terra.cl, US$7 pp, US$13 s, US$17 d) has small but clean budget quarters but also larger, comfier rooms with private baths and cable TV, and is sometimes willing to bargain the price. It has a huge swimming pool (closed when lifeguards are not available), abundantly productive apricot trees, sprawling grape arbor, and loads of free parking.

One block east of the Plaza de Armas,

Residencial O'Higgins (O'Higgins 430, tel. 053/551108, US$8 pp, US$25 d) provides simple but good accommodations with either shared or private bath and garden frontage; breakfast costs extra.

Four blocks east of the plaza, **Hostal Vasco** (Bulnes 120, tel. 053/551119, hostalvasco@hotmail.com, US$30–42 s or d) is an immaculate facility offering spacious, comfortable rooms with private baths, breakfast, cable TV, and a pool; rates vary according to size.

At the southeast corner of the Plaza de Armas, **Restaurant American** (Bulnes 499, tel. 053/551361) serves excellent fish and seafood for around US$7–11, with attentive service—sometimes overpoweringly so.

Getting There and Around

Salamanca has frequent bus service to Illapel and Los Vilos with **Pullman Bus** (Montepío 294, tel. 053/552438) and **TACC Vía Choapa** (O'Higgins 500, tel. 053/551111), which also goes to La Serena and Santiago. **Buses Intercomunal** (O'Higgins 510) goes frequently to Los Vilos, Viña del Mar, and Valparaíso.

THE CHILEAN LAKES DISTRICT

South of the Río Biobío, popularly known as the "Lakes District" for the scenic finger lakes left by receding Pleistocene glaciers, the Sur Chico ("Lesser South") has long enticed Chileans and Argentines with its matchless scenery of ice-capped volcanic cones soaring above dense native forests. Only in the past decade-plus have significant numbers of them, plus adventurous foreigners, begun to venture beyond conventional lakeside resorts into the Andean backcountry for hiking, horseback riding, and white-water rafting. National parks and reserves cover large swaths of the cordillera.

Politically, the Sur Chico comprises the Araucanía (Region IX), he newly designated Los Ríos (Region XIV), and Los Lagos (Region X), which includes the Chiloé archipelago

and, on the mainland across the Golfo de Ancud and the Golfo de Corcovado, what is colloquially known as continental Chiloé. Economically diverse cities such as Temuco, Osorno, and Puerto Montt, which rely on forestry, agricultural services, and manufacturing in addition to tourism, are the gateways, but smaller lakeside towns such as Villarrica, Pucón, and Puerto Varas make better bases for excursions. There are several trans-Andean routes to Argentina, which has its own Lakes District centered on the city of Bariloche; Puerto Montt, the de facto terminus of the continental Panamericana, is the hub for air, land, and sea access to Chilean Patagonia and also a gateway to the Argentine side.

Southeast of Temuco, Lago Villarrica is a beehive of activity for access to national parks

HIGHLIGHTS

◀ Sector Conguillío: The monkey-puzzle tree's fame was such that, nearly a century ago, the famous conservationist John Muir went far out of his way to visit the part of Parque Nacional Conguillío that now protects much of southern South America's endemic araucaria forests (page 340).

◀ Volcán Villarrica: Every summer, hundreds of hikers slog the snow-covered slopes of Chile's most active volcano, in its namesake national park immediately south of Pucón, for the views and the thrills (page 354).

◀ Sendero Lago Verde: Just northwest of Pucón, Parque Nacional Huerquehue is the place for shaded woodland hikes alongside rushing streams over ruggedly scenic terrain (page 356).

◀ Anticura: Its remaining forests resemble the rainforest woodlands north and south of it, but Parque Nacional Puyehue's most impressive sight is the barren high country wrought by the lava flows and ash from its namesake volcano's 1960 eruption (page 372).

◀ Puerto Varas Historic District: On Lago Llanquihue's western shore, studded with shingled houses that recall its early settlers' Middle European origins, Puerto Varas has the Sur Chico's finest services and restaurants, making it the ideal gateway to the bus/boat crossing to the Argentine lakes district city of Bariloche (page 378).

◀ Sector Volcán Osorno: On Lago Llanquihue's eastern shore, in Parque Nacional Vicente Pérez Rosales, Osorno is a beacon of

Fuji-like perfection. Ski facilities have been upgraded, but it's also a summer favorite for climbers and hikers (page 388).

◀ Parque Nacional Chiloé: Only on Chiloé's wild west coast can hikers traipse through dense dwarf woodlands where, according to legend, the troll-like Trauco awaits the unwary (page 414).

LOOK FOR **◀** TO FIND RECOMMENDED SIGHTS, ACTIVITIES, DINING, AND LODGING.

such as Villarrica and Huerquehue, but the district's heart is farther south, where Lago Todos los Santos is widely considered Chile's single most beautiful body of water. Near the picturesque town of Puerto Varas, Volcán Osorno, an almost perfectly symmetrical cone rising above Lago Llanquihue, offers some of the most breathtaking views anywhere. Still, there are dozens of other high volcanic summits, scenic lakes and rivers, and shores and estuaries to fill weeks or months of sightseeing and activities.

Like the Araucanía, Los Lagos has a vigorous tourist industry and infrastructure, but there's a tension between the natural landscape and resource-based industries such as forestry and fisheries—water pollution from large-scale salmon farming in both freshwater lakes and saltwater estuaries continues to cause concern.

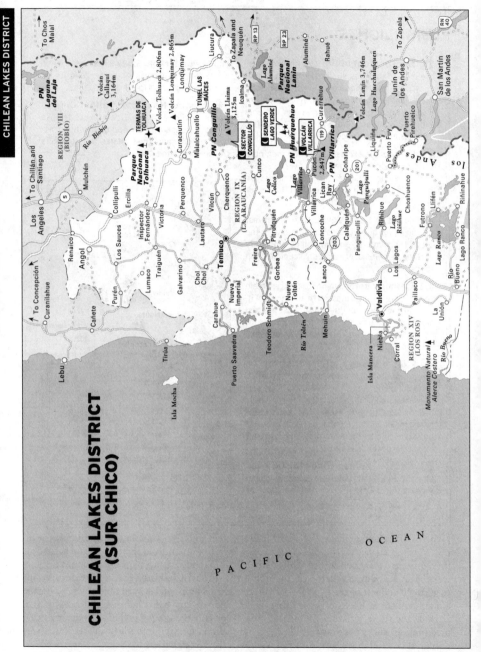

CHILEAN LAKES DISTRICT (SUR CHICO)

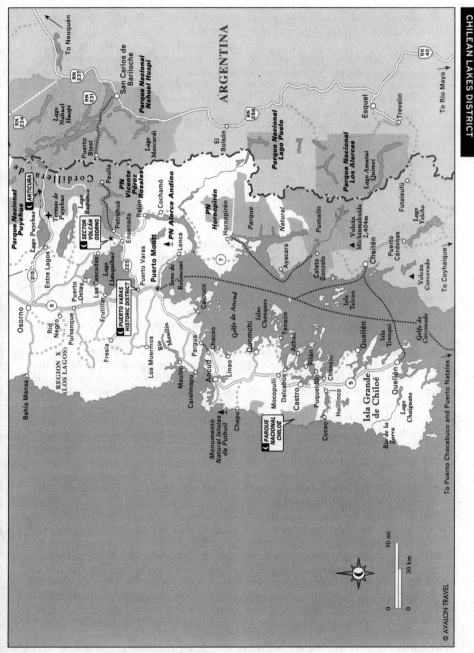

Exploitation of valuable native finfish, as well as shellfish such as abalone and giant mussels, is also a problem.

This chapter also includes insular Chiloé, easily reached by shuttle ferries, and parts of continental Chiloé, south to the town of Hornopirén (also known as Río Negro), where a summer-only ferry usually sails to the tiny cove of Caleta Gonzalo, the de facto start of the Carretera Austral. Because of continental Chiloé's physical isolation from the rest of Region X, only air taxis, catamarans, slow-moving ferries, and roundabout buses through Argentina connect it to Puerto Montt and Castro.

PLANNING YOUR TIME

Because the Lakes District is relatively compact, with excellent highways and secondary roads, and abundant public transportation, travel is normally straightforward. Still, in the summer tourism peak, hotel and rental-car reservations are advisable, though accommodations are abundant enough that something's usually available.

For visitors, the best bases are the Lago Villarrica resorts of Villarrica and Pucón to the north, and the Lago Llanquihue town of Puerto Varas or the mainland city of Puerto Montt to the south. For visitors with vehicles, staying at any of these locales keeps driving to a minimum, but good public transportation means that a car is rarely necessary. For those staying outside town, though, it's helpful to have one.

Seeing the main sights in either of these two clusters requires around a week. This would permit a day trip to Parque Nacional Conguillío and perhaps an overnight near the thermal-baths complex at Malalcahuello, or looping around the park from Temuco via the upper Biobío. In Villarrica or Pucón, there would be ample time for hiking in Parque Nacional Huerquehue, climbing Volcán Villarrica, rafting the Río Trancura, or simply relaxing on the black-sand beaches.

From either Puerto Varas or Puerto Montt,

attractions such as Parque Nacional Vicente Pérez Rosales, the wild Cochamó backcountry, the seafood port of Angelmó, and the Chiloé archipelago are almost equally accessible. Many visitors prefer Puerto Varas, which is quieter and more picturesque and has better services in a more compact area.

HISTORY

Human presence in the region dates from at least 13,000 years ago, when hunter-gatherers roamed the area around Monte Verde, 35 kilometers west of Puerto Montt. One of the continent's oldest archaeological sites, Monte Verde offered ideal conditions for preservation: Despite the humid climate, more than a meter of volcanic ash and peat covered the remains of mastodons, shellfish, seeds, fruits, and roots consumed by the dozen or so families who lived there. From the remaining refuse, researchers have determined that these bands hunted and foraged within a radius of about 100 kilometers.

Unlike the central Andean highlands of Peru and Bolivia, the pre-Columbian Sur Chico never developed cities or monuments—its people developed agricultural skills, but they were shifting cultivators in dispersed settlements, lacking centralized political authority. In practice, this benefited their resistance to the Inka empire and, later, Spanish invaders; the Mapuche used guerrilla tactics to harass their opponents. More egalitarian than hierarchical, their leadership was interchangeable rather than irreplaceable.

Thus, by the early 1600s, Mapuche resistance had reduced most Spanish settlements south of the Biobío to ashes and ruin. Except for the river port of Valdivia, reestablished in the mid-17th century, the area remained precarious for settlers until a series of treaties between the Chilean government and indigenous forces in the 1880s. Several northerly cities and towns—Victoria, Curacautín, Lonquimay, Temuco, Cunco, Villarrica, and Pucón— were originally a string of fortresses along the Mapuche frontier.

Chile counts more than a million Mapuche among its 15 million citizens. Many have left for the cities, but large numbers still remain in the countryside where, in the more liberal political climate following the Pinochet dictatorship, they have become more assertive of their rights to ancestral lands.

Part of the controversy dates from the officially encouraged immigration that took place after the mid-19th century, when Santiago recruited German émigrés to settle on and around Lago Llanquihue. In the ensuing years, Llanquihue and other lakes to the north became the region's highways, linking towns like Puerto Varas and Puerto Octay via sail and steamer until the railroad's advent in the early 20th century.

German immigrants have left a palpable imprint on the economy (through commerce and manufacturing), landscape (through dairy farming and other agricultural pursuits), architecture (some of the country's finest European-style houses), and food (Germanic goodies known collectively as *kuchen* are almost universal). Many other nationalities, mostly Spaniards and Italians, also flowed into the region.

Temuco

Fast-growing Temuco is the gateway to the lakes, numerous national parks, and many other attractions, though its own tourist appeal is limited—while it's a Mapuche market town, the architecture is largely utilitarian and economically it relies on agricultural and forest products. Unfortunately, like Santiago, it suffers air-pollution problems, especially in winter, as widespread use of low-quality wood-burning stoves has contributed to a growing incidence of respiratory infections.

HISTORY

Temuco dates from February 24, 1881, when President Aníbal Pinto sent Interior Minister Manuel Recabarren, veteran general Gregorio Urrutia, engineer Teodoro Schmidt, and the Chilean army to found Fuerte de Temuco (originally Fuerte Recabarren). Later that year, the Chileans averted an attack on the fortress by reaching a treaty agreement, and within 15 years the railroad had arrived. Before the turn of the century, colonists had flooded into the region, their farmers displacing the aboriginal Mapuche, and the population exceeded 7,000. The early push from the railroad sustained that growth well into the 20th century, providing easy access to metropolitan markets and technology.

ORIENTATION

On the north margin of the braided Río Cautín, Temuco (population 232,528) is 677 kilometers south of Santiago and 339 kilometers north of Puerto Montt via the Panamericana, which bypasses the city center; the former Panamericana, known as Avenida Caupolicán, divides the city into a compact original grid to the east and an irregular residential area to the west.

SIGHTS

Temuco's focal point is the lushly landscaped **Plaza de Armas Aníbal Pinto,** whose showpiece is the massive **Homenaje a la Región de la Araucanía,** a sculpture representing a Mapuche *machi* (female healer), the euphemistically titled *Soldado de la Pacificación* (Soldier of the Pacification), a *Colono* (Early Colonist), the conquistador and epic poet Alonso de Ercilla, and the Mapuche *toqui* (leader) Kallfulifán. The bandshell gallery hosts rotating cultural exhibits.

Most other landmarks are scattered, such as the gingerbread-style **Iglesia Anglicana Santa Trinidad** (Vicuña Mackenna and Lautaro), the century-old Anglican church, as well as several museums and markets.

Chile's national flower, the *copihue*

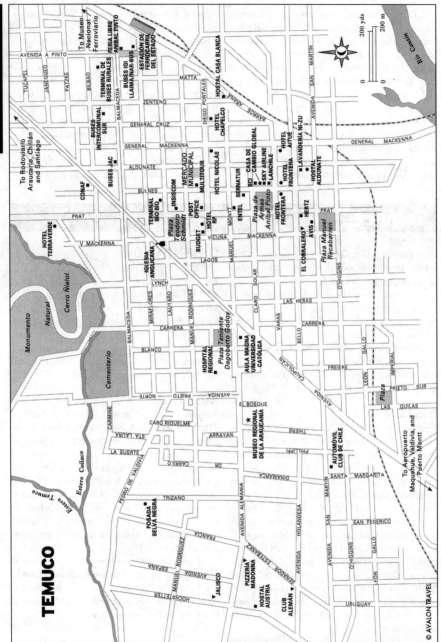

TEMUCO

To Museo
Nacional
Ferroviario

To Rodoviario
Araucaria, Chillán
and Santiago

AVENIDA A PINTO

TUCAPEL
JANEQUEO
PAITKE
BILBAO
BALMACEDA

TERMINAL DE
BUSES RURALES

BUSES IGI
LLAIMA/NAR-BUS

FERIA LIBRE
ANIBAL PINTO

ESTACIÓN DE
FERROCARRIL
DEL ESTADO

MATTA

BARROS ARANA

HOSTAL CASA BLANCA

SAN MARTIN

AVENIDA SAN MARTIN

Río Cautín

200 yds
200 m

ZENTENO

DIEGO PORTALES

HOTEL
CHAPELCO

AVENIDA NI-ZU

GENERAL MACKENNA

BUSES
INTERCOMUNAL
SUR

GENERAL CRUZ

GENERAL   MACKENNA

ALDUNATE

BUSES JAC

CONAF

BULNES

MERCADO
MUNICIPAL

HOTEL NICOLÁS

SERNATUR

BCI
SKY AIRLINE
LANCHILE

CASA DE
CAMBIO GLOBAL
MULTITOUR

HOTEL
FRONTERA

HOTEL
AITUE

LAVANDERIA NI-ZU

HOSTAL
ALDUNATE

PRAT

INSISCOM

TERMINAL
BIO BIO

POST
OFFICE

HOTEL
RP

ENTEL

MONTT

MANUEL

Plaza de
Armas
Anibal Pinto

HOTEL
FRONTERA

HERTZ

AVIS

PRAT

HOTEL
TERRAVERDE

V MACKENNA

IGLESIA
ANGLICANA

Plaza
Teodoro
Schmidt

BUDGET

VICUÑA

MACKENNA

EL CORRALERO

Plaza Manuel
Recabarren

Monumento

Cerro Ñielol

Natural

Cementerio

LAGOS

LYNCH

MIRAFLORES

LAUTARO

MANUEL RODRIGUEZ

CARRERA

BALMACEDA

BLANCO

CLARO

SOLAR

LAS HERAS

VARAS

BELLO

CARRERA

O'HIGGINS

Plaza Teniente
Dagoberto Godoy

HOSPITAL
REGIONAL

AULA MAGNA
UNIVERSIDAD
CATÓLICA

CAUPOLICAN

FREIRE

GALLO

LEON

PRIETO

SUR

Plaza

NORTE

PRIETO

AVENIDA

EL BOSQUE

CABO RIQUELME

ARRAYAN

MUSEO REGIONAL
DE LA ARAUCANÍA

THIERS

PHILLIPI

DINAMARCA

SALVADOR ESTEBANEZ

AUTOMOVIL
CLUB DE CHILE

SANTA   MARGARITA

SAN MARTIN

LAS QUILAS

To Aeropuerto
Maquehue, Valdivia, and
Puerto Montt

CARMINE

STA LAURA

LA SUERTE

CARRILO

DR

Estero Coilaco

Estero Temuco

POSADA
SELVA NEGRA

TRIZANO

PEDRO DE VALDIVIA

FRANCIA

AVENIDA ALEMANIA

AVENIDA

HOLANDESA

SAN FEDERICO

SAN

O'HIGGINS

GALLO

LEON

HOCHSTETTER

MANUEL RODRIGUEZ

ESPAÑA

FRANCIA

JALISCO

PIZZERÍA
MADONNA

HOSTAL
AUSTRIA

CLUB
ALEMÁN

AVENIDA

URUGUAY

© AVALON TRAVEL

(*Lapageria rosea),* flaunts its autumn blooms in the deciduous lowland forest of **Monumento Natural Cerro Ñielol,** a 90-hectare reserve that rises barely 200 meters above sea level on the north side of Temuco. Several short trails thread among the park's mixed woodlands, but it's also a historical site—under the shade of the so-called **La Patagua del Armisticio,** in 1881, Mapuche leaders finally acceded to the founding of the city. For most of its tens of thousands of yearly visitors, though, it's a place for weekend picnics and similar recreation.

Reached by strolling north on Prat from the Plaza de Armas for about one kilometer, Cerro Ñielol (8:30 A.M.–11 P.M. daily) charges US$1.50 admission per pedestrian, US$0.75 for each child.

Museo Regional de la Araucanía

Housed in the former Carlos Thiers residence (1924), a German immigrant-style national monument, Temuco's regional museum has been undergoing a seemingly endless rehab and reorganization and, as of summer 2009, was only informally open. The early results are encouraging, with exhibits on little-known topics such as the immigration of South African Boers in the early 20th century. In the past, though, the museum has seen frequent clashes of philosophy in a region where the indigenous presence is so strong.

The Museo Regional (Av. Alemania 084, tel. 045/735592, www.museoregionalaraucania.cl, 10 A.M.–5:30 P.M. Mon.–Fri., 11 A.M.–5 P.M. Sat., and 11 A.M.–2 P.M. Sun. and holidays, free admission) is about 10 blocks west of the Plaza de Armas.

Museo Nacional Ferroviario Pablo Neruda

Soon after the railroad's arrival from Angol in 1893, Temuco became a key rail hub, where long-distance trains changed locomotives; its original *casa de máquinas* (roundhouse) opened in 1920, housed locomotives used on several branch lines, and also held repair facilities. By the 1930s, though, these installations were inadequate; the current roundhouse was

completed between 1937 and 1941. Temuco was the last Chilean base for steam locomotives; Empresa de los Ferrocarriles del Estado (EFE) maintained it as a repair and reserve center for them until 1983—there were no permanent diesel facilities here until the 1980s—but it closed soon after.

In the aftermath, EFE officials wanted to tear down the roundhouse and sell off its 14 antique steam engines and other rolling stock for scrap, but the persistent Asociación Chilena de Conservación del Patrimonio Ferroviario (ACCPF, Chilean Association for Conservation of Railroad Patrimony) managed to get all of them declared national monuments. Finally, in February 2004, President Ricardo Lagos dedicated the new museum to Pablo Neruda during the poet's centennial year (Neruda's father was a railroad laborer, and Neruda himself wrote many poems about rail travel).

In a 19-hectare facility that includes the roundhouse and extensive lawns with additional stock elevated on rails, the highlights include a luxury presidential railcar that was in service until 2003, an antique sleeper also in service until 2003, and President Carlos Ibáñez del Campo's 1928 Packard limousine—custom-designed so that it could use the rails as well as Chile's then-rudimentary roads.

The Museo Ferroviario (Av. Barros Arana 0565, tel. 045/937940, www.museoferroviariotemuco.cl, 9 A.M.–6 P.M. Tues.–Sun., US$1.50 for adults, US$0.50), about one kilometer north of the station, also features an art gallery. Northbound buses and *taxi colectivos* on Barros Arana go within two short blocks of the site, saving an unappealing walk through a grubby neighborhood. An occasional summer steam train does a five-hour excursion to and from Victoria (US$8 pp).

Mercado Municipal

Replacing an earlier market that the city had outgrown, the municipal bazaar (1928) is a high-ceilinged landmark that draws tourists with its accomplished crafts and typical restaurants, which vary from the plain and simple to, if not quite sublime, at least good enough.

Locals take advantage of abundant fresh produce and utilitarian commodities such as manufactured household goods and clothing.

Two blocks north of the Plaza de Armas, the Mercado Municipal (Manuel Rodríguez 960, tel. 045/203345, www.mercadotemuco.cl, 8 A.M.–8 P.M. Mon.–Sat. and 8 A.M.–4 P.M. Sun. in summer, 8 A.M.–6 P.M. Mon.–Sat. and 8 A.M.–4 P.M. Sun. and holidays the rest of the year) fills most of the eastern two-thirds of the block bounded by Diego Portales, Bulnes, Manuel Rodríguez, and Aldunate.

Feria Libre Aníbal Pinto

Comprising more than 700 different stalls, this lively, mainly Mapuche and sometimes disagreeably fragrant produce market fills several blocks south along Avenida Aníbal Pinto and Avenida Barros Arana from the Terminal de Buses Rurales south to the EFE railroad station. In July 2001, members of the indigenous Asociación de Productores de Verduras Ñuke Mapu protested their possible eviction from the market, resisting what they claimed were the mayor's plans to remodel the entire area to their detriment, but the project nevertheless went forward. The Aníbal Pinto sector is now a roofed pedestrian area that, still under construction, looks pretty handsome and is tidier (and more hygienic) than in past years.

In addition to fruits and vegetables, there are cheap eateries and assorted Mapuche crafts. Hours are roughly 8 A.M.–5 P.M. daily.

ENTERTAINMENT AND EVENTS

Temuco isn't exactly a 24-hour city, but there's usually something going on at local cultural facilities or its two universities. The biggest single celebration is February's **Aniversario de la Ciudad,** commemorating the city's founding—at the time, it was really a fortress—on February 24, 1881. During the festivities, a high-quality crafts fair nearly fills the Plaza de Armas.

The **Aula Magna Universidad Católica** (Manuel Montt 56, tel. 045/205421) has an annual event schedule including live theater and films.

SHOPPING

There's a good crafts selection at the **Mercado Municipal** (Diego Portales and Aldunate), but also lots of kitsch.

ACCOMMODATIONS

Budget accommodations are only so-so, but travelers spending just a little more can get better value. Upper-range choices are generally good.

US$10-25

Hostal Aldunate (Aldunate 864, tel. 045/642438, hostalaldunate864@hotmail.com, US$13–17 s, US$20–25 d private bath, breakfast included) occupies a quiet but still central neighborhood; rates vary according to shared or private bath. At gracefully aging **Hostal Casa Blanca** (Manuel Montt 1306, tel./fax 045/272677, www.hostalcasablancatemuco.cl, US$15–22 s, 27–32 d), all rates include breakfast, but only the pricier rooms with private baths have cable TV.

US$25-50

Hotel Chapelco (General Cruz 401, tel. 045/749393, www.hotelchapelco.cl, US$25s, US$37 d) is a respectable option, with private bath, breakfast, and parking, near the train tracks at the east end of downtown.

In the residential west side of Temuco, (**Posada Selva Negra** (Tirzano 110, tel. 045/236913, www.hospedajeselvanegra.cl, US$30s, US$45 d) is a German-run B&B with quiet garden rooms—some singles are small but have enough room to contain a writing desk and there's WiFi—plus unexpected touches like a soft bathrobe (unusual in this price range). The breakfast nook has a world-class collection of Teutonic kitsch.

Near the Mercado Municipal, **Hotel Nicolás** (General Mackenna 420, tel. 045/210020, www.hotelnicolas.cl, US$42s, US$50 d with private bath and TV) is undistinguished but more central.

US$50-100

C Hostal Austria (Hochstetter 599, tel./fax 045/247169, www.hostalaustria.cl, US$35s, US$60 d) offers quiet, comfortable, spotless, and tobacco-free accommodations with private bath, cable TV, and genuine *Gemütlichkeit* (warmth and personal attention), not to mention a well-above-average breakfast.

Hotel Aitué (Antonio Varas 1048, tel. 045/212512, www.hotelaitue.cl, US$65s, US$75 d but ask for IVA discount) is a business-oriented facility with responsive service.

C Hotel Frontera (Bulnes 733, tel. 045/200400, www.hotelfrontera.cl, US$79–91 s, US$91–/104 d) is a complex of two facing buildings that include one business-oriented hotel and convention center. The one across the street has greater amenities—swimming pool, gym, and the like—but its only advantage is easier access, as guests at either building are entitled to use all facilities.

More than US$100

Downtown's best new accommodations in at least a decade, the **RP Hotel** (Portales 779, tel. 045/977777, www.hotelrp.cl, US$105) is a 23-room boutique hotel that includes one suite.

At the foot of Cerro Ñielol, **Hotel Terraverde** (Prat 0220, tel. 045/239999, www.panamericanahoteles.cl, US$130 s, US$137 d, up to US$192 s or d) is a five-star choice by local standards, but not demonstrably superior to the Frontera.

FOOD

Known best as a crafts market and a sight in itself, the **Mercado Municipal** (Portales and Aldunate) is an equally good choice for straightforward seafood—try **La Caleta** (Puesto 27, tel. 045/213002). Figure about US$7–10 for a good, filling meal; the market, though, is primarily a lunch venue, and most eateries close by 7 P.M.

Downtown's **El Corralero** (Vicuña Mackenna 811, tel. 045/401355, lunch and dinner daily) is the downtown choice for beef.

In residential Temuco, though, only a couple blocks west of Hochstetter and just south of Avenida Alemania, **Restaurant Oregon** (Recreo 530, tel. 045/385776, lunch and dinner daily except for Sun. night) is a popular *parrilla* that is a step-plus above most of its competitors, with fish and pastas to supplement its beef specialties. Most entrées fall into the US$7–10 range, the service is attentive and good-natured, and they're flexible about wine by the glass selections.

The popular **Pizzería Madonna** (Av. Alemania 0660, tel. 045/329393, lunch and dinner daily) has fine pastas and a greater diversity of pizzas, in portions ranging from individual to family-size, than most Chilean pizzerias.

Jalisco (Hochstetter 435, tel. 045/243254, lunch and dinner daily) is a pub with a selection of Tex-Mex options. **Die Pinte** (Recreo 691, tel. 045/245431) is a German-style pub/restaurant operated by the owner of Posada Selva Negra, but it's a free-fire zone for smokers. The **Club Alemán** (Senador Estébanez 772, tel. 045/240034, lunch and dinner daily) is a more traditional option.

INFORMATION

On the north side of the Plaza de Armas, **Sernatur** (Claro Solar 899, tel. 045/211969, infoaraucania@sernatur.cl) distributes free city maps and regional leaflets; it usually has an English speaker on hand. Summer hours are 8:30 A.M.–7:30 P.M. Monday–Saturday and 10 A.M.–2 P.M. Sunday. March–December, hours are 9 A.M.–1 P.M. and 3–5:30 P.M. Monday–Thursday and 9 A.M.–1 P.M. and 3–4:30 P.M. Friday.

For motorists, the **Automóvil Club de Chile** (Acchi, San Martín 0278, tel. 045/910522) is west of the former Panamericana.

Conaf (Av. Bilbao 931, 2nd floor, tel. 045/298114) provides national parks information.

SERVICES

Though it's primarily an administrative and commercial center, Temuco has a full complement of traveler's services as well. **BCI** (Bulnes 615) has one of many ATMs; the nearby **Casa de Cambio Global** (Bulnes 655, Local 1) is an exchange house.

Correos de Chile (Diego Portales 801) is the post office. **Entel** (Prat 505) has a long-distance call center, while **Insiscom** (Prat 283) has Internet connections.

For laundry, try **Lavanderías Ni-Zu** (Aldunate 842, tel. 045/236893).

The expanding **Hospital Regional** (Manuel Montt 115, tel. 045/212525) is west of the former Panamericana.

GETTING THERE

Temuco is Araucanía's major transportation hub, with air connections north and south, and abundant bus connections north and south along the Panamericana, and east into and over the Andes. Technically it's the terminus of the railroad from Santiago, but services were suspended in the summer of 2009, apparently temporarily, due to operational problems. (Check EFE's website, www.efe.cl, for updated information.)

Air

LAN (Bulnes 687, tel. 045/211339) flies several times daily to Santiago and once or twice daily to Puerto Montt. **Sky Airline** (Bulnes 677, tel. 045/747300) flies four times weekly to Santiago and to Puerto Montt.

Bus

The chaos of long-distance carriers that once congested downtown streets has been relieved by construction of the **Rodoviario Araucario** (Vicente Pérez Rosales 01609, tel. 045/225005), at the eastern foot of Cerro Ñielol. This has not completely concentrated services—the **Terminal de Buses Rurales** (Av. Aníbal Pinto 032, tel. 045/210494) hosts regional carriers, and several long-distance companies have ticket offices and even terminals around the axis formed with the perpendicular Avenida Balmaceda.

Among the regional carriers at Buses Rurales are **Flota Erbuc** (tel. 045/272204), which goes several times daily to Curacautín via Lautaro or Victoria, continuing to Malalcahuello and Lonquimay; **Nar-Bus** (tel. 045/407740) and **Intercomunal Sur** (Av. Balmaceda 1371, tel. 045/214864) to Cherquenco (for the Llaima sector of Parque Nacional Conguillío), Icalma, Cunco, and Melipeuco; and **Buses Jac** to Villarrica and Pucón, though departures are more frequent from its other office. From its own terminal, **Buses Biobío** (Lautaro 853, tel. 045/210599) links Temuco to Angol.

From the Rodoviario, many carriers connect Temuco with Panamericana destinations from Santiago to Puerto Montt and Chiloé. Some have, as indicated, downtown ticket offices: **Tur-Bus** (Claro Solar 598, tel. 045/230979); and **Igi Llaima,** which shares facilities with **Nar-Bus** (Miraflores 1535, tel. 045/407777). **Buses Jac** (Av. Balmaceda 1005, tel. 045/210313) shuttles frequently to Villarrica and Pucón, with fewer trips to Lican Ray and to Coñaripe (changing buses in Villarrica in off-season), and a daily service to Curarrehue.

Sample domestic destinations, with approximate fares and times, include Villarrica (US$3, 1 hour), Pucón (US$4, 1.5 hours), Curacautín (US$4, 1.5 hours), Osorno (US$7, 4 hours), Puerto Montt (US$10, 5.5 hours), Santiago (US$14–20, 9 hours).

Most Argentina-bound buses use the Paso Mamuil Malal crossing southeast of Pucón (to Junín de los Andes and San Martín de los Andes), but some take the Paso Pino Hachado route, directly east of Temuco via Curacautín and the upper Biobío town of Lonquimay (to Zapala and Neuquén). In addition, there are connections to Bariloche via the Panamericana to Osorno and Ruta 215 east over Paso Cardenal Samoré.

Since the distances are long, the terrain mountainous, and the roads partly gravel, some trans-Andean buses leave early—sometimes as early as 3 A.M. Carriers serving Junín de los Andes and San Martín de los Andes (US$20, 6 hours) include **Buses San Martín** (tel. 045/258626) and **Buses Ruta Sur** (Miraflores

1151, tel. 045/210079). **Igi Llaima** and **Nar-Bus** (both at Miraflores 1535, tel. 045/407777) alternate daily 5 A.M. services to Zapala and Neuquén (US$25, 10 hours) and also go to San Martín. **Vía Bariloche** (tel. 045/257904) also goes to Neuquén.

Train
The **Estación de Ferrocarriles del Estado** (Av. Barros Arana 191, tel. 045/233416) is eight blocks northeast of the Plaza de Armas, but all services were suspended in mid-2009. Consult www.efe.cl for updated information.

GETTING AROUND
City transport is frequent and cheap, with both buses and *taxi colectivos.*

To the Airport
Just 6 kilometers south of town and west of the Panamericana, Temuco's **Aeropuerto Maquehue** (tel. 045/554801) will eventually move to Freire, 30 kilometers south. **Transfer**

Araucanía (tel. 045/339900) arranges airport transfers (around US$7.50), as do taxis from the northeast corner of the Plaza de Armas.

To the Bus Terminal
From downtown to the Rodoviario, catch northbound Micro 7 Troncal or Micro 9 from Portales and Bulnes, or *taxi colectivo* 11-P from the corner of Prat and Claro Solar.

Car Rental
For excursions into the backcountry in and around Temuco, especially the circuit through Parque Nacional Conguillío or the upper Biobío, scarce public transportation makes car rental the most convenient option. Rental agencies include the **Automóvil Club de Chile** (Acchi, San Martín 0278, tel. 045/248903), **Avis** (San Martín 755, tel. 045/237575, tel. 045/337715 at the airport), **Budget** (Vicuña Mackenna 399, tel. 045/232715), and **Hertz** (Andrés Bello 792, tel. 045/318585, tel. 045/337019 at the airport).

Vicinity of Temuco

There are worthwhile excursions in all directions, but most visitors focus on the Andes to the east. Temuco's **Multitour** (Bulnes 307, Oficina 203, tel. 045/237913, www.chile-travel.com/multitur.html) has English-speaking guides and a good track record for excursions in and around Temuco—primarily toward the Andean national parks and reserves, but also to westerly Mapuche villages.

PARQUE NACIONAL TOLHUACA
Native woodlands of Araucarias and other species adorn the foothill slopes of Parque Nacional Tolhuaca, where the Río Malleco drains south/southwest into marshy Laguna Malleco before plunging toward the coast. Improved access roads have increased visitation, especially in summer and on weekends,

but most people stay in the immediate vicinity of Laguna Malleco—the rest of the park is still ideal for camping, hiking, and fishing.

Geography and Climate
In the Andean precordillera, ranging from 1,000 meters above sea level around Laguna Malleco to 1,821 meters on the summits and ridgelines of Reserva Nacional Malleco to the north, Tolhuaca is a compact 6,374-hectare unit on the north bank of Malleco, which flows northwest toward the town of Collipulli. It has a cool humid climate, with an average annual temperature of 9°C and 2,500–3,000 millimeters of rainfall, but enjoys mild, relatively dry summers. The park's namesake peak, 2,806-meter Volcán Tolhuaca, lies beyond its boundaries to the southeast.

Flora and Fauna

At higher elevations, Tolhuaca has nearly pure Araucaria forests in well-drained soils, but the dense gallery forests along the Río Malleco consist of *coigüe, olivillo,* and other evergreen species, along with deciduous *raulí* and roble. *Quila* forms almost impenetrable bamboo thickets in some areas. *Junquillos* (reeds) grow in the lakeside sediments, while rhubarb-like *nalcas, chilco* (firecracker fuchsia), ferns, mosses, and other water-loving plants grow on the riverbanks.

Except for waterfowl and coypu in Laguna Malleco, Tolhuaca's fauna are inconspicuous, but puma, *pudú* (miniature deer), foxes, and skunks all exist here.

Sights and Recreation

As ash and other sediments from the surrounding ridges and peaks sluice into the river and downstream, water-loving reeds are colonizing the shoreline of 76-hectare **Laguna Malleco,** a glacial remnant where Conaf keeps a loaner rowboat for anglers and birders. It's an easy walk from the campground, and swimming is possible in several nearby pools.

From Laguna Malleco's north shore, the 1,800-meter **Sendero El Salto** winds through thick native forest to **Salto Malleco,** a 50-meter cascade that plummets over rugged basalt into the river's lower drainage. Also from Laguna Malleco, **Sendero Prados de Mesacura** switchbacks up the north shore to intersect the **Sendero Lagunillas,** which follows the contour east through nearly waterless Araucaria woodlands (the porous volcanic soil absorbs almost all precipitation). From a spot about five kilometers east of Laguna Malleco, toward Termas de Tolhuaca, the eight-kilometer **Sendero Laguna Verde** skirts 1,606-meter Cerro Laguna Verde's southwestern slope to arrive at its namesake lake.

Accommodations and Food

At Laguna Malleco, Conaf's shady **Camping Inalaufquén** (tel. 02/1960480, US$20 per site) has 25 sites with barbecue pits, picnic tables, running water, and clean bathrooms with flush toilets and cold showers. Single travelers can appeal for a discount if it's not crowded. For visitors with their own vehicles and more money, Curacautín's Hotel Termas de Tolhuaca is an option.

Tolhuaca lacks a formal visitors center, but Conaf rangers at Laguna Malleco offer daily chats at the outdoor amphitheater. No supplies whatsoever are available here—bring everything you need.

Information

Tolhuaca lacks a formal visitors center, but rangers at Laguna Malleco offer daily chats at the outdoor amphitheater. Park admission costs US$5 for adults, US$2.50 for children.

Getting There and Around

From Curacautín, 87 kilometers northeast of Temuco via Lautaro or 119 kilometers via Victoria, an improved gravel road reaches the hot-springs resort of Termas de Tolhuaca, 33 kilometers to the north. From Termas de Tolhuaca, a once hazardous four-wheel-drive road to Laguna Malleco is now passable for ordinary vehicles, at least in summer. *Taxi colectivos* from Curacautín go as far as Termas de Tolhuaca, but it's another nine kilometers to Malleco.

The Upper Cautín and Biobío

From Victoria, 58 kilometers north of Temuco on the Panamericana, a smooth and scenic two-lane highway goes to Curacautín, Lonquimay, and the upper Biobío, a little-visited and underappreciated area north of Parque Nacional Conguillío. Blessed with its own native forests, rushing rivers, and volcanic grandeur, the upper Biobío is, along with Conguillío, part of a UNESCO World Biosphere Reserve declared to protect its remaining Araucaria stands.

In addition to the main road, this area is also accessible via a shorter paved alternative that heads northeast from Lautaro (30 kilometers north of Temuco). From the upper Biobío, it's also possible to loop back around on good gravel roads to Melipeuco (Conguillío's southern gateway) or back to Temuco.

CURACAUTÍN
Dating from 1882, when the military established Fuerte Ultra Cautín in Pehuenche territory, Curacautín (population 12,812) is now the northern access point to Parque Nacional Conguillío and gateway to the upper Río Cautín and upper Biobío. It is 87 kilometers northeast of Temuco via Lautaro or 119 kilometers via the Panamericana and Victoria.

Accommodations and Food
Facing the highway, **Hospedaje Aliwen** (Manuel Rodríguez 540, tel. 045/881437, US$30–33 d with breakfast) has rooms with either shared or private baths. There are few places to eat, the best of which is probably Hotel Central's **La Cabaña** (Yungay 157, tel. 045/881256), opposite the plaza. **Café Vizzio's** (Serrano 248, tel. 045/881653) has sandwiches, desserts, and coffee.

Information and Services
On the north side of the Plaza de Armas, the **Oficina de Informaciones Turísticas**

© WAYNE BERNHARDSON

Curacautín is vulnerable to an eruption of Volcán Llaima.

(Manuel Rodríguez s/n, tel. 045/464858) is open 8 A.M.–9 P.M. weekdays, 9 A.M.–5 P.M. Saturday, and 9 A.M.–2 P.M. Sunday.

Supermercado Bryc (O'Higgins 515) has an ATM. **Correos de Chile** (Yungay 285) is the post office. **Telefónica** (O'Higgins 640-B) has both long-distance service and Internet access, but there are several new Internet outlets.

Getting There and Around

Three blocks west of the Plaza de Armas, Curacautín's **Terminal Rodoviario** (Ruta 89 and Arica) is directly on the Lonquimay highway. **Tur-Bus** (Serrano 101, tel. 045/882542) has direct Santiago service.

Flota Erbuc has five buses daily to and from Temuco (US$3) via Victoria and four via Lautaro; there are five to Lonquimay. Getting to Parque Nacional Conguillío is only possible with a taxi.

Igi Llaima and **Nar-Bus** pass through town daily en route to Zapala and Neuquén, Argentina (US$23), as does **Buses Plaza;** make reservations in Temuco to guarantee a seat.

TERMAS DE TOLHUACA

Reached by an improved gravel road that heads north out of Curacautín for 35 kilometers, the once-humble hot-springs resort of Termas de Tolhuaca has morphed into a spa. Having recently changed hands, it's an alternative for those who want to visit Parque Nacional Tolhuaca but don't want to camp in the park, which is nine kilometers farther on by road. The resort was founded in 1898, but today's facility is a dramatic improvement over the rustic Russian-built original.

Accommodations at the 100-bed **Hotel Termas de Tolhuaca** (Calama 240, Curacautín, tel. 045/881164, www.termasde-tolhuaca.cl, US$80 pp with full board) include unlimited access to pools and baths; it has its own restaurant. Camping costs US$13 per site for up to six people; public-pool access is US$13 per person (US$6.50 for children), and there are limited supplies on-site.

MANZANAR AND VICINITY

Barely a wide spot in the road, 18 kilometers east of Curacautín and 680 meters above sea level, Manzanar is home to **Hotel Termas de Manzanar** (tel./fax 045/881200, www.termas-demanzanar.cl), a riverside spa resort set back from the south side of the highway. It offers accommodations options ranging from simple rooms with private baths (US$56 s, US$91 d for B&B) to suites with private baths and whirlpool tubs (US$160 s or d for B&B). Full-board packages are also available, and non-guests can use the pools for US$12 pp.

About five kilometers west of Manzanar, Bavarian-run **Hostal Andenrose** (Km 68.5, cel. 09/9869-1700, www.andenrose.com, US$36–45 s, US$51–60 d) is an immaculate bed-and-breakfast/restaurant which, though it's walking distance from the highway, is shielded from any noise or visual pollution by the rushing Río Cautín and the dense woods along its banks. English-speaking owner Hans Schöndorfer will pick up guests from the Curacautín bus terminal and also offers a verdant riverside campground (US$7 pp) for backpackers, with separate toilets and showers.

MALALCAHUELLO AND VICINITY

Ten kilometers east of Manzanar, the hamlet of Malalcahuello occupies a high valley in the shadow of 2,865-meter Volcán Lonquimay (known also as Volcán Mocho). At upwards of 980 meters, Malalcahuello is cooler than areas to the west, and nights can get chilly even in summer. Its newest asset is the hot-springs resort Centro Termal Malalcahuello.

Thanks to accessibility to its namesake national reserve—trailheads start near the highway itself—Malalcahuello makes an ideal destination for hikers and riders.

Reserva Nacional Malalcahuello

Combined with the contiguous Reserva Las Nalcas to the north, the Malalcahuello reserve comprises 25,000 hectares of wild high country that also serves as a key forestry research center.

Higher than nearby Parque Nacional Tolhuaca, Malalcahuello contains an overlapping forest flora of Araucarias with deciduous Andean forest with evergreen *coigüe* and *lenga,* and Araucaria with *coigüe* mixed with *ñire.* The fauna resembles Tolhuaca's, though the Andean condor and the *carpintero negro* (black woodpecker) are more common here.

Its summit crater filled by a glacier that spills onto the adjoining flanks, symmetrical **Volcán Lonquimay** is the reserve's focal point. Slightly northeast of town, it dates from the late Pleistocene but erupted as recently as 1933, almost simultaneously with nearby Volcán Llaima, and lava flows spilled down its northeastern flanks in 1990. Trails to nearby Cerro Cautín (2.5 hours) and Lonquimay's summit start here, and the Sendero de Chile rounds Lonquimay before descending into town and then continuing toward the Sierra Nevada and Conguillío; new trekking maps, for sale at La Suizandina, make hiking here easier.

On the site of an older ski area that was nearly in ruins, Malalcahuello also has a sparkling new resort, the **Corralco Centro de Montaña** (Av. Apoquindo 6275, Las Condes, Santiago, tel./fax 02/2029325, www.corralco .com), open for two-night to weeklong packages. Business hasn't been as good as hoped, though, because access is difficult when it snows heavily and investment to improve the facilities has lagged; lift tickets cost about US$40 per day during the entire mid-June–October season.

Accommodations and Food

Swiss-run ◖ **La Suizandina** (Camino Internacional Km 83 tel. 045/1973725 or cell tel. 09/9884-9541, fax 045/1973724, www .suizandina.com, US$22 pp for hostel accommodations, US$47–65 s, US$59–74 d) is a combination hostel, cabaña, and guesthouse west of town on the north side of the highway. Multilingual founder Tom Buschor is only a part-time presence now, but his Swiss managers and staff still provide a Swiss-style breakfast (Tom is a professional baker) and also serve Swiss specialties such as fondue and raclette for

reasonably priced lunches or dinners, accompanied by fresh desserts and Chilean wines. While they no longer promote Suizandina as a campground, it's still possible to camp here economically (US$7 pp, breakfast optional for US$7). Guests get a 15 percent discount at nearby hot-springs resorts.

The **Malalcahuello Thermal Resort & Spa** (Recabarren 03160, Temuco, tel. 045/1973556, www.malalcahuello.cl, US$220–287 s or d for hotel accommodations) is a hot-springs megaproject that fits surprisingly well into its natural setting, about two kilometers south of the highway via a soon to-be-paved road. With state-of-the-art indoor pools, spa treatments, and physical therapists, it also has a handful of cabañas and bungalows (US$192 for up to five people, including access to baths but not breakfast), and a so-so restaurant. Outside peak season (summer and ski season), rates drop by about 25 percent.

Admission to the pools costs US$17 per adult, US$10 per child aged 3–12, and US$5 for those younger than age 3. Additional services include massages, mud baths, steam baths, and the like.

Conaf's Malalcahuello ranger station is a good source for advice; speakers of English, German, French, and Italian can try La Suizandina. There is free "Bibliored" Internet access at the library at the old train station, but also long waits and no WiFi.

Getting There

Biobío and **Flota Erbuc** buses between Temuco and Lonquimay go directly past the gates of La Suizandina and the ranger station.

LONQUIMAY

From Malalcahuello, the highway heads southeast to enter the 1930s' **Túnel Las Raíces,** where the Púa–Lonquimay railway ran a tourist train as recently as the 1990s. Now open to vehicle traffic (toll US$2), the one-lane, 4.5-kilometer tunnel has been upgraded with new pavement and a reinforced roof, but a second parallel tunnel (to permit two-way rather than alternating traffic at present) remains in the planning stages. This would simplify access to the Pino Hachado border crossing.

Beyond the tunnel, the highway turns northeast to the village of Lonquimay, in the placid upper Biobío drainage—the traditional starting point for descending what was Chile's wildest white-water river until a series of downstream dams submerged the rapids.

Instead of a standard grid, Lonquimay (population 3,435) has a peculiar ovoid city plan, though still centered on the usual Plaza de Armas. For information, it also has an obliging **Parador Turístico** (O'Higgins and Colón, tel. 045/464842, ofiturlonqui@gmail.com) and restaurants and hotels that traditionally close by March. From Malalcahuello, a steep eastbound dirt road over Cuesta las Raíces is a shorter alternate route to Lonquimay, which is 900 meters above sea level, but it's open in summer and autumn only.

Eight kilometers west of town, **Los Arenales de Lonquimay** (Casilla 5, Lonquimay, tel. 045/891911 for lodging, cell tel. 09/9313-2208 for service) is a struggling ski area with erratic management. **Lonco Patagonia** (Ruta 89 Km 106.5, cell tel. 09/9283-0846, www.loncopatagonia.galeon.com) offers horseback excursions in the vicinity.

Hostería Folil Pewenche (Ignacio Carrera Pinto 110, cel. 09/8407-4301) has both shared-bath (US$13 s, US$23 d) and private-bath (US$30 s or d) accommodations. **Donde Juancho Hostería** (O'Higgins 1130, tel. 045/891140, www.dondejuancho.cl, US$17 pp, US$42 s or d) also offers accommodations and has a 50-seat restaurant with a good reputation for beef and traditional Chilean dishes.

At least five **Biobío** and **Flota Erbuc** buses daily connect Lonquimay with Temuco.

ALTO BIOBÍO

South of Lonquimay, a gravel road tracks south past Lago Galletué, the Biobío's official source and part of Conaf's **Reserva Nacional Galletué;** it continues southeast past the border post of Icalma (for the Argentine town of Aluminé), but there is no public transport across this route. There are numerous simple campgrounds along this main road, which then turns west toward Melipeuco and Parque Nacional Conguillío. From Lonquimay, newly paved Ruta 181 crosses Conaf's **Reserva Nacional Alto Biobío** via the 1,884-meter Paso Pino Hachado, the route used by buses to the Argentine cities of Zapala and Neuquén.

MELIPEUCO

In the Río Allipén Valley, sited on an ancient mudflow 92 kilometers east of Temuco via Cunco and 45 kilometers west of Icalma, the Mapuche town of Melipeuco is Parque Nacional Conguillío's southern access point and an alternative route into the upper Biobío loop around Lonquimay. In the 1970s, this was a conflictive area in the agrarian reform movement, and the issue remains alive today.

Melipeuco (population 2,333) operates a summer-only tourist office on Pedro Aguirre Cerda, across from the YPF gas station. There's a crafts market here as well.

The cheapest accommodations are at cozy

At Melipeuco, a sign indicates the evacuation route in case of Llaima's eruption.

Hospedaje Icalma (Pedro Aguirre Cerda 729, cel. 09/9280-8210, US$12 pp with private bath and breakfast), which also arranges Conguillío excursions. **Hostería Huetelén** (Pedro Aguirre Cerda 1, tel. 045/581005, US$33 s or d with private bath and breakfast) is a more formal option, but its restaurant is mediocre; for standard Chilean food, try **Ruminot** (Pedro Aguirre Cerda 496, tel. 045/581087, lunch and dinner daily).

Nar-Bus runs around seven buses daily to and from Temuco's Terminal de Buses Rurales (US$2, 1.5 hours). There is no scheduled public transport to Conguillío, but taxis or pickup trucks will take passengers to the visitors center for about US$12–15.

Parque Nacional Conguillío

Directly east of Temuco, 3,125-meter Volcán Llaima's smoldering crater is Parque Nacional Conguillío's most eye-catching feature; since colonial times, Chile's second most active volcano has recorded dozens of violent eruptions. On New Year's Day 2008, in fact, a sudden eruption and lava flow closed the northern access road from Curacautín and forced evacuation of 150 tourists.

Within its 60,833 hectares, though, this UNESCO biosphere reserve also abounds with dozens of other lava flows, secondary cones, alpine lakes, river canyons, and the Araucaria forest that it was created to protect—the name Conguillío derives from the Mapudungun *kongüijim,* "to enter the *pewen* forest."

The *pewen*'s fame was such that, in late 1911, the aging pioneer U.S. conservationist John Muir traveled here simply to see, sketch, and photograph the tree in its native habitat— "A glorious and novel sight, beyond all I had hoped for." As he so often did in California's Sierra Nevada, Muir slept in the open air, beneath the trees he had come to visit.

For foreigners and Chileans alike, Conguillío is one of Temuco's most popular excursions. It justifies a day trip but merits at least an overnight.

GEOGRAPHY AND CLIMATE

From Temuco, Conguillío's western limit is only about 80 kilometers away via Cherquenco, but by either Curacautín or Melipeuco it's about 120 kilometers. Altitudes range from around 900 meters in the Río Truful Truful Valley to 3,125 meters on Llaima's summit. In its northeastern corner, the ruggedly glaciated Sierra Nevada averages above 2,500 meters.

Since most of Conguillío's 2,500 millimeters of precipitation falls as snow between May and September, the mild summers, averaging around 15°C, make its numerous lakes and streams popular recreational destinations. Even in summer, though, occasional heavy rains—if not lava flows—can make the Curacautín road impassable even with four-wheel drive.

FLORA AND FAUNA

Conguillío originally was two separate parks, the other named Los Paraguas after the umbrella shape of the mature Araucaria that, above 1,400 meters, mixes with the southern beeches *coigüe, ñire,* and *lenga. Coigüe* is also common at lower elevations, around 900 meters, but mixed with roble; above 1,200 meters, *raulí* succeeds roble.

Traditionally, Pewenche Indians collected the coniferous Araucaria's nuts, much as indigenous groups gathered piñon nuts in western North America. The name Pewenche means "people of the *pewen,*" the local species of an endemic Southern Hemisphere genus that once enjoyed a greater distribution throughout the Americas.

Because much of Conguillío's terrain consists of barren volcanic slopes, lava fields, and open woodlands, prime wildlife habitat is scarce and so is wildlife. Birds are most common and resemble those at Tolhuaca or Malalcahuello, but the small reptile *lagartija* flourishes in drier environments.

An Araucaria seedling sprouts on the flanks of Volcán Llaima.

VOLCÁN LLAIMA

Towering just west of the park's geographic center, glacier-covered Llaima is a Holocene structure of accumulated lava flows within an eight-kilometer-wide caldera that exploded about 7,200 years ago. It has two active craters, one on the summit and another on its south-eastern shoulder. Its early 2008 eruption closed the park for a time, but in good weather the northern access road is passable for almost any motor vehicle.

◖ SECTOR CONGUILLÍO

In **Sector Conguillío,** east of Llaima, the sprawling lava flows of **El Escorial** dammed the Río Truful Truful to form **Laguna Arco Iris** and **Laguna Verde;** to the north, beneath the Sierra Nevada, **Laguna Conguillío** has a similar origin.

Near Conaf's Centro de Información at the southwest corner of Laguna Conguillío, the **Sendero Araucarias** is a short woodland nature trail suitable for any hiker. For a longer

and more challenging excursion try walking from **Playa Linda** at the east end of Laguna Conguillío, to the base of the **Sierra Nevada,** which rewards the hiker with overwhelming views through nearly pure Araucaria wood-land. This extension across the mountains to Termas Río Blanco is a hazardous one on which hikers have died.

At **Laguna Captrén,** at the park's northern entrance, the **Sendero de Chile** was the ini-tial section of the nonmotorized trail intended to unite the country from the Peruvian bor-der to Tierra del Fuego. At Laguna Arco Iris, to the south, an early settler built the wooden **Casa del Colono** as a homestead cabin. From Laguna Verde, also known as Laguna Quililo, a short wooded footpath reaches the beach at **La Ensenada.**

Conaf's **Sendero Cañadon Truful-Truful,** a 900-meter nature trail, follows the river's course where erosion has uncovered the rain-bow chronology of Llaima's eruptions and ash falls. Along the 800-meter **Sendero Los Vertientes,** subterranean springs emerge from the volcanic terrain.

SECTOR LOS PARAGUAS

From Sector Los Paraguas, on the park's west side, well-equipped climbers can scale Llaima; camping is possible in summer, and there is also a *refugio.* There is an alternative route from Captrén, which has better public transport, on the north side. Before climbing, get permission from Conaf in Temuco.

Skiing takes place at Los Paraguas's upgraded **Centro de Ski Las Araucarias** (tel. 045/562313, www.skiaraucarias.cl); it has Temuco offices at Bulnes 351, Oficina 47 (tel. 045/239999). Lift tickets cost about US$25–30 per day.

ACCOMMODATIONS AND FOOD

Along Laguna Conguillío's south shore, Conaf has five campgrounds under private conces-sion: The campground administration is at **Los Ñirres** (44 sites), while there are smaller clus-ters at **Los Carpinteros** (12 sites), **La Caseta**

(12 sites), **El Estero** (10 sites), and **El Hoyón** (10 sites). Rates are US$25 per site for up to six people in summer and during Semana Santa, US$17 the rest of the year. Conaf also sets aside a handful of El Estero sites for bicyclists and backpackers (US$5 pp).

Ten kilometers northwest of Laguna Conguillío, there are 12 more sites at **Laguna Captrén**, which are due to reopen after repair of damage from the 2008 eruption. For more information or reservations in Temuco, contact Conaf (tel. 045/298114).

The former cabañas built around massive Araucaria trees have been dismantled, but newer and better ones are now available just one kilometer west of park headquarters for US$75 for up to three guests, US$91 for up to seven; off-season rates are about 20 percent lower. For details and reservations, contact Cristián Pérez (tel. 045/841710 in Victoria, cell tel. 09/9050-2654, cristianevans@hotmail.com).

At Laguna Verde, 18 kilometers northeast of Melipeuco, the private **Cabañas La Baita Conguillío** (Casilla 492, Villarrica, tel. 045/416410, cell tel. 09/9733-2442, www.labaitaconguillio.cl, US$58 s, US$66 d) has cabañas sleeping 4–8 people.

The modern **Centro de Ski las Araucarias** (tel. 045/562313, www.skiaraucarias.cl) has a variety of accommodations. Its **Refugio Paraguas** has dorm beds (US$17 pp with your own sleeping bag) and one six-bed apartment (US$110), while the **Refugio Pehuén** also has dorms (US$17 pp) and doubles with shared bath (US$44) and private bath (US$50). Facilities at the **Apartment Hotel Llaima** (US$108) can sleep up to four.

INFORMATION

At Laguna Conguillío, Conaf's **Centro de Información Ambiental** (tel. 02/1960850, parque.conguillio@conaf.cl), has good natural-history exhibits and a cozy fireplace; it's open 9 A.M.–1 P.M. and 2–6 P.M. daily except in January and February, when it does not close at midday and stays open until 7:30 P.M. It organizes children's programs and hiking excursions and provides evening naturalist talks.

Conaf also has ranger stations at the Laguna Captrén and Truful Truful park entrances, where park admission costs US$8 pp. At the Paraguas ski area, it costs US$2.

GETTING THERE AND AROUND

Because public transportation is inconvenient to almost every sector of the park, it's worth considering a car rental, but it's not absolutely essential. Even with a car, the steep, narrow, and sometimes muddy road between Laguna Captrén and the park administration can be difficult.

Reaching Curacautín and Melipeuco, the northern and southern gateways to the main park loop, is easy enough by public bus. From either Curacautín or Melipeuco, it's possible to hire a taxi or pickup truck to Conguillío.

Sector Los Paraguas is most difficult to reach by public transportation. At Temuco's Terminal de Buses Rurales, **Nar Bus** (Pinto 032, tel. 045/407740) goes to the village of Cherquenco (US$2) at 11:30 A.M. and 12:30, 4:30, and 5:30 P.M., but from there it's 17 kilometers farther to the Los Paraguas ski lodge. An alternative route goes from Captrén to Los Paraguas.

Villarrica

Volcán Villarrica's fiery eruptions may have deterred some settlers, but Mapuche resistance to the Spaniards and Chileans was more effective. In 1552, 50 colonists under Gerónimo de Alderete's command established Santa María Magdalena de Villarrica, but the Mapuche forced its abandonment several times despite speculation about precious metals nearby (the overly optimistic founding name Villarrica means "Rich Town"). After expelling the Spaniards in 1602, the Mapuche enjoyed nearly three centuries of uninterrupted possession until, in 1883, Chilean colonel Gregorio Urrutia reached an agreement with the Mapuche chief Epuléf to regularize the Chilean presence.

Villarrica's 1897 declaration of city status brought an influx of immigrants, many of them German, who transformed the area into a dairy zone and, eventually, a durable resort area with an international reputation.

ORIENTATION

Some 87 kilometers southeast of Temuco via the Panamericana and Ruta 199, an international highway to Argentina, Villarrica (population 30,859) lies at Lago Villarrica's southwestern edge, at its Río Toltén outlet. While the town has a regular grid pattern, the focus of activity is not the Plaza de Armas but rather the lakeshore, along with the commercial thoroughfare Avenida Pedro de Valdivia and its perpendicular Camilo Henríquez.

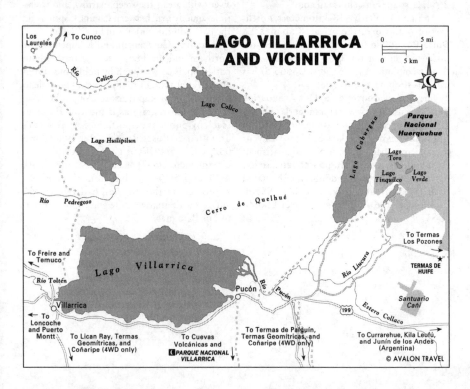

SIGHTS AND RECREATION

Stone tools, early Mapuche ceramics, and contemporary indigenous jewelry, silver, and leatherwork constitute the collections of the **Museo Histórico y Arqueológico de Villarrica** (Pedro de Valdivia 1050, tel. 045/413445, 9 A.M.–1 P.M. and 6–10 P.M. daily except Sunday morning, US$0.20). Directly in front stands a **ruca,** a traditional Mapuche dwelling thickly thatched with *junquillo* and *totora* reeds.

The lakefront **Embarcadero,** with a cluster of small jetties toward the foot of General Körner, is the starting point for water-based excursions.

ENTERTAINMENT AND SHOPPING

In recent years, **The Travellers** (Valentín Letelier 753, tel. 045/412830, www.thetravellers.cl) has morphed from a diverse fusion restaurant into a bar that serves primarily pub grub, but it remains popular; smoking prevails throughout.

El Otro Sur (Valentín Letelier 836) is the direct descendent of Pub del Sur, which burned down a couple years ago; it opens early (around 7 P.M.), stays open late (until around 5 A.M.), and also has live music. **Dinners** (Pedro Montt 390, tel. 045/416745) draws a younger crowd.

Immediately behind the tourist office, the **Feria Artesanal** showcases Mapuche crafts and food in summer, but the rest of the year it's moribund. The daily market opens around midday and closes in late afternoon. **Tejidos Ray-Ray** (Anfión Muñoz 386, tel. 045/412006) is a clothing store strong on woolens.

ACCOMMODATIONS

As in other Lakes District resorts, accommodations prices peak in January and February, but Semana Santa, September's Fiestas Patrias, and the ski season can all see higher prices, as well.

For shoestring backpackers only, the barebones **Hotel Fuentes** (Vicente Reyes 665, tel. 045/411595, US$8–11 pp) has varying rates depending on whether the room has a shared or private bath; some rooms lack windows. Its bar/restaurant has long been a gathering place.

Cyclists in particular flock to the immaculate Swiss-run hostel ☖ **La Torre Suiza** (Bilbao 969, tel./fax 045/411213, www.torresuiza.com, US$12–14 pp for dorms, US$33–42 d), with firm, comfortable beds, easily regulated hot showers, and a tobacco-free interior, but squeaky floors. The higher rates are for larger rooms with private baths in a new wing; everyone shares a substantial European-style breakfast. Owners Béat and Claudia Zbinden also help plan self-guided cycling trips, and rent bikes.

Rates at **Hotel Villa Linda** (Av. Pedro de Valdivia 678, tel. 045/411392, www.villalinda.tk, US$20 pp) include private bath, breakfast, and cable TV.

Modern **Hotel Montebianco** (Pedro de Valdivia 1011, tel. 045/411798, marpack@tie.cl, US$50 s, US$53 d) also has an outstanding restaurant, but it's on Villarrica's busiest street. **Hotel Villarrica** (Körner 255, tel./fax 045/411641, villahotel@corfo.cl, US$44 s, US$54 d) offers good value for its tranquil lakeside location in a residential area.

Comfy, rustically styled **Hostería Bilbao** (Camilo Henríquez 43, tel. 045/411186, US$58 d) enjoys a lakeshore site. The renovated **Hotel Yachting Kiel** (Körner 153, tel. 045/411631, www.restaurantkiel.cl, US$67 d) also offers rooms with lakeview balconies, satellite TV, and WiFi, plus its namesake fish-and-seafood restaurant.

Set among lush gardens, **Hotel El Ciervo** (Körner 241, tel. 045/411215, www.hotelelciervo.cl, US$77 s, US$97 d) is a traditional favorite; some rooms have fireplaces, and rates include an ample European-style breakfast.

Overlooking the lake from secluded high ground, the Oregonian owners at TV-free ☖ **Hostería de la Colina** (Las Colinas 115, tel./fax 045/411503, www.hosteriadelacolina.com, US$65 s, US$85 d, up to US$130 s or d) provide a full American-style breakfast, attractive gardens with a hot tub, and a large English-language book exchange on the honor system; the homemade ice cream alone makes the restaurant worth a visit. On the downside, new construction nearby has obstructed most (though not all) volcano views. The highest rates correspond to spacious garden cabañas.

Midway between Villarrica and Pucón, the area's only legitimate five-star hotel is the lakeside **(Villarrica Park Lake Hotel** (Camino Villarrica Pucón, Km 13, tel. 045/450000, www.villarricaparklakehotel.cl, US$200–515 s or d), a tasteful contemporary place with expansive rooms (nearly all with balconies), all of which face the lake. Its relatively small private beach is rockier than it is sandy, but it compensates partly with indoor and outdoor pools, as well as a spa, two bars, and a restaurant. Serious high rollers choose the presidential suite (US$1,200 per night, usually reserved well ahead of time).

FOOD

For coffee, hot chocolate, kuchen, and other desserts, **Il Golosso** (Urrutia 837, tel. 045/416563, www.ilgolosso.cl) stays open 24 hours in January and February. At the Mercado Fritz crafts market, inexpensive **La Cocina de María** (Aviador Acevedo 600) is a good lunch option for typical Chilean dishes such as chicken with rice, fried chicken, and empanadas.

The unpretentious **Tejuelas** (Gerónimo de Alderete 632, tel. 045/410619) delivers great value for the price, especially with some of the country's finest homemade bread for sandwiches. The pizza is less rewarding, its crust a little heavy despite a diversity of appetizing toppings.

In a lakeside setting, **El Rey del Marisco** (Valentín Letelier 1030, tel. 045/412093, lunch and dinner daily) remains popular for fish and shellfish dishes in the US$9–12 range, but it's been up and down lately. More often than not, the ambitious **Mesa del Mar** (Gerónimo de Alderete 835, tel. 045/419515, www.mesadelmar.cl, lunch and dinner daily) is very good, but on a bad night it's forgettable at best.

Hotel Montebianco's **La Vecchia Cucina** (Pedro de Valdivia 1011, tel. 045/411798, lunch and dinner daily) offers fine pasta entrées for

US$8–10, with slightly cheaper pizzas and homemade ice cream, all with professional service.

The carnivore's choice, Villarrica's most sophisticated option is **(La Cava de Roble** (Valentín Letelier 658, tel. 045/416446, www .lacavaderoble.cl, lunch and dinner daily), which specializes in beef and tasty game dishes such as venison (with a sweet and sour blueberry sauce, US$13) and wild boar. A limited pasta menu is creative—think ravioli stuffed with smoked salmon and abalone (US$7). Unlike most Chilean restaurants outside Santiago, it offers a choice of quality wines by the glass, and there's a spacious terrace for sunny afternoons or fine evenings.

Under the same management, **Restaurant Kiel** (General Körner 153, tel. 045/411631, www.restaurantkiel.cl, lunch and dinner daily) serves a more traditional fish and seafood menu at slightly lower prices, with dishes such as trout stuffed with crab and vegetables. Here, though, only house wines are available by the glass.

Friatto (Camilo Henríquez 387, tel. 045/414534) is a decent ice creamery that's also a WiFi hotspot.

INFORMATION

Well-stocked with maps, brochures, and a roster of accommodations but no prices, Villarrica's municipal **Oficina de Turismo** (Pedro de Valdivia 1070, tel. 045/206619, turis@villarrica.org) keeps long hours in January and February: 8 A.M.–11 P.M. daily; the rest of the year, the schedule's only slightly shorter: 9 A.M.–10 P.M. daily.

SERVICES

Turcamb (Camilo Henríquez 576, Local 6) is the only exchange house. There are multiple ATMs along Avenida Pedro de Valdivia.

Correos de Chile (Anfión Muñoz 315) is the post office. **Entel** (Camilo Henríquez 446) has both long-distance telephone and Internet service. **PuntoNet** (Valentín Letelier 754, tel. 045/414907) keeps long hours for Internet access.

For laundry service, try **Todo Lavado**

(General Urrutia 699, Local 7, tel. 045/414452).

It used to be necessary to organize excursions such as climbing Volcán Villarrica in Pucón, but **Turismo Villarrica Extremo** (Pedro de Valdivia 910, tel. 045/410900, www .villarricaextremo.com) works with Pucón agencies.

For medical assistance, there's the **Hospital Villarrica** (San Martín 460, tel. 045/411169).

GETTING THERE AND AROUND

Villarrica has a central **Terminal de Buses** (Av. Pedro de Valdivia 621), but some carriers have individual offices nearby. **Buses Regionales Villarrica** (Vicente Reyes 619, tel. 045/411871) has frequent buses to Pucón (US$1.50, 45 minutes), where there are connections to other regional destinations such as Curarrehue (US$2) and Puesco.

Buses Jac (Bilbao 610, tel. 045/467777) shuttles at least every 15–30 minutes between Temuco (US$3, 1 hour) and Pucón.

Northbound services to Santiago and intermediates on the Panamericana are frequent, but some southbound services require backtracking to Temuco; alternatively, transfer at Freire from any Temuco-bound bus.

Many companies go to Santiago, including Pullman Bus (Bilbao 598, tel. 045/414217, and Buses Jac and **Tur-Bus** (Anfión Muñoz 657, tel. 045/411534), which have the only direct services to Osorno, Puerto Varas, and Puerto Montt.

Santiago fares start around US$20, with *salón cama* sleepers around US$35. Other sample destinations, fares, and times include Osorno (US$9, 3.5 hours) and Puerto Montt (US$12, 5 hours).

Local carriers also serve the Argentine cities of Junín de los Andes, with connections to San Martín de los Andes; these buses leave from Temuco and board additional passengers in Villarrica and Pucón. **Buses San Martín** (tel. 045/411584) and **Igi Llaima** (tel. 045/412733), both at the main terminal, alternate daily services. For services to Bariloche, it's necessary to return to Temuco or make connections in Osorno.

Castillo Rent A Car (Anfión Muñoz 415, tel. 045/411618, www.castillorentacar.cl) is the only car-rental option.

Pucón

At the foot of ominously smoldering Volcán Villarrica, Pucón has gained a name over the past decade as *the* destination for hikers, climbers, mountain bikers, windsurfers, and white-water rafters and kayakers. Still popular with conventional Chilean holidaymakers, it enjoys a longer season than most Lakes District resorts because hordes of youthful international travelers frequent the area from November to April. It has no sights of its own because almost everything worth seeing or doing is outside town, but at the end of the day everyone swarms to local hotels, restaurants, and bars to party.

That doesn't mean Pucón lacks a serious side. Over the past several years, the landmark cooperative Hostería ¡Ecole!, along with the affiliated Fundación Lahuen, has actively promoted regional forest conservation.

ORIENTATION

Where the Río Pucón enters the lake, 25 kilometers east of the town of Villarrica via Ruta 119, Pucón (population 13,837) occupies a compact grid bounded by the lakeshore to the north and west, Avenida Colo Colo to the east, and Volcán Villarrica's lower slopes to the south. Its main commercial axis is Avenida Bernardo O'Higgins, which continues as Ruta 119 toward Curarrehue and the Argentine border at Paso Mamuil Malal.

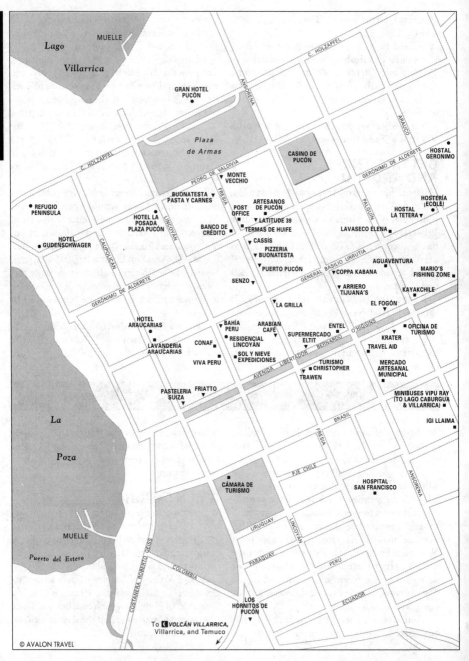

Lago Villarrica

MUELLE

GRAN HOTEL PUCÓN

C. HOLZAPFEL

Plaza de Armas

CASINO DE PUCÓN

HOSTAL GERONIMO

REFUGIO PENINSULA

MONTE VECCHIO

BUONATESTA PASTA Y CARNES

POST OFFICE

ARTESANOS DE PUCÓN

HOSTERÍA ¡ECÒLE!

HOTEL LA POSADA PLAZA PUCÓN

LATITUDE 39

HOSTAL LA TETERA

BANCO DE CRÉDITO

TERMAS DE HUIFE

LAVASECO ELENA

HOTEL GUDENSCHWAGER

CASSIS

PIZZERIA BUONATESTA

AGUAVENTURA

PUERTO PUCÓN

COPPA KABANA

MARIO'S FISHING ZONE

SENZO

ARRIERO TIJUANA'S

KAYAKCHILE

LA GRILLA

EL FOGÓN

HOTEL ARAUCARIAS

BAHÍA PERU

ARABIAN CAFÉ

ENTEL

OFICINA DE TURISMO

LAVÁNDERIA ARAUCARIAS

CONAF

RESIDENCIAL LINCOYÁN

SUPERMERCADO ELTIT

KRATER

TRAVEL AID

VIVA PERU

SOL Y NIEVE EXPEDICIONES

TURISMO CHRISTOPHER

MERCADO ARTESANAL MUNICIPAL

TRAWEN

PASTELERIA SUIZA

FRIATTO

AVENIDA LIBERTADOR

MINIBUSES VIPU RAY (TO LAGO CABURGUA & VILLARRICA)

BRASIL

IGI LLAIMA

La Poza

PJE CHILE

CÁMARA DE TURISMO

HOSPITAL SAN FRANCISCO

MUELLE

URUGUAY

Puerto del Estero

PARAGUAY

COLOMBIA

PERÚ

ECUADOR

LOS HORNITOS DE PUCÓN

To **VOLCÁN VILLARRICA**, Villarrica, and Temuco

© AVALON TRAVEL

ENTERTAINMENT AND EVENTS

There's little in terms of formal entertainment venues, but somehow Pucón has plenty to do.

The shell of the colossal Casino de Pucón burned nearly to the ground in late 2007, costing the city its main performing-arts venue and a cinema, but the new **Enjoy Pucón** (Ansorena 121, tel. 045/550000, www.enjoy.cl) casino imports performers of the stature of Spain's Joan Manuel Serrat.

There's a lot of turnover in bars, but several have managed to last more than a few seasons, most notably **Krater** (O'Higgins 447, tel. 045/441339) and **Mama's & Tapas** (O'Higgins 587, tel. 045/449002). Both places serve food as well, but that's not their forte.

Early February's **Ironman Internacional de Pucón** (Pucón International Triathlon) grows in popularity every year. February 27's **Aniversario de Pucón** celebrates the city's founding.

SHOPPING

The **Mercado Artesanal Municipal** (Ansorena 445, daily) and **Artesanos de Pucón** (Alderete 370, daily) both have ample crafts selections. There are also abundant street vendors.

ACCOMMODATIONS

Pucón has abundant budget accommodations, but the best values are a bit more expensive.

US$25-50

New in 2007, **La Posada del Embrujo** (Colo Colo 361, tel. 045/443840, www.laposadadelembrujo.cl, US$10–12 pp, US$20 s, US$25 d, mostly with private bath) occupies a spacious house with two to six firm beds per room, WiFi, and kitchen access. The location is easy walking distance to bars and restaurants, but far enough for nighttime peace and quiet.

In a quiet site only about 100 meters north of the Tur-Bus terminal, Swiss-run **Casa Satya** (Blanco Encalada 190, tel. 045/444093, cpassavant@gmail.com, US$17 pp, US$53 d with breakfast) has spacious rooms with kitchen privileges; the higher rates correspond to

Pucón's new casino

doubles with private baths. Owner Cristina Passavant also offers massage options ranging from reiki to Thai.

It's a little ragged in some aspects—the rooms have irregular shapes, for instance, and the bathroom linoleum undulates across the floor—but family-run HI affiliate **Refugio Península** (Holzapfel 11, tel. 045/443398, www.refugiopeninsula.cl, US$30 s, US$42 d) compensates with coziness and a quiet lakeshore location. HI members get a small discount.

Residencial Lincoyán (Lincoyán 323, tel. 045/441144, www.lincoyan.cl, US$21 pp with shared bath) is a plain but friendly family-style place with good beds but no other amenities.

Down the block from ¡Ecole!, **The Tree House Hostel** (General Urrutia 660, tel. 045/444679, www.treehousechile.cl, US$13 pp, US$42 s or d) is an Anglo-Chilean venture occupying two adjacent houses on the same property, with both dorms and private rooms. The beds and other furnishings are both sturdy and stylish, but its actual tree

house is just a place to grab a view of Volcán Villarrica.

More than just a comfy bed, **Hostería ¡Ecole!** (General Urrutia 592, tel. 045/441675, www.ecole.cl, US$12–28 pp with shared bath, US$50–72 s or d with private bath) has become a destination in itself. Owned and operated by a cooperative of Chilean and international environmental advocates, it provides informally stylish B&B-style accommodations (breakfast extra). In addition, it has an exceptional but moderately priced, mostly vegetarian restaurant, a bar, and a book exchange; operates its own excursions; and provides information and advice to independent travelers. On the downside, it's become so popular that reservations are essential in summer and advisable the rest of the year. The cheapest choice are backpackers' bunks for which you need your own sleeping bag.

US$50-100

Alongside ¡Ecole!, the more subdued **Hostal La Tetera** (General Urrutia 580, tel./fax 045/441462, www.tetera.cl, US$37 s, US$40 d with shared bath, US$47 s, US$52 d with private bath) offers equally stylish, comfortable rooms with good beds and individual reading lights. Under new ownership, it attracts a quiet clientele and has some of Pucón's best breakfasts; there's also a good book exchange. Rates include IVA discounts.

Completely renovated, **Hostal Gerónimo** (Gerónimo de Alderete 665, tel. 045/443762, www.geronimo.cl, US$48 s, US$57 d, up to US$67 s or d) offers immaculate small-to-mid-sized rooms, some with terrace views of the volcano. The personnel are gracious and helpful, and there's also a pasta-oriented restaurant.

With its spa and other upgrades, **Hotel & Spa Araucarias** (Caupolicán 243, tel. 045/441286, www.araucarias.cl, US$60 s, US$90 d) is an exceptional value with IVA discounts. It also has a small but impressive museum of Mapuche artifacts.

Set on ample grounds, with a large pool, **Hotel La Posada Plaza Pucón** (Pedro de Valdivia 191, tel. 045/441088, www

.hotelplazapucon.cl, US$55–84 s, US$69–92 dd) has midsized rooms in an older upgraded building. The management is very accommodating.

More than US$100

Fronting directly on the lake, the classically aging ◖ **Hotel Gudenschwager** (Pedro de Valdivia 12, tel./fax 045/442025, www.hogu .cl, US$87 s, US$104 d) has reinvented itself as a B&B with modernized rooms (all have private baths) and Wi-Fi throughout. That lakefront location may expose it to roaring Jet Skis at times. Special discount rates of US$45 single, US$70 double with breakfast make it a possible backpacker splurge off-season, but it's worth asking about discounted rates at other times, as well.

The main shortcoming at **Hotel Malalhue** (Camino Internacional 1615, tel. 045/443130, www.malalhue.cl, US$84–97 s, 95–106 d) is that it fronts on the eastbound road out of town and, consequently, has traffic day or night. Still, it's an impressive structure with luminous rooms and contemporary Euro-Andean style.

Two kilometers west of town on the Villarrica road, poised among wooded hillside gardens with immaculate flower beds, pools, and cascades, the Bauhaus-style ◖ **Hotel Antumalal** (tel. 045/441011 www.antumalal .com, US$280 s or d) prides itself on personal service; when you arrive, staff members place a fresh fruit basket in every room and even wash your car. Each of its 22 rooms boasts lake views and a fireplace; the common areas have panoramic views through giant plate-glass windows, as well as a strong WiFi signal. In addition to a heated pool and a private beach, it's also added a spa with a hot tub, sauna, and massage services. Half-board rates are also available; the restaurant has been gaining clientele from nonguests as well.

Enjoying its own black-sand beach, the mammoth lakefront **Gran Hotel Pucón** (Holzapfel 190, tel./fax 045/441001, www .granhotelpucon.cl, US$178 and up s, US$237 and up d) dates from the 1930s, when the state railroad agency Ferrocarriles del Estado chose Pucón as Chile's next great tourist destination. In recent years, it's been declining; recently acquired by the Enjoy group, which also operates the new casino and thus has money to invest in improvements, it focuses on packages lasting from two or three days to a week.

FOOD

Pucón's food ranges from simple regional cuisine and fast food—no greasy chain outlets, thankfully—to sophisticated international fare. A good example of the former is **Coppa Kabana** (Urrutia 407, tel. 045/444371), which serves sandwiches and plain lunches at reasonable prices. **Pastelería Suiza** (O'Higgins 112, tel. 441241) is the classic breakfast spot for tasty pastries.

Latitud 39 (Gerónimo de Alderete 324, cell tel. 09/7430-0016) is a new U.S.-run café with a diverse menu that includes sandwiches, and Mexican and Thai dishes, and serves breakfast all day. Prices are moderate, but the pisco sours are from store-bought bottles. It's introduced a novelty—shaved ice—for hot summer days.

Even if there's no room at the inn, don't miss the mostly vegetarian meals at tobacco-free ◖ **Hostería ¡Ecole!** (Urrutia 592, tel. 045/441675, lunch and dinner daily). For about US$5–10 for lunch or dinner, this is some of the country's best-value food.

Having seemingly taken a page from ¡Ecole!'s book, the menu at ◖ **Trawen** (O'Higgins 311, tel. 045/442024, lunch and dinner daily) does a lot with standards such as ravioli (stuffed with prosciutto, for instance), creative vegetarian dishes, and the freshest ingredients. There's also a respectable selection of wines by the glass.

El Fogón (O'Higgins 480, tel. 045/444904) is a traditional *parrilla,* but Avenida Fresia has sprouted a gaggle of new *parrillas* over the past couple of years. The one that's drawn the most attention is **La Grilla** (Fresia 315, tel. 045/444937, www.lagrilla.cl, lunch and dinner daily), which grills slabs of varied beef cuts in the US$12–15 range and up, as well as pricier game dishes such as wild boar and venison.

There are several adventure tourism operators on Pucón's main drag.

The Argentine-style ☾ **Pizzería Buonatesta** (Fresia 243, tel. 045/441434, lunch and dinner daily) is outstanding. ☾ **Senzo** (Fresia 284, tel. 045/449005, lunch and dinner daily except Tues.) is also highly regarded for pastas and risottos. The trilogy of pastas (US$11) is a sampler of their agnolotti, ravioli, and tortellini, with diverse sauces, but the kitchen is perhaps a little too quick to deliver the goods.

Opposite the plaza, **Monte Vecchio** (Pedro de Valdivia 311, tel. 045/444722, lunch and dinner daily) has a more ambitious but also far more expensive Italian menu; with both stuffed and dried pastas in the US$10–12 range, it's drawn some praise, but it arguably has more style than substance.

Pucón has a pair of Mexican options: the upscale **Puerto Pucón** (Fresia 246, tel. 045/441592, lunch and dinner daily) and the more modest **El Arriero de Tijuana's** (Ansorena 303, tel. 045/444144, lunch and dinner daily). The **Arabian Café** (Fresia 354, tel. 045/443469, lunch and dinner daily) serves Middle Eastern specialties.

Bahía Perú (General Urrutia 211, tel. 045/443820, www.bahiaperu.cl, lunch and dinner daily) falls short of the top echelon of Chile's Peruvian restaurants, but the prices (US$7–10 for most entrées) are fair, the pisco sours suitably tart, and the service exceptional.

Only half a block away, **Viva Perú** (Lincoyán 372, tel. 045/444025) serves arguably lighter versions of Peruvian dishes such as *ají de gallina,* plus ceviche and Peruvian-style pisco sours. Entrées fall into the US$8–10 range.

Cassis (Fresia 223, tel. 045/449088) serves sandwiches, coffee, juices, and particularly exquisite desserts, including homemade ice cream and crepes, as well as artisanal chocolates. **Friatto** (O'Higgins 136-B) also serves very fine ice cream.

INFORMATION

In summer, Pucón's **Oficina Municipal de Turismo** (O'Higgins 483, tel. 045/293002, www.municipalidadpucon.cl) is open 8:30 A.M.–10 P.M. daily; the rest of the year, hours are 8:30 A.M.–7 P.M.

The private **Cámara de Turismo** (Brasil 115, tel. 045/441671, www.puconturismo .cl) is open 9 A.M.–midnight in January and February, 10 A.M.–1:30 P.M. and 4–7 P.M. the rest of the year.

For national parks, **Conaf** (Lincoyán 336, 1st floor, tel. 045/443781) now has centrally convenient offices.

SERVICES

Turismo Christopher (O'Higgins 335) and **Supermercado Eltit** (O'Higgins 336) change U.S. and Argentine cash. The supermarket now has an ATM, as does **BCI** (Fresia 174).

Correos de Chile (Fresia 183) handles the mail. **Entel** (O'Higgins 392) has long-distance telephone and Internet services, but many restaurants and cafés have WiFi.

Speaking Spanish, English, and German, Swiss-run **Travel Aid** (Ansorena 425, Local 4, tel. 045/444040, www.travelaid.cl) is a well-informed travel agency and tour broker that also sells books and maps of the area, region, and country. It's also the local agent for Navimag and Cruce de Lagos.

Lavaseco Elena (General Urrutia 520-B, tel. 045/441019) charges about US$6 per load, washed, dried, and folded. **Lavandería Araucarias** (General Urrutia 108, Local 4) is equally efficient.

For medical services, contact **Hospital San Francisco** (Uruguay 325, tel. 045/441177).

GETTING THERE

In the past there have been occasional summer flights into Pucón, but that seems unlikely to continue, especially because a new airport is opening 30 km south of Temuco within a few years.

Long-distance bus service is an extension of Villarrica service. The three main carriers have their own terminals: **Tur-Bus** (O'Higgins 910, tel. 045/443328), **Buses Jac** (Uruguay 505, tel. 045/990880), and **Pullman Bus** (Palguín 555, tel. 045/443331). **Intersur** shares the Tur-Bus terminal, while other companies have separate terminals around the east end of town.

Buses Jac, Tur-Bus, Intersur, and **Igi Llaima** (Palguín 598, tel. 045/441676) go frequently to Santiago, while Tur-Bus also goes to Puerto Montt. Igi Llaima and **Buses San Martín** (Colo Colo 612, tel. 045/443595) both cross the cordillera to Junín de los Andes and San Martín de los Andes, Argentina.

Minibuses Vipu Ray (Palguín 550, tel. 045/413449) and Buses Jac both go frequently to Villarrica (US$1.50, 45 minutes); Vipu Ray has nine buses daily to Caburgua (US$1), while Jac has three or four daily to Curarrehue (US$2.50). In summer, Buses Caburgua has four daily to Parque Nacional Huerquehue (US$3); the rest of the year, there are at least two per day.

GETTING AROUND

Several adventure travel companies on Avenida O'Higgins also rent mountain bikes.

For rental cars, try **Pucón Rent A Car** (Colo Colo 340, tel./fax 045/443052, www.puconrentacar.cl).

Vicinity of Pucón

The locus of adventure travel in the Andean Lakes District, Pucón offers activities ranging from climbing Volcán Villarrica to rafting the Río Trancura, hiking at Huerquehue, horseback riding, fly-fishing, skiing, and visits to nearby thermal baths. Competition—often cutthroat competition—can keep prices low and temperatures high among local operators. Occasionally, though, they manage to cooperate in putting groups together, especially outside the summer peak.

Commercial operators include French-run **Aguaventura** (Palguín 336, tel. 045/444246, www.aguaventura.com), **Kayakchile** (O'Higgins 524, tel. 045/441584, www.kayakchile.net), **Politur** (O'Higgins 635, tel./fax 045/441373, www.politur.com), and **Sol y Nieve Expediciones** (Lincoyán 361, tel./fax 045/444761, www.solynievepucon.cl).

Best known as a place to stay, noncommercial **Hostería ¡Ecole!** (General Urrutia 592, tel. 045/441675, www.ecole.cl) organizes groups to visit the Fundación Lahuén's nearby Santuario Cañi forest reserve, and other alternative excursions; the staff also offers suggestions for independent excursions.

Mario's Fishing Zone (O'Higgins 590, cell tel. 09/7607280, www.flyfishingpucon.com) is a fly-fishing operator.

CUEVAS VOLCÁNICAS

On Volcán Villarrica's southern slopes, but outside the national park, the misleadingly named "volcanic caves" are really lava tubes that descend 340 meters into the mountainside (unless you're a bat, the darkness at the bottom is absolute). Unfortunately, what was once a once professional introduction to volcanism, with bilingual guides and informative displays, has declined and is hard to recommend with any enthusiasm.

Reached by a fork off the road to Parque Nacional Villarrica, the Cuevas Volcánicas (tel. 045/442002, cuevasvolcanicas@hotmail.com) are 14.5 kilometers south of the main Villarrica–Pucón highway. Some guides can manage English if necessary; admission and the one-hour tour cost US$17 per person for adults, US$10 per person for children.

RÍO TRANCURA

Barely half an hour east of Pucón, the Trancura is not one of Chile's premier white-water rivers—there are long calm floats between rapids—but the Class IV waterfalls make parts of the upper river a wild ride indeed. Heavy competition has kept prices down to about US$38 per person for the Alto Trancura, US$23 for the calmer Bajo Trancura. Both are morning or afternoon excursions, but the Alto Trancura means a little longer on the water.

KILA LEUFÚ

At Palguín Bajo, east of Pucón, Kila Leufú is a working Mapuche farm that offers horseback riding, the chance to participate (or not) in farm activities, a *ruca* for socializing, and accommodations, all at reasonable prices. Half-day horseback rides cost US$36 per person, full-day rides cost US$48 per person, and there are also multi-day trips to Termas de Panqui and Parque Nacional Villarrica.

Kila Leufú (cel. 09/97118064, www.kilaleufu.cl) is 23 kilometers east of Pucón on the Curarrehue road, just beyond the Cabedañe Bridge and the Termas de Palguín turnoff. Camping costs US$6.50 per person with breakfast. Comfortable accommodations with shared baths cost US$12.50 per person with breakfast, while rooms with private baths cost US$16.50 per person. Regular lunches (US$6) and dinners (US$8) include vegetarian options, while there are also samples of Mapuche cuisine (US$8). For more details, contact Kila Leufú's Margot Martínez, who speaks English, German, and French in addition to Spanish (while Margot is Mapuche, her husband Peter Krenner is Austrian).

From Pucón, Curarrehue-bound Buses Jac services pass by Kila Leufú's front door.

HOT SPRINGS

The entire volcanic cordon of the Sur Chico is dotted with *termas*, but there's a particularly dense concentration around Pucón. Several have been turned into retreats or resorts that vary from basic day-use facilities to upmarket but not-quite-lavish hotels.

On the Río Liucura northeast of Pucón, **Hotel y Termas Huife** is the most upscale option, a modern chalet-style resort with spa facilities in 40°C waters and massage therapy. For US$19 in summer, US$13 the rest of the year, day-trippers can use the outdoor pools. The resort provides its own transportation from Pucón for US$25 round-trip, but infrequent buses also pass near the entrance. Restaurant and cafeteria meals are available.

Termas Huife (Gerónimo de Alderete 324, Pucón, tel./fax 045/445970, www.termashuife .cl, US$118–133 s, US$170–200 d) is 30 kilometers northeast of Pucón via Paillaco, on the road to Parque Nacional Huerquehue. The higher rates are in effect mid-December–mid-March only.

Just two kilometers beyond Huife, the minimalist **Termas Los Pozones** (tel. 045/1972350) is a backpacker's alternative; admission to a series of riverside pools ranging 30–40°C costs US$7 per person in the daytime, and US$9 per person at night (when some Pucón travel agencies run tours). Bring food and other supplies, as there's little on-site. There are usually one or two buses daily.

On the highway to Argentina, the **Parque Termal Menetué** (Camino Internacional Km 30, tel. 045/441817, www.menetue .com) has the best indoor installations in the area. Rates for using the pools are US$16 pp in summer, US$12.50 the rest of the year, but there are also mud baths and massages. Cabaña accommodations cost US$145 d in summer, US$133 d the rest of the year; full-board packages cost around US$90 pp. Menetué now runs its own transfers from Pucón, which includes access to the mud baths, for US$25 in summer, US$22 the rest of the year.

RANCHO DE CABALLOS

At Palguín Alto, near Termas de Palguín, the German-run Rancho de Caballos offers a series of three-hour to 10-day riding tours of the backcountry in and around Parque Nacional Villarrica for about US$75 per person per day. In addition to tours, Rancho de Caballos (Casilla 142, Pucón, tel./fax 045/441575, www.ranchodecaballos.com) provides simple cabaña accommodations (US$13–25 pp with breakfast).

CORRAL DEL AGUA

At Currarehue, about 40 kilometers east of Pucón, a narrow gravel road leads northeast toward Reigolil, and at about the 14-kilometer point an even narrower road dead-ends 11 kilometers later at Corral del Agua, a small private nature reserve and lodge that organizes hiking and horseback excursions into the much larger backcountry of Reserva Nacional Villarrica, along the Argentine border.

One of Corral del Agua's most impressive sights is the **Salto Malal-co,** a waterfall that spills vertically over a columnar basalt wall that resembles California's Devil's Postpile. There's abundant birdlife, including nesting condors and many lacustrine and riverine species.

For information on programs and accommodations, contact Corral del Agua (cel. 09/8398-9774, www.corraldelagua.cl). On the same property, **The Lodge** (General Urrutia 123, Pucón, tel. 045/441029, cell tel. 09/8920-6749) is an autonomous enterprise that focuses on climbing in particular but also has accommodations.

SANTUARIO CAÑI

In a high roadless area about 21 kilometers east of Pucón, the Fundación Lahuen administers 400 hectares of mixed Araucaria forest in the Santuario Cañi, Chile's initial private nature reserve. A project is underway to create a "Sendero Pehuén" to connect the reserve with Parque Nacional Huerquehue, as part of the ambitious Sendero de Chile project; it will have campgrounds, *refugios*, trail markers, and hygienic facilities.

For the moment, access is limited to guided hikes (around US$25 pp) under the auspices of the Fundación Lahuen through Hostería ¡Ecole! (Urrutia 592, Pucón, tel. 045/441675, www.ecole.cl) and other local operators. For information in the United States, contact Ancient Forests International (Box 1850, Redway, CA 95560, tel./fax 707/923-3001).

PARQUE NACIONAL VILLARRICA

Dominating the skyline south of Pucón, 2,847-meter Volcán Villarrica's glowing crater is a constant reminder that what Spanish conquistador poet Alonso de Ercilla called its "great neighbor volcano" could, at any moment, bury the town beneath a cloud of ash or a lahar of lava and melting snow—or set it aflame in a cataclysm of volcanic bombs. Closely monitored and occasionally closed to climbers, its summit remains one of Pucón's most popular excursions.

More than just the volcano, the park comprises 63,000 hectares of mostly wooded Andean cordillera stretching from Pucón to the 3,746-meter summit of Volcán Lanín, most of which lies within Argentina's Parque Nacional Lanín (would-be climbers must cross the border to the Argentine side).

Geography and Climate

Immediately south of Pucón, the park ranges from 600 meters above sea level on the lower slopes to 3,746 meters at Volcán Lanín. Barren lava flows and volcanic ash cover much of its surface, but unaffected areas are lushly forested. The other major summit is 2,360-meter Volcán Quetrupillán, halfway to the Argentine border; from Quetrupillán to the east, several alpine lakes are accessible by foot.

Summertime temperatures range from a minimum of about 9°C to a maximum of around 23° C, while wintertime lows average 4°C. Most precipitation falls between March and August, when Pacific storms can drop up to two meters of snow, but rain can fall at any time. The park receives about 2,500–3,500 millimeters rainfall per year.

Flora and Fauna

At lower elevations, up to about 1,500 meters, mixed Araucaria and *Nothofagus* woodlands cover the slopes—the Araucaria reaches its most southerly at Volcán Quetrupillán. The *mañío,* an ornamental in the Northern Hemisphere, also makes an appearance here. Native bunch grasses have colonized some volcanic areas.

Among the mammals are puma, *pudú,* foxes, and skunks, as well as the aquatic coypu. Waterfowl such as coots and ducks inhabit the lakes and other watercourses, while large raptors such as the black-shouldered kite and peregrine falcon are occasionally sighted in the skies.

◖ Volcán Villarrica

Chile's most active volcano, Villarrica is a cauldron of bubbling lava and venting steam that's erupted dozens of times, including a 1971 event that expelled 30 million cubic meters of lava in a flow that spread over 14 kilometers.

Pucón's Volcán Villarrica is probably Chile's most popular volcano for climbing.

A strenuous but nontechnical climb, Villarrica requires crampons, an ice ax, rain- and windgear, high-energy snacks, and a guide—except for those who manage to wrangle one of Conaf's few individual private permits. For those who contract a tour with one of Pucón's adventure travel agencies, it involves a crash course in mountaineering; in good weather, the summit's about six hours from the ski area, but bad weather sometimes forces groups to turn back. When the sulfurous crater is especially active, Conaf closes the route.

While the ascent can be a slog through wet snow, the descent involves body-sledding down the volcano's flanks with only an ice ax for braking. With devaluation, rates for the trip (US$70 pp) have fallen slightly.

When winter snows cover the lower slopes, the **Centro de Ski Volcán Villarrica** operates four lifts with nine runs ranging 500–1,500 meters in length, but there have been many complaints. Lift tickets cost around US$30 per day in peak season, US$22 per day in the shoulder season; there are also three-day, one-week, and season passes. For more information, contact **Pucón Ski** (Holzapfel 190, tel. 045/441901, www.skipucon.cl) in the Gran Hotel Pucón.

Sector Quetrupillán

About midway between Volcán Villarrica and **Volcán Quetrupillán,** a rough summer-only road crosses the park from Termas de Palguín to the hot-springs town of Coñaripe. Best suited to four-wheel-drive or at least high-clearance vehicles, though some daring (or foolhardy) Chileans attempt it with ordinary passenger cars, it passes through a scenic Araucaria forest that includes the park's only campground.

From Volcán Villarrica's southern slopes, hiking trails cross the park to Termas de Palguín and continue to Puesco, where Buses Jac has a daily bus back to Pucón. For more detail on this hike, which has some hard-to-follow segments, see Tim Burford's *Chile and Argentina: The Bradt Trekking Guide* (Bradt, 2001) or the late Clem Lindenmayer's *Trekking in the Patagonian Andes* (Lonely Planet, 2003).

Conaf now levies a US$12 fee for hikers on this trail.

Accommodations and Food

In Sector Quetrupillán on the park's southern boundary, on the steep, narrow road between Termas de Palguín and Coñaripe, Conaf's **Camping Chinay** (US$13 for up to five persons) lies in the midst of an Araucaria forest, but it sometimes suffers water shortages.

At the ski area, the **Refugio Villarrica** serves cafeteria meals, but skiers stay in Pucón.

Information

On the road to the ski area, eight kilometers from Pucón, Conaf's Guardería Rucapillán is the best source for information; rangers collect a US$5 per person admission charge (US$2.50 for children) here. There are ranger stations at Sector Quetrupillán and Sector Puesco.

Getting There and Around

Transportation is limited except for organized tours. To Sector Rucapillán, only a few kilometers south of Pucón, taxis are the only non-tour option.

PARQUE NACIONAL HUERQUEHUE

In the scenic Andean precordillera, dotted with alpine lakes, rushing rivers, and waterfalls set among dense native forest, 12,500-hectare Huerquehue has become one of the area's most popular parks. Its proximity to Pucón and a small but accessible network of hiking trails make it ideal for day trips, but overnights are also possible.

Geography and Climate

Huerquehue is 35 kilometers northeast of Pucón via the hamlet of Paillaco. Elevations range from about 720 meters above sea level near Lago Tinquilco to the 2,000-meter summit of Cerro Araucano, but glaciers and rivers have eroded deep canyons. It receives just over 2,000 millimeters of rainfall per year, mostly between May and September, some falling as snow at higher elevations. While temperatures are generally mild, rain can fall at any time.

Flora and Fauna

On the park's lower slopes, the dominant forest species is the *coigüe,* while *lenga* gives way gradually to Araucaria at higher elevations. Birds, ranging from woodpeckers to thrushes, flit within the forest, while Andean condors sometimes soar among the ridgetops and summits.

◖ Sendero Lago Verde

Huerquehue is a hiker's park, with a good trail network beginning at the north end of Lago Tinquilco. From here, the well-watered Sendero Lago Verde (Lago Verde Trail) zigzags from 700 meters altitude at the trailhead to 1,300 meters at its namesake lake. Light gaps in the *coigüe* woodlands yield glimpses of Volcán Villarrica to the south, while the surrounding ridges sport Araucaria forests.

From Tinquilco, it's about two or more hours of steady hiking to **Lago Chico,** where the terrain levels off; at a trail junction beyond Lago Chico, the left fork goes to **Lago Verde,** while the right fork goes to **Lago El Toro** and continues to Conaf's simple **Refugio Renahue,** where camping is also possible. From here an eastbound trail continues to **Termas de Río Blanco,** thermal springs linked by gravel road to Cunco, Lago Colico, and Lago Caburgua's north end.

Accommodations and Food

On Lago Tinquilco's eastern shore, near the park gate, Conaf's 18-site **Camping Tinquilco** (US$25 per site) can accommodate up to five persons on each of its wooded sites.

Just beyond the park entrance, near the Lago Verde trailhead, the rustically chic Canadian-Chilean ◖ **Refugio Tinquilco** (cel. 09/9539-2728, tel. 02/7777673 in Santiago, www.tinquilco.cl) charges US$14 for hostel-type bunks (with a US$2 surcharge for sheets, if necessary); it also has rooms with king-sized beds (US$33 d with shared bath, US$41 d with private bath). Set on densely wooded grounds, it has its own beach and offers fixed-price breakfasts, lunches, and dinners to guests or nonguests; more elaborate multicourse dinners include aperitifs and wine.

En route to the park, on quiet grounds west of the Pucón–Lago Caburgua road from a turnoff at kilometer 18 (follow the signs), the expanded German-run **Landhaus San Sebastián** (tel. 045/1972360 or 09/94431786, www.landhaus-chile.com, US$66 s or d) can be an ideal escape from Pucón's hyperactivity. In addition to accommodations, it has a restaurant that serves exquisite *onces* and desserts.

Information

At the Lago Tinquilco entrance, Conaf's **Centro de Educación e Intepretación Ambiental** is open 10 A.M.–8 P.M. daily in summer. Rangers at the park gate collect a US$7 admission fee (US$3.50 for children). Refugio Tinquilco is also a good source of information for hiking alternatives beyond the main Lago Verde route.

Getting There and Around

Thanks to increasing demand, **Buses Caburgua** now offers summer service from Pucón to Huerquehue (US$3) four times daily; the rest of the year, though, it's just twice daily. Most Pucón travel agencies also offer Huerquehue excursions.

Valdivia and Vicinity

At the confluence of two major watercourses, Valdivia's major economic and recreational feature is its namesake river while, downstream, several colonial historical monuments are excursion destinations. The Universidad Austral and its many students contribute to an active cultural life, with frequent performing-arts events.

In recent years, though, Valdivia garnered unfortunate publicity because waste from the nearby Celco pulp mill devastated black-necked swans at the Río Cruces nature sanctuary—a disaster that's raised environmental awareness here. Small numbers of birds have recently returned.

In 2007, the province of Valdivia became Chile's 14th region, the Región de los Ríos, separating from Region X (Los Lagos). Valdivia is now the regional capital.

HISTORY
Founded by Pedro de Valdivia himself, the Ciudad de los Ríos dates from 1552, but a late-16th-century Mapuche uprising razed it to the ground. The Peruvian viceroy sent a 900-man naval contingent to establish fortifications at the Río Valdivia's mouth and refound the city in the 17th century; in the 18th century it built fortifications against European powers and pirates, as well as the restive Mapuche.

From colonial times to the present, Valdivia has exported timber from the region's namesake Valdivian forests. It saw substantial Middle European immigration from the mid-19th century to the early 20th century, and its most distinctive architecture dates from this period—though repeated fires and the calamitous 1960 earthquake have wiped out many landmarks.

ORIENTATION
Where the Río Cau Cau joins the winding Río Calle Calle to form the Río Valdivia, the city of Valdivia (population 129,952) is 162 kilometers southwest of Temuco and 35 kilometers west of the Panamericana via Mafil; it is 107 kilometers north of Osorno and 46 kilometers from the Panamericana via Paillaco.

Shaped by the shifting rivers, Valdivia's central core is more irregular than those of most Chilean cities, but most points of interest lie within a roughly triangular zone bounded by the Río Valdivia to the west, the Río Calle Calle from the north to the southeast, and the streets Yerbas Buenas and Beauchef to the south. Eastbound Avenida Ramón Picarte links the city to the Panamericana, while the Puente Pedro de Valdivia crosses the river to the suburb of Isla Teja, site of the Universidad Austral. The road continues to the historic Pacific beach towns of Niebla and Corral.

SIGHTS
Along the Costanera Prat north of the Sernatur office, the **Feria Fluvial** is a colorful riverside fish, fruit, and vegetable market that's also the departure point for downstream riverboat floats to Niebla and Corral. Southern sea lions hang out here and, because of biting incidents that probably resulted from human provocations, a screen now separates them from direct contact.

Valdivia's massive 1960 earthquake destroyed many landmarks, but there remain two small national colonial monuments: the 18th-century **Torreón de los Canelos** (Yerbas Buenas and General Lagos), which guarded the southern approach along the Río Valdivia, and the **Torreón del Barro** (Costanera Prat between José Martí and Condell). In practice, though, these watchtowers served as jail cells, powder magazines, and even windmills. From San Carlos south, beyond the Torreón de los Canelos, Calle General Lagos constitutes a *zona típica* national monument for its typical European-style houses.

Across the river on Isla Teja, the **Museo de Arte Contemporáneo** (Los Laureles s/n, tel. 063/221968, www.macvaldivia.uach.cl) is Valdivia's modern art showcase. It sits on

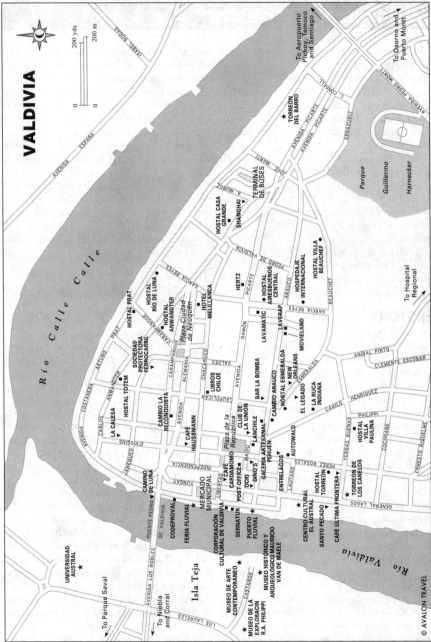

VALDIVIA

200 yds
200 m

To Aeropuerto
Pichoy, Temuco
and Santiago

To Osorno and
Puerto Montt

ISABEL RODAS

AVENIDA ESPAÑA

Rio Calle Calle

Parque
Guillermo
Harnecker

To Hospital
Regional

TORREÓN
DEL BARRO

AVENIDA PICARTE

C. CONDELL

ERRAZURIZ

AVENIDA PEDRO MONTT
LÍNEA PEDRO MONTT

A. MUÑOZ

TERMINAL
DE BUSES

HOSTAL CASA
GRANDE
SHANGHAI

JOSÉ MARTÍ

PEDRO DE VALDIVIA

HOSTAL VILLA
BEAUCHEF

HOSPEDAJE
INTERNACIONAL

HERTZ
PICARTE

HOSTAL
AIRESBUENOS
CENTRAL

ARAUCO

BEAUCHEF

GARCÍA REYES

ANÍBAL PINTO

CLEMENTE ESCOBAR

HOSTAL PRAT

HOSTAL
RÍO DE LUNA

HOSTAL
ANWANDTER

Plaza Ciudad
de Neuquén

HOTEL
MELILLANCA

GARCÍA REYES

PRAT

ARTURO

CARAMPANGUE

RAMÓN

LAVAMATIC

LAVERAP

MOVIELAND

SOCIEDAD
PROTECTORA
FERROCARRIL

ALEMANA

CHACABUCO

VALDÉS

AVENIDA

BAR LA BOMBA

NEW
ORLEANS

HOSTAL ESMERALDA

EL LEGADO

ESMERALDA

COSTANERA

ANWANDTER

HOSTAL TOTEM

CARLOS

O'HIGGINS

CAMBIO LA
RECONQUISTA

AVENIDA

CAPUCHÍN

LIBROS
CHILOÉ

CAMBIO ARAUCO

LA RUCA
INDIANA

CAMILO
HENRÍQUEZ

PHILIPPI

HOSTAL
VILLA
PAULINA

COCHRANE

ERNESTO RIQUELME

LA CALESA

CAFÉ
HAUSSMANN

Plaza de la
República

CLUB DE
LA UNIÓN

LANCHILE

AUTOWALD

YERBAS BUENAS

JANEQUEO

AVENIDA

INDEPENDENCIA

YUNGAY

LIBERTAD

CAFÉ
CARDAMOMO

OCIO

DINO'S

MAIPÚ

GALERÍA ARTESANAL
PEHUÉN

ENTRELAGOS

LAUTARO

PÉREZ ROSALES

HOSTAL
TORREÓN

TORREÓN DE
LOS CANELOS

GENERAL LAGOS

CAMINO
PEDRO DE LUNA

PUENTE PEDRO DE VALDIVIA

MERCADO
MUNICIPAL

POST OFFICE

CODEPROVAL

FERIA FLUVIAL

CORPORACIÓN
CULTURAL DE VALDIVIA

SERNATUR

PUERTO
FLUVIAL

CENTRO CULTURAL
EL AUSTRAL

SANTO PECADO

CAFÉ ÚLTIMA FRONTERA

AVENIDA LOS ROBLES

To Parque Saval

UNIVERSIDAD
AUSTRAL

Isla Teja

LOS LAURELES

CASTAÑOS

MUSEO DE ARTE
CONTEMPORÁNEO

MUSEO DE LA
EXPLORACIÓN
R.A. PHILIPPI

MUSEO HISTÓRICO Y
ARQUEOLÓGICO MAURICIO
VAN DE MAELE

To Niebla
and Corral

Río Valdivia

© AVALON TRAVEL

the foundations of the former Cervecería Anwandter, destroyed by the 1960 earthquake, and is open 10 A.M.–2 P.M. and 4–8 P.M. daily except Monday. Admission costs US$2 for adults, half that for children.

Also on Isla Teja, immediately south of the modern art museum, the **Museo Histórico y Arqueológico Mauricio van de Maele** (Los Laureles 47, tel. 063/212872, www.museosaustral.cl) occupies the Casa Anwandter, a two-story mansion and national monument built by brewer Carlos Anwandter, a German immigrant who arrived around 1850. The museum displays collections from paleo-Indian times to the historic and contemporary Mapuche and the German colonization, and offers guided tours in Spanish only. Open 10 A.M.–1 P.M. and 2–6 P.M., it charges US$1.50 admission for adults, US$0.60 for children. There are launches across the river to the museum, but it's also accessible via the Pedro de Valdivia Bridge.

New in 2008, the **Museo de la Exploración R. A. Philippi** (Los Laureles 47, tel. 063/292723, www.museosaustral.cl, US$1.50) honors the memory of pioneer Chilean naturalist Rudolph A. Philippi, a German immigrant who traveled nearly the entire length of Chile in his research. Seven exhibition rooms cover the development of natural history in Chile and, especially, Philippi's travels. Originally located three kilometers away, the house itself dates from 1914; it was dismantled into 80,000 pieces and reassembled here. It's open 10 A.M.–6 P.M. daily except Monday, but stays open until 8 P.M. in summer.

Also reached by the bridge, Isla Teja's **Parque Saval** (Av. Miguel Agüero s/n, tel. 063/221313) is a 30-hectare botanical garden that once belonged to the immigrant Prochelle family and is now a favorite outing for local families; its centerpiece is lily-padded **Laguna de los Lotos.** Hours are 8 A.M.–6 P.M. daily; admission costs US$0.60.

© WAYNE BERNHARDSON

a pedestrian mall in Valdivia

ENTERTAINMENT AND EVENTS
Bars
Valdivia has a lively pub scene. Among the options are **El Legado** (Esmeralda 657, tel. 063/207546), which features live jazz and blues; and **Ocio** (Arauco 102, tel. 063/345090, www.ociorestobar.cl), which doubles as a fashionable restaurant.

Cinema and Performing Arts
On the 3rd floor of the Plaza de los Ríos mall, **Movieland** (Arauco 561, tel. 063/278757) shows current films.

The **Centro Cultural El Austral** (Yungay 733, tel. 063/213658, ccultural@surnet.cl) is a key performing-arts venue. The **Corporación Cultural de Valdivia** (Prat 549, tel. 063/219690, www.ccmvaldivia.cl) includes the **Sala Ainilebu,** which hosts live theater. There's also the **Teatro Municipal Lord Cochrane** (Independencia 455, tel. 063/220209).

Events
February 9's **Aniversario de la Ciudad** is the biggest local holiday, celebrating the city's founding in 1552, but it's only part of the summer-long **Verano en Valdivia,** which includes many other events.

SHOPPING
Valdivia has numerous crafts outlets, such as the **Galería Artesanal Pehuén** (Arauco 340, tel. 063/251412) and the Mapuche store **La Ruca Indiana** (Camilo Henríquez 772, tel. 063/214946).

Libros Chiloé (Caupolicán 410, tel. 063/219120) is a quality bookstore.

ACCOMMODATIONS
Valdivia budget options are improving, thanks to the presence of several hostels; the quality of accommodations is pretty good in all categories.

US$10-25
Two blocks south of the bus terminal, rates at homey **Hostal Villa Beauchef** (Beauchef 844, tel./fax 063/216044, www.villabeauchef.cl, US$13–19 s, US$22–26 d with private bath) include breakfast.

The more central **Hospedaje Internacional** (García Reyes 660, tel. 063/212015, www.valdiviachile.cl/internacional.php, US$17–25 s, US$23–33 d with breakfast) has rooms with either shared or private baths.

US$25-50
Half a block west of the bus terminal, **Hostal Casa Grande** (Carlos Anwandter 880, tel./fax 063/202035, www.hostalcasagrande.tk, US$20 s, US$30 d) has river-view rooms with private bath and cable TV.

Well-located, worn but not frayed, **Hostal Torreón** (Pérez Rosales 783, tel. 063/212622, mrprelle@gmail.com, US$21/33–25/42 s/d with breakfast) is an older but well-kept building that enjoys an ample setback from the street.

At the north end of town, **Hostal Anwandter** (Anwandter 601, tel./fax 063/218587, www.valdiviachile.cl/anwandter.php, US$25–33 s, US$30–42 d, breakfast extra) has 10 rooms with either shared or private baths; the latter also have cable TV, and WiFi is available.

Down the block, **Hostal Totem** (Carlos Anwandter 425, tel. 063/292849, www.turismototem.cl, US$27 s, US$33 d) has spacious, luminous rooms with private baths and cable TV. It also has WiFi but lacks parking.

Under congenial, multilingual Argentine ownership, the HI representative is **Hostal Airesbuenos** (García Reyes 550, tel. 063/222202, www.airesbuenos.cl, US$13 pp in dorms, US$28 s, US$33 d in private rooms) is a refurbished townhouse, with a secluded garden on a quiet block midway between the bus terminal and Plaza de la República.

In a good residential neighborhood, staffed by responsive personnel, **Hostal Villa Paulina** (Yerbas Buenas 389, tel. 063/212445, leha@surnet.cl, US$25 s, US$37 d with private bath) occupies a handsome historic building.

The handsome **Hostal Esmeralda** (Esmeralda 651, tel. 063/215659, hostal-esmeralda@chile.com, US$20 pp with private bath) occupies a site on the same block with several popular restaurants and pubs.

Facing the Calle Calle, renovated **Hostal Prat** (Av. Prat 595, tel./fax 063/222020, US$30 s, US$42 d with private bath and breakfast) has undergone a recent renovation and expansion that's made it far more attractive than before. The cheerful management is a big plus as well.

US$50-100

Well-located **Hotel Di Torlaschi** (Yerbas Buenas 283, tel. 063/224103, www.aparthotelitaliano.cl, US$53 s, US$59 d) is one of the best choices in its range. Another is the Calle Calle riverfront's ☾ **Hostal Río de Luna** (Av. Prat 695, tel. 063/253333, www.hostalriodeluna.cl, US$43 s, US$63 d), an inviting place with friendly management and bright natural light in nearly all the rooms. Amenities include cable TV and WiFi; with off-season discounts, this is a particularly good value.

All rooms face the river at ☾ **Hotel Naguilán** (General Lagos 1927, tel. 063/212851, www.hotelnaguilan.com, US$65–78 s, US$81–97 d), just beyond the downtown bustle, but those in the newer northern building are more spacious and less institutional. (In a previous incarnation, the older southern building was a shipbuilder's offices, but its common areas, including the reception area, bar, and restaurant, have undergone a tasteful remodel that makes excellent use of natural wood.)

At **Hotel Melillanca** (Av. Alemania 675, tel. 063/212509, www.melillanca.cl, US$60–74 s, US$82–98 d), a modern, central high-rise whose windows feature flower-filled planter boxes, rates include a buffet breakfast. The busy location, though, is a drawback.

US$100-150

Across the Pedro de Valdivia Bridge, Isla Teja's **Hotel Puerta del Sur** (Av. Los Lingues 950, tel. 063/224500, www.hotelpuertadelsur.com, US$147–151 s, US$152–170 d) is more a rural resort than an urban hotel, but it's barely beyond downtown.

FOOD

In the riverfront **Mercado Central,** bounded by the Costanera, Chacabuco, Yungay, and Libertad, several *marisquerías* serve fish and shellfish at bargain prices. Just north of the Pedro de Valdivia Bridge, the floating **Camino de Luna** (Prat s/n, tel. 063/213788) is a more formal seafood venue.

Near the bus terminal, **Shanghai** (Anwandter 898, tel. 063/212577) remains popular even if Chinese food is no longer as fashionable as it once was. **Guacamole** (Esmeralda 693, tel. 063/250714) serves huge portions of Tex-Mex dishes such as burritos. It's arguable whether **New Orleans** (Esmeralda 682, tel. 063/218771) has true Creole and Cajun food, but the local versions add some variety and the portions are abundant.

La Última Frontera (Pérez Rosales 787, tel. 063/235363) is a casual café in a historic district house that also has an outdoor deck for a variety of afternoon and evening sandwiches (mornings are usually a little cool and damp for sitting outside).

Dino's (Maipú 191, tel. 063/213061) is a franchise operation but will do in a pinch for breakfast or sandwiches. The reasonably priced **La Protectora** (Janequeo 491, tel. 063/212715) is a popular beef and seafood locale that belongs to the railroad workers' union.

Overlooking the Plaza de la República, the traditional **Club de la Unión** (Camilo Henríquez 540, tel. 063/213377) serves fixed-price meals at lunch and more elaborate dishes for dinner.

With woodsy riverview seating for fine weather, **Santo Pecado** (Yungay 745, tel. 063/239122, www.santopecado.cl) offers good to excellent lunch specials for US$6; at night, it's more of a pub scene. The downside is that it provides no tobacco-free zone.

In handsome new quarters that lack the riverside views it once enjoyed, **La Calesa** (O'Higgins 160, tel. 063/225467, closed Sun. dinner) still serves Peruvian specialties such as a surprisingly spicy *aji de gallina* and an inventive *chupe de corvina* in the US$10 range. With side orders and drinks, the bill can add up, but it's Valdivia's best splurge.

Entrelagos (Pérez Rosales 640, tel. 063/218333) is the best choice for tasty desserts, *onces,* and ice cream; its next-door branch, **Chocolatería Entrelagos** (Pérez Rosales 622, tel. 063/212047) offers takeaway items. **Café Haussmann** (O'Higgins 394, tel. 063/213878) is also worth a try.

INFORMATION
In summer, the riverfront office of **Sernatur** (Prat 555, tel. 063/239060, infovaldivia@sernatur.cl) is open 8:30 A.M.–7 P.M. daily; the rest of the year, it's open weekdays only and half an hour earlier on Friday. At the bus terminal, the **Oficina de Informaciones** (Anfión Muñoz 360, tel. 063/220498) is open 8 A.M.–10 P.M. daily.

The private **Codeproval** office (Prat 243, tel. 063/278100) is open 9 A.M.–7:30 P.M. daily in summer, but 10 A.M.–4 P.M. weekdays only the rest of the year.

SERVICES
Exchange houses include **Cambio Arauco** (Arauco 331, Local 24) and **Cambio La Reconquista** (Carampangue 325), which keeps long weekday hours and is also open 10 A.M.–2 P.M. Sunday. **Banco Santander** (Pérez Rosales 585) has one of many ATMs.

Correos de Chile (O'Higgins 575), at the southwest corner of Plaza de la República, handles the mail. **Café Cardamomo** (Libertad 127) is a spacious long-distance telephone office that also has inexpensive Internet access, including WiFi.

Within the Único supermarket, **Laverap** (Arauco 697, Local 2, tel. 063/200099) handles the washing.

The **Hospital Regional** (Av. Simpson 850, tel. 063/297000) provides medical services.

GETTING THERE
Valdivia has air and road connections to the rest of Chile, and the railroad may someday return.

Air
LanExpress (Maipú 271, tel. 063/246490) flies twice daily to Santiago, via either Temuco or Concepción. **Sky Airline** (Walter Schmidt 303, tel. 063/222681) also flies to Santiago.

Bus
Valdivia's **Terminal de Buses** (Anfión Muñoz 360, tel. 063/212212) is about eight blocks west of Plaza de la República. There are frequent services along the Panamericana from Santiago to Puerto Montt and intermediate points, and on to Chiloé.

Regionally, **Buses Jac** (tel. 063/212925) goes to Temuco and to Villarrica and Pucón. Other regional carriers include **Buses Pirehueico** (tel. 063/218609) to Panguipulli and **Buses Cordillera Sur** (tel. 063/229533) to other interior Andean lake destinations.

Internationally, **San Martín Centenario** (tel. 063/251062) crosses the Argentine border to San Martín de los Andes, and **Tas Choapa** (tel. 063/213124) and **Igi Llaima** (tel. 063/213542) go to Bariloche (US$24, 8 hours) via Osorno.

Sample destinations, times, and fares include Panguipulli (US$4, 1.5 hours), Temuco or Pucón (US$5, 2 hours), Puerto Montt (US$7, 3 hours), Concepción (US$14, 6 hours), Talca (US$21, 9 hours), and Santiago (US$20–27, 11 hours).

Train
EFE has been due to commence service to Temuco from Estación Valdivia (Ecuador 2000, tel. 063/214978), but progress has nearly stopped.

GETTING AROUND
To the Airport
Aeropuerto Pichoy (tel. 063/272236) is 29 kilometers north of Valdivia, on the road to San José de Mariquina, via the Puente Calle Calle. **Transfer Valdivia** (tel. 063/225533) offers door-to-door service (US$5).

To the Bus Terminal
Buses marked "Plaza" go directly from the bus terminal to Plaza de la República; return buses use Arauco and Picarte. *Taxi colectivos* follow the same routes.

Car Rental
Rental agencies include **Autowald** (Pérez Rosales 660, tel. 063/212786) and **Hertz** (Picarte 640, tel. 063/218316).

CERVECERÍA KUNSTMANN
The most popular excursions follow the Río Valdivia west to its mouth, both by road and by water. About five kilometers west of Valdivia via Isla Teja, open for guided tours, the Cervecería Kunstmann (Camino a Niebla 950, tel. 063/292969, www.lacerveceria .cl) is a major brewery that features a **Museo de la Cerveza** (Beer Museum, open noon–midnight daily).

Kunstmann's pub/restaurant features preposterously large sandwiches (around US$7) and specialties such as Lomo Kassler (pork chops) in the style of *Mitteleuropa*. For US$1.50, lunch- or dinner-goers can sample its seven different varieties of beer. Niebla-bound buses and *taxi colectivos,* leaving from the Pedro de Valdivia Bridge, pass by the front door.

THE RÍO VALDIVIA FORTIFICATIONS
Where the Río Valdivia and the Río Tornagaleones empty into the Pacific, Spain's 17th-century government built elaborate fortifications at Niebla, Corral, and Isla Mancera to protect the refounded city of Valdivia from European privateers and interlopers such as Britain, France, and the Netherlands. In their heyday, these comprised the largest fortified complex on the Pacific coast of the Americas; they played a major role in Chilean independence when, in 1820, the audacious British mercenary Lord Thomas Cochrane captured them from Spanish forces.

There are frequent buses from the corner of Chacabuco and Yungay to Corral, which is 17 kilometers west of Valdivia, but many visitors prefer floating downstream from the Puerto Fluvial, returning by bus in the afternoon. Among the options are the 108-passenger *Orion III* (tel. 063/247896, www.islahuapi.cl), the 130-passenger *Reina Sofía* (tel. 063/212021, reinasofia@surnet.cl), the 200-passenger *Río*

Calle Calle (tel. 063/202223), and the 280-passenger *Neptuno* (tel. 063/218952). Departures are fewer outside the peak summer season; the excursions take about 2.5 hours from Valdivia to Corral via Isla Mancera, Amargos, and Niebla. Fares generally cost US$22–42 with lunch included, but some cheaper options provide transportation only.

Niebla
Combined with the south-shore fortifications at Corral and the midriver base at Isla Mancera, the north shore's **Fuerte Niebla** would catch invaders in a three-way crossfire. Nothing remains of the original 1645 structure, but the battlements of the **Castillo de la Pura y Limpia Concepción de Monfort de Lemus** (1671) are the complex's oldest surviving ruins; 7 of its 14 cannon are original. The restored commander's house serves as the **Museo de Sitio Fuerte Niebla** (Antonio Duce 120, tel. 063/282084); hours are 10 A.M.–7 P.M. daily except Monday. Admission costs US$1 for adults, US$0.50 for children, but it's free Wednesdays.

Hostería Riechers (Antonio Duce 795, tel. 063/282043, hosteria_riechers@eodoramail.cl, US$42 d) has cabaña-style accommodations with private baths and kitchenettes.

Every half hour, from Niebla, inexpensive launches shuttle across the river to Corral.

Corral
Across the river from Niebla, Corral's original **Castillo San Sebastián de la Cruz** (tel. 063/471828) dated from 1645, but the surviving structures are later 17th- and 18th-century bulwarks such as the **Batería de la Argolla** (1764) and the **Batería de la Cortina** (1767), the cannon batteries guarding the harbor. It's open 10 A.M.–7 P.M. daily except Monday; admission costs US$1.

North of Corral, built entirely of stone at Punta de Amargos, the **Castillo San Luis de Alba** was considered the equal of Europe's best. From mid-December to the end of February, a costumed demonstration of late colonial Spanish military maneuvers takes place at 4:30 and 6:15 P.M. daily.

Isla Mancera

Isla Mancera's strategic location at the confluence of the Río Valdivia and the Tornagaleones gave it a critical backup position opposite Niebla. Dating from 1645, its **Castillo San** **Pedro de Alcántara** (tel. 063/212872) later served as the military governor's residence; there were several other constructions on the island. It's open 10 A.M.–8 P.M. daily in summer; admission costs US$1.

Panguipulli and Vicinity

At the northwest corner of its eponymous lake, tranquil Panguipulli is the gateway to the "Siete Lagos," a relatively seldom-visited series of lakes that lie east toward the Argentine border.

East of Panguipulli, the area features a cluster of small towns and hot-springs resorts on or near elongated glacial lakes beneath the 2,422-meter summit of Volcán Mocha Choshuenco, a glacier-filled crater whose last major eruption took place in 1864.

Near Pullingue, paved Ruta 203 turns southeast along Lago Panguipulli's north shore toward Choshuenco but, after about 20 kilometers, the pavement ends (though the work continues). It passes through Neltume, to Puerto Fuy, where a ferry crosses Lago Pirehueico to the Argentine border at Paso Hua Hum for San Martín de los Andes; from the Pullingue junction, graveled Ruta 201 follows Lago Calafquén's south shore to Coñaripe, Liquiñe, and the Carririñe pass to Junín de los Andes. A narrow gravel road covers the 23 kilometers between Carriringue, on Ruta 201, and the south end of Lago Neltume, on Ruta 203, making it possible to loop through the area.

PANGUIPULLI

By a sort of half-truth, Panguipulli (population 15,888) is known as the Ciudad de las Rosas (City of Roses)—with so few inhabitants, though, it's more a small town, 114 kilometers northeast of Valdivia and 49 kilometers from Lanco, the Panamericana junction. Commemorating Panguipulli's 1946 founding, early February's **Semana de las Rosas** does manage to support the claim of its slogan.

Accommodations

Only 200 meters north of the central Plaza Prat, **Camping El Bosque** (tel. 063/311489, US$5 pp) has 15 tent sites (no drive-ins) with picnic tables, hot showers, and lighting. Otherwise, there are several simple lodgings with shared baths and breakfast, such as **Hostal Eva Ray** (Los Ulmos 62, tel. 063/311483, eva_ray50@hotmail.com, US$10 pp). In new quarters, **La Casita del Centro** (Pedro de Valdivia 318, tel. 063/311812, casitacentro@ze.cl, US$13 s, US$25 d, up to US$33 s or d) has rooms with either shared or private baths, and serves a good Germanic *onces* (US$4).

Hostal España (O'Higgins 790, tel. 063/311166, www.hostalespana.cl.kz, US$23 s, US$37 d) was formerly considered the best in town, but **Hotel Le Français** (Martínez de Rosas 880, tel. 063/312496, www.hotelelfrances.cl, US$50 s, US$56 d), with nine nearly-new midsized rooms in excellent condition, now claims the top spot.

Food

Panguipulli has good dining, even if the variety is limited to standard Chilean specialties, beef, and seafood.

For full meals, try **El Chapulín** (Martínez de Rozas 639, tel. 063/312925), **Rincón Criollo** (Matta 131, tel. 063/311603), or especially **Gardylafquen** (Martínez de Rozas 722, tel. 09/4587612). There are also excellent lunchtime specials at the **Hotel Le Français** (Martínez de Rosas 880, tel. 063/312496).

Open in January and February only, **La Escuela** (Freire 394, tel. 063/312040) is where Chilean culinary students come to practice what they've learned in front of a paying public; except for service, which can range from distracted to hyper-attentive, they've learned well. The dishes, such as gnocchi with a chestnut sauce, are creative and visually appealing, and prices are reasonable (around US$10).

Information

One of Chile's best-organized municipal tourist offices, Panguipulli's **Dirección de Turismo** (O'Higgins s/n, tel. 063/310436, www.visitpanguipulli.cl) is on the north side of Plaza Arturo Prat. Summer hours, December to mid-March, are 9 A.M.–11 P.M. daily; the rest of the year, it's open 9 A.M.–1 P.M. and 2:30–5:30 P.M. weekdays only.

Services

BCI (Martínez de Rozas 894) has an ATM.

Correos de Chile (Alessandri s/n) faces Plaza O'Higgins, a block north of Plaza Prat.

Hospital Panguipulli (Cruz Coke s/n, tel. 063/311325) provides medical assistance.

Getting There and Around

Most carriers use Panguipulli's **Terminal de Buses** (Gabriela Mistral 100, tel. 063/311055), but **Tur-Bus** (Carrera 784, tel. 063/311377) has its own terminal. North–south services along the Panamericana are frequent.

Regionally, **Buses Pirehueico** (tel. 063/311497) goes several times daily to Valdivia (2.5 hours) and Puerto Montt, and once to Liquiñe.

Expreso Villarrica circles Lago Calafquén to Coñaripe, with connections to Lican Ray, Villarrica, and Valdivia. **Buses Carrasco** goes to Coñaripe and Liquiñe, while **Buses Lafit** (tel. 063/311647) goes to Choshuenco, Neltume, and Puerto Fuy, the staging point for the bus/ferry crossing to Puerto Pirehueico and San Martín de los Andes, Argentina.

COÑARIPE AND VICINITY

It seems placid enough now, but the eastern Lago Calafquén beach community of Coñaripe has seen its share of disruption—not from war or political violence, but from Volcán Villarrica,

whose March 1964 eruption triggered a lahar (mud flow) that killed 22 people. It may owe those dazzling black-sand beaches to the volcano, but it's paid a price for its proximity.

While Coñaripe is just 37 kilometers east of Panguipulli via Ruta 201, it gets most of its traffic from Villarrica, thanks to the smooth paved road between the two towns, and makes a better day trip than an overnight. From the corner of the main thoroughfare Beck de Ramberga and Los Olivillos, a scenic but narrow and bumpy road, open in summer only, crosses the Quetrupillán sector of Parque Nacional Villarrica to Termas de Palguín and Pucón. While some Chileans take low-clearance vehicles on this hazardous route, even skilled drivers with high-clearance four-wheel-drive vehicles may find it challenging—not least because of others rounding blind curves in the opposite direction.

From Coñaripe, this road is also the gateway to the **Termas Geométricas** (Km 16,

© WAYNE BERNHARDSON

Coñaripe's Termas Geométricas is Chile's most fashionable new hot springs option, though it has no accommodations as yet.

tel. 09/94425420, www.termasgeometricas
.cl), a Zen-like hot-springs retreat that's
drawing raves for its 17 thermal pools,
linked by wooden walkways in a lush sylvan
setting. There's also a café, but no accommodations; hours are 10 A.M.–10 P.M. daily
in summer, 11 A.M.–8 P.M. daily the rest of
the year. Admission costs US$23 for adults,
US$10 for children under age 15. Alcohol is
forbidden.

On international Ruta 201, about 15 kilometers southeast of Coñaripe at the east end
of Lago Pellaifa, the **Centro Turístico Termal
Coñaripe** offers swimming pools, a spa, tennis courts, footpaths, and bridle trails, plus a
120-seat restaurant serving home-grown trout.
It charges US$133–160 d with breakfast for
each of its eight hotel rooms, but also offers
full-board packages. In addition, there are cabañas that can work out to be cheaper on a
per-person basis.

Pools are open to nonguests (US$12 pp,
US$7 for children 2–10); access to the indoor
pool/spa costs US$3 more. For day visitors, it
provides its own transportation (US$23 pp)
from its Villarrica business office (Pedro Montt
525, Villarrica, tel. 045/411111, www.termas-
conaripe.cl), at 11:30 A.M., returning at 6 P.M.

CHOSHUENCO

About 38 kilometers from Panguipulli,
at the southeast end of the lake, the town
of Choshuenco is home to **Rucapillán
Expediciones** (San Martín 85, tel. 063/318220,
www.rucapillan.cl), which offers one-hour,
Class 3 descents of the Río Fuy (US$25) every
summer; in the spring runoff, the Fuy can
reach a rugged Class 5.

Under the same management, with the same
contacts, **Hostería Rucapillán** (US$47 s or d
with breakfast) is a budget alternative to Puerto
Fuy's more elaborate accommodations.

PUERTO FUY AND VICINITY

About 62 kilometers east of Panguipulli, the
lakeside village of Puerto Fuy isn't exactly the
end of the road, but it is the departure point
for the ferry *Hua Hum,* which sails southeast to

Puerto Pirehueico, where the road continues to
the border at Paso Hua Hum. Both the upper
and lower Río Fuy have long been popular with
white-water rafters and kayakers, but the area
has recently gained an offbeat attraction in the
Reserva Biológica Huilo Huilo, which is also a
summer ski and snowboard area.

Reserva Biológica Huilo Huilo

Midway between Neltume and Puerto Fuy,
Huilo Huilo is a sprawling private reserve on
the east side of Volcán Choshuenco, whose permanent snow cover provides an ample area for
what, normally, would be winter-only activities. Most visitors, though, make just a short
detour off the international highway to visit
the **Saltos Huilo Huilo,** a 37-meter waterfall
that tumbles through a volcanic notch to the
river below.

Admission to visit the falls at the Reserva
Biológica Huilo Huilo (Ruta 203, Km 60, tel.
063/1972651, www.huilohuilo.cl) costs US$4
per person; for information on skiing and other
activities, consult the website. At the entrance,
Café del Duende offers short orders, while
Don Quincho prepares *parrillada.*

Accommodations and Food

For those awaiting the ferry, Puerto Fuy has
several basic *hospedajes* and restaurants. Huilo
Huilo's 14-room **La Montaña Mágica Lodge**
(Ruta 203, Km 60, tel. 063/1970121, www
.huilohuilo.cl, US$90–135 d with breakfast)
is a steep-sided pseudo-volcano whose summit
spouts water, in lieu of lava, that cascades down
the building's walls. In truth, this Disneyfied
dreck looks as if it might have been airlifted intact from Anaheim or Orlando, but the oddly-
shaped rooms seem comfortable enough.

Sharing the same reception area and some
other facilities, the new 55-room **Hotel
Baobab** (Ruta 203, Km 60, tel. 063/1970121,
www.huilohuilo.cl, US$153–455 d with break-
fast) is almost equally outlandish—an inverted
seven-story pyramid that resembles a massive
tree house. In a rustic style, the rooms are
larger and more luxurious than at the Montaña
Mágica, but both have access to the new spa

under construction as of summer 2009. It has an excellent restaurant.

At Puerto Fuy itself, under the same ownership but different management, the 22-room **Hotel Marina del Fuy** (Ruta 203, Km 63, tel. 063/1972426, www.marinadelfuy.com, US$83–193 d with breakfast) has some shortcomings—a couple rooms are tiny and their bathrooms even tinier—and not all of the walls are adequately soundproofed. Still, it has its charms and an ideal lakeside location.

Getting There and Around
Buses serving Panguipulli also reach Puerto Fuy; contact individual bus companies for details.

In January and February, the ferry to Puerto Pirehueico departs daily at 8 A.M. and 1 and 6 P.M., returning at 10 A.M. and 3 and 8 P.M. The last fortnight of December and the first fortnight of March, it operates at 8 A.M. and 3 P.M. daily, returning at 10 A.M. and 5 P.M. The rest of the year, departures are at 12:30 P.M., returning at 4 P.M.

Since the *Hua Hum* (tel. 063/1971585) can carry only 24 vehicles, reservations are a good idea at any season; Panguipulli's **Dirección de Turismo** (tel. 063/310436) also handles reservations. Passenger cars pay US$33; pickup trucks, jeeps, and vans US$42; pedestrians US$2.50; bicyclists US$5; motorcyclists US$7. The *Hua Hum* accepts U.S. dollars and Chilean or Argentine pesos, but not euros or credit cards.

Osorno

More a crossroads than a destination, Osorno relies on dairying, forestry, and manufacturing for its livelihood, but it's the gateway to destinations such as Lago Puyehue, Parque Nacional Puyehue, and Argentina's Andean Lakes District. The city dates from 1558, but the Mapuche uprising of 1599 destroyed it and six other cities within five years, even resulting in the death of Spanish governor Oñez de Loyola.

Spanish authorities needed nearly two centuries to refound the city in 1793 with the construction of Fuerte Reina Luisa, a riverside fortification that helped keep out the Mapuche. It failed to flourish until the mid-19th century, as overland communications were too arduous—even hazardous—to permit rapid growth of internal markets. This began to change with the mid-19th-century arrival of German immigrants; it accelerated after the "pacification" of the area south of the Biobío in the 1880s, followed by the railroad's arrival in 1895 and its extension to Puerto Montt by 1911. Through most of the 20th century, it achieved steady growth.

ORIENTATION
Osorno (population 132,245) is 913 kilometers south of Santiago and 109 kilometers north of Puerto Montt via the Panamericana. Also an east–west crossroads, it's 126 kilometers from the Argentine border at Paso Cardenal Samoré via paved Ruta 215.

Central Osorno, about two kilometers west of the Panamericana, has a slightly irregular grid bordered by the Río Damas to the north, Calles Angulo and Eduvijes to the east, Manuel Rodríguez to the south, and the Río Rahue to the west.

SIGHTS
Despite its colonial origins, Osorno has few venerable sights—the so-called **Distrito Histórico** west of the Plaza de Armas includes mostly early-20th-century landmarks such as the restored Francophile **Estación de Ferrocarril** (1912); it now houses the **Museo Interactivo de Osorno** (Portales 901, tel. 064/221916, 10:30 A.M.–12:45 P.M. and 3:30–7:30 P.M. daily except Monday, with shorter winter hours, free), a hands-on science museum.

Other area sights include the restored **Sociedad Molinera de Osorno,** a flour mill now occupied by a pasta factory, and many weathered private residences. The ramparts and towers of **Fuerte Reina Luisa** (1793) modestly stand out—these are all that remains of the erstwhile colonial fortress at the foot of Eleuterio Ramírez.

The de facto historic district, though, is on Juan Mackenna between Avenida Matta and Freire, where half a dozen pioneer houses are national monuments: the **Casa Mohr Pérez** (Mackenna 939), **Casa Enrique Schüller** (Mackenna 1011), **Casa Sürber** (Mackenna 1027), **Casa Germán Stückrath** (Mackenna 1047), **Casa Federico Stückrath** (Mackenna 1069), and **Casa Conrado Stückrath** (Mackenna 1095).

The **Museo Histórico Municipal** (Av. Matta 809, tel. 064/238615, free) exhibits diverse materials ranging from Paleo-Indian archaeology and Mapuche culture to Osorno's colonial founding, its destruction by the Mapuche and subsequent refounding, the 19th century city and immigration, and naval hero Eleuterio Ramírez. A natural-history room and a child-oriented interactive basement display round out the features.

Occupying the former Schilling Buschmann residence (1929), a handsome neocolonial building, the municipal historical museum is open 9 A.M.–5 P.M. Monday–Friday and 3–6 P.M. Saturday. Summer hours are 9:30 A.M.–6 P.M. weekdays except Friday, when it closes an hour earlier, and 2–7 P.M. weekends, with shorter winter hours.

SHOPPING

Detalles Hecho a Mano (Mackenna 1100, tel. 064/238462) sells regional crafts, but the biggest selection is at **Alta Artesanía** (Mackenna 1069, tel. 064/232446), including wood carvings, woolens, ceramics, copper, and jewelry. At the **Pueblito Artesanal** (Mackenna between Freire and Prat), artisans sell directly to the public along a block of the city's most heavily traveled street.

ENTERTAINMENT

Cine Lido (Ramírez 650, tel. 064/233890) is a two-screen movie theater. The municipal **Centro Cultural** (Av. Matta 556, tel. 064/238898, 8:30 A.M.–1:45 P.M. and 4–5:15 P.M. daily) hosts theater and music events, along with rotating art exhibits.

ACCOMMODATIONS

Except in the upper categories, Osorno's accommodations are so-so at best.

East of the bus terminal, **Hospedaje Sánchez** (Los Carrera 1595, tel./fax 064/232560, ximenitasanchez@hotmail.com, US$10 pp) is a modest but passable shoestring choice.

Two blocks east of the Plaza, standard rates at shingled **Residencial Schulz** (Freire 530, tel. 064/237211, US$23–33 s or d) include private baths and breakfast; the cheaper rooms, with shared baths, are on the uppermost floor.

Four blocks south of the terminal, **Hotel Villa Eduviges** (Eduviges 856, tel./fax 064/235023, www.hoteleduviges.cl, US$27 s, US$44 d with breakfast) occupies a rambling older building that's undergone a haphazard modernization; the shower stalls, in particular, are tiny, but it enjoys a less congested and quieter neighborhood than some other places. It does provide WiFi.

Under the same ownership, **Hostal Bilbao** (Bilbao 1019, tel./fax 064/262200, US$33 s, US$47 d, www.hotelbilbao.cl) and the **Hotel Bilbao** (Juan Mackenna 1205, tel./fax 064/264444, www.hotelbilbao.cl, US$37 s, US$53 d) are among the best in their range; the latter has WiFi in all rooms.

Rates at **Hostal Rucaitué** (Freire 546, tel. 064/239922, hrucaitue@surnet.cl, US$45 s, US$58 d) include breakfast, TV, and private bath. **Hotel Pumalal Express** (Bulnes 630, tel./fax 064/242477, hotelpumalal@gmail.com, US$45s, US$62 d) is a contemporary business-oriented hotel.

Since its original 1930 incarnation as the Hotel Burnier, the 65-room **Gran Hotel Osorno** (O'Higgins 615, tel. 064/232171, hoteleraaustral@telsur.cl, US$38 s, US$64 d) has seen better days, but the deco landmark still has ample rooms and standard amenities such as private baths, telephones, and cable TV.

Hotel Lagos del Sur (O'Higgins 564, tel. 064/245222, www.hotelagosdelsur.cl, US$87 s, US$107 d) is a nearly new hotel with handsomely decorated rooms. The well-preserved, deco-style **Hotel Waeger** (Cochrane 816, tel. 064/233721, www.hotelwaeger.cl, US$81 s, US$111 d) is a classic regional hotel where German speakers get special attention.

The contemporary **Hotel García Hurtado de Mendoza** (Mackenna 1040, tel. 064/237111, www.hotelgarciahurtado.cl, US$119 s, US$147 d) is one of the city's best, but it is questionable whether it's worth the rapidly rising prices—despite the peso devaluation.

FOOD

For real budget meals, nothing's better than the seafood at the numerous *comedores* in the **Mercado Municipal** (Prat and Errázuriz)—avoid the *fried* fish, though.

Upstairs from its namesake bakery, **Pastelería Rhenania** (Ramírez 977, tel. 064/235457) serves sandwiches and pastries. **Dino's** (Ramírez 898, tel. 064/233880) also specializes in sandwiches and light meals, as does its franchise rival **Bavaria** (O'Higgins 743, tel. 064/231302). **Bocatto** (Ramírez 938, tel. 064/238000) has similar offerings but also pizza and Osorno's best ice cream.

The **Club Alemán,** also known as the **Deutscher Verein** (O'Higgins 563, tel. 064/232784), reflects the German community's significance more in name than in menu, which is fairly standard Chilean. The **Club de Artesanos** (Juan Mackenna 634, tel. 064/230307) is a labor-union restaurant with a good Chilean menu.

Del Piero (Manuel Rodríguez 1081, tel. 064/256767) offers pizza and pasta. In the historic Casa Conrado Stückrath, **La Parrilla de Pepe** (Mackenna 1095, tel. 064/239653) lacks ambience but serves meats cooked to order, has diligent service, and is tobacco-free.

INFORMATION

On the west side of the Plaza de Armas, **Sernatur** (O'Higgins 667, tel. 064/234104, infosorno@sernatur.cl) occupies a ground floor office at the Edificio Gobernación Provincial. Hours are 8:30 A.M.–1 P.M. and 2:30–5:30 P.M. weekdays. Sernatur also supports a private information office at the long-distance **Terminal de Buses** (Errázuriz 1400, tel. 064/234149).

At the Plaza's southwest corner, the municipal **Departamento de Turismo's** (tel. 064/212740) is an information kiosk open mid-December–mid-March 8:30 A.M.–8 P.M. weekdays, 11 A.M.–6 P.M. Saturday. The rest of the year, it keeps a shorter, weekdays-only schedule.

The **Automóvil Club de Chile** (Acchi, Manuel Bulnes 463, tel. 064/540080) can help motorists. For national-parks information, contact **Conaf** (Martínez de Rozas 430, tel. 064/221301).

SERVICES

Turismo Frontera (Ramírez 959, Local 12) changes cash and travelers checks, while **Banco de Chile** (Juan Mackenna and Av. Matta) has an ATM.

On the west side of the Plaza de Armas, **Correos de Chile** (O'Higgins 645) is the postal service. **Ciber O'Higgins** (O'Higgins 526) has long-distance and Internet service.

Lavandería Limpec (Arturo Prat 678, tel. 064/238966) offers prompt laundry service.

For medical assistance, contact the **Hospital Base** (Av. Bühler 1765, tel. 064/230977); Avenida Bühler is the southward extension of Arturo Prat.

GETTING THERE

Osorno has limited air connections, but it's a hub for bus services along the Panamericana, throughout the region, and across the Andes to Argentina. **LAN** (Ramírez 802, tel. 064/314900) flies at least daily to Santiago, usually via Temuco or Concepción. **Sky Airline** (Cochrane 651, Local 109, tel. 064/230186) flies less often.

The **Terminal de Buses** (Av. Errázuriz

1400, tel. 064/234149) is the long-distance facility. Some but not all regional buses use the Mercado Municipal's **Terminal de Buses Rurales** (Errázuriz 1300, tel. 064/201237).

From the Terminal de Buses Rurales, two companies go to Puyehue and Aguas Calientes: **Buses Expreso Lago Puyehue** (tel. 064/243919) and **Buses Barría** (tel. 064/230628). From 7 A.M. to 9 P.M., there are departures about every half hour on a route that's also served by *taxi colectivos* across the street.

At the main terminal, **Transur** (tel. 064/234371) goes to the eastern Lago Llanquihue destination of Las Cascadas (US$2.50). **Buses Vía Octay** (tel. 064/237043) and **Octay Bus** (tel. 064/213065) go frequently to the northern Lago Llanquihue town of Puerto Octay (US$2); Vía Octay goes to the western lakeside village of Frutillar (US$2).

Many carriers connect Osorno with Panamericana destinations between Santiago in the north and Puerto Montt to the south. Sample destinations, fares, and times include Puerto Montt (US$2.50, 1.5 hours), Valdivia (US$4, 2 hours), Temuco (US$7, 3 hours), and Santiago (US$20–32, 14 hours).

Services to Punta Arenas (US$67, 28 hours) and to Coyhaique (US$58, 19 hours) start in Puerto Montt and pick up passengers here. Note that buses to Chilean Patagonian destinations such as Coyhaique and Punta Arenas use Paso Cardenal Samoré, east of Osorno, but carry through-passengers only—Chilean domestic bus lines may not drop passengers within Argentina.

Most buses across the Andes to Bariloche (US$21, 5 hours) and other Argentine destinations also begin in Puerto Montt and use Paso Cardenal Samoré.

EFE trains between Temuco and Puerto Montt normally stop at **Estación Osorno** (Juan Mackenna and Portales), but were temporarily suspended as of summer 2009. For more information, check www.efe.cl.

GETTING AROUND

Aeropuerto Carlos Hott Siebert (tel. 064/232559), also known as Cañal Bajo, is seven kilometers east of Osorno via Avenida Buschmann. It's off the city bus routes, but cabs cost only about US$5.

Full Travel (Bilbao 1011, tel. 064/235579, www.fulltravel.cl) provides rental cars.

VICINITY OF OSORNO

As a land transport hub, Osorno offers excellent access to some of the Lakes District's most popular summer resort areas. Among them are Lago Puyehue, Termas de Puyehue and other lesser-known hot-springs resorts in its vicinity, Parque Nacional Puyehue, and the northern and western shores of Lago Llanquihue, including the picturesque towns of Puerto Octay and Frutillar.

Auto Museum Moncopulli

Opened in 1995, this private automotive museum contains more than 80 historic vehicles, many restored and others awaiting restoration, along with supplementary advertising and marketing materials and other artifacts of the early- to mid-20th century. German collector Bernardo Eggers, its creator, specializes in the now-obscure Studebaker from its 1850s beginnings as a horsecart manufacturer in South Bend, Indiana, to its first electric automobile (1902) and the plant's closure (1966). With its futuristic design in the late 1940s and early 1950s, the Studebaker was one of the most distinctive automobiles ever manufactured, but it never really caught on with the public.

Professionally arranged, the museum has one shortcoming: a failure to provide any narrative beyond its creator's enthusiasm. That said, for anyone traveling the highway to Parque Nacional Puyehue and the Argentine border, it's well worth at least a brief stop. Classic car fans may want to go out of their way to see it.

East of Osorno, the Auto Museum Moncopulli (Ruta 215, Km 25, tel. 064/210744, www.moncopulli.cl, US$3.50 adults, US$1.50 students, US$0.85 children) is generally open 10 A.M.–6 P.M. daily; in summer, it closes two hours later.

Parque Nacional Puyehue

Barely an hour from Osorno, accessible Puyehue still has plenty of untamed wilderness among its 106,772 hectares of Valdivian rainforest—at least where lava flows and ash from its volcanic vents and summits have not left it as barren as the Atacama Desert. Statistically, it's one of Chile's most visited parks, but statistics can deceive—the highly developed hot-springs resort at Aguas Calientes and its Antillanca ski area draw its mostly Chilean crowds. Except for trails near its hotels and campgrounds, the backcountry gets only small numbers of hikers, and the park is under threat from a proposed hydroelectric project.

GEOGRAPHY AND CLIMATE

Ranging from the Lower Río Golgol Valley, about 250 meters above sea level, to the 2,240-meter summit of **Volcán Puyehue,** the park is about 80 kilometers east of Osorno and extends to the Argentine border. **Volcán Casablanca** (1,980 meters) is another major landmark, and the park has abundant creeks, rivers, and lakes that are ideal for fishing.

The annual rainfall, about 5,000 millimeters (with snow at higher elevations), supports verdant Valdivian forest. Temperatures are relatively mild at lower elevations, averaging about 14°C in summer and 5°C in winter, with highs near 25°C and lows around freezing.

FLORA AND FAUNA

Puyehue's lush lower Valdivian forest is a mixed woodland of species such as *ulmo,* which can reach 40 meters or more in height, along with *olivillo, tineo, mañío,* and *coigüe.*

Beneath the dense canopy grow smaller trees such as the myrtle relative *arrayán,* while the solid bamboo *quila* forms impassable thickets; the endemic *chilco,* along with intensely green ferns and mosses, provides spots of color. The striking *nalca* sports umbrella-sized leaves at the end of edible stalks up to two meters in height.

At some higher elevations, though, lava flows and ash from Volcán Puyehue's 1960 eruption have left the landscape so barren that grasses and shrubs have only recently begun to colonize the area, despite substantial rainfall.

Pudú may inhabit the dense forest, but it's difficult to see them or other woodland and riverine species such as foxes, otters, and coypu. Some 100 or so bird species flit from tree to tree, along with waterfowl such as the *pato cortacorriente* (torrent duck) that fishes in the river rapids, and the condors that soar on the thermals overhead.

SIGHTS AND RECREATION

Puyehue consists of three distinct sectors: Aguas Calientes at its southwestern border, Antillanca at its southeastern border, and Anticura, mostly north of Ruta 215.

Aguas Calientes

From the Termas de Puyehue junction, a paved road leads four kilometers south to **Termas Aguas Calientes** (tel. 064/331710, www .termasaguascalientes.com), whose highlight is its namesake thermal baths, open to hotel guests, campers, and day-trippers alike. Under the same management as Termas de Puyehue, its rates are more affordable.

Several short nature trails and one longer hike start here. The six-kilometer **Sendero El Pionero** switchbacks through dense Valdivian forest to a ridgetop with panoramic northern vistas of Lago Puyehue, the wooded Río Golgol Valley, and Volcán Puyehue's barren cone, before continuing to Lago Espejo and then returning along the Antillanca road. Along its namesake river, the **Sendero Rápidos del Chanleufú** traverses 1,200 meters of gallery forest. The 11-kilometer **Sendero Lago Bertín** climbs steadily to its namesake lake, where backcountry camping is possible.

Antillanca

Beyond Aguas Calientes, the road becomes a gravel surface leading another 18

© WAYNE BERNHARDSON

lodging in Termas de Puyehue, Parque Nacional Puyehue

kilometers to the base of Volcán Casablanca, where Antillanca is a popular hotel and ski resort from early June to late October; in summer it's open for hikers, mountain bikers, anglers, and general recreationists even though there's no campground nearby.

Where the public road ends, the Club Andino Osorno maintains a toll road (US$5 per vehicle) to the 1,262-meter **Cráter Raihuén,** an extinct volcanic crater, and **Cerro Mirador,** the starting point for several high-country trails. Pay at the hotel office, which opens the gate and provides a helpful topographic map.

Ranging from 1,050 meters at its base to 1,514 meters above sea level on Cerro Haique, the ski area itself has beginner, intermediate, and expert slopes. For more details, contact the Centro Turístico Deportivo Antillanca at the **Club Andino Osorno** (Casilla 765, O'Higgins 1073, Osorno, tel. 064/235114, www.skiantillanca.com).

◖ Anticura

From Termas de Puyehue, Ruta 215 leads northeast up the Golgol Valley for 17 kilometers to Anticura, before continuing to Chilean customs and immigration at Pajaritos and on to the Argentine border. At Anticura, there is camping and access to several short trails and some longer ones.

The 950-meter **Sendero Educativo Salto del Indio** is a signed nature trail leading to a waterfall on the Golgol; its name comes from a local legend that a fugitive Mapuche hid to avoid forced labor in a colonial gold mine. An overnight excursion up the Río Anticura Valley leads to **Pampa Frutilla,** now part of the Sendero de Chile. Areas east of Pajaritos, the Chilean border post, require Conaf permission to hike or otherwise explore because it's a legal no-man's-land and, unfortunately, this means limited access to large parts of the park.

From El Caulle, two kilometers west of Anticura, a 16-kilometer trail climbs the abrupt flanks of **Volcán Puyehue,** where there's a simple *refugio* and camping is also possible; alternatively, continue through a barren volcanic landscape of fumaroles and lava flows to rustic thermal pools where it's also possible to camp. At the trailhead, though, ex-UDI senator Marcos Cariola's **Turismo El Caulle** (Ruta 215, Km 90, cell tel. 09/9920-3244, www.elcaulle.com) demands a US$12 toll for the right to pass through his property; this includes use of the *refugio*, but Cariola's cattle have badly eroded parts of the trail. It's possible to hike through to Riñinahue, at Lago Ranco's south end (where there's a US$3.50 toll), rather than return to El Caulle.

Volcán Puyehue itself is a flat-topped Holocene caldera, measuring 2.4 kilometers in diameter; it sits within a larger caldera measuring five kilometers across. The most recent eruptions have come not from the summit caldera, but from vents on its western, southern, and eastern flanks, and a small cone on the southern flank.

ACCOMMODATIONS AND FOOD

Some visitors stay at Termas de Puyehue, but accommodations also include campgrounds and cabañas.

Aguas Calientes

Termas Aguas Calientes (tel. 064/331710, www.termasaguascalientes.cl) operates the 36-site **Camping Chanleufú** (US$20 for up to four persons, open all year). Fees at Chanleufú include firewood and electricity), but access to the pools is additional.

Accommodations at **Cabañas Aguas Calientes** (tel. 064/331710, US$145 for up to four persons) include access to the baths. It also has a cafeteria with a sandwich menu, the more elaborate restaurant **Los Canelos,** and an outdoor *parrilla* in summer only.

Antillanca

At the ski area, the 73-room **Hotel Antillanca** (Ruta 215, Km 98, tel. 064/235114, www.ski-antillanca.cl) has a contemporary sector and an older but more-than-acceptable *refugio*. In the peak season, July–mid-August hotel "ski week" rates reach US$1,413 pp weekly with accommodations, full board, and lift tickets. In the shoulder ski season, prices drop by about 25 percent and, in summer, rooms are available

for for US$46 s, US$67 d in the hotel, US$28 s, US$41 d in the refugio.

In Osorno, contact the Centro Turístico Deportivo Antillanca through the Club Andino Osorno (Casilla 765, O'Higgins 1073, tel. 064/235114).

Anticura

Etnoturismo Anticura (cell tel. 09/9177-4672, etnoturismoanticura@gmail.com) has taken over the eight-site **Camping Catrué** (US$13 d, US$3 each additional person), whose basic facilities include running water, picnic tables, fire pits, and pit toilets; there's also a hostel (US$10 pp with shared bath and kitchen facilities) and cabañas (around US$53 d).

Just west of Anticura, **El Caulle** (Ruta 215, Km 90, cel. 09/9641-2000, www.elcaulle.com) operates a *parrilla* just off the highway and has recently added accommodations (US$12 pp, US$15 pp with breakfast).

INFORMATION

At Aguas Calientes, Conaf's **Centro de Información Ambiental** (tel. 064/1974572, www.parquepuyehue.cl, 9 A.M.–1 P.M. and 2–6 P.M. daily, until 7 P.M. in summer) offers daily slide talks in late afternoon during the summer; permanent exhibits focus on natural history (flora and fauna) and topics such as vulcanism. Conaf also maintains an information center at Antillanca, generally open in ski season only.

GETTING THERE AND AROUND

Paved all the way to the border, Ruta 215 passes directly through the park. From Osorno's Mercado Municipal (Errázuriz 1300), **Buses Expreso Lago Puyehue** (tel. 064/243919) and **Buses Barría** (tel. 064/230628) serve Termas de Puyehue and Aguas Calientes with buses and *taxi colectivos,* with additional service to Anticura and the Chilean border post at Pajaritos.

In winter, the **Club Andino Osorno** (O'Higgins 1073, tel. 064/235114) shuttles between Osorno and the Antillanca ski area.

Puerto Octay and Vicinity

From prosaic 19th-century beginnings as a port at Lago Llanquihue's north end, idyllic Puerto Octay has become one of the region's most picturesque locales, with magnificent views across the lake to Volcán Osorno. Local pleasure boats, though, have supplanted the steaming freighters that once connected Octay with Puerto Varas, and it's become a low-key destination for summer holidaymakers who arrive by paved road from Osorno, 50 kilometers northwest. The German immigrant presence is palpable in its architecture, food, the checkerboard landscape of dairy farms and woodlands, and in its apparent middle-class contentment.

Puerto Octay (population 3,403) also includes Península Centinela, a wooded spit protruding into the lake that's home to hotels and campgrounds. From town, it's possible to travel Llanquihue's western shore to the resort village of Frutillar, or its eastern shore to Ensenada and Parque Nacional Vicente Pérez Rosales, via a road whose northern half is now paved.

SIGHTS

Puerto Octay dates from 1852, but its architectural legacy of European-style neoclassical and chalet houses dates from the early 20th century. While no structure within Puerot Octay is a recognized national monument, at least a dozen private residences and other buildings contribute to the town's captivating ambience.

One of those buildings is the **Casa de la Cultura Emilio Winkler** (Independencia 591, tel. 064/643327, www.museopuertooctay.cl, 10:15 A.M.–1 P.M. and 3–5 P.M. daily), housing part of the **Museo El Colono,** a well-organized collection of maps, photographs, and other materials on early German colonization. The building is too small, though, to contain an assortment of antique farm equipment that spills out of a barn and onto the grounds of a separate facility (at the point where the gravel road to Península Centinela splits off the paved road to Frutillar). Personnel from the Universidad Austral have helped the facilities and reorganized the exhibits. Admission (US$1.50) is valid for both sites.

Puerto Octay Hostal Zapato Amarillo

About two kilometers north of town on the Osorno road, the Swiss-Chilean Zapato Amarillo has become a destination in its own right as much as a place to stay. It provides transfers to La Picada for a five-hour hike to Petrohué (US$37 pp for a minimum of four people, with stops at Saltos del Petrohué and Ensenada on the ride back), hiking excursions from Lago Rupanco to nearby hot springs (US$50 pp), and day trips to Parque Nacional Puyehue (US$47 pp).

Comfortably stylish hostel-type accommodations on ample grounds, with kitchen facilities, cost US$14 per person with breakfast and shared bath October–April, slightly less the rest of the year. It has recently added several doubles with shared or private bath (US$38–49).

In addition, Zapato Amarillo (tel./fax 064/210787, www.zapatoamarillo.cl) offers initial transfers from Puerto Octay, information, WiFi, laundry service (US$6), rental bikes (US$10 per day), and a small sailboat (US$34 per day). Spanish, German, English, and French are all spoken.

ACCOMMODATIONS

Downtown has camping and basic *hospedajes,* but Avenida Andrés Schmoelz leads south out of Puerto Octay proper for about two kilometers to dead-end on Península Centinela, which has more upscale lodgings but also affordable alternatives. The Puerto Octay Hostal Zapato Amarillo is another reasonable option a short distance north of town.

Five hundred meters south of the Plaza de Armas, **Camping El Molino** (Costanera Pichi Juan 124, tel. 064/391375, US$20) has lakefront campsites for up to five persons.

The most interesting option is the recently

reopened **Hotel Haase** (Pedro Montt 344, tel. 064/391302, www.hotelhaase.cl, US$17–20 pp), an architectural monument whose common areas are approaching their onetime grandeur; the rooms, mostly with shared bath, lag a little behind, and the floors are squeaky. The management is friendly, but the restaurant is hit-and-miss.

The peninsula's most affordable choice is the spic-and-span **Hostería La Baja** (tel. 064/391269, irisbravo1@hotmail.com, US$13 pp, breakfast included), though some rooms have low ceilings, and a couple lack exterior windows.

At road's end, the peninsula's showpiece is the renovated and expanded 【 **Hotel y Cabañas Centinela** (tel./fax 064/391326, www.hotelcentinela.cl, US$129–202 s or d with breakfast), a chalet-type structure that, in its 1930s heyday, hosted guests such as the Prince of Wales. The 12 rooms retain their original natural wood, but the furniture and baths have been upgraded.

The hotel proper has greater personality than its nearby A-frame cabañas, whose rates start around US$119 d. Off-season rates March–mid-December are about 15–20 percent lower; nonguests may use the restaurant here.

FOOD

Puerto Octay has little out of the ordinary—it's mostly Chilean standbys such as **Baviera** (Germán Wulf 582, tel. 064/391460, lunch and dinner daily). The well-regarded *parrilla* **El Fogón de Anita** (tel. 064/391455, lunch and dinner daily) is about one kilometer north of town on the Osorno highway. **Puerto Muñoz Gamero** (Muñoz Gamero 107, tel. 064/391485, lunch and dinner daily) is a fish and seafood venue in a traditional German colonial house.

Another option is the **Rancho Espantapájaros** (Camino a Frutillar, Km 6, tel. 065/339141, lunch and dinner daily), whose specialty is barbecued boar as the centerpiece of a US$20 buffet that includes wine or beer. There's also a sandwich menu for those who don't care to gorge themselves, but recent visitors suggest inconsistency.

The restaurant at **Hotel Centinela,** on the peninsula, is open to the public, with three-course fixed-price dinners (around US$20–25 pp).

INFORMATION

On the east side of the Plaza de Armas, the **Oficina Municipal de Turismo** (Esperanza 555, tel. 064/391491) is a small freestanding office alongside the Municipalidad. Theoretical hours are 9 A.M.–9 P.M. daily, December–February only.

A more reliable choice is the private **Oficina La Rueda** (Prat and Germán Wulf), across the plaza, operated by an aging but exceptionally helpful gentleman who knows Octay as well as or better than anyone else.

GETTING THERE AND AROUND

Buses and minibuses leave from the **Terminal de Buses** (La Esperanza and Balmaceda), half a block south of the Plaza de Armas. **Via Octay** (tel. 064/230118) and **Octay Bus** go to Osorno's main bus terminal (US$2) several times daily, while **Thaebus** goes half a dozen times daily to Puerto Montt (US$2.50) via Frutillar and Puerto Varas. Four times daily, **Arriagada** goes south to Las Cascadas, roughly halfway to Ensenada.

LAS CASCADAS

Midway to Ensenada, on Llanquihue's eastern shore, bucolic Las Cascadas sits precariously on a mudflow from looming Volcán Osorno; its primary assets are its black-sand beaches and broad vistas of Osorno. Bike touring companies often follow this route south to the village of Ensenada, the gateway to Parque Nacional Vicente Pérez Rosales and junction to Puerto Varas.

Accommodations and Food

Where the pavement ends at the south end of town, forested **Camping Las Cascadas** (tel. 064/247177 message only, US$12 for up to five people) has shady sites near the lake. The only noncamping budget accommodation (it also serves meals) is friendly **Hostería Irma** (tel. 064/396227, cell tel. 09/8852-6413, US$7 pp with shared bath), one kilometer south of town toward Ensenada, which has a certain decrepit charm.

Getting There and Around

Buses from Puerto Octay are more frequent than they used to be—four per day, at 11 A.M., noon, and 4 and 7 P.M.—instead of just one. To Ensenada, it's another 22 kilometers that involves walking, hitching, or cycling (this is a popular mountain-bike route).

FRUTILLAR

The region's most self-consciously immaculate example of German colonization, the western Llanquihue village of Frutillar can seem a caricature of Teutonic orderliness—a sign on the beach that says *Deporte, Picnic y Camping Prohibido* (Sports, Picnicking, and Camping Prohibited) seems as if it *should* say *Sport, Picknick, und Camping Verboten*. The lakefront is so tidy that, when a thoughtless smoker flips a cigarette butt, some burgher might well materialize to catch it before it hits the ground.

Still, with its almost perfectly preserved European-style houses, Frutillar exudes both style and charm; for a *Dorf* its size, it also has cultural resources in a fine museum, a state-of-the-art theater, and one of Chile's most important music festivals. Mirrored in Llanquihue's waters, Volcán Osorno soars symmetrically to the east.

Orientation

Frutillar (population 9,118) is 63 kilometers south of Osorno and 50 kilometers north of Puerto Montt via the Panamericana. It comprises two separate sectors: Frutillar Alto's busy commercial zone adjoins the Panamericana, while Avenida Carlos Richter leads to tranquil Frutillar Bajo, pinched between the sandy lakeshore and a steeply rising hill, about two kilometers east. Avenida Philippi runs north–south along the lakeshore, linked to the parallel Vicente Pérez Rosales by a series of block-long streets; most services and other

points of interest face the lake from the west side of Philippi.

Sights

Middle European–style architecture is Frutillar Bajo's trademark, in structures such as the 1911 **Iglesia Luterana** (Lutheran Church, Philippi 1000), but German-style houses and other handsome buildings face the entire lakefront.

The highlight is the Universidad Austral's **Museo Colonial Alemán de Frutillar,** an indoor-outdoor facility set among immaculate gardens at the base of the hill. Antique farm machinery in mint condition adorns the grounds; buildings such as the **Molino** (a water-powered mill), the **Casa del Herrero** (a working smithery), the **Campanario** (a storage structure with a conical roof supported by a central pillar), and the **Casa del Colono** (a residence filled with period furniture and household implements) are precise historical reconstructions.

Built partly with German aid, the museum (Vicente Pérez Rosales s/n, tel. 065/421142, www.museosaustral.cl, 10 A.M.–7 P.M. daily) is at the west end of Arturo Prat, one short block from the lakeshore. Admission costs about US$3.50 for adults, US$1 for children.

The museum shop sells souvenirs such as horseshoes forged in the Casa del Herrero and wood carvings of museum buildings.

Events

Frutillar's major annual event is the **Semanas Musicales de Frutillar** (www.semanas musicales.cl), a 10-day extravaganza that has showcased classical, jazz, and ethnic music since 1968. From January 27 to February 5, events take place both during the daytime and at night, when performances are both more formal and more expensive. Some recitals take place at the **Teatro del Lago** (tel. 065/422900, www.teatrodellago.cl), where the last stages of construction continue on lakeshore landfill between Antonio Varas and Manuel Rodríguez. The series also includes concerts in regional cities such as Osorno and Puerto Montt.

The second-largest event is November's

Semana Frutillarina, celebrating its founding as a lakeport in 1856.

Accommodations

Frutillar's accommodations scene is strong at the mid- to upscale range, but budget alternatives are limited; during the music festival, prices can spike even higher than regular summer rates. All listings provided here are in Frutillar Bajo, but Frutillar Alto has a handful of cheaper *residenciales.*

Only a block from the beach, **Hospedaje Tía Clarita** (Vicente Pérez Rosales 743, tel. 065/421806, claritaalmonacid@msn.com, US$13–17 pp, breakfast US$3 more) is a friendly, family-run place that lacks the elaborate German colonial style of Frutillar's more expensive options, but it compensates in other ways. Rates vary according to shared or private bath; rooms with private baths have cable TV.

Also notable for its teahouse, **Hospedaje Trayén** (Philippi 963, tel. 065/421346, tttrayen33@hotmail.com, US$25–33 pp with breakfast) has rooms with private baths and cable TV; some have balconies with lake views. Down the block the **Hostería Winkler** (Philippi 1155, tel. 065/421388, US$17–25 pp) is comparable.

On a hillock with colorful flower gardens, **Hotel Frau Holle** (Antonio Varas 54, tel. 065/421345, frauholle@surnet.cl, US$79 d) embodies traditional Frutillar—a lovingly maintained family-run hotel with no frills but utterly reliable.

Hotel Residenz am See (Philippi 539, tel. 065/421539, US$83–100 d, www.hotelamsee.cl) offers rooms with lake views, WiFi, private baths, a European-style breakfast, and parking.

With just eight tasteful rooms, in an historic house dating from 1911, **((Hotel Kaffee Bauernhaus** (Philippi 663, tel. 065/420003, www.hotelbauernhaus.cl, US$83–100 s or d) is more a B&B than a hotel, but it's a very fine one. Rates vary according to view, and the most expensive rooms have balconies.

At the southern edge of town, the 14 rooms at **Hotel Elun** (Camino Punta Larga, Km 2, tel. 065/420055, www.hotelelun.cl, US$100 s or d) feature natural wood interiors, with lake and volcano views, surrounded by lush gardens. Set back from the street, it's quiet and attractive, with friendly ownership and staff. The restaurant is normally open in summer only, but will serve meals on request the rest of the year.

((Hotel Ayacara (Philippi 1215, tel./fax 065/421550, www.hotelayacara.cl, US$145–180 s or d) occupies a gabled century-old lakefront mansion; each of its eight rooms—the more expensive enjoy lake views—is distinctive. Rates include a full German-style breakfast, with homemade kuchen.

Food

In summer, look along the lakeshore for stands with fresh raspberries, raspberry jam, and raspberry kuchen, all area specialties. Along the lakefront, Frutillar has several breakfast and *onces* places, starting with the **Salón de Té Trayén** (Philippi 963, tel. 065/421346).

For fixed-price meals around US$8, try the firehouse restaurant **Tierra del Fuego** (Philippi 1065, tel. 065/421588, lunch and dinner daily). The traditional **Club Alemán** (San Martín 22, tel. 065/421249, lunch and dinner daily) is more formal and more expensive, but not unreasonable. **Guten Apetit** (Balmaceda 98, tel. 065/421145, lunch and dinner daily) is a *parrilla* with excellent lunchtime specials and assiduous service.

On the southern outskirts of town, **Lavanda** (Camino Quebrada Honda Km 1.5, cell tel. 09/9269-1684, www.lavandacasadete.cl) is a new teahouse that's drawn widespread praise, but reservations are obligatory. Only a short distance beyond it, **Se Cocina** (Camino Totoral Km 2, cell tel. 09/9577-7152, www.secocina.cl) is a full-service gourmet restaurant that's also new on the scene, and also requires reservations.

Information

Tourist information has been a black hole for years, but the private Corporación Turística

Frutillar (www.frutillarchile.cl) is opening a new office at the corner of Av. Philippi and Pedro Montt.

Services

Frutillar has no exchange houses, but **Banco Santander** (Philippi 555) has an ATM.

Correos de Chile (Pérez Rosales and San Martín) delivers the mail and also has good Internet service. For long-distance phone calls, there's a **Centro de Llamados** (Av. Philippi and Manuel Rodríguez) in Frutillar Bajo.

Frutillar Alto's **Lavandería Laveli** (San Pedro 436, tel. 065/421555) washes clothes.

For medical services, contact the **Hospital de Frutillar** (Las Piedras s/n, tel. 065/421386).

Getting There and Around

Buses arrive at and leave from Frutillar Alto; *taxi colectivos* shuttle back and forth to Frutillar Bajo. The major long-distance carriers are **Tur-Bus** (Diego Portales 150, tel. 065/421390) and **Cruz del Sur** (Alessandri 32, tel. 065/421552); both run north (Santiago and intermediates) and south (to Puerto Montt) along the Panamericana. **Thaebus,** at the Alessandri terminal, runs half a dozen buses daily to Puerto Octay.

Puerto Varas

North of Puerto Montt, picturesque Puerto Varas appeals to conventional tourists who loll on Lago Llanquihue's beaches, admire its century-old mansions, sup in some of Chile's best restaurants, and follow the bus-boat crossing to the Argentine resort of Bariloche. Increasing numbers of more adventurous visitors also appreciate the nearby Río Petrohué's white-water rafting, Volcán Osorno's snow-clad slopes, Cochamó's wild backcountry, and other outdoor attractions. To the southeast, beyond Cochamó, a new bridge over the Río Puelo also provides an alternate route to Hornopirén and the Carretera Austral.

Varas's architectural heritage, stemming from its German colonization as a 19th-century lake port, lends it its character. A recent building boom has resulted in nondescript housing developments on the outskirts, but it's also brought more stylish infill downtown; many visitors prefer Varas to nearby Puerto Montt, and not just as a base for excursions.

ORIENTATION

On Llanquihue's southwestern shore, Puerto Varas (population 24,309) is 996 kilometers south of Santiago, 20 kilometers north of Puerto Montt, and a short distance east of Ruta 5, the Panamericana. The boundaries of its compact central grid are the lakeshore to the east, Diego Portales to the north, San Bernardo to the west, and Del Salvador to the south. On all sides except the shoreline, hills rise steeply toward quiet residential neighborhoods that include many places to stay.

From the corner of Del Salvador, the Costanera becomes paved Ruta 225 to the village of Ensenada, the lakeport of Petrohué in Parque Nacional Vicente Pérez Rosales, and toward the Cochamó backcountry.

◖ PUERTO VARAS HISTORIC DISTRICT

Other than the lake and its inspiring views toward Volcán Osorno, Varas's main attraction is its Germanic colonial architecture. The most imposing single structure is the **Iglesia del Sagrado Corazón** (1915), a national monument whose steeple soars above the town from the corner of San Francisco and María Brunn. When lit at night, it's best seen from the corner of Imperial and Santa Rosa.

Numerous private residences are national monuments, mostly in residential neighborhoods northwest and west of downtown, including the **Casa Kuschel** (1910) at Klenner 299, the **Casona Alemana** (1914) at Nuestra Señora del Carmen 788, the deteriorating

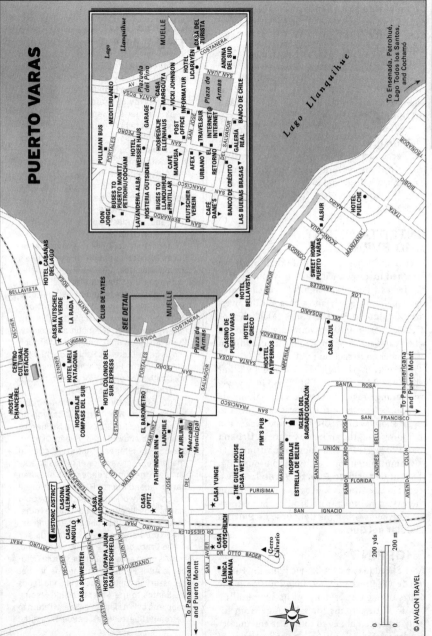

PUERTO VARAS

© AVALON TRAVEL

Casa Maldonado (1915) at Quintanilla 852, Casa Angulo (1910) at Miraflores 96, Casa Opitz (1913) at Terraplén 861, Casa Gotschlich (1932) at Dr. Otto Bader 701-05, and Casa Yunge (1932) at San Ignacio 711. A couple of impressive non-monuments are *hospedajes:* the Casa Schwerter (1941–1942) at Nuestra Señora del Carmen 873, and the Casa Hitschfeld (1930) at Arturo Prat 107.

For some years after the Santiago–Puerto Montt railroad closed, the former Estación del Ferrocarril (Klenner s/n) sat empty, but it's been revamped into the Centro Cultural Estación, a gallery and events center. Rail service, after a brief revival, has been suspended as of 2009.

ENTERTAINMENT AND EVENTS

Puerto Varas has less nightlife than might be expected in a town with so much tourist traffic. It has filled an unsightly vacant lot with the equally unsightly and pharaonically oversized Casino de Puerto Varas (Del Salvador 21, tel. 065/346600), crammed with roulette wheels and slot machines, and a hotel addition was under construction in 2009.

Far better, though, is Garage (Walker Martínez 220, cell tel. 09/9235-3340, www.restaurantgarage.cl), a low-key bar (alongside the Copec gas station) that was once an auto repair shop. While it often has fine live music, including jazz, the air quality is toxic. Urbano (San Pedro 418) is also popular for drinks.

Commemorating the city's 1854 founding, the Aniversario de Puerto Varas lasts two weeks in late January and early February. Soon thereafter, painters from around the country display their work at the Concurso de Pintura El Color del Sur.

SHOPPING

At the headquarters for Parque Pumalín, Puma Verde (Klenner 299, tel. 065/250079) is the crafts outlet for residents of its surrounding communities. Items for sale range from locally produced honey to souvenirs and quality woolens; in addition, there's a good selection of

CROSSING THE LAKES

In Walter Salles's 2004 film *The Motorcycle Diaries,* a youthful Ernesto (Che) Guevara and his friend Alberto Granados push their dying motorcycle through a freak summer snowstorm around Lago Frías en route to Chile. In the early 1950s, the Argentines were following the Cruce de Lagos, a route that's become one of the South American continent's classics since it opened in the early 20th century. Former U.S. president Theodore Roosevelt crossed the Andes from Lago Llanquihue to San Carlos de Bariloche in 1913, and countless thousands of tourists have followed suit.

Connecting the Chilean and Argentine Lakes Districts, passing through Chile's Parque Nacional Vicente Pérez Rosales and Argentina's Parque Nacional Nahuel Huapi, the Cruce Andino is a boat-bus-boat shuttle between Puerto Montt and Bariloche. While many people do it in a day, passively enjoying the mountain scenery, there are hotels and campgrounds at each end of Lago Todos los Santos, on the Chilean side of the border, which provide opportunities for exploratory hikes, though the trail system is not extensive.

The more active can go white-water rafting on the Río Petrohué, canyon up Vicente Pérez Rosales's steep ravines, or even scale snowcapped Volcán Osorno, a 2,652-meter peak that's a technical challenge. There are fewer places to stay on the Argentine side, except between Bariloche and Puerto Pañuelo, but there is a good network of footpaths that would make it possible to hike part of the route. Quite a few cyclists pedal the roads between the water segments of the trip.

The Cruce de Lagos (www.cruceandino.com) is open all year but is best from October to April. From the Chilean side, it's not necessary to continue beyond Lago Todos los Santos to the Argentine side – some people go only as far as Peulla and return to Petrohué, Puerto Varas, or Puerto Montt.

books on Chilean conservation topics, mostly in Spanish.

For chocoholics, **Vicki Johnson** (Santa Rosa 318, tel. 065/232240) fashions exquisite takeaway truffles in addition to a substantial crafts selection.

ACCOMMODATIONS

Puerto Varas has abundant accommodations, some of them very distinctive, in all categories. Some of the cheapest are seasonal, but there are always good options.

US$10-25

Though it's immaculate, in an excellent neighborhood, the dorms-only **Hostel Patiperros** (Mirador 135, tel. 065/235050, www.jardinsa@ entelchile.net, US$8–12 pp) lacks the vibes of other Varas hostels—for better or worse. Calling it lifeless might be an exaggeration, but something's lacking despite firm beds and glistening common areas, including a kitchen and dining room.

Newly affiliated with Hostelling International, the **Pathfinder Inn** (Walker Martínez 561, tel. 065/312515, www.path-finderinn.com, US$11–14 pp) is a cozy three-bedroom hostel (only 14 beds) in an attractive German-colonial house on the edge of the downtown business district. Rates include breakfast, kitchen privileges, and WiFi.

New in early 2009, **Sweet Home Puerto Varas** (Imperial 092, tel. 065/234570, sweet-homeptovaras@gmail.com, US$12 pp–US$48 d) is a quirky hostel with fluent English-speaking Chilean management that also offers yoga classes twice weekly. Campers can pitch their tents in the spacious back yard (US$8 pp), and climbers can work out, even in wet weather, on its basement wall and ceiling.

US$25-50

Casa Margouya (Santa Rosa 318, tel. 065/511648, www.margouya.com, US$13 pp, US$22 s, US$28 d) can lodge up to 17 guests in a variety of singles, doubles, and dorms, which share just two bathrooms. Rates include a buffet breakfast, free tea and coffee, and free Internet

access, with Spanish, English, and French spoken. This is one of Varas's livelier accommodations—not for the early-to-bed crowd.

Easy walking distance from downtown, but in a quiet barrio opposite the old railway station, **Hospedaje Compass del Sur** (Klenner 467, tel. 065/232044, www.compass-delsur.cl, US$15 pp in dorms, US$28 s, US$35 d) occupies a German colonial–style house with large rooms and kitchen privileges; rates include a standard breakfast, but extras such as muesli, eggs, and real coffee (not Nescafé) cost more. Moderately priced laundry service is also available.

Downtown's labyrinthine **Hospedaje Ellenhaus** (San Pedro 325, tel. 065/233577, www.ellenhaus.cl, US$14 pp with shared bath, US$38 d with private bath) is a step above most other budget places.

In a quiet hilltop neighborhood about ten minutes' walk from the Plaza de Armas, German-run **Casa Azul** (Manzanal 66, tel. 065/232904, www.casaazul.net, US$12 pp in dorms, US$30 d with shared bath, US$42 d with private bath) has become a favorite for its rustically stylish and comfortable rooms. Rates include kitchen access, but the huge breakfast of muesli and homemade bread costs US$4 extra. The garden includes a bonsai-bounded koi pond, and a Weimaraner named Bodo provides good company.

Since its arrival in late 2007, alongside the Iglesia Sagrado Corazón, **Hospedaje Estrella de Belén** (Verbo Divino 422, tel. 065/716551, www.hospedaje-estrelladebelen.cl, US$23–28 s, US$42–45 d) has drawn enthusiastic praise. Services include cable TV and WiFi; rates vary according to shared or private bath.

The brown-shingled Casa Hitschfeld, a national monument, is home to **Hostal Opapa Juan** (Arturo Prat 107, tel. 065/232234, www .opapajuan.cl, US$33 s, US$50 d with private bath and breakfast).

Still nearly pristine, **Hostería Outsider** (San Bernardo 318, tel./fax 065/232910, www .turout.com, US$40 s, US$50 d) has consistently provided some of Varas's best value for the price, and has done it with style.

US$50-100

It may look remote on the map, but **Hostal Chancerel** (Decher 400, tel./fax 065/234221, www.turismochancerel.com, US$42 s, US$60 d) is still less than 15 minutes' walk from the Plaza de Armas. Rates include spacious rooms with private bath, breakfast, cable TV, WiFi, and central heating. Other meals and German-style *onces* are available.

One of Varas's most distinctive accommodations, featuring natural wood walls enhanced with work by regional artists, the boutique-style **Hotel El Greco** (Mirador 134, tel. 065/233880, www.hotelelgreco.cl, US$62 s, US$80 d) might be the world's greenest hotel in terms of building materials. When the nearby German school moved to new quarters, El Greco's owners salvaged everything from the building and converted what was once a single story hotel into a four-story building with legitimately traditional style. The current floors, for instance, were once part of the school's gymnasium, and the room doors once opened into classrooms.

Its exterior restored to its pioneer style, ◖ **The Guest House** (O'Higgins 608, tel. 065/231521, www.vicki-johnson.com/guesthouse, US$75 s, US$80 d) occupies the German-colonial Casa Wetzel, a national monument. With smartly furnished rooms and ample, well-lighted common spaces, it provides Varas's most intimate accommodations.

New in 2007, **Hotel Weisser Haus** (San Pedro 252, tel. 065/346479, www.weisserhaus.cl, US$81 d) is a 10-room bed-and-breakfast that consists of a handsome and architecturally suitable addition to a traditional German -colonial–style residence. A couple rooms are small but still well designed, and slightly cheaper.

US$100-150

Directly on the Costanera, **Hotel Licarayén** (San José 114, tel. 065/232305, www.hotelicarayen.cl, US$95–115 s, US$115–145 d) hasn't quite kept up with competitors in its price range but does offer amenities such as a sauna and gym.

In quiet surroundings, some rooms at

Hotel Colonos del Sur Express (Estación 505, tel./fax 065/235555, www.colonosdelsur.cl, US$105–US$133 s, US$120–145 d with breakfast) have truly grand views.

On the lakeshore just south of the casino, the rapidly modernizing **Hotel Bellavista** (Vicente Pérez Rosales 60, tel. 065/232011, www.hotelbellavista.cl, US$125–184 s or d) has outstanding lake views and improved amenities. Popular with foreign tour groups, it's substantially cheaper off-season.

Stretching impressively above the lakeshore, the hillside **Hotel Cabañas del Lago** (Klenner 195, tel. 065/232291, www.cabanasdellago.cl, US$160 s, US$170 d, up to US$220 s or d with breakfast) has equally impressive views and a heated pool. The more expensive corner suites, though, offer views of Osorno as well as the lake and Calbuco.

Across from the train station, the Spanish Meliá chain has rehabbed the rundown casino that sat empty for several years into the glistening **Hotel Meliá Patagonia** (Klenner 349, tel. 065/201000, www.melia-patagonia.cl), with 91 contemporary rooms with elaborate common areas and gardens. Some of the rooms, though, suffer minor limitations associated with the remodeling of an existing building, but this still takes its place among Varas's best hotels.

Hotel Puelche (Itata 695, tel. 065/233600, www.hotelpuelche.com, US$175 d) is a handsome 21-room boutique hotel, in a rustically sophisticated style of stone and wood, on a hill just above the lakeshore. Under the same ownership as Hotel Petrohué, in Parque Nacional Vicente Pérez Rosales, it includes a gym and spa, and is easy walking distance to Varas's best restaurants.

FOOD

Puerto Varas has some of Chile's best food, and even run-of-the-mill restaurants can be pretty good. **Café Dane's** (Del Salvador 441, tel. 065/232371) wins no style points, but its breakfasts, *onces,* and Chilean specialties such as *pastel de choclo* are more than a step above similar fare elsewhere.

El Barómetro (Walker Martínez 584, tel.

© WAYNE BERNHARDSON

Hotel Puelche is one of several new accommodations options in Puerto Varas.

065/346100, lunch and dinner daily) has graduated from a popular meeting place with good sandwiches, desserts, and coffee to a full-fledged restaurant with a more elaborate menu, but loses points for its smoky ambiance.

Café Mamusia (San José 316, tel. 065/233343, lunch and dinner daily) serves fine Chilean specialties, especially *pastel de choclo,* in the US$6–10 range, with a fixed-price *menu de casa* for US$6; the pisco sours are strong and the kuchen sweet with fresh fruit, but service is erratic. The very traditional **Deutscher Verein** (German Club, San José 415, tel. 065/232246, lunch and dinner daily) offers fixed-price midday meals.

In the Mercado Municipal, **Donde El Gordito** (San Bernardo 560, Local 7, tel. 065/233425) is a modest seafood venue that's good value for the price. **Don Jorge** (San Bernardo 240, tel. 09/6559759) is a no-frills locale specializing in beef and Chilean dishes.

The lakeside **Mediterráneo** (Santa Rosa 068, tel. 065/237268, lunch and dinner daily) does a fine leg of lamb (US$15) and has good fish dishes, mostly in the US$10–13 range, but

with wine and dessert it's easy to spend upwards of US$30. For fine summer afternoons and evenings, it has outdoor seating.

Across the street from Mediterráneo, **Govinda** (Santa Rosa 218, tel. 065/233080, www.govinda.cl) is not the Hare Krishna niche restaurant its name might imply, but rather a sophisticated bar/restaurant that uses the freshest ingredients in dishes such as baked hake with a garlic-tinged wheat risotto (US$16). Its bar (which has local brews on tap, and suitably tart pisco sours) is a smoking area, but the dining room is effectively tobacco-free.

A short walk north, extending into the lake on its pylons, the **Club de Yates** (Santa Rosa 0161, tel. 065/232000, lunch and dinner daily) is an upscale seafood option that's more conventional than some of the newer places.

One of the best values is ❰ **Las Buenas Brasas** (San Pedro 543, tel. 065/230953, www.lbb.cl, lunch and dinner daily). From its name (The Good Coals), it sounds like a *parrilla,* but the restaurant is proudest of its fish dishes, especially conger eel (around US$10) and seafood sauces (which cost extra). The service can be a little distracted, but it's so well intentioned that this is a minor flaw.

Trattoria Di Carusso (San Bernardo 318, tel. 065/233478, lunch and dinner daily) makes tremendous pizza (the crust is especially notable) and seafood. The best pizza choice, with the most diverse toppings, is moderately priced **(El Retorno** (San Pedro 465, tel. 065/346441, lunch and dinner daily). If you can put up with zero decor and shaky service, **El Reloj** (San Francisco 310, tel. 065/312475) has excellent pastas and sauces at moderate prices.

Pim's Pub (San Francisco 712, tel. 065/233998, lunch and dinner daily), a popular meeting place, serves pretty good Tex-Mex dishes such as enchiladas and fajitas, and credible margaritas for aperitifs. Prices, though, are about twice what they would be for comparable food in California. Despite a planned building project on the site, it's managed to stave off relocation.

On the lakefront southeast of downtown, **Color Café** (Los Colonos 1005, tel. 065/234311, lunch and dinner daily) is a friendly wine bar, with an appealing natural wood interior; though a little pricey, pasta dishes such as ravioli are excellent. Nearby **Da Alessandro** (Av. Costanera 1290, tel. 065/310583, lunch and dinner daily) gets good reviews from knowledgeable locals for its pizzas, pastas, and seafood.

For fish and seafood, **La Olla** (Pérez Rosales 1071, tel. 065/233540, lunch and dinner daily) falls into the upmarket end of the "hearty Chilean cooking" category, with all traditional dishes plus a few, such as corvina with walnut sauce (US$10), that transcend the stereotype. It gets crowded, especially on weekends.

Almost alongside La Olla, **(Ibis** (Vicente Pérez Rosales 1117, tel. 065/232017, www.ibis-restaurant.cl, dinner only) is one of southern Chile's finest dining experiences, with prices to match. Appetizers cost around US$6–7, and most entrées are in the US$10-and-up range; with drinks and side orders, it's easy to spend upwards of US$30 per person. Still, it's one of the best splurges outside of Santiago for midsized portions of dishes such as *corvina al*

cheff, with a sauce made of shrimp, scallops, and crab; it's also one of only a few Chilean restaurants to offer *criadillas*—often known as Rocky Mountain oysters in North America.

The most impressive recent addition to the dining scene, **(La Rada** (Santa Rosa 040, tel. 065/718316, www.larada.cl) specializes in fish such as vidriola (imported from the Juan Fernández archipelago, US$12) but also exceptional side dishes including superior salads. What the portions lack in size, they more than compensate with flavor, and the service is remarkably good.

INFORMATION

At the foot of the pier on the Avenida Costanera, Puerto Varas's **Casa del Turista** (Piedraplén s/n, tel. 065/237956, www.puertovaras.org, 9 A.M.–10 P.M. daily Dec.–Feb., 9 A.M.–1:30 P.M. and 3–7 P.M. Mar.–Nov.) usually has an English speaker available.

Informatur (San José and Santa Rosa, tel. 065/338542, www.informatur.com), sponsored by an alliance of various service operators, keeps a selective accommodations database.

SERVICES

Afex (San Pedro 414, tel. 065/232377) is the local exchange house; **TravelSur** (San Pedro 451, tel./fax 065/236000) is a general travel agency that also changes money. **Banco de Chile** (Del Salvador 201) and **Banco de Crédito** (Del Salvador 305) have ATMs.

Correos de Chile (San José 242) is the post office. There are numerous downtown phone and cyber outlets, such as **Internet@Internet** (Del Salvador 264, Local 102).

Lavandería Alba (Walker Martínez 511, tel. 065/232908) washes the clothes.

Atop Cerro Calvario in southwestern Puerto Varas, the **Clínica Alemana** (Dr. Otto Bader 810, tel. 065/232336) provides medical assistance.

GETTING THERE

Puerto Varas is close enough to the area's principal airport (Puerto Montt), has good regional and long-distance bus connections, and also lies on the classic bus-boat route to Argentina.

Air

LAN (Av. Gramado 560, tel. 065/234799) flies out of Puerto Montt, as does **Sky Airline** (San Bernardo 430, tel. 065/231039).

Bus

Rather than a central terminal, both regional and long-distance **bus** companies use their own (sometimes shared) offices near the Plaza de Armas. Some long-distance carriers from Puerto Montt pick up passengers here; some regional carriers have no fixed offices but pick up and drop off passengers en route through the city.

Santiago carrier **Pullman Bus** (Portales 318, tel. 065/234612) has its own central terminal, while **Cruz del Sur** (Walker Martinez 239-B, tel. 065/231925; terminal at San Francisco 1317, tel. 065/236969) shares offices with **Buses Norte Internacional,** which goes daily to San Carlos de Bariloche, Argentina (US$20–25, six hours). **Buses Jac** and **Cóndor Bus** (both at Walker Martínez 227, tel. 065/237255) also go to Santiago.

Other northbound carriers to Santiago (US$26–42, 12–13 hours) and intermediates include **Intersur** and **Tur-Bus** (both at San Pedro 210, tel. 065/233787) and **Tas Choapa** (Walker Martínez 230, tel. 065/233831). Santiago fares can even be a little higher, depending on the service level; the most expensive are nighttime buses with fully reclining seats.

Puerto Montt–based **Thaebus** shuttles frequently to Puerto Varas, stopping at the corner of San Bernardo and Walker Martínez, as does **Expresos Puerto Varas** (tel. 065/232253) also goes frequently to Puerto Montt (US$1.20); it is commonly known as "Mitsubishi" for its minibus fleet. From 8:30 A.M.–6 P.M. daily, Expreso Petrohué goes half-hourly to Ensenada (US$2) and Petrohué, on Lago Todos los Santos (US$3). **Buses J.M.** (cell tel. 09/9647-1716) and Thaebus also go to Ensenada and Petrohué, but with fewer frequencies.

From Puerto Montt, **Vía Lago Sur** (cell tel. 09/9224-8109) goes to Cochamó (US$3) and Río Puelo (US$6), at 8 A.M., noon, and 5 P.M. daily. **Buses Río Puelo** (tel. 065/342004) also goes to Cochamó (US$3) at 4 and 4:30 P.M. daily, with the latter continuing to Río Puelo; Varas departures are about half an hour later.

Train

EFE services between Temuco and Puerto Montt, via the **Estación del Ferrocarril** (Klenner 350, tel. 065/232210), were suspended as of summer 2009. For updates, check www.efe.cl.

Bus-Boat

Puerto Varas is one of the intermediate points on the bus-boat shuttle from Puerto Montt to Bariloche (Argentina) via Lago Todos los Santos, so it's possible to purchase tickets and board the bus to Petrohué here. Most of the year, buses leave Puerto Montt at 7:45 A.M. daily for Petrohué; April–mid-September, though, they run Wednesday–Sunday only, leaving Puerto Montt at 9 A.M. For details, contact **Turismo Peulla** (San Juan 430, 2nd floor, tel. 065/236150, www.turismopeulla.cl).

GETTING AROUND
To the Airport

There are no regularly scheduled airport departures, but **Pacific** (tel. 065/237790) will drop off or pick up Varas passengers for US$28 for up to four persons. Otherwise it's necessary to make the connection indirectly via ETM bus from Puerto Montt.

Vicinity Of Puerto Varas

Puerto Varas is the gateway for sights such as Volcán Osorno and Lago Todos los Santos, in Parque Nacional Vicente Pérez Rosales, and the Cochamó backcountry. It's also the staging point for adventure activities such as white-water rafting, hiking, climbing, mountain biking, horseback riding, and fishing. Paved Ruta 225 follows the lakeshore east to Ensenada; at a fork two kilometers farther east, the main road goes northwest to Petrohué, while another paved route heads southeast to Ralún, Cochamó, and Puelo.

Conventional travel agencies include **Andina del Sud** (Del Salvador 72, tel./fax 065/232811, www.andinadelsud.cl) and **TravelSur** (San Pedro 451, tel./fax 065/236000, www.travelsur .cl). For activities-oriented operators, try **Alsur** (Aconcagua 8, tel. 065/232300, www.alsurexpeditions.cl) or **Aqua Motion** (San Francisco 328, tel. 065/232747, www.aqua-motion .com).

Most adventure-travel agencies rent mountain bikes and other outdoor-sports equipment. Just north of the pier, **Canoas Tour** (Av. Costanera s/n, tel. 065/346928, 09/9294-0543) rents kayaks for lake use, but **KoKayak** (Ruta 225, Km 40, cell tel. 09/9310-5272, www .kokayak.com) organizes more ambitious kayak trips on the Río Petrohué.

ENSENADA

At Lago Llanquihue's east end, 45 kilometers from Puerto Varas, the shoreline village of Ensenada lies midway between Volcán Osorno's symmetrical cone, to the northeast, and Volcán Calbuco's serrated caldera to the southwest. Most services are at or near the junction with the northbound road to Las Cascadas and Puerto Octay.

Just north of the Las Cascadas junction, 【 **Hotel Ensenada** (tel. 065/212028, www .hotelensenada.cl, US$200 d with half board) is a century-old classic that oozes character out of the woodwork—all the rooms are spacious, even the third-floor rooms with shared baths, and museum pieces fill the common areas. Rates include bicycles, kayaks, and WiFi, among other recreational options. It's closed April–September.

In a class of its own, built by Seattle tech entrepreneur Michael Darland, the punning 【 **Yan Kee Way Lodge** is an over-the-top luxury resort with whimsical (even kitschy) decor targeting big-bucks travelers for expedition holidays and/or fly-fishing (considerably more expensive). Accommodations include regular hotel rooms and two-unit bungalows (which share a wall). The dining room and elaborate kitchen at its **Latitude 42** draw gourmets from around the country. For more information, contact **Southern Chile Expeditions** (Casilla 149, Puerto Varas, tel. 065/212030, tel. 866/881-9215 in the U.S., www.southern-chilexp.com).

Several buses daily use Ruta 225 between Puerto Varas, Ensenada, and Petrohué; others continue to Ralún, Cochamó, and Puelo.

From Ensenada, a narrow gravel road follows the eastern lakeshore for 22 kilometers to Las Cascadas, where it becomes a paved road to Puerto Octay. There is no public transportation on this route, but four buses daily link Las Cascadas to Puerto Octay.

PARQUE NACIONAL VICENTE PÉREZ ROSALES

Established in 1926, Chile's first national park is a geographical extravaganza whose dominant features are Volcán Osorno, a symmetrical snowcapped cone often called the "Fujiyama of South America," and fjordlike Lago Todos los Santos, which forms an elongated lacustrine highway toward the Argentine border. The 251,000-hectare park also contains rushing rivers, steep forested canyons, and a scattering of alpine lakes.

It takes its name from Vicente Pérez Rosales, an adventurer and explorer whose mid-19th-century travels literally cleared the way for European pioneers—he hired the indigenous

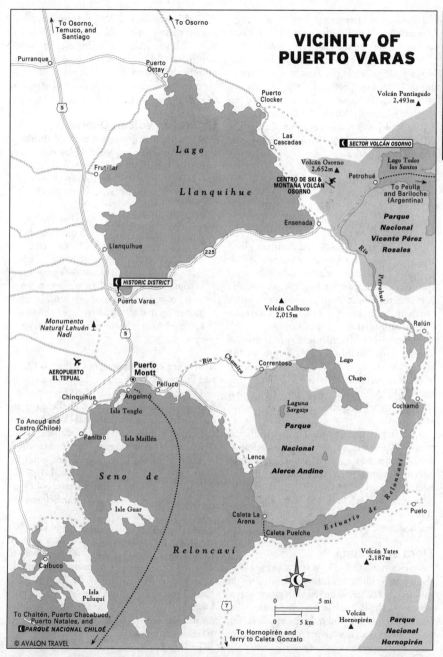

VICINITY OF PUERTO VARAS

To Osorno, Temuco, and Santiago

To Osorno

Purranque

Puerto Octay

Puerto Clocker

Volcán Puntiagudo 2,493m

Las Cascadas

SECTOR VOLCÁN OSORNO

Frutillar

Lago

Llanquihue

Volcán Osorno 2,652m

CENTRO DE SKI & MONTAÑA VOLCÁN OSORNO

Petrohué

Lago Todos los Santos

To Peulla and Bariloche (Argentina)

Ensenada

Parque Nacional Vicente Pérez Rosales

Llanquihue

225

Río Petrohué

HISTORIC DISTRICT

Puerto Varas

Volcán Calbuco 2,015m

Ralún

Monumento Natural Lahuén Nadi

5

AEROPUERTO EL TEPUAL

Puerto Montt

Pelluco

Río Chamiza

Correntoso

Lago Chapo

Laguna Sargazo

Cochamó

Chinquihue

Angelmó

Isla Tenglo

Parque

To Ancud and Castro (Chiloé)

Panitao

Isla Maillén

Nacional

Lenca

Alerce Andino

Seno   de

Isle Guar

Estuario de Reloncaví

Caleta La Arena

Puelo

Caleta Puelche

Reloncaví

Volcán Yates 2,187m

Calbuco

Isla Puluqui

To Chaitén, Puerto Chacabuco, Puerto Natales, and PARQUE NACIONAL CHILOÉ

7

0   5 mi

0   5 km

Volcán Hornopirén

Parque Nacional Hornopirén

To Hornopirén and ferry to Caleta Gonzalo

© AVALON TRAVEL

Huilliche to set fire to the forests near Lago Llanquihue. Pérez Rosales later made a name for himself during the California gold rush.

Boat traffic began to cross Todos los Santos around 1890, with the first tourists arriving in 1903. Long before Europeans saw the area, though, indigenous peoples had used the southerly Paso de Vuriloche to traverse the Andes, and Jesuit missionaries used a slightly different route south of Volcán Tronador, the area's highest peak.

Geography and Climate

Some 50 kilometers northeast of Puerto Varas via Ruta 225, Parque Nacional Vicente Pérez Rosales ranges from 50 meters above sea level near Ensenada to about 3,460 meters on the summit of Cerro Tronador, a dormant glaciated volcano on the Argentine border. Volcán Osorno's 2,652-meter summit is its most conspicuous feature; other high peaks include 2,493-meter Volcán Puntiagudo on the park's northern border and 1,710-meter Cerro La Picada, northeast of Volcán Osorno.

Several rivers drain into Lago Todos los Santos, most notably the Río Negro; at 191 meters above sea level, the lake is the source of the Río Petrohué, diverted southward into the Golfo de Reloncaví by lava flows that reached Lago Llanquihue's shores just north of Ensenada.

The park receives about 2,500 millimeters of rainfall per year at lower elevations but up to 4,000 millimeters, much of it as snow, near the Argentine border. The lake moderates the ambient temperature, which averages about 16°C in summer and 6.5°C in winter, though it gets colder at higher altitude. Summertime highs reach about 25°C.

Flora and Fauna

Ecologically, up to 1,000 meters above sea level, the dense Valdivian rainforest consists of the southern beech *coigüe* mixed with glossy-leaved *ulmos* and the dense bamboo *quila,* as well as ferns and climbing vines. At higher elevations *coigüe* mixes with the related *lenga;* the rare coniferous *alerce* grows in a few steep areas.

Within the park are 33 mammal species, among them puma, *pudú,* foxes, and skunks, and 117 bird species, including torrent ducks, kingfishers, coots, woodpeckers, and hummingbirds. Rainbow and brown trout have been introduced into its lakes and streams, though there are also native trout.

◖ Sector Volcán Osorno

While it hasn't erupted since the mid-19th century, Volcán Osorno's youthful Holocene crater has active fumaroles and is potentially dangerous. From the deck of the *Beagle,* Darwin observed its eruption of January 19–20, 1835:

At midnight the sentry observed something like a large star, which gradually increased in size until about three o'clock, when it presented a very magnificent spectacle. By the aid of a glass, dark objects, in constant succession, were seen, in the midst of a great glare of red light, to be thrown up and to fall down. The light was sufficient to cast on the water a long bright reflection.

Adventure travel operators in Puerto Octay and Puerto Varas offer one-day guided climbs of Osorno, from about US$200 per person. Starting around 4 A.M., it's a challenging ascent, requiring either technical skills on snow and ice or guides with those technical skills, especially to cross crevasses. Conaf, which regulates climbing here, requires one guide for every three climbers on commercial trips; for independent climbers, it requires proof of experience and presentation of gear before issuing permits.

Recent improvements have made Osorno's ski area a viable recreational option in both summer and winter, though it's not likely to draw big crowds away from more elaborate ski areas such as Portillo and Valle Nevado. As it has no accommodations of its own (though a local ski club operates a simple nearby *refugio*), most skiers stay in either Puerto Varas or other lakeside communities.

Facilities include a pair of decent lifts that

carry skiers nearly 500 meters above the base elevation of 1,200 meters. At the base, reached by a paved road just north of Ensenada, there's a small cafeteria and a larger restaurant, seating up to 150 patrons for lunch. Lift tickets are moderately priced, and rental gear is available; outside ski season, visitors can still take the lifts (US$15 pp) for access to the views and high country walks.

For more information on the ski area in both winter and summer, contact **Centro de Ski & Montaña Volcán Osorno** (San Francisco 333, 2nd floor, Puerto Varas, tel. 065/233445, www.volcanosorno.com). **CTS Turismo** (Santa Rosa 560, Local 15, tel. 065/237330, Puerto Varas) provides round-trip transportation (US$25 pp, including a sandwich and drink).

Sector Petrohué

At the west end of Lago Todos los Santos, the source of its namesake river, **Sector Petrohué** is most popular as the port for the passenger ferry to Peulla, which leaves mid-morning and returns in early afternoon. Turismo Peulla, which operates the ferry, also runs a daily excursion to **Isla Margarita,** an island that rears its head above the middle of the lake, in January and February only.

Since most of Sector Petrohué lacks an integrated trail network, visiting remote areas requires either hiring a private launch or contracting an activities-oriented tour, but there are a few accessible options. From **Playa Larga,** the black-sand beach north of Hotel Petrohué, the five-kilometer **Sendero Rincón del Osorno** follows the lake's western shore. Six kilometers southwest of Petrohué, on the south side of the highway, Conaf charges US$2 admission for the **Sendero Saltos del Petrohué,** a short riverbank trail that follows a series of basalt bedrock rapids and falls too rough for rafting or kayaking. Below the falls, Puerto Varas operators start their Class III–IV descents of the **Río Petrohué** (US$45), which is suitable for novice rafters but interesting enough for those with more experience. Sites suitable for rock climbing are nearby.

Sector Peulla

Where the Río Negro and the Río Peulla empty into Todos los Santos, 20 nautical miles east of Petrohué, the hamlet of **Peulla** traditionally earns its livelihood from tourist traffic that patronizes Hotel Peulla and its restaurant, whether overnight, on day excursions from Petrohué, or en route to Bariloche; there is also a new luxury hotel to supplement the Peulla. Chilean customs and immigration is only a short distance east of here.

Day-trippers and through travelers have time enough to walk to **Cascada de Los Novios,** a waterfall just a few minutes from Hotel Peulla. Only overnighters will have time for the eight-kilometer climb of the **Sendero Laguna Margarita.**

Accommodations and Food

Park accommodations and food are limited; hotel reservations are advisable.

Just below Volcán Osorno's permanent snow line, 1,200 meters above sea level, the 40-bunk **Refugio Teski Ski Club** (tel. 09/9700-0370, www.teskiclub.cl, US$24 pp) also serves meals. From a turnoff three kilometers north of the Ensenada junction, the *refugio* is a 13-kilometer climb on a smoothly paved road.

On the Río Petrohué's south bank, reached by rowboat shuttle from the visitors center, the no-frills **Hospedaje Küschel** charges US$13 per person for beds, half that for camping. North of the visitors center, Conaf's 24-site **Camping Playa Petrohué** charges US$13 for up to five persons.

Rebuilt after a 2002 fire, the Middle European–style **◖ Hotel Petrohué** (tel./fax 065/212025, www.petrohue.com, US$164 s, US$229 d with breakfast) is at least the equal of what had always been a fine hotel. Other rate options include half board (US$180 s, US$260 d) and packages with excursions included (US$266 s, US$427 d). Its small restaurant and bar are open to the public; otherwise, only limited supplies at high prices are available at Petrohué's only shop.

In 1913, when the venerable **Hotel Peulla** (tel. 065/212053, www.hotelpeulla.cl, US$140 s, US$170 d with buffet breakfast) opened at the east end of the lake, Theodore Roosevelt was among the first-year contingent of visitors. Though many rooms have been renovated, it retains a Euro-Andean style and squeaky floors; many Cruce Andino passengers take the buffet lunch (US$17) at its restaurant, **Tejuela,** en route to Bariloche. If space is available, the hotel offers a backpackers' special of US$45 pp with half-board.

Hotel Peulla's ownership has also built the new, separately managed **Hotel Natura** (tel. 065/560485, www.hotelnatura.cl, US$220 s, US$269 d with buffet breakfast) in the manner of an Andean design hotel, with spacious four-star rooms and magnificent natural light throughout. Lunch or dinner costs an extra US$30 pp. Both hotels have agonizingly but unavoidably slow Internet connections.

For the truly financially challenged, tent camping is possible near the Conaf cabin on the road that leads from the boat dock to the hotels.

Information

At Petrohué, Conaf's **Centro de Visitantes** contains exhibits on the park's geography, geology, fauna, flora, and history.

Getting There and Around

Regular bus service connects Petrohué with Puerto Varas and Puerto Montt.

Mid-September–mid-April, Monday–Saturday, Puerto Montt's Turismo Peulla operates 7:45 A.M. buses to Ensenada and Petrohué via Puerto Varas, connecting with its own bus-boat crossing to Bariloche (Argentina). The rest of the year, the Bariloche crossing takes two days, with an obligatory overnight at Hotel Peulla; buses run Monday–Friday only, leaving Puerto Montt at 8:30 A.M.

At Petrohué, a dockside kiosk sells tickets for the three-hour voyage to Peulla, where it connects with the bus to the Argentine border at Puerto Frías and a relay of bus-boat links to Bariloche. Hikers and cyclists can also take this route; round-trip tickets to Peulla cost US$37

for adults, slightly less for children; lunch at Hotel Peulla costs an additional US$14 per person. From Puerto Varas, the fare is US$45; for more details, contact **Turismo Peulla** (San Juan 430, 2nd floor, Puerto Varas, tel. 065/236150, www.turismopeulla.cl).

COCHAMÓ AND VICINITY

Two kilometers east of Ensenada, where international Ruta 225 continues to Petrohué, another paved road follows the Río Petrohué southeast for 30 kilometers, where it forks as the river enters the Estuario de Reloncaví. While the right fork heads south to Canutillar, the graveled left fork crosses the bridge over the Petrohué and continues to **Ralún,** where another gravel road forks north to **Cayutué,** on the south arm of Lago Todos los Santos.

The main road, though, continues another 15 kilometers to Cochamó, where the 2,111-meter Volcán Yates provides a backdrop for the shingled **Iglesia Parroquial María Inmaculada** and its soaring steeple. The area's big attraction, though, is the yet untamed grandeur of the upper Río Cochamó, where ribbon-like waterfalls tumble over exfoliated granite domes that rise above the luxuriant rainforest.

Still, only small numbers of hikers, dedicated technical climbers, and horseback riders challenge the muddy trail, part of which follows a 19th-century log road that crossed the Andes to Argentina, to the scenic valley of **La Junta** and beyond. Though landowner opposition has stopped a road up the valley to La Junta, the Spanish utility company Endesa has acquired water rights that could lead to road-building and construction of hydroelectric turbines.

From the Río Cochamó's outlet, the gravel road continues south over a new bridge across the Río Puelo and then joins Ruta 7, the Carretera Austral, to **Caleta Puelche.** Here it's possible to double back north toward Puerto Montt via the ferry shuttle to Caleta La Arena, or continue south to Hornopirén, the vehicle ferry port for southbound travelers.

Campo Aventura Eco-Lodge

Cochamó is the base for **Campo Aventura,** an eco-lodge and horse-trekking company that offers one- to ten-day horseback trips to its backcountry camp at La Junta, 17 kilometers east and 300 meters above sea level. Recently sold to new U.S. ownership, it's likely to expand its hiking programs.

The present trail follows the river's north bank as far as La Junta, where it's necessary to ford the river to Campo Aventura's southbank camp, which has comfortable lodging, camping (US$7 pp with shower access), and its own network of hiking trails. If the river is high, the crossing can be dangerous for hikers and, on rare occasions, even riders, but Campo Aventura has installed its own cable car to simplify the process. Its classic four-day, three-night horseback-riding package costs US$389 per person; for more details, especially on the longer excursions, contact Campo Aventura's Puerto Varas office (San Bernardo 318, tel./fax 065/232910, www.campo-aventura.com). In addition, the company offers boat trips to nearby thermal baths and a sea lion colony, sea kayaking, and fishing and trekking.

Accommodations and Food

Cochamó proper has cozy, well-heated **Residencial Edicar** (tel. 065/216256, US$13 pp with shared bath, breakfast, and cable TV), a lodging with good views over the estuary.

Both horseback-tour clients and nonriders stay overnight (US$42 pp with half board) at the three tasteful cabañas at **◖ Campo Aventura Eco-Lodge,** five kilometers south of Cochamó proper and 500 meters east of the Puelo road, on the south side of the bridge over the Río Cochamó. Along with breakfast, seafood and vegetarian lunches and dinners are available at its restaurant, **La Mesa de los Sabores.**

Open mid-September–mid-May, Campo Aventura has equally stylish if simpler dormitory accommodations at La Junta, with wood-fired hot showers and a campground as well. Meals, wine, and fresh bread are available, but it's best to make advance arrangements for meals at the ecolodge.

Getting There and Around

From Puerto Montt, **Vía Lagos Sur** (cell tel. 09/9224-8109) and **Buses Río Puelo** (tel. 065/342004) go to Cochamó (US$3) four or five times daily via Puerto Varas. Confirm schedules at Campo Aventura's Varas office, which is near the bus stop and can also arrange transfers by private vehicle or even kayak (even for nonkayakers).

Puerto Montt

No Chilean city enjoys a more impressive setting than Puerto Montt, where a cordon of forested mountains and snowcapped volcanoes stretches south along Chile's island-studded "Inside Passage." While the midsize port can't match the prosperity and cultural diversity of cities in comparable surroundings, such as Seattle and Vancouver, B.C., improvements are underway. Part of the waterfront, with its dramatic views, has become a park; anchor businesses are helping make downtown a retail Mecca; handsome high-rise apartments are filling once-vacant lots; pedestrian malls are sprouting chic sidewalk cafés; and pubs and bars are proliferating.

Puerto Montt owes part of this growth to shipbuilding, extractive industries such as forestry, and the burgeoning fish-farming sector. As a city whose potential, to this point, exceeds its achievements, the capital of Region X (Los Lagos) remains primarily a gateway to the Andean Lakes District, the Chiloé archipelago, Chilean Patagonia, and parts of Argentina. As a transport hub where mainland Chile ends

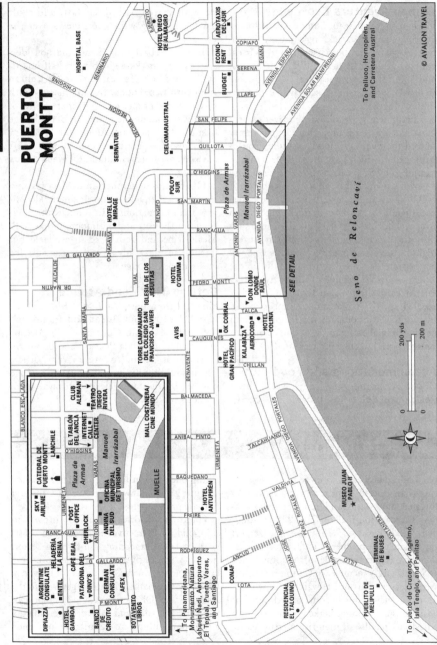

PUERTO MONTT

© AVALON TRAVEL

Seno de Reloncaví

SEE DETAIL

To Peulluco, Hornopirén, and Carretera Austral

To Panamericana, Monumento Natural Lahuen Nadi, Aeropuerto El Tepual, Puerto Varas, and Santiago

To Puerto de Cruceros, Angelmó, Isla Tengló, and Pantiao

200 yds
200 m

CHILE'S INSIDE PASSAGE

Even in the darkest days of the 1970s, as Chile chafed under dictatorship and foreign travelers were few, the occasional adventurer went south in search of a sailing passage through the labyrinth of its southern canals.

Today, fortunately, it's easier than ever to find a berth on "the poor man's cruise," a three-day voyage through western Aisén and Magallanes. The *Magallanes*, which shuttles the 900 nautical miles between Puerto Montt and Puerto Natales, is not a cruise ship. Rather, it's a cargo ferry that also carries passengers in reasonable comfort through some of South America's finest scenery – at least when the weather clears in one of the earth's stormiest regions.

Schedule permitting, the *Magallanes* pauses at **Puerto Edén,** a fishing hamlet where the last remaining Kawéskar (Alacaluf) reside, long enough for an optional landing and walk through town (the US$6 fee per person goes entirely to the community). Beyond Puerto Edén, the enthralling scenery includes emerald forests, countless waterfalls, and glaciers that don't quite reach the sea but still glisten when the sun burns through the clouds. Southbound, the ship detours for a view of Glaciar Pío XI, with its five-kilometer face, before resuming the journey. Approaching Puerto Natales, passengers grab their backpacks and prepare to head for *hospedajes* and hotels to make their plans for Torres del Paine and Patagonia.

PRACTICALITIES

Because the *Magallanes* is faster than the *Puerto Edén,* which used to run this route, the frustration that many passengers felt when weather or mechanical problems caused delays has diminished. For contact information, details on booking, and rates, see *Getting There* in the *Puerto Montt* section. The boat sails Monday afternoons all year, returning from Puerto Natales on Thursday, but longer summer days usually mean good visibility even with changeable weather.

A Japanese ferry remodeled in Chile, the *Magallanes* can carry 337 passengers versus the *Puerto Edén*'s maximum of 175 or so. The former needs only about 60 hours between Puerto Montt and Puerto Natales, even with a stop at Puerto Edén and a detour to Pío XI, while the slower *Puerto Edén* often took longer. When demand falls in the off-season, though, the smaller *Puerto Edén* sometimes substitutes for the *Magallanes*.

The *Magallanes* has a pub, self-service cafeteria and dining room, and spacious upper decks and terraces. Its eight AAA cabins have two bunks each with individual reading lights (with a separate outlet suitable for charging cell phones or computers), private baths, writing desk, chair, locking closet, regulated heat, and an exterior window. Sixteen AA cabins have two upper and two lower bunks and the same amenities except for desk and chair. Fourteen A cabins have identical amenities but lack exterior windows. The 132 C *literas* (berths) have locking closets and shared baths. If you're susceptible to seasickness, medication is available from the bar; take it well before crossing the Golfo de Penas.

The food is cafeteria food, but it has improved in quality and increased in quantity. Both bridge and cabin staff are friendly, even the food servers, and bar prices (notable for the "Happy Sour" promotion) are moderate. Some people bring their own wine, as the selection is limited. Smoking is permitted outdoors only.

Navimag carries twice as many foreigners as Chileans on the Puerto Montt–Puerto Natales route, which can still be delayed by bad weather. At the outset, there is an orientation and safety talk. Videos, including exceptional Chilean films, and other entertainment, including a closing-night party, take place on board.

In the course of the voyage, many people make acquaintances and enduring friendships, and even some marriages have resulted. There's easy access to the bridge, the crew are personable and informative, and it's possible to follow the route on their charts. Some passengers, though, bring their own GPSs and charts, the most comprehensive of which is British Admiralty Chart 561, *Cabo Pilar to Golfo Coronados* (scale 1:750,000).

and archipelagic Chile begins, it enjoys air, land, or sea connections in all directions but west. Increasing numbers of cruise ships are calling at its port of Angelmó, though there's barely room for them to maneuver in and out of the congested harbor; the largest vessels have to anchor offshore and shuttle passengers to the pier.

HISTORY

Puerto Montt dates from 1853, when German colonists landed at the north end of the Seno de Reloncaví in what was then called Melipulli, a Huilliche word whose definition—Four Hills—aptly described the site. It grew slowly until 1912, when the railroad cut travel time to Santiago to only 26 hours and it became the jumping-off point for southbound colonists headed for continental Chiloé, Aisén, and Magallanes.

In 1960, a massive earthquake destroyed the port and most of what Jan Morris called "structures in the Alpine manner, all high-pitched roofs and quaint balconies." Rebuilt in a mostly utilitarian style, Puerto Montt is only now beginning to sport newer buildings of distinction; the earlier style survives in nearby Puerto Varas.

ORIENTATION

Puerto Montt (population 155,895) is 1,016 kilometers south of Santiago via the Panamericana, which bypasses the city center en route to the Chiloé archipelago. Like Valparaíso, it occupies a narrow shelf at the foot of a series of hills, but not so high nor so steep as those at Valparaíso. Westbound Avenida Diego Portales becomes Avenida Angelmó, the main approach to the ferry, fishing, and forest-products port of Angelmó, which draws tourists to its crafts fair and seafood restaurants; eastbound, it becomes Avenida Soler Manfredini, the starting point for the discontinuous Carretera Austral, a series of both paved and gravel highways linked, where necessary, by ferries. This highway ends at Villa O'Higgins, 1,240 kilometers to the south in Region XI (Aisén), but most travelers cover

at least part of the route via air or ferry from Puerto Montt or Chiloé.

SIGHTS

Puerto Montt's strength is its magnificent setting, but it also has a handful of architectural monuments and other sights. On the south side of **Plaza Manuel Irarrázaval,** built of *alerce,* the copper-domed, Parthenon-styled **Catedral de Puerto Montt** (1856) is the city's oldest building. Surrounded by woods, the hillside **Torre Campanario del Colegio San Francisco Javier** (1894) rises behind the **Iglesia de los Jesuitas** (1872), at the corner of Guillermo Gallardo and Rengifo.

Recently upgraded, the waterfront **Museo Juan Pablo II** (Av. Diego Portales 991, tel. 065/223029, museojp@yahoo.com, 10 A.M.–7 P.M. weekdays, 10 A.M.–6 P.M. weekends, US$0.85 adults, US$0.35 children) lies directly east of the bus terminal. It holds collections on natural history, archaeology (including dioramas of the Monte Verde early-man site 35 kilometers west of town), and anthropology,

Catedral de Puerto Montt

early Spanish and 19th-century German colonization, and the city's history from its origins as the hamlet of Melipulli to the 1960 earthquake and up to the present. For locals, history's high point is the 1987 visit from Pope John Paul II, also documented here, which resulted in the museum's renaming.

Puerto Montt and **Angelmó,** two kilometers west, have gradually merged along the waterfront, but the port retains its own identity and attracts more visitors than other parts of town, thanks to its sprawling crafts market and gaggle of *marisquerías,* always jammed with lunch and dinner patrons. *Taxi colectivos* out Avenida Diego Portales go directly to the port area, which is also the departure point for southbound ferries.

Monumento Natural Lahuén Ñadi

Little native forest remains near Puerto Montt, but substantial stands of *alerce, ulmo, mañío, coigüe,* and other species survive in this 200-hectare woodland between the city and Aeropuerto El Tepual, despite the steady encroachment of trophy houses surrounded by high fences and guarded by Rottweilers.

Located on the private Fundo El Rincón, the Conaf-administered park features a small visitors center, a cafeteria, a short nature trail, and one slightly longer hiking trail. Midway between the Panamericana and the airport, a bumpy gravel road leads to the park, about three kilometers north; water can cover parts of the road when rains are heavy, but the surface is firm gravel and vehicles without four-wheel drive pass easily.

Any airport-bound bus will drop you at the junction, which is about 30 minutes' walk from the park. Admission costs about US$2.50.

ENTERTAINMENT

Built with Mexican aid after the 1960 quake, named for the famous muralist, the **Centro de Arte Diego Rivera** (Quillota 116, tel. 065/261817) is Montt's main venue for theater, dance, and the occasional film. Upstairs in the same building, named for a mid-20th century Chilean painter, the **Sala Hardy Wistuba**

(9 A.M.–8 P.M. Mon.–Fri., 11 A.M.–6 P.M. Sat.–Sun., free) is a gallery with rotating exhibits of painting, sculpture, and photography.

Puerto Montt has a smattering of pubs and bars, including the superficially Western-themed **OK Corral** (Cauquenes 128, tel. 065/266287) and the popular **Sherlock** (Antonio Varas 452, tel. 065/288888).

In the former train station, miraculously transformed into the Mall Costanera, the **Cine Mundo** (Illapel 10, Local 303, tel. 065/348055) shows current movies.

SHOPPING

Directly opposite the bus terminal, the **Pueblito de Melipulli** (Diego Portales s/n, tel. 065/263524) is a permanent artisans' market, but crafts stalls also line both sides and cover the sidewalks of Avenida Angelmó west of Independencia. Typical items include woolens, copperware, and standard souvenirs.

Sotavento Libros (Diego Portales 580, tel. 065/256650) specializes in local and regional history and literature.

ACCOMMODATIONS

Puerto Montt has abundant accommodations, but many lower-end options are unremarkable if not quite dire; even most at the top lack distinction. Many visitors prefer to stay in Puerto Varas, 20 minutes north, and visit Puerto Montt for the afternoon.

US$10-25

Uphill from the bus terminal, **Residencial El Talquino** (Pérez Rosales 114, tel. 065/253331, eltalquino@hotmail.com, US$10 pp without breakfast) also offers breakfast (US$3) and kitchen privileges for a small additional charge.

US$25-50

Northwest of the terminal, **◖ Casa Perla** (Trigal 312, tel. 065/262104, www.casaperla .com, US$13 pp with breakfast) offers rooms with shared bath, hot showers, kitchen privileges, and laundry facilities; while it's not Puerto Montt's most appealing neighborhood, the sociable owners speak English, and the cozy common areas include a small library.

Hotel Gamboa (Pedro Montt 157, tel. 065/252741, US$17–20 pp) is a vintage hotel with character but distracted management. The sizable rooms retain most of their original style, though some of the modern furniture is tacky; rates vary according to shared or private baths.

Nearer the port, **Hospedaje Rocco** (Pudeto 233, tel./fax 065/272897, www.hospedaje-rocco.cl, US$20 pp in dorms, US$33 s, US$42 d with breakfast) also gets high marks for hospitality, but the rates are high for a place that has shared baths only.

The contemporary **Hotel Le Mirage** (Rancagua 350, tel. 065/255125, fax 065/256302, www.hotellemirage.cl, US$42 s, US$50 d) often fills with groups; rates include private bath, cable TV, and most other conveniences, but it's worn for its age.

US$50-100

Near the waterfront, under new ownership, the renovated **Hotel Colina** (Talca 81, tel./fax 065/253501, www.hotelcolina.cl, US$47 s, US$53 d) has undergone a facelift that's compromised its original deco style; the busy nearby avenue makes it not the quietest location. Rates include a buffet breakfast.

Business-oriented **Hotel Antupirén** (Freire 186, tel. 065/367800, reservas@hotelantupiren.cl, US$70 s, US$75 d) has attentive, efficient service and a good buffet breakfast. Some smaller, slightly cheaper rooms offer less value for the price.

Up the hill from downtown, with expansive views of the sound and surrounding volcanoes, **Hotel Diego de Almagro** (Ejército 516, tel. 065/320200, www.dahoteles.com, US$75 s, US$85 d) is, at its best, as good or better than the pricier O'Grimm and Gran Pacífico.

More than US$100

Hotel O'Grimm (Gallardo 211, tel. 065/252845, www.ogrimm.com, US$100 s, US$110 d) has attentive service and large rooms with all-modern conveniences. Its attractive bar also has an acoustically insulated basement pub with occasional live music.

The business-oriented **Hotel Gran Pacífico** (Urmeneta 719, tel. 065/482100, www.hotelgranpacifico.cl, US$115 s, US$130 d) has spacious, comfortable, and immaculate rooms that are also soundproofed; those facing southeast have the best views. Amenities include a gym and sauna.

FOOD

With only a few exceptions, downtown Puerto Montt restaurants include reasonably priced but run-of-the-mill places such as **Dino's** (Antonio Varas 550, tel. 065/252785, lunch and dinner daily), with its chain predictability; and **Don Lomo Donde Raúl** (Talca 84, tel. 065/254597, lunch and dinner daily). Figure about US$5–8 for lunch, more for dinner.

DiPiazza (Pedro Montt 181, tel. 065/254174, lunch and dinner daily) makes good thin-crust pizza at moderate prices—individual-sized pizzas start around US$6, and inexpensive pasta plates are also on the menu. The rejuvenated **Club Alemán** (German Club, Antonio Varas 264, tel. 065/252551, lunch and dinner daily) is a step up in both price and quality. So is the seafood at the Centro Español's **Polo Sur** (O'Higgins 233, 2nd floor, tel. 065/343753, lunch and dinner daily). **El Tablón del Ancla** (Antonio Varas 350, lunch and dinner daily) is a cheerful bar/restaurant that's worth a look.

Any of numerous *palafito marisquerías* clustered at the port of Angelmó are worth trying for fish, shellfish, and *curanto*, but streetside restaurants like the flashy **Marfino** (Av. Angelmó 1856, tel. 065/259044) deserve consideration. One of the best options is the steadily improving **El Cuento del Mar** (Av. Angelmó 2476, tel. 061/271500), with fine fish and shellfish entrées starting at US$8. The management, in particular, is congenial and accommodating.

For sandwiches, *onces*, coffee, and desserts such as German-style kuchen, try **Café Real** (Rancagua 137, tel. 065/253750), **Patagonia Deli** (Antonio Varas 486, tel. 065/482898), and **Kalabaza** (Antonio Varas 629, tel.

065/266010). **Heladería La Reina** (Urmeneta 508, tel. 065/253979) continues to produce Puerto Montt's finest ice cream.

INFORMATION

Mid-January–mid-March, Puerto Montt's **Oficina Municipal de Turismo** (Varas and O'Higgins, tel. 065/261823, www.puertomonttchile.cl), just south of the Plaza de Armas, is open 8:30 A.M.–9 P.M. daily; the rest of the year, hours are 8:30 A.M.–7 P.M. Monday–Saturday.

Within the hilltop Intendencia Regional, **Sernatur** (tel. 065/254580) is open 8:30 A.M.– 5:30 P.M. Monday–Thursday, 8:30 A.M.– 4:30 P.M. Friday.

Puerto Montt has **consulates** of Argentina (Pedro Montt 160, 6th floor, tel. 065/253996, 8 A.M.–1 P.M. Mon.–Fri.) and Germany (Antonio Varas 525, Oficina 306, tel. 065/252828).

Conaf's **Patrimonio Silvestre** unit (Urmeneta 977, 5th floor, tel. 065/486115) can provide national park information.

SERVICES

Exchange houses include **Afex** (Diego Portales 516, tel. 065/256604) and the bus terminal's **La Moneda de Oro** (Diego Portales s/n, tel. 065/255108). **Banco de Crédito** Antonio Varas 560) has one of many downtown ATMs.

Correos de Chile (Rancagua 126) is the post office. For long-distance services, **Entel** (Pedro Montt and Urmeneta) also has a small office just outside the Angelmó ferry port. Downtown, try the **Internet Call Center** (Antonio Varas 318), which also has Internet access.

The **Hospital Regional** (Seminario s/n, tel. 065/261134) is northeast of the hilltop Intendencia Regional, reached via O'Higgins and the zigzag Avenida Décima Región.

GETTING THERE

Other than Santiago, Puerto Montt is the main gateway for air, land, and sea connections to Chilean Patagonia and across the Andes to Argentina. Only in summer can overland travelers begin the entire Carretera Austral

by heading southeast from here, as Naviera Austral's Hornopirén–Caleta Gonzalo ferry link operates in January and February only; otherwise, it's necessary to take the ferry or catamaran from Puerto Montt to Chaitén— presuming the route is open after the May 2008 eruption of Volcán Chaitén.

Air

LAN (O'Higgins 167, Local 1-B, tel. 065/253315) flies several times daily to Santiago, usually nonstop but sometimes via Valdivia, Temuco, or Concepción, or a combination of those. It also flies at least twice daily to Balmaceda/Coyhaique and three or four times daily to Punta Arenas. One Saturday-morning Punta Arenas flight continues to the Falkland Islands (sometimes via Río Gallegos, Argentina), while another stops in Balmaceda/Coyhaique. Once a week, usually Sunday, it flies from Santiago to Puerto Montt and on to San Carlos de Bariloche, Argentina.

Sky Airline (Benavente 405, Local 4, tel. 065/437555) flies three times daily to Santiago, once to Balmaceda/Coyhaique, and to Punta Arenas and Puerto Natales.

No carrier has lasted long on the air-taxi route to Chaitén, a major starting point for overland trips on the Carretera Austral, and flights were suspended as of early 2009 because of the town's evacuation. Should conditions change, try contacting **Cielomaraustral** (Quillota 254, Local 1, tel. 065/266666, cschu-wirth@hotmail.com) or **Aerotaxis del Sur** (Antonio Varas 70-A, tel. 065/252523, aero-taxisdelsur@entelchile.net). **Aerocord** (Talca 81, tel. 065/262300) also operates this route.

Bus

Puerto Montt's **Terminal de Buses** (Av. Portales and Lota, tel. 065/283000) is about one kilometer southwest of the Plaza de Armas. Services are frequent to rural, regional, and most long-distance destinations, as well as to Bariloche, Argentina. Buses to the Chilean Patagonia destinations of Coyhaique and Punta Arenas, which pass through Argentina, are less frequent but reliable.

Several companies go to Puerto Varas (US$1.10, 30 minutes), including **Expresos JM, Expreso Puerto Varas,** and **Thaebus** (tel. 065/420120, less frequently). Thaebus also passes through Varas en route to Frutillar and Puerto Octay.

Fierro also goes to Lenca (US$1.50), the southerly access point to Alerce Andino, five times daily except on weekends, when it goes only twice. **Buses J.B.** (tel. 065/290850) goes to Correntoso (US$1.50), the northern access point to Parque Nacional Alerce Andino, six times daily between 7:40 A.M. and 5:15 P.M. except Sunday, when it goes at 9:10 A.M., and 12:30 and 8:30 P.M.

Monday–Saturday at 8 A.M. and at 1:30, 3, and 5 P.M., **Buses Jordán** (tel. 065/254938) goes to Hornopirén, also known as Río Negro (US$6, 3.5 hours), the summer ferry port to Caleta Gonzalo, the gateway to Parque Natural Pumalín and most of the Carretera Austral. Transportation between Caleta Gonzalo and the mainland port of Chaitén, 56 kilometers to the south, was suspended in early 2009 because of volcanic ash and flooding, but should resume in 2010. Still, many more visitors use the ferry from Puerto Montt or from Quellón, on insular Chiloé, to reach Chaitén.

Numerous carriers serve the capital city of Santiago (US$23–39, 12–13 hours) and intermediates. **Turismo Futaleufú** goes to Futaleufú (US$41, 11 hours) via Argentina Thursday at 7 A.M. **Trans Austral** (tel. 065/270984, www .transaustralbus.cl) goes to Coyhaique (US$33, 18 hours) Sunday and Thursday via Argentina. Several companies operate between Puerto Montt and Punta Arenas (US$68, 28 hours) via Argentina, including **Buses Pacheco** (tel. 065/252926), **Pullman Bus** (tel. 065/316561), **Quellen Bus** (tel. 065/253468), and **Turibús** (tel. 065/253245), all of which normally begin in Castro (Chiloé) and pick up passengers here and in Osorno. These are through-buses, not permitted to drop passengers in Argentina.

Four companies cross the Andes to San Carlos de Bariloche, Argentina (US$22–25, 6 hours), via Osorno and the Cardenal Samoré pass: **Andesmar** (tel. 065/252926), **Buses**

Norte Internacional (tel. 065/254731), **Tas Choapa** (tel. 065/254828), and **Vía Bariloche** (tel. 065/253841).

Andina del Sud (Antonio Varas 437, tel. 065/257797) sells tickets for the bus-boat relay to Bariloche (US$230) via Puerto Varas, Ensenada, Petrohué, and Peulla. These leave Puerto Montt in the morning, arriving early evening in Bariloche; summer departures are daily, but the rest of the year they're weekdays only and require an overnight stay in Peulla.

Train

Puerto Montt has a nearly new **Estación de Ferrocarriles** (Cuarta Terraza s/n, tel. 065/480787, www.efe.cl), opposite Aeródromo La Paloma on the heights above downtown, but service was temporarily suspended as of summer 2009.

Sea

From Puerto Montt there are passenger and passenger/vehicle ferries or bus-ferry combinations to Chiloé and Chaitén in Region X, Puerto Chacabuco (the port of Coyhaique) in Region XI (Aisén), and Puerto Natales in Region XII (Magallanes). Since these routes follow the sheltered inland sea, seasickness is usually a minor problem except on the open-ocean crossing of the Golfo de Penas (literally, Gulf of Sorrows), en route to Puerto Natales.

Puerto Montt's **Terminal de Transbordadores** (Av. Angelmó 2187) is the ferry port. To Puerto Chacabuco, **Navimag** (tel. 065/432300, www.navimag.com) sails the passenger/vehicle ferry *Puerto Edén* Wednesday at midnight with extensions to Laguna San Rafael; to Puerto Natales, the faster, larger *Evangelistas* sails Monday afternoons except in winter, when demand is lower and the smaller *Puerto Edén* replaces it. While weather can still cause problems with the Puerto Natales schedule, as both ships must cross the exposed Golfo de Penas, problems are fewer than in the past.

Navimag cabins to Puerto Chacabuco range US$71–239 per person with breakfast included; other meals are available in the cafeteria. Bicycles cost an additional US$50, motorcycles US$100, and private vehicles (automobiles or light trucks) US$225. Larger vehicles pay a per-meter rate.

Substitution of the *Evangelistas* for the smaller *Puerto Edén* has reduced some of the passenger pressure on the Puerto Montt–Puerto Natales route, but reservations are still advisable in the summer peak; if in Santiago, visit the Navimag office there. Still, it's worth trying for a last-minute berth or cabin. Fares depend on the season and the quality of the accommodations but range US$510–2,470 per person with full board; in the 2009 season, though, there were discounts off the lowest fares. Bicycles cost an additional US$50, motorcycles US$127, passenger cars US$417, and light trucks US$492; other vehicles pay a linear meter rate.

Also at the Terminal de Transbordadores, **Naviera Austral** (tel. 065/270430, www.navieraustral.cl) runs shorter ferry routes between Puerto Montt and Chaitén (nine hours) on the ferries *Don Baldo* or *Mailén* three times weekly. Fares range from US$27 per person for fixed seats to US$34 per person for reclining seats and US$48 for bunks. Vehicle rates are US$137 for passenger vehicles and small trucks, and US$35 per linear meter for other vehicles; bicycles cost US$15 and motorcycles US$30.

September–May, **Cruceros Marítimos Skorpios** (Av. Angelmó 1660, tel. 065/252996, fax 065/275660, www.skorpios.cl) operates **luxury cruises** to Laguna San Rafael that begin in Puerto Montt; rates on the 140-passenger *Skorpios II* start at US$1,050 per person and range up to US$2,850 per person.

GETTING AROUND
To the Airport
From the bus terminal, **Buses ETM** (tel. 065/256253) connects to inbound and outbound flights at **Aeropuerto El Tepual** (tel. 065/252019), which is 16 kilometers west via the Panamericana and a paved lateral. The fare is US$2.50.

Car Rental
For car rentals, try **Avis** (Urmeneta 783, tel. 065/255155), **Budget** (Antonio Varas 162, tel. 065/286277), **Full Fama's** (Diego Portales 506, tel. 065/258060, fax 065/259840), **Econorent** (Antonio Varas 126, tel. 065/481261), or **Travi** (Cardonal 2010, tel. 065/257137). Note that taking a vehicle into Argentina requires notarial permission, which local agencies are best at arranging.

Vicinity of Puerto Montt

From Puerto Montt, travelers can head southwest toward the Chiloé archipelago or southeast on the northernmost sector of the Carretera Austral. Only in summer is it possible to commence the full Carretera Austral in this direction, as the Hornopirén–Caleta Gonzalo ferry link operates only in January and February; otherwise, it's necessary to take the ferry from Puerto Montt or Chiloé to Chaitén.

PARQUE NACIONAL ALERCE ANDINO
Occupying most of the peninsula only a short distance east of Puerto Montt and south of Lago Chapo, adjoining the Carretera Austral, Alerce Andino takes its name from the Andean false larch, which survives in and around the 39,255-hectare unit. Hiking its rugged woodland trails and camping on the shores of several alpine lakes are its main attractions; because of its proximity to Puerto Montt, it makes an ideal day trip but is also suitable for an overnight.

Geography and Climate
Park altitudes range from sea level just east of La Arena, on the Estuario de Reloncaví, to 1,558 meters above on Cerro Cuadrado, in the

easternmost sector. While altitudes are not extreme, the precipitous terrain and dense forest make off-trail travel difficult. At upper elevations, there are more than 50 lakes and tarns of glacial origins.

The park consists of three distinct sectors. From the village of Chamiza, 10 kilometers east of Puerto Montt via the Carretera Austral, a gravel road leads 19 kilometers east to the northerly Sector Correntoso and, 9 kilometers farther south, to Sector Sargazo. The Carretera Austral passes near the westerly entrance to Sector Chaicas, about 32 kilometers southeast of Puerto Montt.

With its maritime west coast climate, Alerce Andino gets up to 4,500 millimeters of rainfall per year at lower elevations and substantial snowfall above 700–800 meters. Temperatures are mild, averaging about 7°C in winter and 15°C in summer.

Flora and Fauna

Officially designated a national monument, the long-lived *alerce* spurred the park's creation in 1982. Ranging about 400–700 meters above sea level, it mixes with other species such as *coigüe, tineo, mañío,* and *canelo.* Evergreen rainforest of *coigüe, tepa,* and *ulmo* reaches from sea level up to 900 meters or more, while nearly prostrate *lenga* covers the highest areas.

In such dense forest, wildlife is rarely seen, but there are puma, *pudú,* gray fox, and skunks (*pudú* have been seen in Sector Correntoso's Pangal campground). Birdlife includes the Andean condor, the kingfisher, and waterfowl such as the *pato real* (Chiloé wigeon).

The most conspicuous wildlife, abundant in early summer, is the large but slow-moving biting fly known as the *tábano.* Insect repellent, long trousers, light-colored clothing, and long sleeves are all good precautions, but they're no guarantee of invulnerability.

Sights and Recreation

Because of deadfalls and landslides, the footpath that once connected the Sargazo and Chaicas sectors is no longer viable, but shorter

© WAYNE BERNHARDSON

Barely a half hour from Puerto Montt, Parque Nacional Alerce Andino is home to gems such as tranquil Laguna Sargazo.

hikes through dense forests to lakeside campgrounds are still feasible at both.

From Sector Sargazo, **Sendero Laguna Frías** climbs 9.5 kilometers up the Río Sargazo Valley to **Laguna Frías** (tent camping allowed, but it's a feasible day hike with an early start). There are several shorter spur trails, including a 45-minute climb to placid **Laguna Sargazo** itself, where there's a picnic site with rustic tables (no camping allowed).

At Sector Chaicas, the **Sendero Laguna Chaiquenes** up the Río Chaicas Valley leads to **Laguna Chaiquenes** (5.5 kilometers), where the **Sendero Laguna Triángulo** continues another four kilometers to its namesake lake.

For the most up-to-date information on park trails, contact Conaf's Patrimonio Silvestre office in Puerto Montt or rangers at the park entrances.

Accommodations and Food

At Sector Correntoso, Conaf's **Camping Correntoso** (US$5 for up to six persons)

THE REDWOOD OF THE SOUTH

Like the California redwoods, the coniferous *alerce* is long-lived (up to 4,000 years), tall (up to 70 meters), and a water- and insect-resistant timber. In colonial times, Spanish shipwrights built vessels from it, and some of Chile's historical monuments – most notably Chiloé's churches – consist of *alerce* timber. Much of the south's vernacular architecture, from Puerto Varas's German colonial houses to Chiloé's *palafitos*, also uses its lumber.

The *alerce*'s natural habitat ranges from coastal Valdivia south to archipelagic and continental Chiloé. Although it grows mostly between 400 and 700 meters above sea level, it also occurs in poorly drained *ñadi* marshlands. The branches of younger specimens touch the ground, but the reddish-barked trunks of mature trees are barren.

Known to the Mapuche as the *lawen*, the species is a national monument thanks to the efforts of the conservation organization Codeff, which somehow persuaded the Pinochet dictatorship to protect the remaining *alerce* forests in 1976, a time when any activism was risky.

has six wooded sites with reasonable privacy but only two toilets and (cold) showers for all of them. At the Sector Sargazo entrance, **Refugio Laguna Sargazo** (US$3 pp with kitchen privileges and hot showers) makes a good base for day hikers. There is backcountry camping near Laguna Fría, about 3.5 hours' walk from Sargazo.

At the head of the Río Chaica Valley, the walk-in **Camping Chaica** (US$1.50 pp) is the only option in the southern sector.

By the southern approach, on the highway to Hornopirén, Austrian-run **Hostal Mozart** (Carretera Austral, Km 25, cell tel. 09/8378-7566, hostalmozart@gmail.com, US$18 pp, US$52 d) is a comfortable guesthouse with spacious rooms that range from a five-bed dorm

with a shared bath to a sea-view double with its own small deck. The Austrian owners will shuttle guests to Sector Chaicas (US$20 pp round-trip).

Just outside the park boundaries, the secluded **Alerce Mountain Lodge** (Carretera Austral, Km 36, tel. 065/286969, www.mountainlodge.cl) is a luxury lodge that specializes in multiday packages, including activities such as hiking and horseback riding. Off-season rates (May–October) are about 15–20 percent lower.

En route to Sector Chaicas, a popular choice with guests at Hostal Mozart, **Los Rosales de Pichi Quillaipe** (Carretera Austral, Km 20, cell tel. 09/9920-3692) is a view restaurant that serves Pantagruelian portions of quality regional specialties, such as smoked pork or baked salmon, in the US$10 range. Light eaters might consider sharing a main dish.

Other Practicalities

Conaf has ranger posts at Sector Correntoso, Sector Sargazo, and Sector Chaicas; park admission costs US$1.50 except at Correntoso, where there's no charge.

From Puerto Montt, **Buses J.B.** (tel. 065/290850) goes to the village of **Correntoso** (US$1.50, one hour), the park's northern access point, six times daily except Sunday, when it goes only thrice (early in the morning and late in the evening). There is no public transport to Sector Sargazo, which means a nine-kilometer walk for those without their own vehicles.

Southbound on the Carretera Austral, **Buses Jordán** will drop passengers at **Lenca** (US$1.50), where a seven-kilometer gravel road ascends the Río Chaica Valley to the park. As at Sargazo, there is no public transport along this route.

HORNOPIRÉN (RÍO NEGRO) AND VICINITY

At La Arena, 45 kilometers southeast of Puerto Montt, the mouth of the Estuario de Reloncaví interrupts the graveled Carretera Austral, but frequent ferries cross the water to Puelche and continue to Hornopirén (also known as Río Negro), 48 kilometers farther south. Hornopirén (population 6,583) is the access point for its little-visited namesake national park, only a few kilometers east; it is also the northern port for the summer vehicle/passenger ferry to Caleta Gonzalo and Parque Natural Pumalín.

Parque Nacional Hornopirén

Only a short distance east of town, Parque Nacional Hornopirén is an almost totally undeveloped 48,232-hectare park surrounded by several volcanoes, including 1,210-meter Apagado, 1,572-meter Hornopirén, and 2,187-meter Yates. Access is difficult, though, because of bad roads.

Accommodations and Food

Rates at the aging but charming **Hotel Hornopirén** (Ignacio Carrera Pinto 388, tel. 065/217256, US$20 pp with shared bath) include breakfast; lunch and dinner are optional. In addition, there's a cluster of inexpensive *hospedajes* opposite the ferry ramp, as well as the more developed **Hostería Catalina** (Ingenieros Militares s/n, tel. 065/217359, www.hosteriacatalina.cl, US$15 pp with shared bath, US$32–40 d with private bath).

At the ferry ramp, several simple *cocinerías* prepare fresh fish for those awaiting the *Mailén*.

Other Practicalities

From Puerto Montt, **Buses Jordán** (tel. 065/254938) and **Kémelbus** (tel. 065/256450) each go to Hornopirén (US$6, 3.5 hours) three or four times daily except Sunday, when they go only twice. In summer, the scheduled 2:30 P.M. departures from Hornopirén wait for the ferry from Caleta Gonzalo.

Both buses and private vehicles must cross from La Arena to Puelche over the Estuario de Reloncaví, where **Naviera Puelche** (tel. 065/270000) shuttles the ferry *Trauco* 7:15 A.M.–9:30 P.M. The half-hour voyage costs US$16 for cars, US$18 for light trucks, US$11 for motorcycles, US$4 for bicycles; passengers pay US$2 per person.

In January and February only, Naviera's Austral's ferry *Mailén* (cel. 09/9939-7895) normally sails daily from Hornopirén to **Caleta Gonzalo** (five hours) at 3 P.M.; the rest of the year, it has only one service monthly, but in 2009 this service went to Chaitén because of flood damage to the southbound highway at Caleta Gonzalo. Passengers pay US$20 pp, cyclists an extra US$13 and motorcyclists US$25. Automobiles and light trucks pay US$125, while larger vehicles cost US$32 per linear meter.

Insular Chiloé

The heartland of Chilean folklore, greener than Washington and Oregon, Chiloé is a rain-soaked archipelago whose wild western woodlands are darker than the Black Forest and traversed by trails leading to secluded ocean beaches with rolling dunes. Its cultural landscape is a mosaic of field and forest, and its seas yield some of Chile's most diverse seafood.

Chiloé is the archipelago and the associated mainland area that is inaccessible overland. The main island is the Isla Grande de Chiloé. Some 180 kilometers long and 50 kilometers wide, one of about 40 islands in the group,

the Isla Grande is not only Chile's largest island but South America's second largest—only Tierra del Fuego is larger. The sheltered inlets on its more densely populated east coast are ideal for sea kayaking, linking peasant villages with a unique vernacular architecture of elaborately shingled houses—a handful of them stilted *palafitos*—and churches.

Though it can rain in any season, summer is the best time to visit, as days are long enough at least to hope for a break in the drizzle. On the Pacific side, penguins—the ranges of the Humboldt and Magellanic species overlap here—also breed in summer.

HISTORY

Pre-Columbian Chiloé was the province of the Huilliche, the southernmost branch of the Mapuche, who netted and trapped fish, gathered shellfish such as sea urchins, and cultivated maize and especially potatoes in its cool, damp climate. Their insularity bred a self-reliance that persists to the present, as residents have ingeniously adapted native materials into technologically simple but useful artifacts.

Spain founded the city of Castro in 1567, but Jesuit missionaries soon established a circuit around what they called the "last outpost of Christianity." Before their 1767 expulsion from the Americas, the Jesuits encouraged the construction of churches and chapels that were predecessors of the 50-plus scattered around the archipelago that led to its designation as a UNESCO World Heritage Site.

Refugees fleeing the mainland Mapuche insurrection of the early 17th century found a haven here, creating the first permanent European presence. Their geographical isolation took political form in a conservatism that made them the Spanish empire's last holdouts in Chile, which failed to conquer the fortress of Ancud until 1826.

Economically, isolation meant poverty, though not starvation. Darwin remarked, a few years after Spain's expulsion, that "there is no demand for labour, and consequently the lower orders cannot scrape together money sufficient to purchase even the smallest luxuries," and that barter was pervasive. Emigration for employment became a way of life—buses still leave the Isla Grande for southern Patagonia every day—but developments of the past two decades have improved the economy and reduced isolation. Ferries constantly shuttle across the Canal Chacao to the mainland, and salmon farming, despite serious environmental drawbacks, has brought a measure of prosperity. In summer, the tourist trade also makes a substantial contribution.

ANCUD

On a sheltered harbor with good ocean access, the late colonial outpost of San Carlos de Ancud defended Spain's Pacific coastline from foreign powers and privateers so well that it held out for nearly a decade after Chile's 1818 declaration of independence. Only the Peruvian port of Callao held out longer.

The former fortress was once a major port of entry, but the 1912 arrival of the railroad to Puerto Montt undercut its economic base, and it now relies on fishing for its livelihood. It is now Chiloé's largest town, and its headlands provide exceptional coastal views.

Orientation

On the Isla Grande's northern coast, facing the Canal Chacao, which divides the archipelago from the mainland, San Carlos de Ancud (population 27,292) is 90 kilometers southwest of Puerto Montt, 27 kilometers west of the Pargua–Chacao ferry crossing, and 87 kilometers north of Castro via the Panamericana, which skirts the city's eastern approach. It occupies a hilly peninsular site whose irregular terrain has generated an equally irregular but compact city plan around the roughly trapezoidal Plaza de Armas.

Sights

At the southwest corner of the Plaza de Armas, the recently remodeled **Museo Azul de las Islas de Chiloé,** alternatively known as the **Museo Aurelio Bórquez Canobra,** is the regional museum. Colloquially known as the Museo Chilote, it focuses on the archipelago's natural environment and wildlife, regional archaeology, European settlement, ecclesiastical art and architecture, the 1960 earthquake (which literally shook the island into the present), the Castro–Ancud railway (destroyed by the quake), and a vivid relief map of the archipelago. The patios also include sculptures of folkloric figures such as the sinister, forest-dwelling Trauco and the siren mermaid La Pincoya.

In January and February, the **Museo Chilote** (Libertad 370, tel. 065/622413, US$1 for adults, US$0.50 for children) is open 10 A.M.–7 P.M. weekdays and 10 A.M.–5 P.M.

weekends and holidays. The rest of the year, hours are 10 A.M.–5:30 P.M. Tuesday–Friday, 10 A.M.–2 P.M. weekends and holidays.

Guarding the harbor from a promontory just west of the intersection of Cochrane and San Antonio, the colonial **Fuerte San Antonio** (1770) was Spain's last Chilean stronghold during the independence struggles—revolutionary forces finally lowered the Spanish flag and raised their own in 1826. Its cannon emplacements are still intact. It's now fenced and open 9 A.M.–8 P.M. daily; there is no admission charge.

Entertainment and Events

Performing-arts events take place at the **Teatro Municipal de Ancud** (Blanco Encalada 660), on the east side of the Plaza de Armas, and the **Casa de la Cultura** (Libertad 663, tel. 065/628164), alongside the museum.

Late January's **Semana Ancuditana** (Ancud Week) celebrates the city's founding, the island's folkloric music and dance, and traditional food. Throughout December and January, though, there are similar events in nearby communities.

For drinks, try the **Retro Pub** (Maipú 615) or the nearby **Lumiere Bar** (Ramírez 278).

Shopping

Chiloé's crafts offerings include ceramics, wood carvings, and woolens. Outlets include the **Museo Chilote** and the **Mercado Municipal** (Dieciocho between Libertad and Blanco Encalada). A permanent **Feria Artesanal** (Arturo Prat and Pedro Montt) occupies the site of the old rural bus terminal, but it focuses on fruits, vegetables, and seafood.

Accommodations

Ancud has plenty of accommodations ranging from camping to mostly midrange choices, with a handful of not-quite-upmarket alternatives.

Surveying the shoreline from its location above Playa Gruesa, about 600 meters north of downtown, **Camping Arena Gruesa** (Costanera Norte 290, tel. 065/623428, arenagruesa@yahoo.com, US$6 pp) has 60 lighted

sites with improved privacy, hot showers, firewood, and other conveniences; in a residential neighborhood, its major drawbacks are barking dogs and crowing roosters.

Crammed with kitschy decor, friendly **Hospedaje Alto Bellavista** (Bellavista 449, tel. 065/622384, US$24 d with private bath) has reasonably spacious, comfy rooms and serves an abundant breakfast; parking is limited.

Thanks to its gracious, responsive management, **Hospedaje Germania** (Pudeto 357, tel./fax 065/622214, roseminiortloff@hotmail.com, US$18/25 s/d with shared bath, US$27 s, US$30 d with private bath) is worth consideration.

The best budget choice is immaculate **Hostal Terramar** (Bellavista 457, tel. 065/620493, terramarancud@gmail.com, US$24 s, US$34 d), engagingly decorated with painted flowers on its doors, walls, and even furniture in a style that resembles Argentine *filete,* derived from an Italian signpainting tradition. The rooms aren't large, but they're well furnished, and those with private baths are only slightly more expensive; the common areas are spacious and inviting. It lacks parking.

Just downhill from the Terramar, all rooms at **Hotel Madryn** (Bellavista 491, tel. 065/622128, US$25 s, US$37 d) come with private baths, cable TV, and breakfast, and some have sea views. Some rooms are a little irregular in shape but still functional.

Hostal Vista al Mar (Av. Salvador Allende 918, tel./fax 065/622617, www.vistaalmar.cl, US$13 pp, US$24 s, US$42 d) has moderately priced accommodations with shared baths but has added others with private baths and even some cabañas.

Arguably Ancud's best value, the nearly pristine, Swiss-run ◖ **Hostal Mundo Nuevo** (Av. Costanera Salvador Allende 748, tel. 065/628383, www.newworld.cl, US$13 pp in dorms, US$35–52 d) provides spacious rooms, firm new beds, panoramic sunsets through the glassed porch, a fine breakfast, an ample kitchen for the budget-conscious, and secure parking. Given its popularity, reservations are advisable.

For the best views, there's **Hotel Ancud** (San Antonio 30, tel. 065/622340, tel. 02/2349610 in Santiago, www.hosteriaancud.cl, US$70 d), but the rooms are on the small side in a hotel that needs modernization.

Hotel Galeón Azul (Libertad 751, tel. 065/622567, www.hotelgaleonazul.cl, US$65 s, US$79 d) is cheerful and central, but wins no point for truth in labeling—the "Blue Galeon" sports a bright yellow paint job.

Food

Most restaurant menus are similar in content—fish and shellfish—and in price, mostly in the US$7–10 range for most items. Salads are easily large enough for two. **Chiloé** (Pudeto 43, tel. 065/622952, lunch and dinner daily) is a local favorite. Slightly more elaborate seafood venues include **La Pincoya** (Prat 61, tel. 065/622613, lunch and dinner daily) and the improved **Polo Sur** (Av. Salvador Allende 630, tel. 065/622200, lunch and dinner daily).

The **Retro Pub** (Maipú 615, tel. 065/626410, lunch and dinner daily) breaks the local mold by daring to serve pizza and even some Mexican dishes. For a relatively elegant splurge, **Casa Mar** (Costanera Salvador Allende and Errázuriz, tel. 065/624481, lunch and dinner daily) has a more elaborate menu that includes more sophisticated versions of traditional fish and seafood but also extends to sushi.

Information

Sernatur (Libertad 665, tel. 065/622800, infochiloe@sernatur.cl) is the island's best-equipped office in terms of maps, brochures, and up-to-date accommodations data. In summer, it's open 8:30 A.M.–7 P.M. Monday–Friday, 10 A.M.–6 P.M. Saturday–Sunday. The rest of the year, hours are 8:30 A.M.–5:30 P.M. Monday–Thursday, 8:30 A.M.–4:30 P.M. Friday.

Upstairs at the Mercado Municipal, the Oficina Municipal de Turismo (Dieciocho s/n, tel. 065/628163, turismomuniancud@gmail.com) is a helpful new office open 8 A.M.–1 P.M. and 2–5:15 P.M. Monday–Thursday, 8 A.M.–1 P.M. and 2–4:30 P.M. Friday.

In summer, the private **Asociación de Turismo de Ancud** (ATA, Libertad and Blanco Encalada, tel. 065/622957, www.ancudmagico.cl) is open 9:45 A.M.–12:45 P.M. and 2:15–7:30 P.M. Monday–Friday, 9:30 A.M.–1 P.M. Saturday. The rest of the year, hours are 10:30 A.M.–1 P.M. and 3–7:30 P.M. Monday–Friday, 10 A.M.–1 P.M. Saturday.

Services

Ancud has no exchange houses, but **Banco de Crédito** (Ramírez 257) has an ATM.

For postal services, **Correos de Chile** is at Pudeto and Blanco Encalada. **Entel** (Ramírez 294, Local 21) has long-distance calling and Internet services, but **Zona PC** (Pudeto 276, Local 2) has more and better machines.

Clean Center (Pudeto 45, tel. 065/623838) does the washing.

Hospital de Ancud (Almirante Latorre 301, tel. 065/622355) can handle medical matters.

Getting There and Around

Ancud's long-distance **Terminal de Buses** (Aníbal Pinto and Marcos Vera), about 1.2 kilometers east of downtown, is relatively new but increasingly rundown. **Cruz del Sur** (Los Carrera 850, tel. 065/622249, www.busescruzdelsur.cl) has opened its own glistening new terminal, which is more convenient to downtown.

There are many northbound buses to Puerto Montt and on to Santiago and intermediates, southbound buses to Castro and Quellón, and services to Punta Arenas via Argentina with **Queilen Bus** (tel. 065/621140) and **Turibús** (tel. 065/622289).

Typical destinations, times, and fares include Castro (US$3, 1 hour), Chonchi (US$4.50, 1.5 hours), Puerto Montt (US$6, 2 hours), Temuco (US$15, 7 hours), Santiago (US$40–57, 15 hours), and Punta Arenas (US$68, 32 hours).

For buses to destinations other than those on or along the Panamericana, the **Terminal de Buses Rurales** is at Pedro Montt and Colo Colo.

Transmarchilay and Cruz del Sur ferries sail between Pargua and Chacao, charging US$15 for light trucks, US$10 for motorcycles,

US$2.50 for bicycles; foot passengers go for US$1.

VICINITY OF ANCUD

Ancud's U.S.-Peruvian **Austral Adventures** (Avenida Costanera 904, tel./fax 065/625977, www.austral-adventures.com) conducts multiday hikes along the island's wild northwest coast and custom sea kayak trips. Its specialty, though, is extended explorations of the archipelago's inner waters and points south on the 15-meter *Cahuella,* whose exterior resembles a traditional Chilote fishing boat but whose interior has contemporary comforts.

At the Cruz del Sur bus terminal, **Aki Turismo** (Los Carrera 850, tel. 065/545253, www.akiturismochiloe.cl) arranges local excursions, such as trips to the Puñihuil penguin colony and to the island's churches and chapels. It also has a kiosk at the Mercado Municipal.

Monumento Natural Islotes de Puñihuil

About 27 kilometers southwest of Ancud, the offshore islets of Puñihuil are home to summer breeding colonies of both Magellanic and Humboldt penguins, whose ranges overlap here. Aki Turismo and other operators arrange overland excursions to the sandy beach opposite, where Chilote fishermen shuttle penguin-watchers into the surrounding waters in comfortable boats.

Bahía Puñihuil, one of several restaurants along the beach, serves simple but artful fish and seafood dishes at modest prices (around US$6 with a side dish).

Chepu

About 40 km southwest of Ancud via Ruta 5 and a gravel road, set among Chiloé's rugged western mountains, the village of Chepu has a nascent kayak scene on wetlands created by the massive 1960 tsunami that struck the area. Today its "sunken forest" is a prime birding destination. Here a relocated Santiago couple has created an eco-campground, with wind turbines, solar-powered hot water, and toilets overlooking the river. There are also simple but

stylish cabañas, using the campground's toilets, and meals at the campground.

Children under 18 are not permitted because of safety concerns about the river. For more information, contact English-speaking Fernando Claude at Chepu Adventures (P.O. Box 402, Ancud, cell tel. 09/9379-2482, www.chepuadventures.com).

NORTHEASTERN CHILOÉ

East of the Panamericana and north of the Dalcahue turnoff, several isolated villages are truly off-the-beaten-track destinations, but the government's loosely organized rural tourism network has helped create an infrastructure network that can be surprisingly good. It is invariably hospitable.

Quemchi

On the sheltered east coast of the Isla Grande, Quemchi is a quaint 19th-century village that began as a timber port but now relies on fishing and salmon farming for its livelihood. It is 63 kilometers southeast of Ancud via the Panamericana and a good paved road that leads east from the hamlet of Degán.

The inexpensive **Hospedaje Costanera** (Bahamonde 141, tel. 065/691230, US$10 pp) is one of few choices in town. There are a couple of restaurants, including the waterfront **El Chejo** (Bahamonde 251, tel. 065/691490).

A small tourist kiosk on the Plaza de Armas provides information in summer only. Rural bus terminals in both Ancud and Castro have services to Quemchi.

Tenaún

About 27 kilometers south of Quemchi and 37 kilometers east of Dalcahue via gravel roads, tiny Tenaún is a remote fishing village with an attractive waterfront park, opposite Isla Mechuque. Its 19th-century church, regrettably, seems to be riding a wave—the floors, walls, and columns are all out of plumb, the foundations are sagging precariously, and the next earthquake or tsunami seems likely to knock it to the ground. In the 1920s, locals replaced its *alerce* shingles with galvanized iron cladding. To visit the interior, which has a small ecclesiastical museum, ask for the keys at the house across the street, next to the fire station.

Affiliated with the Red de Agroturismo, the recommended and inexpensive **Hospedaje Vásquez Montaña** (cell tel. 09/9647-6750, US$17 pp) is just east of the church. Its four rooms, sharing baths with hot water, sleep a maximum of seven people; the proprietors also have their own launch for excursions to Isla Mechuque, which has a church worth visiting.

From Quemchi, it's necessary to drive or hitch to Tenaún, but there are buses from Castro's rural bus terminal.

CASTRO

The Isla Grande's first urban settlement, Castro dates from 1567, when Martín Ruiz de Gamboa made it the base for evangelizing the southern Huilliche and Chonos. Despite the activities of Franciscan, Mercedarian, and Jesuit missionaries, it remained a poor and isolated backwater, subject to earthquakes, tsunamis, fires, and sacking by privateers.

In 1834, barely two decades after Chilean independence was declared, Charles Darwin found Castro to be "a most forlorn and deserted place." Even in the early 20th century, it had barely a thousand inhabitants, and its isolation had fostered a distinctive townscape still characterized by its surviving *palafitos,* the stilted waterfront houses with their elaborately carved shingles. By 1912, a narrow-gauge railroad linked it with Ancud and the rest of the country, as farm products increased port activity.

The 1960 earthquake devastated the city, but salmon farming sparked a recovery that has continued to this day. Improved ferry services have brought regular tourist traffic of Chileans and foreigners, especially Argentines.

Orientation

Castro (population 29,148), 88 kilometers south of Ancud via the Panamericana, is a central location for Isla Grande excursions. Its

© WAYNE BERNHARDSON

At high tide, the water reaches more than half way up Castro's *palafitos.*

compact central grid occupies a broad plain above the Estero de Castro, a sheltered ocean inlet, while Avenida Pedro Montt curves around the shoreline at sea level.

Sights

Castro's sights give it greater tourist appeal than any other city on the island, but it's also a fine base for excursions.

On the north side of the refurbished Plaza de Armas, the landmark **Iglesia San Francisco** represents both change and continuity in Chiloé's architectural tradition. After fire destroyed its Franciscan-built predecessor in 1902, ecclesiastical authorities broke with tradition in hiring an Italian architect, Eduardo Provasoli, who incorporated both neo-Gothic and classical elements into the twin-tower structure. At the same time, employing local master builders and artisans ensured that Chilote elements would survive in the ironclad wooden building, which was begun in 1906 but not completed until 1912.

Now a national monument, the church has changed its colors without surrendering its flamboyance—instead of salmon and violet, its galvanized-iron exterior is now banana yellow with violet towers and dashes of reddish trim—but its repainting is long overdue. The burnished-wood interior is more somber, embellished with traditional Catholic statuary—some of it grisly renderings of the crucifixion.

Half a block south of the Plaza de Armas, the **Museo Regional de Castro** (Esmeralda 255, tel. 065/635967) displays Huilliche artifacts and ethnographic materials, "appropriate technology" from the surrounding countryside, accounts of the island's urban development, and greatly improved photographic exhibits. As of 2009, it looks like its move to new waterfront quarters for Chile's 2010 bicentennial may have to wait until the tricentennial; in the meantime, summer hours are 9:30 A.M.–7 P.M. Monday–Saturday, 10:30 A.M.–1 P.M. Sunday. The rest of the year, hours are 9:30 A.M.–1 P.M. and 3–6:30 P.M. Monday–Saturday. Admission is free, but donations are welcome.

Now sitting in the newly developed **Plazuela**

El Tren, a waterfront park on Avenida Pedro Montt, the **Locomotora Ancud-Castro** hauled passengers and freight on the narrow-gauge railroad between 1912 and 1960, when an earthquake and tsunami ended the island's train service. The route either followed or paralleled the present-day Panamericana.

Occupying airy, well-lighted quarters that once were warehouses, the **Museo de Arte Moderno de Chiloé** (MAM, Galvarino Riveros s/n, tel. 065/635454, www.mam-chiloe.cl, free) stresses up-and-coming Chilean, mostly Chilote, painters, sculptors, and multimedia specialists. On the grounds of the Parque Municipal, the MAM is open 10 A.M.–6 P.M. daily in January and February, when invited artists show their latest work. In November, December, and March, hours are 11 A.M.–2 P.M. daily, but it's closed the rest of the year except by appointment.

Until the 1960 earthquake and tsunami, shingled, stilted *palafitos* lined nearly all the Isla Grande's eastern shore estuaries, but only a handful survive today, most notably in Castro and its vicinity. Traditionally, Chilote fishermen would tie their vessels to the pilings out their back doors, but the houses themselves front on city streets.

Castro has the largest remaining assortment of this unique vernacular architecture, along the Costanera Avenida Pedro Montt at the northern approach to town, only two blocks from the Plaza de Armas at the Costanera's south end, and on both sides of the Río Gamboa Bridge, southwest of the city center via the Panamericana.

At the south end of the Costanera, the waterfront **Feria Artesanal** integrates tourist appeal—typical woolens, souvenir basketry, and *palafito marisquerías*—with practical items such as food (including edible algae) and fuel (blocks of peat). While Dalcahue's Sunday crafts market gets more hype, this daily market rates nearly as highly.

Entertainment and Events

For exhibitions, the **Centro Cultural de Castro** (Serrano 320, tel. 065/635531) is open

11 A.M.–1 P.M. and 4–9 P.M. daily, but it also serves as a performing-arts venue; part of it is the **Cine Star,** which shows commercial movies.

Late January's **Festival de Huaso Chilote** is an excuse for high-speed horse races at the Parque Municipal. Mid-February's **Festival Costumbrista** is a weekend event with island crafts, folkloric music and dance, traditional foods such as *curanto* and *yoco* (a pork dish), and liquors such as *chicha* (cider, usually made from apples).

Shopping

In addition to the Feria Artesanal, the **Almacén de la Biodiversidad** (Lillo 1) carries a large selection of quality handicrafts, such as woolens and even scale models of Chilote churches, by island artisans.

Castro has two excellent bookstores, **El Tren Libros** (Thompson 299, tel. 065/633936) and **Anay Libros** (Serrano 437, tel. 065/630158).

Accommodations

Of several budget accommodations, the best central value is **Hospedaje Mirador** (Barros Arana 127, tel. 065/633795, maboly@yahoo.com, US$15 pp, US$35 d with breakfast), an immaculate place on a pedestrian staircase overlooking the port; the more expensive rooms have private baths.

Hostal Quelcún (San Martín 581, tel. 065/632396, quelcun@telsur.cl, US$12 s and US$20 d with shared bath, US$25 s and US$37 d with private bath) has carpeted, centrally heated rooms with breakfast included.

Castro's most distinctive new accommodations can be found at the **Palafito Hostel** (Ernesto Riquelme 1210, tel. 065/531008, www.palafitohostel.com, US$13 pp, US$30 s, US$42 d), near the Gamboa Bridge. The owners have completely rebuilt and expanded an existing palafito house and turned it into a luminous eight-room designer hostel that's more of a B&B—all rooms, even the dorms, have private baths, and the building incorporates elements of the island's maritime heritage, such as curved walls. Even travelers normally wary of a hostel should consider staying here.

Hostal Casablanca (Los Carrera 308, tel./fax 065/632726, nelysald@surnet.cl, US$31 s, US$42 d with breakfast) is spotless and has free Wi-Fi, but the yippy toy poodle is a big minus. Some cubicle-sized singles are cheaper.

One of Castro's best-kept secrets is **Hostal Casa Kolping** (Chacabuco 217, tel. 065/633273, www.kolping.cl, US$30 s, US$42 d), an immaculate and architecturally notable place in a quiet location south of the Plaza, but enough people know about it that reservations are advisable. Off-season rates, about 25 percent lower, are a steal.

Embellished with native wood and carpeted floors, **Hostal Casita Española** (Los Carrera 359, tel. 065/635186, www.hosteriadecastro.cl, US$37 s, US$50 d) is operated under the same management as the more elite Hostería de Castro.

Dating from 1910, a hotel only since 1986, the quirky **Hotel Unicornio Azul** (Pedro Montt 228, tel. 065/632359, www.hotelunicornioazul.cl, US$65 s, US$79 d) was once a budget hotel, but steady improvements have driven prices upward. Rooms vary in size, shape, and view, so don't take anything without seeing it first.

Behind its hideous pink facade, **Hotel Esmeralda** (Esmeralda 266, tel. 065/637900, www.hotelesmeralda.cl, US$56 s, US$82 d with private bath) has large modern rooms. Other amenities include breakfast, WiFi, parking, a restaurant, and a pool hall.

Despite its offbeat chalet design (on an island that rarely gets snow), the **Hostería de Castro** (Chacabuco 202, tel. 065/632301, www.hosteriadecastro.cl, US$70 s, US$89 d) traditionally vies for the honor of being Castro's best hotel in its price range. Amenities include seaviews, a restaurant and bar, an indoor pool, and Wi-Fi. It's recently remodeled two rooms into more elaborate (and expensive) suites.

Food

For breakfasts, sandwiches, coffee, and desserts, try **Café La Brújula del Cuerpo** (O'Higgins 308, tel. 065/633229), which even has Mexican dishes such as fajitas.

Most of the best are seafood venues, such as **Sacho** (Thompson 213, tel. 065/632079, lunch and dinner daily), **Dónde Eladio** (Lillo 97, tel. 065/635285, lunch and dinner daily), and **El Bucanero** (Lillo s/n, tel. 065/637260, lunch and dinner daily).

Widely considered one of the city's best, **Octavio** (Av. Pedro Montt 261, tel. 065/632855, lunch and dinner daily) offers waterfront dining with style and fine service at moderate prices with a diverse menu. Entrées range from US$5 (chicken) to US$15 (king crab). On the minus side, the pisco sours are a little small, and switching off the TV would enhance the experience.

The ambitious **Hicamar** (Gamboa 413, tel. 065/532655, lunch and dinner daily) has a large menu of meat, game, and fish dishes that tops out near US$50 for turbot, but most items fall into the US$8–20 range. The portions are not excessive but neither are they tiny—rather, they strike a happy medium. The service is exemplary.

On the east side of the plaza, **(Años Luz** (San Martín 309, tel. 065/532700, lunch and dinner except Sunday) sets the standard for more creative Chilote cuisine in a hipper atmosphere than any other Castro restaurant. The native potatoes, preferably sautéed in olive oil, reflect the fact that Chiloé is a center of biodiversity for one of the world's most important crops. Several nights a week, after the dinner hour, it offers live music (for which there's a cover charge, about US$2 pp).

Information

In summer, the new municipal **Oficina de Información Turística** is a long-overdue contribution to raising the city's visitor profile, open 8:30 A.M.–9 P.M. daily except Sunday, when it opens half an hour later. The rest of the year, though, visitors are on their own.

Conaf (Gamboa 424, tel. 065/532501) can provide information on Parque Nacional Chiloé.

Services

Cambio Julio Barrientos (Chacabuco 286)

changes foreign money. **Banco de Crédito** (Gamboa 393) has an ATM.

Correos de Chile (O'Higgins 388) handles the mail. **Entel** (O'Higgins 480) is one of many long-distance telephone and Internet providers.

The **Clean Center** (Balmaceda 230, tel. 065/633132) does laundry for about US$2 per kilo.

For medical assistance, contact the **Hospital de Castro** (Freire 852, tel. 065/632445).

Getting There and Around

Most local and long-distance bus companies use the deceptively named **Terminal de Buses Rurales** (San Martín 667). **Cruz del Sur** (San Martín 486, tel. 065/632389) has its own terminal, also used by **Turibús** (tel. 065/632389) and **Transchiloé** (tel. 065/635152). Some companies have ticket agents at both locales.

Cruz del Sur goes south to Chonchi and north to Ancud and Puerto Montt, offering continuing service to Santiago and intermediates. Transchiloé has similar routes. Several carriers go to Punta Arenas, including **Queilen Bus** (tel. 065/632173), **Buses Pacheco** (tel. 065/631188), and Turibús.

At the Terminal de Buses Rurales, **Buses Arroyo** (tel. 065/635604) goes up to five times daily to Cucao, the gateway to Parque Nacional Chiloé; **Ojeda** and **Interlagos** have additional services on the same route. **Dalcahue Expreso** (tel. 065/635164) goes at least half hourly to Dalcahue weekdays, but less frequently on weekends. **Buses Lemuy** and **Buses Gallardo** (tel. 065/634521) serve Chonchi (US$1.50). *Taxi colectivos* to Chonchi leave from the corner of Chacabuco and Esmeralda.

Sample destinations, fares, and times include Ancud (US$3, 1 hour), Puerto Montt (US$9, 3 hours), Temuco (US$18, 8 hours), Santiago (US$43–60, 17 hours), and Punta Arenas (US$68, 34 hours).

VICINITY OF CASTRO

Several companies conduct day trips and longer tours, including destinations such as Dalcahue, Chonchi, Parque Nacional Chiloé, and offshore islands. Among them are **Turismo Quelcún** (San Martín 581, tel. 065/632396), **Turismo Queilen Bus** (San Martín 667, tel. 065/632173), at the Terminal de Buses Rurales, and **Pehuén Turismo** (Blanco 208, tel. 065/635254, www.turismopehuen.cl).

Dalcahue

Artisans from around Chiloé customarily present their best at Dalcahue's Sunday market, still its biggest attraction, but this modest fishing village (population 4,933), about 20 kilometers northeast of Castro, is gaining importance as a base for sea kayaking among the islands off the archipelago's sheltered eastern shore.

Nothing remains of Dalcahue's original *palafitos,* obliterated by the 1960 tsunami, but a handsome new construction, comprised of a gaggle of seafood eateries, puts a modern twist on the typical Chilote style. Alongside it, the vendors and their clients at the sharp new **Mercado Artesanal** no longer have to dodge the rain squalls that pass through here. The 19th-century **Iglesia Parroquial** is one of the architectural monuments that helped the island's wooden churches gain UNESCO World Heritage Site status.

Mid-February's **Semana Dalcahuina** is the town's major festival.

Dalcahue makes a better day trip than an overnight, as its modest accommodations are inferior to their counterparts in Ancud and Castro. The exception is the stylishly Chilote **Hotel La Isla** (Av. Mocopulli 113, tel. 065/641246, hotellaisla@hotmail.com, US$35 s, US$42 d), which has some modern comforts. Mostly interchangeable, the new *palafito* restaurants have fried and grilled fish, and empanadas.

Frequent Dalcahue Expreso **buses** to and from Castro stop at both the main bus terminal (Freire and O'Higgins) and the waterfront Feria Artesanal. There are also *taxi colectivos* to and from Castro.

Ferry service from Dalcahue to Isla Quinchao costs US$6.50 round-trip for automobiles but is free for pedestrians.

Woolens are popular purchases at Dalcahue's new Mercado Artesanal.

© WAYNE BERNHARDSON

ISLA QUINCHAO

Across Canal Dalcahue, a newly paved road follows the center of elongated Isla Quinchao as far as Achao, where it continues as a gravel road to its southeastern tip. Buses from Castro to Achao use the ferry to cross to the island.

Curaco de Vélez

Ten kilometers south of Dalcahue via the ferry crossing of the Canal de Dalcahue and the paved road, Curaco de Vélez is a village of traditional Chilote houses, some of which were moved to higher ground by oxcart after the 1960 tsunami. Its contemporary church, on the north side of the Plaza de Armas, replaced an older landmark destroyed by fire in 1971.

The crypt of Galvarino Riveros Cárdenas, a local naval hero of the Guerra del Pacífico, occupies a place of honor on the Plaza de Armas, though Riveros's actual birthplace was in nearby Changuitad, where there's a reconstruction of the building. On the plaza's east side, Curaco's Centro Cultural has a mediocre museum, but there are several well-restored water mills in the vicinity.

Curaco has no accommodations, but there are a few seafood restaurants, most notably the beachfront **La Bahía,** downhill from the plaza.

Achao

About 15 kilometers east of Curaco de Vélez, accessible Achao has more sights and better services than any other offshore island town in the archipelago. Famous for its February folk festival, it dates from the mid-18th century, when the Jesuits built a mission to the Chonos Indians.

Achao's Plaza de Armas occupies a site at the east end of the town's rectangular grid, which reaches only about three blocks inland from the shoreline. Most services are along Calle Serrano, which ends at the **Embarcadero** (fishing jetty), while its sights are in the vicinity of the plaza.

Small but professionally arranged, the Fondart-sponsored **Museo de Achao** (Delicias and Amunátegui) has exhibits of Chilote basketry, weaving, pottery, boatbuilding, and videos on Chilote culture. It's open 10 A.M.–6 P.M. daily in summer; admission costs US$0.75.

On the Plaza's south side, dating from 1764, the **Iglesia Santa María de Achao** (Pedro Montt and Zañartu) is the archipelago's oldest standing church; only three years later, the Jesuit builders were expelled from the continent. Built of *alerce* and cypress, covered with *alerce* shingles and firmly fixed with wooden pegs in lieu of nails, this national monument has undergone a major restoration to save it from dry rot and termites.

Achao's biggest annual event is early February's **Encuentro Folklórico de las Islas del Archipiélago,** which draws vocal and instrumental groups from throughout Chiloé. At the same time, the best of Chilote cuisine is on the table at the **Muestra Gastronómica y Artesanal,** where the archipelago's artisans also sell their handiwork.

Several economical but acceptable shared-bath accommodations offer bed and breakfast, such as **Hospedaje São Paulo** (Serrano 052, tel. 065/661245, US$8–12 pp), which has a diverse restaurant menu. Friendly **Hostal Plaza** (Amunátegui 20, tel. 065/661283, US$13 s, US$23 d) is a fine choice with private bath and breakfast, if you can ignore the hideous bedspreads.

Best of the bunch, though, is cozy **Hospedaje Sol y Lluvia** (Ricardo Jara 09, tel. 065/661383, US$13–20 pp) which offers an elaborate breakfast.

At the foot of the Embarcadero, **Mar y Velas** (Serrano 02, tel. 065/661375) serves fine seafood.

Banco del Estado (Miranda and Delicias) has an ATM. **Correos de Chile** (Delicias and Velásquez) is the post office. **Centro de Llamados Paola** (Progreso 022) has long-distance phone service, while **T@my Web** (Serrano 059-A) has Internet service. The **Hospital de Achao** (tel. 065/661244) is at the corner of Progreso and Riquelme.

Achao's helpful **Oficina de Información Turística** (Serrano and Ricardo Jara, www .islaquinchao.cl) keeps long hours in January and February but closes the rest of the year.

From Achao's **Terminal de Buses** (Miraflores and Zañartu), at the east end of town, several minibuses and *taxi colectivos* go to Castro via Dalcahue.

CHONCHI

Nicknamed the Ciudad de los Tres Pisos (City of Three Levels) for its sheer hillsides and steep streets, San Carlos de Chonchi (population 4,588) was one of Chiloé's first Jesuit missions, thanks to its strategically central location. Not founded officially until 1767, it managed to keep its own spontaneous street plan and avoid the imposition of the regulation Spanish colonial grid, which would have played havoc with its hilly topography. It is 23 kilometers south of Castro.

Sights

Even if the 1960 tsunami split Chonchi's *palafitos* into toothpicks, the accompanying

© WAYNE BERNHARDSON

Chonchi's new Mercado Municipal holds both a cultural center and seafood restaurants.

earthquake spared its historic **Iglesia San Carlos de Chonchi** (1900) and many houses along **Calle Centenario,** an area designated a *zona típica* national monument; the church's exterior has undergone restoration—though its tower fell in 2008 and had to be replaced, the improvements to the interior are part of an ongoing process. The **Museo de las Tradiciones Chonchinas** (Centenario 116, 9:30 A.M.–1 P.M. and 3–7 P.M. Mon.–Sat. 9 A.M.–2 P.M. Sun., US$0.85) replicates a typical Chilote kitchen and displays impressive photographs of the 1960 tsunami.

New in 2008, the **Mercado Municipal** has helped renovate Chonchi's waterfront, where regular cleanups are keeping the beach presentable. Like its counterpart in Dalcahue, the market blends the traditional and the contemporary, and contains a clutch of seafood restaurants with ocean views.

Events and Shopping
Early February's **Semana Verano Chonchi** is the city's summer festival, featuring folkloric music, dance, and art, along with rural skills such as rodeo.

Chonchi is renowned for its *licor de oro,* a milk-based liqueur resembling Drambuie.

Accommodations and Food
Having undergone substantial restoration, the classic **Hotel Huildín** (Centenario 102, tel. 065/671388, www.hotelhuildin.cl, US$20–23 pp with breakfast and shared bath) once again deserves consideration.

Set on spacious grounds with fruit trees and a gazebo, the seaside **⟨ Hospedaje La Esmeralda** (Irarrázabal s/n, tel. 065/671328, www.esmeraldabythesea.cl, US$12–17 pp with shared bath, US$17–25 pp for more spacious rooms with private bath and in-room heating) is a backpackers' favorite that also has more private rooms. An elaborate breakfast costs US$3; other meals—salmon dinners and on-the-beach *curantos*—are also available, along with rental bikes, a rowboat, fishing gear, and boat tours.

Chonchi's seafood restaurants include **El Trébol** (Irarrázaval s/n, tel. 065/671203) and **La Quila** (Andrade 183, tel. 065/671389). **Los Tres Pisos** (O'Higgins 359, tel. 065/671433) serves sandwiches, empanadas, and kuchen.

Information and Services
The municipal **Oficina de Información Turística** (Sargento Candelaria and Centenario) is open 9:30 A.M.–9 P.M. daily in

summer only, with a branch at the Mercado Municipal.

Banco del Estado (Centenario 28) has an ATM. **Correos de Chile** (Sargento Candelaria and Centenario) is the post office. **Cyber-Café Tronko's** (Sargento Candelaria 392) provides Internet access.

Getting There and Around

In shared offices, **Cruz del Sur** and **Transchiloé** (Pedro Montt 233, tel. 065/671218) have frequent services between Castro and Chonchi; *taxi colectivos* to Castro (US$1) are also frequent. Buses from Castro bound for Cucao (Parque Nacional Chiloé) stop at Chonchi's Terminal Municipal (Alonso de Ercilla s/n).

◖ PARQUE NACIONAL CHILOÉ

South of Ancud and west of the Panamericana, Chiloé's Pacific coast is an almost roadless area of abrupt headlands, broad sandy beaches, and sprawling dunes at the foot of forested mountains dissected by transverse rivers. Much of this landscape, in fact, differs little from Darwin's description in *The Voyage of the Beagle* as he rode west toward Cucao, now the gateway to Parque Nacional Chiloé:

> At Chonchi we struck across the island, following intricate winding paths, sometimes passing through magnificent forests, and sometimes through pretty cleared spots, abounding with corn and potato crops. This undulating woody country, partially cultivated, reminded me of the wilder parts of England, and therefore had to my eye a most fascinating aspect. At Vilinco [Huillinco], which is situated on the borders of the lake of Cucao, only a few fields were cleared....

Since its creation in 1982, Parque Nacional Chiloé has protected a representative sample of the Isla Grande's natural habitat and wildlife, while providing recreational access to growing numbers of outdoors enthusiasts, both Chileans and foreigners. For many years, the Conaf administration failed to integrate the area's indigenous Huilliche residents into its activities—matters had changed little from the 19th century when Darwin observed "they are very much secluded from the rest of Chiloé, and have scarcely any sort of commerce...."—but substantial areas of former parkland are now under Huilliche control.

Geography and Climate

On the thinly settled, densely forested Pacific coast, the park comprises 42,567 hectares in five discrete sectors: **Sector Anay,** west of Chonchi near the village of Cucao; **Sector Chepu,** southwest of Ancud; **Sector Cole Cole,** north of Chanquín; the 50-hectare **Sector Islote Metalqui,** a rugged offshore island; and the Conaf administration area west of Cucao.

Altitudes range from sea level to 850 meters in the Cordillera de Piuchén. Annual rainfall varies from about 2,000 millimeters on the coast to 3,000 millimeters at the highest elevations. Temperatures are mild, averaging about 10°C over the course of the year, with few extremes of either heat or cold.

Flora and Fauna

At some lower elevations, mixed evergreen forest of the endemic *coigüe* or *roble de Chiloé* covers the valleys and slopes, along with the coniferous *mañío* and climbing vines; in others, enormous ferns cover the soil beneath the *ulmo, arrayán,* and the twisted *tepu.* Near its northern limit, the world's most southerly conifer, the *ciprés de los Guaitecas* grows in swampy soils alongside the *tepu;* the *alerce* reaches the southern limit of its geographical range at altitudes above 600 meters.

In such dense forest, it's rare to see mammals, though the *pudú* and the Chiloé fox (*Dusicyon fulvipes,* first identified by Darwin) survive here. Both sea otters and sea lions inhabit coastal areas, while the 110 bird species include Magellanic and Humboldt penguins, oystercatchers, and cormorants on the coast. The dense forest is home to the elusive *chucao.*

THE CHURCHES AND CHAPELS OF CHILOÉ

Chileans have always acknowledged Chiloé's uniqueness, but formal global recognition finally arrived in 2001, when UNESCO named 14 of the archipelago's churches a collective World Heritage Site. These buildings are prime examples of what Chilean architects call the Escuela Chilota de Arquitectura Religiosa en Madera (Chilote School of Religious Architecture in Wood), but they're just a few of the archipelago's 150 or so churches and chapels.

Originally inhabited by Chonos and Huilliche Indians, aboriginal Chiloé quickly converted to Christianity after the Jesuit order succeeded the initial Franciscan and Mercedarian missionaries in 1608. In more than a century and a half, the Jesuit system of itinerant missions, with their skillfully built wooden chapels, literally and figuratively laid the foundation for the archipelago's architecture. Even after their expulsion from the Americas in 1767, the style they pioneered survived.

The UNESCO designation brings recognition, but authorities hope it will also encourage donations toward the millions of dollars still needed to help restore the churches and promote interest in the archipelago. According to Sernatur chief Oscar Santelices, Chiloé's churches are not a historic anachronism, but reflect "the unique nature of the island, its people, and their culture and landscape."

Sights and Recreation

Chanquín is the base for visiting Sector Anay, the park's most accessible area, which has several hiking trails of varying length. Because of the damp climate, wool socks and water-resistant boots are advisable for hikers.

From Conaf's Centro de Visitantes at Chanquín, just across the river from the village of Cucao, the **Sendero Dunas de Cucao** winds through vestigial forest and traverses a broad dunefield to arrive at a long white sandy beach, 1.4 kilometers to the west. Violent surf, treacherous currents, and frigid Pacific waters make it unsuitable for swimming, so the scenery is the main attraction.

Near Conaf's Chanquín campground, winding through boggy, slippery terrain, the 750-meter **Sendero Interpretivo El Tepual** makes as many twists and turns as the *tepu* trunks over which it passes.

North of Cucao, the road continues eight kilometers past **Lago Huelde** to the Río Chanquil; from there, it's necessary to walk to the **Río Cole Cole,** which has a 10-site campground administered by the community of Huentemó. Eight kilometers beyond Cole Cole, Conaf has a new *refugio* on the north bank of the **Río Anay,** but hikers should verify whether there's a boat to shuttle them across the river.

For nonhikers, inexpensive rental horses are available at Chanquín, but they're not suitable for forest trails such as El Tepual, and because they're untrained for amateur riders, there have been accidents.

Accommodations and Food

In and around Chanquín, several Huilliche-run campgrounds charge around US$2–3 per person, but Conaf's **Camping Chanquín** and nearby cabañas have recently been closed. At *refugios* or along trails, camping is free of charge.

Noncampers can try any of several Cucao *hospedajes,* such as **Hospedaje El Paraíso** (cel. 09/9296-5465, US$13 pp with breakfast), which also serves meals.

At Chanquín, just across the bridge, **Parador Darwin** (cell tel. 09/9799-9923, paradordarwin@hotmail.com, US$15 pp) has decent accommodations and excellent fish and seafood, as well as homemade bread and spreads made from local ingredients such as seaweed. A bit farther west, **El Fogón de Cucao** (cell tel. 09/9946-5685, elfogondecucao@hotmail.com, US$30–58 d) has simple accommodations with shared baths, and more elaborate rooms with private baths, including one suite, plus a restaurant.

Cucao has a minimarket, and it's possible to buy fresh fish, potatoes, and the like from local fisherfolk and farmers, but supplies are more diverse and cheaper in Castro and Chonchi.

Information

About one kilometer west of the concrete bridge over the Río Cucao, rangers collect a US$1.50 per person admission charge at Chanquín, where Conaf's **Centro de Visitantes** park is open 9 A.M.–7:30 P.M. daily; they also provide an informative map (Spanish only). It contains exhibits on the park's flora and fauna, the aboriginal Huilliche, mining history, and regional legends and traditions. The surrounding grounds contain samples of Chilote technology, including a cider press and wooden sleighs used to drag heavy loads over boggy ground.

Getting There and Around

Cucao, the park's easiest access point, is 52 kilometers southwest of Castro via the Panamericana and a gravel road (almost always passable but which never seems to improve) and 32 kilometers west of Chonchi, but public transportation now continues to Chanquín. From Castro to Cucao and Chanquín, there are 2–5 or even more buses daily, depending on the season, with **Buses Arroyo** (tel. 065/635604), **Ojeda,** and **Interlagos.** Normally these stop at Chonchi en route.

QUELLÓN

Unlike many Isla Grande settlements, the port of Quellón is a 20th-century town that really only came into its own after an alcohol and acetone distillery, using native woods from dense nearby forests, installed itself here in 1905. After the 1960 tsunami, most inhabitants moved to higher ground away from the port, which is home to a small fishing fleet and regular ferries to continental Chiloé and Aisén. It is technically the Chilean terminus of the Panamericana, though an alternative route goes farther south in Argentine Patagonia.

Quellón is hoping for a tourist influx because of the presence of a large blue whale feeding colony in the waters to the southwest, but there are no commercial operators yet. To the west, center-right presidential candidate Sebastián Piñera has created Parque Tantauco, a conservation project similar to Doug Tompkins's Parque Pumalín. For the moment, though, it's the ferries that bring the tourists.

Orientation

On the southeastern coast of the Isla Grande, Quellón (population 13,656) is 92 kilometers south of Castro via the Panamericana, which becomes Calle Ladrilleros as it enters town. The townsite rises steeply above the harbor. Most points of interest and services are on or near the Costanera Pedro Montt, which runs along the shoreline.

Accommodations and Food

Inexpensive options, with shared baths and breakfast, include waterfront **Hotel Playa** (Pedro Montt 427, tel. 065/681278, US$10 pp, breakfast US$2.50), which also has a restaurant, and **Residencial Esteban** (Aguirre Cerda 353, tel. 065/681438, US$13 pp with shared bath, US$23 s, US$33 d with private bath, with breakfast and cable TV), on a quiet block. It also has a fine and economical downstairs restaurant.

Hotel Los Suizos (Ladrilleros 399, tel. 065/681787, US$25 s, US$30 d) is away from the water. On the waterfront, **Hotel Tierra del Fuego** (Pedro Montt 445, tel. 065/682079, US$30 s, US$45 d with private bath) has an upstairs restaurant with a unique boat-shaped bar.

Hotel El Chico Leo (Pedro Montt 325, tel. 065/681567, elchicoleo@turismoquellon.cl, US$12 pp, US$33 d) has a choice of rooms with shared or private baths, and a restaurant with good seafood and service.

In addition to hotel dining rooms, seafood restaurants dot the waterfront, with a handful of venues elsewhere. Among the choices are **Hostería Romeo Alfa** (Capitán Luis Alcázar 554, tel. 065/680177), which has respectable food but a slow kitchen and even slower service, and **La Quila** (La Paz 385, tel. 065/681206). **Café Nuevo Amanecer** (22 de Mayo 344, tel.

065/682026) serves snacks, sandwiches, and desserts; it also becomes a popular evening hangout.

Information

Two blocks north of the waterfront, staffed by interns whose knowledge varies considerably, Quellón's **Caseta de Información Turística** (Gómez García and Santos Vargas) is theoretically open 8:30 A.M.–8 P.M. daily December–February only.

Services

Services are fewer than in Ancud or Castro. **BCI** (22 de Mayo 343) has an ATM. **Correos de Chile** (22 de Mayo and Ladrilleros) handles the mail. **Entel** (Ladrilleros 405) has long-distance phone service. **Hotel Suizo** (Ladrilleros 399) offers Internet access.

For medical help, try the **Hospital de Quellón** (Dr. Ahués 305, tel. 065/681443).

Getting There and Around

Cruz del Sur and **Transchiloé** (both at Aguirre Cerda 52, tel. 065/681284) have frequent service to Chonchi, Castro, Ancud, and Puerto Montt. There are also *taxi colectivos* to Castro.

Naviera Austral (Pedro Montt 457, tel. 065/682207, www.navieraustral.cl) sails to Chaitén Wednesday and Sunday on either of two ferries, the *Alejandrina* or *Pincoya*. Fares range from US$23 pp for fixed seats to US$40 pp for bunks. Vehicle rates are US$127 for passenger vehicles and small trucks, and US$34 per linear meter for other vehicles; bicycles cost US$12 and motorcycles US$27.

NORTHERN PATAGONIA

Ever since Europeans first saw the extreme southern latitudes of the Americas, Patagonia has held a legendary, even romantic allure. Most accounts, from Darwin's *Voyage of the Beagle* to Bruce Chatwin's classic *In Patagonia,* deal with sprawling Argentine Patagonia, not the lesser-known narrow strip of Pacific Chile in the same latitudes.

Chilean Patagonia's boundaries are imprecise because, in a sense, the region exists in the imagination. It has no juridical reality, though nearly everybody would agree that both Region XI (Aisén) and Region XII (Magallanes) are part of it. More northerly areas would like to be included, if only to partake of the Patagonian mystique.

Part of the problem in defining Patagonia may stem from the fact that, in Argentina, it

is broadly agreed to be the area south of the Río Colorado, an enormous territory comprising Neuquén, Río Negro, Chubut, Santa Cruz, and Tierra del Fuego provinces. Neuquén's most northerly point is only slightly southeast of Chile's heartland city of Talca, which nobody would consider Patagonia. Drawing any line, though, is sure to engender controversy.

This chapter and the next take a utilitarian approach. While Puerto Montt, the formal starting point for the Carretera Austral Longitudinal (Southern Longitudinal Highway) may be the gateway, in practice Patagonia is that continental and insular area accessible only by long-distance ferry or airplane, or overland through Argentina. This excludes insular Chiloé, easily reached by shuttle ferries; it includes most of "continental Chiloé,"

HIGHLIGHTS

◖ Parque Nacional Laguna San Rafael: Southwest of Coyhaique, the ice still reaches the sea at Laguna San Rafael – though it's receding alarmingly fast (page 433).

◖ Puyuhuapi Lodge & Spa: It's not really an island, but this surprisingly affordable hot-springs resort might as well be, due to its splendid isolation opposite the northern Carretera Austral (page 440).

◖ Futaleufú: Almost every rafter and kayaker places the Río Futaleufú among the world's top 10 white-water rivers, and many put it atop the list (page 442).

◖ Parque Natural Pumalín: It's been politically controversial, but South America's largest private conservation project is winning acceptance for its commitment to preserving huge extents of midlatitude rainforest and making them accessible to the public (page 446).

◖ Reserva Nacional Cerro Castillo: Growing in popularity, the trekking beneath the spires of this readily accessible reserve on the southern Carretera Austral makes it second only to Torres del Paine, probably, in its popularity with multiday hikers. It's a distant second, though, so there's no Paine gridlock (page 449).

◖ Capilla de Mármol: Accessible by water only, the sinuous walls of these blue/white grottos line the western shores of Lago General Carrera (page 452).

◖ Caleta Tortel: A road reaches its outskirts now, but the only ways to get around this quaint seaside fishing village are still the boardwalks and staircases that connect its waterfront and scattered houses and businesses (page 460).

◖ Villa O'Higgins: In scenic mountain surroundings, this orderly outpost of bureaucracy is almost the end of the road – the Carretera Austral stops just south of here – but it's also the starting point for the new "Cruce de Lagos" to Argentina's trekking capital of El Chaltén (page 461).

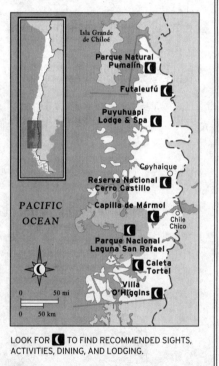

LOOK FOR ◖ TO FIND RECOMMENDED SIGHTS, ACTIVITIES, DINING, AND LODGING.

south of the town of Hornopirén, where a summer-only ferry sails to the tiny port of Caleta Gonzalo, the *real* start of the Carretera Austral. The *Southern Patagonia and Tierra del Fuego* chapter also includes both Chilean and Argentine Tierra del Fuego, and southwestern Santa Cruz province, which is part of a popular circuit that includes Chile's Parque Nacional Torres del Paine.

Throughout Chilean Patagonia, overland transportation schedules change from season to season and year to year, and may be disrupted by weather—or volcanic eruptions—on the Carretera Austral.

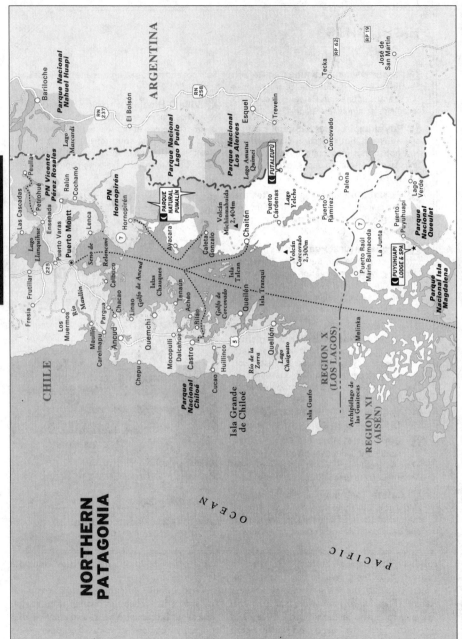

NORTHERN PATAGONIA

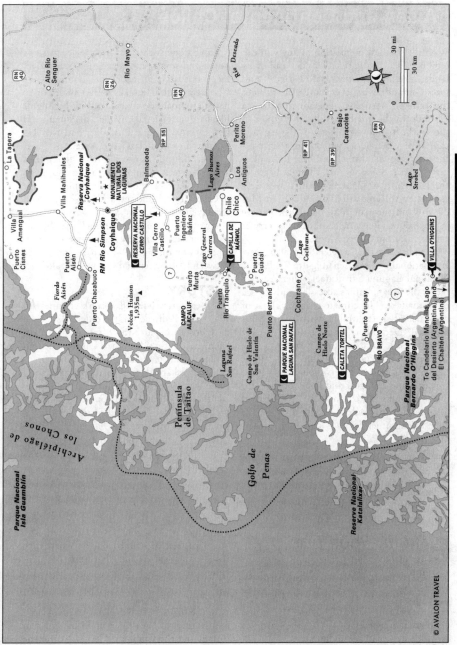

© AVALON TRAVEL

Aisén and Continental Chiloé

With the smallest population of any Chilean region, Aisén is a natural wonderland of islands, mountains, fjords, lakes, rivers, and forests. It is drawing ever more visitors since the Carretera Austral's completion from Caleta Gonzalo in the north to Villa O'Higgins in the south. Its only sizable city is the regional capital of Coyhaique, which has a state-of-the-art airport and is a good base for exploring the area. Some visitors, though, begin at the ferry port of Chaitén—which was devastated by volcanic ash and flooding in May 2008—and move south by road. Others arrive at Coyhaique's Puerto Chacabuco, via ferry or catamaran from Puerto Montt.

In addition to the Carretera Austral and several national parks, Aisén's big draw is Parque Nacional Laguna San Rafael, where the ice meets the ocean, but it's accessible only by sea or by air taxi. The climate resembles that of coastal British Columbia, with the seasons reversed (December, January, and February are summer). Consequently, weather can be wet, windy, and cool at any time, especially at higher elevations, so hikers should carry good trekking and rain gear and hope for the best. Summer highs can climb above 25°C around Coyhaique, but cooler temperatures are the rule. Midsummer days are long, with sunsets around 10 P.M.

Thanks to tourism, Aisén is increasingly prosperous, but agriculture, forestry, and mining are also important. The salmon-farming industry has brought both prosperity and controversy, as its environmental cost is greater than some residents believe it's worth.

PLANNING YOUR TIME

Because distances are great, public transport is limited, and roads are few and slow, Aisén justifies a rental car, preferably with high clearance. Vehicles are also few, so rental reservations are advisable for visitors flying into Balmaceda/Coyhaique, which is the Carretera Austral's approximate midpoint.

Coyhaique is the best base for excursions north and south, and to Laguna San Rafael by catamaran or air taxi. Northbound on the Carretera Austral, it takes at least a week or 10 days to see roadside or near-roadside highlights like Parque Nacional Queulat, the Puyuhuapi hot springs, Parque Pumalín, and the Río Futaleufú's world-class white water.

Southbound on the highway, it requires at least a week to enjoy Cerro Castillo, Lago General Carrera, the singular fishing village of Caleta Tortel, and the wild end-of-the-road scenery at Villa O'Higgins.

For visitors heading south from Puerto Montt, with rental cars, ferry reservations are advisable, especially for the January–February-only service between Hornopirén and Caleta Gonzalo.

HISTORY

Europeans first viewed Aisén's channels in 1553, when Pedro de Valdivia ordered Francisco de Ulloa to explore the Strait of Magellan from the Pacific side. When Ulloa landed on Península Taitao, though, the forerunners of today's Kawéskar (Alacaluf) had been navigating those waterways for millennia; on the nearby continent, the Tehuelche (Aónikenk) and their predecessors had long stalked the steppes for guanaco and the forests for *huemul.*

Aisén's thinly populated, rugged recesses held little for the Spaniards. At first, tales of "Trapananda" drew a few fortune hunters in search of the wealthy but literally fantastic "City of the Caesars" (tales of hidden riches persist to the present, and a small Conaf reserve near Coyhaique still bears the name Trapananda). As gold fever subsided, the Spaniards settled temperate areas where they could extract tribute and labor from the indigenous population, a more dependable source of wealth until introduced diseases greatly reduced their numbers.

In the 1670s, both Bartolomé Díaz Gallardo and Antonio de Vea came upon Laguna San Rafael and the Campo de Hielo Norte, the northern continental ice sheet. The most dedicated explorers, though, were Jesuit missionaries, working their way south from insular Chiloé, by land and sea until their expulsion from the Americas in 1767. The list of non-Spaniards reads like a who's who: John Byron, grandfather of poet George Gordon (Lord Byron), suffered a shipwreck in the late 18th century, and Fitz Roy and Darwin saw Laguna San Rafael on board the *Beagle* a few decades later. Under Admiral Sir Thomas Baker, commanding the British Navy's South American Squadron, the latter charted much of the area's waters, their work supplemented by Chilean naval officer Enrique Simpson in the 1870s.

In 1798, Spain made the region's first land grant, an enormous tract between the northern Río Yelcho and the southern Río Bravo, but Argentine overland explorers were the first non-indigenous travelers to see much of the area. Despite concern about the Argentine presence, which led to territorial disagreements only recently resolved, Chile had trouble enough controlling areas south of the Biobío, let alone remote Aisén. Consequently, settlement lagged until the early 20th century, when it granted the Valparaíso-based Sociedad Industrial Aisén a huge concession for sheep ranching and forestry near present-day Coyhaique.

News of the concession set off a land rush, from the heartland and Argentina's Chubut province, by settlers who challenged the company's state-sanctioned dominance. While these smallholders held their own against the company, both of them, along with the Chilean state, bear responsibility for massive deforestation under a misguided law that encouraged cutting and burning to establish land titles. Today, when hillsides of deciduous *ñirres* turn red in autumn, it's a pale reminder of what the entire region must have looked like seven decades ago, before both deliberate and unintentional wildfires denuded countless slopes, leaving pale trunks scattered among pasture grasses, from Mañihuales in the north to Puerto Ibáñez in the south. Silt carried by the Río Simpson, from erosion triggered by deforestation and grazing, clogged the harbor of Puerto Aisén, the region's main port, necessitating its shift to Puerto Chacabuco.

Since the 1970s, the major development has been construction of the Carretera Austral, parts of which are now being paved, to Villa O'Higgins. Thanks to improved relations with Argentina, cross-border contacts have improved, and pressure has increased to open up the area to controversial hydroelectric projects on the Futaleufú, Baker and Pascua Rivers, all of them prime recreational resources. While Aisén seems likely to grow, it seems unlikely to attract the large-scale immigration advocated by some regional politicians.

NORTHERN PATAGONIA

Coyhaique

Originally known as Baquedano, today's regional capital was once so remote and obscure that letters addressed here could end up in an eponymous Atacama Desert rail junction. After a decade of confusion following its 1929 founding, its name became Coyhaique, but it did not become the provincial capital until it succeeded Puerto Aisén in 1973.

Founded as a service center for the Sociedad Industrial Aisén, its growth spurred by the colonists who flooded the region in its wake, Coyhaique is a mostly modern city whose infrastructure hasn't quite matched its growth—in heavy rain, streets drain poorly and the flow of water is so broad that city workers place temporary pedestrian bridges across the gutters. Recent improvements, though, include a redesigned Plaza de Armas and conversion of congested Calle Horn into Paseo Horn, a pedestrian mall that's become a popular gathering place.

Still the region's only substantial city, Coyhaique has a complete array of services, including fine restaurants, pubs, and travel agencies. The virtual midpoint of the Carretera

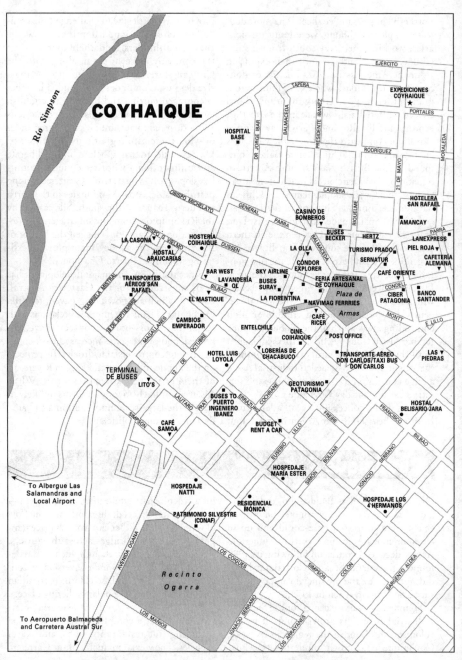

Austral, it also offers an alternate route into Argentina.

ORIENTATION

Beneath the basaltic barricade of Cerro Macay, Coyhaique (population 44,850) sits at the confluence of the Río Simpson and the Río Coyhaique, 455 kilometers south of Caleta Gonzalo and 566 kilometers north of Villa O'Higgins. It is 634 kilometers from Puerto Montt via the Carretera Austral.

Westbound, a paved highway leads to Puerto Aisén and Puerto Chacabuco, while another leads southeast to Balmaceda and the Argentine border at Paso Huemules. On the Argentine side, the mostly paved road continues to the Atlantic port of Comodoro Rivadavia, 600 kilometers east on the so-called Corredor Bioceánico (Bi-Oceanic Corridor) with Puerto Chacabuco.

Based on a pair of concentric pentagons, the inner one surrounding the Plaza de Armas, Coyhaique's street plan is not for the geometrically challenged. Beyond this, it's more regular and less disorienting but still presents problems for anyone unaccustomed to irregular angles at intersections.

Avenida Baquedano, on the northeast edge of town, connects the paved Puerto Chacabuco road with the gravel road leading east to the border at Coyhaique Alto. Avenida Ogana is the main route to the southbound Carretera Austral and Balmaceda.

SIGHTS

Nearly all first-time visitors to the disorienting **Plaza de Armas,** where 10 streets radiate like spokes from a hub, get lost returning to their hotels. Bewildered walkers can blame policeman Luis Marchant González who, in 1929 chose the Carabineros' five-sided badge as a city-planning template. Recently relandscaped, the plaza still boasts many mature trees, but the sightlines are better and new fountains add a touch of distinction.

The **Museo Regional de la Patagonia** (Eusebio Lillo 23, tel. 067/213174, 8:30 A.M.–6 P.M. weekdays, US$0.65), in the Casa de la

© WAYNE BERNHARDSON

the city of Coyhaique, Aisén

Cultura, documents regional history through a well-presented series of historical photographs and early settlers' household implements.

Nearby, on the Baquedano median strip, the **Monumento al Ovejero** commemorates Aisén's pioneer sheep farmers. The series of statues consists of a mounted shepherd, his flock, and his dogs.

ENTERTAINMENT AND SHOPPING

Coyhaique has a growing number of bars, but their aspirations surpass their appeal. **Piel Roja** (Moraleda 495, tel. 067/236635), for instance, has pizza and pub grub, psychedelic decor that probably infringes Fillmore copyrights, and a 7–9 P.M. happy hour, but something's lacking.

Despite its pioneer-style house, swinging doors, pistols on the wall, and cold beer on tap, **Bar West** (Bilbao 110, tel. 065/210007) serves mediocre pisco sours and plays too much insipid pop music.

The liveliest place is **El Cuervo** (General Parra 72, tel. 067/215015), a karaoke bar and WiFi hotspot, but the air quality is deadly. **Peña Quilantal** (Baquedano 791, tel. 065/234394) sometimes showcases live folkloric music but is just as likely to offer run-of-the-mill pop.

Cine Coihaique (Cochrane 321) shows occasional recent films.

At the **Feria Artesanal de Coyhaique,** on the west side of the Plaza de Armas, local horse gear is the main attraction, supplemented by wood carvings and woolens. **Amancay** (21 de Mayo 340, tel. 067/216099) has custom chocolates.

ACCOMMODATIONS

Coyhaique's accommodations scene is unusual, with plenty of budget and midrange choices and few upmarket options. With some exceptions, budget accommodations are only so-so.

US$10-25

Reached by a staircase so narrow your elbows can touch both walls, some rooms at **Hospedaje Los 4 Hermanos** (Colón 495, tel. 067/232647, US$8–10 pp without breakfast) can be claustrophobic, but it's often full and singles are at a premium—phoning ahead is a good idea. The comparable **Hospedaje Natti** (Almirante Simpson 417, tel. 067/231047, US$8 pp) is a good alternative.

For the price, it's hard to find anything better than pristine, friendly **Hospedaje María Ester** (Lautaro 544, tel. 067/233023, www.hospedajemariaester.cl, US$12 pp). Breakfast costs US$2.50 extra.

US$25-50

The backpackers' best is Spanish-run **(Albergue Las Salamandras** (Sector los Pinos s/n, tel. 067/211865, www.salamandras.cl, US$15–21 pp with kitchen access), on piney grounds about two kilometers southwest of town on the old airport road. Most rooms in this attractive building, with large communal spaces, are dorms, but there are a few doubles. Camping (US$6–8 pp) is also possible.

Cheerful **Residencial Mónica** (Eusebio Lillo 664, tel. 067/234302, US$10–15 pp with breakfast) has shared and private bath options, but in some rooms too many beds nearly cover all of the floor space.

In a quiet north-end location, **Hospedaje Baquedano** (Baquedano 20, tel. 067/232520, pguzmanm@entelchile.net, US$17 pp with breakfast and private bath) has English-speaking ownership—with traces of Maine and Tennessee in the accent.

It's spacious and well kept, on a quiet block, but the open floor plan at **Hostal Araucarias** (Obispo Vielmo 71, tel. 067/232707, US$25 s, US$42 d) lets sounds carry upstairs.

(Hostal Gladys (General Parra 65, tel. 067/245288, patagoniagladys@hotmail.com, US$18–25 pp with cable TV) is quiet, well-located, spotless, and tobacco-free, though it has a couple drawbacks: The shared-bath rooms have too many beds, the lurid red bedspreads are distracting, and the private-bath rooms have skylights rather than windows. Breakfast (US$4–6 extra) varies in quality.

US$50-100

Hotelera San Rafael (Moraleda 343, tel. 067/233733, www.hotelerasanrafael.cl, US$49

s, US$58 d without IVA) has added tasteful, spacious, and sunny hotel rooms to a property that once provided just cabaña-style accommodations. New in 2006, **Hostal Español** (Sargento Aldea 343, tel./fax 067/242580, www.hostalcoyhaique.cl, US$40 s, US$60 d with continental breakfast) is a polished product with upstairs view rooms, though it lacks some details.

Hotel Luis Loyola (Prat 455, tel./fax 067/234200, hotelloyolacoyhaique@chile.net, US$49 s, US$62 d) is modern, central, and comfortable.

In some rooms at **Hotel Los Ñires** (Av. Baquedano 315, tel./fax 067/232261, www.doncarlos.cl, US$53 s, US$64 d), large beds occupy almost all the floor space, but the baths are spacious, the hot water abundant, and the water pressure steady.

Despite its unimpressive streetside exterior—hard to see unless you're really looking for it—**Hotelera San Sebastián** (Av. Baquedano 496, tel. 067/233021, US$51 s, US$64 d) has large comfortable rooms with views over the Río Coyhaique.

On a site overlooking the Río Coyhaique, genial **(Hotel El Reloj** (Baquedano 828, tel./fax 067/231108, www.elrelojhotel.cl, US$60 s, US$78 d with breakfast and without IVA) is one of Coyhaique's best values, with an outstanding restaurant as well.

Over US$100

Overseas tour operators often choose **Hostal Belisario Jara** (Bilbao 662, tel./fax 067/234150, www.belisariojara.itgo.com, US$98 s, US$115 d), which has more architectural distinction and personality than most hotels here.

On sprawling west-side grounds, motel-style **Hostería Coihaique** (Magallanes 131, tel. 067/231137, www.hotelsa.cl, US$100 s, US$116 d) is recovering from a fire and may become the new casino.

FOOD

Cafetería Alemana (Condell 119, tel. 065/231731) makes outstanding sandwiches, *onces,* and desserts; down the block is its sister **Café Oriente** (Condell 201, tel. 065/231622). For inexpensive light meals, try **Café Samoa** (Prat 653, tel. 065/232864).

For home cooking with class, try the lunches (US$5) at **El Mastique** (Bilbao 141, tel. 067/235594); its dinner menu is more limited. Despite an almost foreboding exterior, **Lito's** (Lautaro 147, tel. 067/254528) has a spacious dining area with an attractive bar and above-average versions of Chilean beef (US$6–8), fish, and seafood.

With a Chilean menu enhanced by top-quality ingredients, the **Casino de Bomberos** (General Parra 365, tel. 065/231437) is an institution, but it's one of the country's more expensive fire-station restaurants. **La Fiorentina** (Prat 230, tel. 065/238899) has good pizza, *pastel de choclo,* and crisp service at moderate prices.

Loberías de Chacabuco (Prat 386, tel. 067/239786) is a seafood venue that seems to be slumming these days, though it has maintained quality and kept prices reasonable, its clientele is not what it used to be and the locale is less attractive than it once was. **La Olla** (Prat 176, tel. 065/234700) has become one of Coyhaique's better restaurants, with choice pastas (around US$10), but the budget-conscious can enjoy moderately priced (around US$6) lunches. The *pollo al ajillo* (garlic chicken) is excellent, but the service can be slow and the pisco sours sugary.

New in 2007, **Las Piedras** (21 de Mayo 655, tel. 067/233243) bakes a blended *pastel de jaiva y centolla,* a casserole of common and king crab (US$13). For light cooking to international standards, Hotel El Reloj's **El Ovejero** (Baquedano 828, tel./fax 065/231108) comes highly recommended for entrées such as *congrio al ajillo* (conger eel with garlic, US$12) and Patagonian desserts including rhubarb mousse; grab a window table for views over the river.

On the west side of the Plaza de Armas, a favorite with locals and visitors alike, **Café Ricer** (Paseo Horn 48, tel. 067/232920, www.historicoricer.cl) has some of Coyhaique's best food and drink, including Patagonian specialties like barbecued lamb (about US$10) and even Middle Eastern items like stuffed grape leaves; humongous sandwiches and snacks are cheaper. Most people dine in the downstairs café, but the upstairs restaurant has more style, its walls lined with historic photographs (it's now the last refuge of smokers, though).

Another good option, popular with tour operators, is **La Casona** (Obispo Vielmo 77, tel. 067/238894) for lamb, *pastel de jaiva* (crab soufflé), and other regional entrées in the US$8–11 range. The service equals or surpasses the food.

INFORMATION

Sernatur (Bulnes 35, tel. 067/240290, infoaisen@sernatur.cl) is open 8:30 A.M.–8 P.M. Monday–Friday and 10 A.M.–6 P.M. Saturday–Sunday December–February; the rest of the year, hours are 8:30 A.M.–5 P.M. Monday–Friday only. It has English-speaking staff, and when it's not open accommodations and transportation details are posted outside.

Conaf's **Patrimonio Silvestre** (Los Coihues s/n, tel. 067/212125) provides information on national parks and reserves.

SERVICES

Coyhaique has the region's most complete services. Changing money, in particular, is easier than elsewhere on the Carretera Austral.

Turismo Prado (21 de Mayo 417) and **Cambios Emperador** (Freire 171) both exchange cash and travelers checks. **Banco Santander** (Condell 184) and several other banks have ATMs.

For postal services, **Correos de Chile** (Cochrane 202) is near the Plaza de Armas. **Entelchile** (Arturo Prat 340) has phones and Internet connections, but other Internet outlets keep longer hours and will hook up your laptop for around US$1 per hour: **Ciber Patagonia** (21 de Mayo 525, tel. 067/254700) and **Trapananda Cyber** (General Parra 86).

Intensive **Spanish classes** with room and full board cost US$375–400 per week or US$950 per month at **Baquedano**

International Language School (Baquedano 20, tel. 067/232520, www.balasch.cl); rates include four hours of instruction Monday–Saturday, primarily in summer when the main instructor does not have local teaching obligations.

For laundry, try **Lavandería QL** (Bilbao 160, tel. 067/232266) or **Lavandería All Clean** (General Parra 55, Local 2, tel. 067/219635), alongside Residencial Gladys.

For medical attention, contact the **Hospital Base** (J. M. Carrera s/n, tel. 067/231286).

GETTING THERE

Coyhaique is the region's transportation hub, with flights north and south, and bus service along the Carretera Austral, to Region X (Los Lagos) and Region XII (Magallanes) via Argentina, and to Argentina itself. Chilean

---

THE DICTATOR'S HIGHWAY?

The highway where Santiaguinos come to test their SUVs, rather than on the avenues of Las Condes and Vitacura, the **Carretera Austral** is so crucial to Aisén that Coyhaique's modest museum used to devote its largest exhibit to it. Many residents still give General Pinochet the credit – one conspicuous photo showed a grandfatherly Pinochet, in civilian dress, beaming at a local schoolboy. A frequent comment is that the military regime was "the last one to pay attention to the region," and one Pinochet partisan claimed that "the politicians would never have built this highway. There are no votes here."

But Pinochet may get more credit than he deserves. The original highway studies date from 1968, during President Eduardo Frei Montalva's Christian Democrat government, and the project advanced during Salvador Allende's successor Socialist administration. Work accelerated during the dictatorship, but civilian contractors actually did more than the military.

The Carretera's final irony is that the man who finished it, President Ricardo Lagos (2000-2006), is the man who boldly stared down Pinochet in 1988, through a TV camera: "You promise the country another eight years of torture, disappearances, and human rights violations." Lagos's bravery probably turned the tide in a plebiscite that ended Pinochet's reign. Maps once labeled "Carretera Longitudinal Austral Presidente Pinochet" now say "Carretera Longitudinal Austral."

Not so long ago, Villa O'Higgins, the end-of-the-road hamlet, was governed by the far-right UDI (Unión Demócratica Independiente). Still, the entire town showed up in April 2000, when the newly elected Lagos, Pinochet's nemesis, formally dedicated the Río Bravo-Villa O'Higgins segment, the final piece in the puzzle.

The notoriously timid *huemul*, the emblematic, endangered Andean deer that graces Chile's coat-of-arms (along with the Andean condor and the motto "by reason or force") is surprisingly common and even docile along this last segment. In a sense, it's a tangible symbol of change and the openness that the highway represents – not force alone, but reason as well. The highway that began as a military exercise now belongs to everyone.

Some pioneer settlements along the Carretera Austral are acquiring an air of permanence, but this is still wild country, with just enough creature comforts for those on bigger budgets. Prices are highest and public transport most frequent in January and February, when most Chileans take their vacations. The spring months of October and November and the autumn months of March and April can be good times to travel, though public transport is less frequent.

While the Carretera Austral may be one of the continent's loveliest roads – there's no bad scenery – it's also one of the most hazardous. Blind curves in dense forests and sheer mountains, narrow segments with steeply sloping shoulders, and frequent loose gravel all require drivers to pay the closest attention to avoid head-on collisions, rollovers, and other accidents.

buses to destinations in other regions may not drop passengers in Argentina.

Air
Commercial jets land at modern **Aeropuerto Balmaceda,** 50 kilometers southeast of Coyhaique. Small planes still use convenient **Aeropuerto Teniente Vidal,** only five kilometers southwest of town.

LAN (Moraleda 402, tel. 065/231188) flies several times daily to Puerto Montt and Santiago, Saturday only to Punta Arenas. **Sky Airline** (Prat 203, tel. 067/240825) flies daily to Puerto Montt and the Chilean capital, and south to Punta Arenas.

Transporte Aéreo Don Carlos (Subteniente Cruz 63, tel./fax 067/231981, www.doncarlos.cl) flies air-taxi charters to destinations including Chile Chico, Cochrane, and Villa O'Higgins, but its recent safety record is problematic. **Transportes Aéreos San Rafael** (18 de Septiembre 469, tel. 067/233408, transrafael@patagoniachile.cl) flies to the remote island settlement of Melinka (US$42) and on to Quellón, Chiloé (US$44) on Thursday. In addition to Don Carlos and San Rafael, **Aerohein** (Baquedano 500, tel. 067/252177, tel./fax 067/232772) offers charters to Parque Nacional Laguna San Rafael and elsewhere in the region.

Bus
More carriers have begun to use the upgraded **Terminal de Buses** (Lautaro and Magallanes), but several still use their own offices elsewhere. Services north and south along the Carretera Austral are most frequent in summer and may be considerably reduced in winter.

To Puerto Aisén (US$2) and Puerto Chacabuco (US$3, one hour), there are frequent departures with **Buses Suray** (Prat 265, tel. 067/238387).

At the main terminal, **Buses São Paulo** (tel. 067/255726) goes north to Mañihuales (US$3, one hour) daily at 12:30 P.M. via the paved Viviana junction, and to off-highway destinations such as Villa Ortega and La Tapera.

Because of the eruption, northbound services to Chaitén are in flux. **Buses Daniela**

(Baquedano 1122, tel. 099/5123500) normally goes there four times weekly but, as of early 2009, it was going Tuesday and Sunday at 8 A.M. to Futaleufú (US$33, 10.5 hours) via Puerto Puyuhuapi (US$13), La Junta (US$17, 7 hours), and Villa Santa Lucía (US$25, 8.5 hours).

Buses Becker (General Parra 329, tel. 067/232167) covers the same route on Saturdays, and also goes to Puerto Cisnes (US$12, six hours) three times weekly.

At the main terminal, **Terra Austral** (tel. 067/254335) goes to Puerto Cisnes Monday–Saturday at 6 A.M.

To Puerto Ingeniero Ibáñez (US$7, two hours), on Lago General Carrera's north shore, **Buses Carolina** (tel. 067/255726) connects with the Chile Chico ferry; a combined ticket costs US$10. Ibáñez-bound minibuses usually pick up passengers at their homes or hotels; carriers include **Darío Figueroa Castro** (tel. 09/8977-9737) and **Miguel Acuña** (Manuel Rodríguez 143, tel. 067/251579). Some of these also stop at the corner of Prat and Errázuriz.

Other southbound minibuses go as far as Villa Cerro Castillo (US$7, 1.5 hours), where the pavement ends on the Carretera Austral: **Minibuses Amin Alí** (tel. 09/9313-1402) and **Minibuses Tomás Urreta** (cel. 09/9950-0276); these leave from Prat and Lautaro, near the restaurant Moneda de Oro, but with a day's notice they'll come to your hotel.

From the main terminal, **Acuario 13** (tel. 067/255726) goes beyond Cerro Castillo to Cochrane (US$18, 9 hours) and intermediates at 9:30 A.M. Wednesday and Sunday; **Buses São Paulo,** at the same office, goes Tuesday, Thursday, and Saturday. **Don Carlos** (Subteniente Cruz 63, tel. 067/232981) goes Wednesday and Friday.

Other southbound fares include Puerto Río Tranquilo (US$11, 5.5 hours), Puerto Guadal (US$15, 7 hours), and Puerto Bertrand (US$17, 8 hours).

From the main terminal, **Queilen Bus** (tel. 067/240760) goes daily at 5 P.M. to Puerto Montt (US$37, approx. 20 hours) via Argentina.

In the same main terminal office (tel. 067/232067), **Transaustral** serves Comodoro Rivadavia (US$33, 9 hours), Argentina, via Río Mayo and Sarmiento, with northbound connections to Esquel and Bariloche. Departures take place Monday and Friday at 8 A.M.

Sea

Coyhaique is not a seaport, but the local office of **Navimag Ferries** (Paseo Horn 47-D, tel. 067/223306) sells ferry berths from Puerto Chacabuco to Puerto Montt, and to Parque Nacional Laguna San Rafael.

Geoturismo Patagonia (Eusebio Lillo 315, tel. 067/573461; www.geoturismopatagonia.cl) is the agent for Catamaranes del Sur, which has high-speed service to Parque Nacional Laguna San Rafael.

GETTING AROUND
To the Airport

Taxis to **Aeropuerto Teniente Vidal** are cheap enough (about US$4), but air-taxi companies usually provide their own transfers. To **Aeropuerto Balmaceda** about 45 minutes away, door-to-door minivan services (US$7 pp) include **Transfer Coyhaique** (tel. 067/210495), **Transfer AM** (tel. 067/250119), and **Transfer Valencia** (tel. 067/233030).

Car Rental

Even shoestring travelers indulge themselves on car rentals in Aisén, since public transport is less frequent than elsewhere and some sights are off the main north–south route. Because vehicles are limited and demand can be high, summer reservations are advisable—even essential.

Among Coyhaique's rental agencies are **Andes Patagónicos** (Paseo Horn 48, tel. 067/232920), **Avis/Traeger** (Avenida Baquedano 457, tel. 067/231648, traeger@patagoniachile.cl), **Budget** (Errázuriz 454, tel. 067/255171), and **Hertz** (General Parra 280, tel. 067/245780).

Vicinity of Coyhaique

Coyhaique is an ideal base for activities like hiking, fly-fishing, rafting and even winter skiing. Fishing probably tops the list, as the season runs November–May in the numerous lakes and rivers.

Among reliable operators are fly-fishing specialist **Aisén Bridges Travel** (tel./fax 067/233302, www.aisen.cl), which is easiest to contact by phone (English spoken); **Andes Patagónicos** (Paseo Horn 48, Local 11, tel. 067/216711, www.andespatagonicos.cl); **Expediciones Coyhaique** (Portales 195, tel./fax 067/232300, www.expecoy .es.vg), also fly-fishing-oriented; **Cóndor Explorer** (Dussen 357, tel. 067/670349, www.condorexplorer.com); U.S.-run, Puerto Bertrand–based **Patagonia Adventure Expeditions** (Casilla 8, Cochrane, tel./ fax 067/411330, www.adventurepatagonia .com), which offers daily white-water rafting on the Río Baker in addition to longer fishing and backcountry trips; and U.S.–Chilean **Salvaje Corazón** (21 de Mayo 748, tel. 067/211488, www.salvajecorazon.com). English, Hebrew, Portuguese, and some French are also spoken).

RESERVA NACIONAL COYHAIQUE

Few cities anywhere have so much wild country so near as this mountainous 2,676-hectare reserve, with its top-of-the-world views of Coyhaique, Cerro Macay, and Cerro Castillo to the south, the Río Simpson Valley to the west, and the Patagonian plains sprawling eastward. Local residents enjoy weekend picnics and barbecues here, only five kilometers north of town, but there's always space away from the crowds, and weekdays are almost empty.

Altitudes range from 400 meters to 1,361 meters on Cerro Cinchao's summit. More than a meter of rain and snow falls throughout the year, but summers are mild and fairly dry, with an average temperature of 12°C.

While the reserve is wild and almost undeveloped, it's not exactly pristine. Forests of *coigüe (Nothofagus betuloides)* and *lenga (Nothofagus pumilio)* blanket the hillsides, but plantations of exotic pines and larches have supplanted some of the native forest devastated in the 1940s. So close to the city, birds are the most conspicuous wildlife.

The main sights are literally that—the seemingly infinite panoramas in every direction. Several trails offer different perspectives on those panoramas: the 800-meter **Sendero Laguna Verde,** the four-kilometer **Sendero Laguna Venus,** and the **Sendero Las Piedras,** which leads to Cerro Cinchao's summit.

Most visitors stay in town, but Conaf (tel. 067/212125 in Coyhaique) has a rustic six-site campground at **Laguna Verde** and a 10-siter at **Casa Bruja.** Each charges US$7.50 for up to six persons; two of the Laguna Verde sites have roofed shelters. All have picnic tables, freshwater, and fire pits; Casa Bruja has toilets and hot showers. Bring as much food as necessary. At the entrance, Conaf collects an admission fee of US$3 for adults, US$0.50 for children.

Three kilometers north of town via the paved highway to Puerto Chacabuco, a dirt lateral climbs steeply east to the reserve. The road is passable for most vehicles in summer but difficult or impossible with rain. It's close enough to the city, though, that anyone in decent physical condition should be able to hike from the highway to the park entrance in about half an hour.

RESERVA NACIONAL RÍO SIMPSON

Northwest of Coyhaique, midway to Puerto Chacabuco, paved Ruta 240 passes through the Río Simpson Valley, flanked by the steep walls and canyons that form this accessible 41,634-hectare forest reserve.

Altitudes are about 100 meters along the river but rise to 1,878 meters in the cordillera.

Because it's mostly lower than Reserva Nacional Coyhaique, the weather is milder (15–17°C in summer), but it's also wetter, as westerly storms drop up to 2,500 millimeters of precipitation en route inland.

As at Coyhaique, Río Simpson's forests are mostly native southern beeches (*Nothofagus* species), but the rainfall fosters verdant undergrowth of ferns, fuchsias, and the like. *Huemul* are found in the more remote areas, as are puma and *pudú*. Bird species, which include the Andean condor, diminish in autumn and winter, returning in spring.

Opposite the visitors center, at kilometer 37, look for the **Cascada La Virgen,** a waterfall that plunges vertically through intense greenery on the highway's north side. At the center itself, a trail descends to the beach, where both swimming and fishing are possible.

Five kilometers east of park headquarters, Conaf's eight-site **Camping San Sebastián** (Ruta 240, Km 32, US$7.50 per tent) has bathrooms with hot showers.

Conaf's **Centro de Información Ambiental** (Ruta 240, Km 37) boasts a small natural-history museum (8:30 A.M.–5:30 P.M. daily, admission US$1.50) and botanical garden. As of 2009, it's due to move to a new location at Las Chimeneas (Km 30), but progress has been slow.

From Coyhaique, Don Carlos or Suray buses will drop passengers at the campground, museum, or anywhere along the route.

PUERTO CHACABUCO AND VICINITY

The forests that existed here before the 1940s wildfires were more than just embellishments on the landscape; their foliage softened the impact of heavy storms and impeded soil erosion. One effect of the fire-fed devastation was to increase the Río Simpson's sediment load and silt up Puerto Aisén's harbor, forcing authorities to build new port facilities at Puerto Chacabuco, 14 kilometers west.

Now the region's main maritime gateway, Chacabuco is also the departure point for excursions to Parque Nacional Laguna San

Rafael and a stopover on some voyages between Puerto Montt and Laguna San Rafael.

Parque Aiken del Sur

Just 10 kilometers east of Puerto Chacabuco, Aiken del Sur (www.parqueaikendelsur.cl) is a private 250-hectare nature preserve and botanical garden, with several hiking trails at Lago Riesco's south end. Owned by the same company as Catamaranes del Sur and Hotel Loberías del Sur, it's most often visited as part of a hotel stay, including a midday lamb barbecue.

Accommodations and Food

Just beyond the port, the so-so **Hotel Moraleda** (O'Higgins 82, tel. 067/351155, US$11 pp) is cheap but otherwise undistinguished.

With 60 rooms in three separate modules, ◖ **Hotel Loberías del Sur** (J. M. Carrera 50, tel. 067/351115, www.catamaranesdelsur .cl, US$250 s, US$300 d with buffet breakfast) may be the region's best pure hotel (as opposed to lodges and resorts). Everything runs like clockwork, including a first-rate restaurant, catamaran excursions to Laguna San Rafael, and its own 250-hectare forest reserve nearby. The rooms are spacious, with bay windows and king-sized beds; amenities include a gym and sauna, and lobby WiFi reaches some (but not all) of the rooms.

Getting There and Around

Buses shuttle frequently between Puerto Chacabuco and Coyhaique, 82 kilometers east via Ruta 240.

Both long-distance ferries and excursions to Parque Nacional Laguna San Rafael leave from the **Terminal de Transbordadores,** part of the port complex. **Navimag Ferries** (tel. 067/351111, fax 067/351192) operates passenger/vehicle ferries from Puerto Montt to Puerto Chacabuco, with extensions to the national park. Otherwise, simple transportation to Puerto Montt costs from US$62 (with breakfast) to US$238 pp. Shipping a vehicle costs US$215.

◖ PARQUE NACIONAL LAGUNA SAN RAFAEL

Flowing ice meets frigid sea at Parque Nacional Laguna San Rafael, where frozen pinnacles tumble from the crackling face of Ventisquero San Rafael, a 60-meter-high glacier that descends from the Campo de Hielo Norte, to become bobbing icebergs. Misleadingly named, Laguna San Rafael is really an ocean inlet, though its salinity is low as the icebergs slowly thaw and the receding glacier—a palpable victim of global warming that may no longer touch the water within a few years—discharges freshwater into it.

One of Chile's largest national parks (1,742,000 hectares of rugged terrain), Laguna San Rafael is a UNESCO World Biosphere Reserve for its extraordinary scenery and environments. While remote from any settlement, it's a popular summer excursion for Chileans and foreigners, accessible all year.

History

For a place so thinly populated and rarely visited, Laguna San Rafael has an intriguing history. Its first European visitor was Spaniard Bartolomé Díaz Gallardo, who crossed the low-lying Istmo de Ofqui (Isthmus of Ofqui) from the Golfo de Penas. Jesuit missionaries visited in 1766 and 1767, bestowing its present name, but the Spanish king soon expelled them from the continent.

During the voyage of the *Beagle,* Darwin made extensive observations here, while Chilean naval officer Enrique Simpson delivered the first official report in 1871. In 1940, the government started a canal across the isthmus to improve communications with the far south but soon gave up the project. In 1959 it declared the area a national park, but as late as the 1980s it entertained proposals to build a road for cargo transshipments.

Geography and Climate

Laguna San Rafael is 225 kilometers southwest of Puerto Chacabuco via a series of narrow channels, but only 190 kilometers from Coyhaique as the air taxi flies. To the east rises the rugged Patagonian mainland; to the west lie the myriad islands of the Archipiélago de Chonos and the Península de Taitao.

Altitudes range from sea level to 4,058-meter Monte San Valentín, the southern Andes's highest peak. Sea-level temperatures are fairly mild, about 8°C, with upwards of 2,500 millimeters of rainfall per year; at higher elevations, precipitation doubles, temperatures are colder, and the snowfall feeds 19 major glaciers that form the 300,000-hectare Campo de Hielo Norte. Pacific storms can darken the skies for weeks on end, but views are stunning when the overcast lifts.

Flora and Fauna

In areas not covered by ice, up to about 700 meters, grows mixed Valdivian forest so dense that, in Darwin's words, "our faces, hands and shin-bones all bore witness to the maltreatment we received, in attempting to penetrate their forbidding recesses." The main trees are two species of the southern beech *coigüe*, the coniferous *mañío macho (Podocarpus nubigena), tepu,* and other species, with a dense understory of shrubs, ferns, mosses, and vines. Above 700 meters, there is almost equally dense forest of the southern beeches *lenga* and *ñire,* with occasional specimens of the coniferous Guaiteca cypress.

Most of the easily visible wildlife congregates around the shoreline, beginning with eye-catching seabirds such as the flightless steamer duck and Magellanic penguin, the soaring black-browed and sooty albatrosses, and various gulls. Marine mammals include the southern elephant seal, southern sea lion, and southern sea otter.

Forest-dwelling animals are harder to see, but *pudú* and *huemul* graze the uplands, while foxes and pumas prowl for their prey.

Sights and Recreation

Calving off the face of **Ventisquero San Rafael,** indigo icebergs bob and drift in the waters of **Laguna San Rafael,** an oval body of water measuring six to nine kilometers in width and connected to the southern canals by the narrow Río Témpanos. The world's lowest-latitude tidewater glacier, Ventisquero San Rafael may not be so much longer; in continuous retreat since 1960, it could be a casualty of global warming.

Few visitors set foot in the park, as most arrive by ferry or catamaran, transferring to inflatables to meander among the bergs and approach the glacier's face. Those who manage to land can hike through seven kilometers of evergreen forest on the **Sendero al Ventisquero** to a glacial overlook.

Accommodations and Food

At park headquarters, Conaf's three-site **Camping Laguna Caiquenes** (US$6 per site for up to six campers) allows no campfires. Its **Casa de Huéspedes Laguna Caiquenes** (US$117), with kitchen facilities, accommodates up to six persons, park admission included. For reservations, contact Conaf's Coyhaique Patrimonio Silvestre office (Los Coihues s/n, tel. 067/212125).

No supplies except freshwater are available—bring everything from Coyhaique or Puerto Chacabuco. Ferries and catamarans feed their passengers; the catamarans usually have an open bar and chill the whisky with ice chipped off passing bergs.

Information

Conaf's administration and ranger station is on Laguna San Rafael's northeastern shore. Anyone who literally sets foot in the park pays a US$5 admission fee, but boat people do not, as offshore waters fall under naval rather than Conaf jurisdiction; according to Conaf statistics, which exclude maritime passengers, the park hosted only 72 visitors, 17 of them foreigners, in 2008.

Getting There

Air and sea transportation, the only practical means of reaching the park, both have their drawbacks—air travel is expensive and does not afford much time in the park, while sea travel can be moderately priced but slow, or relatively fast and expensive. From the town of Puerto Río Tranquilo, on the north arm of Lago General Carrera, a new gravel road is advancing slowly toward Bahía Exploradores, only about 65 kilometers north of the glacier, but its completion will not eliminate the need for boat travel, only shorten it.

Air taxis can land at the 775-meter gravel airstrip; several Coyhaique-based companies can carry up to five passengers for around US$1,200, remaining only about an hour at the park. The current options are **Transporte Aéreo Don Carlos** (Subteniente Cruz 63, tel./fax 067/231981, www.doncarlos.cl), and **Transportes Aéreos San Rafael** (18 de Septiembre 469, tel./fax 067/573080).

Navimag Ferries offers slow-moving ferries to Laguna San Rafael, while other operators offer options ranging from small cruise ships to high-speed catamarans. For ferries and cruise ships, the overnight voyage can take 12–16 hours from Puerto Chacabuco, while catamarans return the same day. Ferries and cruise ships, though, spend 5–6 hours at the glacier, while catamarans have 2–3 hours at most. While excursions are most frequent in summer, they may take place all year.

Navimag ferries begin in Puerto Montt and call in Puerto Chacabuco before continuing to Laguna San Rafael. From Puerto Montt, summer fares for the five-day, four-night voyage on the *Puerto Edén* range from US$465 per person for berths with exterior baths to US$1,580 s, US$1900 d in private cabins with external views; from Puerto Chacabuco, the comparable round-trip fares are US$380 per person to US$1,325 s, US$1,580 d. Off-season fares are about 15 percent lower; for more detail, contact Navimag offices in Santiago, Puerto Montt, Coyhaique, or Puerto Chacabuco, or see its website (www.navimag.com).

September–May, **Cruceros Marítimos Skorpios** (Augusto Leguía 118, Las Condes, Santiago, tel. 02/2311030, www.skorpios.cl) offers four-day, three-night cruises from Puerto Chacabuco on the 74-passsenger *Skorpios I*. Rates range from US$1,050 per person in low season to US$2,850 per person in high season (mid-December–mid-March), depending on the cabin; some voyages include a side trip to hot springs in the Quitralco fjord. Skorpios also has a Coyhaique office.

Rates on **Catamaranes del Sur**'s *Chaitén* (US$340 pp) include full meals and an open bar; Coyhaique's **Geoturismo Patagonia** (Eusebio Lillo 315, tel. 067/573461, www .geoturismopatagonia.cl) can make reservations, but they're not very knowledgeable about details.

The Northern Carretera Austral

From Coyhaique, the paved Carretera Austral is briefly contiguous with Ruta 240 to Puerto Aisén and Puerto Chacabuco, but after nine kilometers it becomes a gravel road veering northeast to Villa Ortega. Ruta 240 continues west and, passing through the **Túnel Farellón** above the Río Simpson, it reaches the Viviana junction after 39 kilometers. Here, a smooth paved highway turns northeast up the Río Mañihuales Valley and intersects the Carretera Austral about 13 kilometers southeast of Villa Mañihuales.

Heavy rains can and do close the highway north to Chaitén, sometimes for several days.

VILLA MAÑIHUALES

Villa Mañihuales, a pioneer village 76 kilometers north of Coyhaique via the roundabout Viviana junction, is the headquarters for **Reserva Nacional Mañihuales,** a 3,596-hectare forest reserve that takes its name from the native *mañío* (Podocarpus) forest.

Facilities at Conaf's five-site **Camping Las Lavanderas** (US$7.50 for up to six persons) include picnic tables and toilets, but cold showers only. **Residencial Mañiguales** (Ibar 280, tel. 067/431403, US$13 pp with breakfast) has rooms with shared baths; there are a few simple eateries.

All buses from Coyhaique pass through town en route to northbound Carretera Austral destinations.

VILLA AMENGUAL

About 58 kilometers north of Villa Mañihuales, overlooking the Río Cisnes Canyon beneath 2,095-meter Cerro Alto Nevado, Villa Amengual dates from 1983; it owes its existence to the Carretera Austral. A few kilometers south, an eastbound gravel road climbs the valley to the settlement of La Tapera and a rarely used border crossing to Argentina.

Distinguished by its shingled chapel, built in the Chilote immigrant style, Amengual is an important stop for cyclists, as one of few places with food and accommodations between Mañihuales and Puerto Puyuhuapi, another 60 kilometers north over rugged terrain.

Practicalities

Residencial El Encanto (Castro 33-A, US$7 pp) and **Residencial El Paso** (Arias 12, US$10 pp with breakfast) both have simple rooms with shared baths and serve meals.

Amengual has a spiffy new **Oficina de Información Turística,** open in summer only, that doubles as a crafts shop.

All northbound buses from Coyhaique pass through Amengual, but some turn west toward Puerto Cisnes from a junction just a few kilometers north of town.

PUERTO CISNES

At the mouth of its namesake river, Puerto Cisnes (population 2,507) owes its origins to a 1920s lumber mill but still serves as a key port for scattered fishing hamlets in and around Canal Puyuhuapi; rarely visited Parque Nacional Isla Magdalena is just across the water to the west.

Construction of a link to the Carretera Austral has partially reoriented the town inland, and in recent years the economy has diversified with salmon farming and tourism (primarily fly-fishing).

One of Aisén's architectural oddities is the **Biblioteca Pública Genaro Godoy,** a wooden structure with hexagonal neoclassical columns and a pediment with bas reliefs based on Greek mythology.

Visitors can hire a launch to the 157,616-hectare **Parque Nacional Isla Magdalena,** occupying most of its namesake island and several smaller islands, but it costs around US$100 for a day trip. Contact Alberto Miranda (tel. 067/346752), Raúl Rogel Vargas (Gabriela Mistral 165, tel. 067/346600), or Héctor Parra (Dr. Steffens 212, tel. 067/346548).

Accommodations and Food

Puerto Cisnes has several passable accommodations, starting with the reasonably priced **Hospedaje Bellavista** (Séptimo de Línea 112, tel. 067/346408, US$12 pp with shared bath). **Hostería El Gaucho** (Holmberg 140, tel. 067/346514), US$13 pp) is slightly dearer.

Well-kept (**El Guairao** (Piloto Pardo 58, tel. 067/346473, US$67 for up to four persons) has motel-style rooms with satellite TV; it also has the best restaurant, but there are other options along the waterfront.

Information

For information, visit the **Biblioteca Pública** (Sotomayor s/n, tel. 067/346423, ext. 23, 10 A.M.–7 P.M. Mon.–Fri. in summer only), the public library on the south side of the Plaza de Armas.

Getting There and Around

Several companies go to Coyhaique (US$12, six hours), including **Transportes Terra Austral** (Piloto Pardo 368, tel. 067/346757) and **Patagonia Norte** (Arturo Prat s/n, cel. 09/8226-3651), but schedules are in flux.

Buses Entre Verdes (Gabriela Mistral, cel. 09/8426-0959) goes to La Junta (US$7) at 4 P.M. Monday and Friday; otherwise, for northbound connections, wait at the highway junction or backtrack toward Coyhaique.

PARQUE NACIONAL QUEULAT

From the Cisnes junction, the Carretera Austral zigzags over the 500-meter Portezuelo Queulat

© WAYNE BERNHARDSON

The hanging glacier at Parque Nacional Queulat has receded rapidly during historic times.

of Cerro Alto Nevado. Up to 4,000 millimeters of precipitation, evenly distributed throughout the year, feeds its upper snowfields and glaciers, rushing rivers, and peaceful finger lakes; the more westerly areas are wettest. The mean annual temperature is around 8°C.

Flora and Fauna

At lower elevations, Queulat's humid climate fosters dense evergreen forests of the southern beech *coigüe* and *tepa,* which reaches heights of 30 meters or more, with a dense understory of bamboo-like *quila,* fuchsia, and ferns. On some slopes, the coniferous Guaiteca cypress shades massive specimens of the broad-leaved shrub *nalca,* while at higher altitudes the *coigüe* mixes with the related *lenga.*

Even along the highway, look for the timid *pudú,* no bigger than a border collie, as it emerges from the forest. Foxes, pumas, and Patagonian skunks are also present. The seldom-seen *chucao* is a solitary songbird that, legend says, brings good luck if it sings on your right, but bad luck if it sings on your left. The elegant black-necked swan paddles the fjords and even some lakes.

Sights and Activities

Many points of interest are on or near the Carretera Austral; the best operations base is **Sector Ventisquero,** where Conaf's Centro de Información, 22 kilometers south of Puerto Puyuhuapi via the highway and a short eastbound lateral, marks the start of several dead-end trails. Even the most sedentary can walk the 200-meter **Sendero El Mirador** to a vista point that looks up the valley to the **Ventisquero Colgante,** a hanging glacier that suggests what California's Yosemite Valley must have looked like before the ice melted. The trail winds through rainforest so dark that you nearly need a flashlight at midday, even when the sun shines bright.

Crossing its eponymous river on a suspension bridge, the 600-meter **Sendero Río Guillermo** trail arrives at **Laguna Témpanos** (Iceberg Lake); despite the name, it's iceberg-free. On the turbulent river's north bank, the

as it enters 154,093-hectare Parque Nacional Queulat, which rises from the ocean fjords of Canal Puyuhuapi through nearly impenetrable evergreen forests that, except on a few well-kept trails, deter all but the most resolute hikers. Beneath snowcapped summits, meltwater cascades off hanging indigo glaciers into frigidly limpid rivers that have cut deep canyons en route to the sea.

Queulat's accessibility has made it a popular destination for those exploring the Carretera Austral, but most see only a sample of its attractions. Many visitors come to enjoy the fishing in particular, but Queulat could be a poster child for climate change—as late as 1837, its hanging glacier came within 100 meters of the sea, but that distance is now 7.8 kilometers. Much of this change dates from a 1960 flood.

Geography and Climate

Roughly midway between Chaitén and Coyhaique, Queulat ranges from sea level on Canal Puyuhuapi to the 2,225-meter summit

NORTHERN PATAGONIA

3.5-kilometer **Sendero Ventisquero Colgante** climbs unrelentingly to even more breathtaking views of the hanging glacier. As the afternoon sun warms the atmosphere, ice chunks tumble onto the rocks below.

West of the bridge crossing, on the south bank, the 350-meter **Sendero Interpretativo El Aluvión** loops through part of the valley where the 1960 flood carried huge boulders and flattened tall trees. It's signed in Spanish and pretty good English.

Just beyond Guardería Pudú, the park's southern entrance, the 1.7-kilometer **Sendero Río de las Cascadas** trail winds through dripping rainforest before arriving at a granite amphitheater where ribbons of glacial meltwater mark the river's source. Farther on, where the highway begins to switchback into the Río Queulat Valley, a short staircase trail approaches the **Salto Río Padre García,** a waterfall named for the Chiloé-based Jesuit who, in 1766–1767, may have been the first European to see the area.

Queulat's numerous rivers and lakes, particularly the northern **Lago Risopatrón** and **Lago Rosselot,** are prime fly-fishing destinations.

Accommodations and Food

Accommodations are decentralized, to say the least, but there are options from La Junta in the north to the Río Ventisquero and vicinity in the south. Other nearby accommodations can be found in Puerto Puyuhuapi and La Junta.

Near the main trailheads, Conaf's **Camping Ventisquero** (US$8 for up to 10 persons) has 10 relatively barren sites with sheltered cooking areas and immaculate toilets, but if the shower water were any colder the pipes would freeze. Firewood is available for US$1.50.

On Lago Risopatrón's western shore, 12 kilometers north of Puerto Puyuhuapi, Conaf's 10-site **Camping Angostura** (US$8 for up to six persons) has similar facilities in a humid temperate rainforest with soggy soils.

About 17 kilometers south of Puerto Puyuhuapi and five kilometers north of the Sector Ventisquero turnoff, a garden of technicolor lupines marks **ℂ Hospedaje Las Toninas** (US$15 pp with breakfast and shared bath), a shingled roadside inn where cyclists, campers, and backpackers can sleep cheaply and ingest prodigious plates of fresh crab salad at giveaway prices. Inexpensive campsites are also available.

Thirty kilometers south of Puerto Puyuhuapi, fly-fishing is the focus at **Fiordo Queulat Ecolodge** (tel. 067/233302 in Coyhaique, www.aisen.cl, US$250 s or d with half board), but it has branched out to include other activities such as hiking and sea-kayaking, leaving directly from its own property. Formerly just a cluster of cabañas, it has added a handsome new clubhouse with a fireplace and comfortable common areas, and it has 24-hour electricity from a water-driven turbine. Lunches and dinners cost US$28 each per person.

About half an hour north of Puerto Puyuhuapi on Lago Risopatrón, **ℂ Cabañas El Pangue** (Km 240, tel. 067/325128, www.elpangue.cl, US$62 pp) offers spacious cabins with natural wood, large double beds, and sunken tubs in a woodsy setting; off-season rates are about 40 percent lower. Larger units, sleeping up to seven, cost less on a per-person basis; breakfasts and other meals, including lamb barbecues, are also available. The management also rents canoes, rowboats, motorboats, and horses. A sauna and hot tub are available.

Other Practicalities

At Conaf's new and informative **Centro de Información Ambiental** at Sector Ventisquero, rangers provide guidance on hiking and other activities. Visitors can also consult with rangers at Guardería Pudú (the park's southern entrance) and Guardería El Pangue (northern entrance).

Conaf collects a US$5 admission charge (US$1.50 for children) at Sector Ventisquero only.

Buses from Coyhaique to Puerto Puyuhuapi and Chaitén pass directly through the park, though they drop passengers at least half an hour's walk west of Sector Ventisquero.

PUERTO PUYUHUAPI

Thanks to its history as a pioneer port established by Sudeten German immigrants in the 1930s, Puerto Puyuhuapi has a greater air of permanence than any other Carretera Austral settlement between Coyhaique, 225 kilometers to the south, and Chaitén, 195 kilometers to the north. Many of its streets, residents, and businesses still bear names like Hopperdietzel, Grosse, Ludwig, Rossbach, and Übel.

At the north end of Seno Ventisquero, a sheltered extension of the larger Canal Puyuhuapi, Puerto Puyuhuapi (population 505) is also a gateway to Parque Nacional Queulat and the hot-springs resort of Termas de Puyuhuapi.

Alfombras de Puyuhuapi

Since its 1940 founding by textile engineer Walter Hopperdietzel, Alfombras de Puyuhuapi has produced handmade woolen carpets, tinted with Swiss dyes, for both local and export markets. Some sell for upwards of $1,000, but there are smaller, more affordable pieces as well. Most of the 20 employees are female weavers from Chiloé. The benchmark price is about US$150 per square meter.

© WAYNE BERNHARDSON

typical carpet at Alfombras de Puyuhuapi, Puerto Puyuhuapi

The factory is open for tours 8:30 A.M.–noon and 3–7 P.M. Monday–Friday; admission is free. The sales office keeps identical hours but is also open 9:30 A.M.–noon Saturday.

For more information, contact Alfombras de Puyuhuapi (Ernesto Ludwig s/n, tel. 067/325131, www.puyuhuapi.com).

Termas Ventisquero de Puyuhuapi

Six kilometers south of town, nestled between the road and the shoreline, Ventisquero de Puyuhuapi (tel. 067/325228, 9 A.M.–11 P.M. daily) is an upstart hot-springs center with outdoor pools suitable for a hot soak and, for the more daring, a plunge into the sea. Thanks to its accessibility, Ventisquero is drawing visitors who otherwise might spend the day at upscale Puyuhuapi Lodge & Spa (reached only by boat).

Ventisquero de Puyuhuapi charges US$23 per person for use of the baths. Upstairs, it has a handsome café that prepares espresso, quality teas, sandwiches, and kuchen.

Accommodations and Food

Residencial Elizabeth (Circunvalación s/n, tel. 067/325106, US$7–10 pp for B&B) also serves lunch and dinner. After being closed for many years, the classic **La Casona** (Avenida Otto Übel 1, tel. 067/325221, US$17 pp) is once again open to the public. Set among delightful gardens, **Hostería Alemana** (Av. Übel 450, tel. 067/325118, US$17 pp, US$45 d) is good enough but otherwise lacks charm.

Now open all year, with exceptional management, tobacco-free (**Casa Ludwig** (Av. Übel 850, tel./fax 067/325220, www.casaludwig.cl, US$21 s, US$22–48 s, US$31–67 d) is a 10-room bed-and-breakfast in a cavernous four-story landmark house. Attic rooms with shared baths are cheaper than the downstairs rooms (some of which have sea views) but are still comfy and cozy, and the breakfast is excellent. English and German are spoken; the sitting room has a German-language library with a few English titles.

If you wish to venture from hotel dining

rooms, salmon dinners and kuchen are served with inconsistent quality at **Café Rossbach** (Ernesto Ludwig s/n), alongside the carpet factory.

Information

The privately run **Oficina de Información Turística** (Otto Übel s/n, www.puertopuyuhuapi .cl) is open 10 A.M.–2 P.M. and 3–9 P.M. daily in summer.

Getting There and Around

Because of the volcanic chaos in Chaitén, services are changing rapidly here, but as of early 2009 **Buses Becker** (Übel s/n, tel. 067/325195) and **Buses Daniela** (O'Higgins 39, tel. 067/325130) were passing through here from Coyhaique (US$13) en route to Villa Santa Lucía and Futaleufú.

Starting from Puerto Cisnes, **Buses Entre Verdes** (O'Higgins 39, tel. 067/325130) stops here Monday, Wednesday, and Friday en route to and from La Junta.

❰ PUYUHUAPI LODGE & SPA

South of Puerto Puyuhuapi, sumptuous in style but more affordable than it looks, Puyuhuapi Lodge & Spa (Bahía Dorita s/n, tel. 067/325129) is a secluded spa that's not literally an island, but since there's no road and the only access is by launch across the Seno Ventisquero (Glacier Sound), it might as well be. Both hotel guests and day visitors can enjoy naturally heated outdoor pools and hiking trails that veer through the forest understory of dense *quila* (solid bamboo) thickets, *chilco* (firecracker fuchsia), rhubarb-like *nalcas* with leaves the size of umbrellas, and colossal tree ferns.

Hotel guests only, though, have access to spa facilities, including a gym, heated indoor pool, and massage room (perched in a tower, it enjoys 360-degree views of its scenic surroundings). When the weather lifts, the panorama is Queulat's Andean front range, where snow lingers even at summer's end.

Spacious waterfront rooms, stocked with genteel touches like terrycloth robes and individual umbrellas, look onto the dock where the catamaran *Patagonia Express* starts its weekly run to Parque Nacional Laguna San Rafael, on the final day of package holidays that range from four days and three nights to six days and five nights. Activities like hiking, fly-fishing, and excursions along the Carretera Austral are additional.

While the hotel works mainly with packages, overnight accommodations are possible on a space-available basis, normally Thursday and Friday only. In peak season (Christmas–mid-March), rates start at US$118 s or d with buffet breakfast; the rest of the year, they're about 20 percent lower. Spa access costs US$13 per person more. Fixed-price lunches and dinners from the recently remodeled kitchen and dining room, which include salmon from the lodge's own hatchery, cost US$27, while deluxe buffet dinners cost US$32.

While it sounds exclusive, Puyuhuapi also lets the riffraff in for day use of the outdoor pools and baths (US$17 per adult, US$8 pp per child) and of the spa (US$33 per adult, US$17 per child). The cafeteria at the outdoor pools, open only in daytime, has a cheaper but more limited menu than the restaurant.

Launches from its mainland information center on the Carretera Austral, 14 kilometers south of Puerto Puyuhuapi, are free for package guests; otherwise they cost US$8 per adult, US$4 per child round-trip. Scheduled departures from the hotel are at 8:30 A.M., and 1, 5, and 6:30 P.M., returning at 10 A.M. and 5, 5:30, and 7 P.M., but there are occasional unscheduled crossings as well.

Termas de Puyuhuapi's main office is **Patagonia Connection** (Fidel Oteíza 1951, Oficina 1006, Providencia, Santiago, tel. 02/2256489, www.patagonia-connection .com).

LA JUNTA

At the crossroads town of La Junta, new penetration roads proceed west along the Río Palena toward the port of Raúl Marín Balmaceda and east up the Río Figueroa Valley toward the Argentine border. Local businesses, thus, are placing themselves as a "place of encounter" for exploring the "Cuenca de Palena," the Río Palena drainage.

On a broad plain at the confluence of the two rivers, just south of the regional border between Aisén and Los Lagos, La Junta (population about 1,200) is the main access point to **Reserva Nacional Lago Rosselot,** a 12,725-hectare forest reserve whose longitudinal finger lake is known for its fishing.

La Junta gained a measure of notoriety when, in 2001, local authorities erected an unauthorized monument to General Pinochet—still popular with some residents for building the north–south highway. Others, though, find this embarrassing; with a project to widen the highway through town, they may have an excuse to remove it without ruffling feathers—or raising hackles.

Accommodations and Food
Rates at **Residencial Valderas** (Antonio Varas s/n, tel. 067/314105, luslagos@hotmail.com, US$12 pp with shared bath) include breakfast. The elite choice, though, is **(C Hostal Espacio y Tiempo** (Carretera Austral s/n, tel. 067/314141, www.espacioytiempo.cl, US$75 s, US$108 d with breakfast and private bath), where a cordon of conifers encloses the lawns and gardens of a small but appealing roadside inn whose restaurant is also open to the public. It offers fishing and other excursions.

For breakfasts, lunches, and desserts, **Mi Casita de Té** (Carretera Austral and Patricio Lynch, tel. 067/314206) makes an ideal break.

Information
West of the highway, La Junta's summer-only **Oficina de Información Turística** (Antonio Varas s/n, www.cuencadelpalena.cl) is open 10 A.M.–1 P.M. Monday–Saturday, 3–7:30 P.M. Monday–Friday, and 3–5 P.M. Saturday.

Getting There and Around
Like other Carretera Austral villages, La Junta is a regular stop for buses en route between Coyhaique and continental Chiloé. **Entre Verdes** (Antonio Varas s/n, tel. 067/314725)

goes to Puerto Cisnes at 7 A.M. Monday and Friday. Monday and Wednesday at 6 A.M., **Transportes Altamirano** (Moraleda 13, tel. 067/314143) goes to Futaleufú and on to Puerto Montt (US$37, 13 hours) via Argentina.

LAGO YELCHO
About 30 kilometers north of La Junta, where the highway bridges the Río Palena, lies the boundary between Region XI (Aisén) and Region X (Los Lagos). Los Lagos's first major attraction is elongated Lago Yelcho, stretching from Puerto Cárdenas in the north to Puerto Ramírez in the southeast, which formed the lacustrine part of the highway between Chaitén and Futaleufú until the overland route eliminated the need for ferries. Kayakers, though, can still paddle from Puerto Ramírez to Puerto Cárdenas and even to the Pacific.

At **Villa Santa Lucía,** 70 kilometers north of La Junta and 78 kilometers south of Chaitén, the main highway continues north but the eastbound lateral Ruta 235 drops steeply to the lakeshore and **Puerto Ramírez,** continuing southeast toward Palena and a minor border crossing. The alternative Ruta 231 proceeds northeast toward the white-water-rafting and kayaking capital of Futaleufú and a far more efficient crossing.

Midway between Villa Santa Lucía and Puerto Cárdenas, on the west side of the Carretera Austral, the north side of the **Puente Ventisquero** (Glacier Bridge) is the trailhead for a two-hour hike through soggy evergreen forest to the **Ventisquero Cavi,** a hanging glacier. **Camping Ventisquero** (www.ventisqueroyelcho.cl) is a no-frills facility with a token per-person charge. It also operates a summer café, with sandwiches and fresh fruit kuchen.

Across the highway from the Ventisquero Cavi, the lakeside **Hotel Yelcho en la Patagonia** (tel. 065/731337, www.yelcho.cl, US$122 s, US$135 d) is a fashionable fishing lodge whose comfortable upstairs rooms offer lake views through groves of *arrayanes;* the ground-level bar/restaurant has high-beamed ceilings and decent-enough food for a place that specializes in fly-fishing holidays. On the same grounds, it also has 15 campsites (US$44 for up to four persons) with electricity, roofed shelters, and hot showers.

At the north end, where Lago Yelcho becomes the Río Yelcho, the 250-meter suspension bridge that crosses the river at **Puerto Cárdenas** was the first of its kind in Chile. In summer only, there are two simple places to stay, both reachable by the same message number (tel. 065/264429): **Hospedaje Lulú** and the rather better **Residencial Lago Yelcho.** New cabañas are going up as well.

⟨ FUTALEUFÚ

With its reputation for world-class white-water rafting—some say it's *the* best—Futaleufú draws outdoor recreationists like a magnet. But what works for this tidy village, its forested mountains, and its namesake river—spectacular natural beauty, cleanliness, and isolation—also works against it. The 1,153 people here may be on borrowed time, possibly powerless to fend off Endesa, the powerful Spanish electric utility company that wants to build three massive dams where at least three international rafting and kayaking enterprises have elaborate summer camps and several Chilean operators spend at least part of the season. More recent threats have been a gold mine in the upper reaches of the Río Espolón drainage, and the 2008 eruption of Volcán Chaitén, which left substantial amounts of ash in and around the town.

As of 2009, though, the "Fu" remains one of the world's cleanest and most challenging rivers. Both foreign and Chilean operators hope to kindle local and national enthusiasm for preserving the river and its surroundings, and the March 2000 Whitewater Challenge World Championships brought rafters and kayakers from 14 different countries. Fly-fishing has also had a substantial impact on the economy.

Orientation

Only eight kilometers west of the Argentine border, at the confluence of the Río Espolón and the Río Futaleufú, the village is 155 kilometers southeast of Chaitén via the Carretera Austral, Ruta 235 from Villa Santa Lucia, and Ruta 231 from Puerto Ramírez.

Futaleufú's plan is a rectangular grid whose focus, if not its precise center, is the manicured Plaza de Armas. On the plaza's south side, Bernardo O'Higgins leads east toward the Argentine border, while Arturo Prat, on the west side, leads south toward westbound Ruta 231.

Recreation

White water is the major attraction, but hiking, climbing, mountain biking, and horseback riding are also grabbing attention. Several U.S. **rafting/kayaking** operators maintain summer camps in the vicinity October–April.

The Class III Espolón is a good starter river, though the 2008 eruption of volcanic Chaitén has affected it more than any other river here. Even parts of the Fu are suitable for those with limited experience, but rapids like the Class V Terminator can be a challenge even for professionals.

According to former U.S. Olympic kayaker Chris Spelius, who runs a camp here, "Big water can be forgiving to a certain extent, but this river's so big that it can take a normal human being with a life jacket and hold him under water longer than he can hold his breath." Even on commercially rafted Class IV stretches there are "Death Spots" that need a professional guide to be avoided. According to Lawrence Alvarez, another U.S. operator, about 10 percent of Fu rafters become "swimmers" at some point.

A leisurely float or a Class III raft descent on the Espolón costs about US$35 per person. For a half-day Class IV descent on the Fu, figure about US$75 per person; a full-day Class IV–V experience costs about US$100. The former involves descent of the river "between the bridges," a nonstop succession of Class III–IV rapids; novices get out before tackling the Class V Casa de Piedra rapid.

For **hikers,** one of the best trails follows the Fu's south bank, starting on an undulating oxcart road opposite the Expediciones Chile camp about 10 kilometers west of town; ask for directions at **Expediciones Chile** (Gabriela Mistral 296, tel. 065/721386). The trail continues past peasant homesteads above rapids like the Terminator before continuing through southern beech forest so dense that in midafternoon on a sunny day, it's as dark as dusk. The trail eventually emerges onto a terrace with new trophy houses; a nearby bridge recrosses the river to Ruta 231.

For river rafting and other activities, drop-in visitors can try local operators and offices including **Austral Excursiones** (Hermanos Carrera 500, tel. 065/721239), which specializes in floats and rafting on the Espolón; **Cara del Indio** (Arturo Prat s/n, tel. 02/1964239, www.caradelindio.cl), which has a camp and cabañas on the Fu 35 kilometers west of town; **Futaleufú Explore** (O'Higgins 772, tel. 045/450286 in Pucón, www.futaleufu-explore.com), which concentrates on the Río Futaleufú; and **Expediciones Chile** (Gabriela Mistral 296, tel. 065/721386, www.exchile .com), which does both rivers.

For **horseback riding,** contact **Rancho las Ruedas** (Piloto Carmona 337, tel. 065/721294), in the woods at the north end of Arturo Prat.

Accommodations

Futaleufú has more and better accommodations than any other place its size on or along the Carretera Austral; most are utilitarian, but several have both character and style.

Just south of town on Ruta 231, prior to crossing the bridge over the river, **Camping Puerto Espolón** (US$10 per tent) has shady sites with grass, clean toilets, and hot showers.

Affordable accommodations with breakfast and shared baths include **Residencial Carahue** (O'Higgins 332, tel. 065/721221, US$8 pp) and **Hotel Continental** (Balmaceda 595, tel. 065/721222, US$12 pp). WiFi-equipped **Hospedaje Adolfo** (O'Higgins 302, tel. 065/721256, US$12 pp shared bath,

US$15 pp private bath) is a step above the others, though some rooms have low ceilings. **Posada Ely** (Balmaceda 409, tel. 065/721205, US$20 pp with breakfast) has rooms with private baths.

Hostería Río Grande (O'Higgins 397, tel. 065/721320, US$50 s, US$83 d, www.exchile .cl) primarily handles Expediciones Chile clients but will take drop-ins on a space-available basis; contact the Expediciones Chile office (Gabriela Mistral 296, tel. 065/721386). It has pleasant common areas, a bar/restaurant, and a dozen simple, tastefully decorated rooms with twin beds.

Rooms at rustically styled, family-run **Hotel El Barranco** (O'Higgins 172, tel. 065/721314, www.elbarrancochile.cl, US$101 s, US$112 d with breakfast) look into lush woods. While attractive enough, it's overpriced for this market.

Food

Like the accommodations, the food is a bit better than in most other towns of Futaleufú's size, though Chilean standards like beef, chicken, and sandwiches are the rule. In addition to Hostería Río Grande's dining room, choices include **El Encuentro** (O'Higgins 633, tel. 065/721247, lunch and dinner daily), **Escorpio** (Gabriela Mistral 255, tel. 065/721228, lunch and dinner daily), and the rather bland **Futaleufú** (Pedro Aguirre Cerda 407, tel. 065/721295, lunch and dinner daily).

Sur Andes (Aguirre Cerda 308, tel. 065/721405, lunch and dinner daily) has varied espresso drinks, rich desserts, and homemade chocolates. Though overbuilt for a burg of Futa's size, the ambitious **(Martín Pescador** (Balmaceda 603, tel. 065/721279, lunch and dinner daily) offers a cozy living-room style atmosphere for an aperitif, good salmon, and a small English-language library (not a book exchange).

Information and Services

Futaleufú's **Oficina de Turismo Municipal** (O'Higgins 536, tel. 065/721241, www .futaleufu.cl, 9 A.M.–9 P.M. daily Dec.–Mar.)

is on the south side of the Plaza de Armas. **Sernatur** (Sargento Aldea s/n, tel. 061/731082) also has a local representative, but he's often out in the field.

For visitors arriving from or bound for Argentina, the border is open 8 A.M.–8 P.M. daily.

Banco del Estado (O'Higgins and Manuel Rodríguez) is the only place to change money. Bring cash to Futa, as there's no ATM, cashing travelers checks for services is complicated and expensive, and few places accept credit cards.

Telefónica del Sur (Balmaceda 419) has long-distance telephone service, while **Hostería Río Grande** (O'Higgins 397) and several other places have Internet access.

Señora Vicky (Sargento Aldea 273, tel. 067/721276) does the washing.

Getting There and Around

Since the eruption of Volcán Chaitén, services to and from Futaleufú via Argentina are more abundant, but subject to abrupt changes. There is no bus terminal, and companies will either pick you up or tell you where to wait, especially as services often begin in La Junta.

Transporte Cordillera (O'Higgins 234, tel. 067/721248) shuttles passengers to the border, eight kilometers east, for connections to the Argentine towns of Trevelin and Esquel. Departures are at 8:45 A.M. and 6:15 P.M. Monday, Wednesday, and Friday.

Several companies now operate between Futaleufú and Puerto Montt (US$37, 11 hours) via Argentina: **Transportes Altamirano** (tel. 065/721360) Monday and Wednesday, **Buses Transaustral** (tel. 065/714319), **Ferival** (tel. 065/721426), and **Lago Espolón** (tel. 065/721215).

Buses Daniela (tel. 065/721360) has been connecting Futaleufú with Coyhaique (US$33) and intermediates Wednesday and Sunday at 8 A.M.

PALENA

From the Puerto Ramírez junction, where Ruta 231 leads northeast toward Futaleufú, Ruta 235 veers southeast to the hamlet of Palena, which is less frequented but no less scenic. While lacking Futaleufú's critical mass of services, it compensates with a pastoral integrity that manifests itself in events like late January's rodeo. It also provides an alternative route into Argentina.

In the namesake river valley, Palena is 43 kilometers southeast of Puerto Ramírez and five kilometers east of Argentina's Carrenleufú border post. The Carabineros, who manage the Chilean crossing, can be agonizingly slow.

Palena has a pair of simple, affordable accommodations almost side by side: **Hospedaje La Chilenita** (Pudeto 681, tel. 065/741212, US$12 pp with breakfast) and **Hospedaje El Passo** (Pudeto 661, tel. 065/741226, US$12–14 pp with breakfast), which has some rooms with private baths. Both also serve meals, as does **Café Los Pioneros** (Pérez Rosales 663, tel. 065/741262).

Palena's **Oficina de Información Turística** (O'Higgins 740, tel. 065/741217, tur-muni@entelchile.net) keeps long hours in summer only.

Buses Río Palena (Pedro Montt 853, tel. 065/741319) connects to Chaitén (US$13, four hours) via Villa Santa Lucía, Monday, Wednesday, and Friday at 8 A.M., connecting with ferry arrivals and departures.

CHAITÉN

Between the snowy volcanic cones of Michinmahuida and Corcovado, the modest port of Chaitén has been the main gateway to continental Chiloé. Receiving regular ferries and occasional catamarans from Puerto Montt and insular Chiloé, it's the starting point for many trips down the Carretera Austral and the year-round access point for Parque Natural Pumalín, U.S. entrepreneur Douglas Tompkins's controversial conservation initiative.

In May 2008, though, a nearby volcanic eruption and subsequent flooding forced the evacuation of the port of Chaitén and the downwind village of Futaleufú, Chile's whitewater kayaking and rafting capital, where several inches of ash fell.

As of early 2009, ferries were arriving here,

but other services, including accommodations and food, were limited. The Chilean government has been attempting to buy out the remaining residents and relocate the settlement in a less vulnerable location, but has met resistance from a handful of holdouts. Before traveling along the northernmost Carretera Austral, readers should inquire locally and look for updates at the author's blog (www.southernconetravel.com).

Orientation

Chaitén is 46 kilometers north of Puerto Cárdenas by a Carretera Austral segment that is paved almost to Termas de Amarillo, and 56 kilometers south of Caleta Gonzalo, a summer-only ferry port that's also the headquarters of Parque Pumalín.

Accommodations and Food

Because of the eruption, accommodations and food service are truly precarious, with water and electricity supplies uncertain. Nevertheless, in early 2009, several accommodations remained opened and offered meals to their guests. It is unlikely that the settlement will continue where it is, and that services such as Hotel Schilling and Cabañas Pudú will continue.

Getting There and Around

Chaitén has sea links with Puerto Montt and Chiloé, and roads south to Futaleufú and Coyhaique and north to Caleta Gonzalo. After the 2008 eruption, though, services were in flux, and included a summer connection to Hornopirén.

Chaitén's ferry dock is a short distance northwest of town via the Costanera. **Naviera Austral** (www.navieraustral.cl) normally sails twice weekly to Quellón, and three times weekly to Puerto Montt (nine hours) with the vehicle ferries *Don Baldo* or *Mailén*. Fares range from US$27 per person for fixed seats to US$34 per person for reclining seats and US$48 for bunks. Vehicle rates are US$137 for passenger vehicles and small trucks, and US$35 per linear meter for other vehicles;

bicycles cost US$15 and motorcycles US$30. Rates to Quellón are slightly lower.

In January and February only, Naviera Austral normally sails the ferry *Mailén* from Caleta Gonzalo, 56 kilometers north of Chaitén, to the town of Hornopirén, but road damage after the eruption cut this service at least temporarily.

Nearly all buses stop at the main **Terminal de Buses** (O'Higgins 67, tel. 067/731429), but some services are also in flux here. The main destinations are Futaleufú, Coyhaique, and intermediates, but occasional services go north to Caleta Gonzalo (Parque Pumalín). Schedules change frequently; for monthly updates, check the Chaitur website (www.chaitur.com).

When full service resumes, buses to Coyhaique (US$34, 12 hours) are once or twice daily in summer, three or four times weekly the rest of the year, with **Buses Becker** and **Buses Daniela.** Departure time is usually around 9–10 A.M.

When the northbound road reopens, **Chaitur** (O'Higgins 67, tel. 065/731429, cel. 09/7468-5608, www.chaitur.com) and other companies may go to Caleta Gonzalo (US$6, 2 hours), linking up with the Hornopirén ferry.

Transporte Río Palena (tel. 065/741319) goes to and from Palena (US$12, 3.5 hours), connecting with ferries to and from Puerto Montt, Quellón, and Hornopirén (though the latter may disappear when the road to Caleta Gonzalo reopens).

VICINITY OF CHAITÉN

Tourist services in Chaitén are limited, but visitors with their own transportation can still see the sights.

Casa Avión

About 20 kilometers southeast of Chaitén, on the south side of the Carretera Austral, stands one of the region's most offbeat landmarks. In 1974, well before the highway's completion, the Chilean Air Force crashed a DC-3 in the vicinity; unable to fly it out, they salvaged the engine and left the fuselage. Using two oxcarts, farmer Carlos Anabalón hauled it to his roadside property, divided it into three rooms, and lived in the Casa Avión (Airplane House) until the year 2000, when he traded it to a Chaitén policeman for a four-wheel-drive Jeep. At present, though, the interior has been gutted and there are no apparent plans to remodel it.

Termas El Amarillo

At a highway junction about 25 kilometers southeast of Chaitén, a gravel road turns north for five kilometers to the forested, no-frills hot springs of Termas El Amarillo. Admission to the outdoor pools costs US$5 per person; it also has walk-in campsites (US$7 per tent).

◖ PARQUE NATURAL PUMALÍN

In 1991, U.S. businessman Douglas Tompkins and his wife Kristine McDivitt cashed out their equity from the Esprit and Patagonia clothing empires to purchase blocks of temperate rainforest to create the region's largest destination—literally so—in Parque Pumalín, a 317,000-hectare private nature reserve straddling the highway north of Chaitén. Since then, says the *New York Times,* only General Pinochet's name has appeared more in the Chilean press than Tompkins, who's even received death threats from ultranationalists who accuse him of trying to split the country in half. Tompkins has many Chilean supporters, though, and most criticisms are far less extreme.

Tompkins has allayed much of that criticism by building trails, cabins, campgrounds, and a restaurant and visitors center that have lured visitors from Chaitén to the summer ferry port of Caleta Gonzalo, on the Reñihué fjord, and other points along the highway and the park's extensive shoreline. In late 2004, at a ceremony in Santiago, Pumalín finally received formal legal recognition from President Ricardo Lagos's government. Recently, though, a plan to reroute the Carretera Austral and run a 2,300-km power line from a proposed hydroelectric project in southern Aisén to Puerto Montt and farther north has threatened Pumalín's ecological integrity.

Geography and Climate

Pumalín stretches from 42° S, where it's contiguous with Parque Nacional Hornopirén, to nearly 43° S, east of Chaitén in the south. Most visitors, though, see the areas along both sides of the Carretera Austral between Chaitén and Caleta Gonzalo.

Elevations range from sea level to snow-capped 2,404-meter Volcán Michinmahuida, in the park's southernmost sector, but even these statistics are misleading—the topography rises so steeply in some areas that trails require ladders rather than switchbacks.

Pumalín wouldn't look like it does without rain—lots of rain. While there are no reliable statistics, probably more than 4,000 millimeters of rain falls every year. At higher elevations, of course, it accumulates as snow.

Flora and Fauna

Pumalín takes its name from the puma or mountain lion, but the main reason for its creation was to protect the temperate southern rainforest, whose single most significant species is the *alerce* (false larch). There are also several species of southern beech, not to mention numerous other rainforest species common to southern Chile.

In addition to the puma, the *pudú* inhabits the sopping woodlands, while foxes prowl along the shoreline and other open areas. Southern sea lions inhabit headlands and rookeries, stealing salmon from the fish farms that float just beyond the park boundaries—and placing themselves at risk from the powerful companies that bring in much of the region's income.

Hikers here and in other parts of the southern rainforests should watch for tiny *sanguijuelas* (leeches), which can work their way into boots and trousers (some leeches are used for medical purposes in Chile).

Sights and Activities

Because of the eruption of Volcán Chaitén, within the park boundaries, Pumalín was closed for the summer season in 2009. Barring another major event, the park and its roads and trails should reopen in 2010.

THE PUMALÍN SAGA

In the 15 years or so since he bought 17,000 hectares of temperate rainforest on continental Chiloé's Fiordo Reñihué, Californian **Douglas Tompkins** has become the gringo Chile knows best – or at least the one many Chileans think they know best. During that time, as Tompkins acquired a total of about 360,000 hectares in southernmost Region X (Los Lagos), his name appeared constantly in the Chilean press.

One of Chile's largest landholders, Tompkins is a polarizing figure, but not in the usual sense. Objections to large landholdings usually come from the political left, which fought to redistribute *latifundios* to peasants until the 1973 coup. The right, by contrast, upheld the private property status quo, and their position seemingly triumphed after 1973.

Tompkins, founder of the Esprit clothing empire, turned conventional Chilean politics on its head. Taking advantage of openness toward foreign investors, he used the proceeds from selling Esprit to consolidate undeveloped properties not for profit, but for preservation. As other entrepreneurs were clear-cutting native forest and replanting with fast-growing exotics to turn a quick profit, Tompkins formed a Chilean trust to turn his lands into a private *santuario de la naturaleza* (nature sanctuary).

Tompkins expected that his Proyecto Pumalín, in a thinly populated and once-inaccessible area south of Hornopirén and north of Chaitén, would make him a hero. In fact it did – among the small but growing Chilean environmental movement for whom forest preservation was a hot-button issue, and who distrusted the growing power of multinationals. For them, the millionaire capitalist who believed in philanthropy and biodiversity was a real, if improbable, hero.

On the other hand, Tompkins's actions aroused the distrust and hostility of conservative sectors with whom, economically at least,

he would seem to have much in common. He ran afoul of business, military, and religious interests, all with different but overlapping objections for opposing the project.

Tompkins has many local and national supporters, though. Both Christian Democrat deputy Gabriel Ascensio, of Chiloé, and PPD deputy Leopoldo Sánchez, of Chaitén, favored the park and its tourist potential. PPD deputy Guido Girardi, an outspoken conservationist, said that opposition to Pumalín was a combination of "extreme nationalism" and lobbying by forestry companies. The Lagos administration was supportive, though, and on August 19, 2005, it granted final approval to convert Pumalín into a natural sanctuary administered by a seven-member, all-Chilean board of directors.

Even some of Tompkins's supporters agree his actions have not been so transparent as they might have been – his earliest purchases, in particular, seemed almost surreptitious. As the project has developed, though, public access has improved through hiking trails, campgrounds, cabañas, a very good restaurant, and a visitors center, not to mention small-scale sustainable agriculture experiments and other features to benefit the small local population.

So successful has Pumalín been that, in 2005, center-right businessman Sebastián Piñera – a good bet to be Chile's next president – followed Tompkins's model in creating **Parque Tantauco** (www.parquetantauco.cl) through his own Fundación Futuro. At the southern tip of the Isla Grande de Chiloé, Tantauco has limited access, but this should improve in the coming years.

For more details on Pumalín in Chile, contact **Parque Pumalín** (Klenner 299, Puerto Varas, tel. 065/250079 or 065/251911, www.parquepumalin.cl); in the U.S., contact the Foundation for Deep Ecology (Building 1062, Fort Cronkhite, Sausalito, CA 94965, tel. 415/229-9339, www.deepecology.org).

From a trailhead near Café Caleta Gonzalo, the **Sendero Cascadas** climbs and winds through thick rainforest to a high falls; figure about 1.5 hours each way. At the Centro de Información, it's possible to arrange a tour of

the apiaries at **Fundo Pillán,** across the Fiordo de Reñihué, and to obtain fishing licenses.

From a trailhead about 12 kilometers south of Caleta Gonzalo, west of the highway, the **Sendero Laguna Tronador** crosses a *pasarela* (hanging bridge) before ascending a string of slippery stepladders to the **Mirador Michinmahuida,** a platform where, on clear days, there are astounding views of the volcano's wintry summit. The trail continues through nearly pristine forest, dropping gradually to the amphitheater lake where Tompkins's employees have built a stylish two-site campground with picnic tables, a deck, and an outhouse. It's about 1.5 hours to or from the trailhead.

A short distance farther south, on the highway's east side, **Sendero los Alerces** crosses the Río Blanco to a large *alerce* grove. Just a little farther south on the west side, the **Sendero Cascadas Escondidas** is longer and more strenuous than the signposted three hours would suggest. It's mostly boardwalk—through the swampy, soggy forest—and catwalk along precipitous rock walls, with some steep stepladders as well. The hardest part, though, is boulder-hopping the river on slippery granite or, better and perhaps safer, wading across. On the other side, the trail climbs steeply another 15–20 minutes, then drops into a narrow canyon where, on a dangerous-looking stepladder anchored by a rope, the bravest hikers can continue around the rock to get the best view of the "hidden" falls.

Seventeen kilometers south of Caleta Gonzalo, at its namesake campground, **Sendero Lago Negro** leads 800 meters through dense forest to reed-lined Lago Negro. Just north of the park entrance on the Chaitén–Caleta Gonzalo road, the **Sendero de Interpretación** is a 1.8-kilometer walk in the woods starting from the Volcán ranger station, which provides an explanatory map.

From Chaitén, it's now relatively easy to reach the southern **Sendero Ventisquero Amarillo,** via an eight-kilometer northbound road at the highway's junction of the turnoff to Termas El Amarillo. The hike itself is a full-day excursion from road's end and involves fording the Río Amarillo.

Organized Tours

Al Sur Expediciones (Aconcagua 8, Puerto Varas, tel./fax 065/232300, www .alsurexpeditions.com) arranges activity-oriented excursions—hiking, sea kayaking, and sailing—throughout the park.

Chiloé-based **Austral Adventures** (Avenida Costanera 904, Ancud, tel./fax 065/625977, www.austral-adventures.com) offers customized cruises on the 15-meter motor vessel *Cahuella.*

Accommodations and Food

At Caleta Gonzalo, the walk-in **Camping Río Gonzalo** (US$3 pp) has forested sites with fire pits (firewood is for sale), clean toilets, and cold showers. There's a separate large shelter for cooking. Those without tents can rent one of three *fogones* (US$10), roofed shelters with fire pits normally reserved for picnickers during the daytime; *fogón* No. 3 has wide benches that can sleep three tentless campers comfortably, presuming they have their own sleeping pads.

Fourteen kilometers south of Caleta Gonzalo, **Auto-Camping Cascadas Escondidas** has four drive-in sites (US$10) with clean toilets, cold showers, and roofed decks for pitching tents and eating without having to sit on soggy ground.

Seventeen kilometers south of Caleta Gonzalo, **Camping Lago Negro** (US$3 pp, US$10 per roofed site) resembles Cascadas Escondidas, with four roofed sites and an open tent-camping area. Accessible by an 800-meter footpath, **Camping Punta del Lago** has two lakeside sites. Three kilometers farther south, **Camping Lago Blanco** (US$10) resembles Camping Lago Negro, with half a dozen roofed sites. Slightly beyond, near the park entrance, **Camping El Volcán** (US$3 pp, US$10 per roofed site) has a small store at the ranger station.

Tompkins's nine stylish ⦗ **Cabañas Caleta Gonzalo** (tel. 065/250079 in Puerto Varas, info@ parquepumalin.cl, US$92 s, US$117 d) accommodate up to six people each. All have private baths and hot water, but no kitchen facilities.

Dignified by a stone fireplace with a copper vent, the airy tobacco-free ⦗ **Café Caleta Gonzalo** (near the ferry port, 7:30 A.M.–11:30 P.M. daily) has the only menu in Chile with a culinary exhortation from celebrity foodie Alice Waters, thanks to its quality organic fruit, vegetables, dairy products, meat, and seafood. The breakfast (US$7) really shines with homemade bread, local honey, butter, and cheese; there's also a sandwich menu and juices. Four-course lunches or dinners, with fresh bread, cost around US$12.

Information

At Caleta Gonzalo, Pumalín's **Centro de Visitantes** (tel. 1712/1964151) distributes brochures, provides information, and displays informational panels with large black-and-white photographs of the park; it also sells books, maps, film, park products like organic honey and jam, and local crafts. If it's not open, café personnel can unlock it on request.

Pumalín maintains additional **information** offices in Puerto Varas (Klenner 299, tel. 065/250079, info@parquepumalin.cl); and in the United States (The Conservation Land Trust, Building 1062, Fort Cronkhite, Sausalito, CA 94965, tel. 415/229-9339, www.theconservationlandtrust.org).

Pumalín also has a detailed website (www.parquepumalin.cl, in Spanish and English) and publishes the monthly magazine *Puma Verde*.

Getting There

In January and February only, one of **Naviera Austral's** two ferries *Mailén* or *Pincoya* sails daily to Hornopirén (six hours) at 4 A.M.; vehicle reservations are advisable. Passengers pay US$25 per person, while cyclists pay an extra US$12 and motorcyclists US$23. Automobiles and light trucks pay US$117, while larger vehicles pay US$28 per lineal meter.

The Southern Carretera Austral

Even more thinly settled than north of Coyhaique, southern Aisén is wild country, with few and scattered services; barely 10,000 people live in nearly 46,000 square kilometers. The only towns with more than a thousand residents are Chile Chico, near the Argentine border on Lago General Carrera, and Cochrane, directly on the Carretera Austral.

The highway is now paved to Villa Cerro Castillo, 98 kilometers south of Coyhaique, as is the Puerto Ibáñez lateral. In late 1999, it finally reached its terminus at Villa O'Higgins, though the last 100 kilometers still requires a ferry shuttle from Puerto Yungay to Río Bravo.

◖ RESERVA NACIONAL CERRO CASTILLO

Straddling the Carretera Austral beyond the Balmaceda turnoff, marking the divide between the Río Simpson and Río Ibáñez drainages, Cerro Castillo is a 179,550-hectare unit whose map boundaries look like jigsaw puzzle pieces. Its signature landmark is Cerro Castillo itself, whose soaring basaltic battlements, above the tree line, truly resemble a medieval castle.

Elevations range from about 500 meters to Cerro Castillo's 2,320-meter summit, embellished by three south-facing glaciers. Like most of the region, it gets substantial rainfall and snow at higher altitudes, but some east-facing areas enjoy a rain-shadow effect.

Nearly pure stands of the southern beech *lenga* dominate the forest landscape up to about 1,200 meters, along with the related *coigüe, ñire,* and many shrubs. Steppe-like grasslands typify the rain shadow areas.

Mammals include the puma, *huemul,* two fox species, and skunks. Birds are common, including the Andean condor, various owls, the *tordo* (austral blackbird), and the *cachaña* (austral parakeet).

Sights and Activities

About eight kilometers south of Laguna Chiguay, a faint westbound road from a crumbling construction camp is the starting point for **Sendero Las Horquetas,** a

© WAYNE BERNHARDSON

NORTHERN PATAGONIA

Reserva Nacional Cerro Castillo is increasingly popular with Patagonia-bound hikers.

four-day backpacking trail that climbs the Estero la Lima Valley to pass beneath the spires of Cerro Castillo before descending to the roadside village of Villa Cerro Castillo. This is easier from the north than from the south, where the approach is steeper and more rugged.

Practicalities
At the reserve's northeastern edge, Conaf's woodsy **Camping Laguna Chiguay** (Km 67, US$6 per site) is just west of the highway. At the southern approach, there are simple accommodations at Villa Cerro Castillo, just outside the reserve boundary.

Conaf maintains a ranger station on the highway opposite the Laguna Chiguay campground.

All public transportation between Coyhaique, to the north, and Puerto Ibáñez and Villa Cerro Castillo to the south, passes through the reserve's northern sector.

PUERTO INGENIERO IBÁÑEZ
Prior to the Carretera Austral's completion, Puerto Ibáñez was a major lake port, connecting Coyhaique with Chile Chico and other settlements on Lago General Carrera's south shore. Its current livelihood derives from agriculture, both livestock and tree fruit like apples and pears.

Since completion of the highway bypass, it's lost economic clout, but the ferry from here to Chile Chico, for an easy border crossing to Argentina, is quicker and cheaper than the roundabout roads. It's about 110 kilometers south of Coyhaique via the Carretera Austral and a paved lateral that bears south about 10 kilometers east of Villa Cerro Castillo. There's also a rugged road but scenic border crossing along the lake's north shore (in Argentina, it's called Lago Buenos Aires).

Accommodations and Food
Lodging is available at simple **Residencial Vientos del Sur** (Dickson 283, tel. 067/423208, US$7 pp). Two blocks north, the similar **Residencial Ibáñez** (Ronchi 04, tel. 067/423227, US$13 pp) also serves meals. The top choice, though, is Swiss-Chilean ◖ **Shehen Aike** (Risopatrón 055, tel. 067/423284, tel. 02/3567064 in Santiago, www.aike.cl, US$58 s or d). In addition to comfortable cabañas, it organizes local activities.

Getting There and Around
Several companies operate minibuses to Coyhaique (US$7, two hours): **Transportes Yamil Alí** (tel. 067/250346), **Darío Figueroa Castro** (cel. 09/8977-9737), and **Minibus Eben Ezer** (tel. 067/423203).

Mar del Sur (Baquedano 146, Coyhaique, tel. 067/231255) sails the ferry *Pilchero* to Chile Chico (two hours) at 10 P.M. Tuesday, Wednesday, and Friday, 11 A.M. Saturday, and 3 P.M. Sunday; schedules are subject to change. Fares are US$8 per adult, US$4 for children. Bicycles pay an additional US$4,

THE ERUPTION OF VOLCÁN HUDSON

In the vicinity of Lago General Carrera, which continues east across the Argentine border as Lago Buenos Aires, travelers can see the results of the August 1991 eruption of the 1,935-meter Volcán Hudson, northwest of Villa Cerro Castillo. Chile's second-largest 20th-century eruption deposited more than one cubic kilometer of ash in Chile, about two cubic kilometers in Argentine Patagonia, and another two cubic kilometers over the South Atlantic; in some areas, the ashfall reached a depth of more than 1.5 meters.

Northwesterly winds carried the ash plume southeast to the Falkland Islands and South Georgia, in the South Atlantic, and eventually as far as Australia. Fierce winds, in excess of 100 kilometers per hour, also remobilized already-fallen ash to cover pasture and watercourses, resulting in the deaths of tens of thousands of cattle and sheep. Today, though, plantlife is slowly recolonizing parts of Aisén's Hudson ashfall.

motorcycles US$9. Passenger vehicles and light trucks pay US$45; larger vehicles pay US$15 per linear meter.

VILLA CERRO CASTILLO

Founded in 1966, under the Frei Montalva administration, the frontier outpost of Villa Cerro Castillo is finally acquiring an air of permanency, though its exposed site makes it one of the Carretera Austral's bleaker settlements. Just south of here, 89 kilometers from Coyhaique, the pavement ends and the gravel begins. Hikers who begin the trek through Reserva Nacional Cerro Castillo at Las Horquetas will exit the reserve here.

Alero de las Manos

Five kilometers south of town, via a lateral off the highway, the positive and negative hands of the pre-Columbian rock art at Alero de las Manos resemble those of the famous Argentine site at Cueva de las Manos. Beneath a volcanic overhang, these paintings differ in that they are fewer, younger (only about 3,000 years old), and include no animals. In some cases, rocks have split from the overhang and fallen to the ground, probably concealing even more images.

Alero de las Manos (admission US$1.50 pp including a guided tour) is open 10 A.M.–6 P.M. daily. There's a small visitors center with clean toilets.

Practicalities

Though improving, accommodations other than inexpensive campgrounds are limited and fill up fast.

Hospedaje La Querencia (O'Higgins 522, tel. 067/411610, US$8.50 pp) has firm beds, good food, and improved bathroom facilities (all of them shared). **Hospedaje Villarrica** (O'Higgins s/n, tel. 067/419500, US$30 d) has upgraded its rooms, runs a cheerful restaurant, and has added cabañas (US$58 d).

Open long hours November–March only, the helpful **Oficina de Información Turística** (O'Higgins s/n, www.rioibanez.cl) provides a town map and list of services.

All leaving around 7 A.M., several **minibus** services connect Cerro Castillo with Coyhaique (US$7, 1.5 hours); all regularly scheduled services between Coyhaique, to the north, and Puerto Río Tranquilo and Cochrane, to the south, pass by the entrance to town.

BAHÍA MURTA AND VICINITY

West of Villa Cerro Castillo, the Carretera Austral climbs above the Río Ibáñez Valley before veering south to Lago General Carrera and the lakeside hamlet of Bahía Murta, one of the best areas to see fall colors. Murta's also the gateway to **Puerto Sánchez,** 23 kilometers south, for boat trips to the **Cavernas** de Mármol, a series of small islands opposite Puerto Río Tranquilo's Capilla de Mármol.

From early November to late March, Murta's **Oficina de Información Turística** (5 de Abril s/n, www.rioibanez.cl) keeps long hours.

Accommodations and Food

There are several simple in-town accommodations, including **Hostería Lago General Carrera** (Av. 5 de Abril 314, US$7 pp) and **Residencial Patagonia** (Pasaje España 64, US$7 pp); the latter has a convenient branch at the highway junction (US$9 pp), with good beds, a small museum, and squeaky floors. All use the same community telephone (tel. 067/419600) and charge around US$3 more for breakfast.

PUERTO RÍO TRANQUILO AND VICINITY

Until the Carretera Austral's completion, Puerto Río Tranquilo was a port with a weekly supply boat from Puerto Ibáñez; today it's a small but steadily growing settlement at Lago General Carrera's west end, 25 kilometers south of Puerto Murta. At the north end of town, a new road toward Bahía Exploradores, an inlet of the larger Estero Capquelán, is being built; eventually, with a boat connection and an hour's hike, you'll reach Laguna San Rafael.

◖ Capilla de Mármol

The area's best excursion is a launch trip to Capilla de Mármol, a string of swirling marble grottos on the shoreline. The 1.5-hour trip costs around US$40 for up to five persons, but it's difficult if winds are high. It's best in late summer or fall, when water levels permit launches to approach more closely and explore more thoroughly.

Ask at Hostal Los Pinos to hire a launch, or contact Pedro Contreras (tel. 067/258168, pedrocmarmol@hotmail.com).

Valle Exploradores

Westbound from Río Tranquilo, a smooth but narrow penetration road will eventually reach the Pacific, but at present it goes only about 60 kilometers, past Lago Bayo and the Glaciar Exploradores, an impressive but receding continental glacier that's scoured the mountainside, leaving lateral and terminal moraines; small icebergs still calve off its face and float down its namesake river.

While the road will eventually reach Parque Nacional Laguna San Rafael, most of the land is private property. **El Puesto** (Km 52, tel. 02/1964555 in Tranquilo) charges US$4 for climbing the trail to its Mirador Exploradores, a 20-minute woodland walk that yields spectacular views from a hilltop deck. More ambitious hikers can arrange for a full-day ice hike (US$50 pp) at Tranquilo or here, if guides are available.

Accommodations and Food

Río Tranquilo has above-average accommodations for a town its size; unless otherwise indicated, all use the same community telephone (tel. 067/419500) for messages.

Two blocks west of the highway, local favorite **Residencial Darka** (Los Arrayanes 330, US$10 pp) has smallish rooms with twin beds and shared baths.

Right on the highway, **Hostería Costanera** (Carretera Austral s/n, tel. 067/411121, US$10 pp) is friendly enough but suffers the shortcomings of many cheap hotels—too many beds in too many rooms. Some rooms are claustrophobically tiny, others spacious; some beds are firm, others sag like hammocks.

Also on the highway, **Hostal Carretera Austral** (Carretera Austral s/n, lopezpinuer@ yahoo.es, US$13 pp) also has cabañas that can work out cheaper for a group. In addition, it has a modest restaurant.

With 10 rooms divided by a corridor, friendly, family-run **Hostal Los Pinos** (Godoy 51, tel. 067/411576, US$15 pp, US$42 s or d) has spotless accommodations with breakfast and either shared or private baths. Low-season prices are about 10–15 percent cheaper. Its restaurant is also above average, serving fixed-price lunches or dinners for US$8–10 in a tobacco-free dining room.

Los Pinos is no longer the best, though, since

© WAYNE BERNHARDSON

Capilla de Mármol (Marble Chapel), Lago General Carrerra

the opening of **Hostal El Puesto** (Pedro Lagos 258, tel. 02/1964555, www.elpuesto.cl, US$92 s or d), which is closer in style to high-priced fishing lodges than to traditional roadside accommodations (actually, it's a couple blocks west of the highway).

In the Valle Exploradores, German-owned **Albergue Campo Alacaluf** (Km 44, www.backpackerschile.com, US$30–40 pp) has four rooms with either shared or private baths in a rustically handsome house with 24-hour electricity from its own water-driven turbine. Rates include breakfast, and other simple home-cooked meals cost US$10.

Information and Getting There

From November to March, there's a helpful **Oficina de Información Turística** (9 A.M.–9 P.M. daily) directly on the highway, across from the gas station.

Scheduled buses between Coyhaique and Cochrane drop and pick up passengers here. Many backpackers try hitching here, which means heavy competition for a handful of rides.

CRUCE EL MAITÉN AND VICINITY

Cruce El Maitén, about 50 kilometers south of Puerto Río Tranquilo at Lago General Carrera's westward outlet, is only a crossroads with the eastbound highway to Puerto Guadal and Chile Chico. Nevertheless, there are important services in the vicinity.

Almost at the junction, **◖ Hacienda Tres Lagos** (Km 274, tel./fax 067/411323, from US$269 s, US$300 d) is one of the highway's best accommodations options. Oriented toward packages of three days or more, its spacious, well-lighted cabañas are appealing enough, but its newer suites, separated from the main building, are even more so. Amenities include WiFi and a sauna, while activities include horseback riding, fishing, and excursions to sights on and off the highway. Its restaurant, **El Parador Austral,** open to the public, has a superb kitchen. In Santiago, contact Hacienda Tres Lagos (Zurich 255, Oficina 24, Las Condes, Santiago tel./fax 02/3334122, www.haciendatreslagos.com).

One kilometer north, **Mallín Colorado** (Km 273, tel. 02/2341843, tel. 02/3609743 in Santiago, www.mallincolorado.cl, US$320 d) has several log-style cabañas with similar amenities. It primarily works with excursion-oriented packages, though.

About 14 kilometers north of the junction, near the handsome suspension bridge at the lake outlet, the **Pasarela Sur Lodge** (Km 260, tel. 067/411425, www.pasarelasurlodge .cl, US$75 s or d) primarily attracts fishing-oriented visitors but can also arrange other activities like rafting, hiking, and horseback riding. It also has a decent restaurant.

PUERTO GUADAL

Another former lake port, at Lago General Carrera's west end, Puerto Guadal is more picturesque than most area towns. It lies 13 kilometers east of El Maitén; from here, a rugged and narrow road leads northeast to Chile Chico and the Argentine border at Los Antiguos.

Puerto Guadal has upgraded its free lakeshore campground. The next cheapest accommodations are **Hostería Huemules** (Las Magnolias 382, tel. 067/411202, US$8.50 pp), which also has a restaurant. **Cabañas Antué** (Los Pinos 456, tel. 067/431215, US$58 for up to five persons) has hot showers, full kitchens, and wood stoves; check in at Supermercado Plaza (Las Camelias 147).

On Guadal's eastern outskirts, the wooded grounds at elegantly simple **◖ Terra Luna** (tel. 067/431263, fax 067/431264, www.terra-luna .cl) enjoy lake panoramas. While the French-run resort specializes in weeklong activities-oriented packages, it also rents "ministudio" accommodations (US$30 s or d in the off-season, US$40 s or d in summer); rooms in the main lodge go for US$80 off-season, US$130 in summer. Breakfast is included, but other meals are extra; the kitchen can do a lot with a little, even on short notice. English and French are spoken; the Santiago contact is Azimut 360 (General Salvo 159, Providencia, tel. 02/2363880, www.azimut360.com).

Other than the Terra Luna, **Café de la**

Frontera (Los Lirios 399, tel. 067/431234, lunch and dinner daily) is the best place for standard Chilean food.

To Chile Chico (US$10), try **Turismo Seguel** (Los Notros 560, tel. 067/431214) Monday and Thursday at 4 P.M. and **Transporte Ale** tel. 067/522242), which passes through here en route from Cochrane. Seguel also goes to Coyhaique (US$15) and intermediates.

CHILE CHICO AND VICINITY

Settled from Argentina in the early 20th century, on Lago General Carrera's south shore, Chile Chico developed in isolation from the rest of Chile, and connections are still better with Argentina. One of the region's easiest border crossings, it also enjoys access to remote protected areas like Reserva Nacional Jeinimeni and is the starting (or finishing) point for the wild rugged highway to or from Puerto Guadal.

Despite brief mining booms, Chile Chico's enduring economic base has been the production of temperate fruits, thanks to its mild lakeshore microclimate. This has not exactly brought prosperity, though—even after the 1952 completion of the first motor road from Coyhaique to Puerto Ibáñez, it remained remote from any sizable market. Ashfall from Volcán Hudson's 1991 eruption depressed fruit production, which has only recently recovered.

Improvements are under way, with many more paved streets, a refurbished Plaza de Armas, and a newly paved road to the border town of Los Antiguos. From Los Antiguos, travelers can make connections to the town of Perito Moreno and the Atlantic-coast city of Caleta Olivia, the northern Argentine Patagonian cities of Esquel and Bariloche, and southern Argentine Patagonian destinations such as El Chaltén and El Calafate.

Motorists may be able to fill the tank more cheaply in Los Antiguos, but Argentine pricing policies have eliminated cheaper diesel for vehicles with foreign license plates; the policy does not extend to gasoline, however.

Orientation

Only five kilometers west of the border, Chile Chico (population 3,042) is 122 kilometers northeast of Cruce El Maitén via the narrow, precipitous road along Lago General Carrera's south shore. Avenida O'Higgins, one block south of the lakeshore, is the main thoroughfare; the central grid extends about 10 blocks east–west, and four blocks north–south. The Plaza de Armas is in the northwest corner of town.

Museo de la Casa de la Cultura

Improved, but still lacking interpretive panels, Chile Chico's museum (O'Higgins and Lautaro, tel. 067/411268, free admission) displays regional painting and sculpture along with paleontological materials, historical artifacts from early colonists, and, connected to the second story by a walkway leading straight to its deck, the restored *Los Andes,* which once ferried passengers and cargo around the lake. Hours are supposedly 10 A.M.–7 P.M. Monday–Saturday, December–March only, but the actual schedule can be erratic.

Reserva Nacional Lago Jeinemeni

South of Chile Chico, a four-wheel-drive-only road parallels the border to Reserva Nacional Lago Jeinemeni, an infrequently visited protected area of 161,000 hectares. There is little infrastructure except a campground (US$6 per tent); Conaf rangers collect US$1.50 admission for adults, US$0.75 for children.

Accommodations

The quantity of accommodations is increasing and their quality is improving, but there are no luxury lodgings. Half a block south of the plaza, **Hospedaje Don Luis** (Balmaceda 175, tel. 067/411384, US$8–21 pp with breakfast) is one of the best values. Traditional budget choice **Hospedaje Brisas del Lago** (Manuel Rodríguez 443, tel. 067/411204, US$12.50 pp) has added cabañas (US$40 s or d).

On quiet grounds about one kilometer east of town, rustic but friendly **Hospedaje No Me Olvides** (Camino Internacional s/n, tel.

098/8338006, US$13 pp) also has camping (US$3.50 pp). In season, it has fresh honey and fruit.

In a distinctive deco-style brick structure, run by an obliging family, **Hotel Plaza** (Balmaceda 102, tel. 067/411215, US$13 pp) has cheerful rooms but no frills (shared bath only, no breakfast). Some interior walls are a bit thin, but the major downside is that one exterior wall adjoins a thunderous Saturday disco (the hotel proprietors are candid about potential noise). On other nights, it's fine.

Hotel Ventura (Carrera 290, tel. 067/411311, US$17 pp with private bath) is good and central. **Hotel Austral** (O'Higgins 501, tel. 067/411815, US$30 s, US$45 d with private bath) is also worth consideration.

On the eastern outskirts, the Belgian-Chilean **◖ Hostería de la Patagonia** (Camino Internacional s/n, tel./fax 067/411337, US$27 s, US$43 d) is an ivy-covered inn with large, rustically decorated but cozy rooms with private baths and breakfast (excellent homemade bread); there's one tiny single with shared bath for US$15 and some slightly larger ones for US$17. Camping and additional meals are available.

Food

There's nothing exceptional, though the dining room at **Hostería de la Patagonia** is pretty good. On the east side of the plaza, **Café Loly y Elizabeth** (González 25, tel. 067/411288) serves reliable breakfasts, sandwiches, and *onces.*

Café Refer (O'Higgins 416, tel. 067/411225, lunch and dinner daily) is a pub/restaurant that serves sandwiches and also specializes in salmon (US$6–7), embellished with a variety of sauces.

Information and Services

The privately run **Oficina de Información Turística** (O'Higgins s/n, tel. 067/411638, www.chilechico.cl) is open 8 A.M.–10 P.M. daily except weekends, when it opens at 10 A.M. For national parks information, contact **Conaf** (Blest Gana 121, tel. 067/411325).

Expediciones Patagonia (O'Higgins 333, tel. 09/8595-7934, www.expeditionspatagonia .com) leads excursions to Jeinemeni and other nearby attractions, rents cars, and posts additional information on the town and vicinity on its website.

Banco del Estado (González 112, 10 A.M.–1 P.M. weekdays only) is slow to change both U.S. cash and travelers checks, but it now has an ATM (MasterCard only).

Correos de Chile (O'Higgins 223) is the post office. **Entel** (O'Higgins 426) provides long-distance telephone and Internet connections. **Conect@t** (O'Higgins 408, Local 3) has Internet service.

Opposite the Copec gas station near the ferry dock, **Lavandería Ayken** (Rodríguez s/n, cel. 09/9575-8134) does the laundry.

Hospital Chile Chico (Lautaro 275, tel. 067/411334) provides medical services.

Getting There and Around

Except for minibus shuttles to Los Antiguos, transportation out of town can be difficult. Bus and boat capacity are limited, so reserve as early as possible.

Minibuses to Los Antiguos (US$4, 30 minutes) leave from in front of Entel long-distance offices (O'Higgins 426); carriers include **Transporte Jaime Acuña** (Augusto Grosse 150, tel. 067/411590) and **Transporte Castillo** (tel. 067/411388), at the passenger pier. There are four or five Monday–Saturday, and only one or two on Sunday.

Transportes Seguel (O'Higgins 394, tel. 067/411443) goes to Puerto Guadal (US$9, three hours) Monday and Thursday at 7 A.M., and continues to Coyhaique and intermediates. **Transportes Ale** (Rosa Amelia 880, tel. 067/411739) goes Wednesday and Saturday at 1:15 P.M. to Puerto Guadal and Cochrane (US$20, six hours).

From new dockside quarters, **Mar del Sur** (Manuel Rodríguez s/n, tel. 067/411864) sells tickets for the vehicle-passenger ferry *Pilchero,* which sails north to Puerto Ibáñez at 8 A.M. Monday, 3 P.M. Tuesday, 1 P.M. Thursday,

and 3 P.M. Friday and Sunday; schedules are subject to change. For fares, see the Puerto Ibáñez entry.

PUERTO BERTRAND AND VICINITY

Separated from Lago General Carrera by a short and narrow channel, Lago Bertrand is the source of the Río Baker, Chile's largest river in terms of its flow. Beautifully sited on the lake's southeastern shore, the village of Puerto Bertrand is a convenient base for exploring the area, though there are several handsome lodges in the vicinity. It is 11 kilometers south of Cruce El Maitén.

Sights and Activities

For water sports—rafting, kayaking, and fly-fishing—the **Río Baker** itself is the big draw. Because it has few rocks and play spots, the Class II and III rapids draw fewer rafters and kayakers than the rugged Futaleufú, but its fast current, huge flow, large waves, and occasional deep holes make it lively enough for beginners. Fly-fishing lodges line the highway south of town, beneath the glistening backdrop of the northern Patagonian ice field.

October–April, Bertrand-based, U.S.-run **Patagonia Adventure Expeditions** (postal address Casilla 8, Cochrane, tel./ fax 067/411330, www.adventurepatagonia .com) arranges adventure excursions in the vicinity; there is also a specialist fly-fishing guide. It no longer does half-day trips down the Baker, but does more more ambitious expeditions such as the 212-kilometer, eight-day descent to the ocean. Its specialty, though, is the Aysén Glacier Trail, a 10-day trek with porters that goes through nearly uncharted territory on the eastern edge of Parque Nacional Laguna San Rafael and ends with a float down the Río Baker to Caleta Tortel.

Meanwhile, based at Hostería Bertrand, **Baker Patagonia Adventure** (Costanera s/n, tel. 067/419900) has taken over the half-day rafting trips on the Baker for US$28 pp.

Practicalities

There are primarily budget accommodations in Bertrand itself and package-oriented fishing lodges in the vicinity; if space is available, lodges will take drop-in guests.

The upstairs front room at **Hostería Bertrand** (Costanera s/n, tel./fax 067/419900, US$13 pp shared bath, US$35 d private bath) has central heating of a sort—the chimney pipe from the 1st-floor woodstove rises directly through the room. Rates include an adequate breakfast, and its restaurant is decent enough for other meals.

Also in town, Argentine-run ◖ **Lodge Río Baker** (tel./fax 067/411499, US$83 s or d) enjoys a stunning riverside location with great fly-fishing possibilities. It has contact numbers in Buenos Aires (tel. 54/11/4863-9373) and Mendoza (tel. 54/261/4202196).

At the highway junction, **Cabañas Campo Baker** (tel./fax 067/411447, campobaker@hotmail.com, US$92 for up to four persons) is a low-key Hare Krishna outpost with an incomprehensible—to carnivorous locals at least—vegetarian restaurant, **Govinda.**

Three kilometers south of town, the **Cabañas Rápidos Río Baker** (tel. 067/411150, www.rapidosdelriobaker.cl, US$100 for up to six persons) is one of several places of its type. It caters primarily to fly-fishing groups but will accommodate passersby on a space-available basis.

Also south of town, the six-room **Patagonia Baker Lodge** (tel. 067/411903, US$108 s, US$133 d with breakfast, slightly more for a larger suite) is a new but sterile riverside facility that stresses fly-fishing. In Santiago, contact Patagonia Baker Lodge (Av. del Parque 5455, D84, Ciudad Empresarial, Huechuraba, tel. 02/7280018, www.pbl.cl).

In summer, the **Red de Turismo Rural Río Baker** (Costanera s/n, tel. 067/419900) operates a Spanish-only information kiosk at the campground entrance, fairly well stocked with brochures.

Buses between Coyhaique and Cochrane, and between Chile Chico and Cochrane, stop at Hostería Bertrand for about 15 minutes.

CRUCE PASO ROBALLOS AND VICINITY

At the confluence of the Río Baker and Río Nef, 15 kilometers south of Puerto Bertrand, the **Cascada Nef Baker** is a thunderous waterfall but, since the highway was rerouted it's no longer visible from the road. Property owner Jonathan Leidich, though, allows free foot access to the river on the condition that people carry out their trash and do not start fires; no camping is allowed. There's clearly signed parking and a trail down to the river.

The highway continues south to Cochrane and Villa O'Higgins, while an eastbound lateral ascends the Río Chacabuco Valley to 647-meter Paso Roballos, the region's most southerly border crossing for motor vehicles (others farther south are for nonmotorized transport only). Across the border, at the bleak crossroads of Bajo Caracoles (where gasoline sometimes runs out), Argentina's dusty Ruta Nacional 40 leads south to El Calafate and Chile's Parque Nacional Torres del Paine.

Between the highway junction and the border, **Estancia Valle Chacabuco** is a large sheep farm recently purchased by conservationist Doug Tompkins and his wife Kris McDivitt, who outbid Chilean interests concerned—or obsessed—with his Patagonian property acquisitions. Tompkins and McDivitt plan to donate the land to Conaf, the state conservation agency, for a national park.

Should Tompkins's plan proceed, Aisén will have a large, nearly unbroken swath of national park and reserve land stretching from Reserva Nacional Jeinemeni, just south of Chile Chico, through the Chacabuco Valley to Reserva Nacional Cochrane. At present, though, the only parts of Valle Chacabuco open to the public are along the highway.

COCHRANE AND VICINITY

Once literally the end of the road, the tidy town of Cochrane may still have more horses than automobiles, but, says one immigrant, "If you park your horse in front of the bar now, you'll get a ticket for shitting on the sidewalk." Tidy

the elusive and endangered huemul

enough for a frontier settlement, thanks to a neatly landscaped Plaza de Armas and broad paved streets, its main appeal lies in the surrounding countryside of **Reserva Nacional Lago Cochrane,** north and northeast of town. If and when Valle Chacabuco achieves protected status, Cochrane could see a major outdoor recreation boom.

Cochrane is still an obligatory stop for southbound wanderers, partly because it's the last accommodations and food for nearly 300 kilometers and partly because it's home to **Casa Melero,** Patagonia's greatest general store. It's *the* place to buy camping gear, canoes, chainsaws, chocolate, fine wines, fishing gear, and almost anything else you can't find between here and Antarctica. Cochrane was also, apparently, the end of the line for the traveling salesman who peddled the lurid red bedspreads to so many cheap hotels.

Orientation

Cochrane (population 2,217) is 345 kilometers south of Coyhaique and 225 kilometers north of Villa O'Higgins. Its core is a rectangular grid that's only about three blocks from north to south but about nine blocks from west to east, where the Río Cochrane marks its limit.

Recent changes have meant inconsistencies in street numbers, but the town is small enough that orientation remains fairly simple.

Reserva Nacional Lago Cochrane

Informally known as Reserva Nacional Tamango, Reserva Nacional Lago Cochrane is most notable as home to the endangered *huemul,* the south Andean deer that appears on Chile's coat of arms. On the north shore of its namesake lake, the 6,925-hectare reserve is six kilometers northwest of Cochrane. Admission at the Guardería Húngaro entrance costs US$5 per adult, US$1.50 per child.

Huemul-watching excursions to the east end of the lake, by launch, cost US$45–70 for up to seven people. While there is no regular public transportation to the reserve, it's close enough that hitching is possible, and even a taxi's not that expensive.

On the Río Cochrane's north bank, Conaf's **Camping Las Correntadas** (US$13) has four sites with picnic tables, wash basins, and fire pits. A four-person cabaña (US$42) has a bathroom and hot shower. For reservations, contact the **Red de Turismo Rural** (tel. 067/522646, gp_tamango@hotmail.com).

Accessible only by a 45-minute boat ride (US$28) or an eight-kilometer hike, Conaf's lakeside **Camping Playa Paleta** has four campsites and three cabañas with baths but without shower. Prices are identical to Las Correntadas.

Accommodations

Residencial El Fogón (San Valentín 651, tel. 067/522240, US$8 pp) has one of Cochrane's better restaurants. The simple **Residencial Cochrane** (Dr. Steffens 451, tel. 067/522377, US$10 pp) also offers camping space (US$4 pp).

A steep rickety staircase leads to six simple rooms with shared baths at **Residencial El Arriero** (San Valentín 750, tel. 067/522137, US$10 pp with an above-average breakfast). The beds are comfortable, the shared baths are tidy and the showers excellent, and some rooms even have balconies, but the doors and floors are creaky. Ask at the downstairs supermarket to see the rooms.

Friendly, family-run **Residencial Paola** (Lago Brown 150, tel. 067/522215, US$10 pp) and **Residencial Cero a Cero** (Lago Brown 464, tel. 067/522158, ceroacero@hotmail.com, US$12–17 pp) are similar.

Rooms vary at **Residencial Sur Austral** (Arturo Prat 334, tel. 067/522150, US$12 pp), but the best are comfortable and spacious. Another budget favorite is family-run **Hostal Latitude 47° Sur** (Lago Brown 564, tel. 067/522280, turislat47sur@hotmail.com, US$13 pp).

Popular with cycling groups, comfortably furnished **Residencial Rubio** (Teniente Merino 871, tel. 067/522173, US$12–20 pp) has spacious, spotless rooms with twin beds, private baths, and breakfast (some cheaper rooms have shared baths).

Across the street from El Arriero, **Residencial Lago Esmeralda** (San Valentín

141, tel. 067/522621, US$12 pp with breakfast) has some legitimate singles, rather than the closet-sized partitions that often pass for singles in the region. The mattresses, though, are getting soft and the shower fixtures in the shared baths can be awkward.

Directly across the street from Cero a Cero, on barren grounds long awaiting landscaping, Spanish-run **❰ Hotel Ultimo Paraíso** (Lago Brown 455, tel./fax 067/522361, US$63 s, US$77 d) is otherwise exceptional, with eight well-heated, spacious, and attractive rooms with private baths. The guests-only restaurant serves lunch and dinner.

Food

Part of its namesake accommodations, **El Fogón** (San Valentín 651, lunch and dinner daily) is no longer the best, but it's still not bad. The name implies a *parrilla*, but the menu is more diverse than that, with fish (including conger eel, hake, and salmon) and fowl, in the US$7–10 range. The specialty, though, is the so-called *doble infarto* (double heart attack) of steak, eggs, onions, and French fries smothered in a pepper cream sauce.

Thanks to outstanding homemade meals, family-run **❰ Ñirrantal** (O'Higgins 650-C, tel. 067/522604, lunch and dinner daily) has taken over the top spot, with diverse entrées ranging from sandwiches and salmon to beef and everything in between; entrées cost as little as US$6 including a side dish. While the service can be erratic, it's so well intentioned and the food is so good that's only a minor drawback.

Information and Services

December–March only, the municipal **Oficina de Información Turística** (www.cochranepatagonia.cl, 9 A.M.–9 P.M. daily) works from a kiosk at the southeast corner of the Plaza de Armas; the staff can be indifferent. For information on nearby parks and reserves, visit **Conaf** (Río Nef 417, tel. 067/522164).

On the east side of the Plaza de Armas, **Banco del Estado** (Esmeralda 460) now has an ATM. **Correos de Chile** (Esmeralda 199)

handles postal needs. The best phone service is at **El Encargo** (Teniente Merino and Arturo Prat), while the **Cibercentro Cochrane** (Río Maitén s/n) provides fast Internet access.

In addition to its accommodations, **Hostal Latitude 47° Sur** (Dr. Steffen 576, tel. 067/522280) arranges fly-fishing and other excursions. **La Lavandería** (Los Helechos 336) washes and irons for about US$8.

Hospital Cochrane (O'Higgins 755, tel. 067/522131) provides medical assistance.

Getting There

Buses Don Carlos (Prat 281, tel. 067/522150) goes overland to Coyhaique (US$17, nine hours) and intermediates Wednesday, Friday, and Sunday at 9:30 A.M., and to Villa O'Higgins (US$18, seven hours) Tuesday and Friday at 8 A.M. The latter is a subsidized route on which locals have priority.

Buses São Paulo (Río Baker 349, tel. 067/255726) goes to Coyhaique (US$18) daily except Monday at 8 A.M., while **Buses Acuario 13** (Río Baker 349, tel. 067/522143) goes Tuesday and Saturday at the same hour. (US$18); between them, Acuario 13 and **Buses Becerra** have daily service to Caleta Tortel (US$10, three hours) at 9:30 A.M.

Transportes Ale (Las Golondrinas 399, tel. 067/522448) goes to Puerto Guadal and Chile Chico (US$20, six hours) Thursday and Sunday at 1:15 P.M.

◖ CALETA TORTEL

Where the Río Baker greets the sea, Caleta Tortel is a distinctive fishing village with no streets in the traditional sense—boardwalks and staircases link its houses and businesses. For nearly half a century the only access to this isolated hamlet (founded 1955) was slow or expensive—or both—by air, river, or sea. Since the road link opened from the Carretera Austral, though, it's accessible overland.

In addition to the town itself—a real charmer—there is hiking to destinations such as **Cerro La Bandera** or, more ambitiously, to **Cascada Pisagua,** which requires hiring a launch to the trailhead.

Caleta Tortel (population about 500) is roughly 130 kilometers southeast of Cochrane via the Carretera Austral and a westbound lateral along the Río Baker's south bank. Motor vehicles arrive at a parking lot at the Rincón Alto sector, from which it's necessary to wheel or haul your luggage down the steep staircases (and back up when you leave).

For accommodations, backpackers' choice **Hospedaje Celes Salom** (US$8 pp) also serves meals. Traditionally the town's best, **Hostal Costanera** (Antonio Ronchi 141, tel. 067/234815, US$17 pp with shared bath) has one exceptional room with high ceilings and sea views, but all the others are more than acceptable. It's getting competition, though, from two bright new places: across-the-boardwalk **Hospedaje Estilo** US$13 pp), which also serves meals, and **Hospedaje Don Adán** (hospedaje_donadan@chile.com, US$11 pp).

For the freshest fish, head to **El Mirador** (Sector Base s/n, lunch and dinner daily), whose picture windows provide broad panoramas of the harbor and mountains. This is river salmon, not farmed, and while the preparation may be unsophisticated, the quality is high; there are often catch-of-the-day specials such as *merluza* (hake) and *reineta*. A three-course meal costs around US$8.

At the parking lot, the Municipalidad maintains a small but helpful tourist office that has sometimes has maps and offers suggestions for hikes and excursions. They can also help arrange six-hour boat trips to nearby glaciers (around US$300 for up to 10 people).

Transporte Aéreo Don Carlos flies Wednesdays to Coyhaique (US$42) from the airstrip immediately east of town.

From the parking lot above town, **Buses Acuario 13** and **Buses Becerra** alternate daily service to Cochrane (US$10, three hours) at 3:30 P.M.

PUERTO YUNGAY

Until 1999 Puerto Yungay, on Fiordo Mitchell, was the highway's end point, but now it's the port for a free car and passenger ferry to a ramp at Río Bravo and Villa O'Higgins, the highway's most southerly outpost. When the road opened late that year, according to Sergeant Eduardo Martínez of the Cuerpo Militar de Trabajo (CMT, Chile's Army Corps of Engineers), it was the site of the highway's biggest traffic jam waiting: "There were so many cars backed up that we were working from 7 A.M. until midnight. Some days we couldn't handle all of them, so they had to camp and wait until the next day."

The CMT may someday carve a road along the sheer rock wall of the fjord's north side, but it will never be as fast as the half-hour ferry to Río Bravo, where the road resumes. There, some visionary (or hallucinatory) politicians envision a further southern link to Parque Nacional Torres del Paine, a project that could take decades and still require eight or nine ferry crossings (already, though, a segment of this road is under construction).

In November 2005, the sparkling new car ferry *Padre Antonio Ronchi* replaced the tiny old CMT ferry on this run; space is available free on a first-come, first-served basis. Summer departures are at 10 A.M., noon, and 6 P.M. daily; return times from Río Bravo are at 11 A.M., 1 P.M., and 7 P.M. The rest of the year, services may be reduced; for more information, contact Cochrane's Departamento de Vialidad (Av. O'Higgins and Esmeralda, tel. 067/521242).

There are no other services at Puerto Yungay except for a small kiosk that, in season, prepares hot tea or coffee and has a small selection of groceries and snacks, including tasty raspberry kuchen.

Ⓒ VILLA O'HIGGINS

For decades, the frontier outpost of Villa O'Higgins was accessible only by air taxi from Coyhaique or by water from Argentina. It depended on Argentine supplies, and highway construction materials entered via Argentine roads and ferries on Lago O'Higgins (Lago San Martín to Argentines). Now, though, the Puerto Yungay ferry drops passengers and vehicles at Río Bravo, a boat ramp 100 kilometers to the northwest, for the Carretera Austral's last leg.

When the new road finally opened, said ex-policeman Arturo Gómez, curious tourists overran the town. "We were at full capacity, and most of the people here have scarce resources and couldn't arrange things so soon." People camped, slept in spare rooms, and rented a handful of cabañas. "We didn't evolve step-by-step," said then-mayor Alfredo Runín. "We went from horseback to jet."

Villa O'Higgins (population 463) is booming with new construction, and the town has big plans. The idea, added Runín, "is to promote the ice, because that's what we've got the most of." Thanks to work on the new Sendero de Chile trail, and the motor launch that helps link the town with remote parts of the lake and the Argentina trekking capital of El Chaltén, the backcountry is increasingly hiker-friendly.

A new road has also been built to Río Mayer, on the Argentine border to the northeast, for a probable future border crossing. Still, Villa O'Higgins's services are about 15 years behind El Chaltén's (not everyone thinks that's a bad thing).

Sights and Recreation

Directly east of town, a footpath leads to a scenic overlook that's part of **Parque Cerro Santiago,** Chile's first municipal nature reserve. Hoping to attract adventurous hikers and climbers, local authorities have patched together a trail by signing existing forest paths to a backwoods shelter near the **Ventisquero Mosco** (Mosco Glacier).

Villa O'Higgins lies in the broad valley of the **Río Mayer,** a prime trout stream. Just outside town, a southbound secondary road crosses the river on the **Puente Colgante August Grosse,** a 123-meter suspension bridge; from the bridge's south side, an exposed zigzag trail leads west above **Lago Ciervo,** a scenic route that eventually drops onto the shore of **Lago Negro,** where camping is possible. With an early start, this can also be a long day hike, but the trail is tiring because it conserves altitude poorly and is difficult to follow in some spots.

THE NEW CRUCE DE LAGOS

The traditional lake-land-lake crossing from Chile to Argentina goes from Puerto Montt to Bariloche, but if Aisén and Santa Cruz authorities have their druthers, the next big thing will be the route from Villa O'Higgins to El Chaltén.

Increasing numbers of hardy travelers are making the journey from Villa O'Higgins to the Lago O'Higgins port of Bahía Bahamóndez for the twice-weekly, 50-kilometer, 3.5-hour journey (US$42) by the 60-passenger motor launch *Quetru* to the Chilean border post of Candelario Mancilla. From Candelario Mancilla, the *Quetru* makes an optional excursion to **Glaciar O'Higgins** and **Glaciar Chico** before returning to Mancilla (to pick up arrivals from Argentina) and return to Bahamóndez.

At Candelario Mancilla, where there are simple accommodations (US$10 pp), camping (US$2 per tent), and meals, Chilean Carabineros handle immigration and customs procedures. By foot, bicycle, horseback, or vehicle, it's another 15 kilometers to the international border and 7.5 kilometers more to the Argentine Gendarmería, who handle customs and immigration there. In some cases, hikers may need to ford the appropriately named Río Obstáculo (Obstacle River); beyond the borderline, the existing road becomes a foot-path unsuitable for cyclists, who will have to push or even carry their bikes. At Candelario Mancilla, it's possible to hire a guide (US$20) and horses (US$27 pp plus US$27 for each pack animal).

From the Gendarmería post, at the north end of Laguna del Desierto, there are passenger launches (US$32, 30-45 minutes, plus US$3 per bicycle) to the south end of the lake at 1:30 and 4:45 P.M. Alternatively, hikers can walk the 15 kilometers in about five hours. At the south end, where the launches leave for the border at 10:45 A.M. and 2 P.M., there is also **Camping Laguna del Desierto** (US$2 pp).

From Laguna del Desierto, there are buses to El Chaltén (US$22, one hour) at 2:30 and 8:30 P.M. Buses from El Chaltén to Laguna del Desierto leave at 8:30 A.M. and 3 P.M.; schedules are subject to change.

There are environmental issues here – deforestation, erosion, etc. – and romantics may deplore the loss of frontier feeling as buses replace bicycles. Whatever the ultimate result, though, crossing the borders here is a huge improvement over the days when Chilean and Argentine forces exchanged gunfire – including an incident that killed a Carabinero in 1965 – over what was one of the last outstanding border disputes between the two countries.

To the west, the steeply rising peaks of the **Campo de Hielo Sur,** the southern Patagonian icecap, may be the next big thing for hikers for whom Torres del Paine is too tame. Beyond the bridge, the road continues south to **Bahía Bahamóndez,** where a launch carries tourists up Lago O'Higgins to the **Glaciar O'Higgins** in a full-day excursion.

It is possible, however, to cross the Argentine border by taking the boat to the south end of **Lago O'Higgins** and making a long and sometimes difficult hike through rugged country to **Laguna del Desierto.** From this point there's a road to the Argentine village of **El Chaltén,** in Parque Nacional Los Glaciares.

Accommodations and Food

Until not so long ago, Villa O'Higgins had only one permanent lodge, the simple but well-kept **Hospedaje Patagonia** (Río Pascua 191, tel. 067/431818, US$10 pp), opposite the Plaza de Armas, with comfortable beds and a decent breakfast. In summer, it serves lunch and dinner as well.

Hospedaje Carretera Austral (Río Colorado 40, tel. 067/431819, US$8.50 with breakfast) is a friendly family-run hostelry with good meals, but the walls seem a little thin if it's really crowded.

Run by the former mayor, **Hostal Runín** (Pasaje Vialidad s/n, tel. 067/431870, hostal-runin@yahoo.com, US$41 s, US$53 d with private bath and breakfast) has comfortable rooms with hot showers and good meals for about US$9. When it's crowded in town, he allows garden camping.

There are now a couple restaurants, serving Chilean standards, including seafood.

Information and Services

Local guide Hans Silva's **Hielo Sur** (Carretera Austral 267, tel. 067/431821, www.villaohiggins.com) maintains an informative Spanish-language website that should at some point appear in English. Silva also operates the twice-weekly excursion to Glaciar O'Higgins (US$83 pp), one leg of which also transports passengers to Candelario Mancilla (US$68 pp) for the crossing to Argentina.

Half a block south of the plaza, the **Biblioteca Pública** (Public Library) has free Internet access in half-hour blocks, by reservation only (the wait is rarely long). Across the street, there's a long-distance telephone office.

Getting There and Around

From the airstrip directly opposite the main drag, **Transportes Aéreos Don Carlos** flies to Coyhaique (US$60, one hour) Monday and Thursday, but locals have priority.

Buses to Cochrane (US$20, 6.5 hours) remain infrequent and subject to change, with preference for local residents. Presently the only carrier is **Don Carlos** (tel. 067/431829) at 9 A.M. Wednesday and Saturday.

SOUTHERN PATAGONIA AND TIERRA DEL FUEGO

Thanks to the Torres del Paine, the magnificent granite needles that rise above the Patagonian plains, Chile's most southerly region has acquired international fame. Pacific storms drench the nearly uninhabited western cordillera, feeding alpine and continental glaciers and rushing rivers, but relentless winds buffet the rolling eastern grasslands of the Andean rain shadow. Along the Strait of Magellan, the city of Punta Arenas is the center for excursions to various attractions, including easily accessible penguin colonies and Tierra del Fuego's remote fjords. The region has no direct road connections to the rest of Chile—travelers arrive by air, sea, and through Argentine Patagonia.

Administratively, Region XII (Magallanes) includes all Chilean territory beyond 49° south latitude—technically to the South Pole, as Chile claims a slice of Antarctica between 53° and 90° west longitude. It also takes in the Chilean sector of the Tierra del Fuego archipelago.

Over the past decade, improved communications have meant that many visitors to southern Argentina also visit Chile to see Puerto Natales, Torres del Paine, and other attractions. With the recent weakness in the Chilean peso, it is now cheaper in Chile, but as of 2009 the economic situation is unstable and this could change.

January and February are the peak months, but the season is broadening. Prices drop in winter, though many places also close.

For convenience, this chapter also covers southeasterly parts of Argentina's Santa Cruz province and the Argentine sector of Tierra del

HIGHLIGHTS

◖ Casa Braun-Menéndez (Museo Regional de Magallanes): Magallanes's regional museum now occupies what was originally the mansion of Patagonia's wool aristocracy (page 470).

◖ Monumento Natural Los Pingüinos: In the summer season, penguins occupy every square centimeter of Isla Magdalena, also home to a historic lighthouse (page 481).

◖ The Fjords of Fuegia: Even backpackers sometimes splurge for a leg of this unforgettable itinerary (page 487).

◖ Torres del Paine: The granite needles that rise above the Patagonian steppe are a beacon drawing travelers from around the world to Chile's premier national park, Parque Nacional Torres del Paine (page 507).

◖ Cuernos del Paine: This jagged interface between igneous and metamorphic rock, also in Parque Nacional Torres del Paine, comprises some of the world's most breathtaking alpine scenery (page 508).

◖ Glaciar Perito Moreno: The constantly calving 60-meter face of groaning Glaciar Moreno, east of El Calafate in Parque Nacional Los Glaciares, is one of the continent's most awesome sights (and sounds) (page 526).

◖ Sector Fitz Roy: Near the hamlet of El Chaltén, this sector of Parque Nacional Los Glaciares offers some of the Andes' most exhilarating scenery, hiking, and climbing (page 527).

◖ Museo Marítimo de Ushuaia: Much more than its name suggests, Ushuaia's best museum needs more than one visit to absorb its maritime heritage and appreciate the way in which one of the world's most remote prisons affected the city's development (page 549).

◖ Estancia Harberton: East of Ushuaia, this historic *estancia* is, arguably, the nu-

cleus of the "uttermost part of the earth." (page 559).

◖ Glaciar Martial: Whether entirely by foot or partly by chairlift, the climb to Ushuaia's nearby glacier, part of Parque Nacional Tierra del Fuego, rewards visitors with panoramic views of the city and the storied Beagle Channel (page 560).

LOOK FOR ◖ TO FIND RECOMMENDED SIGHTS, ACTIVITIES, DINING, AND LODGING.

SOUTHERN PATAGONIA

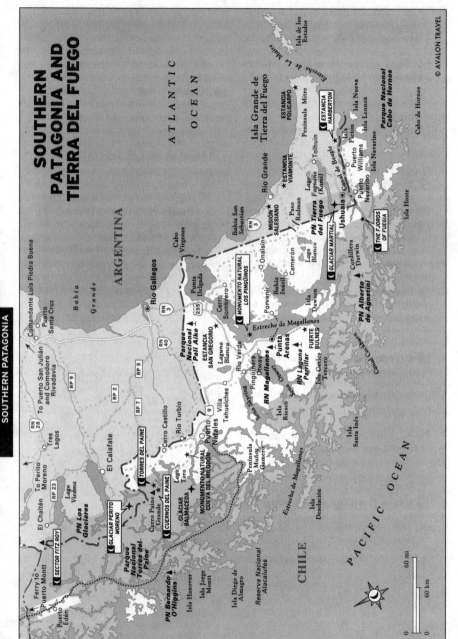

Fuego, both of which pull many visitors over the border.

PLANNING YOUR TIME

Punta Arenas can be a sightseeing base, but only for a day or two; for those who haven't seen Magellanic penguins elsewhere, it's worth scheduling or waiting for the boat to Isla Magdalena. It's also home port for the spectacular cruise to Tierra del Fuego's remotest fjords and Cape Horn via Ushuaia (Argentina), a three- or four-day excursion in either direction. Based on an island in the western Strait of Magellan, summer whale-watching is drawing a small but growing crowd on three-day excursions.

Exploring the thinly populated Chilean sector of Tierra del Fuego requires a vehicle or an airplane—connections to Puerto Williams, though it's not far from Ushuaia as the crow flies, are haphazard except by air from Punta Arenas. Once you're there, hiking the Dientes circuit takes at least a week.

Puerto Natales, the urban gateway to Torres del Paine, is mainly a place to prepare for trekking, but its seaside setting, youthful exuberance, and nearby hiking excursions can extend the stay. The park deserves no less than a week, for day-hikers and overnight trekkers alike, but even an abbreviated day trip—some people do it, despite the time and difficulty of getting here—is worth the trouble.

Another attraction is the *Skorpios III* cruise through the fjords on the west side of the Campos de Hielo Sur, across the ice from Torres del Paine. In summer, this five-day, four-night excursion visits many otherwise inaccessible areas.

Like the rest of the region, Tierra del Fuego deserves all the time you can give it, but most visitors have to make choices. The Argentine city of Ushuaia is the best sightseeing base in Tierra del Fuego proper, given its access for excursions to the nearby national park, the Beagle Channel, and Estancia Harberton, with a minimum of three days. Hikers may wish to spend several days more, and fly-fishing aficionados—who prefer the vicinity of Río Grande—can easily stay a week or two.

HISTORY

Some of the continent's oldest archaeological evidence for human habitation comes from volcanic rock shelters in and near Parque Nacional Pali Aike, along the Argentine border. Pleistocene hunter-gatherers once stalked now-extinct species such as giant ground sloths and native American horses, but they later switched to a broader subsistence that included marine and coastal resources. These peoples were the predecessors of the few surviving Tehuelche and Kawéskar (Alacaluf) peoples and the nearly extinct Selknam (Ona) and Yámana (Yahgan), who gathered shellfish and hunted guanaco and rhea with bows and arrows and *boleadoras*.

The European presence dates from 1520, when Portuguese navigator Fernando Magalhaes, under the Spanish flag, sailed through the strait that bears his name (Magallanes in Spanish, Magellan in English). Ranging 3–25 kilometers in width, the strait became a major maritime thoroughfare en route to the Pacific.

Spain's colonization attempts failed miserably, as did early Chilean and Argentine efforts, but the city of Punta Arenas took hold after 1848—thanks partly to the fortuitous discovery of gold in California just a year later. Gold fever soon subsided, but the introduction of sheep brought a wool and mutton boom that benefited from the 1870s Franco-Prussian War and helped create sprawling *estancias* that dominated regional political, social, and economic life for nearly a century.

While the livestock industry hangs on, commercial fisheries, the state-run oil industry, and the tourist trade have superseded it in the economy. Even these industries have proved vulnerable to fluctuations, declining reserves, and international developments beyond their control, but Chile's energy shortages have spurred new exploration and investment. The Zona Franca free-trade zone, which once drew immigrants from central Chile, has largely stagnated, but Magallanes still has Chile's lowest unemployment rate.

SOUTHERN PATAGONIA

Punta Arenas

Patagonia's largest city, Punta Arenas is also the regional capital and the traditional port of entry, whether by air, land, or sea. Stretching north–south along the Strait of Magellan, the city boasts an architectural heritage that ranges from the Magellanic vernacular of metal-clad houses with steeply pitched roofs to elaborate Francophile mansions commissioned by 19th-century wool barons. Home to several museums, it's a good base for excursions to historical sites and nearby penguin colonies.

The diverse economy depends on fishing, shipping, petroleum, duty-free retail, and tourism. Historically, it's one of the gateways to Antarctica for both research and tourism, but the Argentine port of Ushuaia has absorbed much of this traffic. Ironically, in a region that grazes millions of sheep, it's hard to find woolens here because of the influx of artificial fabrics through the duty-free Zona Franca.

HISTORY

After the collapse of Chile's initial Patagonian settlement at Fuerte Bulnes, Governor José Santos Mardones relocated north to a site on the western shore of the Strait of Magellan, long known to British seamen as "Sandy Point." Soon expanded to include a penal colony, the town adopted that name in Spanish translation.

The timing was propitious, as California's 1849 Gold Rush spurred a surge of shipping that helped keep the new city afloat—even if supplying sealskins, coal, firewood, and lumber did not exactly portend prosperity. A mutiny that resulted in Governor Benjamín Muñoz Gamero's death did not improve matters, and traffic soon fell off.

What did bring prosperity was Governor Diego Dublé Almeyda's introduction of breeding sheep from the Falkland Islands. Their proliferation on the Patagonian plains, along with a vigorous immigration policy that brought entrepreneurs such as the Portuguese José Nogueira, the Spaniard José Menéndez,

and the Irishman Thomas Fenton—not to mention the polyglot laborers who made their fortunes possible—helped transform the city from a dreary presidio to the booming port of a pastoral empire. Its mansions matched many in Buenos Aires, though the maldistribution of wealth and political power remained an intractable issue well into the 20th century.

As the wool economy declined after World War II, petroleum discoveries on Tierra del Fuego and commercial fishing sustained the economy. Creation of Zona Franca duty-free areas gave commercial advantages to Punta Arenas in the 1970s, and tourism has flourished since Pinochet's dictatorship ended in 1989.

ORIENTATION

Punta Arenas (population 116,105) is 210 kilometers southwest of Río Gallegos via the Argentine RN 3 and the Chilean Ruta 255 and Ruta 9; it is 241 kilometers southeast of Puerto Natales via Ruta 9. A daily vehicle ferry connects Punta with Porvenir, while a gravel road, the continent's most southerly, leads to Fuerte Bulnes and Cabo San Isidro.

On the Strait of Magellan's western shore, Punta Arenas occupies a narrow north–south wave-cut terrace, but the ground rises steeply farther west. Only in recent years has the city begun to spread eastward rather than north to south.

Most landmarks and services are within a few blocks of the central Plaza Muñoz Gamero; street names change on each side of the plaza, but the numbering system is continuous.

SIGHTS

For a panoramic overview of the city's layout, the Strait of Magellan, and the island of Tierra del Fuego in the distance, climb to **Mirador La Cruz,** four blocks west of Plaza Muñoz Gamero via a staircase at the corner of the Fagnano and Señoret.

© WAYNE BERNHARDSON

Plaza Muñoz Gamero, Punta Arenas

SOUTHERN PATAGONIA

Plaza Muñoz Gamero and Vicinity

Unlike plazas founded in colonial Chilean cities, Punta Arenas's central plaza was not the initial focus of civic life, but thanks to European immigration and wealth generated by mining, livestock, commerce, and fishing, it became so by the 1880s. Landscaped with Monterey cypress and other exotic conifers, the plaza and surrounding buildings constitute a *zona típica* national monument; the plaza proper underwent a major renovation in 2004.

It takes its name from early provincial governor Benjamín Muñoz Gamero, who died in an 1851 mutiny. Among its features are the Victorian kiosk (1910), which now houses the municipal tourist office, and sculptor Guillermo Córdova's elaborate monument sponsored by wool magnate José Menéndez on the 400th anniversary of Magellan's 1520 voyage. Magellan's figure, embellished with a globe and a copy of his log, stand above a Selknam Indian representing Tierra del Fuego, a Tehuelche symbolizing Patagonia, and a

mermaid with Chilean and regional coats-of-arms. According to local legend, anyone touching the Tehuelche's now well-worn toe—enough have done so to change its color—will return to Punta Arenas.

After about 1880, the city's burgeoning elite began to build monuments to their own good fortune, such as the ornate **Palacio Sara Braun** (1895), a national monument in its own right, at the plaza's northwest corner. Only six years after marrying José Nogueira, Punta's most prominent businessman, the newly widowed Sara Braun contracted French architect Numa Mayer, who applied contemporary Parisian style in designing a two-story mansard building that helped upgrade the city's earlier utilitarian architecture. Now home to the Club de la Unión and Hotel José Nogueira, the building retains most original features, including the west-facing winter garden that now serves as the hotel's bar/restaurant.

Mid-block, immediately east, the **Casa José Menéndez** belonged to another of Punta's wool barons, while at the plaza's northeast corner, the Comapa travel agency now occupies the former headquarters of the influential **Sociedad Menéndez Behety** (Magallanes 990). Half a block north, dating from 1904, the **Casa Braun-Menéndez** (Magallanes 949) houses the regional museum.

At the plaza's southwest corner, the **Iglesia Matriz** (1901) now enjoys cathedral status. Immediately north, both the **Residencia del Gobernador** (Governors' Residence) and the **Gobernación** date from the same period, filling the rest of the block with offices of the Intendencia Regional, the regional government. On the south side, directly opposite the Victorian tourist kiosk, the former **Palacio Montes** now holds municipal government offices; at the southeast corner, the **Sociedad Braun Blanchard** belonged to another powerful commercial group (as should be obvious from the names, Punta Arenas's first families were, commercially at least, an incestuous bunch).

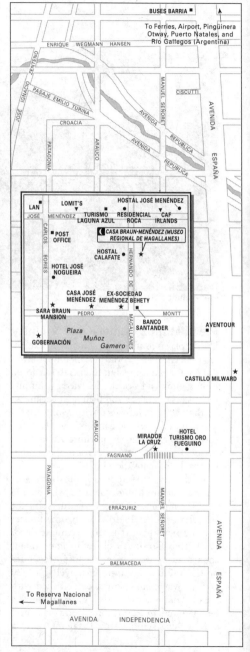

◖ Casa Braun-Menéndez (Museo Regional de Magallanes)

Like European royalty, Punta's first families formed alliances sealed by matrimony, and the Casa Braun-Menéndez (1904) is a classic example: the product of a marriage between Mauricio Braun (Sara's brother) and Josefina Menéndez Behety (daughter of José Menéndez and María Behety, a major wool-growing family in Argentina—though international borders meant little to wool barons).

Still furnished with the family's belongings, preserving Mauricio Braun's office and other rooms virtually intact, the house boasts marble fireplaces and other elaborate architectural features. The basement servants' quarters expose the early-20th-century's upstairs–downstairs divisions.

Today, the Casa Braun-Menéndez (Magallanes 949, tel. 061/244216, www.museodemagallanes.cl, 10 A.M.–5 P.M. daily except Sun., when it closes at 2 P.M., US$1.50 adults, US$0.75 children) serves as the regional museum, replete with pioneer settlers' artifacts

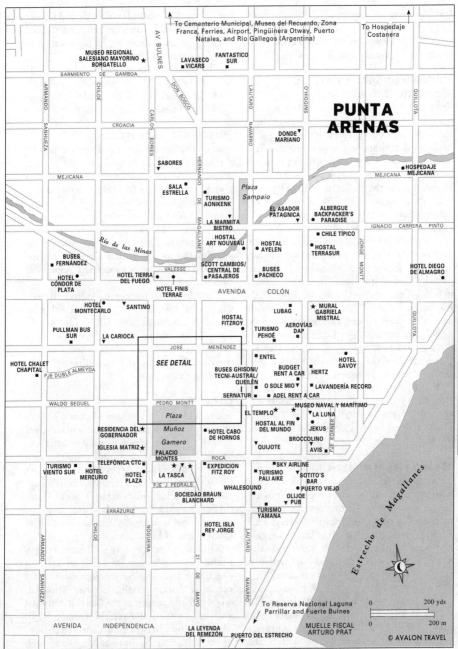

SOUTHERN PATAGONIA

and historical photographs. There are imperfect but readable English descriptions of the exhibits. On some days, a pianist plays beneath the atrium's stained-glass skylight.

Museo Regional Salesiano Mayorino Borgatello

From the 19th century, the Salesian order played a key role in evangelizing southern Patagonia and Tierra del Fuego, on both sides of the border. Punta Arenas was their base and, while their rosy view of Christianity's impact on the region's native people may be debatable, figures such as the Italian mountaineer priest Alberto de Agostini (1883–1960) made key contributions to both physical geography and ethnographic research.

Agostini left a sizeable collection of photographs in the museum, which also has a library and a regionally oriented art gallery. Permanent exhibits deal with regional flora and fauna, a handful of early colonial artifacts, regional ethnography, the missionization of Isla Dawson and other nearby areas, cartography, and the petroleum industry. For Darwinians, there's a scale model of the *Beagle* and, for Chilean patriots, one of the *Ancud,* which sailed from Chiloé to claim the region in 1843.

The Museo Regional Salesiano (Avenida Bulnes 336, tel. 061/221001, www.museomaggiorinoborgatello.cl, US$3 adults, US$0.30 children) is open 10 A.M.–6 P.M. Tuesday–Sunday.

Museo Naval y Marítimo

Pleasantly surprising, Punta Arenas's naval and maritime museum provides perspectives on topics like ethnography—in the context of the Strait of Magellan's seagoing peoples—even while stressing its military mission. It features interactive exhibits, such as a credible warship's bridge, a selection of model ships, and information on the naval history of the southern oceans.

The most riveting material, though, concerns Chilean pilot Luis Pardo Villalón's 1916 rescue of British explorer Ernest Shackleton's crew at Elephant Island, on the Antarctic peninsula. On the cutter *Yelcho,* with neither

heat, electricity, nor radio in foggy and stormy winter weather, Pardo soon returned the entire crew to Punta Arenas; he later served as Chilean consul in Liverpool.

The Museo Naval (Pedro Montt 981, tel. 061/205479, terzona@armada.cl, US$1.50 adults, US$0.85 children) is open 9:30 A.M.–5 P.M. Tuesday–Saturday.

Museo del Recuerdo

Run by the Instituto de la Patagonia, part of the Universidad de Magallanes, the Museo del Recuerdo is a mostly open-air facility displaying pioneer agricultural implements and industrial machinery, reconstructions of a traditional house and shearing shed, and a restored shepherd's trailer house (hauled across the Patagonian plains on wooden wheels). In addition to a modest botanical garden, the institute has a library/bookshop with impressive cartographic exhibits.

The Museo del Recuerdo (Avenida Bulnes 01890, tel. 061/207056, 8:30 A.M.–11 A.M. and 2–5 P.M. weekdays, US$2 adults, free for children) can be reached from downtown Punta Arenas by *taxi colectivos* (duty-free to the Zona Franca), which stop directly opposite the entrance.

Other Sights

Four blocks south of Plaza Muñoz Gamero, at the foot of Avenida Independencia, naval vessels, freighters, cruise ships, Antarctic icebreakers, and yachts from many countries dock at the **Muelle Fiscal Arturo Prat,** the city's major port facility until recently. It's still a departure point for cruises to the fjords of Tierra del Fuego and to Antarctica but, unfortunately, international security hysteria has closed it to spontaneous public access.

The late, gifted travel writer Bruce Chatwin found the inspiration for his legendary vignettes of *In Patagonia* through tales of his eccentric distant relative Charley Milward, who built and resided at the **Castillo Milward** (Milward's Castle, Avenida España 959). Described by Chatwin as "a Victorian parsonage translated to the Strait of Magellan," with "high-pitched gables and gothic windows," the building features a square street-side tower and an octagonal one at the rear.

At the corner of Avenida Colón and O'Higgins, gracing the walls of the former **Liceo de Niñas Sara Braun** (Sara Braun Girls' School), and honoring Chile's Nobel Prize poetess, the weathering seven-meter **Mural Gabriela Mistral** has undergone a recent restoration.

Ten blocks north of Plaza Muñoz Gamero, the **Cementerio Municipal** (Avenida Bulnes 029) is home to the extravagant crypts of José Menéndez, José Nogueira, and Sara Braun; the multinational immigrants who worked for them—English, Scots, Welsh, Croat, German, and Scandinavian—repose in more modest circumstances. A separate monument honors the vanished Selknam (Ona) Indians who once flourished in the Strait, while another memorializes German fatalities of the Battle of the Falklands (1914).

ENTERTAINMENT

Except on Sunday, when the city seems deader than the cemetery, there's usually something to do.

Punta Arenas has one surviving cinema, the **Sala Estrella** (Mejicana 777, tel. 061/241262).

El Templo (Pedro Montt 951, tel. 061/223667) is primarily a dance club. The stylish **Olijoe Pub** (Errázuriz 970) has the feel of an upscale English pub, with paneled walls, ceiling, and bar, and reasonably priced drinks; the music, though, can get a little loud for conversation. The Sara Braun mansion's basement **Taberna Club de la Unión** (Plaza Muñoz Gamero 716, tel. 061/617133) is popular on weekends.

Santino (Avenida Colón 657, tel. 061/710882, www.santino.cl) is a spacious and informal pub where everyone (except non-smokers) feels welcome; there's also food, but it's not the star.

At the north end of town, **Makanudo** (El Ovejero 474, cel. 09/6492031) has 7–10 P.M. happy hours Monday–Thursday, and live music Friday and Saturday nights from around 1:30 A.M.

The **Club Hípico** (municipal racetrack) fronts on Avenida Bulnes between Coronel Mardones and Manantiales, north of downtown. Professional soccer matches take place at the **Estadio Fiscal** (stadium), a few blocks north at Avenida Bulnes and José González.

SHOPPING

Though it's faltered in recent years, Punta Arenas's major shopping destination is the duty-free **Zona Franca,** four kilometers north of downtown but easily reached by taxi *colectivo* from Calle Magallanes. Consumer electronics were once the big attraction—Santiaguinos even flew here for the bargains—but price differentials are smaller now.

Puerto del Estrecho (O'Higgins 1401, tel. 061/241022) is a good if fairly pricey souvenir shop; in addition, it has an upstairs café, Internet access, and long-distance telephone service.

For crafts such as metal (copper and bronze), semi-precious stones (lapis lazuli), and woolens, visit **Chile Típico** (Ignacio Carrera Pinto 1015, tel. 061/225827). For books (including some local guidebooks and travel literature in English), maps, and keepsakes, try **Southern Patagonia Souvenirs & Books,** which has outlets at the airport (tel. 061/211591) and at the Zona Franca (tel. 061/216759).

ACCOMMODATIONS

Sernatur maintains a complete list of accommodations with up-to-date prices. What in many other parts of Chile would be called *residenciales* are *hostales* (B&Bs) here. Some relatively expensive places have cheaper rooms with shared baths that can be excellent values.

US$10-25

With the Chilean peso's recent depreciation, finding truly shoestring accommodations has become easier. Under new ownership, the improved **Albergue Backpacker's Paradise** (Ignacio Carrera Pinto 1022, tel. 061/240104, backpackersparadise@hotmail.com, US$8 pp) is still a crowded hostel, but for the price it has its attributes: adequate common spaces with cable TV, cooking privileges, and Internet access.

Economical **Hospedaje Mejicana** (Mejicana 1174, tel. 061/227678, yoya_h@hotmail.com, US$7 pp, US$13 s, US$23 d) has also made good impressions. East of the racetrack at the foot of Quillota, the shoreline **Hospedaje Costanera** (Rómulo Correa 1221, tel. 061/240175, hospedajecostanera@hotmail.com, US$10–12 pp, US$27 d) has drawn favorable commentary. The doubles have private baths.

US$25-50

Often full despite mixed reviews, **Hostal Dinka's House** (Caupolicán 169, tel./fax 061/244292, www.dinkaspatagonia.com, US$12 pp, US$33 d) has rooms with either private or shared baths.

⊂ Hostal Fitz Roy (Lautaro Navarro 850, tel./fax 061/240430, www.hostalfitzroy.com, US$13 pp, US$25 s, US$33 d with shared bath) is an old-fashioned B&B offering some modern comforts—notably cable TV and phones in each room—along with peace and quiet, thoughtful English-speaking ownership, and an excellent breakfast that includes fresh homemade bread and eggs. Returned to their original configuration, the rooms are spacious, but buildings of this vintage still have creaky floors and staircases. There are separate cabañas with private bath (US$50 d) and ample parking.

In a large old house that's been subdivided, rooms at **Hostal al Fin del Mundo** (O'Higgins 1026, tel. 061/710185, alfindelmundo@123.cl, US$13 pp with shared bath, US$20 s, US$37 d) vary in size and quality, but it has its good points (including proximity to some of the city's best restaurants).

Only a block from the plaza, creaky **Residencial Roca** (Magallanes 888, 2nd floor, tel./fax 061/243903, franruiz@entelchile.net, US$13 pp, US$25 s, US$42 d) has rooms with either shared or private baths, cable TV, laundry service, and a book exchange.

Hostal Ayelen (Lautaro Navarro 763, tel. 061/242413, www.ayelenresidencial.com, US$31 s, US$43 d) is a friendly family-run

hostelry with small but efficient singles, and larger doubles and triples. Rates include satellite TV, WiFi, and parking but, at midday, the yippy poodles in the garden can be a nuisance (they're indoors, and quiet, at other hours).

Rehabbed **Hotel Montecarlo** (Avenida Colón 605, tel. 061/222120, administracion@h-montecarlo.com, US$20–30 s, US$37–50 d) is once again worth consideration; the more expensive rooms have private baths.

Thanks to the weakening peso, prices have slipped a notch at well-regarded, cul-de-sac **Hostal Sonia** (Pasaje Darwin 175, tel. 061/248543, www.hostalsk.cl, US$37 s, US$50 d with breakfast), which has rooms with private baths.

US$50-100

Though it's well kept, some rooms are small at **Hostal José Menéndez** (José Menéndez 882, tel. 061/221279, www.chileaustral.com/josemenendez, US$25–42 s, US$33–57 d). Still, it's friendly and central, arranges tours, has parking, and offers a decent breakfast; rates vary according to shared or private bath.

Across from Hostal Ayelen, **Hostal Art Nouveau** (Lautaro Navarro 762, tel. 061/228112, www.hostalartnouveau.cl, US$41 s, US$63 d) is less pretentious than it sounds— a lovingly restored period house with attractive common spaces and a breakfast. Some of the rooms, though, lack exterior windows.

Low-key **Hostal Terrasur** (O'Higgins 723, tel. 061/225618, www.hostalterrasur.cl, US$50 s, US$67 d) is one of the more appealing B&B-style places in its range. Rates include cable TV, telephone, and continental breakfast.

Hotel Cóndor de Plata (Avenida Colón 556, tel. 061/247987, US$59 s, US$70 d, www.condordeplata.com) has always been a good choice, and the weakening pesos has once again made its price competitive.

⊂ Hostal Turismo Oro Fueguino (Fagnano 356, tel. 061/249401, www.orofueguino.com, US$60 s, US$74 d) is still a good hotel, but the cheap aluminum siding and faux brick have marred its deco-style exterior. Rates include cable TV, telephone, central heating, breakfast,

© WAYNE BERNHARDSON

In Punta Arenas, the Hotel José Nogueira occupies the former Sara Braun mansion.

and private bath; some rooms are windowless but have skylights.

Hotel Savoy (José Menéndez 1073, tel./fax 061/247979, www.hotelsavoy.cl, US$60 s, US$77 d) lacks style—some interior walls have cheap plywood paneling—but the rooms are large and comfortable, and the staff is responsive. Still, there are better values.

New in late 2007, the 11-room **Hotel Chalet Chapital** (Sanhueza 974, tel. 061/730100, www.hotelchaletchapital.cl, US$62 s, US$78 d) occupies a handsomely restored historic building, with contemporary furnishings, WiFi, and whirlpool tubs in every room.

Despite its misleadingly small street-side facade, **Hostal Calafate** (Magallanes 926, www.calafate.cl, tel./fax 061/241281, US$29–64 s, US$–79 d) is a rambling building with spacious rooms that once held the former Hotel Oviedo; remodeled just a few years ago, it keeps a couple so-called *celdas de castigo* ("prison cells") for backpacker clients for about US$15 per person—a pretty good deal in a well-kept, central facility. It also has some of Punta's best Internet facilities, also open to nonguests.

The stylishly modernized **Hotel Mercurio** (Fagnano 595, tel./fax 061/242300, www.chileaustral.com/mercurio, US$67 s, US$82 d) offers both convenience and charm, with gracious staff to boot.

US$100-200

Half a block south of Plaza Muñoz Gamero, **Hotel Plaza** (Nogueira 1116, tel. 061/241300, www.hotelplaza.cl, US$89 s, US$108 d) is a classic of its era. The contemporary **Hotel Tierra del Fuego** (Avenida Colón 716, tel./fax 061/226200, www.puntaarenas.com, US$125 s, US$140 d) is a business-oriented facility. **❮ Hotel Isla Rey Jorge** (21 de Mayo 1243, tel. 061/222681, www.islareyjorge.com, US$119 s, US$146 d) is a favorite with foreign tour groups, but it's showing signs of deferred maintenance.

Punta's newest hotel, overlooking the rejuvenated waterfront, **Hotel Diego de Almagro** (Avenida Colón 1290, tel. 061/208800, www.dahoteles.com, US$126 s, US$147 d) is a welcome addition to Punta's accommodations roster. **Hotel Finis Terrae** (Avenida Colón 766, tel. 061/228200, www.hotelfinisterrae.com, US$154 s, US$185 d) is another fine newer hotel.

The most historic accommodations, though, can be found at the [**Hotel José Nogueira** (Bories 959, tel. 061/711000, www.hotel-nogueira.com, US$170 s, US$190 d), which occupies part of the Sara Braun mansion. Its greenhouse bar/restaurant, with its snaking grape arbor, merits a visit even if you can't afford to book a room.

Built by the Sociedad Ganadera Tierra del Fuego, the 1960s high-rise **Hotel Cabo de Hornos** (Plaza Muñoz Gamero 1025, tel. 061/715000, www.hoteles-australis.com, US$180 s, US$200 d) has undergone not just a face-lift but a full-scale makeover under new ownership—the same as the Cruceros Australis cruise line. The public spaces are spectacular and the rooms attractive, but they have their shortcomings—the Ethernet cables, for instance, are short and remote from the any potential workspace.

FOOD

Punta Arenas's gastronomic scene ranges from fast food to haute cuisine, with regional twists. Despite the depreciating Chilean peso, dining out here is no bargain.

Quijote (Lautaro Navarro 1087, tel. 061/241225) serves inexpensive lunches. Upstairs in the Casa del Turista, at the entrance to Muelle Prat, **Café Puerto del Estrecho** (O'Higgins 1401, tel. 061/241022) has a variety of espresso-based specialty coffees, such as mocha and amaretto, plus snacks and desserts to accompany them.

The best fast-food alternative is [**Lomit's** (José Menéndez 722, tel. 061/243399), a dependable sandwich-and-beer chain that's almost always packed. Sandwiches cost around US$5. **La Carioca** (José Menéndez 600, tel. 061/224809), by contrast, is a one-of-a-kind sandwich outlet that also serves passable pizza, pasta, and draft beer. The **Café Irlandés** (José Menéndez 848, tel. 061/246082) is similar but more spacious and comfortable, though there's little Irish about it except a long bar.

Dónde Mariano (O'Higgins 504, tel. 061/245291, lunch and dinner daily) delivers on its modest pretensions, serving simply prepared fish entrées, including a side order, in the US$8–12 range. The decor has improved, and the service is adept.

On the former site of the landmark restaurant La Luna (and under the same management), **O Sole Mio** (O'Higgins 974, tel. 061/242026, lunch and dinner daily) serves a diversity of pastas with seafood sauces, but the quality varies. Prices are moderate, around US$8 per entrée, and it's kept most of La Luna's informal atmosphere.

In new quarters half a block south, [**La Luna** (O'Higgins 1017, tel. 061/228555, www.laluna.cl, lunch and dinner daily) still buzzes with activity—pins stuck on wall maps indicate the origins of the clientele—but the transition seems to have cost it some of its informality. Even the *chupe de centolla* (king crab casserole, US$12) isn't quite what it was, and they may be trying a little too hard.

New in late 2007, alongside La Luna, **Jekus** (O'Higgins 1021, tel. 061/245851, jekus.patagonia@gmail.com, lunch and dinner daily) has a sunken bar and dining room of natural woods, with a separate upstairs for smokers. The food is demonstrably Patagonian in dishes such as the tender lamb chops (US$14) flavored with a spicy *merkén*. Some reports suggest uneven initial results but, at its best, it's outstanding.

[**La Marmita Bistro** (Plaza Sampaio 678, tel. 061/222056, lunch and dinner daily) has risen to near the top of Punta's restaurant scene for creative seafood (no Italian would recognize the scallop appetizer as "lasagna," but it's outstanding) and roast lamb (US$13) with a Mapuche *tomaticán* sauce of mushroom, onion, and tomato. With a atmosphere that is both historic and casual, it also serves unusual vegetarian plates and varied desserts.

For US$22, **Sabores** (Mejicana 702, 2nd floor, tel. 061/227369, www.restaurantsabores

.com, lunch and dinner daily) serves a four-course "Magellanic menu" that includes both king crab and salmon, as well as a pisco sour and half bottle of wine; Wednesdays are all-you-can-eat pasta nights (US$6 pp).

Expanding from its Puerto Natales base, **El Asador Patagónico** (O'Higgins 694, tel. 061/222463, lunch and dinner daily) opened here in late 2008, and the early returns are mixed. The menu is virtually identical to that of the original, it's a little cheaper and a little smaller, but the service is erratic even when it's not crowded.

In expanded quarters, the nautically themed **Puerto Viejo** (O'Higgins 1166, tel. 061/225103) continues doing bang-up business with an almost exclusively seafood menu, but the service has deteriorated dramatically. Open for lunch and dinner, it serves specialties such as *centolla* (king crab) and *merluza* (hake).

Under the same management, a couple kilometers north of the plaza, **Los Ganaderos** (Avenida Bulnes 0977, tel. 061/214597, www.parrillalosganaderos.cl, lunch and dinner daily) is a classy *parrilla* specializing in succulent Patagonian lamb grilled on a vertical spit—for US$15 *tenedor libre* (all-you-can-eat), per person. There is also a more diverse *parrillada* for two (about US$25), and pasta dishes in the US$8–10 range. Try the regional Patagonian desserts, such as *mousse de calafate* and *mousse de ruibarbo* (rhubarb).

Four blocks south of the plaza, the creative **La Leyenda del Remezón** (21 de Mayo 1469, tel. 061/241029, lunch and dinner daily) serves game dishes (beaver and guanaco are now being farmed in the region) in the US$25 and up range—not cheap, obviously, but unique. Seafood specialties include krill, king crab, and spider crab, and most dishes are substantially cheaper than the game.

In the old Centro Español, the upstairs **La Tasca** (Plaza Muñoz Gamero 771, tel. 061/242807, lunch and dinner daily) has been reborn as a cheerful midrange-to-upmarket Spanish restaurant with creative variants on traditional dishes, such as *merluza* (hake) stuffed with king crab and avocado (US$12).

The pisco sours are excellent, and the wine list greatly improved, but it's also become a smokers' refuge.

Broccolino (O'Higgins 1049, tel. 061/710479, lunch and dinner daily) serves a fine risotto with *centolla* and scallops, along with beef, lamb, and pastas in the US$10–12 range. Traditionally, **Sotito's Bar** (O'Higgins 1138, tel. 061/245365, lunch and dinner daily) has set the seafood standard here, and it still deserves consideration.

INFORMATION

In new quarters one block east of the plaza, **Sernatur** (Lautaro Navarro 999, tel. 061/225385, infomagallanes@sernatur.cl, 8:30 A.M.–7 P.M. weekdays all year, 9 A.M.–6 P.M. weekends summer only) is one of Chile's better regional offices, with English-speaking personnel and up-to-date accommodations and transportation information.

In summer, Plaza Muñoz Gamero's municipal **Kiosko de Informaciones** (tel. 061/200610, informacionturistica@puntaarenas.cl) is open 8 A.M.–5:30 P.M. weekdays except Monday, when it closes an hour earlier, and 9 A.M.–6 P.M. Saturday.

Conaf (Avenida Bulnes 0309, 4th floor, tel. 061/238581) provides information on the region's national parks.

SERVICES

Punta Arenas is one of the easier Chilean cities in which to change both cash and travelers checks, especially at travel agencies along Lautaro Navarro. Most close by midday Saturday, but **Scott Cambios** (Avenida Colón and Magallanes, tel. 061/245811) will cash travelers checks then.

Several banks in the vicinity of Plaza Muñoz Gamero have ATMs, such as **Banco Santander** (Magallanes 997).

Just north of Plaza Muñoz Gamero, **Correos de Chile** (Bories 911) is the post office.

Long-distance call centers include **Telefónica CTC** (Nogueira 1116), at the southwest corner of Plaza Muñoz Gamero, and **Entel** (Lautaro Navarro 931). Try also **Hostal Calafate**

(Magallanes 922), which has expanded its hotel business with an Internet café and call center, now the best in town.

The **Argentine consulate** (21 de Mayo 1878, tel. 061/261912) is open 10 A.M.–3:30 P.M. weekdays only.

For clean clothes, try **Lavandería Record** (O'Higgins 969, tel. 061/243607) or **Lavaseco Vicars** (Sarmiento de Gamboa 726, tel. 061/241516).

Punta Arenas's **Hospital Regional** (Arauco and Angamos, tel. 061/244040) is north of downtown.

GETTING THERE

Punta Arenas has good air links with mainland Chile, frequent air service to Chilean Tierra del Fuego, infrequent flights to Argentine Tierra del Fuego, and regular weekly service to the Falkland Islands. There are roundabout overland routes to mainland Chile via Argentina, regular bus service to Argentine Tierra del Fuego via a ferry link, direct ferry service to Chilean Tierra del Fuego, and expensive (but extraordinarily scenic) cruise-ship service to Ushuaia, in Argentine Tierra del Fuego.

Air

LAN (Bories 884, tel. 061/241232) flies four times daily to Santiago, normally via Puerto Montt, but some flights stop at Balmaceda, near Coyhaique. It also flies three times weekly to Ushuaia, Argentina, and Saturday to the Falkland Islands; one Falklands flight per month stops in the Argentine city of Río Gallegos.

Sky Airline (Roca 935, tel. 061/710645) now flies north to Balmaceda/Coyhaique, Puerto Montt, and Santiago, with connections to northern Chilean cities.

Aerovías DAP (O'Higgins 878, tel. 061/616100, www.aeroviasdap.cl) flies seven-seat Cessnas to and from Porvenir (US$34), in Chilean Tierra del Fuego, at least once a day except Sunday, more often in summer. Daily except Tuesday and Sunday, it flies 20-seater Twin Otters to and from Puerto Williams on Isla Navarino (US$92). In addition, it has extensive charter services and occasionally goes to Antarctica.

Bus

Punta Arenas has no central terminal, though some companies share facilities and the **Central de Pasajeros** (Avenida Colón and Magallanes, tel. 061/245811) sells tickets for all of them. Most terminals are within a few blocks of each other, north of Plaza Muñoz Gamero. Services vary seasonally but are most numerous in January and February.

Carriers serving Puerto Natales (US$7–10, three hours) include **Pullman Bus Sur** (José Menéndez 552, tel. 061/614224, www.bus-sur .cl), with four buses daily; **Buses Fernández** (Armando Sanhueza 745, tel. 061/242313, www.busesfernandez.com), seven daily; and **Buses Pacheco** (Avenida Colón 900, tel. 061/225527, www.busespacheco.com), four daily.

In addition to its Puerto Natales services, Buses Pacheco goes to the Chilean cities of Osorno (US$64, 28–30 hours), Puerto Montt, and Castro Wednesday at 9 A.M., via Argentina. **Queilen Bus** (Lautaro Navarro 975, tel. 061/222714) and **Turibús** (Armando Sanhueza 745, tel. 061/227970) alternate services to Puerto Montt and Castro most mornings at 9:30 A.M. In addition to its Puerto Natales services, Bus Sur goes to Coyhaique (US$50, 20 hours) Monday at 10:30 A.M.

Several carriers go to Río Gallegos (US$12, 4 hours): **Buses Pingüino** (Armando Sanhueza 745, tel. 061/223898), **Buses Ghisoni** (Lautaro Navarro 975, tel. 061/613420, busesghisoni@123.cl), and Buses Pacheco.

Tecni-Austral (Lautaro Navarro 975, tel. 061/222078) goes to Río Grande (US$33, 8 hours) and Ushuaia (US$50, 11.5 hours) in Argentine Tierra del Fuego, Tuesday, Thursday, and Saturday at 8:30 A.M. **Buses Pacheco** goes Monday, Wednesday, and Friday at 9 A.M. to Río Grande, with connections to Ushuaia.

Sea

Transbordadora Austral Broom (Avenida Bulnes 05075, tel. 061/218100, www.tabsa.cl)

AIR ANTARCTICA

The Aerovías DAP comes in for a landing at Isla Rey Jorge, Antarctica.

For many visitors, one of the great disincentives to Antarctic travel is the fact that, even though southern South America offers the closest approach to the frozen continent, it usually involves a stomach-churning two-day crossing of the stormy Drake Passage – in each direction. If Chilean entrepreneurs have their way, though, well-heeled travelers will soon skip the seasickness.

In the summer of 2004, Punta Arenas-based **Antarctica XXI** organized the first commercial air-sea excursion to the Antarctic Peninsula, eliminating the Drake Passage segment.

Arriving at the Base Aérea Presidente Eduardo Frei Montalva, the Chilean air force's main Antarctic base on Isla Rey Jorge, passengers almost immediately board the Russian research vessel *Professor Multanovskiy* for a five-day cruise among the peninsula's relatively sheltered waters.

The convenience comes at a price, though; the cheapest rate for the all-inclusive tour is US$8,990 per person, double occupancy. For more details, contact Antarctica XXI (Lautaro Navarro 987, 2nd floor, Punta Arenas, tel. 061/614100, www.antarcticaxxi.com).

sails from Punta Arenas to Porvenir (2.5 hours) at 9 A.M. daily except Sunday, when sailing time is 9:30 A.M. Adult passengers pay US$7.50 per person except for the drivers, whose fare is included in the US$48 charge per vehicle (motorcyclists pay US$14 but bicyclists board for free). The rate for children is half the adult fare. Given limited vehicle capacity, reservations are a good idea on the *Crux Australis,* which leaves from Terminal Tres Puentes, at the north end

of town but easily reached by *taxi colectivo* from the Casa Braun-Menéndez, on Magallanes half a block north of Plaza Muñoz Gamero.

Broom also operates the ferry *Bahía Azul* to Puerto Williams (32 hours) every Wednesday at 6 P.M., returning Friday at 10 P.M. The fare is US$210 for a bunk, US$175 for a reclining seat.

It's neither cheap nor a conventional way of getting to Argentina, but the luxury cruisers

MV *Mare Australis* and MV *Via Australis* shuttle to Ushuaia as part of a weeklong circuit through the fjords of Chilean Tierra del Fuego, and passengers can disembark in Ushuaia (or board there, for that matter). Normally both ships require reservations well in advance.

GETTING AROUND
Aeropuerto Presidente Carlos Ibáñez del Campo is 20 kilometers north of town on Ruta 9, the Puerto Natales highway. **Transfer Austral** (Lautaro Navarro 975, tel. 061/617202) arranges door-to-door transfers (US$5 pp).

Buses returning from Puerto Natales will normally drop passengers at the airport to meet outgoing flights on request, but make arrangements before boarding. Natales-bound buses will also pick up arriving passengers, but again make arrangements in advance.

Punta Arenas has numerous car-rental options, including **Adel Rent a Car** (Pedro Montt 962, tel. 061/224819, www.adel.cl), **Budget** (O'Higgins 964, tel./fax 061/241696, budget@ctcinternet.cl), **Avis** (Roca 1044, tel./fax 061/241182, rentacar@viaterra.cl), **Hertz** (O'Higgins 931, tel. 061/613087), and **Lubaq** (Avenida Colón 975, tel./fax 061/710484, luis_barra@entelchile.net).

Vicinity of Punta Arenas

Punta Arenas's myriad travel agencies operate a variety of excursions to nearby destinations such as Reserva Nacional Magallanes, Fuerte Bulnes, the Seno Otway penguin colony, Río Verde, Estancia San Gregorio, and even Parque Nacional Torres del Paine. The most popular half-day excursions, such as Fuerte Bulnes and Otway, cost US$21–30 per person, while full-day trips such as Pali Aike can cost up to US$112 per person, with a three-person minimum.

Among the established operators are **Aventour** (Patagonia 779-A, tel. 061/241197, www.aventourpatagonia.com), **Turismo Aónikenk** (Magallanes 619, tel. 061/221982, www.aonikenk.com), **Turismo Laguna Azul** (José Menéndez 786, tel. 061/225200, www.lagunaazul.cl), **Turismo Pali Aike** (Lautaro Navarro 1125, tel. 061/615750, www.turismopaliaike.com), **Turismo Viento Sur** (Fagnano 585, tel. 061/222590, www.vientosur.com), and **Turismo Yámana** (Errázuriz 932, tel. 061/710567, www.yamana.cl).

RESERVA NACIONAL MAGALLANES
Only eight kilometers west of downtown, 13,500-hectare Reserva Nacional Magallanes is a combination of Patagonian steppe and southern beech forest which, in good winters, amasses enough snow for skiing. Despite its proximity to Punta Arenas, official statistics say it gets barely 11,000 visitors per year, and barely 1,300 of those are foreigners.

Westbound Avenida Independencia, a good gravel road that may require chains in winter, climbs gradually to a fork whose southern branch leads to the **Sector Andino,** where the local Club Andino's **Centro de Esquí Cerro Mirador** includes a *refugio* that serves meals, as well as a ski school and a single well-maintained chairlift. In summer, try the **Sendero Mirador,** a two-hour loop hike that winds through the forest and crosses the ski area; there's also a mountain-bike circuit.

The northwesterly **Sector Las Minas,** which includes a gated picnic area, charges US$1.50 per person for adult admission, but nothing for kids. A longer footpath links up with the trail to the El Mirador summit, which offers panoramas east toward Punta Arenas, the strait, and Tierra del Fuego, and west toward Seno Otway.

Though some travel agencies offer tours to the reserve, it would also be a good mountain-bike excursion from town.

PINGÜINOS AND PINGÜINERAS

Chilean Patagonia's largest city is close to two breeding colonies of the **burrowing Magellanic penguin,** *Spheniscus magellanicus*. The Otway Sound colony is about a 45-minute drive from the city, and is interesting enough, but the larger colony on Isla Magdalena, an island in the Strait of Magellan, is two hours away by ferry or slightly less by bus and rigid inflatable.

Also known to English speakers as the jackass penguin because its call resembles that of a braying burro, the Magellanic is present October through April. It's most numerous in January and February, when the chicks hatch in the sandy burrows that the birds have dug beneath the coastal turf. After the chicks have hatched, the parents alternate fishing trips in search of food that they later regurgitate to their young (combined with the scent of bird droppings, this makes any visit to a penguin colony an olfactory as well as a visual and auditory experience).

While the birds appear tame, they are wild animals and their sharp beaks can draw blood – maintain a respectful distance for photography. Though both the Otway and Magdalena colonies have fenced walking routes to restrain tourists, the birds themselves frequently cross these routes.

Besides the countless seabirds and dolphins en route, the Magdalena trip has the added bonus of a historic lighthouse that now serves as a visitor center on an island that's one big warren of penguin burrows. While neither trip is strenuous, any walk in Patagonia's roaring winds can be a workout.

PINGÜINERA SENO OTWAY

Burrowing Magellanic penguins abound along Argentine Patagonia's Atlantic shoreline, but they are fewer in Chile. Barely an hour from Punta Arenas, though, the Otway colony of *Spheniscus magellanicus* is the closest to any major city on the continent. Under the administration of the nonprofit Fundación Otway, it grew in a decade from no more than 400 penguins to about 11,000 at present. From October, when the first birds arrive, to April, when the last stragglers head to sea, it draws up to 40,000 visitors. The peak season is December–February.

While the site is fenced to keep human visitors out of critical habitat, the birds are relatively tame and easy to photograph; on the downside, this fence did not prevent stray dogs from killing more than a hundred birds in 2001. The landowning Kusanovic family has taken over management from the Fundación Otway.

During the season, any number of Punta Arenas operators shuttle visitors to and from Otway for about US$20 per person, not including the US$7.50 per person admission charge. Half-day tours take place either in morning (which photographers may prefer) or afternoon. For visitors with private vehicles, there's also a US$1.50 toll.

Otway is only about 60 kilometers northwest of Punta Arenas via Ruta 9 and a gravel road that leads west from a signed junction at Parque Chabunco, about 19 km north of the city.

While Otway is a worthwhile excursion, visitors with flexible schedules and a little more money should consider the larger Isla Magdalena colony in Monumento Natural Los Pingüinos, in the Strait of Magellan.

◖ MONUMENTO NATURAL LOS PINGÜINOS

From early October, more than 60,000 breeding pairs of Magellanic penguins paddle ashore and waddle to burrows that cover nearly all of 97-hectare Isla Magdalena, 20 nautical miles northeast of Punta Arenas, before returning to sea in April. Also the site of a landmark lighthouse, Isla Magdalena is the focal point of Monumento Natural Los Pingüinos, one of Conaf's smallest but most interesting reserves.

While the mainland Otway colony gets upwards of 40,000 visitors per year, Isla Magdalena gets fewer than 20,000—90

SOUTHERN PATAGONIA

THE WHALES OF MAGALLANES

For decades, the great whales have drawn travelers to Mexico's Baja California lagoons, the shallows of Argentina's Península Valdés, and other breeding and feeding sites. From late December to April, the latest entry in the whale-watching sweepstakes is Parque Marino Francisco Coloane, in the Strait of Magellan southwest of Punta Arenas.

Established in July 2003, named in honor of a Chilean author who chronicled the southern seas, the 67,000-hectare park is the result of five years' research that pinpointed the waters near Isla Carlos III as feeding grounds for the southern humpback whale *(Megaptera novaeangliae)* from mid-December to late April. In addition to the humpbacks, which migrate south from Colombia, the park's seas and shorelines are home to breeding populations of Magellanic penguins, cormorants, many other southern seabirds, fur seals, and sea lions. Orcas are also present.

The Punta Arenas company Whalesound operates the motor yacht *Esturión,* which sails south through the strait; as it spies Isla Dawson to the east, black-browed albatrosses, giant petrels, and Magellanic penguins circle the ship above and in the water. It then passes the Cabo Froward lighthouse where, by tradition, Pacific and Atlantic waters mix beneath the **Cruz de los Mares,** an illuminated hilltop cross that marks the terminus of an overland trek from the road's end at Cabo San Pedro. Construction materials for the cross arrived by boat and, after being beached here, were helicoptered to the summit.

Turning west into the Strait, the ship reaches Carlos III by late afternoon and, after unloading luggage at the camp, usually takes a spin around nearby rocks to see breeding colonies of fur seals and sea lions, as well as Magellanic oystercatchers, kelp geese, and small birds. The main attraction, though, is the humpbacks that dive and breach in the open strait.

Carlos III itself is a sheltered island of bonsai beeches that's also home to the world's southernmost conifer, the *ciprés de las Guaitecas* (Guaiteca cypress, *Pilgerodendron uviferum*). At low tide, a fur seal colony is only 20 minutes away on foot.

After trolling for whales the next morning, the boat circumnavigates wooded **Isla Rupert,** with a breeding colony of 22,000 Magellanic penguins. Unfortunately, the burrowing Magellanics have undermined the southern beech forest and, with their excrement and urine, are putting the woodland under serious stress.

From Isla Rupert, the *Esturión* sails west to **Isla Santa Inés** and its **Canal Ballena,** where the water shifts from deep blue to a blue-gray that it owes to sediments from a glacier that, though it reaches the sea, is receding quickly. In an area as scenic as Tierra del Fuego's fjords, there is little wildlife except for nesting rock cormorants and, surprisingly, a clutch of condors in an area with little carrion.

Leaving Santa Inés, where Whalesound offers sea kayaking and intends to build a trail for overnight treks, the ship returns to Carlos III by early evening. The next morning, it returns to the continent via **Fiordo Jerónimo,** part of southernmost **Isla Riesco**'s wild scenery, in Conaf's **Reserva Nacional Alacalufes.** At Seno Otway, passengers meet a vehicle for the return to Punta Arenas.

PRACTICALITIES

Whalesound (Lautaro Navarro 1163, 2nd floor, Punta Arenas, tel. 061/710511, cel. 09/9349-

---

percent of them foreigners—because of limited accessibility. In summer, though, the ferry *Melinka* visits the island daily from Punta Arenas. Though more expensive than Otway tours, these excursions also offer the chance to see penguins and dolphins in the water, as well as black-browed albatrosses, cormorants, kelp gulls, skuas, South American terns, and other seabirds in the surrounding skies.

From a floating dock on the east side of the island, a short trail leads along the beach and up the hill to Scottish engineer George Slight's **Faro Magdalena** (1901), a lighthouse whose iron tower rises 13.5 meters above the island's

© WAYNE BERNHARDSON

a humpback whale surfaces near Carlos III, in the western Strait of Magellan

3862, www.whalesound.com) offers three-day expeditions (US$750 pp, minimum two persons) to Isla Carlos III, where guests sleep in geodesic dome tents, with comfortable Japanese beds and solar-powered electricity. The cost includes daily excursions with specialized bilingual guides and gourmet meals from a French-trained Chilean chef. There is also a four-day program (US$1,300 pp) that includes sea kayaking.

The *Esturión II* sails from Fuerte Bulnes, an hour south of Punta Arenas by road; if seas are too rough, they may go overland via Isla Riesco and then a shorter hop to Carlos III on rigid inflatables. For those with more money than time, there are half-day helicopter trips.

Purchased in Buenos Aires after service on the calmer Río de la Plata, the Esturión is an 11-meter launch that does just eight knots. It carries up to ten passengers and can sleep seven in close quarters; in addition, it has a galley, sofa, and an open-air observation deck (which served it better on the balmy River Plate than the stormy Strait of Magellan).

Carlos III's sturdy dome tents are spacious but unheated; sleeping bags with fitted mummy sheets cover their single-sized platform beds. Boardwalks connect them to separate baths (hot showers with a view!) and the combination kitchen/dining room/bar, but it can be a wet, cold walk if you need the toilet in the middle of the night.

Food is excellent both on board and on land, with exceptional ceviche, fresh fish, beef, fruit, and Chilean wines. The boat's crew is friendly, the guides are knowledgeable, and the service is attentive.

New in 2008, **Expedición Fitz Roy** (Roca 825, Oficina 3, tel. 061/613933, www.expedicionfitzroy.com) offers similar services but passengers sleep on board the reconditioned M/V *Forrest*, which once hauled wool around the Falkland Islands. Rates start at US$900 pp for three-day, two-night packages.

highest point; still functioning, the light has a range of 10 nautical miles. A narrow spiral staircase ascends the tower.

In the building's first five decades, a resident caretaker maintained the acetylene light, but after its automation in 1955 the building was abandoned and vandalized. In 1981, though, the Chilean navy entrusted the building to Conaf; declared a national monument, it has since become a visitors center. It boasts remarkably good exhibits on the island's history, including discovery, early navigation, cartography, and the lighthouse's construction, and natural history in both Spanish and English (though the English text is less complete). U.S. archaeologist Junius Bird, best known for his 1930s work at the mainland site of Pali Aike, also undertook excavations here.

For ferry excursions to Isla Magdalena, contact **Turismo Comapa** (Magallanes 990, tel. 061/200200, tcomapa@entelchile.net). In December, January, and February, after its regular Tuesday/Thursday/Saturday run to Porvenir, the *Melinka* makes a passengers-only trip to Isla Magdalena (US$33 pp, US$17 for children) from Terminal Tres Puentes; sailing time is 4 P.M. (bring food—the *Melinka's* snack bar is pretty dire). Visitors spend about 1.5 hours on the island, returning to Punta Arenas around 9:30 P.M.

Passengers on the luxury *Mare Australis* and *Via Australis* cruises through Tierra del Fuego's fjords stop here on the return leg of the trip, but there's also an intermediate alternative that's more frequent than either of the above. Since 2005, **Solo Expediciones** (José Nogueira 1255, tel. 061/710219, www.solo-expediciones.com) offers half-day excursions (US$76 pp) that shuttle passengers from the mainland in Zodiacs and include an approach to nearby Isla Marta, where the overflow from penguin-saturated Magdalena has migrated.

FUERTE BULNES

In 1584, Spanish explorer Pedro Sarmiento de Gamboa organized an expedition of 15 ships and 4,000 men to control the Strait of Magellan, but after a series of disasters only three ships with 300 colonists arrived to found **Ciudad del Rey don Felipe,** at Punta Santa Ana south of present-day Punta Arenas. Even worse for the Spaniards, the inhospitable climate and unsuitable soils made agriculture impossible; when British privateer Thomas Cavendish landed three years later, in 1587, he found only a handful of survivors and gave it the name Port Famine, which has survived as the Spanish **Puerto del Hambre.**

For many years, the consensus was that starvation alone determined the fate of Puerto Hambre, but regional historian Mateo Martinic has suggested that disease, mutual acts of violence, Tehuelche attacks, and a simple sense of anguish or abandonment contributed to its demise. Unfortunately, the Chilean military control much of the area, making archaeological excavations that might resolve the question difficult.

The area remained unsettled until 1843, when President Manuel Bulnes ordered the cutter *Ancud* south from Chiloé with tools, construction materials, food, and livestock to take possession for the expansionist Chilean state. The result was Fuerte Bulnes, a military outpost that survived only a little longer than the original Spanish settlement before being relocated to Punta Arenas in 1848.

Modern Fuerte Bulnes, on the site of the first Chilean settlement, is a national monument more for its site than for its reconstructions of 19th-century buildings and the defensive walls—with sharpened stakes—that surround them. Among the structures were residences, stables, a blockhouse, a chapel, a jail, and warehouse.

Archaeologists located nearby remnants of Ciudad del Rey don Felipe in 1955, and later excavations turned up human remains, bullets, tombs, and ruins of Puerto Hambre's church. A more recent plaque (1965) celebrates the 125th anniversary of the Pacific Steam Navigation Company's ships *Chile* and *Perú* and their routes around the Horn.

Puerto Hambre and Fuerte Bulnes are 58 kilometers south of Punta Arenas via Ruta 9, which is paved about halfway; the rest is bumpy but passable. There is no regular public transportation, but most Punta Arenas tour operators offer half-day excursions. Admission is free of charge.

PARQUE MARINO FRANCISCO COLOANE

Established in July 2003, named for a Chilean author who chronicled the southern seas, this 67,000-hectare maritime park is the result of five years' biological investigations that pinpointed the area around Isla Carlos III, in the southwestern Strait of Magellan, as summer feeding grounds for the southern humpback whale. In addition to the humpbacks, which migrate the length of the South American coast from Colombia, the park's seas and shores are home to breeding Magellanic penguins, cormorants, many other southern seabirds, fur seals, and sea lions. Orcas are also present.

From mid-December to late April, **Whalesound** (Lautaro Navarro 1175, 2nd floor, Punta Arenas, tel. 061/710511, ext. 201, cel. 09/9349-3862, www.whalesound.com) offers three-day expeditions (US$750 pp, minimum two persons) to the park, where guests sleep in geodesic dome tents, with comfortable Japanese beds and solar-powered electricity, on Isla Carlos III. The cost includes daily excursions with specialized bilingual guides and gourmet meals from a French-trained Chilean chef. Sea kayaks are also available.

RÍO VERDE

Some 43 kilometers north of Punta Arenas on Ruta 9, a gravel road loops northwest along Seno Otway to Seno Skyring and Estancia Río Verde, which has seemingly made the transition from a shipshape sheep farm to a model municipality of exquisitely maintained public buildings in the Magellanic style. Note particularly the manicured gardens surrounding the **Escuela Básica,** the local boarding school.

Off to a good start, in one wing of the boarding school, the **Museo Comunal Río Verde** (10 A.M.–5 P.M. daily, US$1) has exhibits on local history, natural history (taxidermy), ethnology, and local and regional literature.

Unfortunately, only the foundations of the recently created *Municipalidad* remain, after it burned to the ground a couple years back and museum exhibits were lost; municipal offices have since moved to the former Hostería Río Verde, 90 kilometers from Punta Arenas and six kilometers south of the *estancia.*

Across from the former *hostería,* a small ferry shuttles vehicles and passengers to **Isla Riesco** (warning: it's free to the island, but costs US$30 to get your vehicle back to the mainland). Nearby, Paola Vizzani González's *Escultura Monumental,* a beached whale built of concrete and driftwood, honors the region's

early colonists. Also nearby, the **Hito El Vapor** marks the final resting place of the steamer *Los Amigos,* which carried coal to outlying farms until it ran aground in a storm.

The loop road rejoins Ruta 9 at Villa Tehuelches, a wide spot in the road about 90 kilometers from Punta Arenas. This makes a good alternative route north or south for both motorists and mountain bikers.

While the *hostería* at the ferry crossing no longer provides accommodations, the Chilean-Uruguayan ❬ **Estancia Río Verde** (Km 98 Norte, tel. 061/311123 or 061/311131, jmma@ entelchile.net, US$83 s, US$107 d) offers stylish accommodations (one suite has a sunny tower with sea and pampas views), day tours that can include horseback riding and fishing, and *asados,* lunches, and tea in its restaurant. Open November to March, it is a bargain by *estancia* standards and has gracious English-speaking ownership.

ESTANCIA RÍO PENITENTE

Founded by Falkland Islands immigrants in 1891, Río Penitente has turned one of the best-preserved historic houses on any Patagonian sheep ranch into a guesthouse that feels like a step back in time, but still has essential comforts such as private baths. Most guest rooms in this two-story Victorian have period furniture, in immaculate condition, and fireplaces for heat. Activities include horseback riding and fly-fishing in its namesake river, but it's an ideal place for just relaxing. The restaurant serves lamb-on-a-stake barbecues to tour groups on weekends.

Hostería Estancia Río Penitente Ruta 9 Km 137, tel. 061/331694, www.hosteriariopenitente.com, US$92 s, US$113 d with breakfast) is open October to Semana Santa (Holy Week).

RÍO RUBENS

About halfway between Villa Tehuelches and Puerto Natales, Río Rubens is a prime trout stream that flows northeast into Argentina. At Km 183 on Ruta 9, the nearby **Hotel Posada Río Rubens** (cel. 09/9433-4727, www .hotelrubens.cl) has resisted the temptation to upgrade itself from a modest rural inn, with a decent restaurant at modest prices, though it has added *cabañas* and camping. Hotel rates are US$20 s, US$30 d with private bath and breakfast.

ESTANCIA SAN GREGORIO

From a highway junction about 45 kilometers north of Punta Arenas, paved Ruta 225 leads east/northeast to the Argentine border at Monte Aymond, passing the former Estancia San Gregorio, once one of Chilean Patagonia's largest landholdings. Part of the Menéndez wool empire, San Gregorio dates from the 1890s, though it reached its peak between 1910 and 1930. Besides wool, it produced frozen mutton, hides, and tallow.

Now run as a cooperative, 120 kilometers from Punta Arenas, San Gregorio is a *zona típica* national historical monument. It exemplified the Anglo-Scottish model of the Patagonian sheep *estancia,* in which each unit was a self-sufficient hierarchy with a nearly omnipotent administrator at the top. Geographically, it consisted of discrete residential and production sectors: The former included the administrator's house, employee residences, shearers' dormitories, chapel, and the like, while the latter comprised the shearing shed, warehouses, a smithery, company store, and similarly functional buildings. It had its own pier and railroad to move the wool clip directly to freighters.

Most of San Gregorio's constructions date from the 1890s, but a descendent of the Menéndez dynasty still occupies French architect Antoine Beaulier's **Casa Patronal** (1925). The farm featured an extensive system of windbreaks ranging upwards of five meters in height, later planted with Monterey cypress for beautification.

While technically not open to the public, many of San Gregorio's buildings line both sides of the highway to Monte Aymond. Beached on shore are the corroded hulks of the British clipper *Ambassador* (a national monument) and the company steamer *Amadeo,* which gave up the ghost in the 1940s.

PUNTA DELGADA

About 30 kilometers east of San Gregorio, paved Ruta 257 leads southeast to **Punta Delgada,** the port for the ferry crossing to Tierra del Fuego via the Primera Angostura narrows. Depending sometimes on tidal conditions, the ferries *Patagonia, Fueguino* and *Pionero* shuttle across the channel every 1.5 hours 8:30 A.M.–11 P.M. Fares are US$2.50 per person for passengers, US$1.25 for kids ages 10–14, US$23 for automobiles, and US$7 for motorcycles. Most buses to Argentine Tierra del Fuego use this route because the longer ferry to Porvenir goes only once daily and is subject to delay or cancellation for rough seas.

PARQUE NACIONAL PALI AIKE

Hugging the Argentine border north of Kimiri Aike and west of the Monte Aymond border crossing, little-visited Pali Aike is an area of volcanic steppe and rugged lava beds that once supported megafauna such as the ground sloth milodon and the native American horse, both of which disappeared soon after humans first inhabited the area some 11,000 years ago.

While Paleo-Indian hunters may have contributed to their extinction, environmental changes after the last major glaciation may also have played a role. In the 1930s, self-taught archaeologist Junius Bird, of New York's American Museum of Natural History, conducted the earliest systematic excavations of Paleo-Indian sites such as Cueva Pali Aike, within the park boundaries, and Cueva Fell, a short distance west. These archaeologically rich volcanic shelters (not caves in the strictest sense of the word) are the prime reason Chilean authorities have nominated the area as a UNESCO World Heritage Site.

Findings at Pali Aike include human remains that have yielded insights on Paleo-Indian funerary customs, while materials from Cueva Fell have helped reveal the transition from relatively simple hunting to more complex forms of subsistence. These include sophisticated hunting tools such as the bow and arrow and *boleadoras,* and a greater reliance on coastal and marine resources. There are also indicators of ceremonial artifacts.

Geography and Climate

Part of arid eastern Magallanes, 5,030-hectare Pali Aike consists of rolling steppe grasslands whose porous volcanic soils and slag absorb water quickly. Almost constant high winds and cool temperatures make it a better summer or autumn excursion.

Flora and Fauna

While the milodon and native horse may have disappeared, the park's grasslands swarm with herds of wild guanaco and flocks of rheas, upland geese, ibis, and other birds. Pumas and foxes are the major predators.

Sights and Recreation

Accessible by road, **Cueva Pali Aike** is a volcanic tube seven meters wide and five meters high at its mouth; it is 17 meters deep but tapers as it advances. In the 1930s, Bird discovered both human and megafauna remains, at least 8,600 years old and probably much older, in the cave.

Tours from Punta Arenas visit Cueva Pali Aike and usually hike the 1.7-kilometer trail through the **Escorial del Diablo** (the appropriately named Devil's Slag Heap, which is hell on hiking boots). The trail ends at the volcanic **Crater Morada del Diablo.**

From Cueva Pali Aike, a nine-kilometer footpath leads to **Laguna Ana,** where waterfowl are abundant, and the main road, five kilometers from the park entrance. Mountain bikes should be ideal for this sort of rolling terrain, but it could be even tougher on tires than it is on boots.

Practicalities

As of 2009, campground is supposedly in the works, but there are no tourist services as yet, so bring supplies.

At the main entrance, Conaf has a ranger station but collects no admission fee. A great destination for solitude seekers, Pali Aike officially gets fewer only about 1,600

visitors per year, barely a quarter of them foreigners.

Parque Nacional Pali Aike is 196 kilometers northeast of Punta Arenas via Ruta 9, Ruta 255, and a graveled secondary road from the hamlet of Cooperativa Villa O'Higgins, 11 kilometers beyond Kimiri Aike. Just south of the Chilean border post at Monte Aymond, a hard-to-follow dirt road also leads to the park.

There is no public transportation, but Punta Arenas travel agencies can arrange visits. Hiring a car, though, is probably the best option, especially if shared among several people.

◖ THE FJORDS OF FUEGIA

Short of Antarctica itself, some of the Southern Hemisphere's most awesome scenery occurs in the Beagle Channel and southern Tierra del Fuego. And as usual, Charles Darwin left one of the most vivid descriptions of the channel named for the vessel on which he sailed:

> The scenery here becomes even grander than before. The lofty mountains on the north side compose the granitic axis, or backbone of the country, and boldly rise to a height of between three and four thousand feet, with one peak above six thousand feet. They are covered by a wide mantle of perpetual snow, and numerous cascades pour their waters, through the woods, into the narrow channel below. In many parts, magnificent glaciers extend from the mountain side to the water's edge. It is scarcely possible to imagine anything more beautiful than the beryl-like blue of these glaciers, and especially as contrasted with the dead white of the upper expanse of the snow. The fragments which had fallen from the glacier into the water, were floating away, and the channel with the icebergs presented, for the space of a mile, a miniature likeness of the Polar Sea.

Even today, few visitors see Tierra del Fuego's splendid fjords, barely changed since Darwin described them in 1833; many of those do so onboard weeklong excursions from Punta Arenas to the Argentine port of Ushuaia and back on the twin Chilean vessels *Mare Australis* and *Vía Australis*. Unlike the Navimag ferry from Puerto Montt to Puerto Natales, these are cruises in the traditional sense—the passengers are waited on hand and foot, and they're not cheap. Yet for the foreseeable future, this remains the only way to see the area short of sailing your own yacht or chartering someone else's, and for that reason it's worth consideration even for those with limited finances.

One common alternative is to do either leg of the voyage separately—either four days and three nights from Punta Arenas to Ushuaia, or five days and four nights from Ushuaia to Punta Arenas. The boats sometimes undertake variants that involve four nights from Punta Arenas and three from Ushuaia, and there's usually some duplication; both legs, for instance, visit the western Beagle Channel's **Glaciar Pía,** and sometimes the boats are there simultaneously.

Routes can vary depending on weather conditions in this notoriously capricious climate. After an evening departure from Punta Arenas's Muelle Prat, the vessel crosses the Strait of Magellan to enter the **Seno del Almirantazgo** (Admiralty Sound), a westward maritime extension of the freshwater Lago Fagnano trough. Passengers usually go ashore at **Bahía Ainsworth,** near the **Glaciar Marinelli,** where there's a short hiking trail through what was once forest until feral beavers dammed the area into a series of ponds; the most interesting site for most visitors is a small elephant seal colony. Farther west, at **Isla Tucker,** there's a small Magellanic penguin colony (usually observed from an inflatable Zodiac) and it's also possible to see the rare striated caracara, *Phalcoboenus australis.*

After a night's sailing, the ship may enter the **Fiordo D'Agostini,** a glacial inlet named for the early 20th-century Italian priest and mountaineer who explored the Cordillera Darwin's farthest recesses. When high winds make it

Chilean Tierra del Fuego's Glaciar Pía is one of the top shore excursions for Cruceros Australis.

© WAYNE BERNHARDSON

impossible to approach the **Glaciar Serrano** (named for Chilean naval Lieutenant Ramón Serrano Montaner, who charted the Strait in 1879), an option is the more sheltered **Glaciar D'Agostini.** Even here, though, seracs crack off the glacier's face, touching off a rapid surge of water and ice that runs parallel to a broad gravel beach and, when it subsides, leaves the beach littered with boulders of ice.

Darwin, again, described the dangers of travel in a land that sea kayakers are just beginning to explore:

> The boats being hauled on shore at our dinner hour, we were admiring from the distance of half a mile a perpendicular cliff of ice, and were wishing that some more fragments would fall. At last, down came a mass with a roaring noise, and immediately we saw the smooth outline of a wave traveling toward us. The men ran down as quickly as they could to the boats; for the chance of their being dashed to pieces was evident. One of the seamen just caught hold of the bows, as the curling breaker reached it: he was knocked over and over, but not hurt; and the boats, though thrice lifted on high and let fall again, received no damage.... I had previously noted that some large fragments of rock on the beach had been lately displaced; but until seeing this wave, I did not understand the cause.

After navigating Canal Cockburn, where open ocean swells can rock the boat at least briefly, the vessel turns into the calmer **Canal Ocasión** and eventually enters the Beagle Channel's north arm, sailing past the so-called **Avenida de los Glaciares,** a series of glaciers named for various European countries; passengers normally disembark at **Glaciar Pía.** Traditionally, after sailing through the night, the ship has spent a few hours at **Puerto Williams** as Chilean authorities came aboard to process passports before it continued to Argentina, but emigration formalities now take place at **Puerto Navarino,** at the western end of **Isla Navarino.**

Proceeding to **Ushuaia,** all passengers spend the night aboard; those returning to Punta Arenas have the day free in Ushuaia before returning to the ship, while new passengers check their bags downtown before boarding in late afternoon.

After reentering Chile at Puerto Navarino, the ship sails south to **Cabo de Hornos** (Cape Horn) and, wind permitting (less than 45 knots), passengers disembark to visit the small Chilean naval detachment and hike to the stylized albatross sculpture that symbolizes sailors who lost their lives "rounding the Horn."

Again, if weather permits, the captain can choose to round the Horn himself before proceeding north to **Bahía Wulaia,** on Isla Navarino's western shore. Here passengers visit the site of an early mission where, in a notorious incident, the Yámana massacred all but one of the Anglicans and their crew. There is then the option of a short but steep hike with panoramic views of the bay, or an easier shoreline walk to see birdlife including Magellanic oystercatchers.

Returning to the Beagle Channel, the ship veers westward through the Beagle Channel's north arm, again passing the Avenida de los Glaciares and entering Fiordo Pía (Pía Fjord), where dozens of waterfalls cascade down sheer metamorphic slopes from the **Glaciar Pía** and passengers take a short hike. Proceeding through the afternoon and the night, the boat starts the last full day navigating the **Fiordo Chico** (Little Fjord), where passengers board Zodiacs to approach but not land at **Glaciar Plüschow,** named for a German pioneer aviator who took the first aerial photos of the Cordillera Darwin.

In the afternoon, the **Glaciar Águila** is the site of an easy shoreline walk or a more demanding slog through knee-deep mud in a southern beech forest (the video footage of this hike, shown the night before in an orientation session, is priceless). On the final morning, the boat sails north to **Isla Magdalena** (see *Monumento Natural Los Pingüinos*) before returning to Punta Arenas.

SOUTHERN PATAGONIA

Practicalities

Well-organized without being regimented, the cruise is informal in terms of dress and behavior. As the start, passengers sign up for meal tables; places are fixed for the duration except at the buffet breakfast, when people tend to straggle in at different times. In general, passengers are grouped according to language, though they often place together people who speak English as a second language. The staff themselves can handle Spanish, English, German, French, and occasionally other languages.

After introduction of the captain and crew, and an obligatory safety drill, there's a welcome drink and a brief folklore show (in Punta Arenas) or tango demonstration (in Ushuaia). Smoking is prohibited everywhere except outdoors and at the rear of the fourth deck pub; bar consumption is now included in the package.

The cabins themselves are reasonably spacious, with either a double or twin beds, built-in reading lights, a closet with hangers and a small lock box for valuables, and a private bath with excellent hot showers. Some rooms also have a fold-down bunk for children or a third person. The food is abundant and occasionally excellent, though breakfasts are a little monotonous; the wine is superb, and the service exceptional. Vegetarian menus are available on request.

For those who tire of the landscape or when the weather is bad, onboard activities include karaoke, slide lectures on flora and fauna, engine-room tours, and culinary demonstrations of carved cucumbers, peppers, zucchinis, and other vegetables, in the shapes of birds and flowers.

The farewell dinner is a fairly gala affair, followed by champagne on the topmost deck.

Punta Arenas is the homeport for fjord-bound cruises; check-in takes place at Turismo Comapa (Magallanes 990, tel. 061/200200) 1–5 P.M., while boarding takes place 5–6 P.M. at the entrance to Muelle Prat. Some passengers begin or end the trip in Argentine Tierra del Fuego, where check-in takes place at Comapa's Ushuaia office (San Martín 245, tel. 02901/430727, 9 A.M.–4 P.M.); boarding takes place at the Muelle Prat 5–6 P.M.

Usually this popular cruise runs full October–April, except for the last trip before Christmas, which may be only half full; in this case, it may be possible to negotiate a deal in Punta Arenas, getting a private cabin without paying a single supplement, for instance. In addition, at this time of year, days are so long that it's possible to enjoy the landscape until after 11 P.M., and there's sufficient light to read by 4 A.M.

Make reservations through **Cruceros Australis** (Avenida Bosque Norte 0440, 11th floor, Las Condes, Santiago, tel. 02/4423110, fax 02/2035173, www.australis.com), which also has offices in Buenos Aires (Carlos Pellegrini 989, 6th floor, Retiro, tel. 011/4325-8400) and in Miami (4014 Chase Ave., Suite 202, Miami Beach, FL 33140, tel. 305/695-9618 or 877/678-3772). Per-person rates for four days and three nights start at US$960–1,680 in low season and go up to US$1,140–1,980 in high season. For five days and four nights, the comparable rates are US$1,110–1,940 in low season to US$1,310–2,290 in high season.

Puerto Natales

In the past 20 years, Puerto Natales has changed from a sleepy wool and fishing port on what seemed the aptly named Seno Última Esperanza—"Last Hope Sound"—to a bustling tourist town whose season has lengthened well beyond the traditional summer months. Its proximity to the famous Torres del Paine, coupled with its status as the southern terminus for the scenic ferry route from Puerto Montt, has placed it on the international travel map, utterly transforming the local economy.

While Natales has no knockout attractions in its own right, the town enjoys a magnificent seaside setting, with the snow-capped Cordillera Sarmiento and Campo de Hielo Sur, the southern Patagonian ice cap, visible over the water to the west, and the waterfront is more presentable than in the past. For visitors to Paine and other regional sights, it has abundant services, including tour operators and rental equipment, plus convenient connections to the Argentine town of El Calafate and Parque Nacional Los Glaciares. The strength of the Chilean peso had reduced its competitiveness with nearby Argentine attractions such as the Moreno Glacier, but depreciation in late 2008 has made the city a good value again.

Another possible strong point is the possible construction of a 150-meter cruise-ship pier, which would simplify land transfers from both the ferry (which does have an improved dock) and visiting cruisers, but it in early 2009 this remained at the talking stage. Meanwhile, private initiative has built a smaller jetty for local cruises near Puerto Bories, north of town.

HISTORY

Última Esperanza acquired its name because expeditions led by 16th-century explorers Juan Ladrilleros and Pedro Sarmiento de Gamboa failed to find a westbound route to the Pacific here. Puerto Natales proper dates from the early 20th century, a few years after German explorer Hermann Eberhard founded the area's first sheep *estancia* at Puerto Prat. Within a few years, the Sociedad Explotadora de Tierra del Fuego had built a slaughterhouse at nearby Bories to process and pack mutton for the export market. While the livestock economy declined in the second half of the 20th century, the tourist boom has reactivated and diversified the economy.

ORIENTATION

On the eastern shores of Seno Última Esperanza, Puerto Natales (population 16,978) is 250 kilometers northwest of Punta Arenas via paved Ruta 9. It is 150 kilometers south of Parque Nacional Torres del Paine, also by Ruta 9, which is paved for 13 kilometers north of the city.

Entering town from the north, Ruta 9 becomes the roughly north–south Costanera Pedro Montt; most services and points of interest are within easy walking distance to the east. The principal commercial streets are east–west Manuel Bulnes and north–south Avenida Baquedano. A new northwesterly route has cut the distance to the park border.

SIGHTS

The Sociedad Explotadora de Tierra del Fuego, owner of large pasture tracts in both Chile and Argentina, financed construction of Natales' gingerbread-style **Municipalidad,** dating from 1929 (the powerful Sociedad Explotadora was, in some ways, the region's de facto government). Immediately east, the **Iglesia Parroquial María Auxiliadora** dates from the same era and shares its Magellanic style.

In the same exterior fashion but with a roomier interior that displays its holdings to advantage, the **Museo Histórico Municipal** (Bulnes 285, tel. 061/411263, muninata@ ctcinternet.cl, 8 A.M.–7 P.M. weekdays, 10 A.M.–1 P.M. and 3–6 P.M. weekends, US$0.85 for Chileans, US$1.50 for foreigners) offers displays on natural history, archaeology,

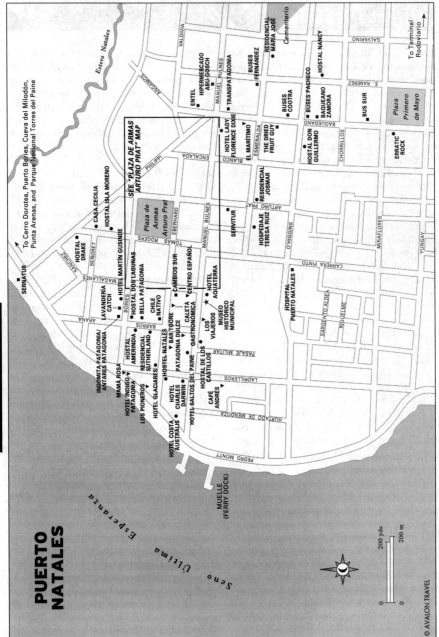

PUERTO NATALES

SOUTHERN PATAGONIA

To Cerro Dorotea, Puerto Bories, Cueva del Milodón,
Punta Arenas, and Parque Nacional Torres del Paine

Estero Natales

Seno Última Esperanza

SERNATUR

VALDIVIA

ANDSMOS

PHILIPPI

ENCALADA

BLANCO

Cementerio

GALVARINO

To Terminal
Rodoviario

HIPERMERCADO
ABU-GOSCH

MANUEL BULNES

TRANSPATAGONIA

RESIDENCIAL
MARIA JOSÉ

HOSTAL NANCY

E. RAMIREZ

ENTEL

BUSES
FERNÁNDEZ

HOTEL LADY
FLORENCE DIXIE

EL MARITIMO

ESMERALDA

BUSES PACHECO

BAQUEDANO

BUSES
COOTRA

BAQUEANO
ZAMORA

BUS SUR

Plaza
Primero
de Mayo

SEE "PLAZA DE ARMAS ARTURO PRAT" MAP

THE DRIED
FRUIT GUY

HOSTAL DON
GUILLERMO

CHORRILLOS

ERRATIC
ROCK

CASA CECILIA

HOSTAL ISLA MORENO

Plaza de
Armas
Arturo Prat

ROGERS

EBERHARD

RESIDENCIAL
JOSMAR

TOMAS ROGERS

MANUEL BULNES

SERVITUR

HOSPEDAJE
TERESA RUIZ

ARTURO PRAT

O'HIGGINS

MIRAFLORES

YUNGAY

HOSTAL
DRAKE

SENORET

SANCHEZ

HOTEL MARTIN GUSINDE

MAGALLANES

ARANA

BORIES

LAVANDERIA
CATCH

HOSTAL DOS LAGUNAS

BELLA PATAGONIA

CHILE
NATIVO

CAMBIOS SUR

CENTRO ESPAÑOL

HOTEL
AQUATERRA

BARROS

MUSEO
HISTÓRICO
MUNICIPAL

CALETA

HOSPITAL
PUERTO NATALES

CARRERA PINTO

SARGENTO ALDEA

RIQUELME

INDOMITA PATAGONIA/
ANTARES PATAGONIA

MAMÁ ROSA

HOTEL INDIGO
PATAGONIA

LOS PIONEROS

HOTEL GLACIARES

HOSTAL
AMERINDIA

RESIDENCIAL
SUTHERLAND

HOSTEL NATALES

BAR TOORE

PATAGONIA DULCE

GASTRONOMICA

LOS
VIAJEROS

PASAJE MILITAR

HOTEL COSTA
AUSTRALIS

HOTEL
CHARLES
DARWIN

HOTEL SALTOS DEL PAINE

HOSTAL DE LOS
CASTILLOS

CAFÉ
ANDRÉS

LADRILLEROS

HURTADO DE MENDOZA

PEDRO MONTT

MUELLE
(FERRY DOCK)

200 yds
200 m

0
0

© AVALON TRAVEL

and the region's aboriginal peoples, European settlement, and the rural economy (including the Sociedad Explotadora), Natales' own urban evolution, and the Carabineros police, who played a role in the museum's creation. Noteworthy individual artifacts include a Yámana (Yahgan) dugout canoe and Aónikenk (Tehuelche) *boleadoras,* plus historical photographs of Captain Eberhard and the town's development.

ENTERTAINMENT

Nightlife is limited mostly to dining out and to low-key bars such as **Bar Toore** (Eberhard 169), a new entrant in the nightlife sweepstakes. The well-established **El Bar de Ruperto** (Bulnes 371) takes its name from the pisco-swilling burro once popular on Chilean TV ads.

Upstairs at the restaurant **PezGlaciar** (Ladrilleros 105), a separate **PiscoSour Café & Bar** has snacks, a diversity of pisco sours including one made with the Mapuche spice *merkén,* WiFi, occasional slide shows on the park and other travel-related topics, and even movies, projected onto a wall screen, to watch from comfortable sofas. In summer, these start late because sunset falls after 10 P.M.

SHOPPING

In new quarters, **Ñandú Artesanía** (Eberhard 301, tel. 061/414382) sells maps and books in addition to a selection of quality crafts. Across the street, with more style, **El Emporio de la Pampa** (Eberhard 302, tel. 061/413279) also sells crafts, but it's also a deli with gourmet cheeses, finer wines than usually found in Natales, and real coffee (as opposed to Nescafé).

World's End (Blanco Encalada 226, tel. 061/414725, www.patagoniax.com) is a map specialist that also carries a big selection of used books in English and other languages, available on a purchase-or-exchange basis.

The **Pueblo Artesanal Ehterh Aike** (Philippi 660) has a variety of crafts but is also the best place in town to buy fresh fruit and other produce.

ACCOMMODATIONS

Over the past two decades-plus, Natales has developed one of Chile's densest offerings of accommodations. This is especially true in the budget category, where competition keeps prices low, and in exceptional new upscale options—but there are plenty of mediocre and ordinary places in all ranges. Off-season rates can drop dramatically at upscale places.

US$10-25

In new quarters, **Residencial María José** (Esmeralda 869, tel. 061/412218, juan_lasa@hotmail.com, US$8 pp) is the Israeli favorite, and has opened a second branch **Residencial María José II** (Magallanes 638, tel. 061/414312) with identical prices.

Hospedaje Teresa Ruiz (Esmeralda 463, tel. 061/410472, freepatagonia@hotmail.com, US$10 pp) gets high marks for congeniality, cleanliness, and outstanding breakfasts with homemade rhubarb preserves.

Residencial Josmar 2 (Esmeralda 517, tel. 061/413796, www.josmar.cl, US$8 pp) has added a spacious campground (US$5–6 pp) with clearly delineated sites, privacy from the street, electricity, and hot showers. Campers can use the hotel's common spaces.

Among the most traditional of budget accommodations, **Residencial Sutherland** (Barros Arana 155, tel. 061/410359, US$10 pp, US$27 d) has recently added rooms with private bath.

Magallania Backpacker (Tomás Rogers 255, tel. 061/414950, magallania@yahoo.com, US$10 pp) is an informal hostel with spacious dorms and a few doubles (US$25) including breakfast, kitchen privileges, a TV room, and *buena onda* (good vibes).

Friendly **Residencial Patagonia Aventura** (Tomás Rogers 179, tel. 061/411028, www.apatagonia.com, US$15 pp, US$35 d) provides a bit more privacy than others in its range, with knowledgeable operators who also rent equipment. It has WiFi, but no kitchen access (though it has a good café).

Operated by expat Oregonians, the informal hostel **Erratic Rock** (Baquedano 719, tel. 061/410355, www.erraticrock.com, US$13–17 pp) occupies a creaky house with character. It also serves a better-than-average breakfast, has a large book exchange, and rents quality gear for Paine-bound travelers. It also has a unique special: Anyone who can do 150 pushups nonstop gets one free night.

US$25-50

Relocated in improved quarters, **Hostal Nancy** (Ramírez 540, tel. 061/410022, www.nataleslodge.cl, US$30 d with breakfast) has long been a popular choice in its price range.

At friendly **Hostal Dickson** (Bulnes 307, tel. 061/411871, patagoniadickson@hotmail.com, US$17 d with shared bath, US$20 s, US$30 d with private bath), look at the rooms closely—some have windows so small that they feel like jail cells. On the other hand, there's central heating, the beds are good, the shared baths are numerous, and rates include breakfast.

Open all year, in an older house with substantial character and attentive ownership, the five-room ◖ **Hostal Dos Lagunas** (Barros Arana 104, tel. 061/415733, doslagunas@hotmail.com, US$25 s, US$33 d with shared bath) is slowly but steadily upgrading, and is due to add some private baths. Rates include an ample and varied breakfast; owner Alejandro Cárdenas, who speaks English and German, conducts off-season trips to Paine.

Hostal Isla Morena (Tomás Rogers 68, tel. 061/414773, www.islamorena.cl, US$21 p) enjoys fine natural light in modern rooms with private bath; a couple lack exterior windows but have skylights.

In an off-the-beaten-sidewalk location, looking more expensive than it is, the immaculate ◖ **Hostal Don Guillermo** (O'Higgins 657, tel./fax 061/414506, www.hostaldonguillermo.cl, US$20 s, US$37–50 d) is underpriced compared to nearby competitors. Though the singles are small, some rooms now have private baths and the breakfast is excellent; rates vary according to whether the room has cable TV.

With what may be Natales's most colorful garden—the summer roses are a sight—**Hostal de los Castillos** (Bulnes 241, tel. 061/413641, www.hostalcastillos.com, US$33 s, US$50 d with breakfast) is also a popular teahouse. The rooms themselves are comfortable and spacious, though one picture-window double faces the street (heavy curtains give it sufficient privacy).

US$50-100

Now a Natales institution, █ **Casa Cecilia** (Tomás Rogers 60, tel. 061/613560, www .casaceciliahostal.com, US$21–42 s, US$37–53 d) deserves credit for improving accommodations standards here—it's such a legend that, on occasion, nonguests even ask for tours of the Swiss-Chilean B&B. The rooms are simple, and some are small, but all enjoy central heating and some have private baths and cable TV. The cheerful atrium is a popular gathering place. Rates include a diverse breakfast and WiFi.

Rehabbed **Hostal Drake** (Philippi 383, tel./ fax 061/411553, www.hostalfrancisdrake.com, US$48 s, US$58 d) is a comfortable hostelry in a quiet location that tour operators often choose for their clients. Rates include breakfast, and it's more attuned to IVA discounts than in the past.

New in early 2006, the artfully decorated **Hostal Amerindia** (Barros Arana 135, tel. 061/411945, www.hostelamerindia.com, US$47 s, US$59 d, with a six percent surcharge for credit cards) is a B&B that's added rooms and upgraded with private baths. Its major shortcoming is that three slightly cheaper, otherwise comfortable rooms share one bath; the other four have private baths. It also has WiFi and serves a buffet breakfast.

Nearly new, **Hostal South Wind** (Eberhard 568, tel. 061/412766) www.southwindhostel.cl, US$40 s, US$60 d) offers spacious and comfortable rooms, with contemporary furnishings and private baths; the rooms mostly lack windows but get ample illumination from skylights. The upside to the windowless rooms is that they get almost no street noise.

Hostel Natales (Ladrilleros 209, tel. 061/410081, www.hostelnatales.cl, US$25 pp, US$50 s, US$65 d) has transformed the dreary Hotel Palace into warm, luminous accommodations with private baths; some rooms have two or four bunk beds—a little expensive by hostel standards—while others have doubles for couples. The lobby and atrium (which includes a fountain) are spacious and inviting, with comfortable chairs and sofas, but the rooms are sparsely furnished and sounds carry from the lobby (which is also an Internet café) to the nearest ones.

US$100-200

If only for honoring history's greatest scientist, **Hotel Charles Darwin** (Bulnes 90, tel. 061/412478, www.hotelcharlesdarwin.com, US$108 s, US$114 d) deserves some attention; painted in pastels, the 22 rooms range from smallish to midsize, but they're flooded with natural light and have state-of-the-art baths. Management is accommodating, and the restaurant has an interesting menu as well.

The striking **Hotel Lady Florence Dixie** (Manuel Bulnes 659, tel. 061/411158, florence@chileanpatagonia.com, US$82–98 s, US$100–115 d) has expanded and upgraded what was already a good hotel, but prices have risen in dollar terms even as the peso has slipped in value. **Hotel Glaciares** (Eberhard 104, tel./fax 061/411452, www.hotelglaciares .com, US$107 s, US$119 d) is comparable.

Just a few years ago █ **Hotel Aquaterra** (Bulnes 299, tel. 061/412239, www.aquaterra patagonia.com, US$107 s, US$122 d), a purpose-built hotel that combines style (native woods) and substance (comfortable furnishings), was almost unique. Though the competition has more than caught up, it's still worth consideration, as is its unconventional restaurant menu.

Atop a bluff on the Paine road just north of town, **Weskar Patagonian Lodge** (Ruta 9 Km 1, tel. 061/414168, www.weskar.cl, US$120 s, US$160 d) has panoramic views of the sound from its bar/restaurant and slightly less panoramic views from its upstairs rooms, some of whose windows are triangular. The rooms themselves are midsize but get fine natural light, and the beds and other furnishings are excellent.

Recently acquired by the neighboring casino, the expanding **Hotel Martín Gusinde** (Bories 278, tel. 061/412770, www.martingusinde.cl, US$127 s, US$154 d) may undergo a change in character. The handsome **Hotel Saltos del Paine** (Bulnes 156, tel. 061/413607, www.saltosdelpaine.cl, US$150 s, US$165 d) is more spacious than the Darwin.

Natales's most distinctive new accommodations are at the subtly landscaped **Hotel Altiplánico del Sur** (Ruta 9 Norte, Huerto 258, tel. 061/412525, www.altiplanico.cl, US$170 s, US$180 d), which has built all its rooms into the hillside along the Paine highway about two km north of town. Only the windows and roof rise above ground level, while blocks of peat insulate the concrete structure and help adapt it to its site. The common areas, the rooms, and the furnishings all display an elegant simplicity.

Over US$200

After suffering a serious fire that cost it the entire 2009 summer season, the waterfront classic **Hotel Costa Australis** (Costanera Pedro Montt 262, tel. 061/412000, www.hoteles-australis.com, US$220/248–470/490 s/d) is due to reopen; standard rates depend on whether the room has a city or sea view, and the highest rates correspond to suites. It's hard-pressed to keep up with newer choices such as the Altiplánico and Indigo, though the new addition may close the gap at least partially.

New in late 2006, on the site of what was once a modest B&B, **❰ Hotel Indigo Patagonia** (Ladrilleros 105, tel. 061/413609, www.indigopatagonia.com, US$280–378 s or d) is a minimalist-design hotel and spa with 29 rooms, including half a dozen suites. Most rooms are surprisingly small but efficient and striking—the glassed-in shower, for instance, has a huge copper showerhead. The design theme extends to the public computers, which are iMacs.

FOOD

Known for seafood, Natales has several moderately priced eateries and improving midrange-to-upscale choices.

To stock up on supplies for that Paine trek, visit **Hipermercado Abu-Gosch** (Bulnes 742). More specialized, for your trail mix, is **The Dried Fruit Guy** (Baquedano 443).

Decor-free **Masay** (Bulnes 427, tel. 061/415008) has decent inexpensive sandwiches and pizzas. **Café Evasión** (Eberhard 595-B, tel. 061/414605) is a moderately priced café with daily lunch specials. Basic Chilean dishes outshine the Italian at **La Repizza** (Blanco Encalada 294, tel. 061/410361).

Patagonia Dulce (Barros Arana 233, tel. 061/415285, www.patagoniadulce.cl) serves several varieties of hot chocolate (expensive at around US$4–5 each, but welcome on a cold morning) and desserts, including kuchen and mousses, along with rich homemade chocolate candies by weight. Unfortunately it doesn't open until 11 A.M.

On the east side of the Plaza de Armas, the British-run vegetarian **❰ El Living** (Arturo Prat 156, tel. 061/411140, 11 A.M.–11 P.M. daily, closed May–mid-Oct., US$4–5 for sandwiches) also serves breakfast, economical sandwiches and desserts (try especially the Sachertorte). Its owner arrived here by way of Torres del Paine's extravagant Hotel Salto Chico, but his food is more upmarket than his prices.

In the same style, the cozy **Café Cielo de Palo** (Tomás Rogers 179, tel. 061/411028, lunch and dinner daily) serves tasty vegetarian dishes such as falafel and a variety of fine desserts, not to mention freshly brewed coffee, tea, juices, and sandwiches.

El Marítimo (Baquedano 379-A, tel. 061/413166, www.restaurantelmaritimo.com, lunch and dinner daily) and **Los Pioneros** (Pedro Montt 166, tel. 061/410783, lunch and dinner daily) set the standard in quality fish and seafood at moderate prices, but lack flair. For better atmosphere, try the casual **La Tranquera** (Bulnes 579, tel. 061/411039, lunch and dinner daily).

La Caleta Gastronómica (Eberhard 261, tel. 061/413969, lunch and dinner daily) is a moderately priced (US$6–10) locale that offers excellent value—try the salmon with king crab sauce. Another well-established option is **Café Andrés** (Ladrilleros 381, tel. 061/412380, lunch and dinner daily), for cooked-to-order seafood.

Don Jorge (Bories 430, tel. 061/410999, lunch and dinner daily) and **El Asador**

Patagónico (Prat 158, tel. 061/413553, lunch and dinner daily) are both *parrillas* facing the Plaza de Armas. The latter prepares meat to order, including lamb on a stake, provides a selection of by-the-glass wines that's uncommonly flexible for the provinces, and features assiduous service.

La Burbuja (Bulnes 300, tel. 061/414204, lunch and dinner daily) specializes in seafood and meats, but also has vegetarian offerings; try the *ostiones al pil pil* (US$7), a mildly spicy scallops appetizer, and the *congrio* (conger eel) for an entrée.

In a relaxed setting, (**La Casa de Pepe** (Tomás Rogers 131, tel. 061/410950, lunch and dinner daily) prepares refined versions of Chilean standards such as *pastel de choclo* (US$10) and *cazuela de ave* (US$7.50) with the freshest ingredients. On the Plaza de Armas, it's also tobacco-free (though the owner himself is an occasional smoker).

Rarely does Chilean pizza merit special mention, but the thin-crusted pies at (**Mesita Grande** (Arturo Prat 196, tel. 061/411571, www.mesitagrande.cl, lunch and dinner daily) do. Individual pizzas (US$5–9), of four ample slices, range from simple mozzarella to spinach and garlic to ground lamb and just about everything in between; diners sit at either of two long but solid tables that promote conversation with neighboring parties.

Greatly improved, opposite the plaza, (**La Oveja Negra** (Tomás Rogers 169, tel. 061/415711, US$8–12, lunch and dinner daily) is the choice for a quiet meal in relaxed, if not quite intimate, surroundings. For either seafood or beef, its upscale aspirations make for more elaborate dining than at most of its competitors, but it's also a free-fire zone for tobacco junkies.

Part of its eponymous hotel, **Aquaterra** (Bulnes 299, tel. 061/412239, lunch and dinner daily, US$9–12 for entrées) is an upscale restaurant with menu items such as Mexican fajitas and Japanese *gyoza* (pot stickers) rarely seen in this part of the world. For more conservative palates, it offers traditional beef dishes.

Underrated (**Última Esperanza** (Eberhard 354, tel. 061/413626, lunch and dinner daily) deserves more attention than it gets for exceptional seafood at reasonable prices with outstanding service. **Los Viajeros** (Bulnes 291, tel. 061/411156, lunch and dinner daily) is a recent entry in the seafood category but also serves grilled Patagonian lamb. The **Centro Español** (Magallanes 247, tel. 061/411181, lunch and dinner daily) promises Spanish cuisine, but it remains a work in progress.

The surprising **Afrigonia** (Eberhard 343, tel. 061/412232, lunch and dinner daily) attempts to fuse Patagonian standards with East African touches in dishes such as lamb with a mint sauce (US$12), plus curry and tandoori. Early signs are positive, but whether it can survive the low season, when the critical mass of foreign tourists that form its clientele shrinks, is open to question. The service is uneven and the kitchen can be slow, but reservations are advisable because it's small.

Reopened and relocated after an unfortunate absence, **Angélica's** (Bulnes 501, tel. 061/410007, lunch and dinner daily) has great fish and seafood such as king crab cannelloni (US$13), but the service is an anomaly—often great when it's crowded, but distracted when it's barely a third full. Still, this would be a good restaurant just about anywhere.

Hotel Indigo's adjacent restaurant **Mamá Rosa** (Ladrilleros 105, tel. 061/413609, ext. 218, lunch and dinner daily) offers bayview dining on sophisticated versions of Chilean seafood standards such as hake and salmon, in the US$8–12 range. The flavors are delicate and the side orders thoughtfully assembled, and service has improved.

At Natales's best ice creamery, **Helados Bruna** (Bulnes 585), calafate and rhubarb are the regional specialties.

INFORMATION

In a freestanding waterfront chalet, the local delegation of **Sernatur** (Pedro Montt 19, tel./fax 061/412125) is open 8:15 A.M.–7 P.M. weekdays all year; December–March, it's also open 10:30 A.M.–1:30 P.M. and 3–6 P.M. Saturday–Sunday. It has helpful personnel, occasionally English-speaking, and fairly thorough

SOUTHERN PATAGONIA

information on accommodations, restaurants, and transportation.

Two relocated Oregonians publish the monthly freebie tabloid *Black Sheep* (www .patagoniablacksheep.com), with engaging articles and frequently updated information on Natales, Torres del Paine, and services throughout the region. It's widely available around town.

SERVICES

Puerto Natales has several exchange houses, including **Cambio Mily** (Blanco Encalada 266) and **Cambios Sur** (Eberhard 285). **Banco Santander Santiago** (Bulnes 598) has an ATM.

Correos de Chile (Eberhard 429), at the southwest corner of Plaza Arturo Prat, is the post office.

Long-distance operators include **Telefónica CTC** (Blanco Encalada and Bulnes) and **Entel** (Baquedano 270).

Internet connections are improving and cheapening, with new outlets appearing all the time and WiFi ubiquitous at places like **Coffee Pl@net** (Bulnes 555).

Lavandería Catch (Bories 218) can do the washing.

Hospital Puerto Natales (Ignacio Carrera Pinto 537, tel. 061/411582) handles medical emergencies.

GETTING THERE
Air

LAN no longer keeps a separate office here, but **Turismo Comapa** (Eberhard 555, tel. 061/414300, www.comapa.com) handles reservations and tickets. Punta Arenas–bound buses will drop passengers at that city's Aeropuerto Presidente Carlos Ibáñez del Campo.

Up to three times weekly, **Sky Airline** (Bulnes 692, Local 4, tel. 061/410646, www .skyairline.cl) offers service from Santiago, stopping here before continuing to Punta Arenas and then back to Santiago.

Bus

As of 2009, Puerto Natales was building a new Terminal Rodoviario at Santiago Bueras (the eastward extension of Yungay) and Santiago Bueras, destined to be more efficient but less convenient than individual companies' scattered, but mostly central, bus terminals. There's frequent service to and from Punta Arenas and Torres del Paine, and regular but less frequent service to the Argentine destinations of Río Turbio, Río Gallegos, and El Calafate.

Carriers serving Punta Arenas (US$7–10, 3 hours) include **Bus Sur** (Baquedano 668, tel. 061/614220, www.bus-sur.cl), **Buses Fernández** (Ramírez 399, tel. 061/411111), and **Buses Pacheco** (Baquedano 500, tel. 061/414513). Round-trip tickets offer small discounts, but less flexibility. Pacheco goes to Ushuaia (Argentina) daily except Saturday at 7:30 A.M. (US$60, 14 hours), which involves changing buses just outside Punta Arenas.

Services to Torres del Paine (US$13, 2.5 hours) vary seasonally, and there is frequent turnover among agencies; again, there are small discounts for round-trip fares. Carriers include **Buses J.B.** (Prat 258, tel. 061/410242), **Buses Gómez** (Arturo Prat 234, tel. 061/411971), **Buses María José** (Bulnes 386, tel. 061/412218), and **Trans Vía Paine** (Bulnes 518, tel. 061/413672). **Vía Terra** (061/613840, puertonatales@vientosur.com) operates a door-to-door service (US$35 pp) as far as Hostería Lago Grey as part of its full-day tours.

For the Argentine border town of Río Turbio (US$6, one hour), where there are connections to El Calafate and Río Gallegos, try **Buses Cootra** (Baquedano 454, tel. 061/412785), which has five to seven daily except on weekends, when there are only two or three. Bus Sur has fewer departures.

To the Argentine town of El Calafate (US$17, five hours), the carriers are Buses Cootra, Bus Sur, and **Turismo Zaahj** (Prat 236, tel. 061/412260, www.turismozaahj .co.cl). Services are frequent in high season, but in winter they may be weekly only.

Ferry

Turismo Comapa/Navimag (Eberhard 555, tel. 061/414300, www.navimag.cl) operates the weekly car/passenger ferry MV *Magallanes* to the mainland Chilean city of Puerto Montt. In early season, it's fairly easy to get a northbound berth, but later in the season reservations are advisable.

Northbound departures are normally Friday at 6 A.M., but weather and tides can change schedules. Passengers usually spend the night on board before these early-morning departures, but Navimag also has a Sala de Espera (waiting room) immediately across from the new pier.

GETTING AROUND

The selection of rental cars is growing, though it's better in Punta Arenas. Agencies include **Transpatagonia** (Blanco Encalada 330, tel. 061/414930, www.transpatagonia.cl) and **Punta Alta** (Blanco Encalada 244, tel. 061/410115, www.puntaalta.cl).

World's End (Blanco Encalada 226, tel. 061/414725) rents bicycles and motorcycles.

Vicinity of Puerto Natales

A growing number of operators arrange excursions to nearby sites of interest and, of course, to Parque Nacional Torres del Paine and even Argentina's Parque Nacional Los Glaciares. Day tours of Paine, more feasible since completion of a new road permits loops rather than time-consuming backtracking to return to Natales, cost around US$33 pp (plus the park entrance fee, of course). The most reliable are **Tour Express** (Manuel Bulnes 769, tel. 061/410734, www.tourexpress.cl) and **Kipaventour Patagonie** (Bulnes 90-B, tel. 061/413615, www.kipaventourpatagonie.com).

Several operators supply services, including accommodations and meals at park refugios, and activities within the park. These include **Fantástico Sur** (Sanhueza 579, Punta Arenas, tel./fax 061/613410, www.fantasticosur.com), with its own accommodations; **Turismo Stipe** (Baquedano 571, tel./fax 061/411125, turismostipe@entelchile.net); **Chile Nativo** (Eberhard 230, tel. 061/411385, www.chilenativo.com) for riding, trekking, and birding; **Fortaleza Patagonia** (Tomás Rogers 235, tel. 061/410595, www.fortalezapatagonia.cl); and **Servitur** (Prat 353, tel./fax 061/411858, www.servitur.cl). **Baqueano Zamora** (Baquedano 534, tel. 061/613530, www.baqueanozamora.com) specializes in horseback trips in the park and is also the concessionaire for Posada Río Serrano and Hostería El Pionero.

Three companies have united to form the **Centro de Turismo Aventura de Patagonia** (Bories 206), all with different contacts: **Antares Patagonia** (tel. 061/414611, www.antarespatagonia.com) for trekking; **Indómita Patagonia** (tel. 061/414525, www.indomitapatagonia.com) for kayaking and sea kayaking; and **Big Foot Patagonia** (tel. 061/414525, www.bigfootpatagonia.com) for expeditions.

Several other companies work together on sea kayaking in particular, including Fortaleza Patagonia; **Bella Patagonia** (Barros Arana 160, tel. 061/412489, www.bellapatagonia.com); **Sendero Aventura** (Tomás Rogers 179, tel. 061/415636, www.senderoaventura.com), in the same building as Residencial Patagonia Aventura; and **La Maddera** (Arturo Prat 297, tel. 061/413318), though the latter is more a gear rental place.

FRIGORÍFICO BORIES

Four kilometers north of Puerto Natales, the Sociedad Explotadora de Tierra del Fuego built this state-of-the-art (for its time) meat freezer to process livestock, primarily sheep, for shipment to Europe. Built of brick between 1912 and 1914, in the Magellanic style, it's the only plant of its kind in a reasonable state of preservation. After its 1971 expropriation by the Allende government, the plant was partially dismantled and finally shut down a few years back.

Among the remaining structures are the rendering plant, which converted animal fat into tallow; the tannery, which prepared hides for

SOUTHERN PATAGONIA

shipment; and the main offices, smithery, locomotive repair shop (Bories had its own short line), freight jetty, power plant, and boilers. The power plant still works.

Accommodations and food are available at **Hotel Cisne Cuello Negro** (tel. 061/411498, US$91 s, US$130 d); make reservations through **Turismo Pehoé** (José Menéndez 918, Punta Arenas, tel. 061/244506, www.pehoe.com). Rates include private bath and breakfast; there is also a restaurant.

PUERTO PRAT AND VICINITY

About 15 kilometers northwest of Puerto Natales via a gravel road, sheltered Puerto Prat is the nearest thing to a beach getaway for Natalinos—on rare hot days, its shallow waters warm up enough to let the truly intrepid dip their toes into the sea. It's also the paddling point for half-day sea kayak trips to **Fiordo Eberhard** (about US$75 pp); for details, contact any of several kayaking companies in Puerto Natales.

A short distance north, settled by Captain Hermann Eberhard, **Estancia Puerto Consuelo** was the area's first sheep farm. It's open to the public, but usually only those on horseback excursions.

DIFUNTA CORREA SHRINE

About six kilometers east of Puerto Natales, on the south side of Ruta 9, the spreading mountain of water-filled plastic bottles at this spontaneous roadside shrine suggests one of two things: Either many Argentines are traveling here, or Chileans are becoming devoted to Argentina's favorite folk saint. Or it may be a changing combination of the two, as the Argentine economic crisis reversed the traditional flow of Argentine tourists into Chile.

CERRO DOROTEA

About seven kilometers east of town on Ruta 9, nudging the Argentine border, the hike to the Sierra Dorotea ridge makes an ideal half-day excursion, offering some of the area's finest panoramas. Well-marked with red blazes and signs, the route to Cerro Dorotea's 549-meter summit is, after the initial approach, unrelentingly uphill but never exhaustingly steep. This is not pristine nature—much of the lower slopes are cutover *lenga* forest, some of which has regenerated itself into an even-aged woodland. The ridge itself is barren, with a telephone relay antenna on the top.

Trailhead access is over private property, where farmer Juan de Dios Saavedra Ortiz collects US$8 per person. The fee, though, includes a simple but welcome Chilean *onces* (afternoon tea with homemade bread, butter, ham, and cheese) on your return from the hike.

MONUMENTO NATURAL CUEVA DEL MILODÓN

Northwest of present-day Puerto Natales, on the shores of a small inlet known as Fiordo Eberhard, the giant Pleistocene ground sloth known as the mylodon *(Mylodon darwini)* took shelter in this wave-cut grotto some 30 meters high and 80 meters wide at its mouth, and 200 meters deep. While the mylodon has been extinct for nearly as long as humans have inhabited the area—some 11,000 years—the discovery of its remains caused a sensation, as their state of preservation induced some European scientists to speculate the animal might still be alive.

German pioneer Hermann Eberhard gets credit for discovering the cave in 1895, but Erland Nordenskjöld (1900) was the first scientist to study it, taking sample bones and skin back to Sweden. Its manure has been carbon-dated at roughly 10,400 years before the present, meaning the large herbivore coexisted with humans, but it was most definitely *not* a domesticate. In all probability, hunting pressure contributed to its demise (and that of other Pleistocene megafauna). Oddly enough, no complete skeleton has been found.

The mylodon has gained a spot in the Western imagination, both among scientists and the lay public. U.S. archaeologist Junius Bird described the animal in his journals, published as *Travel and Archaeology in South Chile* (University of Iowa Press, 1988), edited by John

Hyslop of the American Museum of Natural History. Family tales inspired Bruce Chatwin to write his masterpiece *In Patagonia,* which relates far-fetched legends that Paleo-Indians penned the mylodon in the cave and that some animals survived into the 19th century.

Conaf's **Museo de Sitio** (8 A.M.–8 P.M. daily) has excellent information on the 192-hectare park, which attracted nearly 68,702 visitors in 2008, about half of them foreigners. A tacky life-sized statue of the mylodon stands in the cave itself.

Summer admission costs US$5 for adult foreigners, US$2.50 for Chilean residents, with nominal rates for children. Many Natales-based tours take in the sight, but there is no regular public transport except for Paine-bound buses that pass on Ruta 9, five kilometers east. Mountain-bike rental could be a good option. In addition to the park's picnic area, **Café Restaurant Caverna** is a view restaurant directly opposite the visitors center.

GLACIAR BALMACEDA (PARQUE NACIONAL BERNARDO O'HIGGINS)

Chile's largest national park, covering 3,525,901 hectares of islands and icecaps from near Tortel in Region XI (Aisén) to Última Esperanza in Region XII (Magallanes), has few easy access points, but the Balmaceda Glacier at the Río Serrano's outlet is one of them. From Puerto Natales, the closest approach is a four-hour sail northwest—where Juan Ladrilleros and Pedro de Sarmiento de Gamboa ended their futile quests for a sheltered route to the Pacific—past Puerto Bories, several wool *estancias* reachable only by sea, and nesting colonies of seabirds and breeding colonies of southern sea lions, among U-shaped valleys with glaciers and waterfalls. Andean condors have been sighted in the area.

At the end of the cruise, passengers disembark for an hour or so at **Puerto Toro,** where a half-hour walk through southern beech forest leads to the fast-receding **Glaciar Balmaceda.** Visitors remain for about an hour before returning to Natales, unless they take advantage of the option to travel upriver to Torres del Paine, which may be visible in the distance.

A new option for visiting remote parts of the park, in comfort, is the five-day, four-night *Skorpios* cruise of the so-called "Ruta Kawéskar."

Accommodations and Food

The park lacks formal accommodations. Across the sound from Puerto Toro, though, in virtually the most peaceful location imaginable—but for the wind—the nearly new **Hostería Monte Balmaceda** (c/o Turismo 21 de Mayo, Eberhard 560, Puerto Natales, tel. 061/411978, 21demayo@chileaustral.com) charges US$150 s, US$180 d with breakfast; lunch and dinner cost another US$25 each.

As it's mostly accessible by sea, a stay here is usually part of a package including a visit to the park and/or Torres del Paine. There is, however, a footpath suitable for a two-day trek to or from Torres del Paine.

Transportation

Natales operators sail up the sound to the Balmaceda Glacier, usually daily in summer, less frequently the rest of the year. Bad weather and high winds may cause cancellations at any time of year.

The traditional operator is **Turismo 21 de Mayo** (Eberhard 560, tel. 061/411978, www .turismo21demayo.cl), which sails its eponymous cutter or the yacht *Alberto de Agostini* to the park. Fares are US$90 per person; on the return the boat stops for lunch at Hostería Monte Balmaceda, sometimes an *asado,* at Estancia Los Perales.

Recently, though, Punta Alta (Blanco Encalada 244, tel. 061/410115, www.puntaalta .cl) has provided competition with a newer catamarans that cover the route faster, in greater comfort (US$92–112 pp), and good food is provided on board.

Instead of returning to Puerto Natales, it's possible to continue upriver to Torres del Paine with either Turismo 21 de Mayo or Punta Alta. In open Zodiac rafts, supplying all passengers with warm raingear, the route traverses scenic areas not normally seen by Paine visitors, makes a lunch stop, and requires a brief portage around the Serrano rapids before arriving at the Río Serrano campground. The total cost is about US$108 with lunch; the excursion can also be done in the opposite direction, or as a round-trip from either Puerto Natales or the park.

PUERTO EDÉN AND VICINITY

Thanks to nearly incessant rains, Puerto Edén is as verdant as Adam and Eve's Biblical garden, but red-tide conditions have placed the shellfish livelihood of the remaining 15 or so Kawéskar Indians at risk. Their only other income sources are government hand-outs and some crude crafts—tiny carved canoes and shells, for instance. Alcoholism is sadly common.

Vicinity is a relative term with respect to Puerto Edén (population about 300), the last outpost of the Kawéskar, which is about 400 kilometers northwest of Puerto Natales. It is on the weekly Navimag ferry route to and from Puerto Montt and also gets *Skorpios III* cruise-ship passengers and private yachts, which can explore the ice fields of the Campo de Hielo Sur, in Parque Nacional Bernardo O'Higgins, from the west.

Cruise passengers typically spend a couple hours on shore, where the subsidized Proyecto Yekchal has built a boardwalk over soggy terrain to an overlook where, on clear days, the view is magnificent. There's also a replica of a traditional Kawéskar house, but nobody lives in these sorts of dwellings anymore.

Puerto Edén's only accommodations and meals are available at **Hospedería Yekchal,** on the boardwalk north of the boat dock. Ships of any size cannot get close to shore and need to shuttle passengers on smaller boats.

CERRO CASTILLO AND VICINITY

North of Natales, one of Chile's most thinly populated municipalities, the *comuna* of Torres del Paine has only 739 inhabitants according to the 2002 census; more than half reside in

© WAYNE BERNHARDSON

Puerto Edén is the only stop on the Navimag ferry between Puerto Montt and Puerto Natales.

the hamlet of Cerro Castillo, 60 kilometers north of Puerto Natales on Ruta 9, alongside the Río Don Guillermo border crossing. Called Cancha Carrera on the Argentine side, this is the most direct route from Parque Nacional Torres del Paine to El Calafate (Argentina) and Parque Nacional Los Glaciares. Previously seasonal, it is now open all year.

Formerly an *estancia* of the powerful Sociedad Explotadora de Tierra del Fuego, Cerro Castillo has an assortment of services, including a dismal museum at the municipal **Departamento de Turismo** (Avenida Bernardo O'Higgins s/n, tel. 061/691932) and the only gas station north of Puerto Natales (if continuing to Argentina, gasoline—but not diesel—is cheaper on the Argentine side).

En route to and at Cerro Castillo, there are several accommodations options. The most southerly, on the site of an older namesake that burned to the ground, **Hotel Tres Pasos** (Km 38 Norte, tel. 02/1969630 or 02/1969631, www.hotel3pasos.cl, US$100 s, US$123 d) is a contemporary roadside inn that's above average for the area. Lunch or dinner costs US$17 at its restaurant.

At Cerro Castillo itself, there are basic accommodations at **Residencial Loreto Belén** (tel. 061/691932, Anexo 728, US$17 pp) and more elaborate lodgings at **Hostería El Pionero** (Baquedano 534, Puerto Natales, tel. 061/613531, www.baqueanozamora.com, US$32 pp, US$97 s, US$117 d); the cheaper rates correspond to an annex *refugio*. Open September–April only, it also serves meals to nonguests and rents horses.

On what is still a working sheep ranch on Estancia Cerro Guido, about midway between Cerro Castillo and Torres del Paine, **Lodge**

Cerro Guido (tel. 02/1964807, tel. 061/227716 in Punta Arenas, www.lodgecerroguido.cl, US$236–305 s or d) has rehabbed and modernized its historic *casco* and another structure into attractive guesthouses with 10 total rooms. About 12 km north of the road that leads to the park's Laguna Amarga entrance, Cerro Guido gets less traffic than Paine's accommodations, but its facilities equal or better most of them; there's also a restaurant/bar whose wines come from the ownership's own Matetic family vineyards near Valparaíso. Rates include breakfast, while lunch or dinner costs about US$30 extra. Activities include horseback riding (multi-day excursions are possible), hiking, and observing farm activities such as summer shearing.

Parque Nacional Torres del Paine

Several years ago, when a major Pacific Coast shipping company bought a two-page spread in Alaska Airlines' in-flight magazine, the landscape chosen to represent Alaska's grandeur was…Parque Nacional Torres del Paine! While an uninformed photo editor was the likely culprit—fittingly enough for a Southern Hemisphere destination, the image was reversed—the soaring granite spires of Chile's premiere national park have truly become an international emblem of alpine majesty.

But there's more—unlike many South American parks, Torres del Paine has an integrated network of hiking trails suitable for day trips and backpack treks, endangered species such as the wild guanaco in a UNESCO-recognized World Biosphere Reserve, and accommodations options from rustic campgrounds to cozy trail huts and five-star luxury hotels. So popular that some visitors prefer the shoulder seasons of spring (November–December) or fall (March–April)—the park receives more than 140,000 visitors annually, about 70 percent of them foreigners. While Torres del Paine has become a major international destination, it's still wild country.

Almost everybody visits the park to behold

extraordinary natural features such as the **Torres del Paine,** the sheer granite towers that defy erosion even as the weaker sedimentary strata around them have weathered, and the jagged **Cuernos del Paine,** with their striking interface between igneous and metamorphic rocks. Most hike its trails uneventfully, but for all its popularity, this can still be treacherous terrain. Hikers have disappeared, the rivers run fast and cold, the weather is unpredictable, and there is one documented case of a tourist killed by a puma.

ORIENTATION

Parque Nacional Torres del Paine is 112 kilometers northwest of Puerto Natales via Ruta 9 through Cerro Castillo; 38 kilometers beyond Castillo, a westbound lateral traces the southern shore of Lago Sarmiento de Gamboa to the park's isolated Laguna Verde sector. Three kilometers beyond the Laguna Verde junction, another westbound lateral leaves Ruta 9 to follow Lago Sarmiento's north shore to Portería Sarmiento, the main gate; it continues southwest for 37 kilometers to the Administración, the park headquarters at the west end of Lago del Toro.

SOUTHERN PATAGONIA

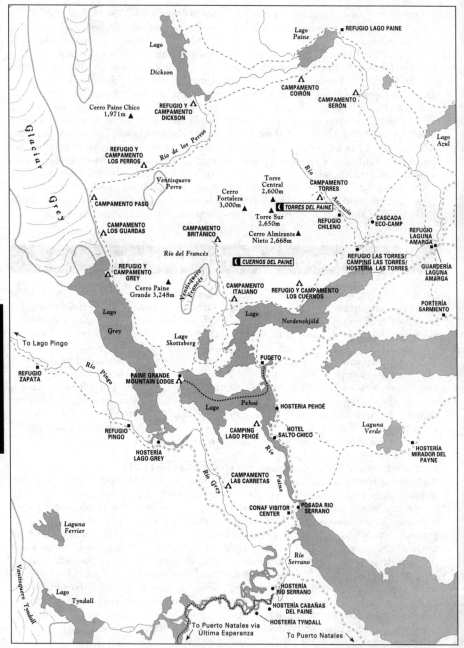

CAMPING
LAGUNA AZUL

GUARDERÍA
LAGUNA AZUL

PARQUE NACIONAL
TORRES DEL PAINE

Laguna
Amarga

Lago Sarmiento

Sierra del Toro

To Cerro Castillo
and Puerto Natales

Lago Toro

0   4 mi

0   4 km

© AVALON TRAVEL

Twelve kilometers east of Portería Sarmiento, another lateral branches northwest and, three kilometers farther on, splits again; the former leads to Guardería Laguna Azul, in the little-visited northern sector, while the latter enters the park at Guardería Laguna Amarga, the most common starting point for the popular Paine Circuit, and follows the south shore of Lago Nordenskjöld and Lago Pehoé en route to the Administración visitors center. Most public transportation takes this route.

Recently completed, a new bridge over the Río Serrano now permits access to park head-quarters via Cueva del Milodón and Lago del Toro's western shore, but this has not affected regular public transportation.

GEOGRAPHY AND CLIMATE

Parque Nacional Torres del Paine comprises 181,414 hectares of Patagonian steppe, low-land and alpine glacial lakes, glacier-fed torrents and waterfalls, forested uplands, and nearly vertical granite needles. Altitudes range from only about 50 meters above sea level along the lower Río Serrano to 3,050 meters atop Paine Grande, the central massif's tallest peak.

Paine has a cool temperate climate characterized by high winds, especially in spring and summer. The average summer temperature is about 10.8°C, with highs reaching around 23°C, while the average winter minimum is around freezing. Average figures are misleading, though, as the weather is changeable. The park lies in the rain shadow of the Campo de Hielo Sur, where westerly storms drop most of their load as snow, so it receives only about 600 millimeters rainfall per year. Still, snow and hail can fall even in midsummer. Spring is the windiest season; in autumn, March and April, winds tend to moderate, but days are shorter.

It should go without saying that at higher elevations temperatures are cooler and snow is likelier to fall. In some areas it's possible to hut-hop between *refugios,* eliminating the need for a tent and sleeping bag—but not for warm clothing and impermeable raingear.

SOUTHERN PATAGONIA

THE CHANNELS OF THE KAWÉSKAR

From the Golfo de Penas to Tierra del Fuego, southwestern Patagonia is one of the planet's most thinly peopled, least visited areas. Its pre-Columbian inhabitants were "Canoe Indians," a term applied to the Yámana and Kawéskar Indians who used precarious vessels to hunt seals and gather shellfish. Never numerous, they prospered on local resources until catastrophic contact with Europeans – first violence and then disease – nearly obliterated them.

Today, ironically enough, it's possible to explore the dramatically scenic channels and icy fjords of the Kawéskar – also known as the Alacaluf – on a comfortable cruiser. Long known for its voyages from Puerto Montt to Laguna San Rafael, the Skorpios line has incorporated the glacial fjords between Puerto Natales and Puerto Edén into a five-day, four-night **Ruta Kawéskar** itinerary that pays symbolic homage, at least, to the last sad survivors.

The *Skorpios III* normally sails late Saturday from the company's new jetty, four kilometers north of Puerto Natales. At the beginning, it follows Navimag's northbound ferry route as far as Isla Chatham, where it turns east to enter **Parque Nacional Bernardo O'Higgins** and anchor briefly at the remote fishermen's camp of **Caleta Villarrica**. It then enters **Fiordo Amalia,** where **Glaciar Amalia**'s floating tongue protrudes from the southern continental ice field, almost directly opposite Torres del Paine. Here passengers transfer onto double-hull, flat-bottomed boats that are really mini-icebreakers, slicing through pack ice to approach the glacier's face (flat roofs keep off the rain and snow – except when wind makes the rain horizontal).

From Amalia, the ship sails north to **Fiordo Calvo,** a site of magnificent hanging glaciers, a sea-lion colony, and a rock-cormorant colony. Unfortunately, when the icebreakers' noisy diesels approach too closely, the lions and their pups scramble over the rocks and into the sea.

Retracing its route and then sailing north, the ship eventually turns northeast into **Fiordo Eyre** and steams to **Glaciar Pío XI,** the continent's largest glacier – 62 kilometers long and 6 kilometers wide. Here passengers approach the glacier in smaller, quieter lifeboats, floating past indigo icebergs that are constantly calving off the face. Before reversing direction south, the vessel pays a brief visit to **Puerto Edén,** home of the surviving Kawéskar.

The area's finest scenery, arguably, is the return trip's **Fiordo de la Montaña,** a sheer-sided canyon between the Cordillera Sarmiento and Cordillera Riesco, just west of Puerto Natales. Also reachable by day trips from Natales, it includes the cruise's only other shore-based excursion – a hike to the relatively small **Glaciar Bernal.** The last night on board, which includes a dinner-dance, is spent in the lee of **Isla Focus,** within sight of Natales.

Accommodating only 110 passengers in 48 cabins, *Skorpios III* is small for a cruise ship. Decorated with handsome wood veneer, with view windows rather than portholes, the cabins also have excellent bathrooms and showers. Some beds, though, are on the soft side. The food and wine are excellent, and the service personalized.

The Kochifas family, Greek-Chilean shipbuilders based in Puerto Montt, have pioneered an appealing itinerary. What the Ruta Kawéskar trip lacks is information: The guides' main task seems to be pointing out photo opportunities – already obvious enough in this extraordinary landscape. The *Skorpios III* would benefit from a library of books on the region, and presentations on history, environment, and ecology – instead, it's simply "eat well, sip your pisco sours, and snap your shutter."

The *Skorpios III* operates early September-mid-May, leaving late Saturday night or Sunday morning; high-season is mid-December-mid-March. Rates range from US$2,150 to US$4,300 pp, depending on the season and level of accommodations. For more detail, contact **Cruceros Skorpios** (Augusto Leguía Norte 118, Las Condes, Santiago, tel. 02/4771900, www.skorpios.cl; tel. 305/484-5357 in Miami).

FLORA AND FAUNA

Less diverse than in areas farther north, Paine's vegetation still varies with altitude and distance from the Andes. Bunch grasses of the genera *Festuca* and *Stipa,* known collectively as *coirón,* cover the arid southeastern steppes, often interspersed with thorny shrubs such as the calafate *(Berberis buxifolia),* which produces edible fruit, and *neneo.* There are also miniature ground-hugging *Calceolaria* orchids such as the *zapatito* and *capachito.*

Approaching the Andes, deciduous forests of southern beech *(Nothofagus)* species such as *lenga* blanket the hillsides, along with the related evergreen *coigüe de Magallanes* and the deciduous *ñirre.* At the highest elevations, little vegetation of any kind grows among alpine fell fields.

Among Paine's mammals, the most conspicuous is the llama-relative guanaco, whose numbers—and tameness—have increased dramatically over two decades. Many of its young, known as *chulengos,* fall prey to the puma. A more common predator, or at least a more

visible one, is the gray fox, which feeds off the introduced European hare and, beyond park boundaries, off sheep. The endangered *huemul* (Andean deer) is a rare sight.

The monarch of South American birds, of course, is the Andean condor, not a rare sight here. Filtering the lake shallows for plankton, the Chilean flamingo summers here after breeding in the northern altiplano. The *caiquén* (upland goose) grazes the moist grasslands around the lakes, while the black-necked swan paddles peacefully on the surface. The fleet flightless rhea or *ñandú* scampers over the steppes.

C TORRES DEL PAINE

Some of the Andes' youngest peaks, the Torres del Paine are among the most emblematic in the entire range. Some 10 million years ago, a magma intrusion failed to reach the earth's surface, cooling underground into resistant granite; in the interim, water, ice, and snow have eroded softer terrain to liberate the spires as one of the world's most dramatic landscapes.

© WAYNE BERNHARDSON

A hiker contemplates the Cuernos del Paine.

SOUTHERN PATAGONIA

So strong a draw are the Torres that some visitors pressed for time settle for day tours that allow only a few hours in the park. Others walk to the base of the Torres from Hostería Las Torres, a relatively easy day hike where it's hard to avoid the crowds. A longer and more tiring alternative, up the steep canyon of the Río Bader, provides a different perspective and the Andean solitude that many hikers seek.

◀ CUERNOS DEL PAINE

Many park visitors misidentify the Cuernos del Paine (Horns of Paine) as the Torres. Located almost immediately south of the Torres proper, the saw-toothed Cuernos retain a cap of darker but softer metamorphic rock atop a broader granitic batholith that, like the Torres, never reached the surface before cooling. It's the contrast between the two that gives the Cuernos their striking aspect.

As with the Torres, day-trippers can admire the Cuernos from the highway through the park. The best views, though, come from the "W" trail along the north shore of Lago Nordenskjöld, between Hostería Las Torres and Lago Pehoé.

PAINE CIRCUIT

Nearly three decades ago, under a military dictatorship, Chile attracted few foreign visitors, and hiking Torres del Paine was a solitary experience—on a 10-day trek over the now-famous circuit, the author met only three other hikers, two Americans and a Chilean. Parts of the route were easy-to-follow stock trails (the park was once an *estancia*), while others, on the east shore of Lago Grey and into the Río de los Perros Valley in particular, were barely boot-width tracks on steep slopes, or involved scrambling over granite boulders and fording waist-deep glacial meltwater.

In the interim, as raging rivers have destroyed bridges at the outlets of Lago Nordenskjöld and Lago Paine, the original trailhead on Lago Pehoé's north shore no longer exists. Completion of a trail along Lago Nordenskjöld's north shore several years back, though, created a new loop and simultaneously

THE TORRES DEL FUEGO

In February 2005, in an incident that will have consequences for years to come, a careless Czech camper overturned his campstove, starting a fire that burned for nearly a month in Parque Nacional Torres del Paine. The conflagration scorched 15,470 hectares of native vegetation, including forest, scrubland, and steppe, in the park's popular northeastern sector.

Most of the burned area consisted of steppe grasses and shrubs that are recovering nicely, but the 2,400 hectares of slow-growing southern beech forest are more problematic. West of the Río Paine and the Lago Paine road, Conaf is placing priority on restoring 800 hectares of *lenga* and *ñire*. Some parts of the fire area will be fenced off to prevent humans from trampling on, and guanacos from feeding off, the newly planted trees.

Some parts of the park may be off limits to hikers indefinitely, though it's possible trails may be rerouted. While the fire came perilously close to the (since relocated) Cascada EcoCamp and the Hostería Las Torres, it damaged no major structures.

provided access to the Torres' south side, offering easier access up the Río Ascencio and Valle del Francés on the shorter "W" route to Lago Pehoé. Where the former circuit crossed the Río Paine and continued along its north bank to the Laguna Azul campground, the new circuit now follows the river's west bank south to Laguna Amarga (a Laguna Azul exit or entrance is still feasible, though, by crossing the Río Paine by a cable raft at the river's Lago Dickson outlet, with help from the staff at Refugio Dickson).

In the interim, trail maintenance and development have improved, rudimentary and not-so-rudimentary bridges have replaced fallen logs and traversed stream fords, and comfortable concessionaire *refugios* and organized campgrounds have supplanted the lean-tos and *puestos* (outside houses) that once sheltered shepherds. Though it's theoretically possible to complete most of the circuit without a tent or even a sleeping bag, showering and eating at the *refugios,* hikers must remember that this is still rugged country with unpredictable weather.

Most hikers now tackle the circuit counterclockwise from Guardería Laguna Amarga, where buses from Puerto Natales stop for passengers to pay the park admission fee. An alternative is to continue to Pudeto and take a passenger launch to Refugio Pehoé, or else to the park's Administración (involving a longer and less interesting approach); both of these mean doing the trek clockwise.

At least a week is desirable for the circuit; before beginning, registration with park rangers is obligatory. Camping is permitted only at designated sites, a few of which are free. Purchase supplies in Puerto Natales, as only limited goods are available with the park, at premium prices.

Accommodations and Food

For counterclockwise hikers beginning at Laguna Amarga, there is no *refugio* until Lago Dickson (roughly 11 hours), though there is a fee campground at **Campamento Serón** (4–5 hours).

All the *refugios* are presently under concession to Puerto Natales's **Vértice Patagonia** (Esmeralda 671, tel. 061/412742, Puerto Natales, www.verticepatagonia.cl) including **Refugio Lago Grey** and **Refugio Lago Dickson,** where there are also campgrounds and backpackers still crash at the old *puesto,* plus the **Campamento Río de los Perros.**

Both *refugios* resemble each other, with 32 bunks charging US$25 per person, with kitchen privileges and hot showers, but without sheets or sleeping bags, which are technically available for rental but sometimes scarce. Breakfast costs US$8, lunch US$12, dinner US$15; a bunk with full board costs US$57 per person. Campers pay US$6 each (*refugio* guests, though, have shower priority). Rental tents, sleeping bags, mats, and camp stoves are also available.

Replacing the cramped and overcrowded Refugio Lago Pehoé, the **Paine Grande Mountain Lodge** (tel. 02/1960051) is the newest option along the Paine Circuit. Rates are US$37–50 per person without breakfast (US$9 extra); lunch (US$12) and dinner (US$16) are available separately, but full-board packages (US$73–85 pp) mean a small savings. Camping costs US$7 pp (US$42 with full board), with rental tents, pads, and sleeping bags available. There's also phone and even (expensive) Internet access.

THE "W" VARIANT

From Guardería Laguna Amarga, a narrow undulating road crosses the Río Paine on a narrow suspension bridge to the grounds of **Estancia Cerro Paine,** at the foot of 2,640-meter Monte Almirante Nieto. The *estancia* operates a hotel, *refugios,* and campgrounds, and staff also shuttles hikers back and forth from Laguna Amarga for US$4 per person.

From Estancia Cerro Paine, a northbound trail parallels the route from Guardería Laguna Amarga, eventually meeting it just south of Campamento Serón. The *estancia* is more notable, though, as the starting point for the "W" route to Lago Pehoé, a scenic and popular option for hikers lacking time for the full circuit. On the western edge of the grounds, the trail crosses the Río Ascencio on a footbridge to a junction where a northbound lateral climbs the river canyon to Campamento Torres, where a short but steep trail ascends to a nameless glacial tarn at the foot of the Torres proper. This is an easy day hike from the *estancia,* though many people prefer to camp or spend the night at the *refugio.*

From the junction, the main trail follows Lago Nordenskjöld's north shore, past another *refugio* and campground, to the free Campamento Italiano at the base of the **Río del Francés** Valley. While the main trail continues west toward Lago Pehoé, another northbound lateral climbs steeply up the valley, between the striking metamorphic Cuernos del Paine to the east and the 3,050-meter granite summit of Paine Grande to the west, to the free Campamento Británico.

Hikers in search of peace and quiet can make a strenuous detour up the **Valle Bader,** a steep rugged river valley that's home to a climber's camp at the base of the Cuernos. The route is mostly unmarked, but experienced cross-country walkers can handle it.

Accommodations and Food

Technically outside park boundaries, most of the "W" route belongs to **Fantástico Sur** (Sarmiento 846, Punta Arenas, tel./fax 061/360360, www.lastorres.com), which runs the 96-bunk **Refugio Las Torres Norte** and the new, nearby **Refugio Las Torres Central** on the *estancia's* main grounds; the 36-bunk **Refugio Chileno** in the upper Río Ascencio Valley; and the 28-bunk **Refugio Los Cuernos,** all of which also have campgrounds. Fantástico Sur's *refugios* are more spacious, diverse, and attractive in design than the Conaf *refugios,* and the food is better as well.

Bunks at Fantástico Sur *refugios* cost US$32 per person (US$64 pp with full board), except for the slightly mor expensive Las Torres Central (US$35 pp, US$68 with full board). Camping costs US$7 per person with hot showers. Refugio Los Cuernos also has two-person cabañas (US$105 d with breakfast and hot tub, US$142 s, US$175 d with full board).

Separately, breakfast costs US$8, lunch US$12, or dinner US$15; a full meal package costs US$33. Rental tents, sleeping bags, mats, and stoves are also available.

OTHER TRAILS

After heavy runoff destroyed the once-sturdy bridge at Lago Paine's outlet in the early 1980s, the Río Paine's north shore became, and has remained, isolated from the rest of the park. A good road, though, still leads from Guardería Laguna Amarga to Laguna Azul's east end, where there are a campground and *cabañas,* and the **Sendero Lago Paine,** a four-hour walk to the lake and a simple *refugio.* A trekkers' alternative is the **Sendero Desembocadura,** which leads north from Guardería Laguna Amarga

through open country to Laguna Azul's west end and continues to Lago Paine, but this takes about 8 hours. From the north shore of Lago Paine, the **Sendero Lago Dickson** (5.5 hours) leads to the Dickson Glacier.

Several easy day hikes are possible near Guardería Lago Pehoé, directly on the road from Laguna Amarga to the Administración visitors center. The short **Sendero Salto Grande** trail leads to the thunderous waterfall, at Lago Sarmiento's outlet, that was the Circuit's starting point until unprecedented runoff swept away the iron bridge to Península Pehoé in 1986. From Salto Grande, the **Sendero Mirador Nordenskjöld** is a slightly longer but still easy walk to a lakeshore vista point, directly opposite the stunning Cuernos.

From Guardería Lago Grey, 18 kilometers northwest of the Administración by road, a short footpath leads to a sandy beach on Lago Grey's south shore, where steady westerlies often beach icebergs from Glaciar Grey. The longer and less visited **Sendero Lago Pingo** ascends the Río Pingo Valley to its namesake lake (5.5–6 hours); there are a basic *refugio* and two free campgrounds along the route.

FURTHER RECREATION

Though popular, hiking is not Paine's only recreational option.

Despite similar terrain, Paine attracts fewer climbers than Argentina's neighboring Parque Nacional Los Glaciares, perhaps because fees for climbing permits have been high here. At present, permits are free of charge; before being granted permission, though, climbers must present Conaf with climbing résumés, emergency contacts, and authorization from their consulate.

When climbing in sensitive border areas (meaning most of Andean Chile), climbers must also have permission from the Dirección de Fronteras y Límites (Difrol, www.difrol.cl) in Santiago. It's possible to do this through a Chilean consulate overseas or at Difrol's Santiago offices or, preferably, online; if you arrive in Puerto Natales without permission, it's possible to request it through the **Gobernación Provincial** (tel. 061/411423, fax 061/411992), the regional government offices on the south side of Plaza Arturo Prat. The turnaround time is 48 hours.

While climbing and mountaineering activities may be undertaken independently, local concessionaires can provide training and lead groups or individuals with less experience on snow and ice. **Rutas Patagonia** (tel. 061/613874, www.rutaspatagonia.com) has a Refugio Grey base camp, where it leads half-day traverses of Glaciar Grey's west side (US$112 pp). Except for warm, weatherproof clothing, the company provides all equipment.

Kayaking specialist **Indómita** (Bories 206, tel./fax 061/414525, www.indomitapatagonia.com) arranges guided three-day, two-night descents of the Río Serrano (US$500–667 pp, depending on group size).

The only concessionaire offering horseback trips is Río Serrano–based **Baqueano Zamora** (Baquedano 534, Puerto Natales, tel. 061/613531, www.baqueanozamora.com). Just outside the park boundaries, though, Hostería Las Torres has its own stables.

ACCOMMODATIONS AND FOOD

Park accommodations range from free trailside campgrounds to first-rate luxury hotels with just about everything in between; in summer, reservations are almost obligatory at hotels and advisable at campgrounds and *refugios*.

Camping

At Estancia Cerro Paine, **Camping Las Torres** (US$7 pp, US$32 pp with full board) draws hikers heading up the Río Ascencio Valley to the Paine overlook and/or west on the "W" route to Lago Pehoé, or finishing up the circuit here. Formerly insufficient shower and toilet facilities have improved.

On a bluff above Refugio Las Torres, the **Cascada EcoCamp** (www.ecocamp.travel) is a geodesic dome-tent facility designed for minimum-impact accommodations; on raised platforms, each tent is five meters wide, with

The Cascada EcoCamp's Dome Suites offer fine views of the Torres del Paine.

© WAYNE BERNHARDSON

wooden floors and two single beds, with towels and bedding including down comforters. Two larger domes contain a common living area, dining rooms, and kitchen; the separate bathrooms have hot showers and composting toilets (from some domes, it's a long walk for middle-of-the-night toilet visits). Electricity comes from solar collectors, windmills, and a small hydroelectric turbine. Cascada's organized tour clients have priority, but its half-dozen luxury "Dome Suites" with woodstoves, king-size beds, private bath and shower, and exterior decks with views of the Torres, are available to private parties on a space-available basis. Contact them through the website or, alternatively, through their Puerto Natales office (Barros Arana 166, tel. 061/414442).

On the small peninsula on its namesake lake's eastern shore, just west of the road to the Administración, sites at concessionaire-run **Camping Lago Pehoé** (tel. 02/1960377, asoto@sodexho.cl, US$7) hold up to six people; fees include firewood and hot showers. About six kilometers south of park headquarters,

Camping Río Serrano (US$7 pp) has reopened with considerable improvements, including cooking shelters at each site.

In Paine's remote northeastern sector, which some visitors prefer, is **Camping Laguna Azul** (tel. 061/613531 in Puerto Natales, www.baquedanozamora.cl, US$7 pp).

Hosterías, and Hotels
Posada Río Serrano (tel. 061/613531 in Puerto Natales, tel. 02/1960338, baquedanoz@tie.cl, US$87–117 d) is a former *estancia* house retrofitted as a B&B. Rates, which include breakfast, depend on whether the room has shared or private bath; there is a restaurant/bar for so-so meals and drinks. While it's improved under new management, and quadruples (US$42 pp) and sextuples (US$37 pp) can be cheaper, it's overpriced for what it offers.

Reachable by road along Lago Sarmiento's south shore or by foot or horseback from the Río Paine, well-regarded **Hostería Mirador del Payne** (tel. 061/410498, www.miradordelpayne.com, US$158 s, US$195 d) lies in the isolated southeastern Laguna Verde sector.

Where Lago Grey becomes the Río Grey, the 30-room **Hostería Lago Grey** (US$251 s, US$290 d with breakfast) hosts visitors to the park's lesser-visited western sector; it also has a restaurant open to the public. For reservations, contact the hotel through **Turismo Lago Grey** (tel. 061/712100, www.lagogrey.cl).

The park's oldest hotel, on a five-hectare island linked to the mainland by a footbridge, the 25-room **Hostería Pehoé** (US$225–271 s, US$271–318 d) has improved since the operator began to reinvest in what had been a run-down facility, with substandard service, in an undeniably spectacular setting. For reservations, contact **Turismo Pehoé** (José Menéndez 918, Punta Arenas, tel. 061/241373, www.pehoe.com).

At Estancia Cerro Paine, seven kilometers west of Guardería Laguna Amarga, the sprawling but well-run **◀ Hostería Las Torres** (Sarmiento 846, Punta Arenas, tel. 061/360360, www.lastorres.com, US$165–232 s, US$199–265 d) is a gem for its setting

beneath Monte Almirante Nieto, its professionalism, the recent addition of a spa offering saunas and massages, and even WiFi access (expensive because of a costly satellite link). While it's an elite option, it's conscientiously ecofriendly in terms of waste disposal, and management is constantly seeking feedback from guests. It now offers all-inclusive packages as well as just lodging. Off-season hotel rates are about half. Open to both guests and nonguests, the tobacco-free restaurant prepares quality food in cruise-ship quantities.

Open for packages only, **◀ Hotel Salto Chico** is a mega-luxury resort that, somehow, manages to blend inconspicuously into the landscape while providing some of the grandest views on the globe. Rates start at US$3,748 s, US$5,220 d for four nights in the least expensive room, ranging up to US$11,360 s, US$14,032 d for eight nights in the costliest suite, including transfer to and from Punta Arenas and unlimited excursions. Low-season rates are about 20 percent cheaper. For details and/or reservations, contact **Explora Hotels** (Américo Vespucio Sur 80, 5th floor, Las Condes, Santiago, tel. 02/2066060, www.explora.com).

Just beyond park boundaries, reached by launch over the Río Serrano, the stylish **Hotel Lago Tyndall** (tel. 061/614682, www.hoteltyndall.cl, US$187–253 s, US$220–275 d) enjoys peace, quiet, and magnificent views. Nearby is the less stylish **Hostería Cabañas del Paine** (tel. 061/210179 in Punta Arenas, www.cabanasdelpaine.cl, US$240 s, US$250 d).

INFORMATION
Conaf's principal facility is its **Centro de Informaciones Ecológicas** (tel. 061/691931, ptpaine@conaf.cl, 8:30 A.M.–8 P.M. daily in summer), at the Administración building on the shores of Lago del Toro near the Río Paine outlet, with good natural-history exhibits.

Ranger stations at Guardería Laguna Amarga, Portería Lago Sarmiento, Guardería Laguna Azul, Guardería Lago Verde, and Guardería Lago Grey can also provide information.

The private Hostería Las Torres has an excellent audiovisual salon with sophisticated environmental exhibits.

Entry Fee

For foreigners, Torres del Paine is Chile's most expensive national park—the entry fee is US$25 per person except May 1–September 30, when it's US$12.50. Rangers at Portería Lago Sarmiento, Guardería Laguna Amarga (where most inbound buses now stop), Guardería Lago Verde, or Guardería Laguna Azul collect the fee, issue receipts, and provide a 1:100,000 park map suitable for trekking.

Books and Maps

Still serviceable, Tim Burford's *Chile & Argentina: The Bradt Trekking Guide* (Bradt Publications, 2001) is overdue for a new edition; the maps are only so-so. Also overdue for an update, Clem Lindenmayer and Nick Tapp's 3rd edition of *Trekking in the Patagonian Andes* (Lonely Planet, 2003) has significantly better maps than the Bradt guide's and expanded coverage compared to its own previous editions. Only a few of those maps, though, are as large as the 1:100,000 scale that's desirable for hiking, though the rest are suitable for planning hikes.

Climbers should look for Alan Kearney's *Mountaineering in Patagonia* (Seattle: The Mountaineers, 1998), which includes both historical and practical information on climbing in Torres del Paine and Argentina's Parque Nacional Los Glaciares. Gladys Garay N. and Oscar Guineo N. have collaborated in *The Fauna of Torres del Paine* (1993), a locally produced guide to the park's animal life.

GETTING THERE

Most people find the bus the cheapest and quickest way to and from the park, but the more expensive trip up Seno Última Esperanza and the Río Serrano by cutter and Zodiac is a viable, more interesting alternative.

The new road from Puerto Natales has opened, so tour companies usually enter the park at Laguna Amarga and loop back on the new road, but bus companies continue to use the old highway.

Bus

Bus companies enter the park at Guardería Laguna Amarga, where many hikers begin the Paine circuit, before continuing to the Administración at Río Serrano and then returning by the same route. Round-trips from Natales are slightly cheaper, but companies do not accept each others' tickets.

In summer only, there may be direct bus service to El Calafate, Argentina, the closest town to that country's Parque Nacional Los Glaciares. Inquire in Puerto Natales at Calafate Travel (Baquedano 459, tel. 061/414456).

River

Transportation up and down the Río Serrano, between the park and Puerto Natales, has become a popular if more expensive alternative to the bus; see *Transportation* under *Glaciar Balmaceda (Parque Nacional Bernardo O'Higgins)* in this chapter. Visitors who only want to see this sector of the river, without continuing to Puerto Natales, can do so as a day trip to Puerto Toro and back.

GETTING AROUND

Buses to and from Puerto Natales will also carry passengers along the main park road, but as their schedules are similar, there are substantial periods with no public transportation. Hitching is common, but competition is heavy and most vehicles are full with families. There is a regular shuttle between Guardería Laguna Amarga and Estancia Cerro Paine (Hostería Las Torres, US$2 pp) that meets arriving and departing buses.

October–April, reliable transportation is available from Pudeto to Refugio Pehoé (US$18 one-way, 30 minutes; US$30 round-trip) with the catamaran *Hielos Patagónicos* (tel. 061/411380 in Puerto Natales). The first two weeks of October and in April, there is one departure daily, at noon, from Pudeto, returning at 12:30 P.M. From mid-October to mid-November and the last fortnight of

March, there's an additional service at 6 P.M., returning at 6:30 P.M. From mid-November to mid-March, there are departures at 9:30 A.M., noon, and 6 P.M., returning at 10 A.M., 12:30 P.M., and 6:30 P.M. Schedules may be postponed or canceled due to bad weather, and there are no services on Christmas and New Year's Day.

Also in season, the catamaran *Grey II* goes daily from Hotel Lago Grey to Glaciar Grey (US$34 one-way, US$78 round-trip) at 9 A.M. and 3 P.M. daily; on the return, it cruises the glacier's face, so the reverse direction costs US$52 one-way. There is a US$16 shuttle between the Administración and Hotel Lago Grey that connects with the excursion.

El Calafate, Argentina

Spreading along the south shore of Lago Argentino, a giant glacial trough fed by meltwater from the Campo de Hielo Sur, fast-growing El Calafate is the poster child for Argentina's tourism boom. The gateway to Parque Nacional Los Glaciares and its spectacular Moreno Glacier, it has few points of interest in itself. Still, it has increasing and improving services, including hotels and restaurants, and it's southwestern Santa Cruz's transport hub.

Calafate owes its growth to 1) a new international airport that's nearly eliminated the overland route from Río Gallegos for long-distance passengers; 2) the competitive Argentine peso; 3) the fact that former Argentine president Néstor Kirchner, a Santa Cruz native, built a home here and invited high-profile international figures, such as Brazilian president Luis Inácio da Silva (Lula) and former Chilean president Ricardo Lagos, to admire the Moreno Glacier with him.

The boom has had drawbacks, though. As the population has more than doubled in a decade, real-estate prices have skyrocketed. Sadly, a prime downtown location that used to house the old power plant—admittedly a noisy eyesore—has become the site of a hideously pharaonic casino.

ORIENTATION

El Calafate (population 6,439) is 320 kilometers northwest of Río Gallegos and 32 kilometers west of northbound RP 40, which leads to the wilder El Chaltén sector of Parque Nacional

Los Glaciares and an adventurous overland route back to Chile. While only about 50 or 60 kilometers from Torres del Paine as the crow flies, El Calafate is 215 kilometers from the Cerro Castillo border crossing and about 305 kilometers from Puerto Natales via Argentine highways RN 40, RP 5, and RP 11, plus a small additional distance on the Chilean side.

A former stage stop, El Calafate has an elongated city plan that has spread only a few blocks north and south of its main east–west thoroughfare, the pompously named Avenida del Libertador General José de San Martín (for Argentina's independence hero). Most services and points of interest are close to "Avenida Libertador" or "San Martín," as the street is variously called, but explosive hotel growth is taking place to the east, on and near the former airfield.

SIGHTS

After years of near abandonment, the **Museo Regional El Calafate** (Avenida Libertador 575, tel. 02902/491924, 10 A.M.–5 P.M. weekdays) has reopened, but it's hard to say that the sparse and poorly presented exhibits on paleontology, natural history, geology, and ethnology were worth the wait. The photographic histories of pioneer families show promise, but it's long needed an explanation of the 1920s labor unrest that led to several shooting deaths on the *estancias*.

More promising is the **Centro de Interpretación Histórica** (Almirante Brown and Bonarelli, tel. 02902/492799, calafatecentro@cotecal.com.ar, 10 A.M.–8 P.M. daily Sept.–Semana Santa, 10 A.M.–6 P.M. the rest of the year, US$5.50), whose sophisticated timeline puts southern Patagonian natural, cultural and historical events in context; it has many photographs, good English translations, and a quality library. Admission includes *remise* transportation from downtown.

At the north edge of town, municipal authorities have transformed a onetime sewage pond into **Reserva Municipal Laguna Nimez,** a freshwater body now frequented by more than 100 bird species. It's fenced, but locals and others often squeeze through gaps for a walk through the wetlands and along the lakeshore.

One sight that locals know but few foreigners recognize is the **Casa Kirchner** (Los Gauchos and Namuncurá), the home of Argentina's first couple, ex-president Néstor Kirchner and current president Cristina Fernández de Kirchner.

ENTERTAINMENT

El Calafate is surprisingly light on nightlife, which consists mostly of dining out and drinking at venues such as **Don Diego de la Noche** (Avenida Libertador 1603, tel. 02902/493270). On Calafate's western outskirts, the best place for drinks is the **Shackleton Lounge** (Avenida Libertador 3287, tel. 02902/493516), which has lake views but suffers excesses of electronica.

Tradiciones Argentinas (Avenida del Libertador 351, tel. 02902/491281) is a folkloric music venue.

SHOPPING

Downtown Avenida del Libertador is lined with souvenir shops such as **Open Calafate** (Avenida Libertador 996, tel. 02902/491254), which also sells books and maps. **Keokén** (Avenida Libertador 1311, keoken@cotecal. com.ar) has a more representative selection of Patagonian crafts.

Boutique del Libro (Avenida Libertador 1033, tel. 02902/491363) carries a broad selection of books (many in English) on Antarctica, Argentina, and Patagonia, including Moon Handbooks and novels.

For premium homemade chocolates, try **Ovejitas de la Patagonia** (Avenida Libertador 1118, tel. 02902/491736), **Laguna Negra** (Avenida Libertador 1250, tel. 02902/492423), or any of several similar locales.

Recently, trendy Buenos Aires design and fashion shops have installed themselves here. **Cardón** (Emilio Amado 835, tel. 02902/492074), for instance, is a casual clothing counterpart to Esprit or Patagonia. **Pampa** (Avenida Libertador 1179, tel. 02902/491305) and **Pueblo Indio** (Avenida Libertador and 9 de Julio, tel. 02902/491965, www.puebloindio .com.ar) carry high-end crafts from around the country, including ceramics, silverwork, and tapestries.

ACCOMMODATIONS

El Calafate has diverse accommodations of generally high standards, ranging from camping to five-star extravagance. Its custom-built hostels, with stylish architecture, engaging common areas with stunning views, and even restaurants and bars, far surpass the dingy no-frills reputation that the word sometimes implies. In addition to dorms, several have excellent private rooms that shame some hotels.

Occupancy rates are at all-time highs, and places that once stayed open in summer only now stay open all year. Unless otherwise indicated, prices below are for high season, usually October–April, but dates vary and, if business is slow, rates can be negotiable. Every place in categories over US$50 includes breakfast; less expensive places may or may not provide it. Argentine hotels, unlike those in Chile, do not discount IVA to foreign visitors.

Camping

Flanking the Arroyo Calafate, the municipal **Camping El Ovejero** (José Pantín s/n, tel. 02902/493422, campingelovejero@hotmail. com, US$4 pp) has reopened under a private concessionaire. Fenced and forested, it has good common toilets and hot showers, and each site has its own fire pit; areas east of the creek are for walk-in campers only.

On the grounds of its namesake

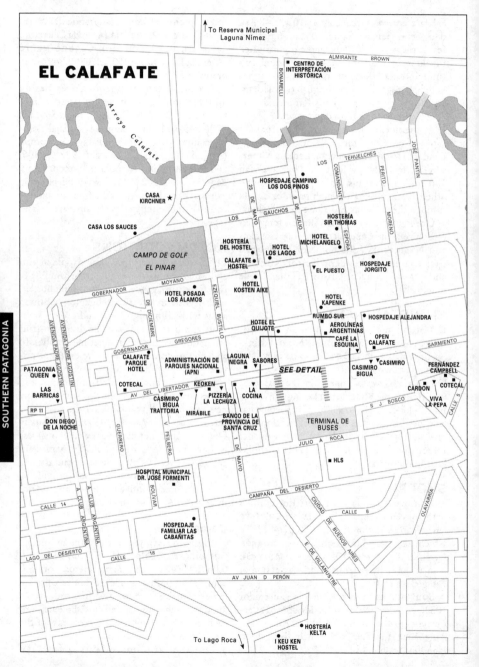

EL CALAFATE

To Reserva Municipal
Laguna Nímez

ALMIRANTE   BROWN

CENTRO DE
INTERPRETACIÓN
HISTÓRICA

BONARELLI

Arroyo   Calafate

JOSÉ PANTIN

PERITO

COMANDANTE

TEHUELCHES

LOS

MORENO

ESPORA

9 DE JULIO

GAUCHOS

LOS

25 DE MAYO

CASA
KIRCHNER ★

HOSPEDAJE CAMPING
LOS DOS PINOS

HOSTERÍA
SIR THOMAS

CASA LOS SAUCES

HOSTERÍA
DEL HOSTEL

HOTEL
LOS LAGOS

HOTEL
MICHELANGELO

*CAMPO DE GOLF
EL PINAR*

CALAFATE
HOSTEL

EL PUESTO

HOSPEDAJE
JORGITO

GOBERNADOR

MOYANO

HOTEL POSADA
LOS ÁLAMOS

HOTEL
KOSTEN AIKE

HOTEL
KAPENKE

RUMBO SUR

HOSPEDAJE ALEJANDRA

7 DE DICIEMBRE

EZEQUIEL   BUSTILLO

HOTEL EL
QUIJOTE

AEROLÍNEAS
ARGENTINAS

OPEN
CALAFATE

SARMIENTO

GREGORES

CAFÉ LA
ESQUINA

GOBERNADOR

LAGUNA
NEGRA

SABORES

SEE DETAIL

CASIMIRO
BIGUÁ

CASIMIRO

FERNÁNDEZ
CAMPBELL

PATAGONIA
QUEEN

CALAFATE
PARQUE HOTEL

ADMINISTRACIÓN DE
PARQUES NACIONAL
(APN)

AVENIDA PADRE AGOSTINI

AVENIDA PADRE AGOSTINI

COTECAL

KEOKEN

LA
COCINA

CARDON

COTECAL

LAS
BARRICAS

LIBERTADOR

AV DEL

PIZZERÍA
LA LECHUZA

VIVA
LA PEPA

CALLE 5

RP 11

CASIMIRO
BIGUÁ
TRATTORIA

MIRÁBILE

GUERRERO

DON DIEGO
DE LA NOCHE

BANCO DE LA
PROVINCIA DE
SANTA CRUZ

S J BOSCO

FELBERG

TERMINAL DE
BUSES

1 DE MAYO

JULIO   A   ROCA

BOLIVAR

HOSPITAL MUNICIPAL
DR. JOSÉ FORMENTI

HLS

CAMPAÑA   DEL   DESIERTO

OLAVARRÍA

A   CLUB   ARGENTINA

CALLE 14

CALLE   8

CIUDAD

DE   BUENOS   AIRES

HOSPEDAJE
FAMILIAR LAS
CABAÑITAS

LAGO   DEL   DESIERTO

CALLE   18

E   DE   VILLANUSTRE

AV   JUAN   D   PERÓN

HOSTERÍA
KELTA

To Lago Roca

I KEU KEN
HOSTEL

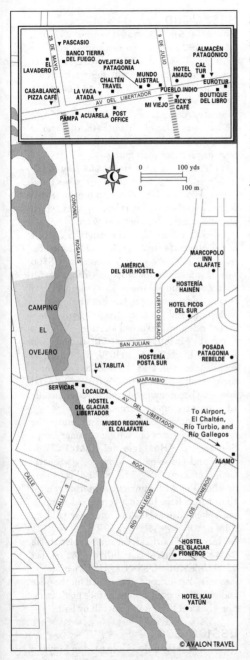

© AVALON TRAVEL

hospedaje, **Camping Jorgito** (Moyano 943, tel. 02902/491323, US$4 pp) is decent enough. **Camping Los Dos Pinos** (9 de Julio 218, tel. 02902/491271, www.losdospinos.com, US$4 pp plus US$2 per car) has improved and expanded.

US$10-25

Friendly **Hospedaje Jorgito** (Moyano 943, tel. 02902/491323, US$11 pp) has good multibed rooms with shared or private baths.

Expanded **Hospedaje los dos Pinos** (9 de Julio 358, tel./fax 02902/491271, www.losdospinos.com, US$10–12 pp, US$52 d) provides a variety of plain but spacious and immaculate rooms—ranging from hostel dorms to private doubles and cabañas (its tours, though, have drawn some criticism). Breakfast costs extra.

Calafate's best new hostel is the custombuilt **Che Lagarto** (25 de Mayo 311, tel. 02902/496670, www.chelagarto.com, US$12 pp, US$42 d) with large and luminous common areas, though some of the dorms are a cramped with up to a dozen beds. Even some of the dorms have balconies, though, and it's a triumph of style as well as amenities.

Only a few years old, the **I Keu Ken Hostel** (Pontoriero 171, tel. 02902/495175, www.patagoniaikeuken.com.ar, US$13 pp, US$37 d) is a purpose-built hostel in the Magellanic style, with truly inviting common areas. All rooms are quadruple dorms, with lockers and shared baths; rates include breakfast. It's a bit uphill from downtown, but there are free transfers from the bus terminal.

Among the best in its non-hostel class, family-run **Hospedaje Alejandra** (Espora 60, tel. 02902/491328, US$20 s, US$24 d) has small but spotless rooms with twin beds and shared baths, but serves no breakfast.

"Think big" seems the motto at **Calafate Hostel** (Gobernador Moyano 1296, tel. 02902/492450, www.calafatehostels.com, US$12 pp), which has dorms with shared baths and balconies, in a stylish building with vast common areas; it also has better rooms with private baths (US$40 s, US$51 d with breakfast).

East of the arroyo, open October–mid-April, the HI affiliate **(Hostel del Glaciar Pioneros** (Los Pioneros 251, tel./fax 02902/491243, www.glaciar.com, US$12–14 pp, US$31–36 s, US$38–45 d) has extensive common spaces, including a large lounge with WiFi, kitchen space, and laundry facilities. The higher rates are for larger and comfortable but no-frills hotel-style rooms with breakfast; it also offers its own Moreno Glacier excursions.

Under the same management, with identical prices, the nearly new **(Hostel del Glaciar Libertador** (Avenida Libertador 587, tel./fax 02902/491792, www.glaciar.com) has 22 rooms with private baths; some are four-bed dorms, while others are twins or doubles. Both hostels offer roughly 15 percent discounts for HI members, and 30 percent low-season discounts in October and April (except for Semana Santa).

Near the old airfield, a short walk from América del Sur, the **Marco Polo Inn** (Calle 405 No. 82, tel. 02902/493899, www.marcopoloinncalafate.com, US$12–14 pp, US$57–63 d, with breakfast) has just opened a new hostel here to complement its others in Puerto Iguazú and Bariloche. Amenities include a kitchen, a bar, and a restaurant, and there are half a dozen private rooms in addition to the dorms.

US$25-50

Several hostels in the previous category also have private accommodations that are excellent values in this price range, which otherwise has few options, or slightly above.

On the hilltop immediately east of the municipal campground, custom-built **(América del Sur Hostel** (Puerto Deseado s/n, tel. 02902/493525, www.americahostel.com.ar, US$14 pp, US$63 d) has friendly management, spectacular common spaces with panoramic views, and well-designed rooms in which the toilet and shower are separate, and the vanity outside of both. Rates include breakfast and free transfers from the bus terminal; off-season rates are about 20 percent less.

US$50-100

Hostería Sir Thomas (Espora 257, tel. 02902/492220, www.sirthomas.com.ar, US$43 s, US$51 d without breakfast) is reliable. Reservations are advisable at the chalet-style **Hospedaje Familiar Las Cabañitas** (Valentín Feilberg 218, tel. 02902/491118, lascabanitas@cotecal.com.ar, US$43 s, US$52 d), which offers some of Calafate's most *simpático* management, taking a personal interest in and responsibility for their guests.

Tidy, well-regarded **Hotel Los Lagos** (25 de Mayo 220, tel. 02902/491170, www.loslagoshotel.com.ar, US$60 d with breakfast) has come up in the world—as have its rates, which also include free Internet and WiFi.

Directly across from the América del Sur hostel, **Hostería Hainén** (Puerto Deseado 118, tel. 02902/493874, www.hainen.com, US$66 s or d) is a handsome wooden structure with wainscoted midsize rooms in soothing colors. It lacks elaborate amenities but compensates with peace and quiet (except for nearly incessant winds at this exposed location).

Nearby **Hotel Picos del Sur** (Puerto San Julián 271, tel. 02902/493650, www.hotelpicosdelsur.com.ar, US$71 s or d) has overcome some service problems—it's truly congenial now—to become a good choice. Rates include an airport pickup and dropoff.

Alongside the Calafate Hostel, under the same management but with a separate reception area, the **Hostería del Hostel** (25 de Mayo and Gobernador Moyano, www.calafatehostels.com, US$55 s, US$72 d) is a smart new building with immaculate midsize rooms, all of which have Internet-connected computers. When business is slow, rates may fall by a third or so.

Near the old airfield, the rooms at **Hostería Posta Sur** (Puerto San Julián 490, tel./fax 02902/492406, US$89 s, US$95 d, www.hosteriapostasur.com.ar) are small for the price and some lack even closets, but it's no desperation choice. Off-season rates fall by half.

US$100-200

Hotel Michelangelo (Gobernador Moyano

1020, tel. 02902/491045, www.michelangelo hotel.com.ar, US$87 s, US$100 d) includes breakfast, but its restaurant draws raves for lunch or dinner as well. Some rooms are small, but the management and service are professional, and it's now tobacco-free.

The hillside (**Hostería Kelta** (Portoriero 109, tel. 02902/491966, www.kelta.com.ar, US$94 s, US$116 d) is a handsome hotel with views across the lake; the larger lakeview rooms are no more expensive than the smaller interior rooms and, on request, the staff will shift guests to better rooms as they open up.

Hotel Kapenke (9 de Julio 112, tel. 02902/491093, www.kapenke.com.ar, US$115 s, US$130 d) has added a handsome new wing to an already attractive hotel, but rates continue to rise.

At first glance, the interior of (**Posada Patagonia Rebelde** (José R. Haro 442, tel. 02902/494495, www.patagoniarebelde.com, US$118 s or d) seems more a well-stocked antiques shop than a boutique hotel in a distinctive Patagonia style. Ironically, much of the recycled material that built the building came from the Buenos Aires barrio of La Boca, and its own rustic sophistication contrasts dramatically with the sophisticated design hotels elsewhere in town. Though it's not for everyone, everyone who's read *In Patagonia* is likely to love it.

Its exterior handsomely rehabbed in wood and glass, the pastel rooms at **Hotel El Quijote** (Gregores 1191, tel. 02902/491017, www.quijotehotel.com.ar, US$137 s, US$166 d) make it one of El Calafate's most stylish hotels. A recent remodel enlarged the rooms and made them more comfortable, but it's also meant thinner walls that conduct noise more easily.

New in late 2007, **Patagonia Queen** (Avenida Padre Agostini 49, tel. 02902/496701, www.patagoniaqueen.com.ar, US$165–186 s or d) is a 20-room boutique hotel, done in stunning natural wood, with earnest Korean-Argentine management. The rooms are only midsized, but all the baths have whirlpool tubs, and it's tobacco-free throughout.

Hotel Mirador del Lago (Avenida Libertador 2047, tel. 02902/493176, www.miradordellago

.com.ar, US$117–167 s, US$126–176 d) is two decades old, but a recent rehab and expansion have left it looking like new. Rooms in the newer wing are slightly larger and more expensive, but even the older rooms are good and, from its knoll on the east side of the road, it has fine lake views. The staff often anticipates (rather than reacts to) its guests' needs.

When El Calafate was smaller, (**Hotel Kau Yatún** (tel. 02902/491259, www.kauyatun.com, US$145/170 s/d–260 s or d with breakfast) was part of Estancia 25 de Mayo; the older part was the *casco,* whose suites have a whirlpool tub, fireplace, and other amenities, including a full buffet breakfast. Note that its business address of Avenida Libertador 1190 is not the same as the property itself, which is east of the arroyo and up the hill from the Albergue del Glaciar.

The 60-room **Hotel Kosten Aike** (Gobernador Moyano 1243, tel. 02902/492424, www.kostenaike.com.ar, US$184 s or d) is an impressive four-star facility with every modern convenience, including gym and spa, modem access, and even handicapped facilities. The large and comfy quarters have drawn uniformly positive comments.

More than US$200

Upping the stakes in Calafate's competitive hotel scene, the architecturally audacious (**Design Suites Calafate** (Calle 94 No. 190, tel. 02902/494525, www.designsuites .com, US$210–275 s or d plus taxes) enjoys spectacular panoramas from a blustery bluff north of the old airfield. The higher-priced suites have lake views, while slightly smaller standard rooms face the steppe, but all rates are discriminatory against foreign visitors.

Hotel Posada Los Álamos (Gobernador Moyano 1355, tel. 02902/491144, www.posadalosalamos.com, from US$211 s, US$230 d) may be Calafate's most complete hotel, with a pool, spa, and convention center. Breakfast takes place in the restaurant across the street, where it also operates the compact nine-hole (three holes with three different tees each) Campo de Golf Pinar.

It's drawn some attention, but it's questionable whether the midsized rooms at the **Calafate Parque Hotel** (7 de Diciembre and Gobernador Gregores, tel. 02902/492970, www.calafateparquehotel.com.ar, US$236 s or d) justify the rack rates. The facilities, including a third-floor gym and spa, as well as a fairly elaborate restaurant, are good enough, but does it justify more than double the price of, say, the Hainén (with admittedly fewer amenities)? Discounted rates may be possible through its website.

New in 2005, atop a hill near the eastern approach to town, is the **Hotel Alto Calafate** (RP 11 s/n, tel. 02902/494110, www.hotelaltocalafate.com.ar, US$247 s or d), where upper-midsized rooms command views of the entire Lago Argentino basin and the Andes to the southwest, or of the "Balcón de Calafate" that rises immediately behind it. The service is exemplary, and its bar/restaurant precludes the need to dine or drink in town (though a free hourly shuttle is available). There are no neighbors to make any noise, but the wind can wail at this exposed location.

In a sense, every room is a presidential suite at **Casa Los Sauces** (Los Gauchos 1352, tel. 2902/495854, www.casalossauces.com, from US$1,200 d), as it's the property of President Cristina Fernández and her husband, ex-President Néstor Kirchner. Its 36 rooms, in several buildings over three willow-studded hectares, adjoin the presidential weekend house, and the rates seem more suitable for kings.

FOOD

El Calafate has Santa Cruz province's best restaurants and, in southernmost Argentine Patagonia, only Ushuaia can match it for quality. Prices have risen considerably, though the quality remains high.

Unfortunately, unlike Ushuaia, it's not yet banished tobacco from the food scene; some individual restaurants have done so and others have tobacco-free areas, though some of those are merely symbolic.

The best breakfast spot is **Cafetería Don Luis** (9 de Julio 265, tel. 02902/491550), with the best coffee, the most succulent croissants, and many other treats to try throughout the day.

Several decent *confiterías* offer *minutas* (short orders), sandwiches, coffee, and the like. Among them are **Café La Esquina** (Avenida Libertador 1000, tel. 02902/492334) and the tobacco-heavy, WiFi-equipped **Casablanca Pizza Café** (Avenida Libertador 1202, tel. 02902/491402). For sandwiches including smoked venison or wild boar on homemade bread (US$8), don't miss tobacco-free **Almacén Patagónico** (Avenida Libertador 1044), flooded with natural light and, moreover, fresh-made chocolates.

(**Pizzería La Lechuza** (Avenida Libertador and 1° de Mayo, tel. 02902/491610, lunch and dinner daily) deserves special mention for its *super cebolla y jamón crudo* (onion and prosciutto), and its empanadas. The pastas-only **La Cocina** (Avenida Libertador 1245, tel. 02902/491758, lunch and dinner daily) has slipped a notch but still has its public. New on the scene, **Mirábile** (Avenida del Libertador 1329, tel. 02902/492230, closed Mon.) has plenty of tough competition in the pastas category, but has moderate prices (most entrees less than US$10) and excellent service.

(**Viva la Pepa** (Emilio Amado 833, Local 1, tel. 02902/491880, lunch and dinner daily) offers a variety of outstanding sweet and savory crepes (US$7–12) that are an ideal antidote for anyone who's overdosed on beef, lamb, or other Patagonian staples. The small wine list stresses Patagonian vintages.

In one of Calafate's oldest buildings (1957), **El Puesto** (Gobernador Moyano and 9 de Julio, tel. 02902/491620, lunch and dinner daily) has three snug little dining rooms, one glassed-in to enjoy garden views, with decor that reflects the theme of a outside house on a sheep estancia. The Patagonian lamb dishes are the most sophisticated, but there are also fine pizzas and pasta, and a variety of baked empanadas. The posted sentiment "Enjoy our aromas and flavors—don't smoke" is a welcome one, but they don't enforce it strictly.

La Vaca Atada (Avenida Libertador 1176, tel. 02902/491227, lunch and dinner daily) is a popular *parrilla* that also has fine soups and pasta, at moderate prices. **Mi Viejo** (Avenida Libertador 1111, tel. 02902/491691, lunch and dinner daily) is comparable but a bit dearer. Remodeled **Rick's Café** (Avenida Libertador 1105, tel. 02902/492148, lunch and dinner daily) and **La Tablita** (Coronel Rosales 28, tel. 02902/491065, lunch and dinner daily) are both well-regarded *parrillas*.

◖ **Casimiro** (Avenida Libertador 963, tel. 02902/492590, www.casimirobigua.com, lunch and dinner daily) would be a good choice almost anywhere in the world; the plate of smoked Patagonian appetizers is exquisite. Other entrées, in the US$9–15 range, are close behind but less interesting, though portions are large in pastas, trout, and lamb. It's also a by-the-glass wine bar, with an imposing list reaching upwards of US$600 per bottle (there are other more affordable, and more than palatable, choices).

A few doors west, under the same ownership, **Casimiro Biguá** (Avenida del Libertador 993, tel. 02902/493993, www.casimirobigua .com, lunch and dinner daily) has an overlapping menu but it's best to stick with its *parrilla* specialties of grilled beef and lamb.

In the same vein as Casimiro, **Pascasio** (25 de Mayo 52, tel. 2902/492055, lunch and dinner daily) is a gourmet restaurant with starters such as lamb carpaccio (US$8), pastas with a regional touch, a lamb risotto (US$16), and occasional game dishes such as Patagonian hare.

A spinoff from its near namesakes, new in late 2007, **Casimiro Biguá Trattoria** (Avenida Libertador 1359, tel. 02962/492993, lunch and dinner daily) specializes in Patagonian-inspired pastas, such as lamb ravioli (US$15). The flavors are rich and portions generous, the wine list diverse, but the service can border on indifferent or inattentive.

Often accommodating tour groups, **Las Barricas** (Avenida Libertador 1610, tel. 02902/493414, www.barricasdeenopio. ar, lunch and dinner daily) prepares a variety of meat, fish, and game dishes, plus smoked meats. Desserts are only so-so, but there's a big list of premium wines in the US$20–50 range;

decent by-the-glass house wines are moderately priced.

Two blocks west of Barricas, an open secret to locals, ◖ **Pura Vida** (Avenida Libertador 1876, tel. 02902/493356, lunch and dinner daily) gets few foreigners for quality versions of traditional Argentine and Patagonian dishes such as gnocchi (US$8) with a saffron sauce, *carbonada* (a motley stew large enough for two hungry diners, US$13), and *cazuela de cordero* (a lamb casserole, US$16). Self-consciously casual—no two chairs nor menu cards are alike—it has mezzanine seating with views over Laguna Nimes and, in the distance, Lago Argentino; the main floor, though, is cozier. The menu rarely changes, though, and the wine list is modest (with nothing by the glass).

El Calafate went nearly a decade without a quality ice creamery, but now it has three outstanding ones. **Acuarela** (Avenida Libertador 1177, tel. 02902/491315) can aspire toward Buenos Aires's best, but **Sabores** (Avenida Libertador 1222, tel. 02902/492422) and **Tito** (Espora 65) are also fine. For a local treat, try Sabores' fresh *calafate* flavor, slightly better than Acuarela's.

INFORMATION

At the bus terminal, the **Secretaría de Turismo de la Municipalidad de El Calafate** (Avenida Roca 1004, tel. 02902/491090, www .elcalafate.gov.ar, 8 A.M.–10 P.M. Nov.–Mar., 8 A.M.–8 P.M. Apr.–Oct.) maintains a database of hotels and other services; it has English-speaking personnel, maps, brochures, and a message board.

The **Administración de Parques Nacionales** (APN, Avenida Libertador 1302, tel. 02902/491755 or 02902/491545, losglaciares@apn.gov.ar) is open 7 A.M.–2 P.M. weekdays only.

There is a useful private website, www.losglaciares.com, that contains considerable information on El Calafate and surroundings.

SERVICES

Cambio Thaler (Avenida del Libertador 963, tel. 02902/493245) is the only exchange house.

Both **Banco Santa Cruz** (Avenida Libertador 1285) and **Banco Tierra del Fuego** (25 de Mayo 40) have ATMs.

Correo Argentino (Avenida Libertador 1133) is the post office.

The **Cooperativa Telefónica de Calafate** (Cotecal, Avenida Libertador 1486, tel. 02902/491900) has the best and cheapest Internet service; there are no collect phone calls, though. **Open Calafate** (Avenida Libertador 996, tel. 02902/491254) provides some competition in both telephone and Internet, but its connections are slower.

El Lavadero (25 de Mayo 43, tel. 02902/492182) charges around US$5 per laundry load.

The **Hospital Municipal Dr. José Formenti** (Avenida Roca 1487, tel. 02902/491001, 02902/491173) handles medical matters.

GETTING THERE

El Calafate is the transport hub for western Santa Cruz, thanks to its new airport, road connections to Río Gallegos, and improving links north and south along RN 40.

Air

Aerolíneas Argentinas (9 de Julio 57, tel. 02902/492815) normally flies north to Trelew and Buenos Aires's Aeroparque, and south to Ushuaia, but it sometimes has service to or from Bariloche as well. LAN Argentina has an increasing number of flights; travel agencies such as **Rumbo Sur** (9 de Julio 81, tel. 02902/492155, rumbosur@cotecal.com.ar) can arrange seats.

LADE (tel. 02902/491262, ladecalafate@cotecal.com.ar) keeps an office at the bus terminal (Avenida Roca 1004). It flies northbound to Comodoro Rivadavia and Buenos Aires, and southbound to Río Gallegos, Río Grande, and Ushuaia.

Bus

El Calafate's **Terminal de Ómnibus** overlooks the town from its perch at Avenida Roca 1004; for pedestrians, the easiest approach is a staircase from the corner of Avenida Libertador and 9 de Julio. There's been little progress on plans to move it to the former airfield terminal just west of the bridge over the arroyo, so that buses would no longer enter town. For long-distance connections to most of the rest of the country, it's necessary to backtrack to Río Gallegos, but there are services to Puerto Natales and Torres del Paine, Chile.

Interlagos (tel. 02902/491179) and **Taqsa** (tel. 02902/491843, www.taqsa.com.ar) shuttle between El Calafate and the Santa Cruz provincial capital of Río Gallegos (US$13, 4 hours), where there are northbound connections to Buenos Aires and intermediates, and southbound connections to Punta Arenas (Chile). These buses will also drop passengers at the Río Gallegos airport.

Three carriers connect El Calafate with El Chaltén (US$18–20, 4.5 hours) in the Fitz Roy sector of Parque Nacional Los Glaciares: **Cal Tur** (tel. 02902/491842), **Chaltén Travel** (tel. 02902/492480), and Taqsa. Most services leave around 7:30–8 A.M., though there are sometimes afternoon buses around 5–6 P.M. Winter services are fewer, but normally at least daily among the three companies.

From September to April, Taqsa now has a daily 3 P.M. service to Perito Moreno (the town, not the glacier) and Los Antiguos (US$52, 16 hours), along desolate RN 40, for connections to Chile Chico. While this is more expensive than comparable distances elsewhere, it's also more direct, quicker, and even cheaper than the roundabout routes via coastal RN 3, especially if you factor in accommodations.

December–April or so, Chaltén Travel also provides alternate-day bus service from El Calafate to Perito Moreno and Los Antiguos (US$57, 14 hours). Passengers from El Chaltén can board the northbound bus from El Calafate at the junction of RN 40 and RP 23 without having to return to El Calafate. Buses depart Calafate on odd-numbered days and return from Los Antiguos on even-numbered days.

In summer, **Turismo Zaahj/Bus Sur** (tel. 02902/491631, www.turismozaahj.co.cl) and **Cootra** (tel. 02902/491444) alternate daily services to Puerto Natales, Chile (US$15, 4.5

hours); occasionally there are direct services to Parque Nacional Torres del Paine. In winter, these services may operate only weekly.

GETTING AROUND

For US$7.50 pp, **Ves Patagonia** (tel. 02902/494355, www.vespatagonia.com.ar) provides door-to-door shuttles to **Aeropuerto Internacional El Calafate** (tel. 02902/491220, aerocal@cotecal.com.ar), 23 kilometers east of town, just north of RP 11. A *remise* costs about US$23 for up to four passengers.

Car rental agencies include **Alamo** (Avenida Libertador 290, tel. 02902/493707, calafate@alamoargentina.com.ar), **Hertz** (Avenida Libertador 1822, tel. 02902/492525), **Localiza** (Avenida Libertador 687, tel. 02902/491398, localizacalafate@hotmail.com), **Nunatak** (Gobernador Gregores 1075, tel. 02902/491987, nunatakrentacar@cotecal.com.ar), and **Servicar** (Avenida del Libertador 695, tel. 02902/492301, servicar@cotecal.com.ar).

Half a block south of the bus terminal, **HLS** (Buenos Aires 173, tel. 02902/493806) rents bicycles.

Vicinity of El Calafate

Tours and transport to the Moreno Glacier and other nearby attractions are possible with a variety of competent operators. In alphabetical order, they include **Aventura Andina** (Avenida del Libertador 761, Local 4, tel. 02902/491726, aventuraandinafte@cotecal.com.ar), **Cal Tur** (Avenida Libertador 1080, tel. 02902/492217, caltur@cotecal.com.ar), **Cordillera del Sol** (25 de Mayo 43, tel. 02902/492822, www.cordilleradelsol.com), **Eurotur** (Avenida del Libertador 1025, tel. 02902/492190), **Mundo Austral** (Avenida Libertador 1114, tel. 02902/492365, mundoaustral@cotecal.com.ar), and **Rumbo Sur** (9 de Julio 81, tel. 02902/492155, rumbosur@cotecal.com.ar).

ESTANCIA ALICE

Formerly the *casco* (big house) of Estancia Alice, west of El Calafate en route to the Moreno Glacier, **El Galpón del Glaciar** (RP 11 Km 22) is open for day tours that may include activities such as birding and horseback riding, as well as exhibitions of sheep herding and shearing, afternoon tea, and a barbecued-lamb dinner. Rates are around US$53 pp with transportation to and from the farm; horseback rides (US$20 per hour) are additional.

El Galpón also offers accommodations for US$410 s, US$460 d for a two-night minimum, with limited activities included). For details, contact Agroturismo El Galpón (Avenida Libertador 761, El Calafate, tel. 02902/497793, www.elgalpondelglaciar.com.ar).

EOLO LODGE

On the 4,000-hectare Estancia Alice, Eolo is an exclusive mountainside lodge with 17 spacious suites and equally spacious common areas, all with "Big Sky" views that include either Lago Argentino to the east, the Valle de Anita immediately south, the Brazo Rico to the west, or a combination of them. On a clear day, there are even glimpses across the border to Torres del Paine.

Eolo owes its style to the *cascos* of the great Patagonian wool *estancias,* with corrugated metal siding and antique furnishings, and English tea settings. Contemporary technology such as double-paned windows, though, allows far greater natural light and better views than the poorly insulated buildings of the late 19th and early 20th centuries. The baths are modern.

Like those houses, though, the suites at Eolo lack modern conveniences such as television and Internet (though there's a satellite TV and DVD lounge, as well as WiFi in common areas). All suites take their names from typical Patagonian fauna—the Cóndor, for instance, is a corner suite with views to both the south and west (naming a room Zorrino [Skunk] may be a minor faux pas). There's a sheltered interior patio studded with Technicolor lupines in summer, and a small indoor pool.

Eolo helps arrange excursions to the Moreno Glacier and other nearby sights, but does not organize them itself. The property offers hiking to a bird-rich lagoon and to the summit of Cerro Frías, mountain biking, and horseback rides (contracted separately on the property).

Perched on the south slope of Cerro Frías, Eolo normally sells multi-night packages reserved well in advance but, if space is available, they're open to phone-ahead guests on short notice. Likewise, three-course lunches and dinners in the Francophile restaurant are open to nonguests, but by reservation only. Smoking is allowed in the bar only.

Open mid-September through April, Eolo (RP 11 Km 23, tel. 2902/492042, www.eolo.com.ar, US$995 s, US$1420 d for a two-night minimum) also has a Gran Buenos Aires contact (Laprida 3278, Oficina 39, San Isidro, tel. 011/4700-0705).

HOSTERÍA ALTA VISTA

Once a separate *estancia*, since absorbed by adjacent Estancia Anita, **Hostería Alta Vista** (RP 15 Km 35, tel./fax 02902/499902, www.hosteriaaltavista.com.ar, US$366 s, US$483 d) is an outpost of the Braun-Menéndez dynasty that dominated the Patagonian wool industry of Chile and Argentina. As such, its seven-room *casco*, which includes one luxury suite, is the place to be spoiled; surrounded by luxuriant gardens in a sheltered location at the foot of 1,294-meter Cerro Freile, it has a first-rate bar/restaurant open to guests only, a separate *quincho* for lamb *asados*, and flawless service from its English-speaking staff.

In addition to accommodations, Alta Vista offers excursions that include horseback riding in the hills immediately behind the *estancia*, offering a small lagoon full of wildfowl, with condors soaring above, and distant views of the Moreno Glacier. Two-night packages that include excursions to the glacier and other more remote sights are slightly more expensive.

Near Estancia Anita's entrance stands a memorial to the "Patagonia Rebelde" strikers of 1921–1922; erected by the provincial legislature, it reads "If the winners write history, that means there's another history: the Santa Cruz strikers, their stories present in our memory."

Accommodations are all-inclusive except for incidentals such as telephone charges and laundry. In addition to accommodations, it offers activities-oriented packages at rather higher prices.

Parque Nacional Los Glaciares

On the eastern slope of the Andes, Parque Nacional Los Glaciares comprises more than 759,000 hectares of slowly flowing ice that give birth to clear, frigid rivers and vast lakes, interspersed with Magellanic forests, along the Chilean border east and north of El Calafate. A UNESCO World Heritage Site, it's famous for the Moreno Glacier, which draws thousands of visitors for day trips but also pulls in scientists absorbed in glaciology and climate studies. The northern sector—a 3.5-hour bus trip from El Calafate—attracts those seeking to spend several days in vigorous exercise, either trekking or the far more demanding and dangerous technical climbing. Wildlife includes the endangered, rarely seen Andean *huemul*.

GEOGRAPHY AND CLIMATE

When the Campo de Hielo Sur receded at the end of the Pleistocene, it left behind the two huge glacial troughs that are now Lago Argentino and, to the north, the roughly parallel Lago Viedma. While these lakes lie only about 250 meters above sea level, the Andean summits along the border rise to 3,375 meters on Cerro Fitz Roy and nearly as high on pinnacles such as 3,102-meter Cerro Torre,

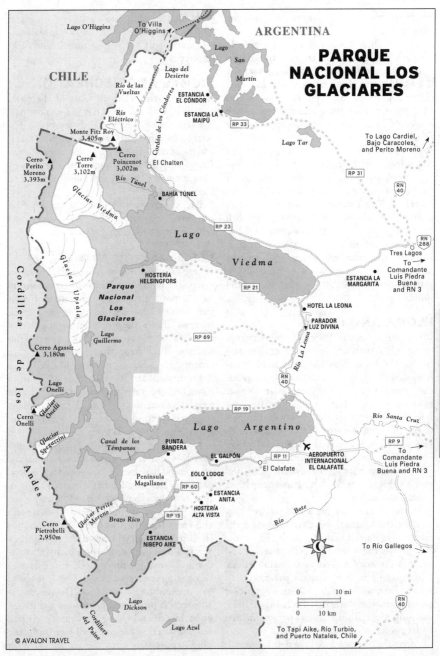

SOUTHERN PATAGONIA

which matches Chile's Torres del Paine for sheer majesty.

Most of these bodies of water lie outside the park boundaries, but the eastern Andean slopes still contain their remnants, some of the world's most impressive, and accessible, glaciers. Thirteen major glaciers flow toward the Argentine side, including the benchmark Moreno Glacier; ice covers 30 percent of the park's surface.

Despite its accumulated snow and ice, the Argentine side is drier than the Chilean, receiving only about 400 millimeters of precipitation on the eastern steppe, rising to about 900 millimeters at higher western elevations, where it's forested. The warmest month is February, with an average maximum temperature of 22°C and a minimum of 9°C; the coolest is August, when the maximum averages only 5°C and the minimum -1°C. As elsewhere in Patagonia, it gets ferocious winds, strongest in spring and summer.

FLORA AND FAUNA

Where rainfall is insufficient to support anything other than *coirón* bunch grasses and thorny shrubs such as the *calafate (Berberis buxifolia)* that gave the nearby town its name, the guanaco grazes the Patagonian steppe. Foxes and Patagonian skunks are also conspicuous, the flightless rhea or *ñandú* scampers across the open country, the *bandurria* (buff-necked ibis) hunts invertebrates, and flocks of upland geese browse the swampy lakeshores. The Andean condor soars above the plains and even the highest peaks, but occasionally lands to feast on carrion.

In the forests, the predominant tree species are the southern beeches *lenga* and the *coigüe,* also known here as *guindo.* The puma still prowls the forest, while the *huemul* and perhaps the *pudú* survive near Lago Viedma. Squawking flocks of austral parakeets flit among trees, while the Patagonian woodpecker pounds on their trunks. Perching calmly, awaiting nightfall, the austral pygmy owl is a common late-afternoon sight.

Along the lakeshores and riverbanks, aquatic birds such as coots and ducks are abundant. The most picturesque is the Patagonian torrent duck, which dives for prey in the rushing creeks.

SIGHTS AND RECREATION

In general, the southerly part of the park, east of El Calafate, gets day visitors for passive sightseeing. The northerly sector—a 3.5-hour bus trip from El Calafate—attracts hikers and mountaineers. Gregory Crouch's *Enduring Patagonia* (Random House, 2001) details one mountaineer's experiences on Fitz Roy and Cerro Torre.

Backpackers should note that no campfires are permitted within the park—carrying a campstove is obligatory for cooking.

◖ Glaciar Perito Moreno

Where a low Andean pass lets Pacific weather systems cross the cordillera, countless storms have deposited hundreds of meters of snow that, over millennia, have compressed into the Moreno Glacier, the groaning, rasping river of ice that's one of the continent's greatest sights and sounds. Fifteen times during the 20th century, the advancing glacier blocked Lago Argentino's **Brazo Rico** (Rico Arm) to form a rising body of water that eventually, when the weight became too great for the natural dam, triggered an eruption of ice and water toward the lake's main glacial trough.

No such event took place from 1988 until March 14, 2004, when the avalanche of ice and water could have been a metaphor for the flood of tourists that invaded El Calafate in anticipation. On any given day, though, massive icebergs still calve off the glacier's 60-meter face and crash into the **Canal de los Témpanos** (Iceberg Channel) with astonishing frequency. Perched on newly modernized catwalks and overlooks, many visitors spend entire days either gazing at or, eyes closed, simply listening to this rumbling river of ice. Descending to lake level is prohibited because of the danger of backwash and flying ice chunks; it's possible, though, to contract full-day "minitrekking" excursions onto the ice (US$129 pp with transport from El Calafate) with **Hielo y Aventura** (Avenida Libertador 935, El Calafate, tel. 02902/491053, www.hieloyaventura.com). Hielo y Aventura also offers a more strenuous "Big Ice" trip (US$150 pp) and a passive "Safari Náutico" boat trip (US$10 pp, one hour) that approaches the glacier's face.

Organized tours to the glacier, 80 kilometers southwest of El Calafate via RP 11, leave every day, as does scheduled transport; transport is usually extra for everything except bus tours.

Glaciar Upsala

Even larger than the Moreno Glacier, 50 kilometers long and 10 kilometers wide at its foot, the Upsala Glacier is accessible only by crowded catamaran trips from Puerto Bandera via Lago Argentino's Brazo Norte (North Arm). Impressive for its sheer extent, the sizeable bergs that have calved off it, and their shapes and colors, it's the trip's outstanding sight.

At midday, the boat anchors at Bahía Onelli, but bring a bag lunch (skipping the restaurant) to hike to ice-clogged **Lago Onelli.** The land portion of this excursion is regimented, and the guide-suggested pace—30 minutes from dock to lakeshore—is suitable for those on crutches. Smoking is prohibited on the forest trail.

Visitors should realize that this is a mass-tourism excursion that may frustrate hikers accustomed to freedom of the hills. If you take it, choose the biggest available ship, which offers the most deck space to see the Spegazzini and Upsala Glaciers. On board, the freshest air is within the cabin of the *ALM,* whose seats are cramped but where smoking is prohibited; on deck, smokers congregate even in freezing rain. Reasonably priced cakes, sandwiches, coffee, tea, and hot chocolate are available on board.

Puerto Bandera is 45 kilometers west of Calafate via RP 11 and RP 8. For information and reservations, contact concessionaire Fernández Campbell (Avenida Libertador 867, El Calafate, tel. 02902/491155 or 02902/491428, www.fernandezcampbell.com.ar). The full-day trip costs about US$85 per person; this now includes transfers to Puerto Bandera but not the US$17 park fee for non-Argentines.

A new alternative is an overnight trip, with onboard accommodations and meals, through **Cruceros Marpatag** (9 de Julio 57, Local 10, El Calafate, tel. 02902/492118, www.crucerosmarpatag.com), which visits the Upsala and Spegazzini Glaciers the first day and the Moreno Glacier on the second before returning to Puerto Bandera. Rates are US$625 pp, double occupancy.

Lago Roca

Also known as La Jerónima, the park's seldom-visited southwesterly sector along Lago Roca's Brazo Sur (South Arm) offers camping and cross-country hiking—there are no formal trails, only routes such as the one from the campground to the summit of **Cerro Cristal,** 55 kilometers from El Calafate. The landscape's most striking feature is the high shoreline—dry from the days when the lake backs up behind the advancing Moreno Glacier. Unlike other sectors, Lago Roca charges no admission fee.

Sector Fitz Roy

In the park's most northerly sector, the Fitz Roy Range has sheer spires to match Torres del Paine, but even if you're not a top technical climber, trails from the village of El Chaltén to the base of summits such as Fitz Roy and Cerro Torre make for some of the southern hemisphere's most exhilarating hikes. It's even possible to traverse the southern Patagonian icefields, but visitors seeking a sedate outdoor experience will find a handful of former sheep *estancias,* onetime Patagonian wool producers that have reinvented themselves as tourist accommodations.

From a signposted trailhead at El Chaltén's north end, just south of the former Camping Madsen, the **Sendero Laguna Torre** is an 11-kilometer track gaining about 200 meters in elevation as it winds through southern beech forests to the climbers' base camp for Cerro Torre; figure about 3–3.5 hours. At the lake, in clear weather, there are extraordinary

© WAYNE BERNHARDSON

the Fitz Roy Range, Parque Nacional Los Glaciares, Argentina

views of Cerro Torre's 3,102-meter summit, crowned by the so-called ice-and-snow "mushroom" that technical climbers must surmount. While Italian Cesare Maestri claimed that he and Austrian Toni Egger reached the summit in 1959 (Egger died in an avalanche, taking the expedition's camera with him), Italian Casimiro Ferrari made the first undisputed ascent (1974).

From the Madsen pack station, the more demanding **Sendero Río Blanco** trail rises steeply at the outset before leveling out through boggy beech forest and continuing to the Cerro Fitz Roy base camp, climbing about 350 meters in 10 kilometers. About midway to Río Blanco, a signed lateral leads south to **Laguna Capri,** which has backcountry campsites.

From Río Blanco, a vertiginous zigzag trail ascends 400 meters in just 2.5 kilometers to **Laguna de los Tres,** a glacial tarn whose name commemorates three members of the French expedition—René Ferlet, Lionel Terray, and Guido Magnone—who reached Fitz Roy's summit in 1952. Truly a top-of-the-world

experience, Laguna de los Tres offers some of Patagonia's finest Andean panoramas.

From the Río Blanco campground (reserved for climbers), a northbound trail follows the river's west bank north to **Laguna Piedras Blancas,** whose namesake glacier continually calves small icebergs. The trail continues north to the Río Eléctrico, beyond the park boundaries, where a westbound trail climbs the river to Piedra del Fraile and a possible circuit of the Campo de Hielo Sur, only for experienced snow-and-ice trekkers. At the Río Eléctrico, it's also possible to rejoin the road from El Chaltén to Lago del Desierto.

Another worthwhile hike, starting at the park visitors center, is the four-hour climb to **Loma del Pliegue Tumbado,** a 500-meter elevation gain that yields some of the area's finest panoramas to the north. From the same trailhead, a shorter ascent (about 45 minutes) leads to the **Mirador de los Cóndores,** for good views of El Chaltén and the confluence of the Río de las Vueltas and the Río Fitz Roy.

Glaciar Viedma

From Lago Viedma's north shore, south of El Chaltén, the park's best lake excursion is the catamaran *Viedma Discovery's* full-day voyage to the Viedma Glacier, which includes an iceclimbing component.

Sailing from Bahía Túnel, the vessel rounds the ironically named **Cabo de Hornos** (Cape Horn) to enter an iceberg-cluttered area before anchoring in a rocky cove. After disembarking, visitors hike to an overlook of the glacier (Argentina's largest, though its lakeside face is small) and of 2,677-meter Cerro Huemul. Those who wish can strap on crampons and continue onto the glacier for about 2.5 hours (even some pretty sedentary city dwellers do so).

The bilingual guides know glaciology and provide more personalized service than the Fernández Campbell excursion from Puerto Bandera. While the price here does not include lunch, they do provide an aperitif on the glacial rocks.

Departure time from El Chaltén is 8:30 A.M., while the boat sails from Bahía Túnel at 9 A.M.;

the cost is US$100 per person including transportation from El Chaltén. For details, contact **Patagonia Aventura** (Güemes s/n, tel. 02962/493110, El Chaltén, www.patagonia-aventura.com).

Lago del Desierto

Elongated Lago del Desierto, 37 kilometers north of El Chaltén, is a scenic end-of-the-road destination with hiking trails, boat excursions, and even a challenging border crossing to the Chilean settlement of Villa O'Higgins.

From the lake's south end, a short trail winds west through dense southern beech forest to a vista point and the hanging glacier at **Laguna Huemul;** a longer route follows the eastern shore to the border, a 20-kilometer trek over gentle terrain. Every year, a few hundred people cross the Argentine-Chilean border in a place that was once so contentious that, decades ago, a Chilean Carabinero even lost his life in a firefight with Argentine border guards.

Despite objections by a handful of Chilean nationalists, the matter is resolved, the border is peaceable, and determined hikers or even mountain bikers can readily reach Villa O'Higgins. Before attempting it, though, verify the latest details with Argentina's Gendarmería (Border Patrol) in El Chaltén.

From El Chaltén, **Transporte Las Lengas** (Viedma 95, tel. 02962/493023) minibuses go to El Pilar (US$10 pp) and Lago del Desierto (US$22 one-way or round-trip) at 8:30 A.M. and 3 P.M. daily, returning at 2:30 and 8:30 P.M. Hitching is feasible but vehicles are few and often full. At the lake itself, the *Viedma 1* carries passengers to the north end and back (US$32 pp).

ACCOMMODATIONS AND FOOD

Since most Moreno Glacier visitors stay at El Calafate, the park's southern sector has only limited accommodations, but they're increasingly abundant in and around El Chaltén, at the Fitz Roy sector.

Hikers should note that campfires are prohibited—campstoves are obligatory for cooking. Rangers assert that park water is potable throughout.

Glaciar Moreno

The only accommodations near the glacier, multi-day packages with full board and excursions are the rule at the lavish **◖ Hostería Los Notros** (tel. 02902/499510) rivals Torres del Paine's Hotel Salto Chico in the "room-with-a-view" competition; all 32 rooms face the ice. Minimum two-night packages start at US$1,826 s, US$2,574 d; for details, contact Hostería Los Notros (Arenales 1457, 7th floor, Buenos Aires, tel. 011/4814-3934, www.losnotros.com).

Also at the glacier, **Nativos de la Patagonia** operates both a snack bar (sandwiches for US$5–7, plus coffee and desserts) and a separate restaurant with set meals (around US$20); there's also an à la carte menu. A couple kilometers east of the park entrance, highly recommended by Calafate-based guides, **Los Ventisqueros** serves a limited lunchtime menu of pasta, chicken, lamb, and beef.

Lago Roca

La Jerónima's **Camping Lago Roca** (tel. 02902/499500, lagoroca@yahoo.com.ar, US$6 pp) also has four-bed dorm-style *cabañas* US$37 d, US$48 q), with exterior baths. Hot showers are available, and its restaurant *confitería* serves decent meals.

At the terminus of RP 15, 56 kilometers southwest of El Calafate, the *casco* at Croatian-founded **Estancia Nibepo Aike** (tel./fax 02966/422626 in El Calafate, www.nibepoaike.com.ar) preserves its original rustic style but is now a five-room guesthouse with contemporary conveniences. Rates are US$389 s, US$510 d with half board, for a minimum two-night stay. Open October 1–April 30, it also has a newer **Quincho Don Juan** for day-trippers to lunch or dine; overnight guests can choose to dine there or in the main house's dining room. "Day-in-the-country" excursions cost around US$45 pp including lunch or dinner and transportation.

INFORMATION

At the Río Mitre entrance, the main Moreno Glacier approach, the Administración de Parques Nacionales (APN) collects a US$17 admission fee (payable in pesos only) for nonresidents of Argentina. At present, the Lago Roca and El Chaltén sectors continue fee-free.

At the southern approach to El Chaltén, the **Administración de Parques Nacionales** (tel. 02962/493004, 9 A.M.–8 P.M. daily) has turned a former *hostería* into a visitors center. In addition to natural history exhibits, it provides a decent trail map (scale 1:75,000) and also issues climbing permits (free).

Hikers may want to consult Tim Burford's *Chile and Argentina: The Bradt Trekking Guide* (Bradt Travel Guides, 2001), or Clem Lindenmayer's and Nick Tapp's *Trekking in the Patagonian Andes* (Lonely Planet, 2003); the former has thorough text, but the latter has better maps. There is also Miguel A. Alonso's locally available, bilingual *Trekking en Chaltén y Lago del Desierto* (Los Glaciares Publishers, 2003), which covers numerous hikes in the vicinity. Alonso has also written *Lago Argentino & Glaciar Perito Moreno Handbook* (Buenos Aires: Zagier & Urruty, 1997), a more general guide that's available in English, Italian, German, and French.

For an informed guide who leads backcountry trips in the El Chaltén sector, contact retired ranger Adrián Falcone (tel. 02962/493064, aefalcone@gmail.com), who speaks English and even a smattering of Japanese.

GETTING THERE AND AROUND

The Moreno Glacier is about 80 kilometers west of El Calafate by RP 11, which is paved to the park entrance; the trip takes slightly over an hour. Both **Cal Tur** (tel. 02902/491842) and **Taqsa** (tel. 02902/491843, www.taqsa.com.ar), at El Calafate's bus terminal, have scheduled services at 9 A.M. daily (US$23 r/t), returning in the afternoon.

In addition to regularly scheduled services, guided bus tours are frequent, but both are less frequent in winter; for suggested operators, see *Vicinity of El Calafate*. El Calafate's **Albergue del Glaciar** runs its own guided minivan excursions (US$50 pp), leaving about 8:30 A.M. and returning about 5 P.M. These include more hiking and a navigation for a waterside view of the lake.

El Chaltén

Billing itself as "Capital Nacional del Trekking," Argentina's national trekking capital, El Chaltén has become popular for easy access to Fitz Roy–range trailheads in Parque Nacional Los Glaciares. Many trails are suitable for overnight backpacks, but access is so good that day hikers can cover nearly as much ground.

Exposed to fierce westerly winds and to potential floods from the Río de las Vueltas, El Chaltén has still managed to achieve a sense of permanence in what, just a few years back, seemed a bleak outpost of government offices aimed to uphold Argentina's presence in a disputed border zone (the last of many Chilean-Argentine territorial quarrels, over Lago del Desierto to the north, was finalized a few years ago). With the highway from the RN 40 junction recently paved, it's growing so rapidly that some fear it will become the next El Calafate, where real estate development (and speculation) are rampant.

When the last 17 km of the RN 40 link are paved, travel time from El Calafate will fall from four hours to three or so. Meanwhile, the town is enjoying improvements as the streets are paved to keep down the dust, and a new bus terminal is due to begin construction.

El Chaltén (population about 500) is 220 kilometers northwest of El Calafate via eastbound RP 11 to the Río Bote junction, northbound RN 40, and westbound RP 23 along Lago Viedma's north shore. It's worth mentioning

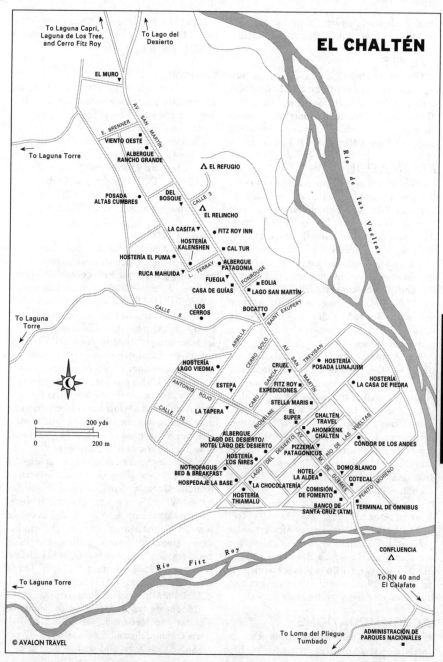

EL CHALTÉN

To Laguna Capri, Laguna de Los Tres, and Cerro Fitz Roy

To Lago del Desierto

EL MURO

AV SAN MARTÍN

E. BRENNER

VIENTO OESTE

To Laguna Torre

ALBERGUE RANCHO GRANDE

EL REFUGIO

POSADA ALTAS CUMBRES

DEL BOSQUE

CALLE 3

EL RELINCHO

LA CASITA

FITZ ROY INN

HOSTERÍA KALENSHEN

CAL TUR

HOSTERÍA EL PUMA

ALBERGUE PATAGONIA

TERRAY

FONROUGE

RUCA MAHUIDA

FUEGIA

EOLIA

CASA DE GUÍAS

LAGO SAN MARTÍN

CALLE 8

LOS CERROS

BOCATTO

SAINT EXUPERY

To Laguna Torre

ARBILLA

CERRO SOLO

AV SAN MARTÍN

TREVISAN

HOSTERÍA LAGO VIEDMA

CRUEL

HOSTERÍA POSADA LUNAJUIM

GARCIA

ANTONIO ROJO

ESTEPA

FITZ ROY EXPEDICIONES

HOSTERÍA LA CASA DE PIEDRA

CABU

CALLE 10

LA TAPERA

RIQUELME

STELLA MARIS

EL SUPER

CHALTÉN TRAVEL

0 200 yds

0 200 m

AHONIKENK CHALTÉN

ALBERGUE LAGO DEL DESIERTO/ HOTEL LAGO DEL DESIERTO

AV DEL DESIERTO

LAGO I DEL DESIERTO

RÍO DE LAS VUELTAS

CÓNDOR DE LOS ANDES

PIZZERÍA PATAGONICUS

HOSTERÍA LOS ÑIRES

NOTHOFAGUS BED & BREAKFAST

DOMO BLANCO

HOTEL LA ALDEA

COTECAL

HOSPEDAJE LA BASE

LA CHOCOLATERÍA

M. DE GÜEMES

PERITO MORENO

HOSTERÍA THIAMALU

COMISIÓN DE FOMENTO

BANCO DE SANTA CRUZ (ATM)

TERMINAL DE ÓMNIBUS

Río Fitz Roy

To Laguna Torre

CONFLUENCIA

To RN 40 and El Calafate

Río de las Vueltas

SOUTHERN PATAGONIA

To Loma del Pliegue Tumbado

ADMINISTRACIÓN DE PARQUES NACIONALES

© AVALON TRAVEL

that, while street addresses are increasingly common, locals pay little attention to them.

EVENTS

El Chaltén celebrates several events, including October 12's **Aniversario de El Chaltén,** marking its formal founding in 1985; November 10's **Día de la Tradición,** celebrating the gaucho heritage; and early February's weeklong **Fiesta Nacional del Trekking.**

RECREATION

From here, it's possible to arrange a one-day trek and ice climb on Glaciar Torre (US$85 pp) with **Fitz Roy Expediciones** (Avenida San Martín 56, tel. 02962/493017, www.fitzroyexpediciones.com.ar), which also offers lengthier guided hikes—nine-day expeditions, really—on the Campo de Hielo Sur, the Southern Continental Ice Field. **Oscar Pandolfi Expediciones** (Calle 2 No. 23, tel. 02962/493043, www.caminoabierto.com) and **Alta Montaña** (Lionel Terray 55, tel. 02962/493018, altamont@infovia.com.ar) are additional guides.

NYCA Adventure (Cabo García 122, tel. 02962/493185, www.nyca.com.ar) offers half-day excursions including activities such as climbing, hiking, mountain biking, rafting, and rappelling. **Lago San Martín** (Avenida San Martín 275, tel. 02962/493045) arranges excursions to and from Lago San Martín, across the mountains to the northeast, with *estancia* accommodations. The **Casa de Guías** (Avenida San Martín 310, tel. 02962/493118) is another possibility.

Just north of Albergue Rancho Grande, **Viento Oeste** (San Martín 898, tel. 02962/493200, vientooeste@infovia.com.ar) rents and sells climbing, camping, and wet-weather gear, as does **La Brecha** (Costanera Sur 246, tel. 493151). **Eolia** (Pasaje Fonrouge 45, tel. 02962/493066, www.patagoniamagica.com) also rents gear and provides guide service.

ACCOMMODATIONS

El Chaltén has a reasonable selection of accommodations, some of them very good, but high demand in summer makes reservations advisable. Many places close in winter, but there's usually something available.

Camping

Directly across from the APN office, on the Río Fitz Roy's banks, **Camping Confluencia** is free, but sheltered sites are few here, and toilet facilities are rustic.

Commercial campgrounds, which offer hot showers and shelter for cooking, include **Camping El Refugio** (Calle 3 s/n, tel. 02962/493221, US$6 pp) and **Camping El Relincho** (San Martín 505, tel. 02962/493007, elrelincho@cotecal.com.ar, US$6 pp).

US$10-25

Of several hostel-style accommodations, three are HI affiliates. Open all year except June, expanding 【 **Albergue Patagonia** (San Martín 493, tel. 02962/493019, www.elchalten.com/patagonia, US$14 pp, US$40–60 s, US$66 d) provides utilitarian dorms—four beds per room—but also has shared bath doubles and a separate wing of more spacious and comfortable doubles and twins with private bath; the latter include continental breakfast. On the hostel side, it also provides cooking facilities, laundry service, meals, a book exchange, and bike rentals, and organizes excursions. Its main drawback is that the hostel toilet and shower facilities, while good enough, are arguably too few. English and Dutch are spoken.

Having more than doubled its capacity by adding a second floor, the 90-bed **Albergue Rancho Grande** (San Martín 635, tel./fax 02962/493005, www.ranchograndehostel.com.ar, US$12 pp, US$57 s or d) has drawn some flak for failing to insulate the gap between floors for sound. It does offer B&B packages with transportation from El Calafate; for reservations, contact Chaltén Travel (Avenida Libertador 1174, El Calafate, tel. 02902/492212, www.chaltentravel.com).

Cóndor de los Andes (Avenida Río de las Vueltas and Halvorsen, tel. 02962/493101, www.condordelosandes.com, US$14–17 pp, US$63 d) has four- and six-bed dorms, each with its own bath, kitchen facilities, and spacious common areas with exceptional views. It has also added private rooms.

Comparably priced non-HI hostels are opening all the time, including **Ahonikenk Chaltén** (Güemes 23, tel. 02962/493070, ahonikenkchalten23@yahoo.com.ar, US$12 pp, US$40 d) and **Albergue Lago del Desierto** (Lago del Desierto 135, tel. 02962/493010, hosteldellago_elchalten@yahoo.com.ar, US$12 pp).

US$25-50

Like El Calafate, El Chaltén has little or nothing exclusive to this range, but several hostels also offer private rooms that are excellent values for around the same price or a little more.

US$50-100

Family-run **Hospedaje La Base** (Lago del Desierto 97, tel./fax 02962/493031, labase@elchaltenpatagonia.com.ar, US$52 s or d) has two firm beds per room, which are two-bedroom *cabañas* that share a kitchen but have private baths. Like many other places, it closes June–November.

The no-frills **Hostería Los Ñires** (Lago del Desierto 120, tel. 02962/493009, www.losnireschalten.com.ar, US$45 s, US$50 s, US$57 d with a middling breakfast) has tiny but functional singles (some with thin walls), larger but awkwardly shaped doubles that lack closet space, and more standard rooms with traditional amenities. All have private baths. Separated from its bar/restaurant by a long corridor, the sleeping quarters are normally quiet.

Cozy, friendly and tobacco-free, **◖ Nothofagus Bed & Breakfast** (Calle 10 No. 40, tel. 02962/493087, www.nothofagusbb.com.ar, US$37–57 s, US$40–60 d with breakfast) has seven rooms in a handsome house with convivial common areas; rates vary according to whether the room has a shared or a private bath.

Friendly **Hostería Thiamalu** (Lago del Desierto 99, tel. 02962/493736, www.thiamalu.com.ar, US$60 s, US$70 d with breakfast) isn't up to the level of the Nothofagus, though all of its rooms do have private baths.

Hotel Lago del Desierto (Lago del Desierto 137, tel. 02962/493010, hotellagodeldesierto@yahoo.com.ar, US$71 s or d with breakfast) also rents six-bed *cabañas* with kitchen facilities for US$130, and has camping facilities (US$6 pp).

Open October–March, **Hostería Lago Viedma** (Arbilla 71, tel. 02962/493089, hosterialagoviedma@hotmail.com, US$74 s or d) has just four small but well-designed rooms with private bath and breakfast, but is closed May–October; it may add more rooms.

Recently expanded **Posada Altas Cumbres** (Lionel Terray 342, tel. 02962/493060, altas_cumbres@hotmail.com, www.elchalten.com/altascumbres, US$71 s, US$77 d) has a dozen spacious new rooms and a restaurant.

US$100-200

At the southern approach to town, **Hotel La Aldea** (Avenida Güemes 95, tel. 02962/493040, www.hotellaaldea.com.ar, US$92 s, US$103 d with breakfast) is more of a motel-style complex, with the rooms separate from a two-story reception area that includes a restaurant and bar.

Rates at the venerable (by Chaltén standards) **Fitz Roy Inn** (San Martín 520, tel. 02962/493062, fitzroyinn@hotmail.com, US$100 s, US$105 d) drop considerably outside the November–March high season; it also has multi-day packages with half or full board, but the full-board option would preclude eating at other good places.

Hostería Kalenshen (Lionel Terray 30, tel. 02962/493108, www.kalenshen.com, US$100 s, US$110 d with breakfast) has 17 rooms with handmade furniture and another six cabañas.

Rates have risen at **Hostería La Casa de Piedra** (Lago del Desierto 423, tel./fax 02962/493015, hosterialacasadepiedra@yahoo.com.ar, www.elchalten.com/lacasadepiedra, US$112–290 s, US$120–330 d), which provides large and comfy but tackily decorated rooms with private baths. It has well-tended grounds and is quiet, though the nearby power plant might bother some guests.

North of town, in an out-of-the-way location bordering the Lago del Desierto road,

Hostería El Pilar (tel./fax 02962/493002, tel. 011/5031-0755 in Buenos Aires, www.hosteriaelpilar.com.ar, US$120 s, US$143 d with breakfast) has the classic style of a Patagonian *casco*, but it's really a recent construction (1996). Reservations are essential for this cozy and increasingly popular place (open October–April); it's possible to dine in the restaurant without being a guest, but reservations are advisable. Shuttle transportation from El Chaltén is free for guests.

With improved landscaping, **Hostería Posada Lunajuim** (Trevisan 45, tel. 02962/493047, posadalunajuim@yahoo.com.ar, US$121 s, US$148 d) continues to make a good impression with appealing common areas (including a bar/restaurant) and rooms with private baths, central heating, and breakfast.

The eight-room **Hostería El Puma** (Lionel Terray 212, tel. 02962/493095, www.hosteriaelpuma.com.ar, US$130 s, US$160 d) and its Terray restaurant make another impressive addition to Chaltén's accommodations scene.

More than US$200

Atop a hillock with panoramic views of the Río de la Vueltas, under the same ownership as Hostería Los Notros, **Los Cerros** (tel. 02962/493182, tel. 011/4814-3934 in Buenos Aires, www.loscerrosdelchalten.com, from US$362 s, US$452 d) works mainly with multi-day packages but takes other guests on a space-available basis. Spacious and luminous, with baths all featuring whirlpool tubs, the rooms have massive picture windows; the common areas (many of them decorated with historic maps) have soaring cathedral ceilings that flood them with natural light.

FOOD

Hikers and climbers stock up on supplies at **El Super** (Lago del Desierto 248), **El Gringuito** (Cerro Solo 108), and **Stella Maris** (Avenida San Martín 36). Otherwise, for its size, El Chaltén offers a fine and improving restaurant selection.

La Chocolatería (Lago del Desierto 105, tel. 02962/493008) is more than it sounds—the desserts are good enough, but the breakfasts and pizzas are also excellent, and the Bailey's-spiked hot chocolate is comforting on a cold night. **Domo Blanco** (Avenida Güemes 71, tel. 02962/493036) serves exceptional ice cream, with local ingredients such as raspberries and strawberries from a nearby estancia, and will also deliver to your hotel.

Bocatto (Avenida San Martín s/n) makes the best takeaway empanadas, in several varieties, all a little larger than the Argentine standard. **Cruel** (San Martín 84, tel. 02962/493167) is best for a quick sandwich.

La Tapera (Antonio Rojo 76, tel. 02962/493138, lunch and dinner daily) is a cozy (four tables) and exceptionally friendly restaurant/tapas bar with a small but excellent menu of fixed-price dinners (US$13) that includes soup and a choice among four entrées.

New in 2007, **Del Bosque** (San Martín 591) is a combination teahouse and ice cream parlor. **El Bodegón** (San Martín 320, tel. 02962/493109, lunch and dinner daily) is a pizza pub with its own microbrewed beer (US$2 per pint); it also prepares an outstanding *locro* (US$5.50), a meal-in-itself northwestern Argentine stew that's ideal for a cool Chaltén evening.

Open in summer only, **Ruca Mahuida** (Lionel Terray 55, tel. 02962/493018, lunch and dinner daily) is one of Chaltén's most imaginative eateries and also sends smokers outdoors, but the service can be forgetful. Lamb is the specialty at **La Casita** (San Martín 430, tel. 02962/493042, lunch and dinner daily), which otherwise serves a standard Argentine menu—beef, pizza, pasta, and the like—its major downside is the cramped and tobacco-heavy atmosphere. In mid-summer, it can be hard to get a table at popular **Pizzería Patagonicus** (Güemes 57, tel. 02962/493025, lunch and dinner daily), one of few Argentine eateries to have lamb on the pizza menu; the decor, with natural wood and mountaineering photos, embodies Chaltén's evolving style.

Reservations are advisable for tobacco-free **⟨** **Fuegia** (San Martín 342, tel. 02962/493019, lunch and dinner daily), Albergue Patagonia's bistro-style restaurant, though it's expanded to accommodate demand for dishes like rack of lamb and Patagonian trout (US$15). Likewise, plan ahead for the unpretentious **⟨** **Estepa** (Cerro Solo 86, tel. 02962/493069, lunch and dinner daily), a snug, tobacco-free, nine-table place with views of Fitz Roy. Offering home-style cooking at a high level, its specialty is *cordero estepa*, lamb with *calafate* sauce, but there are also pizzas and empanadas, with most entrées in the US$8–15 range.

Also tobacco-free, at the north end of town, tiny **El Muro** (San Martín 912, tel. 02962/493248, www.chaltencocinademontana .com.ar, lunch and dinner daily) is a bistro-style restaurant where the kitchen pays minute attention to diners' tastes, but the service can be distracted when it gets busy. Dishes such as lamb loin with a fresh raspberry-and-cherry sauce (US$15), though, are well worth minor inconveniences. The light-crusted empanadas, including lamb and beef, deserve special mention.

INFORMATION AND SERVICES

El Chaltén's **Comisión de Fomento** (Avenida Güemes 21, tel. 02962/493011, www .elchalten.com, 8 A.M.–8 P.M. daily in summer, 9 A.M.–5 P.M. weekdays only the rest of the year), just north of the bridge across the Río Fitz Roy, has maps and other information.

Cotecal (Güemes 109) has long-distance phone and fax service. **Chaltén Travel** (Avenida Güemes 7) has relatively but not outrageously expensive Internet connections, but they're agonizingly slow.

Visitors *must* appreciate that El Chaltén has only informal money exchange—no banks, ATMs, or exchange houses—and they need to bring cash for the duration of their stay.

Some places will accept US dollars or euros in exchange for services, but few handle credit cards. Banco de Santa Cruz has finally placed an ATM (Güemes s/n) in El Chaltén, just north of the bridge over the Río Fitz Roy, but it's still a good idea to bring Argentine cash to town, just in case it runs out.

GETTING THERE

Several companies connect El Chaltén with El Calafate (US$18–20, 3.5 hours): **Cal Tur** (San Martín 451, tel. 02962/493062); **Chaltén Travel** (San Martín 724, tel. 02962/493005); and **Taqsa** (Antonio Rojo 88, tel. 02962/493294). Departures are usually in late afternoon, around 5–6 P.M. There are several buses daily in summer, but this falls to about one daily in winter.

With Chaltén Travel, it's possible to travel north on gravel RN 40 to the towns of Perito Moreno and Los Antiguos in Chubut province (US$55, 13 hours). Chaltén Travel leaves Chaltén on alternate days in summer; passengers from El Calafate can board the bus at at the RN 40 junction. The rest of the year, there may be only one bus weekly. **Corredor Patagónico** also does this route.

Transporte Las Lengas (Viedma 95, tel. 02962/493023) goes to Comandante Luis Piedra Buena (US$37, 6 hours) at 5:30 A.M. Monday, Wednesday and Friday in summer.

Also in summer, at 5 A.M. Monday, Thursday, and Saturday, **Transpatagonia Servicios** (Cerro Solo 95, tel. 02962/493160) provides door-to-door service to Río Gallegos (US$36, 5 hours), which makes it feasible to connect with buses to Argentine Tierra del Fuego and to Punta Arenas, Chile.

GETTING AROUND

When the national park shuttles don't meet your needs, consider a meterless taxi service such as **Remises Chaltén Móvil** (tel. 02962/493061), an economical option if shared by several riders.

Tierra del Fuego

If Patagonia is exciting, Tierra del Fuego—the "uttermost part of the earth"—is electrifying. In the days of sail, its sub-Antarctic weather and ferocious westerlies obsessed seamen whether or not they had ever experienced the thrill—or terror—of "rounding the Horn." After Richard Henry Dana survived the southern seas en route to California in 1834, he vividly recounted conditions that could change from calm to chaos in an instant:

> "Here comes Cape Horn!" said the chief mate; and we had hardly time to haul down and clew up, before it was upon us. In a few moments, a heavier sea was raised than I had ever seen before, and...the little brig... plunged into it, and all the forward part of her was under water; the sea pouring in through the bow ports and hawse-hole, and over the knight-heads, threatening to wash everything overboard.... At the same time sleet and hail were driving with all fury against us.

In Dana's time, that was the price of admission to the earth's most spectacular combination of sea, sky, land, and ice. In a landscape whose granite pinnacles rise nearly 2,000 meters straight out of the ocean, only a handful of hunter-gatherers foraging in the fjords and forests knew the area with any intimacy. Today, fortunately, reaching the Fuegian archipelago involves less hardship—not to mention motion sickness—than Dana and his shipmates suffered.

In his memoirs, pioneer settler Lucas Bridges labeled Tierra del Fuego the "Uttermost Part of the Earth" for its splendid isolation at the continent's southern tip. The "Land of Fire" is still a place where fur seals, sea lions, and penguins cavort in the choppy seas of the strait named for the celebrated navigator Ferdinand Magellan, where Darwin sailed on the *Beagle* and the first '49ers found their route to California. From the seashore, behind the

Argentine city of Ushuaia, glacial horns rise like sacred steeples. The beaches and southern beech forests of Parque Nacional Tierra del Fuego, west of the city, are the terminus of the world's southernmost highway.

Tierra del Fuego may be an archipelago, but the Isla Grande de Tierra del Fuego is South America's largest island. Chile shares the territory with Argentina; while parts of the Argentine side are urbanized, the Chilean side has just a few small towns and isolated *estancias*. Roads are few but improving, especially on the Argentine side; the unpaved roads, though, can be hell on windshields, which are most cheaply replaced in the Chilean mainland city of Punta Arenas.

Though it has much in common with other parts of Patagonia, Tierra del Fuego retains its own distinctive identity. Most attractions and services—at least the most accessible ones—are on the Argentine side.

There are two ferry routes from the Chilean mainland: a shuttle from Punta Delgada, only 45 kilometers south of the Argentine border, across the Primera Angostura narrows to Puerto Espora, and a daily service from Punta Arenas to Porvenir, one of the strait's widest parts.

HISTORY

Prior to Magellan's "discovery," southern South America's insular extremes were inhabited by dispersed bands of hunter-gatherers such as the Selknam (Ona), Kawéskar (Alacaluf), and Yámana (Yahgan), who lived off maritime and terrestrial resources that they considered abundant—only in European eyes was this a land of deprivation. The archipelago acquired its name from the fires set by the "Canoe Indians," the Kawéskar and Yámana, for heating and cooking; in this soggy region, though, it might more accurately have been Tierra del Humo (Land of Smoke).

Early navigators dreaded Cape Horn's wild seas, and their reports gave their countrymen little reason to settle or even explore the area. In the early 1830s, Captain Robert Fitz Roy of the *Beagle* abducted several Yámana, including the famous Jemmy Button, to England, subjecting them to missionary indoctrination before returning them years later. On that voyage, a perplexed Charles Darwin commented on the simplicity of their society: "The perfect equality among the individuals composing the Fuegian tribes, must for a long time retard their civilization."

The first to try to bring civilization to the Yámana, rather than the opposite, were Anglican missionaries from the Falkland Islands, some of whose descendants still live here. After abortive attempts that included both Fuegian assaults and the starvation death of missionary Allen Gardiner, the Anglican Thomas Bridges settled at present-day Ushuaia, on the Argentine side of the Isla Grande, where he compiled an English–Yahgan dictionary. His son Lucas, who grew up with Yámana playmates, wrote the extraordinary memoir *The Uttermost Part of the Earth,* published a few years before his 1950 death.

In the meantime, both Chile and Argentina established a presence, and gigantic sheep *estancias* occupied the sprawling grasslands where native peoples once hunted guanaco and other game. As the guanaco slowly disappeared, the desperate Fuegians began to hunt domestic sheep and often found themselves facing the wrong end of a rifle. Introduced European diseases such as typhoid and measles, though, killed more native people than did bullets.

The archipelago's borders were never clearly defined, and the two countries nearly warred over three small Beagle Channel islands in 1979. Positions were uncompromising—one Argentine poster audaciously proclaimed "We will never surrender what is ours!"—but papal mediation averted open warfare and brought a settlement within a few years. Chilean director Alex Bowen's 2005 film *Mi Mejor Enemigo* ("My Best Enemy") depicts a tragicomic confrontation between Chilean and Argentine forces on the mainland border north of Punta Arenas at this time.

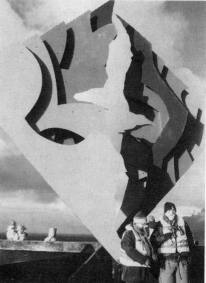

albatross monument to shipwrecked sailors, Isla Cabo de Hornos, Chilean Tierra del Fuego, by sculptor José Balcells

© WAYNE BERNHARDSON

SOUTHERN PATAGONIA

Since then, travel to Tierra del Fuego has boomed, especially on the Argentine side in the summer months, but there are lingering issues such as transportation across the channel from Ushuaia to Puerto Williams. Other important economic sectors are sheep farming and petroleum, on both sides of the border.

PORVENIR

Chilean Tierra del Fuego's main town, Porvenir sits on a sheltered harbor on the Strait of Magellan's eastern shore. It dates from the 1880s, when the area experienced a brief gold rush, but stabilized with the establishment of wool *estancias* around the turn of the 20th century. After the wool boom fizzled in the 1920s, it settled into an economic torpor that, appropriately enough, has left it a collection of corroding metal-clad Magellanic buildings. Recent construction of a salmon-processing plant has jump-started the local economy, and it's more presentable than in the recent past.

Porvenir's inner harbor is a great place for

spotting kelp geese, gulls, cormorants, steamer ducks, and other seabirds, but the lack of public transportation to the Argentine border has marginalized the tourist sector—all buses from the mainland to Argentine Tierra del Fuego take the longer Primera Angostura route, with a shorter and more frequent ferry crossing. Small local enterprises have begun to offer access to parts of the archipelago that, up to now, have only been accessible through expensive cruises.

Only 30 nautical miles east of Punta Arenas, Porvenir (population 4,734) occupies a protected site at the east end of Bahía Porvenir, an inlet of the Strait of Magellan. Its port, though, is three kilometers west of the town proper.

From Porvenir, Ruta 215 (a smooth gravel road) leads south and then east along the Bahía Inútil shoreline to the Argentine border at San Sebastián, 150 kilometers away; an interesting alternate route leads directly east through the Cordón Baquedano before rejoining Ruta 215 about 55 kilometers to the east. If it's too late to catch the ferry back to Punta Arenas, another gravel road follows the coast to Puerto Espora, 141 kilometers northeast.

Sights

Directly on the water, **Parque Yugoslavo** memorializes the earliest gold-seeking immigrants, mostly Croats; it's also one of Porvenir's best birding spots. The tourist office provides a small map/brochure, in English, of the city's architectural heritage; many of its houses and other buildings were also Croatian-built.

Most public buildings surround the neatly landscaped **Plaza de Armas,** two blocks north of Parque Yugoslavo. Among them is the expanded and improved **Museo de Tierra del Fuego Fernando Rusque Cordero** (Zavattaro 402, tel. 061/581800, 8 A.M.–5:30 P.M. weekdays, 10 A.M.–1:30 P.M. and 3–5 P.M. weekends $0.85), a regional museum dealing with the island's natural history, indigenous heritage, the early gold rush, the later but longer-lasting wool rush, and even cinematography—German-born local filmmaker José Bohr went to Hollywood in 1929, and enjoyed a long if inconsistent career. It has added a skillfully produced replica of an early rural store, and a good photographic display on local architecture.

The museum takes its name from a Carabineros officer who helped found it—and was no doubt responsible for the permanent exhibit on police uniforms.

Accommodations and Food

There's no sign outside homey **Hospedaje Shinká** (Santos Mardones 333, tel. 061/580491, US$20 s, US$33 d), but it offers better facilities and amenities—immaculate midsize rooms with comfortable beds, private bath, and cable TV—for less money than any other place in town. The breakfast is forgettable, but that's a minor fault for a place this good.

All rooms now have private baths at upgraded, expanded **Hotel España** (Croacia 698, tel. 061/580160, www.hotelespana.cl, US$20–25 s, US$30–42 d), whose utilitarian addition masks large new rooms; the cheapest rooms, in the older section, are smaller but still adequate. It also has a restaurant.

All rooms at **Hotel Rosas** (Philippi 269, tel. 02901/580088, US$30 s, US$40 d) have private bath and include breakfast; its restaurant is one of Porvenir's better values in a town with, admittedly, few other choices.

Other than hotel restaurants, the main dining options include the basic **Puerto Montt** (Croacia 1199, tel. 061/580207, lunch and dinner daily, closed Sun. evenings) and the **Club Social Catef** (Zavattaro 94, tel. 061/581399, lunch and dinner daily, closed Sun. evenings). **El Chispa** (Señoret 202, tel. 061/580054, lunch and dinner daily, closed Sun. evenings) is a *picada* with good home cooking at moderate prices.

At Bahía Chilote, **La Picá de Pechuga** (cel. 099/8886380, lunch and dinner daily, closed Sun. evenings) is a moderately priced seafood *picada* that gets its fish fresh off the boat. The waterfront **Club Social Croata** (Señoret 542, tel. 061/580053, lunch and dinner daily, closed Sun. evenings) is more formal and has good fish and wine by the glass, though service can be erratic.

Information and Services

In the same offices as the museum, Porvenir's efficient **Oficina Municipal de Turismo** (Padre Mario Zavattaro 434 (tel. 061/581800, muniporvenir@terra.cl) keeps the same hours as the museum.

Banco del Estado (Philippi 263) now has an ATM.

Correos de Chile (Philippi 176) is at the southwest corner of the Plaza de Armas. Near the bank, the **Centro de Llamados** (Philippi 277) has long-distance telephones.

For medical assistance, try **Hospital Porvenir** (Carlos Wood s/n, between Señoret and Guerrero, tel. 061/580034).

Getting There and Around

Porvenir has regular but infrequent connections to the mainland but none to the Argentine border crossing at San Sebastián; those with their own vehicles (including bicyclists) will still find this a shorter route from Punta Arenas to Ushuaia.

Aerovías DAP (Manuel Señoret s/n and Muñoz Gamero, tel. 061/580089) operates air-taxi service to Punta Arenas (US$34) at least daily except Sunday, often more frequently.

Tuesday and Friday at 4 P.M., there's a municipal bus from the DAP offices on Señoret to Camerón and Timaukel (US$2.50, 2 hours), in the island's southwestern corner; another goes to **Cerro Sombrero** (US$4, 1.5 hours) at 5 P.M. Monday, Wednesday, and Friday from Zavattaro 432.

In the same office as DAP, **Transbordadora Broom** (Manuel Señoret s/n, tel. 061/580089) sails the car-passenger ferry *Melinka* to Punta Arenas (2.5 hours) Tuesday–Sunday, seas permitting. The ferry leaves from Bahía Chilote, about three kilometers west of town. Fares are US$7.50 per person except for the driver, whose fare is included in the US$48 vehicle charge; the children's fare is US$3.75. Motorcycles pay US$15, while bicycles are free.

VICINITY OF PORVENIR

Vicinity is a relative term on Tierra del Fuego, as some fascinating locales are difficult or expensive—or both—to reach. **Cordillera Darwin, Ltda.** (Croacia 675, tel. 061/50167, 09/6407204, www.explorepatagonia.cl) does brief dolphin-watching tours around Bahía Chilote, vehicle tours of the Cordón Baquedano, three-day horseback excursions to the Río Cóndor, and a six-day Cordillera Darwin trip that's substantially cheaper than the only other option, the luxury cruises on the *Mare Australis* and *Via Australis*.

Monumento Natural Laguna de los Cisnes

International birding groups often detour to this 25-hectare saline lake reserve, which sometimes dries out, just north of Porvenir. While it takes its name from the elegant black-necked swan, it's home to many other species.

Cordón Baquedano

After Chilean naval officer Ramón Serrano Montaner found gold in the rolling hills east of Porvenir in 1879, panners from Chile and Croatia flocked to the Río del Oro Valley, between the Cordón Baquedano and the Sierra Boquerón. Living in sod huts that shielded them from the wind and cold, hoping to eke out a kilogram per year, more than 200 worked the placers until they gave out. By the turn of the century, California miners introduced dredges and steam shovels, but decreasing yields ended the rush by 1908–1909. A century later, a few hardy panners hang on.

From Porvenir, the eastbound road through the Cordón Baquedano passes several gold-rush sites, some marked with interpretive panels; the literal high point is the **Mirador de la Isla,** an overlook 500 meters above sea level. In many places guanacos, which seem to outnumber sheep, gracefully vault the same meter-high fences that stop the sheep cold.

Onaisín

About 100 kilometers east of Porvenir, a major north–south road crosses Ruta 215 at Onaisín, a former Sociedad Explotadora *estancia* whose **Cementerio Inglés** is a national historical monument. Northbound, the road goes to the petroleum company town of Cerro Sombrero, while southbound it goes to Camerón and Lago Blanco.

Lago Blanco

Some 50 kilometers southwest of Onaisín, the road passes through **Camerón,** an erstwhile picture-postcard *estancia* that is now a municipality. The road then angles southeast to Lago Blanco, an area known for its fishing and, until recently, a speculative and controversial project for native forest exploitation by the U.S.-based Trillium Corporation. In summer, there's a bumpy border crossing to Río Grande, Argentina, via a dirt road, with many livestock gates, and a ford of the Río Rasmussen. The Argentine border post is called Radman.

Estancia Yendegaia

Visited primarily by Chilean cruise ships and private yachts, Yendegaia conserves 44,000 hectares of Fuegian forest in the Cordillera Darwin between the Argentine border and Parque Nacional Alberto de Agostini. While the owners hope to establish a private national park and create an unbroken preservation corridor along the Beagle Channel (Yendegaia borders Argentina's Parque Nacional Tierra del Fuego), there's government pressure to pave the *estancia's* airstrip at Caleta María, at the property's north end, and a road south from Lago Blanco has reached the Chilean side of Lago Fagnano. The owners, for their part, would rather see the border opened to foot traffic from Argentina, but they have consulted with public-works officials to minimize the road's environmental impact.

In the meantime, the *estancia* is open to visitors—though access is difficult without chartering a plane or boat, or taking an expensive tour like the *Mare Australis* cruise through the Fuegian fjords; even this cruise stops here only occasionally. Naval boats between Punta Arenas and Puerto Williams may drop passengers here but are so infrequent that getting back could be problematic.

CERRO SOMBRERO

About 70 kilometers north of Onaisín and 43 kilometers south of the Puerto Espora ferry landing, Cerro Sombrero is a company town where employees of Chile's Empresa Nacional de Petróleo (ENAP, National Petroleum Company) reside in orderly surroundings with remarkable amenities for a town with only about 150 houses. Dating from the early 1960s, it boasts an astronomical observatory, a bank, a botanical garden, a cinema, a hospital, recreational facilities including a heated swimming pool, and restaurants. Buses between Río Grande and Punta Arenas take a meal break at **Restaurant El Conti,** just outside town.

Overnighters will find accommodations at vastly improved **Hostería Tunkelén** (Arturo Prat 101, tel. 061/296696, www.hosteriatunkelen.cl, US$53 s, US$66 d), which also has a good (but expensive) restaurant.

PUERTO WILLIAMS

On Isla Navarino's north shore, across the Beagle Channel from Argentine Tierra del Fuego, Puerto Williams is the so-called "Capital of Antarctica" and gateway to the rugged Los Dientes backcountry circuit, a five-day slog through soggy mountainous terrain. Local residents look forward to a permanent ferry link to nearby Argentina, but there is much political opposition across the channel because myopic Ushuaia impresarios fear losing business to tiny Williams—however unlikely that possibility.

Founded in the 1950s, formerly known as Puerto Luisa, the town (population 1,952) has paved sidewalks but gravel streets. Most residents are Chilean naval personnel living in relatively stylish prefabs, but there are also some 60 remaining Yámana descendents, only a few of whom speak the language—now a hybrid including many Spanish and English words—among themselves.

Sights

Overlooking the harbor is the **Proa del Escampavía Yelcho,** the prow of the cutter that, under Luis Pardo Villalón, rescued British explorer Edward Shackleton's crew from Elephant Island, on the Antarctic Peninsula, in 1916. A national monument, the bow survived collisions with icebergs to get to its destination; returning to Punta Arenas, the entire ship makes a cameo appearance in original newsreel footage in British director George Butler's *Endurance,* an extraordinary documentary of Shackleton's expedition.

Very professional for a small-town museum, Williams's **Museo Martin Gusinde** (Aragay 1, tel. 061/621043, www.museoantropologicomartingusinde.cl, 9 A.M.–1 P.M. and 2:30–7 P.M. weekdays, 2:30–6:30 P.M. weekends, free) has exhibits on geology, economic plants and taxidermy, a marker for the former post office, and a sign for the coal mine at Caleta Banner, on nearby Isla Picton, which provisioned the *Yelcho* on its rescue mission. Nearby is the **Parque Botánico Omora,** an organized selection of native plants.

Built in Germany for operations on the Rhine, the **MV *Micalvi*** shipped supplies between remote *estancias* and other settlements before sinking in Puerto Williams' inner harbor in 1962; the upper deck and bridge remain as the yacht club's bar/restaurant.

Accommodations, Food, and Entertainment

At **Residencial Pusaki** (Piloto Pardo 242, tel. 061/621116, pattypusaki@yahoo.es, US$14–18 pp), rates vary according to shared or private bath. **Refugio Coirón** (Ricardo Maragaño 168, tel. 061/621227, www.hostalcoiron.cl, US$30–37 s, US$42–65 d) has good accommodations with kitchen privileges and shared baths; it has also added rooms with private baths.

The top choice is the utterly transformed, 24-room **Hotel Lakutaia** (tel. 061/621733, www.lakutaia.cl, US$200 s, US$250 d), which is more a destination than just a hotel; it also has a fine restaurant. Off-season rates (May–mid-October) are about 25 percent lower.

South America's southernmost bar/restaurant, the **Club de Yates Micalvi,** occupies the main deck and bridge of the historic vessel that lies grounded in the inner harbor.

The **Pingüino Pub** is at the Centro Comercial.

Services

Nearly all services are concentrated around the Centro Comercial, a cluster of storefronts just uphill from the Muelle Guardián Brito, the main passenger pier. These include the post office, several telephone offices, Banco de Chile, the Cema-Chile crafts shop, and Manualidades, which rents mountain bikes.

Transportation

Aerovías DAP (tel. 061/621051), at the Centro Comercial, flies 20-seat Twin Otters to Punta Arenas (US$92) daily except Tuesday and Sunday, April–October. The rest of the year, flights leave Monday–Saturday. DAP flights are often heavily booked, so make reservations well in advance.

Regular connections between Puerto Williams and Ushuaia, on Argentine Tierra del Fuego, continue to be problematic, but hitching a lift across the channel with a yacht is feasible—for a price. For up-to-date information, contact the **Gobernación Marítima** (tel. 061/621090), the **Club de Yates** (tel. 061/621041, Ext. 4250), or **Turismo Sim** (tel. 061/621150). There are occasional charter flights as well.

In summer, the **ferry** *Bahía Azul* sails to Punta Arenas (32 hours) Friday at 10 P.M. Fares are US$210 for a bunk, US$175 for a reclining seat.

VICINITY OF PUERTO WILLIAMS

The Williams-based, German-Venezuelan **Sea & Ice & Mountains Adventures Unlimited** (Austral 74, tel./fax 061/621150, tel. 061/621227, coiron@simltd.com, www.simltd.com) organizes trekking, climbing, and riding expeditions on Isla Navarino and the Cordillera Darwin; weeklong yacht excursions around the Beagle Channel and to Cape Horn;

and even trips to Antarctica. Advance booking is essential.

The Coastal Road

From Puerto Williams, a coastal road runs 54 kilometers west to the village of Puerto Navarino, now a legal port of entry, and 28 kilometers east to Caleta Eugenia; only two kilometers east of Williams, **Villa Ukika** is the last Yámana refuge. From Caleta Eugenia, the road is gradually advancing southeast to **Puerto Toro,** where some 60 boats employ about four persons each in search of *centolla* (king crab).

Cordón de los Dientes

Immediately south of Puerto Williams, Cordón de los Dientes is a range of jagged peaks rising more than 1,000 meters above sea level that offers the world's southernmost trekking opportunities. There are, however, few trails through this rugged countryside—anyone undertaking the four- to five-day "circuit" should be experienced in route finding.

Río Grande, Argentina

Most visitors who stay in and around Río Grande, on the Isla Grande's blustery Atlantic shoreline, do so for the fishing. For the rest, this once-desolate city is more a transit point than a destination in itself, but thanks to smoothly paved streets, the huge dust clouds that once blew through the wool and oil burg have subsided. There are limits to beautification, though, as all the trees planted in Plaza Almirante Brown are stiffly wind-flagged.

Bus schedules used to dictate that travelers pass the night here, but recent improvements mean quicker overland connections to Ushuaia. Still, services have improved, and there's enough to do that an afternoon spent here need not be a wasted one.

On the north bank of its namesake river, Río Grande (population 52,786) is 79 kilometers southeast of the Chilean border post at San Sebastián and 190 kilometers northeast of Ushuaia via RN 3, which is now completely paved (though some deteriorating segments south toward Tolhuin will need repaving in the future).

SIGHTS AND ENTERTAINMENT

The **Museo de La Ciudad Virginia Choquintel** (Alberdi 555, tel. 02964/421767, 9 A.M.–7 P.M. weekdays, 3–7 P.M. Sat., free admission) does a lot with a little, with good materials on natural history, surprisingly sophisticated exhibits on ethnology and aboriginal subsistence, and historic displays on maps and mapmaking, the evolution of island communications, and astronomy. The museum occupies the former storehouses of the Asociación Rural de Tierra del Fuego.

Río Grande has few architectural landmarks—or few buildings of any antiquity for that matter—but the **Obras Sanitarias** waterworks tower (Lasserre 386), at the Plaza's northeast corner, dates from the Juan Perón era (circa 1954).

El Cine 1 & 2 (Perito Moreno 211, tel. 02962/433260) shows current films in modern facilities, but it sometimes cranks up the volume to excruciating levels—bring or improvise ear plugs, just in case.

ACCOMMODATIONS

Accommodations are few, particularly at the budget end, where quality varies dramatically. Nearly every midrange-to-upscale place offers a 10 percent discount for cash payment.

Río Grande's first backpacker hostel, at the south end of town, **Hotel Argentino** (San Martín 64, tel. 02964/422546, hotelargentino@hotmail.com, US$12 pp) gets high marks for hospitality, good beds, and good common

FISHING IN FUEGIA

Fishing for Atlantic salmon, brown trout, and rainbow trout is a popular pastime throughout Argentine Tierra del Fuego, but fees differ according to the period of time, the lake or river in question, and residence status.

Daily rates range US$17-100 for foreigners; there's a weekly license for US$67-200, and seasonal rates are US$100-333. Fuegian and Argentine residents pay a fraction of these rates.

In Ushuaia, licenses are available at the **Asociación Caza y Pesca** (Maipú 822, tel. 02901/423168, cazpescush@infovia.com.ar). In Río Grande, contact **El Tano** (Rivadavia 675, tel. 02964/424324).

areas including kitchen access. Prices with shared or private bath are acceptable, but make reservations for the latter; a couple of rooms are run-down and it sometimes suffers water shortages. Staff will fetch guests from the bus terminals for free.

The simple but spotless, family-run **Hospedaje Noal** (Obligado 557, tel. 02964/427516, US$14 pp, US$34 d) has spacious rooms with shared bath but plenty of closet space and good beds, and some rooms with private bath. **B&B El Puesto** (Juan Bautista Thorne 345, tel. 02964/420923, bybelpuesto@yahoo.com.ar US$28 s, US$34 d), the only one of its kind, is one of Río Grande's best values.

Around the corner from the former bus terminal, the seaside **Hotel Isla del Mar** (Güemes 936, tel. 02964/422883, isladelmar@arnet.com.ar, US$44 s, US$52 d) is frayed, not just worn around the edges, with loose doorknobs, scuffed walls, and slowly eroding wooden built-ins. Still, it exudes a certain funky charm, even if "sea view" is a relative term here—with Río Grande's enormous tidal range, the Atlantic tides sometimes seem to be on the distant horizon. Rates include breakfast, and there's a small discount for cash payments.

Possibly Río Grande's best value for money, rehabbed **Hotel Villa** (San Martín and Espora, tel. 02964/424998, hotelvillarg@hotmail.com, US$57 s, US$69 d) has cheerful contemporary rooms and assiduous service. It offers 10 percent cash discounts.

A glass palace that's an architectural sore thumb, **Hotel Atlántida** (Avenida Belgrano 582, tel./fax 02964/431914, www.atlantidahotel.com.ar, US$71 s, US$87 d) has improved its accommodations, and offers a 10 percent discount for payment in cash. Likewise, with its rooms and public areas upgraded, **Hotel Federico Ibarra** (Rosales 357, tel. 02964/430071, www.federicoibarrahotel.com.ar, US$79 s, US$94 d) is well worth consideration with breakfast and similar cash discounts.

Río Grande's most professional operation, **(Posada de los Sauces** (Elcano 839, tel. 02964/432895, www.posadadelossauces.com.ar, US$80–96 s, US$94–118 d) is easily top of the line. One of the suite bathrooms could hold a hot-tub party, and the restaurant is the city's most elegant.

FOOD

La Nueva Piamontesa (Belgrano and Mackinlay, tel. 02964/424366) is a longstanding favorite for varied baked empanadas and the pizzas in its deli. An inexpensive sit-down restaurant as well, it's open 24/7.

Leymi (25 de Mayo 1335, tel. 02964/421683, lunch and dinner daily) serves inexpensive fixed-price lunches and has a broad *parrillada* and pasta menu, plus other short orders. **El Rincón de Julio** (Elcano 805, tel. 02964/15-604261, lunch and dinner daily) is a hole-in-the-wall *parrilla,* highly regarded by locals, with lunch-counter-style service.

Mamá Flora (Avenida Belgrano 1101, tel. 02964/424087, breakfast and lunch daily) is a good breakfast choice that also has coffee and exquisite chocolates. At the plaza's northwest corner, **Limoncello** (Rosal and Fagnano, tel. 02964/420134) is an exceptional ice creamery.

Several hotels have their own restaurants, most notably the ◖ **Posada de los Sauces** (Elcano 839, tel. 02964/430868, lunch and dinner daily), which deserves special mention for superb service, the cooked-to-order *lomo a la pimienta* (pepper steak, US$10) and its complimentary glass of wine. There's also a 10 percent cash discount.

INFORMATION

On Plaza Almirante Brown, Río Grande's **Oficina de Información Turística** (Rosales 350, tel. 02964/431324, www.riogrande.gov.ar, 9 A.M.–5 P.M. daily in summer, 9 A.M.–5 P.M. weekdays the rest of the year) is exceptionally helpful.

The provincial **Instituto Fueguino de Turismo** (Infuetur, Espora 533, tel. 02962/422887) is open 9 A.M.–6 P.M. weekdays only.

SERVICES

Cambio Thaler (Rosales 259, tel. 02964/421154) is the only exchange house. Banks with ATMs include **Banco de Tierra del Fuego** (San Martín 193) and **HSBC** (San Martín 194).

Correo Argentino (Rivadavia 968) is two blocks west of San Martín; the postal code is 9420. **Locutorio Cabo Domingo** (San Martín 458) has both long-distance telephone and Internet services.

El Lavadero (Perito Moreno 221) handles the washing.

For medical services, contact the **Hospital Regional** (Ameghino s/n, tel. 02964/422088).

GETTING THERE

Aerolíneas Argentinas (San Martín 607, tel. 02964/422748) flies daily to Río Gallegos and Buenos Aires. **LADE** (Lasserre 425, tel. 02964/422968) flies with some frequency to Río Gallegos, less often to Comodoro Rivadavia.

La Terminal (Obligado and Sinocchio) is Río Grande's new bus terminal, but companies retain their old offices, some of them more central, as well. **Lider** (Perito Moreno 635, tel. 02964/420003, www .lidertdf.com.ar) and **Transportes Montiel** (25 de Mayo 712, tel. 02964/420997) have multiple departures to Tolhuín (US$10) and Ushuaia (US$17). At the new terminal, **Buses Pacheco** (cel. 02964/15-408717, www.busespacheco.com) goes to Punta Arenas, Chile (US$33, eight hours) Tuesday, Thursday, and Saturday at 10 A.M. and has summer connections to Puerto Natales, Chile.

Tecni-Austral (Moyano 516, tel. 02964/430610) goes to Punta Arenas Monday, Wednesday, and Friday at 8 A.M., to Río Gallegos (US$34, eight hours) via Chile Monday–Saturday at 8:30 A.M., and to Ushuaia (US$17, four hours) at 4 P.M. daily.

Buses Marga (Mackinlay 545, tel. 02964/426180) goes daily to Río Gallegos (US$34, nine hours).

GETTING AROUND

City bus Línea C goes directly to **Aeropuerto Internacional Río Grande** (tel. 02964/420600), a short distance west of downtown on RN 3, for US$0.50. It's also a reasonable cab ride.

Europcar (Avenida Belgrano 423, tel. 02964/432022) rents cars and light trucks.

Vicinity of Río Grande

As the surrounding area lacks a well-developed transport infrastructure, hiring a vehicle is worth consideration.

RESERVA PROVINCIAL COSTA ATLÁNTICA DE TIERRA DEL FUEGO

From Cabo Nombre, at the north end of Bahía San Sebastián, to the mouth of the Río Ewan southeast of Río Grande, the Isla Grande's entire shoreline is a bird sanctuary because of the abundant plovers and sandpipers, some of which migrate yearly between the Arctic and South America. Near the San Sebastián border post is the privately owned **Refugio de Vida Silvestre Dicky,** a prime wetland of 1,900 hectares.

MISIÓN SALESIANA

One exception to Río Grande's lack of historic sites is the Salesian mission (RN 3 Km 2980, tel. 02964/421642, www.misionrg.com.ar), founded by the order to catechize the Selknam; after the aboriginals died out from unintentionally introduced diseases and intentional slaughter, the fathers turned their attention to educating rural youth in their boarding school. The well-preserved **Capilla** (chapel), a national historic monument, and similar Magellanic buildings make up part of the mission's **Museo de Historia, Antropología y de Ciencias Naturales** (3–5:45 P.M. daily, US$0.60 for adults, half that for children), whose facilities display their natural history and ethnography exhibits far better than in the not-too-distant past.

From Río Grande, Línea D goes hourly to the Misión Salesiana, about 11 kilometers north of Río Grande, 7:30 A.M.–8:30 P.M.

HISTORIC *ESTANCIAS*

Several of the region's largest and most important *estancias* are in the vicinity of Río Grande. Founded by the Menéndez dynasty's Sociedad Explotadora de Tierra del Fuego,

Estancia María Behety, 17 kilometers west via gravel RC-c, is home to the world's largest shearing shed.

Also Sociedad Explotadora property, **Estancia José Menéndez,** 25 kilometers southwest of town via RN 3 and RC-b, is one of the island's most historic ranches. RC-b continues west to an obscure border post at **Radman,** where few visitors of any kind cross the line to Lago Blanco on the Chilean side (Nov.–Mar. only).

For potential overnighters, though, the Sea View Guest House at the Simon and Carolina Goodall family's **Estancia Viamonte** (tel. 02964/430861, www.estanciaviamonte.com, US$145 pp with half board, US$175 pp with full board) is the only place on the island that can offer the opportunity to sleep in Lucas Bridges' bedroom. Directly on RN 3, about 42 kilometers southeast of Río Grande, it fronts on a bird-rich beach; the house itself can sleep up to six people with two shared baths, plus living and dining rooms. There are extensive gardens, and chances for fishing, riding, and farm activities.

LAGO FAGNANO (KAMI)

Named for the priest who spearheaded Salesian evangelism among the Selknam, this elongated body of water fills a structural depression that stretches across the Chilean border to the west. Also known by its Selknam name Kami, its shoreline is nearly 200 kilometers long and its surface covers nearly 600 square kilometers.

The lake's most westerly part, along the Chilean border, lies within Parque Nacional Tierra del Fuego but is virtually inaccessible except by boat. As might be expected, the lake is popular with fishing enthusiasts.

At the east end, about midway between Río Grande and Ushuaia, pilgrims pause at the town of **Tolhuin** to sample the goods at ◖ **Panadería la Unión** (www.panaderialaunion.com), a legendary bakery whose celebrity visitors have ranged from ex-President Carlos Menem to folk-rocker León Gieco, hard-rockers Los Caballeros de la Quema, and actress China Zorrilla. It has the usual fine bread but also loads of *facturas* (pastries), *alfajores*, and sandwiches; what it lacks, astonishingly for Argentina, is any coffee other than machine-dispensed instant.

For a full meal, there's nearby **La Posada de los Ramírez** (Avenida de los Shelk'nam 411, tel. 02901/492382, lunch and dinner daily), which has excellent pastas at bargain prices, but also meats and, on occasion, local specialties such as trout.

Ushuaia, Argentina

Beneath the Martial range's serrated spires, on the Beagle Channel's north shore, the city of Ushuaia is both an end (virtually the terminus of the world's southernmost highway) and a beginning (the gateway to Antarctica). The surrounding countryside is increasingly popular with activities-oriented visitors for hiking, mountain biking, fishing, and skiing. In the summer season, the city gets hundreds of thousands of foreign visitors, though many are merely day-trippers from the hundreds of cruise ships that anchor here.

After more than two decades of economic growth and physical sprawl, the provincial capital is both declining and improving. On the one hand, the duty-free manufacturing, fishing, and tourist boom that transformed a onetime penal colony and naval base into a bustling city has weakened. On the other, it's spruced up the waterfront and restored historic buildings that gave the town its personality, some of them becoming hotels or B&Bs. The streets are cleaner (though Avenida San Martín is tourist-trap ugly) and there are more parks, plazas, and green spaces. Still, Ushuaia has particulate pollution problems because high winds kick up dust in its unpaved newer neighborhoods.

HISTORY
Ushuaia dates from 1870, when the Anglican South American Missionary Society decided to place the archipelago's first permanent European settlement here. Pioneer missionary Thomas Bridges and his descendants have left an enduring legacy in Bridges' Yahgan (Yámana) dictionary, his

son Lucas's memoir, and the family *estancia* at nearby Harberton (the Yahgans whom Thomas Bridges hoped to save, though, succumbed to introduced diseases and conflict with other settlers).

Not long after Ushuaia's settlement, Argentina, alarmed by the British presence, moved to establish its own authority at Ushuaia and did so with a penal settlement for its most infamous criminals and political undesirables. It remained a penal settlement until almost

SOUTH TO THE ICE

Since the Soviet Union's demise, Ushuaia has become the main jumping-off point for Antarctic excursions on Russian icebreakers that, despite being chartered under American officers, sometimes still show the hammer and sickle on their bows. For travelers with flexible schedules, it's been possible to make last-minute arrangements at huge discounts – no ship wants to sail with empty berths – but heavy demand has made it difficult to pay anything less than about US$3,500-4,000 for a trip of about 9-14 days, including several days' transit across the stormy Drake Passage (medication advisable).

On the waterfront Muelle Comercial, Ushuaia's **Oficina Antártida Infuetur** (tel. 02901/424431, antartida@tierradel-fuego.org.ar) has the latest information. At present, even last-minute arrangements normally go through Ushuaia travel agencies for the mid-November-mid-March season.

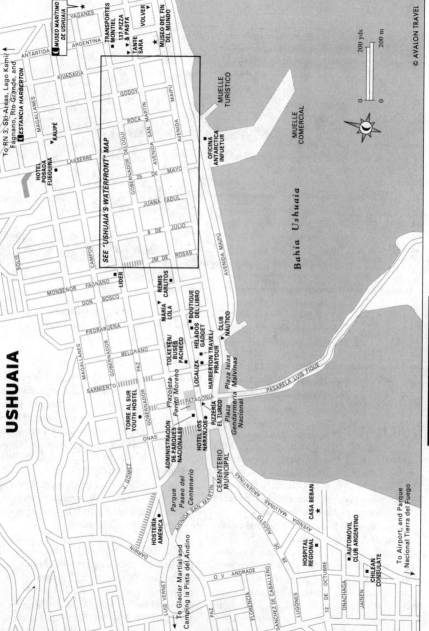

SOUTHERN PATAGONIA

Ushuaia's Beagle Channel setting is one of the most spectacular in South America.

1950, when Juan Domingo Perón's government created a major naval base to support Argentina's Antarctic claims. Only since the 1976–1983 military dictatorship ended has it become a tourist destination, visited by countless cruise ships as well as overland travelers and air passengers who come to see the world's southernmost city.

ORIENTATION

Stretching east–west along the Beagle Channel's north shore, Ushuaia (population 64,107, an almost 40 percent increase over the 2001 census) is 3,220 kilometers south of Buenos Aires and 190 kilometers southwest of Río Grande, the island's only other city.

Bedecked with flowerbeds, the main thoroughfare is Avenida Maipú, part of RN 3, now expanded into a divided boulevard; it continues west to Bahía Lapataia in Parque Nacional Tierra del Fuego. The parallel Avenida San Martín, one block north, is the main commercial street; the focus of Ushuaia's nightlife, it gets gridlocked on summer nights as surely as any avenue in Buenos Aires. From

the shoreline, the perpendicular northbound streets rise steeply—some so steeply that they become staircases.

SIGHTS

Even if it's leveled off, Ushuaia's economic boom provided the wherewithal to preserve and even restore some of the city's historic buildings. Two of them are now museums: Dating from 1903, the waterfront **Casa Fernández Valdés** (Avenida Maipú 175) houses the historical Museo del Fin del Mundo, while the 1896 **Presidio de Ushuaia** (Yaganes and Gobernador Paz) is now the misleadingly named Museo Marítimo (while not insignificant, its maritime exhibits are less interesting than those on the city's genesis as a penal colony).

Three blocks west of the Casa Fernández Valdés, dating from 1894, the classically Magellanic **Poder Legislativo** (Maipú 465) once housed the provincial legislature, and is now part of the Museo del Fin del Mundo. Five blocks farther west, prisoners built the restored **Capilla Antigua** (Avenida Maipú and Rosas), a chapel dating from 1898. A branch of the municipal tourist office occupies the **Biblioteca Sarmiento** (1926) at San Martín 674, the city's first public library. At the west end of downtown, the waterfront **Casa Beban** (Avenida Malvinas Argentinas and 12 de Octubre) is a reassembled pioneer residence dating from 1913; it now houses the municipal Casa de la Cultura, a cultural center.

Museo del Fin del Mundo

Its block-style exterior handsomely restored, Ushuaia's evolving historical museum contains exhibits on the Yámana, Selknam, and other Fuegian Indians, and on early European voyages. There remain permanent exhibits on the presidio, the Fique family's early general store, the original branch of Banco de la Nación (which occupied the building for more than 60 years), and natural history, including run-of-the-mill taxidermy. Its celebrity artifact is a rare copy of Thomas Bridges' Yámana–English dictionary.

An open-air sector re-creates a Yámana encampment and dwellings, alongside machinery used in early agriculture and forestry projects. The Museo del Fin del Mundo (Avenida Maipú 175, tel. 02901/421863, www.tierradelfuego .org.ar/museo, US$6.50 for adults, US$2.50 for students and retired people, free for children

14 and under) also contains a bookstore/souvenir shop and a specialized library on southernmost Argentina, the surrounding oceans, and Antarctica. The exceptional website places much of this material online.

November–April, hours are 9 A.M.–8 P.M. daily, with guided tours at 11 A.M., and 2, 4, and 6 P.M.; the rest of the year, hours are noon–7 P.M. daily except Sunday, with guided tours at 2 and 5 P.M. There is no additional charge for tours.

Admission to the museum includes access to the ex–Poder Legislativo (Provincial Legislature, Maipú 465).

◖ Museo Marítimo de Ushuaia

Misleadingly named, Ushuaia's maritime museum (Yaganes and Gobernador Paz, tel. 02901/437481, www.museomaritimo .com, US$13, US$8.50 for foreign students, Argentines and locals get a discount) most effectively tells the story of Ushuaia's inauspicious origins as a penal settlement for both civilian and military prisoners. Alarmed over the South American Missionary Society's incursions among the Beagle Channel's indigenous peoples, Argentina reinforced its territorial claims by building, in 1884, a military prison on Isla de los Estados (Staten Island), across

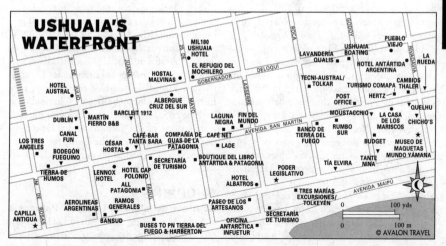

the Strait of Lemaire at the southeastern tip of the Isla Grande.

Barely a decade later, in 1896, it established Ushuaia's civilian Cárcel de Reincidentes for repeat offenders; after finally deciding, in 1902, that Isla de los Estados was a hardship post even for prisoners, the military moved its own facility to Ushuaia. Then, in 1911, the two institutions fused in this building that, over the first half of the 20th century, held some of the country's most famous political prisoners, celebrated rogues, and notorious psychopaths.

Divided into five two-story pavilions, with 380 cells intended for one prisoner each, it held up to 600 prisoners at a time before closing in 1947. Its most famous inmates were political detainees such as Russian anarchist bomber Simón Radowitzsky, who killed Buenos Aires police chief Ramón Falcón in 1909; Radical politicians Ricardo Rojas, Honorio Pueyrredón, and Mario Guido (in reality, the deceptively named Radicals are an ineffectual middle-class party); and Peronist politician Héctor Cámpora, who was briefly president in the 1970s.

Many if not most prisoners, though, were long-termers or lifers such as the diminutive strangler Cayetano Santos Godino, a serial killer dubbed "El Orejudo" for his oversized ears (the nickname also describes a large-eared bat native to the archipelago). Julio Ordano has written a play, performed in Buenos Aires, about Santos Godino, *El Petiso Orejudo.*

Life-sized figures of the most infamous inmates, modified department-store dummies clad in prison stripes, occupy many cells. One intriguing exhibit is a wide-ranging comparison with other prisons that have become museums, such as San Francisco's Alcatraz and South Africa's Robben Island.

The museum does justify its name with a collection of scale models of ships that have played a role in local history, such as Magellan's galleon *Trinidad,* the legendary *Beagle,* the South American Missionary Society's three successive sailboats, each known as the *Allen Gardiner,* and Antarctic explorer and conqueror Roald Amundsen's *Fram.* In addition,

there are materials on Argentina's Antarctic presence since the early 20th century, when the corvette *Uruguay* rescued Otto Nordenskjöld's Norwegian expedition, whose crew included the Argentine José María Sobral. On the grounds stands a full-size replica of the Faro San Juan de Salvamento, the Isla de los Estados (Staten Island) lighthouse that figures in Jules Verne's story "The Lighthouse at the End of the World."

In addition, the museum contains a philatelic room, natural history exhibits, and admirable accounts of the region's aboriginal peoples. It has only two drawbacks: There's too much to see in a single day, and the English translations could use some polishing—to say the least.

The Museo Marítimo is open 9 A.M.–8 P.M. daily October through April; the rest of the year, it opens an hour later.

On request, staff will validate your admission ticket for another day; since there's so much here, splitting up sightseeing sessions is a good idea. It has an excellent book and souvenir shop, and a *confitería* for snacks and coffee.

Museo de Maquetas Mundo Yámana

While both the Museo del Fin del Mundo and Museo Marítimo do a creditable job on Tierra del Fuego's indigenous heritage, this small private museum (Rivadavia 56, tel. 02901/422874, mundoyamana@infovia.com.ar, 10 A.M.–8 P.M. daily, US$4 for adults, US$2 for students and retired people, free for children under 13) consists of skillfully assembled dioramas of pre-European life along the Beagle Channel, at a scale of 1:15. It also includes cartographic representations of the Yámana and their neighbors, interpretations of the European impact, and panels of historical photographs. The staff speak fluent English.

SHOPPING

Boutique del Libro Antártida & Patagonia (25 de Mayo 62, tel. 2901/432117, www .antartidaypatagonia.com.ar) carries a wide choice of Argentine and imported books, in Spanish, English, and other languages, on the "uttermost part of the earth" and its surroundings, including current Moon Handbooks at moderate markups; there are also novels for that long voyage across the Drake Passage to Antarctica. Relocated to more spacious quarters, its other **Boutique del Libro** (San Martín 1120, tel. 02901/424750) offers an excellent selection of Spanish-language books and a smaller choice of English-language titles.

Along with many similar venues along Ushuaia's main shopping street, **Fin del Mundo** (San Martín 505, tel. 02901/422971) has many kitschy souvenirs but also maps and books. Nearby **Laguna Negra** (San Martín 513, tel. 02901/431144) specializes in locally produced chocolates.

Tierra de Humos (San Martín 861, tel. 02901/433050, www.tierradehumos.com.ar) stocks locally produced leather, fleeces, handicrafts, and silverwork. For purchases directly from the artisans, there's the **Paseo de los**

Artesanos (Maipú and Lasserre), at the entrance to the Muelle Comercial port.

Quelhué (San Martín 214, tel. 02901/435882, www.quelhue.com.ar) carries a fine selection of Argentine wines and imported duty-free liquors.

ENTERTAINMENT

Ushuaia has sprouted a plethora of pubs, some but not all with Irish aspirations or pretensions, such as **Dublin** (9 de Julio 168, tel. 02944/430744), with a standard menu of *minutas* (short orders).

ACCOMMODATIONS

Ushuaia has abundant accommodations, but it's long been one of the most expensive destinations in what was, until recently, an expensive country. Demand is also high, though, in the summer months of January and February, when prices rise and reservations are advisable. One heartening development is the proliferation of good but moderately priced backpacker

Ramos Generales is a bar and restaurant that recreates the atmosphere of old Ushuaia – except that it's tobacco-free.

© WAYNE BERNHARDSON

SOUTHERN PATAGONIA

hostels and the arrival of several bed-and-breakfasts—known by the semi-English acronym ByB—some of them excellent alternatives.

US$10-25

Eight kilometers west of Ushuaia on the Lapataia road, the **Camping Municipal** has free but limited facilities (fire pits and pit toilets only). A stiff climb to the northwest of downtown, **La Pista del Andino** (Alem 2873, tel. 02901/435890, 02901/15-568626, www.lapistadelandino.com.ar, US$5 pp) has slightly sloping sites at its ski area; the first transfer from downtown or the airport is free. Guests with sleeping bags can crash in the *refugio* above its bar/restaurant but shouldn't expect get to sleep early.

US$25-50

The HI affiliate ◖ **Albergue Los Cormoranes** (Kamshen 788, tel. 02902/423459, www.loscormoranes.com, US$12–15 pp in dorms, US$46–57 d with private bath, with breakfast) has attractive common areas, including a wind-sheltered garden, and arguably better sleeping facilities than Torre al Sur. Most easily reached by climbing Don Bosco to its end and then taking a left, it's about eight steep blocks north of the waterfront (arrival transfers are free).

Perched at downtown's western edge, with spectacular Beagle Channel views, HI affiliate **Torre al Sur Youth Hostel** (Gobernador Paz 1437, tel. 02901/430745, www.torrealsur.com.ar, US$14–15 pp) has been one of Argentina's finest backpacker facilities, but overcrowding and noise have gotten it mixed reviews recently. Rooms have two or four beds, with lockers; there's hot water, Internet access, and free luggage storage.

The more central **Albergue Cruz del Sur** (Deloqui 636, tel. 02901/434099, www.xdelsur.com.ar, US$15 pp) is an independent hostel with four-, six-, or eight-bed rooms; there is also cable TV, Internet access, two kitchens, and a free initial pick-up. Guests also get a series of discounts and specials at various services around town.

Half a block from the Lider bus terminal,

the fast-expanding **Freestyle Backpackers Hostel** (Gobernador Paz 866, tel. 02901/432874, www.ushuaiafreestyle.com, US$15 pp) is a gleaming purpose-built hostel with a youthful ambience, a spacious lounge and kitchen facilities, and secondary amenities including laundry service and parking.

Pueblo Viejo (Deloqui 242, tel. 02901/432098, www.puebloviejo.info, US$40 s, US$47 d with shared bath) is a B&B built on the foundations of an early Ushuaia house; replicating the traditional Magellanic style, it's added innovative contemporary touches. The street level rooms are more luminous than their semi-basement counterparts.

US$50-100

On the hillside, the contemporary ◖ **Martín Fierro B&B** (9 de Julio 175, tel. 02901/430525, www.martinfierrobyb.com.ar, US$40 s, US$57 d) has two bunks in each of several small but well-designed rooms with shared baths. Host Javier Jury has created tasteful common areas that are simultaneously spacious and cozy, and the breakfast is varied and filling; the tiny shower stalls, though, make bathing with a friend impossible without being *really* intimate. Two downstairs "aparthotel" rooms (US$52 s, US$71 d), with separate kitchens, sleep up to four people each.

Responsive **Hostería América** (Gobernador Paz 1665, tel. 02901/423358, www.hosteriaamerica.com.ar, US$57 s, US$71 d) is a decent choice in a fine location above the Parque Paseo del Centenario.

Hostal Malvinas (Gobernador Deloqui 615, tel./fax 02901/422626, www.hostalmalvinas.net, US$70 s, US$80 d) provides simple but quiet and immaculate rooms with large baths and no frills—not even TV—but croissants and coffee are free all day.

Rehabbed **Hotel César** (Avenida San Martín 753, tel. 02901/421460, www.hotelcesarhostal.com.ar, US$56 s, US$86 d) has become one of the better values in a congested central area.

Just uphill from Martín Fierro, the best choice in its price range, **Hotel Austral** (9 de Julio 250, tel. 02901/422223, www.hotel-austral.com.ar, US$85 s, US$95 d) is a 10-room hotel with soaring, light-filled common areas that offer panoramic views of the Beagle Channel (at least until new constructions block them some years from now). Painted in pastels, the rooms themselves are spacious and comfortable.

Only a short distance walk from downtown, in an oasis neighborhood of sheltered gardens, (Galeazzi-Basily B&B (Gobernador Valdés 323, tel. 2901/423213, www.avesdelsur .com.ar, US$37/52 s/d with shared bath, US$69 s or d with private bath d) is a comfortable family house that also has exterior cabañas. The hosts speak English fluently, and are a great source of information on the rest of the island, including Estancia Harberton.

US$100-200

Hillside **Hotel Ushuaia** (Lasserre 933, tel. 02901/430671, www.ushuaiahotel.com.ar, US$90 s, US$120 d with breakfast) is a good value in its price range.

Though it's not really a view hotel, the **Mi180 Ushuaia Hotel** (25 de Mayo 245, tel. 02901/437710, www.hotel1810.com, US$101--149 s or d) is a central boutique hotel that occupies a prominent hillside site just a couple blocks from the waterfront, close enough to walk everywhere but just beyond the congested center.

Only its busy location detracts from the bright and cheerful **Hotel Cap Polonio** (San Martín 746, tel. 02901/422131, www.hotel-cappolonio.com.ar, US$135 s or d with breakfast). All rooms are carpeted, with cable TV; the private baths have tubs as well as showers, and there's a good restaurant *confitería* (breakfast is included in the rate).

From its cul-de-sac perch, (**Hotel Posada Fueguina** (Lasserre 438, tel. 02901/423467, www.posadafueguina.com.ar, US$100--126 s, US$140--169 d) offers awesome views plus cable TV, and similar amenities. It has added cabañas to handle any overflow.

At the west end, one of Ushuaia's tallest buildings, the nearly new **Hotel Los Naranjos** (San Martín 1446, tel. 02901/435862, www

.losnaranjosushuaia.com, US$156 s or d) offers comfortable midsize rooms with either Channel or glacier views, at least from the uppermost floors. The restaurant menu is worth a look.

Downtown's nearly new **Lennox Hotel** (San Martín 776, tel./fax 02901/436430, www.lennox hotel.com.ar, US$143 s or d) has midsized rooms with either Channel or mountain views, but even with amenities such as whirlpool baths and WiFi it's hard to think it's worth more than double the price of, say, Hotel César. It also follows the dubious practice of charging foreigners more than Argentines.

In dense woods about 1.5 km northeast of downtown, (**Patagonia Villa Lodge** (Bahía Buen Suceso 563, tel. 02901/435937, www.patagoniavilla.com, US$200--240 s, US$260--300 d) has just five rooms in luminous semi-detached cabins with a magnificently rustic architecture and comforts such as whirlpool tubs (in some, at least) and WiFi. There is one double (US$110 s, US$130 d) that lacks significant natural light but suffers only by comparison with the others; elsewhere, it would count among the best in town. Owner Luciana Lupotti, a former Florida exchange student, speaks fluent English. Rates include airport pick-up/drop-off; the most expensive rooms have whirlpool tubs.

The spacious, rejuvenated **Hotel Albatros** (Avenida Maipú 505, tel. 02901/433446, www .albatroshotel.com.ar, US$195 s or d) is the pick of the waterfront accommodations.

More than US$200

The interior is more impressive than the surprisingly plain exterior at the luxury **Hotel del Glaciar** (Luis Martial 2355, tel. 02901/430640, www.hoteldelglaciar.com, US$209--229 s or d). At Km 3.5 on the road to the Martial Glacier, each room has either a mountain or an ocean view, but it's questionable whether staffing is sufficient for a hotel of its category—and price.

About four km west of downtown, in a still developing neighborhood that's mostly residential, family-run (**Hostería Tierra de Leyendas** (Tierra de Vientos 2448, tel.

02901/443565, www.tierradeleyendas.com.ar, US$195–235 s or d) is a new five-room boutique hotel, with expansive views of the Beagle Channel. There are plans to add no more than two additional rooms. Owner Sebastián García Cosoleto, who cooked for eight years at the Buenos Aires Marriott Plaza Hotel, is also chef of its French-influenced restaurant (open for dinner only, reservations obligatory for nonguests).

At Km 3 on the glacier road, the **Hotel y Resort Las Hayas** (Luis Martial 1650, tel. 02901/430710, www.lashayas.com.ar, US$317 s or d) enjoys nearly all conceivable luxuries, including an elaborate buffet breakfast, gym, sauna, hot tub, and a heated indoor pool; it picks up guests at the airport and offers a regular shuttle to and from downtown. Behind its surprisingly utilitarian exterior, some of its 93 rooms and suites suffer from hideous decor—the wallpaper is to cringe at—but all are comfortable and its staff members are highly professional.

FOOD

Ushuaia has always been an expensive place to eat, though the 2001–2002 peso collapse reined in prices. Over the last couple years, though, prices have rebounded and there are some truly expensive choices; the financially challenged should look for *tenedor libre* specials, or be cautious with extras like dessert and coffee.

Hotel Cap Polonio's **Marcopolo** (San Martín 730, tel. 02901/430001) is a café/restaurant that serves excellent coffee, chocolate, and croissants for breakfast—try the *submarino* for a cold morning's pickup. **Café de la Esquina** (Avenida San Martín 602, tel. 02901/423676) is a popular meeting place with similar offerings, as well as sandwiches for late-afternoon tea.

Open for lunch only Weekdays, but with Saturday evening hours, **Pizzería El Turco** (San Martín 1440, tel. 02901/424711) is good and moderately priced, but it lacks variety. Well-established **Barcleit 1912** (Fadul 148, tel. 02901/433105, lunch and dinner daily) has fallen a step behind some of the other pizzerias, but also offers a variety of moderately priced short orders.

In luminous new quarters, **Tante Sara** (San Martín 175, tel. 02901/424118, lunch and dinner daily) made its name in sweets and snacks, which are still abundant, but it also produces a limited menu of well-crafted lunch and dinner dishes, such as a rib eye with a Malbec sauce (US$11). For breakfast, coffee, sandwiches, and desserts, try its **Café-Bar Tante Sara** (San Martín 701, tel. O2901/423912).

Formerly part of Tante Sara, now under new ownership, **137 Pizza & Pasta** (San Martín 137, tel./fax 02901/435005, lunch and dinner daily) still sets the pace in diverse pastas with a broad selection of imaginative sauces, as well as pizza. Most entrées, such as ravioli with king crab, fall into the US$7–10 range, with sauces extra.

New in 2006, **Ramos Generales** (Maipú 749, tel. 02901/424317, www.ramos-generalesushuaia.com, noon–11 P.M. daily) is a bar and restaurant that re-creates a pioneer general store with humor and museum-quality artifacts. It may romanticize the era, but its snacks (including sandwiches) and sweets reinforce the style to make it a must for any Ushuaia visitor. The menu is not elaborate, but the quality is outstanding.

Also in an artfully restored historic house, **Bodegón Fueguino** (San Martín 859, tel. 02901/431972, lunch and dinner daily) specializes in Fuegian lamb, prepared in a variety of styles for around US$10, but it also has seafood dishes, tangy beef empanadas, and good desserts.

La Rueda (San Martín 193, tel. 02901/436540, lunch and dinner daily) charges only slightly more for its own buffet *parrillada*. The well-established **Moustacchio** (Avenida San Martín 298, tel. 02901/423308, lunch and dinner daily) stresses seafood but also serves beef and other meats.

Ushuaia has a wider choice of seafood restaurants than most any other Argentine provincial city. **La Casa de los Mariscos** (San

Martín 232, tel. 02901/421928, lunch and dinner daily) specializes in *centolla* (king crab) but has many other fish and shellfish options in the US$10–15 range. Looking like a Buenos Aires antique shop housed in a classic Magellanic residence, tango-themed **Volver** (Avenida Maipú 37, tel. 02901/423977, lunch and dinner daily) doesn't quite live up to its potential—the fish and seafood dishes can be disappointingly bland.

With a 30-year history and portside views, **Tante Nina** (Gobernador Godoy 15, tel. 02901/432444, www.tanteninarestaurant.com.ar, lunch and dinner daily) focuses on Fuegian fish and seafood; the food is fine and the service is efficient, but the ambience feels institutional. **Chicho's** (Rivadavia 72, tel. 02901/423469, lunch and dinner daily) also handles large crowds efficiently, serving dishes such as king crab (US$16), hake (US$16), and Fuegian trout stuffed with crab and shrimp (US$12).

Other possibilities include the **El Náutico** (Avenida Maipú and Belgrano, tel. 02901/430415, lunch and dinner daily), where entrées start around US$10–12; **Tía Elvira** (Avenida Maipú 349, tel. 02901/424725); and (**Kaupé** (Roca 470, tel. 02901/422704, lunch and dinner daily), which serves an exclusively (and exclusive) à la carte menu. The latter has specialties such as king crab, exquisite lemon ice cream, carpaccio, and wine by the glass. Even post-devaluation, a full meal here can cost well upwards of US$35 pp, but some knowledgeable locals suggest the menu has stagnated.

Equally top-of-the-line—both literally and geographically—is the dining-room-with-a-panoramic-view at (**Chez Manu** (Luis Martial 2135, tel. 02901/423253, lunch and dinner daily), immediately below the Hotel del Glaciar. Using local ingredients such as king crab and lamb, the French-run restaurant is *the* place for a truly elaborate meal at equally elaborate prices: US$30 and up. This is one Ushuaia restaurant with food to match its views, though portions are on the small side.

On a promontory, in a recycled building that once transmitted Argentina's first-ever color TV program—the 1978 World Cup—(**María Lola** (Deloqui 1048, tel. 02901/421185, www.marialolaresto.com.ar) may be Ushuaia's best restaurant, period. For items ranging from relatively simple but delicate pastas to more elaborate dishes such as stir-fried Patagonian lamb with vegetables, prices range US$10–25. The bar serves a diversity of mixed drinks at moderate prices. Open for lunch and dinner, it's closed Monday.

Helados Gadget (Avenida San Martín 621) has all the conventional Argentine ice-cream flavors—good enough in their own right—but also incorporates regional specialties such as *calafate* and, occasionally, rhubarb.

INFORMATION

Ushuaia's well-organized municipal **Secretaría de Turismo** (Maipú s/n, tel. 02901/437666, www.e-ushuaia.com, muniush@speedy.com.ar) has moved its main office to a spacious new building opposite the tourist pier but will keep its other office (San Martín 674, tel. 02901/424550) in operation. Hours are 8 A.M.–10 P.M. weekdays and 9 A.M.–8 P.M. weekends and holidays. English-speaking staff are normally present. There's also a subsidiary airport office (tel. 02901/423970) that's open for arriving flights only.

The provincial **Instituto Fueguino de Turismo (Infuetur)** has ground-floor offices at Hotel Albatros (Avenida Maipú 505, tel. 02901/423340, info@tierradelfuego.org.ar).

Motorists can consult the **Automóvil Club Argentino** (ACA, Malvinas Argentinas and Onachaga, tel. 02901/421121).

The **Administración de Parques Nacionales** (APN, Avenida San Martín 1395, tel. 02901/421315, tierradelfuego@apn.gov.ar) is open 9 A.M.–noon Monday–Friday.

At the waterfront Muelle Comercial, the **Oficina Antártica Infuetur** (tel. 02901/421423, antartica@tierradelfuego.org.ar, 8 A.M.–5 P.M. daily in summer, 9 A.M.–4 P.M. Mon.–Fri. the rest of the year) has the latest information on Antarctic sailings and tours.

SERVICES

Several banks have ATMs, including **BanSud** (Avenida Maipú 781) and **Banco de Tierra del Fuego** (San Martín 396); the latter accepts travelers checks at a 3 percent commission. **Cambio Thaler** (Avenida San Martín 209, tel. 02901/421911) also takes 3 percent on travelers checks but keeps longer hours: 9:30 A.M.–1:30 P.M. and 4–8 P.M. Monday–Friday, 10 A.M.–1:30 P.M. and 5:30–8 P.M. Saturday and 5:30–8 P.M. Sunday.

Correo Argentino (San Martín 309) is the post office.

Café Net (San Martín 565, tel. 02901/422720) provides telephone, fax, and Internet access, including WiFi.

The **Chilean consulate** (Jainén 50, tel. 02901/430970) is open 9 A.M.–1 P.M. weekdays only.

The **Dirección Nacional de Migraciones** (Beauvoir 1536, tel. 02901/422334) is open 9 A.M.–5 P.M. weekdays only.

Los Tres Angeles (Juan Manuel de Rosas 139, tel. 02901/422687) offers quick and reliable laundry service but can be overwhelmed in high season; try instead **Lavanderías Qualis** (Deloqui 368, tel. 02901/421996).

The **Hospital Regional** (Maipú and 12 de Octubre, tel. 02901/422950, tel. 107 for emergencies) handles medical issues.

GETTING THERE

Ushuaia has good air connections to Buenos Aires and intermediate points, and improving overland transportation from mainland Argentina and from Chile. Maritime transportation is either tenuous or expensive.

Air

Aerolíneas Argentinas (Maipú 823, tel. 02901/421218) normally flies two or three times daily to Aeroparque, sometimes via Río Gallegos, El Calafate, or Trelew. Occasional Buenos Aires–bound flights land at the international airport Ezeiza instead of Aeroparque.

The Chilean carrier LAN flies several times weekly to Punta Arenas, Chile (Ushuaia's only scheduled international service), while its affiliate LAN Argentina serves Aeroparque and other destinations. LAN's local representative is **Rumbo Sur** (San Martín 342, tel. 02901/422441).

In the Galería Albatros, **LADE** (Avenida San Martín 564, Local 5, tel. 02901/421123) flies irregularly to Río Gallegos, El Calafate, Comodoro Rivadavia, Bariloche, and Buenos Aires.

For Puerto Williams, across the Channel in Chile, it may be possible to arrange a private charter through the **Aeroclub Ushuaia** (tel. 02901/421717 or 02901/421892, www.aeroclubushuaia.org.ar).

Bus

Ushuaia lacks a central bus terminal. **Lider** (Gobernador Paz 921, tel. 02901/436421) goes to Tolhuín (US$7, 1.5 hours) and Río Grande (US$13, 3.5 hours) eight times daily except Sunday and holidays, when it goes only six times. **Transportes Montiel** (Deloqui 110, tel. 02901/421366) goes to Tolhuin and Río six or seven times daily except Sundays and holidays, when it goes five times only.

Represented by Tolkar Turismo (Roca 157, tel. 02901/431408), **Tecni-Austral** goes Monday–Saturday at 5 A.M. to Río Grande, sometimes continuing to Río Gallegos (US$42, 13 hours) and others to Punta Arenas, Chile (US$52, 12 hours). At the same office, **Buses Marga** goes daily at 6 A.M. to Río Gallegos. Buses Pacheco (San Martín 1267, tel. 02901/430727) goes to Punta Arenas Tuesday, Thursday, and Saturday, with connections to Puerto Natales.

Sea

The Chilean cruisers MV *Mare Australis* and *Via Australis* offer luxury sightseeing cruises to Puerto Williams, Cape Horn, and through the fjords of Chilean Tierra del Fuego to Punta Arenas; while not intended as simple transportation, they can serve that purpose for those who can afford them. It's possible to either disembark in Punta Arenas (four days) or return to Ushuaia (in a week).

These cruises are usually booked far in advance, but on occasion—normally just before Christmas—it may be possible to make on-the-spot arrangements.

International political obstacles continue to complicate regular transportation across the Beagle Channel to Puerto Williams, even though in December 2001 Chile and Argentina agreed to open Puerto Navarino, at the east end of Isla Navarino, as a port of entry to Chile. Nevertheless, **Ushuaia Boating** (Godoy 190, tel. 02901/436193, www.ushuaiaboating.com.ar) occasionally shuttles passengers across the Channel to Puerto Navarino and then overland to Puerto Williams (US$130 pp, two hours; US$240 r/t).

GETTING AROUND
To the Airport
A causeway links the city with **Aeropuerto Internacional Malvinas Argentinas,** which has the country's highest airport taxes: US$5 for elsewhere in Argentina, and US$20 for international flights. Taxis and *remises* cost about US$6 with **Remiscar** (San Martín 995, tel. 02901/422222, www.remiscar.com.ar).

Bus
From a new staging point at Avenida Maipú and Juana Fadul, several bus companies all charge around US$14 round-trip per person to Parque Nacional Tierra del Fuego; it's normally possible to camp in the park and return the following day. The most frequent services are with **Pasarela Tour** (tel. 02901/424582) and **Buses Eben-Ezer** (tel. 02901/431862) which between them have 18 buses daily to the park between 8 A.M. and 7 P.M., returning between 9 A.M. and 8 P.M. There are also services to the chairlift at the Glaciar Martial (US$7 pp), normally with a minimum of two passengers, and to Estancia Harberton (US$42 pp r/t).

Car Rental
Car rentals start around US$38 per day and range up to US$143 per day for four-wheel-drive vehicles. Some agencies offer unlimited mileage within Tierra del Fuego province, but others limit this to as few as 100 kilometers per day, so verify before signing any contract.

Rental agencies include **Budget** (Gobernador Godoy 45, 1st floor, tel. 02901/437373, ushuaia@budgetargentina.com), **Hertz** (San Martín 245, tel. 02901/437529, hertzushuaia@infovia.com.ar), and **Localiza** (Sarmiento 81, tel. 02901/437780, localizaush@speedy.com.ar).

Vicinity of Ushuaia

Ushuaia has more than a dozen travel agencies offering excursions in and around Ushuaia, ranging from double-decker-bus city tours (US$8, 1 hour) to Parque Nacional Tierra del Fuego (US$30, 4–5 hours) and historic Estancia Harberton (US$65, 8 hours). They also organize activities such as hiking, climbing, horseback riding, fishing, and mountain biking.

Local operators include **All Patagonia** (Juana Fadul 60, tel. 02901/433622, www.all-patagonia.com), which is the AmEx representative; **Canal Fun** (9 de Julio 118, Local 1, tel. 02901/437395, www.canalfun.com); **Rumbo Sur** (San Martín 350, tel. 02901/421139, www.rumbosur.com.ar); **Tolkar** (Roca 157, Local 1, tel. 02901/431408, www.tolkarturismo.com.ar); and **Tolkeyén** (San Martín 1267, tel. 02901/437073, www.tolkeyenpatagonia.com).

The **Compañía de Guías de Patagonia** (San Martín 628, tel. 02901/437753, www.companiadeguias.com.ar) specializes in trekking.

BEAGLE CHANNEL BOAT EXCURSIONS
From the Muelle Turístico, at the foot of Lasserre, there are boat trips to Beagle Channel wildlife sites such as **Isla de los Lobos,** home

to the southern sea lion *(Otaria flavescens)* and the rarer southern fur seal *(Arctocephalus australis)*, and **Isla de Pájaros,** a nesting site for seabirds, mostly cormorants. These excursions cost around US$40 per person for a 2.5-hour trip on oversized catamarans such as the *Ana B, Ezequiel B,* and *Luciano Beta.* With extensions to the penguin colony at Estancia Harberton and a visit to the *estancia* itself, the cost is about US$68.

Rumbo Sur and Tolkeyén sell tickets for these excursions from offices at the foot of the Muelle Turístico, where Héctor Monsalve's **Tres Marías Excursiones** (tel./fax 02901/421897, www.tresmariasweb.com) operates four-hour trips (US$43–52 pp) on smaller vessels (four passengers minimum, ten maximum) that can approach Isla de Lobos more closely than the large catamarans. They also land on Isla Bridges, a small but diverse island with cormorant colonies, shell mounds, and even the odd penguin.

FERROCARRIL AUSTRAL FUEGUINO

During Ushuaia's early days, prison labor built a short-line, narrow-gauge steam-driven railroad west into what is now Parque Nacional Tierra del Fuego to haul the timber that built the city. Only a few years ago, commercial interests rehabilitated part of the roadbed to create an antiseptic tourist version of the earlier line that pretty much ignores the unsavory aspects of its history to focus on the Cañadon del Toro's admittedly appealing forest scenery.

The train leaves from the **Estación del Fin del Mundo** (tel. 02901/431600, www .trendelfindelmundo.com.ar), eight kilometers west of Ushuaia at the municipal campground. October–mid-April, there are three departures daily, while the rest of the year only one, or perhaps two, are provided if demand is sufficient. The two-hour-plus excursion costs US$24 per person in tourist class, US$46 per person in first class, and US$64–86 per person with food service. Fares do not include the US$14 park entry fee.

SKI AREAS

Most visitors see Ushuaia in summer, but it's becoming a winter sports center as well, thanks to its proximity to the mountains. Downhill skiing, snowboarding, cross-country skiing, and even dogsledding are possibilities.

The major ski event is mid-August's **Marcha Blanca,** which symbolically repeats Argentine liberator José de San Martín's heroic winter crossing of the Andes from Mendoza to assist his Chilean counterpart Bernardo O'Higgins against the Spaniards. Luring upwards of 400 skiers, it starts from the Las Cotorras cross-country area and climbs to Paso Garibaldi, the 430-meter pass between the Sierra Alvear and the Sierra Lucas Bridges. Ideally, it takes place August 17, the anniversary of San Martín's death. (Argentine novelist Tomás Eloy Martínez has called his countrymen "cadaver cultists" for their apparent obsession with celebrating death rather than birth dates of their national icons.)

There are two downhill ski areas. The aging **Centro de Deportes Invernales Luis Martial** (Luis Martial 3995, tel. 02901/15-613890 or 02901/15-568587, esquiush@tierradelfuego. org.ar), seven kilometers northwest of town at the end of the road, has a single 1,130-meter run on a 23-degree slope, with a double-seat chairlift capable of carrying 224 skiers per hour.

East of Ushuaia, **Cerro Castor** (RN 3 Km 27, www.cerrocastor.com) has up-to-the-minute facilities, including four lifts and 15 different runs. In mid-season, lift tickets cost US$25–37 per day, with discounts for multi-day packages; in low and shoulder seasons, there are additional discounts.

Other areas east of town, along RN 3, are for cross-country skiers. These include **Tierra Mayor** (Km 21, tel. 02901/437454, tierra-mayor@tierradelfuego.org.ar), **Las Cotorras** (Km 26, tel. 02901/499300), **Haruwen** (Km 35, tel./fax 02901/424058, haruwen@tierradel-fuego.org.ar), and several newer options. All of them rent equipment and offer transfers from Ushuaia.

⟨ ESTANCIA HARBERTON

Historic Harberton dates from 1886, when missionary Thomas Bridges resigned from Ushuaia's Anglican mission to settle at his new *estancia* at Downeast, later renamed for the Devonshire hometown of his wife Mary Ann Varder. Thomas Bridges, of course, was the author of the famous English–Yámana dictionary, and their son Lucas continued the family literary tradition with *The Uttermost Part of the Earth,* an extraordinary memoir of a boyhood and life among the indigenous Yámana and Ona (Selknam).

Harberton continues to be a family enterprise—its present manager and part-owner, Tommy Goodall, is Thomas Bridges' greatgrandson. While the wool industry that spawned it has declined in recent years, the *estancia* (which still has about 1,000 cattle) has opened its doors to organized English- and Spanish-language tours of its grounds and outbuildings; these include the family cemetery, flower gardens, woolshed, woodshop, boathouse, and a native botanical garden whose Yámana-style lean-tos are far more realistic than their Disneyfied counterparts along the Ferrocarril Austral Fueguino tourist train. Photographs in the woolshed illustrate the process of cutting firewood with axes and transporting it by raft and oxcart, and the tasks of gathering and shearing sheep.

In addition, American biologist Rae Natalie Prosser (Tommy Goodall's wife) has created the **Museo Acatushún de Aves y Mamíferos Marinos Australes** (www.acatushun.com, 10 A.M.–7 P.M. daily mid-Oct.–mid-Apr., US$3 pp), a bone museum stressing the region's marine mammals but also seabirds and a few shorebirds. It's also possible to visit Magellanic penguin rookeries at Isla Martillo (Yecapasela) with Piratour for US$18 per person; a small colony of gentoo penguins has established itself on the island, making this a more intriguing trip for those who've seen Magellanic penguins elsewhere.

Estancia Harberton (contact Alejandro Galeazzi, tel. 02901/423123 in Ushuaia, alejandrogaleazzi@speedy.com.ar, ngoodall@tierradelfuego.org.ar, www.estanciaharberton.com) is 85 kilometers east of Ushuaia via paved RN 3 and gravel RC-j, but work has stopped on a new coastal road from Ushuaia that would shorten the distance. Mid-October–mid-April, the *estancia* is open for guided tours (US$7 pp) 10 A.M.–7 P.M. daily except Christmas, New Year's Day, and Easter. Because of Harberton's isolation, there is no telephone, and email communications—which require a trip to Ushuaia—can be slow.

With written permission, free **camping** is permitted at unimproved sites; the *estancia* has also remodeled the former cookhouse (two rooms with 4–5 beds each and shared bath, US$70–90 pp) and shepherds' house (two rooms of three beds with private bath, US$90–110 pp). Dinner or lunch costs an additional US$30 pp.

Harberton's teahouse **Mánacatush** serves a three-course lunch without drinks for US$30. A separate afternoon tea (US$7 pp) is offered for nonguests, with a four-guest minimum. Its restaurant **Parrilla Acawaia** serves clients on the penguin tour.

In summer, several companies provide round-trip transportation from Ushuaia (around US$40 pp), but services change frequently. From Ushuaia's Muelle Turístico, **Piratour** (tel. 02901/15-604646, www.piratour.com.ar) offers a US$70 package with overland transportation and a visit to the penguin colony.

Catamaran tours from Ushuaia are more expensive and spend less time at Harberton but do include the farm-tour fee.

Parque Nacional Tierra del Fuego

For pilgrims to the uttermost part of the earth, Mecca is Parque Nacional Tierra del Fuego's Bahía Lapataia, where RN 3 ends on the Beagle Channel's north shore. It's a worthy goal, but, sadly, most visitors see only the area in and around the highway because most of the park's mountainous interior, with its alpine lakes, limpid rivers, blue-tinged glaciers, and jagged summits, is closed to public access.

GEOGRAPHY AND CLIMATE

About 18 kilometers west of Ushuaia, Parque Nacional Tierra del Fuego hugs the Chilean border as its 63,000 hectares stretch from the Beagle Channel north across Lago Fagnano (Kami). Elevations range from sea level on the channel to 1,450 meters on the summit of Monte Vinciguerra.

The park has a maritime climate, with frequent high winds. Rainfall is moderate, about 750 millimeters per year, but humidity is high, as cool temperatures inhibit evapotranspiration—the summer average is only about 10°C. The record maximum temperature is 31°C, while the minimum is a fairly mild -12°C. At sea level, snow rarely sticks, but higher elevations have permanent snowfields and glaciers.

FLORA AND FAUNA

As in southernmost Chile, thick southern beech forests cover the Argentine sector of Tierra del Fuego. Along the coast, the deciduous *lenga (Nothofagus pumilio)* and the Magellanic evergreen *coigüe (Nothofagus betuloides)* are the main tree species; at higher elevations, the stunted, deciduous *ñirre (Nothofagus antarctica)* forms nearly pure stands. In some low-lying areas, where cool annual temperatures inhibit complete decomposition, dead plant material compresses into *sphagnum* peat bogs with a cover of ferns and other moisture-loving plants; the insectivorous *Drosera uniflora* swallows unsuspecting bugs.

Until recently Argentina's only coastal national park, Parque Nacional Tierra del Fuego has a seashore protected by thick kelp beds that serve as incubators for fish fry. Especially around Bahía Ensenada and Bahía Lapataia, the shoreline and inshore waters swarm with cormorants, grebes, gulls, kelp geese, oystercatchers, flightless and flying steamer ducks, snowy sheathbills, and terns. The maritime black-browed albatross skims the Beagle's waters, while the Andean condor sometimes soars overhead. Marine mammals, mostly sea lions but also fur seals and elephant seals, cavort in the ocean. The rare southern sea otter *(Lutra felina)* may exist here.

Inland areas are fauna-poor, though foxes and guanacos are present in small numbers. The most conspicuous mammals are the European rabbit and the Canadian beaver, both of which were introduced for their pelts but have proved to be pests.

◖ GLACIAR MARTIAL

Technically within park boundaries but also within walking distance of Ushuaia, the Glaciar Martial is the area's best single hike, offering expansive views of the Beagle Channel and across to the jagged peaks of Chile's Isla Navarino. Reached not by RN 3 but rather by the zigzag Camino al Glaciar (also known as Luis Martial) that climbs northwest out of town, the trailhead begins at the Aerosilla del Glaciar, the ski area's chairlift, which operates 9 A.M.–7 P.M. daily. The 1.2-kilometer chairlift (US$6 pp) reduces the two-hour climb to the foot of the glacier by half. In summer there are occasional buses to the lift (US$4 r/t) with Pasarela, Eben Ezer, and Bellavista, leaving from the corner of Avenida Maipú and 25 de Mayo, 9 A.M.–9 P.M. Though easy to follow, the trail—especially the middle segment—is steep, and the descent requires particular caution because of loose rocks and soil. There is no admission charge to this sector.

OTHER SIGHTS AND ACTIVITIES

Where freshwater Lago Roca drains into the sea at Bahía Lapataia, the park's main sector has several short nature trails and a handful of longer ones; most of the backcountry is off-limits to casual hikers. Slightly less than one kilometer long, the **Senda Laguna Negra** uses a boardwalk to negotiate boggy terrain studded with ferns, wildflowers, and other water-tolerant species. The 400-meter **Senda de los Castores** (Beaver Trail) winds among southern beeches gnawed to death to form dams and ponds where the beavers themselves occasionally peek out of their dens.

The five-kilometer **Senda Hito XXIV** follows Lago Roca's northeastern shore to a small obelisk that marks the Chilean border. If, someday, Argentine and Chilean authorities can get it together, this would be an ideal entry point to Estancia Yendegaia's wild backcountry, but at present it's illegal to continue beyond the marker. From a junction about one kilometer up the Hito XXIV trail, **Senda Cerro Guanaco** climbs four kilometers northeast up the Arroyo Guanaco to its namesake peak's 970-meter summit.

From Bahía Ensenada, near the park's southeastern edge, there are boat shuttles to **Isla Redonda** (10 A.M.–5:30 P.M., US$27 pp).

PRACTICALITIES
Accommodations and Food

Camping is the only option in the park itself, where there are free sites with little or no infrastructure at **Camping Ensenada, Camping Río Pipo, Camping Las Bandurrias, Camping Laguna Verde,** and **Camping Los Cauquenes.** While these are improving, they're less tidy than the commercial **Camping Lago Roca** (tel. 02901/433313, lagoroca@speedy.com.ar, US$4 pp), which has hot showers, a grocery, and the restaurant *confitería* **La Cabaña del Bosque.**

Information

At the park entrance on RN 3, the APN has a Centro de Información where it collects a US$14 pp entry fee. Argentine residents pay half.

Several books have useful information on the park, including William Leitch's *South America's National Parks* (Seattle: The Mountaineers, 1990), which is now out of print. Two good hiking guides are the fifth edition of Tim Burford's *Backpacking in Chile & Argentina* (Bradt Publications, 2001); and the third edition of Clem Lindenmayer and Nick Tapp's *Trekking in the Patagonian Andes* (Lonely Planet, 2003, overdue for an update), but locals criticize the latter vociferously.

Birders may want to acquire Claudio Venegas Canelo's *Aves de Patagonia y Tierra del Fuego Chileno-Argentina,* Ricardo Clark's *Aves de Tierra del Fuego y Cabo de Hornos* (Buenos Aires: Literature of Latin America, 1986), or Enrique Couve and Claudio Vidal Ojeda's bilingual *Birds of the Beagle Channel* (Punta Arenas: Fantástico Sur Birding & Nature, 2000).

Getting There and Around

The transportation details provided for Ushuaia apply to the park as well.

SOUTHERN PATAGONIA

THE CHILEAN PACIFIC ISLANDS

By quirks of geography and history, Chile possesses two of the world's most fascinating island outposts: the Juan Fernández archipelago, several hundred kilometers off the coast of Valparaíso, and Easter Island (known to its Polynesian islanders as Rapa Nui), in the vast subtropical Pacific. Administratively, both belong to Region V (Valparaíso), but geographically and culturally they are worlds apart.

Chile annexed Easter Island, the most remote inhabited piece of land on the globe, in the late 19th century. It is a UNESCO World Heritage Site for the stunning stone statues that have become global icons.

Rarely visited and even less appreciated by either Chileans or foreigners, the Juan Fernández archipelago has become a UNESCO World Biosphere Reserve mainly for its singular flora, but it gained global fame in the early 18th century when the Scotsman Alexander Selkirk—by consensus, the *real* Robinson Crusoe—returned to Britain after spending four solitary years on what, then, was an uninhabited island.

PLANNING YOUR TIME

The Juan Fernández archipelago and Easter Island are different places, but they have their remoteness and inaccessibility in common; together they make a rare and unforgettable mix. The former, though closer to the South American continent, presents greater logistical challenges.

Small planes fly regularly to Isla Robinson Crusoe, the Juan Fernández group's main destination, where the village of San Juan Bautista

© WAYNE BERNHARDSON

HIGHLIGHTS

(Museo Antropológico Padre Sebastián Englert: Despite some faults, Hanga Roa's museum bridges the gap between archaeology and ethnology (page 572).

(Parque Nacional Rapa Nui: In the entire world, it's not just the best of its kind, it's the *only* one of its kind (page 581).

(San Juan Bautista: Even if a handful of unnecessary automobiles and motorcycles now scoot along its few streets, this friendly village remains the staging point for most hikes into Parque Nacional Juan Fernández (page 589).

(Mirador de Selkirk: From this saddle atop the Cordillera de Chiflones, hikers can enjoy the vast Pacific views that brought the real "Robinson Crusoe" to the point of despair (page 594).

(Bahía Tierras Blancas: Just a short descent from the island's airstrip, this is the place to meet the endemic Juan Fernández fur seal up close and personal (page 595).

LOOK FOR **(** TO FIND RECOMMENDED SIGHTS, ACTIVITIES, DINING, AND LODGING.

is the base for exploring Parque Nacional Juan Fernández. A minimum of three full days would allow for exploring the village and vicinity, hiking to Selkirk's lookout, and even hiring a launch to circumnavigate the island. At the same time, visitors need to appreciate that flight schedules from Santiago can be hard to keep because of changeable weather, and it's sometimes necessary to stay an extra day or more (which, of course, requires more money on an island with no bank or other formal exchange facilities). There's plenty to do, but bad weather can also reduce access to parts of the park.

Visiting the even more remote Isla Alejandro Selkirk, a full-day's sail to the west, is so logistically complex that it might be considered a true expedition. While there's regular if infrequent boat service, and fishermen will also carry passengers when they're looking for lobsters, the landing is difficult and supplies are few—visitors need to bring everything along. It's also possible to charter a boat, but this is very expensive. In sum, visiting Alejandro Selkirk is for adventurous travelers for whom time is no factor, and money only secondary.

THE CHILEAN PACIFIC ISLANDS

Rapa Núi (Easter Island)

More than 1,000 years ago, some of history's most truly intrepid travelers sailed east on Polynesian outriggers to the Pacific's most remote outpost, where their descendants carved colossal *moai* from volcanic quarries, transported them over rugged terrain without the wheel and without damage, and hoisted them onto massive platforms known as *ahu*. It's still possible to reach Easter Island by boat—freighter, anyway—but almost everyone nowadays prefers the five-hour flight from Santiago in order to spend more time wandering among the world-famous monuments.

The world's most isolated inhabited place—the next closest settlement is more than 1,900 kilometers to the west—Rapa Nui acquired its English name indirectly through Dutchman Jacob Roggeveen, the first European to see the island. Sighting land on Easter Sunday, April 5, 1772, he named it for the date after the custom of his era, and his designation spread to every European language.

Chileans commonly refer to the island as Isla de Pascua, but there is a broad consensus for using indigenous Polynesian terminology whenever possible with regard to territory, ethnology, and linguistics. Within this consensus, though, there are conflicting opinions about usage of the terms "Rapa Nui," which some consider a European invention, and "Rapanui," which is closer to other Polynesian languages. This book uses "Rapa Nui" to describe the territory and "Rapanui" for the islanders and their language.

GEOGRAPHY AND CLIMATE

Only a few degrees south of the Tropic of Capricorn, oceanic Rapa Nui is one of a handful of islands to emerge from a submarine volcanic chain that stretches west from the Chilean mainland; the others, with no permanent inhabitants, are San Félix, San Ambrosio, and Sala y Gómez. The closest populated land is Pitcairn Island, 1,900 kilometers west, beyond which are the Polynesian outposts of the Mangarevas or Gambier Islands (2,500 kilometers west) and the Marquesas Islands (3,200 kilometers northwest).

Even farther from the Chilean coast—about 3,700 kilometers west of the mainland port of Caldera—Rapa Nui consists of lava flows from three distinct cones that fused to form a triangular landmass of just 171 square kilometers, resting on a subterranean platform that plunges abruptly into the depths of the Pacific. It is nowhere longer than 24 kilometers and nowhere wider than 12 kilometers.

All these volcanoes are dormant; the most recent eruption, at the northerly 507-meter Maunga Terevaka, occurred 10,000 years ago. The water-filled, 410-meter crater of Rano Kau, to the southwest, and the 400-meter Pu A Katiki are both nearly three million years old, with their last eruptions more than 180,000 years ago.

standing *moai* at Rano Raraku, Parque Nacional Rapa Nui

© WAYNE BERNHARDSON

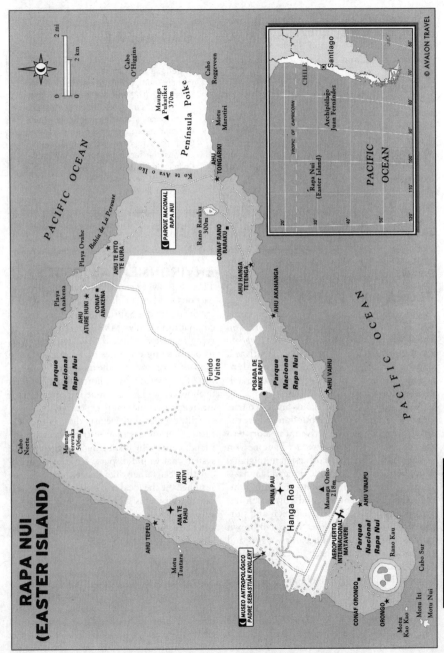

RAPA NUI (EASTER ISLAND)

THE CHILEAN PACIFIC ISLANDS

PACIFIC OCEAN

Cabo O'Higgins

Cabo Roggeveen

Maunga Pukatikei 370m

Península Poike

Motu Marotiri

Ko te Ava o Iko

AHU TONGARIKI

PARQUE NACIONAL RAPA NUI

Rano Raraku 300m

CONAF RANO RARAKU

AHU HANGA TETENGA

AHU AKAHANGA

AHU VAIHU

Playa Ovahe

Bahía de La Perouse

Playa Anakena

AHU TE PITO TE KURA

CONAF ANAKENA

AHU ATURE HUKI

Fundo Vaitea

POSADA DE MIKE RAPU

Parque Nacional Rapa Nui

Cabo Norte

Maunga Terevaka 500m

Parque Nacional Rapa Nui

AHU AKIVI

PUNA PAU

ANA TE PAHU

AHU TEPEU

Motu Tautara

Hanga Roa

MUSEO ANTROPOLÓGICO PADRE SEBASTIÁN ENGLERT

Maunga Orito 218m

AHU VINAPU

AEROPUERTO INTERNACIONAL MATAVERI

Parque Nacional Rapa Nui

Rano Kau

CONAF ORONGO

ORONGO

Cabo Sur

Motu Iti

Motu Nui

Motu Kao Kao

PACIFIC OCEAN

PACIFIC OCEAN

CHILE

Santiago

TROPIC OF CAPRICORN

Archipiélago Juan Fernández

Rapa Nui (Easter Island)

© AVALON TRAVEL

0 2 mi

0 2 km

THE CHILEAN PACIFIC ISLANDS

In addition to these major craters, there are several smaller but significant craters and other volcanic landforms, including sprawling surface lava fields and subterranean tubes that extend for considerable distances. Much of the island's perimeter consists of rugged headlands, with no truly sheltered anchorages and only a few sandy beaches. There are no surface streams, as rainfall percolates quickly into the porous terrain, but a few areas have sufficient soil for horticulture.

As a subtropical oceanic island, Rapa Nui experiences relatively minor seasonal variations—the mean summer maximum temperature is 27.3°C, the mean winter minimum 15.5°C, and the annual average 20.7°C. The average annual precipitation is 1,126 millimeters; most rain falls between late autumn and early spring, but cloudbursts can occur at any time of year.

FLORA AND FAUNA

Hundreds of years of human occupation have totally transformed Rapa Nui's flora and fauna; where native forests of *toromiro (Sophora toromiro)* and stands of palms once flourished, dense plantations of introduced eucalyptus now cover the slopes of Rano Kau crater. Grasses cover most of the hillsides.

Most remote oceanic islands are, of course, flora- and fauna-poor. Abundant when the first Polynesian settlers arrived, the sooty tern *(Sterna fuscata)* survives in reduced numbers on offshore islets. The first Polynesian immigrants brought their own domestic flora and fauna—crops such as the sweet potato and edible animals such as the chicken and Polynesian rat. Europeans brought both accidental and purposeful introductions—the Norway or brown rat that hitched a lift on oceanic voyages and the horses, cattle, and sheep that they brought as economic domesticates.

There is a good synopsis of Rapa Nui's native and introduced flora and their uses—both horticultural and medicinal—in Conaf's well-illustrated *Vegetación de Rapa Nui: Historia y Uso Tradicional* (1996), by Marcos Rauch, Patricia Ibáñez, and José Miguel Ramírez. Available

---

BUG ALERT

It's not cause for panic, but an outbreak of dengue fever, probably arrived from French Tahiti, occurred on Easter Island in early 2002, and there were 25 confirmed cases in 2008 (but no deaths, and no instances of the deadlier dengue hemorrhagic fever). Long-sleeved shirts and long trousers, or else appropriate applications of insect repellent, are advisable. Chilean health authorities are undertaking measures to eradicate the white-spotted mosquito vector.

---

from Conaf both here and in Santiago, it costs US$5.

ENVIRONMENTAL ISSUES

There is growing concern about tourism's impact on the island's cultural resources and quality of life, and a Santiago consulting firm is conducting a study of the island's tourist "carrying capacity." While the evaluation appears to be focusing on issues of water, land, and food, water is probably the most important factor—few people rely on horticulture for their livelihoods, and food can be imported even if air freight becomes more expensive.

Still, the possibility exists that, in the near future, authorities may restrict access to the island, perhaps by instituting a staggered price system that would disperse business throughout the year rather than concentrate it in the summer. At the local end, relative affluence is causing problems such as the proliferation of automobiles, with their associated pollution, and the accumulation of solid waste on an island with little land to spare.

HISTORY

Rapa Nui's dramatically improbable *moai* have attracted global attention, and deservedly so—their iconic appeal is undeniable, and to contemplate how such an isolated people could create them and, without benefit of the wheel or draft animals, transport them across rugged terrain and erect them on massive platforms excites the imagination. These matters, though, often distract visitors from even bigger but ultimately related questions—the regularity and direction of cultural contacts across the Pacific, how and when the first immigrants arrived at this remote speck of land, and how an apparent handful of people created a society with monuments that seem far likelier in empires with millions of inhabitants.

The peopling of the Pacific is a complex topic, and its relationship to the Americas even more complex. In the remote past, as humans spread out of Africa to inhabit Europe and Asia, they eventually reached North America via a land bridge across the Bering Strait before dispersing throughout the Caribbean and South America; by at least 12,000 years ago, when melting continental glaciers and rising seas closed the land bridge, humans had occupied the entire Western Hemisphere, even if their density was low. Over succeeding millennia, societies and civilizations in the Eastern and Western Hemispheres developed in geographical isolation.

Columbus's voyages across the Atlantic ended this isolation forever, though the isolation had never been complete. Vikings had reached Greenland and Labrador around the end of the first millennium A.D., but Polynesians may have reached South America even earlier. Or vice-versa, according to speculations by the likes of Norwegian adventurer Thor Heyerdahl, who claimed pre-Columbian South Americans sailed west to Polynesia.

In this larger context, Rapa Nui fits into the long-standing academic controversy between advocates of "independent invention," who emphasize the parallel development of cultures separated by the oceans, and adherents of "diffusionism," who argue the importance of pre-Columbian contacts. As in many academic debates, there are political overtones, as diffusionists often stand accused of disparaging the ostensibly derivative achievements of New World peoples.

In 1947, on his famous *Kon-Tiki* raft voyage, Heyerdahl proved it possible to sail west from

South America to Polynesia with the help of prevailing currents. Still, he never really proved that was how it happened; the pre-Columbian sailing tradition in the Americas, although it covered distances as great as those from Peru to Mexico, was primarily coastal. Still, there is material evidence of movement in both directions—key economic plants, most notably the tropical coconut and sweet potato (the latter an American domesticate), were present in both hemispheres in pre-Columbian times.

It is likelier that, with their elaborate seafaring tradition, Polynesian islanders reached Rapa Nui first (though it's conceivable they did so *after* crossing the Pacific to Peru). What seems clear is that voyages across the Pacific, in spacious double outriggers capable of carrying food, water, and domestic animals, took place on a basis of knowledge and skill. They were not fortuitous—trans-Pacific sailors were unlikely to have survived a long voyage for which they had not planned. By observing currents, winds, clouds, and the flight patterns of birds, they could often infer the existence of land at great distances.

The Peopling of Rapa Nui
Besides the diffusionism controversy, in which Rapa Nui plays a part because of its geographical position as the most easterly inhabited point for voyages from Polynesia and the most westerly for voyages from South America, the other great issue in local history is population. While it may not be immediately obvious, it directly touches the creation and destruction of the *moai*.

According to oral tradition, Rapa Nui received two waves of immigration starting around the 5th century A.D., though the first material evidence is far more recent, about A.D. 800. Playa Anakena, the north shore's sandy beach, was the ostensible landing place of Hotu Matua, leader of the eastern *hanau eepe,* while the *hanau momoko* arrived from the west. Many accounts portray these warring groups as "Long Ears" and "Short Ears," because of the practice of earlobe elongation, but this is the result of Heyerdahl's erroneous translation of terminology that, according to Georgia Lee, would more correctly be "corpulent people" and "thin people."

In the aftermath of internal and external conflicts that nearly annihilated the population by the mid-19th century, oral testimony passed through a handful of survivors is, to say the least, an imprecise means of tracking local history. What seems clear, though, is that a growing population led to a remarkably complex and specialized society that produced the great monuments but which, when its limited land and sea base could support no further growth, disintegrated into a series of clan-based resource conflicts.

In its early centuries, Rapa Nui was a thinly populated island with a redistributive economy, but as the population grew its *akiri* (kings) and priests presided over a society where artisans fashioned the enormous *moai* and commoners performed the dangerously laborious process of moving the megaliths to the imposing *ahu* (altars or platforms) on which they would stand. This consumed enormous amounts of resources, including food and forests, until shortages ignited a series of wars; by A.D. 1600 or so, these conflicts had divided the island, toppled many of the *moai* that symbolically represented the lineages, and even degenerated into ritual cannibalism. In a situation that many modern scientists might interpret as a classic imbalance between population and resources, the society seen by the first Europeans was a precarious one, and things would get far worse before getting better.

The European Voyages

For more than two centuries after Magellan's global circumnavigation, Rapa Nui remained unknown to Europeans. Then, on Easter Sunday of April 1722, Dutch admiral Jacob Roggeveen's expedition became the first Europeans to sight and set foot on the island. Roggeveen's crew arrived, apparently, at a time of relative peace and prosperity; one member, Carl Behrens, published an account in which he remarked on the productive gardens, noted the *moai* and the religious ceremonies

associated with them, and described islanders' appearance in detail. In 1770, claiming the island for Spain, the expedition of Felipe González de Haedo made similar observations, noting abundant produce and the presence of cave dwellings and *hare paenga,* the boat-shaped houses whose foundations are still visible today.

The most noteworthy European voyage, though, was that of the famous Englishman, Captain James Cook, in 1774. Cook's familiarity with Polynesia made him the first European to link the Rapanui explicitly to the rest of Oceania, and he was also the first to report damaged *ahu,* toppled, broken *moai,* and a ragged populace that bore the scars of conflict. He also remarked that the *moai* seemed to have lost their ritual significance, perhaps an indicator of the transition from a lineage-based tradition of ancestor worship to the Tangata Manu (birdman) cult of the creator Makemake.

While Cook's reports contrasted with the apparent stability, harmony, and prosperity seen by the Roggeveen and González expeditions, in all likelihood neither of the earlier voyages provided a thorough assessment. Later visits, by the Frenchman Jean François de Gallup, Comte de la Perouse, in 1786, and by the Russian ship *Neva* under Yuri Lisiansky in the early 19th century, present contradictory visions, suggesting that the fortunes of the islanders, in peace and war, ebbed and flowed. As frictions periodically intensified, *moai* were toppled and broken, and only a handful remained standing. Even before the indigenous population felt the full impact of imperialism and colonialism, the population had declined rapidly from a maximum that may have reached 20,000 (though most estimates are lower).

Contact, Conflict, and Chileanization

Rapidly expanding commercial activities— first whaling, then the systematic planting of tropical crops such as coffee, copra, rubber, and sugar—transformed the Pacific by the mid-19th century. While Rapa Nui, with its limited agricultural potential, did not experience this transformation immediately, the population suffered a major Peruvian slave raid and subsequent forced emigration that, when it did not kill the individuals either abducted or forced into signing one-sided labor contracts, disrupted local society and separated them from their kin. The arrival of missionaries, and of European diseases to which locals had little or no natural immunity, subjected the island to a simultaneous cultural and biological assault.

Nearly 1,000 Rapanui, many of them royalty and priests, may have died as a result of the 1862 Peruvian raid, which transported them to the South American mainland to become indentured servants. By the time Catholic missionaries settled permanently, in 1866, perhaps only a few hundred Rapanui remained on the island itself.

While the Rapanui remained politically autonomous for some years more, commercial and ecological exploitation arrived by 1870, in the person of Jean-Baptiste Dutroux-Bornier, a French sailor who took advantage of the nearly depopulated island to graze sheep at Mataveri, site of the present-day airport. Dutroux-Bornier seemingly planned to declare himself sovereign of his own mini-kingdom, expelling the islanders to Tahiti; the missionaries, to their credit, opposed his plans, but they were unable to prevent a violent deportation that left only about 100 residents on the island.

Dutroux-Bornier died at the hands of the remaining Rapanui in 1877, but by 1888 naval officer Policarpo Toro had annexed the island for Chile. While Chile may have been flexing its naval muscle in the aftermath of the War of the Pacific (1879–1884), it really had no clear intentions for Rapa Nui and finally leased the island to Valparaíso merchant Enrique Merlet, who continued to graze sheep for wool. Merlet in turn sold out to the Valparaíso-based Williamson, Balfour & Company, the Chilean subsidiary of a British-held company, whose Compañía Explotadora de la Isla de Pascua (Cedip) was the de facto sovereign from 1888 to 1952.

As the population recovered from the 19th-century demographic catastrophe, it became, despite its Polynesian heritage, a polyglot mix of South Pacific, European, and Asian peoples dramatically different, at least in the strictest genetic sense, from its predecessors. The paternalistic Cedip regime continued until 1953, when the Chilean navy assumed control, marking Rapa Nui's definitive incorporation into the modern state.

The Modernization of Rapa Nui

Rapa Nui was a de facto naval base into the 1960s, but an event that would change the island forever occurred in 1951, when Roberto Parragué Singer flew the *Manutara* from the Norte Chico city of La Serena to Hanga Roa in 20 hours—the first flight ever from the continent. By 1967, the new Aeropuerto Mataveri became a refueling depot on the first-ever commercial flight from Santiago to Papeete, definitively incorporating the island into the Chilean—and international—political and economic orbit.

These dramatic developments, and the navy's withdrawal from administration, addressed a variety of local issues: Islanders could now travel, vote, and have a voice in local and national matters—in Rapanui (whose usage had been suppressed) as well as Spanish. The Christian Democrat administration of President Eduardo Frei Montalva (1964–1970) paid greater attention than ever to islanders' concerns, including education, medical care, and infrastructure projects such as electrical power, potable water, and roads.

Even during the Pinochet dictatorship, improvements continued, but since the return to democracy islanders have become even more outspoken—and prosperous. At the same time they have argued vigorously for return of ancestral lands on an island where, for many decades, their residence was confined to a small area in and around Hanga Roa.

Many Rapanui have taken advantage of other opportunities. Some have traveled to the mainland and around the world for education, while others have remained to profit from the tourist trade. According to some statistics, every year upward of 20,000 tourists now visit the island, only five hours by jet from Santiago.

GOVERNMENT AND POLITICS

While Rapa Nui is administratively subject to Region V (Valparaíso), with a governor (usually a local) appointed from Santiago, it is also a separate municipality with an elected mayor.

The current local administration distrusts both the central and regional governments, resents the inability to raise revenue locally, and argues that islanders should have autonomy within the Chilean state. Dissenters, though, argue that recognition as a separate people means second-class citizenship. Land rights also continue to be a hot issue, as some oppose government "grants" on the rationale that Chile cannot give away what it never rightfully acquired.

ECONOMY

Tourism, having grown by 20 percent over the past decade, is the backbone of the economy. While the numbers may not seem impressive by global standards, more than 24,000 tourists saw the island in 2004—nearly seven times the local population. Europeans, mostly French, German, British and Italian, account for about half the visitors; the French figures may be misleading, since many of them are Tahitian residents on long weekends. U.S. citizens compose about 10 percent of the total, and mainland Chileans about 20 percent.

Tourism is making some people wealthy—the symbols of affluence, such as automobiles, color TVs, and computers are becoming abundant. Many who do not rely directly on the tourist trade—by providing accommodations, serving meals, and renting cars, for instance—still depend on it indirectly; gardeners, for instance, grow fruit and vegetables, ranchers raise sheep and cattle, and fisherfolk net fish and trap lobster.

Still, many services depend on government subsidies, and the island has a substantial bureaucracy. Ironically, many locals depend on central government for their employment.

PEOPLE

Almost all of Rapa Nui's 3,791 residents live in Hanga Roa, the island's only town. More than two-thirds can claim Polynesian ancestry, but many Rapanui also live in mainland Chile and overseas. At the same time, nearly 200 mainland Chileans settle on the island every year, straining its health, education, and social services.

HANGA ROA

On Rapa Nui's eastern shore, the island's only town is the base for all visitors. Most spend several days exploring the island on foot, bicycle, horseback, or by car. The more adventurous can take their chances surfing (there are good breaks even in town despite the lack of sandy beaches) or diving.

Orientation

Sprawling Hanga Roa has street names painted on most curbs, but these fade fast in the subtropical sun. There is no numbering system for houses or any other buildings—all of them are s/n (*sin número,* without a number)—so consult the map when in doubt. Even the map can be deceptive, as most hotels, *residenciales,* and other businesses lack identifying signs. For orientation, locals often refer to landmarks such as the airport, the church, the *Feria Municipal* (Municipal Market), the *Gobernación* (Government Offices), and the harbor at Caleta Hanga Roa.

Sights

Except for **Ahu Tautira** and **Ahu Tahai** (for both see *Parque Nacional Rapa Nui*), **Ahu Vai Uri,** and **Ahu Akapu,** Hanga Roa proper has only a handful of typical tourist sights. Its vigorous village life is a very real if intangible asset, though; one of its foci is **Avenida Atamu Tekena.** At the corner of Atamu Tekena and Te Pito Te Henua, **Plaza Policarpo Toro** contains side-by-side busts of its namesake naval officer, who claimed the island for Chile in 1888, and of Atamu Tekena, who ostensibly ceded Rapanui sovereignty to the Chileans.

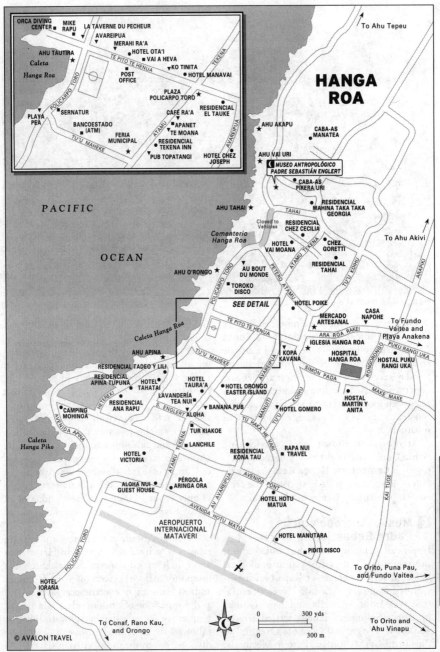

Detail (inset map):

ORCA DIVING CENTER
MIKE RAPU
LA TAVERNE DU PECHEUR
AVAREIPUA
MERAHI RA'A
HOTEL OTA'I
VAI A HEVA
KO TINITA
HOTEL MANAVAI
AHU TAUTIRA
Caleta Hanga Roa
TE PITO TE HENUA
TEKENA
POST OFFICE
PLAZA POLICARPO TORO
RESIDENCIAL EL TAUKE
PLAYA PEA
SERNATUR
CAFÉ RA'A
BANCOESTADO (ATM)
FERIA MUNICIPAL
APANET
TE MOANA
RESIDENCIAL TEKENA INN
PUB TOPATANGI
HOTEL CHEZ JOSEPH
POLICARPO TORO
TU'U MAHEKE
ATAMU
AVAREIPUA

Main map:

PACIFIC
OCEAN

HANGA ROA

To Ahu Tepeu

AHU AKAPU
CABA-AS MANATEA
AHU VAI URI
MUSEO ANTROPOLÓGICO PADRE SEBASTIÁN ENGLERT
CABA-AS PIKERA URI
RESIDENCIAL MAHINA TAKA TAKA GEORGIA
AHU TAHAI
TAHAI
RESIDENCIAL CHEZ CECILIA
CHEZ GORETTI
To Ahu Akivi
Cementerio Hanga Roa
Closed to Vehicles
HOTEL VAI MOANA
ATAMU TEKENA
RESIDENCIAL TAHAI
TU'U KOIHU
AHU O'RONGO
AU BOUT DU MONDE
TOROKO DISCO
SEE DETAIL
PETERO ATAMU
HOTEL POIKE
MERCADO ARTESANAL
CASA NAPOHE
ARAPIKI
POLICARPO TORO
TE PITO TE HENUA
TU'U MAHEKE
ARA ROA RAKEI
IGLESIA HANGA ROA
To Fundo Vaitea and Playa Anakena
Caleta Hanga Roa
AHU APINA
RESIDENCIAL TADEO Y LILI
RESIDENCIAL APINA TUPUNA
HOTEL TAHATAI
HOTEL TAURA'A
LAVANDERÍA TEA NUI
HOTEL ORONGO EASTER ISLAND
BANANA PUB
KOPÁ KAVANA
AVAREIPUA
HOSPITAL HANGA ROA
RONGORONGO
PUKU RANGI UKA
HOSTAL PUKU RANGI UKA
HETEREKI
S. ENGLERT
ALOHA
TUR KIAKOE
LANCHILE
CAMPING MOHINOA
RESIDENCIAL ANA RAPU
TU'U KOIHU
SIMÓN PAOA
MAKE MAKE
HOSTAL MARTÍN Y ANITA
AVENIDA APINA
Caleta Hanga Piko
HOTEL VICTORIA
ATAMU TEKENA
MANUTTI
TU HAKA HE VARI
RESIDENCIAL KONA TAU
RAPA NUI TRAVEL
KAI TUOE
ALOHA NUI GUEST HOUSE
PÉRGOLA ARINGA ORA
AVENIDA PONT
TU'U KOIHU
AVENIDA
HOTEL HOTU MATUA
AEROPUERTO INTERNACIONAL MATAVERI
AV. AVAREIPUA
AVENIDA HOTU MATUA
HOTEL MANUTARA
PIDITI DISCO
To Orito, Puna Pau, and Fundo Vaitea
POLICARPO TORO
HOTEL IORANA

© AVALON TRAVEL

To Conaf, Rano Kau, and Orongo

0   300 yds
0   300 m

To Orito and Ahu Vinapu

© WAYNE BERNHARDSON

Hanga Roa from the air

On a rise at the eastern end of Te Pito Te Henua, the **Iglesia Parroquial de la Santa Cruz** (Tu'u Koihu s/n) is the island's Catholic church and a focus of the colorful Easter Sunday services, when the priest arrives and departs on horseback. Its airy interior is decorated with spectacular carved wooden statues, a syncretic vision of Christianity and indigenous spirituality.

At the north end of town, overlooking Bahía Cook, artificial flowers festoon headstones at **Cementerio Hanga Roa,** the mostly Polynesian cemetery. At Eastertime, the cemetery is particularly vivid with decorations.

◖ Museo Antropológico Padre Sebastián Englert

Improved in many ways, but not without shortcomings, Hanga Roa's anthropological museum sets the stage for Rapa Nui by dividing the South Pacific into "Near Oceania" (the area from Australia and New Guinea up to the Solomon Islands), settled around 40,000 years ago, and "Remote Oceania" to the northeast (Micronesia, Eastern Melanesia,

and Polynesia), colonized from about 2000 B.C. to A.D. 1000.

Its displays provide valuable information on island geography, traditional navigation in the Pacific, immigration and population, the island's half-dozen *mata* or tribes (which later became 10), religion and the *moai,* subsistence activities (mainly fishing and horticulture), the birdman cult, body decoration (tattoos) and clothing, and rock art. There are also wood carvings, *rongorongo* tablets, weapons, and a case full of stone tools. Among the more unusual items are a female *moai,* one of only about 10 found on the island, and an eye of a *moai* made of white coral and volcanic scoria.

Its name a tribute to the Catholic priest and scholar who lived many years in Hanga Roa and who is buried just outside the church, the museum's major shortcoming is its failure to address historical or contemporary topics such as the imposition of Chilean rule, the impact of tourism, or even the demographic decline that followed the arrival of Europeans and their diseases, not to mention Peruvian slavers. On the other hand, the important Mulloy library has recently moved here from Viña del Mar's Museo Fonck.

Midway between Ahu Tahai and Ahu Akapu, the Museo Antropológico (tel. 032/2551020, www.museorapanui.cl) is open Tuesday–Friday 9:30 A.M.–12:30 P.M. and 2–5:30 P.M., weekends and holidays 9:30 A.M.–12:30 P.M. only. Admission costs US$1.75 for adults, half that for children 8–18, and is free to children under eight years old.

Recreation

There are two diving operations at Caleta Hanga Roa: the **Mike Rapu Diving Center** (www.mikerapu.cl, tel. 032/2551055) and the **Orca Diving Center** (tel. 032/2550375 or 032/2550877, www.seemorca.cl). Diving excursions cost in the US$50–65 per person range.

Caleta Hanga Roa is also the island's best surf site, busiest on weekends when local surfers line up for waves.

Cabalgatas Pantu (tel. 032/2100577, www.rapanuiturismopantu.cl) organizes horseback excursions, mostly half- and full-day, but there's also one overnight option that includes camping and a cookout.

ISLAND EVENTS

The island's biggest major annual event is early February's **Tapati Rapa Nui,** a ten-day cultural celebration that resembles the Heiva of French Polynesia. March 19's **Día de San José** commemorates the Catholic saint.

It's briefer than Tapati Rapa Nui, but **Semana Santa** (Holy Week) is crowned by Easter Sunday, when the Rapanui fill the church to overflowing to acknowledge the Christian holiday that gave the island its Europeanized identity.

June 21's **Ceremonia Culto al Sol** observes the winter solstice. In late November, **Día de la Lengua Rapanui** promotes the Polynesian linguistic heritage.

Entertainment

Hanga Roa has a pair of discos, both of which stay open very late on weekends. You can hear the lively, youthful **Toroko** (Policarpo Toro s/n), near Ahu O'rongo, from far off; near the airport, **Piditi** (Av. Hotu Matua s/n) draws a more mature public.

Bars include the **Banana Pub** (Atamu Tekena s/n), which sometimes features live music; **Pub Topatangi** (Atamu Tekena s/n, tel. 032/2551694), which has live music Thursday–Sunday evenings; **Aloha** (Atamu Tekena s/n, tel. 032/2551383); and **Mahatu Pub** (Te Pito Te Henua s/n), near Caleta Hanga Roa.

Now lighted, the soccer field at the corner of Policarpo Toro and Te Pito Te Henua is the site of spirited Sunday matches.

Shopping

The most popular souvenirs are carved replicas of *moai* (in both stone and wood), and of *moai kavakava* and *rongorongo* tablets (both in wood). The level of workmanship varies but can be remarkably high. Numerous souvenir shops line Atamu Tekena and Te Pito Te Henua, occupy the lobbies of the best hotels, and fill the departure lounge at Mataveri.

For size and variety, the best outlet is the **Mercado Artesanal** (Tuukoihu and Ara Roa Rakei), across from the church; the **Feria Municipal** (Atamu Tekena and Tuumaheke) is a distant second.

At the Museo Antropológico, the **Museum Store** (tel. 032/2551020) carries books and jewelry. Profits from the locally run souvenir shop **Vai a Heva** (Atamu Tekena s/n) go to a scholarship fund operated by the nonprofit Easter Island Foundation.

With sufficient notice, it's possible to hire a carver to create a custom stone *moai* and have it packed for shipping. The Sernatur office on Policarpo Toro can put you in touch with the carvers, who are tough negotiators.

Accommodations

Compared with other Polynesian islands, Rapa Nui is a bargain, but price levels are higher than most of mainland Chile. With over 600 rooms and more than 1,300 beds, accommodations are abundant for such a small place, so reservations are generally unnecessary except during the summer peak, particularly during the Tapati festival. Polynesian hospitality is the norm, but some places are substantially better than others. While several hotels are near the airport, the infrequent air traffic—one or two flights a day—is rarely disruptive.

For passengers lacking reservations, finding a first night's lodging is a more orderly process than it once was, since the airport arrival area now features a series of booths for each hotel or *hostal*. All provide transport into town, a welcome service in sprawling Hanga Roa. Nearly all include breakfast and private bath, and some offer additional meals, but full board is not recommended for anyone exploring the more distant archaeological sites—it can be a nuisance to have to return to Hanga Roa for lunch. Also, while Hanga Roa may not be a gourmet ghetto, its independent restaurants are outstanding for a community of its size.

Camping: At Caleta Hanga Piko, **Camping Mihinoa** (Av. Pont s/n, tel. 032/2551593, www.mihinoa.com, US$6–8 pp) has grassy but treeless sites with access to bathrooms, showers, a kitchen and dining room, laundry service, and even Internet access; rental tents are available for US$3.50–5 per person. The higher prices correspond to the November–April high season. In addition, a few Hanga Roa *residenciales* permit garden camping for a small charge.

US$25-50

It's a little remote for an easy restaurant stroll, but **Cabañas Manatea** (Ahu Akapu s/n, cel. 09/7746-2432, www.rapanuiweb.com/manatea, US$30 s, US$42 d) has four pleasant rooms in an almost unpopulated area with dramatic ocean views. At **Residencial Ana Rapu** (Apina Iti s/n, tel./fax 032/2100540, www.anarapu.cl, US$35 s, US$45 d), the newer rooms offer better value, but it's even cheaper if you camp in the garden (US$15 d).

The affable HI affiliate **Residencial Kona Tau** (Avareipua s/n, tel. 032/2100321, hieasterisland@hostelling.cl, US$20–25 pp) has 16 beds in dorms and other rooms with greater privacy, and guests can collect free mangos from its gardens. The lower rates are for HI members, the higher ones for nonmembers.

Surfers congregate at **Residencial Apina Tupuna** (Apina Nui s/n, tel. 032/2100763, www.apinatupuna.com, US$20 pp, US$50 d), whose best accommodations are cabañas with private bath. Camping in its palm-studded garden costs US$8 per person.

Comparable places include **Hotel Vai Kapua** (Te Pito Te Henua s/n, tel./fax 032/2100377, vaikapua@entelchile.net, US$25 pp with private bath and breakfast), which also has some new rooms, and **Residencial El Tauke** (Te Pito Te Henua s/n, tel. 032/2100253, US$22 pp with private bath), which charges an extra US$5 for breakfast.

US$50-100

Staying at **Residencial Mahina Taka Taka Georgia** (Tahai s/n, tel. 032/2100452, www.mahinatakataka.com, US$33/58 s/d) is a real Polynesian experience, almost like being adopted into Lucía Riroroko's family. Though it falls well short of luxurious, the rooms are spacious, and its slightly out-of-town location, in a wooded setting near Ahu Tahai, is a bonus.

In a quiet location at the northern Tahai sector, longtime stalwart **Residencial Chez Cecilia** (Atamu Tekena s/n, tel./fax 032/2100499, www.rapanuichezcecilia.com, US$40 s, US$60 d) also offers garden camping (US$10 pp).

The basic **Hostal Tekena Inn** (Atamu Tekena s/n, tel./fax 032/2100289, www.hostaltekenainn.com, US$45 s, US$65 d) is drab but friendly and central, with good beds, private bath, and a decent breakfast. While the walls are a little thin, it's not a rowdy place, and rates may be negotiable.

East of the church, the newish **Hostal Puku Rangi Uka** (Puku Rangi Uka s/n, tel. 032/2100405, pukurangiuka@entelchile.net, US$35 s, US$65 d) has plain rooms but some attractive common spaces.

In a quiet area uphill from the church, **Casa Napohe** (Ara Roa Rakei s/n, tel. 032/2551169,

TOURING RAPA NUI

Hanga Roa has an abundance of operators who offer tours around the island. Some have offices in Santiago where excursions can be arranged in advance, but this is more expensive – and rarely necessary except for those seeking specific hotels or those on a very compressed time schedule.

Partly because many mainlanders have moved to the island and offered their services as guides, whether or not they have formal qualifications, locals have organized an Asociación de Guías de Turismo de Isla de Pascua (Easter Island Tourist Guides Association) to regulate the industry. While it may not be quite perfect, it's a good start toward establishing and maintaining standards.

- **Aku Aku Tour** (Av. Tu'u Koihu s/n, tel./fax 032/2100770)

- **Aku Aku Tour** (Estado 115, Oficina 703, Santiago Centro, tel./fax 02/6328173, www.akuakuturismo.cl)

- **Haumaka Tour** (Puku Rangi Uka s/n, tel./fax 032/2100411, www.haumakatours.com)

- **Kia Koe Tour** (Policarpo Toro s/n, tel./fax 032/2100282)

- **Kia Koe Tour** (Napoleón 3565, Oficina 201, Las Condes, Santiago, tel. 02/2037209, www.kiakoetour.cl)

- **Mahinatur Services** (Atamu Tekena s/n, tel./fax 032/2551513, www.mahinatur.cl)

- **Manu Iti** (Hotel Sofia Gomero, Av. Tu'u Koihu s/n, tel./fax 032/2100313, www.hotelgomero.com)

- **Ota'i Tour** (Hotel Ota'i, Te Pito o Te Henua s/n, tel. 032/2100250, www.hotelotai.com)

- **Rapa Nui Travel** (Tu'u Koihu s/n, tel./fax 032/2100548, www.rapanuitravel.com)

www.napohe.com, US$33 pp) has modest but decent bungalows with kitchenettes. Around the corner from the Mercado Artesanal, **Hotel Poike** (Petero Atamu s/n, tel. 032/2100283, fax 032/2100366, US$33 pp) is also a decent choice.

Not bad for the price, but a bit out of the way, **Residencial Tahai** (Atamu Tekena s/n, tel. 032/2100395, www.aotour.cl, US$33 pp with breakfast and private bath) has upgraded, and no longer offers garden camping.

Cozy **Hotel Orongo Easter Island** (Atamu Tekena s/n, tel./fax 032/2100294, US$47 s, US$70 d) is a ten-room garden hotel with all the advantages, and drawbacks, of centrally located accommodations.

The exceptional 【 **Aloha Nui Guest House** (Atamu Tekena s/n, tel./fax 032/2100274, haumaka@entelchile.net, US$58 s, US$70 d) has sizable rooms with private bath in a lush garden setting. Hosts Ramón Edmunds and Josefina Mulloy, a granddaughter of the pioneering archaeologist William Mulloy, manage English, German, and Spanish well, and operate a variety of excursions.

Just uphill from the church and across from the hospital, rooms at **Hostal Martín y Anita** (Simón Paoa s/n, tel. 032/2100593, www.hostal.co.cl, US$50 s, US$80 d) come with a substantial breakfast, private bath, and air-conditioning. The owners handle English well.

US$100-150

In a quiet zone near the airport, **Hotel Hotu Matua** (Av. Pont s/n, tel. 032/2100242, www.hotelhotumatua.com, US$70 s, US$100 d) features 53 large, comfortable rooms, a swimming pool, and sprawling subtropical gardens, but it's slipped a notch, and seems understaffed for its size.

Set among spacious lawns, **Hotel Gomero** (Tu'u Koihu s/n, tel. 032/2100313, fax 032/2551662, www.hotelgomero.com, US$90 s, US$105 d) has sizable rooms, a pool, and other attractive common areas.

Nearby, the 18-room **Hotel Vai Moana**

THE CHILEAN PACIFIC ISLANDS

THE ART AND ARCHITECTURE OF RAPA NUI

Famous for its *moai*, Rapa Nui boasts other kinds of archaeological, artisanal, and artistic artifacts: the *ahu* (platforms) on which some *moai* stand (or stood), the *pukao* (topknots) that crowned some of the *moai*, the *hare paenga* (elliptical houses) whose scattered foundations are still common, and the petroglyphs that adorned sacred sites such as Orongo. In different circumstances, using the medium of *toromiro*, the ancestors of today's Rapanui carved the wooden *rongorongo* tablets and the *moai kavakava*, or "statues of ribs."

Unfortunately, many artifacts reside elsewhere. Only a handful of *moai* have left the island – perhaps they were even harder to load onto ships than move to their *ahu*-but mainland Chilean and overseas museums, as well as private collections, hold more portable items such as *rongorongo* tablets, stone tools, and stone weapons.

Long after the clan wars that toppled the *moai*, local events took a toll on the island's material legacy – the Rapanui themselves recycled ancient stonework into newer, less distinguished structures. The Cedip administration, for its part, turned ruined *ahu* into boat docks at Caleta Hanga Roa and into cattle walls on the grasslands outside town.

AHU

All around the island's circumference, one is rarely out of sight of the 350 or so *ahu;* their very density suggests how large the zenith population must have been. Very few, most notably Maunga Terevaka's Ahu Akivi, occupy inland sites.

The term *ahu* actually describes three distinct types of structures, sited above a plaza or similar open space. All share common elements, being elevated earth platforms with a paved, level upper surface, enclosed by tightly fitted retaining walls of larger stones. The most conspicuous are the elaborate *ahu moai*, on which the stone statues stood. Some plazas contained circular ceremonial areas known as *paina;* in some cases, *apapa* (stone) ramps descend from the *ahu* to the ocean.

Others were semipyramidal *ahu*, some of which were ruined *ahu moai* that became funerary structures from the 16th century until the 19th; others appear to have been built specifically for this purpose. A later style, which probably appeared after Europeans saw the island, was the *ahu poe poe*, an elongated structure whose raised extremities resembled the bow and stern of a European sailing ship. Few in number, largely confined to the north coast, these were also funerary.

MOAI

Numbering about 887, the great stone *moai* are Rapa Nui's most emblematic achievement. Of these, 288 were erected on *ahu*, 397 remain at Rano Raraku, and 92 were in transport. This leaves about 110 unaccounted for.

According to archaeologist Joanne van Tilburg, the average *moai* was 4.05 meters high and weighed 12.5 tons with a volume of 5.96 cubic meters. Mostly male, though about 10 specimens reveal breasts and vulva, they generally range 2-10 meters in height. Some even larger ones remained attached to bedrock at Rano Raraku when quarry work suddenly ceased; shortages of wood to transport and raise them probably contributed to cessation of work.

In style, all *moai* have much in common. Nearly all begin at the torso, and nearly all their features are elongated: bodily appendages such as arms, hands, and fingers, and facial features such as noses and earlobes. Resembling statues elsewhere in Polynesia, they consist of volcanic tuff that was carved with harder basalt *toki*.

On completion, carvers separated the *moai* from its pit and, in all likelihood, laborers lowered it down the crater's outer slopes with ropes. Once it arrived at the base – avoiding breakage or, even worse, fatalities from slippage – an even greater task remained: moving the statue overland and raising it onto an *ahu*.

The precise mechanism for moving the *moai* across the island has been the subject of prolonged debate, but there is no question that it required a large labor force over prolonged periods – one standard for a complex society. Oral tradition says the *moai* moved by the priestly power of *mana*, but researchers from the amateur Heyerdahl to accomplished archaeologists such as William Mulloy, Vince Lee, and Joanne van Tilburg have all agreed that some means of wooden transport – sledges, runners, or rollers – was responsible for getting the statues across the island. Whichever was correct, all these explanations help account for environmental deterioration that contributed to conflict on the island.

Most recently, Van Tilburg recruited robotics expert Zvi Shiller to devise a route for moving the *moai* from Rano Raraku to Ahu Akivi with a three-dimensional model, which van Tilburg corroborated with subsequent field research. According to Shiller's model, 75-150 people could have moved the *moai* in 4.5-9 days. In arguing for rollers as the main means of transport, Van Tilburg suggests that the flat backs of the *moai* indicate they were intended to be moved horizontally.

Once at the *ahu*, there remained the task of raising the *moai*. All researchers are consistent that wooden poles or levers helped lift the heavy statues; in the course of doing so, islanders stabilized them by wedging rocks underneath until the *moai* stood vertically. Most observers have interpreted the large numbers of loose stones near Ahu Akahanga and Ahu Te Pito Te Kura as evidence of this.

Pulling the statues down was easier than carving, transporting, and erecting them on *ahu*. While the islanders themselves inflicted most damage, natural hazards – earthquakes and tsunamis – may well have contributed. The only standing *moai* are late-20th-century restorations.

PUKAO

Quarried from the soft volcanic scoria at Puna Pau, the fitted cylindrical topknots atop some *moai* were apparently a late development – fewer than 100 of them exist, not nearly enough for all the *moai*. Some believe they were hats, but it seems likelier that they represent a male hairstyle in fashion when Europeans first arrived. With their hollow undersides, they were probably attached by rope to their *moai* and raised simultaneously, though they may have been rolled separately to their *ahu*. Even then, moving, tying, and raising an 11-ton *pukao* was no easy task.

HARE PAENGA

On Rapa Nui, these elliptical or boat-shaped houses were built on basalt foundations with small, regularly spaced hollows that supported its superstructure of arched poles, all tied to a central ridge pole that fitted into a hollow at each end. Entered by low, narrow doorways at the midpoint of one side of the house, these houses belonged to high-rank families. Walled with thatch, most were 10-15 meters long and 1.5-2.5 meters wide, but some reached 40 meters long.

RONGORONGO TABLETS

Still common in the mid-19th century, only a few of these original *toromiro* tablets – inscribed with minute symbols in orderly rows and shaped like elongated rectangular paddles – survive today. First described by missionary Eugene Eyraud, they ranged 30-50 centimeters in length, but even when Eyraud took an interest in them, the Peruvian slave trade and subsequent smallpox epidemic had eliminated nearly all the islanders capable of communicating their meaning.

Many originals are now in overseas collections, but anthropologist Steven Fischer has succeeded in bringing them alive in two recent books. Intended for the general public, his *Glyphbreaker* (1997) contends that surviving tablets are sacred chants whose 120 different pictograms signify a sequence of sexually explicit creation myths. His more erudite *Rongorongo, the Easter Island Script: History, Traditions, Text* (1997) appeals to academics and specialists.

The resourceful Rapanui, meanwhile, have turned carved replica *rongorongo* into one of the island's favorite souvenirs.

MOAI KAVAKAVA

Frequently found as souvenirs, the *moai kavakava* ("statues of ribs") probably date from the period when demographic pressure triggered the conflict that resulted in destruction of the giant *moai* – certainly these emaciated wooden figures symbolize starvation. Oral tradition, though, attributes their origin to an encounter by King Tu'u Koihu with two *aku aku* (sleeping spirits) at Puna Pau Crater.

(Atamu Tekena s/n, tel./fax 032/2100626, www.vai-moana.cl, US$84 s, US$108 d) has lustrous common spaces and larger, better appointed rooms than others in its price range.

The management can be brusque at Tahai's **Chez Goretti** (Atamu Tekena s/n, tel./fax 032/2100459, www.chezmariagoretti.com, US$80 s, US$110 d), but its 20 rooms enjoy a quiet setting among expansive subtropical gardens, and the main building, with a central dining room and other common spaces, is a treasure.

Near Caleta Hanga Roa, the Rapanui-French **Residencial Tadeo y Lili** (Av. Policarpo Toro s/n, tel./fax 032/2100422, www.tadeolili.bizland .com, US$91 s, US$110 d) has cabaña-style accommodations with breakfast; the attractively decorated main house has a good library on island themes, though much of it is in French. The owners also offer two-, three-, or six-night packages with full board and excursions, and can manage French, English, or Spanish.

Though perilously proximate to Hanga Roa's Mormon missionary church, **Hotel Chez Joseph** (Avareipua s/n, tel. 032/2100373, fax 032/2100281, www.hotelrapanui.cl, US$80 s, US$120 d) enjoys a hilltop location with fine views from its front porch and spacious bedrooms with cool tile floors.

Atop a grassy knoll, offering large rooms with private bath and breakfast, underrated **Hotel Victoria** (Av. Pont s/n, tel./fax 032/2100272, www.rapanui-victoria.com, US$90 s, US$120 d) enjoys fine views in all directions.

Across from the museum near Ahu Vai Uri, **Cabañas Pikera Uri** (tel. 032/2100577, www .pantupikerauri.cl, US$105 s, US$125 d) enjoys splendid isolation, without being too remote from town, and more than a modicum of style.

Possibly Hanga Roa's best value, in terms of price-quality ratio, may be **Hotel Otai** (Te Pito Te Henua s/n, tel. 032/2100560, www .hotelotai.com, US$95–115 s, US$125–150 d), with motel-style rooms set among lush tropical gardens in the midst of town.

US$150-200

Centrally located **Hotel Manavai** (Te Pito Te Henua s/n, tel. 032/2100670, fax 032/2100658, www.hotelmanavai.cl, US$110 s, US$153 d) has beautiful veranda rooms facing subtropical gardens that reflect its name ("sunken gardens" in Rapanui), as well as a small pool and an outdoor bar. It is, however, perilously close to sound waves from the Toroko disco.

Across from the airport, **Hotel Manutara** (Hotu Matua s/n, tel./fax 032/2100297, www .hotelmanutara.cl, US$125 s, US$156 d) ranks highly in both service and facilities, including a pool.

Its ample rooms embellished with Rapanui carvings, family-run **Hotel Taura'a** (Atamu Tekena s/n, tel. 032/2100463, www.tauraahotel.cl, US$157 d) serves an Australian-style cooked breakfast—with real coffee—and has fine new baths with up-to-date appliances such as hair dryers.

On sprawling grounds just south of Caleta Hanga Roa, the not-so-new but still sparkling **Hotel Tahatai** (Apina Nui s/n, tel./fax 051/551193, www.hoteltahatai.cl, US$150-200 s or d) has spacious, well-lighted accommodations with private bath, breakfast, and a swimming pool.

More than US$200: Enjoying an isolated waterfront site west of the airport, **Hotel Iorana** (Policarpo Toro s/n, tel./fax 032/2100312, www.hoteliorana.cl, US$205 s, US$231 d, up to 371 s or d) is certainly one of Hanga Roa's best. It may be overpriced for the level of service, but celebrity guests such as Kevin Costner and even Axl Rose (who behaved himself) have found it satisfactory.

Food

While most hotels and *residenciales* include breakfast and offer additional meals as well, travelers on a budget can buy produce and fish at the open-air Feria Municipal, on Atamu Tekena, or groceries at any of several supermarkets.

Otherwise, Hanga Roa has restaurants ranging from the utilitarian to above average to truly exceptional. Always, however, ask for the Spanish-language menu, which has prices in pesos rather than dollars and is often substantially cheaper.

For light meals, friendly **Café Ra'a** (Atamu Tekena s/n, tel. 032/2551530, www.caferaa .com) offers shady sidewalk seating, German-style sweets, omelettes, salads, juices, and lemonade, as well as a book exchange and Internet access. It's open for lunch and dinner daily except Tuesday.

Open for lunch and dinner, with enthusiastic and gracious service in simple but agreeable surroundings at Caleta Hanga Roa, ◖ **Avareipua** (Policarpo Toro s/n, tel. 032/2551158) serves a tasty *toremo,* which holds its moisture better than tuna, for US$9 with salad—about what a good fish dish would cost on the mainland. More elaborate meals, such as lobster, run about US$50 for two diners. Since Rapa Nui gets so many German visitors, the new German ownership is planning to introduce German dishes.

Around the corner, across from the soccer field, **Merahi Ra'a** (Te Pito Te Henua s/n, tel. 032/2551125) has simply prepared seafood lunches and dinners, around US$11 with a salad, with more variety than most places. Very friendly, it has veranda seating and very good service even when busy.

◖ **Kopa Kavana** (Avareipua s/n, tel. 032/2100447) serves a more Polynesian-style menu with items such as *remo-remo,* which has darker meat and stronger flavor than tuna, and fried sweet potatoes.

Pea (Policarpo Toro s/n, tel. 032/2100382) went through some tough times, but its fish-oriented menu (most entrées around US$10) is once again a good value for the price. Its oceanside veranda makes it the best restaurant to watch the surfers and the sunset.

On restaurant row, **Te Moana** (Atamu Tekena s/n, tel. 032/2551578) is a pub/restaurant with fine food but erratic service and a slow kitchen when things get busy. The tuna ceviche (US$11) is an excellent starter, and the house *caipirinha* (US$6) is deadly. A Rapanui band plays reggae-tinged Polynesian music some nights.

The kitchen is also a bit slow at **Kaimana** (Atamu Tekena s/n, tel. 032/2551740), but it has very fine fish, gracious service, and an attractive veranda looking toward the sea. It's open noon–midnight daily except Monday.

At its best, French-run ◖ **Taverne du Pecheur** (Caleta Hanga Roa, tel. 032/2100619) is the hands-down winner for Hanga Roa's finest (and dearest) food, with entrées starting around US$13 and ranging up to US$40–60 for lobster, depending on the size; drinks and wine are also expensive. Still, the food is worth the price if—and it's a big if—the service is at its most attentive and responsive, even creative. If the mood deteriorates, though, expect friction and even a lecture–"this is not McDonald's!"—from the chef.

More simpatico, the Belgian-run ◖ **Au Bout du Monde** (Policarpo Toro s/n, tel. 032/2552060, closed Tues.) prepares and presents *matahuira* (US$16) in a vanilla and saffron sauce, accompanied by a salad of tomato, cucumber, and carrot—ideally climaxed with spectacular chocolate mousse.

Other eateries include **Iorana** (Atamu Tekena s/n near Plaza Policarpo Toro, tel. 032/2100265), where fixed-price lunches or dinners cost around US$7; **La Tinita** (Te Pito Te Henua s/n, tel. 032/2100813, for seafood; **Ki Tai** (Policarpo Toro s/n at Caleta Hanga Roa, tel. 032/2100641); and **Pérgola Aringa Ora** (Hotu Matua s/n, tel. 032/2100394).

Information

In new quarters opposite Caleta Hanga Roa, **Sernatur** (Policarpo Toro s/n, tel. 032/2100255, ipascua@sernatur.cl) is open 8:30 A.M.–5 P.M. weekdays only; an airport booth meets arriving flights. Its personnel can normally handle English and French in addition to Spanish and Rapanui.

Next door, the private **Cámara de Turismo** (Policarpo Toro s/n, tel. 032/2550055, www .visitrapanui.cl) also provides information, but progress on its web portal has advanced at a moai's pace.

Services

The ATM at **Banco del Estado** (Tuumaheke

s/n) is a better option than changing either U.S. cash or travelers checks, as rates are poorer and commissions higher than on the mainland. The gas station on Avenida Hotu Matua also has an ATM.

Local merchants generally accept U.S. dollars for accommodations (Sernatur maintains a dollars-only database), meals, and many other items though they will, of course, accept Chilean pesos. Credit cards are becoming more widely accepted as well, even at some surprisingly modest accommodations, but it's still a good idea to carry some cash.

Correos de Chile (Te Pito Te Henua s/n), the post office, is half a block east of Caleta Hanga Roa. A few doors south of Plaza Policarpo Toro, **Apanet** (Atamu Tekena s/n) is a combination cybercafé/call center with reasonable prices by island standards. It's open 10 A.M.–10:30 P.M. daily. Since Rapa Nui is part of Region V. its area code is 032, the same as Viña del Mar and Valparaíso, both of which are local calls.

For laundry services, **Lavandería Tea Nui** (Atamu Tekena s/n, tel. 032/2100580) is directly opposite the Banana Pub.

For medical assistance, **Hospital Hanga Roa** (Simón Paoa s/n, tel. 032/2100215) is about 500 meters southeast of the church.

Getting There

Rapa Nui is easily and regularly (but not cheaply) reached by air, and more economically (but less easily and frequently) reached by sea.

Aeropuerto Mataveri (Av. Hotu Matua s/n, tel. 032/2100277) is at the south end of town; getting to and from the airport is not a problem, since virtually every hotel or residencial provides free transfers, but there is also taxi service.

LAN (Atamu Tekena s/n, tel. 032/2100279) is the only commercial carrier with regular flights to and from Santiago. There are at least two international flights per week that continue to Tahiti and return to Santiago the following day; in the peak summer season, there is at least one additional domestic flight and sometimes two or even more.

Moai-bound passengers disembark at Hanga Roa's Aeropuerto Mataveri.

© WAYNE BERNHARDSON

Note that, for nonislanders, round-trip tickets from Santiago are expensive—up to US$900—but travelers who use LAN for their international flights can often get major discounts to Rapa Nui.

Quarterly naval supply ships, which carry passengers for about US$33 per person per day, connect Rapa Nui with the mainland port of Valparaíso; for details, contact the Comando de Transporte at the **Primera Zona Naval** (Plaza Sotomayor 592, Valparaíso, tel. 032/2506354); travel between the island and the mainland takes about a week-plus.

Getting Around
Hanga Roa has both formal rental agencies and many people who rent out their vehicles casually—look for window signs. Be aware that there is no insurance on any vehicle on the island; you're on your own. Among the agencies are **Insular Rent A Car** (Atamu Tekena s/n, tel. 032/2100480); **Kia Koe Tour** (Atamu Tekena s/n, tel. 032/2100852); and **Oceanic Rent A Car** (Atamu Tekena s/n, tel. 032/2100985). Oceanic and Insular both have motorcycles, while Insular has bicycles as well.

Hanga Roa's only gas station—a seemingly out-of-place convenience store—is at the west end of Avenida Hotu Matua.

There are now two moderately priced taxi services: **Radio Taxi Avareipua** (tel. 032/2100700) and **Radio Taxi Petero Atamu** (tel. 032/2100399).

◖ PARQUE NACIONAL RAPA NUI
Created in 1935, now under Conaf administration, Parque Nacional Rapa Nui comprises about 40 percent of the island's surface. Declared a UNESCO World Heritage Site in 1995, it protects all the island's archaeological sites as part of a *museo al aire libre* (open-air museum).

Orientation
Visiting the park entails getting around the entire island, though precise park boundaries are in flux as land is returned to the islanders. The

DEFENDING THE MOAI

All the monuments on Rapa Nui, from the smallest petroglyphs to the largest *moai* and *ahu*, are vulnerable enough to natural weathering without having to suffer the depredations of enthusiastic but shortsighted tourists. Even a single step, multiplied a million times over years, contributes to the deterioration of this irreplaceable heritage.

Make a special effort not to climb upon the *ahu* anywhere on the island, gently inform anyone doing so that it is inappropriate, and especially do not walk on the *in situ* statues in and around the quarry at Rano Raraku. Marked trails suggest a safe distance.

roads, fortunately, are much improved—the highway to Anakena is smoothly paved, and the south coast road is mostly paved as far as Rano Raraku and Ahu Tongariki. Most of the remainder of the loop across the Poike isthmus and along the north coast to Ovahe and Anakena is still a bumpy dirt surface, however.

Because Rapa Nui is so compact, and the roads improved, it's possible to see a great deal in a day, but rather than hopscotching around the island it's better to explore in a systematic manner by following logical geographical routes.

The Hanga Roa Loop
Many of the island's archaeological sites are accessible from Hanga Roa—indeed, some of them are in Hanga Roa itself—via a loop that begins in town, climbs to Rano Kau crater and the Orongo ceremonial village, visits Ahu Vinapu at the east end of the airport, detours to Puna Pau crater before continuing north to the southwestern slope of Maunga Terevaka, and then returns to Hanga Roa via the coast. It is, of course, possible to do the loop in reverse order or break it up into almost any number of segments.

The most easily accessible *ahu*, **Ahu Tautira** overlooks the harbor at Caleta Hanga Roa. Two broken *moai* stand atop the platform, which was restored in 1980.

Just north of the cemetery, restored in 1968 under the supervision of William Mulloy (whose ashes are buried nearby), **Ahu Tahai** was a ceremonial center with three separate *ahu*, as well as *hare paenga*, a boat ramp, and several *umu* (earth ovens). The central **Ahu Tahai** has a single *moai*, while the flanking **Ahu Ko Te Riku** sports another with its top-knot in place. Nearby, five *moai* stand atop the especially large **Ahu Vai Uri.**

South of Hanga Roa, a meandering road and a rather more direct trail climb the north slope of **Rano Kau** to the island's greatest remaining natural sight, the high crater rim that offers spectacular views, across its *totora*-lined fresh-water lake, to a scattering of offshore islets and the infinite sea in the distance.

The trail, known as the **Ruta Patrimonial Te Ara o Rapa Nui,** actually starts at Hanga Roa's Museo Antropológico and passes through town. For the most part, it parallels the coastal road, passing several major *ahus* and shoreline caves before emerging onto the road and entering Conaf grounds south of town. It then climbs steeply through eucalyptus woods and open grassland before reaching the crater's rim. From there, another trail drops into the steep-sided crater, where citrus trees and grapevines grow wild, and follows the muddy lakeshore, but this is now off-limits.

Farther along the rim via either road or footpath, suspended 400 meters above the sea between Rano Kau's south rim and a nearly vertical plunge into the ocean, **Orongo** was a ceremonial site for the so-called "birdman" cult that flourished in the 18th and 19th centuries, long after the *moai* had been sculpted, raised, and even toppled. Superseding the ancestor worship associated with the giant *moai*, the cult venerated the creator Makemake; its annual highlight was a contest to retrieve the season's first sooty tern egg from the offshore *motu*, or islets. The winner or his sponsor spent a year as the

birdman, gaining great status but restricted to one of the ritual houses.

Visited by a looping signed footpath, Orongo's 53 restored houses are among the world's most curious constructions, their walls and roofs formed by thin, overlapping horizontal wedges. Covered by earth, they were entered by doorways so small that, in the words of an English visitor in 1926:

> The only method of procedure is a most un-dignified snake-like wiggling, which makes one appreciate the full significance of that primeval curse, "Upon thy belly shalt thou go, and dust shalt thou eat."

Today, though, visitors should refrain from even attempting to enter the houses and should also avoid walking on their roofs, which are sometimes difficult to distinguish from the rest of the terrain. Do keep an eye out for the 1,700 or so petroglyphs, some of them faint, that decorate the rocks on the crater rim.

Orongo is the only site where Conaf collects an admission charge, about US$9 per person for adults, US$4.50 per person for children. There is a small museum here.

During the years of the birdman cult, the islets of **Motu Nui, Motu Iti,** and **Motu Kao Kao** were nesting sites for the *mahohe*, or frigate bird, and the sooty tern; the former disappeared and the latter declined under human pressure for their eggs. By contracting a fishing launch at Caleta Hanga Roa, it's possible to approach Motu Nui, where there are cave paintings and remains of an *ahu*, but landings are no longer permitted.

Known for its finely fitted stonework, which led some overly zealous researchers to assume connections to pre-Columbian South American sites such as Tiwanaku (Bolivia) and Cuzco (Peru), **Ahu Vinapu** actually consists of three separate *ahu*, prosaically known as Vinapu I, II, and III. Vinapu II does outwardly resemble those Andean sites, but instead of large stone blocks it is merely an attractive facade for an otherwise rubble-filled platform.

All the *moai* at Ahu Vinapu lie broken and

scattered in the immediate vicinity after being overturned during the islandwide conflicts of the 18th and 19th centuries. Some of the ruins were later used for shelters.

To get to Ahu Vinapu, follow Avenida Hotu Matua to the east end of Aeropuerto Mataveri's runway, then follow the lateral that leads south between the runway and fuel storage tanks to the beachfront parking lot.

Reached by a southbound trail about 1.4 kilometers east of Hanga Roa on the road to Anakena, **Maunga Orito** was a quarry site for the glossy black obsidian that the Rapanui once used for cutting and drilling tools, and for spear points such as the *mataa.* Today, though, Rapanui artisans use the stone for souvenir jewelry.

From a junction about 700 meters beyond the fork to the south coast road, a gravel road leads north toward the southern slopes of Maunga Terevaka; about 500 meters north of the junction, a dirt lateral leads west to **Puna Pau,** whose quarry produced the reddish scoria that forms the *pukao,* or topknots, of the *moai.*

From the Puna Pau turnoff, the main road continues north to Maunga Terevaka's southwestern base, where **Ahu Akivi** is the site of the "Seven Moai," restored in 1960 under the direction of William Mulloy and Chilean archaeologist Gonzalo Figueroa. Much has been made of the fact that these *moai* appear to look out to sea, rather than inland like all the island's other *moai,* but archaeologist Georgia Lee considers this a coincidence—most importantly, they look onto the ceremonial area. It does seem significant, though, that these seven *moai* stare directly into the setting sun on the spring and autumn equinoxes.

Rapa Nui's volcanic landscape features a large number of so-called "caves" that are, in fact, tubes formed as the lava from various eruptions cooled. Some are large, others small; while they served many purposes—shelter, defense, storage—one of the most interesting is **Ana Te Pahu,** colloquially known as the "banana cave" because its moisture and accumulated soil made it possible to cultivate tropical and subtropical crops at its sheltered subsurface

entrance, despite limited sunlight. The local term for these sunken gardens is *manavai.*

Only a short distance west of Ahu Akivi, Ana Te Pahu is an inconspicuous landmark but is well-signed. The road continues northwest toward Ahu Tepeu before turning south along the coast toward Tahai and Hanga Roa.

About 10 kilometers north of Hanga Roa, **Ahu Tepeu** has stonework that resembles that of Ahu Vinapu, but the Heyerdahl expedition of 1960 literally undermined its walls by excavating under their base. The foundation of one of the island's largest boat-shaped houses is nearby.

While there is no road north of Ahu Tepeu, it's possible to follow the coastline to Cabo Norte and then west to Playa Anakena where, though there is no regular public transportation, it's possible to ask someone for a lift back to Hanga Roa. Also feasible in the other direction, this route can be done on mountain bike or horseback as well.

Anakena and Vicinity

From Hanga Roa, a smooth paved road goes northeast to Anakena, the island's best beach and one of its major and best-restored archaeological sites. Several other points of interest dot the north coast road as it bumps eastward toward Península Poike.

In the approximate geographical center of the island, and roughly midway between Hanga Roa and Anakena, **Fundo Vaitea** contains Rapa Nui's best cultivable land. Both Dutroux-Bornier and Williamson, Balfour & Company used it for crops and livestock, but the government development agency Corfo eventually took it over.

At present, some of the land is being redistributed to islanders in five-hectare plots that are now being cultivated for pineapple, mango, and similar crops—transforming the island's contemporary cultural landscape. While some Rapanui have objected to government "land grants," on the rationale that Chile has no right to grant lands that never belonged to it, one local has reached an agreement with the luxury

© WAYNE BERNHARDSON

Most of the *moai* at Ahu Nau Nau, at Playa Anakena, still have their topknots.

hotel chain Explora to build elite accommodations nearby.

Legendary as the ostensible landing point for Hotu Matua (logical enough despite a lack of evidence), **Playa Anakena** is the island's only significant sandy beach, a popular spot for swimming, sunbathing, and Sunday picnics. Backed by a plantation of palms, it also has picnic tables, fire pits, and toilets.

Anakena is more notable, though, for its two substantial *ahu*. Heyerdahl's Norwegian expedition reerected the single *moai* on **Ahu Ature Huki**, while Rapanui archaeologist Sergio Rapu oversaw the 1979 restoration of **Ahu Nau Nau** and its seven *moai*, four of which sport *pukao* (two of the other three are badly damaged). In the course of restoration, the researchers found fragments of inlaid coral eyes, which they were able to reconstruct.

A short distance east of Anakena, **Playa Ovahe** is the island's next-best beach, sandy with hidden caves. Much smaller than Anakena, it gets many fewer visitors.

On the west side of the rocky Bahía La Perouse, out of sight but indicated by a signpost, **Ahu Te Pito Kura** is the site of the largest *moai* (9.8 meters long, weight 82 tons, with an 11.5-ton *pukao*) ever transported and erected on an *ahu*. According to Georgia Lee, this may have been the last standing *moai*, having been toppled some time after 1838. The site takes its name from a large rounded rock that, according to legend, Hotu Matua brought from overseas (geologically it is of local origin). The term *te pito te kura* means "navel of the world" or "navel of light."

South Coastal Road

A short distance east of Hanga Roa, where the paved highway continues northeast toward Anakena, a southern fork follows the coast past a series of ruined coastal *ahu* en route to the magnificent Rano Raraku quarry, the restored and almost equally impressive Ahu Tongariki, and Península Poike, the island's most easterly point.

On the bay of Hanga Tee, **Ahu Vaihu** is the

site of eight fallen *moai* and their *pukao,* which were recovered from the ocean in 1986.

Sometimes claimed to be Hotu Matua's burial site, **Ahu Akahanga** is a large *ahu* that clearly has royal connections. A dozen *moai* lie fallen in the vicinity, along with many *pukao,* though William Mulloy thought the large amount of rubble in the vicinity indicated that stones were used to help raise the *moai* onto the *ahu.* Ruins of a village, primarily *hare paenga* foundations and earth ovens, are also nearby.

Just beyond the shattered **Ahu Hanga Tetenga,** where a pair of *moai* lie in ruins, a dirt track forks north to the parking lot for **Rano Raraku,** the crater where the ancestors of the present-day Rapanui chiseled all the mighty *ahu* before liberating them from the volcanic bedrock and transporting them to their *ahu.* About 390 remain in and around the crater, in all stages of completion. Many of them stand erect, buried to their waists or shoulders in alluvium, while others patiently recline, seemingly waiting to be released from their attachment to the crater.

From the parking area on the south slope of the crater, a series of signed footpaths switchback up the slope to figures such as the kneeling **Moai Tukuturi,** one of few to have visible buttocks, and the reclining 21-meter Goliath, measuring four meters across, still joined to the tuff from which it was carved. Unfortunately, intentional but unattributed fires have denuded some of the slopes around the crater, potentially damaging the sites but also exposing the *moai* transport routes to view.

To the west, several parallel trails climb the contour into the crater, where *totora* reeds line the shore of the freshwater lake that fills the lower basin; in late summer, fruit from the feral guava trees still make a tasty snack. One measure of the cataclysmic warfare that hit the island is the fact that more than 300 unfinished *moai* populate the crater and its outer slopes. The crater's craggy eastern rim offers some of the island's best views.

At the parking area ranger station, there are picnic tables, fire pits and toilets.

Its *moai* toppled in the chaos of intertribal warfare and its base destroyed by a tsunami in 1960, **Ahu Tongariki** underwent a major restoration when, in 1992, the Japanese Tadano company brought a crane, cash, and personnel to show how to manage it. Under the supervision of Chilean archaeologist Claudio Cristino, an island resident, about 40 Rapanui worked six-day weeks for nearly four years to finish the project. Some 15 *moai* now stand atop the *ahu,* which measures 98 meters long, 6 meters wide, and 4 meters high—the largest on the island. There are also numerous nearby petroglyphs, including a turtle, a tuna fish, a birdman, and *rongorongo* tablets.

Where the south coast road turns north toward Anakena, the eastern end of Rapa Nui's **Península Poike** is the site of the 400-meter Maunga Pu A Katiki, a dormant volcano almost entirely surrounded by steep volcanic cliffs except along its western isthmus, the narrowest point on the island, which parallels the north–south road. Directly across the isthmus runs the depression known as **Ko te Ava o Iko** (Iko's Ditch), once thought to be a defensive fortification, set afire to prevent an invasion from the west. Recent research has indicated the ditch to be a natural feature; although there is evidence of natural fires, there is no evidence of weapons.

Information

South of town on the Rano Kau road, **Conaf** (tel. 032/2100827) is open 8:30 A.M.–6 P.M. weekdays only; there are also ranger posts at Orongo (which has a small museum), Anakena, and Rano Raraku.

Conaf's well-illustrated English-language brochure *Archaeological Field Guide, Rapa Nui National Park,* by Claudio Cristino, Patricia Vargas, and Roberto Izaurieta, is an outstanding summary of the park's monuments.

For US$30 per year, real Rapanuiphiles can subscribe to the quarterly *Rapa Nui Journal,* c/o the Easter Island Foundation (P.O. Box 6774, Los Osos, CA 93412-6774, tel. 805/528-8558, www.islandheritage.org). In addition to serious scholarly articles, it also provides the latest island gossip, travel information, and even "*moai* sightings" around the world.

The best, most easily available map is the third edition of ITM's *Easter Island* (scale 1:30,000), readily found at bookstores in the United States and Canada; it can also be ordered through International Travel Maps & Books (530 W. Broadway, Vancouver, BC V5Z 1E9, Canada, tel. 805/879-3621, www.itmb.com).

The Juan Fernández Archipelago

In his classic 1830s seafaring adventure *Two Years before the Mast*, Richard Henry Dana called Robinson Crusoe's island "the most romantic spot of earth that my eyes had ever seen." Dana's impression owed much to novelist Daniel Defoe, who had placed fiction's most famous castaway in the Caribbean, but the real-life Crusoe was Alexander Selkirk, a Scotsman marooned more than four years on a tiny but mountainous island—then known as Isla Masatierra—in the Pacific.

In what is now almost entirely national park land, visitors to what is now called Isla Robinson Crusoe, in what is now part of Chile, can hike to Selkirk's lookout through forests of rare endemic plant species and observe endangered fur seal colonies in local launches. Air access from Santiago is easy and there's an infrequent maritime connection with Valparaíso.

GEOGRAPHY AND CLIMATE

Almost directly west of Valparaíso, 667 kilometers from the continent, three subterranean mountains break the Pacific surface to form the Archipiélago de Juan Fernández. The only permanently inhabited one is Isla Robinson Crusoe (ex-Masatierra). Isla Santa Clara (known to early buccaneers as "Goat Island") is only a few kilometers off its southwesterly tip, while Isla Alejandro Selkirk (ex-Masafuera) is 167 kilometers farther west. The original Spanish names are geographical references—Masatierra means "closer to land" (the South American continent), Masafuera means "farther out."

All are mere dots in the Pacific: Robinson Crusoe's area is only 93 square kilometers, Santa Clara's only 5 square kilometers, and Alejandro Selkirk's only 85 square kilometers. All are ruggedly mountainous, though: Robinson Crusoe's Cerro El Yunque rises 915 meters above sea level, Alejandro Selkirk's Cerro Los Inocentes reaches 1,480 meters, and even tiny Santa Clara sticks 375 meters above the ocean. Because the islands are so small—Robinson Crusoe is 22 kilometers long and only 7.3 kilometers wide— the terrain is even more abrupt than these relatively modest elevations might suggest. Because it sits atop a subterranean mountain range, the land plunges swiftly into the Pacific depths.

In an area where subtropical Pacific seas blend with sub-Antarctic flows from the northerly Humboldt or Peru Current, the archipelago has a Mediterranean oceanic climate resembling that of Chile's continental heartland. Temperatures are mild: On Robinson Crusoe, the annual average is 15.2°C, with an average summer maximum of 21.8°C and a winter minimum of 10.1°C. More than two-thirds of the 1,000 millimeters annual precipitation falls between April and October; less than 10 percent falls in the summer, from December to February.

Rainfall statistics are misleading, though, because the steep east–west ridge of Robinson Crusoe's Cordón Chifladores causes a strong rain-shadow effect; its north side is verdant rainforest, while the south side and Isla Santa Clara are as barren as the Atacama coastline. Even then, like the Atacama, the arid south side gets convective fogs like the *camanchaca*.

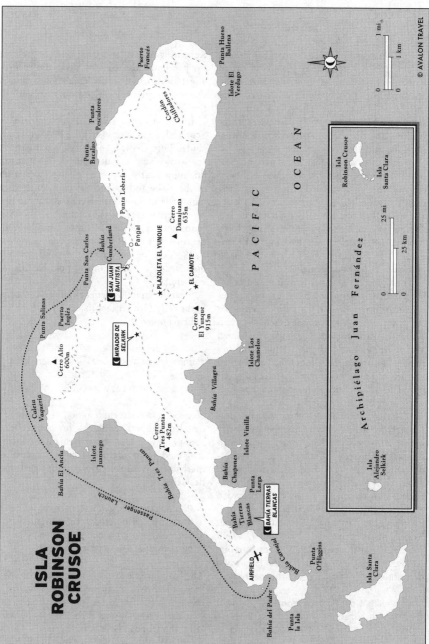

ISLA ROBINSON CRUSOE

Punta Hueso Ballena

Islote El Verdugo

Puerto Francés

Cordón Chifladores

Punta Pescadores

Punta Bacalao

Punta Lobería

Pangal

Cerro Damajuana 635m

★ PLAZOLETA EL YUNQUE

★ EL CAMOTE

Bahía Cumberland

Punta San Carlos

🏠 SAN JUAN BAUTISTA

Puerto Inglés

Punta Salinas

★ MIRADOR DE SELKIRK

Cerro Alto 600m

Cerro El Yunque 915m

Islote Los Chamelos

Bahía Villagra

Caleta Vaquería

Bahía El Ancla

Islote Juanango

Cerro Tres Puntas 482m

Bahía Tres Puntas

Islote Vinilla

Bahía Chupones

Punta Larga

Bahía Tierras Blancas

🏠 BAHÍA TIERRAS BLANCAS

✈ AIRFIELD

Bahía Carvajal

Punta O'Higgins

Bahía del Padre

Punta la Isla

Isla Santa Clara

Passenger Launch

P A C I F I C   O C E A N

© AVALON TRAVEL

0   1 mi
0   1 km

Archipiélago Juan Fernández

Isla Robinson Crusoe

Isla Santa Clara

Isla Alejandro Selkirk

0   25 mi
0   25 km

HISTORY

While a group of Australian and New Zealand archaeologists have recently sought evidence of a pre-Columbian presence on Juan Fernández, all the unusual items they found appear to have been from historic times. Certainly when Spanish navigator Juan Fernández named them the "Islas Santa Cecilia" after the date of their sighting in November 1574, they were uninhabited, and they had no permanent residents until the mid-18th century.

Even if there was no regular human presence on the islands until then, there was plenty of activity. Foreign navies and privateers regularly took R&R and filled their water casks here, and even after Spain finally founded the settlement of San Juan Bautista in 1750, North American sealers continued to slaughter the endemic Juan Fernández fur seal *(Arctocephalus phillippi)* for its valuable pelt.

The closest claim to permanent residence belonged to the impulsive Selkirk. In 1704, after continual quarrels with Captain Stradling of the privateer *Cinque Ports,* the irascible seaman demanded to be put ashore; though he repented almost immediately, the departing Stradling rebuked him with the admonition "Stay where you are and may you starve!" Overcoming his initial despair, Selkirk endured more than four years in nearly utter isolation.

Masatierra was no tropical paradise but, fortunately for Selkirk, it was a temperate, partly man-made one. Wood and water were plentiful, wild cabbages abounded, and, most important, the Spaniards had introduced goats. These feral beasts, while they inflicted incalculable damage on the native flora, provided meat and clothing for the solitary exile until his rescue, in 1709, by Commander Woodes Rogers of the privateers *Duke* and *Duchess.* Rogers, whose famous pilot William Dampier had earlier gone to sea with Selkirk, left a vivid description of his first sight of the castaway:

Immediately our Pinnace return'd from the shore, and brought abundance of Crawfish, with a man Cloth'd in Goat-Skins, who look'd wilder than the first Owners of them.

Returning to Scotland, Selkirk recounted his story to journalist Richard Steele and eventually it found its way into Defoe's novel, though Defoe changed the location from the Pacific to the Caribbean.

In the decades after Selkirk's return to Scotland, figures to visit Juan Fernández included Lord George Anson, who commanded the Royal Navy's South American squadron during a nearly four-year circumnavigation of the globe and named the main anchorage Cumberland Bay. Spanish concerns about foreign interlopers led to the establishment of San Juan Bautista, at Bahía Cumberland, by mid-century, but it was mainly a penal colony—in 1814, during the wars of independence, the Spaniards sent 42 prominent political prisoners here.

Even the establishment of Chilean authority in the early 19th century made little difference, as Dana noted that:

All the people there, except the soldiers and a few officers, were convicts sent from Valparaíso.... The island...had been used by the government as a sort of Botany Bay.

Nor did it stop the exploitation of the island's natural wealth: The valuable fur seal declined so rapidly that U.S. sealer Benjamin Morrell remarked, in an instance of either the most remarkable naïveté or transparent disingenuousness, that:

Perhaps the moral atmosphere may have been so much affected by the introduction of three hundred felons as to become unpleasant to these sagacious animals.

The islands came to world notice again in 1915 when the British navy, once again a factor in the South Pacific, forced the scuttling of the massive German cruiser *Dresden.* Two decades later, the Chilean government created the national park that, in 1977, became a UNESCO

World Biosphere Reserve. The only parts of the island not belonging to the national park are the airfield and the village of San Juan Bautista, which thrives on the high-value local lobster, flown daily to Santiago restaurants, and a modest tourist trade.

◖ SAN JUAN BAUTISTA

All of Isla's Robinson Crusoe's 635 inhabitants live in or near the village of San Juan Bautista. Nearly all of them depend directly or indirectly on fishing for the so-called Juan Fernández lobster, in reality a crayfish, and on the modest tourist trade. Both of these are seasonal activities, from October to April or May, though the tourist season peaks in January and February.

Though still one of Chile's most isolated settlements, San Juan Bautista has modern infrastructure, with comfortable guesthouses, a state-of-the-art phone system, satellite TV, and even roads capable of handling an increasing fleet of motor vehicles—in a town where it's impossible to work up enough speed to get out of second gear. For all of this, few islanders visit the "continent" except for education or medical emergencies; even then the Chilean air force pays literal "flying visits" to deal with routine medical and dental care on the island's airstrip.

The outstanding contemporary travel essayist Thurston Clarke describes San Juan, its people, and surroundings in the opening chapter of his *Searching for Crusoe: A Journey Among the Last Real Islands* (Ballantine, 2001).

Orientation

On Robinson Crusoe's well-watered north shore, at the foot of the precipitous Cordón Chifladores, San Juan Bautista sits on a narrow wave-cut terrace facing the sheltered Bahía Cumberland. One curving main street, Larraín Alcalde, runs nearly the length of the village; toward its south end it becomes the pedestrian Costanera El Palillo. Other streets, and footpaths, rise at right angles from Larraín Alcalde.

Launches to and from the airfield at Bahía

THE SCUTTLING OF THE *DRESDEN*

En route to Europe in 1914, Captain Fritz Lüdecke of the German cruiser *Dresden* received news of the outbreak of World War I and orders to meet the German South Pacific squadron under Admiral Graf von Spee. After participating in the battle of Coronel (near Concepción) on November 1, the *Dresden* escaped a surprise British attack at the Falkland Islands on December 8 – in which Von Spee died – and fled around Cape Horn to the southern Chilean fjords. After reprovisioning at Punta Arenas with help from the local German colony, it came under pursuit by the British vessels *Glasgow, Kent,* and *Orana* before eventually attempting to take refuge at Bahía Cumberland. In a hopeless situation, Captain Lüdecke scuttled the ship; the surviving crew was taken into Chilean custody and remained on Isla Quiriquina (near Concepción) until 1919.

---

del Padre use the Embarcadero immediately east of the plaza. There is also a ramp for the Chilean navy's roll-on, roll-off cargo ferry a short distance to the south.

Sights

Best known as the site of Selkirk's solitary exile, San Juan is home to several historical landmarks, all just a short distance from the plaza.

In 1749, alarmed that British privateer Lord Anson had spent three months at Bahía Cumberland preparing to attack the ports of El Callao (Peru), Acapulco (Mexico), and Manila (Philippines), Spain tried to discourage incursions by sending 200 colonists to the island. Less than two years later, a tsunami destroyed the settlement, but in 1770 the Spanish crown sent engineer José Antonio Birt to plan the fortifications of **Fuerte Santa Bárbara,** with mortar-covered stone walls and gun emplacements with several cannon each. Partially dismantled in 1817, then damaged by

© WAYNE BERNHARDSON

San Juan Bautista and Bahía Cumberland, from Parque Nacional Archipielago Juan Fernandez

earthquakes in 1822 and 1835, the fortress was reconstructed in 1974.

After Chilean rebels suffered the so-called "Desastre de Rancagua" in 1814, Spanish commander Mariano Osorio raided the homes of 42 key figures who, transported to Valparaíso, were shipped to Masatierra aboard the corvette *Sebastiana.* Juan Egaña, Manuel de Salas, U.S. consul Matthew Arnold Hoevel, and the others spent three years in the damp grottos now known as the **Cuevas de los Patriotas,** now a national monument, before the ultimate Chilean victory freed them.

The German headstones at **Cementerio San Juan Bautista,** near the lighthouse at the north end of town, recall the World War I odyssey of the German cruiser *Dresden,* which lies beneath the offshore waters where fur seals now cavort (British shells that missed their target are embedded in nearby headlands). Other gravestones bear mostly Spanish but also French inscriptions from the islands' colonists.

At the top of Vicente González, open for tours on request, the **Vivero Conaf** is a nursery that grows native species for reforesting the park and ecological exotics for planting near the village. Two *invernaderos* (greenhouse) nurture the seedlings.

Accommodations and Food

The cheapest accommodations alternative is camping, but San Juan Bautista also has a handful of B&B accommodations that consistently serve local lobster for dinner. Since accommodations are limited, reservations are important in January and February. Nowhere except perhaps Pangal will visitors be able to avoid barking dogs at night.

Just above the shoreline, the municipal **Camping Los Cañones** (Vicente González s/n) has cheap sites with basic bathrooms and cold showers. Uphill from the gymnasium, just north of the Embarcadero, **(Residencial Barón de Rodt** (La Pólvora s/n, tel. 032/2751109, baronderodt@yahoo. es, US$20 pp) has just two double rooms, so reservations are almost essential; its tobacco-free restaurant prepares superb fish and other dishes at reasonable prices.

Just uphill from Fuerte Santa Barbará, **(Residencial Mirador de Selkirk** (El Castillo 251, tel. 032/2751028, mfernandeziana@hotmail.com, US$33 pp with half-board, US$42 pp with full board) is an attractive three-room B&B (shared bath only) that's also one of the best places to eat—fish doesn't get any fresher, nor any better prepared, than it does here. The deck has ocean views.

Hostal Charpentier (Ignacio Carrera Pinto 256, tel. 032/2751070, fax 032/2751020, www.hostalcharpentier.cl, US$50 s, US$83 d with half board, US$58 s, US$100 d with full board) also rents a separate cabaña (US$50 without meals) that sleeps up to three people.

Directly across from the police station, run by an ex-Carabinero, **Hostal Petit Breuilh** (Vicente González 84, tel. 032/2751107, www.hostalpetit.cl, US$30 s, US$50 d with breakfast, US$37 s, US$67 d with half board, US$46 s, US$83 d with full board) is another good choice; the first night's dinner includes lobster. Some suggest, though, that its recent expansion has focused on quantity before quality.

Set back from the plaza, **Hostería Martínez-Green** (Larraín Alcalde s/n, tel./fax 032/2751039, US$42 pp with half board) is a decent choice.

With its rickety exterior and shoreline location, the quirky **Aldea Daniel Defoe** (Daniel Defoe 449, tel./fax 032/2751075, www.robinsoncrusoeisland.cl, from US$50 pp with half board, US$67 pp with full board) will be the first to go in the next tsunami, but it remains a decent choice for both accommodations and food.

New on the scene, on the waterfront footpath to El Palillo, tobacco-free **(Hostería Refugio Náutico** (Ignacio Carrera Pinto s/n, tel. 032/2751077, www.islarobinsoncrusoe.cl, US$58 s, US$75 d with breakfast, US$67 s, US$85 d with half board, US$75 s, US$92 d with full board) has added an element of style to San Juan's accommodations—while not luxurious, it's bright and cheerful, and the private baths have tubs as well as showers. The restaurant has an ocean-view deck for sunny days and warm evenings.

Reached by a shuttle launch from the Embarcadero or a scenic 45-minute hike that switchbacks up the slope from El Palillo before following the road the rest of the way, **Hotel Isla Robinson Crusoe** (tel. 02/6345300 in Santiago, www.robinson-crusoe-island.com, from US$350 s, US$500 d with breakfast) has reinvented itself an isolated spa hotel that emphasizes all-inclusive activities packages, but will take overnighters for accommodations only.

San Juan has few places to eat other than its accommodations, and at these, it's almost imperative to give some notice—preferably at least a day for lobster. **El Nocturno** (Larraín Alcalde s/n, tel. 032/2751113) is more a sandwich place, while **(El Bahía** (Larraín Alcalde s/n) prepares outstanding lobster despite its modest appearance.

Information

Opposite the plaza, Conaf's **Caseta de Informaciones** (Larraín Alcalde s/n) has brochures with maps and information about the village and the national park, and collects park admission fees; hours are 8:45 A.M.–12:30 P.M. and 2–5:30 P.M. weekdays, 8:30 A.M.–noon and 2–5:30 P.M. weekends.

About 500 meters uphill from the shoreline, Conaf's **Centro de Información Ambiental Eduardo Paredes** (Vicente González s/n, tel. 032/2751004 or 032/2751022), the visitors center for Parque Nacional Juan Fernández, has professional displays on the park's geography, environment, and history, including topics such as the endangered fur seal and the scuttled *Dresden*. Built and organized with Dutch assistance, its English is as good as its Spanish; hours are 8 A.M.–12:50 P.M. and 2–6 P.M. weekdays, though it keeps longer hours and opens on weekends when the tourist presence is heavy.

Services

Bring money from the continent, in small bills. San Juan has no exchange facilities, relatively little cash circulates, and shopkeepers have trouble making change. Hotels and *hospedajes* will accept U.S. dollars, and a handful of places now handle credit cards.

On the plaza's south side, **Correos de Chile** (Larraín Alcalde 352-A) is the post office; for long-distance telephone calls, try **Minimercado Nenuco** (Larraín Alcalde s/n), alongside the Brújula discotheque.

Free public Internet access is possible at the **Casa de la Cultura** (Larraín Alcalde s/n), but a new private office has opened as well.

For medical treatment, the only option is the government-run **Posta Rural** (Vicente González s/n, tel. 032/2751067).

Getting There

For most visitors, air taxis from Santiago are the only practicable means of transportation, but for those with plenty of time or particularly good timing, sea travel from Valparaíso is conceivable.

Two companies provide air-taxi service from Santiago; flights are frequent in January and February, few outside the November to March period, and windy or rainy weather can abort takeoffs and landings at any time of year. Visitors should arrange their itineraries and finances to be able to stay a day or two extra in case of adverse weather. Round-trip fares are about US$650, but there are occasional discounts and packages that include hotel stays and full board.

Many carriers have come and gone, but **Lassa** (Av. Larraín 7941, La Reina, tel. 02/2735209 or 02/2731458, lassa@tie.cl; Alcalde Larraín s/n, San Juan Bautista) has shown the greatest durability and reliability. It flies out of Aeródromo Tobalaba, in Santiago's eastern suburbs; in addition to seven-seater taxis, it uses 18-passenger Dornier 220s when demand is high.

A recent entry into the market, **Aerolíneas ATA** (Av. 11 de Septiembre 2155, Oficina 1107, Providencia, tel. 02/2343389, www.aerolineas-ata.cl; Larraín Alcalde s/n, San Juan Bautista, tel. 032/2751059, teresamaldonado@gmail.com) flies seven-seaters out of Santiago's international airport at Pudahuel.

San Juan Bautista is about 1.5 hours by motor launch from the passenger pier at Bahía del Padre, an ocean-flooded caldera reached by a short but precipitous dirt road from the renovated airfield, which occupies one of few relatively level sites on the entire island (and now has toilets as well). The boat transfer, usually included in the air ticket, is scenic, but the seas can be rough on visitors unaccustomed to relatively small ships; consider medication.

Sailing from Valparaíso to Juan Fernández requires patience and good timing. It is, for instance, easier to get information on the quarterly naval vessels than it once was, but sailings are not any more frequent and usually require reservations a month or more in advance.

For naval vessels, contact the **Comando de Transporte** at the Primera Zona Naval (Plaza Sotomayor 592, Valparaíso, tel. 032/2506354), whose infrequent supply ships carry civilian passengers for about US$35 per person per day; the round-trip takes five days, but if spending any significant time on the island you'll need to fly back from San Juan Bautista. They're hard to reach by phone; it's best to go in person between 8 A.M. and noon weekdays.

Getting Around

Walking is the best way to get around San Juan and most of the national park, but some sights are most easily accessible by launch—ask at the Municipalidad, around the Embarcadero, or your accommodations may be able to arrange something. The Municipalidad maintains a list of prices for launch excursions around the island.

Endémica Expediciones (tel. 032/2751003, www.endemica.com) has an extensive offering of diving, hiking, fishing, and other excursions from San Juan.

PARQUE NACIONAL ARCHIPIÉLAGO JUAN FERNÁNDEZ

Almost contiguous with the archipelago—excluding only San Juan Bautista and the airfield at Robinson Crusoe's southeast corner—Parque Nacional Archipiélago Juan

Fernández comprises 9,571 hectares of protected land that varies from barren desert to dense endemic forest on Isla Robinson Crusoe, Isla Santa Clara, and Isla Marinero Alejandro Selkirk. From a wildlife perspective, it's noteworthy for what it excludes: All the surrounding offshore areas fall under jurisdiction of the navy's Gobernación Marítima.

Flora and Fauna

Having evolved in oceanic isolation, about 70 percent of the archipelago's plant species are endemic, despite broad similarities with flora from tropical Hawaii, the Andean highlands, temperate New Zealand, and sub-Antarctic Magallanes. Even at the genus level, nearly 20 percent of the flora is endemic.

There exist three principal plant communities: the evergreen rainforest, an evergreen heath, and an herbaceous steppe. In all likelihood, the lushly diverse evergreen forest once reached to the shoreline, but aggressive introduced plant species, imported both intentionally and accidentally, and damage from non-native grazers such as goats and cattle have squeezed it out of the lower elevations. On higher slopes, climbing vines cover the trunks of endemic trees such as the *luma (Nothomyrcia fernandeziana)* and the *chonta* palm *(Juania australis),* which shade a verdant understory of tree ferns such as *Dicksonia berteroana* and *Thyrsopteris elegans.* In Selkirk's time, visiting mariners gathered forest products such as the fruits of the wild cabbage tree *Dendroseris litoralis,* which Woodes Rogers praised as "very good."

On shallow soils at higher elevations, or on nearly sheer gradients, the evergreen heath features smaller trees of the genus *Robinsonia* and tree ferns such as *Blechnum cyadifolium.* In the drier southeastern part of Isla Robinson Crusoe and on Isla Santa Clara, bunch grasses such as *Stipa fernandeziana* provide a patchy cover on the steppe.

The replacement of native flora was well under way even during colonial times, when privateers planted their own gardens. When Maria Graham visited the island with Lord Cochrane in 1823, they found apples, cherries, pears, and quinces, and mint and parsley. Barely a decade later, wrote Richard Henry Dana,

> Ground apples, melons, grapes, strawberries of an enormous size, and cherries, abound here. The latter are said to have been planted by Lord Anson.

Other species have been less benevolent and even invasive, such as the wild blackberry *(Rubus ulmifolius)* and the *maqui (Aristotelia chilensis),* a shrub that has displaced native forest but has an important economic use for lobster traps.

The Juan Fernández group has no native land mammals, but 60 percent of its land bird species are endemic, most notably the strikingly red male Juan Fernández hummingbird *(Sephanoides fernandensis),* which feeds on the native cabbage trees. Ground-nesting seabirds, most notably Cook's petrel *(Pterodroma cookii defilippiana),* have suffered depredations from exotic mammals such as the Norway rat, the domestic cat, and the South American coatimundi.

Morrell and his contemporaries pursued the Juan Fernández fur seal to near extinction, a recent Conaf census counted nearly 30,000 individuals (admittedly a small fraction of the hundreds of thousands killed by 19th-century sealers) on the archipelago's three islands. The near absence of a continental shelf provides little habitat for inshore fauna, but the misleadingly named Juan Fernández lobster (*Jasus frontalis* is really a crayfish) fetches premium prices in Santiago's finest restaurants.

Sights and Recreation

Many of the park's attractions are within walking distance of San Juan Bautista, but often only via a rugged hike. Its signature excursion is the **Mirador de Selkirk,** on a scenic trail that continues to **Bahía Tierras Blancas** (site of a large fur seal colony) and the airstrip where flights from the mainland arrive.

At the south end of San Juan, swimmers dive off the rocks at **El Palillo,** where Conaf has a wooded 15-site picnic ground (no camping, though) with fire pits and trash collection;

THE CHILEAN PACIFIC ISLANDS

this is also the officially designated site of the **Sendero de Chile**'s only submarine sector (accessible to divers). From El Palillo, a trail switchbacks up the hillside before leveling out and joining the road to Hostería Pangal.

At the foot of the island's highest peak, **Plazoleta El Yunque** is a shorter, easier hike than Selkirk's lookout. Beginning at the village power plant and gaining only 257 meters in three kilometers, the road becomes a footpath that leads to this placid forest clearing where Hugo Weber, who escaped the *Dresden*'s sinking, built a house whose foundations still survive. Conaf maintains a picnic area here, and permits one night's camping.

From Plazoleta El Yunque, Conaf permission and a guide are necessary to ascend the steep rugged route to **El Camote**, a saddle with views to equal or surpass those of Selkirk's lookout, particularly the sight of **El Verdugo**, a sheer volcanic needle that rises 157 meters out of the sea. The climb to El Camote, through thick native forest, requires at least as much arm strength as hiking ability, as it often requires pulling yourself up by tree limbs. **Cerro El Yunque** itself, a 915-meter pinnacle, is not unattainable, but it's not for dilettantes either; a Conaf-approved local guide is imperative.

Only a short shot north of San Juan Bautista by launch, **Puerto Inglés** is the site of Selkirk's replica shelter; camping is possible here. For non-hikers, the launch to Puerto Inglés costs about US$35 for a minimum five persons; in rough seas, the landing is tricky and the rocks are slippery.

Puerto Inglés is about two hours away starting at the zigzag **Sendero Salsipuedes,** which climbs from the west end of Calle La Pólvora; passing through nonnative forest of acacia, eucalyptus, Monterey cypress, and Monterey pine, the newly rerouted trail to the Salsipuedes ridge provides some of the best village and harbor views. Beyond the ridge, though, the descent to Puerto Inglés requires a local guide.

On a small inlet on Crusoe's north shore, **Puerto Vaquería** features a small fur seal colony and a Conaf *refugio*. The landing is equally

if not more awkward than that at Puerto Inglés. Camping is possible, a local guide obligatory.

On Robinson Crusoe's eastern shore, about half an hour by launch from San Juan Bautista, **Puerto Francés** is a desert area where the presence of French pirates led Spain to build a now-ruined set of ramparts overlooking the sea. From the Conaf *refugio* here, a trail climbs the **Quebrada Los Picos** through thickening forest to *Cerro La Piña;* a longer trail connects Quebrada Los Picos with Pangal (local guide obligatory).

Rarely visited except by lobsterers, Conaf's seasonal ranger, and the odd cruise ship, **Isla Marinero Alejandro Selkirk** (ex-Isla Masafuera) must be one of the earth's loneliest places—even more so, in Selkirk's time, than Masatierra (Selkirk had no connection whatsoever with the island that now bears his name). The municipal launch *Blanca Luz* discourages passengers and travels there only infrequently; landings are difficult as there is no pier. Special excursions are very expensive.

Mirador de Selkirk

The park's single most popular destination, the Mirador de Selkirk (Selkirk's Lookout) is a stiff hike starting at Subida El Castillo, at the south end of San Juan's plaza. Over a distance of 2,700 meters, it gains 565 meters in altitude—an average grade of nearly 21 percent. The initial segment passes through a badly eroded area that quickly becomes covered with blackberry vines and nonnative scrub before finally entering a dense native forest with a verdant undergrowth of ferns—some the size of trees. This is a designated nature trail, and Conaf's inexpensive booklet *Sendero Interpretativo Mirador Alejandro Selkirk* describes the native and nonnative plants and wildlife and explains what environmental damage the area has suffered.

From a saddle on the ridge between the two sides of the island, the hiker's reward is a series of views from Bahía Cumberland and San Juan on the north to the airfield to Isla Santa Clara on the south. On the saddle itself, two plaques honor Selkirk's memory. Royal Navy officers placed the first, cast by John Child & Son of Valparaíso, which says:

In memory of Alexander Selkirk, Mariner, a native of Largo, in the county of Fife, Scotland, who lived on this island in complete solitude for four years and four months.

He was landed from the Cinque Ports galley, 96 tons, 16 guns, A.D. 1704 and was taken off in the Duke, privateer, 12th Feb., 1709.

He died lieutenant of HMS Weymouth, A.D. 1723, aged 47 years.

This tablet is erected near Selkirk's lookout, by Commodore Powell and the officers of HMS Topaze, A.D. 1868.

The second, placed nearby by a Scottish relative, reads:

Tablet placed here by Allan Jardine of Largo, Fife, Scotland, direct descendant of Alexander Selkirk's brother David. Remembrance 'Till a' the seas gang dry and the rocks melt in the sun.' January 1983.

From the saddle, where wind and fog can make the weather far cooler than at sea level, the trail descends through densely vegetated Sector Villagra before emerging onto the desert side of the island; it's about 10 kilometers farther to the airfield on a path that, for most of its length, is wide enough for a Hummer. Villagra has a ranger station and campground where islanders gather for the summer rodeo, in early February.

Through hikers should carry water, as the only reliable sources en route are a conspicuous pipe where the trail crosses Estero El Castillo (San Juan's water supply) and begins to switchback toward Selkirk's lookout, and a spring that drops over a rock outcrop just west of the Villagra turnoff.

◖ Bahía Tierras Blancas

Just before reaching the airfield, the trail from San Juan passes an unmarked but conspicuous lateral that descends to the island's principal fur seal colony at Bahía Tierras Blancas. The zigzag trail is wide, but it has loose volcanic rock and many eroded gullies that require scrambling to reach the seashore. Figure about two hours down and back, including time to photograph the seals (keep a respectful distance from the animals).

Some visitors hike to the airfield to catch their flights back to the mainland, but this requires an early departure and might limit your time at the seal colony. On the other hand, if the flight is delayed for weather conditions, it might entail camping a night at the barren airfield. Another option is to hike from the airfield to San Juan; it's possible to do this on arrival, as the boat to San Juan will normally deliver your baggage to your accommodations.

It's also possible to spend the first night or more in San Juan, then catch a boat to Bahía del Padre for a hike back to the village on another day; this ensures an earlier arrival at San Juan, with more time for sightseeing breaks. The western approach is also more gradual, though it also climbs steeply to Selkirk's lookout. Still, it takes 4–5 hours, even longer with wet weather.

Information

At its San Juan information kiosk, Conaf now collects a US$5 per person park admission charge (US$3 for Chileans), and more for those who come with specific activities in mind. Senior citizens pay US$0.85 and children US$0.85 per person except for foreign kids (US$1.50).

Getting Around

The boat trip from Bahía del Padre to San Juan Bautista is a good introduction to Robinson Crusoe's geography—it covers nearly half the island's circumference—but hiring a launch in San Juan offers greater flexibility and the option, if seas permit, of going ashore in otherwise inaccessible areas. Figure about US$165 for a five-hour circumnavigation of the island; expenses can be shared by up to five or six people.

THE CHILEAN PACIFIC ISLANDS

BACKGROUND

The Land

Chile's diverse geography, stretching from the desert tropics to the sub-Antarctic, rises from sea level to alpine and altiplano areas well above 4,000 meters. It contains nearly every South American environment *except* tropical rainforest.

GEOGRAPHY

At about 800,000 square kilometers, Chile is slightly larger than Texas, but that statistic can be misleading: It stretches more than 4,300 kilometers from the border with Peru and Bolivia, at a tropical latitude of 17° 30' south, to sub-Antarctic Cabo de Hornos (Cape Horn), at 56° south. On the other hand, it is never wider than about 285 kilometers, between the Pacific Ocean and the Bolivian border.

Lying where the Nazca and South American tectonic plates collide, Chile is one of the world's most seismically active countries. In 1906, only a few months after earthquake and fire rocked and scorched San Francisco, its Chilean counterpart Valparaíso suffered a similar disaster. A tsunami triggered by the massive 1960 earthquake, near the southern city of Valdivia, devastated coastal areas from Concepción to Chiloé, and left many thousands homeless. Seismic safety has improved, but earthquakes are not going away.

© WAYNE BERNHARDSON

Mountains

Chile's most imposing feature is the longitudinal Andean range, which extends from its northern borders to southern Patagonia, where it gradually disappears beneath the oceans. Along the Pacific "ring of fire," it has numerous active volcanoes—some of them *very* active.

The highest point is the 6,885-meter summit of Ojos del Salado, east of the city of Copiapó, but much of the northern Andes and altiplano (high steppe) exceeds 4,000 meters. To the south, the Andes are lower but still spectacular.

Throughout most of the country, there is a lower coastal range, but even some parts of it exceed 2,000 meters. From Puerto Montt south, it forms an intricate series of channels and fjords.

Rivers

From the Andes, transverse rivers flow generally west toward the Pacific; in the desert north, they rarely reach the sea, but even then they often provide irrigation water. From Santiago south, several carry enough volume for good to world-class white-water rafting and kayaking, and some still irrigate the fields of the Central Valley.

The largest rivers are the Biobío, whose lower stretches are navigable (its upper basin, once a magnet for white-water daredevils, now lies mostly submerged beneath hydroelectric reservoirs); the Futaleufú, still providing recreational thrills but also threatened with major dam projects; and the remote but equally threatened Baker, which carries the largest flow of any Chilean river.

Lakes

Chile is famous for its southern Lakes District, where receding Pleistocene glaciers have left a legacy of indigo bodies of water. Even in the desert north, there are surprises such as Lago Chungará, home to a wealth of birdlife. The remote Aisén region has countless lakes barely touched by anglers.

CLIMATE

Because Chile stretches from the desert tropics, where solar intensity and daylight vary little over the year, to southern latitudes where blustery maritime conditions prevail and seasonal variations can be dramatic, it's difficult to generalize about climate. Moreover, altitude plays a major role almost everywhere.

As a rule, the Norte Grande is rainless, but cool ocean currents and coastal fogs keep temperatures mild. Rainfall increases west to east, where the precordillera and altiplano experience a summer rainy season (December–March or April), paradoxically known as the *invierno altiplánico* (altiplano winter) or *invierno boliviano* (Bolivian winter, as storms come from that direction). Afternoon thundershowers, common at that time of year, can make secondary roads impassable.

The arid Norte Chico gets a brief winter rainy season that, after rare downpours, brings a vivid explosion of wildflowers to the desert floor. Its altiplano has bitterly cold winters.

The heartland has a Mediterranean climate, with wet winters and dry summers; the rainy season runs roughly May–October, the dry season November–April. About 500 kilometers south of Santiago, the city of Los Ángeles marks the transition to a marine west coast climate with cool temperatures and evenly distributed annual rainfall.

Its receding glaciers sensitive to warming, Chilean Patagonia is a living laboratory for climate-change studies. While it's the country's wettest and coolest region, its inclemency is often overstated—despite its geographical position at the continent's southern tip, it's far from Antarctica. Eastern parts of it are even arid steppe, with low rainfall but high winds, especially in summer.

Flora and Fauna

With latitudinal limits comparable to those between Havana and Hudson's Bay, and elevations ranging from oceanic to alpine, one would expect a diversity of flora and fauna. While this is true to a degree, it's also misleading: Tropical northern Chile, for instance, is desert rather than rainforest, and the southern rainforests contain large single-species stands. Still, the high Andes and the arid Atacama make Chile a biogeographical island; much of its biota will be novel to foreign visitors, especially those from the Northern Hemisphere.

CONSERVATION ORGANIZATIONS

In charge of national parks and other protected areas, the Corporación Nacional Forestal (Conaf, Avenida Bulnes 291, Santiago, tel. 02/3900282, 02/3900125, www.conaf.cl) provides information and also sells maps, books, and pamphlets at its Santiago offices. It also has offices in every regional capital and some other cities, and visitors centers and/or ranger stations at nearly all its units.

Renace (Seminario 774, tel. 02/2234483, Ñuñoa, Santiago, www.renace.cl) is a loose alliance of environmental organizations. The highly professional Fundación Terram (General Bustamante 24, 5-I, Providencia, Santiago, tel. 02/2694499, www.terram.cl) emphasizes sustainable development.

The best-known forest preservation organization is Defensores del Bosque Chileno (Defenders of the Chilean Forest, Alvaro Casanova 613, Peñalolén, Santiago, tel. 02/2780237, www.elbosquechileno .cl). Headed by founder/botanist Adriana Hoffman, its focus is native forest preservation and restoration.

Ever since 1968, the Comité de la Defensa de Flora y Fauna (Committee for the Defense of Flora and Fauna, or Codeff, Ernesto Reyes 035, Providencia, Santiago, tel. 02/7772534, www.codeff.cl) has focused on practical projects to preserve and restore native plants and animals, often in cooperation with government agencies such as Conaf.

VEGETATION ZONES

Floral associations are correlated with latitude and altitude.

Coastal Deserts

Much of northernmost Chile is barren. Even in the river valleys that descend from the Andes, water may reach the ocean only during major floods, but subsurface aquifers support desert scrub and even irrigated agriculture.

One exception to this arid sterility is the Pampa del Tamarugal, a forested plain east of the city of Iquique. These woodlands of *tamarugo,* a relative of the common mesquite, are mostly plantations, but they represent restoration of a native species that flourished on fossil Andean water before their deforestation for the colonial silver-mining industry.

Precordillera

As rainfall increases with altitude and distance from the coast, the hillsides sprout stands of the appropriately named candelabra cactus. Eventually, the cacti yield to several species of low-growing shrubs known collectively as *tola* but also stands of stunted *queñoa,* one of the world's highest-altitude trees.

Altiplano

The altiplano, also known as the *puna,* consists mostly of patchy perennial grasses interspersed with *tola,* though there are a few signature species such as the rock-hard *llareta (Laretia compacta),* a shrub so densely branched that it resembles a spreading moss. The altiplano also contains patches of well-watered marshlands known collectively as *bofedales* or *ciénagas,* which provide year-round pasture for domestic llamas, alpacas, and sheep. In some cases, indigenous pastoralists have expanded the *bofedales* through an ingenious system of canals.

nalca (Gunnera chilensis) flowers in Parque Nacional Puyehue

Valdivian Cloud Forest

In scattered parts of the Norte Chico, drip from the *camanchaca* (coastal fog) supports a verdant forest whose closest geographical counterpart occurs in the well-watered Sur Chico. The best place to see this is Parque Nacional Bosque de Fray Jorge, west of the city of Ovalle.

Mediterranean Scrub

From the Norte Chico through most of the heartland, the native flora consists mostly of sclerophyllous (glossy-leaved) shrubs that evolved to survive long dry summers. Their Northern Hemisphere analogue is the California chaparral.

Some southern beech *(Nothofagus)* species appear at higher elevations in the heartland coast range. Once common, the native palm *Jubaea chilensis* is slowly declining because of overexploitation for economic ends.

Broadleaf and Coniferous Forest

South of the Río Biobío, various broad-leaved southern beeches, both evergreen and deciduous, are the most abundant trees. Several conifers also grow here, particularly the coniferous *paraguas* (umbrella) or monkey puzzle tree, so called because its crown resembles an umbrella and its limbs a monkey's curled tail; the Mapuche call it *pewen*. Also coniferous, the long-lived *alerce* or *lawen* is endangered because of its high timber value, though most stands are now protected. Both the *pewen* and *lawen* are national monuments.

Temperate Rainforest

In western Chilean Patagonia, heavy rainfall supports dense coastal and upland southern beech forests, though there are many other broadleaf trees and even the occasional conifer such as the *ciprés del los Guaitecas* (Guaytecas cypress). In some areas, though, this forest has suffered at the hands of corporations and colonists.

Patagonian Steppe

On the eastern plains of Magallanes, Tierra del Fuego, and parts of Aisén, in the rain shadow of the Andes, decreased rainfall supports extensive grasslands. In some areas, thorn scrub such as the fruit-bearing barberry *calafate* is abundant. From the late 19th century, sheep grazing for wool denuded these natural pastures.

The Pacific Islands

While greatly transformed by nonnative invaders, the Juan Fernández archipelago exhibits such great floral diversity that it's a UNESCO World Biosphere Reserve. Easter Island (Rapa Nui), however, has a badly impoverished flora partly because of its deforestation for rollers to move its famous stone monuments. The native tree *toromiro (Sophora toromiro),* for instance, no longer exists in its natural environment; efforts to reintroduce it from mainland botanical gardens have so far failed.

FAUNA

Like its flora, Chile's fauna is largely correlated with altitude. In a sense, the entire country is an island—the high Andes separate it from the rest of the continent, while the northern deserts impede the easy southward migration of plants and animals.

Marine, Coastal, and Aquatic Fauna

Paralleling the coastline, the Peru–Chile Trench reaches depths exceeding 8,000 meters; upwelling nutrients and the north-flowing Peru or Humboldt Current make this one of the world's richest fishing grounds.

Seafood distinguishes Chilean cuisine—so much so that one North American foodie wrote that he felt he was observing the marine life of another planet.

In the Norte Grande, the indigenous Chango fished from rafts crafted from southern sea lion hides, found from the Peruvian border all the way to Tierra del Fuego. The southern elephant seal and southern fur seal are both classified as threatened or regionally endangered. The Juan Fernández fur seal is a narrow endemic found only on its namesake archipelago.

Several other Chilean marine mammals are in danger of immediate extinction without remedial action, including several whale species and the *chungungo* (sea otter). The bottlenose dolphin and its relatives are common sights.

Terrestrial and Freshwater Fauna

Chile is poor in terms of land fauna, especially large mammals.

Mammals: The only large carnivore is the puma (mountain lion). Other wild felines include the smaller Andean cat and the jaguarundi, both endangered species. Two otter species, the long-tailed otter and the southern river otter, are also endangered. There are no wolves, but fox species include the threatened Argentine gray fox.

Wild grazing mammals include the northern altiplano's vicuña, an endangered camelid related to the domestic llama and alpaca. Its more widely distributed cousin, the wild guanaco, is most abundant on the Patagonian steppe but also found in parts of the Andes. Domestic

Feral horses are responsible for substantial environmental damage at Rano Raraku, Parque Nacional Rapa Nui.

© WAYNE BERNHARDSON

livestock such as cattle, horses, burros, sheep, and goats are of course very common.

The South Andean *huemul,* a cervid that appears on Chile's coat-of-arms, is the subject of a joint Argentine-Chilean conservation effort. The related North Andean *huemul* occurs only in the Norte Grande. The territory of the *pudú,* a miniature deer, extends from the Sur Chico well into Chilean Patagonia.

Two noteworthy rodent species, the Andean vizcacha and its smaller nocturnal cousin the chinchilla, inhabit the northern altiplano. The former occupies large rookeries and is easy to spot.

Reptiles and Amphibians: Chile is not quite snake-free, but they are rare and there are no venomous species. Even lizards are a rare sight.

Freshwater Fish and Crustaceans: Crustaceans are particularly uncommon, though the Salar de Atacama is home to a tiny brine shrimp.

Birds

What it lacks in other wildlife, Chile more than compensates for in birds, especially in the Norte Grande and southern Patagonia's steppes and oceans. For Northern Hemisphere visitors and especially dedicated birders, the great majority are novelties on their life lists.

In the altiplano east of Arica, Parque Nacional Lauca (a UNESCO World Biosphere Reserve) and its vicinity are home to more than 150 bird species. Among them are the signature Andean condor, the ostrich-like *ñandú* or *suri,* the Andean flamingo, the Chilean flamingo, the James flamingo, the peregrine falcon, the *tagua gigante* (giant coot), the Andean gull, and many waterfowl species.

Some 240 species inhabit the Magellanic region, including the wandering albatross (with its awesome four-meter wingspan), the black-necked swan, the Coscoroba swan, the flightless steamer duck, the kelp gull, and several penguin species, most commonly the Magellanic or jackass penguin; its endangered relative, the Humboldt penguin, ranges far to the north. The greater rhea, also known as *ñandú,* roams the Patagonian steppes.

Invertebrates

For purely practical purposes, pay attention to pests and dangers such as mosquitoes, flies, and ticks, which can be disease vectors, even though maladies such as malaria and dengue are almost unheard of—the mosquito vector for dengue has been found on Easter Island (Rapa Nui). The disease itself was detected in 2002, and there were three cases in 2007.

The reduvid, or assassin bug, which bears trypanosomiasis (Chagas' disease), is present in Chile, but hardly cause for hysteria.

The Cultural Landscape

Chile's natural landscapes, flora, and fauna are fascinating and enchanting, but the country also has a cultural landscape, transformed by human agency over the millennia. Few areas are truly pristine, but their landscapes are no less intriguing for all that.

As outliers of the great Andean civilizations, the Norte Grande and Norte Chico, and even parts of the heartland, still show tangible evidence of those times. Many *pukarás* (fortresses),

pircas (walls), and pre-Columbian roads survive, along with geoglyphs covering entire hillsides along ancient trade routes.

In the southern heartland, the Sur Chico, and Patagonia, shifting cultivators and nomadic pre-Columbian peoples left less-conspicuous landmarks, but there are aboriginal rock art sites. One of the continent's most important early human sites is at Monte Verde, near Puerto Montt.

AGRICULTURE AND THE LANDSCAPE

In some areas, such as the precordillera of Region I (Tarapacá), local communities have retained control of their better lands and constructed durable terrace systems to conserve soil and maintain productivity. Native crops such as quinoa are still grown in some areas.

While *bofedales* may appear to be natural marshes, and do support abundant wildfowl, today's Aymara llama and alpaca herders continue to expand the area covered by these valuable grasslands with ingenious irrigation canals that are only obvious on close inspection.

Because the southern pre-Columbian peoples were shifting cultivators, their impact on the landscape is less obvious. Although they cut the forest and used fire to clear the fields before planting, long fallow periods allowed the woodlands to recover; what seems to be virgin forest is often secondary growth.

The Spaniards' arrival brought major changes. At first content to collect tribute from the indigenous population, they became landholders as that population declined through introduced diseases and other causes. Their large rural estates, known as haciendas or *fundos,* consisted of cultivated land surrounded by larger areas that pastured cattle, horses, and other European livestock. In Patagonia, the sprawling sheep *estancia,* producing wool for Europe and North America, was the dominant institution.

SETTLEMENT LANDSCAPES

After the Spaniards took control of Chile, they instituted a policy of *congregación* or *reducción,* which concentrated native populations in villages or towns for the purposes of political control and religious evangelization. At best inconvenient for most indigenous peoples, this contributed to land disputes within indigenous communities, and between indigenous communities and Spaniards.

Still, in many areas, the need to be close to one's fields or animals has reinforced a dispersed rural settlement pattern—in the altiplano, for instance, apparently deserted villages have become ceremonial sites where people gather for their patron saint's festival. The traditional house is an adobe, usually with a thatched or tiled roof, and small windows to conserve heat; earthquakes, though, have encouraged concrete-block construction, and galvanized roofing is simpler to install and easier to repair.

Some vernacular architecture survives in the south. Many Mapuche still inhabit traditional *rucas,* plank houses with thatched roofs customarily erected with community labor. On parts of the Chiloé archipelago, some neighborhoods of *palafitos* (houses on stilts or pilings) have withstood earthquakes and tsunamis. In Patagonia, 19th-century "Magellanic" houses affect a Victorian style, with wooden framing covered by metal cladding and topped by corrugated metal roofs.

Cities, of course, differ from the countryside. Traditionally, colonial houses fronted directly on the street, with an interior patio or garden for family use; any setback was almost unheard of. This pattern survives, though building materials have changed from adobe to concrete. Many wealthier Chileans, though, have built houses with large gardens, on the suburban model, but surrounded by high fences and state-of-the-art security.

Northern mining towns like Iquique are notable for their Georgian-style gingerbread architecture, but the most distinctive urban style belongs to the spontaneous city of Valparaíso, which has adapted itself admirably to the contours of its hilly terrain.

Environmental Issues

Chile faces a multitude of environmental issues, both urban and rural, including air, water, and noise pollution, garbage disposal, wildland conservation, and soil degradation. According to a study by the nonprofit Fundación Terram, the mining, fishing, and forestry industries are major environmental culprits.

The official environment agency is the Comisión Nacional del Medio Ambiente (Conama, www.conama.cl), which reports directly to the president. Many conservationists, though, consider it weak and incapable of withstanding industry pressures.

AIR POLLUTION

One of Chile's most intractable problems is air pollution. In 2001, the journal *Science* ranked Santiago as the Americas' second most polluted city, after only Mexico City, and matters have not improved.

Like Los Angeles (California), Santiago lies in a basin between the coastal range and high mountains that block the dispersal of pollutants from smokestack industries and automobile emissions, and dust from unpaved streets and roads outside the central city. Rain washes some pollutants out of the sky, but the long, dry summer and the stagnant autumn air often result in heavy haze.

Except in summer, there are weekday restrictions on vehicles without catalytic converters. Still, when the Lagos administration placed limited restrictions on vehicles with catalytic converters on truly extreme days, rightist politicians and automobile owners protested vociferously.

Residents of the wealthy eastern suburbs argue that their new vehicles pollute less than older automobiles and buses used by other commuters. While not entirely false, this argument overlooks the congestion created by numerous private vehicles, which increases the time that internal combustion engines spend idling.

The new Transantiago public bus system has gotten the worst diesel-polluting offenders off the streets, but clumsy implementation has driven some commuters back to their cars.

Other antipollution measures include bus-only lanes on the Alameda, the city's major thoroughfare, and some other streets, as well as higher-quality, lower-sulfur diesel fuel.

Even the countryside is not free of pollution. Agricultural burning is widespread and summer forest fires are common, especially in the heartland's dry Mediterranean climate. In mining areas such as Chuquicamata, Pacific westerlies billow toxic clouds across the desert. In the Sur Chico, the main source is ash from firewood, used for heating and cooking even in cities the size of Temuco.

In far southern Chile, depletion of the Antarctic ozone layer has exposed both humans and livestock to summer ultraviolet radiation. The gaping ozone hole is a global problem, but Chileans suffer the consequences of its aerosol-triggered deterioration.

WATER POLLUTION

Most municipalities have sewer systems, but wastewater treatment is inconsistent. Rivers, lakes, and oceans themselves can become open sewers.

Current legislation, though, requires Santiago to become the first Latin American capital to treat all its wastewater, and a major project to reclaim malodorous Río Mapocho has begun. More than half of the country's industry is in Santiago, and additional legislation requires private factories to draft wastewater management plans and implement them within a few years.

Nonmetropolitan industries such as agriculture, forestry, and mining also contribute to the contamination of streams and seas. Many commercial fruit growers rely on far more chemical fertilizers and pesticides than necessary to augment their flourishing exports, while pulp mills pump toxic waste into the rivers. Salmon farming causes chemical runoff problems in the Sur Chico and Patagonia.

NOISE POLLUTION

Antique diesel buses are not the nuisance they once were, but 18-wheel trucks are still a

THE CHILEAN PATH TO CONSERVATION

One of Latin America's most far-sighted conservation projects is the Lagos administration's **Sendero de Chile,** a foot-, bicycle-, and horse path linking the Norte Grande's altiplano, near the Peruvian border, with southern Patagonia's sub-Antarctic tundra. Intended for both environmental and recreational purposes, its initial segments opened in 2001, but the ambitious goal is to finish the project by 2010, the bicentennial of Chilean independence.

Comparable to the United States' Pacific Crest Trail in the terrain it covers, but more like the older Appalachian Trail in that authorities hope to encourage community maintenance, the trail will pass through a representative sample of precordillera and upper Andean ecosystems. There is even the unprecedented possibility of cooperation with Argentina, where the route passes through the vicinity of the Campo de Hielo Sur, the southern Patagonian ice sheet that once engendered a bitter border dispute between the two countries.

Conama, the state environmental agency entrusted with the project, permits no motorized transport whatsoever on the two-meter-wide dirt and gravel trail. Mostly following the Andean foothills, the route provides detours to important natural, cultural, or even commercial features such as archaeological sites, wineries, and crafts markets.

Conama hopes the trail will attract both urban day-trippers and Chilean and foreign outdoor enthusiasts to hike some or all of its length. Along the route there will be rustic cabins and campsites, built in locally appropriate styles, as well as mileage markers and informational panels on flora and fauna. Because one project goal is to encourage local development, there will be special emphasis on local place-names and cultural monuments.

Since early 2001, when Ricardo Lagos himself inaugurated the first kilometer at Parque Nacional Conguillío, thousands of kilometers have opened to the public. This progress may not be so great as it implies, though – parts of it link preexisting trails in national parks, reserves, and monuments. Some segments will pass through private land, and private companies and individuals will become involved.

Conama and its tourism counterpart, Sernatur, are now promoting this as the world's longest hiking trail, in excess of 8,500 kilometers by its presumed completion in 2010. To follow its progress, visit the Sendero de Chile website (www.senderodechile.cl), which details access, services, and routes.

---

problem. Other contributors include cars and motorcycles with inadequate mufflers, "personal watercraft" on otherwise placid lakes, and public performances of amplified music.

SOLID WASTE

Poor solid-waste management also contributes to air pollution and health problems, not to mention its aesthetics—at Lampa, on Santiago's northern outskirts, productive farmland is disappearing beneath unregulated dumping. Chile also has many informal rubbish dumps.

Despite disposal problems, city streets are relatively clean even if, in the course of Chile's rush toward "development," disposable beverage containers and other undesirable packaging have proliferated.

Metropolitan residents produce an average of one kilogram of solid waste daily, and recycling is limited—by 2010, according to Conama, only about 10 percent of this will be recovered. The big culprit, though, is mining—99 percent of Chile's solid waste comes from that sector.

ENERGY

Energy shortages are the factor that most threatens to derail the economy—the southernmost Magallanes region has crude oil in small amounts only, so the country must purchase nearly everything on the international market.

It has a little more natural gas (recent discoveries in remote Tierra del Fuego are promising, but unlikely to satisfy the shortfall); neighboring Bolivia and Argentina have ample supplies but are politically unreliable.

Chile has some sustainable energy resources, primarily hydroelectricity, but projects such as damming the Río Biobío have not come close to satisfying growing demand. The remaining potential hydroelectric sites—continental Chiloé's Río Futaleufú and Aisén's Río Baker—are remote and would involve serious environmental disruption, but they may well be developed.

In the Sur Chico, which lacks natural gas infrastructure, even cities the size of Temuco (population 233,000) and Valdivia (population 130,000) still use firewood for domestic heating and cooking). This is theoretically sustainable, but it brings serious air pollution problems—after Santiago, Temuco probably has the worst air quality of any Chilean city.

Alternative energy sources have not yet been seriously explored—even though the northern deserts, where the mining industry is the major user, have almost unlimited solar potential. The Patagonian steppes of Aisén and Magallanes have wind power potential; a new wind farm has recently appeared on Coyhaique's outskirts.

DEFORESTATION AND SOIL CONSERVATION

According to Conaf, the country possesses 13.4 million hectares of native forest, 3.9 million of which enjoy government protection as part of the Sistema Nacional de Áreas Silvestres Protegidas (Snaspe, or National System of Protected Wild Areas). The remaining 9.5 million hectares are in private hands, 80 percent of whom are small or medium-sized landowners. Most of these forests are in southern Chile.

Native forest conservation is a hot-button issue for Chilean activists, who have led successful opposition to the Cascada Chile wood chip project in Region X (Los Lagos), which was canceled in early 2001, and a similar effort by the U.S.-based Trillium Corporation in Region XII (Magallanes).

According to the industry-oriented Corporación de Madera (Corma), 90 percent of the wood arriving at Chilean factories comes from forest plantations and only 10 percent from native forests. This figure is misleading, though, in that eucalyptus and Monterey pine plantations have often replaced heavily logged native woodlands. Moreover, 70 percent of the 10 million cubic meters of wood used annually for heating and cooking in Chilean households comes from native forests.

Some foreign environmental organizations, such as the Sierra Club, question free trade agreements because they believe Chile's environmental legislation, particularly on native forests, to be weak. In late 2008, Congress passed a Ley de Recuperación del Bosque Nativo (Native Forest Recovery Law) designed to provide economic incentives for owners of native forest properties, promote sustainable harvest with subsidies, and discourage nonnative plantations, but many environment advocates are dissatisfied with the details.

NATIONAL PARKS AND OTHER PROTECTED AREAS

While Chile has an impressive roster of national parks, reserves, and monuments, covering a remarkably large area, it has been criticized for not doing more to conserve environmentally significant areas close to population centers, especially when conservation conflicts with established economic interests such as forestry and mining.

The main conservation agency is the Corporación Nacional Forestal (Conaf, National Forestry Corporation, www.conaf .cl), which manages the Sistema Nacional de Áreas Silvestres Protegidas (Snaspe, National Protected Areas System). Within Snaspe, Chile has three principal categories of protection: *parques nacionales* (national parks), *reservas nacionales* (national reserves), and *monumentos naturales* (natural monuments). In addition, Chilean law allows the establishment of private natural reserves (*reservas naturales privadas* or *santuarios de la naturaleza*), which are growing in number and importance.

History

On the periphery of the continent's pre-Columbian civilizations, Chile cannot match renown and colossal monuments of those in other nations, but its history has an epic intensity all its own. Integrating that past with the present is a challenge, and it's hard for many analysts to avoid polemic.

PREHISTORY

Human occupation of the Americas, unlike that of Africa, Europe, and Asia, is relatively recent. The earliest immigrants reached North America from East Asia more than 12,500 years ago, when sea levels fell during the last major continental glaciation and united the two continents via the Bering Strait land bridge. Some researchers believe this migration, interrupted by interglacials during which rising sea levels submerged the crossing, began tens of thousands of years earlier. Nevertheless, by the time the bridge last closed about 10,000 years ago, the entire Western Hemisphere was populated, at least thinly, with hunter-gatherer bands in environments that varied from barren, torrid deserts to sopping rainforests to frigid uplands and everything in between.

Evidence of Paleo-Indian hunter-gatherers is scarce in Chile, but one of the continent's oldest archaeological sites is at Monte Verde, just north of Puerto Montt. Radiocarbon dating there has given a figure of 13,000 years at a site that, according to archaeologist Tom Dillehay, has some of the continent's earliest evidence of architecture, as well as use of wild potatoes and other native tubers. The most geographically proximate early man sites—later than Monte Verde—are at least 900 kilometers north. Dillehay's research, while generally accepted, has earned some criticism for its early dates.

As important as hunting was to the first Americans, wild plants probably contributed more to the diet. As the population gradually reached its saturation point under hunter-gatherer technology, people began to rely on so-called incipient agriculture. In the process

of gathering, these early farmers had acquired knowledge of seed plant cycles, and they selected, scattered, and harvested them in a lengthy domestication process. The earliest domesticates may have been Amazonian root crops such as manioc, but as these are perishable tubers rather than durable seeds, there is little supporting evidence.

In any event, starting about 6000 B.C., beans, squash, and potatoes became the staples of an agricultural complex that, as population grew, supported a settled village life and then the Andean civilizations. When the Spaniards finally arrived, according to one scholar, they found "the richest assemblage of food plants in the Western Hemisphere." Domestic animals were few, though—just the dog (sometimes raised for food), the guinea pig (definitely raised for food), and the llama and alpaca (both raised for food and fiber, with the llama also serving as a pack animal).

Slower to develop than the Andean region, southern mainland society remained semi-sedentary and more egalitarian until shortly before the Spanish invasion. In Patagonia, some indigenous peoples sustained a hunter-gatherer way of life even into the 20th century.

PRE-COLUMBIAN CIVILIZATION AND CULTURES

In Pre-Columbian times, then, what is now Chile comprised a diversity of native peoples ranging from small isolated bands of hunter-gatherers to semiurbanized outliers of Tiwanaku (in present-day Bolivia) and Inka Cuzco (in present-day Peru).

Inhabiting the westward-sloping precordillera and the altiplano of today's Norte Grande, politically subordinate to the Inka, the Aymara were part of an exchange system between peoples occupying different ecological niches. The coastal Chango, for instance, moved products such as fish and guano up the transverse river valleys in return for agricultural and livestock products such as maize, *chuño* (freeze-dried potatoes), *ch'arki* (freeze-dried meat), and llama and alpaca wool. Llamas, of course, carried the goods from sea level to the *puna*.

South of the Río Loa, the Atacameño practiced a similar subsistence, but both they and the more southerly Diaguita operated on a looser tether from the Inka state and its tributary obligations. South of the heartland, where the Inka had an equally tenuous control over the sedentary Picunche, other Araucanian peoples—the semisedentary Mapuche and the closely related Pehuenche, Huilliche, and Puelche, as well as the Cunco—withstood both the Inka expansion and, for over three centuries, the Spanish invasion. Among the reasons they survived were their mobility, as shifting cultivators, and their decentralized political structure—not easily dominated by the bureaucratic Inka.

In Patagonia, hunting, fishing, and gathering were the primary means of subsistence for peoples such as the Chonos, Tehuelche, Kawéskar (Alacaluf), Yámana (Yahgan), and Selkn'am (Ona), who proved unconquerable until sheep occupied their hunting grounds and introduced European diseases nearly obliterated them.

The Inka Empire and Its Collapse

At the time of the Spanish invasion, the Inka ruled a centralized but unwieldy empire; their hold was especially tenuous on the southern Araucanian (Mapuche) frontier. Though Inka political achievements were impressive, they were relative latecomers, only consolidating their power around A.D. 1438. Building on earlier Andean advances in mathematics, astronomy, and other sciences, they were literate and sophisticated, but their hierarchical organization, like that of the modern Soviet Union, proved unsustainable.

As the 16th century approached, because of internal divisions after the premature deaths of the Inka ruler Huayna Capac and his immediate heir, there developed a struggle between potential successors Atahualpa and Huáscar. The fact that the Inka empire was a house divided

against itself helps explain why a small contingent of Spanish invaders could overcome vastly superior numbers, but it's only part of the story.

THE SPANISH INVASION AND COLONIAL CHILE

Christopher Columbus's so-called "discovery" of the "New World" was one of the signal events of human history. While he may have bungled his way into fame—according to geographer Carl Sauer, "The geography in the mind of Columbus was a mixture of fact, fancy and credulity"—the audacious Genovese sailor excited the interest and imagination of Spaniards and others who, within barely half a century, brought nearly all of present-day Latin America under at least nominal control.

Europeans had roamed the Caribbean for more than three decades after Columbus's initial voyage, but the impulse to conquer South America came from Mexico and especially Panama, which Francisco Pizarro and his brothers used as a base to take Peru. From Peru, in 1535, Pizarro's partner and rival Diego de Almagro made the first attempt to take Chile, but his poorly organized expedition ended in failure as most of his personnel, retainers, and even livestock died. Four years later, after defeating an uprising by Almagro, Pizarro designated Pedro de Valdivia to undertake the conquest of Chile.

By 1541, Valdivia had founded Santiago and, in short order, La Serena, Concepción, Valparaíso, Villarrica, and his namesake city, Valdivia. He finally met his match, his own former Araucanian slave Lautaro, at the Battle of Tucapel, but before dying he had laid the groundwork for today's Chile.

The Spanish Imposition

From the beginning, Spain's presence had contradictory goals. Most invaders just meant to get rich, but others were Christian idealists who sought to save the souls of millions of Indians (putting aside for the moment the fact that these millions already had their own elaborate religious beliefs).

Consequently, the Spanish crown obliged its forces to read a statement known as the *requerimiento,* which offered their opposition the option to accept papal and Spanish authority over their lands in lieu of military subjugation. Whether or not they accepted, the indigenes became subject to a Spanish colonial system that, if less overtly violent than military conquest, was stacked against them.

Many prisoners of war became Spanish slaves and were shipped elsewhere in the Americas. Others who remained had to provide labor for individual Spaniards through the *repartimiento,* an ostensible wage system not always distinguishable from slavery. The *repartimiento,* in turn, is not easy to distinguish from the *encomienda,* a grant of Indian labor and tribute within a given geographical area. In principle, the Spanish *encomendero* was to provide reciprocal instruction in the Spanish language and catechization in Catholicism, but Spain's distant administration could rarely enforce these requirements. The *encomienda,* it should be emphasized, was *not* a land grant, though many *encomenderos* became large landholders.

Spanish institutions were most easily imposed in those areas that had been under Inka influence, as a tradition of hierarchical government let the Spaniards to place themselves atop the pyramid. Subjects accustomed to paying tribute to the Inka's representative now paid it to the *encomendero,* the Spanish crown's agent. This was different, however, with the unsubjugated Araucanians.

The Demographic Collapse and Its Consequences

One of the invasion's apparent mysteries was how so few Spaniards could dominate such large populations in so little time. Spanish weapons were not markedly superior—it took longer to reload a harquebus than a bow, for instance, and bow and arrow were probably more accurate. Mounted cavalry gave Spaniards a tactical edge in open terrain, but this was only occasionally decisive. The Spaniards took advantage of local factionalism, but that was not the entire story either. The Spaniards' greatest allies may have been microbes.

Ever since rising sea levels closed the Bering land bridge, the Americas had been geographically isolated from Europe and Asia. Diseases that had evolved in the Old World, such as smallpox, measles, plague, and typhus, no longer took a catastrophic toll there, but when the Spaniards inadvertently brought them to the New World, the diseases encountered immunologically defenseless human populations and spread like wildfire. One statistically sophisticated study concluded that introduced European diseases reduced highland Mexico's population from 25.2 million in 1518 to just a little over one million in 1605.

Similar disasters occurred throughout the Americas. In general the effect was heaviest in the humid tropical lowlands; in the cooler, drier highlands, disease spread more slowly, but was still overwhelming. In some parts of South America, it even preceded direct contact with the Spaniards—Huayna Capac's death may have been the indirect result of smallpox. For this reason, historian Murdo Macleod has called introduced diseases "the shock troops of the conquest."

The demographic collapse strongly influenced the development of Chilean society, especially in the Norte Grande and the heartland. While the population was large, *encomiendas* brought wealth to those who held them (including the Catholic church). As the population plummeted, *encomiendas* lost value—dead Indians paid no tribute.

Meanwhile, the *encomienda* came under political, legal, and judicial assault, as pro-Indian clergy such as the Mexico-based Dominican Bartolomé de las Casas argued for the institution's reform. The result was Charles V's so-called "New Laws" of 1542, which theoretically dissolved *encomiendas* on the *encomendero's* death. While local enforcement was lax, the days of the *encomienda* days were numbered.

In the absence of large populations to exploit, Spaniards took economic refuge in large rural estates, or haciendas, but lacked labor to work them. Over time, though, unattached Spanish men formed unions—formal and informal—with indigenous women; their resulting mestizo offspring brought a demographic rebound.

As long as the indigenous or mestizo population was small, land conflicts were few; as numbers recovered, though, the oligarchy's *latifundia* (large landholdings) contrasted dramatically with the *minifundia* (smallholdings) of peasant cultivators who struggled to eat, especially as average farm size declined with recovering populations. This divided the country into haves and have-nots, based on their access to land—a situation that would contribute to late-20th-century upheavals.

South of the heartland, the situation was different—the mobile Araucanians, assisted by their adoption of the Spanish-introduced horse, staved off the Spaniards and their Chilean successors for more than three centuries. In fact, the area south of the Río Biobío was widely known as a separate country called "Arauco." In far-off Patagonia, Spanish colonization efforts failed disastrously because of poor planning and extreme environmental conditions.

© WAYNE BERNHARDSON

bell tower and shrine at Parinacota

The Dissolution of Colonial Chile

Colonial Chile was an *audiencia* subdivision of the Viceroyalty of Peru; Spain had three other viceroyalties, in New Spain (based in Mexico), Nueva Granada (Colombia), and the Río de la Plata (Buenos Aires). The Audiencia of Chile was larger than the current republic, as it included the trans-Andean Cuyo region (now Argentine) and much of present-day Argentine Patagonia. Its capital was Santiago del Nuevo Extremo, now known as Santiago de Chile.

Appointed by the Spanish crown, major viceregal officials governed from the capital, and economic power was also concentrated there. Even Santiago formally depended on distant Madrid for legitimacy, but provincial bosses created their own power bases. With Napoleon's early 19th-century invasion of Spain, the glue that held the colonies together began to dissolve.

Contributing to this tendency was a changing sense of identity among Chile's people. In the early generations, people identified themselves as Spaniards, but *criollos* (American-born Spaniards) began to differentiate themselves from *peninsulares* (European-born Spaniards). While the mestizos and even the remaining indigenous population may have identified more closely with Chile than Spain, independence appealed most to the *criollo* intelligentsia.

The South American independence movements commenced on the periphery, with figures such as Argentina's José de San Martín, Venezuela's Simón Bolívar, and, of course, Chile's Bernardo O'Higgins. Chile marks its independence from 1810, when a local junta took over government in the name of Spain's Fernando VII, but it was nearly eight years more before a formal declaration. As Bolívar and San Martín converged on Lima for final victory over the Spaniards, O'Higgins remained in Santiago to consolidate Chile's self-determination.

REPUBLICAN CHILE

As heir to the *intendencias* of Santiago and Concepción, administrative subdivisions of the Viceroyalty of Peru, independent Chile comprised only the area from around Copiapó in the north to Concepción, in the south. A few other outliers, such as the city of Valdivia and the Chiloé archipelago, were under nominal Chilean control, but the Araucanians (Mapuches) still ruled the countryside.

To some degree, this worked to Chile's advantage. Compared to sprawling Argentina, where provincial warlords fought a weak central government, the compact Chilean polity and its fairly homogenous population were easy to govern. Nevertheless, despite Chile's reputation for liberal democracy, nearly all its 19th-century leaders (and many in the 20th) were military men.

O'Higgins was the first of these, but his own authoritarian tendencies and opposition from the landholding oligarchy undercut his position. After his resignation and exile in 1823, there were several years of instability before the wealthy merchant Diego Portales emerged as the power behind the executive, under a constitution that he himself wrote. Portales's constitution, which created a unitary state with Roman Catholicism as the official religion and instituted a property requirement for voting, even survived his death in a military mutiny in 1837. Until 1925, when Chile adopted a new constitution, Portales's document remained in force.

Favorable economic developments assisted Chile's stability. In the 1830s, a bonanza silver mine at Chañarcillo, near Copiapó, helped make the country solvent. Shortly thereafter, the California gold rush kindled demand for Chilean wheat, making Valparaíso one of Pacific America's premier ports. Simultaneously, Chile developed a navy to project its power elsewhere on the continent.

The Guerra del Pacífico and Territorial Consolidation

By the last quarter of the 19th century, Chile's population had roughly tripled to about 2.5 million, its economy had grown, and its commercial influence expanded beyond its borders. In 1879, after Chilean nitrate mining interests

protested unfair taxation by Bolivian authorities in the vicinity of Antofagasta (then part of Bolivia), Chilean forces occupied the port city, sparking the Guerra del Pacífico (War of the Pacific).

Despite Bolivia's strategic alliance with Peru, within four years Chile's well-organized forces had taken not only Antofagasta (landlocked Bolivia's only maritime outlet) but also Peru's southern provinces of Tacna, Arica, and Tarapacá, and even Lima. Eventually the Chileans returned everything but nitrate-rich Tarapacá and the port of Arica, where they granted Bolivia a railroad to the Pacific.

Like the silver strikes at Chañarcillo, nitrate shipments from the docks of Antofagasta, Iquique, and other ports that no longer exist earned enormous revenues and made some Chileans fabulously wealthy. At the same time, the proliferation of mining towns in the Norte Grande created a militant working class whose significance would not become obvious until the following century. One omen, though, was a march on Iquique by nitrate strikers, hundreds of whom—men, women and children—died when the army fired upon their refuge in the Escuela Santa María.

While disposing of Peru and Bolivia, Chile also managed to turn its attention to the Araucanian frontier and then the southern oceans. In 1881, treaties with the Mapuche paved the way for European, mostly German, immigration south of the Biobío; in 1888 the country participated in imperialism's classic age by annexing the volcanic speck of Easter Island, 3,700 kilometers west.

Meanwhile, Chile had consolidated its hold on its Patagonian territories, the city of Punta Arenas grew with the California gold rush, and the subsequent wool boom contributed to the country's newfound prosperity. The glitch in this trajectory was the 1891 civil war, which began as President José Manuel Balmaceda, a reformist, attempted to spread the benefits of that prosperity to the population at large. Ending the era of presidential supremacy, Balmaceda's suicide left a huge gap between haves and have-nots.

The Modern Republic and Its Demise

The early 20th century looked bright as nitrate income filled the state coffers, foreign freighters called at busy harbors, and the nascent copper industry advanced with North American investment. Soon, though, synthetic nitrates superseded Chile's northern ores, the Panama Canal reduced traffic around the Horn, and World War I cut commerce with Chile's British and German trading partners. Copper came to dominate the economy, as it still does in the present day.

As the Norte Grande's nitrate towns closed and large but underused rural estates pushed laborers off the land, heavy industry was unable to absorb urban immigrants. Increasingly well represented in government, the democratic left took a more interventionist role in industry and agriculture through the state development corporation Corfo, but it could never overcome the landed elite's entrenched power.

The electorate, meanwhile, fragmented into an alphabet soup of political parties in which the centrist Democracia Cristiana (DC) and its allies held the balance of power between a reactionary right that coalesced around the Partido Nacional (PN) and a multiplicity of leftist parties that included the relatively moderate Partido Comunista (PC, Communist Party) and the more militant Partido Socialista (PS, Socialist Party). Organizations such as the Movimiento de Izquierda Revolucionario (Revolutionary Leftist Movement, MIR) advocated the state's overthrow and made common cause with labor activists, Mapuche militants, and other land reform crusaders.

DC reformist president Eduardo Frei Montalva's 1964 election was a hopeful sign, but his six-year term failed to defuse the increasing polarization that resulted in the 1970 election, by a small plurality, of Socialist president Salvador Allende Gossens. Heading a leftist coalition known as the Unidad Popular (UP, Popular Unity), Allende became famous as the world's first freely elected Marxist head of state.

Allende, the Unidad Popular, and the *Golpe de Estado*

Despised by the political right, distrusted by the DC center, and viewed suspiciously by U.S. president Richard Nixon and his adviser, Henry Kissinger, Allende faced the task of redistributing Chile's wealth by constitutional means (Allende's friendly relations with Cuba's Fidel Castro did not improve his standing with Nixon and Kissinger). The government nationalized the copper industry and began a land reform program that enraged the right but failed to satisfy the revolutionary left.

In this confrontational milieu, political violence increased, the government's policy of printing money to cover its obligations brought triple-digit inflation, and conservative truckers paralyzed the economy with a transport strike. Finally, on September 11, 1973, a little-known army general, Augusto Pinochet Ugarte, unleashed a ferocious *golpe de estado* (coup d'etat) that began one of the most durable military dictatorships ever, on a continent notorious for such regimes.

Under orders from Pinochet and fellow plotters in the navy, air force, and Carabineros (national police), soldiers stormed Santiago's colonial La Moneda presidential palace. As planes bombed and straffed the building, Allende and his supporters made their last stand. Finally, according to Allende's personal physician Patricio Guijón, the president killed himself with a machine gun given him by Fidel Castro. Like Balmaceda in 1891, Allende ended his life to make a statement rather than go into exile.

The aftermath was nightmarish, as police and military rounded up thousands of Allende partisans and sympathizers, incarcerating them in locales such as Santiago's Estadio Nacional (National Stadium) and clandestine torture centers. At least 3,000 died, many more were tortured, and the term "disappeared" entered the global vocabulary to describe known opponents of the military whose remains were never found. Army general Sergio Arellano Stark toured northern Chilean cities to identify leftist figures for execution in the "Caravan of Death."

Pinochet emerged as the strongman of a four-member junta that included the heads of the other services. While intimidating Chileans at home, his agents also conducted a state-sponsored terror campaign that used car bombs to assassinate exiles such as constitutionalist general Carlos Prats in Buenos Aires (1974) and former diplomat Orlando Letelier in Washington, D.C. (1976), and they seriously injured Christian Democrat politician Bernardo Leighton in a shooting in Italy (1975).

The Pinochet Dictatorship

While the Pinochet dictatorship was a murderous police state, it was much more. Compared with neighboring Argentina, which experienced a bloodless 1976 coup with a bloody aftermath that continued for years, the Pinochet regime did its worst at the beginning. While suspending civil liberties, banning political parties, and enforcing measures such as a curfew that required citizens to be off the street by 11 P.M. well into the 1980s, it also undertook a coherent, if controversial, economic program that transformed the way Chileans live and work.

Inspired by the "Chicago School" of economists, the regime instituted the most radical free-market transformation ever implemented. It auctioned off state enterprises to balance the budget, reduced regulatory functions, promoted private health and pension plans, and encouraged foreign investment with favorable legislation. Despite some glitches—high inflation persisted for years, an unanticipated devaluation decimated salaries, and low copper prices slowed recovery—nontraditional exports such as off-season temperate fruits helped diversify the economy. By 1980, the recovery was impressive enough that Pinochet could hold—and win—a plebiscite that ratified a new constitution and confirmed his "presidency" until 1989. Many voters, though, abstained from the plebiscite, whose options were a simple "yes" or "no."

Confident of public support, Pinochet permitted political parties to operate openly again in 1987. Under his customized constitution, drafted by lawyer Jaime Guzmán, Pinochet held another plebiscite to extend his mandate until 1997. In this instance, though, an alliance of centrist and center-left parties that became known as the Concertación para la Democracia (Consensus for Democracy) opposed him.

The turning point in the "No" campaign occurred when Socialist Ricardo Lagos, in a television appearance on April 25, 1988, challenged the dictator with a *dedazo* (pointing finger) and an accusation: "You promise the country another eight years of torture, disappearances, and human rights violations" (two years earlier, Pinochet's "security forces" had ordered Lagos's assassination, but the Policía de Investigaciones [Investigations Police] ironically enough saved the politician by taking him into protective custody).

Despite widespread expectations that Lagos (elected president in 2000) would be arrested, the regime's failure to respond emboldened the Concertación, and the electorate rejected the extension of Pinochet's term by a healthy majority. Conservative businessman Sebastián Piñera (a presidential candidate in 2005 and 2009) also supported the democratic restoration by publicly announcing his "no" vote despite vicious verbal attacks by pro-Pinochet elements.

The Democratic Restoration

In 1989, Christian Democrat Patricio Aylwin easily won a four-year transitional presidency as the Concertación's candidate. Nevertheless, certain provisions of the Pinochet–Guzmán constitution perpetuated a dictatorial legacy.

In the 1993 elections, Christian Democrat Eduardo Frei Ruiz-Tagle, son of the late president Eduardo Frei Montalva, won a six-year presidential term. Both presidents only tweaked the economic model they inherited, as Chile experienced strong and steady growth, while arguing for constitutional reforms that would abolish its antidemocratic features.

Events overtook this moderate reformism in October 1998, when British officials arrested

Pinochet for human rights violations at the behest of Spanish judge Báltazar Garzón for deaths and disappearances of Spanish citizens after the 1973 coup. Despite public support from Frei's government, which felt it had to honor its part of the transition agreement and argued that only Chilean courts could deal with crimes alleged to have occurred in Chile, Pinochet suffered a series of legal reverses in British courts. The general's ordeal—if one can describe house arrest in a suburban London mansion by such a word—ended in March 2000, when British Home Secretary Jack Straw released him on grounds of ill health.

Though Pinochet went home, he was not home free. Unexpectedly, Santiago judge Juan Guzmán undertook an aggressive investigation of human rights complaints that resulted in the loss of Pinochet's senatorial immunity and his indictment in the Caravan of Death and other cases. Unfortunately, a divided appeals court ruled that the general's ostensibly deteriorating health prevented his mounting a defense and it suspended the proceedings.

Pinochet, though, undercut his own case by giving TV interviews in which he appeared more cogent that his attorneys and supporters claimed. On top of that, in 2005, investigators discovered more than a hundred questionable overseas bank accounts, totaling US$27 million, and false passports that implicated Pinochet and close family members. Daughter Lucía Pinochet Hiriart suffered the worst humiliation as she sought asylum in the United States, only to be strip-searched, shackled, and imprisoned for having an invalid visa; on being informed she would have to wait in prison indefinitely as U.S. authorities considered her request, she chose to return to Chile.

The "Riggs Bank" case destroyed Pinochet apologists' arguments that, even if the general was tough on his foes, he was honest. Things got worse in May 2006, though, when a Santiago judge filed charges against Pinochet in the 1993 murder of DINA chemist Eugenio Berríos in Uruguay. Berríos, suspected of having poisoned former Chilean president Eduardo Frei Montalva with sarin gas in 1982, was apparently ready to reveal the dictatorship's secrets in return for immunity (the cause of Frei's death after minor surgery is still under investigation).

The general successfully avoided prosecution before dying on December 10, 2006, at the age of 91. Once again under house arrest, he failed to enjoy the statesmanlike retirement he envisioned. Meanwhile, recent reforms have eliminated some of Jaime Guzmán's more unsavory provisions.

CONTEMPORARY CHILE

Even if Pinochet escaped final judgment, his 16-month detention in London, followed by indictment in Chilean courts, released political dialogue from the straitjacket it had worn since 1973. One measure of this new openness was the election to the presidency, in early 2000, of Pinochet critic Ricardo Lagos—the first Socialist to occupy the office since Salvador Allende. Current military leaders, for their part, appear embarrassed by the revelations of the past few years and seem more than willing to resume an apolitical role. General Juan Emilio Cheyre, the army commander-in-chief, even apologized to Chileans for his institution's role in the coup and its aftermath.

Another positive indicator was a public apology by rightist legislator María Pía Guzmán for having been aware of and ignoring human rights abuses committed during the dictatorship—though she drew fire from her unreconstructed colleagues. Leftist commentator Tomás Moulián, in response, called Guzmán's apology an example to Chilean society; at the same time, Moulián denounced those who continue to deny such abuses as a "Taliban" unwilling to give up their holy war against the left.

Nevertheless, most Chileans have moved on. According to editor Patricio Fernández of the iconoclastic weekly *The Clinic*:

> [T]he day they indicted the former unconstitutional president [Pinochet], after the

surprise of it all, no one really gave a hoot. With the exception of those who lost family members during the military government, or those who are political fanatics, or their accomplices, or three or four strange devils who went out to shout in the streets–the rest of us took the news in stride.

Still, in Fernández's words:

> We are left uncomfortable knowing that the Chilean state would much more forcefully prosecute a chicken thief than it would someone responsible for thousands of atrocities.

Government and Politics

Traditionally, Chilean politics is highly centralized, the ongoing legacy of Diego Portales in a country whose sprawling capital holds more than a third of the population. The 1980 constitution, written by Pinochet's lawyer Jaime Guzmán, changed this only slightly, moving the legislature to the port city of Valparaíso. The central government appoints governors and other officials of the 13 regions (recently increased to 15), but municipalities or *comunas* elect their own mayors and councilors.

ORGANIZATION

Chile's national government consists of separate and legally independent executive, legislative, and judicial branches. The popularly elected president works out of Santiago's La Moneda presidential palace but no longer resides there (there is no official presidential residence).

Based in Valparaíso, the bicameral Congreso Nacional (National Congress) consists of a 38-member Senado (Senate) and a 120-member Cámara de Diputados (Chamber of Deputies). Recent constitutional reform has eliminated eight so-called "institutional" senators, a Pinochet–Guzmán legacy that included ex-presidents and former armed forces heads. Based in Santiago, the 21-member Corte Suprema (Supreme Court) is the highest judicial authority.

POLITICAL PARTIES

Chile has many political parties, but Guzmán's cleverly crafted electoral system rewards coalitions that pool their votes rather than parties that stand alone. There are two major coalitions: the center-left Concertación para la Democracia (Consensus for Democracy) and the center-right Alianza por Chile (Alliance for Chile). Even within these coalitions, there are ideological and practical tensions that obstruct their efficient collaboration.

The Concertación, which has won every presidential election since the return to democracy, consists of the centrist Democracia Cristiana (DC, Christian Democrats), the more leftist Partido Socialista (PS, Socialist Party, less radical than in the Allende days) and Partido por la Democracia (PPD, Party for Democracy), and the Partido Radical Socialista Demócrata (PRSD, Radical Socialist Democratic Party). There is considerable ideological overlap among these parties.

The Alianza por Chile consists of the center-right Renovación Nacional (RN, National Renovation) and the ultra-right Unión Demócrata Independiente (UDI, Independent Democratic Union), but there is also ideological overlap between them. Founded by Jaime Guzmán, the more cohesive UDI has managed to make inroads into poorer neighborhoods with a populist approach, but has struggled to distance itself from its identification with the military dictatorship.

Several less-influential parties lack congressional representation: the Partido Comunista (PC, Communist Party), the Partido Humanista (Humanist Party), and the Partido Liberal (Liberal Party).

ELECTIONS

Following major 2005 reforms, Chile's constitution establishes a four-year term for a popularly elected president, who is not eligible for immediate reelection (he or she may run again after a four-year hiatus). If no candidate obtains a majority, the top two finishers stage a runoff.

In the January 2006 runoff, Concertación candidate Michelle Bachelet, a Socialist, became Chile's first female head of state by defeating the RN's Sebastián Piñera, a conservative but maverick businessman who broke early and publicly with the dictatorship. In the December 2005 primary, Piñera had defeated UDI candidate Joaquín Lavín, who finished a strong second to Ricardo Lagos in a 2000 runoff.

Under the 1980 Pinochet–Guzmán constitution, the Congreso has a binomial electoral system by which each district (60 for deputies and 19 for senators) elects two officials, but a list or coalition must double its rivals' votes to take both seats. In practice, this favored the conservative Alianza, whose total vote has always been smaller than that of the Concertación, though the difference is narrowing. The Congreso renews the 120-strong Chamber of Deputies and half the 38 Senate members every four years. Voting is obligatory for citizens registered, but registration itself is not.

As of mid-2009, the Concertación held a precarious majority in the Senate and a larger majority in the Cámara de Diputados, but the Alianza seemed likely to win the presidency and improve its legislative standing.

BUREAUCRACY

Unlike most other Latin American countries, Chile enjoys a reputation for integrity in public administration—regularly, the country receives the region's highest rating from the anticorruption organization Transparency International.

For the year 2008, using standards of general corruption in the political arena, bribery in the public sector, irregular payment practices, and obstacles to business, Transparency gave Chile a 6.9 rating on a 10-point scale, making it the 23rd-cleanest of 180 states evaluated in the study and the best, along with identically ranked Uruguay, in Latin America; the 18th-ranked United States, by way of comparison, received a slightly higher rating of 7.3.

The government agencies most travelers are likely to come into contact with are immigration, customs, and police, all of which are trustworthy as institutions. There are, however, instances of renegade cops who rob, steal, and intimidate, especially in lower-class neighborhoods.

THE MILITARY

Only a few years ago, it would have been impossible to write about Chilean politics without emphasizing the role of the military, whose impunity was the single greatest menace to domestic tranquility. After Pinochet's arrest in London, his prosecution in Santiago, revelations of human rights abuses, imprisonment of individuals such as former intelligence officer Manuel Contreras, and evidence of money laundering, the military leadership has kept its distance from the former regime. Many retired officers, though, remain unrepentant.

Under the constitution, the heads of the army, navy, air force, and Carabineros form a large part of the Consejo Nacional de Seguridad (Cosena, or National Security Council), but since the 2005 reforms, Cosena merely advises the president and the military has no voting role in the institution.

The army has 51,000 active members, about 10 percent of them women. About half the total are youthful conscripts; the remainder is about 10 percent officers 30 percent NCOs. Military service is obligatory but not universal; President Michelle Bachelet pledged to end the draft, but has failed to do so.

The navy contingent is roughly 22,000, about 14 percent of them women; its hardware consists of 29 vessels, only six of which are combat ships, plus four Talcahuano-based submarines. The 13,500-strong air force (FACh) has bases at Iquique, Antofagasta, Santiago, Puerto Montt, and Punta Arenas, and on

Antarctica's King George Island; 16 percent of its personnel are female. There are about 43,000 Carabineros (nationwide paramilitary police), about 10 percent of them women.

Educational changes in the military are tentatively encouraging. Since 2001, cadets at the army's Escuela Militar (War College) have studied human rights and international humanitarian law. Cadets also pursue civilian courses parallel to their military studies, graduating with a major in military science and a minor in humanities or science. In total, about 15 percent of the Chilean military are female.

Chile devotes more of its GDP (about 2.7 percent) to military spending than any other South American country except Colombia. Neighboring Argentina, by contrast, spends only about 1.2 percent of its GDP on its armed forces. The law stipulates that military spending cannot fall below 1989 levels nor drop in real terms, and guarantees it 10 percent of profits from Codelco's state copper sales.

Economy

While not large, Chile's economy remains one of the region's most stable and dynamic. For nearly two decades, it has enjoyed almost uninterrupted growth, though growth rates have fallen from upwards of 7 percent into the 4–5 percent range, and it's likely to have fallen even more in 2009. For 2007, estimated GDP was US$164 billion (about US$9,980 per capita), though an overvalued peso may have exaggerated the figure; it also disguises considerable income disparities. Inflation for 2008 was only 7.1 percent, but would have been higher if it were not for falling energy prices.

According to the Banco Central (Central Bank), the total foreign debt is about US$82 billion; the publicly held portion is about 12 percent of GDP. Recently, though, the peso has fallen against both the U.S. dollar and the euro, which increases the debt balance.

In 2009, the World Economic Forum's competitiveness evaluation rated Chile among the region's top economies. In addition to a global rating of 28th among 134 countries, Chile ranked 14th in macroeconomic stability, 37th in institutions, and 30th in infrastructure. It ranked lower in technology, but telephones are so reasonably priced that even Chileans of limited means have them (but not necessarily Internet connections, as home computers are often beyond their budgets).

Perhaps the economy's most obvious weakness is its dependence on mining, particularly copper. It's also vulnerable to energy shortages, getting less than 5 percent of its petroleum and natural gas from domestic sources; also in addition, Chile depends on erratic rainfall to fill its hydroelectric reservoirs, which produce 60 percent of the energy in the Central Interconnected Power System (SIC), which delivers electricity to 93 percent of the population. South-central Chile's heavy rainfall and extensive rivers make hydroelectricity the cheapest energy source, but at enormous environmental cost.

Despite its macroeconomic achievements, contemporary Chile has its critics. Journalist María Monckeberg's polemic *El Saqueo de Los Grupos Económicos al Estado de Chile* (*The Plundering of the Chilean State by Economic Groups*), published in 2001, took a muckraking approach toward the dictatorship's privatizations. According to Monckeberg, Pinochet's cronies:

> appropriated the big state-owned companies at a time when there were no freedoms, no real parliament, no unions and not a single newspaper that realized what was going on or was free to print it. Given those circumstances, the bottom line is they were free to do whatever they wanted.

SALVAGING CHILE'S RIVERS

Over the past decade-plus, the only environmental issue to rival forest preservation has been Chile's wild rivers, and the struggle over water rights and development will likely continue well into the future. This complex matter encompasses indigenous rights, energy use, air and water pollution, and economic development, and there's no easy answer.

Chile is poor in fossil-fuel resources, obtaining less than 10 percent of its own crude petroleum consumption and a small amount of coal from domestic sources in the southern region of Magallanes. Both industry and transportation rely on imported fuels, and the capital of Santiago has paid the price with some of the world's most polluted urban skies.

For both economic and environmental reasons, Chile would like to increase its supply of relatively clean hydroelectricity by building dams to hold the spring snowmelt from its transverse rivers. In the course of constructing a series of dams on the Río Biobío, though, the Spanish-Chilean utility Endesa ran afoul of a few determined Pehuenche Indian families who, backed by the 1992 Ley Indígena (Indigenous Law), vowed that "The only way we will be taken away from here, is once we are dead." In their opposition to the Ralco dam, one of half a dozen planned for the area, the Pehuenche were backed by conservationists and recreationists who saw the Biobío as one of the world's top streamside habitats and white-water rivers, even after construction of Endesa's Pangue dam a few years ago.

Endesa won that battle with an enormous buyout, but the Biobío was not the last threatened Chilean river. Many rafters and kayakers consider the Futaleufú, in southern Region X near the Argentine border, the world's greatest white-water challenge, but Endesa and other energy companies have options on its water rights, despite its isolation. Near the Region XI town of Cochrane, Endesa has plans to build a series of four massive dams on the nearly pristine Río Baker and Río Pascua; these would not only affect the local environment, but would require clear-cutting large swaths of forest for more than a thousand kilometers of transmission lines to connect them to the national grid.

Environmental advocates argue that sustainable activities, such as rafting and kayaking, fly-fishing, and even salmon farming (a bogeyman to some conservationists) are more appropriate uses. To promote their cause, Chilean conservation organizations such as the **Grupo de Acción Biobío** (Biobío Action Group) have made common cause with overseas affiliates such as the **International Rivers Network** (1847 Berkeley Way, Berkeley, CA 94703, tel. 510/848-1155, www.irn .org) and **FutaFriends** (349 Park Forest Way, Wellington, FL 33414, tel. 831/440-8650, www.futafriends.org). U.S. conservationist Robert F. Kennedy Jr. has brought several high-profile groups to raft the "Fu" and has questioned the long-term viability of Endesa's plans.

EMPLOYMENT, UNEMPLOYMENT, AND UNDEREMPLOYMENT

In a survey by the International Institute for Management Development, Chile displayed many strengths, but its labor force was a mixed bag—Chileans worked the longest hours on average of any country in the world, but per-hour productivity was low. According to another survey, per-worker productivity was about one-sixth that of U.S. workers. Many cities, for instance, employ a platoon of human parking meters—dead-end jobs that, whatever their merits in providing a paycheck, contribute little to economic development.

At the end of 2008, according to the Instituto Nacional de Estadística (INE, National Statistics Institute), the unemployment rate had risen to 7.5 percent, a 6.6 percent increase over the previous year, and 0.3 percent higher than the previous quarter's rate. It remained low in the southernmost regions of X (Los Lagos,

3.1 percent), XI (Aisén, 4.4 percent), and XII (Magallanes, 2.8 percent), but was distressingly high in regions XIII (Arica and Parinacota, 8.6 percent), V (Valparaíso, 10.1 percent), and IX (Araucanía, 10.2 percent).

Employment statistics can be misleading, though, as figures are significantly higher among young people. At the same time, the standard for calculating unemployment is whether an individual worked at all; anyone who spends even an hour in casual labor counts among the employed. Many individuals also labor as street vendors hawking ice cream, newspapers, and music cassettes, but their earnings are low and they often run afoul of the police. Because of seasonal agricultural work, unemployment figures fall in the spring and rise after the autumn harvest.

AGRICULTURE

Chile's agriculture is as diverse as its geography—from peasant cultivation of native grains and tubers on the Norte Grande's precordillera terraces to Sur Chico's dairy farms, Chiloé's potato fields, the sprawling wool *estancias* of Magallanes and Tierra del Fuego, and even the Polynesian horticultural complex of Easter Island (Rapa Nui). In the narrowest economic sense, though, the most valuable lands lie in the Mediterranean heartland.

Pedro de Valdivia himself painted Middle Chile as "the most abounding land in pastures and fields, and for yielding every kind of livestock and plant imaginable." With its fertile alluvial soils, mild temperatures, and lengthy growing season, it yielded plenty to support the Spaniards—in fact, well into republican times, the land was underused despite its suitability for wine grapes, temperate fruits, and abundant grains. It first attracted global attention when Chilean wheat fed the '49ers who scrambled over the Great Plains and sailed around the Horn en route to California's gold fields.

Today, Chile's US$2.7 billion fresh-fruit export industry provides much of the off-season wintertime fruit consumed in Northern Hemisphere countries, but it's facing competition from other Southern Hemisphere producers such as Argentina, New Zealand, and South Africa—though Chile's weaker peso has made Chilean produce less expensive overseas. With government encouragement, growers are attempting to maintain their leadership by reducing dependency on agricultural chemicals and meeting Good Agricultural Practices (GAP, www.chilegap.com) standards for environmental friendliness and safety; about 1,200 participate in a variety of such programs.

Chile has produced wine since colonial times, but only the 19th-century influx of French varieties gave it commercial significance; the great export boom has occurred in the past decade-plus. Commercial vines stretch from the northern Region III (Atacama), where the crop primarily consists of pisco grapes, to the southern Region IX (Araucanía), where production is precarious; the prime wine district runs from Region V (Valparaíso) through Region VII (Maule). The United States is the largest market, and, though fine wine exports have grown in recent years, some experts worry that production is unsustainably dependent on chemicals.

One interesting development is a plan to establish organic standards for all of Region XI (Aisén), which would simplify the export of products such as beef to the European Community. This could also apply to fruit-growing in the "banana belt" around Lago General Carrera, and even to fish farming.

INDUSTRY

If tropical Latin American nations have been "banana republics," 20th-century Chile was a "copper republic," and mining remains its major foreign exchange earner. For 2008, copper revenues exceeded US$34 billion and accounted for more than half of all exports. Skyrocketing prices, from US$0.82 per pound in 2000 to more than US$3 per pound by mid-2006 because of strong Chinese demand, fortified the economy. With the global slowdown of late 2008, though, prices had fallen to around US$1.50 in early 2009, demonstrating the vulnerability of reliance on a single commodity.

Copper's share of total exports has dropped

by half since the early 1970s but has remained stable since the early 1990s. Private mining companies now outproduce Codelco, the powerful state copper corporation, but even Pinochet's dictatorship dared not privatize Codelco—likely because the law designates 10 percent of its profits to the military.

Mining as a whole accounts for about 13 percent of GDP; other minerals include iron ore, nitrates, precious metals, lithium, and molybdenum. The greatest mines are in the Norte Grande—Chuquicamata has been the world's largest open pit mine, but others of more recent vintage are making substantial progress. El Teniente mine east of Rancagua is the world's largest subsurface mine.

Other industrial activities include mineral refining and metal manufacturing, food and fish processing, forest products industries including paper and wood, and textiles. In addition to Santiago, the main industrial centers are the Concepción–Talcahuano and Valparaíso–Viña del Mar conurbations.

FORESTRY

After mining, the single most important export is forest products; in 2005, it accounted for US$3.5 billion, 13 percent of exports. Most exports consist of wood pulp, but finished furniture is increasing.

The forestry sector is controversial for environmental reasons, as overexploitation of native forests and their replacement by exotics such as eucalyptus and Monterey pine have created biological deserts—about 90 percent of commercial woodlands are non-native plantations. Pollution from pulp plants, meanwhile, has been implicated in the deaths of black-necked swans near the southern city of Valdivia.

Forestry is also controversial for social and political reasons, as lumber companies have occupied ancestral lands of the Mapuche, who are increasingly vocal in seeking the return of the lands.

FISHING AND FISH FARMING

Thanks to the rich north-flowing Humboldt or Peru Current, which parallels the coast, Chile has become one of the world's leading fishing industry countries. Northern cities such as Iquique and Antofagasta are major fishmeal producers, but the entire coastline is historically productive, and, because Chile's market is relatively small, it has brought an export boom.

The boom, though, has meant overfishing of species such as Chilean sea bass, more properly known as the Patagonian toothfish *(Dissostichus eleginoides)*. While the toothfish in Chile's territorial waters appears to be well-managed, uncontrolled pirate fishing boats in both the South Pacific and South Atlantic have placed its viability in question. U.S. Customs now routinely checks certification of any toothfish imports.

Another development is salmon farming in the cool ocean inlets and lakes from the southern Sur Chico south through Aisén and into Magallanes. According to the Asociación de Productores de Salmón y Trucha (Association of Salmon and Trout Producers), in 2007, Chile exported 397,000 tons of farmed salmon and trout with a total value of US$2.24 billion; two-thirds of this goes to Japan and the United States.

This flourishing industry and its profits, however, have grown at the expense of environmental quality. Salmon feces, waste feed, and antibiotics have contaminated previously pristine lakes and waterways, and escaped fish have flourished at the expense of native stock. Some salmon farmers have also been responsible for killing sea lions that find easy pickings around the floating cages. At the same time, small-scale fishermen unable to live off declining toothfish stocks have resorted to providing salmon farms with the smaller seafood that the predatory toothfish requires.

DISTRIBUTION OF WEALTH

The gap between rich and poor, once an issue of the landed and the landless, is more complex today. The issue has not disappeared, especially among the Mapuche who hope to reclaim ancestral lands from forestry companies and *fundos;* in general, though, agrarian reform and land redistribution is a matter of the past.

More important is the difference between hereditary wealth and a nouveau riche plutocracy on the one hand, and a struggling working class on the other. The gap between rich and poor remains an intractable problem despite the country's macroeconomic successes: According to 2006 statistics, the wealthiest 10 percent of Chileans receive 44.7 percent of all income; by contrast, the lowest 10 percent earned only 1 percent of total income. The income ratio of the highest to lowest 10 percent is roughly 45 to 1.

The wealth gap has geographical as well as social dimensions; the lowest poverty rates are in the Región Metropolitana (which, incidentally, accounts for 40 percent of the country's GDP) and in the northern mining areas of Region I (Tarapacá) and Region II (Antofagasta), and in the thinly populated Patagonia of Region XI (Aisén) and Region XII (Magallanes). Even the north's apparent prosperity is a bit misleading, since capital-intensive mining has been responsible for much of its relative prosperity.

The poorest regions are those with redundant miners and industrial workers, such as Region VIII (Biobío), and large peasant populations, such as Region IX (La Araucanía). Rural poverty is supposedly decreasing, but some of that decrease may be attributed to a redefinition of poverty levels.

EDUCATION

Literacy is formally high, upward of 95 percent, but many more Chileans may be functionally illiterate, unable to understand instructions, prescriptions, warning labels, and even classified advertisements. Education is free through high school and compulsory to age 12, but more than 20 percent of the labor force of five million have not completed secondary school. Many schoolchildren lack complementary educational resources at home, such as books and computers, and scores on international math and science tests are low.

While university education is generally of high quality, it traditionally generates too many high-status degrees in fields such as law or intellectually stimulating—but less clearly practical—subjects such as sociology. Meanwhile, there are shortages in fields such as engineering and computer science.

At the same time, there is little respect for technical or vocational skills, even when those jobs pay more than white-collar positions or office work. Many workers lack initiative and require supervision to go beyond narrowly prescribed duties.

TOURISM

Tourism is a growing sector, employing more than 135,000 Chileans, about 2.2 percent of the work force. According to Sernatur, the state tourism agency, the number of foreign visitors in 2008 was 2.15 million. Total revenues for the year were about US$1.7 billion.

Most visitors come from other South American countries. In 2008, the largest numbers came from Argentina (688,000), Bolivia (253,000), Brazil (225,000), and Peru (207,000). From overseas, the greatest numbers came from the United States (170,000), Germany (55,000), Spain (47,000), the United Kingdom (51,000), France (48,000), Canada (37,000), Australia (31,000), Italy (22,000) and Switzerland (14,000). The greatest increases have come from Argentina, Australia, and Canada.

North American and European travelers stay for longer periods and spend about five times as much money per capita than those from neighboring countries. According to Sernatur's 2007 statistics, for example, Argentines spent only US$32 per day, while U.S. visitors averaged US$62, Canadians US$60, Spaniards US$61, and Britons US$68. Brazilians spent the most, US$98 per day, probably because many come during ski season.

Compared to other countries, though, Chile spends little on promotion; in 2007, the total was about US$4.5 million. Peru, by contrast, spent about US$20 million and Argentina US$32 million. There are few tourist offices outside the country—in Washington, D.C., Miami, and Madrid only.

One advantage, in addition to Chile's natural and cultural attractions, is that it may well be the hemisphere's safest country. Unfortunately, its international profile is low except for negative publicity such as the Pinochet controversy.

People and Culture

According to the 2002 census, Chile's population is 15,116,435, but in 2008 it was estimated at 16.8 million. Growing at roughly 0.9 percent per year, it would take 80 years to double and thus the country is getting older: At present, the population under age 15 and over 65 is roughly equal.

Birth rates are decreasing, infant mortality decreasing, and life expectancy increasing (the average is now 75 years, 72 for males and 78 for females). The Instituto Nacional de Estadística (INE, National Statistics Institute) calculates that by 2020 more than 3 million of the predicted 18.7 million Chileans will be over 60 years old. This, of course, will require major changes in health care.

According to the last INE survey, several years ago, about 880,000 Chileans live beyond its borders. Other countries with substantial Chilean populations include Argentina (429,700), the United States (113,394), Sweden (42,396), Canada (37,577), Australia (33,626), Brazil (28,371), Venezuela (27,106), Spain (23,911), France (15,782), and Germany (10,280). As of mid-2007, more than 55,000 Peruvians purportedly lived in Chile, but even this figure may be an understatement.

POPULATION GEOGRAPHY

The population distribution is complex, both regionally and in urban/rural terms. Nearly 87 percent of all Chileans live in cities or towns, almost 39 percent of them in Santiago and its suburbs. Santiago's metropolitan population is at least 10 times greater than Valparaíso–Viña del Mar or Concepción–Talcahuano, the next largest urban areas.

At the other extreme, about 91,000 people, barely half a percent of the population, live in the remote Aisén region (about a third of the country's territory). In the desert north, almost everyone lives in a handful of large cities, such as Antofagasta, Iquique, and Arica; in the heartland and the Sur Chico, rural population density is high.

Indigenous Peoples

Chile's population is largely mestizo, of mixed Spanish and indigenous heritage, but nearly a million Mapuche inhabit the mainland south of the Biobío as well as Santiago boroughs such as Cerro Navia, La Pintana, El Bosque, Pudahuel, and Peñalolén, where some community leaders are concerned that the younger generation is losing contact with its heritage.

The Mapuche constitute about 90 percent of Chile's total indigenous population. About 5 percent are Aymara in Region I (Tarapacá), with smaller numbers of Kolla (Quechua) and Atacameños in Region II (Antofagasta), Rapanui on their namesake island, and remnants of Kawéskar (Alacaluf) and Yámana (Yahgan) in the southern fjords and rainforests of Patagonia.

Eighty percent of the indigenous population lives in cities and towns, only 20 percent in the countryside, but urban indigenous populations are getting less assistance in buying property than those who remain on the land. Still, some feel optimistic about developments in the country—in the words of one Aymara woman, because of the sympathetic Concertación governments, "it's a good time to be an indigenous person in Chile."

Ethnic Minorities

The surnames of Chile's nonindigenous populations suggest a potpourri of nationalities—Spanish, Basque, Italian, German, Anglo, and many others—but they do not form such obvious ethnic communities as, say, Italian-Americans in New York or Irish-Americans in Boston.

Chile has a small Jewish community in Santiago and Viña del Mar, and a somewhat larger population of Palestinian origin; the two appear to live without animosity. In the Norte Grande, once part of Peru, there exists a small Afro-Chilean minority in the rural communities of Azapa, Lluta, and Camarones, who have formed an organization called Oro Negro (Black Gold) and are trying to determine the number of Chileans with African ancestry.

Language Groups

Spanish is the dominant language, but English is widely spoken in business circles and the tourist industry. The next most widely spoken language is Mapundungun, the Mapuche vernacular, followed by Aymara, Kolla, Rapanui, Yámana, and Kawéskar.

Several languages have disappeared since the arrival of the Europeans: Chango, Atacameño, Diaguita, Selk'nam, and Chono. Both Yámana and Kawéskar have only a handful of native speakers and may disappear; there are, however, projects to preserve Kawéskar and Yámana, including the creation of alphabets and dictionaries and studies of their grammar.

Rapanui is at risk because of the island's curious demographic history, which has caused it to be mixed with Tahitian, French, English, and Spanish (which is now universal). Only about 800 people speak the language fluently, but a committee is working on a dictionary and also promoting language use among island youth.

RELIGION

Once nearly exclusively Roman Catholic, Chile's religious landscape has become a complex mosaic. Orthodox Roman Catholicism was the invaders' religion and is still the most widespread faith, though there are conservative and liberal, even radical, factions. Evangelical Protestantism has made tremendous inroads in recent decades. A small Jewish community practices in Santiago, while the Mapuche,

---

WHAT'S IN A NAME?

Like many other Latin Americans, Chileans customarily use double surnames to identify themselves; a child takes both the paternal and maternal surnames, in that order. In the case of Salvador Allende Gossens, for instance, Allende comes from the father's side, while Gossens comes from the mother's. Normally, Salvador would go by the surname Allende, but he would sign legal documents as Allende Gossens.

Marriage complicates the issue somewhat. After marrying Salvador Allende, Hortensia Bussi Soto became Hortensia Bussi de Allende. Their daughter Isabel (not the novelist, but a current Chilean legislator), in turn, goes by the surnames Allende Bussi. Hortensia's own surname would be lost in the succeeding generation.

There are exceptions even to these rules, especially when elite families want to retain conspicuous evidence of their heritage – the late president Eduardo Frei Montalva (1964-1970) married María Ruiz-Tagle Jiménez, whose hyphenated first surname dates well back into Chilean history. The children of their son, former president Eduardo Frei Ruiz-Tagle (1994-2000), have lost the prestigious Ruiz-Tagle surname, however.

Aside from knowing which surname to use when dealing with locals, visitors to Chile may find a more practical application – don't be surprised to hear Chilean officials, at immigration offices or elsewhere, use your middle name on the assumption that it's really your father's surname.

Aymara, and other indigenous peoples practice their own, sometimes syncretic, rituals.

The Indigenous Heritage

The Spaniards effectively destroyed the institutional religion of the Andean civilizations, but they failed to eradicate the pantheistic beliefs that persist in the northern altiplano. Certain Aymara individuals, for instance, are *yatiri* (healer or diviner), and natural features such as mountain peaks may be *wak'a* (shrines or spirits). Even meteorological events such as lightning may have spiritual significance. Possessing and chewing coca leaves (supposedly illegal in Chile) and sacrificing llamas are common practices. An un-self-conscious syncretism is routine: Phallic statuary, for instance, adorns the perimeter walls of the colonial church at the hamlet of Parinacota.

Mapuche religious practices differ from those of the Aymara, as they are more clearly oriented toward a supreme being, but the antiquity of this belief is unclear. Shamanism is also widespread, and the *machi* combine the roles of seer and healer. Since the 18th century, women have normally been *machis,* but male transvestites are not unheard of; the *machis* also participate in public rituals.

Roman Catholicism

Ever since Pedro de Valdivia entered the Mapocho Valley, Roman Catholicism has played an influential role here. The church has also influenced the cultural landscape; despite the ravages of earthquakes, colonial churches have left a lasting imprint in Santiago and other cities and towns, along with chapels in the altiplano. Chiloé's unique churches and chapels have made the archipelago a UNESCO World Heritage Site.

Starting with the famous Dominican Bartolomé de las Casas in Mexico, factions within the church have wrestled with the contradictions between its official mission—recruiting and saving souls—and its duty to alleviate the misery caused by secular injustice and persecution. Chile is no exception—the priest Miguel Hasbun, for instance, is still a Pinochet apologist, but others, such as the church's Vicaría de la Solidaridad, worked against the dictatorship. Some more militant clergy toiled in the slums under the influence of "liberation theology," some losing their lives in the coup's aftermath.

While most observers laud the church's human rights efforts, it is doctrinally one of Latin America's most conservative. Though Catholicism ceased to be the official state religion in 1925, for instance, church lobbying prevented civil divorce until 2004. This exposed it to charges of hypocrisy, as it often tolerated "annulments" of longstanding marriages for technical reasons.

As elsewhere in Latin America, the church has had problems in staffing its widespread dominion, and many towns lack resident priests. This is one of many factors contributing to the rise of evangelical Protestantism.

In both geographical and theological areas, folk beliefs overlap into the official. One of these is the pilgrimage site at La Tirana, east of the Norte Grande city of Iquique; here, according to legend, an Inka princess who had resisted the Spaniards but took a Spanish captive as her lover was executed by her followers for accepting his spiritual beliefs.

Protestantism

Chilean Protestantism dates from the 19th century, when European merchants established themselves in Valparaíso, Santiago, and other cities after independence. The first "nonconformist" cemetery was in the Norte Chico port of Caldera, and other cities soon had *"cementerios de disidentes."* While it would be fair to say that most Chileans looked upon Anglicans, Lutherans, and other conventional Protestant denominations with distrust and even disdain for decades, Ricardo Lagos's Protestant affiliation was no issue in the 1999–2000 presidential election.

Chilean evangelical Protestantism boomed in the late 20th century as the Catholic church neglected many isolated rural communities. It skyrocketed as desperate Chileans sought spiritual solace in the turmoil of the 1970s and 1980s. Evangelical Protestantism is especially strong among low-income communities and in rural areas, where the official Catholic presence is weak. A study by the Universidad Católica admits that about 14 percent of Chileans are evangelicals, but this rises to 21 percent among low-income populations. Among upper-income

Chileans, more than 80 percent are Catholic and fewer than 10 percent evangelical.

The particularly aggressive Church of Jesus Christ of Latter-day Saints is a controversial presence, and Mormon churches were, until a few years ago, targets of repeated bombings.

Other Religions

The Chilean constitution guarantees freedom of religion, and adherents of non-Christian faiths are no longer rare, if not exactly widespread or numerous. Among those represented are Judaism, Islam, the Baha'i faith, Sikhism, and Buddhism. Even unconventional "New Age" faiths have found a niche in places such as Cochiguaz (Region IV) and Pucón (Region IX). President Michelle Bachelet is agnostic.

LANGUAGE

Spanish is the official language and the language of commerce. In the tourist sector, it's not unusual to find English speakers, but it's better to gain a working knowledge of Spanish than to depend on finding them. Even if your linguistic skills are limited, making an effort earns goodwill and respect.

While Spanish is nearly universal, many indigenous Chileans are bilingual or even multilingual.

Language Study

The major language study institutions are in Santiago, but there are also possibilities in Valparaíso, Pucón, and other cities.

Arts and Entertainment

Chile's contributions to the fine arts are remarkable for a country its size. In literature, in particular, the results have been extraordinary—with a pair of Nobel Prize–winning poets. Chileans have also had a glboal impact on art, architecture, cinema, music, and other fields.

LITERATURE

Chile is famous for its poets. The progenitor of them all was conquistador Alonso de Ercilla (1533–1594), who paid his indigenous adversaries tribute in the 16th-century epic *La Araucana*. The first notable Chilean-born poet was Pedro de Oña (1570–1643), whose *Arauco Domado* (Arauco Tamed) extols the Spaniards' martial achievements.

The dean of modern Chilean poets was Paris-based Vicente Huidobro (1893–1948), whose French contemporaries included Rimbaud, Verlaine, and Mallarmé. Chile's most famous literary figure, though, was the flamboyant, politically committed poet Pablo Neruda (1904–1973), who earned the 1971 Nobel Prize for a body of work including *Las Alturas de Macchu Picchu* (*The Heights of Machu Picchu,* first published 1948) and *Canto General* (1950). Neruda's work is widely available in English translation.

Despite her 1945 Nobel Prize, Gabriela Mistral (1889–1957) is less widely known, perhaps because she left Chile at age 30 and rarely returned, possibly because she was a woman, and maybe even for (a)political reasons—the Communist writer Volodia Teitelboim left her out of his and Eduardo Anguita's *Antología de la Poesía Chilena* (Anthology of Chilean Poetry, 1953). Translations of her work are fewer than of Neruda's, but look for Langston Hughes's *Selected Poems of Gabriela Mistral* (Indiana University Press, 1957).

The Chilean novel didn't really find its voice until the late 20th century, though Alberto Blest Gana's 19th-century work has historical interest. Though not a novelist, the Venezuelan polymath Andrés Bello (1781–1865) influenced Chilean intellectual life through his essays and his transformation of the educational system.

The most famous contemporary Chilean writer is novelist Isabel Allende (born 1942), a niece of the late president. Though she now lives in Marin County, California, she continues to write on Chilean (and Californian-Chilean) themes.

Antonio Skármeta (born 1940) is a novelist who became known as the author of *Burning Patience* (New York: Random House, 1987), which served as a *very* rough template, cleansed of its political content, for director Michael Radford's Oscar-winning film *Il Postino* (1995); Pablo Neruda was a key character in the story.

Marco Antonio de la Parra (born 1952) is a playwright, novelist, and psychiatrist whose *The Secret Holy War of Santiago de Chile* (New York: Interlink, 1994) uses Chile's capital city as the backdrop for a "magical realist" interpretation of the Pinochet dictatorship's last years. California-raised Alberto Fuguet (born 1964) is the author of *Bad Vibes* (New York: St. Martin's, 1997), a tale of disaffected affluent youth whose families profited from the dictatorship.

Roberto Ampuero's place-oriented mystery novels explore locales such as Valparaíso and San Pedro de Atacama, but unfortunately none of his Cayetano Brulé novels have yet appeared in English. Ampuero's unadorned style makes his books a good choice for neophytes easing their way into Spanish-language literature.

Over the past few years, the most conspicuous Chilean writer has been the late Roberto Bolaño (1953–2003), whose unconventional novels *The Savage Detectives* (1998; translated in English 2007) and *2666* (2004; translated in English 2008) have gained an international following. The outspoken Bolaño, who led an erratic lifestyle mostly in Spain and Mexico, once dismissed Isabel Allende as "a typist."

VISUAL ARTS

The earliest Chilean art was, of course, ecclesiastical, evident in museums such as the Museo de Arte Colonial in Santiago's 17th-century Iglesia San Francisco. With independence, the tendency was toward pompous portraits of military men such as O'Higgins and their contemporaries in the war against Spain, and most provincial museums contain dreary works of this sort.

Nevertheless, there is adventurous contemporary work in Santiago's Museo de Bellas Artes, Museo de Artes Visuales, Castro's Museo de Arte Moderno, and Providencia's open-air Museo Parque de las Esculturas, on the Mapocho's banks. One of the most noteworthy sites is Chillán's Escuela México, its library walls adorned with murals by the famous artist David Alfaro Siqueiros and his contemporary Xavier Guerrero.

Northern European influences began to appear with landscapes by 19th-century Englishman Thomas Somerscales (1842–1927), who spent 23 years in Valparaíso and its vicinity. The most influential modern painter, also a sculptor and engraver, is the late surrealist Roberto Matta (1911–2002), who lived mostly in Paris but also in Mexico and New York. The versatile Mario Irarrázaval (born 1940) erected the roadside sculpture *Mano del Desierto* (*Hand in the Desert*) on the Panamericana south of Antofagasta; he is also the sculptor of the *Tabernáculo* (*Tabernacle*) at the Templo Votivo de Maipú, a pilgrimage site in Santiago, and the painter of *El Juicio* (*The Judgment*), a harsh portrayal of military "justice."

Chilean photography is not widely known, but Marcos Chamudes (1907–1989) joined the U.S. Army in World War II and photographed the European theater before returning to Chile for the rest of his life.

ARCHITECTURE

Indigenous architecture survives in the northern altiplano's Aymara adobes and the thatched Mapuche *rucas* of the south. In the heartland, Spanish culture has left an enduring imprint on official and vernacular architecture, as buildings with thick adobe walls and tiled roofs are common among all social classes; because of repeated earthquakes, these generally were larger structures of lower proportions.

In older cities and towns, there is little or no setback from the street; houses usually have a central patio surrounded by the various rooms, and share walls with their neighbors. Rural houses are similar but freestanding. In newer subdivisions, though, single-family houses fronted by lawns are becoming more common.

Norte Grande cities such as Iquique and Antofagasta, dating from the late-19th- and early-20th-century nitrate era, are distinguished by their balconied Georgian and Victorian buildings. Many consist of Douglas fir imported from California and Oregon (Douglas fir is widely but incorrectly known in Chile as *pino oregón,* Oregon pine).

In Sur Chico settlements such as Puerto Varas, 19th-century German immigration has left a legacy of shingled houses seemingly straight out of Bavaria. The Chiloé archipelago has become a UNESCO World Heritage Site for its churches and chapels—the diversity of shingle designs is truly extraordinary—but its remaining *palafitos* (houses on stilts or pilings) are another treasure of vernacular architecture.

Southernmost Chile, especially the city of Punta Arenas, is notable for wool-boom mansard mansions from the late 19th and early 20th centuries, but also for its simpler wooden-framed, metal-clad "Magellanic" houses. Some of the best are in the town of Porvenir, on the Chilean side of Tierra del Fuego, but many also remain in Argentine Patagonia and Tierra del Fuego.

In Santiago, many dignified French-style buildings remain from the 19th century, but contemporary architecture tends toward the functional and utilitarian. At its worst, it's a clutter of shopping malls, but the newest office and apartment buildings are taking advantage of new design techniques. Throughout the country, a handful of design hotels are pushing the architectural envelope.

MUSIC

Globally, the most famous musical figures are folk artists such as Violeta Parra, her children Ángel and Isabel, Patricio Manns, Víctor Jara, and other contributors to the *Nueva Canción Chilena* (New Chilean Song Movement) of the 1950s and 1960s, known for its committed leftist politics and *peñas* (cultural centers). Both Violeta Parra (1917–1967) and Víctor Jara (1932–1973) met unhappy ends; Parra committed suicide, and Jara died at the hands of the military.

In addition to singer-songwriters, Chile has many folk-oriented bands whose work adapted Andean music and instrumentation, such as the *zampoña* (panpipes), *charango* (a stringed instrument resembling the mandolin), and others, along with traditional guitars. Among them are Inti-Illimani, Quilapayún, and Illapu.

In popular music, the Mexico-based Chilean band La Ley won a 2001 Grammy for best alternative Latin rock album and has toured the United States, playing at San Francisco's legendary Fillmore Auditorium. The massively popular rock band Los Prisioneros, which expressed Chilean youth's frustration during the Pinochet dictatorship, disbanded in the aftermath of its greatest popularity. Based in France, Los Jaivas tour Chile every summer with their blend of Chilean folk themes, Pink Floydish technological prowess, and an enviable rapport with their public.

A handful of classical musicians have earned a worldwide reputation. Chillán-born Claudio Arrau (1903–1991) was Chile's best-known classical pianist, an artistic descendant of Franz Liszt through Lizst's student Martin Krause. Oscar Gacitúa (1926–2001), who committed suicide by throwing himself in front of the Santiago Metro, was an Arrau piano disciple who had earned an honorable mention at 1955's Warsaw Chopin competition.

Punta Arenas tenor Tito Beltrán (born 1965), a Swedish resident considered one of the world's dozen best opera singers in his range, has sung alongside Luciano Pavarotti. Sergio Ortega (born 1938), who composed the anthem for Allende's Unidad Popular, adapted Pablo Neruda's verses to opera in *Muerte y Fulgor de Joaquín Murieta,* about the legendary (but probably fictional) Chilean outlaw in gold rush–era California.

CINEMA

Chileans have played a greater role in global cinema than most people realize, though it's best not to exaggerate. It has its origins, surprisingly enough, in the Tierra del Fuego town of Porvenir, where German-born José Bohr made an early movie before eventually finding an erratic Hollywood career. Many recent Chilean films are available on video or DVD.

With state support in the late 1960s and early 1970s, talented but noncommercial filmmakers did some truly audacious work, most notably Alejandro Jodorowsky's esoteric Mexican western *El Topo* (*The Mole,* 1971). Miguel Littín's crime melodrama *El Chacal de Nahueltoro* (*The Jackal of Nahueltoro,* 1968) was a Chilean hit, but he's best known for *Alsino and the Condor* (1983), filmed in exile in Nicaragua, which earned an Academy Award nomination for Best Foreign Film. His *Tierra del Fuego* (2000) is, in the director's words, an "existentialist western."

The France-based Raúl Ruiz has directed many films, but only the psychological whodunit *Shattered Image* (1998) has appeared in English. Ruiz took on Marcel Proust in *Time Regained* (1999), based on the last volume of *Remembrance of Things Past,* which starred Catherine Deneuve, John Malkovich, and Vicente Pérez.

Documentarist Patricio Guzmán (born 1941) earned a certain fame for *La Batalla de Chile* (*The Battle of Chile,* 1975–1979), about the Unidad Popular and its overthrow by Pinochet. More recently, he produced *The Pinochet Case* (2001), on the dictator's arrest and its aftermath, and *Salvador Allende* (2004), about the man Pinochet overthrew.

Chilean-born but Spanish-bred, Alejandro Amenábar wrote and directed *The Others* (2001), a subtle haunted-house story with a twist. The youthful (born 1973), multitalented Amenábar also wrote the musical score. Gustavo Graef-Marino (born 1965) directed *Johnny Cien Pesos* (1993), a character-driven Santiago crime story based on true events, and the Hollywood action movie *Diplomatic Siege* (1999).

Other films to look for include Alex Bowen's *Mi Mejor Enemigo* (*My Best Enemy,* 2005), a tragicomedy about an encounter between Argentine and Chilean forces in the Patagonian near-war of 1978; Andrés Wood's (born 1963) *Historias de Fútbol* (*Soccer Stories,* 1997) and *Machuca* (2004), a tale of growing up in Chile's early 1970s turmoil; Cristián Galaz's *El Chacotero Sentimental* (*The Sentimental Teaser,* 1999), about a sympathetic radio talk show host; and Orlando Lubbert's (born 1945) *Taxi para Tres* (*Taxi for Three,* 2001), an action comedy with social undertones set in a poor Santiago neighborhood. The latter earned a "Concha de Oro" best-picture award at Spain's San Sebastián Film Festival.

THEATER

Santiago's theater scene is among the continent's liveliest, but even in the regions live theater has an audience. Conventional theater plays venues such as Santiago's Teatro Municipal and Providencia's Teatro de la Universidad de Chile, but there's an alternative theater scene elsewhere in Barrio Bellavista, parts of Providencia, and even otherwise staid, middle-class Ñuñoa.

One of Chile's most popular plays is *La Negra Ester,* a prostitute's story written by Roberto Parra (1921–1995), a musician brother of Violeta and Nicanor Parra. Since its debut in 1988, more than three million theatergoers have seen the play in various venues.

DANCE

Chile's national dance is the *cueca,* an innocently suggestive cock-and-hen courtship ritual that's a staple of mid-September's patriotic holidays and many rural festivals. While tango is an Argentine import, it has devoted adherents in Santiago, Valparaíso, and some other cities.

Performances of classical and modern dance, such as ballet, take place at formal venues such as Santiago's Teatro Municipal or Providencia's Teatro de la Universidad de Chile.

ARTS AND CRAFTS

Chile may lack the colorful indigenous markets of its Andean neighbors Peru and Bolivia, but it compensates with artisanal *ferias* in both urban and rural areas, especially in summer.

CHILEAN HOLIDAYS

Government offices and most businesses close on national holidays, more than half of which are religious observations. Traditionally, many Chileans take "sandwich holidays" between actual holidays and the weekend, but the government is attempting to eliminate the practice by moving some holidays to the nearest Monday.

- January 1: **Año Nuevo** (New Year's Day)
- March/April (moveable): **Semana Santa** (Easter Week)
- May 1: **Día del Trabajo** (International Labor Day)
- May 21: **Glorias Navales** (naval Battle of Iquique)
- May 30: **Corpus Christi**
- June 29: **Día de San Pedro y San Pablo** (Saint Peter and Saint Paul's Day)
- August 15: **Asunción de la Virgen** (Assumption)
- September 18: **Día de la Independencia Nacional** (Independence Day)
- September 19: **Día del Ejército** (Armed Forces Day)
- October 12: **Día de la Raza** (Columbus Day)
- November 2: **Todo los Santos** (All Saints' Day)
- December 8: **Inmaculada Concepción** (Immaculate Conception)
- December 25: **Navidad** (Christmas Day)

Certain crafts are similar and nearly universal: basketry, stone and wood carvings, copperware, lapis lazuli jewelry and statuary, and cotton and woolen weavings. There are also regional specialties.

Santiago's Barrio Bellavista is one of the best urban areas for crafts, but Valparaíso and Viña del Mar also have good selections. On Valparaíso's Plaza O'Higgins, the Sunday antiques market is the country's best.

In the Norte Grande, especially in the altiplano, Aymara weavers produce llama and alpaca caps, sweaters, and other clothing, but much of this material arrives from Peru and Bolivia. Throughout the heartland and well into the south, *huaso* horsegear is unique—look for the elaborately carved stirrups in particular.

Mapuche communities, which produce exquisite silverwork, and Sur Chico resorts do have good selections of indigenous crafts, and the towns of Angelmó (Puerto Montt), and Dalcahue and Castro (both on the Isla Grande de Chiloé) have picturesque waterfront markets. Chiloé carvers produce model *dalcas* (dugouts), *palafitos* (houses on pilings), and dolls, while weavers in the entire Sur Chico and into Patagonia create sweaters and caps (from sheep's wool rather than llama or alpaca).

The Polynesian Easter Islanders (Rapanui) produce souvenir *moai* of both wood and stone, modeled after the massive pre-Columbian stone statues but also in the style of later indigenous carvings. While there's plenty of ready-made stuff to buy, it's also possible to order a larger custom *moai;* since this may take several days, do it soon after arrival.

Throughout Chile, bargaining is less common and aggressive than it is in the Central Andean highlands, but it's not completely inappropriate; just don't make insultingly low offers. In souvenir shops and other businesses with an obvious overhead, such as suburban shopping malls, bargaining is inappropriate.

HOLIDAYS, FESTIVALS, AND EVENTS

The year's first major event is **Semana Santa** (Holy Week), culminating in **Pascua** (Easter Sunday), but it's a relatively sober and earnest observation compared with, say, its colorful counterpart in Guatemala. From Maundy Thursday through Sunday, though, it's a major travel time, when prices rise for accommodations and demand can be high—reservations are advisable.

Chileans celebrate mid-September's patriotic holidays with parades, military marches, and gatherings in public parks.

November 2's **Día de Todos los Santos,** also known as **Día de los Muertos** (Day of the Dead), is when Chileans visit the graves of their departed and leave them elaborate flower arrangements, among other tributes. Though less spectacular than its Mexican counterpart, it can still be impressive.

Several unofficial festivals take place throughout the year. One worth special attention is mid-July's weeklong **Festival de la Virgen del Carmen,** when tens of thousands of celebrants converge on the Norte Grande hamlet of La Tirana for the country's most important popular religion fiesta. Another colorful event is December 26's **Fiesta de la Virgen de Andacollo** in the Norte Chico, though it's more official than La Tirana.

ESSENTIALS

Getting There

Most overseas visitors arrive by air, though many also arrive overland from Argentina, Bolivia, and Peru. Almost all of the latter arrive by bus or private vehicle; the only international rail service is the short line from Arica to Tacna (Peru).

BY AIR

Most passengers arrive at Santiago's **Aeropuerto Internacional Arturo Merino Benitez** (SCL, tel. 02/6901753, www.aeropuertosantiago.cl), one of the world's most modern and well-monitored facilities; according to Chile's Dirección General de Aeronáutica Civil (DGAC, Civil Aeronautics Commission), it's so secure that it may become a regional security checkpoint for U.S.-bound flights.

More than nine million passengers used SCL in 2008, a six percent increase over the previous year; more than half of that traffic was international. New technology should allow increased traffic without disrupting flight activity.

Most major international airlines fly out of the capital, while regional airports at Arica, Iquique, Antofagasta, La Serena, Temuco, Puerto Montt, and Punta Arenas have occasional flights to neighboring countries only.

For the cheapest fares, avoid the Christmas–New Year's period, when flights fill with Chileans returning home for the holidays.

Chilean patriotic holidays in mid-September are also busy. Going and returning just before or after holiday periods will produce better fares, as will shoulder-season travel in the southern spring or autumn.

From North America

From North America, the main gateways to Santiago are Miami; Washington, D.C. (Dulles); Atlanta; New York; Chicago; Dallas; and Los Angeles. Canadian passengers may also use Toronto.

Chile's LAN is the traditional flag carrier (though now private). Other options include Aerolíneas Argentinas, American Airlines, Copa, Delta, Grupo Taca, Mexicana, Transportes Aéreos Mercosur (TAM), and Varig. American, Delta, and LAN have the only nonstop or direct services; others require changing planes either in Central or South America. Non-Canadians can avoid the hassle of getting a U.S. transit visa by taking Air Canada's triangle route from Toronto to Buenos Aires and Santiago.

From Mexico, Central America, and the Caribbean

Services from Mexico usually require changing planes in Central America or elsewhere in South America; the main exception is LAN, which flies nonstop from Mexico City.

Other carriers from Mexico City include Copa (via Panama) and Grupo Taca (via Lima, Peru). Colombia's Avianca has connections via Bogotá from the Caribbean, Central America, and Mexico.

Copa flies daily from Panama, with connections throughout the region.

Within South America

Santiago has connections to neighboring countries of Peru, Bolivia, and Argentina, and elsewhere on the continent.

LAN and Grupo Taca compete on the Lima–Santiago route. LAN flies four times weekly from La Paz to Santiago via Arica and/or Iquique.

LAN flies several times daily from Buenos

Aires, less frequently from Mendoza, Córdoba, and Rosario, and occasionally from Bariloche via Puerto Montt. Aerolíneas Argentinas also flies several times daily from Buenos Aires. The Buenos Aires–Santiago route is highly competitive because many European carriers lose most passengers at Buenos Aires and, consequently, sell the empty seats at bargain prices.

Except for the Guianas, Santiago has service from all other South American capitals, including the Falkland Islands. LAN serves all of these, often continuing to North America or Europe. Other carriers include Avianca from Bogotá, Colombia; Grupo Taca from Caracas, Venezuela, via Lima; TAM Mercosur from Asunción, Paraguay, and from the Brazilian cities of São Paulo and Rio de Janeiro; Varig and Gol from Brazil; and Pluna from Montevideo, Uruguay. LAN offers one flight weekly (Saturday) from the Falklands to Punta Arenas, continuing to Santiago.

OVERLAND

Chile has a few border crossings with Peru and Bolivia, but many with Argentina. Only a handful have scheduled transportation: the Peruvian crossing from Tacna; the Bolivian roads from La Paz to Arica via Parque Nacional Lauca, and from Oruro to Iquique via Colchane; the crossing from Uyuni to Calama via Ollagüe, and the overland four-wheel-drive excursion from Uyuni to San Pedro de Atacama via Laguna Verde.

From Argentina, there are buses from Salta and Jujuy to San Pedro de Atacama and Calama via the Paso de Jama, now paved on both sides of the border. The busiest crossing, though, is the Los Libertadores tunnel between Mendoza and Santiago.

In the Sur Chico there are buses from Neuquén to Temuco over the Paso de Pino Hachado via Curacautín and Lonquimay; the alternative Paso de Icalma is slightly to the south. Other routes include a regular bus service from San Martín de los Andes to Temuco via the Paso de Mamuil Malal (Paso Tromen to Argentines); a bus-boat combination from San Martín de los Andes to Panguipulli via

Paso Huahum and Lago Pirehueico; a paved highway from Bariloche to Osorno via the Paso de Cardenal Samoré that's the second-busiest crossing between the two countries; and the bus-boat shuttle from Bariloche to Puerto Varas and Puerto Montt.

Patagonia has many crossings, but mostly bad roads and little public transport. Those with scheduled services include the mostly gravel road from Esquel (local buses only) to Futaleufú, for connections to Chaitén; Comodoro Rivadavia to Coyhaique on a mostly paved road via Río Mayo on comfortable coaches; Los Antiguos to Chile Chico (shuttles with onward connections); El Calafate to Puerto Natales via Río Turbio on a mostly paved route; Río Gallegos to Punta Arenas via paved highway; and Ushuaia and Río Grande to Punta Arenas.

In addition, many border crossings are suitable for private motor vehicles and mountain bikes, and a few by foot.

Bus and *Taxi Colectivo*

International bus service is available from the neighboring republics Argentina, Bolivia, and Peru, and from more distant destinations such as Uruguay, Brazil, Paraguay, Ecuador, and Colombia.

Both international and domestic bus services normally have comfortable reclining seats (with every passenger guaranteed a seat), toilets, air-conditioning, and on-board meals and refreshments, at least on the longest trips. If not, they make regular meal stops. Between Santiago and Mendoza, shared *taxi colectivos* are slightly more expensive but faster than buses.

Rail

Repaired after floods in 2001, a short line connects the northern city of Arica with the Peruvian city of Tacna, but there are many faster, cheaper buses and shared taxis on this route. The freight line from the Argentine city of Salta to the Chilean border at Socompa, connecting to the Chilean rail graveyard of Baquedano, may carry truly determined passengers with plenty of time, patience, and grit.

Car, Motorcycle, and Bicycle

Overland travel from North America or elsewhere is problematic because Panama's Darien Gap to Colombia is impassable for motor vehicles, difficult and dangerous even for walkers, and passes through areas controlled by smugglers, guerrillas, and/or brutal Colombian paramilitaries. Fortunately, with its minimal bureaucracy, Chile is probably the continent's best option for shipping a vehicle; the author has twice retrieved vehicles from Chilean customs in less than two hours. Even with shipping expenses, anyone traveling for at least a three- to four-month period will probably find it competitive with, or cheaper than, renting a vehicle for the same amount of time.

To locate a shipper, check the local Yellow Pages under Automobile Transporters, who are normally freight consolidators rather than the company that owns the ship (which will charge higher container rates). Since more people ship vehicles to Europe than to South America, finding the right shipper may take patience; one reliable U.S. consolidator is **McClary, Swift & Co.** (360 Swift Ave., South San Francisco, CA 94080, tel. 650/872-2121, www.mcclaryswift.com), which has affiliates at many U.S. ports.

BY SEA

Cruise ships and private yachts call at Chilean ports, but scheduled passenger shipping is rare. The scenic crossing from the Argentine city of Bariloche to Chile's Puerto Varas and Puerto Montt involves shuttling over several lakes on tourist ships whose ports are linked by buses. The Chilean fjords cruise with Cruceros Australis allows passengers to board in Punta Arenas and disembark in Ushuaia, on Argentine Tierra del Fuego, or vice versa. There are occasional shuttles from Ushuaia to Chile's Isla Navarino.

Getting Around

Chilean air services are well-developed, but connecting the desert north with the humid south will always involve changing planes in Santiago. Bus is the primary means of overland transport; the passenger rail, which theoretically reaches the southern mainland cities of Concepción and Puerto Montt, is problematical. There is also commuter rail from Santiago south to San Fernando, and from Valparaíso to nearby communities.

BY AIR

Besides the airports mentioned above, commercial flights also serve Calama, Copiapó, El Salvador, Pucón, Valdivia, Osorno, Chaitén, Balmaceda (Coyhaique), and Puerto Natales. Smaller airfields are also in Santiago for flights to the Juan Fernández archipelago, and in Coyhaique for flights to Laguna San Rafael.

LAN is Chilean civil aviation's 800-pound gorilla, dominating the domestic market through its independently operated subsidiary LanExpress. In a country whose longest domestic flight is only about three hours, its Boeings and Airbuses are comfortably spacious.

No competitor has had much luck challenging LAN's supremacy, especially because the company is professionally operated and has deeper pockets than its rivals, but the budget carrier Sky Airline has managed to grow its market share in recent years.

Chilean domestic airfares are generally reasonable, but buying tickets a few days ahead of time can often result in substantial discounts. While LAN has discontinued its "Visit Chile" pass, it now offers a separate "Visit South America" pass that covers both Chile and other South American countries.

For student discounts on both international and domestic flights, try the Student Flight Center (Hernando de Aguirre 201, Oficina 401, Providencia, Santiago, tel. 02/4112000, www.sertur.cl).

BY BUS

Buses along the main longitudinal highways, and those connecting other main cities and resorts, are frequent, spacious, and comfortable, sometimes luxurious. On backroads routes, some are infrequent and only slightly better

© WAYNE BERNHARDSON

Minibuses to Parque Nacional Tierra del Fuego leave from the new bus terminal, ostensibly to be covered at Ushuaia's waterfront.

than Central American "chicken buses," but distances are short.

"Pullman" buses have reclining seats, and for short-to-medium runs, up to six or seven hours, they're adequate. Seats are guaranteed. For the longest trips, *semi cama* or *salón cama* service provides greater legroom in seats that recline almost horizontally. Fares are moderate—the 26-hour Santiago–Arica marathon—roughly equivalent to the distance between Los Angeles and Vancouver B.C.—costs about US$90 in *salón cama,* including onboard or roadside meal service.

Most cities have a central *terminal de buses* (bus terminal) or *terminal rodoviario,* but some towns have multiple terminals for long-distance, regional, and rural services, or for individual companies. Some companies have separate ticket offices in more central locations than the terminals themselves—in Santiago, for instance, some Metro stations have ticket outlets.

Reservations are rarely necessary except for infrequently traveled routes and some international services, or during holiday periods such as mid-September's independence celebrations, the Semana Santa (Holy Week) and Christmas–New Year's periods, and occasionally during the January–February summer vacation season.

According to transport regulations, bus tickets may be returned for 85 percent of face value up to four hours before departure. Exchanges are free of charge.

BY RAIL
Once the primary means of interurban transportation, domestic rail service is now limited to the longitudinal line that runs from Santiago to Temuco—though even that was suspended, supposedly temporarily, in early 2009—and a relic narrow-gauge short line that runs from the heartland city of Talca to the port of Constitución.

When they run, trains are cheap. Ticket holders in need of a refund can get 85 percent of the fare returned up until two hours before departure.

As of 2009, commuter trains serve on the longitudinal line as far as Rancagua and San Fernando, and plans have been in the works to open a new commuter line on the 70 kilometers between Santiago and the southwestern town of Melipilla, and to the northerly town of Tiltil.

Construction of a high-speed line to Valparaíso, at a cost of US$800 million, is under consideration; if built, it would cut travel time from the capital to 50 minutes at speeds of up to 180 kilometers per hour. Valparaíso and Viña del Mar have their own Metro system, the recently modernized Merval, used by up to 12 million passengers per year.

BY CAR AND MOTORCYCLE
Stretching from the Peruvian border to Puerto Montt and the Isla Grande de Chiloé, the Panamericana (Ruta 5) is Chile's main transport artery, though the shorter and more scenic coastal Ruta 1 has superseded it between Iquique and Antofagasta. The Panamericana is entirely paved; from La Serena south to Puerto Montt, it is a four-lane divided highway. Even so, despite the presence of call boxes, rest areas, and *peajes* (toll booths), there are occasionally loose livestock, wandering pedestrians, and even vendors hawking items ranging from sweets and ice cream to fresh produce and cheese to dressed kid goat, ready for the grill.

Many more roads are paved or smoothly graded, though the Aisén region's Ruta 7, the Carretera Austral (Southern Highway), is often narrow, mostly gravel, and occasionally precarious (the author has wrecked two four-wheel-drive vehicles on it, amidst extenuating circumstances). Heavy truck traffic can make all these routes dangerous, but most Chileans are courteous and cautious drivers. Watch for Argentine license plates, as many trans-Andean visitors drive far more aggressively.

Congested Santiago can be a madhouse, the routes out of the capital can be difficult for drivers without local experience, and there's a complex toll system that penalizes drivers who stumble into it without electronic tags. It's better to park the car, preferably in a guarded lot, and use public transport. Avoid leaving conspicuous valuables in the car.

In both the city and the countryside, watch for *lomas de burro* (speed bumps, also known as *pacos acostados,* sleeping policemen). Night driving is inadvisable in some rural areas, as domestic livestock and inebriated *campesinos* may roam freely.

Police checkpoints are less common than they were under the dictatorship, but always stop when the Carabineros police signal you to do so; this is usually a routine document check. Carabineros have been trained to refuse bribes, so don't even think about offering one; if you've committed an *infracción* (traffic violation), try to reason with them and you may get off unless your offense is flagrant or truly dangerous. Note that the slang term *paco* is an insult—never use it to a cop's face.

Speed limits are generally around 100 kilometers per hour, but the maximum is 120 kilometers per hour on four-lane divided roads. Carabineros with radar guns are common sights along all highways.

In remote areas where gas stations are few, such as Aisén or the altiplano east of Arica and Iquique, carry additional fuel. Note that members of the American Automobile Association (AAA), Britain's Automobile Association (AA), and other similar clubs are often eligible for limited roadside assistance and towing through the Automóvil Club de Chile (Acchi, Av. Andrés Bello 1863, Providencia, Santiago, tel. 02/4311000, www.acchi.cl). It has affiliates in the larger cities.

Vehicle Documents and Driver's License

Most South American countries have dispensed with the cumbersome *Carnet de Passage en Douanes,* which required depositing a large bond to import a motor vehicle. Officials at Chilean ports of arrival issue a 90- to 180-day *Título de Importación Temporal de Vehículos* upon presentation of the title, registration, bill of lading, and your passport. There may be relatively small port charges (which grow if the vehicle has been stored more than a few days).

It's not possible for the vehicle owner to leave the country without the vehicle except by transferring responsibility to a legal Chilean resident. Nor is it possible to sell a used vehicle except in the Zona Franca (duty-free zone) of either Iquique or Punta Arenas, where vehicles are so abundant that prices are depressed.

Some visitors obtain an International or Interamerican Driving Permit, available through the American Automobile Association (AAA) or its counterpart in your home country; these are normally valid for one calendar year from date of issue. Chilean police normally acknowledge other national or state drivers' licenses, however.

Expenses

Operating a gasoline-powered vehicle is more expensive than in the United States but still cheaper than in Europe, even though Chile imports more than 90 percent of its oil. Prices generally increase with distance from the capital. Unleaded fuel is available everywhere; higher octane fuel is only slightly more expensive. Diesel fuel prices have risen and are comparable to those for regular gasoline. Gasoline has been cheaper in Argentina, but prices have risen there except in southern Patagonia, where it is subsidized. Argentina also charges vehicles with foreign plates higher prices, at least in border areas.

If importing a car as a tourist, be sure to obtain Chilean insurance, which is available in major cities. *Seguro mínimo,* a cheap no-fault policy with limited personal injury coverage, is obligatory but inadequate for any serious accident.

Repairs are cheap in terms of labor but expensive in terms of parts, nearly all of which must be imported. Fortunately, Chilean mechanics are skilled at rehabilitating almost any salvageable part.

Car Rental

Rental cars are widely available in Santiago and other major cities and tourist centers; rates start around US$39 per day or US$240 per week for the smallest vehicles and around US$75 per day or US$509 per week or up for twin-cab pickups. More expensive are four-wheel-drive vehicles, commonly referred to as *doble tracción* or *cuatro por cuatro* (usually written "4X4"). On the other hand, if shared among a group, they can be fairly reasonable.

Local agencies are usually cheaper than major international franchises, and monthly rates can be relative bargains. All car rentals pay 19 percent IVA (value added tax). Taking a Chilean vehicle into Argentina involves additional paperwork and a surcharge, as well as supplementary insurance. Returning a vehicle to an office other than the one you rented from, which is impossible with the cheapest local companies, means a hefty surcharge.

To rent a vehicle, you must have a valid driver's license and a credit card, and be at least 25 years old. Rental insurance may not completely cover you against losses—there is almost always a substantial deductible (higher in case of serious damage, total destruction, or vehicle theft).

RVs ranging from camper pickups to fully equipped motor homes are available through Holiday Rent (Suecia 734, Providencia, Santiago, tel. 02/2582000, www.chile-travel.com/holiday.htm) or Trekker Chile (Viña Andrea s/n, Sector Alto Lircay, Talca, tel. 071/1970096, cel. 09/9419-0625, www.trekkerchile.com).

Buying a Vehicle

If visiting Chile and other parts of South America for several months, buying a vehicle is worth consideration; there are plenty of good used vehicles, even if you can't quite name your price. Santiago has the largest selection; be cautious if buying a vehicle in Region I (Tarapacá) or Region XII (Magallanes), where Zona Franca duty-free regulations limit purchases of many vehicles to permanent residents. Only a vehicle that is legally *liberado* may be sold in and taken outside those regions.

To buy a car, you need a RUT (Rol Unico Tributario) Chilean tax ID number, which takes only a few minutes at any office of the Servicio de Impuestos Internos (SII, Internal Revenue Service); you need not be a Chilean resident but must have a Chilean address. The SII issues a provisional RUT, valid for any purpose, and sends the permanent card to the address you designate.

Before buying the vehicle, request a *Certificado de Inscripción y Anotaciones Vigentes* at any office of the Registro Civil (Civil Registry); this document, which costs a couple dollars, will alert you to title problems if any, as well as any pending legal issues (such as accident settlements). To be licensed, the vehicle needs an up-to-date *revisión técnica* (safety and emissions test).

Registering the sale is relatively straightforward at any Registro Civil office, involving a notarized *compraventa* (bill of sale, about US$15); an official *Giro y Pago del Impuesto a la Transferencia de Vehículos Motorizados* (Proof of Payment of Motor Vehicle Transfer Tax, made at a local bank, variable depending on the vehicle's value but modest for a used car); and a *Solicitud Registro Nacional de Vehículos Motorizados* (Application to the National Registry of Motorized Vehicles, about US$25). The Registro then issues a provisional title and mails the permanent title, usually within a month, to the address on your RUT.

Theoretically, the *compraventa* and other documents entitle you to take the vehicle across borders, but since the purchase of a Chilean vehicle by nonresidents is uncommon, try making a special request to accelerate the permanent title's issuance. This requires a brief letter to the head of the Registro, whose personnel may help with this.

HITCHHIKING

Chile and Argentina, where private cars are more abundant than in the Andean republics of Peru and Bolivia, are probably the continent's best countries for hitchhiking. Buses are so few in some rural areas that thumbing may be the only option. Unlike in Peru and Bolivia, drivers normally do not expect to be paid.

Hitching has the advantage of flexibility, but it can also be unpredictable; carry food, water, and appropriate clothing for the climate and season. Many young Chileans hit the Panamericana north and south in summer, so there's plenty of competition—but it can also be unsafe. Solitary women, in particular, should pay attention to security.

BY BICYCLE

For the physically fit, or those intending to become physically fit, cycling is an ideal way to see Chile. Because so many roads are unpaved in scenic areas, a *todo terreno* (mountain bike) is better than a touring bike. Cyclists should know how to do basic repairs, though parts and bicycle mechanics are easier to find than they once were. In an emergency, it's easy to load a bicycle onto a bus.

Some cyclists dislike the busy Panamericana, much of which is relatively uninteresting, but its completion as a four-lane divided highway with broad paved shoulders should make it safer. There are many alternatives, however, including really exciting ones such as the rarely used route along the former Norte Chico rail line

BY FERRY AND CATAMARAN

From Puerto Montt south through the Aisén and Magallanes regions, lacustrine and maritime transportation links gaps in the highway network. Even in the Sur Chico, ferries on finger lakes such as Lago Pirehueico and Lago Todos los Santos (carrying passengers only) form part of routes to Argentina.

Navimag Ferries (Av. El Bosque Norte 0440, 11th floor, Las Condes, Santiago, tel. 02/4423120, www.navimag.cl) and **Naviera Austral** (Av. Angelmó 2187, Puerto Montt, tel. 065/270400, www.navieraustral.cl) operate ferries from Puerto Montt to Chaitén and Puerto Chacabuco. Navimag continues to the ice fields of Parque Nacional Laguna San Rafael, a route also traveled by the tourist cruise ship *Skorpios* and the luxury passenger catamarans *Iceberg Expedition* and *Patagonia Connection*.

Navimag's ferries *Puerto Edén* and *Magallanes* connect Puerto Montt with, respectively, Puerto Chacabuco (an overnight trip) and Puerto Natales (a three-day journey

through the scenic fjords of Aisén and northern Magallanes).

Transmarchilay also runs a shuttle ferry across the mouth of the Reloncaví estuary, from La Arena to Puelche, about 45 kilometers southeast of Puerto Montt. The village of Hornopirén, 60 kilometers farther southeast, is the port for Naviera Austral's summer-only ferry to Caleta Gonzalo, the gateway to Chaitén and the Carretera Austral.

Transmarchilay and **Cruz del Sur** ferries connect Pargua, on the mainland Sur Chico, with Chacao, on the Isla Grande de Chiloé. Naviera Austral also connects Quellón, on the Isla Grande, to Chaitén.

Mar del Sur sails the *Pilchero* from the Aisén village of Puerto Ingeniero Ibáñez, on Lago General Carrera's north shore, to the south shore border town of Chile Chico; Chile Chico is also accessible by a road around the lake, but the ferry is faster and cheaper than driving.

In Magallanes, a daily ferry crosses the Strait of Magellan from Punta Arenas to Porvenir, in Chilean Tierra del Fuego; a more frequent shuttle ferry crosses the strait from Primera Angostura, northwest of Punta Arenas.

LOCAL TRANSPORTATION

Even as automobiles clog the streets of Santiago and other cities, most Chileans still rely on public transportation.

Metro

Now in its fourth decade, carrying more than 2.2 million passengers per day, Santiago's privately operated Metro (www.metrosantiago .cl) looks almost as good as when it opened in 1975. It's steadily expanding service through the sprawling capital, and government expects ridership to nearly double over the next several years.

The Metro runs 6:30 A.M.–10:30 P.M. Peak "normal" hours are now 7:15–9 A.M. and 6–7:30 P.M., while all other hours, including weekends, are *económico*. Peak fares are about US$0.70, while *económico* fares are about US$0.65; rechargeable "Multivía" or "Bip" tickets may be used by more than one person, legally, by passing them back across the turnstile (no ticket is necessary to exit the system). There is a charge, however, for the initial electronic ticket; this may make it less useful for one-time visitors.

Rail

The state-run Empresa de Ferrocarriles del Estado (EFE, www.efe.cl) operates a southbound commuter line to the cities of Rancagua and San Fernando. EFE's Metro de Valparaíso (Merval) links the port city to nearby Viña del Mar and Viña's outer suburbs; it has recently been modernized, with both new and rejuvenated stations, and undergrounded through Viña's densely built downtown.

Buses

Santiago, other large cities, and even most small towns have local bus systems that cover their farthest extents. City buses are usually known as *micros,* but smaller ones carrying only about 20–25 passengers are often referred to as *liebres* (literally, hares). In the capital, the new Transantiago system (www .transantiago.cl) has replaced many antiquated vehicles with fewer, but larger and more comfortable, articulated buses, but the change has been awkward.

Routes can and do change, but most buses are numbered and have obvious placards indicating the major streets. If in doubt, ask the driver, as identically numbered buses sometimes follow slightly different routes. Fares are about US$0.65 in Santiago, a little less elsewhere. In Santiago, authorities have mandated automatic ticket machines to spare the driver the distraction of making change.

Taxi

Taxis are moderately priced in Santiago but more expensive in resorts and other towns. Painted black with yellow roofs, all have meters; fares start around Ch$150–200 (US$0.25–0.35) to *bajar la bandera* (literally, drop the flag), then cost Ch$100–120 (US$0.17–0.20) per 200 meters.

In Santiago, there's a separate radio taxi system, and hotels and restaurants usually call these cabs for clients. Slightly cheaper than metered taxis, they offered fixed fares agreed upon in advance and look like ordinary automobiles, with no identification except that they are invariably new with large antennae.

Taxi Colectivo

One of public transport's great conveniences is the *taxi colectivo,* which operates like a city bus on a numbered route. Slightly more expensive than buses, they are usually faster and guarantee seats. They are identifiable by the illuminated plastic signs on their roofs, which show major destinations.

Airport Buses and Shuttles

Santiago enjoys inexpensive airport bus service (US$1.50–2 pp), but getting to the bus stop can be a nuisance for those with more than a backpack. Most regional airports also have bus service; if not, a shuttle or taxi is necessary.

In Santiago and several other cities, there are inexpensive door-to-door shuttles (US$8–10 pp, depending on distance from the airport) that are ideal if your baggage is substantial. It's best to arrange this the day before your flight, but they can often accommodate passengers on short notice.

Bicycle

Because of heavy traffic and uneven pavement, cycling may not be the safest way of navigating traffic, but the number of cyclists is growing rapidly. When riding around Santiago or other cities, side streets may be safer than fast-moving avenues, but they are also narrower, with less room to maneuver. Weekend traffic is milder than on weekdays, and parts of downtown Santiago are virtually deserted on Sunday. There are a handful of dedicated bike paths, mostly through city parklands, but there are plans to increase them.

Ciclistas Furiosos (Raging Cyclists, www .furiosos.cl) is a Santiago organization that promotes cycling as a partial solution to the traffic and pollution problems, lobbies strongly for new bike routes, and also leads high-profile events resembling "Critical Mass" rides in North America.

Walking

Most cities are compact enough that walking suffices for sightseeing and other activities, and in congested areas pedestrians often move faster than automobiles. Drivers generally defer to pedestrians, though the rule is not universal—Santiago bus drivers are notorious for inattention to foot traffic. Take particular care in crossing wide busy streets like Santiago's Alameda and Avenida Providencia.

Visas and Officialdom

Entry requirements are straightforward. Argentines, Brazilians, Uruguayans, and Paraguayans need only national identity cards, but every other nationality needs a passport. Citizens of the United States and Canada, along with those of the European Community, Switzerland, Norway, Israel, Mexico, Australia, and New Zealand need passports but not advance visas.

Nationalities that *must* obtain advance visas include Indians, Jamaicans, Koreans, Poles, Russians, and Thais.

Chile routinely grants 90-day entry permits, on a tourist card that must be surrendered upon departure. Formally, visitors should have a return or onward ticket, but the author has entered Chile dozens of times over many years, at the international airport and remote border posts, without ever having been asked for a return or onward ticket.

One unpleasant surprise, though, is the hefty *arrival* tax that Chile's Ministerio de Relaciones Exteriores (Foreign Ministry) imposes on certain nationalities: US$23 for Mexicans, US$90 for Australians, US$131 for U.S. citizens, and US$159 for Canadians. These are one-time fees, valid for the life of the user's passport, and collected only at airports.

The rationale behind the *gasto administrativo de reciprocidad* (administrative reciprocity charge) is that those countries' governments require Chilean citizens to pay the same amounts simply to apply for a visa (with no guarantee of being issued one). That's a reasonable argument, but the misunderstandings provoked when officials direct unsuspecting arrivals to a special line to pay those fees often generates ill will.

Ninety-day extensions can take several days and cost roughly US$100, plus two color photos, at the **Departamento de Extranjería** (Moneda 1342, Santiago Centro, tel. 02/6725320) or in regional capitals. Visitors close to the Argentine, Peruvian, or Bolivian borders may find it quicker and cheaper to dash across the line and return. For lost tourist cards, request a replacement from the **Policía Internacional** (General Borgoño 1052, Independencia, Santiago, tel. 02/7371292) or from offices in regional capitals.

Always carry identification, since the Carabineros (national police) can request it at any moment, though they rarely do so capriciously. Passports may be necessary for routine transactions such as checking into hotels and cashing travelers checks.

LOST OR STOLEN PASSPORTS

Visitors who suffer a lost or stolen passport must obtain a replacement at their own embassy or consulate. After obtaining a replacement passport, visit the Policía Internacional (General Borgoño 1052, Independencia, Santiago, tel. 02/7371292) to replace the tourist card.

TAXES

For international flights or more than 500km, Chile's international departure tax recently rose to US$30, normally included in the price of the ticket; for shorter flights, it's only US$8. The domestic airport departure tax (US$8 for flights of more than 270 km) is likewise included in the ticket. At land borders, immigration officials sometimes collect a token fee for agricultural inspections.

CUSTOMS

Visitors may import personal effects including clothing, jewelry, medicine, sporting gear, camping equipment and accessories, photographic and video equipment, personal computers and the like, and wheelchairs for disabled individuals. They may also bring 500 grams of tobacco, three liters of wine or alcoholic beverages (adults only), and small quantities of perfume.

Customs inspections are usually routine, but at Santiago's international airport and some land borders, incoming baggage must pass through X-rays; do not put photographic film in your bag en route from Mendoza, Argentina, to Santiago, for instance. At the Peruvian and Bolivian borders, inspectors pay special attention to illegal drugs; at the international airport, there are drug-sniffing beagles.

Travelers bound from Region I (Tarapacá) and Region XII (Magallanes) will undergo internal customs checks because those regions have Zona Franca duty-free status. At many borders, the Servicio Agrícola Ganadero (SAG, Agriculture and Livestock Service) conducts agricultural inspections—fresh food will be confiscated—and sometimes levies a small charge. At some remote borders, the Carabineros handle all border formalities.

BORDER CROSSINGS

Chile has a handful of border crossings from Peru and Bolivia, and many from Argentina, but relatively few have regular public transportation. Some crossings are seasonal, especially in the high Andes and Patagonia, and others have limited hours.

Bad weather can close the passes across the Andes from Bolivia and Argentina at times, but many stay open all year. In addition to the Peruvian crossing from Tacna to Arica, all-year crossings include the Bolivian routes from La Paz to Arica, from Oruro to Iquique, Uyuni to Calama, and Uyuni to San Pedro de Atacama.

From Argentina, all-year routes include Salta and Jujuy to San Pedro de Atacama and Calama; the Los Libertadores tunnel between Mendoza and Santiago; the San Martín de los Andes to Temuco route via Paso de Mamuil Malal (Paso Tromen to Argentines); the Bariloche–Osorno highway; and the bus-boat shuttle from Bariloche to Puerto Varas.

There are many Patagonian crossings. Those open all year include the road from Esquel (local buses only) to Futaleufú; Comodoro Rivadavia to Coyhaique via Río Mayo; Los Antiguos to Chile Chico; El Calafate to Puerto Natales via Río Turbio; Río Gallegos to Punta Arenas; and Ushuaia and Río Grande to Punta Arenas.

POLICE AND MILITARY

Chile's Carabineros are probably the continent's most professional police, with a reputation for integrity and a low tolerance for corruption. (Argentine motorists, accustomed to bribing their own cops to avoid traffic tickets, have had vehicles confiscated for trying to do so in Chile.) Known popularly but scornfully—yet privately—as *pacos* by some Chileans, the Carabineros are normally polite and helpful in public but can be stern with lawbreakers, or individuals they suspect of being lawbreakers.

Chile's figure of 240 police officers per million inhabitants is below the world average of 286, but somehow there always seems to be an officer within sight.

During Pinochet's dictatorship, the military were feared, but since the return to constitutional government and especially since his detention and arrest in London, military personnel keep a low public profile. The current leadership appears committed to constitutional rule.

Accommodations

In the main tourist centers, there are alternatives for every budget, but some remote areas have only shoestring sleeping quarters.

Sernatur publishes an annually updated accommodations brochure with approximate prices; often, but not always, it excludes budget options and even omits some midrange and high-end places. Prices may be negotiable, especially outside the January–February peak. Travelers should not take hotel ratings literally as they often represent an ideal rather than a reality, and some one- or two-star places are better than others that theoretically rank higher.

Prices often rise in January and February—Chileans and Argentines (the most numerous foreign visitors) usually take their vacations after the school year ends in December—and during holiday periods such as Semana Santa (Holy Week) and patriotic holidays (mid-September).

Midrange to top-end hotels levy 19 percent in Impuesto de Valor Agregado or IVA (Value Added Tax or VAT), but they will discount that to bona fide tourists with appropriate documentation—passport and tourist card. Foreign residents of Chile are *not* eligible for this discount. At the same time, the discount can be smaller than expected if the hotel exchange rate is unfavorable.

While this book's rates for accommodations are quoted for both single and double occupancy, they are grouped in price categories according to the double occupancy cost.

CAMPING

Organized camping is a common alternative, especially in the mainland Lakes District, and it's a popular family option throughout the country. In wilder, more remote areas such as Aisén and Magallanes, it's possible to camp almost anywhere for free except in the most popular places, such as Parque Nacional Torres del Paine. Note that many Chilean campgrounds charge per site (for up to five or six people) rather than per person, which can make camping less appealing economically for single

people or couples, who may stay equally cheaply at pretty good budget accommodations.

HOSTELS

While Chile has only one dedicated Hostelling International facility, in Santiago's Barrio Brasil, there are several affiliates throughout the country that give discounts to HI members. With few exceptions, they are usually not dramatically cheaper than some more conventional budget options, but they do offer the opportunity to meet like-minded travelers.

For up-to-the-minute information on official hostels, contact Hostelling International Santiago (Cienfuegos 151, Santiago Centro, tel. 02/6718532, www.hostelling.cl) or the Asociación Chilena de Albergues Turísticos Juveniles (Hernando de Aguirre 201, Oficina 602, Providencia, Santiago, tel. 02/2333220, fax 02/2322555).

There are also many unofficial hostels, some of them outstanding. Some are affiliated with Backpacker's Best (www.backpackersbest.cl) and others with Backpackers Chile (www.backpackersbest.cl), and often have private rooms in addition to dorm-style accommodations.

OTHER BUDGET ACCOMMODATIONS

Budget accommodations, as cheap as US$5 per person but generally costing around US$8–10, go by a variety of names that may disguise their quality—they can vary from dingy fleabag hotels with sagging mattresses to simple but cheerful and tidy places with firm new beds. Some even have parking, except in densely built areas such as central Santiago.

Among the budget lodgings are *hospedajes* (generally family-run accommodations with a few spare rooms), *pensiones,* and *casas de huéspedes,* terms that are virtually interchangeable. All may have long-term residents as well as overnight guests. *Residenciales* are generally constructed with short-stay accommodations in mind but may also have semipermanent inhabitants. Generally a step up, an *hostería* often refers to a country hotel with a restaurant. All of these places may even use the term *hotel,* though usually that belongs to a more formal category.

That said, there are also some exceptional values in all categories. Many places will have shared bath and toilet *(baño general* or *baño compartido),* or offer a choice between shared and private bath *baño privado;* showers are the norm and bathtubs are rare. In some cases, rooms will have ceiling fans and even cable TV, but they may charge extra for cable and almost always do so for air-conditioning.

Budget travelers should consider bringing their own towels and, if traveling in the colder regions, perhaps even their own sleeping bags. Many accommodations, but by no means all, include breakfast in their rates; ask to be certain.

Showers
Rarely, today, hot water will come from an electric in-line heater that's capable of rendering a startling shock to unsuspecting users— *never* touch the fixture or the shower head while water's flowing. Generally, these showers work best with relatively low flows; as the flow increases, heating the volume of water becomes more difficult.

MIDRANGE ACCOMMODATIONS
Midrange hotels generally offer larger, more comfortable, and better furnished rooms, almost always with private bath, than even the best budget places. Ceiling fans, cable TV, and air-conditioning are common, but these hotels may lack on-site parking. Some have restaurants. Rates can range from US$30 up to US$100 d; some are better values than their high-end counterparts.

HIGH-END ACCOMMODATIONS
Some of this category's best options are country inns and hot-springs resorts, offering traditional hospitality and ambience with style unmatchable at other high-end places. Prices may be upward of US$100, often substantially higher, and some are gems of contemporary design.

Luxury hotels with top-flight service, in the same range, are few outside the capital and major resort areas. In the capital, these usually offer amenities such as restaurants, swimming pools, gym facilities, office space, wireless Internet connections, and conference rooms; outside the capital, these are mostly resorts and may lack business facilities. Invariably they offer secure parking.

Food and Drink

Chile's long coastline and rich farmland provides seafood, meat, fresh fruit, and vegetables in abundance. While the everyday local diet may have some shortcomings, in most areas visitors will easily find appealing food and drink.

According to historian John C. Super, whatever the Spanish invasion's negative consequences, it actually improved a pre-Columbian diet that was, by some accounts, nutritionally deficient (often protein-poor).

When the Europeans first set foot in South America, the Andean staples were beans, squash, and a variety of potatoes and other tubers, but the diet was low in animal protein—only the llama, alpaca, guinea pig, and wild game were readily available, and these not in all areas. Cultivation of tubers stretched into high latitudes such as archipelagic Chiloé, one of the areas of greatest diversity for potatoes. This, of course, spread across the Atlantic, but so did nonstaples such as chiles and avocados. Spanish introductions such as wheat and barley, yielding only a four-to-one harvest ratio in Europe, were significantly more successful in the Americas.

The Spanish introductions blended with the

indigenous base to create many edibles found on Chilean tables today. The abundant seafood, combined with the increase of European livestock and the high productivity of temperate European fruits such as apples, apricots, grapes, and pears, resulted in a diverse food production and consumption system that, however, is changing today.

Several government surveys have worried that the Chilean diet is deteriorating and obesity growing because of increased fats and cholesterol, partly because of fast food and a more sedentary lifestyle; there is particular concern over young schoolchildren and pregnant women. Red meat consumption has grown among lower classes but has decreased among the affluent. On the other hand, it's a third lower than in neighboring Argentina, and chicken, pork, and turkey consumption are increasing more rapidly. Lamb and mutton are stable, but despite Chile's wealth of marine resources, seafood consumption is lower than in Europe.

Cereal and vegetable consumption has decreased in all classes; that of vegetables is about half of the internationally recommended quantities. While consumption rates of mayonnaise, alcohol, and soft drinks have all tripled, Chileans are also eating greater quantities of fresh fruit.

WHERE TO EAT

Places to eat vary from hole-in-the-wall *comedores* or *cocinerías* (both roughly translatable as "eateries") with no formal menu to elegant *restaurantes*. About the only hard and fast rule is to avoid those in which solitary men—or groups of men—sit and drink beer.

There is, however, an elaborate but inconsistent terminology. Though *restaurante* generally means a place with sit-down service, it can cover a range of possibilities. *Fuente de soda* (literally "soda fountain") signifies a place with a modest menu that lacks a liquor license. *Cafeterías* provide plain meals, usually without table service, but the misleadingly named *salón de té* (literally "teahouse") can be more like a European-style café, sometimes with sidewalk

> ### WARNINGS
>
> Many Chileans slather high-fat *mayonesa* (mayonnaise) on almost anything, including sandwiches, salads, and seafood. If you don't like mayonnaise, ask whether your dish comes with it; even if you like the stuff yourself, you may prefer to ask for a side dish and apply it in the desired quantity. Similarly, fresh-fruit drinks are often oversugared; if the fruit alone is sweet enough for your taste, request it *sin azúcar, por favor.*
>
> Note also that the preferred terms for waiters are *garzón* and *mesero*. The term *mozo*, widely used and totally innocuous in neighboring Argentina, is an insult in Chile.

seating. *Hosterías* are generally country-style restaurants serving crowds of customers on weekend or holiday outings; if they're open weekdays, numbers will be smaller. *Hostería* can also mean a type of accommodation, though such places will usually have restaurants as well.

The most common term for menu is *la carta; el menú* is almost equally common but can also mean a fixed-price lunch or dinner. The bill is *la cuenta.*

Another option is the *picada,* generally a small family-run eatery that begins informally, often with just a couple of tables in a spare streetside room, that may develop into something more elaborate. In beachfront towns north of Viña del Mar, for instance, seafood *picadas* offer excellent food at modest prices.

In places other than *comedores* or *cocinerías,* a 10 percent tip is the norm. At *comedores,* tips are unexpected, but that doesn't mean they're unwelcome or inappropriate.

WHAT TO EAT

For those who read Spanish and enjoy cooking, the *Gran Libro de la Cocina Chilena* (Santiago: Editorial Bibliográfica, 1990) contains more than 500 pages of recipes for drinks, appetizers, soups, salads, meats, poultry, pasta, seafood, and many other specialties from the Chilean kitchen.

Cereals

Maíz (maize or corn) is a main ingredient in many dishes including *pastel de choclo,* the tasty traditional casserole of chicken, ground beef, olives, and other ingredients. Maize leaves serve as a wrapping for dishes such as *humitas,* similar to Mexican tamales.

Trigo (wheat), a Spanish introduction, is primarily for *pan* (bread), but it's also common as pasta. *Arroz* (rice) is a common *agregado* (side dish), but the native Andean grain quinoa is making a comeback, especially at creative restaurants.

Legumes, Vegetables, and Tubers

Salads are generally safe, but short-term visitors with tender stomachs might verify whether the greens have been washed with purified water. The *ensalada chilena* (Chilean salad) of tomato and onion, sometimes garnished with cilantro, is one of the best options.

Porotos (beans) are the traditional working class protein, but all Chileans eat them. Other legumes include *porotos verdes* (green beans), *arvejas* (peas), *lentejas* (lentils), and *habas* (fava beans).

In many varieties, *zapallo* (squash) remains part of the diet, as does the *tomate* (tomato). Old World vegetables include *acelga* (chard), *berenjena* (eggplant), *coliflor* (cauliflower), *lechuga* (lettuce), and *repollo* (cabbage). Despite the country's name, spicy *chiles* (peppers) are uncommon; most Chilean cuisine is fairly bland despite the presence of chile-based *ají* or *pebre* at most meals.

Native to the Andes, *papas* (potatoes) grow in well-drained soils at higher elevations or higher latitudes such as the Chiloé archipelago; *papas fritas* (French fries) are universal, but spuds also appear as *purée* (mashed) and in other forms. Other common tubers include *zanahorias* (carrots) and *rábanos* (radishes).

Vegetarianism

Except in Santiago, vegetarian restaurants are few, but the ingredients for quality vegetarian meals are easy to obtain, and many eateries prepare vegetarian versions of dishes such as pasta. Before ordering pasta, clarify whether it comes with a meat sauce: *Carne* means beef, and waiters or waitresses may consider chicken, pork, and similar items as *carne blanca* (literally, white meat). Faced with a reluctant cook, try claiming *alergia* (allergy).

Fruits

Its seasons reversed from those of the Northern Hemisphere, temperate Chile produces the same fruits and fresh juices. Items such as *manzana* (apple), *pera* (pear), *naranja* (orange), *ciruela* (plum), *sandía* (watermelon), *membrillo* (quince), *durazno* (peach), *frambuesa* (raspberry), and *frutilla* (strawberry) will be familiar to almost everyone.

Also widely available, mostly through import, are tropical and subtropical fruits such as banana, chirimoya, and *piña* (pineapple). Less commonly consumed locally, but often exported, are nontraditional temperate fruits such as *arándano* (blueberry) and kiwi.

The *palta* (avocado), known as *aguacate* in its Central American region of origin, often appears in salads and sandwiches.

Meats and Poultry

Before the Spaniards, South America's only domesticated animals were the *cuy* (guinea pig), the llama and alpaca, and the dog (sometimes used for food). The Spaniards enriched their diet with domestic animals, namely cattle, sheep, pigs, and poultry, including chicken and ducks.

Cuts of *carne,* often modified as *carne de vacuno,* or *bife* (beef) is the most common menu item. The widest selection is usually available in the *parrillada* or *asado,* a mixed grill that includes prime cuts but also offal such as *chunchules* (small intestines), *morcilla* (blood sausage), and *riñones* (kidneys). *Asado* can also mean a simple roast.

Cordero (lamb), often roasted on a spit over an open fire, is common in the Sur Chico and Chilean Patagonia. *Cerdo* (pork) appears in many forms, from *chuletas* (chops) to *tocino* (bacon) and *chicharrones* (rinds).

Ave (poultry) most often means *pollo* (chicken), which sometimes appears on menus as *gallina* (literally, hen). *Pavo* (turkey) is becoming more common. Eggs are *huevos*.

Fish and Seafood

Seafood includes both *pescado* (fish) and *mariscos* (shellfish and crustaceans), in abundance. The most common fish are *congrio* (conger eel, covering a variety of species), *corvina* ("sea bass"), *lenguado* (sole or flounder), and *merluza* (hake); *salmón* (salmon) comes from controversial fish farms on the inlets, fjords, and freshwater lakes of the Sur Chico and Aisén.

The cheapest restaurants can ruin quality fish by preparing it *frito* (overpoweringly deep fried), but on request almost all will prepare it *a la plancha* (grilled, usually with butter) or *al vapor* (steamed). Some restaurants may add elaborate sauces, often with shellfish.

Chilean cuisine really distinguishes itself in its *mariscos*. Most visitors will recognize the relatively commonplace *almejas* (clams), *calamares* (squid), *camarones* (shrimp), *cangrejo* or *jaiva* (crab), *centolla* (king crab), *cholgas* and *choritos* (different varieties of mussels), *machas* (razor clams), *ostiones* (scallops), *ostras* (oysters), and *pulpo* (octopus). Less familiar will be the *choro zapato* ("shoe mussel," so called for its enormous size); *erizos* (sea urchins, often exported to Japan); the oddly named *locos* (giant abalone, literally "crazies"); *picoroco* (giant barnacle); and *piure* (resembling a dirty sponge, according to food writer Robb Walsh). Many of these have closed seasons, when they may not be taken, so be aware.

Seafood often appears as **ceviche,** raw fish or shellfish heavily marinated in lime juice and spiced with cilantro. River trout from Patagonia is also common. On the Juan Fernández archipelago and Easter Island, *langosta* (meaning "lobster," but really a crayfish) is a premium menu item.

Among seafood specialties worth looking for are *chupes* (thick, buttery stews) of *congrio, jaiva,* and *locos,* and *curanto,* a kitchen-

© WAYNE BERNHARDSON

conger eels hang for sale at Angelmó

sink stew that can include fish, shellfish, beef, chicken, lamb, pork, potato, and vegetables.

Desserts

Helado (ice cream) is popular, but quality is only so-so except in the capital and major beach resorts, where *elaboración artesanal* (small-scale production) is more common. *Arroz con leche* (rice pudding) and *flan* (egg custard) are better choices except in the Sur Chico, Patagonia, and scattered places elsewhere, where German immigrants have left a legacy of *kuchen* (pastries such as apple strudel and raspberry tarts). Chileans also adore *manjar*, the caramelized milk spread known as *dulce de leche* in Argentina.

International and Ethnic Food

Santiago, an underappreciated gastronomic center, has the greatest variety of international food, though some tourist-oriented areas also have good selections. Italian and Chinese are the most common foreign cuisines—*chifa* is a common term for inexpensive Chinese restaurants in the Norte Grande—but French, German, and Spanish food are also plentiful. Brazilian, Mexican, and Middle Eastern cuisines are less common; some world food cuisines, such as Thai and especially Japanese sushi, are gaining popularity.

MEALS AND MEALTIMES

By North American and European standards, Chileans are late risers and late eaters. Even in hotels, it may be difficult to get breakfast before 8 A.M. Lunch *(almuerzo* or *colación)* often starts around 2 P.M., *cena* (dinner) around 9 P.M. or later—sometimes much later. Chileans bide their time between lunch and dinner with a late afternoon *onces* ("elevenses," afternoon tea) consisting of a sandwich or some sort of pastry, but it can be a more substantial meal.

Breakfast

Most Chileans eat a light breakfast of tea and *pan tostado* (toast), perhaps with eggs. Eggs may be either *fritos* (fried) or *revueltos* (scrambled), occasionally *duros* (hard-boiled).

Avena (oatmeal) is common in wintertime, but dry breakfast cereals such as cornflakes have also made inroads.

Lunch

Lunch is often the main meal, usually including an *entrada* (appetizer), followed by a *plato de fondo* (entrée), accompanied by an *agregado* (side dish) and a *bebida* (soft drink) or *agua mineral* (mineral water), and followed by *postre* (dessert).

Upscale Santiago restaurants sometimes offer fixed-price lunches that make it possible to eat well and stylishly without busting the budget, but elsewhere that's unusual. Fast-food items such as *hamburguesas* (hamburgers), sandwiches, pizza, and pasta are easy to find.

Onces

The late afternoon *onces* can vary from a sandwich to the equivalent of afternoon tea, with elaborate cakes and cookies, and it's often a social occasion as well. Presumably intended to tide people over until their late dinner, it's often larger and more elaborate than that would imply.

Dinner

Dinner resembles lunch, but in formal restaurants it may be much more elaborate (and expensive); it can be a major social occasion. Chileans dine late—9 P.M. is early, and arriving earlier may earn "What are you doing here?" stares from waiters.

BUYING GROCERIES

Virtually every city, town, village, and hamlet has a central market where it's possible to buy fresh produce. Even in locales without central markets, there are always small shops where groceries are available.

In larger cities, supermarkets carry a wide selection of processed foods but a lesser variety (and quality) of fresh produce than is available in produce markets.

BEVERAGES
Coffee, Tea, and Chocolate

Chilean coffee can be a disappointment for caffeine addicts—powdered Nescafé is the norm, and espresso is rare except in the capital and some tourist spots. *Café negro* is Nescafé mixed with hot water; *café con leche* (coffee with milk) is usually Nescafé dissolved in warm milk.

Té negro (black tea), usually in bags, is insipid by most standards. Those wanting tea with milk in the British manner should ask for tea first and cold milk later; for most Chileans, *té con leche* is a tea bag steeped in hot water with *leche en polvo* (powdered milk). Herbal teas, from the nearly universal *té de manzanilla* (chamomile) and *rosa mosqueta* (rose hips) to native specialties such as *llantén* (plantain), *cedrón* (lemon verbena), *paico* (saltwort), and *boldo,* are often better alternatives. In the far south, some Chileans follow the Argentine custom of sipping *yerba mate,* the so-called "Paraguayan tea."

It's possible to get a good cup of *chocolate* (hot chocolate) in Santiago and much of the southern lake district, where Swiss-German influence is most significant. Elsewhere, it will be powdered chocolate mixed with hot water.

Water, Juices, and Soft Drinks

Agua de la llave (tap water) is almost always potable; for ice, request it *con hielo.* Visitors on brief vacations where stomach upset can be disastrous might consider bottled water. Ask for *agua pura* or *agua mineral;* for carbonated water, add *con gas.* Sometimes these are known by brand names such as Cachantún.

Gaseosas (in the plural) are sweetened, bottled soft drinks. Only Mexicans consume more of these than Chileans, who average more than 90 liters per person in a market estimated at US$1 billion per year.

Licuados are fruit-based drinks mixed with water or blended with *leche* (milk). Unless your sweet tooth is insatiable, have them prepared without sugar *(sin azúcar, por favor).* Fresh-squeezed *jugos* (fruit juices) can be exceptional but, again, watch the sugar. This is usually not a problem with orange juice, but it is with others.

Alcoholic Drinks

While Chile is famous for its wines, Chileans themselves lean more toward beer. The most widely available are Cristal, Becker, and similar lagers, which are palatable but unexceptional. They taste best as *chopp,* direct from the tap, rather than from bottles or cans. In recent years, microbrews have made an impact, especially in Santiago, the Sur Chico, and Patagonia.

Chile is a major wine producer, and exports have boomed since the end of the dictatorship, during which many people boycotted Chilean products. Specialists such as James Molesworth and Jancis Robinson have acknowledged improvements in Chilean wines, even though Molesworth compared the industry to a young baseball player "hitting the occasional home run, sometimes striking out."

Wine lists rarely indicate the source region or the vintage, so diners may have to ask to see the bottle itself. Only the best restaurants have a wide selection, usually in full bottles though sometimes it's possible to get a *media botella* (half bottle) or, occasionally, wine by the glass. The common *botellín* or *vino individual* is a small bottle that's slightly more than a single glass, but these are not premium wines.

Wine tourism is developing rapidly, though less spontaneously than in locales such as California's Napa Valley. While it's better to call ahead for reservations or book a tour, drop-ins are not unheard of. There are fast-developing "Rutas del Vino" (Wine Routes) in the Aconcagua, Casablanca, Colchagua, and Maule Valleys.

Chile is also, along with Peru, a major producer of the potent grape brandy known as pisco, the base of the legendary pisco sour. The Norte Chico valleys of Copiapó, Huasco, and Elqui are the major producing areas, and pisco has also spawned a small tourist industry.

Another popular aperitif is the *vaina,* a concoction of port, cognac, cocoa, and egg white that some Chileans consider a "woman's drink."

Conduct and Customs

Proper conduct and respect for local mores require special attention from travelers unaccustomed to traveling among indigenous peoples. When greeting Chileans, it's good form to offer the appropriate polite greeting *buenos días* (good morning), *buenas tardes* (good afternoon), or *buenas noches* (good evening or good night, depending on the time of day).

In terms of general conduct, both women and men should dress conservatively and inconspicuously when visiting churches, chapels, and sacred sites. This, again, is an issue of respect.

Photographic Etiquette

It's highly inappropriate to take an in-your-face approach to photographing indigenous peoples, particularly the Mapuche. If the inclusion of people is incidental to, say, a landscape, that's usually not a problem, but when a person is the primary subject it is best, if you manage Spanish or have another language in common, to try to establish a relationship before asking permission. If you have negotiated a crafts market purchase, for instance, there should be no problem; still, when in doubt ask, and respect your subject's decision.

If photographing an individual with his or her consent, offer to send him or her a copy of the photo.

Tips for Travelers

WHAT TO TAKE
Luggage

For shoestring travelers planning months in Chile and neighboring countries, for instance, a spacious lightweight backpack is the best choice; a small daypack for local excursions is also a good idea.

Even for nonbackpackers, light luggage and a small daypack for excursions are advisable. Small but sturdy lightweight locks are advisable for all sorts of luggage, if only to discourage temptation.

Clothing

Because of Chile's altitudinal and latitudinal variation, clothing can vary from light cottons to heavy woolens. Much depends on the season and the activity; a good rule of thumb is appropriately seasonal clothing for comparable Northern Hemisphere latitudes and altitudes—though only the highest peaks in North America or Europe can match Andean altitudes that are readily reached by car in Chile.

Both hikers and city walkers should have a wide-brimmed hat for protection from the sun; Patagonia's thinning ozone layer makes sunburn a serious hazard. In the Lakes District, an umbrella is useful at any season—but in Patagonia, squalls can shred your *paraguas* in an instant, so heavier rain gear is desirable.

Camping Gear

Quality camping gear, for sale or rental, is more easily available than it once was, especially in Santiago and outdoorsy towns such as Pucón and Puerto Natales. Bring a lightweight tent with a rain fly for shedding the showers and, at the highest altitudes, keeping out the cold. A three-season sleeping bag is sufficient for most weather—unless you're camping or bivouacking on the Patagonian icefields or the altiplano's massive volcanoes.

For those hiking either the highlands or the lowland forests, lightweight rain gear is also a good idea, along with fabric hiking boots that dry out quickly.

Since some places lack fresh water—many volcanic areas have no surface streams—sturdy plastic water bottles, a water filter, and even iodine drops or tablets are indispensable. Carry insect repellent, not just for mosquitoes but also for the Lakes District's large biting *tábanos* (horseflies).

Odds and Ends

Public toilets sometimes lack toilet paper, so travelers should always carry a roll. Many budget hotels have thin walls and squeaky floors, so earplugs are a good idea.

Leg pouches and money belts are good options for securing cash, travelers' checks, and important documents. Compact binoculars are a good idea for birders and others who enjoy wildlife and the landscape.

EMPLOYMENT OPPORTUNITIES

Many foreigners work informally on tourist visas. Among the options are teaching English or another foreign language, work in the tourist industry, or casual labor in bars or restaurants. The problem with such jobs is that they either require time to build up a clientele (in the case of teaching), are seasonal (tourism), or poorly paid (in bars or restaurants, except the few places where tips are high).

Legal residence, permitting eligibility for more and better-paying jobs, usually requires local or foreign sponsorship, a substantial investment, marriage to a Chilean or other permanent resident, or a reliable retirement income. There are three types of working visas: a temporary visa for professionals and trained technicians, whose qualifications must be evaluated by an appropriate Chilean institution; a contract-specific visa with an employer, valid up to two years and primarily for low-skilled workers, who must have a return ticket to their country of origin; and a visa for exchange students seeking part-time work. In theory, temporary working visas can lead to residence, but the Interior Ministry bureaucracy moves slowly.

STUDY

Most people who undertake study programs are Spanish-language students in Santiago. While a student visa is supposedly obligatory, in practice virtually everyone arrives and registers on a tourist visa.

Several U.S. universities also have undergraduate exchange programs with the Universidad de Chile, the Universidad Católica, and other schools; for more information, contact your own university's overseas programs department.

BUSINESS TRAVEL

For many years now, Chile's economy has been the continent's most productive, and its institutional stability and low corruption levels have made it an investors' favorite—in 2008, according to the Latin Business Index, Chile was the region's best country. Chile and the United States have a bilateral free-trade agreement that has eliminated tariffs on nearly all imported goods, and their trade has more than doubled through the first decade of the new millennium (though the global economic crisis that began in 2008, and declining copper prices, could affect these statistics in the long run).

That, however, does not eliminate the need to understand the cultural and legal context of business or investment here; before signing any deal, consult a local lawyer recommended by your embassy, consulate, or a truly trusted friend.

Good background sources on business, for those who read Spanish, are financial dailies such as *Estrategia* (www.estrategia.cl). Exporters should consult the U.S. Commercial Service's Chile page (www.buyusa.gov/chile/en) for suggestions.

Business Etiquette

Conducting business is as much a personal and social activity as an economic one. Initial contacts may be formal, with appointments arranged well in advance, but topics such as family and sports are often part of the conversation. Formality in dress and appearance is less rigid than it once was, but in sectors like banking it's still the rule.

Spanish-language skills are a plus, though many Chilean business figures speak English well (more than a few have been educated in English-speaking countries). The best months for business travel are April–November; in January and February, when school lets out and Chileans take their summer vacations, Santiago can seem almost deserted. Many people also leave for winter holidays, the last two weeks of July.

Useful Organizations

Nearly all important business-oriented organizations are in Santiago. One critically important contact is the national customs headquarters, the Servicio Nacional de Aduanas (Plaza Sotomayor 60, Valparaíso, tel. 0322/200513, www.aduana.cl). If importing equipment for permanent use, it's essential to deal with them through an *agente de aduanas* (private customs broker).

U.S. citizens can get advice at the **Cámara Chileno Norteamericana de Comercio** (U.S. Chamber of Commerce, Av. Presidente Kennedy 5735, Oficina 201, Torre Poniente, Las Condes, tel. 02/2909700, www.amcham-chile.cl). Its Chilean counterpart is the **Cámara de Comercio de Santiago** (Santiago Chamber of Commerce, Monjitas 392, tel. 02/3607000, www.ccs.cl).

Chile's stock exchange is the **Bolsa de Comercio de Santiago** (La Bolsa 64, tel. 02/3993000, www.bolsadesantiago.com).

For agricultural contacts, visit the **Sociedad Nacional de Agricultura** (National Agricultural Society, Tenderini 187, Santiago, tel. 02/5853310, www.sna.cl).

ORGANIZED TOURS

Because of Chile's complex travel logistics, organized tours can be useful for visitors with limited time. Many reputable U.S. and Chilean operators offer and even coordinate tours. Sometimes these take in sights in neighboring countries, usually Argentina but sometimes Peru or Bolivia. Within each category, the following companies appear in alphabetical order. For the latest prices, consult them individually.

U.S.-Based Operators

Primarily but not exclusively oriented toward cyclists, **Backroads** (801 Cedar St., Berkeley, CA 94710, tel. 510/527-1555 or 800/462-2848, www.backroads.com) offers a nine- or ten-day hiking and/or biking excursions in the Chilean and Argentine Lakes District around Puerto Varas, and Argentina's Bariloche and San Martín de los Andes. Its "Patagonian Walking and Hiking" trip stays at luxury lodgings in Parque Nacional Torres del Paine and Argentina's Parque Nacional Los Glaciares; a similar trip uses less opulent accommodations.

Bio Bio Expeditions (P.O. Box 2028, Truckee, CA 96160, tel. 800/246-7238, www.bbxrafting.com) offers weeklong trips from Puerto Montt to its Río Futaleufú base camp for kayaking and multisport trips.

Based at its own deluxe camp, **Earth River Expeditions** (180 Towpath Rd., Accord, NY 12404, tel. 845/626-2665 or 800/643-2784, www.earthriver.com) offers similar 10-day rafting and kayaking trips on and around the Futaleufú.

The **Earthwatch Institute** (3 Clocktower Pl., Maynard, MA 01754, tel. 978/461-0081, tel. 800/776-0188, www.earthwatch.org) arranges a variety of volunteer programs in which participants pay for the privilege of assisting university faculty and independent researchers in archaeological, environmental, or similar projects. Chilean projects have included Easter Island archaeological digs, Río Toltén river otters, and *huemul* (Andean deer) in the Aisén region.

For travelers at least 55 years old, **Elderhostel** (11 Avenue de Lafayette, Boston, MA 02111, tel. 877/426-8056, www.elderhostel.org) operates theme-oriented trips that range from relatively sedentary ("History and Culture from Santiago to Rio," by cruise ship) to active ("The Atacama Desert and Easter Island: Different Worlds").

A pioneer on the Río Futaleufú, former U.S. Olympian Chris Spelius's **Expediciones Chile** (P.O. Box 752, Sun Valley, ID 83353, tel. 888/488-9082, www.exchile.com) has its own sprawling and secluded camp on the river's south bank. While they specialize in kayaking the Fu, they also offer rafting and multi-sport holidays that include birding, fly-fishing, hiking, and horseback riding. Weeklong stays include plenty of time and instruction on the river, and transfers from the Argentine city of Esquel; there are also shorter programs at lower prices.

Far Horizons Archaeological and Cultural Trips (P.O. Box 2546, San Anselmo, CA 94979, tel. 800/552-4575, www.farhorizon .com) offers archaeologically oriented trips, guided by top academics, to Rapa Nui (Easter Island) and the Atacama Desert.

Mountain Travel Sobek (1266 66th St., Emeryville, CA 94608, tel. 888/687-6235, www.mtsobek.com) does a variety of Patagonian adventure trips, including an 11-day "Trekking the Paine Circuit," a 12-day "Aysén Glacier Trail," and a 15-day "Patagonia Explorer" that includes the glacier cruise from Punta Arenas, Chile, to Ushuaia, Argentina.

Nature Expeditions International (7860 Peters Rd., Suite F-103, Plantation, FL 33324, tel. 954/693-8852 or 800/869-0639, www .naturexp.com) operates "soft adventure" and culture-oriented tours to Argentina and Chile, among other destinations. Their 15-day "Chile: Land of Extremes" takes in San Pedro de Atacama, Pucón, Puerto Varas, Laguna San Rafael, and Torres del Paine, while the 16-day "Chile and Argentina: the Southern Cone" includes both countries' northern lake districts, as well as Argentina's El Calafate and vicinity, and Buenos Aires. It also does a nine-day "Undiscovered Rapa Nui" trip to Easter Island.

Fly-fishing specialist **Orvis** (4200 Route 7A, Manchester Center, VT 05255, tel. 802/362-3750 or 800/547-4322, www.orvis.com) arranges angling holidays in the Andean lake district and the more southerly Aisén region, and sometimes has celebrity guests such as author Peter Mathiessen.

Powderquest Tours (7108 Pinetree Rd., Richmond, VA 23229, tel. 804/285-4961 or 888/565-7158, www.powderquest.com) runs five or six ski and snowboard tours annually. Resorts visited include Portillo, Valle Nevado,

Termas de Chillán, and Antillanca; some trips cross to Argentina.

REI Adventures (P.O. Box 1938, Sumner, WA 98390, tel. 800/622-2236, www.rei.com/ adventures) offers a 10-day "Wine Roads of the Andes Cycle" (including parts of Argentina), a 10-day "Northern Patagonia" visit to the lake district, and a 13-day "Fitzroy & Paine Trek" that also takes in parts of Argentina.

Affiliated with the Smithsonian Institution, **Smithsonian Journeys** (P.O. Box 23293, Washington, DC 20026-3293, tel. 202/357-4700 or 877/338-8687, www.smithsonianjourneys.org) offers the 13-day "Patagonia and the Natural Wonders of Argentina and Chile," which starts and ends in Buenos Aires, but also visits Puerto Varas and vicinity, Punta Arenas, Puerto Natales and vicinity, and Torres del Paine.

Its South American services focus on Buenos Aires and Argentina, but **Travel Jewish** (P.O. Box 6771, Ithaca, NY 14851, tel. 949/307-9231, www.traveljewish.com) also offers a selection of tours to Santiago, Viña del Mar and Valparaíso, and as far afield as La Serena and Temuco (home to Chile's oldest synagogue).

Wilderness Travel (1102 Ninth St., Berkeley, CA 94710, tel. 510/558-2488 or 800/368-2794, www.wildernesstravel.com) offers a selection starting with a nine-day "Chile Private Journey" that takes in the Lakes District and Torres del Paine, and a nine-day "Futaleufú Adventure" (US$3,095), also primarily a hiking trip. Other trips include the 16-day "In Patagonia" excursion that focuses mostly on Argentina but also visits Torres del Paine, and a 15-day "Undiscovered Patagonia" that takes in the Lakes District and Argentina's Moreno Glacier and Fitz Roy areas.

Wildland Adventures (3516 NE 155th St., Seattle, WA 98155, tel. 800/345-4453, www .wildland.com) operates small group tours (2–8 persons) through locally based guides. The 14-day "In the Wake of Magellan" trip includes both Torres del Paine and a segment of the luxury cruise between Punta Arenas and Ushuaia, as well as Argentina's Moreno Glacier. Other options include the 10-day "Chile Adventure

Land of Contrasts," covering the Lakes District as well as Torres del Paine; the nine-day "Torres del Paine Base Camp Trek"; and the eight-day "Explora Travesía," which involves crossing the Andes from San Pedro de Atacama to Salta, Argentina.

Chile-Based Operators

All the following operators are permanently based in Chile, though not all are Chilean. When phoning or faxing an operator from outside Chile, use the Chilean country code 56 as a prefix.

AlSur Expediciones (Aconcagua and Imperial, Puerto Varas, tel./fax 065/232300, www.alsurexpeditions.com) operates tours and activities in the Andean lake district and specializes in Parque Pumalín, Douglas Tompkins's private nature reserve.

Based in summer only at Dalcahue, on the Isla Grande de Chiloé, **Altué Sea Kayaking** (Encomenderos 83, Las Condes, Santiago, tel. 09/9419-6809, www.seakayakchile.com).

Antares Patagonia Adventure (Bories 206, Puerto Natales, tel. 061/414611, www.antarespatagonia.com) operates activities-oriented trips to Patagonia—ice hiking, kayaking, and mountaineering—mostly but not exclusively in Parque Nacional Torres del Paine. Its U.S. representative is Americas Travel (348 Hayes St., San Francisco, CA 94102-4421, tel. 415/703-9955, mdiaz@antarespatagonia.com).

U.S./Peruvian-run **Austral Adventures** (Avenida Costanera 904, Ancud, tel./fax 065/625977, www.austral-adventures.com) offers six-day custom boat tours from Ancud south to Parque Pumalín, as well as land-based programs on the Isla Grande de Chiloé.

French-owned **Azimut 360** (General Salvo 159, Providencia, Santiago, tel. 02/2351519, www.azimut360.com) offers Patagonian excursions ranging from traditional lake district trips to northern Patagonian ice fields and technical climbs of summits such as Aisén's 4,058-meter Monte San Valentín. It's also recently begun programs in the Norte Grande precordilla hamlet of Codpa.

Putre-based, U.S.-run **Birding Altoandino** (cel. 09/9890-7291, www.birdingaltoandino .com) conducts birding, botany, and even archaeological tours of the Norte Grande, with special options available for those who cannot or prefer not to deal with very high elevations. Operator Barbara Knapton has an exceptional library of Andean natural-history books at her Putre headquarters.

Campo Aventura (San Bernardo 318, Puerto Varas, tel./fax 065/232910, www.campoaventura.com) offers four-day, three-night horseback explorations of the spectacularly scenic Cochamó backcountry southeast of Puerto Varas, but shorter and longer options are possible.

German-Austrian **Casa Chueca** (tel. 071/1970096, tel./fax 071/1970097, cel. 09/9419-0625 or 09/9837-1440, www.trekkingchile.com) organizes backcountry trips in the vicinity of Talca and Curicó, an area that gets fewer visitors than it deserves, and elsewhere in the country and in Argentine Patagonia.

Santiago-based **Cascada Expediciones** (Don Carlos 3219, Las Condes, tel. 02/2329878, www.cascada.travel) offers activity-oriented excursions from the city and, during the summer season, trips farther afield to destinations such as Pucón, Futaleufú, San Pedro de Atacama, and Torres del Paine (where its domed EcoCamp is the most distinctive accommodations option).

Aisén-based **Catamaranes del Sur** (Pedro de Valdivia 0210, Providencia, Santiago, tel. 02/2311902, www.catamaranesdelsur.cl) goes to Laguna San Rafael from its hotel at Puerto Chacabuco, and has multi-day programs that include other excursions in the region.

October–April, **Cruceros Australis** (Av. Bosque Norte 0440, 11th floor, Las Condes, Santiago, tel. 02/4423110, www.australis .com) offers three-, four-, and seven-day cruises from Punta Arenas through southern Tierra del Fuego's fjords to Ushuaia and Cape Horn on its twin luxury vessels *Mare Australis* and **Via Australis.** Rates change from low-season (October and April) to midseason (November–mid-December and all of March) and high-season (mid-December–February). Cruceros Australis also has offices in Miami (4014 Chase Ave., Ste. 202, Miami Beach, FL 33140, tel. 305/695-9618 or 877/678-3772).

September–May, **Cruceros Marítimos Skorpios** (Augusto Leguía 118, Las Condes, Santiago, tel. 02/2311030, www.skorpios .cl) operates small cruise ships (around 100 passengers) from Puerto Montt and Puerto Chacabuco to Laguna San Rafael, and from Puerto Natales to the fjords of the Campo de Hielo Sur, the southern continental ice field.

Explora Hotels (Américo Vespucio Sur 80, 5th floor, Las Condes, Santiago, tel. 02/2066060, www.explora.com) offers expensive packages, ranging from three days to a week, at its magnificently sited hotel in Parque Nacional Torres del Paine. It also has permanent facilities in San Pedro de Atacama and on Rapa Nui (Easter Island). The San Pedro facility, in particular, has drawn criticism on environmental grounds (it has four swimming pools), but visitors have praised the all-inclusive accommodations and especially the excursions.

In the Norte Chico east of Ovalle, German-operated **Hacienda Los Andes** (Correo Hurtado, tel. 053/691822, www.haciendalosandes.com) runs horseback and other excursions through a truly off-the-beaten-track part of the Andes. Bed-and-breakfast accommodations in colonial-style rooms are also available.

Hotel Awasi (Tocopilla 4, San Pedro de Atacama, tel. 02/9472049, www.awasi.cl) is an eight-room boutique hotel that, like Explora, offers all-inclusive packages, but it's more central and fits better into the local scene. Tours here are individual—one or two persons per guide, rather than Explora's slightly larger groups.

Chile's flagship airline also operates **LAN Vacations** (toll-free tel. 877/219-0345 in the United States, www.lanvacations.com), with individually crafted itineraries in its home country and other destinations that it serves.

Navimag Ferries (Av. El Bosque Norte 0440, Las Condes, 11th floor, tel. 02/4423120, www.navimag.com) sails between the Patagonian town of Puerto Natales and the mainland city of Puerto Montt. While these are not cruises in the traditional sense, they are more than just transportation as they pass through Pacific Chile's spectacular fjordlands. For details and fares, visit www .navimag.com.

Pachamama by Bus (Agustinas 2113, Santiago, tel. 02/6888018, www.pachamamabybus.com) is a weekly hop-on, hop-off backpackers' bus between Santiago and San Pedro de Atacama (to the north) and Santiago and Puerto Montt (to the south), which visits and even stays at destinations such as Parque Nacional Pan de Azúcar and Pichilemu. While it's more expensive than regular buses, it has English-speaking guides, stops at roadside attractions, permits clients to stop over and board a subsequent bus at no additional charge, and has no time limit. Scheduled trips leave even with one passenger; the maximum is 13.

Patagonia Connection (Fidel Oteíza 1951, Oficina 1006, Providencia, Santiago, tel. 02/2256489, www.patagonia-connection .com) offers four-day and three-night, as well as six-day and five-night packages based at its Termas de Puyuhuapi hot-springs resort in Aisén; these include a full-day catamaran excursion to Parque Nacional Laguna San Rafael. Prices are lower in the fall and spring shoulder seasons than in the January–February summer peak.

Puerto Williams–based, German-run **Sea & Ice & Mountains Adventures Unlimited** (tel./ fax 061/621150, tel. 061/621227, www.simltd .com) operates summer yacht tours through Tierra del Fuego and Cape Horn.

Terrantai Lodge (Tocopilla 411, San Pedro de Atacama, tel. 055/851045, www.terrantai .com) offers packages with full board, transfers from Calama airport, and specialized tour guides. For tours in English, rates are slightly higher.

Based in Puerto Montt, British-run **Travellers** (Bulnes 1009, tel./fax 065/262099, www.travellers.cl) is an experienced resource for the southernmost Sur Chico, setting up adventure travel excursions with the most reliable local operators.

TRAVELERS WITH DISABILITIES

For visitors with disabilities, Chile can be more problematic than other parts of the world. The narrow, uneven city sidewalks, fast-moving traffic, and rugged backcountry are unkind to people with certain physical disabilities, especially those who need wheelchairs. Picturesque Valparaíso's winding pathways and staircases can be nightmarish for wheelchair users.

Public transportation can rarely accommodate passengers with disabilities, though Santiago's newer Metro stations have elevators. Santiago's **Servicio Tixi** (tel. 800/372300 toll-free) has specially equipped cabs.

Few older buildings are specifically equipped for people with disabilities, but the prevalence of earthquakes means they are low and can often accommodate them. At newer hotels, often high-rises, wheelchair accessibility is obligatory.

TRAVELING WITH CHILDREN

In most ways, Chile is child-friendly. In fact, since many Chileans enjoy large extended families, they may feel little in common with people in their late 20s and older who do *not* have children, and traveling with kids can open doors.

There are also practical advantages to traveling with children. On buses, for instance, small children who do not occupy a separate seat do not pay, and budget hotels often make no additional charge for kids.

FEMALE TRAVELERS

Like other Latin American societies, Chile has a strong *machista* (chauvinist) element. Women are traditionally mothers, homemakers, and caregivers, while men are providers and decision-makers, though this is changing subtly in contemporary times. Domestic violence is a serious problem, especially among the lower classes, but it is not unique to that part of society.

Many Chilean men view foreign women as sexually available, and this can lead to harassment. Harassment is usually verbal, but it can turn ugly. If you receive unwanted attention, try to ignore it, and the odds are that the problem will go away on his own. If not, the next best option is to return to your hotel, a restaurant, or some other public place where harassment will be more conspicuous and you're likely to find support. Some women have suggested wearing a bogus wedding ring, but truly persistent suitors might see this as a challenge.

Despite problems, women have begun to acquire political prominence. The most noteworthy is President Michelle Bachelet, elected in 2006 after serving as both Health Minister and Defense Minister. Longtime activist Gladys Marín, who died in 2005, was the 1999 Communist presidential candidate (during the campaign, though, a TV interviewer remarked that Marín had the best legs of any candidate—to which she responded with her most *simpática* smile).

GAY AND LESBIAN TRAVELERS

While there may be no legal prohibition on homosexual behavior, in a country where machismo is the rule, it can be risky in public, and police harassment is possible. Things are definitely better, however, than during General Carlos Ibáñez del Campo's authoritarian presidency (1924–1931), when government agents rounded up homosexuals and threw them into the sea with concrete weights on their feet. Playwright Andrés Pérez turned this period into *La Huida,* produced in Santiago several years ago.

Santiago has an active gay scene centered around Barrio Bellavista, and there are enclaves elsewhere, most notably in Viña del Mar.

Health and Safety

As a mostly midlatitude country, Chile presents relatively few health problems—even in the north, which lies within tropical latitudes, the arid climate precludes malaria and most tropical diseases.

A good general source is Dr. Richard Dawood's *Travelers' Health* (New York: Random House, 1994), a small encyclopedia on the topic. Dr. Stuart R. Rose's regularly updated *International Travel Health Guide* (Northampton, MA: Travel Medicine Inc., 2001) is regionally focused. Try also the fifth edition of Dirk G. Schroeder's *Staying Healthy in Asia, Africa, and Latin America* (Emeryville, CA: Avalon Travel Publishing, 2000).

For up-to-date information on health issues throughout the Southern Cone, see the U.S. Centers for Disease Control (CDC) Temperate South America regional page (www.cdc.gov/travel/temsam.htm). Another good source is the United Kingdom's Department of Health (www.dh.gov.uk), which provides a chart of recommended prophylaxis by country.

BEFORE YOU GO

Theoretically, Chile has no vaccination requirements, but if you are coming from a tropical country where yellow fever is endemic, authorities could ask for a certificate.

Traveling without adequate medical insurance is risky. Before leaving your home country, obtain insurance that includes evacuation in case of serious emergency. Foreign health insurance may not be accepted, so you may be required to pay out of your own pocket for later reimbursement. Often, however, private medical providers accept international credit cards in return for services.

Numerous carriers provide medical and evacuation coverage; an extensive list, including Internet links, is available at the U.S. State Department's website (www.travel.state.gov/travel/tips/health/health_1185.html).

© WAYNE BERNHARDSON

At Puerto Natales, regional authorities post warnings about solar radiation due to the thinning ozone layer.

GENERAL HEALTH MAINTENANCE

Common-sense precautions can reduce the possibility of illness. Washing hands frequently with soap and water, and drinking only bottled, boiled, or carbonated water help diminish the likelihood of contagion for short-term visitors—though Chilean tap water is potable almost everywhere.

Where purified water is unobtainable, pass drinking water through a one-micron filter and then purify it with iodine drops or tablets (but avoid prolonged consumption of iodine-purified water). Nonpasteurized dairy products, such as goat cheese, can be problematic.

FOOD- OR WATER-BORNE DISEASES

Relatively few visitors run into problems of this sort, but contaminated food and drink are not unheard of. In many cases, it's simply exposure to different bugs to which your body becomes accustomed, but if symptoms persist the problem may be more serious.

Traveler's Diarrhea

Often colloquially known as *turista,* the classic traveler's diarrhea (TD) rarely lasts longer than a week. Besides "the runs," symptoms include nausea, vomiting, bloating, and general weakness. The usual cause is the *Escherichia coli* bacterium from food or water; *E. coli* infections can be fatal.

Fluids, including juices, plus small amounts of bland foods such as cooked rice or soda crackers, may help relieve symptoms and restore strength. Dehydration is a serious problem, especially for children, who may need an oral rehydration solution (ORS) of carbohydrates and salt.

Over-the-counter remedies such as Pepto-Bismol, Lomotil, and Immodium may relieve symptoms but can also cause problems. Prescription drugs such as doxycyline and trimethoprim/sulfamethoxazole can also shorten the cycle. These may not be suitable for children, and it's better for everyone to avoid them if possible.

Continuing and worsening symptoms, such as bloody stools, may mean dysentery, which requires a physician's attention.

Dysentery

Bacterial dysentery, resembling a more intense form of TD, responds to antibiotics, but amoebic dysentery is more serious, sometimes leading to intestinal perforation, peritonitis, and liver abscesses. Like diarrhea, its symptoms include soft and bloody stools, but some people may be asymptomatic even as they pass on *Entamoeba hystolica* through unsanitary toilet and food preparation practices. Metronidazole, known by the brand names Flagyl or Protostat, is effective treatment, but a physician's diagnosis is advisable.

Cholera

Resulting from poor hygiene, inadequate sewage disposal, and contaminated food, contemporary cholera is less devastating than its historic antecedents, which produced rapid dehydration, watery diarrhea, and imminent death (without rapid rehydration). While today's cholera strains are infectious, most carriers do not even come down with symptoms. Existing vaccinations are ineffective, so health authorities now recommend against them.

Treatment can only relieve symptoms. On average, about 5 percent of victims die, but those who recover are immune. It's not common in Chile, but it's not unheard of either.

Hepatitis A

Usually passed by fecal–oral contact under conditions of poor hygiene and overcrowding, hepatitis A is a virus. The traditional gamma globulin prophylaxis has limited efficacy and soon wears off. New hepatitis A vaccines, however, are more effective and last longer.

Typhoid

Typhoid is a serious disease common under unsanitary conditions, but the recommended vaccination is an effective prophylaxis.

INSECT-BORNE DISEASES

Chile is malaria-free, but a few other insect-borne diseases are present if not prevalent.

Chagas' Disease

Also known as South American trypanosomiasis, Chagas' disease is most common in Brazil but affects about 18 million people between Mexico and Argentina; 21,000 people die from it every year. Not a tropical disease per se, it has a discontinuous distribution—Panama and Costa Rica, for instance, are Chagas-free.

Since it is spread by the bite of the *vinchuca* (conenose or assassin bug), which lives in adobe structures and feeds at night, avoid such structures; if it's impossible to do so, sleep away from the walls. DEET-based inspect repellents offer some protection. Chickens, dogs, and opossums may help spread the disease, but the insect vector may be near eradication in Chile.

Chagas' initial form is a swollen bite that may be accompanied by fever, which soon subsides. In the long run, though, it may cause heart damage leading to sudden death, intestinal constipation, and difficulty in swallowing; there is no cure. Charles Darwin may have been a chronic Chagas sufferer.

Dengue

Like malaria, mosquito-borne dengue is a disease of the lowland tropics, but it's less common and only rarely fatal. Debilitating in the short term, its symptoms include fever, headache, joint pain, and skin rashes, but most people recover quickly although there is no treatment. Uncommon but often fatal, the more severe dengue hemorrhagic fever sometimes occurs in children, particularly those infected previously.

Mainland Chile has not recorded any dengue, but the arrival of the white-spotted mosquito vector *Aëdes aegypti* on Easter Island (Rapa Nui)—an apparent arrival from tropical French Polynesia—caused an outbreak there. This mosquito bites during the daytime, making the usual malarial recommendation for long sleeves and long trousers harder to live up to—if you must wear shorts and short sleeves, make sure you're covered with insect repellent.

HANTAVIRUS

Since 2001, according to Chile's health ministry, there have been nearly 600 cases of hantavirus, an uncommon but very deadly disease contracted by breathing, touching, or ingesting feces or urine of the long-tailed rat; more than 200 victims have died. Primarily a rural phenomenon and most prevalent in the south, the virus thrives in enclosed areas; when exposed to sunlight or fresh air, it normally loses potency. Avoid places frequented by rodents, particularly abandoned buildings, but note that there have been cases in which hikers and farm workers have contracted the disease in open spaces.

RABIES

Rabies, a virus transmitted through bites or scratches by domestic animals (such as dogs and cats) and wild mammals (such as bats), is a concern; many domestic animals go unvaccinated. Human prophylactic vaccination is possible but may be incompatible with malaria medication.

Untreated rabies is painful and usually fatal. In case of an animal bite or scratch, immediately clean the affected area with soap and running water, and then with antiseptics such as iodine or 40 percent–plus alcohol. If possible, try to capture the animal for diagnosis, but not at the risk of further bites; in areas where rabies is endemic, painful post-exposure vaccination may be unavoidable.

SNAKEBITE

Herpetophobes can breathe easy. Chile has no poisonous snakes—except perhaps in zoos—and only a few nonpoisonous ones. Neighboring Argentina does have poisonous snakes, but not in areas covered in this book.

ALTITUDE SICKNESS

Above about 3,000 meters, *apunamiento* or *soroche* can be an annoyance and even a danger, especially to older people with respiratory problems. Even among young, robust individuals, a quick rise from sea level to the altiplano can cause intense headaches, vertigo, either drowsiness or insomnia, shortness of breath, and other symptoms. Combined with hypothermia, it can be life-threatening.

For most people, rest and relaxation help relieve symptoms as the body adapts to the reduced oxygen at higher altitudes; aspirin or a comparable painkiller will combat headache. If symptoms persist or worsen, moving to a lower elevation should have the desired effect. Some individuals have died at elevations above 4,000 meters; it is better to stay at an intermediate altitude than to climb directly from sea level to such high elevations. Do not overeat, avoid or limit alcohol consumption, and drink extra fluids.

Stephen Bezruchka's *Altitude Illness, Prevention & Treatment* (Seattle: The Mountaineers, 1994) deals with the topic in detail; the fifth edition of James A. Wilkerson's edited collection *Medicine for Mountaineering & Other Wilderness Activities* (Seattle: The Mountaineers, 2001) discusses other potential problems.

HYPOTHERMIA

Hypothermia is a dangerously quick loss of body heat, most common in cold and damp weather at high altitudes or high latitudes—areas with major temperature variations between day and night, or between sun and shade. Symptoms include shivering, disorientation, loss of motor functions, skin numbness, and exhaustion. The best remedy is warmth, shelter, and food; unlike cottons, woolen clothing retains warmth even when wet. Avoid falling asleep; in truly hazardous conditions, you may not regain consciousness. Carry high-energy snacks and drinking water.

SUNBURN

Sunburn is potentially serious. In the northernmost tropical and subtropical deserts, nearly vertical solar rays are intense; in the oxygen-poor altiplano, sunburn can combine with altitude sickness to be life-threatening. Wearing a baseball cap or similar head covering is advisable; at lower altitudes, long-sleeved cotton shirts and long trousers help protect your skin. If you dress for the beach, use a heavy sunblock.

In southernmost Chile, where aerosols have damaged the ozone layer, ultraviolet radiation has caused skin problems for people and even for livestock such as cattle and sheep. Again, wear head coverings and a heavy sunblock.

SEXUALLY TRANSMITTED DISEASES

AIDS is the deadliest of sexually transmitted diseases (STDs), but other STDs are more prevalent and also serious if untreated. All are spread by unprotected sexual contact; use of latex condoms can reduce the possibility of infection but not eliminate it.

Most STDs, including gonorrhea, chlamydia, and syphilis, are treatable with antibiotics, but some strains have developed immunity to penicillin and alternative treatments. If taking antibiotics, complete the prescribed course—an interrupted treatment may not kill the infection and could even help it develop immunity.

Herpes, a virus that causes small but irritating ulcers in the genital area, has no effective treatment. It is likely to recur, easily spread when active, and can contribute to cervical cancer. **Hepatitis B,** though not exclusively an STD, can spread through the mixing of bodily fluids such as saliva, semen, and menstrual and vaginal secretions. It can also spread through unsanitary medical procedures, inadequately sterilized or shared syringes, during body piercing, and similar circumstances. Like hepatitis A, it can cause liver damage but is more serious; vaccination is expensive but advisable for high-risk individuals.

HIV/AIDS

According to Chile's Health Ministry, in early 2008 the country reported about 6,400 full-blown AIDS cases, more than 30,000 HIV-infected individuals, plus others who are likely unaware they are infected. About 1,000 Chileans died of AIDS in 2007.

HIV/AIDS is not just an STD (intravenous drug users can get it by sharing needles), but unprotected sexual activity is a common means of transmission; latex condoms can reduce the possibility of infection. While many consider it a disease prevalent among homosexual men, females—particularly prostitutes—may also be infected.

Despite the problem and the Concertación government's open-mindedness, many would still prefer to turn a blind eye. Several years ago, for instance, protests from Valparaíso Bishop Gonzalo Duarte de Cortázar forced health workers to stop handing out free condoms at

Viña del Mar on the grounds that it gave the impression that Viña was a "city of promiscuous people."

Vivo Positivo (San Isidro 367, Santiago, tel. 02/6353591, www.vivopositivo.cl) is an advocacy organization for AIDS/HIV sufferers. The Health Ministry has a toll-free AIDS hotline, Fonosida (tel. 800/202120).

SMOKING

Tobacco use is more prevalent in Chile than in the United States, but less so than in Europe. It is prohibited on public transportation, including airplanes, long-distance buses, the subway, and city buses (though in some neighborhoods the odd smoker may light up in the back). A new but confusing tobacco control law is almost toothless, as it does not even require restaurants and bars to set aside smoke-free areas, unless they serve individuals under age 18. Some restaurants have nonsmoking areas, and Chileans are generally considerate and observant of these.

LOCAL DOCTORS

Top-quality medical services are available in Santiago and other cities, though simple clinics make do in the smallest settlements. Foreign embassies sometimes maintain lists of English-speaking doctors, who may have overseas training.

Public emergency facilities, such as Santiago's Posta Central, are often understaffed and underfunded; it's better to patronize private clinics rather than demand services that, in any event, are geared toward poorer people with no alternatives. That said, public staff do their best in an emergency.

PHARMACIES

Pharmacies play an important role in public health, but they also carry risks. Pharmacists may provide drugs on the basis of symptoms that they may not completely comprehend, especially through a language barrier; while the cumulative societal impact may be positive, individual recommendations may be erroneous.

Many medications available only by prescription in North America or Europe are available over the counter here. Travelers should be cautious about self-medication even when drugs are available; check expiration dates, as many expired drugs are never cleared off the shelf.

In large cities and some smaller towns, pharmacies remain open all night for emergencies on a rotating basis. The *farmacia de turno* and its address will usually be posted in other pharmacies' windows, or advertised in the newspaper.

CRIME

Many Chileans believe assaults, rapes, homicide, and crimes against property are increasing, but Chile is a safe country by most standards. According to one United Nations study, Chile has one of the world's lowest robbery rates, only slightly higher than Jordan (Bahamas has the highest).

Most crimes are crimes of opportunity. Never leave luggage unattended, be sure to store valuables in the hotel safe, keep watch on your belongings at sidewalk cafés, and carry a photocopy of your passport with the date of entry into the country. Do not carry large amounts of cash (money belts or leg pouches are good alternatives for hiding cash), leave jewelry at home, and keep conspicuous items such as photo and video cameras out of sight as much as possible. Do not presume that any area is totally secure.

If you should be accosted by anyone with a firearm or other potentially lethal weapon, do not resist. While guns are uncommon—knives are the weapon of choice—and truly violent crime is unusual, the consequences of a misjudgment can be fatal.

Information and Services

MONEY

Travelers checks are the safest way to carry money, since they're refundable in case of loss or theft, but banks keep limited hours and in some remote areas they're simply nonexistent. Because ATMs are open 24 hours, many visitors prefer this alternative, but the same problem holds for remote destinations.

International credit cards are widely accepted except again in remote areas, so it makes sense to carry Chilean cash and an emergency cash reserve in U.S. dollars, preferably hidden in an inconspicuous leg pouch or money belt (not the bulky kind that fits around the waist, which thieves or robbers easily recognize, but a zippered leather belt that looks like any other).

Currency

Chile's currency is the peso (Ch$). Coins with denominations of Ch$5, Ch$10, and Ch$50 all display profiles of liberator Bernardo O'Higgins. Ch$100 coins issued by the former dictatorship, with the inscription "Libertad" (Freedom) breaking chains and the coup date of September 11, 1973, are still in circulation, but newer coins are gradually replacing them. The most recent contains an image of a Mapuche woman. The Ch$500 coin honors the late Cardinal Raúl Henríquez Silva, one of the country's most beloved religious figures.

Banknotes come in values of Ch$1,000 (with a portrait of Ignacio Carrera Pinto), Ch$2,000 (Manuel Rodríguez), Ch$5,000 (Gabriela Mistral), Ch$10,000 (Arturo Prat), and Ch$20,000 (Andrés Bello).

Exchange Rates

In February 2009, rates for the U.S. dollar, the benchmark foreign currency, were around Ch$620. Rates tend to be higher in Santiago and lower in the regions, but this is less meaningful than it once was because of ATM access. There is no black market.

For the most up-to-date exchange rates,

consult the business section of your daily newspaper or an online currency converter such as www.oanda.com; in Chile, the best source on exchange rate trends is the financial daily *Estrategia*.

Changing Money

Money can be changed at banks and *casas de cambio* (exchange houses), though not every bank cashes travelers checks. ATMs, universal except in a few remote areas, match the best bank rates and are accessible 24/7.

Before heading into the countryside, where many smaller villages do not even have banks, change enough money to get you to the next major town. At the same time, carry plenty of smaller bills—for a small shopkeeper with limited resources, changing a Ch$5,000 note may be impossible.

Travelers Checks and Refunds

Travelers checks may be the safest means of carrying money, but changing them at banks can be exasperating. Banks and *cambios* also pay lower rates for travelers checks than for cash.

For assistance in replacing lost or stolen American Express checks, contact its local representative, Travel Security (Av. Apoquindo 3180, Las Condes, Santiago, tel. 02/5843400, www.travelsecurity.cl).

Bank Transfers

It's fairly simple to send money from overseas because many exchange houses are affiliated with Western Union (www.westernunion.com), whose website lists Chilean affiliates.

In an emergency, it's also possible to forward money to U.S. citizens via Santiago's U.S. embassy by establishing a Department of State trust account through its Overseas Citizens Services (Washington, DC 20520, tel. 202/647-5225); there is a US$30 service charge for setting up the account. It is possible

CHILEAN EMBASSIES AND CONSULATES ABROAD

- **Argentina:** San Martín 439, 9th floor, Buenos Aires, tel. 011/4327-2435

- **Australia:** 10 Culgoa Circuit, O'Malley, ACT 2606, tel. 02/6286-2430
  Consulates: 80 Collins St., Level 43, Melbourne, Victoria 3000, tel. 03/9654-4982; 44 Market St., Level 18, Sydney, NSW 2000, tel. 02/9299-2533

- **Bolivia:** Calle 14 No. 8042, Calacoto, La Paz, tel. 2/2797331

- **Brazil:** Praia do Flamengo 344, 7th floor, Flamengo, Rio de Janeiro, tel. 21/2552-5349; Avenida Paulista 1009, 10th floor, São Paulo, tel. 11/3284-2148

- **Canada:** 50 O'Connor St., Suite 1413, Ottawa, Ontario K1P 6L2, tel. 613/235-4402
  Consulates: 2 Bloor St. West, Suite 1801, Toronto, Ontario M4W 3E2, tel. 416/924-0106; 1010 Sherbrooke St. West, Suite 710, Montréal, Québec H3A 2R7, tel. 514/499-0405; 1250-1185 West Georgia St., Vancouver, British Columbia V6E 4E6, tel. 604/681-9162

- **France:** 64 Blvd. de la Tour Maubourg, Paris, tel. 4705-4661

- **Germany:** Mohrenstrasse 42, Berlin, tel. 30/726-203-901
  Consulate: Humboldtstrasse 94, Frankfurt-am-Main, tel. 69/550194

- **Mexico:** Ejército Nacional 423, 3rd floor, Colonia Granada, Mexico City, tel. 55/5545-1043

- **Netherlands:** Stadhouderskade 2, 5th floor, 1054 Es, Amsterdam, tel. 20/612-0086

- **New Zealand:** 7th floor, Willis Corroon House, 1-3 Welleston St., Wellington, tel. 4/471-6270

- **Peru:** Javier Prado Oeste 790, San Isidro, Lima, tel. 1/611-2200

- **Switzerland:** Eigerplatz 5, 12th floor, Bern, tel. 31/370-0058

- **United Kingdom:** 12 Devonshire St., London W1N 2DS, tel. 20/7580-1023

- **United States of America:** 1736 Massachusetts Ave. NW, Washington, DC 20036, tel. 202/785-3159
  Consulates: 6100 Wilshire Blvd., Suite 2140, Los Angeles, CA 90048, tel. 323/933-3697; 870 Market St., Suite 1062, San Francisco, CA 94105, tel. 415/982-7662; 800 Brickell Ave., Suite 1230, Miami, FL 33131, tel. 305/373-8623; 875 N. Michigan Ave., Suite 3352, Chicago, IL 60611, tel. 312/654-8780; 79 Milk St., Suite 600, Boston, MA 02109, tel. 617/426-1678; 866 United Nations Plaza, Suite 601, New York, NY 10017, tel. 212/355-0612; Public Ledger Building, Suite 1030, 6th St. & Chestnut St., Philadelphia, PA 19142, tel. 215/829-9520; Edificio American Airlines, Suite 800, 1509 López Landrón, Santurce, San Juan, PR 00911, tel. 809/725-6365; 1360 Post Oak Blvd., Suite 2330, Houston, TX 77056, tel. 713/621-5853

- **Uruguay:** Andes 1365, 1st floor, Montevideo, tel. 2/902-6316

to arrange this as a wire or overnight mail transfer through Western Union (tel. 800/325-6000); for details see the Department of State's website (www.travel.state.gov).

Credit and Debit Cards

Credit cards are widely accepted in the capital and major tourist centers but less so in the remote countryside. The mostly reliably used are Visa and MasterCard, though American Express is possibly accepted in some areas. Many banks provide cash advances on either Visa or MasterCard.

Services such as hotels, restaurants, and car

rental agencies rarely, but occasionally, impose a *recargo* (surcharge) on credit card purchases; ask before paying.

For lost or stolen credit cards there are local contacts for Visa and MasterCard (tel. 02/6317003); Diner's Club (tel. 02/2320000); and American Express (tel. 800/201022 toll-free).

Costs

By global standards, Chilean travel is moderately priced, but much depends on the traveler's expectations and where in the country he or she goes. There are suitable services for everyone, from bare-bones budget backpackers to pampered international business travelers.

The countryside is cheaper than the cities, and truly disciplined travelers in rural areas might get away with as little as US$25 or less per day by staying in the cheapest basic accommodations, buying groceries and cooking for themselves, or eating market food. Public transportation is moderately priced, especially given the long distances on some routes, but the fact that Chile imports nearly all its oil makes the sector vulnerable to fluctuations.

In the capital, the cities, and main tourist areas, however, costs are higher. Budget travelers will find beds or bunks under US$12 per person scarce, though there are some excellent values for just a little more money. Hotels and resorts of international stature, such as the Hyatt and Sheraton chains, charge corresponding prices. Likewise, meals are a few dollars or even less at the simplest *comedores,* but restaurants with sophisticated international cuisine can charge a lot more; even the latter, however, often serve moderately priced lunchtime specials.

Taxes

Chile imposes a 19 percent *impuesto de valor agregado* (IVA, value added tax or VAT) on goods and services, though this is normally included in the advertised price; if in doubt, ask for clarification *(¿Incluye los impuestos?).* Most

midrange to upscale hotels can legally discount IVA for foreign visitors who receive a *factura de exportación* (export receipt) along with their hotel bill.

Tipping

In restaurants with table service, a 10 percent gratuity is customary, but in family-run *comedores* the practice is rare. Taxi drivers are customarily not tipped, but rounding off the fare to the next highest convenient number is appropriate. Where there is no meter, this is not an issue.

Bargaining

Bargaining is not the way of life that it is in some other countries, but in crafts markets the vendor may start at a higher price than he or she expects to receive—avoid insultingly low offers, or such a high offer that the vendor will think you a fool. Depending on your language and bargaining skills, you should achieve a compromise that satisfies everybody. It's best to keep this practice at the market or the roadside stand; in shopping malls, souvenir shops, restaurants, and similar establishments, bargaining is considered inappropriate.

Student and Senior Discounts

Student discounts are few, and prices are so low for most services that it's rarely worth arguing the point. In the case of foreign travel, though, students may be eligible for discount airfares. Senior discounts may be available for those over 60 years of age, but some providers grant these only to Chilean nationals and residents.

COMMUNICATIONS
Postal Services

Since the privatization of Correos de Chile, postal service is more reliable. Domestic mail is generally cheap, international post more expensive. Major international couriers, such as DHL, provide fast, reliable services at premium prices.

General delivery at Chilean post offices is

lista de correos, quite literally a list arranged in alphabetical order. Because Chileans use both paternal and maternal surnames, postal employees may confuse foreign middle names with paternal surnames—a letter to Michelle Bachelet Jeria would be found under "B," while one to "Barack Hussein Obama" might be found under "H" rather than "O."

In Spanish-language street addresses, the number follows rather than precedes the name; instead of "1343 Washington Avenue," for example, a comparable Chilean address would read "Avenida Bilbao 272." Spanish speakers normally omit the word *calle* (street) from addresses; where an English speaker might write "499 Jones Street," a Chilean would simply use, say, "Carrera 272." It's not unusual for street addresses to lack a number, as indicated by *s/n* (*sin número,* without a number).

Telephone and Fax

Chile's country code is 56; there are area codes for individual cities and, in some cases, entire regions. All telephone numbers in the Región Metropolitana have seven digits, while those in the other regions generally have six, but in some rural areas they have seven digits beginning with 1. When dialing a local number (i.e. within the same area code), dial only the number. Beyond the local area code and with cell phones, you must dial a zero before the area code. From outside Chile, it's necessary to dial the country code (56) and the local area code (without a zero), and the number.

Cellular phones all have eight digits, prefixed by 09; however, calls between cell phones do not require the prefix. Certain toll-free and other specialty numbers have six digits with a three-digit prefix.

Public telephones are abundant; some operate with coins only, but most also accept rechargeable account cards. The basic pay phone rate is Ch$100 (about US$0.15) for five minutes or so; domestic long-distance rates are not much more expensive.

For long-distance and overseas calls, and fax services, it's simplest to use *centros de llamados* (call centers), which are ubiquitous. Prices are cheaper than placing *cobro revertido* (collect) or *tarjeta de crédito* (credit card) calls to the United States or any other country.

Internet Access

In the last few years, public Internet access has become both abundant and cheap—rarely does it cost more than about US$2 per hour, and it's often cheaper. Many *centros de llamados* offer access, but there are also numerous Internet cafés with *banda ancha* (broadband) and wireless Internet. Laptop hookups are routine but not universal.

Media

Chile may have emerged from dictatorship, but freedom of expression still has its limits. A study by the Universidad de Chile has criticized the concentration of print media, in particular, in the hands of large consortia such as Agustín Edwards' El Mercurio group, which owns its influential namesake daily *El Mercurio* along with the daily tabloids *La Segunda* and *Las Ultimas Noticias,* and the Consorcio Periodistico de Chile (Copesa), which owns the tabloids *La Tercera, La Hora,* and the particularly sensationalist *La Cuarta.*

The study noted not just the business aspects of the oligopoly—the El Mercurio group earns about 70 percent of all advertising revenue for print media—but also the "ideological monopoly" of the country's most conservative elements. The Copesa group, in particular, consists of a daily newspaper and three magazines controlled by former officials of the Pinochet regime. Ironically enough, Pinochet's political departure in 1990 made times harder for critical journalists, who lost their easiest editorial target.

Pinochet's arrest and subsequent legal troubles, however, opened up a whole new space for irreverently satirical papers such as *The Clinic* (the paper named itself for the London clinic where the former dictator was detained). Another constraint on freedom of expression disappeared when, in early 2001, Congress repealed a clause of the Pinochet-era National Security Law that permitted imprisonment for anyone who would "defame, injure, or slander members of the high courts."

For an English-language summary of the Chilean daily press, plus occasional original reporting, look at the Internet-only *Santiago Times* (www.chip.cl).

MAPS AND TOURIST INFORMATION

Chile has good sources for maps and tourist information, but others are available overseas.

Maps

International Travel Maps and Books (ITMB, 530 W. Broadway, Vancouver BC, V5Z 1E9, tel. 604/879-3621, fax 604/879-4521, www.itmb.com) publishes a series of maps that cover all or parts of Chile at a variety of scales.

Recently taken over by the Copec oil retailer, the former *Turistel* guidebook series (Spanish only) contains the most current road maps at the back of its *Norte* (North), *Centro* (Center), and *Sur* volumes, along with numerous useful city maps, which, unfortunately, lack scales.

JLM Cartografía (General del Canto 105, Oficina 1506, tel./fax 02/2364808, Providencia, Santiago, jmatassi@interactiva.cl) publishes regional and local maps at varying scale (even within the same map), in both Spanish and imperfect but generally serviceable English. Some cover parts of neighboring countries.

Chile's official **Instituto Geográfico Militar** (IGM, Dieciocho 369, Santiago Centro, tel. 02/4606800, fax 02/4608924, www.igm.cl) publishes detailed topographic maps covering the entire country at a scale of 1:50,000; some of these, however, are "proprietary" as they adjoin what the military consider to be sensitive border areas. They are also expensive at about US$15 and up. The Instituto also sells city maps, road atlases, and books that are useful to the everyday visitor, and the staff is professional and efficient.

In addition to being a reliable adventure tour operator, Talca-based **Trekking Chile** (www.trekkingchile.com) produces a series of magnificent hiking maps for their own signature "Condor Circuit" in the nearby Andes, as well as for San Pedro de Atacama, Termas de Chillán, or other localities.

Tourist Offices

Sernatur (www.sernatur.cl), the national tourism service, maintains public information offices in Santiago and all regional capitals, and also in Chillán, Valdivia, Futaleufú, and Puerto Natales. Most are normally open weekdays only, but in summer and in some localities they open on weekends.

In addition to Sernatur's offices, some municipalities have their own offices, especially in southern lake-district resorts such as Villarrica, Pucón, and Puerto Varas, which keep long summer hours but are limited the rest of the year. Many smaller towns have summer-only (January–February) offices.

FILM AND PHOTOGRAPHY

For those who haven't switched to digital, print film is widely available, slide film somewhat less so. Price differences are less than they used to be, but if buying film here, check the expiration date to make sure it's current—especially in out-of-the-way places. In the capital and larger tourist centers, competent print film processing is readily available and moderately priced, but take slide film to specialists or store under cool, dark, and dry conditions until your return to your home country.

WEIGHTS AND MEASURES
Time

Chile is four hours behind GMT most of the year, but it does observe daylight saving time (summer time), though dates for the changeover vary from year to year. When the U.S. Eastern Standard Time zone is on daylight saving time, during the Northern Hemisphere summer, and Chile is on standard time, the hour is identical in New York and Santiago.

All of continental Chile goes on daylight saving time despite latitudes that range from about 18° to 56° S, and this causes some anomalies. In summer, northern cities such as Arica, where the length of day is relatively equal throughout the year, do not see daylight until almost 8 A.M.; at this time of the year, they are two hours ahead of nearby Peru. In the far south, by contrast, midsummer daylight can last until nearly 11 P.M. or later. Because most of Argentina (except Buenos Aires and a few other provinces) does not observe daylight saving time, there is no summer time difference between the two countries.

Easter Island (Rapa Nui) is two hours behind the continent.

Electricity

Throughout the country, nearly all outlets are 220 volts, 50 cycles, but many North American electronics, such as computers and electric razors, are now dual voltage appliances. Plugs are two rounded prongs. Electrical supply stores on Santiago's Calle San Pablo, north of the Plaza de Armas, sell plug adapters and adequately powered converters if necessary, but it's harder to find these outside the capital.

Measurements

The metric system is official, but this doesn't completely eliminate vernacular measures. In rural areas, people often use the *legua* (league) of about five kilometers as a measure of distance, and the *quintal* of 46 kilos is also widely used, especially in wholesale markets and statistics.

At airports, the Chilean military measures altitude in feet above sea level. Tire pressure is often measured in pounds per square inch.

RESOURCES

Glossary

albergue juvenil youth hostel

altiplano high Andean steppe of the Norte Grande

anexo telephone extension

apunamiento altitude sickness

ascensor literally an "elevator," but a term often applied to the funiculars of the city of Valparaíso

avenida avenue

ayllu an Andean moiety or kinship unit, also a geographical entity

bahía bay

bajativo after-dinner drink

balneario bathing or beach resort

baño compartido shared bath (in a hotel or other accommodations)

baño general shared or general bath (in a hotel or other accommodations)

baño privado private bath

barrio neighborhood

bencina gasoline

bodega winery storage cellar

bofedal marshy pasture of the altiplano, used primarily to graze alpacas; also known as *ciénaga*

boldo the leaf, used as herbal tea, of its namesake tree

boleadoras round stone weights, linked by a leather strap, used for hunting by Patagonian Indians. When thrown, they would tie themselves around the legs of, say, a guanaco or rhea, immobilizing the animal; later, they would be used to capture wild cattle.

botellín individually sized bottle of wine, usually mediocre in quality

butaca reclining seat

cajero automático automatic teller machine (ATM)

calafate a Patagonian shrub with dark blue berries with large seeds

calefón hot-water heater

caliche hardpan clay from which mineral nitrates were extracted in the Norte Grande

callampas "mushrooms," spontaneous squatter settlements on the periphery of large cities

calle street

camanchaca dense convective fog that forms on the Chilean coastline, especially in the northern desert

camioneta pickup truck

campo minado minefield

carretera highway

casa de cambio money exchange facility, often just *"cambio"*

casa de huéspedes guesthouse, usually a modest family-run place

casilla post office box

cerro hill

chifa Chinese restaurant, a term used mostly in the Atacama Desert and in Peru

Chilote in the strictest sense, a native of the Chiloé archipelago; in a discourteous sense, a "bumpkin"

chopp draft beer

cobro revertido collect telephone call

cocinería simple eatery, often in a market

colación lunch, especially during the work day

colectivo in Chile, a shared-route taxi; in Argentina, a city bus

comedor simple family-style restaurant

comuna borough, a unit of municipal government; in Chile, some of these are totally urban, while others take in huge rural areas

confitería in Argentina, a restaurant/café with a menu of *minutas* (short orders)

congregación Spanish colonial policy of concentrating indigenous peoples in nucleated settlements for purposes of taxation and tribute

costanera any road along a seashore, lakeshore, or riverside

criollo in colonial times, a Chilean-born Spaniard; today, normally a descriptive term meaning "traditionally" Chilean

cueca traditional Chilean folk dance

curanto seafood stew of Chiloé and Patagonia

desierto florido "flowering desert" of the Norte Chico, an ephemeral explosion of wildflowers after substantial rains

doble tracción four-wheel drive (4WD), also known as *cuatro por cuatro* (the latter written as "4X4")

edificio building

encomienda in colonial times, a grant of Indian labor and tribute within a given geographical area. The *encomendero* (holder of the *encomienda*) incurred the reciprocal obligation to provide instruction in the Spanish language and Christian religion, though such obligations were rarely honored

estancia cattle or sheep ranch controlling large extents of land, most often in Patagonia, often with an absentee owner, dominant manager, and resident employees

estero estuary

ex-voto a gift to a saint in exchange for a favor or miracle

feria artisans' market

farmacia de turno pharmacy open all night for emergencies

ficha token that circulated instead of cash in nitrate *oficinas*

fundo large rural estate, nearly synonymous with hacienda

garúa coastal fog; see also *camanchaca*

garzón waiter

golfo gulf

golpe de estado coup d'etat

hacienda large rural estate, usually assembled by Spaniards in areas where indigenous populations disappeared because of introduced diseases

hipódromo horserace track

hospedaje inexpensive accommodation, usually family-run

huaso Chilean counterpart to Argentine gaucho

icchu high Andean bunch grasses

indigenismo exaggerated romantic appreciation of indigenous history and heritage, common in art, literature, and rhetoric

infracción traffic violation

invierno altiplánico "altiplano winter," the summer rainy season at high altitudes in the Norte Grande; also known as *invierno boliviano* (Bolivian winter) for the direction from which rains come

isla island

islote islet

istmo isthmus

IVA *impuesto de valor agregado,* value-added tax (VAT)

lago lake

laguna lagoon

latifundio large landholding, either a *fundo* or a hacienda

liebre small city bus, literally "hare"

local numbered office or locale, at a given street address

lonko traditional Mapuche leader

machi Mapuche seer/healer

machista male chauvinist

marisquería fish and seafood restaurant, often on the beach or in a market

media pensión half board, at a hotel or guesthouse

menú menu; also, a fixed-price meal

mesero waiter

mestizo individual of mixed indigenous and Spanish ancestry

micro city bus or small backroads bus

minifundio peasant landholding

minuta in Argentina, a short-order meal such as pasta

mirador overlook or viewpoint

monumento nacional national monument, usually an archaeological site or historical building

monumento natural a category of state-protected land

municipalidad city hall; by extension, city government

museo museum

nevado snow peak

oficina nitrate mining company town in the Norte Grande

onces afternoon tea ("elevenses")

paco "cop," a term to be used circumspectly when discussing Carabineros, the Chilean national police force, and never to be used to their faces

pajarete Norte Chico dessert wine

palafito fisherman's house on stilts or pilings, once common in Chiloé

pampa broad, flat desert expanse in the Norte Grande

pan amasado kneaded bread

parada bus stop

parque nacional national park

pasarela hanging bridge or walkway

paseo pedestrian mall

peaje toll booth

penquista native or inhabitant of Concepción

pensión inexpensive family-style accommodations

pensión completa full board, at a hotel or guesthouse

peña traditional folk-music venue

picada informal, usually family-run restaurant that often begins as a neighborhood hangout and becomes more elaborate

pingüinera penguin colony

pisco potent grape brandy

playa beach

plazuela small plaza

porteño native or resident of Valparaíso (in Argentina, a native or resident of Buenos Aires)

posta clinic, usually but not always in a small town that lacks a full-service hospital

precordillera foothills of the Andes

propina tip, as at a restaurant

puente bridge

puerto port

puesto "outside house" on a sheep or cattle *estancia;* also, a market food stall

pukará pre-Columbian, often Inka, fortress

Pullman first-class bus, with reclining seats

and luggage storage underneath

puna synonym for altiplano

quebrada ravine or canyon

recargo surcharge on credit card purchases

reducción synonym for *congregación*

refugio rustic or occasionally more formal shelter, usually in wild country such as a national park

remise meterless taxi

repartimiento Spanish forced-labor system

requerimiento formal Spanish obligation to offer peace to indigenous armies on condition that they accept crown and papal authority

reserva nacional national reserve, a category of state-protected land

río river

rodeo annual cattle roundup on an *estancia;* also a festival of horsemanship

ruca thatched Mapuche house

ruta route or highway

salar high-altitude salt lake

salón de té European-style café, often with sidewalk seating

sendero trail or footpath

seno sound or fjord

soroche altitude sickness

s/n *sin número,* a street address without a number

tábano aggressive horsefly of the Sur Chico

tajamares colonial dikes built to control floods on Santiago's Río Mapocho

tejuela shingle, common form of siding in archipelagic Chiloé; usually made of *alerce* or other native wood

tenedor libre all-you-can-eat, literally "free fork," restaurant, more common in Argentina than in Chile

termas hot springs

todo terreno mountain bike

toque de queda curfew, under military dictatorship

toqui Mapuche war leader

totora a sort of reed used for weaving mats

ventisquero glacier; also *glaciar*

volcán volcano

zona típica "typical area," a legal designation intended to preserve a neighborhood's historic character

Spanish Phrasebook

Spanish is the official language, but the local variant, which often drops terminal and even internal consonants, can confuse those who have learned Spanish elsewhere. At tourist offices, airlines, travel agencies, and upscale hotels, English is often spoken. But out on the road, it's the exception.

Visitors spending any length of time in Chile, especially students and business people, should look for John Brennan's and Alvaro Taboada's *How to Survive in the Chilean Jungle* (Santiago: Dolmen Ediciones, 1996), which has gone through multiple hilarious editions of explaining everyday Chilean expressions. Usage of these may require *great* caution for those unaware of their every meaning.

PRONUNCIATION GUIDE

Spanish pronunciation is much more regular than that of English, but there are still occasional variations in pronunciation.

Consonants

c as c in "cat," before a, o, or u; like s before e or i

d as d in "dog," except between vowels, then like th in "that"

g before e or i, like the ch in Scottish "loch"; elsewhere like g in "get"

h always silent

j like the English h in "hotel," but stronger

ll like the y in "yellow"

ñ like the ni in "onion"

r always pronounced as strong r

rr trilled r

v similar to the b in "boy" (not as English v)

y similar to English, but with a slight j sound; when standing alone, it's pronounced like the e in "me"

z like s in "same"

b, f, k, l, m, n, p, q, s, t, w, x as in English

Vowels

a as in "father," but shorter

e as in "hen"

i as in "machine"

o as in "phone"

u usually as in "rule"; when it follows a q the u is silent; when it follows an h or g, it's pronounced like w, except when it comes between g and e or i, when it's also silent (unless it has an umlaut, ü, when it again is pronounced as English w)

Stress

Native English speakers frequently make errors of pronunciation by ignoring stress. Any Spanish vowel – a, e, i, o, and u – may carry an accent that determines which syllable gets emphasis. Often, stress seems unnatural to nonnative speakers – the surname Chávez, for instance, is stressed on the first syllable – but failure to observe this rule may make it difficult for native speakers to understand you.

NUMBERS

0 *cero*
1 *uno (masculine)*
1 *una (feminine)*
2 *dos*
3 *tres*
4 *cuatro*
5 *cinco*
6 *seis*
7 *siete*
8 *ocho*
9 *nueve*
10 *diez*
11 *once*
12 *doce*
13 *trece*
14 *catorce*
15 *quince*
16 *diez y seis*
17 *diez y siete*
18 *diez y ocho*
19 *diez y nueve*
20 *veinte*
21 *veinte y uno*
30 *treinta*

40 *cuarenta*
50 *cincuenta*
60 *sesenta*
70 *setenta*
80 *ochenta*
90 *noventa*
100 *cien*
101 *ciento y uno*
200 *doscientos*
1,000 *mil*
10,000 *diez mil*
1,000,000 *un millón*

DAYS OF THE WEEK

Sunday *domingo*
Monday *lunes*
Tuesday *martes*
Wednesday *miércoles*
Thursday *jueves*
Friday *viernes*
Saturday *sábado*

TIME

Chileans mostly use the 12-hour clock, but in some instances, usually associated with plane or bus schedules, they may use the 24-hour military clock. Under the latter, for example, *las nueve de la noche* (9 P.M.) would be *las 21 horas* (2100 hours).

What time is it? *¿Qué hora es?*
It's one o'clock *Es la una.*
It's two o'clock *Son las dos.*
It's ten to three *Son tres menos diez.*
It's ten past three *Son tres y diez.*
It's three fifteen *Son las tres y cuarto.*
It's two forty-five *Son tres menos cuarto.*
It's two-thirty *Son las dos y media.*
It's six A.M. *Son las seis de la mañana.*
It's six P.M. *Son las seis de la tarde.*
It's ten P.M. *Son las diez de la noche.*
Today *hoy*
Tomorrow *mañana*
Morning *la mañana*
Tomorrow morning *mañana por la mañana*
Yesterday *ayer*
Week *la semana*
Month *mes*

Year *año*
Last night *anoche*
The next day *el día siguiente*

USEFUL WORDS AND PHRASES

Spanish speakers consider formalities important. When approaching anyone for information or some other reason, do not forget the appropriate salutation: good morning, good evening, etc. Standing alone, the greeting *hola* (hello) can sound brusque.

Most of the words listed below are fairly standard, common to all Spanish-speaking countries. Many, however, have more idiomatic Chilean equivalents.

Hello. *Hola.*
Good morning. *Buenos días.*
Good afternoon. *Buenas tardes.*
Good evening. *Buenas noches.*
How are you? *¿Cómo está?*
Fine. *Muy bien.*
And you? *¿Y usted?*
So-so. *Más o menos.*
Thank you. *Gracias.*
Thank you very much. *Muchas gracias.*
You're very kind. *Muy amable.*
You're welcome. *De nada.* (literally, "It's nothing.")
Yes *sí*
No *no*
I don't know. *No sé.*
It's fine; okay *Está bien.*
Good; okay *Bueno.*
Please *por favor*
Pleased to meet you. *Mucho gusto.*
Excuse me (physical) *Perdóneme.*
Excuse me (speech) *Discúlpeme.*
I'm sorry. *Lo siento.*
Goodbye *adiós*
See you later *hasta luego* (literally, "until later")
More *más*
Less *menos*
Better *mejor*
Much, a lot *mucho*
A little *un poco*

Large *grande*
Small *pequeño, chico*
Quick, fast *rápido*
Slowly *despacio*
Bad *malo*
Difficult *difícil*
Easy *fácil*
He/She/It is gone; as in "She left," "He's gone" *Ya se fue.*
I don't speak Spanish well. *No hablo bien el español.*
I don't understand. *No entiendo.*
How do you say...in Spanish? *¿Cómo se dice...en español?*
Do you understand English? *¿Entiende el inglés?*
Is English spoken here? (Does anyone here speak English?) *¿Se habla inglés aquí?*

TERMS OF ADDRESS

When in doubt, use the formal *usted* (you) as a form of address. If you wish to dispense with formality and feel that the desire is mutual, you can say *Me puedes tutear* (you can call me "tú").

I *yo*
You (formal) *usted*
you (familiar) *tú*
He/him *él*
She/her *ella*
We/us *nosotros*
You (plural) *ustedes*
They/them (all males or mixed gender) *ellos*
They/them (all females) *ellas*
Mr., sir *señor*
Mrs., madam *señora*
Miss, young lady *señorita*
Wife *esposa*
Husband *marido* or *esposo*
Friend *amigo* (male), *amiga* (female)
Sweetheart *novio* (male), *novia* (female)
Son, daughter *hijo, hija*
Brother, sister *hermano, hermana*
Father, mother *padre, madre*
Grandfather, grandmother *abuelo, abuela*

GETTING AROUND

Where is...? *¿Dónde está...?*
How far is it to...? *¿A cuanto está...?*
from...to . . . *de...a . . .*
Highway *la carretera*
Road *el camino*
Street *la calle*
Block *la cuadra*
Kilometer *kilómetro*
North *norte*
South *sur*
West *oeste; poniente*
East *este; oriente*
Straight ahead *al derecho; adelante*
To the right *a la derecha*
To the left *a la izquierda*

ACCOMMODATIONS

Is there a room? *¿Hay cuarto?*
May I (we) see it? *¿Puedo (podemos) verlo?*
What is the rate? *¿Cuál es el precio?*
Is that your best rate? *¿Es su mejor precio?*
Is there something cheaper? *¿Hay algo más económico?*
Single room *un sencillo*
Double room *un doble*
Room for a couple *matrimonial*
Key *llave*
With private bath *con baño*
With shared bath *con baño general; con baño compartido*
Hot water *agua caliente*
Cold water *agua fría*
Shower *ducha*
Towel *toalla*
Soap *jabón*
Toilet paper *papel higiénico*
Air conditioning *aire acondicionado*
Fan *ventilador*
Blanket *frazada; manta*
Sheets *sábanas*

PUBLIC TRANSPORT

Bus stop *la parada*
Bus terminal *terminal de buses*
Airport *el aeropuerto*
Launch *lancha*

Dock *muelle*
I want a ticket to . . . *Quiero un pasaje a . . .*
I want to get off at . . . *Quiero bajar en . . .*
Here, please. *Aquí, por favor.*
Where is this bus going? *¿Adónde va este autobús?*
Round-trip *ida y vuelta*
What do I owe? *¿Cuánto le debo?*

FOOD

Menu *la carta, el menú*
Glass *taza*
Fork *tenedor*
Knife *cuchillo*
Spoon *cuchara*
Napkin *servilleta*
Soft drink *agua fresca*
Coffee *café*
Cream *crema*
Tea *té*
Sugar *azúcar*
Drinking water *agua pura, agua potable*
Bottled carbonated water *agua mineral con gas*
Bottled uncarbonated water *agua sin gas*
Beer *cerveza*
Wine *vino*
Milk *leche*
Juice *jugo*
Eggs *huevos*
Bread *pan*
Watermelon *sandía*
Banana *banano*
Plantain *plátano*
Apple *manzana*
Orange *naranja*
Meat (without meat) *carne (sin carne)*
Beef *carne de res*
Chicken *pollo; gallina*

Fish *pescado*
Shellfish *mariscos*
Shrimp *camarones*
Fried *frito*
Roasted *asado*
Barbecued *a la parrilla*
Breakfast *desayuno*
Lunch *almuerzo*
Dinner (often eaten in late afternoon) *comida*
Dinner, or a late-night snack *cena*
The check, or bill *la cuenta*

MAKING PURCHASES

I need . . . *Necesito . . .*
I want . . . *Deseo...or Quiero . . .*
I would like...(more polite) *Quisiera . . .*
How much does it cost? *¿Cuánto cuesta?*
What's the exchange rate? *¿Cuál es el tipo de cambio?*
May I see . . .? *¿Puedo ver . . .?*
This one *ésta/ésto*
Expensive *caro*
Cheap *barato*
Cheaper *más barato*
Too much *demasiado*

HEALTH

Help me please. *Ayúdeme por favor.*
I am ill. *Estoy enfermo.*
It hurts. *Me duele.*
Pain *dolor*
Fever *fiebre*
Stomachache *dolor de estómago*
Vomiting *vomitar*
Diarrhea *diarrea*
Drugstore *farmacia*
Medicine *medicina*
Pill, tablet *pastilla*

Suggested Reading

ARCHAEOLOGY, ETHNOGRAPHY, AND ETHNOHISTORY

Dillehay, Tom D. *Monte Verde: A Late Pleistocene Settlement in Chile*, 2 vols. Washington, D.C. and London: Smithsonian Institution Press, 1989–1997. Exhaustive treatment of a crucially important site of early human culture west of Puerto Montt, one of the continent's oldest.

McEwan, Colin, Luis A. Borrero, and Alfredo Prieto, eds. *Patagonia: Natural History, Prehistory and Ethnography at the Uttermost End of the Earth.* Princeton University Press, 1997. First published under the auspices of the British Museum, this is a collection of academic but accessible essays on topics ranging from Patagonia's natural environment to early human occupation, first encounters between Europeans and indigenes, the origins of the Patagonian "giants," and even Patagonian travel literature.

Pringle, Heather. *The Mummy Congress.* New York: Hyperion, 2001. Using a congress of mummy specialists in the city of Arica as its starting point, this is a lively synthesis of cultural traditions of preserving human bodies, the accidental preservation of bodies under specific environmental conditions, and their significance in the contemporary world—including research ethics. While Pringle's research and travels take her around the world, there's a focus on the Atacama and the central Andes.

GUIDEBOOKS AND TRAVELOGUES

Allende, Isabel. *My Invented Country: A Nostalgic Journey through Chile.* New York: HarperCollins, 2003. The best-selling California-based novelist, niece of the late president Salvador Allende, reconnects with her homeland and its customs after more than a decade of exile.

Burford, Tim. *Chile and Argentina: The Bradt Trekking Guide,* 5th ed. Guilford, CT: The Globe Pequot Press, 2001. A greatly improved hiking guide that covers much of both countries with diligence; its maps, though also improved, could still be better and it would benefit from photographs of the spectacular scenery it covers.

Chatwin, Bruce. *In Patagonia.* New York: Summit Books, 1977. One of the continent's classic travelogues, even if—perhaps because—Chatwin blurs the line between experience and fiction.

Chatwin, Bruce. *What Am I Doing Here?* New York: Viking, 1989. This collection of Chatwin miscellanea contains an essay on Chiloé and, specifically, the village of Cucao.

Darwin, Charles. *Voyage of the Beagle* (many editions). Possibly the greatest travel book ever written, Darwin's narrative of his 19th-century journey brims with insights on the people, places, and even politics he saw while collecting the plants and animals that led to his revolutionary theories. His accounts of Tierra del Fuego, Chiloé, Concepción, Cerro La Campana, and Copiapó are so vivid they might have been written yesterday.

Dorfman, Ariel. *Desert Memories: Journeys through the Chilean North.* Washington D.C.: National Geographic, 2004. In his first dedicated venture into the travel genre, Dorfman revisits a region he overlooked in his youth and finds the keys to understanding his country. It includes a poignant visit to Pisagua, where a university friend died at the hands of Pinochet's executioners.

Dorfman, Ariel. *Heading South, Looking North.* New York: Farrar, Strauss and Giroux, 1998. Overlapping the travel literature genre, this is a memoir of reflections on the second half of the 20th century by a bilingual activist and major Chilean literary figure; one critic, though, has termed the author's self-criticism of his role in Unidad Popular as *mea minima culpa.*

Green, Toby. *Saddled with Darwin.* London: Phoenix, 1999. Audacious, if uneven, account by a talented writer of his attempt to retrace the tracks—not the footsteps—of Darwin's travels through Uruguay, Argentina, and Chile. Self-effacing but still serious, the author manages to compare Darwin's experience with his own and stay almost completely off the gringo trail.

Guevara, Ernesto. *The Motorcycle Diaries: A Journey around South America.* New York and London: Verso, 1995. Translated by Ann Wright, this is an account of an Argentine drifter's progress across the Andes and up the Chilean coast by motorcycle and, when it broke down, by any means necessary. The author is better known by his nickname, "Che," a common Argentine interjection.

Muir, John. *John Muir's Last Journey.* Washington, D.C.: Island Press, Shearwater Books, 2001. Edited by Michael P. Branch, this annotated collection of Muir's correspondence and notes on his eight-month odyssey through South America and Africa includes his search for native araucaria forests in the Lake District.

Murphy, Dallas. *Rounding the Horn.* New York: Basic Books, 2004. A hybrid of historical and contemporary navigation in the world's wildest waters, Murphy's travelogue conveys the travails of advancing against the winds of the "Furious Fifties." But it also communicates the mystique of South America's southernmost tip.

Reding, Nick. *The Last Cowboys at the End of the World.* New York: Crown Publishing, 2001. Anthropological in its approach, this account of isolated gauchos in Chilean Patagonia's Upper Río Cisnes rings true for the author's admirable refusal to romanticize people with whom he clearly sympathizes and empathizes.

Roosevelt, Theodore. *A Book Lover's Holiday in the Open.* New York: Scribner's, 1916. After retiring from politics, the still-vigorous U.S. president undertook numerous overseas adventures; this collection includes his crossing of the Andes from Chile into the lake district of northern Argentine Patagonia, and his meeting with legends such as Perito Moreno.

Sagaris, Lake. *Bone and Dream: Into the World's Driest Desert.* Toronto: Alfred A. Knopf Canada, 2000. Written by a Chile-based Canadian journalist, this literary travelogue conflates the legend of an Inka princess in the Norte Grande and the country's post-Pinochet development.

Schubert, Franz, and Malte Siebert. *Adventure Handbook Central Chile.* Santiago: Viachile Editores, 2002. This professionally produced and well-illustrated book covers recreational activities, primarily but not exclusively backcountry hikes, in the area between the Aconcagua and the Biobío rivers. An excellent complement to this Moon Handbook, it also contains a great deal of useful practical and cultural information.

Symmes, Patrick. *Chasing Che: A Motorcycle Journey in Search of the Guevara Legend.* New York: Vintage, 2000. Symmes follows the tiretracks of Che's legendary trip through Argentina and Chile in the early 1950s.

Torres Santibáñez, Hernán, and Marcela Torres Cerda. *Los Parques Nacionales de Chile: una Guía para el Visitante,* 2nd ed. Santiago:

Editorial Universitaria, 2004. Well illustrated with maps and color photographs, this concise guide features 24 of Chile's most accessible national parks, reserves, and monuments.

Wheeler, Sarah. *Travels in a Thin Country.* New York: The Modern Library, 1999. A lively travelogue that even includes the Chilean sector of Antarctica, but occasionally irritating for the unwarranted plugs for a well-known international rental car company that underwrote part of her trip.

HISTORY

Bauer, Arnold. *Chilean Rural Society from the Spanish Conquest to 1930.* Cambridge: Cambridge University Press, 1975. A complex, comprehensive, and systematic analysis of the continuities and discontinuities in rural history that led to upheaval in the 1960s and 1970s.

Crow, John A. *The Epic of Latin America,* 3rd ed. Berkeley: University of California Press, 1980. A comprehensive history of the region, told more through narrative than analysis, in an immensely readable manner. Several chapters deal with Chile.

Lockhart, James, and Stuart Schwartz. *Early Latin America.* Cambridge: Cambridge University Press, 1983. A creative interpretation of colonial history that treats the region's aboriginal inhabitants as active agents rather than mere victims. There is substantial coverage of Chile, particularly the Araucanian frontier.

McBride, George McCutcheon. *Chile: Land and Society.* New York: American Geographical Society, 1936. Based on personal observations, this account of life on Chilean *fundos* and haciendas presents the conditions that led to agrarian discontent in the following decades, though the author may have overestimated these institutions' durability.

Mavor, Elizabeth, ed. *The Captain's Wife: The South American Journals of Maria Graham, 1821–23.* London: Weidenfeld and Nicolson, 1993. An edited version, with commentary, of Maria Graham's lengthy account of residence in Valparaíso and travels in Chile and elsewhere in South America, and her acquaintance and friendship with historic figures such as Bernardo O'Higgins and Lord Cochrane.

Nadelson, Reggie. *Comrade Rockstar.* New York: Walker Books, 2006. Difficult to categorize, this true tale of Colorado-born singer and actor Dean Reed, who became a partisan of Salvador Allende and the Unidad Popular before spending the rest of his career in the Soviet Union and East Germany, has been optioned for a Tom Hanks movie.

Slatta, Richard. *Cowboys of the Americas.* New Haven and London: Yale University Press, 1990. Spectacularly illustrated comparative account of New World horsemen, including both Argentine gauchos and Chilean *huasos.*

GOVERNMENT AND POLITICS

Branch, Taylor, and Eugene Propper. *Labyrinth.* New York: Penguin, 1982. Narrative of the assassination of Chilean diplomat Orlando Letelier, in Washington, D.C., by agents of the Pinochet dictatorship.

Caviedes, César. *Elections in Chile: The Road to Redemocratization.* Boulder, Colo.: Lynne Rienner, 1991. Analysis of the elections that brought the Concertación to power.

Constable, Pamela, and Arturo Valenzuela. *A Nation of Enemies: Chile under Pinochet.* New York and London: W. W. Norton, 1991. A journalistic and academic account of the Pinochet coup, its aftermath, and the transition to democracy.

Hauser, Thomas. *The Execution of Charles Horman: An American Sacrifice.* New York:

Simon and Schuster, 1988. Hauser recounts the fate of a young U.S. journalist during the Pinochet coup in a book that implicated U.S. authorities and served as the basis of Costa-Gavras's film *Missing*.

LITERATURE

Allende, Isabel. *The House of the Spirits*. New York: Knopf, 1985. Set amidst the tumult of the agrarian reform of the author's uncle's presidency, this novel is perhaps her most political.

Allende, Isabel. *Daughter of Fortune*. New York: Harper Collins, 1999. Set in North and South America, Allende's 19th-century romance fashions a vivid portrait of early Valparaíso, illuminates the underappreciated role of Chileans in the California gold rush, and even offers an imaginative speculation on the Joaquín Murieta legend.

Bolaño, Roberto. *The Savage Detectives*. New York, Farrar, Straus & Giroux, 2007. Stream-of-consciousness novel by Chile's late literary wild man, a Williams Burroughs counterpart who derided Isabel Allende as "a typist."

Donoso, José. *Curfew*. New York: Weidenfeld and Nicholson, 1988. An end-of-the-dictatorship novel from the viewpoint of a folk musician who has returned from exile.

Fuguet, Alberto. *Bad Vibes*. New York: St. Martin's Press, 1997. Tale of apolitical alienation in Pinochet's Chile by an author whose motto is "I am not a magical realist."

Skármeta, Antonio. *Burning Patience*. New York: Pantheon, 1987. The fictional account of Pablo Neruda's counsel to a childishly infatuated postman, later transformed into the Oscar-winning film *Il Postino* (*The Postman*).

ENVIRONMENT AND NATURAL HISTORY

Araya M., Braulio. *Guía de Campo de las Aves de Chile,* 4th ed. Santiago: Editorial Universitaria, 1991. A Spanish-language field guide, with English and Linnean nomenclature as well, to birds throughout the country.

Bahre, Conrad. *Destruction of the Natural Vegetation of North Central Chile*. Berkeley: University of California Press, 1978. A workmanlike analysis of the human impact on the environment of the Norte Chico, including mining and agriculture, but its argument is weakened by inattention to socioeconomic factors such as lopsided land tenure.

Couve Montané, Enrique, and Claudio Vidal-Ojeda. *Aves del Canal Beagle/Birds of the Beagle Channel*. Punta Arenas: Fantástico Sur Birding, 2000. A bilingual field guide, with excellent photographs, of southernmost archipelagic Chile.

Wilcox, Ken. *Chile's Native Forests*. Redway, Calif.: Ancient Forests International, 1996. Comprehensive survey of Chilean forests and forestry from an activist, conservation-oriented perspective.

Internet Resources

AmeriSpan
www.amerispan.com
Information on language instruction throughout the Americas, including Chile.

Automóvil Club de Chile
www.acchi.cl
Motorists' organization that also provides services to members of overseas affiliates.

Backpacker's Best
www.backpackersbest.cl
More than the name suggests, this is a guide to quality budget accommodations, not just hostels, and other services.

Backpacker's Best
www.backpackerschile.com
Similar to Backpacker's Best, with some overlap, this is another guide to quality budget accommodations and other services.

Black Sheep Patagonia
www.patagoniablacksheep.com
Puerto Natales–based monthly, in English, with cleverly written features and useful practical info; also available in a free print version in southernmost Chile and Argentina.

Centers for Disease Control
www.cdc.gov
U.S. government page with travel health advisories.

Chile Information Project
www.chip.cl
English-language site with daily Chilean news summaries and a useful travel section.

Ciclistas Furiosos
www.furiosos.cl
Site for Chile's militant bicyclists.

Codelco
www.codelcochile.cl
Home page for the state-run copper industry, the country's most important single exchange earner, in Spanish and English; includes information on tourist visits to Chuquicamata and the historic company town at Sewell.

Comité de la Defensa de Flora y Fauna
www.codeff.cl
Well-established group oriented toward wildlife and habitat conservation.

Conservación Patagónica
www.patagonialandtrust.com
Projects of environmental philanthropists Doug Tompkins and Kris McDivitt.

Corporación Nacional de Desarrollo Indígena
www.conadi.cl
Official government page for indigenous affairs, in Spanish only.

Corporación Nacional Forestal
www.conaf.cl
Official page of quasi-governmental agency in charge of Chile's national parks and other protected areas; in Spanish only.

Corrugated City
www.corrugatedcity.com
Informative blog about the city of Valparaíso, by an English resident who dabbles in real estate.

Currency Converter
www.oanda.com
Present and historic exchange rate information.

Defensores del Bosque Chileno
www.elbosquechileno.cl
NGO devoted to native forest conservation.

Department of Health
www.dh.gov.uk
British government agency with country-by-country health advice.

Department of State
www.travel.state.gov
Travel information and advisories from the U.S. government; its warnings are often exaggerated.

Easter Island Foundation
www.islandheritage.org
The source for everything to do with Chile's remote Pacific landmark.

El Mercurio
www.emol.com
Santiago's traditional daily newspaper, with conservative editorial line; in Spanish.

Empresa de los Ferrocarriles del Estado (EFE)
www.efe.cl
Official site of the erratic state railway company, with info on passenger services.

Escalada en Chile
www.escalando.cl
Site devoted to hiking, rock climbing, and ice climbing in Chile; in Spanish and English.

Estrategia
www.estrategia.cl
Santiago financial daily; in Spanish.

Federación de Andinismo
www.feach.cl
Site devoted to climbing, including bureaucratic obstacles in sensitive border areas.

Fundación Terram
www.terram.cl
Nonprofit promoting sustainable development.

FutaFriends
www.futafriends.org
Nonprofit organization dedicated to preserving the Río Futaleufú.

Hostelling International Santiago
www.hostelling.cl
Chilean affiliate of Hostelling International, with information on hostels and activities throughout the country.

Instituto Geográfico Militar
www.igm.cl
Chilean government agency in charge of mapping, map sales, and general geographic information.

La Tercera
www.latercera.cl
Best of the Chilean tabloid dailies, serious but with a rigidly conservative editorial policy.

Latin American Network Information Center–LANIC
http://lanic.utexas.edu
Organized by the University of Texas, this outstanding site has a huge collection of quality links to Chile and other Latin American countries.

Metro Santiago
www.metrosantiago.cl
Site of Santiago's state-of-the-art subway system.

Mercopress
www.falkland-malvinas.com
Montevideo-based news digest for the entire Southern Cone.

Punto Gay
www.puntogay.cl
Portal oriented toward gays, lesbians, and bisexuals, including visitors to Chile.

Renace
www.renace.cl
Alliance of Chilean environmental organizations.

Revolver
www.revolver-magazine.com
Santiago-based online culture and nightlife magazine, in English.

Sernatur
www.sernatur.cl
Chilean government tourism bureau; in Spanish and English.

Transantiago
www.transantiago.cl
Site of Santiago's rapidly reforming public bus system.

Trekking Chile
www.trekkingchile.com
Probably the best all-around site about exploring Chile's mountains, in English, Spanish, and German.

Turismo Chile
www.turismochile.travel
Public/private Chilean site in English and Spanish.

USENET DISCUSSION GROUPS
Soc.culture.chile
No-holds-barred discussion group that touches on many issues besides travel.

Rec.travel.latin-america
Regional discussion group dealing with all Latin American countries, with a steady amount of postings on Chile.

Index

JK

L

List of Maps

Acknowledgments

As do my previous Moon Handbooks, this title owes its existence to numerous individuals in North America, Chile, Argentina, and elsewhere. Once again, the highest praise to Bill Newlin and his staff at Berkeley's Avalon Travel Publishing, now part of Perseus Books Group.

In the course of nearly 30 years' experience in Chile, more than half that as a guidebook writer, I owe enormous unpayable debts to friends, acquaintances, and officials throughout the country. My apologies to anyone I may have overlooked or perhaps omitted because of an errant keystroke.

In Santiago and vicinity, thanks to Pablo Moll and Kristina Schreck of Turismo Chile, Santiago; Steve Anderson of the Chile Information Project; Harold Beckett of the *Guía Aérea Oficial*; Pablo Fernández and Rodrigo Vásquez of Hostelling International; Yerko Ivelic, Javier López, and the rest of the staff at Santiago's Cascada Expediciones; Eduardo Núñez of Conaf for once again smoothing access to national parks and other reserves; and Marco Vergara of Cruceros Australis.

Elsewhere in the Heartland, my appreciation to Christian Güntert of Valparaíso; Julian Arellano of Vina del Mar; Paola Lara of Sernatur, Viña del Mar; Todd Temkin of the Fundación Valparaíso; Jorge Espinoza Bustos of Sernatur, Rancagua; Andrea Ilabaca of Viña MontGras, Santa Cruz; Verónica Morgado Saldivia of Sernatur, Talca; Doris Sandoval Gutiérrez of Sernatur, Chillán; and Nelson Oyarzo Barrientos of Sernatur, Concepción; and Winfried and Elke Lohmar of Los Angeles.

In the Norte Grande, thanks to Charlie Dekeyser of Arica; Barbara Knapton of Putre; Hugo Cerda of Desértica, Antofagasta; Gustavo Herrera Soto of Sernatur, Antofagasta; and Martín Beeris of Cosmo Andino, San Pedro de Atacama.

In the Norte Chico, thanks to Solange Fuster, Luis Canales Leyton, and Leila Manterola of Sernatur, Copiapó; Ted Stevens of La Serena; Alicia Díaz Fraile of Sernatur, La Serena; and Clark Stede and Manuela Paradiser of Hurtado.

In the Sur Chico, my regards to Javier Ibar Muñoz of the Municipalidad de Angol; Carolina Morgado of Parque Pumalín; Gina Rubio of Sernatur, Temuco; Tom Buschor of Malalcahuello; Matthias Holzmann of Puerto Varas; Raúl Richard Villegas of Sernatur, Puerto Montt; Béat and Claudia Zbinden of Villarrica; Glen and Bev Aldrich of Villarrica; Patricio Yáñez Strange of Sernatur, Valdivia; Armin and Nadia Dübendorfer of Puerto Octay; superintendent Javier Labra of Parque Nacional Puyehue; Iván Vargas of Parque Nacional Alerce Andino; Margot Martínez of Pucón; Franz Schirmer of Puerto Varas; Britt and Sandra Lewis of Ancud, Chiloé; and Carl Grady of Chonchi, Chiloé.

In Chilean Patagonia, thanks to Nicholas La Penna of Chaitén; Chris Spelius of Expediciones Chile, Futaleufú; Richard Figueroa of Sernatur, Futaleufú; Gabriela Neira Morales of Sernatur, Coyhaique; Jonathan Leidich of Puerto Bertrand; Francisco Sánchez Aguilar of Sernatur, Punta Arenas; British Consul John Rees Jones of Punta Arenas; Werner and Cecilia Ruf-Chaura, of Casa Cecilia, Puerto Natales; and Hernán Jofré of Indómita Patagonia, Puerto Natales.

In Hanga Roa, Rapa Nui, special mention to Josefina Nahoe and to Conny Martin of Rapa Nui Travel.

In Argentine Patagonia and Tierra del Fuego, thanks to Javier Jury, Elsa Zaparart, Alejandro Galeazzi, and Natalie Prosser de Goodall of Ushuaia, Tierra del Fuego; Rubén Vásquez and Ricardo Brondo of El Chaltén, Santa Cruz; and my cousin Elisa Rodríguez of El Calafate.

Stateside, thanks to Georgia Lee of Los Osos, CA, for once again helping out on Rapa Nui; Fernando Varela and Pablo Retamal of the Chilean Embassy in Washington, DC; and Verónica Mellado and Ursula Velarde of LAN Airlines, Miami, who helped arranged international and internal flights.

Thanks also to those whom I encountered along the way or who sent me information that has been incorporated into this book, including specifically but not exclusively Lode Peeters of Belgium; Bruce and Laurie Lakin of Cuenca, Ecuador; and Kuenley Chiu of Pasadena. My apologies for deadline pressures that have caused any omissions.

www.moon.com

DESTINATIONS | ACTIVITIES | BLOGS | MAPS | BOOKS

MOON.COM is all new, and ready to help plan your next trip! Filled with fresh trip ideas and strategies, author interviews, informative blogs, a detailed map library, and descriptions of all the Moon guidebooks, Moon.com is all you need to get out and explore the world—or even places in your own backyard. As always, when you travel with Moon, expect an experience that is uncommon and truly unique.

MAP SYMBOLS

Expressway	**(** Highlight	✗ Airfield	⌀ Golf Course
Primary Road	○ City/Town	✗ Airport	▯ Parking Area
Secondary Road	◉ State Capital	▲ Mountain	⬟ Archaeological Site
Unpaved Road	✳ National Capital	✦ Unique Natural Feature	⛪ Church
Trail	★ Point of Interest		
Ferry	• Accommodation	⚑ Waterfall	Gas Station
Railroad	▼ Restaurant/Bar	▲ Park	Glacier
Pedestrian Walkway	■ Other Location	◨ Trailhead	Mangrove
Stairs	▲ Campground	✗ Skiing Area	Reef
			Swamp

CONVERSION TABLES

$$°C = (°F - 32) / 1.8$$
$$°F = (°C \times 1.8) + 32$$

1 inch = 2.54 centimeters (cm)
1 foot = 0.304 meters (m)
1 yard = 0.914 meters
1 mile = 1.6093 kilometers (km)
1 km = 0.6214 miles
1 fathom = 1.8288 m
1 chain = 20.1168 m
1 furlong = 201.168 m
1 acre = 0.4047 hectares
1 sq km = 100 hectares
1 sq mile = 2.59 square km
1 ounce = 28.35 grams
1 pound = 0.4536 kilograms
1 short ton = 0.90718 metric ton
1 short ton = 2,000 pounds
1 long ton = 1.016 metric tons
1 long ton = 2,240 pounds
1 metric ton = 1,000 kilograms
1 quart = 0.94635 liters
1 US gallon = 3.7854 liters
1 Imperial gallon = 4.5459 liters
1 nautical mile = 1.852 km

MOON CHILE

Avalon Travel
a member of the Perseus Books Group
1700 Fourth Street
Berkeley, CA 94710, USA
www.moon.com

Editors: Michelle Cadden, Shaharazade Husain
Series Manager: Kathryn Ettinger
Copy Editor: Maura Brown
Graphics Coordinator: Lucie Ericksen
Production Coordinator: Lucie Ericksen
Cover Designer: Lucie Ericksen
Map Editor: Albert Angulo
Cartographers: Chris Markiewicz & Kat Bennett
Indexer: Jean Mooney

ISBN: 978-1-59880-181-1
ISSN: 1540-3394

Printing History
1st Edition – 2002
3rd Edition – October 2009
5 4 3 2 1

KEEPING CURRENT

If you have a favorite gem you'd like to see included in the next edition, or see anything
that needs updating, clarification, or correction, please drop us a line. Send your
comments via email to feedback@moon.com, or use the address above.